ELEVENTH EDITION

LITERATURE
THE HUMAN EXPERIENCE

RICHARD ABCARIAN
MARVIN KLOTZ
California State University, Northridge, Emeriti

SAMUEL COHEN
University of Missouri

D0112073

BEDFORD/ST. MARTIN'S
Boston ◆ New York

For Bedford/St. Martin's

Senior Executive Editor: Stephen A. Scipione
Developmental Editor: Alicia Young
Senior Production Supervisor: Jennifer Peterson
Marketing Manager: Stacey Propps
Project Management: DeMasi Design and Publishing Services
Permissions Manager: Kalina K. Ingham
Senior Art Director: Anna Palchik
Text Design: Joan O'Connor
Cover Design: Marine Miller
Cover Art: Copyright © 2012 by Elizabeth Rosen/Morgan Gaynin, Inc.
Composition: Cenveo Publisher Services
Printing and Binding: RR Donnelley and Sons

President, Bedford/St. Martin's: Denise B. Wydra
Presidents, Macmillan Higher Education: Joan E. Feinberg and Tom Scotty
Editor in Chief: Karen S. Henry
Director of Marketing: Karen R. Soeltz
Production Director: Susan W. Brown
Associate Production Director: Elise S. Kaiser
Manager, Publishing Services: Andrea Cava

Library of Congress Control Number: 2012942002

Manufactured in the United States of America.

7   6   5   4
g   f   e   d

For information, write: Bedford/St. Martin's, 75 Arlington Street, Boston, MA 02116
(617-399-4000)

ISBN 978-1-4576-0429-4

Acknowledgments

Again,

for Joan.

And for David, Dan, Jennifer and Steve,

Robin, Sara, Peter and Vivianne,

Rick and Marie, and all their children

that are and may be. And for Kristin, Ben,

and Henry.

PREFACE FOR INSTRUCTORS

> We all suffer alone in the real world; true empathy's impossible. But if a piece of fiction can allow us imaginatively to identify with a character's pain, we might then also more easily conceive of others identifying with our own. This is nourishing, redemptive; we become less alone inside. It might just be that simple.
>
> —David Foster Wallace

While committed readers would agree that they read literature because they find it delightful, instructive, or both, many of your students may read literature because it has been assigned to them in a required class. We've prepared every edition of *Literature: The Human Experience* for such students. For them, we choose literature that's entertaining and thought-provoking enough to capture the interest of indifferent or uncommitted readers. We organize that literature to address cradle-to-grave thematic concerns that are compelling and inescapable. Finally, we show students how to connect with what they encounter in the literature through their reading, discussion, and writing. As David Foster Wallace's epigraph suggests, reading literature can forge empathetic links that are consoling, sustaining, and even redemptive. We believe that students' experience of literature in a course should leave them feeling connected, not only to the writing they read and the writers who wrote it, but also to one another—indeed, to the multitudes of others, past and present, whose lives comprise the human experience.

Everything that's new in the eleventh edition furthers these goals. New works by young writers extend our effort to bring students to literature by including writing that speaks, in voices more like theirs, of experiences to which they can connect. New examples of classic literature on timeless themes continue to represent the best that's been thought and said and as well the perennial need for humans to represent their experiences through imaginative work and storytelling. New pairs and clusters of literary works juxtapose classic and recent writing, encouraging critical comparative thinking. Creative new writing topics strengthen the book's emphasis on getting students to see literature—and life—as writers.

FEATURES

A THEMATIC ORGANIZATION THAT CONNECTS LITERATURE TO LIFE.

We believe that students are most immediately engaged by works in which they can see themselves. The ability of students to connect their experiences to those they read about does not mean they should be assigned nothing but literature about students or Americans or Westerners or young people from anywhere; it does mean that the human experience, in its dazzling variety, can be represented in art and that students can respond to it no matter the different circumstances of reader and writer. In gathering these works, we tried to meet students where they live and take them to places they have never seen. The best way to do this is to concentrate on different themes drawn from human experience and to ask students to read divergent perspectives on these themes. Thus, the anthology is organized into five thematic sections: "Innocence and Experience," "Conformity and Rebellion," "Culture and Identity," "Love and Hate," and "Life and Death." Each section opens with a short introductory essay and questions that invite students to reflect on their own experiences with the chapter's theme.

To enhance teaching flexibility, the thematic structure features two subordinate arrangements of the literature. Embedded in each thematic section, the stories, poems, plays, and essays are grouped by genre; within each genre, selections are arranged chronologically by author's birth date. (The date following the title indicates the selection's first appearance in a book; a designation in parentheses indicates the date of either composition or appearance in a publication other than a book. We have not attempted to date traditional ballads.) The dates, together with an appendix containing biographical notes on the authors, provide students with a brief historical context for each work. So whether you teach literature thematically, generically, or historically—or some combination of the three—the organization of *Literature: The Human Experience* accommodates your approach.

The thematic sections are also punctuated with twenty-six short units that pair or cluster literary works—often classic with contemporary. While promoting comparative critical thinking with their accompanying questions and writing assignments, these compact clusters provide engaging reading for students. For example, "Connecting Stories: Superantiheroes" features works by Harlan Ellison and Jonathan Lethem about alienated and peculiar superheroes. In "Connecting Poems: Poetic Identities," five poets of a range of canonical status—old members (Walt Whitman), new members (Billy Collins), and future members (Timothy Yu)—connect what they write to who they are in powerful and surprising ways. In "Connecting Nonfiction: Closer to Death," a classic essay by E. B. White is joined by a new classic piece of brief creative nonfiction by Brian Doyle and a beautiful and affecting personal reflection by novelist Chang-rae Lee, offering students the opportunity to compare both their thoughts on life and death and their different ways of turning those thoughts into art.

SUPPORT FOR READING AND WRITING ABOUT LITERATURE. Two introductory chapters, "Responding to Literature" and "Writing about Literature," give students the tools to think about and appreciate what they read and to put those thoughts into words. In these chapters, we discuss the formal elements of each genre and provide descriptions and samples of various forms of written response and documentation. Throughout the thematic sections, study questions challenge students to analyze works, to make connections between them, and to write about them in a variety of ways. At the end of the book, the "Glossary of Critical Approaches" and the "Glossary of Literary Terms" provide additional resources for students learning about how to approach literature.

NEW TO THIS EDITION

WIDE-RANGING CONTEMPORARY LITERATURE ANCHORED BY A STURDY SELECTION OF CLASSICS.

- *Fiction:* Chimamanda Ngozi Adichie's "Birdsong" and Lydia Millet's "Girl and Giraffe" are among this edition's recent stories, while classics like Kate Chopin's "The Story of an Hour" make new appearances.
- *Poetry:* Classic poems by John Donne, Allen Ginsberg, William Shakespeare, and Frank O'Hara are new to the eleventh edition, as are the modern voices of Alexandra Teague, Natasha Trethewey, Terrance Hayes, Daisy Fried, and Maggie Nelson.
- *Drama:* Two new selections include a short contemporary play and a full-length classic: Lynn Nottage's *Poof!* and Sophocles' *Antigonê.*
- *Nonfiction:* Recent essays by Lacy M. Johnson, David Sedaris, and Brian Doyle stand alongside vintage work by Jamaica Kincaid, Rachel Carson, and Katha Pollitt.

A NEW THEMATIC CHAPTER ON LIFE AND DEATH. This final chapter combines literary works about human mortality with explorations of the mutable but enduring natural world of which we are part yet against which we often define ourselves.

TWO NEW CASE STUDIES. Flannery O'Connor's story "A Good Man Is Hard to Find" is followed by critical essays that illustrate the significance and limitations of interpreting texts, and Shakespeare's *Othello* is accompanied by a collection of documents that highlight the racial contexts of the play.

MORE SUPPORT FOR ACTIVE AND CRITICAL READING. "Responding to Literature" shows students the importance of learning to read actively and become truly engaged, critical readers. New "Questions for Exploring" also provide genre-specific questions to consider when reading stories, poems, plays, or essays.

YOU GET MORE RESOURCES FOR *LITERATURE: THE HUMAN EXPERIENCE*

Literature: The Human Experience doesn't stop with a book. Online, you'll find both free and affordable premium resources to help students get even more out of the book and your course. You'll also find convenient instructor resources, and even a nationwide community of teachers. To learn more about or order any of the products below, contact your Bedford/St. Martin's sales representative, e-mail sales support (sales_support@bfwpub.com), or visit the Web site at **bedfordstmartins.com/experience_literature/catalog**. Visit *Re:Writing for Literature* **bedfordstmartins.com/rewritinglit** and supplement your print text with our free and open resources for literature (no codes required) and flexible premium content.

GET FREE ONLINE HELP FOR YOUR STUDENTS. *Re:Writing for Literature* provides close reading help, reference materials, and support for working with sources.

- *VirtuaLit Interactive Tutorials* for close reading (fiction, poetry, and drama)
- *AuthorLinks* and biographies for 800 authors
- Quizzes on poetic elements and hundreds of literary works
- Glossary of literary terms
- MLA-style student papers
- A sampler of author videos and additional literature
- Help for finding and citing sources, including access to Diana Hacker's *Research and Documentation Online*

LITERATURE: THE HUMAN EXPERIENCE NOW COMES WITH VIDEO. At no additional cost to students, this book can be packaged with *VideoCentral: Literature*, our growing library of more than fifty video interviews with today's writers. It includes Ha Jin on how he uses humor and T. Coraghessan Boyle on how he works with language and style. Biographical notes and questions make each video an easy-to-assign module. See **bedfordstmartins.com/videolit/catalog**. To order *VideoCentral: Literature* with this print text, use ISBN 978-1-4576-4205-0.

ACCESS YOUR INSTRUCTOR RESOURCES

You have a lot to do in your course. Bedford/St. Martin's wants to make it easy for you to find the support you need—and to get it quickly. Go to bedfordstmartins.com/experience_literature/catalog.

DOWNLOAD YOUR INSTRUCTOR'S MANUAL. *Editor's Notes for Teaching Literature: The Human Experience* offers teaching ideas for each selection in the anthology as well as additional thematic connections and writing topics. To download the PDF, go to bedfordstmartins.com/experience_literature/catalog.

GET TEACHING IDEAS YOU CAN USE TODAY. Are you looking for professional resources for teaching literature and writing? How about some help with planning classroom activities?

- **TeachingCentral.** We've gathered all of our print and online professional resources in one place. You'll find landmark reference works, sourcebooks on pedagogical issues, award-winning collections, and practical advice for the classroom—all free for instructors and available at **bedfordstmartins .com/teachingcentral**.

- **LitBits: Ideas for Teaching Literature and Creative Writing.** Our new *LitBits* blog—hosted by a growing team of instructors, poets, novelists, and scholars—offers a fresh, regularly updated collection of ideas and assignments. You'll find simple ways to teach with new media, excite your students with activities, and join an ongoing conversation about teaching. Go to **bedfordstmartins.com/litbits/catalog** and **bedfordstmartins.com/litbits**.

- *Order content for your course management system.* Our content cartridges for the most common course management systems—Blackboard, WebCT, Angel, and Desire2Learn—allow you to easily download Bedford /St. Martin's digital materials for your course. For more information, visit **bedfordstmartins.com/coursepacks**.

- *Package one of our best-selling brief handbooks at a discount.* Do you need a pocket-sized handbook for your course? Package *Easy Writer* by Andrea Lunsford or *A Pocket Style Manual* by Diana Hacker and Nancy Sommers with this text at a 20% discount. For more information go to **bedfordstmartins.com/easywriter/catalog** or **bedfordstmartins.com/pocket /catalog**.

- *Teach longer works at a nice price.* Our literary reprints series—the Case Studies in Contemporary Criticism series, Bedford Cultural Editions series, and the Bedford Shakespeare series—can be shrink-wrapped with *Literature: The Human Experience.* For a complete list of available titles, visit **bedfordstmartins.com/literaryreprints/catalog**.

- *Package works from our video and DVD library.* Qualified adopters can choose from selected videos and DVDs of plays and stories included in *Literature: The Human Experience.* To learn more, contact your Bedford/St. Martin's sales representative, or e-mail sales support (**sales_support@bfwpub.com**).

- **TradeUp *and save 50%.*** Add more value and choice to your students' learning experiences by packaging their Bedford/St. Martin's textbook with one of a thousand titles from our sister publishers such as Farrar, Straus and Giroux and St. Martin's Press—at a discount of 50% off the regular price.

ACKNOWLEDGMENTS

We would like to thank the professors who generously took time to share their ideas about the previous edition of this anthology. They are Deborah F. Barnard, Middle Tennessee State University; DeMisty Bellinger-Delfeld, University of Nebraska-Lincoln; Emily A. Bernhard Jackson, University of Arkansas; Kevin A. Brown, Middle Tennessee State University; Marie Brown, Middle Tennessee State University; Shahara Drew, Assumption College; Ellen Feig, Bergen Community College; Deborah Garfinkle, College of San Mateo/De Anza College; Seamus A. Gibbons, Bergen Community College; Tokeya C. Graham, Monroe Community College (Damon City Campus); Timothy B. Messick, Mohawk Valley Community College; Melanie Springer Mock, George Fox University; Barbara Nave, Limestone College; Ryan Reed, Middle Tennessee State University; Timothy Rogers, University of Massachusetts at Lowell; Stephan Schaffrath, Indiana University of Pennsylvania; Celeste M. Sherry, SUNY Rockland Community College; Christopher J. Stephens, Northeastern University; Brad Sullivan, Western New England College; Robert Vettese, Southern Maine Community College; Frederick White, Slippery Rock University; and our reviewer from Siena College who wishes to remain anonymous.

We wish to thank Karissa Lagos, whose precocious writing skills provided us with a superb research paper. We also wish to thank Anita Zubère, who helped untangle some knotty lines of poetry; Roy Merrens for explaining some of the arcane features of the urban London landscape; and Bainbridge Scott, whose knowledge of music made our task easier. Our thanks also go to Mary Lawless for her thoughtful contributions to the introductory chapters on reading and writing and to Sara Eaton Gaunt for her smart and detailed updates to the biographical notes.

Experienced and wise people at Bedford/St. Martin's have guided this book along the way. We thank Joan Feinberg, co-president of Macmillan Higher Education, and Denise Wydra, president of Bedford/St. Martin's, for supporting this eleventh edition. As well, we are grateful to Kalina Ingham and Caryn Burtt for procuring permissions and Linda DeMasi and Andrea Cava for shepherding the book through production. We thank Marine Miller for her persistence in creating the design of a new cover and Jenna Bookin Barry for providing expert marketing advice. We thank editor in chief Karen Henry for her encouraging and nurturing leadership. As ever, we owe many thanks to senior executive editor Steve Scipione, as well as heaps of gratitude to editor Alicia Young, for her vision, hard work, and endless patience and good humor. This book would simply not be what it is without their contributions—it would not exist at all. Some of this labor (there's certainly enough to go around) must surely be credited to editorial assistant Bethany Gordon—to her, many thanks as well.

Richard Abcarian
Marvin Klotz
Samuel Cohen

CONTENTS

INNOCENCE AND EXPERIENCE 76

QUESTIONS FOR THINKING AND WRITING 78

FICTION 79

CONNECTING STORIES: CRUSHES 122

CONNECTING POEMS:
REVISITING FAIRY TALES   208

CONNECTING POEMS: VOICES OF EXPERIENCE 214

CONNECTING POEMS: HAPPY HOLIDAYS 220

DRAMA 228

CULTURE AND IDENTITY   548

CONNECTING POEMS: POETIC IDENTITIES   705

LOVE AND HATE   832

POETRY   896

LIFE AND DEATH 1104

CASE STUDY

POEMS ABOUT PAINTINGS   1231

ALTERNATE CONTENTS

Arranged by genre and alphabetically by the author's last name

FICTION

POETRY

DRAMA

NONFICTION

ART

DOCUMENTS

EXCERPTS FROM LONGER WORKS

INTRODUCTION

RESPONDING TO LITERATURE

There is no Frigate like a Book
To take us Lands away
Nor any Coursers like a Page
Of prancing poetry—

This Traverse may the poorest take
Without oppress of Toll—
How frugal is the Chariot
That bears the Human soul.
　　　　—Emily Dickinson (ca. 1873)

WHY WE READ LITERATURE

The epigraph from poet Emily Dickinson promotes reading as an escape, a way for us to take a vacation from our lives. If we think about our experiences with literature—and with other forms of entertainment, such as movies and TV shows—that probably sounds about right. Most of us have enjoyed forgetting about the cares of the world with a page-turning thriller or a tear-jerking melodrama. But literature can also help us get closer to life, to understand it in a new way when we get back from our literary journey. We understand what Dickinson means because we can connect to it—we think about our experiences as readers and that helps us understand the poem while, at the same time, the poem clarifies something about how reading makes us feel. The best literature helps us to understand ourselves, one another, and our world in new ways and to make connections that had never occurred to us or that we might have sensed but were unable to express.

Of course, you may not feel this way about reading the kind of literature you expect to find in a textbook. It may be that opening a textbook signals to you that the fun is over. And certainly reading and responding to serious literature requires concentrated attention and is not relaxing in the way that kicking back and watching a TV show might be. But what you may not realize is that you likely respond critically to literature without even realizing that you are doing so. Inevitably, when you encounter any kind of literature, you distinguish good from evil, right from wrong—and you do so based on your own experiences and knowledge of the world. When writers convey cultural ideas about the nature of love, of duty, of heroism—sometimes broadly, sometimes with subtlety—you agree or disagree, are moved or are not. You may not now be moved by the same literature that entranced you when you were a child, or you may have come to appreciate that literature in a fuller, more nuanced way. But you may be surprised, when you turn your attention to "serious" literature, to find how much these works have in common with the books, movies, and TV shows you have turned to for entertainment. Some "popular" authors—Janet Evanovich, Lee Child, John Grisham, Dorothy Sayers, and others—who write spy novels and detective fiction are routinely read in college courses that celebrate literature. Their exciting and suspenseful novels are often made into films, but so, too, are the classic works of William Shakespeare, Jane Austen, Edith Wharton, F. Scott Fitzgerald, and Ernest Hemingway.

Serious literature, no less than popular literature, embodies thrilling adventure. Serious literature is replete with monsters (consider the Old English epic *Beowulf*), ghosts (at the outset of Shakespeare's *Hamlet* and in the middle of *Macbeth*), witches, supernatural spirits, magical transformations, unspeakably brutal wars, terrible murders, and bloody vengeance. Given the close ties between popular and serious literature, scholars, teachers, and readers frequently debate what should be included in textbooks like this one, what literature best represents the "literary canon." Here things get a bit murky. *Canon* is derived from the Latin word meaning "measuring line or rule" and is used in religious discourse to signify "sacred writings admitted to the catalog according to the rule." Early theologians decided which books were the authentic word of God and which were not. But, much like today's literary scholars, they did not always agree. Although it attempts to establish the body of literature that humans need to study and master, the literary canon changes in response to political and social changes. Further, a literary canon is bound to reflect the cultural tradition that produces it. The literary canon of China will differ markedly from the literary canon of the United States. And both will change with the eruptions of history and the demands of fashion.

For example, although American literary history is replete with women writers, they have often been undervalued by the literary canon's guardians. But a century of political struggle—which led, first, to enfranchising women as voters and, later, to a feminist movement that demanded equality for women and their works—has allowed some women authors to gain entry to the canon, forever changing it. Writers like Kate Chopin and Charlotte Perkins Gilman are now routinely included in university courses and women writers are broadly represented in this anthology. Further, the political struggles of Native American, African American, Latino/a, and Asian American citizens have drawn considerable attention to a large and diverse body of writing that was often overlooked by critics who prized European authors. Skillful literary artists from these groups are also represented here.

You might reasonably ask, What difference does broadening the literary canon make? Consider: if you love books and movies, then you know how influential they can be and you'll probably agree that what we read makes a tremendous difference to the world we live in. You learn a great deal about your society from reading—what it values, what it condemns, how it expects you to behave, what constitutes success both economically and morally, what it sees as the very nature of good and evil. If your reading were limited to, say, European works and you were embedded in a non-European social group, you might not discover yourself or your peers in the books you read. Thus, schools and anthologies that project a narrow literary canon would present a world foreign to your experience. The resulting sense of anomie—a rootless lack of purpose, identity, and values—could be terribly damaging. At the same time, ignorance of your neighbors' lifestyles could also seriously impair your life by giving you a skewed, incomplete vision of the world. Conversely, reading widely could help you avoid the baleful consequences of racism, hypernationalism, and ignorance.

The stories, poems, plays, and essays in this textbook have been selected from a diverse array of important authors, some of them very popular, others often most appreciated by scholars and critics. Some of these writers have been read and studied in schools and colleges for centuries while others, especially from historically underrepresented groups, may be entirely new to you. We hope that you enjoy reading the works by the authors and thinkers in this book. We also hope that you find surprising commonalities among these very different writers and between them and you. The units are organized around universal themes and are designed to help you connect your own life and the things you are reading to the many literary traditions that join us to each other, to our collective history, and to the world at large. The literature in this volume will take you out of your comfort zone to "lands away" while giving you new tools for understanding yourself and your immediate world. The only "toll" required is an open mind and an attentive eye.

READING ACTIVELY AND CRITICALLY

In a well-ordered universe, you would enjoy all your reading—and your delight would derive from your complete absorption in and understanding of what you read. But just as sports require physical conditioning in order for you to perform at your best, you may need to build up your stamina as an effective reader. First of all, pay attention to *how* you read. Can you read fifty pages in one sitting, or do you find your mind wandering after a page or two? If you fall into the latter category, don't worry—we all succumb to the allure of distractions once in a while. But it is up to you to train yourself not to let it diminish your reading experience. If you feel your attention beginning to wander, stop and look back to the place in the text where you began to drift. When you come back to your reading, commit yourself to reading another portion of the passage that's longer than the last one you read. You can hold yourself accountable by writing a short summary—from memory—of what you've read every few sentences, paragraphs, or pages. When you deliberately "train" your mind in this way, your ability to focus and concentrate—and think—will be enhanced, and you will be a better reader for your efforts.

Equally important to reading actively is paying attention to *what* you read. It can be easy to get bogged down by the sheer volume of words on a page, but you can help make sense of them by keeping a pencil in hand and interacting with the page. Mark words you don't recognize and look them up in the dictionary. Note when you feel a protest rising in your throat. Jot down places where the text reminds you of something in your own life or in another work of art—any kind of connection. Active reading takes you beyond the role of an observer, removed and separate from the things you read, and makes you a participant in a conversation with the author or even with the characters. So don't be shy—speak up!

Beyond being an active reader of literature, you must also become a critical reader. Beyond simply perceiving the words on the page, critical reading invites you to question those words in profound, meaningful ways. When we ask you to read critically, we ask that you use the complex set of experiences that define you as a human being—as well as a sense of the cultural imperatives among which you live—to analyze the work you encounter. As a critical reader, you learn to address your biases, enlarge your universe, and test your comfortable convictions. Thus, when you adopt a critical position toward a piece of literature, you need to test and question that position. Ask, What perspective does the author have that led him or her to write this work? What social, cultural, or historical conditions influenced the production of the work? What other ways might the author have presented the ideas or subjects of the work? Are the author's values different from my own? How do my views and experiences affect whether I like or dislike the work? Such questions are stepping stones toward being able to write about literature meaningfully and compellingly (a process that is discussed in greater detail on pp. 31–75).

READING FICTION

Fiction creates imaginary worlds by telling stories written in *prose* (ordinary, unrhymed language), about realistic characters, set in physical environments, and with sustained attention to descriptive detail.

Works of fiction *narrate,* or tell, stories. Of course, narrative is not specific to fiction or to any other literary genre: telling stories pervades almost every aspect of our daily lives. We learn very early on how to recognize and tell stories, and we rely heavily on narrative to organize and make sense of our experience. For example, when we study history, we mostly study stories of various events. Likewise, an astronomer's account of the universe's origins may take the shape of a narrative. Even in our sleep, we tell ourselves stories in the form of dreams. It is impossible to imagine our lives without these narratives; in fact, every culture uses them to order and make sense of lived experience. Narrative fiction is not meant to recount actual events, of course, though it may refer to real events or real persons. Rather than relate actual experiences, fiction uses narrative to shape imaginary ones.

Works of fiction, however, cannot be reduced to a listing of their narrative events any more than paintings can be replaced by diagrams. Such summaries diminish a work's realism, which is produced by careful description of characters, settings, and actions, as well as its depths of meaning. For example, the emotional impact of James Joyce's "Araby" cannot be captured by summarizing its simple plot. Without suspending critical judgment, readers of fiction have to be willing to suspend disbelief, that is, to enter the imaginary world of the novel or short story.

The Methods of Fiction

In order to examine the methods of fiction—tone, setting, plot, theme, characterization, point of view, and irony—let us look more closely at James Joyce's "Araby" (p. 122).

TONE One of the things most readers first respond to in a short story is its *tone*. Because it is like a *mood*, tone is difficult to talk about. It can be defined as an author's implicit attitude toward the characters, places, and events in the story and toward the reader of the work. Tone depends for its substance on delicate emotional responses to language and situation. Notice how a distinct tone is established in the language of the opening lines of "Araby":

> North Richmond Street, being blind, was a quiet street except at the hour when the Christian Brothers' School set the boys free. An uninhabited house of two storeys stood at the blind end, detached from its neighbours in a square ground. The other houses of the street, conscious of decent lives within them, gazed at one another with brown imperturbable faces.

Is this scene cheerful? Vital and active? Should we expect this story to celebrate the joys of growing up in Dublin? Negative responses to these questions arise from the tone of the opening description. Notice, for example, that the dead-end street is "blind"; that the school is said to "set the boys free," which makes it sound like a prison; that the uninhabited house is "detached from its neighbours"; and that the other houses, personified, gaze at one another with "brown imperturbable faces"—*brown* being a nondescript color and *imperturbable* reinforcing the still, lifeless, somber quality of the passage as a whole.

PLOT Through the series of events that make up a story's *plot*, an author presents us with a carefully created fictional world. In "Araby," the plot, or the arrangement of a connected sequence of narrative events, can be simply stated. A young boy who lives in a drab but respectable neighborhood develops a crush on his playmate's sister. She asks him if he intends to go to a charity fair that she cannot attend. He resolves to go and purchase a gift for her. He is tormented by the late and drunken arrival of his uncle, who has promised him the money he needs. When the boy finally arrives at the bazaar, he is disappointed by the difference between his expectation and the actuality of the almost deserted fair. He perceives some minor events, overhears some minor conversation, and the climax occurs when he confronts the darkened fair and the banal expression of sexual attraction between two gentlemen and a young woman. This sequence of events prompts the boy to see himself "as a creature driven and derided by vanity."

CHARACTERIZATION   One of the obvious differences between short stories and novels is that story writers develop *characters* rapidly and limit the number of developed characters. Many stories have only one fleshed-out, or *round*, character; the other characters are frequently two-dimensional, or *flat*. Rarely does a short story have more than three developed characters.

One feature that distinguishes "Araby" is its *characterization*, or the process by which the characters are rendered to make them seem real to the reader. Characterization, however, cannot easily be separated from the other elements of fiction; that is, it depends heavily on tone, plot, theme, setting, and so on. It is part of the boy's character, for example, that he lives in a brown imperturbable house on North Richmond Street, that he does the things he does (which constitute the plot of the story), and that he learns about what he does (which is the theme). Much of this characterization in "Araby" emerges from Joyce's rich *style*, or the way he uses language and images. Consider how the boy's character is revealed in the following paragraph:

> Her image accompanied me even in places the most hostile to romance. On Saturday evenings when my aunt went marketing I had to go to carry some of the parcels. We walked through the flaring streets, jostled by drunken men and bargaining women, amid the curses of labourers, the shrill litanies of shopboys who stood on guard by the barrels of pigs' cheeks, the nasal chanting of street-singers, who sang a *come-all-you* about O'Donovan Rossa, or a ballad about the troubles in our native land. These noises converged in a single sensation of life for me: I imagined that I bore my chalice safely through a throng of foes. Her name sprang to my lips at moments in strange prayers and praises which I myself did not understand. My eyes were often full of tears (I could not tell why) and at times a flood from my heart seemed to pour itself out into my bosom. I thought little of the future. I did not know whether I would ever speak to her or not or, if I spoke to her, how I could tell her of my confused adoration. But my body was like a harp and her words and gestures were like fingers running upon the wires.

In this passage, character is revealed through *diction*, or choice of words. By using the words *litanies, prayers,* and *adoration,* the narrator draws heavily from the distinctive vocabulary of the Roman Catholic Church. (The reference to the harp also reinforces the religious tone of the passage.) *Chalice* and *throng of foes* are related to this tradition as well; a chalice is a cup for the consecrated wine of the Eucharist, and throngs of foes often confronted the Christian martyrs whose deeds are immortalized in religious literature. At the same time, however, these last two phrases call up the world of chivalric romance, which is alluded to in the first line of the paragraph. The narrator's diction casts his awakening sexuality in the mold of high romance on the one hand and Christian devotion on the other. This sense of holy chivalry (reinforced by the earlier reference to the priest who owned a chivalric novel) stands in sharp contrast to the humdrum experience of carrying groceries home from the market.

SETTING   Unlike novels, short stories usually work themselves out in a restricted geographical *setting*—in a single place and within a short period of time. Any consideration of setting should include the historical time when a story takes place and the social situation set in the story, as well as the physical location of the events. In "Araby," the dreary details of Dublin are significantly described in the story's very first lines.

POINT OF VIEW   A character's or narrator's diction raises important questions about who is narrating the story. What is the narrator like? Is he reliable or unreliable? How can we judge? These questions help us distinguish another element of fiction, *point of view*. "Araby" is a *first-person narrative*; that is, the story is told from the perspective of a narrator who speaks in the first person. Most of the time, first-person narrators use the singular (*I, my*); in "A Rose for Emily" (p. 649), however, Faulkner's narrator uses the first person plural (*we, our*).

Third-person point of view—in which the narrator does not appear as a character in the story—is the most common perspective used to tell stories. Using third-person point of view, a narrator tells a story from the outside, referring to the characters as *she, he,* and *they*. A narrator who knows everything, can tell us what the characters are thinking, and can move around in space and time at will is an *omniscient narrator*. Alternatively, a narrator who chooses to focus on the thoughts, feelings, and actions of a single character is called a *limited omniscient narrator*. Generally, the brevity of the short story makes the first-person or limited omniscient narrations the most frequently used points of view for these works, while the lengthy and comparatively complex narrative of novels is more suited to the omniscient point of view.

A less frequently employed point of view is that of the second person, in which the author addresses the action to a character identified as *you*. For example, "You ask the clerk for change; he gives you four quarters. You go outside and wait for the bus." Although it evokes a rare intimacy with the reader, second-person point of view is difficult to sustain even in a short story.

IRONY   Authors' decisions about point of view create powerful narrative effects. Throughout "Araby," we sense a gap between the boy's sensibility and that of the more mature narrator, who refers at various times to his "innumerable follies" and "foolish blood." That is, we see the events of "Araby" from the boy's perspective, even though the language is that of an adult. The gap between the boy's knowledge and the narrator's creates *irony*.

There may be more than one level of irony at work in a story. When the narrator calls himself "a creature driven and derided by vanity," whose eyes "burned with anguish and anger," this overstatement is known as *verbal irony*. Some critics have maintained that the romanticized language of the story's conclusion itself invites an ironical reading—that is, we readers may know something about the narrator that he does not know himself—that he idealizes disenchantment as fervently as the boy idealized romance and religion.

In short, Joyce may be using *dramatic irony,* encouraging the reader to see things about the first-person narrator that he does not see about himself. Both kinds of irony hinge on differing levels of knowledge and the author's skillful manipulation of narrative perspective.

THEME   *Theme* is an underlying idea, a statement that a work makes about its subject. This tiny stretch of experience out of the boy's life introduces him to an awareness of the differences between imagination and reality, between his romantic infatuation and the vulgar reality all about him. The theme of "Araby" emerges from the drab setting and mundane events of the story as a general statement about an intensely idealized and childish love, the shattering recognition of the false sentimentality that occasions it, and the enveloping vulgarity of adult life. By detailing a few events from one boy's life, the story illuminates the painful loss of innocence we all endure. In this case, the *protagonist,* or main character, experiences what Joyce called an *epiphany,* or sudden flash of recognition, that signals the awareness of a set of moral complexities in a world that once seemed uncomplicated and predictable.

We often speak of tone, setting, plot, theme, characterization, and point of view as separate aspects of a story in order to break down a complex narrative into more manageable parts. But this analytic process of identifying various elements is something we have done to the story: the story (if it is a good one) is an integrated whole. The more closely we examine the separate elements, the clearer it becomes that each is integrally related to the others.

In "Araby," Joyce employs the methods of fiction to create a world based on 1895 Dublin and Irish middle-class society. The success or failure of the story depends on Joyce's ability to render that world convincingly and our willingness to enter it imaginatively. We must not refuse to engage that world because the characters do not act as we would have them act or because the events never actually happened. Novelist Henry James urged that readers allow the author to have his or her *donnée,* or "given." When we grant this, the act of reading fiction provides us with much more pleasure and emotional insight.

Here are some questions to ask as you set out to read or write about fiction. Your answers to these questions will help you brainstorm and develop the ideas that form your response to a story.

QUESTIONS FOR EXPLORING FICTION

1. WHAT IS THE TONE OF THE STORY? Does the tone change with the story's events or remain fixed? How does the tone contribute to the effect of the story?

2. WHAT IS THE PLOT OF THE STORY? Does the sequence of events that make up the plot emerge logically from the nature of the characters and circumstances? Or does the plot rely on coincidence and arbitrary events?

3. WHO ARE THE PRINCIPAL CHARACTERS IN THE STORY? What functions do the minor characters serve? Do any characters change during the course of the story? How and why?

4. WHAT IS THE SETTING OF THE STORY? Does it play an important role, or is it simply the place and time where things happen? How would some other setting affect the story?

5. FROM WHAT POINT OF VIEW IS THE NARRATOR TELLING THE STORY? Do you trust him or her?

6. WHAT IS THE THEME OF THE STORY?

7. DO YOU FIND AMBIGUITIES IN THE STORY? Does that ambiguity result in confusion, or does it add to the story's complexity?

8. DOES THE STORY SEEM TO SUPPORT OR CONFLICT WITH YOUR OWN POLITICAL AND MORAL POSITIONS?

9. WHEN WAS THE STORY WRITTEN? Draw on your knowledge of history and contemporary events as you read the story. Does the story clarify, enhance, or contradict your understanding of history?

10. CAN YOU CONNECT THE STORY TO ANYTHING ELSE YOU HAVE READ OR SEEN?

READING POETRY

Reading poetry is unlike the other reading you do. To appreciate the sounds and meaning of a poem, it is best to start by reading it aloud. Some poems are straightforward, requiring little analysis; others are more dense and complex. Try reading the poem "When I Heard the Learn'd Astronomer" (1865) by Walt Whitman out loud.

> When I heard the learn'd astronomer,
> When the proofs, the figures, were ranged in columns before me,
> When I was shown the charts and diagrams, to add, divide, and measure them,
> When I sitting heard the astronomer where he lectured with much
>   applause in the lecture-room,
> How soon unaccountable I became tired and sick,
> Till rising and gliding out I wander'd off by myself,
> In the mystical moist night-air, and from time to time,
> Look'd up in perfect silence at the stars.

Whitman's distinction between mind (intellectual knowledge) and heart (emotion and feelings) is an old but a useful one. Compelled to analyze, dissect, categorize, and classify, the poem's narrator finally yearns for the simple pleasure of unanalytical enjoyment—to look up "in perfect silence at the stars." You may very well enjoy a poem without recognizing its patterns of imagery or the intricate way its author weaves together the past and the present. But understanding the elements of poetry will allow you to use analysis to enhance your emotional response to a poem—and thereby deepen the pleasure a poem can give you.

Poems have to be read with great intensity but without any sense of urgency. Reading with a relaxed but complete mindfulness, try to slow down, pay attention, and allow the language of the poem to work.

Word Choice

Once you have listened to the poem, what should you pay attention to next? Start with the words that make up the poem. *Where* a poem takes the reader is inseparable from *how* it takes the reader. Poets pay especially close attention to diction, or their choice of words; every word in a poem counts. In your everyday reading, you encounter unfamiliar words and phrases, and figure out their meanings from the contexts in which they occur. Reading poetry requires even more scrupulous attention to unusual words and phrases. Here, again, making connections will help you get the most out of your reading. Look for words or images that repeat or change as a poem continues. Finding patterns can be the first step in developing an interpretive reading of a poem.

Critics often describe poetry as "heightened language," meaning that the poet strives for precision and richness in the words he or she uses. For the poet, "precision" and "richness" are not contradictory. Words have dictionary, or *denotative*, meanings as well as associative, or *connotative*, meanings; they also have histories and relationships with other words. The English language is rich in synonyms—words whose denotative meanings are roughly the same but whose connotations vary widely (*excite, stimulate, titillate, inflame; poor, impoverished, indigent, destitute*). Many words are identical in sound and often in spelling but differ in meaning (*forepaws, four paws; lie* ["recline"], *lie* ["fib"]). The meanings of words have changed over time, and the poet may deliberately select a word whose older meaning adds a dimension to the poem.

Figurative Language

Figurative language is the general term we use to describe the many devices of language that allow us to speak nonliterally in order to achieve some special effect. Figurative language makes a comparison between the thing being written about and something else that allows the reader to better picture or understand it. When Robert Burns compares his love to a red rose in his poem "A Red, Red Rose" (p. 909), he abandons literal language because the emotional energy of his thoughts can be expressed more effectively in figurative language.

Figurative language allows us—and the poet—to use *imagery* to transcend both the confinement of the literal and the vagueness of the abstract. The world is revealed to us through our senses—sight, sound, taste, touch, and smell. Through imagery, the poet creates a recognizable world by drawing on this fund of common experiences. The difference between good and bad poetry often turns on the skill with which imagery (or other figurative language) is used. Bad poetry is often bad because the imagery is stale ("golden sunset," "the smiling sun," "the rolling sea") or so skimpy that the poem dissolves into vague and meaningless abstraction.

Consider these familiar old sayings: "The grass is always greener on the other side of the fence"; "A bird in the hand is worth two in the bush"; "The early bird catches the worm." Although these sayings make literal sense (the grass you see from a distance looks greener than the grass under your feet), their meaning to a native speaker of English is clearly not literal. When we use them, we are making general and highly abstract observations about human attitudes and behavior. Yet these generalizations and abstractions are embodied in *concrete* imagery. Try to explain what any of these expressions mean and you will quickly discover that you are using many more words and much vaguer language than the expression itself uses. This is precisely what happens when you try to paraphrase or put into your own words the language of a poem. Like poetry, these sayings rely on the figurative use of language.

METAPHOR   Because poetry is an intense and heightened use of language, it relies on more frequent and original use of figurative language than does ordinary speech. One of the most common figurative devices, *metaphor,* in which one thing is compared to something else, occurs frequently in everyday language. "School is a rat race," or "That issue is a minefield for the mayor," we say, and the meaning is vividly clear. When W. H. Auden, commenting on the death of William Butler Yeats, says, "Let the Irish vessel lie/Emptied of his poetry," he pays a complex tribute to the great Irish poet with a metaphor that compels readers to confront not only the loss of a man but also the loss of his poetic voice.

SIMILE   *Simile* is closely related to metaphor. But where metaphor says that one thing *is* another, simile says that one thing *is like* another, as in Robert Burns's "O My Luve's like a red, red rose" and Frost's "life is too much like a pathless wood" (p. 187). The distinction between simile and metaphor, while easy enough to make technically, is often difficult to distinguish in terms of effect. Frost establishes a comparison between life and a pathless wood and keeps the two even more fully separated by adding the qualifier "too much." Burns's simile maintains the same separation and, in addition, because it occurs in the opening line of the poem, eliminates any possible confusion the reader might experience if the line were "O My Luve is a red, red rose." You can test the difference in effect by changing a metaphor into a simile or a simile into a metaphor to see if the meaning is in any way altered.

PERSONIFICATION   *Personification,* another device of figurative language, attributes human qualities to things or ideas. Personification can make an abstract thing more understandable in terms of human form, emotion, or action. For example, when John Donne, in his poem "Death, Be Not Proud" (p. 1220), exclaims "Death, thou shalt die," he transforms the abstraction of death into a human adversary (while also creating a memorable *paradox*).

ALLUSION   *Allusion* to other literary works, persons, places, or events enables poets to call up associations and contexts that complicate and enrich their poems. Whether these allusions are obvious or subtle, they draw on knowledge shared by the poet and the reader. In T. S. Eliot's dense and difficult "The Love Song of J. Alfred Prufrock" (p. 675), the speaker says at one point, "I have seen my head (grown slightly bald) brought in upon a platter." A reader familiar with the New Testament might recognize this allusion to John the Baptist's decapitation and better understand Prufrock's sense of spiritual desolation. The association Eliot makes brings an added, intensified layer of meaning to the work.

SYMBOLS A *symbol*, in its broadest sense, is anything that stands for some thing else. In this sense, most words are symbolic: the word *tree* stands for an object in the real world. When we speak of a symbol in a literary work, however, we mean something more precise. In poetry, a symbol is an object or event that suggests more than itself. It is one of the most common and powerful devices available to the poet, for it allows him or her to convey economically and simply a wide range of meanings.

It is useful to distinguish between two kinds of symbols: *public symbols* and *contextual symbols*. Public symbols are those objects or events that history has invested with rich meanings and associations—for example, national flags or religious objects such as a cross. Yeats uses such a symbol in his poem "Sailing to Byzantium" (p. 1227), drawing on the celebrated and enduring art of the ancient Byzantine Empire as a symbol of timelessness.

In contrast to public symbols, contextual symbols are objects or events that are symbolic by virtue of the poet's handling of them in a particular work— that is, by virtue of the context. Consider, for example, the opening lines of Robert Frost's "After Apple-Picking" (p. 1229).

> My long two-pointed ladder's sticking through a tree
> Toward heaven still,
> And there's a barrel that I didn't fill
> Beside it, and there may be two or three
> Apples I didn't pick upon some bough.

The apple tree is a literal tree, but it also symbolizes the speaker's life, with a wide range of possible meanings (do the few unpicked apples symbolize the dreams that even the fullest life cannot satisfy?). Contextual symbols tend to present more interpretive difficulties than public symbols do because recognizing them depends on a sensitivity to everything else in the poem.

The Music of Poetry

A number of terms describe the various sound patterns that project the *music* of poetry. Of these, *rhyme*—the repetition of the final stressed vowel sound and any sounds following—is the best known: *brow, now; debate, relate;* and so on. *Alliteration,* or the repetition of a consonant sound, usually at the beginning of words in close proximity, is also common: "*besiege* thy *brow*." Alliteration is frequently used to underscore key words and ideas.

Rhythm, created by the relationship between stressed and unstressed syllables, is another way poets can convey meaning. The pattern formed when the lines of a poem follow a recurrent or similar rhythm is the poem's *meter*. The smallest repeated unit in this pattern is called a *foot*. Looking, for example, at the first line of one of Shakespeare's sonnets, we see that the foot consists of an *iamb*—an unstressed syllable followed by a stressed one:

When forty winters shall besiege thy brow.

Because the line consists of five iambs, or sets of unstressed syllables followed by stressed ones, it is called *iambic pentameter*. (If the line had four iambic feet, it would be in iambic tetrameter; if six, iambic hexameter; and so on.)

Other metrical feet include the *trochee, anapest, dactyl,* and *spondee* (all of which are defined in the "Glossary of Literary Terms"); but such terms are the tools of literary study and not its object. Perhaps the most important thing to remember about meter is that it should not be mistaken for the actual rhythm of the poem. Instead, it is best thought of as a kind of ideal rhythm that the poem can play against. Meter suggests certain patterns that invite expectations that may or may not be satisfied. Much of the poet's art consists of crafting variations of sound and rhythm to create specific effects.

Some of these effects are illustrated nicely in the following passage from Alexander Pope's "An Essay on Criticism," in which the definitions of bad and good *verse* are ingeniously supported by the music of the lines.

These[1] equal syllables alone require,
Though oft the ear the open vowels tire;
While expletives their feeble aid do join;
And ten low words oft creep in one dull line;
While they ring round the same unvaried chimes,
With sure returns of still expected rhymes;
Where'er you find "the cooling western breeze,"
In the next line, it "whispers through the trees";
If crystal streams "with pleasing murmurs creep,"
The reader's threatened (not in vain) with "sleep";
Then, at the last and only couplet fraught
With some unmeaning thing they call a thought,
A needless Alexandrine[2] ends the song
That, like a wounded snake, drags its slow length along.

. . . . .

True ease in writing comes from art, not chance,
As those move easiest who have learned to dance.
'Tis not enough no harshness gives offense,
The sound must seem an echo to the sense:

---

[1] Bad poets.
[2] Twelve-syllable line or a line with six rhythmic feet. As in Pope's example, *alexandrines* often follow lines of pentameter, or lines with five metrical feet.

> Soft is the strain when Zephyr gently blows,
> And the smooth stream in smoother numbers flows;
> But when loud surges lash the sounding shore,
> The hoarse, rough verse should like the torrent roar:
> When Ajax[3] strives some rock's vast weight to throw,
> The line too labors, and the words move slow;
> Not so, when swift Camilla[4] scours the plain,
> Flies o'er the unbending corn, and skims along the main.

When the speaker condemns the use of ten monosyllables, the line contains ten monosyllables: "And ten low words oft creep in one dull line." When he speaks of the wind, the line is rich in hissing sounds that imitate that wind. When he speaks of Ajax striving, clusters of consonants and stressed syllables combine to slow the line; when he speaks of Camilla's swiftness, the final consonants and initial sounds form liaisons that can be pronounced swiftly.

Analysis of this sort can illuminate and enrich our understanding of poetry, but it does not exhaust the significance of a poem. As the poet Dylan Thomas once remarked,

> You can tear a poem apart to see what makes it technically tick and say to yourself when the works are laid out before you—the vowels, the consonants, the rhymes, and rhythms—"Yes, this is it. This is why the poem moves me so. It is because of the craftsmanship." But you're back where you began. The best craftsmanship always leaves holes and gaps in the works of the poem so that something that is not in the poem can creep, crawl, flash, or thunder in.

A truly fine poem not only repays attention to its formal features but also points beyond its technique to something more sensuous and less domesticated.

Here are some questions to ask when you face the task of reading and writing about poetry.

QUESTIONS FOR EXPLORING POETRY

1. WHO IS THE SPEAKER? What does the poem reveal about the speaker's character? Do you think you can trust this speaker? In some poems the speaker may be nothing more than a voice meditating on a theme, while in others the speaker takes on a specific personality.

2. IS THE SPEAKER ADDRESSING A PARTICULAR PERSON? If so, who is that person, and why is the speaker interested in him or her?

3. DOES THE POEM HAVE A SETTING? Is the poem occasioned by a particular event?

4. IS THE THEME OF THE POEM STATED DIRECTLY OR INDIRECTLY? From what particular lines or words can you identify the theme of the poem?

---

[3] A Greek warrior celebrated for his strength.
[4] A swift-footed queen in Virgil's *Aeneid*.

5. FROM WHAT PERSPECTIVE IS THE SPEAKER DESCRIBING SPECIFIC EVENTS? Is the speaker recounting events of the past or events that are occurring in the present? If past events are being recalled, what present meaning do they have for the speaker?

6. DOES A CLOSE EXAMINATION OF THE FIGURATIVE LANGUAGE OF THE POEM REVEAL ANY PATTERNS? See p. 12 and "Glossary of Literary Terms."

7. WHAT IS THE STRUCTURE OF THE POEM? Since narrative poems—those that tell stories—reveal a high degree of selectivity, it is useful to ask why the poet has focused on particular details and left out others. Analyzing the structure of a nonnarrative or lyric poem can be more difficult because it does not contain an obvious series of chronologically related events. The structure of the poem will be revealed through an analysis of patterns of images that embody the theme.

8. WHAT DO SOUND AND METER (SEE "GLOSSARY OF LITERARY TERMS") CONTRIBUTE TO THE POEM?

9. WHAT WAS YOUR RESPONSE TO THE POEM ON FIRST READING? Did your response change after study of the poem or class discussions about it?

READING DRAMA

Drama is fundamentally different from other literary forms. Unlike fiction, for example, most plays are designed to be performed in public and not read in private. The public nature of drama is reflected in the words we use to discuss it. The word *drama* itself is derived from the Greek word for "action, deed, or performance," and *theater* derives from the Greek word for "sight or contemplation." By their nature, plays are more spectacular than poems or works of fiction. Directors and their staffs pay great attention to costumes, set design, lights, and stage movement; the reader, who doesn't experience these elements, must imagine the action on the basis of words alone. Dramatists use words as starting points for, rather than realizations of, their artistic visions.

Although plays typically lack narration and description—they are designed to show, not tell—they can be considered in terms of setting, plot, theme, characterization, and irony. Indeed, these notions are even more important in drama than in fiction, where narrative style and point of view carry great weight, or in poetry, where diction and imagery are central.

As much as possible, the way to read a play is to imagine that you are its director. In this role you must visualize yourself creating the set and the lighting. You will envision people dressed so that their clothes give support to their words. You will think about timing (how long between events and speeches) and blocking (how the characters move as they interact on stage). Perhaps the best way to confront the literature of the stage, to respond most fully to what is there, is to attempt to produce some scenes either in class or after class. If possible, attend the plays or the rehearsals of plays in production on campus. Nothing will provide better insight into the complexities of the theater than attending a rehearsal where the problems are encountered and solved.

As you read any of the opening speeches of any of the plays in this anthology, imagine yourself the director and make decisions. How should the lines be spoken (quietly, angrily, haltingly)? What should the characters do as they speak (remain stationary, look in some direction, traverse the stage)? How should the stage be lit (partially, brightly, in some color that contributes to the mood of the dialogue and action)? What should the characters who are not speaking do? What possibilities exist for conveying appropriate signals solely through gesture and facial expression—signals not contained in the words you read?

Stages and Staging

Although staging is more important to spectators than to readers, some knowledge of staging history can enrich your reading of a play. For example, it helps to know that in the Greek theater of Dionysus in Athens (below), there was no scene shifting. In Sophocles' *Antigonê* (p. 468), which was staged in an open-air amphitheater seating about 14,000 people, actors entered from the *skene,* or a fixed-stage house, which might have had painted panels to suggest a scene. Important events, especially violent ones, occur offstage, and the audience learns of these events from a messenger, who comes onstage to describe them. This convention was partly a matter of taste, but the conditions of the Greek stage also prevented Sophocles from moving the action to another scene. Later dramatists, writing for a more flexible stage and a more intimate theater, exploited the dramatic possibilities of such violence.

The vast outdoor theater imposed restrictions on acting style. Facial expressions played no role in the actor's craft; in fact, the actors wore large masks, which were probably equipped with some sort of megaphone to amplify speech.

The Theatre of Dionysus in Athens

As a result, it was difficult to modulate speech to create subtle effects, and the speeches were probably delivered in formal, declamatory style. In addition to these limitations, the Athenian government made available only three principal actors, all male, as the cast (excluding the *chorus,* a group of citizens that commented on the action and characters) for each play. Consequently, there were never more than three players onstage at once, and the roles were designed so that each actor could take several parts, each signified by a different mask.

Shakespeare's stage was altogether different from Sophocles'. Although both theaters were open-air, the enclosure around the Elizabethan stage was much smaller than the Greek amphitheater, and the theater's capacity was limited to between 2,000 and 3,000 spectators. As in classical drama, men played all the roles, but they no longer wore masks. The stage protruded into the audience, allowing for more intimacy and a greater range of speech, gesture, and expression. Even so, and despite Hamlet's advice to the troupe "to hold as 't were, the mirror up to nature," Shakespearean *tragedy* did not lend itself to a modern realistic style. Those great speeches are written in verse; they are frequently meant to augment the meager set design with verbal imagery; and they are much denser in texture, image, and import than is ordinary speech. Most of the important action was played out on the uncurtained main platform, jutting into the audience and surrounded on three sides by spectators. The swiftly moving scenes followed each other without interruption, doubtless using different areas of the stage to signify different locations. There was some sort of terrace or balcony one story above the main stage, and there was an area at the back of the main protruding stage that could be curtained off when not in use. Although Shakespeare's plays are usually

Interior of the Swan Theatre, London, 1596

Hypothetical reconstruction of the interior of the Globe Theatre in the days of Shakespeare

divided into five separate acts in printed versions, they were played straight through, without intermission, much like a modern motion picture. These characteristics distinguish the Shakespearean stage from the familiar realism of most contemporary theater.

Much current theater uses a *box stage*—essentially a box with one wall removed so that the audience can see into the playing area. The box stage lends itself to realistic settings. It can easily be furnished to look like a room; or, if outdoor scenes are required, painted backdrops and angled sets provide perspective. Shortly after the introduction of the box stage, the possibilities for scenic design produced great set designers and increasingly sophisticated stage machinery. These new possibilities, in turn, freed the dramatist from the physical limitations imposed by earlier stages.

By the late nineteenth century, the versatility of the box stage enabled playwrights such as Henrik Ibsen to write detailed stage settings for the various locations in which the drama unfolds. Further, the furnishing of the stage in Ibsen's plays sometimes functions symbolically to visually reinforce the claustrophobic quality of the bourgeois life depicted in his plays. Later dramatists have relied on realistic settings to convey meaning and to serve symbolic functions. The modern production may take place in a theater that is simply a large empty room (with provisions for technical flexibility in the matter of lighting) that can be rearranged to suit the requirements of specific productions. This ideal of a "theater space" that can be freely manipulated has become increasingly attractive since it frees the dramatist and the performance from limitations built into permanent stage design.

A seventeenth-century French box stage

The Elements of Drama

CHARACTERS Plays usually consist of narratives with plots, settings, themes, characters, and irony, and most plays have no narrators as such. In Greek drama, the chorus functions as a kind of narrator. In Shakespearean drama, the *soliloquy*, in which an actor speaks thoughts aloud, allows the audience to hear what a character is thinking. But in most plays, the story unfolds before our eyes without the intervention of an authorial voice or point of view.

Without a narrator to tell us what a character is thinking, we usually infer a character's thoughts by his or her actions and demeanor, and by *dialogue*, or the words a character speaks to others. Characterization, in plays as in fiction, is a process by which the author establishes the personality of a character, revealed through what the particular character does and says, and by what other characters say. The main character, the hero or *protagonist*, is the center of our attention. He or she is often opposed by another major character, the *antagonist*, whose opposition creates the central conflict of the drama. The protagonist and the antagonist, as well as other characters of major significance in the drama, have a vital interest in the outcome of the action, and grow and develop as the action progresses and are therefore described as *rounded* characters. Those characters who are peripheral to the action, who often supply the kind of exposition a third-person narrator does in fiction, are minor, or *flat*, characters.

DRAMATIC IRONY   *Dramatic irony* allows the audience to know more than the characters do about their own circumstances by letting the audience hear more than the characters hear. Shakespeare's *Othello* (p. 947) provides an excellent illustration of the uses of dramatic irony. At the end of act II, Cassio, who has lost his position as Othello's lieutenant, asks Iago for advice on how to regain favor. Iago, who, unknown to Cassio, had engineered Cassio's disgrace, advises him to ask Desdemona, Othello's adored wife, to intervene. Actually this is good advice; ordinarily the tactic would succeed, so much does Othello love his wife and wish to please her. But Iago explains, in a soliloquy to the audience, that he is laying groundwork for the ruin of all the objects of his envy and hatred—Cassio, Desdemona, and Othello:

> . . . for while this honest fool
> Plies Desdemona to repair his fortunes,
> And she for him pleads strongly to the Moor,
> I'll pour this pestilence into his ear
> That she repeals him for her body's lust;
> And, by how much she strives to do him good,
> She shall undo her credit with the Moor.
> So will I turn her virtue into pitch,
> And out of her goodness make the net
> That shall enmesh them all.

Of course, Desdemona, Cassio, and Othello are ignorant of Iago's enmity. Worse, all of them consider Iago a loyal friend. But the audience knows Iago's design, and that knowledge provides the chilling dramatic irony of act III, scene 3.

All the emotional tautness in the audience results from irony, from knowing what the victims do not know. But dramatic irony is the special tool of the dramatist, well suited to produce an electric tension in a live audience that watches and overhears the action onstage.

PLOT AND CONFLICT   Plays often portray oppositions between characters or groups or even between two aspects of a character's personality. This opposition often takes the form of a *conflict* that drives the plot. In *Othello*, for example, a variety of conflicts shapes the action of the play. Most obviously, Iago's scheming puts Othello in conflict with Cassio, and turns him against Desdemona. But conflicts can be less literal: Othello and Desdemona's marriage puts them at odds with Venetian society, raising larger questions about race and culture. And conflicts can be within a single character: Othello's jealousy triggers conflicting emotions about himself and about his wife.

Understanding the methods of drama can help us analyze a play and its various effects. But such analysis only gestures at the emotional experience produced by successful drama. More than other forms of literature, plays give physical expression to the social and psychological conflicts that define us individually and collectively. As in *Othello*, a play may torment its audience by imposing on admirable characters unfair circumstances that will result in tragic deaths. Or, as in Susan Glaspell's *Trifles* (p. 1050), a play may mock prevalent attitudes and compel an audience to reexamine its values. By giving expression to human impulses and conflicts, plays enact our most persistent concerns with the greatest possible intensity.

A traditional and still useful way of looking at the plot of a play is to see it in five parts: exposition, rising action, climax, falling action, and denouement. *Exposition* provides the audience with information about background matters important to the play. The first part of the plot also includes *rising action*, as the plot progresses toward complexity and conflict, which reaches a crisis, or *climax*, of some sort. This is the turning point of the play, when the protagonist must act decisively or make a critical choice from which there is no turning back. This in turn leads to the *falling action*, as the protagonist confronts the inexorable consequences of his or her act or decision. The play ends with the *denouement* (French for "untying or unraveling"), with the conflict resolved or the mystery solved. Although this template cannot be applied to every play, it comes close enough in describing the structure of many plays to make it a useful tool for analyzing much drama.

Here are some more specific questions to ask when you begin to read or write about drama. Write out your answers to check your understanding of a play or to begin collecting ideas for an essay assignment.

QUESTIONS FOR EXPLORING DRAMA

1. HOW DOES THE PLAY BEGIN? Is the exposition presented dramatically as characters interact, novelistically through long speeches that convey a lot of information, or through some device such as a messenger who delivers long letters or lengthy reports?

2. HOW DOES THE INFORMATION CONVEYED IN EXPOSITION ESTABLISH THE BASIS FOR DRAMATIC IRONY? Does the audience know more than the characters do? How does that irony create tension in the audience?

3. WHO ARE THE PRINCIPAL CHARACTERS? How are the distinctive qualities of each dramatically conveyed? How do they change as the play proceeds? Are they sympathetic? What function do the minor characters serve?

4. WHERE IS THE PLAY SET? Why does it matter that it is set there? Does the setting play a significant role in the drama, or is it merely a place, any place?

5. WHAT IS THE CENTRAL CONFLICT IN THE PLAY? Is the central conflict between characters, between groups, or even between two parts of a character's personality? How is it resolved? Is the resolution satisfying?

6. WHAT IS THE CONTEXT FOR THE PLAY? Do you need to know the historical circumstances out of which the play emerged or something of the life of the author to appreciate the play fully? If so, how does the information enhance your understanding?

7. WHAT VISUAL AND AUDITORY ELEMENTS OF THE PLAY EFFECT YOUR RESPONSE TO THE PLAY? Since plays are usually written to be performed rather than read, place yourself in the position of the director and the actors to respond to this aspect of drama if you are reading a text.

8. WHAT IS THE PLAY'S THEME? How does the dramatic action embody that theme?

9. HOW DOES THE PLAY END? How does the ending connect to the beginning—or any other specific points—of the play?

10. HAS THE PLAY BEEN MADE INTO A FILM? In the adaptation, what has been added and what has been deleted? How does this production compare with your reading of the play?

READING NONFICTION

Essays differ from fiction in that they generally do not create imaginary worlds inhabited by fictional characters. We know, for example, through media accounts and the testimony of his friends, that Martin Luther King Jr. was indeed jailed in Birmingham, Alabama, where he wrote his famous argument for social justice, "Letter from Birmingham Jail" (p. 533). And, although we cannot independently verify that George Orwell actually shot an elephant (p. 816), his work exhibits the formal nonfictional qualities of the essay rather than the imagined world of the short story.

Writers turn to the essay form when they wish to confront their readers directly with an idea, a problem (often with a proposed solution), an illuminating experience, an important definition, or some flaw (or virtue) in the social system. Usually, the essay is relatively short, and almost always embodies the writer's personal viewpoint. And although the essay may share many elements with other literary forms, it generally speaks with the voice of a real person about the real world. The term *essay* derives from the French verb *essayer*—"try, attempt." That verb, in turn, derives from the Latin verb *exigere*—"weigh out, examine."

While the French term calls attention to the personal perspective that characterizes the essay, the Latin verb suggests that an essay can not only examine personal experiences but can also explore and clarify ideas by arguing for or against a position.

As you read an essay, you need to ask yourself, What is the central argument or idea? Sometimes the answer is obvious, sometimes less so. In some cases, essays do not argue for one thing in particular, but rather meditate on human experience and address the inner lives of their readers. John Donne's "Meditation XVII" (p. 1288), for example, does not attack or justify anything.

Rather, it reminds us to be aware of our mortality and thereby to alter our interactions with or perceptions of the people around us.

Types of Nonfiction

If you have taken a composition course, you may have read and written narrative, descriptive, expository, and argumentative essays. While reviewing the characteristics of each of these types, keep in mind that in the real world, authors of essays are more interested in effectiveness than in purity of form, and frequently combine features of different formal types.

NARRATIVE NONFICTION Narrative essays recount a sequence of related events and are often autobiographical. But those events are chosen because they suggest or illustrate some larger insight or problem. In "Shooting an Elephant" (p. 816), for example, George Orwell narrates an episode from his life that led him to an important insight about imperialism. In Maxine Hong Kingston's "No Name Woman" (p. 1073) the narrator's reflections on the significance of her aunt's suicide in China many years ago, a tragic family secret that still haunts her, powerfully illustrate the deep connection between past and present and the troubling idea that family and culture can oppress. In these narrative essays, the writers discover in their own experiences the evidence for generalizations about themselves and their societies.

DESCRIPTIVE NONFICTION Descriptive essays depict sensory observations in words. They evoke in the reader's imagination the sights and sounds, perhaps even the smells, that transport the reader to such places as George Orwell's Burma. The descriptive essay, like the narrative essay, often addresses complex issues that trouble our lives, but it does so by appealing primarily to sensory awareness—sight, sound, touch, taste, smell—rather than to intellect. The power of description is so great that narrative and expository essays often use lengthy descriptive passages to communicate forcefully.

EXPOSITORY NONFICTION Expository essays attempt to explain and elucidate, to organize and provide information. Often they embody an extended definition of a complex conception such as love or patriotism; other times, they describe a process—how to do something. This book's coverage of essays, for example, is clearly not narrative because it doesn't depend for its form on a chronological sequence of meaningful events. It is not descriptive in the pure sense of that type because it does not depend on conveying sensory impressions. It is, in fact, expository. It acquaints its readers with the techniques and types of essays and provides some tips to help students read essays both analytically and pleasurably. Many of these approaches involve making some kind of connection. You may recognize a number of rhetorical strategies from writing courses you may have taken. We *classify* essays by type; we *compare and contrast* them; we use *definition;* we give *examples* to make a point; we imply that there is a *cause-and-effect* relationship between what readers bring to an essay and the pleasure they derive from it. Similarly, the essayists represented in this book use a variety of such rhetorical strategies to achieve their aims.

ARGUMENTATIVE NONFICTION　Although Orwell's "Shooting an Elephant" can be categorized as a narrative essay, we might reasonably assert that it is also argumentative because it is designed to convince readers that imperialism is as destructive to the oppressors as to the oppressed. The argumentative essay wishes to persuade its readers. Thus, it usually deals with controversial ideas, marshals arguments and evidence to support a view, and anticipates and answers opposing arguments. Martin Luther King Jr. accomplishes all these ends in his "Letter from Birmingham Jail" (p. 533). So does Jonathan Swift in "A Modest Proposal" (p. 500), with an approach complicated by his reliance on irony and satire.

Analyzing Nonfiction

THE THESIS　The best way to begin analyzing an essay is to ask, What is the point of this piece of writing; What is the author trying to show, attack, defend, or prove? If you can answer that question satisfactorily and succinctly, then the analysis of the essay's elements (i.e., its rhetorical strategies, structure, style, tone, and language) becomes easier. E. L. Doctorow's "Why We Are Infidels" (p. 517), for example, projects a clear thesis. On the other hand, a much more complex and ambitious essay, such as Virginia Woolf's "What If Shakespeare Had Had a Sister?" (p. 804), does not yield up its thesis quite so easily. We might say that Woolf's examination of the historical record leads her to argue that women did not write during the Elizabethan period because literary talent could not flourish in a social system that made women the ill-educated property of men. This formulation of the essay's thesis, as you will see when you read the essay, leaves a good deal out—notably the exhortation to action with which Woolf concludes the piece.

STRUCTURE AND DETAIL　Read carefully the first and last paragraphs of a number of essays. Note the writers' strategy for engaging you at the outset with an irresistible proposition:

> In Moulmein, in lower Burma, I was hated by large numbers of people—the only time in my life that I have been important enough for this to happen to me.

> If I speak in the tongues of men and of angels, but have not love, I am a noisy gong or a clanging cymbal.

> I was saved from sin when I was going on thirteen.

These opening sentences are startling, hooking readers so that they will eagerly read on to find out what it was that made the writer so hated in Burma, why love is so important, how Langston Hughes was saved from sin. You will find that the opening lines of most well-wrought essays instantly capture your attention.

Endings, too, are critical. And if you examine the concluding lines of any of the essays in this collection, you will find forceful assertions that sharply focus the matter that precedes them. Essayists, unsurprisingly, systematically use gripping beginnings and forceful endings.

What come between those beginnings and endings are often abstract issues—the nature of love, the inevitability of death, the evils of imperialism. Though such abstractions do significantly influence our lives, as subject matter for reading they seem impersonal and distant. Reading about great ideas becomes a sort of academic task, relegated to some intellectual sphere, separate from the pain and passion of our own humanity. The accomplished essay writer, however, entices us to confront such issues by converting abstract ideas into concrete and illustrative detail.

STYLE AND TONE The word *style* refers to all the writing skills that contribute to the effect of any piece of literature. And *tone*—the attitude conveyed by the language a writer chooses—is a particularly significant aspect of writing style. As an illustration of the effect of tone, consider these opening lines of two essays—Martin Luther King Jr.'s "Letter from Birmingham Jail" and Langston Hughes's "Salvation":

> While confined here in the Birmingham city jail, I came across your recent statement calling my present activities "unwise and untimely." Seldom do I pause to answer criticism of my work and ideas. If I sought to answer all the criticisms that cross my desk, my secretaries would have little time for anything other than such correspondence in the course of the day, and I would have no time for constructive work. But since I feel that you are men of genuine good will and that your criticisms are sincerely set forth, I want to try to answer your statement in what I hope will be patient and reasonable terms.

> I was saved from sin when I was going on thirteen. But not really saved. It happened like this. There was a big revival at my Auntie Reed's church. Every night for weeks there had been much preaching, singing, praying, and shouting, and some very hardened sinners had been brought to Christ, and the membership of the church had grown by leaps and bounds. Then just before the revival ended, they held a special meeting for children, "to bring the young lambs to the fold."

Both first-person accounts use provocative openings, immediately hooking the reader. King's tone, however, is formal; consider his grave rhythm ("Seldom do I pause") and diction ("If I sought to answer"), and his mature and studied word choices: *confined, statement, correspondence, constructive, sincerely, patient, reasonable.*

Hughes's tone, in his first-person account, is personal and informal. He uses colloquial diction ("It happened like this," "leaps and bounds") and a sardonic wit ("some very hardened sinners had been brought to Christ"). Although a reminiscing adult describes the event, the writer creates the voice of a child by using simple grammar and a child's vocabulary.

The tone a writer creates contributes substantially to the message he or she conveys. Jonathan Swift might have written a sound, academic essay about the economic diseases of Ireland and how to cure them—but his invention of the speaker of "A Modest Proposal," who ironically and sardonically proposes the establishment of a human-baby meat-exporting industry, jars the readers in ways no scholarly essay could. The high seriousness of Donne's tone in "Meditation XVII" perfectly suits his contemplation of the relationship among the living, the dying, and the dead.

Style is a more difficult quality to define than tone is. Dictionaries define *style* as both "a manner of expression in language" and "excellence in expression." Certainly it is easier to distinguish between various *manners* of expression than it is to describe just what constitutes *excellence* in expression. For example, the manners of expression of John Donne in "Meditation XVII" (p. 1288) and of Judith Ortiz Cofer in "American History" (p. 302) clearly differ. The first muses about death, God, alienation, and community in a style characterized by formality and complex extended images. The second uses the conversational style of a memoirist to evoke a particular moment in her life that has larger resonance in the story of twentieth-century America. Although Cofer considers some of the same broad themes as Donne does, her perspective, focus, and conclusions are entirely different, and this difference is reflected in the tone and style of the piece.

Despite their vast differences, we can describe the excellence of each style. Donne, an Anglican priest, meditates on the community of all living humans and the promise of eternal life in the face of physical death. He evokes a remarkable image when he states that "all mankind is of one author." Not so remarkable, you might argue; God is often called the "author of mankind." But why? This image is powerful not just because it is an apt metaphor but because it is an apt metaphor that famously appears in the opening lines of the Gospel according to John in the Bible tells us that "[i]n the beginning was the Word, . . . and the Word was God." Donne develops this idea, further insisting on the intimate relationship among all people because humankind "is one volume." Then he extends this metaphor by arguing that "when one man dies, one chapter is not torn out of the book, but translated into a better language." The vivid image is further extended. "God," Donne tells us, "employs several translators; some pieces are translated by age, some by sickness, some by war, some by justice." By alluding to the actual making of a book by the bookbinder, Donne elaborates on the central image and reestablishes the idea of community: "God's hand is in every translation, and his hand shall bind up all our scattered leaves again for that library where every book shall lie open to one another." Donne alludes to the Bible repeatedly throughout the essay, adding layers to the significance of the "holy book" image and further demonstrating his own faith by showing the depths of his biblical knowledge. The complexity and aptness of Donne's figurative characterization of death is a remarkable stylistic achievement, and one need not share his beliefs to be impressed by his mastery of his medium.

By contrast, Judith Ortiz Cofer's very specific examination of some apparently irreparable rifts in the "human volume" opens with a reference to *Ripley's Believe It or Not,* hardly an exalted cultural allusion and one whose words suggest anything but faith. While Donne argues—in language some readers might find alienating—that we are all connected by God, Cofer attempts a more earthly connection, using everyday language and popular references that she expects contemporary American readers to recognize and grasp immediately. For many of her readers, the Kennedy assassination became the ultimate where-were-you-when-you-heard moment, and the emotional resonance of the reference is as historically specific as Donne's references are not. While Donne's imagery seems intended to convey timeless religious truths, Cofer's brings to mind worldly divisions: even their shared grief over President Kennedy cannot bridge the various cultural divides between the young narrator and her neighbors. Her Catholicism implicitly separates her from white Protestant America and connects her to the martyred Kennedy, yet teenage heartache is more meaningful to the narrator than the death of Kennedy or any comfort or meaning that faith might provide. Indeed, looking toward heaven for answers is registered as a kind of denial in Cofer's essay: even as the girl looks up into the falling snow, she cannot keep from her mind the knowledge that it will get dirty the minute it touches her urban backyard. The "veil" of snow evokes nuns or even the Virgin Mary's traditional cloak, but Cofer tells us, once one looks around and sees the whole picture, one cannot avoid noticing the dirt of urban life turning that white snow grey. Although these essays have some surprising connections—like many essayists, both authors are struggling with questions about their mortality and their place in the world—their larger points, and thus their styles, are starkly different. Particularly in their uses of allusion—the kinds of works they refer to and why—the two pieces could hardly have less in common. Yet what they do share is that the style of each is ideally suited to its subject matter and position, that it reinforces some larger truth about each piece. These writers exhibit distinctive manners of expression and distinctive varieties of excellence; in short, they have distinctive styles.

Your principal concern, when reading an essay, must always be to discover its central thesis. What does the writer wish you to understand about his or her experience, the world, or yourself? Once you have understood the essay's thesis, you can enhance your understanding by examining the means the author used to convey it and, perhaps, recognize techniques that will enhance the quality of your own writing. To that end, you ought to examine the essay's structure and the rhetorical strategies that shape it. How does it begin and end? What type is it—narrative, descriptive, expository, argumentative? How do rhetorical strategies—definition, cause and effect, classification, exemplification, comparison and contrast—function to serve the author's purposes? Then analyze the sources of the essay's effectiveness by closely analyzing the language of the essay. Watch writers energize abstract ideas with details and moving experience; consider the uses of figurative language—the metaphors and similes that create both physical and emotional landscapes in the prose; respond to the tone of voice and the stylistic choices that create it. When you have done all this successfully, when you have discovered not only *what* the author has said but also *how* the author moved you to his or her point of view— then you will have understood the essay.

Here are some questions to ask when you face the task of reading and writing about essays.

QUESTIONS FOR EXPLORING NONFICTION

1. WHAT IS THE AUTHOR'S THESIS? What evidence or arguments does the author advance to support the thesis? Is the thesis convincing? If not, why not? Does the author rely on any basic but unstated assumptions?

2. WHAT IS THE AUTHOR'S TONE? Select for analysis a passage you consider illustrative of the author's tone. Does the author maintain that tone consistently throughout the essay?

3. HOW WOULD YOU CHARACTERIZE THE AUTHOR'S STYLE? For example, are the syntax, length of sentences, and diction elevated and formal or familiar and informal?

4. WHAT RHETORICAL STRATEGIES DOES THE AUTHOR USE? For example, can you identify the effective use of narration, description, classification, comparison and contrast, analogy, cause and effect, or definition? Note that one of these rhetorical strategies may constitute the unifying idea of the essay or the means of structuring it.

5. WHAT ARE THE MAJOR DIVISIONS IN THE ESSAY? How are they set off? Are the transitions between the divisions effective and easy to follow?

6. HOW DOES THE AUTHOR BEGIN THE ESSAY? Does the opening paragraph effectively gain the reader's attention? Does it clearly state the essay's thesis? If it does not, at what point do the author's thesis and purpose become clear? How does the essay's concluding paragraph connect to the opening paragraph?

WRITING ABOUT LITERATURE

If reading literature offers a way to listen to the surprisingly alive voices of the past, writing about literature affords the opportunity to respond to these voices. Depending on how complicated the piece is or how foreign its world is to your own experiences, your initial responses might just be a jumble of vague impressions. Classroom discussion can help to clarify your thoughts, but the best ideas do not usually come together until you sit down and write. The act of composition often generates a line of thinking. Writing about literature is an invitation to organize your impressions and to check those impressions against the work that prompted them. When you accept this invitation, you undertake a process that helps make sense of the literary work and helps you understand your reactions to it.

RESPONDING TO YOUR READING

As you know from experience, complete essays do not pop into your head immediately after you read a work of literature. The process starts with an impression here, a fragment there, or a question about something that catches your attention, which is why it is important to read actively and annotate while you read.

Annotating While You Read

Each of the discussions of the four literary genres concludes with "Questions for Exploring," a series of questions that you might bring to the reading of any text. As an active and critical reader, you must attempt to answer those questions as you read—and note your responses as you do. Look at the considerations we raise for readers of poetry (pp. 16–17). We asked some students to apply this questioning and annotating technique to Shakespeare's Sonnet 29, a moderately difficult poem. Here is a composite of what they produced:

When, in disgrace with fortune and men's eyes,
— hated by others
— fortune = luck? unlucky?

I all alone beweep my outcast state
— Sorry for self, isolated

And trouble deaf heaven with my bootless cries
— shoeless? as in poor?
  booty like treasure?
  bootless = useless?

And look upon myself and curse my fate,

Wishing me like to one more rich in hope,

Featured like him, like him with friends possessed,
— Wants to be more like someone else—hopeful/attractive/talented

Desiring this man's art and that man's scope,

With what I most enjoy contented least;
— nothing pleases him

Yet in these thoughts myself almost despising,
— tone changes here

Haply I think on thee, and then my state,
— happily? happenstance? both?
— girlfriend!

Like to the lark at break of day arising
— free as a bird

From sullen earth, sings hymns at heaven's gate;
— escape from dark, anger, sadness

For thy sweet love remembered such wealth brings
— no longer feels poor

That then I scorn to change my state with kings.
— rather be self than anyone—he's got the girl!

All in all, the annotations to this sonnet are quite good. The students grasped the poet's design, largely overcame the difficulties created by somewhat archaic language, and recognized the poet's aim to both flatter his love and express the saving grace that love provides.

But curious things happen with language. The deconstructionist critics (see "Glossary of Critical Approaches," p. 1317) have argued that because each reader brings a different set of experiences and assumptions to texts, it is difficult (some say impossible) to confidently understand any text. Put another way, different readers will interpret the same text in vastly different ways. For example, some readers, at the crucial moment when the poet remarks, "Haply I think on thee" (l. 10), might interpret the pronoun not as an *allusion* to a friend or lover but as an allusion to God. In this interpretation the sonnet resolves, not with the saving grace of a love that sets all things right, but with the ineffable saving grace of God that, with the promise of heaven, makes human pain and misery insignificant. Is such a religious reading of the poem simply wrong? And if so, what evidence could we use to show that it is wrong? Are the students who agree that the poet's girlfriend is the agent of his lifted spirits quite right? These are difficult questions, not the least because Shakespeare's sonnets seriously trouble scholars to this day.

At this point (moving away from the formalist critical approach used above—see "Glossary of Critical Approaches"), history comes into play. The edition of Shakespeare's 154 sonnets, published without his permission by Thomas Thorpe roughly ten to eleven years after they were written, was dedicated to "the only Begetter of These Insuing Sonnets Mr. W. H." Alas, we are not sure who Mr. W. H. was. Furthermore, we cannot be certain that the dedication was written by Shakespeare, rather than by Thorpe. Next, we cannot find among Shakespeare's sonnets any others that celebrate God, as some readers might suggest this sonnet does. Also, the sonnets just before and after Sonnet 29 lament that the poet suffers from the separation from his "friend." But that friend is quite possibly a man, not the girlfriend our first group of students found in the text. Literary historians would argue that interpreting this sonnet as a poem praising the restorative power of God cannot be defended given the body of work in which it resides. They would also argue that, although later sonnets (see Sonnet 130, p. 900) clearly are addressed to a woman, this one is more likely addressed to a man. But whether addressed to a woman or a man, the sonnet celebrates love's triumph over the mundane human despair that afflicts us all from time to time. And the modern reader can confidently address it to his or her beloved without being misunderstood.

Here, printed with enough space for your comments, is a dramatic monologue by the British novelist and poet Thomas Hardy (1840–1928). Try annotating it. You will discover that your first notions may have to be modified as you read through the poem. No problem—if this happens, just go back and correct your initial responses. Then compare your annotations to the composite annotations on pages 34–35.

The Man He Killed

"Had he and I but met

    By some old ancient inn,

We should have sat us down to wet

    Right many a nipperkin!

"But ranged as infantry,

    And staring face to face,

I shot at him as he at me,

    And killed him in his place.

"I shot him dead because—

    Because he was my foe,

Just so: my foe of course he was:

That's clear enough; although

"He thought he'd 'list, perhaps,

Off-hand-like—just as I—,

Was out of work—had sold his traps—

No other reason why.

"Yes; quaint and curious war is!

You shoot a fellow down

You'd treat, if met where any bar is,

Or help to half-a-crown."

The Man He Killed

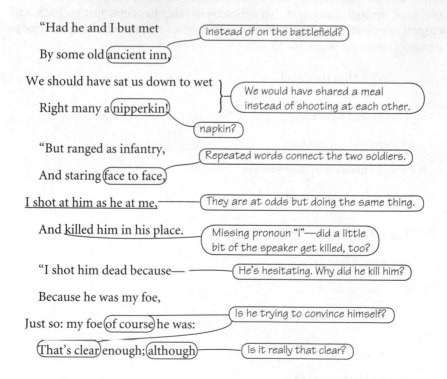

"Had he and I but met   *instead of on the battlefield?*

By some old ancient inn,

We should have sat us down to wet   *We would have shared a meal*
                                         instead of shooting at each other.
Right many a nipperkin!

                                         napkin?

"But ranged as infantry,   *Repeated words connect the two soldiers.*

And staring face to face,

I shot at him as he at me,———   *They are at odds but doing the same thing.*

And killed him in his place.   *Missing pronoun "I"—did a little*
                                         bit of the speaker get killed, too?

"I shot him dead because———   *He's hesitating. Why did he kill him?*

Because he was my foe,

Just so: my foe of course he was: *Is he trying to convince himself?*

That's clear enough; although———   *Is it really that clear?*

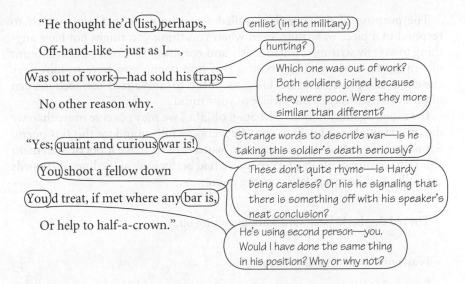

"He thought he'd list, perhaps,   enlist (in the military)

Off-hand-like—just as I—,   hunting?

Was out of work—had sold his traps—

No other reason why.   Which one was out of work? Both soldiers joined because they were poor. Were they more similar than different?

"Yes; quaint and curious war is!   Strange words to describe war—is he taking this soldier's death seriously?

You shoot a fellow down   These don't quite rhyme—is Hardy being careless? Or is he signaling that there is something off with his speaker's neat conclusion?

You'd treat, if met where any bar is,

Or help to half-a-crown."   He's using second person—you. Would I have done the same thing in his position? Why or why not?

Observe how these composite annotations engage with the poem and ask questions of Hardy's poetic structure and language. How do your own annotations compare to these composite annotations? Was there a certain point that you interpreted differently than the composite showed? Can you see how something might be read differently by different people? One of the qualities of literature that makes it so engaging is its openness to interpretation and discussion. Only by asking questions of a piece of literature will it be able to answer you—and the answers it provides are where the process of writing about literature begins.

Freewriting

Another way to ask questions of a piece of writing is to read it and then write a spontaneous response separately from the piece. Imagine this scenario. Your teacher asks you to write an essay about one of the works you've read, and you don't have a clue about where to start. Consider the following very short poem, "The Span of Life" (1936), by Robert Frost:

> The old dog barks backward without getting up.
> I can remember when he was a pup.

Set yourself a limit of five minutes to write a response to the poem. Don't worry about style or grammatical correctness, or even whether your observations necessarily make logical sense—just start writing anything that comes to mind. You may be able to write very little at first. What is there to say? The poem seems to need no explanation; its words are familiar, and the dog image unambiguous. How could someone write even a short essay about this piece? Is this a joke?

The purpose of this practice—called *freewriting*—is to force yourself to respond to a piece of writing, even when you think you might not have anything to say. By writing spontaneously and continuously for a certain amount of time, even when writing about a two-line poem, you have to look very closely at the piece—and in doing so, hitherto-unrealized connections can often work their way to the surface of your mind.

If we look again closely at "The Span of Life," we may observe more than we did on an initial reading. First, the title seems awfully grand for this tiny poem. Somehow, these two lines and sixteen words are to make a poetic statement about the nature of life itself. Perhaps we had better look at the lines and words carefully. As a first step, let's scan the poem:

The óld dóg bárks báckward withóut gétting úp.

Í can remémber whén he wás a púp.

Now, speak the poem aloud. Note that the first half of line 1 seems to move slowly, while line 2 seems to prance. That series of four stressed syllables in line 1 "slows" the line. Further, it seems that the words are hard to say quickly—perhaps because the last letter of each stressed syllable has to be finished before you can speak the first letter of the following word: "old *dog* barks backward *without*." The *meter* and the sound patterns that describe the dog, old and tired as he is, contribute to the lethargy described in line 1. But is this poem about a mere dog's life or, perhaps, life in general?

In the second line, the lilting *anapestic meter* dances across the page. (An *anapest* is a metrical foot consisting of two unaccented syllables followed by an accented syllable. See *Meter* in the "Glossary of Literary Terms.") The final *n* of "can" slides easily into the initial *r* of "remember"; the easy movements between words and in the sound sequences that follow all contribute to the quickness of the line. Thus, the joyful playfulness of a puppy, suggested by the bounding anapestic meter, is reinforced by the sound patterns embodied in the words chosen to evoke the old dog's youth. Since the title of the poem invites the reader to generalize, we could assume that human life spans, like the old dog's, move from the energetic exuberance of youth to the fatigued immobility of advanced age.

Now the title makes sense—and the *poetic* quality of the sixteen-word *couplet* (two consecutive rhyming lines) emerges from the rhythm and the sounds that reinforce the meaning of the words.

Reread your five-minute freewrite. Did you note any of these matters? Did you wonder about the poem's title? Do you have an alternative reading to suggest? After this discussion, could you now write a short essay on Frost's poem? These first jottings do not require that you bring any special knowledge to this poem, just that you attend to what's there on the page—a puzzling title, an unusual variation of metrical patterns, and the sounds that embody the poem.

Writing about literature challenges you to teach yourself. Every element in a literary work has been deliberately put there by the author—the description of the *setting*, the events that form the *plot*, the *dialogue*, the *imagery*. E. M. Forster, a literary critic and novelist, had one of his characters say, "only connect." This notion is a good one to follow when trying to write an essay that analyzes literature. Does what you are reading remind you of anything in your own life? Of anything else you have read? When you slow down and read even more carefully, you will notice connections between words and images that can help you find the key to interpreting the work of literature at hand. Readers experience a mysterious intellectual and emotional event as a result of the writer's purposeful manipulation of language. When you write about what you've read, you confront not only your response to a work but also the elements within the work that cause your response.

Think about a short story or novel that you have read or a movie you have seen recently. Did you like or dislike the story? Try to list the reasons for your general reaction and evaluation: the characters were interesting or dull and lifeless; the ending satisfied expectations or, perhaps, was surprising; the story was easy to understand; it offered new insights about people, or places, or a different society; you couldn't wait to see what would happen next (or found the story so boring that you had trouble finishing it). Your personal impressions, as you jot them down, represent your response to the work.

When you write about literature, you begin with your response to the work. Then you need to consider the writer's purpose. This is not easy; in fact, some critics argue that the reader can never fully recover the writer's purpose. But you can explore the text, try to discover how the plot, setting, *characterizations*—the very words (sometimes *symbolic*)—all conspire to generate the *theme*, and, finally, work on your feelings so that you have some response.

To write about literature is, in one way or another, an attempt to discover and describe how the writer's art created the reader's response. In other words, whatever your assignment, the fundamental task is to answer two questions: How do I respond to this piece? How has the author brought about my response?

Keeping a Journal

Your instructor may require you to keep a journal—a day-by-day account of your reactions to and reflections on your reading. Even if a journal is not required, you might want to keep one for a variety of reasons. From a purely practical perspective, writing in a journal regularly is excellent practice at conquering the blank page and generating ideas. You need not construct grammatical sentences, write cohesive paragraphs, develop your ideas, or even make sense. In a journal you are free to comment on only one aspect of a work or on a personal recollection that something in the work triggered. You are recording your reactions, ideas, feelings, questions. Jotting down personal connections— for example, if a character reminds you of a friend or teacher—can be helpful even if they don't make it in into your essay. If you are conscientious about keeping your journal, you may come to find writing in it a pleasant activity.

A journal's helpfulness extends beyond its use as a place for reflection. When the time comes to write a full-length essay for your class, the journal can provide many possible topics. Use your journal to express in writing the pleasure (or pain) of each reading assignment. Jot down unfamiliar words (which you should then, of course, look up in your dictionary). Note your reactions to characters—that some are nasty, others too saintly, some realistically rendered, still others unbelievable. Some of your journal entries may be confessions of confusion, posing open-ended questions about a reading. Others may be a record of personal feelings and recollections triggered by a work; thinking critically about such reactions might generate an essay that examines the conflict between your own moral values and those embodied in a particular work.

Finally, remember that—unless your instructor has specific guidelines for journal keeping—your journal will be the one place where you can write as much or as little as you please, as often or infrequently as you wish, with care and deliberation or careless speed. Its only purpose is to serve your needs. But if you write fairly regularly, you will probably be surprised not only at how much easier the act of writing becomes but also at how many ideas suddenly pop into your head in the act of writing. Henry Adams was surely right when he observed, "The habit of expression leads to the search for something to express."

Exploring and Planning

ASKING GOOD QUESTIONS Often the best ideas for paper topics begin as questions (possibly from a freewrite) or as responses (perhaps from a journal) that can be turned into questions. In reading James Joyce's "Araby (p. 122)," for example, you may notice that the narrator makes a big deal out of carrying the groceries home. This observation can be converted into a question: Why the big deal about carrying the groceries home? Or, to focus the question a bit, Why and how does the boy idealize these everyday situations? Note that these questions do not lead to a single irrefutable answer. When you write responses to literature, your goal is to pose a good question, answer it clearly, and support the answer with evidence from the work.

While it is important to clear up basic questions—for example, what a word or phrase means, or who did what, or how the characters are related to one another—successful papers usually take up questions that are less easily settled. For example, you would probably not want to ask whether it was a mistake for Shakespeare's Othello to trust Iago, or whether the *tragedy* could have been avoided if he had acted otherwise. Questions such as these do not lend themselves to sustained discussion. Questions of personal taste are not immediately useful for the same reason; if you say you like a particular work, there is little anyone can say to the contrary. Sometimes such assertions can be usefully converted, especially if you begin to ask why you like or dislike a work. In general, however, you should strive to explore open-ended interpretative and thematic questions rather than rehash the facts or declare personal preferences.

ESTABLISHING A WORKING THESIS   Early in the writing process, as you gather ideas about what to write, you should formulate a tentative *working thesis* that states your topic and the point or comment you wish to make about the topic. Although your working thesis will probably change as you collect information, articulating it will help you focus your thoughts and further research. Make your working thesis as specific as possible to limit your topic and keep the scope of the essay manageable. Consider the audience appeal of your working thesis as well.

A *thesis* states the main point you'll make in your final essay. In your opening paragraph, a clear thesis statement should both indicate the position you intend to take and prepare your reader for what follows. The thesis statement should be accompanied by some indication of the *scope* of your argument— the several issues you intend to explore.

For example, generating ideas for an essay about *Othello*, you may be struck by a line uttered by Othello when he is speaking before the Duke in act I: "Rude I am in my speech, / and little blessed with the soft phrase of peace." Despite this line, you notice that Othello's speech is admirably measured and eloquent. Is he being falsely modest? Is he tailoring his rhetoric to his noble audience? Is there a genuine note of insecurity being sounded? Whatever your preliminary answer, it is the beginning of your working thesis. The next step is to re-examine Othello's speeches to see if you can find evidence to support and refine the claim of your working thesis.

GATHERING INFORMATION   Once you have chosen your topic and articulated a working thesis, consider what additional information you will need to explore the issue. This may mean identifying examples from the text of the literary work you are analyzing to support your thesis or gathering information from other sources. The library is likely to be the principal source of additional information, though online research is becoming increasingly reliable.

If you use an electronic source, it is often a simple matter to print online information. If you use print sources in a library, you will need to make a photocopy or take notes. In any case, be sure to indicate on your printout or your note cards the exact publication and location information for all your sources so that you can properly document your sources in the final essay. Even if you are using just one source, you will need to provide information crediting that source in your list of works cited. For more information about crediting sources and creating a Works Cited page, see page 73.

ORGANIZING INFORMATION   Writing an essay would be a much quicker and more straightforward process if you could somehow magically know what you wanted to write about before you began your research and then whipped up a succinct thesis followed by a structured outline in which arguments I, II, and III were supported by points A, B, and C. In the real world, writers research a preliminary topic and then impose order on the information they have amassed. Think about how best to group or organize your points so that they will be persuasive to your readers.

One general approach to organizing an essay requires you to complete this statement: "The purpose of my essay is X. To demonstrate X, I will support it with arguments A, B, and C." In an essay on *Othello,* for example, you might write, "The purpose of this essay is to argue that Othello's fall is a logical consequence of his situation and his character. To demonstrate this thesis, I will examine his age and race, his military life, and his inexperience with European women."

Once you've nailed down the thesis and scope of the essay, you can, in your draft, add layers to support your claim:

> Many writers have argued that the rapid fall of the noble Moor Othello is unbelievable. But consider his situation. He is a black man in a white country; he is much older than his beautiful wife. As a military man, he self-consciously lacks social grace. And his inexperience with European women contributes to the emotional insecurity that finally destroys him.

Where you cite other writers' arguments—as in the first sentence—you must offer documentation for your sources.

The next several paragraphs would follow the organization set up by the opening. First might be a paragraph on Othello's race and age and the attitudes toward him established in act I, followed by a paragraph on Othello's self-conscious unfamiliarity with the behavior of European women. The next paragraph might argue that he sees himself as unappealing to women from his adopted city. Each of these assertions should be supported with dialogue from the play. A conclusion would follow: Othello was never quite as noble as some have suggested and, under the circumstances, was doomed from the start.

One of the intellectual hurdles you'll face as a student of literature is learning to distinguish between a *summary* that recounts events and details and an *analysis* that interprets what events and details might mean. Of course an analysis should provide enough plot summary so that your reader has the context to understand what you are talking about. In fact, if you are confused about the plot of a literary work—what happened, in what order?—then writing a summary may help to clear up your confusion. Moreover, writing a summary is often a first step to writing an analysis and offering an interpretation. As you describe what happens in a work of literature, you begin to ask questions about why those events happened. In choosing the details and events to include in your summary, you are making decisions about which details and events are worth attending to when you try to ascribe meaning to them in the context of analysis and interpretation.

The following summary of Shakespeare's *Othello* reduces the play to its major plot elements. Notice that it does not interpret the play, focusing on particular details and explaining what they mean. (Notice also that it is narrated in the present tense, a conventional practice when you summarize.) This is in contrast to the later analysis of *Othello* in this chapter that answers questions of why things happened in the play and what these events might mean to us as readers.

A Summary of *Othello*

Set in Venice and then Cyprus, *Othello* opens with a scene of the villainous Iago and his henchman Roderigo hatching a vengeful plot against Iago's commanding general Othello, who has passed him over to promote the handsome Michael Cassio to be his Lieutenant. Iago first tries to undermine Othello by anonymously revealing to the father of Othello's new wife that his daughter is now married to a person of a different race (Othello is a Moor—an African). The father, a nobleman named Brabantio, is appalled that his daughter, Desdemona, is married to a Moor, but when he takes his argument to the Duke of Venice, the Duke, who desires Othello's services to protect Venice from an invasion from Cyprus, judges that Othello and Desdemona truly love each other, and approves their wedding. Thwarted in his first attempts at vengeance, Iago contrives to draw Cassio into a drunken street brawl that leads to Othello stripping Cassio of his new rank. Iago then advances his vengeance by leading Othello to believe Desdemona has betrayed him with Cassio. Exploiting his loving wife Emilia, Iago uses a handkerchief that Emilia obtains from Desdemona to fool Othello into believing Desdemona is involved with Cassio. Succumbing to Iago's lies, Othello grows mad with jealousy and asks Iago to help him kill Cassio and Desdemona. Iago continues to weave a series of lies and schemes that ultimately trick Othello into murdering his guiltless wife Desdemona. Believing himself a cuckold, Othello ignores Desdemona's protestations of innocence and strangles her in her bed. Then he discovers through Emilia how he has been duped by Iago. Confronted with Iago's betrayal and the enormity of his own crime against an innocent woman who loved him, Othello chooses to commit suicide rather than try to exculpate himself and live knowing his folly. Iago's vengeance is complete, but his crimes, which include the murder of Roderigo and Emilia, have come to light and he is arrested. Still he vows neither to repent nor ever to speak again of his crimes, even in the face of torture and death.

DRAFTING THE ESSAY

It is important to start writing even if you are unsure about the exact shape or direction of your argument since frequently your ideas develop and become more focused as you proceed. In working through a draft essay on *Othello*, you may initially find yourself interested in, on the one hand, how eloquent you found Othello's address to the court of the Duke of Venice and, on the other hand, his self-characterization as plain-spoken, even ill-spoken. Does Othello really believe he is a "rude" speaker? Is he perhaps manipulating his audience? But as you write your first draft and your thoughts evolve, you may find yourself moving from a thesis that Othello has crafty control of his language to something quite different. Keep writing and stay flexible. A first draft does not have to be perfect. It's a stage for making discoveries and clarifying your ideas.

Refining Your Opening

Once the draft is done and you have a clear idea of your thesis and the passages in the work that best support it, you can begin to shape and refine the essay. In doing so, pay special attention to the introductory paragraph, which should introduce the topic and lead directly to a clear, arguable thesis. While there is no surefire formula for a first paragraph, some strategies are better than others. Avoid the following types of opening sentences:

> Ever since the dawn of time, people have been fascinated by the fall of great men.

> Insecurity is a feeling that can prove harmful in even the most accomplished people.

This kind of throat-clearing generalization is common and even helpful at the draft stage, but it gets the essay off to a slow start. If the working thesis is that Othello is undone not only by treachery but also because of the insecurities that lurk beneath his formidable bearing, a direct approach is more effective:

In Othello's first speech at the court of the Duke, he presents himself as a simple soldier awkwardly attempting to explain how he won the hand of the beautiful Desdemona. In fact his "rude" words are highly eloquent, and a reader may judge that the proud general is using false modesty to advance his case. Such a judgment ignores a more central issue than Othello's pride and eloquence. His words hint at the insecurities—as a military man short on civilian social graces, an older man with a young wife, a black African in a white European culture— that will cloud his judgment and ultimately prove his undoing.

Note that this opening paragraph introduces the topic and moves directly toward an explicit and arguable claim. By doing so, it lets the reader—and the writer—know where the essay is going. That is, once a clear thesis is in place, both writer and reader can use it as a road map for the rest of the essay.

Supporting Your Thesis

The body of the essay will be devoted to supporting the thesis. The best way to establish a claim is to cite and analyze carefully selected passages from the text that relate directly to it. The following paragraph focuses on lines that support our sample claim directly:

As indicated by the preceding examples, numerous passages reveal Othello's various insecurities. But in the following passage, his language manifests them all:

Haply, for I am black,

And have not those soft parts of conversation

That chamberers have, or for I am decline'd,

Into the vale of years—yet that's not much— (3.3 263–66)

Here Othello catalogs his self-perceived flaws: His Africanness ("for I am black"), his rough manners ("I . . . have not those soft parts of conversation"), and his age ("decline'd / Into the vale of years"). He is now tormented by the very qualities and achievements that once set him proudly apart from others in European culture.

The first part of the paragraph tells the reader what to look for in the cited lines, and the subsequent analysis underscores their relevance to the overall argument clearly and convincingly.

If you offer a claim, support it with an analysis of the relevant passages, and consider different interpretations of those passages, you have completed the main task in much writing about literature. Concluding paragraphs can move toward closure by reviewing the claim and its significance, which you should be careful not to overstate. In the essay on *Othello,* for example, it would not be effective to conclude with a sweeping claim that the Moor's insecurities represent Shakespeare's indictment of European culture in his era. Your readers will find your claims more convincing if you do not exaggerate their importance.

REVISING THE ESSAY

After you've completed your draft, it is time to look at the essay more critically, paying special attention to revision. Revision involves taking a fresh look at your essay's thesis and support, as well as its organization and language. Reading your essay aloud, or asking someone else to read it, will help you catch many problems. Revision is most effective if begun well before the paper is due. Start writing early so that you have time to review your decisions, ask for feedback from others, and revise accordingly. Because you cannot always anticipate audience reaction, a preliminary reading of your writing by a friend, a teaching assistant, a tutor, or an instructor can highlight the areas that need attention or additional revision.

The basic guidelines for good style are not mysterious; in fact, you use them every day in conversation. In conversation and in writing, we all rely heavily on cooperation to make sense of exchanges, and a polished practical style makes cooperation easier. Writers develop such a style by acknowledging that readers expect the same things that listeners expect in conversation: clarity, relevance, and proportion. If you listen to someone who is not clear, who cannot stay on the topic, or who offers too much or too little information, you will quickly lose interest in the conversation. Writers, too, need to be clear, stay on the topic, and give information appropriately. In fact, this attention to audience and appropriateness may be even more important in writing than in conversation because writing does not permit the nonverbal communication and immediate feedback that are part of conversation. As writers, we have to anticipate the absent reader's response; in effect, we have to imagine both halves of a virtual conversation.

Begin by evaluating your essay's thesis. Is it clear? Vagueness or tentativeness here may mean problems later in the essay, so make sure your thesis is crystal clear. Second, is the evidence you present relevant to each major point? While it is tempting and sometimes productive to go off on tangents while drafting a paper, in the final essay if the evidence doesn't fit the claim, tinker with the claim, or go back to the early exploratory writing you did and to your sources to look for better evidence. Are there any points that need to be clarified? Check all your quotations, paraphrases, and summaries for their citations and for accuracy.

Next, can you tighten the organization of your draft? Are your claims and evidence unified? Put yourself in your reader's place, and clarify ambiguities. Each detail or piece of evidence in a paragraph should relate back to the claim it supports in the topic sentence of that paragraph. At the same time, avoid oversupporting some points with too much discussion or detail.

Finally, ask yourself if the general proportions of your essay are suitable. A five-page paper should not use three of those pages to introduce the topic or recount a work's plot. If the essay is too short, the trouble might be an unarguable thesis or insufficient evidence. If it is running too long, eliminate or compress the parts that do not bear directly on the main claim, or limit the claim to something more manageable.

Editing Your Draft

After you have evaluated and revised your draft and determined the format for your paper, you are ready to edit it carefully, paying close attention to each sentence and paragraph. These guidelines will help you focus on some common trouble spots.

SELECTING STRONG VERBS Careful selection of lively, active verbs will make your writing more interesting to your audience. Consider the main verb in the following sentence:

> Three conflicts, all of which play crucial roles in the plot, are evident in
>
> Othello.

The core assertion of this sentence is that "[t]hree conflicts . . . are evident." Notice that nothing actually happens in this sentence. To stir things up, borrow the verb *play* from another part of the sentence:

> Three conflicts play crucial roles in the plot of *Othello*.

The revision is better, but the sentence can be made even more concise using *drive:*

> Three conflicts drive the plot of *Othello*.

The revised sentence more clearly gets to the point, an effect that is rarely lost on an audience. It also permits a more direct move to the topic—namely, the conflicts. Finally, in an economical seven words rather than a verbose fifteen, it neither belabors nor omits anything of importance in the first sentence.

Writing that relies too heavily on *be* verbs often produces wordiness and unnecessary abstraction:

> There <u>was</u> opposition to interracial marriage among most of the citizens
>
> of Venice.

Deleting the *be* verb (*was*) and converting the abstract noun *opposition* into a verb make the sentence more active:

> Most Venetians <u>opposed</u> interracial marriage.

This clearer sentence lets the verb do the major work. Of course, a good verb does not always present itself as an abstract noun in an early draft. Sometimes you'll need to consult a thesaurus or a dictionary to find just the right word.

Search your draft for weak verbs and insignificant words and for sentences that begin *There is, There are, It is.* Often, a few words later, a *that, which,* or *who* will appear. Overuse of *There is* and *There are* produces sentences where the action is buried. Edit these sentences by deleting the weak verb constructions and replacing them with strong, precise verbs. For example, change "*There is* a destiny *that* controls the fate of Sam" to "Destiny controls Sam's fate."

Finally, check your draft for passive constructions (the ball *was thrown*), and replace them when possible with active verbs. Passive sentences are often wordier and dull the action of a sentence. For example, change "The essay was read by the class" to "The class read the essay."

ELIMINATING UNNECESSARY MODIFIERS   When choosing or revising a verb, you are also choosing the sentence elements that necessarily accompany it. These other sentence elements are called *complements* because they complete the meaning of the verb. In the following sentences the complements are underlined:

> Iago betrays <u>Othello</u>.
>
> The boy idealized <u>his situation</u>.

Iago cannot just betray; he has to betray something. Likewise, *his situation* completes the meaning of the verb *idealized*. Almost everything else added to these sentences will be *modifiers*—additional elements that will modify, rather than complete, the meaning of the sentences. A writer can add any number of modifiers to a sentence:

> Iago betrayed Othello <u>cold-bloodedly</u>, <u>with a malignity beyond measure,</u>
>
> <u>a malignity that Coleridge characterized as "motiveless."</u>

From a grammatical standpoint, these modifiers are optional; without them the sentence still expresses a complete thought. Unnecessary modifiers can make your writing heavy and murky:

> <u>Basically</u>, the Greeks invented <u>a rather innovative and distinctive form of government known as</u> democracy.

Eliminating the modifiers and making a few other snips result in the following:

> The Greeks invented democracy.

The clearer sentence does not lose much in the way of content. Of course, being able to eliminate modifiers does not mean that you should; sometimes modifiers are the most significant parts of a sentence. You can always use modifiers for nuance or emphasis, but you must ruthlessly trim unnecessary modifiers from wordy, unclear sentences.

GRAMMATICAL CONNECTIONS Make sure your sentences and paragraphs are firmly linked by using explicit transitional phrases such as *however, although, likewise, for example, therefore,* and so on. Note in this sample opening paragraph how the underlined transitional phrases indicate the relationships between the sentences:

> In his speech before the Duke's court, Othello speaks disarmingly to the assembled nobles. He flatteringly describes his audience as being potent, grave, and reverend. He modestly describes himself as being a blunt-spoken soldier hardly qualified to talk of anything but the wars that he has seen and fought. <u>However</u>, Othello's modesty is belied by the deeds of which he speaks. <u>In particular</u> he boldly admits to having won both the love of Desdemona and many battles, dating from when he was but a child. The court is looking for a conqueror, and in his guise of modesty Othello presents himself as that man.

The appearance of *however* halfway through the paragraph signals the contrast between Othello's professed modesty and his powerful deeds. The transitional phrase *in particular* in the next sentence signals that we are narrowing the preceding point and focusing our discussion. Experienced readers look for such transitional phrases that suggest an interpretive path through an argument.

Note that the third sentence of the paragraph repeats a key word from the second one (*describes*); so does the first and fourth sentence (*speaks*). The repetition helps keep the spotlight on Othello's rhetoric, an important notion in the paragraph. Note also the use of *modestly* and *modesty*. By repeating key terms, sometimes with slight variation, you can powerfully illuminate the main idea of a paragraph.

After checking for explicit connections within paragraphs, make sure that the progression of ideas from one paragraph to another is clear. Here again, transitional phrases are useful. A simple transition such as *nevertheless, furthermore,* or *on the other hand* is often adequate. Sometimes the entire opening sentence of a paragraph may provide the transition, including key words, pronouns, or other references to the previous paragraph.

Proofreading Your Draft

Print out, type, or (if your instructor allows it) neatly write in ink the final copy of your essay for submission to your instructor, taking care to follow any special instructions about format that you have been given. Don't rush; be meticulous. When you have finished, proofread the final copy carefully, looking for spelling or punctuation errors, omitted words, disagreement between subjects and verbs or between pronouns and antecedents, and typographical errors that will detract from the essay you have worked hard to write.

For additional advice on checking your use of sources and documenting in your final essay, see "Some Matters of Form and Documentation" (p. 71). Finally, use "A Checklist for Writing about Literature" (p. 75) to help with a quick review of your final draft.

SOME COMMON WRITING ASSIGNMENTS

A writing assignment for a literature course may require any of a variety of kinds of writing. You might be called on to compare and contrast literary works, to analyze the language of a work, to discuss the interaction of a work's parts, to discuss a work's theme, or to articulate your own responses to the work. Sometimes an instructor may ask simply that you write an essay on one of the pieces you have read. This type of assignment requires you to create your own boundaries—to find a specific focus that both suits the piece you choose and is manageable within a paper of the assigned length. Sometimes you may be asked to simply summarize a complex literary work. The summary of *Othello* (pp. 41–42) would be adequate if the assignment was this straightforward. Other times, you may be asked to respond creatively, to come up with original work that reimagines a poem or story from your own point of view and in your own words. However, in many literature courses, assigned essays tend to fall into one of three modes—explication, analysis, and comparison and contrast—or some combination of these. Familiarity with these three kinds of writing about literature will help you not only with full-length essay assignments but also with exams and other in-class writing.

Explication

In an explication essay, you examine a work in much detail. Line by line, *stanza* by stanza, scene by scene, you explain each part as fully as you can and show how the author's techniques produce your response. An *explication* is essentially a demonstration of your thorough understanding of a work.

Here is a sample essay that explicates a relatively difficult poem, Dylan Thomas's "Do Not Go Gentle into That Good Night" (p. 1234).

Dylan Thomas's villanelle "Do Not Go Gentle into That Good Night" is addressed to his aged father. The poem is remarkable in a number of ways, most notably in that contrary to most common poetic treatments of the inevitability of death, which argue for serenity or celebrate the peace that death provides, this poem urges resistance and rage in the face of death. It justifies that unusual attitude by describing the rage and resistance to death of four kinds of men, who each can summon up the image of a complete and satisfying life that is denied to him by death.

The first tercet of the intricately rhymed villanelle opens with an arresting line. The adjective *gentle* appears where we would expect the adverb *gently*. The strange diction suggests that *gentle* may describe both the going (i.e., gently dying) and the person (i.e., gentleman) who confronts death. Further, the speaker characterizes "night," here clearly a figure for death, as "good." Yet in the next line, the speaker urges that the aged should violently resist death, characterized as the "close of day" and "the dying of the light." In effect, the first three lines argue that however good death may be, the aged should refuse to die gently, should passionately rave and rage against death.

In the second tercet, the speaker turns to a description of the way the first of four types of men confronts death (which is figuratively defined throughout the poem as "that good night" and "the dying of the light"). These are the "wise men," the scholars, the philosophers, those who understand the inevitability of death, men who "know dark is right." But they do not acquiesce in death "because their words had forked no lightning," because their published wisdom failed to bring them to that sense of completeness and fulfillment that can accept death. Therefore, wise as they are, they reject the theoretical "rightness" of death and refuse to "go gentle."

The second sort of men—"good men," the moralists, the social reformers, those who attempt to better the world through action as the wise men attempt to better it through "words"—also rage against death. Their deeds are, after all, "frail." With sea imagery, the speaker suggests that these men might have accomplished fine and fertile things—their deeds "might have danced in a green bay." But with the "last wave" gone, they see only the frailty, the impermanence of their acts, and so they, too, rage against the death that deprives them of the opportunity to leave a meaningful legacy.

The "wild men," the poets who "sang" the loveliness and vitality of nature, also learn as they approach death that the sensuous joys of human existence wane. As the life-giving sun moves toward dusk, as death approaches, their singing turns to grieving, and they refuse to surrender gently, to leave willingly the warmth, pleasure, and beauty that life can give.

Finally, with a pun suggestive of death, the "grave men," those who go through life with such high seriousness as never to experience gaiety and pleasure, see all the joyous possibilities that they were blind to in life. And they, too, rage against the dying of a light that they had never properly seen before.

The speaker then calls on his aged father to join these men raging against death. Only in this final stanza do we discover that the entire poem is addressed to the speaker's father and that, despite the generalized statements about old age and the focus on types of men, the poem is a personal lyric. The edge of death becomes a "sad height," the summit of wisdom and experience old age attains includes the sad knowledge of life's failure to satisfy the vision we all pursue. The depth and complexity of the speaker's sadness is startlingly given in the second line, when he calls on his father to both curse and bless him. These opposites richly suggest several related possibilities: "Curse me for not living up to your expectations. Curse me for remaining alive as you die. Bless me with forgiveness for my failings. Bless me for teaching you to rage against death." And the curses and blessings are contained in the "fierce tears"—fierce because you will burn and rave and rage against death. As the poem closes by bringing together the two powerful refrains, the speaker himself seems to rage because his father's death will cut off a relationship that is incomplete.

This explication deals with the entire poem by coming to grips with each element in it.

You can learn a great deal about the technique of drama by selecting a short, self-contained scene and writing a careful description of it. The length of plays will probably require that you focus on a single segment—a scene, for example—rather than the entire play. This method of explication will force you to confront every speech and stage direction and to come to some conclusion regarding its function. Why is the set furnished as it is? Why does a character speak the words he or she does or remain silent? What do we learn of characters from the interchanges among them? Assume that everything that occurs in the play, whether on the printed page or on the stage, is put there for a purpose. Seek to discover the purpose, and you will, at the same time, discover the distinctive nature of drama.

Fiction, too, can be treated effectively in a formal explication. As with drama, it will be necessary to limit the text: you will not be able to explicate a ten-page story in a 1,000-word essay. Choose a key passage—a half page that reflects the form and content of the overall story, if possible. Often the first half page of a story, where the author, like the playwright, must supply information to the reader, will make a fine text for an explication. Although the explication will deal principally with only an excerpt, feel free to range across the story and show how the introductory material foreshadows what is to come. Or perhaps you can explicate the climax of the story—the half page that most pointedly establishes the story's theme—and subject it to a close line-by-line reading that illuminates the whole story.

Analysis

Breaking a literary work down into its elements is only the first step in literary analysis. When you are assigned an analysis essay, you are expected to focus on one of the elements that contributes to the complex compound of a work. This process requires you to extricate the element you plan to explore from the other elements that you can identify, to study this element—not only in isolation but also in relation to the other elements and the work as a whole—and, using the insights you have gained from your special perspective, to make an informed statement about it.

This process may sound complicated, but if you approach it methodically, each stage follows naturally from the stage that precedes it. If, for example, you are to write an analysis essay on characterization in *Othello*, you would begin by thinking about each character in the play. You would then select the character whose development you would like to explore and reread carefully those speeches that help to establish his or her substance. Exploring a character's development in this way involves a good deal of explication: in order to identify the "building blocks" that Shakespeare uses to create a three-dimensional role, you must comb very carefully through that character's speeches and actions. You must also be sensitive to the ways in which other characters respond to these speeches and actions. When you have completed this investigation, you will probably have a good understanding of why you intuitively responded to the character as you did when you first read the play. You will also probably be prepared to make a statement about the character's development: "From a realistic perspective, it is hard to believe that a man of Othello's position could be so gullible; however, Shakespeare develops the role with such craft that we accept the Moor as flesh and blood." At this point, you have moved from the broad *subject* of "characterization in *Othello*" to a thesis, a statement that you must prove. As you formulate your thesis, think of it as a position that you intend to *argue* for with a reader you need to persuade. This approach is useful in any essay that requires a thesis, where you move beyond simple explication and commit yourself to a stand. Note that our sample thesis is *argumentative* on two counts; "characterization in *Othello*" is not remotely argumentative. Further, you have more than enough material to write a well-documented essay of 1,000 words supporting your proposition; you cannot write a well-documented 1,000-word essay on the general subject of characterization in *Othello* without being superficial.

You may be one among the many writers who have trouble finding a starting point. For example, you have been assigned an analysis essay on a very broad subject, such as imagery in love poetry. A few poems come to mind, but you don't know where to begin. You read these poems and underline all the images that you can find. You look at these images over and over, finding no relation among them. You read some more poems, again underlining the images, but you still do not have even the germ of a thesis.

The technique of freewriting might help to overcome your block. You have read and reread the poems you intend to write about. Now, put the assignment temporarily out of your mind, and start writing about one or two of the poems without organizing your ideas, without trying to reach a point. Write down what you like about a poem, what you dislike about it, what sort of person the speaker is, which images seemed striking to you—anything at all about the work. If you do this for perhaps ten minutes, you will probably discover that you are voicing opinions. Pick one that interests you or seems the most promising to explore.

The basic form of the analysis assignment has a few variations. Your instructor might narrow the subject in a specific assignment: analyze the development of Othello's character in act I. This sort of assignment limits the amount of text you will have to study, but the process from this point on is no different from the process you would employ to address a broader subject. Sometimes instructors will supply you with a thesis, and you will have to work backward from the thesis to find supporting material. Again, careful analysis of the text is required. The problem you will have to address when writing an analytical essay remains the same regardless of the literary genre you are asked to discuss. You must find an arguable thesis that deals with the sources of your response to the work.

Suppose your instructor has made the following assignment: write an analysis of Harlan Ellison's story "'Repent, Harlequin!' Said the Ticktockman (p. 401)," in which you discuss the theme of the story in terms of the characters and the setting. Now consider the following opening (taken from a student paper):

> " 'Repent, Harlequin!' Said the Ticktockman" is a story depicting a society in which time governs one's life. The setting is the United States, the time approximately 2400 A.D. somewhere in the heart of the country. Business deals, work shifts, and school lessons are started and finished with exacting precision. Tardiness is intolerable as this would hinder the system. In a society of order, precision, and punctuality, there is no room for likes, dislikes, scruples, or morals. Thus, personalities in people no longer exist. As these "personless" people know no good or bad, they very happily follow in the course of activities that their society has dictated.

At the outset, can you locate a thesis statement? The only sentences that would seem to qualify are the last three in the paragraph. But notice that, although those sentences are not unreasonable responses to the story, they do not establish a thesis that is *responsive to the assignment*. Because the assignment calls for a discussion of theme in terms of character and setting, a thesis statement should argue how character and setting embody the theme. Here is another opening paragraph on the same assignment (also taken from a student paper):

> Harlan Ellison's " 'Repent, Harlequin!' Said the Ticktockman"
>
> opens with a quotation from Thoreau's essay "Civil Disobedience,"
>
> which establishes the story's theme. Thoreau's observations about three
>
> varieties of men—those who serve the state as machines, those who
>
> serve it with their heads, and those who serve it with their consciences—
>
> are dramatized in Ellison's story, which takes place about 400 years in the
>
> future in a setting characterized by machinelike order. The interaction
>
> among the three characters, each of whom represents one of Thoreau's
>
> types, results in a telling restatement of his observation that "heroes, pa-
>
> triots, martyrs, reformers in the great sense, and men . . . necessarily resist
>
> [the state] and . . . are commonly treated as enemies by it."

Compare these two opening paragraphs sentence by sentence for their responsiveness to the assignment. The first sentence of the first opening does not refer to the theme of the story (or to its setting or characterization). In the second sentence, the discussion of the setting ignores the most important aspect—that the story is set in a machine- and time-dominated future. The last three sentences deal obliquely with character, but they are imprecise and do not establish a thesis. The second opening, on the other hand, immediately states the theme of the story. It goes on to emphasize the relevant aspects of the futuristic setting and then refers to the three characters who animate the story in terms of their reactions to the setting. The last sentence addresses the assignment directly and also serves as a thesis statement for the paper. It states the proposition that will be developed and supported in the rest of the paper. The reader of the second opening will expect the next paragraph of the paper to discuss the setting of the story and subsequent paragraphs to discuss the response to the setting of the three principal characters.

The middles of essays are largely determined by their opening paragraphs. However long the middle of any essay may be, each of its paragraphs ought to be responsive to some explicit statement made at the beginning of the essay. Note that it is practically impossible to predict what the paragraph following the first opening will address. Here is the first half of that next paragraph as the first student wrote it:

The Harlequin is a man in the society with no sense of time. His having a personality enables him to have a sense of moral values and a mind of his own. The Harlequin thinks that it is obscene and wrong to let time totally govern the lives of people. So he sets out to disrupt the time schedule with ridiculous antics such as showering people with jelly beans to try to break up the military fashion in which they are used to doing things.

The paragraph then goes on to discuss the Ticktockman, the capture and brainwashing of the Harlequin, and the resulting lateness of the Ticktockman.

Note that nothing in the opening of this student's paper prepared readers for the introduction of the Harlequin. In fact, the opening concluded rather inaccurately that the people within the story "happily follow in the course of activities that their society has dictated." Hence, the description of the Harlequin in the second paragraph is wholly unexpected. Further, because the student has not dealt with the theme of the story (as the assignment asked), the comments about the Harlequin's antics remain disconnected from any clear purpose. They are essentially devoted to what teachers constantly warn against: a mere plot summary. The student has obviously begun to write before analyzing the story sufficiently to understand its theme. With further thought, the student would have perceived that the central thematic issue is resistance to an oppressive state—the issue stated in the epigraph from Thoreau. On the other hand, because the second opening makes that thematic point clearly, we can expect it to be followed by a discussion of the environment (that is, the setting) in which the action occurs. Here is such a paragraph taken from the second student's paper:

Ellison creates a society that reflects one possible future development of the modern American passion for productivity and efficiency. The setting is in perfect keeping with the time-conscious people who inhabit the city. It is pictured as a neat, colorless, and mechanized city. No mention is made of nature: grass, flowers, trees, and birds do not appear. The buildings are in a "Mondrian arrangement," stark and geometrical. The cold steel sidewalks, slowstrips, and expresstrips move with precision. Like a chorus line, people move in unison to board the movers without a wasted motion. Doors close silently and lock themselves automatically. An ideal efficiency so

dominates the social system that any "wasted time" is deducted from
the life of an inefficient citizen.

Once the setting has been established, the writer turns to the characters,
linking those characters to thematic considerations, beginning with a short
transitional paragraph that shapes the remainder of the middle of the essay:

Into this smoothly functioning but coldly mechanized society, Ellison introduces three characters: Pretty Alice, one of Thoreau's
machinelike creatures; the Ticktockman, one of those who "serve the
state chiefly with their heads, and, as they rarely make any moral
distinctions, they are as likely to serve the Devil, without intending it,
as God"; and Everett C. Marm, the Harlequin, whose conscience forces
him to resist the oppressive state.

Following a logical organization, the essay then includes a paragraph devoted
to each of the three characters:

Pretty Alice is, probably, very pretty. (Everett didn't fall in love
with her brains.) In the brief section in which we meet her, we find
her hopelessly ordinary in her attitudes. She is upset that Marm finds it
necessary to go about "annoying people." She finds him ridiculous and
wishes only that he would stay home, as other people do. Clearly, she
has no understanding of what Everett is struggling against. Though her
anger finally leads her to betray him, Everett himself can't believe that
she has done so. His own loyal and understanding nature colors his view
of her so thoroughly that he cannot imagine the treachery that must
have been so simple and satisfying for Pretty Alice, whose only desire is
to be like everybody else.

The Ticktockman is more complex. He sees himself as a servant
of the state, and he performs his duties with resolution and competence.
He skillfully supports a System he has never questioned. The System
exists; it must be good. His conscience is simply not involved in the

performance of his duty. He is one of those who follow orders and expect

others to follow orders. As a result, the behavior of the Harlequin is more

than just an irritant or a rebellion against authority. It is unnerving. The

Ticktockman wishes to understand that behavior, and with Everett's time-

card in his hand, he muses that he has the name of "*what* he is, not *who*

he is. . . . Before I can exercise proper revocation, I have to know *who*

this *what* is." And when he confronts Everett, he does not just liquidate

him. He insists that Everett repent. He tries to convince Everett that the

System is sound, and when he cannot win the argument, he dutifully

reconditions Everett, since he is, after all, more interested in justifying

the System than in destroying its enemies. It is easy to see this man as

a competent servant of the devil who thinks he is serving God.

But only Everett C. Marm truly serves the state because his

conscience requires him to resist. He is certainly not physically heroic. His

very name suggests weak conformity. Though he loves his Pretty Alice,

he cannot resign from the rebellious campaign on which his conscience

insists. So without violence, and mainly with the weapon of laughter, he

attacks the mechanical precision of the System and succeeds in breaking

it down simply by making people late. He is himself, as Pretty Alice points

out, always late, and the delays that his antics produce seriously threaten

the well-being of the smooth but mindless System he hates. He is captured

and refuses, even then, to submit, and so his personality is destroyed by

the authorities that fear him. The Ticktockman is too strong for him.

An appropriate ending emerges naturally from this student's treatment of
the assignment. Having established that the story presents characters who deal
in different ways with the oppressive quality of life in a time- and machine-
obsessed society, the student concludes with a comment on the author's criticisms of such a society:

Harlequin is defeated, but Ellison, finally, leaves us with an

optimistic note. The idea of rebellion against the System will linger in the minds of others. There will be more Harlequins and more disruption of this System. Many rebels will be defeated, but any System that suppresses individualism will give birth to resistance. And Harlequin's defeat is by no means total. The story ends with the Ticktockman himself arriving for work three minutes late.

Comparison and Contrast

An essay in comparison and contrast shows how two works are similar to and different from one another. It almost always starts with a recognition of similarities, often of subject matter. Sometimes you may be asked to connect what you have read with something in your own life, creating an original comparison, for example, between Peter Meinke's "Advice to My Son" (p. 216) and advice you have been given by an adult in your own life. Most comparison-and-contrast assignments involve two works of the same genre. While it is possible to compare *any* two works, the best comparison-and-contrast essays emerge from the analysis of two works similar enough to illuminate each other. Two works about love, or death, or conformity, or innocence, or identity give you something to begin with. The groupings in this book will suggest some ways you might read certain works together. For example, both Emily Dickinson's "Apparently with no surprise" (p. 1225) and Robert Frost's "Design" (p. 1241) are about death, and they both use remarkably similar events as the occasion for their poems. Starting with these similarities, you would soon find yourself noting the contrasts (in tone, for example, and theme) between nineteenth-century and twentieth-century views of the nature of God.

Before you begin writing a comparison-and-contrast essay, it is especially important to have clearly in mind the points of comparison and contrast you wish to discuss and the order in which you can most effectively discuss them. You will need to give careful thought to the best way to organize your paper, jotting down the plan your comparison will follow. As a general rule, it is best to avoid dividing the essay into separate discussions of each work. That method tends to produce two separate, loosely joined analysis essays. The successful comparison-and-contrast essay treats some point of similarity or contrast between the two works, then moves on to succeeding points, and ends with an evaluation of the comparative merits of the works.

Like any essay that goes beyond simple explication, a comparison-and-contrast essay requires a strong thesis statement. However, a comparison-and-contrast thesis is generally not difficult to formulate: you must identify the works under consideration and state clearly your reasons for making the comparison.

Here is a student paper that compares and contrasts Dylan Thomas's "Do Not Go Gentle into That Good Night" with the poetic response it triggered from a poet with different views:

Dylan Thomas's "Do Not Go Gentle into That Good Night" and Catherine Davis's "After a Time" demand comparison: Davis's poem was written in deliberate response to Thomas's. Davis assumes the reader's familiarity with "Do Not Go Gentle," which she uses to articulate her contrasting ideas. "After a Time," although it is a literary work in its own right, might even be thought of as serious parody—perhaps the greatest compliment one writer can pay another.

"Do Not Go Gentle into That Good Night" was written by a young man of thirty-eight who addresses it to his old and ailing father. Perhaps because Thomas had very little of his own self-destructive life left as he was composing this piece, he seems to have more insight into the subject of death than most people his age. He advocates raging and fighting against it, not giving in and accepting it.

"After a Time" was written by Davis at about the same age and is addressed to no one in particular. Davis has a different philosophy about death. She "answers" Thomas's poem and presents her differing views using the same poetic form—a villanelle. Evidently, she felt it necessary to present a contrasting point of view eight years after Thomas's death.

While "Do Not Go Gentle" protests and rages against death, Davis's poem suggests a quiet resignation and acquiescence. She seems to feel that raging against death is useless and profitless. She argues that we will eventually become tame, anyway, after the raging is done.

Thomas talks about different types of men and why they rage against death. "Wise men" desire immortality. They rage against death occurring before they've made their mark on history. "Good men" lament the frailty of their deeds. Given more time, they might have accomplished great things. "Wild men" regret their constant hedonistic pursuits. With more time they could prove their worth. "Grave men" are quite the opposite and regret they never took time for the pleasures in life. Now it is too late. They rage against death because they are not ready for it.

His father's death is painful to Thomas because he sees himself lying in that bed; his father's dying reminds him of his own inevitable death. The passion of the last stanza, in which the poet asks his father to bless and curse him, suggests that he has doubts about his relationship with his father. He may feel that he has not been a good enough son. He put off doing things with and for his father because he always felt there would be time later. Now time has run out and he feels cheated.

Catherine Davis advocates a calm submission, a peaceful acquiescence. She feels raging is useless and says that those of us who rage will finally "go tame / When what we have we can no longer use." When she says "One more thing lost is one thing less to lose," the reader can come to terms with the loss of different aspects of the mind and body, such as strength, eyesight, hearing, and intellect. Once one of these is lost, it's one thing less to worry about losing. After a time, everything will be lost, and we'll accept that, too, because we'll be ready for it.

Thomas's imagery is vivid and powerful. His various men not only rage and rave, they *burn*. Their words "forked no lightning," their deeds might have "danced in a green bay," they "sang the sun in flight," and they see that "blind eyes could blaze like meteors." Davis's images are quiet and generally abstract, without much sensory suggestiveness, as in "things lost," a "reassuring ruse," and "all losses are the same." Her most powerful image—"And we go stripped at last the way we came"—

makes its point with none of the excitement of Thomas's rage. And yet,

I prefer the quiet intelligence of Davis to the high energy of Thomas.

"And we go stripped at last the way we came" can give strange

comfort and solace to those of us who always envied those in high

places. People are not all created equal at birth, not by a long shot. But

we will all be equal when we die. All wealth, power, and trappings will

be left behind, and we will all ultimately be equal. So why rage? It won't

do us any good.

THE RESEARCH PAPER

Research papers depend on secondary sources (the primary source is, of course, the work, the historical event, or the literary theory you are studying). Research assignments send you to the library, to the Web, or to any source of information that bears on your project. Whether you are researching to discover the varied responses to a work, to gain some insight into the author's life and times, or to identify relevant critical principles, you will synthesize what you have read *about* the work into a well-organized paper and provide *proper documentation.* But a research paper is not a mindless recitation of what your secondary sources have said. Nor does it require you to suspend your own critical judgment. By the time you settle into writing your paper, you will have learned some things you didn't know before. You have earned—and ought to exercise—the right to make some judgments. An assigned research topic will probably ask you to come to some conclusions. If you choose your own topic, you must discover in your research support for a clear, focused thesis before you begin to write.

Here is a sample student research paper that illustrates the technique. The marginal notes call attention to some of the details that make this a successful effort. In general, notice that the author has done research, but the paper is not weighed down with it. The opening paragraph provides a historical context for the subject of the paper, Kate Chopin's short story "The Storm" (p. 835). The writer has a point of view about the story, or thesis, stated in the second paragraph. While that thesis is developed throughout, the writer makes interesting observations on such matters as the relationship of other Chopin works to the story, the names of characters, local color, and a notable change in American moral attitudes. Note how the writer concludes with two paragraphs that resolve the issues raised in the opening two paragraphs.

The sample paper employs the Modern Language Association's (MLA) standard documentation and footnote form. The section that follows the research paper provides further samples that will help you manage formal matters and documentation. It concludes with a checklist that you might want to consult both before you begin writing your paper and before you submit your final draft.

AN ANNOTATED STUDENT RESEARCH PAPER

Lagos 1

Krissa Lagos

Professor Richard Abcarian

English 255

Sex and Sensibility

in Kate Chopin's "The Storm"

Kate Chopin's openly erotic depictions of marital infidelity in her literary works separate her from all other American female writers of her time. The adulterous affair of a strong independent woman depicted in her novel *The Awakening* (1899) created a public scandal. And, though she "never flouted convention as strongly as did her fictitious heroine, she did exhibit an individuality and strength remarkable for upper-middle-class women of the time" (Moon). Her honest and direct portrayal of the sexuality of her female characters was rejected until well into the 1900s, when the minds of readers caught up to her advanced thinking (Skaggs 5). Works such as "The Storm"—once shunned (especially by the male community) because of their focus on sexual exploration—are now celebrated as serious literature. In fact, when Chopin wrote "The Storm" in 1898, she knew that no magazine would ever publish such an uninhibited and uncritical account of an adulterous encounter, and so never attempted to have it published (Toth 206).

Margin annotations:

Writer's name and page number.

Use MLA standard style or follow instructor's criteria.

Center title.

First paragraph establishes context.

Documents an Internet source with no page number (see Works Cited).

Documents a book in Works Cited and gives page number.

States the
elements of the
paper's thesis.

    In "The Storm," Chopin utilizes the irony characteristic of her writing to give the story a light, easy feel. She also uses diction and imagery to draw the reader into the emotions of her characters. She ignores the usual implications of unfaithfulness to a spouse, and instead focuses on the pleasure inspired by the instant gratification of physical desire.

Provides
important
context for the
story's events.

    "The Storm" is in fact a sequel to another short story, "At the 'Cadian Ball." In the first tale, which takes place in Louisiana, a favorite setting for Chopin,[1] a farmer named Bobinôt is captivated with spirited, Spanish-blooded Calixta. Calixta, however, has her eyes on a handsome local planter, Alcée Laballière, who is charmed by her attractive features and openly sexual attitude. At the end of the night, however, Clarisse, a woman who is Alcée's social equal (and also happens to be his cousin), suddenly appears and agrees to marry him. Calixta, deserted by Alcée, is "deemed lucky to get anyone, even stodgy Bobinôt" (Ewell 77).

Discusses the
significance of
setting.

    By setting "The Storm" in Louisiana, Chopin is able to take advantage of the unstable, muggy weather of the region to help build up to the story's climax. The events of the tale occur because of the weather: the storm strands Bobinôt and his son Bibi at a store while wife and mother Calixta is at home, and Alcée is driven into Bobinôt and Calixta's house by the approaching rain. More subtle events, nearly all of which carry sensual undercurrents, are also inspired by the weather conditions.

Uses concrete
examples to
bolster
assertions.

Lagos 3

For instance, when Calixta is first mentioned, she is sewing, and Chopin immediately introduces an indirect sexual undertone to her movements: ". . . she felt very warm and often stopped to mop her face on which the perspiration gathered in beads. She unfastened her white sacque at the throat" (Chopin, "The Storm" 835). Except for what follows, there would be no reason at all to interpret this minor event. However, when Alcée arrives, the loosened collar eventually leads to more than one would imagine possible. First, Calixta is driven into his arms by the lightning crashing all around the house. Alcée attempts to ease her fears while at the same time fighting the desire for her that has been reawakened by contact with her body. Her unbuttoned collar is part of what defeats his battle against his desires:

> He pushed her hair back from her face that was
> warm and steaming. Her lips were as red and moist
> as pomegranate seed. Her white neck and a glimpse
> of her full firm bosom disturbed him powerfully. As
> she glanced up at him the fear in her liquid blue
> eyes had given place to a drowsy gleam that
> unconsciously betrayed a sensuous desire. (Chopin,
> "The Storm" 837)

Obviously the sole reason for Calixta and Alcée succumbing to their passions is not that she unbuttoned her shirt collar. However, the accumulation of this and other details—their shared climax with the storm, the correspondence between them lying contented afterward while the storm departs softly—make

Ellipses indicate omission in a direct quote.

Identifies the specific work from the Works Cited list when there is more than one work by the same author.

Shows how Chopin uses details to advance the plot.

this story a powerful work of art. Chopin crafts her sentences to enhance her narrative's power.

The French Louisiana setting of "The Storm" is typical of many of her writings (Ewell 52). The detailed local color is reflected by the French names of the characters. Calixta, Bobinôt, and Bibi speak the 'Cadian dialect of Louisiana, which in Calixta's case occasionally includes a small smattering of French (Ewell 77). Alcée, in contrast, speaks impeccable English, reflective of his better education. Chopin inserts a significant detail at the beginning of the story when Bobinôt purchases "a can of shrimps, of which Calixta was very fond" (Chopin, "The Storm" 835). The small gesture reveals Bobinôt's affectionate appreciation of his wife.

Discusses Chopin's view of the rights of women.

In "The Storm," Chopin conveys the theme of autonomy, something familiar to her female characters, especially in "The Story of an Hour."[2] Both Calixta and Clarisse are happiest in "The Storm" when they are separated from their husbands and free to do as they wish.

> As for Clarisse, she was charmed upon receiving her husband's letter. She and the babies were doing well. The society was agreeable; many of her old friends seemed to restore the pleasant liberty of her maiden days. Devoted as she was to her husband, their intimate conjugal life was something which she was more than willing to forego for a while. (Chopin, "The Storm" 839)

Therefore Clarisse, though far from the actual storm, benefits from its effects. She feels unfettered, pleased at being given space for the first time since she has been married to Alcée. For Calixta, the short time she spends with Alcée during the storm is enough to make her lift "her pretty chin in the air" and laugh with delight (Chopin, "The Storm" 838).

In "At the 'Cadian Ball," the two couples are paired together at the end of the night due to Alcée's notion of honor and propriety (Ewell 77). As Chopin explains in "The Storm," he never intended to marry Calixta, but he did want more from her than what he took in the story's prequel at the ball: "If she was not an immaculate dove in those days, she was still inviolate; a passionate creature whose very defenselessness had made her defense, against which his honor forbade him to prevail" (Chopin, "The Storm" 837). When the ball ended, only Calixta was left unsatisfied, but by the time "The Storm" takes place, only Bobinôt is still utterly content.

Earlier story is used to establish Alcée's character.

The fact that Calixta is now married somehow frees Alcée from his previous restraints, and he is able to satisfy his craving for her at last. As a result, Alcée is also more content with his wife away, which leads him to write the letter to her urging her to prolong her stay in Biloxi. Bobinôt is the most easily pleased of all. He reaches home cringing at what his wife will say to Bibi and him when she notices how dirty they are. Luckily for the father and son, she is still glowing from her brief interlude with Alcée, and "they laughed much and so loud that anyone might have heard them as far away as Laballière's" (Chopin, "The Storm" 838).

Chopin's irony shines through "The Storm" in many parts of the story. One of these moments occurs when she addresses the issue of natural right while Calixta and Alcée are making love: "Her firm, elastic flesh that was knowing for the first time its birthright, was like a creamy lily that the sun invites to contribute its breath and perfume to the undying life of the world" (Chopin, "The Storm" 837). Chopin goes further than condoning the affair between Calixta and Alcée by describing it as something completely natural, an event that was meant to occur.

What would have been most shocking to audiences in the nineteenth century was the fact that when the storm ended, there were no repercussions. Alcée "turned and smiled" at Calixta "with a beaming face" and rode away, Calixta showed "nothing but satisfaction" when her husband and son returned home, Bobinôt and Bibi "began to relax and enjoy themselves" when they saw that Calixta was in good spirits, and Clarisse stayed in Biloxi, enjoying herself. For such severe sins to be committed and go unpunished was unheard of in Chopin's time, and "even today some readers find that conclusion unforgivable" (Skaggs 62).

In truth, this very conclusion elevates "The Storm" to the high level it resides on. Through adultery, deception, and self-indulgence, the characters achieve happiness, a surprise ending that Chopin adopted from Guy de Maupassant.[3] This ironic twist makes the story a unique departure from the norm, even today, and "The Storm" ends on a comic note, the reader left as contented as the story's characters.

Asserts the proven thesis stated in the second paragraph.

Notes

[1]Chopin set many of her stories in the Cane River country of Louisiana; her husband, Oscar, was raised in Louisiana, and they lived there together for twelve years (Toth 92).

[2]In Chopin's "The Story of an Hour," the main character discovers that she prizes individual freedom over all else—even the life and love of her husband.

[3]Guy de Maupassant (1850–1893) was a French writer whose short stories often featured surprise endings.

Works Cited

Abcarian, Richard, Marvin Klotz, and Samuel Cohen, eds. *Literature: The Human Experience*. 11th ed. Boston: Bedford. 2013. Print.

Chopin, Kate. "At the 'Cadian Ball." *The Complete Works of Kate Chopin*. Ed. Per Seyersted. Baton Rouge: Louisiana State UP, 1969. 219–27. Print.

---. "The Storm." Abcarian, Klotz, and Cohen 835–39. Print.

Ewell, Barbara C. *Kate Chopin*. New York: Ungar, 1986. Print.

Moon, Jennifer. "ClassicNote on Kate Chopin." *GradeSaver*. *ClassicNotes by GradeSaver*. GradeSaver LLC, n.d. Web. 30 Mar. 2000.

Skaggs, Peggy. *Kate Chopin*. New York: Twayne, 1985. Print.

Toth, Emily. *Unveiling Kate Chopin*. Jackson: UP of Mississippi, 1999. Print.

SOME MATTERS OF FORM AND DOCUMENTATION

After you have worked hard to draft, revise, and edit an essay, check to be sure you have documented your sources accurately and fairly. A consistent, well-documented essay allows readers to focus on your argument rather than on your document.

Titles

When included in the body of your essay, the first word and all main words of titles are capitalized. Ordinarily (unless they are the first or last word), articles (*a, an,* and *the*), prepositions (*in, on, of, with, about,* and so on), conjunctions (*and, but, or,* and so on), and the *to* in an infinitive ("A Good Man Is Hard to Find") are not capitalized.

The titles of short stories, poems, articles, essays, songs, episodes of television programs, and parts of larger collections are enclosed in quotation marks.

The titles of plays, books, movies, periodicals, operas, television series, recordings, paintings, and newspapers are italicized. If your word-processing program does not produce italic type that is easily distinguishable from non-italic type, use underlining.

The title you give your essay is neither placed in quotation marks nor italicized. However, the title of a literary work used as a part of your title would be either placed in quotation marks or italicized, depending on the type of work it is.

Quotations

Quotation marks indicate that you are transcribing someone else's words; those words must, therefore, appear *exactly* as they do in your source.

As a general rule, quotations of not more than four lines of prose or two lines of poetry are placed between quotation marks and incorporated into your own text:

> Near the end of "Young Goodman Brown," the narrator asks, "Had
>
> Goodman Brown fallen asleep in the forest and only dreamed a wild
>
> dream of a witch-meeting?" (88).

If you are quoting two or three lines of verse in your text, indicate the division between lines with a slash. Leave a space before and after the slash:

> Prufrock hears the dilettantish talk in a room where "the women come
>
> and go / Talking of Michelangelo."

Longer quotations are indented ten spaces from the left margin and are double-spaced. They are not enclosed in quotation marks, since the indention signals a quotation.

BRACKETS AND ELLIPSES   If you insert anything into a quotation—even a word—the inserted material must be placed within brackets. If you wish to omit some material from a passage in quotation marks, the omission must be indicated with ellipsis points—three equally spaced periods. When an ellipsis occurs between complete sentences or at the end of a sentence, a fourth period, indicating the end of the sentence, should be inserted.

Here is an example of a full quotation from an original source:

> As one critic puts it, "Richard Wright, like Dostoevsky before him, sends his hero underground to discover the truth about the upper world, a world that has forced him to confess to a crime he has not committed."

Here is the quotation with insertion and omissions:

> As one critic puts it, "Richard Wright . . . sends his hero [Fred Daniels] underground to discover the truth about the upper world. . . ."

Use a full line of spaced periods to indicate the omission of a line or more of poetry:

> For I have known them all already, known them all—
>
> Have known the evenings, mornings, afternoons,
>
> I have measured out my life with coffee spoons;
>
> . . . .
>
> And I have known the eyes already, known them all—
>
> The eyes that fix you in a formulated phrase.

QUOTATION MARKS AND OTHER PUNCTUATION   Periods and commas are placed *inside* quotation marks:

> In "The Lesson," the narrator describes Miss Moore as someone "who always looked like she was going to church, though she never did."

Other punctuation marks such as colons or semicolons go outside the concluding quotation marks unless they are part of the material being quoted.

> Bartleby repeatedly insists that he "would prefer not to"; eventually these words become haunting.

For poetry quotations, provide the line number or numbers in parentheses immediately following the quotation:

With ironic detachment, Prufrock declares that he is "no prophet" (83).

Documentation

You must acknowledge sources for the ideas you paraphrase or summarize and material you quote. Such acknowledgments are extremely important, for even an unintentional failure to give formal credit to others for their words or ideas can leave you open to an accusation of *plagiarism*—that is, the presentation of someone else's ideas as your own.

In the body of your essay, use parenthetical citations to document those works that you quote, paraphrase, or summarize. A list of your sources should be the last page of your essay, the Works Cited page. If you use other kinds of sources not listed here, consult the *MLA Handbook for Writers of Research Papers*, Seventh Edition (2009), or online at <www.mla.org/style>.

This whimsical paragraph demonstrates the use of parenthetical citations.

Leslie Fiedler's view of the relationship between Jim and Huck

(669–70) uses a method often discussed by other critics (Abcarian,

Klotz, and Cohen 7–10). Cooper's 1971 study (180) raises similar

issues, although such methods are not useful when dealing with such a

line as "North Richmond Street, being blind, was a quiet street except at

the hour when the Christian Brothers' School set the boys free" (Joyce,

"Araby" 122). But when Joyce refers to the weather (*Dubliners* 224), the

issue becomes clouded.

The first citation gives only the page reference, which is all that is necessary because the author's name is given in the text and only one work by that author appears in the list of works cited. The second citation gives the editors' names and thus identifies the work being cited. It then indicates the appropriate pages. The third citation, because the author's name is mentioned in the text, gives only a page reference. The fourth citation must provide the author's name *and* the work cited, because two works by the same author appear in the list of works cited. The last citation, because it refers to an author with two works in the list of works cited, gives the name of the work and the page where the reference can be found.

In short, your parenthetical acknowledgment should contain (1) the *minimum* information required to lead the reader to the appropriate work in the list of works cited and (2) the location within the work to which you refer. Citations give credit whenever it is due and enable your reader to go directly to your sources as quickly and easily as possible.

Works Cited

Abcarian, Richard, Marvin Klotz, and Samuel Cohen, eds. *Literature: The Human Experience*. 11th ed. Boston: Bedford. 2013. Print.

Cooper, Wendy. *Hair, Sex, Society, Symbolism*. New York: Stein, 1971. Print.

Fiedler, Leslie. "Come Back to the Raft Ag'in, Huck Honey." *Partisan Review* 15 (1948): 664–71. Print.

Joyce, James. "Araby." Abcarian, Klotz, and Cohen 122–26.

---. *Dubliners*. Eds. Robert Scholes and A. Walton Litz. New York: Penguin, 1976. Print.

The first of these citations is for this book. Note that the first editor's name is presented surname first, but the second and subsequent names are presented with the surname last. The second entry illustrates the form for citing a book with one author. The third gives the form for an article published in a periodical (note that the title of the article is in quotes and the title of the journal is italicized). The fourth entry shows how to cite a work included in an anthology. The fifth citation, because it is by the same author as the fourth, begins with three hyphens in place of the author's name.

DOCUMENTING ONLINE SOURCES   Until recently, there were few standards governing the citation of electronic sources. However, it has become increasingly common to employ at least some online tools while conducting research. The form suggested below will probably serve for most citations to online books, articles, databases, and other kinds of sites. Keep in mind, however, that if it does not, you will have to decide for yourself the best way to include additional information. The most important thing is that you accurately cite every single source you consult whether that source is a Web site or a more traditional source like a book or an encyclopedia.

1. Author's name
2. Title of the work in quotation marks
3. Title of the Web site (italicized)
4. Sponsor or publisher
5. Date of publication or most recent update

6. Medium of publication

7. Date of access

O'Rourke, Megan. "A Pessimist in Flower." *Slate*. Washington Post.

Newsweek Interactive Co. LLC, 18 Jan. 2007. Web. 9 Mar. 2011

A CHECKLIST FOR WRITING ABOUT LITERATURE

1. Is my essay clearly responsive to the assignment?

2. Does my essay put forward a clearly defined thesis at the outset?

3. Does each paragraph have an identifiable topic sentence?

4. Have I marshaled my paragraphs logically and provided appropriate transitions?

5. Do I support my assertions with evidence?

6. Have I used direct quotations appropriately, and have I transcribed them accurately?

7. Do I document the sources of other people's ideas and the direct quotations I use? Is the documentation in appropriate form?

8. Have I written syntactically correct sentences (no run-ons and no fragments except by design)?

9. Have I eliminated as many passive constructions and forms of the verb *to be* as possible?

10. Have I avoided long sequences (say, three or more) of prepositional phrases?

11. Can I feel good about this essay? Does it embody serious thinking in attractive form (free of typos and other errors)? Can I put my name on the essay with pride?

INNOCENCE AND EXPERIENCE

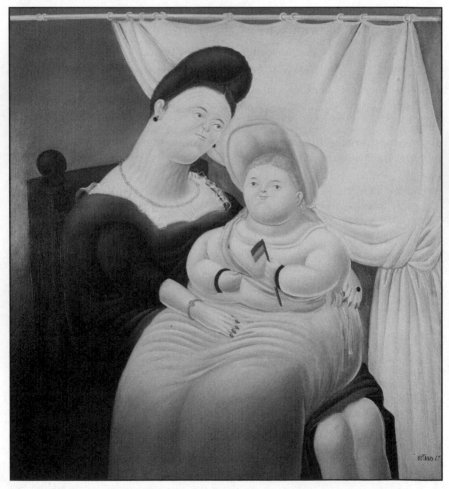

The Grandmother (La Abuela), 1967, by Fernando Botero.

Humans strive to give order and meaning to their lives, to reduce the mystery and unpredictability that constantly threaten them. Life is infinitely more complex and surprising than we imagine, and the categories we establish to give it order and meaning are, for the most part, "a momentary stay against confusion" to borrow Robert Frost's description of poetry. At any time the equilibrium of our lives, the comfortable image of ourselves and the world around us, may be disrupted by something new, forcing us into painful reevaluation. These disruptions create pain, anxiety, and terror but also wisdom and awareness.

The works in this section deal generally with the movement of a central character from moral simplicities and certainties into a more complex and problematic world. Though these works frequently deal with awareness, even wisdom, their central figures rarely act decisively. The main character or protagonist is more often a passive figure who learns the difference between the ideal world he or she imagines and the injurious real world. If the protagonist survives the ordeal, he or she often becomes a better human—better able to wrest some satisfaction from a bleak and threatening world. Many of the works here deal with the passage from childhood to adulthood, the time that certainty gives way to uncertainty.

Almost universally, innocence is associated with childhood and youth, as experience is with age. We teach the young about an ideal world, without explaining that it has not yet been and may never be achieved. As innocents, children are terribly vulnerable to falsehood, to intrusive sexuality, and to the machinations of the wicked, who often triumph.

But the terms *innocence* and *experience* range widely in meaning, and that range is reflected here. Innocence may be social—the innocence of Brown in Nathaniel Hawthorne's "Young Goodman Brown." Or innocence may be seen as the child's ignorance of his or her own mortality, as in Gerard Manley Hopkins's "Spring and Fall" and Dylan Thomas's "Fern Hill." In such works as Nathaniel Hawthorne's "Young Goodman Brown" and Robert Browning's "My Last Duchess," one discovers the tragic consequences of an innocence that is blind.

The contrast between what we thought in our youth and what we have come to know, painfully, as adults stands as an emblem of the passage from innocence to experience. Yet all of us remain, to one degree or another, innocent throughout life, since we never—except with death—stop learning from experience. Looked at in this way, experience is the ceaseless assault life makes on our innocence, moving us to a greater wisdom about ourselves and the world around us.

QUESTIONS FOR THINKING AND WRITING

As you read the selections in this section, consider the following questions. You may want to write out your thoughts informally in a journal or notebook as a way of preparing to respond to the selections, or you may wish to make one of these questions the basis for a formal essay.

1. Innocence is often associated with childhood; responsibility, with adulthood. Were you happier or more contented as a preteen than you are now? Why? Which particular aspects of your childhood do you remember with pleasure? Which with pain? Do you look forward to the future with pleasurable anticipation or with dread? Why?

2. Do you know any adults who seem to be innocents? On what do you base your judgment? Do you know any preteens who seem to be particularly "adult" in their behavior (beyond politeness and good manners—they may, for example, have to cope with severe family difficulties)? On what do you base your judgment?

3. Have you spent your life under the authority of others, such as parents, teachers, and employers? How do you deal with authorities you resent? Do you look forward to exercising authority over others (your own children, your own students, employees under your supervision)? How will your experiences affect your behavior as an authority figure?

4. How does the growth from innocence to experience affect one's sexual behavior? Social behavior? Political behavior?

FICTION

NATHANIEL HAWTHORNE (1804–1864)

YOUNG GOODMAN BROWN 1846

Young Goodman[1] Brown came forth at sunset into the street at Salem village; but put his head back, after crossing the threshold, to exchange a parting kiss with his young wife. And Faith, as the wife was aptly named, thrust her own pretty head into the street, letting the wind play with the pink ribbons of her cap while she called to Goodman Brown.

"Dearest heart," whispered she, softly and rather sadly, when her lips were close to his ear, "prithee put off your journey until sunrise and sleep in your own bed to-night. A lone woman is troubled with such dreams and such thoughts that she's afeared of herself sometimes. Pray tarry with me this night, dear husband, of all nights in the year."

"My love and my Faith," replied young Goodman Brown, "of all nights in the year, this one night must I tarry away from thee. My journey, as thou call-est it, forth and back again, must needs be done 'twixt now and sunrise. What, my sweet, pretty wife, dost thou doubt me already, and we but three months married?"

"Then God bless you!" said Faith, with the pink ribbons; "and may you find all well when you come back."

"Amen!" cried Goodman Brown. "Say thy prayers, dear Faith, and go to bed   5 at dusk, and no harm will come to thee."

So they parted; and the young man pursued his way until, being about to turn the corner by the meeting-house, he looked back and saw the head of Faith still peeping after him with a melancholy air, in spite of her pink ribbons.

"Poor little Faith!" thought he, for his heart smote him. "What a wretch am I to leave her on such an errand! She talks of dreams, too. Methought as she spoke there was trouble in her face, as if a dream had warned her what work is to be done to-night. But no, no; 'twould kill her to think it. Well, she's a blessed angel on earth; and after this one night I'll cling to her skirts and follow her to heaven."

---

[1] Equivalent to *Mr.*, a title given to a man below the rank of gentleman.

With this excellent resolve for the future, Goodman Brown felt himself justified in making more haste on his present evil purpose. He had taken a dreary road, darkened by all the gloomiest trees of the forest, which barely stood aside to let the narrow path creep through, and closed immediately behind. It was all as lonely as could be; and there is this peculiarity in such a solitude, that the traveller knows not who may be concealed by the innumerable trunks and the thick boughs overhead; so that with lonely footsteps he may yet be passing through an unseen multitude.

"There may be a devilish Indian behind every tree," said Goodman Brown to himself; and he glanced fearfully behind him as he added, "What if the devil himself should be at my very elbow!"

His head being turned back, he passed a crook of the road, and, looking forward again, beheld the figure of a man, in grave and decent attire, seated at the foot of an old tree. He arose at Goodman Brown's approach and walked onward side by side with him. 10

"You are late, Goodman Brown," said he. "The clock of the Old South[2] was striking as I came through Boston, and that is full fifteen minutes agone."

"Faith kept me back a while," replied the young man, with a tremor in his voice, caused by the sudden appearance of his companion, though not wholly unexpected.

It was now deep dusk in the forest, and deepest in that part of it where these two were journeying. As nearly as could be discerned, the second traveller was about fifty years old, apparently in the same rank of life as Goodman Brown, and bearing a considerable resemblance to him, though perhaps more in expression than features. Still they might have been taken for father and son. And yet, though the elder person was as simply clad as the younger, and as simple in manner too, he had an indescribable air of one who knew the world, and who would not have felt abashed at the governor's dinner table or in King William's[3] court, were it possible that his affairs should call him thither. But the only thing about him that could be fixed upon as remarkable was his staff, which bore the likeness of a great black snake, so curiously wrought that it might almost be seen to twist and wriggle itself like a living serpent. This, of course, must have been an ocular deception, assisted by the uncertain light.

"Come, Goodman Brown," cried his fellow-traveller, "this is a dull pace for the beginning of a journey. Take my staff, if you are so soon weary."

"Friend," said the other, exchanging his slow pace for a full stop, "having kept covenant by meeting thee here, it is my purpose now to return whence I came. I have scruples touching the matter thou wot'st of." 15

"Sayest thou so?" replied he of the serpent, smiling apart. "Let us walk on, nevertheless, reasoning as we go; and if I convince thee not thou shalt turn back. We are but a little way in the forest yet."

[2] A church in Boston.
[3] Ruler of England from 1689 to 1702.

"Too far! too far!" exclaimed the goodman, unconsciously resuming his walk. "My father never went into the woods on such an errand, nor his father before him. We have been a race of honest men and good Christians since the days of the martyrs;[4] and shall I be the first of the name of Brown that ever took this path and kept—"

"Such company, thou wouldst say," observed the elder person, interpreting his pause. "Well said, Goodman Brown! I have been as well acquainted with your family as with ever a one among the Puritans; and that's no trifle to say. I helped your grandfather, the constable, when he lashed the Quaker woman so smartly through the streets of Salem; and it was I that brought your father a pitch-pine knot, kindled at my own hearth, to set fire to an Indian village, in King Philip's war.[5] They were my good friends, both; and many a pleasant walk have we had along this path, and returned merrily after midnight. I would fain be friends with you for their sake."

"If it be as thou sayest," replied Goodman Brown, "I marvel they never spoke of these matters; or, verily, I marvel not, seeing that the least rumor of the sort would have driven them from New England. We are a people of prayer, and good works to boot, and abide no such wickedness."

"Wickedness or not," said the traveller, with the twisted staff, "I have a very general acquaintance here in New England. The deacons of many a church have drunk the communion wine with me; the selectmen of divers towns make me their chairman; and a majority of the Great and General Court[6] are firm supporters of my interest. The governor and I, too—But these are state secrets."

"Can this be so?" cried Goodman Brown, with a stare of amazement at his undisturbed companion. "Howbeit, I have nothing to do with the governor and council; they have their own ways, and are no rule for a simple husbandman[7] like me. But, were I to go on with thee, how should I meet the eye of that good old man, our minister, at Salem village? Oh, his voice would make me tremble both Sabbath day and lecture day."

Thus far the elder traveller had listened with due gravity; but now burst into a fit of irrepressible mirth, shaking himself so violently that his snake-like staff actually seemed to wriggle in sympathy.

"Ha! ha! ha!" shouted he again and again; then composing himself, "Well, go on, Goodman Brown, go on; but, prithee, don't kill me with laughing."

"Well, then, to end the matter at once," said Goodman Brown, considerably nettled, "there is my wife, Faith. It would break her dear little heart; and I'd rather break my own."

---

[4] A reference to the persecution of Protestants in England (1553–1558) by the Catholic monarch Mary Tudor.

[5] War waged (1675–1676) against the colonists of New England by the Indian chief Metacomet, also known as "King Philip."

[6] The Puritan legislature.

[7] An ordinary person.

"Nay, if that be the case," answered the other, "e'en go thy ways, Goodman   25
Brown. I would not for twenty old women like the one hobbling before us that
Faith should come to any harm."

As he spoke he pointed his staff at a female figure on the path, in whom Goodman Brown recognized a very pious and exemplary dame, who had taught him
his catechism in youth, and was still his moral and spiritual adviser, jointly with
the minister and Deacon Gookin.

"A marvel, truly, that Goody[8] Cloyse should be so far in the wilderness at
nightfall," said he. "But with your leave, friend, I shall take a cut through the
woods until we have left this Christian woman behind. Being a stranger to
you, she might ask whom I was consorting with and whither I was going."

"Be it so," said his fellow-traveller. "Betake you to the woods, and let me
keep the path."

Accordingly the young man turned aside, but took care to watch his companion, who advanced softly along the road until he had come within a staff's
length of the old dame. She, meanwhile, was making the best of her way, with
singular speed for so aged a woman, and mumbling some indistinct words—a
prayer, doubtless—as she went. The traveller put forth his staff and touched
her withered neck with what seemed the serpent's tail.

"The devil!" screamed the pious old lady.   30

"Then Goody Cloyse knows her old friend?" observed the traveller, confronting her and leaning on his writhing stick.

"Ah, forsooth, and is it your worship indeed?" cried the good dame. "Yea,
truly is it, and in the very image of my old gossip, Goodman Brown, the grandfather of the silly fellow that now is. But—would your worship believe it?—my
broomstick hath strangely disappeared, stolen, as I suspect, by that unhanged
witch, Goody Cory, and that, too, when I was all anointed with the juice of
smallage and cinquefoil and wolf's bane"[9]—

"Mingled with fine wheat and the fat of a new-born babe," said the shape of
old Goodman Brown.

"Ah, your worship knows the recipe," cried the old lady, cackling aloud.
"So, as I was saying, being all ready for the meeting, and no horse to ride on,
I made up my mind to foot it; for they tell me there is a nice young man to be
taken into communion to-night. But now your good worship will lend me
your arm, and we shall be there in a twinkling."

"That can hardly be," answered her friend. "I may not spare you my arm,   35
Goody Cloyse; but here is my staff, if you will."

So saying, he threw it down at her feet, where, perhaps, it assumed life, being
one of the rods which its owner had formerly lent to the Egyptian magi.[10] Of
this fact, however, Goodman Brown could not take cognizance. He had cast
up his eyes in astonishment, and, looking down again, beheld neither Goody

---

[8] A polite title for a wife of humble rank.
[9] All these plants were associated with magic and witchcraft.
[10] Allusion to the biblical magicians who turned their rods into serpents (Exodus 7:11–12).

Cloyse nor the serpentine staff, but his fellow-traveller alone, who waited for him as calmly as if nothing had happened.

"That old woman taught me my catechism," said the young man; and there was a world of meaning in this simple comment.

They continued to walk onward, while the elder traveller exhorted his companion to make good speed and persevere in the path, discoursing so aptly that his arguments seemed rather to spring up in the bosom of his auditor than to be suggested by himself. As they went, he plucked a branch of maple to serve for a walking stick, and began to strip it of the twigs and little boughs, which were wet with evening dew. The moment his fingers touched them they became strangely withered and dried up as with a week's sunshine. Thus the pair proceeded, at a good free pace, until suddenly, in a gloomy hollow of the road, Goodman Brown sat himself down on the stump of a tree and refused to go any farther.

"Friend," said he, stubbornly, "my mind is made up. Not another step will I budge on this errand. What if a wretched old woman do choose to go to the devil when I thought she was going to heaven: is that any reason why I should quit my dear Faith and go after her?"

"You will think better of this by and by," said his acquaintance, compos- 40 edly. "Sit here and rest yourself a while; and when you feel like moving again, there is my staff to help you along."

Without more words, he threw his companion the maple stick, and was as speedily out of sight as if he had vanished into the deepening gloom. The young man sat a few moments by the roadside, applauding himself greatly, and thinking with how clear a conscience he should meet the minister in his morning walk, nor shrink from the eye of good old Deacon Gookin. And what calm sleep would be his that very night, which was to have been spent so wickedly, but so purely and sweetly now, in the arms of Faith! Amidst these pleasant and praiseworthy meditations, Goodman Brown heard the tramp of horses along the road, and deemed it advisable to conceal himself within the verge of the forest, conscious of the guilty purpose that had brought him thither, though now so happily turned from it.

On came the hoof tramps and the voices of the riders, two grave old voices, conversing soberly as they drew near. These mingled sounds appeared to pass along the road, within a few yards of the young man's hiding-place; but, owing doubtless to the depth of the gloom at that particular spot, neither the travellers nor their steeds were visible. Though their figures brushed the small boughs by the wayside, it could not be seen that they intercepted, even for a moment, the faint gleam from the strip of bright sky athwart which they must have passed. Goodman Brown alternately crouched and stood on tiptoe, pulling aside the branches and thrusting forth his head as far as he durst without discerning so much as a shadow. It vexed him the more, because he could have sworn, were such a thing possible, that he recognized the voices of the minister and Deacon Gookin, jogging along quietly, as they were wont to do, when bound to some ordination or ecclesiastical council. While yet within hearing, one of the riders stopped to pluck a switch.

"Of the two, reverend sir," said the voice like the deacon's, "I had rather miss an ordination dinner than to-night's meeting. They tell me that some of our community are to be here from Falmouth[11] and beyond, and others from Connecticut and Rhode Island, besides several of the Indian powwows,[12] who, after their fashion, know almost as much deviltry as the best of us. Moreover, there is a goodly young woman to be taken into communion."

"Mighty well, Deacon Gookin!" replied the solemn old tones of the minister. "Spur up, or we shall be late. Nothing can be done, you know, until I get on the ground."

The hoofs clattered again; and the voices, talking so strangely in the empty air, passed on through the forest, where no church had ever been gathered, nor solitary Christian prayed. Whither, then, could these holy men be journeying so deep into the heathen wilderness? Young Goodman Brown caught hold of a tree for support, being ready to sink down on the ground, faint and overburdened with the heavy sickness of his heart. He looked up to the sky, doubting whether there really was a heaven above him. Yet there was the blue arch, and the stars brightening in it.   45

"With heaven above and Faith below, I will yet stand firm against the devil!" cried Goodman Brown.

While he still gazed upward into the deep arch of the firmament and had lifted his hands to pray, a cloud, though no wind was stirring, hurried across the zenith and hid the brightening stars. The blue sky was still visible, except directly overhead, where this black mass of cloud was sweeping swiftly northward. Aloft in the air, as if from the depths of the cloud, came a confused and doubtful sound of voices. Once the listener fancied that he could distinguish the accents of towns-people of his own, men and women, both pious and ungodly, many of whom he had met at the communion table, and had seen others rioting at the tavern. The next moment, so indistinct were the sounds, he doubted whether he had heard aught but the murmur of the old forest, whispering without a wind. Then came a stronger swell of those familiar tones, heard daily in the sunshine at Salem village, but never until now from a cloud of night. There was one voice, of a young woman, uttering lamentations, yet with an uncertain sorrow, and entreating for some favor, which, perhaps, it would grieve her to obtain; and all the unseen multitude, both saints and sinners, seemed to encourage her onward.

"Faith!" shouted Goodman Brown, in a voice of agony and desperation; and the echoes of the forest mocked him, crying, "Faith! Faith!" as if bewildered wretches were seeking her all through the wilderness.

The cry of grief, rage, and terror was yet piercing the night, when the unhappy husband held his breath for a response. There was a scream, drowned immediately in a louder murmur of voices, fading into far-off laughter, as

---

[11] A town near Salem, Massachusetts.
[12] Medicine men.

the dark cloud swept away, leaving the clear and silent sky above Goodman Brown. But something fluttered lightly down through the air and caught on the branch of a tree. The young man seized it, and beheld a pink ribbon.

"My Faith is gone!" cried he, after one stupefied moment. "There is no good on earth; and sin is but a name. Come, devil; for to thee is this world given." 50

And, maddened with despair, so that he laughed loud and long, did Goodman Brown grasp his staff and set forth again, at such a rate that he seemed to fly along the forest path rather than to walk or run. The road grew wilder and drearier and more faintly traced, and vanished at length, leaving him in the heart of the dark wilderness, still rushing onward with the instinct that guides mortal man to evil. The whole forest was peopled with frightful sounds—the creaking of the trees, the howling of wild beasts, and the yell of Indians; while sometimes the wind tolled like a distant church bell, and sometimes gave a broad roar around the traveller, as if all Nature were laughing him to scorn. But he was himself the chief horror of the scene, and shrank not from its other horrors.

"Ha! ha! ha!" roared Goodman Brown when the wind laughed at him. "Let us hear which will laugh loudest. Think not to frighten me with your deviltry. Come witch, come wizard, come Indian powwow, come devil himself, and here comes Goodman Brown. You may as well fear him as he fears you."

In truth, all through the haunted forest there could be nothing more frightful than the figure of Goodman Brown. On he flew among the black pines, brandishing his staff with frenzied gestures, now giving vent to an inspiration of horrid blasphemy, and now shouting forth such laughter as set all the echoes of the forest laughing like demons around him. The fiend in his own shape is less hideous than when he rages in the breast of man. Thus sped the demoniac on his course, until, quivering among the trees, he saw a red light before him, as when the felled trunks and branches of a clearing have been set on fire, and throw up their lurid blaze against the sky, at the hour of midnight. He paused, in a lull of the tempest that had driven him onward, and heard the swell of what seemed a hymn, rolling solemnly from a distance with the weight of many voices. He knew the tune; it was a familiar one in the choir of the village meeting-house. The verse died heavily away, and was lengthened by a chorus, not of human voices, but of all the sounds of the benighted wilderness pealing in awful harmony together. Goodman Brown cried out, and his cry was lost to his own ear by its unison with the cry of the desert.

In the interval of silence he stole forward until the light glared full upon his eyes. At one extremity of an open space, hemmed in by the dark wall of the forest, arose a rock, bearing some rude, natural resemblance either to an altar or a pulpit, and surrounded by four blazing pines, their tops aflame, their stems untouched, like candles at an evening meeting. The mass of foliage that had overgrown the summit of the rock was all on fire, blazing high into the night and fitfully illuminating the whole field. Each pendent twig and leafy festoon was in a blaze. As the red light arose and fell, a numerous congregation alternately shone forth, then disappeared in shadow, and again grew, as it were, out of the darkness, peopling the heart of the solitary woods at once.

"A grave and dark-clad company," quoth Goodman Brown.   55

In truth they were such. Among them, quivering to and fro between gloom and splendor, appeared faces that would be seen next day at the council board of the province, and others which, Sabbath after Sabbath, looked devoutly heavenward, and benignantly over the crowded pews, from the holiest pulpits in the land. Some affirm that the lady of the governor was there. At least there were high dames well known to her, and wives of honored husbands, and widows, a great multitude, and ancient maidens, all of excellent repute, and fair young girls, who trembled lest their mothers should espy them. Either the sudden gleams of light flashing over the obscure field bedazzled Goodman Brown, or he recognized a score of the church members of Salem village famous for their especial sanctity. Good old Deacon Gookin had arrived, and waited at the skirts of that venerable saint, his revered pastor. But, irreverently consorting with these grave, reputable, and pious people, these elders of the church, these chaste dames and dewy virgins, there were men of dissolute lives and women of spotted fame, wretches given over to all mean and filthy vice, and suspected even of horrid crimes. It was strange to see that the good shrank not from the wicked, nor were the sinners abashed by the saints. Scattered also among their pale-faced enemies were the Indian priests, or powwows, who had often scared their native forest with more hideous incantations than any known to English witchcraft.

"But where is Faith?" thought Goodman Brown; and, as hope came into his heart, he trembled.

Another verse of the hymn arose, a slow and mournful strain, such as the pious love, but joined to words which expressed all that our nature can conceive of sin, and darkly hinted at far more. Unfathomable to mere mortals is the lore of fiends. Verse after verse was sung; and still the chorus of the desert swelled between like the deepest tone of a mighty organ; and with the final peal of that dreadful anthem there came a sound, as if the roaring wind, the rushing streams, the howling beasts, and every other voice of the unconcerted wilderness were mingling and according with the voice of guilty man in homage to the prince of all. The four blazing pines threw up a loftier flame, and obscurely discovered shapes and visages of horror on the smoke wreaths above the impious assembly. At the same moment the fire on the rock shot redly forth and formed a glowing arch above its base, where now appeared a figure. With reverence be it spoken, the figure bore no slight similitude, both in garb and manner, to some grave divine of the New England churches.

"Bring forth the converts!" cried a voice that echoed through the field and rolled into the forest.

At the word, Goodman Brown stepped forth from the shadow of the trees   60 and approached the congregation, with whom he felt a loathful brotherhood by the sympathy of all that was wicked in his heart. He could have well-nigh sworn that the shape of his own dead father beckoned him to advance, looking downward from a smoke wreath, while a woman, with dim features of despair, threw out her hand to warn him back. Was it his mother? But he had no power to retreat one step, nor to resist, even in thought, when the minister and good old Deacon Gookin seized his arms and led him to the blazing rock. Thither came also the slender form of a veiled female, led between Goody Cloyse, that pious teacher of the catechism, and Martha Carrier,[13] who had received the devil's promise to be queen of hell. A rampant hag was she. And there stood the proselytes beneath the canopy of fire.

"Welcome, my children," said the dark figure, "to the communion of your race. Ye have found thus young your nature and your destiny. My children, look behind you!"

They turned; and flashing forth, as it were, in a sheet of flame, the fiend worshippers were seen; the smile of welcome gleamed darkly on every visage.

"There," resumed the sable form, "are all whom ye have reverenced from youth. Ye deemed them holier than yourselves, and shrank from your own sin, contrasting it with their lives of righteousness and prayerful aspirations heavenward. Yet here are they all in my worshipping assembly. This night it shall be granted you to know their secret deeds: how hoary-bearded elders of the church have whispered wanton words to the young maids of their households; how many a woman, eager for widows' weeds, has given her husband a drink at bedtime and let him sleep his last sleep in her bosom; how beardless youths have made haste to inherit their fathers' wealth; and how fair damsels—blush not, sweet ones—have dug little graves in the garden, and bidden me, the sole guest, to an infant's funeral. By the sympathy of your human hearts for sin ye shall scent out all the places—whether in church, bed-chamber, street, field, or forest—where crime has been committed, and shall exult to behold the whole earth one stain of guilt, one mighty blood spot. Far more than this. It shall be yours to penetrate, in every bosom, the deep mystery of sin, the fountain of all wicked arts, and which inexhaustibly supplies more evil impulses than human power—than my power at its utmost—can make manifest in deeds. And now, my children, look upon each other."

They did so; and, by the blaze of the hell-kindled torches, the wretched man beheld his Faith, and the wife her husband, trembling before that unhallowed altar.

"Lo, there ye stand, my children," said the figure, in a deep and solemn tone, 65 almost sad with its despairing awfulness, as if his once angelic nature could yet mourn for our miserable race. "Depending upon one another's hearts, ye had still hoped that virtue were not all a dream. Now are ye undeceived. Evil is the nature of mankind. Evil must be your only happiness. Welcome again, my children, to the communion of your race."

"Welcome," repeated the fiend worshippers, in one cry of despair and triumph.

[13] One of the women hanged in Salem in 1697 for witchcraft.

And there they stood, the only pair, as it seemed, who were yet hesitating on the verge of wickedness in this dark world. A basin was hollowed, naturally, in the rock. Did it contain water, reddened by the lurid light? or was it blood? or, perchance, a liquid flame? Herein did the shape of evil dip his hand and pre-pare to lay the mark of baptism upon their foreheads, that they might be par-takers of the mystery of sin, more conscious of the secret guilt of others, both in deed and thought, than they could now be of their own. The husband cast one look at his pale wife, and Faith at him. What polluted wretches would the next glance show them to each other, shuddering alike at what they disclosed and what they saw!

"Faith! Faith!" cried the husband, "look up to heaven, and resist the wicked one."

Whether Faith obeyed he knew not. Hardly had he spoken when he found himself amid calm night and solitude, listening to a roar of the wind which died heavily away through the forest. He staggered against the rock, and felt it chill and damp; while a hanging twig, that had been all on fire, besprinkled his cheek with the coldest dew.

The next morning young Goodman Brown came slowly into the street of 70 Salem village, staring around him like a bewildered man. The good old minis-ter was taking a walk along the graveyard to get an appetite for breakfast and meditate his sermon, and bestowed a blessing, as he passed, on Goodman Brown. He shrank from the venerable saint as if to avoid an anathema. Old Deacon Gookin was at domestic worship, and the holy words of his prayer were heard through the open window. "What God doth the wizard pray to?" quoth Goodman Brown. Goody Cloyse, that excellent old Christian, stood in the early sunshine at her own lattice, catechizing a little girl who had brought her a pint of morning's milk. Goodman Brown snatched away the child as from the grasp of the fiend himself. Turning the corner by the meeting-house, he spied the head of Faith, with the pink ribbons, gazing anxiously forth, and bursting into such joy at sight of him that she skipped along the street and almost kissed her husband before the whole village. But Goodman Brown looked sternly and sadly into her face, and passed on without a greeting.

Had Goodman Brown fallen asleep in the forest and only dreamed a wild dream of a witch-meeting?

Be it so if you will; but, alas! it was a dream of evil omen for young Goodman Brown. A stern, a sad, a darkly meditative, a distrustful, if not a desperate man did he become from the night of that fearful dream. On the Sabbath day, when the congregation were singing a holy psalm, he could not listen because an anthem of sin rushed loudly upon his ear and drowned all the blessed strain. When the minister spoke from the pulpit with power and fervid eloquence, and, with his hand on the open Bible, of the sacred truths of our religion, and of saint-like lives and triumphant deaths, and of future bliss or misery unut-terable, then did Goodman Brown turn pale, dreading lest the roof should thunder down upon the gray blasphemer and his hearers. Often, awakening suddenly at midnight, he shrank from the bosom of Faith; and at morning or eventide, when the family knelt down at prayer, he scowled and muttered to himself, and gazed sternly at his wife, and turned away. And when he had lived long, and was borne to his grave a hoary corpse, followed by Faith, an aged woman, and children and grandchildren, a goodly procession, besides neighbors not a few, they carved no hopeful verse upon his tombstone, for his dying hour was gloom.

FOR ANALYSIS

1. At the end of the story, the **narrator** asks, "Had Goodman Brown fallen asleep in the forest and only dreamed a wild dream of a witch-meeting?" Why, instead of answering the question, does he say, "Be it so if you will"?

2. Examine the seemingly supernatural events Brown experiences as he penetrates ever deeper into the forest. Can the reader determine whether those events are really taking place? If not, what purpose does the **ambiguity** serve?

3. What attitude does this story express toward the church of Puritan New England?

4. What elements of the story can be described as **allegorical** or **symbolic**?

5. What is the "guilty purpose" (para. 41) that has drawn Brown to the forest?

MAKING CONNECTIONS

1. Both this story and Melville's "Bartleby, the Scrivener" (p. 325) deal with **protagonists** who withdraw from life. What similarities and differences do you find in the reasons for their withdrawal, the ways in which they withdraw, and the consequences of their withdrawal?

2. Both Hawthorne's "Young Goodman Brown" and Ellison's "'Repent, Harlequin!' Said the Ticktockman" (p. 401) rely on fantasy. What advantages does the use of fantasy give the authors?

WRITING TOPICS

1. Write an essay in which you argue for or against the proposition that the "truth" Brown discovers during the night in the forest justifies his gloom and withdrawal.

2. Write out a paraphrase of Satan's sermon.

A & P 1961

In walks these three girls in nothing but bathing suits. I'm in the third check-out slot, with my back to the door, so I don't see them until they're over by the bread. The one that caught my eye first was the one in the plaid green two-piece. She was a chunky kid, with a good tan and a sweet broad soft-looking can with those two crescents of white just under it, where the sun never seems to hit, at the top of the backs of her legs. I stood there with my hand on a box of HiHo crackers trying to remember if I rang it up or not. I ring it up again and the customer starts giving me hell. She's one of these cash-register-watchers, a witch about fifty with rouge on her cheekbones and no eyebrows, and I know it made her day to trip me up. She'd been watching cash registers for fifty years and probably never seen a mistake before.

By the time I got her feathers smoothed and her goodies into a bag—she gives me a little snort in passing, if she'd been born at the right time they would have burned her over in Salem—by the time I get her on her way the girls had circled around the bread and were coming back, without a pushcart, back my way along the counters, in the aisle between the checkouts and the Special bins. They didn't even have shoes on. There was this chunky one, with the two-piece—it was bright green and the seams on the bra were still sharp and her belly was still pretty pale so I guessed she just got it (the suit)—there was this one, with one of those chubby berry-faces, the lips all bunched together under her nose, this one, and a tall one, with black hair that hadn't quite frizzed right, and one of these sunburns right across under the eyes, and a chin that was too long—you know, the kind of girl other girls think is very "striking" and "attractive" but never quite makes it, as they very well know, which is why they like her so much—and then the third one, that wasn't quite so tall. She was the queen. She kind of led them, the other two peeking around and making their shoulders round. She didn't look around, not this queen, she just walked straight on slowly, on these long white prima-donna legs. She came down a little hard on her heels, as if she didn't walk in her bare feet that much, putting down her heels and then letting the weight move along to her toes as if she was testing the floor with every step, putting a little deliberate extra action into it. You never know for sure how girls' minds work (do you really think it's a mind in there or just a little buzz like a bee in a glass jar?) but you got the idea she had talked the other two into coming in here with her, and now she was showing them how to do it, walk slow and hold yourself straight.

She had on a kind of dirty-pink—beige maybe, I don't know—bathing suit with a little nubble all over it, and what got me, the straps were down. They were off her shoulders looped loose around the cool tops of her arms, and

I guess as a result the suit had slipped a little on her, so all around the top of the cloth there was this shining rim. If it hadn't been there you wouldn't have known there could have been anything whiter than those shoulders. With the straps pushed off, there was nothing between the top of the suit and the top of her head except just *her*, this clean bare plane of the top of her chest down from the shoulder bones like a dented sheet of metal tilted in the light. I mean, it was more than pretty.

She had sort of oaky hair that the sun and salt had bleached, done up in a bun that was unravelling, and a kind of prim face. Walking into the A & P with your straps down, I suppose it's the only kind of face you *can* have. She held her head so high her neck, coming up out of those white shoulders, looked kind of stretched, but I didn't mind. The longer her neck was, the more of her there was.

She must have felt in the corner of her eye me and over my shoulder Stokesie 5 in the second slot watching, but she didn't tip. Not this queen. She kept her eyes moving across the racks, and stopped, and turned so slow it made my stomach rub the inside of my apron, and buzzed to the other two, who kind of huddled against her for relief, and then they all three of them went up the cat-and-dog-food-breakfast-cereal-macaroni-rice-raisins-seasonings-spreads-spaghetti-soft-drinks-crackers-and-cookies aisle. From the third slot I look straight up this aisle to the meat counter, and I watched them all the way. The fat one with the tan sort of fumbled with the cookies, but on second thought she put the package back. The sheep pushing their carts down the aisle—the girls were walking against the usual traffic (not that we have one-way signs or anything)—were pretty hilarious. You could see them, when Queenie's white shoulders dawned on them, kind of jerk, or hop, or hiccup, but their eyes snapped back to their own baskets and on they pushed. I bet you could set off dynamite in an A & P and the people would by and large keep reaching and checking oatmeal off their lists and muttering "Let me see, there was a third thing, began with A, asparagus, no, ah, yes, applesauce!" or whatever it is they do mutter. But there was no doubt, this jiggled them. A few houseslaves in pin curlers even looked around after pushing their carts past to make sure what they had seen was correct.

You know, it's one thing to have a girl in a bathing suit down on the beach, where what with the glare nobody can look at each other much anyway, and another thing in the cool of the A & P, under the fluorescent lights, against all those stacked packages, with her feet paddling along naked over our check-board green-and-cream rubber-tile floor.

"Oh Daddy," Stokesie said beside me. "I feel so faint."

"Darling," I said. "Hold me tight." Stokesie's married, with two babies chalked up on his fuselage already, but as far as I can tell that's the only difference. He's twenty-two, and I was nineteen this April.

"Is it done?" he asks, the responsible married man finding his voice. I forgot to say he thinks he's going to be manager some sunny day, maybe in 1990 when it's called the Great Alexandrov and Petrooshki Tea Company or something.

What he meant was, our town is five miles from a beach, with a big summer 10
colony out on the Point, but we're right in the middle of town, and the women
generally put on a shirt or shorts or something before they get out of the car into
the street. And anyway these are usually women with six children and varicose
veins mapping their legs and nobody, including them, could care less. As I say,
we're right in the middle of town, and if you stand at our front doors you can
see two banks and the Congregational church and the newspaper store and three
real-estate offices and about twenty-seven old freeloaders tearing up Central
Street because the sewer broke again. It's not as if we're on the Cape; we're north
of Boston and there's people in this town haven't seen the ocean for twenty years.

The girls had reached the meat counter and were asking McMahon something. He pointed, they pointed, and they shuffled out of sight behind a pyra-
mid of Diet Delight peaches. All that was left for us to see was old McMahon
patting his mouth and looking after them sizing up their joints. Poor kids,
I began to feel sorry for them, they couldn't help it.

Now here comes the sad part of the story, at least my family says it's sad,
but I don't think it's so sad myself. The store's pretty empty, it being Thursday
afternoon, so there was nothing much to do except lean on the register and wait
for the girls to show up again. The whole store was like a pinball machine and I
didn't know which tunnel they'd come out of. After a while they come around
out of the far aisle, around the light bulbs, records at discount of the Caribbean Six or Tony Martin Sings or some such gunk you wonder they waste the
wax on, sixpacks of candy bars, and plastic toys done up in cellophane that
fall apart when a kid looks at them anyway. Around they come, Queenie still
leading the way, and holding a little gray jar in her hand. Slots Three through
Seven are unmanned and I could see her wondering between Stokes and me,
but Stokesie with his usual luck draws an old party in baggy gray pants who
stumbles up with four giant cans of pineapple juice (what do these bums *do*
with all that pineapple juice? I've often asked myself) so the girls come to me.
Queenie puts down the jar and I take it into my fingers icy cold. Kingfish Fancy
Herring Snacks in Pure Sour Cream: 49¢. Now her hands are empty, not a ring
or a bracelet, bare as God made them, and I wonder where the money's coming from. Still with that prim look she lifts a folded dollar bill out of the hollow
at the center of her nubbled pink top. The jar went heavy in my hand. Really, I
thought that was so cute.

Then everybody's luck begins to run out. Lengel comes in from haggling
with a truck full of cabbages on the lot and is about to scuttle into that door
marked MANAGER behind which he hides all day when the girls touch his
eye. Lengel's pretty dreary, teaches Sunday school and the rest, but he doesn't
miss that much. He comes over and says, "Girls, this isn't the beach."

Queenie blushes, though maybe it's just a brush of sunburn I was noticing
for the first time, now that she was so close. "My mother asked me to pick up
a jar of herring snacks." Her voice kind of startled me, the way voices do when
you see the people first, coming out so flat and dumb yet kind of tony, too, the
way it ticked over "pick up" and "snacks." All of a sudden I slid right down

her voice into her living room. Her father and the other men were standing around in ice-cream coats and bow ties and the women were in sandals picking up herring snacks on toothpicks off a big glass plate and they were all holding drinks the color of water with olives and sprigs of mint in them. When my parents have somebody over they get lemonade and if it's a real racy affair Schlitz in tall glasses with "They'll Do It Every Time" cartoons stencilled on.

"That's all right," Lengel said. "But this isn't the beach." His repeating this 15 struck me as funny, as if it had just occurred to him, and he had been thinking all these years the A & P was a great big sand dune and he was the head lifeguard. He didn't like my smiling—as I say he doesn't miss much—but he concentrates on giving the girls that sad Sunday-school–superintendent stare.

Queenie's blush is no sunburn now, and the plump one in plaid, that I liked better from the back—a really sweet can—pipes up, "We weren't doing any shopping. We just came in for the one thing."

"That makes no difference," Lengel tells her, and I could see from the way his eyes went that he hadn't noticed she was wearing a two-piece before. "We want you decently dressed when you come in here."

"We *are* decent," Queenie says suddenly, her lower lip pushing, getting sore now that she remembers her place, a place from which the crowd that runs the A & P must look pretty crummy. Fancy Herring Snacks flashed in her very blue eyes.

"Girls, I don't want to argue with you. After this come in here with your shoulders covered. It's our policy." He turns his back. That's policy for you. Policy is what the kingpins want. What the others want is juvenile delinquency.

All this while, the customers had been showing up with their carts but, you 20 know, sheep, seeing a scene, they had all bunched up on Stokesie, who shook open a paper bag as gently as peeling a peach, not wanting to miss a word. I could feel in the silence everybody getting nervous, most of all Lengel, who asks me, "Sammy, have you rung up their purchase?"

I thought and said "No" but it wasn't about that I was thinking. I go through the punches, 4, 9, groc, tot—it's more complicated than you think, and after you do it often enough, it begins to make a little song, that you hear words to, in my case "Hello (*bing*) there, you (*gung*) hap-py *pee*-pul (*splat*)!"—the *splat* being the drawer flying out. I uncrease the bill, tenderly as you may imagine, it just having come from between the two smoothest scoops of vanilla I had ever known were there, and pass a half and a penny into her narrow pink palm, and nestle the herrings in a bag and twist its neck and hand it over, all the time thinking.

The girls, and who'd blame them, are in a hurry to get out, so I say "I quit" to Lengel enough for them to hear, hoping they'll stop and watch me, their unsuspected hero. They keep right on going, into the electric eye; the door flies open and they flicker across the lot to their car, Queenie and Plaid and Big Tall Goony-Goony (not that as raw material she was so bad), leaving me with Lengel and a kink in his eyebrow.

"Did you say something, Sammy?"

"I said I quit."

"I thought you did." 25

"You didn't have to embarrass them."

"It was they who were embarrassing us."

I started to say something that came out "Fiddle-de-doo." It's a saying of my grandmother's, and I know she would have been pleased.

"I don't think you know what you're saying," Lengel said.

"I know you don't," I said. "But I do." I pull the bow at the back of my 30 apron and start shrugging it off my shoulders. A couple customers that had been heading for my slot begin to knock against each other, like scared pigs in a chute.

Lengel sighs and begins to look very patient and old and gray. He's been a friend of my parents for years. "Sammy, you don't want to do this to your Mom and Dad," he tells me. It's true, I don't. But it seems to me that once you begin a gesture it's fatal not to go through with it. I fold the apron, "Sammy" stitched in red on the pocket, and put it on the counter, and drop the bow tie on top of it. The bow tie is theirs, if you've ever wondered. "You'll feel this for the rest of your life," Lengel says, and I know that's true, too, but remembering how he made that pretty girl blush makes me so scrunchy inside I punch the No Sale tab and the machine whirs "pee-pul" and the drawer splats out. One advantage to this scene taking place in summer, I can follow this up with a clean exit, there's no fumbling around getting your coat and galoshes, I just saunter into the electric eye in my white shirt that my mother ironed the night before, and the door heaves itself open, and outside the sunshine is skating around on the asphalt.

I look around for my girls, but they're gone, of course. There wasn't anybody but some young married screaming with her children about some candy they didn't get by the door of a powder-blue Falcon station wagon. Looking back in the big windows, over the bags of peat moss and aluminum lawn furniture stacked on the pavement, I could see Lengel in my place in the slot, checking the sheep through. His face was dark gray and his back stiff, as if he'd just had an injection of iron, and my stomach kind of fell as I felt how hard the world was going to be to me hereafter.

FOR ANALYSIS

1. Describe Sammy's voice as he tells the story. How does Updike's choice to have him **narrate** help us get a sense of Sammy as a **character**? Is he understandable? Is he likable? Can readers sympathize with him?

2. What about "Queenie" is most attractive to Sammy? Is it just her appearance? What else figures in?

3. At the very end of the story, Updike has Sammy describe his customers **figuratively** as pigs and sheep. Why do you think he does this? What does this choice reveal about Sammy's attitude toward them, and toward the adult ways of living he is on the verge of?

4. Sammy describes his quitting as a gesture. For whom is the gesture made—for one audience, or for multiple audiences? What does it say to each audience?

MAKING CONNECTIONS

1. Compare the connections made between work and identity in "A & P" and in Daniel Orozco's "Orientation" (p. 105).

2. Reread the passage in which Sammy imagines the scene in "Queenie's" parents' living room. Compare to the passage in Toni Cade Bambara's "The Lesson" (p. 98) in which Miss Moore asks about the children's desks at home. What does each moment say about the pictures of the social divisions embedded in each story?

WRITING TOPIC

Retell the story with Lengel as **narrator**, showing how that change might affect **point of view**, voice, and meaning.

TONI CADE BAMBARA (1939–1995)

THE LESSON 1972

Back in the days when everyone was old and stupid or young and foolish and me and Sugar were the only ones just right, this lady moved on our block with nappy hair and proper speech and no makeup. And quite naturally we laughed at her, laughed the way we did at the junk man who went about his business like he was some big-time president and his sorry-ass horse his secretary. And we kinda hated her too, hated the way we did the winos who cluttered up our parks and pissed on our handball walls and stank up our hallways and stairs so you couldn't halfway play hide-and-seek without a goddamn gas mask. Miss Moore was her name. The only woman on the block with no first name. And she was black as hell, cept for her feet, which were fish-white and spooky. And she was always planning these boring-ass things for us to do, us being my cousin, mostly, who lived on the block cause we all moved North the same time and to the same apartment then spread out gradual to breathe. And our parents would yank our heads into some kinda shape and crisp up our clothes so we'd be presentable for travel with Miss Moore, who always looked like she was going to church, though she never did. Which is just one of the things the grownups talked about when they talked behind her back like a dog. But when she came calling with some sachet she'd sewed up or some gingerbread she'd made or some book, why then they'd all be too embarrassed to turn her down and we'd get handed over all spruced up. She'd been to college and said it was only right that she should take responsibility for the young ones' education, and she not even related by marriage or blood. So they'd go for it. Specially Aunt Gretchen. She was the main gofer in the family. You got some old dumb shit foolishness you want somebody to go for, you send for Aunt Gretchen. She been screwed into the go-along for so long, it's a blood-deep natural thing with her. Which is how she got saddled with me and Sugar and Junior in the first place while our mothers were in a la-de-da apartment up the block having a good ole time.

So this one day Miss Moore rounds us all up at the mailbox and it's pure-dee hot and she's knockin herself out about arithmetic. And school suppose to let up in summer I heard, but she don't never let up. And the starch in my pinafore scratching the shit outta me and I'm really hating this nappy-head bitch and her goddamn college degree. I'd much rather go to the pool or to the show where it's cool. So me and Sugar leaning on the mailbox being surly, which is a Miss Moore word. And Flyboy checking out what everybody brought for lunch. And Fat Butt already wasting his peanut-butter-and-jelly sandwich like the pig he is. And Junebug punchin on Q.T.'s arm for potato chips. And Rosie Giraffe shifting from one hip to the other waiting for somebody to step on her foot or ask her if she from Georgia so she can kick ass, preferably Mercedes'. And Miss Moore asking us do we know what money is, like we a bunch of retards. I mean real money, she say, like it's only poker chips or monopoly papers we lay on the grocer. So right away I'm tired of this and say so. And would much rather snatch Sugar and go to the Sunset and terrorize the West Indian kids and take their hair ribbons and their money too. And Miss Moore files that remark away for next week's lesson on brotherhood, I can tell. And finally I say we oughta get to the subway cause it's cooler and besides we might meet some cute boys. Sugar done swiped her mama's lipstick, so we ready.

So we heading down the street and she's boring us silly about what things cost and what our parents make and how much goes for rent and how money ain't divided up right in this country. And then she gets to the part about we all poor and live in the slums, which I don't feature. And I'm ready to speak on that, but she steps out in the street and hails two cabs just like that. Then she hustles half the crew in with her and hands me a five-dollar bill and tells me to calculate 10 percent tip for the driver. And we're off. Me and Sugar and Junebug and Flyboy hangin out the window and hollering to everybody, putting lipstick on each other cause Flyboy a faggot anyway, and making farts with our sweaty armpits. But I'm mostly trying to figure how to spend this money. But they all fascinated with the meter ticking and Junebug starts laying bets as to how much it'll read when Flyboy can't hold his breath no more. Then Sugar lays bets as to how much it'll be when we get there. So I'm stuck. Don't nobody want to go for my plan, which is to jump out at the next light and run off to the first bar-b-que we can find. Then the driver tells us to get the hell out cause we there already. And the meter reads eighty-five cents. And I'm stalling to figure out the tip and Sugar say give him a dime. And I decide he don't need it bad as I do, so later for him. But then he tries to take off with Junebug foot still in the door so we talk about his mama something ferocious. Then we check out that we on Fifth Avenue and everybody dressed up in stockings. One lady in a fur coat, hot as it is. White folks crazy.

"This is the place," Miss Moore say, presenting it to us in the voice she uses at the museum. "Let's look in the windows before we go in."

"Can we steal?" Sugar asks very serious like she's getting the ground rules 5 squared away before she plays. "I beg your pardon," say Miss Moore, and we fall out. So she leads us around the windows of the toy store and me and Sugar screamin, "This is mine, that's mine, I gotta have that, that was made for me, I was born for that," till Big Butt drowns us out.

"Hey, I'm goin to buy that there."

"That there? You don't even know what it is, stupid."

"I do so," he say punchin on Rosie Giraffe. "It's a microscope."

"Whatcha gonna do with a microscope, fool?"

"Look at things." 10

"Like what, Ronald?" ask Miss Moore. And Big Butt ain't got the first notion. So here go Miss Moore gabbing about the thousands of bacteria in a drop of water and the somethinorother in a speck of blood and the million and one living things in the air around us is invisible to the naked eye. And what she say that for? Junebug go to town on that "naked" and we rolling. Then Miss Moore ask what it cost. So we all jam into the window smudgin it up and the price tag say $300. So then she ask how long'd take for Big Butt and Junebug to save up their allowances. "Too long," I say. "Yeh," adds Sugar, "outgrown it by that time." And Miss Moore say no, you never outgrow learning instruments. "Why, even medical students and interns and," blah, blah, blah. And we ready to choke Big Butt for bringing it up in the first damn place.

"This here costs four hundred eighty dollars," say Rosie Giraffe. So we pile up all over her to see what she pointin out. My eyes tell me it's a chunk of glass cracked with something heavy, and different-color inks dripped into the splits, then the whole thing put into a oven or something. But for $480 it don't make sense.

"That's a paperweight made of semi-precious stones fused together under tremendous pressure," she explains slowly, with her hands doing the mining and all the factory work.

"So what's a paperweight?" asks Rosie Giraffe.

"To weigh paper with, dumbbell," say Flyboy, the wise man from the East.   15

"Not exactly," say Miss Moore, which is what she say when you warm or way off too. "It's to weigh paper down so it won't scatter and make your desk untidy." So right away me and Sugar curtsy to each other and then to Mercedes who is more the tidy type.

"We don't keep paper on top of the desk in my class," say Junebug, figuring Miss Moore crazy or lyin one.

"At home, then," she say. "Don't you have a calendar and pencil case and a blotter and a letter-opener on your desk at home where you do your homework?" And she know damn well what our homes look like cause she nosys around in them every chance she gets.

"I don't even have a desk," say Junebug. "Do we?"

"No. And I don't get no homework neither," says Big Butt.   20

"And I don't even have a home," say Flyboy like he do at school to keep the white folks off his back and sorry for him. Send this poor kid to camp posters, is his specialty.

"I do," says Mercedes. "I have a box of stationery on my desk and a picture of my cat. My godmother bought the stationery and the desk. There's a big rose on each sheet and the envelopes smell like roses."

"Who wants to know about your smelly-ass stationery," say Rosie Giraffe fore I can get my two cents in.

"It's important to have a work area all your own so that . . ."

"Will you look at this sailboat, please," say Flyboy, cuttin her off and pointin   25 to the thing like it was his. So once again we tumble all over each other to gaze at this magnificent thing in the toy store which is just big enough to maybe sail two kittens across the pond if you strap them to the posts tight. We all start reciting the price tag like we in assembly. "Handcrafted sailboat of fiberglass at one thousand one hundred ninety-five dollars."

"Unbelievable," I hear myself say and am really stunned. I read it again for myself just in case the group recitation put me in a trance. Same thing. For some reason this pisses me off. We look at Miss Moore and she lookin at us, waiting for I dunno what.

"Who'd pay all that when you can buy a sailboat set for a quarter at Pop's, a tube of glue for a dime, and a ball of string for eight cents? It must have a motor and a whole lot else besides," I say. "My sailboat cost me about fifty cents."

"But will it take water?" say Mercedes with her smart ass.

"Took mine to Alley Pond Park once," say Flyboy. "String broke. Lost it. Pity."

"Sailed mine in Central Park and it keeled over and sank. Had to ask my 30 father for another dollar."

"And you got the strap," laugh Big Butt. "The jerk didn't even have a string on it. My old man wailed on his behind."

Little Q.T. was staring hard at the sailboat and you could see he wanted it bad. But he too little and somebody'd just take it from him. So what the hell. "This boat for kids, Miss Moore?"

"Parents silly to buy something like that just to get all broke up," say Rosie Giraffe.

"That much money it should last forever," I figure.

"My father'd buy it for me if I wanted it."   35

"Your father, my ass," say Rosie Giraffe getting a chance to finally push Mercedes.

"Must be rich people shop here," say Q.T.

"You are a very bright boy," say Flyboy. "What was your first clue?" And he rap him on the head with the back of his knuckles, since Q.T. the only one he could get away with. Though Q.T. liable to come up behind you years later and get his licks in when you half expect it.

"What I want to know is," I says to Miss Moore though I never talk to her, I wouldn't give the bitch that satisfaction, "is how much a real boat costs? I figure a thousand'd get you a yacht any day."

"Why don't you check that out," she says, "and report back to the group?" 40 Which really pains my ass. If you gonna mess up a perfectly good swim day least you could do is have some answers. "Let's go in," she say like she got something up her sleeve. Only she don't lead the way. So me and Sugar turn the corner to where the entrance is, but when we get there I kinda hang back. Not that I'm scared, what's there to be afraid of, just a toy store. But I feel funny, shame. But what I got to be shamed about? Got as much right to go in as anybody. But somehow I can't seem to get hold of the door, so I step away for Sugar to lead. But she hangs back too. And I look at her and she looks at me and this is ridiculous. I mean, damn, I have never ever been shy about doing nothing or going nowhere. But then Mercedes steps up and then Rosie Giraffe and Big

Butt crowd in behind and shove, and next thing we all stuffed into the doorway with only Mercedes squeezing past us, smoothing out her jumper and walking right down the aisle. Then the rest of us tumble in like a glued-together jigsaw done all wrong. And people lookin at us. And it's like the time me and Sugar crashed into the Catholic church on a dare. But once we got in there and everything so hushed and holy and the candles and the bowin and the handkerchiefs on all the drooping heads, I just couldn't go through with the plan. Which was for me to run up to the altar and do a tap dance while Sugar played the nose flute and messed around in the holy water. And Sugar kept givin me the elbow. Then later teased me so bad I tied her up in the shower and turned it on and locked her in. And she'd be there till this day if Aunt Gretchen hadn't finally figured I was lyin about the boarder takin a shower.

Same thing in the store. We all walkin on tiptoe and hardly touchin the games and puzzles and things. And I watched Miss Moore who is steady watchin us like she waitin for a sign. Like Mama Drewery watches the sky and sniffs the air and takes note of just how much slant is in the bird formation. Then me and Sugar bump smack into each other, so busy gazing at the toys, 'specially the sailboat. But we don't laugh and go into our fat-lady bump-stomach routine. We just stare at that price tag. Then Sugar run a finger over the whole boat. And I'm jealous and want to hit her. Maybe not her, but I sure want to punch somebody in the mouth.

"Watcha bring us here for, Miss Moore?"

"You sound angry, Sylvia. Are you mad about something?" Givin me one of them grins like she tellin a grown-up joke that never turns out to be funny. And she's lookin very closely at me like maybe she planning to do my portrait from memory. I'm mad, but I won't give her that satisfaction. So I slouch around the store bein very bored and say, "Let's go."

Me and Sugar at the back of the train watchin the tracks whizzin by large then small then gettin gobbled up in the dark. I'm thinkin about this tricky toy I saw in the store. A clown that somersaults on a bar then does chin-ups just cause you yank lightly at his leg. Cost $35. I could see me askin my mother for a $35 birthday clown. "You wanna who that costs what?" she'd say, cocking her head to the side to get a better view of the hole in my head. Thirty-five dollars could buy new bunk beds for Junior and Gretchen's boy. Thirty-five dollars and the whole household could go visit Granddaddy Nelson in the country. Thirty-five dollars would pay for the rent and the piano bill too. Who are these people that spend that much for performing clowns and $1000 for toy sailboats? What kinda work they do and how they live and how come we ain't in on it? Where we are is who we are, Miss Moore always pointin out. But it don't necessarily have to be that way, she always adds then waits for somebody to say that poor people have to wake up and demand their share of the pie and don't none of us know what kind of pie she talking about in the first damn place. But she ain't so smart cause I still got her four dollars from the taxi and she sure ain't gettin it. Messin up my day with this shit. Sugar nudges me in my pocket and winks.

Miss Moore lines us up in front of the mailbox where we started from, seem 45
like years ago, and I got a headache for thinkin so hard. And we lean all over
each other so we can hold up under the draggy-ass lecture she always finishes
us off with at the end before we thank her for borin us to tears. But she just
looks at us like she readin tea leaves. Finally she say, "Well, what did you think
of F.A.O. Schwarz?"

Rosie Giraffe mumbles, "White folks crazy."

"I'd like to go there again when I get my birthday money," says Mercedes,
and we shove her out the pack so she has to lean on the mailbox by herself.

"I'd like a shower. Tiring day," say Flyboy.

Then Sugar surprises me by sayin, "You know, Miss Moore, I don't think all
of us here put together eat in a year what that sailboat costs." And Miss Moore
lights up like somebody goosed her. "And?" she say, urging Sugar on. Only I'm
standin on her foot so she don't continue.

"Imagine for a minute what kind of society it is in which some people can 50
spend on a toy what it would cost to feed a family of six or seven. What do you
think?"

"I think," say Sugar pushing me off her feet like she never done before, cause
I whip her ass in a minute, "that this is not much of a democracy if you ask me.
Equal chance to pursue happiness means an equal crack at the dough, don't
it?" Miss Moore is besides herself and I am disgusted with Sugar's treachery.
So I stand on her foot one more time to see if she'll shove me. She shuts up,
and Miss Moore looks at me, sorrowfully I'm thinkin. And somethin weird is
goin on, I can feel it in my chest.

"Anybody else learn anything today?" lookin dead at me. I walk away and
Sugar has to run to catch up and don't even seem to notice when I shrug her
arm off my shoulder.

"Well, we got four dollars anyway," she says.

"Uh hunh."

"We could go to Hascombs and get half a chocolate layer and then go to the 55
Sunset and still have plenty money for potato chips and ice cream sodas."

"Un hunh."

"Race you to Hascombs," she say.

We start down the block and she gets ahead which is O.K. by me cause I'm
going to the West End and then over to the Drive to think this day through.
She can run if she want to and even run faster. But ain't nobody gonna beat me
at nuthin.

For Analysis

1. What are Sylvia's outstanding traits? How are they reflected in her language and in
her description of her neighborhood?

2. How is Sylvia's **character** revealed through her relationship with Sugar?

3. Describe the lesson Miss Moore tries to teach the children by taking them to visit
F.A.O. Schwarz.

4. How is Sylvia's assessment of Miss Moore at the beginning of the story borne out by the ending?

5. What evidence is there that Sylvia has been changed by the visit to F.A.O. Schwarz?

MAKING CONNECTIONS

1. Compare and contrast the use of the **first-person narrator** in this story with that in John Updike's "A & P" (p. 90).

2. In "Commencement Speech, Kenyon College" (p. 315), David Foster Wallace implies that an individual's moral sense can come not as much from his religion or her upbringing but from a conscious effort to step outside of oneself and empathize, to think about how it feels to be other kinds of people. Sylvia's moral sense is likewise awakened in "The Lesson." Though Wallace's speech is about something else entirely, can we use it to help us think about Sylvia's sense of right and wrong? Where does it come from? How is it awakened? Do you have any sense if this awakening is temporary or longer-lasting?

WRITING TOPICS

1. Write an essay arguing for or against the proposition that the story ends optimistically.

2. In your opinion, is Sylvia a reliable or unreliable **narrator**?

JAMAICA KINCAID (B. 1949)

GIRL (1983)

Wash the white clothes on Monday and put them on the stone heap; wash the color clothes on Tuesday and put them on the clothesline to dry; don't walk barehead in the hot sun; cook pumpkin fritters in very hot sweet oil; soak your little clothes right after you take them off; when buying cotton to make yourself a nice blouse, be sure that it doesn't have gum on it, because that way it won't hold up well after a wash; soak salt fish overnight before you cook it; is it true that you sing benna[1] in Sunday school?; always eat your food in such a way that it won't turn someone else's stomach; on Sundays try to walk like a lady and not like the slut you are so bent on becoming; don't sing benna in Sunday school; you mustn't speak to wharf-rat boys, not even to give directions; don't eat fruits on the street—flies will follow you; *but I don't sing benna on Sundays at all and never in Sunday school*; this is how to sew on a button; this is how to make a button-hole for the button you have just sewed on; this is how to hem a dress when you see the hem coming down and so to prevent yourself from looking like the slut I know you are so bent on becoming; this is how you iron your father's khaki shirt so that it doesn't have a crease; this is how you iron your father's khaki pants so that they don't have a crease; this is how you grow okra—far from the house, because okra tree harbors red ants; when you are growing dasheen,[2] make sure it gets plenty of water or else it makes your throat itch when you are eating it; this is how you sweep a corner; this is how you sweep a whole house; this is how you sweep a yard; this is how you smile to someone you don't like too much; this is how you set a table for dinner with an important guest; this is how you smile to someone you don't like at all; this is how you smile to someone you like completely; this is how you set a table for tea; this is how you set a table for dinner; this is how you set a table for lunch; this is how you set a table for breakfast; this is how to behave in the presence of men who don't know you very well, and this way they won't recognize immediately the slut I have warned you against becoming; be sure to wash every day, even if it is with your own spit; don't squat down to play marbles—you are not a boy, you know; don't pick people's flowers—you might catch something; don't throw stones at blackbirds, because it might not be a blackbird at all; this is how to make a bread pudding; this is how to make doukona;[3] this is how to make pepper pot; this is how to make a good medicine for a cold; this is how to make a good medicine

[1] Calypso music.
[2] Taro root.
[3] Spicy plantain pudding.

to throw away a child before it even becomes a child; this is how to catch a fish; this is how to throw back a fish you don't like, and that way something bad won't fall on you; this is how to bully a man; this is how a man bullies you; this is how to love a man, and if this doesn't work there are other ways, and if they don't work don't feel too bad about giving up; this is how to spit up in the air if you feel like it, and this is how to move quick so that it doesn't fall on you; this is how to make ends meet; always squeeze bread to make sure it's fresh; *but what if the baker won't let me feel the bread?*; you mean to say that after all you are really going to be the kind of woman who the baker won't let near the bread? 40

FOR ANALYSIS

1. What does the title of this piece suggest?

2. Who is the speaker? To whom is she speaking?

3. What kind of "girl" is the advice intended to produce?

4. What is the speaker's biggest fear?

5. Are the girl's two responses spoken aloud to the speaker, or are they only the girl's thoughts? Explain.

6. What do the girl's two responses suggest about her relationship to the speaker?

MAKING CONNECTIONS

1. Compare the girl in this story with Sylvia, the **narrator** of Bambara's "The Lesson" (p. 96).

2. Describe the speaker in this story, and then compare the speaker with the father in Meinke's poem "Advice to My Son" (p. 216). How do they differ? Do they share any qualities?

WRITING TOPICS

1. List the advice you received from your parents and other elders, and write a paragraph in imitation of Kincaid's piece.

2. Examine the details that constitute the advice in this story. What kind of society and culture do these details seem to suggest?

DANIEL OROZCO (B. 1942)

ORIENTATION 1998

Those are the offices and these are the cubicles. That's my cubicle there, and this is your cubicle. This is your phone. Never answer your phone. Let the Voicemail System answer it. This is your Voicemail System Manual. There are no personal phone calls allowed. We do, however, allow for emergencies. If you must make an emergency phone call, ask your supervisor first. If you can't find your supervisor, ask Phillip Spiers, who sits over there. He'll check with Clarissa Nicks, who sits over there. If you make an emergency phone call without asking, you may be let go.

These are your IN and OUT boxes. All the forms in your IN box must be logged in by the date shown in the upper left-hand corner, initialed by you in the upper right-hand corner, and distributed to the Processing Analyst whose name is numerically coded in the lower left-hand corner. The lower right-hand corner is left blank. Here's your Processing Analyst Numerical Code Index. And here's your Forms Processing Procedures Manual.

You must pace your work. What do I mean? I'm glad you asked that. We pace our work according to the eight-hour workday. If you have twelve hours of work in your IN box, for example, you must compress that work into the eight-hour day. If you have one hour of work in your IN box, you must expand that work to fill the eight-hour day. That was a good question. Feel free to ask questions. Ask too many questions, however, and you may be let go.

That is our receptionist. She is a temp. We go through receptionists here. They quit with alarming frequency. Be polite and civil to the temps. Learn their names, and invite them to lunch occasionally. But don't get close to them, as it only makes it more difficult when they leave. And they always leave. You can be sure of that.

The men's room is over there. The women's room is over there. John 5 LaFountaine, who sits over there, uses the women's room occasionally. He says it is accidental. We know better, but we let it pass. John LaFountaine is harmless, his forays into the forbidden territory of the women's room simply a benign thrill, a faint blip on the dull flat line of his life.

Russell Nash, who sits in the cubicle to your left, is in love with Amanda Pierce, who sits in the cubicle to your right. They ride the same bus together after work. For Amanda Pierce, it is just a tedious bus ride made less tedious by the idle nattering of Russell Nash. But for Russell Nash, it is the highlight of his day. It is the highlight of his life. Russell Nash has put on forty pounds, and grows fatter with each passing month, nibbling on chips and cookies while peeking glumly over the partitions at Amanda Pierce, and gorging himself at home on cold pizza and ice cream while watching adult videos on TV.

Amanda Pierce, in the cubicle to your right, has a six-year-old son named Jamie, who is autistic. Her cubicle is plastered from top to bottom with the boy's crayon artwork—sheet after sheet of precisely drawn concentric circles and ellipses, in black and yellow. She rotates them every other Friday. Be sure to comment on them. Amanda Pierce also has a husband, who is a lawyer. He subjects her to an escalating array of painful and humiliating sex games, to which Amanda Pierce reluctantly submits. She comes to work exhausted and freshly wounded each morning, wincing from the abrasions on her breasts, or the bruises on her abdomen, or the second-degree burns on the backs of her thighs.

But we're not supposed to know any of this. Do not let on. If you let on, you may be let go.

Amanda Pierce, who tolerates Russell Nash, is in love with Albert Bosch, whose office is over there. Albert Bosch, who only dimly registers Amanda Pierce's existence, has eyes only for Ellie Tapper, who sits over there. Ellie Tapper, who hates Albert Bosch, would walk through fire for Curtis Lance. But Curtis Lance hates Ellie Tapper. Isn't the world a funny place? Not in the ha-ha sense, of course.

Anika Bloom sits in that cubicle. Last year, while reviewing quarterly reports in a meeting with Barry Hacker, Anika Bloom's left palm began to bleed. She fell into a trance, stared into her hand, and told Barry Hacker when and how his wife would die. We laughed it off. She was, after all, a new employee. But Barry Hacker's wife is dead. So unless you want to know exactly when and how you'll die, never talk to Anika Bloom.

Colin Heavey sits in that cubicle over there. He was new once, just like you. We warned him about Anika Bloom. But at last year's Christmas Potluck, he felt sorry for her when he saw that no one was talking to her. Colin Heavey brought her a drink. He hasn't been himself since. Colin Heavey is doomed. There's nothing he can do about it, and we are powerless to help him. Stay away from Colin Heavey. Never give any of your work to him. If he asks to do something, tell him you have to check with me. If he asks again, tell him I haven't gotten back to you.

This is the Fire Exit. There are several on this floor, and they are marked accordingly. We have a Floor Evacuation Review every three months, and an Escape Route Quiz once a month. We have our Biannual Fire Drill twice a year, and our Annual Earthquake Drill once a year. These are precautions only. These things never happen.

For your information, we have a comprehensive health plan. Any catastrophic illness, any unforeseen tragedy is completely covered. All dependents are completely covered. Larry Bagdikian, who sits over there, has six daughters. If anything were to happen to any of his girls, or to all of them, if all six were to simultaneously fall victim to illness or injury—stricken with a hideous degenerative muscle disease or some rare toxic blood disorder, sprayed with semiautomatic gunfire while on a class field trip, or attacked in their bunk beds by some prowling nocturnal lunatic—if any of this were to pass, Larry's girls would all be taken care of. Larry Bagdikian would not have to pay one dime. He would have nothing to worry about.

We also have a generous vacation and sick leave policy. We have an excellent disability insurance plan. We have a stable and profitable pension fund. We get group discounts for the symphony, and block seating at the ballpark. We get commuter ticket books for the bridge. We have Direct Deposit. We are all members of Costco.

This is our kitchenette. And this, this is our Mr. Coffee. We have a coffee 15 pool, into which we each pay two dollars a week for coffee, filters, sugar, and CoffeeMate. If you prefer Cremora or half-and-half to CoffeeMate, there is a special pool for three dollars a week. If you prefer Sweet'n Low to sugar, there is a special pool for two-fifty a week. We do not do decaf. You are allowed to join the coffee pool of your choice, but you are not allowed to touch the Mr. Coffee.

This is the microwave oven. You are allowed to *heat* food in the microwave oven. You are not, however, allowed to *cook* food in the microwave oven.

We get one hour for lunch. We also get one fifteen-minute break in the morning, and one fifteen-minute break in the afternoon. Always take your breaks. If you skip a break, it is gone forever. For your information, your break is a privilege, not a right. If you abuse the break policy, we are authorized to rescind your breaks. Lunch, however, is a right, not a privilege. If you abuse the lunch policy, our hands will be tied, and we will be forced to look the other way. We will not enjoy that.

This is the refrigerator. You may put your lunch in it. Barry Hacker, who sits over there, steals food from this refrigerator. His petty theft is an outlet for his grief. Last New Year's Eve, while kissing his wife, a blood vessel burst in her brain. Barry Hacker's wife was two months pregnant at the time, and lingered in a coma for half a year before dying. It was a tragic loss for Barry Hacker. He hasn't been himself since. Barry Hacker's wife was a beautiful woman. She was also completely covered. Barry Hacker did not have to pay one dime. But his dead wife haunts him. She haunts all of us. We have seen her, reflected in the monitors of our computers, moving past our cubicles. We have seen the dim shadow of her face in our photocopies. She pencils herself in in the receptionist's appointment book, with the notation: To see Barry Hacker. She has left messages in the receptionist's Voicemail box, messages garbled by the electronic chirrups and buzzes in the phone line, her voice echoing from an immense distance within the ambient hum. But the voice is hers. And beneath her voice, beneath the tidal *whoosh* of static and hiss, the gurgling and crying of a baby can be heard.

In any case, if you bring a lunch, put a little something extra in the bag for Barry Hacker. We have four Barrys in this office. Isn't that a coincidence?

This is Matthew Payne's office. He is our Unit Manager, and his door is 20 always closed. We have never seen him, and you will never see him. But he is here. You can be sure of that. He is all around us.

This is the Custodian's Closet. You have no business in the Custodian's Closet.

And this, this is our Supplies Cabinet. If you need supplies, see Curtis Lance. He will log you in on the Supplies Cabinet Authorization Log, then give you a Supplies Authorization Slip. Present your pink copy of the Supplies Authorization Slip to Ellie Tapper. She will log you in on the Supplies Cabinet Key Log, then give you the key. Because the Supplies Cabinet is located outside the Unit Manager's office, you must be very quiet. Gather your supplies quietly. The Supplies Cabinet is divided into four sections. Section One contains letterhead stationery, blank paper and envelopes, memo and note pads, and so on. Section Two contains pens and pencils and typewriter and printer ribbons, and the like. In Section Three we have erasers, correction fluids, transparent tapes, glue sticks, et cetera. And in Section Four we have paper clips and push pins and scissors and razor blades. And here are the spare blades for the shredder. Do not touch the shredder, which is located over there. The shredder is of no concern to you.

Gwendolyn Stich sits in that office there. She is crazy about penguins, and collects penguin knickknacks: penguin posters and coffee mugs and stationery, penguin stuffed animals, penguin jewelry, penguin sweaters and T-shirts and socks. She has a pair of penguin fuzzy slippers she wears when working late at the office. She has a tape cassette of penguin sounds which she listens to for relaxation. Her favorite colors are black and white. She has personalized license plates that read PEN GWEN. Every morning, she passes through all the cubicles to wish each of us a *good* morning. She brings Danish on Wednesdays for Hump Day morning break, and doughnuts on Fridays for TGIF afternoon break. She organizes the Annual Christmas Potluck, and is in charge of the Birthday List. Gwendolyn Stich's door is always open to all of us. She will always lend an ear, and put in a good word for you; she will always give you a hand, or the shirt off her back, or a shoulder to cry on. Because her door is always open, she hides and cries in a stall in the women's room. And John LaFountaine—who, enthralled when a woman enters, sits quietly in his stall with his knees to his chest—John LaFountaine has heard her vomiting in there. We have come upon Gwendolyn Stich huddled in the stairwell, shivering in the updraft, sipping a Diet Mr. Pibb and hugging her knees. She does not let any of this interfere with her work. If it interfered with her work, she might have to be let go.

Kevin Howard sits in that cubicle over there. He is a serial killer, the one they call the Carpet Cutter, responsible for the mutilations across town. We're not supposed to know that, so do not let on. Don't worry. His compulsion inflicts itself on strangers only, and the routine established is elaborate and unwavering. The victim must be a white male, a young adult no older than thirty, heavyset, with dark hair and eyes, and the like. The victim must be chosen at random, before sunset, from a public place; the victim is followed home, and must put up a struggle; et cetera. The carnage inflicted is precise: the angle and direction of the incisions; the layering of skin and muscle tissue; the rearrangement of the visceral organs; and so on. Kevin Howard does not let any of this interfere with his work. He is, in fact, our fastest typist. He types as if he were on fire. He has a secret crush on Gwendolyn Stich, and leaves a red-foil-wrapped Hershey's Kiss on her desk every afternoon. But he hates Anika Bloom, and keeps well away from her. In his presence, she has uncontrollable fits of shaking and trembling. Her left palm does not stop bleeding.

In any case, when Kevin Howard gets caught, act surprised. Say that he seemed like a nice person, a bit of a loner, perhaps, but always quiet and polite. 25

This is the photocopier room. And this, this is our view. It faces southwest. West is down there, toward the water. North is back there. Because we are on the seventeenth floor, we are afforded a magnificent view. Isn't it beautiful? It overlooks the park, where the tops of those trees are. You can see a segment of the bay between those two buildings there. You can see the sun set in the gap between those two buildings over there. You can see this building reflected in the glass panels of that building across the way. There. See? That's you, waving. And look there. There's Anika Bloom in the kitchenette, waving back.

Enjoy this view while photocopying. If you have problems with the photocopier, see Russell Nash. If you have any questions, ask your supervisor. If you can't find your supervisor, ask Phillip Spiers. He sits over there. He'll check with Clarissa Nicks. She sits over there. If you can't find them, feel free to ask me. That's my cubicle. I sit in there.

FOR ANALYSIS

1. Who is the **narrator** in "Orientation"? What do you know about this person? What do you not know? Why do you think Orozco tells us what he does—and, omits what he does—about the narrator's identity?

2. What kind of workplace is this? What sort of work do the employees do there? How do they seem to feel about their work? How do you know?

3. How is this story structured? What can you say about the **plot**? Does a storyline develop from beginning to end? What drives the story along?

4. How would you describe the **tone** of "Orientation"? Is it uniform, or varied? If varied, between what tones does it move, and to what effect?

5. What **themes** arise in this story? Are they specific to the story's setting, or might they be more widely applied? If so, how?

MAKING CONNECTIONS

1. Compare and contrast "Orientation" to Nathaniel Hawthorne's "Young Goodman Brown" (p. 79) in terms of their commitment to representing reality. How does each draw a picture of life as it really is, or seems to be? How does each diverge from that kind of picture?

2. Read "Orientation" against Jamaica Kincaid's "Girl" (p. 103) for the way both speak in imperatives. What kinds of things are their **narrators** telling their audience to do? What effects do they achieve by addressing their audience in this way?

WRITING TOPICS

1. Describe your feelings about a workplace in which you have been employed. (If you have never worked, describe a place that embodies your ideas about what a workplace might be like—the good things and the things you fear or wish to avoid.) How do your feelings about this real or imagined workplace connect to your ideas about what work should be like? How do you think people should feel about the place in which they spend a significant chunk of their waking hours?

2. Write a short piece in which you orient your readers to a place or situation and tell them what they need to know about it and how to act there. What are the difficulties of such an approach? What does it allow you to do?

HARI KUNZRU (B. 1969)

RAJ, BOHEMIAN 2008

We liked to do things casually. We called at the last minute. We messaged one another from our hand-held devices. Sometimes our names were on exclusive guest lists (though we were poor, we were beautiful, and people liked to have us around), but often we preferred to do something else—attend a friend's opening, drink in after-hours clubs or the room above a pub, trek off to remote suburbs to see a band play in a warehouse. We went dancing whenever we felt like it (none of us had regular jobs), and when we didn't we stayed in, watching movies and getting high. Someone always had something new or special—illegal prereleases of Hollywood blockbusters, dubs of 8-mm shorts from the nineteen-seventies. We watched next summer's exploding airplanes, Viennese Actionists masturbating onto operating tables. Raw meat and Nick Cage. Whatever we watched was, by definition, good, because we'd watched it, because it had belonged—at least, temporarily—to us. By the time the wider world caught up—which always happened, sooner or later—we'd usually got bored and moved on. We had long since given up mourning the loss of our various enthusiasms. We'd learned to discard them lightly. It was the same with clubs and bars. Wherever we went would be written about in magazines three or four months later. A single mention on a blog, and a place that had been spangled with beautiful, interesting faces would be swamped by young bankers in button-down shirts, nervously analyzing the room to see if they were having fun.

I must make it clear that we didn't plan for our lives to be this way. We despised trendies—fashion kids who tried too hard, perennially hoping to get hosed down by the paps or interviewed about their hair. With us, it wasn't a neurotic thing. We put on public events—salons, gigs, parties, shows. But once in a while, in the midst of our hectic social gyrations, we liked to do something for one another, something that didn't drain our energy, that made us feel private again.

My friend Sunita had a sense of theatre. She loved formality, intrigue. She had a certain archaic style, which would have been pompous or tediously ironic if it hadn't been for her cracked sense of humor, her painful, charming earnestness. For Sunita, the world was a kind of tragic game. When she threw one of her dinner parties, there were handmade invitations, a dress code. Once, she held a surrealist dinner, all diving suits and lobsters, over which she presided in a sheer green dress that was almost completely transparent. Another time, her theme was war. You might think it bad taste to hold a war-themed dinner party—now, of all times—but Sunita pulled it off. We arrived carrying toy guns, wearing helmets daubed with bloodthirsty slogans. Some

111

of us sniggered; others muttered about our hostess's poor taste. Yet somehow the evening, which should have been ludicrous, took on an unexpected aura of profundity. How? Sunita turned it into a wake. We raised our glasses to the millions of dead, to all the people who had had to endure what we merely watched on television. We had escaped, and we felt very guilty about it. Our childish carnival costumes were a sign of our shame. Donkeys' ears, dunces' caps.

When word got around that Sunita was holding another dinner, people immediately started angling for invitations. Everyone knew that she and I were close. Friends called, more or less begging me to get them in. I had to apologize and say that there was nothing I could do. It was a rule, an unofficial rule: no liggers and no hangers-on.

Sunita lived in an old textile warehouse, a big, echoing building that was due to be converted into apartments. It had pools of water in the basement and a goods lift that clanked its way up to the third floor, where she'd set up home, plumbing in a kitchen and partitioning off a bedroom and a bathroom. The main space was a studio where she made her drawings, ramified patterns of abstract nested lines that had grown, in the time I'd known her, from tiny quadrants smaller than a paperback into huge things that rambled over sheets of paper in uncertain arcs. The landlord, a Greek named Constantine who had a dozen other properties in the area, was waiting for the market to improve before he redeveloped. In the meantime, Sunita lived rent free. She and Constantine had some kind of deal; I never knew the details. I would occasionally find him there when I went to visit, a portly man in a cashmere coat, sitting at her huge pine table shelling pistachios. He often brought nuts, sometimes cherries or boxes of gluey sweets. Sunita seemed able to handle him well enough.

The card for Sunita's latest dinner was minimal: a thick piece of cream-colored paper, with the words "Eating Is Honest" printed in an old-fashioned cursive font. Date and time, address, the cryptic instruction "Dress sincerely." I spent a long time debating what to wear. Sunita was typically tight-lipped about how her theme should be interpreted. "No, I won't help you," she said. "You know it would ruin everything." So I phoned around. No one had a clue. Vikram was his usual scatological self. "Toilets," he said. "She's going to do the thing out of the Buñuel film with the toilets. She's going to make all of us take a shit around a dining table and then eat in little locked cubicles."

I ended up adopting a sort of ironic nerd look, with thick, plastic-framed glasses and a clip-on tie. I wasn't very satisfied with it. I considered wearing my "own" clothes, on the ground that it would have been the most sincere response—to dress as if there were no dress code—but I couldn't work out what the most neutral choice would be. How to let everyone know that not only was I myself, I was *expressing* myself? Damn Sunita, I thought. Damn her clever ideas.

When I arrived at the warehouse, I found that she'd transformed the place into a kind of kitsch Christian heaven. White sheets were draped over the walls. A long table was arrayed with flowers and candelabra and lavish silver platters of food. When you got up close, you saw that it was all aluminum foil and spray paint, but by candlelight the scene looked sumptuous, romantic.

Next to each place setting was a little hand mirror. Evidently, self-examination was part of the rubric. A number of old-fashioned medical illustrations were tacked incongruously on the wall, demonstrating the digestive system. Sunita was dressed in a white linen shift, and welcomed us with a short speech that, as far as I could tell, was composed of cut-up extracts from diet books. The food was simple and plain—fruit, cheeses, loaves of crusty bread—and while we ate it there was a program of entertainment. Michel read several of his poems. Hengist and Horsa played folk songs. A woman called Kevin did some kind of improvised dance, a flurry of arm-swirling that made me feel embarrassed and slightly uncomfortable. I took that as a good sign. If a piece of art makes me uncomfortable or, better still, angry, that seems to be a reason to pay attention to it.

It was all very pure and calming, an atmosphere that Faye de Way (when we finally managed to steer her away from the perennial topic of her operation) labeled "Baroque detox." If that was the effect our hostess was shooting for, it was slightly spoiled by her guests, who were all smoking like chimneys. "Chew twenty times!" Sunita admonished. "Once for each person at the table." I was seated next to Thanh, who'd cut her hair into a fringe. She looked like a Vietnamese Nico. I told her she was an inscrutable Oriental, and she told me I was a round-eyed pervert who would cry like a little baby when she cut my cock off. How we laughed! I was in a beautiful place, surrounded by talented people. No one was showing off, no one was being pushy, but somehow everyone shone. For one night, we were glorious.

Gradually, we all swapped chairs, clustering in groups to chat. Vikram stood 10 by the record player, putting on seven-inch singles. The table, which had looked so pristine, was strewn with a wreckage of empty bottles and ashtrays and plastic cups. Sunita sat down beside me and asked if I was enjoying myself. I told her I was. She hugged me and I kissed her on the lips. "You should save that for Thanh," she warned. "If you're not careful, Raj will get hold of her."

Raj was one of the few people at the party that I didn't know. He was good-looking, in that conventional way which seems to sabotage any chance of depth or credibility in a person. Are handsome men doomed to become skin-care-obsessed dullards simply because no one talks to them about serious things? Or are looks linked in some genetic way to intelligence? Raj's hair was gelled and teased into spikes. He wore a fussy beard, shaved into a fine line around the contours of his jaw. He was flirting with Thanh, which annoyed me, since I'd weighed things up and decided that I definitely wanted to go home with her. Still, I swallowed my distaste—after all, the guy was a friend of Sunita's—and was gratified to find that when I moved over to sit beside Thanh he ceded possession graciously enough.

As we chatted, I decided that he was actually rather charming. He even ventured an occasional shot at self-deprecation, which I certainly hadn't expected from someone like him. He'd brought along several bottles of vodka, an unfamiliar brand. He poured a shot for each of us, telling us that he'd just discovered it and rhapsodizing about how fragrant it was, how smooth. We talked about a number of other things—I can't remember what—and he took a few pictures with his phone, which I thought was lame. I mean, if you're too busy recording the experience, are you actually having it in the first place? I came away thinking that he was all right. A little suburban, a little bland, but sweet enough.

As I'd hoped, I went home with Thanh, and for a few weeks my memories of Sunita's party were filtered through my new relationship with her. We'd lie for hours on a rug on her studio floor, fucking and listening to music. One evening, while she got dressed to go back to the boyfriend with whom she had a complex but live-in relationship, I was idly typing our names into a search engine—sort of the digital equivalent of scratching initials into the trunk of a tree—when I came across a picture of the two of us, arms around each other, our cheeks mashed together as we blew kisses at the camera. In the foreground was a vodka bottle. For a moment, I couldn't work out where the photograph had been taken. Then, to my surprise, I realized that it was from Sunita's party. The site it was on was a corporate advertorial affair called something like Get-the-Taste, or Feel-the-Refreshment. There was a competition and an unpopulated "community." Across the screen scrolled similar photos of sexy young things in social situations, always with the vodka bottle in the shot. None of the pictures seemed posed.

It took me a minute or two to put it together, and when I did I wasn't happy. The bastard. The two-faced little fucker. Raj had been getting paid to take those pictures. He'd come to our party, and not just any party, to Sunita's party, the most beautiful gathering imaginable, and he'd shamelessly used it to sell us—to sell me—a product. The more I thought about it, the more angry I became. All that trash about the vodka being smooth: his whole conversation had been a sales pitch. It was creepy. More than creepy. It was sinister. Furious, I told Thanh to come over and have a look. She peered at the monitor, doing up her blouse.

"You came out pretty well," she said. "I like your glam-rock pout." 15

"But look at it. That bastard made us into an advert."

"Are we credited?"

"Only our first names."

"Shame. And I look so drunk."

"I suppose you—no, no, no! That's not the point. I mean, don't you feel 20
used?"

"What are you so upset about? You don't look nearly as wasted as me. It's hardly fair. You were downing those shots all night."

"But what about Raj? He never asked us whether we wanted to be on his damn vodka Web site. And all that patter about how smooth it tasted!"

"It was smooth."

"But to talk to people and secretly be trying to sell them something—isn't that, I don't know, unethical? Surely you agree that it's completely out of order."

"He didn't ask us to buy anything. He gave us free drinks." 25

"I know, but the point was to get us to buy something later on. That particular brand. We generate buzz. We recommend it to our friends, it becomes hip, blah-blah-blah."

"He should have given me image approval. Look at my chin! I'm going to have words next time I see him."

"For fuck's sake, Thanh! He was just using us. He wanted to make us into— into early adopters."

"But we *are* early adopters. I got a free phone a few months ago. All I had to do was watch a film and say how it made me feel."

"Jesus, you really are a shallow bitch."   30

Thanh and I more or less stopped seeing each other after that. I couldn't understand why she didn't feel more angry. Something precious to me had been violated, something I'd been holding on to. A secret pleasure that I hadn't wanted to throw into the big commercial vat with all the rest of the stuff—all the other moments and memories that get recycled into processed trends, like so many cheese triangles. Sunita's party had been private. That is the only way I can put it. The party had been private and he'd made it public.

I went to tell Sunita. "That's so Raj," she said.

I was confused. What did she mean, "so Raj"? Didn't she think that he'd betrayed her trust? Wasn't his behavior sleazy and underhanded?

"He was just being himself." She laughed. "He's a hustler. That's something you'll learn about Raj when you get to know him better."

One thing I must admit here: I find anger tricky. Anger is a very sincere 35 emotion. We live under the rule of cool, and we are expected to encounter the vicissitudes of the world with a certain degree of irony. Sincerity, as any hip- ster will tell you, is for awkward teens and people on SSRIs. Think about it— sincerity is gauche, gauche is boring, and boring is rude, so it's only a matter of ordinary politeness not to take things too seriously. But I really couldn't deal with Sunita laughing at me. When you're truly vexed, so vexed that it makes you incoherent and frustrated, there's nothing worse than being laughed at. You cunt, I thought. You fucking cunt. You're not who I thought you were.

Just as I was making up my mind to say something, I was saved by the inter- com. Sunita buzzed up fat Constantine, who was hefting a box of mangoes in his meaty hands. He nodded to me, installed himself at the table, and started to peel and slice them. Sunita sat down beside him. I stood by the sink, my fists balled, so consumed with irritation that I couldn't think of anything to say. Constantine fed Sunita slices of mango, spearing them on the tip of his knife. She took them between her teeth, making eyes at him. Eventually, he looked up at me. "Don't let me interrupt," he said.

"He was talking about my friend Raj," Sunita explained, wiping her mouth with a napkin. "He's a bit of a wheeler-dealer."

"My kind of guy," Constantine said.

Sunita smiled at me. "Raj has the greatest car. Have you seen it?"

No, I hadn't.   40

"It's a big metallic purple thing, with under-floor lighting and 'Rude Mercs' written on the back window. It's hilarious."

"How did you and Raj meet?"

"Oh, around."

That was her standard euphemism for sleeping with someone. There had never been anything serious between Sunita and me, but all the same I felt a pang.

"I can't believe it, Sunny. He's an idiot."   45

"What's the problem?" Constantine asked. "Who is this Raj?"

"No one," Sunita said. "Just a guy who's been treading on someone's little tootsies."

Constantine gestured to his plate. "Try a mango," he said. "They're Alfonsos. Very sweet."

That night, I couldn't get to sleep. Round and round it went in my mind: Raj, vodka. Of course, it wasn't about the vodka. I'd enjoyed the damn vodka. And surely there was nothing intrinsically wrong with accepting a free drink. But there must come a time when you're allowed to stop being a consumer. There has to be some respite from all that choosing, a time, well, just to *be*. Sunita's party had been cool. Add as many quotation marks around the word as you like, but it was true. Most people never get the chance to attend a party like that. And, yes, there had been an element of performance to it. But I'd thought that we were just being cool for one another, to stave off boredom for a few hours, not to make some poor shell-suited kid on a housing estate feel jealous. I mean, jealousy just breeds resentment, right? Violence. People could get mugged because of Raj and his pictures. People could get raped. I started to look at my lifestyle in a new, fearful light. What did I have that people might want to take? Did people get burgled for their cultural capital?

I'd assumed that Raj's betrayal of trust would be obvious to everyone, but, to my   50 shock, none of my friends seemed to see anything wrong. Otto was a long-haired German who shot music promos. "I need information, man," he said, shrugging. We were sitting in a sushi bar, drinking green tea. "I don't care how it gets to me."

"It's not information," I argued, waving my cup around. "The speed of light, the date of the moon landing. That's information."

"Uh, they recently invented this thing called the Internet."

"Piss off, Otto. You know what I mean."

"Get over yourself, man. You're acting so old-fashioned, like some kind of Communist. I have the right to perform acts of rational consumer choice: our ancestors fought wars for it. And I think I'm clever enough to filter a little bit of spin, don't you? Look, why don't you check out this band I'm working with?" He handed me a sleek little music player. I listened for a while, out of politeness.

"They're the final wave of New Wave," he explained. "After this, there will   55 never be another reason to wear a Blondie T-shirt."

I nodded listlessly. I felt too despondent to argue anymore. Otto, smiling at me as he bounced his head to the beat of the music he couldn't hear, seemed not to notice. "I knew you'd like them. Aren't those headphones great, though? Optional noise cancellation. Amazing dynamic range. Particularly the bass—really rich, considering how small they are."

A sudden suspicion crossed my mind. But, no, this wasn't some suburban wide-boy. This was Otto.

And yet . . . Over the next few days, I started to notice something odd. Every time I met a friend, he or she would immediately make a recommendation, urge me to try something new. Lucas had been to a club on the other side of town and insisted that it was the best night out he'd had in ages. Janine almost forced me to take home a bottle of her "new favorite nutritional supplement." At first, I shrugged it off. But, deep down, I knew that it had something to do with Raj and his vodka. Every night, I'd turn the incident over in my mind. I swallowed Ativan and Valium and Paxil (I had a compliant doctor), hoping that my anxiety would pass. It didn't. There was Joe and his new running shoes. Razia's bike. All my friends seemed to be dropping snippets of advertising copy into their conversation, short messages from their sponsors. They were constantly stating preferences for particular brands, dishing out free samples.

Perhaps nothing had changed. We'd always shared new music with one another or recommended places to eat. But now there was something different. A tone? It was hard to say. I found myself wondering if Sasha was telling me that the sushi at Bar Fugu was "to die for" because he meant it or because it was a snappy slogan. Vikram started talking to me at nauseating length about tires. Steel radials, depth of tread. I hadn't even known that Vikram had a car. When Wei Lin began rhapsodizing about the streaming capabilities of his new video projector, I snapped.

"Don't start this shit on me, Wei. I'm sick of it."   60

"What?"

"This sales patter. I can't take it anymore. Frankly, you disgust me."

"I what?"

"It's not even as if you need the money. You're loaded."

"I don't understand why you're being so hostile."   65

"Your daddy in Shanghai owns a fucking construction company. We all know, Wei. It's not a secret. So why do you need to do this? There's no reason! Is it fun? Does it get you laid?"

Afterward, he told everyone that I'd physically threatened him. He said to Thanh that he thought I might be on crack.

I was shaken up. I tried to get on with my life, working on my designs, speaking to people—even going out, just as if things were normal. But they weren't. I felt I was under immense mental pressure, in constant danger of some unforeseen catastrophic event, a psychological bridge collapse. I found parties increasingly traumatic: the bombardment of messages, the pitches coming at me from every side. It was impossible to untangle what was being said because the speaker felt or believed it from what was merely repetition. When were people being themselves and when were they acting? I began, ever so slightly, to doubt the reality of other minds. People seemed to zone in and out of existence. Sometimes they were fully present, animated by something original and real. But mostly they were just zombies, empty vessels operated by corporate remote control.

I tell you, I was afraid. Becoming a hermit was looking like a good option. A cave in the Hebrides. The lonely sea and the sky. I was ready to batten down the hatches and crawl into the submarine of my own paranoia when I met Zoe. She understood me immediately, saw that my life had been stripped of all humor, all scope and playfulness, that it was irising down to the enforced sincerity of the locked ward.

Zoe didn't like being in physical proximity to too many people, because she thought it made her sick, though as far as I could tell she was a perfectly healthy person. She didn't go outside much, and always went to the shops with a tub of antiseptic wipes in her bag. On bad days, she wore a face mask. Despite her eccentricities, she was no introvert, was a lively presence on various online sites and game worlds. We spent a lot of time indoors, smoking and talking. She wasn't physically beautiful, but I didn't want someone beautiful; I wanted someone who made me feel safe, which Zoe did—until the night I mentioned her ring. 70

It was a large copper band with a number of tiny stones set into it, a trashy-looking thing with a vaguely *Lord of the Rings* aesthetic. I asked her what it was.

"This?" she said absent-mindedly, sticking one hand out as she manipulated a joystick with the other, careering through some virtual maze. "It's an appetite-reduction ring. See the tiny gems? There are nine of them. It helps correct biochemical imbalances in the body by reverse-actuating the ionic flow in my bloodstream. You should get one."

Zombie-speech. She had reeled it off without a pause.

"Oh, no, Zoe."

She paused her game. "What?" 75

"Not you, too."

"I don't understand. Are you all right?"

"Zoe, I'm going to ask you something, and you'd better tell me the truth."

"What are you talking about? You look pale."

"Is someone paying you to say that stuff?" 80

She giggled. "Sorry, babe, it just pops out sometimes. I didn't mean to pitch you. I'm supposed only to do it to my girlfriends."

"What?"

"Ignore me. You know how hard it is to keep track of one's placements."

"Placements?"

"Placements. Why are you making that face? You're looking at me like I'm some kind of freak." 85

"You have a lot of—placements?"

"Oh, don't get on your high horse. You don't work, either. What do you do for cash? If a girl doesn't want a straight job, she has to monetize her social network."

I'm not proud of what I did then. I just couldn't control myself. I slapped her. I told her that she was a fake, a zombie. Before I walked out, I took a last look at her, pathetically scrubbing at her cheek with a cloth.

At my flat, I looked at the presents she'd bought me during our short relationship—a pair of shoes, a scarf. I decided to give them to charity. I found a cardboard box, but it was big and the shoes and scarf didn't take up much space, so I added a few more things. The experience was oddly pleasurable.

Once I'd started, it was hard to stop. Soon I'd filled several boxes, then several more. They were too heavy to carry to the charity shop, so I just left them on the street outside my building. For the rest of the day, I watched from the balcony as people stopped to rummage and carry things away. That night, I put the rest of my stuff out. All of it—clothes, books and records, furniture, even the cans of food from my kitchen cupboards. Everything I owned. By the following afternoon, it was all gone.

I spent the next couple of days squatting on my haunches in a corner of my 90 empty flat. Something in me had snapped, was broken beyond repair. My taste had been central to my identity. I'd cultivated it, kept it fed and watered like an exotic flowering plant. Now I realized that what I thought had been an expression of my innermost humanity was nothing but a cloud of lifestyle signals, available to anyone at the click of a mouse. How had this happened?

I couldn't understand. There had to be something else. What was a personality if it wasn't a drop-down menu, a collection of likes and dislikes? And now that my possessions were gone, what would I put in their place? Who was I without my private pressings, my limited editions, my vintage one-offs? How could I signal to potential allies across the vast black reaches of interpersonal space?

It was then that I realized I'd been robbed. I'd been forcibly expropriated from myself. And who had done this to me? Who was the cause of all my loss and pain? I stormed around to Sunita's to ask for Raj's address. The door was opened by Constantine, wearing a quilted paisley dressing gown.

"She's out," he said, tightening the cord around his paunch. "She says don't come around no more." He burped.

"Sunita doesn't want to see me?"

"That's right. She says you have a bad energy."   95

I didn't know quite how to process that information. "Whatever. For now, I just need a number for Raj."

"Raj is it? He's a nice guy."

"So you know him?"

"Sure. Everyone knows Raj."

"So how do I get hold of him?"   100

"I've got his card somewhere."

He disappeared and came back holding a business card. On it was written, in a cheesy futuristic font, "Raj, Bohemian." I couldn't tell if it was a company name or a job description. The office address was close by.

"Thanks."

Constantine looked at me solicitously. "You know your problem?"

"Tell me my problem."   105

"Stress. You should get a massage. I'll give you another number. It's local. The girls are very attentive."

I turned my back on him and pressed the call button on the lift.

The trip to Raj's office passed in a dream. I was a ghost, floating through a world of moving signage, people carrying shopping bags, immigrants handing out flyers for bars and language schools. I went into a department store, dazzled by chrome and glass and brushed steel. It was a palace of mirrors, zombie heaven. Girls at the makeup counter, dressed like slutty pharmacists. Rich men with ski tans fingering cashmere sweaters. In the housewares department was a display cabinet of knives, gleaming with surgical allure. I bought the largest and headed back up the escalator to the teeming street.

Raj's office wasn't what I'd expected. I was imagining—I don't know what I was imagining. A flashy loft. A lifestyle statement. It turned out to be a shared suite, a dreary place with grubby tube lights and contract carpeting, where freelancers rented desks, huddling together to make themselves feel less alone. One or two people looked up from their work as I walked in. I felt dizzy, disoriented, carrying the knife wrapped in a yellow plastic bag.

"Hey, man! Good to see you!" 110

Raj was standing up behind a desk piled high with paper and promotional knickknacks. Across the top of his computer monitor paraded a little line of toys. He looked tired and drab, his eyes rimmed with dark circles, a reddish stain disfiguring his crisp white polo shirt. Raj, my nemesis. So ordinary. I had gone there to kill him, to make him into nothing for having made me into nothing. But now that he stood in front of me he was just a guy with a greasy forehead and a pimple on his top lip. Now that I saw the reality of his life, the plastic bags full of free samples, the half-eaten sandwich balanced on a teetering stack of magazines, I knew that any confrontation would be absurd. I sank down onto a swivel chair and spun in little half circles, while he hovered over me, this person who'd polluted my whole life without even realizing it. Someone else was there. A woman. I think he was trying to introduce her to me. I shook my head mutely. What was I? A sorting device. A filter. A human bivalve, culture accreting in me like a mercury deposit. I looked around the office at the young workers wearing headphones, typing, talking into phones with their feet on their desks. This was the world, just the same indoors and out, a place of total nullity. How could anything make any difference? Unless you managed to keep your head underwater, to immerse yourself in the endless metonymic shuffling of objects, it would be intolerable.

"You look awful," Raj said. "Are you feeling O.K.?"

I stared up at him. He was holding out a glass of water.

"Is it good?" I asked.

He shook his head, not understanding. 115

"Is it better than other brands of water?"

"It's just water. From the tap."

I took a sip.

"Are you sick?" he asked gently.

"No." 120

"What is it, then?"

I closed my eyes. "I'm not sure. I think I might be bored."

"Ah."

"Is there anything going on tonight?"

He smiled and started to tell me about a party, a guest list, a secret venue. I 125
took out my phone to punch in the contact number.

FOR ANALYSIS

1. Why does the **narrator** get rid of all his possessions? At the end of the story, do you think he will continue to live without things?

2. What is it that makes the narrator want to kill Raj? Why does he not follow through with his plan?

3. Why do you think Kunzru chose to use Raj's name in the title? How do you think the second part of the title is meant to be taken?

4. Who is innocent in "Raj, Bohemian"? Who is experienced? What does it mean to be each in the context of this story?

MAKING CONNECTIONS

1. Melville's "Bartleby, the Scrivener" (p. 325) and Kafka's "A Hunger Artist" (p. 353) both feature eponymous **protagonists** who, in the words of Bartleby, "prefer not to." Compare the main character in "Raj, Bohemian" to one or both of these **characters**. How are they similar, and how are they different? Compare especially the things they prefer not to do and their reasons for not doing them.

2. Compare "Raj, Bohemian" to any or all of the selections in "Connecting Poems: Revisiting Fairy Tales" (p. 208). How does each of these works take up the issue of innocence?

WRITING TOPICS

1. Write an essay in which you reflect on how your tastes—the things you wear, carry, listen to, watch—define who you are. How did you come to like these things? What do you think they say about you?

2. Write an essay in which you discuss the workings of identification in this story. How do you feel about the **characters**—the **narrator**, and Sunita, and their circle of friends? Do you find them ridiculous or sad or likable? Do you see yourself in them, or do you see yourself as completely different? What do you think the author wants you to feel about them? Why?

CONNECTING STORIES: CRUSHES

Crush is a funny word. Its literal meaning is "romantic attraction that is somewhere short of love"—something short-lived and superficial. But buried in the word's etymology is a somewhat contradictory sense of intensity, of something pressing or grinding (and even a sense of violence if you consider the word's original meaning, which included a loud crashing or cracking sound). As you read these stories, look for the ways in which a crush, while it lasts only a brief while and then is gone, can also be intense and even overwhelming. One of the reasons crushes are rich subjects for literature is that as powerful infatuations they contain contradiction, expressing something of life's deepest feelings as well as life's mutability—the quick-changing quality that often drives artists to try to capture lost, fleeting moments. In the following stories, James Joyce and Rivka Galchen manage to capture two similar—and similarly lost—moments, but in very different ways.

JAMES JOYCE   (1882–1941)

ARABY   1914

North Richmond Street, being blind, was a quiet street except at the hour when the Christian Brothers' School set the boys free. An uninhabited house of two storeys stood at the blind end, detached from its neighbours in a square ground. The other houses of the street, conscious of decent lives within them, gazed at one another with brown imperturbable faces.

The former tenant of our house, a priest, had died in the back drawing-room. Air, musty from having been long enclosed, hung in all the rooms, and the waste room behind the kitchen was littered with old useless papers. Among these I found a few paper-covered books, the pages of which were curled and damp: *The Abbot*, by Walter Scott, *The Devout Communicant* and *The Memoirs of Vidocq*. I liked the last best because its leaves were yellow. The wild garden behind the house contained a central apple-tree and a few straggling bushes under one of which I found the late tenant's rusty bicycle pump. He had been a very charitable priest; in his will he had left all his money to institutions and the furniture of his house to his sister.

When the short days of winter came dusk fell before we had well eaten our dinners. When we met in the street the houses had grown sombre. The space of sky above us was the colour of ever-changing violet and towards it the lamps of the street lifted their feeble lanterns. The cold air stung us and we played till our bodies glowed. Our shouts echoed in the silent street. The career of our play brought us through the dark muddy lanes behind the houses where we ran the gauntlet of the rough tribes from the cottages, to the back doors of the dark dripping gardens where odours arose from the ashpits, to the dark odorous stables where a coachman smoothed and combed the horse or shook music from the buckled harness. When we returned to the street, light from the kitchen windows had filled the areas. If my uncle was seen turning the corner we hid in the shadow until we had seen him safely housed. Or if Mangan's sister came out on the doorstep to call her brother in to his tea we watched her from our shadow peer up and down the street. We waited to see whether she would remain or go in and, if she remained, we left our shadow and walked up to Mangan's steps resignedly. She was waiting for us, her figure defined by the light from the half-opened door. Her brother always teased her before he obeyed and I stood by the railings looking at her. Her dress swung as she moved her body and the soft rope of her hair tossed from side to side.

Every morning I lay on the floor in the front parlour watching her door. The blind was pulled down to within an inch of the sash so that I could not be seen. When she came out on the doorstep my heart leaped. I ran to the hall, seized my books and followed her. I kept her brown figure always in my eye and, when we came near the point at which our ways diverged, I quickened my pace and passed her. This happened morning after morning. I had never spoken to her, except for a few casual words, and yet her name was like a summons to all my foolish blood.

Her image accompanied me even in places the most hostile to romance. On [5] Saturday evenings when my aunt went marketing I had to go to carry some of the parcels. We walked through the flaring streets, jostled by drunken men and bargaining women, amid the curses of labourers, the shrill litanies of shop-boys who stood on guard by the barrels of pigs' cheeks, the nasal chanting of street-singers, who sang a *come-all-you*[1] about O'Donovan Rossa, or a ballad about the troubles in our native land. These noises converged in a single sensation of life for me: I imagined that I bore my chalice safely through a throng of foes. Her name sprang to my lips at moments in strange prayers and praises which I myself did not understand. My eyes were often full of tears (I could not tell why) and at times a flood from my heart seemed to pour itself out into my bosom. I thought little of the future. I did not know whether I would ever speak to her or not or, if I spoke to her, how I could tell her of my confused adoration. But my body was like a harp and her words and gestures were like fingers running upon the wires.

One evening I went into the back drawing-room in which the priest had died. It was a dark rainy evening and there was no sound in the house. Through one of the broken panes I heard the rain impinge upon the earth, the fine incessant needles of water playing in the sodden beds. Some distant lamp or lighted window gleamed below me. I was thankful that I could see so little. All my senses seemed to desire to veil themselves and, feeling that I was about to slip from them, I pressed the palms of my hands together until they trembled, murmuring: "*O love! O love!*" many times.

---

[1]A street ballad beginning with these words. This one is about Jeremiah Donovan, a nineteenth-century Irish nationalist popularly known as O'Donovan Rossa.

At last she spoke to me. When she addressed the first words to me I was so confused that I did not know what to answer. She asked me was I going to *Araby*. I forgot whether I answered yes or no. It would be a splendid bazaar, she said she would love to go.

"And why can't you?" I asked.

While she spoke she turned a silver bracelet round and round her wrist. She could not go, she said, because there would be a retreat that week in her convent. Her brother and two other boys were fighting for their caps and I was alone at the railings. She held one of the spikes, bowing her head towards me. The light from the lamp opposite our door caught the white curve of her neck, lit up her hair that rested there and, falling, lit up the hand upon the railing. It fell over one side of her dress and caught the white border of a petticoat, just visible as she stood at ease.

"It's well for you," she said. 10

"If I go," I said, "I will bring you something."

What innumerable follies laid waste my waking and sleeping thoughts after that evening! I wished to annihilate the tedious intervening days. I chafed against the work of school. At night in my bedroom and by day in the classroom her image came between me and the page I strove to read. The syllables of the word *Araby* were called to me through the silence in which my soul luxuriated and cast an Eastern enchantment over me. I asked for leave to go to the bazaar on Saturday night. My aunt was surprised and hoped it was not some Freemason affair. I answered few questions in class. I watched my master's face pass from amiability to sternness; he hoped I was not beginning to idle. I could not call my wandering thoughts together. I had hardly any patience with the serious work of life which, now that it stood between me and my desire, seemed to me child's play, ugly monotonous child's play.

On Saturday morning I reminded my uncle that I wished to go to the bazaar in the evening. He was fussing at the hallstand, looking for the hat-brush, and answered me curtly:

"Yes, boy, I know."

As he was in the hall I could not go into the front parlour and lie at the win- 15 dow. I left the house in bad humour and walked slowly towards the school. The air was pitilessly raw and already my heart misgave me.

When I came home to dinner my uncle had not yet been home. Still it was early. I sat staring at the clock for some time and, when its ticking began to irritate me, I left the room. I mounted the staircase and gained the upper part of the house. The high cold empty gloomy rooms liberated me and I went from room to room singing. From the front window I saw my companions playing below in the street. Their cries reached me weakened and indistinct and, leaning my forehead against the cool glass, I looked over at the dark house where she lived. I may have stood there for an hour, seeing nothing but the brown-clad figure cast by my imagination, touched discreetly by the lamplight at the curved neck, at the hand upon the railings and at the border below the dress.

When I came downstairs again I found Mrs. Mercer sitting at the fire. She was an old garrulous woman, a pawnbroker's widow, who collected used stamps for some pious purpose. I had to endure the gossip of the tea-table. The meal was prolonged beyond an hour and still my uncle did not come. Mrs. Mercer stood up to go: she was sorry she couldn't wait any longer, but it was after eight o'clock and she did not like to be out late, as the night air was bad for her. When she had gone I began to walk up and down the room, clenching my fists. My aunt said:

"I'm afraid you may put off your bazaar for this night of Our Lord."

At nine o'clock I heard my uncle's latchkey in the hall door. I heard him talking to himself and heard the hallstand rocking when it had received the weight of his overcoat. I could interpret these signs. When he was midway through his dinner I asked him to give me the money to go to the bazaar. He had forgotten.

"The people are in bed and after their first sleep now," he said.   20

I did not smile. My aunt said to him energetically:

"Can't you give him the money and let him go? You've kept him late enough as it is."

My uncle said he was very sorry he had forgotten. He said he believed in the old saying: "All work and no play makes Jack a dull boy." He asked me where I was going and, when I had told him a second time he asked me did I know *The Arab's Farewell to His Steed*. When I left the kitchen he was about to recite the opening lines of the piece to my aunt.

I held a florin tightly in my hand as I strode down Buckingham Street towards the station. The sight of the streets thronged with buyers and glaring with gas recalled to me the purpose of my journey. I took my seat in a third-class carriage of a deserted train. After an intolerable delay the train moved out of the station slowly. It crept onward among ruinous houses and over the twinkling river. At Westland Row Station a crowd of people pressed to the carriage doors; but the porters moved them back, saying that it was a special train for the bazaar. I remained alone in the bare carriage. In a few minutes the train drew up beside an improvised wooden platform. I passed out on to the road and saw by the lighted dial of a clock that it was ten minutes to ten. In front of me was a large building which displayed the magical name.

I could not find any sixpenny entrance and, fearing that the bazaar would be   25 closed, I passed in quickly through a turnstile, handing a shilling to a weary-looking man. I found myself in a big hall girdled at half its height by a gallery. Nearly all the stalls were closed and the greater part of the hall was in darkness. I recognised a silence like that which pervades a church after a service. I walked into the centre of the bazaar timidly. A few people were gathered about the stalls which were still open. Before a curtain, over which the words *Café Chantant* were written in coloured lamps, two men were counting money on a salver. I listened to the fall of the coins.

Remembering with difficulty why I had come I went over to one of the stalls and examined porcelain vases and flowered tea-sets. At the door of the stall a young lady was talking and laughing with two young gentlemen. I remarked their English accents and listened vaguely to their conversation.

"O, I never said such a thing!"

"O, but you did!"

"O, but I didn't!"

"Didn't she say that?"

"Yes. I heard her."

"O, there's a . . . fib!"

Observing me the young lady came over and asked me did I wish to buy anything. The tone of her voice was not encouraging; she seemed to have spoken to me out of a sense of duty. I looked humbly at the great jars that stood like Eastern guards at either side of the dark entrance to the stall and murmured:

"No, thank you."

The young lady changed the position of one of the vases and went back to   35 the two young men. They began to talk of the same subject. Once or twice the young lady glanced at me over her shoulder.

I lingered before her stall, though I knew my stay was useless, to make my interest in her wares seem the more real. Then I turned away slowly and walked down the middle of the bazaar. I allowed the two pennies to fall against the sixpence in my pocket. I heard a voice call from one end of the gallery that the light was out. The upper part of the hall was now completely dark.

Gazing up into the darkness I saw myself as a creature driven and derided by vanity; and my eyes burned with anguish and anger.

FOR ANALYSIS

1. Reread the opening paragraph. How does it set the **tone** for the story?

2. Why does the **dialogue** the **narrator** overhears at the bazaar trigger the climax of the story and the insight described in the final paragraph?

WRITING TOPICS

1. Write a page describing a romantic infatuation you experienced when you were younger that blinded you to the reality of the person you adored.

2. Analyze the **imagery** of light and vision in this story.

Rivka Galchen (B. 1976)

Wild Berry Blue 2008

This is a story about my love for Roy, though first I have to say a few words about my dad, who was there with me at the McDonald's every Saturday letting his little girl—I was maybe eight—swig his extra half-and-halfs, stack the shells into messy towers. My dad drank from his bottomless cup of coffee and read the paper while I dipped my McDonaldland cookies in milk and pretended to read the paper. He wore gauzy plaid button-ups with pearline snaps. He had girlish wrists, a broad forehead like a Roman, an absolutely terrifying sneeze.

"How's the coffee?" I'd ask.

"Not good, not bad. How's the milk?"

"Terrific," I'd say. Or maybe, "Exquisite."

My mom was at home cleaning the house; our job there at the McDonald's 5 was to be out of her way.

And that's how it always was on Saturdays. We were Jews, we had our rituals. That's how I think about it. Despite the occasional guiltless cheeseburger, despite being secular Israelis living in the wilds of Oklahoma, the ineluctable Jew part in us still snuck out, like an inherited tic, indulging in habits of repetition. Our form of *davenning*. Our little Shabbat.

Many of the people who worked at the McDonald's were former patients of my dad's: mostly drug addicts and alcoholics in rehab programs. McDonald's hired people no one else would hire; I think it was a policy. And my dad, in effect, was the McDonald's–Psychiatric Institute liaison. The McDonald's manager, a deeply Christian man, would regularly come over and say hello to us, and thank my dad for many things. Once he thanked him for, as a Jew, having kept safe the word of God during all the dark years.

"I'm not sure I've done so much," my dad had answered, not seriously.

"But it's been living there in you," the manager said earnestly. He was basically a nice man, admirably tolerant of the accompanying dramas of his work force, dramas I picked up on peripherally. Absenteeism, petty theft, a worker OD-ing in the bathroom. I had no idea what that meant, to OD, but it sounded spooky. "They slip out from under their own control," I heard the manager say one time, and the phrase stuck with me. I pictured one half of a person lifting up a velvet rope and fleeing the other half.

Sometimes, dipping my McDonaldland cookies—Fryguy, Grimace—I'd hold 10 a cookie in the milk too long and it would saturate and crumble to the bottom of the carton. There, it was something mealy, vulgar. Horrible. I'd lose my appetite. Though the surface of the milk often remained pristine I could feel the cookie's presence down below, lurking. Like some ancient bottom-dwelling fish with both eyes on one side of his head.

I'd tip the carton back in order to see what I dreaded seeing, just to feel that queasiness, and also the pre-queasiness of knowing the main queasiness was coming, the anticipatory ill.

Beautiful/Horrible—I had a running mental list. Cleaning lint from the screen of the dryer—beautiful. Bright glare on glass—horrible. Mealworms—also horrible. The stubbles of shaved hair in a woman's armpit—beautiful.

The Saturday I was to meet Roy, after dropping a cookie in the milk, I looked up at my dad. "Cookie," I squeaked, turning a sour face at the carton.

He pulled out his worn leather wallet, with its inexplicable rust stain ring on the front. He gave me a dollar. My mom never gave me money and my dad always gave me more than I needed. (He also called me the Queen of Sheba sometimes, like when I'd stand up on a dining room chair to see how things looked from there.) The torn corner of the bill he gave me was held on with yellowed Scotch tape. Someone had written over the treasury seal in blue pen, "I love Becky!!!"

I go up to the counter with the Becky dollar to buy my replacement milk, and   15 what I see is a tattoo, most of which I can't see. A starched white long-sleeve shirt covers most of it. But a little blue-black lattice of it I can see—a fragment like ancient elaborate metalwork, that creeps down all the way, past the wrist, to the back of the hand, kinking up and over a very plump vein. The vein is so distended I imagine laying my cheek on it in order to feel the blood pulse and flow, to maybe even hear it. Beautiful. So beautiful. I don't know why but I'm certain this tattoo reaches all the way up to his shoulder. His skin is deeply tanned but the webbing between his fingers sooty pale.

This beautiful feeling. I haven't had it about a person before. Not in this way.

In a trembling moment I shift my gaze up to the engraved nametag. There's a yellow M emblem, then *Roy*.

I place my dollar down on the counter. I put it down like it's a password I'm unsure of, one told to me by an unreliable source. "Milk," I say, quietly.

Roy, whose face I finally look at, is staring off, up, over past my head, like a bored lifeguard. He hasn't heard or noticed me, little me, the only person in line. Roy is biting his lower lip and one of his teeth, one of the canines, is much whiter than the others. Along his cheekbones his skin looks dry and chalky. His eyes are blue, with beautiful bruisy eyelids.

I try again, a little bit louder. "Milk."   20

Still he doesn't hear me; I begin to feel as if maybe I am going to cry because of these accumulated moments of being nothing. That's what it feels like standing so close to this type of beauty—like being nothing.

Resolving to give up if I'm not noticed soon I make one last effort and, leaning over on my tiptoes, I push the dollar further along the counter, far enough that it tickles Roy's thigh, which is leaned up against the counter's edge.

He looks down at me, startled, then laughs abruptly. "Hi little sexy," he says. Then he laughs again, too loud, and the other cashier, who has one arm shrunken and paralyzed, turns and looks and then looks away again.

Suddenly these few seconds are everything that has ever happened to me.

My milk somehow purchased I go back to the table wondering if I am green, 25 or emitting a high-pitched whistling sound, or dead.

I realize back at the table that it's not actually the first time I've seen Roy. With great concentration, I dip my Hamburglar cookie into the cool milk. I think that maybe I've seen Roy—that coarse blond hair—every Saturday, for all my Saturdays. I take a bite from my cookie. I have definitely seen him before. Just somehow not in this way.

My dad appears to be safely immersed in whatever is on the other side of the crossword puzzle and bridge commentary page. I feel—a whole birch tree pressing against my inner walls, its leaves reaching to the top of my throat— the awful sense of wanting some other life. I have thought certain boys in my classes have pretty faces, but I have never before felt like laying my head down on the vein of a man's wrist. (I still think about that vein sometimes.) Almost frantically I wonder if Roy can see me there at my table, there with my dad, where I've been seemingly all my Saturdays.

Attempting to rein in my anxiety I try and think: What makes me feel this way? Possessed like this? Is it a smell in the air? It just smells like beefy grease. Which is pleasant enough but nothing new. A little mustard. A small vapor of disinfectant. I wonder obscurely if Roy is Jewish, as if that might make normal this spiraling fated feeling I have. As if really what's struck me is just an unobvious family resemblance. But I know that we're the only Jews in town.

Esther married the gentile king, I think, in a desperate absurd flash.

Since a part of me wants to stay forever I finish my cookies quickly. 30

"Let's go," I say.

"Already?"

"Can't we just leave? Let's leave."

There's the Medieval Fair, I think to myself in consolation all Sunday. It's two weekends away, a Saturday. You're always happy at the Medieval Fair, I say to myself, as I fail to enjoy sorting my stamps, fail to stand expectantly, joyfully, on the dining room chair. Instead I fantasize about running the French fry fryer in the back of McDonald's. I imagine myself learning to construct Happy Meal boxes in a breath, to fold the papers around the hamburgers *just so*. I envision a stool set out for me to climb atop so that I can reach the apple fritter dispenser; Roy spots me, making sure I don't fall. And I get a tattoo. Of a bird, or a fish, or a ring of birds and fish, around my ankle.

But there is no happiness in these daydreams. Just an overcrowded and 35 feverish empty.

At school on Monday I sit dejectedly in the third row of Mrs. Brown's class, because that is where we are on the weekly seating chart rotation. I suffer through exercises in long division, through bits about Magellan. Since I'm not in the front I'm able to mark most of my time drawing a tremendous maze, one that stretches to the outer edges of the notebook paper. This while the teacher reads to us from something about a girl and her horse. Something. A horse. Who cares! Who cares about a horse! I think, filled, suddenly, with unexpected rage. That extra white tooth. The creeping chain of the tattoo. I try so hard to be dedicated to my maze, pressing my pencil sharply into the paper as if to hold down my focus better.

All superfluous, even my sprawling maze, superfluous. A flurry of pencil shavings from the sharpener—they come out as if in a breath—distracts me. A sudden phantom pain near my elbow consumes my attention.

I crumple up my maze dramatically; do a basketball throw to the wastebasket like the boys do. I miss of course but no one seems to notice, which is the nature of my life at school, where I am only noticed in bland embarrassing ways, like when a substitute teacher can't pronounce my last name. The joylessness of my basketball toss—it makes me look over at my once-crush Josh Deere and feel sad for him, for the smallness of his life.

One day, I think, it will be Saturday again.

But time seemed to move so slowly. I'd lost my appetite for certain details 40
of life.

"Do you know about that guy at McDonald's with the one really white tooth?" I brave this question to my dad. This during a commercial break from *Kojak*.

"Roy's a recovering heroin addict," my dad says, turning to stare at me. He always said things to me other people wouldn't have said to kids. He'd already told me about the Oedipus complex and I had stared dully back at him. He would defend General Rommel to me, though I had no idea who General Rommel was. He'd make complex points about the straits of Bosporus. It was as if he couldn't distinguish ages.

So he said that to me, about Roy, which obviously he shouldn't have said. (Here, years later, I still think about the mystery of that plump vein, which seems a contradiction. Which occasionally makes me wonder if there were two Roys.)

"I don't know what the story with the tooth is," my dad adds. "Maybe it's false?" And then it's back to the mystery of *Kojak*.

I wander into the kitchen feeling unfulfilled and so start interrogating my 45
mom about my Purim costume for the carnival that is still two Sundays, eons, away. The Purim carnival is in Tulsa, over an hour's driving distance; I don't know the kids there, and my costume never measures up. "And the crown," I remind her hollowly. I'm not quite bold enough to bring up that she could buy me one of the beautiful ribbon crowns sold at the Medieval Fair, which we'll be at the day before. "I don't want," I mumble mostly to myself, "one of those paper crowns that everyone has."

Thursday night I am at the Skaggs Alpha Beta grocery with my mom. I am lingering amid all the sugar cereals I know will never come home with me. It's only every minute or so that I am thinking about Roy's hand, about how he called me sexy.

Then I see Roy. He has no cart, no basket. He's holding a gallon of milk and a supersized bag of Twizzlers and he is reaching for, I can't quite see—a big oversized box that looks to be Honeycomb. A beautiful assemblage. Beautiful.

I turn away from Roy but stand still. I feel my whole body, even my ears, blushing. The backs of my hands feel itchy the way they always do in spring. Seeking release I touch the cool metal shelving, run my fingers up and over the plastic slipcovers, over the price labels, hearing every nothing behind me. The price labels make a sandy sliding sound when I push them. He's a monster, Roy. Not looking at him, just feeling that power he has over me, a monster.

My mom in lace-up sandals cruises by the aisle with our shopping cart, unveiling to me my ridiculousness. Able now to turn around I see that Roy is gone. I run after my mom and when finally we're in the car again, back door closed on the groceries—I see celery stalks innocently sticking out of a brown paper bag when I turn around—I feel great relief.

I decide to wash my feet in the sink, this always makes me happy. On my dad's 50 shaving mirror in the bathroom, old Scotch tape holding it in place, is a yellowed bit of paper, torn from a magazine. For years it's been there, inscrutable, and suddenly I feel certain that it carries a secret. About love maybe. About the possessed feeling I have because of Roy.

It says *And human speech is but a cracked kettle upon which we tap crude rhythms for bears to dance to, while we long to make music that—*

Next to the scrap is a sticker of mine, of a green apple.

I look again at the quote: the bears, the kettle.

Silly, I decide. It's all very silly. I start to dry my feet with a towel.

For the impending McDonald's Saturday I resolve to walk right past my 55 tattooed crush. I'll have nothing to do with him, with his hi little sexys. This denouncement is actually extraordinarily painful since Roy alone is now my whole world. Everything that came before—my coin collection in the Tupperware, the corrugated cardboard trim on school bulletin boards, the terror of the fire pole—now revealed supremely childish and vain. Without even deciding to, I have left all that and now must leave Roy too. I commit to enduring the burden of the universe alone. The universe with its mysterious General Rommels, its heady straits of Bosporus. I resolve to suffer.

Saturday comes again. My mom has already taken the burner covers off the stove and set them in the sink. I'm anxious, like branches shaking in wind, and I'm trying the think-about-the-Medieval-Fair trick. I picture the ducks at the duck pond, the way they waddle right up and snatch the bread slice right out of my hand. I focus on the fair—knowing that time will move forward in that way, eventually waddle forward to the next weekend.

Buckling myself into the front seat of our yellow Pinto I put an imitation Life Saver under my tongue, a blue one. When my dad walks in front of the car on the way to the driver's side, I notice that he has slouchy shoulders. Horrible. Not his shoulders, but my noticing them.

"I love you," I say to my dad. He laughs and says that's good. I sit there hating myself a little.

I concentrate on my candy, on letting it be there, letting it do its exquisitely slow melt under my tongue. Beautiful. I keep that same candy the whole car ride over, through stop signs, waiting for a kid on a Bigwheel to cross, past the Conoco, with patience during the long wait for the final left turn. In my pocket I have more candies. Most of a roll of wild berry. When I move my tongue just a tiny bit, the flavor, the sugary slur, assaults my sensations. I choke on a little bit of saliva.

When we enter I sense Roy at our left; I walk on the far side of my dad, hoping 60
to hide in his shadow. In a hoarse whisper I tell my dad that I'll go save our table and that he should order me the milk and the cookies.

"Okay," he whispers back, winking, as if this is some spy game I am playing.

At the table I stare straight ahead at the molded plastic bench, summoning all my meager power to keep from looking feverishly around. I think I sense Roy's blond hair off in the distance to my left. I glimpse to the side, but see just a potted plant.

"How's the coffee?" I ask after my dad has settled in across from me.

He shrugs his ritual shrug but no words except the question of how is your milk. Is he mad at me? As I begin dipping my cookies with a kind of anguish, I answer that the milk is delicious.

Why do we say these little things? I wonder. Why do I always want the 65
McDonaldland butter cookies and never the chocolate chip? It seems creepy to me suddenly, all the habits and ways of the heart I have that I didn't choose for myself.

I throw back three half-and-halfs.

"Will you get me some more half-and-halfs?" my dad asks.

He asks nicely. And he is really reading the paper while I am not. Of course I'm going to go get creamers. I'm a kid, I remember. He's my dad. All this comes quickly into focus, lines sharp, like feeling the edges of a sticker on paper.

"I don't feel well," I try.

"Really?" 70

"I mean I feel fine," I say getting out of the chair.

Roy. Taking a wild berry candy from my pocket I resolve again to focus on a candy under my tongue instead of on him. I head first toward the back wall, darting betwixt and between the tables with their attached swiveling chairs. This is the shiniest cleanest place in town, that's what McDonald's was like back then. Even the corners and crevices are clean. It's strange to me in that way. Our house—even after my mom cleans, it's all still in disarray. I'll unfold a blanket and there'll be a stray sock inside. Behind the toilet there's blue lint. That's what makes a home, I think, its special type of mess.

And then I'm at the front counter. I don't look up.

I stand off to the side since I'm not really ordering anything, just asking for a favor, not paying for milk but asking for creamers. Waiting to be noticed, I stare down at the brushed steel counter with its flattering hazy reflection and then it appears, he appears. I see first his palm, reflected in the steel. Then I see his knuckles, the hairs on the back of his hand, the lattice tattoo, the starched shirt cuff that is the beginning of hiding all the rest of the tattoo that I can't see.

Beautiful. 75

A part of me decides I am taking him back into my heart. Even if no room will be left for anything else.

Roy notices me. He leans way down, eyes level with my sweaty curls stuck against my forehead, at the place where I know I have my birthmark—a dark brown mole there above my left eyebrow—and he says, his teeth showing, his strange glowing white canine showing—"D'ya need something?" He taps my nose with his finger.

That candy—I had forgotten about it, and I move my tongue and the flavor—it all comes rushing out, overwhelming, and I drool a little bit as I blurt out, "I'm going to the Medieval Fair next weekend." I wipe my wet lips with the back of my hand and see the wild-berry blue saliva staining there.

"Cool," he says, straightening up, and he interlaces his fingers and pushes them outward and they crack deliciously, and I think about macadamias. I think I see him noticing the blue smeared on my right hand. He then says to me: "I love those puppets they sell there—those real plain wood ones."

I just stare at Roy's blue eyes. I love blue eyes. Still to this day I am always 80 telling myself that I don't like them, that I find them lifeless and dull and that I prefer brown eyes, like mine, like my parents', but it's a lie. It's a whole other wilder type of love that I feel for these blue-eyed people of the world. So I look up at him, at those blue eyes, and I'm thinking about those plain wooden puppets—this is all half a second—then the doors open behind me and that invasive heat enters and the world sinks down, mud and mush and the paste left behind by cookies.

"Oh," I say. "Half-and-half."

He reaches into a tray of much-melted ice and bobbing creamers and he hands three to me. My palm burns where he touched me and my vision is blurry; only the grooves on the half-and-half container keep me from vanishing.

"Are you going to the fair?" I brave. Heat in my face again, the feeling just before a terrible rash. I'm already leaving the counter so as not to see those awful blue eyes and I hear, "Ah I'm workin'" and I don't even turn around.

I read the back of my dad's newspaper. They have found more fossils at the Spiro mounds. There's no explanation for how I feel.

How can I describe the days of the next week? I'd hope to see Roy when I ran 85
out to check the mail. I'd go drink from the hose in our front yard thinking he
might walk or drive by, even though I had no reason to believe he might ever
come to our neighborhood. I got detention for not turning in my book report
of *The Yellow Wallpaper*. I found myself rummaging around in my father's
briefcase, as if Roy's files—I imagined the yellow Confidential envelope from
Clue—might somehow be there. Maybe I don't need to explain this because
who hasn't been overtaken by this monstrous shade of love? I remember walking home from school very slowly, anxiously, as if through foreign, unpredictable terrain. I wanted to buy Roy a puppet at the Medieval Fair. One of the
wooden ones like he'd mentioned. Only in that thought could I rest. All the
clutter of my mind was waiting to come closer to that moment of purchasing
a puppet.

So I did manage to wake up in the mornings. I did try to go to sleep at night.
Though my heart seemed to be racing to its own obscure rhythm, private even
from me.

Friday night before the fair, hopeless for sleep—my bedroom seemed
alien and lurksome—I pulled my maze workbook from the shelf and went
into the brightly lit bathroom. I turned on the overhead fan so that it
would become noisy enough to overwhelm the sound in my mind of Roy
cracking his knuckles, again and again. The whirring fan noise—it was like
a quiet. I sat in the empty tub, set the maze book on the rounded ledge
and purposely began on a difficult page. I worked cautiously, tracing ahead
with my finger before setting pen to paper. This was pleasing, though out
of the corner of my eye I saw the yellowed magazine fragment—*cracked
kettle*—and it was like a ghost in the room with me, though its message,
I felt sure—almost too sure considering that I didn't understand it—had
nothing to do with me.

In the morning my mom found me there in the tub, like some passed-out
drunk, my maze book open on my small chest. I felt like crying, didn't even
know why. I must have fallen asleep there. I reached up to my face, wondering
if something had gone wrong with it.

"Do you have a fever?" my mom asked.

It must have seemed like there had to be an explanation. When she left, 90
assured, somewhat, I tried out those words—*Human speech is like a cracked
kettle*—like they were the coded answer to a riddle.

I was always that kind of kid who crawled into bed with her parents, who
felt safe only with them. If my mom came into my classroom because I had
forgotten my lunch at home, I wasn't ashamed like other kids were, but
proud. For a few years of my life, up until then, my desires hadn't chased
away from me. I wanted to fall asleep on the sofa while my dad watched
The Twilight Zone and so I did. I wanted couscous with butter and so I had
some. Yes, sometimes shopping with my mom I coveted a pair of overalls
or a frosted cookie, but the want would be faint and fade as soon as we'd
walked away.

I had always loved the Medieval Fair. A woman would dress up in an elaborate mermaid costume and sit under the bridge that spanned the artificial pond. I thought she was beautiful. People tossed quarters down at her. She'd flap her tail, wave coyly. It wasn't until years later that I realized that she was considered trashy.

Further on there was a stacked hay maze that had already become too easy by late elementary school but I liked looking at it from a distance, from up on the small knoll. I think every turn you might take was fine. Whichever way you went you still made it out. I remember it being upsetting, being spat out so soon.

We had left the house uncleaned when we went to the fair that Saturday. I was thinking about the wooden puppet but I felt obligated to hope for a crown; that's what I was supposed to be pining for. I imagined that my mom would think to buy me a crown for my Queen Esther costume. But maybe, I hoped, she would forget all about the crown. It wasn't unlikely. What seemed like the world to me often revealed itself, through her eyes, to be nothing.

We saw the dress-up beggar with the prosthetic nose and warts. We crossed 95 the bridge, saw the mermaid. A pale teenage boy in stonewashed jeans and a tank top leaned against the bridge's railing, smoking, and looking down at her. Two corseted women farther along sang bawdy ballads in the shade of a willow and while we listened a slouchy man went by with a gigantic foam mallet. The whole world, it seemed, was laughing or fighting or crying or unfolding chairs or blending smoothies and this would go on until time immemorial. Vendors sold wooden flutes, Jacob's ladders. The smell of funnel cakes and sour mystery saturated the air. In an open field two ponies and three sheep were there for the petting and the overseer held a baby pig in his hands. We ate fresh ears of boiled corn, smothered with butter and cracked pepper. My mom didn't mention the price. That really did make it feel like a day in some other me's life.

But I felt so unsettled. Roy's tooth in my mind as I bit into the corn, Roy's fingers on my palm as I thrummed my hand along a low wooden fence. I had so little of Roy and yet he had all of me and the feeling ran deep, deep to the most ancient parts of me. So deep that in some way I felt that my love for Roy shamed my people, whoever my people were, whomever I was queen of, people I had never met, nervous people and sad people and dead people, all clambering for air and space inside of me. I didn't even know what I wanted from Roy. I still don't. All my life love has felt like a croquet mallet to the head. Something absurd, ready for violence. Love.

I remember once years later, in a love fit, stealing cherry Luden's cough drops from a convenience store. I had the money to pay for them but I stole them instead. I wanted a cheap childish cherry flavor on my tongue when I saw my love, who of course isn't my love anymore. That painful pathetic euphoria. Low-quality cough drops. That's how I felt looking around anxiously for the wooden puppet stand, how I felt looking twice at every blond man who passed, wondering if he might somehow be Roy, there for me, even though he'd said he wouldn't be there. Thinking about that puppet for Roy eclipsed all other thoughts, put a slithery veil over the whole day. How much would the puppet cost? I didn't have my own pocket money, an allowance or savings or anything like that. I wasn't in the habit of asking for things. I never asked for toys. I never asked for sugar cereals. I felt to do so was wrong. I had almost cried that one day just whispering to myself about the crown. But all I wanted was that puppet because that puppet was going to solve everything.

At the puppet stand I lingered. I was hoping that one of my parents would take notice of the puppets, pick one up. My dad, standing a few paces away, stood out from the crowd in his button-up shirt. He looked weak, sunbeaten. My mom was at my side, her arms crossed across an emergency orange tank top. It struck me, maybe for the first time, that they came to this fair just for me.

"I've never wanted anything this much in my whole life," I confessed in a rush, my hand on the unfinished wood of one of the puppets. "I want this more than a crown."

My mom laughed at me, or at the puppet. "But it's so ugly," she said, in 100 Hebrew.

"That's not true," I whispered furiously, feeling as if everything had fallen silent, as if the ground beneath me was shifting. The vendor must surely have understood my mom, by her tone alone. I looked over at him: a fat bearded man talking to a long-haired barefoot princess. He held an end of her dusty hair distractedly; his other hand he had inside the collar of his shirt. He was sweating.

"*Drek.*" My mom shrugged. Junk.

"Grouch," I broke out, like a tree root heaving through soil. "You don't like anything," I almost screamed, there in the bright sun. "You never like anything at all." My mother turned her back to me. I sensed the ugly vendor turn our way.

"I'll get it for you," my dad said, suddenly right with us. There followed an awkward argument between my parents, which seemed only to heighten my dad's pleasure in taking out his rust-stained wallet, in standing his ground, in being, irrevocably, on my side.

His alliance struck me as misguided, pathetic, even childish. I felt like a vil- 105 lain. We bought the puppet.

That dumb puppet—I carried it around in its wrinkly green plastic bag. For some reason I found myself haunted by the word *leprosy*. When we watched the minstrel show in the little outdoor amphitheater I tried to forget the green bag under the bench. We only made it a few steps before my mom noticed it was gone. She went back and fetched it.

At home I noticed that the wood of one of the hands of the puppet was cracked. That wasn't the only reason I couldn't give the puppet to Roy.

Looking at that mute piece of wood I saw something. A part of me that I'd never chosen, that I would never control. I went to the bathroom, turned on the loud fan, and cried, feeling angry, useless, silly. An image of Roy came to my mind, particularly of that tooth. I felt my love falling off, dissolving.

He was my first love, my first love in the way that first loves are usually second or third or fourth loves. I still think about a stranger in a green jacket across from me at the waiting room at the DMV. About a blue-eyed man with a singed earlobe whom I saw at a Baskin-Robbins with his daughter. My first that kind of love. I never got over him. I never get over anyone.

FOR ANALYSIS

1. How old is the **narrator** when the events in the story occur? How old is she when she tells this story about them? Is there a difference between how she felt at the time these events happened and how she feels about them at the time she tells the story?

2. From where does Galchen get the title for her story? What resonance does it have?

MAKING CONNECTIONS

1. Compare the **tone** in "Araby" and "Wild Berry Blue." How would you character-ize each in terms of humor? What does the use or lack of humor tell us about the way each story handles the significance that the adult **narrator** attaches to childhood experience?

2. Carefully examine the language of paragraph 5 of "Araby" (p. 123). What **stylistic** devices allow the narrator to transform a simple shopping trip into a chivalric romance? Can you find a passage in "Wild Berry Blue" in which Galchen uses style to transform her equally everyday setting and situation into something seemingly more significant or more grand?

3. Compare the endings of these two stories. How do the two narrators think of themselves? How do you think these pictures of their past selves relate to their sense of themselves in the present?

WRITING TOPICS

1. Write about a memory of your early years. What details stand out—what sensory images, what facts about place and time, what sense of your feelings and thoughts? Are there connections between this memory and how you think of yourself now?

2. Have you ever been to a fair—a county or state fair, a Medieval or Renaissance festival? If so, write an account of it that tries to capture the experience. If not, imag-ine what the experience might be like. What aspects of the experience stand out? What makes it different from regular daily life? How is it similar?

CASE STUDY

FLANNERY O'CONNOR IN A CRITICAL CONTEXT

The fiction of Flannery O'Connor has become famous to readers for the darkness of its vision, for its vivid picture of the Southern grotesque, for its sharp humor, and for its unyielding religious undergirding. Her fiction has also become famous to critics not only for its excellence and power but also for the critical conundrums it introduces. Those who try to teach or write about O'Connor's work find very quickly that there are tensions in her work that translate into tensions between different ways of interpreting exactly what the work is up to. Readers and critics are further vexed by the fact that O'Connor often offered her own interpretations of her stories (see her comments from *Mystery and Manners* about "A Good Man Is Hard to Find" on p. 150), though this did not always go over smoothly, as the essays in this casebook from Rebecca R. Butler, Hallman B. Bryant, Robert H. Brinkmeyer Jr., and Joseph O'Neill will attest.

As you read "A Good Man Is Hard to Find," keep in mind the fact that these long-running interpretive arguments over O'Connor's stories exist, and that in thinking further after your first reading, you will be well-served to keep your mind open to the possibility of multiple interpretations—and to laughing at what might seem at first like some pretty dark stuff.

FLANNERY O'CONNOR   (1925–1964)

A GOOD MAN IS HARD TO FIND   1953

The grandmother didn't want to go to Florida. She wanted to visit some of her connections in east Tennessee and she was seizing at every chance to change Bailey's mind. Bailey was the son she lived with, her only boy. He was sitting on the edge of his chair at the table, bent over the orange sports section of the *Journal.* "Now look here, Bailey," she said, "see here, read this," and she stood with one hand on her thin hip and the other rattling the newspaper at his bald head. "Here this fellow that calls himself The Misfit is aloose from the Federal Pen and headed toward Florida and you read here what it says he did to these people. Just you read it. I wouldn't take my children in any direction with a criminal like that aloose in it. I couldn't answer to my conscience if I did."

Bailey didn't look up from his reading so she wheeled around then and faced the children's mother, a young woman in slacks, whose face was as broad and innocent as a cabbage and was tied around with a green headkerchief that had two points on the top like a rabbit's ears. She was sitting on the sofa, feeding the baby his apricots out of a jar. "The children have been to Florida before," the old lady said. "You all ought to take them somewhere else for a change so they would see different parts of the world and be broad. They never have been to east Tennessee."

The children's mother didn't seem to hear her but the eight-year-old boy, John Wesley, a stocky child with glasses, said, "If you don't want to go to Florida, why dontcha stay at home?" He and the little girl, June Star, were reading the funny papers on the floor.

"She wouldn't stay at home to be queen for a day," June Star said without raising her yellow head.

"Yes and what would you do if this fellow, The Misfit, caught you?" the 5 grandmother asked.

"I'd smack his face," John Wesley said.

"She wouldn't stay at home for a million bucks," June Star said. "Afraid she'd miss something. She has to go everywhere we go."

"All right, Miss," the grandmother said. "Just remember that the next time you want me to curl your hair."

June Star said her hair was naturally curly.

The next morning the grandmother was the first one in the car, ready to 10 go. She had her big black valise that looked like the head of a hippopotamus in one corner, and underneath it she was hiding a basket with Pitty Sing, the cat, in it. She didn't intend for the cat to be left alone in the house for three days because he would miss her too much and she was afraid he might brush against one of the gas burners and accidentally asphyxiate himself. Her son, Bailey, didn't like to arrive at a motel with a cat.

She sat in the middle of the back seat with John Wesley and June Star on either side of her. Bailey and the children's mother and the baby sat in front and they left Atlanta at eight forty-five with the mileage on the car at 55890. The grandmother wrote this down because she thought it would be interesting to say how many miles they had been when they got back. It took them twenty minutes to reach the outskirts of the city.

The old lady settled herself comfortably, removing her white cotton gloves and putting them up with her purse on the shelf in front of the back window. The children's mother still had on slacks and still had her head tied up in a green kerchief, but the grandmother had on a navy blue straw sailor hat with a bunch of white violets on the brim and a navy blue dress with a small white dot in the print. Her collars and cuffs were white organdy trimmed with lace and at her neckline she had pinned a purple spray of cloth violets containing a sachet. In case of an accident, anyone seeing her dead on the highway would know at once that she was a lady.

She said she thought it was going to be a good day for driving, neither too hot nor too cold, and she cautioned Bailey that the speed limit was fifty-five miles an hour and that the patrolmen hid themselves behind billboards and small clumps of trees and sped out after you before you had a chance to slow down. She pointed out interesting details of the scenery: Stone Mountain; the blue granite that in some places came up to both sides of the highway; the brilliant red clay banks slightly streaked with purple; and the various crops that made rows of green lace-work on the ground. The trees were full of silver-white sunlight and the meanest of them sparkled. The children were reading comic magazines and their mother had gone back to sleep.

"Let's go through Georgia fast so we won't have to look at it much," John Wesley said.

"If I were a little boy," said the grandmother, "I wouldn't talk about my native state that way. Tennessee has the mountains and Georgia has the hills."   15

"Tennessee is just a hillbilly dumping ground," John Wesley said, "and Georgia is a lousy state too."

"You said it," June Star said.

"In my time," said the grandmother, folding her thin veined fingers, "children were more respectful of their native states and their parents and everything else. People did right then. Oh look at the cute little pickaninny!" she said and pointed to a Negro child standing in the door of a shack. "Wouldn't that make a picture, now?" she asked and they all turned and looked at the little Negro out of the back window. He waved.

"He didn't have any britches on," June Star said.

"He probably didn't have any," the grandmother explained. "Little niggers   20
in the country don't have things like we do. If I could paint, I'd paint that picture," she said.

The children exchanged comic books.

The grandmother offered to hold the baby and the children's mother passed him over the front seat to her. She set him on her knee and bounced him and told him about the things they were passing. She rolled her eyes and screwed up her mouth and stuck her leathery thin face into his smooth bland one. Occasionally he gave her a faraway smile. They passed a large cotton field with five or six graves fenced in the middle of it, like a small island. "Look at the graveyard!" the grandmother said, pointing it out. "That was the old family burying ground. That belonged to the plantation."

"Where's the plantation?" John Wesley asked.

"Gone With the Wind," said the grandmother. "Ha. Ha."

When the children finished all the comic books they had brought, they   25
opened the lunch and ate it. The grandmother ate a peanut butter sandwich and an olive and would not let the children throw the box and the paper napkins out the window. When there was nothing else to do they played a game by choosing a cloud and making the other two guess what shape it suggested. John Wesley took one the shape of a cow and June Star guessed a cow and John Wesley said, no, an automobile, and June Star said he didn't play fair, and they began to slap each other over the grandmother.

The grandmother said she would tell them a story if they would keep quiet. When she told a story, she rolled her eyes and waved her head and was very dramatic. She said once when she was a maiden lady she had been courted by a Mr. Edgar Atkins Teagarden from Jasper, Georgia. She said he was a very good-looking man and a gentleman and that he brought her a watermelon every Saturday afternoon with his initials cut in it, E.A.T. Well, one Saturday, she said, Mr. Teagarden brought the watermelon and there was nobody at home and he left it on the front porch and returned in his buggy to Jasper, but she never got the watermelon, she said, because a nigger boy ate it when he saw the initials, E.A.T.! This story tickled John Wesley's funny bone and he giggled and giggled but June Star didn't think it was any good. She said she wouldn't marry a man that just brought her a watermelon on Saturday. The grandmother said she would have done well to marry Mr. Teagarden because he was a gentleman and had bought Coca-Cola stock when it first came out and that he had died only a few years ago, a very wealthy man.

They stopped at The Tower for barbecued sandwiches. The Tower was a part stucco and part wood filling station and dance hall set in a clearing outside of Timothy. A fat man named Red Sammy Butts ran it and there were signs stuck here and there on the building and for miles up and down the highway saying, TRY RED SAMMY'S FAMOUS BARBECUE. NONE LIKE FAMOUS RED SAMMY'S! RED SAM! THE FAT BOY WITH THE HAPPY LAUGH. A VETERAN! RED SAMMY'S YOUR MAN!

Red Sammy was lying on the bare ground outside The Tower with his head under a truck while a gray monkey about a foot high, chained to a small chinaberry tree, chattered nearby. The monkey sprang back into the tree and got on the highest limb as soon as he saw the children jump out of the car and run toward him.

Inside, The Tower was a long dark room with a counter at one end and tables at the other and dancing space in the middle. They all sat down at a board table next to the nickelodeon and Red Sam's wife, a tall burnt-brown woman with hair and eyes lighter than her skin, came and took their order. The children's mother put a dime in the machine and played "The Tennessee Waltz," and the grandmother said that tune always made her want to dance. She asked Bailey if he would like to dance but he only glared at her. He didn't have a naturally sunny disposition like she did and trips made him nervous. The grandmother's brown eyes were very bright. She swayed her head from side to side and pretended she was dancing in her chair. June Star said play something she could tap to so the children's mother put in another dime and played a fast number and June Star stepped out onto the dance floor and did her tap routine.

"Ain't she cute?" Red Sam's wife said, leaning over the counter. "Would you like to come be my little girl?"

"No I certainly wouldn't," June Star said. "I wouldn't live in a broken-down place like this for a million bucks!" and she ran back to the table.

"Ain't she cute?" the woman repeated, stretching her mouth politely.

"Aren't you ashamed?" hissed the grandmother.

Red Sam came in and told his wife to quit lounging on the counter and hurry up with these people's order. His khaki trousers reached just to his hip bones and his stomach hung over them like a sack of meal swaying under his shirt. He came over and sat down at a table nearby and let out a combination sigh and yodel. "You can't win," he said. "You can't win," and he wiped his sweating red face off with a gray handkerchief. "These days you don't know who to trust," he said. "Ain't that the truth?"

"People are certainly not nice like they used to be," said the grandmother.   35

"Two fellers come in here last week," Red Sammy said, "driving a Chrysler. It was a old beat-up car but it was a good one and these boys looked all right to me. Said they worked at the mill and you know I let them fellers charge the gas they bought? Now why did I do that?"

"Because you're a good man!" the grandmother said at once.

"Yes'm, I suppose so," Red Sam said as if he were struck with this answer.

His wife brought the orders, carrying the five plates all at once without a tray, two in each hand and one balanced on her arm. "It isn't a soul in this green world of God's that you can trust," she said. "And I don't count nobody out of that, not nobody," she repeated, looking at Red Sammy.

"Did you read about that criminal, The Misfit, that's escaped?" asked the   40 grandmother.

"I wouldn't be a bit surprised if he didn't attack this place right here," said the woman. "If he hears about it being here, I wouldn't be none surprised to see him. If he hears it's two cent in the cash register, I wouldn't be a tall surprised if he. . . ."

"That'll do," Red Sam said. "Go bring these people their Co'-Colas," and the woman went off to get the rest of the order.

"A good man is hard to find," Red Sammy said. "Everything is getting terrible. I remember the day you could go off and leave your screen door unlatched. Not no more."

He and the grandmother discussed better times. The old lady said that in her opinion Europe was entirely to blame for the way things were now. She said the way Europe acted you would think we were made of money and Red Sam said it was no use talking about it, she was exactly right. The children ran outside into the white sunlight and looked at the monkey in the lacy chinaberry tree. He was busy catching fleas on himself and biting each one carefully between his teeth as if it were a delicacy.

They drove off again into the hot afternoon. The grandmother took cat naps   45 and woke up every few minutes with her own snoring. Outside of Toombsboro she woke up and recalled an old plantation that she had visited in this neighborhood once when she was a young lady. She said the house had six white columns across the front and that there was an avenue of oaks leading up to it and two little wooden trellis arbors on either side in front where you sat down with your suitor after a stroll in the garden. She recalled exactly which road to turn off to get to it. She knew that Bailey would not be willing to lose any time looking at an old house, but the more she talked about it, the more she wanted to see it once again and find out if the little twin arbors were still standing. "There was a secret panel in this house," she said craftily, not telling the truth but wishing that she were, "and the story went that all the family silver was hidden in it when Sherman[1] came through but it was never found. . . ."

"Hey!" John Wesley said. "Let's go see it! We'll find it! We'll poke all the woodwork and find it! Who lives there? Where do you turn off at? Hey Pop, can't we turn off there?"

"We never have seen a house with a secret panel!" June Star shrieked. "Let's go to the house with the secret panel! Hey Pop, can't we go see the house with the secret panel!"

"It's not far from here, I know," the grandmother said. "It won't take over twenty minutes."

Bailey was looking straight ahead. His jaw was as rigid as a horseshoe. "No," he said.

The children began to yell and scream that they wanted to see the house 50 with the secret panel. John Wesley kicked the back of the front seat and June Star hung over her mother's shoulder and whined desperately into her ear that they never had any fun even on their vacation, that they could never do what THEY wanted to do. The baby began to scream and John Wesley kicked the back of the seat so hard that his father could feel the blows in his kidney.

"All right!" he shouted and drew the car to a stop at the side of the road. "Will you all shut up? Will you all just shut up for one second? If you don't shut up, we won't go anywhere."

"It would be very educational for them," the grandmother murmured.

"All right," Bailey said, "but get this: this is the only time we're going to stop for anything like this. This is the one and only time."

"The dirt road that you have to turn down is about a mile back," the grandmother directed. "I marked it when we passed."

"A dirt road," Bailey groaned. 55

After they had turned around and were headed toward the dirt road, the grandmother recalled other points about the house, the beautiful glass over the front doorway and the candle-lamp in the hall. John Wesley said that the secret panel was probably in the fireplace.

"You can't go inside this house," Bailey said. "You don't know who lives there."

"While you all talk to the people in front, I'll run around behind and get in a window," John Wesley suggested.

"We'll all stay in the car," his mother said.

They turned onto the dirt road and the car raced roughly along in a swirl 60 of pink dust. The grandmother recalled the times when there were no paved roads and thirty miles was a day's journey. The dirt road was hilly and there were sudden washes in it and sharp curves on dangerous embankments. All at once they would be on a hill, looking down over the blue tops of trees for miles around, then the next minute, they would be in a red depression with the dust-coated trees looking down on them.

"This place had better turn up in a minute," Bailey said, "or I'm going to turn around."

[1] William Tecumseh Sherman (1820–1891) was a Union Army general during the American Civil War.

The road looked as if no one had traveled on it for months.

"It's not much farther," the grandmother said and just as she said it, a horrible thought came to her. The thought was so embarrassing that she turned red in the face and her eyes dilated and her feet jumped up, upsetting her valise in the corner. The instant the valise moved, the newspaper top she had over the basket under it rose with a snarl and Pitty Sing, the cat, sprang onto Bailey's shoulder.

The children were thrown to the floor and their mother, clutching the baby, was thrown out the door onto the ground; the old lady was thrown into the front seat. The car turned over once and landed right-side-up in a gulch off the side of the road. Bailey remained in the driver's seat with the cat—graystriped with a broad white face and an orange nose—clinging to his neck like a caterpillar.

As soon as the children saw they could move their arms and legs, they 65 scrambled out of the car, shouting, "We've had an ACCIDENT!" The grandmother was curled up under the dashboard, hoping she was injured so that Bailey's wrath would not come down on her all at once. The horrible thought she had before the accident was that the house she had remembered so vividly was not in Georgia but in Tennessee.

Bailey removed the cat from his neck with both hands and flung it out the window against the side of a pine tree. Then he got out of the car and started looking for the children's mother. She was sitting against the side of the red gutted ditch, holding the screaming baby, but she only had a cut down her face and a broken shoulder. "We've had an ACCIDENT!" the children screamed in a frenzy of delight.

"But nobody's killed," June Star said with disappointment as the grandmother limped out of the car, her hat still pinned to her head but the broken front brim standing up at a jaunty angle and the violet spray hanging off the side. They all sat down in the ditch, except the children, to recover from the shock. They were all shaking.

"Maybe a car will come along," said the children's mother hoarsely.

"I believe I have injured an organ," said the grandmother, pressing her side, but no one answered her. Bailey's teeth were clattering. He had on a yellow sport shirt with bright blue parrots designed in it and his face was as yellow as the shirt. The grandmother decided that she would not mention that the house was in Tennessee.

The road was about ten feet above and they could see only the tops of the 70 trees on the other side of it. Behind the ditch they were sitting in there were more woods, tall and dark and deep. In a few minutes they saw a car some distance away on top of a hill, coming slowly as if the occupants were watching them. The grandmother stood up and waved both arms dramatically to attract their attention. The car continued to come on slowly, disappeared around a bend and appeared again, moving even slower, on top of the hill they had gone over. It was a big black battered hearse-like automobile. There were three men in it.

It came to a stop just over them and for some minutes, the driver looked down with a steady expressionless gaze to where they were sitting, and didn't speak. Then he turned his head and muttered something to the other two and they got out. One was a fat boy in black trousers and a red sweat shirt with a silver stallion embossed on the front of it. He moved around on the right side of them and stood staring, his mouth partly open in a kind of loose grin. The other had on khaki pants and a blue striped coat and a gray hat pulled down very low, hiding most of his face. He came around slowly on the left side. Neither spoke.

The driver got out of the car and stood by the side of it, looking down at them. He was an older man than the other two. His hair was just beginning to gray and he wore silver-rimmed spectacles that gave him a scholarly look. He had a long creased face and didn't have on any shirt or undershirt. He had on blue jeans that were too tight for him and was holding a black hat and a gun. The two boys also had guns.

"We've had an ACCIDENT!" the children screamed.

The grandmother had the peculiar feeling that the bespectacled man was someone she knew. His face was as familiar to her as if she had known him all her life but she could not recall who he was. He moved away from the car and began to come down the embankment, placing his feet carefully so that he wouldn't slip. He had on tan and white shoes and no socks, and his ankles were red and thin. "Good afternoon," he said. "I see you all had you a little spill."

"We turned over twice!" said the grandmother. 75

"Oncet," he corrected. "We seen it happen. Try their car and see will it run, Hiram," he said quietly to the boy with the gray hat.

"What you got that gun for?" John Wesley asked. "Whatcha gonna do with that gun?"

"Lady," the man said to the children's mother, "would you mind calling them children to sit down by you? Children make me nervous. I want all you all to sit down right together there where you're at."

"What are you telling US what to do for?" June Star asked.

Behind them the line of woods gaped like a dark open mouth. "Come here," 80 said their mother.

"Look here now," Bailey said suddenly, "we're in a predicament! We're in. . . ."

The grandmother shrieked. She scrambled to her feet and stood staring. "You're The Misfit!" she said. "I recognized you at once!"

"Yes'm," the man said, smiling slightly as if he were pleased in spite of himself to be known, "but it would have been better for all of you, lady, if you hadn't of reckernized me."

Bailey turned his head sharply and said something to his mother that shocked even the children. The old lady began to cry and The Misfit reddened.

"Lady," he said, "don't you get upset. Sometimes a man says things he don't 85 mean. I don't reckon he meant to talk to you thataway."

"You wouldn't shoot a lady, would you?" the grandmother said and removed a clean handkerchief from her cuff and began to slap at her eyes with it.

The Misfit pointed the toe of his shoe into the ground and made a little hole and then covered it up again. "I would hate to have to," he said.

"Listen," the grandmother almost screamed, "I know you're a good man. You don't look a bit like you have common blood. I know you must come from nice people!"

"Yes mam," he said, "finest people in the world." When he smiled he showed a row of strong white teeth. "God never made a finer woman than my mother and my daddy's heart was pure gold," he said. The boy with the red sweat shirt had come around behind them and was standing with his gun at his hip. The Misfit squatted down on the ground. "Watch them children, Bobby Lee," he said. "You know they make me nervous." He looked at the six of them huddled together in front of him and he seemed to be embarrassed as if he couldn't think of anything to say. "Ain't a cloud in the sky," he remarked, looking up at it. "Don't see no sun but don't see no cloud neither."

"Yes, it's a beautiful day," said the grandmother. "Listen," she said, "you 90 shouldn't call yourself The Misfit because I know you're a good man at heart. I can just look at you and tell."

"Hush!" Bailey yelled. "Hush! Everybody shut up and let me handle this!" He was squatting in the position of a runner about to sprint forward but he didn't move.

"I pre-chate that, lady," The Misfit said and drew a little circle in the ground with the butt of his gun.

"It'll take a half a hour to fix this here car," Hiram called, looking over the raised hood of it.

"Well, first you and Bobby Lee get him and that little boy to step over yonder with you," The Misfit said, pointing to Bailey and John Wesley. "The boys want to ast you something," he said to Bailey. "Would you mind stepping back in them woods there with them?"

"Listen," Bailey began, "we're in a terrible predicament! Nobody realizes 95 what this is," and his voice cracked. His eyes were as blue and intense as the parrots in his shirt and he remained perfectly still.

The grandmother reached up to adjust her hat brim as if she were going to the woods with him but it came off in her hand. She stood staring at it and after a second she let it fall to the ground. Hiram pulled Bailey up by the arm as if he were assisting an old man. John Wesley caught hold of his father's hand and Bobby Lee followed. They went off toward the woods and just as they reached the dark edge, Bailey turned and supporting himself against a gray naked pine trunk, he shouted, "I'll be back in a minute, Mamma, wait on me!"

"Come back this instant!" his mother shrilled but they all disappeared into the woods.

"Bailey Boy!" the grandmother called in a tragic voice but she found she was looking at The Misfit squatting on the ground in front of her. "I just know you're a good man," she said desperately. "You're not a bit common!"

"Nome, I ain't a good man," The Misfit said after a second as if he had considered her statement carefully, "but I ain't the worst in the world neither. My daddy said I was a different breed of dog from my brothers and sisters. 'You know,' Daddy said, 'it's some that can live their whole life out without asking about it and it's others has to know why it is, and this boy is one of the latters. He's going to be into everything!'" He put on his black hat and looked up suddenly and then away deep into the woods as if he were embarrassed again. "I'm sorry I don't have on a shirt before you ladies," he said, hunching his shoulders slightly. "We buried our clothes that we had on when we escaped and we're just making do until we can get better. We borrowed these from some folks we met," he explained.

"That's perfectly all right," the grandmother said. "Maybe Bailey has an 100 extra shirt in his suitcase."

"I'll look and see terrectly," The Misfit said.

"Where are they taking him?" the children's mother screamed.

"Daddy was a card himself," The Misfit said. "You couldn't put anything over on him. He never got in trouble with the Authorities though. Just had the knack of handling them."

"You could be honest too if you'd only try," said the grandmother. "Think how wonderful it would be to settle down and live a comfortable life and not have to think about somebody chasing you all the time."

The Misfit kept scratching in the ground with the butt of his gun as if he 105 were thinking about it. "Yes'm, somebody is always after you," he murmured.

The grandmother noticed how thin his shoulder blades were just behind his hat because she was standing up looking down on him. "Do you ever pray?" she asked.

He shook his head. All she saw was the black hat wiggle between his shoulder blades. "Nome," he said.

There was a pistol shot from the woods, followed closely by another. Then silence. The old lady's head jerked around. She could hear the wind move through the tree tops like a long satisfied insuck of breath. "Bailey Boy!" she called.

"I was a gospel singer for a while," The Misfit said. "I been most everything. Been in the arm service, both land and sea, at home and abroad, been twict married, been an undertaker, been with the railroads, plowed Mother Earth, been in a tornado, seen a man burnt alive oncet," and he looked up at the children's mother and the little girl who were sitting close together, their faces white and their eyes glassy; "I even seen a woman flogged," he said.

"Pray, pray," the grandmother began, "pray, pray. . . ."   110

"I never was a bad boy that I remember of," The Misfit said in an almost dreamy voice, "but somewheres along the line I done something wrong and got sent to the penitentiary. I was buried alive," and he looked up and held her attention to him by a steady stare.

"That's when you should have started to pray," she said. "What did you do to get sent to the penitentiary that first time?"

"Turn to the right, it was a wall," The Misfit said, looking up again at the cloudless sky. "Turn to the left, it was a wall. Look up it was a ceiling, look down it was a floor. I forget what I done, lady. I set there and set there, trying to remember what it was I done and I ain't recalled it to this day. Oncet in a while, I would think it was coming to me, but it never come."

"Maybe they put you in by mistake," the old lady said vaguely.

"Nome," he said. "It wasn't no mistake. They had the papers on me." 115

"You must have stolen something," she said.

The Misfit sneered slightly. "Nobody had nothing I wanted," he said. "It was a head-doctor at the penitentiary said what I had done was kill my daddy but I known that for a lie. My daddy died in nineteen ought nineteen of the epidemic flu and I never had a thing to do with it. He was buried in the Mount Hopewell Baptist churchyard and you can see for yourself."

"If you would pray," the old lady said, "Jesus would help you."

"That's right," The Misfit said.

"Well then, why don't you pray?" she asked trembling with delight suddenly. 120

"I don't want no hep," he said. "I'm doing all right by myself."

Bobby Lee and Hiram came ambling back from the woods. Bobby Lee was dragging a yellow shirt with bright blue parrots in it.

"Throw me that shirt, Bobby Lee," The Misfit said. The shirt came flying at him and landed on his shoulder and he put it on. The grandmother couldn't name what the shirt reminded her of. "No, lady," The Misfit said while he was buttoning it up, "I found out the crime don't matter. You can do one thing or you can do another, kill a man or take a tire off his car, because sooner or later you're going to forget what it was you done and just be punished for it."

The children's mother had begun to make heaving noises as if she couldn't get her breath. "Lady," he asked, "would you and that little girl like to step off yonder with Bobby Lee and Hiram and join your husband?"

"Yes, thank you," the mother said faintly. Her left arm dangled helplessly 125 and she was holding the baby, who had gone to sleep, in the other. "Hep that lady up, Hiram," The Misfit said as she struggled to climb out of the ditch, "and Bobby Lee, you hold onto that little girl's hand."

"I don't want to hold hands with him," June Star said. "He reminds me of a pig."

The fat boy blushed and laughed and caught her by the arm and pulled her off into the woods after Hiram and her mother.

Alone with The Misfit, the grandmother found that she had lost her voice. There was not a cloud in the sky nor any sun. There was nothing around her but woods. She wanted to tell him that he must pray. She opened and closed her mouth several times before anything came out. Finally she found herself saying, "Jesus, Jesus," meaning Jesus will help you, but the way she was saying it, it sounded as if she might be cursing.

"Yes'm," The Misfit said as if he agreed. "Jesus thown everything off balance. It was the same case with Him as with me except He hadn't committed any crime and they could prove I had committed one because they had the papers on me.

Of course," he said, "they never shown me my papers. That's why I sign myself now. I said long ago, you get your signature and sign everything you do and keep a copy of it. Then you'll know what you done and you can hold up the crime to the punishment and see do they match and in the end you'll have something to prove you ain't been treated right. I call myself The Misfit," he said, "because I can't make what all I done wrong fit what all I gone through in punishment."

There was a piercing scream from the woods, followed closely by a pis- 130 tol report. "Does it seem right to you, lady, that one is punished a heap and another ain't punished at all?"

"Jesus!" the old lady cried. "You've got good blood! I know you wouldn't shoot a lady! I know you come from nice people! Pray! Jesus, you ought not to shoot a lady. I'll give you all the money I've got!"

"Lady," The Misfit said, looking beyond her far into the woods, "there never was a body that give the undertaker a tip."

There were two more pistol reports and the grandmother raised her head like a parched old turkey hen crying for water and called, "Bailey Boy, Bailey Boy!" as if her heart would break.

"Jesus was the only One that ever raised the dead," The Misfit continued, "and He shouldn't have done it. He thown everything off balance. If He did what He said, then it's nothing for you to do but thow away everything and follow Him, and if He didn't, then it's nothing for you to do but enjoy the few minutes you got left the best way you can—by killing somebody or burning down his house or doing some other meanness to him. No pleasure but meanness," he said and his voice had become almost a snarl.

"Maybe He didn't raise the dead," the old lady mumbled, not knowing what 135 she was saying and feeling so dizzy that she sank down in the ditch with her legs twisted under her.

"I wasn't there so I can't say He didn't," The Misfit said. "I wisht I had of been there," he said, hitting the ground with his fist. "It ain't right I wasn't there because if I had of been there I would of known. Listen lady," he said in a high voice, "if I had of been there I would of known and I wouldn't be like I am now." His voice seemed about to crack and the grandmother's head cleared for an instant. She saw the man's face twisted close to her own as if he were going to cry and she murmured, "Why you're one of my babies. You're one of my own children!" She reached out and touched him on the shoulder. The Misfit sprang back as if a snake had bitten him and shot her three times through the chest. Then he put his gun down on the ground and took off his glasses and began to clean them.

Hiram and Bobby Lee returned from the woods and stood over the ditch, looking down at the grandmother who half sat and half lay in a puddle of blood with her legs crossed under her like a child's and her face smiling up at the cloudless sky.

Without his glasses, The Misfit's eyes were red-rimmed and pale and defenseless-looking. "Take her off and thow her where you thown the others," he said, picking up the cat that was rubbing itself against his leg.

"She was a talker, wasn't she?" Bobby Lee said, sliding down the ditch with a yodel.

"She would of been a good woman," The Misfit said, "if it had been some-   140
body there to shoot her every minute of her life."

"Some fun!" Bobby Lee said.

"Shut up, Bobby Lee," The Misfit said. "It's no real pleasure in life."

FOR ANALYSIS

1. From whose **point of view** is the story told—that is, through whose eyes do we see events unfold? What is the effect of O'Connor's choice of **narrator**?

2. How would you describe the **tone** of this story? Is it uniform, or does it vary? How? Why do you think O'Connor uses tone the way she does?

3. With whom do you identify in this story? One character, or more, or none? How do you think identification works in this story?

4. Describe this story's **setting**. Does it inform the **mood** or tone of the story? How?

MAKING CONNECTIONS

1. Hawthorne's "Young Goodman Brown" (p. 79) and "A Good Man Is Hard to Find" are both in part about religious belief, though they are of course very different stories. In what do the main characters—Brown, The Misfit, and the grandmother—believe, and not believe?

2. An important line in Toni Cade Bambara's "The Lesson" (p. 96) comes near the end: " 'Anybody else learn anything today?' " (para. 52). "The Lesson" is more obviously a story of education, but in what way is "A Good Man Is Hard to Find" also one? What character learns a lesson in the story? What is the lesson? "The Lesson" ends with the **narrator** reflecting on the impact of her lesson. What is the impact of the lesson in O'Connor's story?

WRITING TOPICS

1. Compare and contrast The Misfit and the grandmother. Do they come to seem more different or more alike over the course of the story? In what ways?

2. The story's last line is The Misfit's: he says, "It's no real pleasure in life" (para. 142). While "A Good Man Is Hard to Find" is a sad, violent story, there is pleasure in reading it. Write about some of these pleasures. How do you reconcile them with the story's darkness?

FROM MYSTERY AND MANNERS   1963

It is true that the old lady is a hypocritical old soul; her wits are no match for the Misfit's, nor is her capacity for grace equal to his; yet I think the unpreju-diced reader will feel that the Grandmother has a special kind of triumph in this story which instinctively we do not allow to someone altogether bad.

I often ask myself what makes a story work and what makes it hold up as a story, and I have decided that it is probably some action, some gesture of a character that is unlike any other in the story, one which indicates where the real heart of the story lies. This would have to be an action or a gesture which was both totally right and totally unexpected; it would have to be one that was both in character and beyond character; it would have to suggest both the world and eternity. The action or gesture I'm talking about would have to be on the anagogical level, that is, the level which has to do with the Divine life and our participation in it. It would be a gesture that transcended any neat allegory that might have been intended or any pat moral categories a reader could make. It would be a gesture which somehow made contact with mystery.

There is a point in this story where such a gesture occurs. The Grandmother is at last alone, facing the Misfit. Her head clears for an instant and she realizes, even in her limited way, that she is responsible for the man before her and joined to him by ties of kinship which have their roots deep in the mystery she has been merely prattling about so far. And at this point, she does the right thing, she makes the right gesture.

I find that students are often puzzled by what she says and does here, but I think myself that if I took out this gesture and what she says with it, I would have no story. What was left would not be worth your attention. Our age not only does not have a very sharp eye for the almost imperceptible intrusions of grace, it no longer has much feeling for the nature of the violences which precede and follow them. The devil's greatest wile, Baudelaire has said, is to convince us that he does not exist.

I suppose the reasons for the use of so much violence in modern fiction will 5 differ with each writer who uses it, but in my own stories I have found that violence is strangely capable of returning my characters to reality and preparing them to accept their moment of grace. Their heads are so hard that almost nothing else will do the work. This idea, that reality is something to which we must be returned at considerable cost, is one which is seldom understood by the casual reader, but it is one which is implicit in the Christian view of the world.

I don't want to equate the Misfit with the devil. I prefer to think that, however unlikely this may seem, the old lady's gesture, like the mustard-seed, will grow to be a great crow-filled tree in the Misfit's heart and will be enough of a pain to him there to turn him into the prophet he was meant to become. But that's another story.

This story has been called grotesque, but I prefer to call it literal. A good story is literal in the same sense that a child's drawing is literal. When a child draws, he doesn't intend to distort but to set down exactly what he sees, and as his gaze is direct, he sees the lines that create motion. Now the lines of motion that interest the writer are usually invisible. They are lines of spiritual motion. And in this story you should be on the lookout for such things as the action of grace in the Grandmother's soul, and not for the dead bodies.

MAKING CONNECTIONS

1. How do you understand O'Connor's description of the grandmother's "gesture" as being about grace? Does your interpretation of the story change if you read it as being about a literal moment of salvation?

2. Do you read the story differently than O'Connor does? Is her interpretation helpful? What does it mean about how literature works that a reader can disagree with a writer about her own work?

REBECCA R. BUTLER (B. 1943)

WHAT'S SO FUNNY ABOUT FLANNERY O'CONNOR? 1979

When Flannery O'Connor was asked why the story about the grisly family murder, "A Good Man Is Hard to Find," appeared to be her favorite, she corrected that impression: She chose that story for her public reading engagements, she explained, not because of a special preference for it, but because, she said, it was the only one she could get through out loud without laughing.[1]

Now, if any of you have ever studied or taught that particular O'Connor short story, you may agree with the author that it is entirely possible to read right through it without once being incapacitated by laughter. I know myself that I can keep a perfectly straight face as I read of the children and their mother being marched off into the woods at gunpoint, followed by the sounds of shots. And when the grandmother calls out to The Misfit, " 'You're one of my own children!' " and he shoots her three times in the chest, I don't even smile. On the other hand, I think it would take some practice for me to maintain a deadpan throughout the grandmother's story of her youthful suitor, Mr. Edgar Atkins Teagarden from Jasper, Georgia, whose love-token, a watermelon carved with his initials, E. A. T., and left on the front porch, was eaten by an evidently literate "nigger boy." Similarly, the repartee between the grandmother and her saucy granddaughter, June Star, and the entire episode at Red Sammy Butts's barbecue house do give rise to laughter. To explain just how and why this story, which ends with the grandmother dead in a pool of her own blood, can be called comic is risky. E. B. White gives this warning to would-be analysts of comedy: "Humor can be dissected," he wrote, "as a frog can, but the thing dies in the process and the innards are discouraging to any but the pure scientific mind."[2] O'Connor herself used the same image in voicing a similar complaint about the fate of her stories: "Every time a story of mine appears in a freshman anthology," she said, "I have a vision of it, with its

---

[1] Flannery O'Connor in a conversation with Robert Drake, August, 1963.

[2] "Some Remarks on Humor," in *The Second Tree from the Corner* (1954), rpt. in *The Comic in Theory and Practice*, eds. John J. Enck, Elizabeth T. Fortner, Alvin Whitley (New York: Appleton-Century-Crofts, 1960), p. 102.

little organs laid open, like a frog in a bottle."[3] So it seems that, as an investigator of the comic, I face two alternatives: to step aside now or to proceed with caution. I will take the second route, using as my guide Louis Rubin, himself a masterful analyst of the American comic tradition who, in his Preface to *The Comic Imagination in American Literature*, acknowledged that "writing *about* humor and humorists" is necessarily "an awkward business" which always risks making the analyst look ridiculous.[4] But he went right ahead and wrote, adhering to the principle that understanding heightens enjoyment.

Despite O'Connor's implication that many of her stories were too funny for her to read before an audience, some critics have failed to see the humor in the O'Connor canon. In the first place, of course, some commentators were interested in other aspects of the work than the humorous. For a while, the words most frequently used to describe her writing belonged to one of two groups: Such words as *prophecy, vision, spiritual quest, redemptive grace, vocation,* and *sacrament* belong to one group, and to the other such words as *perverse, demonic, grotesque, insane, hostile,* and *obsessive.* In other words, most of the early criticism has emphasized the religious dimension or the psychological dimension of the work, sometimes both. An articulate appreciation of the comic dimension was slower in coming. When Martha Stephens published a study of the tone of the fiction, entitled *The Question of Flannery O'Connor,* she sparked just such an articulate assessment. In her book Stephens goes so far as to say that O'Connor was not truly a comic writer, that her novels "are not *comic novels* in any accepted sense of the term."[5] In fact, Stephens accepts only "a few stories" as belonging within the category of comedy. This thorough analysis of the fiction in terms of the deep ambivalence it seems to elicit from most readers does address intelligently some of the crucial and most complex issues of O'Connor's method, but, like so many less persuasive commentators before her, Stephens fails to maintain the double vision that O'Connor used in blending the laughable and the serious in her tales. There is an assumption, more or less obviously at work, for instance, that overt references to religion, violence, or death automatically shift the tone to the somber or horrific end of the scale. According to this same frame of reference, O'Connor's personal religious views, as they are discovered in the fiction, are so repugnant and oppressive with their contempt for ordinary human life, that they mar the entire work. As evidence of this contempt, Stephens cites the physical descriptions of characters, their ugliness, their animalistic features.

It was to this one-sided reading of such conventional comic techniques as exaggeration and caricature as indications that "human life is a sordid, almost unrelievedly hideous affair,"[6] that Carter Martin seemed to be addressing his

---

[3] Flannery O'Connor, "On Her Own Work," in *Mystery and Manners*, eds. Sally and Robert Fitzgerald (New York: Farrar, Straus and Giroux, 1957), p. 108.

[4] Louis D. Rubin, ed., *The Comic Imagination in American Literature* (New Brunswick, N.J.: Rutgers Univ. Press, 1973), x.

[5] (Baton Rouge: LSU Press, 1973), pp. 14,18.

[6] *The Flannery O'Connor Bulletin*, IV (1975), 1–12.

analysis of "Comedy and Humor in Flannery O'Connor's Fiction."[7] Equally pertinent was Louis Rubin's contribution to the O'Connor Symposium in Milledgeville in 1977, "Flannery O'Connor's Company of Southerners: or, 'The Artificial Nigger' Read as Fiction Rather than Theology."[8] Martin indicates a corrective direction by reviewing the broad contours of Western comedy from Aristophanes to Jonson to Bergson; what he calls the "comic-cosmic" view of man, that more inclusive view, is certainly the one that O'Connor found most workable and is the context into which her work fits most comfortably. And, in particular, it fits into the American version of that view, as Rubin indicates by reminding us of the wealth of comic writers and characters who belong to the Middle Georgia region where Flannery attended high school and did her mature writing. Uncle Remus, Simon Suggs, Polly Peachblossom, Major Jones, Johnson Jones Hooper all lived in or hailed from this special region. And a comparison of O'Connor's comic characterizations and themes with those of Joel Chandler Harris or Augustus Baldwin Longstreet shows that, no more than they was she ridiculing, disdaining, or demeaning these poor rural folk nor their lives. The conventions of the tradition can be understood through a meaningful perspective.

It is not unusual to be tone-deaf when encountering a new style. My own students, I know, are sometimes unable to see anything comic in Manley Pointer's theft and desertion of Joy-Hulga in "Good Country People," nor do they always laugh at Mrs. Crater's sly campaign to marry her not-entirely-eligible only daughter, Lucynell, to Mr. Shiftlet. For critics to be so unappreciative, however, is disappointing. The students, after all, know little of the stylistics of comedy, and they are only beginning to develop their imaginative "ears." For the benefit of the student or any reader new to O'Connor's fiction, a relatively brief tuning-up period is in order. First on the checklist are titles: occasionally the title will sound a bit peculiar or zany itself, like "The Artificial Nigger" or "You Can't Be Any Poorer Than Dead." More often the title gains comic momentum as it recurs in the story, the way "A Good Man Is Hard to Find," a familiar song title, does as it reappears as a hackneyed expression in Red Sammy Butts's conversation, and is repeated with a twist by The Misfit who, by his own admission is not a good man, but would like to be able to verify the reported goodness of Jesus. The second benchmark, applicable in any comic work, is the name of any character or place. Why name a con artist Manley Pointer, or Hoover Shoats for that matter, if your aim is a primarily sober one? And we have already mentioned Red Sammy Butts, an ideal name for a buffoon-host. Although all of O'Connor's names are actually well-known in certain Southern regions, usually they are uncommon; they seem to be chosen for their suggestiveness or their sound effect: Hooten, Parrum, Turpin, Cheatham, Godhigh, Farebrother, Ham, Block, Fox, Pitts. Place names work in a similar fashion: Taulkinham, Eastrod, Toombsboro,

[7] *The Flannery O'Connor Bulletin*, VI (1977), 47–71.
[8] "Some Remarks on Humor," p. 102.

Timberboro, Partridge. And there are the ladies with three names, for some reason always good for a laugh: Sally Poker Sash, Lucynell Crater, Sarah Ruth Cates. In "The Displaced Person," Mrs. McIntyre's litany of worthless tenants suggests a recital of the plagues of Egypt: there were the Shortleys, Ringfields, Collinses, Garrits, Jarrells, Perkinses, Pinkins, and Herrins. From that same story, the unpronounceable Guizac is rendered "Gobblehook" by Mrs. Short-ley, who also says that she'd as soon call a child Bollweevil as Sledgewig. Such films as "The Displaced Person," televised by the Public Broadcasting System as part of its American Short Story series, demonstrate a third way to over-come quickly the handicap of "wooden ear" which can strike any of us upon encountering a new writer. Because a dramatization allows us to see and hear the characters in action, the imaginative ear does not have to bear the burden of interpretation alone. Furthermore, I have seen illuminating dramatizations of "A Good Man Is Hard to Find," "A View of the Woods," and "Revelation." The rhythm and lilt of O'Connor's dialogue, for instance, can enter through the ear rather than be interpreted on the silent page. This can be especially important to a reader who is not native to the South. Perhaps you remember this little speech by Mr. Shortley, the dairyman whose position is threatened by a new tenant, a refugee from Poland, Mr. Guizac:

> "All men was created free and equal," he said to Mrs. McIntyre, "and I risked my life and limb to prove it. Gone over there and fought and bled and died and come back over here and find out who's got my job—just exactly who I been fighting. It was a hand-grenade come that near to killing me and I seen who throwed it—little man with eye-glasses just like his. Might have bought them at the same store. Small world," and he gave a bitter little laugh. He had the power of making other people see his logic. He talked a good deal to the Negroes.

Comic dialogue is, of course, O'Connor's specialty, and one to which we will return.

Now there's one other element of O'Connor's fiction that perhaps cannot be analyzed and explained as readily as the first three items on our checklist, but it cannot be ignored, and that is the sense of threat, of danger, of vio-lence that, in some form, permeates all of her stories. It is a commonplace, of course, that all accomplished comedy contains or rests upon some deeply serious or horrifyingly repugnant reality. While the underlying seriousness of O'Connor's humor is relatively obvious, a simple definition will not do it jus-tice. I am not convinced that this Southern woman, for example, was evan-gelizing through her fiction. I have found a comment by E. B. White on this topic that sounds so much like something she would have written that I will let it serve. White does not agree with those who say that the humorist is funda-mentally a very sad person. "[I]t would be more accurate, I think," he writes, "to say that there is a deep vein of melancholy running through everyone's life and that the humorist, more sensible of it than some others, compensates for it actively and positively. Humorists fatten on trouble. They have always made trouble pay. They struggle along with a good will and endure pain cheerfully, knowing how well it will serve them in the sweet by and by."⁹ And serve it does! It serves as an antidote to that mind-dulling sentimentality O'Connor attacked at every opportunity. Again and again in her occasional prose we find this word, *sentimentality*, used as a scourge against mindless Catholic readers, mindless critics, mindless writers. A similar favorite phrase was "hazy compassion," and she described one of her reader's affection for [T]he Misfit as "sentimental." In her resistance to heart-warming and uplifting characterization, O'Connor is adhering to one of comedy's oldest purposes—that of dispelling illusion. Sentimentality, as represented by the grandmother and quite a number of upright matrons, is a self-deceit that O'Connor shock tactics are designed to expose. A sentimental comedy, of course, would contain no murders, no abandonments, no strokes, no handicaps nor illnesses of a disfiguring nature. No wooden legs, no coffins too small for the body, no cans of peanut brittle filled with teeth-fracturing springs, no women pregnant in iron lungs, no wheelchair veterans left in the sun beside the Coke machine. The "paraphernalia of suffering," as Nathanael West calls it, serves as unlikely fodder for this "realist of distances," as O'Connor called herself.

Once the checklist has done its work and the newcomer is well-launched on O'Connor's comic seas, he [or she] is ready for more detailed study which could follow any of several approaches. Careful reading of a critical theorist like Northrop Frye, for instance, yields a systematic framework on which to test and measure individual stories and characters. Frye discusses the importance in Shakespearean comedy of the term "grace," a word central to O'Connor's fiction, and he explains why a religious outlook requires the comic mode. Even such a theorist as Freud, who would seem to be an unsuitable companion for O'Connor, produces a characteristically economic definition of the comical as "an unintentional discovery in social relations" that seems to match ideally with her own description of the "totally unexpected" action that serves as the pivot for each of her stories. Manley Pointer's theft of Joy-Hulga's wooden leg is just such an unexpected, unintentional discovery, not only for the reader, according to O'Connor, but for the author as well. The denouement occurred to her only lines before she wrote it! Other similar comic surprises may be profitably compared with O'Connor's from the works of Mark Twain, Eudora Welty, William Faulkner, and Nathanael West.

Consideration of the principles that unify the comic imagination in American letters should be particularly fruitful approaches to this twentieth-century Georgian. What Rubin calls "the Great American Joke" is certainly one that O'Connor was in on. America is a country that cherishes its ideals, but carefully avoids any institution that has traditionally embodied them—thus, no aristocracy, no monarchy, no state church. Ideals without institutions is the Great American Joke that allows for the triumph of the

⁹ Rubin, "Introduction," pp. 8–13.

banal—from Mark Twain's Emmeline Grangerford to Nathanael West's Miss Lonelyhearts to Joseph Heller's Bob Slocum. For O'Connor, the Great American Joke paved the way for numberless religious eccentrics, probably best explored in *Wise Blood,* and for an equal number of abstracted or sentimental idealists, often her matrons, but drawn in greater detail as Rayber the pedant in *The Violent Bear It Away.* Probably more accessible for most readers is a conflict that is very much alive in virtually all American comic writing, and that is what Rubin has identified as the incompatibility of the vulgar and the genteel viewpoints within a single society. "Each persists in making the other look ridiculous," according to Rubin, "and usually that is what is funny."[10] *Huckleberry Finn* is the most widely known, extended example of this clash of cultural modes, and contains some of the most memorable examples of the language that embodies this clash, the vernacular and the refined. O'Connor fits squarely in this tradition, as her dialogue attests. Ripely vernacular, the exchanges between the landed and the servant classes, for example, demonstrate just how incompatible but how interdependent the two verbal styles are. Listen to Mrs. Hopewell, the eternal optimist, and her hired hand, Mrs. Freeman:

> When Mrs. Hopewell said to Mrs. Freeman that life was like that, Mrs. Freeman would say, "I always said so myself."
>
> She was quicker than Mr. Freeman. When Mrs. Hopewell said to her after they had been on the place a while, "You know, you're the wheel behind the wheel," and winked, Mrs. Freeman said, "I know it. I've always been quick. It's some that are quicker than others."
>
> "Everybody is different," Mrs. Hopewell said.
>
> "Yes, most people is," Mrs. Freeman said.
>
> "It takes all kinds to make the world."
>
> "I always said it did myself."
>
> The girl was used to this kind of dialogue for breakfast and more of it for dinner; sometimes they had it for supper too.

When the property-owning Mrs. Cope urges A Higher View in the story, "A Circle in the Fire," her tenant Mrs. Pritchard, parries with sour logic:

> "Every day I say a prayer of Thanksgiving. Think of all we have," she said, and sighed, "We have everything."
>
> Mrs. Pritchard studied the woods. "All I got is four abscess teeth," she remarked.

This verbal dueling is a hallmark of O'Connor's humor, and it illustrates her use of that distinctive American juxtaposition of vernacular and refined speech, each working to make the other sound laughable. Whether it takes on the tone and force of a Punch and Judy routine or the subtle shrewdness of

---

[10] Rubin, "The Barber Kept on Shaving," p. 385.

a horse swap, every conversation in every story is essentially an argument, a contest between rival wills; and for this reason, the dialogue is a good place to take the pulse of her fiction and to discover, first, how alive, indeed, it is, and second, how completely it depends upon the tensions of unresolved opposition. Returning to the question of what place the shocking, the ugly, the violent can have in a work of comedy, in O'Connor's comedy, at least, it provides the frame, the context within which the laughable can be appreciated to full advantage. To return once more to the story, "A Good Man Is Hard to Find," and the question of why and how that story can be called comic, it may now be clearer that the violence of that story is never completely without a humorous coloring. The early dialogue among the grandmother and June Star and Bailey becomes more than trivial bickering. It now becomes intensely significant that the grandmother has dressed so that anyone coming upon her body after a highway accident could see at once that she was a lady. The violence supercharges, in a manner of speaking, the comedy and this is explicitly illustrated in [T]he Misfit's parting tribute: "'She would of been a good woman . . . if it had been somebody there to shoot her every minute of her life.'"

O'Connor accepted philosophically the fact that some of her readers failed to see her humor. About her audience she wrote: "You discover your audience at the same time and in the same way that you discover your subject; but it is an added blow."[11]

MAKING CONNECTIONS

1. Butler highlights the tension between finding humor and reading for the psychological or religious dimensions of O'Connor's fiction. Do you agree that there is a tension here? How can these two seemingly disparate kinds of activities be understood to be complementary?

2. In quoting a number of people on the dangers of analyzing **comic** writing—that is, sucking the funny right out of it—Butler asserts the value of doing so anyway, arguing that "understanding heightens enjoyment" (p. 153). Do you agree? Are there other kinds of analysis beyond the analysis of the comic to which this conversation could be applied? Do you think the process of coming to greater understanding of a work of literature can lead to its denaturing?

HALLMAN B. BRYANT (B. ?)

READING THE MAP IN "A GOOD MAN IS HARD TO FIND"   1981

Flannery O'Connor, remarking on her most famous short story, "A Good Man Is Hard to Find," issues several caveats to critics. She allows that "a certain amount of what is the significance of this" kind of investigation has to go on in teaching and in literary analysis, but she cautions against reducing

What's So Funny about Flannery O'Connor?
[11] *Mystery and Manners*, p. 118.

a story to "a problem to be solved" so that it becomes "something which you evaporate to get Instant Enlightenment."

Without evaporating too much I will try to shed light on the significance of some small details in "A Good Man Is Hard to Find." Although I do not think an analysis of O'Connor's use of place names in the story will create instant enlightenment, I believe that the towns alluded to along the route which the family travels were chosen for two reasons: first, and most obviously, to foreshadow; and second, to augment the theme of the story. Furthermore, because the numerous places mentioned in the story can actually be found on the map, with only one important exception, it is thus possible to estimate within a few miles the physical distance that the family travels.

The first thing one notices about "A Good Man Is Hard to Find" is that it is set in a real place—in the state of Georgia. The opening scene describes an Atlanta family quarreling about their vacation plans. The grandmother is opposed to going to Florida ostensibly because a convict "that calls himself The Misfit is aloose from the Federal pen and headed toward Florida." (Apparently the Federal penitentiary from which The Misfit has escaped is the one in Atlanta, although it is not specified in the story.) Regardless of the threat posed by The Misfit, the family heads south for Florida instead of east Tennessee where the grandmother had tried to persuade them to take her. We are told that the family left Atlanta at 8:35 in the morning with the mileage on the car at 55890, a fact recorded by the grandmother because she "thought it would be interesting to say how many miles they had been when they got back." From this point on one can literally follow the journey of the family with a road map and take the mileage they put on their car before the wreck and the subsequent meeting with The Misfit and his henchmen.

One odd fact about their route emerges immediately to anyone familiar with Atlanta and its environs. Although the family lives in Atlanta and is headed south, we are told that they pass Stone Mountain along the way. This natural phenomenon and tourist attraction is about fifteen or sixteen miles from Atlanta on the northeast side of the city. At the time the story was written, one had to follow U.S. 78 North to get to Stone Mountain, a highly unlikely road to take out of Atlanta if one is going to Florida.[1]

---

[1] The detour by Stone Mountain was probably due to O'Connor's uncertainty about its exact location; she simply found it a convenient allusion since Stone Mountain was for years Georgia's most famous tourist attraction, but perhaps there is more than meets the eye. In 1915 a project was begun by the United Daughters of the Confederacy which called for Robert E. Lee and his lieutenants to be carved in heroic scale on the vertical face of the mountain. Ironically, the artist commissioned for the job was a Yankee sculptor named Gutzon Borglum who blasted and chiseled on the mountain until 1928 when funds and patience ran out. After expenditure of hundreds of thousands of dollars in a vain effort to impose the heroes of the "Lost Cause" on the side of the mountain, the project was dropped. The scarred carvings, empty catwalks and scaffolds were reminders of a long series of errors and frustrations of the U.D.C. ladies who dreamed of keeping the past alive with a memorial that would be "the perpetuation of a vision." (See *The Story of Stone Mountain* by Willard Neal [Atlanta: Neal and Rogers, 1963], 23–33). Flannery O'Connor was amused by the quixotic qualities of the U.D.C., and Stone Mountain would evoke for Georgians of O'Connor's generation the folly of a sentimental project—a project almost as futile as the grandmother's in the story, whose fascination with past grandeur is congruent with that of the U.D.C.'s and has equally unfortunate results.

Although one of the children urges his father to "go through Georgia fast 5 so we won't have to look at it much," there nevertheless are some interesting details of scenery along the roadside, and the grandmother tells us about many of the things they pass by. She notices "a cute little pickaninny" standing in the door of a shanty that she fancies would make a nice study for a sentimental painting, but the same subject disgusts her granddaughter June Star, who comments acidly, "He didn't have any britches on." More significantly, the grandmother points out a graveyard with five or six graves fenced off in the middle of a large cotton field, which is a rather obvious foreshadowing of the fate that will befall the family.

When the grandmother can no longer hold the children's attention with roadside attractions, she tells them a story of one of her girlhood suitors, Mr. Edgar Atkins Teagarden, who was from Jasper, Georgia, a small north Georgia town located in Pickens County and approximately fifty or sixty miles from the Tennessee state line. Although we are not told just where the grandmother is from, only that she has "connections in east Tennessee," it seems that to be consistent with her tale of Mr. Teagarden's courtship, she would have to have lived somewhere near Jasper, since he drove to her house by buggy every Saturday and gave her a watermelon monogrammed with his initials, E. A. T.

The family's journey is interrupted by a stop for a lunch of barbecued sandwiches at a café called The Tower which is located in "a clearing outside of Timothy." For economic effect this is one of the great scenes in all of Flannery O'Connor's fiction; yet here one cannot plot the location of the place on the map for there is no town of Timothy in Georgia. (If there is, it is such a small community it is not listed in the state atlas.) Since the other references to places in the story are to actual localities in the state, why does she create a fictitious name at this point? My theory is that in this scene, which has strong moral intention, O'Connor select[s] the name Timothy for the ironic effect it would produce. The allusion here is not geographical but Biblical, and the Timothy alluded to is almost certainly the book in the New Testament which bears the same name. Usually referred to as the Pastoral Letters, this gospel purports to be letters from Paul addressed to his disciples and through them to the Christian community at large. More than any other writing in the New Testament, the letters to Timothy are concerned with Christian orthodoxy. In this gospel Paul deals essentially with three topics: the opposition of false doctrine; the organization of the church and establishment of ecclesiastical regulations; and exhortations which indicate how to be a good citizen and Christian.

It seems to me that the concerns expressed by Paul in his letter to Timothy are very germane to the concerns expressed by Flannery O'Connor in "A Good Man Is Hard to Find," especially the concern with heretics and the advice on how to be a good Christian. One has only to set the family of six from Atlanta and Red Sammy and his wife (as well as The Misfit)—all of whom Flannery O'Connor considers heretics—against certain passages from Timothy to see that O'Connor's allusion ironically tells us just where these modern-day people are in error. For example, these verses seem to apply especially to Bailey. "He [the husband] must manage his own family well and see that his children obey him with proper respect" (I Tim. 3:4–5).

Also the author of the epistle commands good Christians to keep the faith and avoid "vain discussions" and concern with trivial matters and endless wrangling about genealogies (I Tim. 6:3–10). Further, he admonishes women "to dress modestly, with decency and propriety" and "to learn in quietness and full submission . . . and be silent" (I Tim. 2:9–12). This instruction seems to bear most directly on the grandmother, who is vain about her Old South heritage and certainly conscious of her social standing and what is required to be a lady. This is best brought out in her selection of attire for the trip. She is turned out in white gloves, black purse, a navy blue straw sailor hat with white violets on the brim, a navy blue polka dot dress with collar and cuffs of white organdy trimmed with lace, and on her neck she has pinned a purple spray of cloth violets containing a sachet. Her costume has been prepared so that, in the event of an accident, "anyone seeing her dead on the highway would know at once that she was a lady."

The grandmother's superficial conception of values is ironically under- 10 scored in the vain discussions with her grandchildren about what kind of conduct was once expected from children and her trivial remarks about plantation days and old suitors. Nowhere are her ideas more tellingly satirized than in her conversation with Red Sammy in the café where both complain of misplaced trust in their fellow man, which the grandmother sees as an indication of the general lack of manners in the modern world. She tells Red Sammy, "People are certainly not nice like they used to be." Of course, both Red Sammy and the grandmother are conceited enough to think that they are just as good as they ought to be. When Red Sammy complains of a recent theft of some gasoline by men driving a Chrysler and asks in a puzzled way why he had trusted them, he is quickly told by the grandmother that it was "because you're a good man," to which he candidly assents, "Yes'm, I suppose so."

The grandmother's inability to "learn in quietness" is tragically the cause of the deaths of the entire family. Shortly after Bailey overturns the car in a ditch, they are approached by a bespectacled man who the grandmother feels is "someone she knew" and soon she recognizes the stranger as The Misfit whose picture she has seen, and she blurts out this fact, saying, "You're The Misfit . . . I recognized you at once," to which he replies, "but it would have been better for all of you, lady, if you hadn't of reckernized me."

It is generally agreed that in the traumatic moments that follow in which the grandmother witnesses the deaths of her family and anticipates her own she does learn a lesson she has not heeded previously during her life. This lesson is the central message which Paul attempts to convey to Christians through Timothy and that is, "There is one God and one mediator between God and men, the Lord Jesus Christ, who gave himself to save mankind" (I Tim. 2:5). The evidence for assuming that she has come to a belated awareness that her faith has been misplaced in the pursuit of social graces and a concern with manners is limited to The Misfit's remark, "She would of been a good woman . . . if it had been somebody there to shoot her every minute of her life." Furthermore, in death she appears like a child, and her face is "smiling up at the cloudless sky," suggesting that she has found grace at last.

Another passage from Timothy seems especially applicable at this point: "The Spirit clearly says that in later times some will abandon the faith and follow deceiving spirits and things taught by demons. Such teachings come through hypocritical liars, whose consciences have been seared as with hot iron" (I Tim. 4:1–12). Although the whole cast of characters in the story has abandoned the faith and followed the wrong paths, the indictment of these lines would apply most forcibly to The Misfit who wears glasses and has a scholarly look. He has indeed been taught by demons, and from the Christian point of view that O'Connor takes in "A Good Man Is Hard to Find" he is a hypocritical liar who has no faith in a moral purpose in the universe and teaches that "it's nothing for you to do but enjoy the few minutes you got left the best way you can—by killing somebody or burning down his house or doing some other meanness to him." Thus, according to the ethics of this teacher, goodness is a matter of sadistic gratification. "No pleasure but meanness," he says, indicating how completely his conscience has been seared and his vision warped by his hedonistic atheism.

The numerous ways in which the content of this book of the New Testament dovetails with the characters and the theme of "A Good Man Is Hard to Find" could not be a complete accident. It cannot be demonstrated that Flannery O'Connor conceived of the moral of her story in terms of this specific book, but she made no bones about the fact that she wrote "from the standpoint of Christian orthodoxy"[2]; and there is no doubt that Paul wrote from a similar standpoint, and his letter to Timothy has the same hortatory, moralizing tone that we find just below the surface in "A Good Man Is Hard to Find." Thus, it seems likely that she put the town of Timothy on the map because she wanted the reader to pick up the allusion and perhaps [review] the contents of the New Testament, but more probably she saw the parallel between her modern-day characters who have left the main road of Christian faith and Paul's warning to the church when he feared it was in danger off into the byways of heresy.

Just as the name of the town where the family stops for lunch is carefully 15 chosen, so is the name of Red Sammy's café. In Christian iconography towers are ambivalent symbols, that is, they speak *in bono* or *in malo*, to use the vocabulary of medieval exegetes, and can represent either good or evil qualities. For example, the Tower of Babel is symbolic of man's pride and stands for misbegotten human enterprises. The fate of the tower and its architects shows the consequences of overconfidence in the pursuit of fanciful ideas. (Interestingly enough, Nimrod, who began the construction of the tower, was also a

[2] *The Habit of Being: Letters of Flannery O'Connor*, ed. Sally Fitzgerald (New York: Farrar, 1979), 196.

mighty hunter, and like Red Sammy, a keeper of wild game, if Red Sammy's monkey can be called wild.)

As well as its nugatory meaning, the tower is a traditional symbol of the Virgin Mary and is a token of her purity and powers of transformation. Mary as the "refugee of sinners" according to Catholic doctrine is appropriately represented by the tower, a place associated with safety and sanctuary.

Outside of its Christian meaning the tower in arcane lore is a portent of disaster. In the sixteenth enigma of the Tarot pack of cards, catastrophe is indicated by the image of a tower struck by lightning. Whether O'Connor knew this fact about the meaning of the tower is uncertain, but she could not have been unaware of the former implications of the tower as a symbol, versed as she was in Biblical and church lore. It is appropriate that the conceited owner of this barbecue palace should have called it The Tower; it is ironic that this tower has no capacity to transform or give refuge.

Leaving Timothy and The Tower behind, both in the Biblical and geographical sense, the family [resume] their trip and we are told that just beyond Toombsboro, Georgia, the grandmother awakens from a nap with the recollection, mistaken as it turns out, that there is an old plantation nearby which she had visited as a girl; she even thinks she remembers the road to take to get there and tells Bailey, "It's not far from here, I know. . . . It wouldn't take over twenty minutes." As it so happens there is a Toomsboro (spelled without the "b") on the map and it is only twenty-three miles south of Milledgeville, Flannery O'Connor's home. She surely knew the place and chose to mention it because the name has an ominous ring, and it also would have been a logical terminus for the family's trip in terms of the time and distance they have traveled since leaving Atlanta in the morning. In fact, if one follows the usual route from Atlanta to Milledgeville (Georgia Highway 212), the distance is 93 miles, and if one adds to this the 23 miles further to Toomsboro, plus the estimated 15 or so miles that the detour to the plantation takes, then it can be calculated that the family has come a total of 130 miles. Considering the conditions of Georgia roads in the late 1940s, one had to drive under 50 m.p.h. to keep from knocking the wheels out of line from the numerous potholes that Governor Talmadge's highway people never patched. Thus, if one assumes that Bailey has averaged around 45 m.p.h. and takes account of the lunch stop, they have been on the road four or five hours and their meeting with The Misfit occurs in the early afternoon of a cloudless day with the mileage on the car standing at about 56020 on the meter. Sadly enough, the grandmother will be forever unaware of this "interesting fact," but we as readers should have a better understanding of how carefully O'Connor has used realistic detail for symbolic effects.

In the course of this story, the family's trip takes them from their complacent and smug living room to a confrontation with ultimate evil and ultimate reality as well. They are not prepared for the meeting because, like the heretics who concerned Paul in his epistle to Timothy, they have been occupied with the trivial things and involved in quarrels; and, like the builders of the Tower of Babel, they are preoccupied with vain enterprises.

Flannery O'Connor saw herself as a prophetic writer and her authorial 20 strategy was to shock; her fiction is intended as a rebuke to rationalistic, materialistic and humanistic thought—the heresies of the twentieth century. She believed that people in the modern world were not following the true path and had to be made to see their condition for what it was—a wandering by the wayside. In "A Good Man Is Hard to Find" the family's wayward lives are given direction in their final moments, and from O'Connor's point of view they are at last on the right road.

MAKING CONNECTIONS

1. Bryant's "Reading the Map in 'A Good Man Is Hard to Find'" argues not simply for the significance of the journey taken in the story but for the significance of the place names, real and imagined. Compare his account of the story as meticulously constructed so as to imbed this significance to O'Connor's own account of a writer's activity as about discovering meaning as she goes along. Are these two kinds of journeys—one carefully planned, with a road atlas, the other a journey of discovery— reconcilable? If so, how?

2. Bryant takes "A Good Man Is Hard to Find" very seriously both as a carefully constructed narrative and as a spiritual and moral tale. Do you think it is possible to appreciate the story without reading it in this way? Why or why not?

ROBERT H. BRINKMEYER JR. (B. 1951)

FROM FLANNERY O'CONNOR AND HER READERS 1989

As her letters and essays clearly indicate, O'Connor was very much concerned with her reading audience. Her comments on her audience and how it affected her as an artist, however, were not entirely consistent, and it seems clear that O'Connor was of two minds on the subject.[1] One part of O'Connor downplayed the significance of the audience, saying that artists should be concerned with one thing—their art—and that they bear no responsibility to the audience. By this line of thinking writers concentrate on making their fiction— the characters and their world—come alive, and they make sure that the story works as a story and not as a medium for expressing an abstract statement. The meaning of a piece of fiction, O'Connor insisted, was the entire experience one has with it and was not a statement imposed on it that could then later be extracted and held up as its "message." Such thinking was central to the advice she wrote (December 11, 1956) to A. about writing fiction. O'Connor wrote that a writer should merely "start simply with a character or anything that you can make come alive." She continued, "When you have a character he will create his own situation and his situation will suggest some kind of resolution as

---

[1] The most extensive discussion of O'Connor's interpretation of her audience is in Carol Shloss, *Flannery O'Connor's Dark Comedies: The Limits of Inference* (Baton Rouge, 1980). [Brinkmeyer's note]

you get into it. Wouldn't it be better to discover a meaning in what you write than to impose one?" (*HB*, 188).

Behind O'Connor's thinking is the thought of Saint Thomas Aquinas, whom O'Connor frequently cites. For Aquinas a work of art is, as O'Connor points out in "Catholic Novelists and Their Readers," "a good in itself," being "wholly concerned with the good of that which is made." As such, it "glorifies God because it reflects God," and writers have no cause to put their work to any other end; such endeavors only undermine the integrity of the vision and sully the purity of the art. Modern writers, O'Connor says in this same essay, by and large fail to heed Aquinas's lesson and instead wrench their art to make it fit utilitarian ends. For her, in contrast, "the artist has his hands full and does his duty if he attends to his art. He can safely leave the evangelizing to the evangelists" (*MM*, 171, 173, 171).

Catholic writers, in O'Connor's eyes, were particularly prone to distort their fiction for utilitarian purposes—to make it do something rather than be something. Particularly disturbing to her were those writers, in part goaded by the Catholic press, who wrote in pious language about the pieties of the Church. O'Connor's attitude toward this type of fiction was sharp: "As for the fiction," she wrote (February 19, 1956) to John Lynch, "the motto of the Catholic press should be: We guarantee to corrupt nothing but your taste" (*HB*, 138). In ignoring the realities of the here and now outside the Church, such fiction was for O'Connor little more than religious propaganda, the stuff one expects to find in the vestibules of churches but not in bookstores. These writers, she believed, were too concerned with presenting the Church in a favorable light and tending to their readership's spiritual needs; O'Connor's answer to them was that in writing fiction the Catholic writer "does not decide what would be good for the Christian body and proceed to deliver it" (*MM*, 183). Instead, as we have seen O'Connor stressing, writers must work within the limitations of their vocation to create the best story—not tract—possible. "The writer is only free when he can tell the reader to go jump in the lake," O'Connor said in one of her interviews, stressing the artist's independence from the audience. She added that though the writer of course wants to communicate a personal vision, "whether [the reader] likes it or not is no concern of the writer" (*CFO*, 39).

If in this way O'Connor downplayed the significance of the audience, she also frequently said something quite different. She argued that the audience played a crucial role in artistic creation and that writers always had to be aware of, and to take account of, their audience. She spoke of this connection in "Catholic Novelists and Their Readers," saying that "it takes readers as well as writers to make literature," and she added in "The Catholic Novelist in the Protestant South" that "it is what writer, character, and reader share that makes it possible to write fiction at all." Elsewhere (in "Novelist and Believer") O'Connor wrote that fiction was ultimately an attempt at communication; successful writing, she added, was not merely a rendering of the artist's vision but a rendering of it in such a way that the reader could understand it. "The novelist doesn't write to express himself, he doesn't write simply to render a vision he believes true, rather he renders his vision so it can be transferred, as nearly whole as possible, to his reader," she wrote. "You can safely ignore the reader's taste, but you can't ignore his nature, you can't ignore his limited patience. Your problem is going to be difficult in direct proportion as your beliefs depart from his." She echoes this observation in "Some Aspects of the Grotesque in Southern Fiction," saying that the writer's vision "has to be transmitted and that the limitations and blind spots of his audience will very definitely affect the way he is able to show what he sees" (*MM*, 182, 204-205, 162, 47).

When speaking of her own audience, O'Connor almost always stressed the great distance she felt between herself and her readers and pointed to the ways this gulf pressured and limited her as a writer. She believed that she and other American Catholic writers lacked a significant and responsive audience, and that this situation stifled imaginative growth and artistic expression. O'Connor found several reasons for this development. Central to the Catholic writer's plight, O'Connor believed, was the fact that in America Catholic writers lacked a distinctive social and cultural heritage based on religious identity. In "The Catholic Novelist in the Protestant South" she asserts that "the writer whose themes are religious particularly needs a region where these themes find a response in the life of the people." She then adds: "The American Catholic is short on places that reflect his particular religious life and his particular problems. This country isn't exactly cut in his image." She goes on to say that even in areas where there are large numbers of Catholics, Catholic life there lacks "the significant features that result in a high degree of regional self-consciousness" and so offers the Catholic writer few "exploitable benefits." O'Connor's analysis of Catholic writers continues: "They have no great geographical extent, they have no particularly significant history, certainly no history of defeat; they have no real peasant class, and no cultural unity of the kind you find in the South." She adds that Catholics usually "blend almost imperceptively into the general materialistic background." This lack of a strong cultural tradition and a supportive audience greatly burdens Catholic writers, impoverishing their imaginative life and art. "If the Catholic faith were central to life in America, Catholic fiction would fare better, but the Church is not central to this society." O'Connor continues: "The things that bind us together as Catholics are known only to ourselves. A secular society understands us less and less. It becomes more and more difficult in America to make belief believable" (*MM*, 200, 201).

These final words point to the second reason American Catholics lack a supportive audience: The larger society they write from and to is overwhelmingly secular and materialistic, money based rather than religious based. O'Connor [. . .] was well aware of the trends in modern social and intellectual thought that since the Enlightenment have been validating and valorizing the human consciousness and rationality while undermining and reducing the significance of the religious. In a letter (October 19, 1958) to T. R. Spivey, O'Connor wrote that by and large people in today's society have "no sense of the power of God that could produce the Incarnation and the Resurrection. They are all so busy explaining away the virgin birth and such things, reducing everything to human proportions that in time they lose even the sense of the human itself, what they were aiming to reduce everything to" (*HB*, 300). Because moderns lacked a faith in transcendent values and order, O'Connor, as she said in "Some Aspects of the Grotesque in Southern Fiction," saw the age as one "which doubts both fact and value, which is swept this way and that by momentary convictions" (*MM*, 49). O'Connor found such relativism particularly disturbing, and this in part explains her strong attraction to the fundamentalist imperative that defines all values according to the simple—but total—choice of being for either Christ or the Devil.

Given these trends and developments, O'Connor saw her own position, as well as that of almost all American Catholic writers, as being particularly precarious in terms of communicating with her readership. O'Connor frequently asserted in her letters that she could consistently count on only a handful of informed readers—an assertion largely borne out by the number of vicious and misinformed readings her work received, particularly early on—and that she had to make these readers go a long way in her life as an author. O'Connor knew hers was not the type of fiction that most Catholic readers yearned to read—not, in other words, fiction that was thoroughly positive and that went out of its way to celebrate the life of the Church. She characterized the general Catholic reader as unthinking, and she said that this reader "is so busy looking for something that fits his needs, and shows him in the best possible light, that he will find suspect anything that doesn't serve such purpose" (*MM*, 182). Elsewhere, in a letter (May 4, 1963) to Sister Mariella Gable, she wrote that those Catholic readers who demand that the writer make Christianity look desirable are asking the writer to describe Christianity's essence and not what the writer actually sees. "Ideal Christianity doesn't exist, because anything the human being touches, even Christian truth, he deforms slightly in his own image," she wrote, adding a bit later that the tendency of the Catholic readers she had been discussing "is always toward the abstract and therefore toward allegory, thinness, and ultimately what they are looking for is apologetic fiction. The best of them think: make it look desirable because it is desirable. And the rest of them think: make it look desirable so I won't look like a fool for holding it" (*HB*, 516). Such readers would find little to like in O'Connor's fiction and in all likelihood would see it as a good deal more than suspect—subversive, probably.

O'Connor of course felt an even greater distance from what she saw as the thoroughly secular and unbelieving general reader, the reader to whom she claimed she primarily wrote. In "The Catholic Novelists and Their Readers" she said that Catholic readers make a great mistake in supposing that Catholic writers write exclusively for them. "Occasionally this may happen," she wrote, "but generally it is not happening today" (*MM*, 185), and O'Connor made it clear elsewhere that it was not happening in her fiction. To A., O'Connor wrote (August 2, 1955) of the audience she perceived, saying that "one of the awful things about writing when you are a Christian is that for you the ultimate reality is the Incarnation, the present reality is the Incarnation, and nobody believes in the Incarnation; that is, nobody in your audience. My audience are the people who think God is dead. At least these are the people I am conscious of writing for" (*HB*, 92). Trying to bridge this gap between believing author and unbelieving audience was a terrible burden for O'Connor, and one that haunted her throughout her career. In a review of Caroline Gordon's *The Malefactors*, O'Connor wrote that "making grace believable to the contemporary reader is the almost insurmountable problem of the novelist who writes from the standpoint of Christian orthodoxy," an observation that speaks crucially to O'Connor's own situation in communicating with her audience (*PG*, 16).

O'Connor further perceived her audience as making demands that she was not prepared to meet—ever. She complained in "Some Aspects of the Grotesque in Southern Fiction" that her freedom as a writer was always under pressure, since everywhere "the novelist is asked to be the handmaid of his age." She wrote, "Whenever the public is heard from, it is heard demanding a literature which is balanced and which will somehow heal the ravages of our time." This literature, she said elsewhere in this essay, was based on what she called "a realism of fact"—a realism that associated "the only legitimate material for long fiction with the movement of social forces, with the typical, with the fidelity to the way things look and happen in normal life." Such realism, she added, limited both the scope of the imaginative vision of artists and their fiction. As O'Connor noted here and elsewhere, her own fiction was written with a realism of an altogether different sort—a realism that sought not to mirror the typical but to reveal the spiritual. To this end, she says in "Novelist and Believer," the writer "is bound by the reasonable possibilities, not the probabilities of his culture" (*MM*, 46, 39, 165).

If the overall critical environment established its own orthodoxy for fiction, 10 O'Connor also saw general readers establishing their own expectations and demands for what they should experience in the act of reading. She characterized the general readers as being "tired," of wanting what she called at one point "Instant Uplift"—that is, wanting to have their spirits raised in an act of easy compassion and sentiment. This demand for uplift and the redemptive act, O'Connor notes in "Some Aspects of the Grotesque in Southern Fiction," is a characteristic human need, and one that both the storyteller and the listener find particularly compelling in narrative. What bothers O'Connor is not that the reader seeks this motion in fiction but that the reader "has forgotten the cost of it." She explains that the modern reader's "sense of evil is diluted or lacking altogether, and so he has forgotten the price of restoration. When he reads a novel, he wants either his senses tormented or his spirits raised. He wants to be transported, instantly, either to mock damnation or a mock innocence." To underscore the risks the writer takes in ignoring such readers, O'Connor writes in this same essay that there are those who "say that the serious writer doesn't have to bother about the tired reader, but he does, because they are all tired. One old lady who wants her heart uplifted wouldn't be so bad, but you multiply her two hundred and fifty thousand times and what you get is a book club" (*MM*, 165, 48–49).

ABBREVIATIONS

Abbreviations of works by Flannery O'Connor commonly cited in the text refer to the following editions:

CFO   *Conversations with Flannery O'Connor*. Edited by Rosemary M. Magee. Jackson, Miss., 1987.

HB   *The Habit of Being: Letters*. Edited by Sally Fitzgerald. New York, 1969.

MM   *Mystery and Manners: Occasional Prose*. Edited by Sally Fitzgerald and Robert Fitzgerald. New York, 1969.

PG   *The Presence of Grace and Other Book Reviews by Flannery O'Connor*. Compiled by Leo J. Zuber. Edited by Carter W. Martin. Athens, Ga., 1983.

MAKING CONNECTIONS

1. Does it seem like O'Connor's goal of "making grace believable to the contemporary reader" is compatible with her advice that writers "discover meaning" in what they write rather than imposing meaning? What might it mean if O'Connor did follow her own advice and ended up writing stories that revealed the workings of grace in the world?

2. Read Brinkmeyer's characterization of O'Connor's notion that stories must not be written to convey messages against O'Connor's own reflections from *Mystery and Manners*. Are Brinkmeyer's ideas consistent or inconsistent with O'Connor's? How?

3. Which of these pieces—Brinkmeyer's, Bryant's, Butler's, or O'Connor's own—offers the reading of "A Good Man Is Hard to Find" that most closely matches your initial sense of the story? Which did you find the most eye-opening—that is, which most made you see things about the story that you hadn't at first? Which did you find to be furthest from your initial sense of the story—and did it convince you at all?

JOSEPH O'NEILL   (B. 1964)

TOUCHED BY EVIL   2009

For years I was under the impression that Flannery O'Connor was Irish—a Kerryman, perhaps—and without doubt a male link in the concatenation featuring Flann O'Brien and Frank O'Connor. The delusion belonged to the fog in which one's early and unsystematic encounters with literature, and indeed the world, take place. My own fog was thickened by growing up in a Dutch town. The only sizable store of books in English was the American Book Center, a faintly indecent basement establishment mainly stocked, unless I misremember, with *Mad* comics and X-rated-looking publications. At the far end of the store was a wall of poetry (I now marvel, *Why? Which hero was behind that?*), and it was during half hours spent at that wall, wearing a figurative mackintosh, that I was blown away by *Ariel* without knowing that Sylvia Plath had killed herself, and fell under the spell of *North* clueless as to who Seamus Heaney might be.

The force of such pure shocks of language—made only more blissful by the merely flickering intelligibility, to my immature self, of versified English—features significantly in the work of O'Connor, which gives us characters who are, in their empty-headedness, unusually vulnerable to the thrilling mystery of religious speech. More generally, it's a force that highlights one's natural ambivalence about biography and the cloud it places between the reader and the words. The mystery of the unknown is lost; distractions creep in. It is questionable, for example, that an appreciation of V. S. Naipaul's work is much improved by knowing the particulars of his marital nastiness, or that the value of such improvement exceeds its cost—namely, a diminishment in the autonomy that an artistic text formally, if feebly, claims for itself. Fiction necessarily insists on a separation between itself and an extrinsic world that includes the possibly vile, possibly virtuous author: Why, otherwise, create a self-contained body of words? How, otherwise, can a novel generate its moral authority?

The literary significance of mystery, the interrelations of fictive text and actual text-maker—these are particularly charged issues in the case of Flannery O'Connor. Her work (like that of Plath, a contemporary) is hard for a reader to approach without being dazzled by a high beam of personal myths— the reclusiveness, the lupus, the pathetically short life span (1925–1964). Now we have Brad Gooch's *Flannery*, its subject's first major biography and a more controlled illumination of the background to O'Connor's two novels and two story collections. Note that nine further stories may be found in the Library of America's exemplary *O'Connor*, a single, ingot-like volume that, in addition to the collected fiction, contains select essays, lectures, and letters, not to mention a penetrating chronology of the life. Therefore *Flannery* qualifies *O'Connor*, which is as it should be.

Externally, Flannery O'Connor's life was, except in the matter of her physical travails, uneventful. As she noted with satisfaction, "Lives spent between the house and the chicken yard do not make exciting copy." After all, she was born into the Georgia bourgeoisie, a milieu rarely thought of as action-packed. The O'Connors, descended from mid-nineteenth-century immigrants from Ireland, were unexceptional specimens of the middle class. The Clines, Flannery's maternal line, were also Irish Catholic, but posher and more prosperous, though it is not clear from Gooch's account precisely how their ethnic/religious identity affected their position in the local pecking order (a pity, because social nuances are important in O'Connor's fiction). Flannery grew up—in Savannah and in Atlanta and, from 1938, in the Cline mansion in Milledgeville—with black servants floating around and a sense of herself as part of the genteel, bigoted, spottily educated stratum of landed whites. An only child, she was treated as a brilliant case almost from infancy. Though she was hopeless at math and spelling, everyone seems to have recognized that her confidence and strangeness—the young Flannery was sardonic, marginal, good at cartooning, obsessed with ducks and chickens—were the signs of giftedness. Hers was a well-nurtured, happy childhood, except that in 1941 her gentle, failed-realtor father died from lupus erythematosus, an incurable disease in which the immune system fatally attacks the sufferer's vital organs.

The following year, Flannery went off to Georgia State College for Women— 5
went off being slightly misleading, given that the college was a block from her home. There she began to write with growing seriousness. Although O'Connor is commonly perceived as an outsider artist—the crippled, eccentric scribbler—she was in fact from the beginning very much an insider. Her career ladder, with its institutional rungs, was a prototype of the ladder young writers still seek to scramble up. Indeed, they'd kill for the résumé:

1945–48: University of Iowa Writers' Workshop, winning prizes and fellowships. Magazines begin publishing her stories.

1948–49: Lengthy residence at Yaddo, stories in *Partisan Review*.

1952: First novel, *Wise Blood*, published.

1955: *A Good Man Is Hard to Find* (stories). Finalist, National Book Award, and a commercial hit.

1956 and onward: Fellowships and O. Henry Awards and lecturing invitations and grants (including $8,000 from the Ford Foundation).

1960: *The Violent Bear It Away* (novel). Finalist, National Book Award.

1965: *Everything That Rises Must Converge* (stories). Finalist, National Book Award.

1971: *The Complete Stories*. Winner, National Book Award.

1971–: Literary immortality.

Thus O'Connor never experienced professional hardship. Her belief in herself and sense of vocation were never shaken. She was famous and revered by her early 30s. ("How we did adore and envy them, the idols of our college years—Hemingway and Faulkner, Frost and Eliot, Mary McCarthy and Flannery O'Connor and Eudora Welty!" wrote John Updike. He was seven years younger than O'Connor.) She never lacked for a prestigious mentor (Robert Lowell, Philip Rahv, Robert Penn Warren) or for helpful friends. She never had to take a job. From 1951, she lived at Andalusia, the Georgia property (500 acres of fields and 1,000 acres of woods) co-owned and farmed by her mother, Regina, which turned out to be the perfect habitat for her imagination. Her personal needs were few: she seemingly never wanted, and therefore was never distracted by, children or by her lack thereof. Ditto, pretty much, lovers. Genuinely cerebral, she apparently received ample emotional gratification from her collection of exotic barnyard fowl (peacocks and swans as well as chickens), from her piety, and from her intellectual endeavors. She regularly entertained visitors and was sustained by the friendship of interesting and loyal correspondents, Elizabeth Bishop among them. In sum, she was a great writer but also a fortunate one. This bears emphasizing in light of her exceedingly unfortunate medical history.

To summarize: O'Connor was diagnosed with lupus when she was 25, although she was not told the truth for more than a year. The disease caused her joint pain in the arms, hips, and shoulders; required blood transfusions and ACTH injections and bed rest; weakened her horribly. There was severe hair loss, and at 29 she needed a cane to walk. At 34, she had trouble eating because of necrosis in her jaws; thereafter her ailments became ever more painful and grotesque and immobilizing, as if her well-being had been entrusted to Samuel Beckett. But O'Connor unwell was as purposeful and witty and free of desperation as O'Connor healthy. She was given to dutifulness, religious and artistic, and this strengthened her. She put in two hours a day at the typewriter, even after receiving the sacrament of the dying.

O'Connor was a fervent Roman Catholic—a "thirteenth century" Catholic, as she described herself. She read deeply into theology, with a special interest in Teilhard de Chardin. She went to Mass every day she could, invariably accompanied by her mother. Flannery and Regina's claustrophobic, mutually dependent relationship was inevitably vexing for both women—and mortifying for the daughter when the mother revealed to visitors her own less than edified social attitudes. These domestic circumstances, in combination with Flannery's religiosity and visibly worsening health, hardly form a propitious setup for a gentleman caller. But one did materialize. In 1953, she began to receive visits from Erik Langkjaer, a handsome, thoughtful Dane whose work as a college-textbook salesman regularly brought him to the Milledgeville area. The friendship became, Gooch writes, "at least tinged with romance." On a drive together, they shared a fateful kiss. Langkjaer, in one of the biography's most powerful passages, remembers this:

> She had no real muscle tension in her mouth, a result being that my own lips touched her teeth rather than lips, and this gave me an unhappy feeling of a sort of memento mori, and so the kissing stopped . . . I had a feeling of kissing a skeleton, and in that sense it was a shocking experience.

It is very hard, reading this kind of thing, not to feel great sympathy for O'Connor and mix the feeling into one's evaluation of her work. She herself would have rejected such a mixture. "My lupus has no business in literary considerations," she maintained. This was true not only for critics but for the writer herself. O'Connor's fiction gives few signs of her disease. *Wise Blood* was more or less completed before the diagnosis, and her subsequent writing obviously was cut from the same pre-lupine bolt of obsessions.

Flannery O'Connor's preoccupations are so insistent that it is probably not ideal to read her work from beginning to end in one go, as I did. Again and again, the same dynamic impresses itself: A and B and—why not?—C reveal their more or less cretinous moral natures and slide toward a bizarre, often violent crisis, the whole production unfolding under the auspices of a solar or lunar drama ("A fat yellow moon appeared in the branches of the fig tree as if it were going to roost there with the chickens"). Her settings are agrarian, static, unscientific, largely insulated from modern modes of information and movement. We are given a tragicomic world of dirt roads, pigs, girls who are "practically morons," "trashy" whites, idiotic "niggers," and every stripe of schemer and nitwitted chatterer. The dramatic premises are almost premodern, very easily concerned with religious visionaries or with the arrival, into an unchanging locale, of a stranger. Grassroots evangelical Protestantism and its defective adherents are objects of fascination, though the appearance of an urbane secular party is generally a cue for a particularly grievous display of stupidity and pride. The characters are not "likeable," but my God they are alive. The writing is almost unfairly good:

> She lay her head back and as he watched, gradually her eyes closed and her mouth fell open to show a few long scattered teeth, some gold and some darker than her face; she began to whistle and blow like a musical skeleton.

Or (upon the arrival of refugee Poles at a farm):

> She began to imagine a war of words, to see the Polish words and the English words coming at each other, stalking forward, not sentences, just words, gabble gabble gabble, flung out high and shrill and stalking forward and then grappling with each other. She saw the Polish words, dirty and all-knowing and unreformed, flinging mud on the clean English words until everything was equally dirty. She saw them all piled up in a room, all the dead dirty words, theirs and hers too, piled up like the naked bodies in the newsreel. God save me, she cried silently, from the stinking power of Satan!

The narrating third person hovers in an almost miraculous fusion of proximity and comic distance. With O'Connor, there never seems to be space between the words and their creator's sensibility. You almost never catch a whiff of authorial self-consciousness. About how many writers can this be said?

Of course, you cannot help asking, Are we humans really so awful? Is the world really like this? O'Connor wrote several essays/lectures on these and related questions:

> I am always having it pointed out to me that life in Georgia is not at all the way I picture it, that escaped criminals do not roam the roads exterminating families, nor Bible salesmen prowl about looking for girls with wooden legs.

But her own circumstances, in their sadness and oddness, corroborated her dark fantasies, and, as Gooch shows, many of her stories' outlandish elements were inspired by actual events. O'Connor declared herself a realist, albeit one pushing "toward the limits of mystery." Mystery, in her mind, was concerned with "the ultimate reaches of reality," which is to say, the agency of the divine in human affairs. This is where things become problematic—where the churchgoer glosses her gloriously sullen fiction.

O'Connor was dismissive of any pressure, whether of religious or secular 10 origin, for more "positive" fiction. She saw no contradiction between her faith and her art. Just the opposite: "Because I am a Catholic I cannot afford to be less than an artist." However, she stated,

> the novelist with Christian concerns will find in modern life distortions which are repugnant to him, and his problem will be to make these appear as distortions to an audience which is used to seeing them as natural.

This assertion, taken together with O'Connor's assertion that the central mystery is why human existence "has, for all its horror, been found by God to be worth dying for," constitutes the following argument: (1) from the Christian viewpoint, the modern human condition is filled with a peculiar horror; (2) therefore, to fictionally depict humans in their peculiarly horrifying aspect is necessary in order to explore the mysteries of redemption and grace.

The problem with (1) is that the Christian viewpoint does not necessitate a heightened sensitivity to that which is loathsome about humans or modern times. A heightened love of humans and the lives they create for themselves could just as easily be argued. There is a further problem. The repugnancy of O'Connor's characters is, in *her* portrayal, connected to their poverty and backwardness. Yet in the essays, she is anguished by, and fundamentally hostile to, the forces—ostensibly progressive—that ask us "to form our consciences in the light of statistics." She is hostile, in other words, to the enlightened disturbance of the culture of which the poverty and backwardness are part, and in which characters repugnantly find themselves. Some readers may find that here O'Connor is herself repugnant: that they are faced with one of those people for whom the misery and injustice of human affairs is chiefly a source of egocentric intellectual gratification, and whose political and moral instincts are distorted accordingly. However, it is precisely this troubling feature that gives O'Connor's work its strange power.

One problem with O'Connor the exegesist is that she narrows the scope of her work, even for Catholic readers. To decode her fiction for its doctrinal or supernatural content is to render it dreary, even false, because whatever her private purposes, O'Connor was above all faithful to a baleful comic vision derived, surely, from an ancient, artistically wholesome tradition of misanthropy. Nonetheless, a spiritual drama is playing out. Only it is not the one put forward by the self-explaining author, in which she figures as an onlooker occupying the high ground of piety. On the contrary, Flannery

O'Connor's criticism reveals her as scarily belonging to the low world she evokes. She was touched by evil and no doubt knew it. That is what makes her so wickedly good.

MAKING CONNECTIONS

1. Read O'Neill's account of O'Connor's failings as an interpreter of her own work, then imagine him reading O'Connor's remarks from *Mystery and Manners*. What might O'Neill have to say about O'Connor's self-evaluation as a writer?

2. While admiring O'Connor's writing, O'Neill finds her to be a misanthrope whose view of humankind is confirmed by the misery she sees in the world. Do you agree with his assessment of her? Why or why not?

3. Try to classify the different kinds of approaches taken in the essays in this case study in terms of their critical orientation. Which take biographical information into account? Which take historical information into account? Which put more stock in authorial intention, and which are more concerned with readers' receptions? What is the value in each approach?

POETRY

WILLIAM BLAKE (1757–1827)

THE CHIMNEY SWEEPER 1789

When my mother died I was very young,
And my Father sold me while yet my tongue
Could scarcely cry " 'weep! 'weep! 'weep! 'weep!"
So your chimneys I sweep, and in soot I sleep.

There's little Tom Dacre, who cried when his head,
That curled like a lamb's back, was shaved: so I said,
"Hush, Tom! never mind it, for when your head's bare
You know that the soot cannot spoil your white hair."

And so he was quiet and that very night
As Tom was a-sleeping, he had such a sight!   10
That thousands of sweepers, Dick, Joe, Ned, and Jack,
Were all of them locked up in coffins of black.

And by came an Angel who had a bright key,
And he opened the coffins and set them all free;
Then down a green plain leaping, laughing, they run,
And wash in a river, and shine in the Sun.

Then naked and white, all their bags left behind,
They rise upon clouds and sport in the wind;
And the Angel told Tom, if he'd be a good boy,
He'd have God for his father, and never want joy.   20

And so Tom awoke; and we rose in the dark,
And got with our bags and our brushes to work.
Though the morning was cold, Tom was happy and warm;
So if all do their duty they need not fear harm.

THE LAMB   1789

Little Lamb, who made thee?
Dost thou know who made thee?
Gave thee life, and bid thee feed
By the stream and o'er the mead;
Gave thee clothing of delight,
Softest clothing, wooly, bright;
Gave thee such a tender voice,
Making all the vales rejoice?
Little Lamb, who made thee?
Dost thou know who made thee?   10

Little Lamb, I'll tell thee,
Little Lamb, I'll tell thee:
He is callèd by thy name,
For he calls himself a Lamb.
He is meek, and he is mild;
He became a little child.
I a child, and thou a lamb,
We are callèd by his name.
Little Lamb, God bless thee!
Little Lamb, God bless thee!   20

THE GARDEN OF LOVE   1793

I went to the Garden of Love,
And saw what I never had seen:
A Chapel was built in the midst,
Where I used to play on the green.

And the gates of this Chapel were shut,
And "Thou shalt not" writ over the door;
So I turn'd to the Garden of Love,
That so many sweet flowers bore,

And I saw it was filled with graves,
And tomb-stones where flowers should be: 10
And Priests in black gowns were walking their rounds,
And binding with briars my joys & desires.

FOR ANALYSIS

1. What meanings does the word *love* have in this poem?
2. What is Blake's judgment on established religion?
3. Explain the meaning of *Chapel* (l. 3) and *briars* (l. 12).

WRITING TOPIC

Read the definition of **irony** in "Glossary of Literary Terms." Write an essay in which you distinguish between the types of irony used in "The Chimney Sweeper" and "The Garden of Love."

LONDON   1794

I wander through each chartered[1] street,
Near where the chartered Thames does flow
And mark in every face I meet
Marks of weakness, marks of woe.

In every cry of every man,
In every infant's cry of fear,
In every voice, in every ban,
The mind-forged manacles I hear:

How the chimney-sweeper's cry
Every blackening church appalls,   10
And the hapless soldier's sigh
Runs in blood down palace-walls.

But most, through midnight streets I hear
How the youthful harlot's curse
Blasts the new-born infant's tear,
And blights with plagues the marriage-hearse.

THE TYGER   1794

Tyger! Tyger! burning bright
In the forests of the night,
What immortal hand or eye
Could frame thy fearful symmetry?

London
  [1] Preempted by the state and leased out under royal patent.

In what distant deeps or skies
Burnt the fire of thine eyes?
On what wings dare he aspire?
What the hand dare seize the fire?

And what shoulder, & what art,
Could twist the sinews of thy heart?   10
And when thy heart began to beat,
What dread hand? & what dread feet?

What the hammer? what the chain?
In what furnace was thy brain?
What the anvil? what dread grasp
Dare its deadly terrors clasp?

When the stars threw down their spears,
And water'd heaven with their tears,
Did he smile his work to see?
Did he who made the Lamb make thee?   20

Tyger! Tyger! burning bright
In the forests of the night,
What immortal hand or eye
Dare frame thy fearful symmetry?

ROBERT BROWNING   (1812–1889)

MY LAST DUCHESS   1842

FERRARA

That's my last Duchess painted on the wall,
Looking as if she were alive. I call
That piece a wonder, now: Frà Pandolf's[1] hands
Worked busily a day, and there she stands.
Will't please you sit and look at her? I said
"Frà Pandolf" by design, for never read
Strangers like you that pictured countenance,
The depth and passion of its earnest glance,
But to myself they turned (since none puts by
The curtain I have drawn for you, but I)   10
And seemed as they would ask me, if they durst,

My Last Duchess
    [1] Frà Pandolf and Claus of Innsbruck (who is mentioned in the last line) are fictitious artists.

How such a glance came there; so, not the first
Are you to turn and ask thus. Sir, 'twas not
Her husband's presence only, called that spot
Of joy into the Duchess' cheek: perhaps
Frà Pandolf chanced to say "Her mantle laps
Over my lady's wrist too much," or "Paint
Must never hope to reproduce the faint
Half-flush that dies along her throat": such stuff
Was courtesy, she thought, and cause enough
For calling up that spot of joy. She had　　　　　　　　　20
A heart—how shall I say?—too soon made glad,
Too easily impressed; she liked whate'er
She looked on, and her looks went everywhere.
Sir, 'twas all one! My favor at her breast,
The dropping of the daylight in the West,
The bough of cherries some officious fool
Broke in the orchard for her, the white mule
She rode with round the terrace—all and each
Would draw from her alike the approving speech,　　　30
Or blush, at least. She thanked men—good! but thanked
Somehow—I know not how—as if she ranked
My gift of a nine-hundred-years-old name
With anybody's gift. Who'd stoop to blame
This sort of trifling? Even had you skill
In speech—which I have not—to make your will
Quite clear to such an one, and say, "Just this
Or that in you disgusts me; here you miss,
Or there exceed the mark"—and if she let
Herself be lessoned° so, nor plainly set　　　　　　　taught　40
Her wits to yours, forsooth, and made excuse,
—E'en then would be some stooping; and I choose
Never to stoop. Oh sir, she smiled, no doubt,
Whene'er I passed her; but who passed without
Much the same smile? This grew; I gave commands;
Then all smiles stopped together. There she stands
As if alive. Will't please you rise? We'll meet
The company below, then. I repeat,
The Count your master's known munificence°　　　　generosity
Is ample warrant that no just pretense　　　　　　　50
Of mine for dowry will be disallowed;
Though his fair daughter's self, as I avowed
At starting, is my object. Nay, we'll go
Together down, sir. Notice Neptune, though,

Taming a sea-horse, thought a rarity,
Which Claus of Innsbruck cast in bronze for me!

FOR ANALYSIS

1. To whom is the duke speaking, and what is the occasion?

2. What does a comparison between the duke's feelings about his artwork and his feelings about his last duchess reveal about his character?

3. Does this poem rely on **irony**? Explain.

WRITING TOPIC

Write an essay in which you argue that the reader either is or is not meant to sympathize with the duke's **characterization** of his wife.

EMILY DICKINSON   (1830–1886)

I FELT A FUNERAL, IN MY BRAIN   1861

I felt a Funeral, in my Brain,
And Mourners to and fro
Kept treading—treading—till it seemed
That Sense was breaking through—

And when they all were seated,
A Service, like a Drum—
Kept beating—beating—till I thought
My Mind was going numb—

And then I heard them lift a Box
And creak across my Soul   10
With those same Boots of Lead, again,
Then Space—began to toll,

As all the Heavens were a Bell,
And Being, but an Ear,
And I, and Silence, some strange Race
Wrecked, solitary, here—

And then a Plank in Reason, broke,
And I dropped down, and down—
And hit a World, at every plunge,
And Finished knowing—then—   20

THOMAS HARDY   (1840–1928)

THE RUINED MAID   1902

"O 'Melia, my dear, this does everything crown!
Who could have supposed I should meet you in Town?
And whence such fair garments, such prosperi-ty?"
"O didn't you know I'd been ruined?" said she.

"You left us in tatters, without shoes or socks,
Tired of digging potatoes, and spudding up docks;°   digging herbs
And now you've gay bracelets and bright feathers three!"
"Yes: that's how we dress when we're ruined," said she.

"At home in the barton° you said 'thee' and 'thou,'   farmyard
And 'thik oon,' and 'theäs oon,' and 't'other'; but now   10
Your talking quite fits 'ee for high compa-ny!"
"Some polish is gained with one's ruin," said she.

"Your hands were like paws then, your face blue and bleak
But now I'm bewitched by your delicate cheek,
And your little gloves fit as on any la-dy!"
"We never do work when we're ruined," said she.

"You used to call home-life a hag-ridden dream,
And you'd sigh, and you'd sock; but at present you seem
To know not of megrims° or melancho-ly!"   sick headaches
"True. One's pretty lively when ruined," said she.   20

"I wish I had feathers, a fine sweeping gown,
And a delicate face, and could strut about Town!"
"My dear—a raw country girl, such as you be,
Cannot quite expect that. You ain't ruined," said she.

GERARD MANLEY HOPKINS   (1844–1889)

SPRING AND FALL   1880

TO A YOUNG CHILD

Márgarét, áre you gríeving
Over Goldengrove unleaving?°   losing leaves
Leáves, líke the things of man, you
With your fresh thoughts care for, can you?

182

Áh! ás the heart grows older
It will come to such sights colder
By and by, nor spare a sigh
Though worlds of wanwood leafmeal[1] lie;
And yet you wíll weep and know why.
Now no matter, child, the name: 10
Sórrow's spríngs áre the same.
Nor mouth had, no nor mind, expressed
What heart heard of, ghost° guessed: soul
It ís the blight man was born for,
It is Margaret you mourn for.

FOR ANALYSIS

1. In this poem Margaret grieves over the passing of spring and the coming of fall. What does the coming of fall **symbolize**?

2. Why, when Margaret grows older, will she not sigh over the coming of fall?

3. What are "Sórrow's spríngs" (l. 11)?

A. E. HOUSMAN   (1859–1936)

TERENCE, THIS IS STUPID STUFF[1]   1896

"Terence, this is stupid stuff:
You eat your victuals fast enough;
There can't be much amiss, 'tis clear,
To see the rate you drink your beer.
But oh, good Lord, the verse you make,
It gives a chap the bellyache.
The cow, the old cow, she is dead;
It sleeps well, the hornéd head:
We poor lads, 'tis our turn now
To hear such tunes as killed the cow.   10
Pretty friendship 'tis to rhyme
Your friends to death before their time
Moping melancholy mad:
Come, pipe a tune to dance to, lad."

Spring and Fall
   [1] Pale woods littered with mouldering leaves.

Terence, This Is Stupid Stuff
   [1] Housman originally titled the volume in which this poem appeared *The Poems of Terence Hearsay.*
Terence was a Roman satiric playwright.

Why, if 'tis dancing you would be,
There's brisker pipes than poetry.
Say, for what were hopyards meant,
Or why was Burton built on Trent?[2]
Oh many a peer of England brews
Livelier liquor than the Muse,
And malt does more than Milton can
To justify God's ways to man.[3]
Ale, man, ale's the stuff to drink
For fellows whom it hurts to think:
Look into the pewter pot
To see the world as the world's not.
And faith, 'tis pleasant till 'tis past:
The mischief is that 'twill not last.
Oh I have been to Ludlow fair
And left my necktie God knows where,
And carried halfway home, or near,
Pints and quarts of Ludlow beer:
Then the world seemed none so bad,
And I myself a sterling lad;
And down in lovely muck I've lain,
Happy till I woke again.
Then I saw the morning sky:
Heigho, the tale was all a lie;
The world, it was the old world yet,
I was I, my things were wet,
And nothing now remained to do
But begin the game anew.

Therefore, since the world has still
Much good, but much less good than ill,
And while the sun and moon endure
Luck's a chance, but trouble's sure,
I'd face it as a wise man would,
And train for ill and not for good.
'Tis true the stuff I bring for sale
Is not so brisk a brew as ale:
Out of a stem that scored the hand
I wrung it in a weary land.
But take it: if the smack is sour,
The better for the embittered hour;

---

[2] The river Trent provides water for the town's brewing industry.
[3] In the invocation to *Paradise Lost*, Milton declares that his epic will "justify the ways of God to men."

It should do good to heart and head
When your soul is in my soul's stead;
And I will friend you, if I may,
In the dark and cloudy day.

There was a king reigned in the East:
There, when kings will sit to feast,   60
They get their fill before they think
With poisoned meat and poisoned drink.
He gathered all that springs to birth
From the many-venomed earth;
First a little, thence to more,
He sampled all her killing store;
And easy, smiling, seasoned sound,
Sate the king when healths went round.
They put arsenic in his meat
And stared aghast to watch him eat;   70
They poured strychnine in his cup
And shook to see him drink it up:
They shook, they stared as white's their shirt:
Them it was their poison hurt.
—I tell the tale that I heard told.
Mithridates, he died old.[4]

FOR ANALYSIS

1. What does the speaker of the first fourteen lines object to in Terence's poetry?

2. What is Terence's response to the criticism of his verse? What function of true poetry is implied by his comparison of bad poetry with liquor?

WRITING TOPIC

How does the story of Mithridates (ll. 59–76) illustrate the **theme** of the poem?

WHEN I WAS ONE-AND-TWENTY   1896

When I was one-and-twenty
    I heard a wise man say,
"Give crowns and pounds and guineas
    But not your heart away;

Terence, This Is Stupid Stuff
[4] Mithridates, the King of Pontus (in Asia Minor), reputedly immunized himself against poisons by administering to himself gradually increasing doses.

Give pearls away and rubies
    But keep your fancy free."
But I was one-and-twenty,
    No use to talk to me.

When I was one-and-twenty
    I heard him say again,
"The heart out of the bosom
    Was never given in vain;
'Tis paid with sighs a plenty
    And sold for endless rue."
And I am two-and-twenty,
    And oh, 'tis true, 'tis true.

WILLIAM BUTLER YEATS (1865-1939)

LEDA AND THE SWAN[1]   1928

A sudden blow: the great wings beating still
Above the staggering girl, her thighs caressed
By the dark webs, her nape caught in his bill,
He holds her helpless breast upon his breast.

How can those terrified vague fingers push
The feathered glory from her loosening thighs?
And how can body, laid in that white rush,
But feel the strange heart beating where it lies?

A shudder in the loins engenders there
The broken wall, the burning roof and tower
And Agamemnon dead.
                Being so caught up,
So mastered by the brute blood of the air,
Did she put on his knowledge with his power
Before the indifferent beak could let her drop?

Leda and the Swan
  [1] In Greek myth, Zeus, in the form of a swan, rapes Leda. As a consequence, Helen and Clytemnestra are born. Each sister marries the king of a city-state: Helen marries Menelaus, and Clytemnestra marries Agamemnon. Helen, the most beautiful woman on Earth, elopes with Paris, a prince of Troy, an act that precipitates the Trojan War in which Agamemnon commands the combined Greek armies. The war ends with the destruction of Troy. Agamemnon, when he returns to his home, is murdered by his unfaithful wife.

ROBERT FROST (1874–1963)

THE ROAD NOT TAKEN 1915

Two roads diverged in a yellow wood,
And sorry I could not travel both
And be one traveler, long I stood
And looked down one as far as I could
To where it bent in the undergrowth;

Then took the other, as just as fair,
And having perhaps the better claim,
Because it was grassy and wanted wear;
Though as for that the passing there
Had worn them really about the same,   10

And both that morning equally lay
In leaves no step had trodden black.
Oh, I kept the first for another day!
Yet knowing how way leads on to way,
I doubted if I should ever come back.

I shall be telling this with a sigh
Somewhere ages and ages hence:
Two roads diverged in a wood, and I—
I took the one less traveled by,
And that has made all the difference.   20

BIRCHES 1916

When I see birches bend to left and right
Across the lines of straighter darker trees,
I like to think some boy's been swinging them.
But swinging doesn't bend them down to stay
As ice-storms do. Often you must have seen them
Loaded with ice a sunny winter morning
After a rain. They click upon themselves
As the breeze rises, and turn many-colored
As the stir cracks and crazes their enamel.
Soon the sun's warmth makes them shed crystal shells   10
Shattering and avalanching on the snow-crust—
Such heaps of broken glass to sweep away
You'd think the inner dome of heaven had fallen.
They are dragged to the withered bracken by the load,

And they seem not to break; though once they are bowed
So low for long, they never right themselves:
You may see their trunks arching in the woods
Years afterwards, trailing their leaves on the ground
Like girls on hands and knees that throw their hair
Before them over their heads to dry in the sun.   20
But I was going to say when Truth broke in
With all her matter-of-fact about the ice-storm
I should prefer to have some boy bend them
As he went out and in to fetch the cows—
Some boy too far from town to learn baseball,
Whose only play was what he found himself,
Summer or winter, and could play alone.
One by one he subdued his father's trees
By riding them down over and over again
Until he took the stiffness out of them,   30
And not one but hung limp, not one was left
For him to conquer. He learned all there was
To learn about not launching out too soon
And so not carrying the tree away
Clear to the ground. He always kept his poise
To the top branches, climbing carefully
With the same pains you use to fill a cup
Up to the brim, and even above the brim.
Then he flung outward, feet first, with a swish,
Kicking his way down through the air to the ground.   40
So was I once myself a swinger of birches.
And so I dream of going back to be.
It's when I'm weary of considerations,
And life is too much like a pathless wood
Where your face burns and tickles with the cobwebs
Broken across it, and one eye is weeping
From a twig's having lashed across it open.
I'd like to get away from earth awhile
And then come back to it and begin over.
May no fate willfully misunderstand me   50
And half grant what I wish and snatch me away
Not to return. Earth's the right place for love:
I don't know where it's likely to go better.
I'd like to go by climbing a birch tree,
And climb black branches up a snow-white trunk
Toward heaven, till the tree could bear no more,
But dipped its top and set me down again.
That would be good both going and coming back.
One could do worse than be a swinger of birches.

E. E. CUMMINGS (1894–1962)

IN JUST- 1923

in Just-
spring   when the world is mud-
luscious the little
lame balloonman

whistles   far   and wee

and eddieandbill come
running from marbles and
piracies and it's
spring

when the world is puddle-wonderful   10

the queer
old balloonman whistles
far   and   wee
and bettyandisbel come dancing

from hop-scotch and jump-rope and

it's
spring
and
   the

     goat-footed   20

balloonMan   whistles
far
and
wee

STEVIE SMITH (1902–1971)

NOT WAVING BUT DROWNING 1957

Nobody heard him, the dead man,
But still he lay moaning:
I was much further out than you thought
And not waving but drowning.

Poor chap, he always loved larking
And now he's dead
It must have been too cold for him his heart gave way,
They said.

Oh, no no no, it was too cold always
(Still the dead one lay moaning)   10
I was much too far out all my life
And not waving but drowning.

FOR ANALYSIS

1. Explain the **paradox** in the first and last **stanzas**, where the speaker describes someone dead as moaning. Who do you suppose the *you* of line 3 is? The *They* of line 8?

2. Explain the meaning of line 7. Can it be interpreted in more than one way?

3. Explain the meanings of *drowning*.

4. The only thing we learn about the dead man is that "he always loved larking" (l. 5). Why is this detail significant? What kind of man do you think he was?

5. Does the speaker know more about the dead man than the man's friends do? Explain.

WRITING TOPICS

1. Write an essay describing how you or someone you know suffered the experience of "not waving but drowning."

2. Write an essay describing how you came to the realization that someone close to you was not the person you thought he or she was.

TO CARRY THE CHILD   1966

To carry the child into adult life
Is good? I say it is not,
To carry the child into adult life
Is to be handicapped.

The child in adult life is defenceless
And if he is grown-up, knows it,
And the grown-up looks at the childish part
And despises it.

The child, too, despises the clever grown-up,
The man-of-the-world, the frozen,   10
For the child has the tears alive on his cheek
And the man has none of them.

As the child has colours, and the man sees no
Colours or anything,
Being easy only in things of the mind,
The child is easy in feeling.

Easy in feeling, easily excessive
And in excess powerful,
For instance, if you do not speak to the child
He will make trouble.   20

You would say a man had the upper hand
Of the child, if a child survive,
But I say the child has fingers of strength
To strangle the man alive.

Oh! it is not happy, it is never happy,
To carry the child into adulthood,
Let the children lie down before full growth
And die in their infanthood
And be guilty of no man's blood.

But oh the poor child, the poor child, what can he do,   30
Trapped in a grown-up carapace,
But peer outside of his prison room
With the eye of an anarchist?

COUNTEE CULLEN   (1903-1946)

INCIDENT   1925

Once riding in old Baltimore,
    Heart-filled, head-filled with glee,
I saw a Baltimorean
    Keep looking straight at me.

Now I was eight and very small,
    And he was no whit bigger,
And so I smiled, but he poked out
    His tongue and called me, "Nigger."

I saw the whole of Baltimore
    From May until December: 10
Of all the things that happened there
    That's all that I remember.

DYLAN THOMAS   (1914–1953)

FERN HILL   1946

Now as I was young and easy under the apple boughs
About the lilting house and happy as the grass was green,
    The night above the dingle° starry,   small wooded valley
        Time let me hail and climb
    Golden in the heydays of his eyes,
And honored among wagons I was prince of the apple towns
And once below a time I lordly had the trees and leaves
        Trail with daisies and barley
    Down the rivers of the windfall light.

And as I was green and carefree, famous among the barns   10
About the happy yard and singing as the farm was home,
    In the sun that is young once only,
        Time let me play and be
    Golden in the mercy of his means,
And green and golden I was huntsman and herdsman, the calves
Sang to my horn, the foxes on the hills barked clear and cold,
        And the sabbath rang slowly
    In the pebbles of the holy streams.

All the sun long it was running, it was lovely, the hay
Fields high as the house, the tunes from the chimneys, it was air   20
    And playing, lovely and watery
        And fire green as grass.
    And nightly under the simple stars
As I rode to sleep the owls were bearing the farm away,
All the moon long I heard, blessed among stables, the nightjars[1]
    Flying with the ricks, and the horses
        Flashing into the dark.

And then to awake, and the farm, like a wanderer white
With the dew, come back, the cock on his shoulder: it was all
    Shining, it was Adam and maiden,   30
        The sky gathered again
    And the sun grew round that very day.
So it must have been after the birth of the simple light
In the first, spinning place, the spellbound horses walking warm
    Out of the whinnying green stable
        On to the fields of praise.

[1] Nightjars are nocturnal birds.

And honored among foxes and pheasants by the gay house
Under the new made clouds and happy as the heart was long,
    In the sun born over and over,
        I ran my heedless ways,   40
    My wishes raced through the house high hay
And nothing I cared, at my sky blue trades, that time allows
In all his tuneful turning so few and such morning songs
    Before the children green and golden
        Follow him out of grace.

Nothing I cared, in the lamb white days, that time would take me
Up to the swallow thronged loft by the shadow of my hand,
    In the moon that is always rising,
        Nor that riding to sleep
    I should hear him fly with the high fields   50
And wake to the farm forever fled from the childless land.
Oh as I was young and easy in the mercy of his means,
        Time held me green and dying
    Though I sang in my chains like the sea.

FOR ANALYSIS

1. What emotional impact does the color **imagery** in the poem provide?

2. Trace the behavior of "time" in the poem.

3. Fairy tales often begin with the words "once upon a time." Why does Thomas alter that formula in line 7?

4. Explain the **paradox** in line 53.

WRITING TOPICS

1. Lines 17–18, 30, and 45–46 incorporate religious language and biblical **allusion**. How do those allusions clarify the poet's vision of his childhood?

2. Compare this poem with either Hopkins's "Spring and Fall" (p. 182) or Housman's "When I Was One-and-Twenty" (p. 185).

LAWRENCE FERLINGHETTI   (B. 1919)

CONSTANTLY RISKING ABSURDITY   1958

        Constantly risking absurdity
                        and death
            whenever he performs
                        above the heads
                                    of his audience

                    the poet like an acrobat
                              climbs on rime
                                        to a high wire of his own making
and balancing on eyebeams
                              above a sea of faces   10
              paces his way
                        to the other side of day
performing entrechats[1]
                        and sleight-of-foot tricks
and other high theatrics
                        and all without mistaking
              any thing
                        for what it may not be

        For he's the super realist
                              who must perforce perceive   20
                taut truth
                        before the taking of each stance or step
        in his supposed advance
                              toward that still higher perch
where Beauty stands and waits
                    with gravity
                              to start her death-defying leap

And he
        a little charleychaplin[2] man
                              who may or may not catch   30
              her fair eternal form
                        spreadeagled in the empty air
              of existence

PHILIP LARKIN   (1922–1985)

A STUDY OF READING HABITS   1960

When getting my nose in a book
Cured most things short of school,
It was worth ruining my eyes
To know I could still keep cool,

Constantly Risking Absurdity
   [1] In ballet, a leap straight upward in which the legs are repeatedly crossed or heels struck together.
   [2] Charles Spencer Chaplin (1889–1977) was cinema's most celebrated comedian of the silent-film era. His trademark was the mustachioed Little Tramp, whose pathos and comedy were accompanied by extraordinary acrobatic skills.

And deal out the old right hook
To dirty dogs twice my size.

Later, with inch-thick specs,
Evil was just my lark:
Me and my cloak and fangs
Had ripping times in the dark.   10
The women I clubbed with sex!
I broke them up like meringues.

Don't read much now: the dude
Who lets the girl down before
The hero arrives, the chap
Who's yellow and keeps the store,
Seem far too familiar. Get stewed:
Books are a load of crap.

FOR ANALYSIS

1. What different sorts of books did the speaker read as a schoolchild (stanza 1)?

2. How might reading cure "most things short of school" (l. 2)?

3. Describe the change in the speaker's reading habits revealed in the second **stanza**.

4. Explain why the speaker asserts that he doesn't read much now (l. 13). What experiences led him to the conclusion that "[b]ooks are a load of crap" (l. 18)?

WRITING TOPIC

Describe the poem's metrical pattern and its **rhyme** scheme. See **ballad** in the "Glossary of Literary Terms," read some ballads in this book, and argue for or against the proposition that this poem is a modern ballad.

THIS BE THE VERSE   1974

They fuck you up, your mum and dad.
    They may not mean to, but they do.
They fill you with the faults they had
    And add some extra, just for you.

But they were fucked up in their turn
    By fools in old-style hats and coats,
Who half the time were soppy-stern
    And half at one another's throats.

Man hands on misery to man.
   It deepens like a coastal shelf.
Get out as early as you can,
   And don't have any kids yourself.   10

AUDRE LORDE   (1934–1992)

HANGING FIRE   1978

I am fourteen
and my skin has betrayed me
the boy I cannot live without
still sucks his thumb
in secret
how come my knees are
always so ashy
what if I die
before morning
and momma's in the bedroom   10
with the door closed.

I have to learn how to dance
in time for the next party
my room is too small for me
suppose I die before graduation
they will sing sad melodies
but finally
tell the truth about me
There is nothing I want to do
and too much   20
that has to be done
and momma's in the bedroom
with the door closed.

Nobody even stops to think
about my side of it
I should have been on Math Team
my marks were better than his
why do I have to be
the one
wearing braces   30
I have nothing to wear tomorrow
will I live long enough

to grow up
and momma's in the bedroom
with the door closed.

FOR ANALYSIS

1. How do you think the speaker's skin has "betrayed" her (l. 2)?

2. What does the expression *hang fire* mean? In what ways is the speaker hanging fire?

MAKING CONNECTIONS

Compare the speaker's repeated statements about her fear of death in "Hanging Fire" to the wounded child in Hanan Mikha'il 'Ashrawi's "From the Diary of an Almost-Four-Year-Old" (p. 200). What is different about the attitudes expressed—toward life, toward death, toward growing up—in these two poems?

WRITING TOPICS

1. Look up the origins of the phrase used in the poem's title. Where does it come from? Is there anything about this original meaning that might add to the poem's meaning?

2. Analyze the structure of the poem—how it is divided into parts, how certain lines and images and feelings are repeated. How does the structure enrich the poem's meaning?

JEAN NORDHAUS   (B. 1939)

A DANDELION FOR MY MOTHER   2006

How I loved those spiky suns,
rooted stubborn as childhood
in the grass, tough as the farmer's
big-headed children—the mats
of yellow hair, the bowl-cut fringe.
How sturdy they were and how
slowly they turned themselves
into galaxies, domes of ghost stars
barely visible by day, pale
cerebrums clinging to life   10
on tough green stems.   Like you.
Like you, In the end.   If you were here,
I'd pluck this trembling globe to show
how beautiful a thing can be
a breath will tear away.

LOUISE GLÜCK (B. 1943)

THE SCHOOL CHILDREN 1975

The children go forward with their little satchels.
And all morning the mothers have labored
to gather the late apples, red and gold,
like words of another language.

And on the other shore
are those who wait behind great desks
to receive these offerings.

How orderly they are—the nails
on which the children hang
their overcoats of blue or yellow wool.   10

And the teachers shall instruct them in silence
and the mothers shall scour the orchards for a way out,
drawing to themselves the gray limbs of the fruit trees
bearing so little ammunition.

ALAN FELDMAN (B. 1945)

MY CENTURY 2001

The year I was born the atomic bomb went off.
Here I'd just begun, and someone
found the switch to turn off the world.

In the furnace-light, in the central solar fire
of that heat lamp, the future got very finite,
and it was possible to imagine time-travelers

failing to arrive, because there was no future.
Inside the great dark clock in the hall,
heavy brass cylinders descended.

Tick-tock, the chimes changed their tune   10
one phrase at a time. The bomb became
a film star, its glamorous globe of smoke

searing the faces of men in beach chairs.
Someone threw up every day at school.
No time to worry about collective death,

when life itself was permeated by ordeals.
And so we grew up, beneath an umbrella of acceptance.
In bio we learned there were particles

cruising through us like whales through archipelagoes,
and in civics that if Hitler had gotten the bomb   20
he'd have used it on the inferior races,

and all this time love was etching its scars
on our skins like maps. The heavens
remained pure, except for little white slits

on the perfect blue skin that planes cut
in the icy upper air, like needles sewing.
From one, a tiny seed might fall

that would make a sun on earth.
And so the century passed, with me still in it,
books waiting on the shelves to become cinders,   30

what we felt locked up inside, waiting to be read,
down the long corridor of time. I was born
the year the bomb exploded. Twice

whole cities were charred like cities in the Bible,
but we didn't look back. We went on thinking
we could go on, our shapes the same,

darkened now against a background lit by fire.
Forgive me for doubting you're there,
Citizens, on your holodecks with earth wallpaper—

a shadow-toned ancestor with poorly pressed pants,   40
protected like a child from knowing the future.

FOR ANALYSIS

1. What kinds of **images** appear in this poem? Natural? Man-made? Large? Small?
Why do you think Feldman chose the combination of images that he did?

2. What sense of time does this poem have? What might it be trying to express?

3. What is this poem's central **paradox**? Where is it first named?

WRITING TOPIC

Find a significant historical event that occurred in the year of your birth. In a poem, a short story, or an essay, reflect on the event's significance to you, or to humankind, or simply to the people to whom it happened.

HANAN MIKHA'IL 'ASHRAWI   (B. 1946)

FROM THE DIARY OF AN ALMOST-FOUR-YEAR-OLD   1988

Tomorrow, the bandages
will come off. I wonder
will I see half an orange,
half an apple, half my
mother's face
with my one remaining eye?

I did not see the bullet
but felt its pain
exploding in my head.
His image did not   10
vanish, the soldier
with a big gun, unsteady
hands, and a look in
his eyes
I could not understand.

If I can see him so clearly
with my eyes closed,
it could be that inside our heads
we each have one spare set
of eyes   20
to make up for the ones we lose.

Next month, on my birthday,
I'll have a brand new glass eye,
maybe things will look round
and fat in the middle—
I've gazed through all my marbles,
they made the world look strange.

I hear a nine-month-old
has also lost an eye,

I wonder if my soldier
shot her too—a soldier
looking for little girls who
look him in the eye—
I'm old enough, almost four,
I've seen enough of life,
but she's just a baby
who didn't know any better.

                30

FOR ANALYSIS

1. How was the speaker injured?

2. What words in this poem would not ordinarily be part of the vocabulary of an average four-year-old? Does the use of such language detract from the poem's impact? Explain.

3. Discuss the effect of the words "a look in / his eyes / I could not understand" (ll. 13–15).

4. Discuss the various meanings of "look him in the eye" (l. 33).

5. The speaker contrasts her almost four years of experience with the innocence of a nine-month-old baby. What impact does this have?

WRITING TOPIC

Armed conflict often creates "collateral damage." Define the term. Under what circumstances is such damage morally justified or plainly immoral?

KATHERINE McALPINE (B. 1948)

PLUS C'EST LA MÊME CHOSE[1] 1994

LINES WRITTEN UPON CHAPERONING THE SEVENTH GRADE DANCE

When did these little girls turn into women?
Lip-glossed and groomed, alarmingly possessed
of polish, poise and, in some cases, breasts,
they're clustered at one corner of the gym in
elaborate indifference to the boys,
who, at the other end, convene with cables,

Plus C'est la Même Chose
  [1] The title comes from the French expression *Plus ça change, plus c'est la même chose*, which means "The more things change, the more they remain the same."

adjusting speakers, tuners and turntables
to make the optimum amount of noise.
If nobody plans to dance, what's this dance for?
Finally the boys all gather in formation,   10
tentatively begin a group migration
across the fearsome distance of the floor—
and then retreat, noticing no one's there.
The girls have gone, en masse, to fix their hair.

FOR ANALYSIS

1. What is the **tone** of this **sonnet**? Point to specific elements to support your response.

2. Explain the title.

3. Explain the appropriateness of "elaborate indifference" (l. 5), "gather in formation" (l. 10), and "migration" (l. 11).

WRITING TOPIC

Write an essay in which you use one of the following as a thesis statement: (1) the
poem embodies a traditional, sexist view of gender differences, or (2) the poem
describes, without making a judgment, the culturally determined differences between
males and females. If you disagree with both of these statements, formulate your own.

SANDRA CISNEROS   (B. 1954)

MY WICKED WICKED WAYS   1987

This is my father.
See? He is young.
He looks like Errol Flynn.[1]

He is wearing a hat
that tips over one eye,
a suit that fits him good,
and baggy pants.

He is also wearing
those awful shoes,
the two-toned ones   10
my mother hates.

My Wicked Wicked Ways
[1] Errol Flynn (1909–1959) was a handsome leading man in many Hollywood movies during the
1930s and 1940s.

Here is my mother.
She is not crying.
She cannot look into the lens
because the sun is bright.
The woman,
the one my father knows,
is not here.
She does not come till later.

My mother will get very mad.   20
Her face will turn red
and she will throw one shoe.
My father will say nothing.
After a while everyone
will forget it.
Years and years will pass.
My mother will stop mentioning it.

This is me she is carrying.
I am a baby.
She does not know   30
I will turn out bad.

FOR ANALYSIS

1. Why does the speaker tell us that her mother "is not crying" (l. 13)?
2. What will the speaker's mother "get very mad" about (l. 20)?
3. What is the connection between the last four lines and the rest of the poem?

WRITING TOPIC

Discuss the meaning of the final line of the poem. What does the speaker mean by *bad*?

SANDRA M. CASTILLO   (B. 1962)

CHRISTMAS, 1970   2002

We assemble the silver tree,
our translated lives,
its luminous branches,
numbered to fit into its body.
place its metallic roots
to decorate our first Christmas.
Mother finds herself
opening, closing the Red Cross box

she will carry into 1976
like an unwanted door prize,   10
a timepiece, a stubborn fact,
an emblem of exile measuring our days,
marked by the moment of our departure,
our lives no longer arranged.

Somewhere,
there is a photograph,
a Polaroid Mother cannot remember was ever taken:
I am sitting under Tia Tere's Christmas tree,
her first apartment in this, our new world:
my sisters by my side,   20
I wear a white dress, black boots,
an eight-year-old's resignation;
Mae and Mitzy, age four,
wear red and white snowflake sweaters and identical smiles,
on this, our first Christmas,
away from ourselves.

The future unreal, unmade,
Mother will cry into the new year
with Lidia and Emerito,
our elderly downstairs neighbors,   30
who realize what we are too young to understand:
Even a map cannot show you
the way back to a place
that no longer exists.

FOR ANALYSIS

1. How is the tree described in "Christmas, 1970"? Why do you think it is described in this way?

2. This poem includes a number of details about time, such as dates and ages and references to the past and the future, and about place, such as the different **settings** and the mention of a map. How do place and time intersect in this poem? Why are they important?

3. How does Castillo use verb tense in this poem? How does it change? What do you think it means that it does?

WRITING TOPIC

Recall a significant moment from your childhood when you were "too young to understand" something. What makes you able to understand it now?

SPENCER REECE (B. 1963)

THE MANHATTAN PROJECT 2011

First, J. Robert Oppenheimer wrote his paper on dwarf stars—"What happens to
a massive star that burns out?" he asked. His calculations suggested that instead
of collapsing it would contract indefinitely, under the force of its own gravity.
The bright star would disappear but it would still be there, where there had
been brilliance there would be a blank. Soon after, workers built Oak Ridge, the
accumulation of Cemesto hutments not placed on any map. They built a church,
a school, a bowling alley. From all over, families drove through the muddy ruts.
The ground swelled about the ruts like flesh stitched by sutures. My father, a
child, watched the loads on the tops of their cars tip. Gates let everyone in and out
with a pass. Forbidden to tell anyone they were there, my father's family moved 10
in, quietly, behind the chain-link fence. Niels Bohr said, "This bomb might be
our great hope." My father watched his parents eat breakfast: his father opened
his newspaper across the plate of bacon and eggs, his mother smoked Camel
straights, the ash from her cigarette cometing across the back of the obituaries.
They spoke little. Increasingly the mother drank Wild Turkey with her women
friends from the bowling league. Generators from the Y-12 plant droned their
ambition. There were no birds. General Leslie Groves marched the boardwalks,
yelled, his boots pressed the slates and the mud bubbled up like viscera. My father
watched his father enter the plant. My shy father went to the library, which was
a trailer with a circus tent painted on the side. There he read the definition of 20
"uranium" which was worn to a blur. My father read one Hardy Boys mystery
after another. It was August 1945. The librarian smiled sympathetically at the
12-year-old boy. "Time to go home," the librarian said. They named the bomb
Little Boy. It weighed 9,700 pounds. It was the size of a go-kart. On the battle
cruiser *Augusta*, President Truman said, "This is the greatest thing in history."
That evening, my father's parents mentioned Japanese cities. Everyone was quiet.
It was the quiet of the exhausted and the innocent. The quietness inside my father
was building and would come to define him. I was wrong to judge it. Speak,
Father, and I will listen. And if you do not wish to speak, then I will listen to that.

FOR ANALYSIS

1. Who were J. Robert Oppenheimer, Niels Bohr, and Leslie Groves? Why are they
in this poem? What is the effect of having real people in a poem?

2. How would you describe the form of this poem in terms of **rhythm**, **rhyme**, and
the shape of the lines? Does it look or sound like a poem? What makes it a poem?

3. Why do you think Reece mentions the name of the bomb?

WRITING TOPIC

Write a short essay in which you compare "The Manhattan Project" to Alan
Feldman's "My Century" (p. 198). How do the different poems treat what is almost
the same subject?

EXPERIENCE   2005

When I think of everything I've wanted
I feel sick. There was this night in winter
when Jennifer Scanlon and I were driven
out to the desert to be the only girls there
when the boys got drunk and chose
the weakest among themselves to beat
the living shit out of over and over again
as the dumb night continued in its airy way
to say nothing. I wanted so badly that night
to believe violence was a little bell you could ring   10
and get what you wanted. It seemed to work
for those boys, who'd established order among
the disorderly wilderness using nothing
but a few enthusiastic muscles. Even after
he'd begun bleeding from his nose, the boy
stayed. It was an initiation is what he believed.
Thank god time erases everything
in this steady impeccable way. Now it's like
I never lived that life, never had to, sitting
on a tailgate while Jennifer asked for advice   20
on things she'd already done, watching the stars
waver above us, adoring whatever it was
that allowed those boys to throw themselves
fists first at the world, yell every profanity ever
made into the pried-open ear of the universe.
It often occurred to me then that if only
we could get quiet enough, we'd hear
the universe calling back to us, telling us
what to do next. Of course, if we'd been quiet
we wouldn't have heard anything, and that   30
silence, too, would have ruined us.

SOLIPSISM   1994

I spend days at the gym enclosed by four mirrors,
a silver pole balanced on my shoulders.
I slide keys out of the machines, slot them lower
to lift my weights with increased strain,
to pump the last reps in my personal program.

I watch on television a show that is being taped
in the studio across the hall. It is shown simultaneously
in the green room but will not be broadcast publicly
until next week. I feel very special
yet out of step with the rest of the viewing world.   10

In aerobics class we lie on our backs and pump our hips
repetitively towards the ceiling. Soon lovers will come
to smother us with their bodies, pumping equally.
Now there are only our midriffs rising and lowering,
our shapes contained in lycra and cotton.

I break cold medication out of its blister wrap
in the green room, I swallow sedatives in soothing colours.
The makeup person touches my face with gentle fingers.
She covers me in a smock the colour of roses
and together we watch the changes in the mirror.   20

The faces around me are glazed with perspiration,
their bodies are lovely and plain by turns.
I take my position at the exercise bar between two bodies.
I resume the process of making myself perfect
as they both are, yet not like them, uniquely myself.

I see my body in four funhouse mirrors.
It is shaped exactly like an upended couch.
The gym is a marvel of bodies in motion,
lineups are polite at the popular machines,
active minds are occupied with weight goals, diet instructions.   30

The audience would wave if the camera glanced their way.
It would stampede to the nearest exit in case of fire
or planted bomb, crushing members of its own sex and race.
I am very calm. I have rehearsed my instructions,
not once do I stray from the script or structure.

Journalists declare there are weather and wars
happening outside the fitness-club doors,
but I hear only music and the splash of water fountains.
I only notice how others have tied back their hair.
Rarely do I look outside, for something other or more.   40

FOR ANALYSIS

1. Look up *solipsism* in the dictionary. Is it an appropriate title for this poem?
Explain.

2. Consider the first three lines of the last **stanza**. How do they relate to the central issue of this poem?

3. How might you define *perfect* as it is used in line 24? Can the speaker make herself perfect in the fitness club? Explain.

WRITING TOPICS

1. Describe the circumstances that would allow you to feel that nothing exists or is real but yourself.

2. Using someone you know—or know of—as a model, describe the behavior of a solipsistic person. Do you believe that solipsism is a desirable or an undesirable trait? Explain.

CONNECTING POEMS: REVISITING FAIRY TALES

For centuries, fairy tales were often dark and violent stories that served as warnings to children. More recently, however, they have been tamed, stripped of violence and sexual undertones, and have adopted a new focus on magical worlds and happy endings—seemingly unrealistic views of the human experience. Despite this shift, fairy tales continue to encompass some of the most significant cultural assumptions—fears, beliefs, and ideas about how the world is and should be. The poems in this unit revisit fairy tales that are likely to be familiar to you. As you read the poems, keep the two kinds of fairy tales in mind. Do the poems remain faithful to their innocent models? Do they describe a magical world? Do they end happily? Or do they focus on the darker side of experience? Are they realistic? How does the language in which they are written—the kinds of words and **images** and **tone** they use—reflect their relationship to fairy tales?

ANNE SEXTON   (1928-1974)

CINDERELLA   1971

You always read about it:
the plumber with twelve children
who wins the Irish Sweepstakes.
From toilets to riches.
That story.

Or the nursemaid,
some luscious sweet from Denmark
who captures the oldest son's heart.

From diapers to Dior.
That story.   10

Or a milkman who serves the wealthy,
eggs, cream, butter, yogurt, milk,
the white truck like an ambulance
who goes into real estate
and makes a pile.
From homogenized to martinis at lunch.

Or the charwoman
who is on the bus when it cracks up
and collects enough from the insurance.
From mops to Bonwit Teller.   20
That story.

Once
the wife of a rich man was on her deathbed
and she said to her daughter Cinderella:
Be devout. Be good. Then I will smile
down from heaven in the seam of a cloud.
The man took another wife who had
two daughters, pretty enough
but with hearts like blackjacks.
Cinderella was their maid.   30
She slept on the sooty hearth each night
and walked around looking like Al Jolson.
Her father brought presents home from town,
jewels and gowns for the other women
but the twig of a tree for Cinderella.
She planted that twig on her mother's grave
and it grew to a tree where a white dove sat.
Whenever she wished for anything the dove
would drop it like an egg upon the ground.
The bird is important, my dears, so heed him.   40

Next came the ball, as you all know.
It was a marriage market.
The prince was looking for a wife.
All but Cinderella were preparing
and gussying up for the big event.
Cinderella begged to go too.
Her stepmother threw a dish of lentils
into the cinders and said: Pick them
up in an hour and you shall go.

The white dove brought all his friends;   50
all the warm wings of the fatherland came,
and picked up the lentils in a jiffy.
No, Cinderella, said the stepmother,
you have no clothes and cannot dance.
That's the way with stepmothers.

Cinderella went to the tree at the grave
and cried forth like a gospel singer:
Mama! Mama! My turtledove,
send me to the prince's ball!
The bird dropped down a golden dress   60
and delicate little gold slippers.
Rather a large package for a simple bird.
So she went. Which is no surprise.
Her stepmother and sisters didn't
recognize her without her cinder face
and the prince took her hand on the spot
and danced with no other the whole day.

As nightfall came she thought she'd better
get home. The prince walked her home
and she disappeared into the pigeon house   70
and although the prince took an axe and broke
it open she was gone. Back to her cinders.
These events repeated themselves for three days.
However on the third day the prince
covered the palace steps with cobbler's wax
and Cinderella's gold shoe stuck upon it.

Now he would find whom the shoe fit
and find his strange dancing girl for keeps.
He went to their house and the two sisters
were delighted because they had lovely feet.   80
The eldest went into a room to try the slipper on
but her big toe got in the way so she simply
sliced it off and put on the slipper.
The prince rode away with her until the white dove
told him to look at the blood pouring forth.

That is the way with amputations.
They don't just heal up like a wish.
The other sister cut off her heel
but the blood told as blood will.
The prince was getting tired.   90

He began to feel like a shoe salesman
but he gave it one last try.
This time Cinderella fit into the shoe
like a love letter into its envelope.

At the wedding ceremony
the two sisters came to curry favor
and the white dove pecked their eyes out.
Two hollow spots were left
like soup spoons.

Cinderella and the prince   100
lived, they say, happily ever after,
like two dolls in a museum case
never bothered by diapers or dust,
never arguing over the timing of an egg,
never telling the same story twice,
never getting a middle-aged spread,
their darling smiles pasted on for eternity.
Regular Bobbsey Twins.[1]
That story.

FOR ANALYSIS

1. Where does one usually find the first four "stories" mentioned in the poem? Why
do such stories interest readers?

2. Do you remember your feelings as a child in response to the story of Cinderella—
particularly Cinderella's success? How are those feelings modified by the last **stanza**?

WRITING TOPIC

The language and formal structure of this poem resemble **prose**. Through examination of
the **image** patterns and individual lines, describe the qualities that make the piece a poem.

BRUCE BENNETT (B. 1940)

THE TRUE STORY OF SNOW WHITE   1989

Almost before the princess had grown cold
Upon the floor beside the bitten fruit,
The Queen gave orders to her men to shoot
The dwarfs, and thereby clinched her iron hold

Cinderella
[1] The ever-cheerful central figures in a series of children's books.

Upon the state. Her mirror learned to lie,
And no one dared speak ill of her for fear
She might through her devices overhear.
So, in this manner, many years passed by,
And now today not even children weep
When someone whispers how, for her beauty's sake,   10
A child was harried once into a grove
And doomed, because her heart was full of love,
To lie forever in unlovely sleep
Which not a prince on earth has power to break.

FOR ANALYSIS

1. Describe the **allusion** at the center of this poem, and explain how it contributes to the poem's force.

2. Note that the poem is a **sonnet**. Explain how this choice of form contributes an **ironic** element that reinforces the poem's grim message.

3. Why would the mirror learn "to lie" (l. 5)? What "devices" (l. 7) might frighten the Queen's subjects?

WRITING TOPIC

Compare and contrast this **sonnet** (see "Glossary of Literary Terms") with two others from the text, and characterize each. How do they differ, and how do they resemble one another? Are they personal **lyrics**, political statements, or psychological insights?

MARILYN HACKER   (B. 1942)

CONTE   1981

(CINDERELLA, SOMETIME AFTER THE AFFAIR

OF THE GLASS/FUR SLIPPER)

First of all, I'm bored. It's not
what you'd think. Every day, meetings
I can't attend, I sit and sit and stick
my fingers with petit-point needles. Ladies
ignore me, or tell me all their petty secrets
(petty because *they* can't attend meetings)
about this man or that. Even his mistress—
you would have assumed he had a mistress—
gritted her teeth and had me come to lunch
and whined about the way she was mistreated.   10
And I suppose she's right, she was mistreated.

The plumbing is appalling, but I won't
go into that. He is forever brooding
on lost choices he might have made; before
three days had passed, I'd heard, midnight to dawn,
about the solitary life he craved.
Why *not* throw it all up, live on the coast
and fish, no, no, impossible with wives!
Why *not* throw it all up, live on the coast,
or cut my hair, teach (what?) little girls   20
and live at home with you? I schooled myself
for this, despised *you* for going to meetings,
reading instead of scrubbing, getting fat
(scorn of someone who burns off bread and puddings).
I made enduring tedium my virtue.
I'll have to keep my virtue. I could envy
you, but I'm sick of envy. Please allow
me now, at least, to call you sisters. Yours, C.

FOR ANALYSIS

1. This poem turns out to be a letter. To whom do you think it was written?

2. How does the original fairy tale of Cinderella end? When does this poem's narrative take place? Does it end the same way?

3. A *conte* is a short tale of adventure. Is this poem a short tale of adventure? Why do you think Hacker chose that word for the title?

WRITING TOPIC

Write two of your own letters from one character in a well-known story to another. Make sure the first set of characters you choose is from a story in which things have turned out as expected, and the second set is from a story in which they have not.

KATHARYN HOWD MACHAN (B. 1952)

HAZEL TELLS LAVERNE   1976

last night
im cleanin out my
howard johnsons ladies room
when all of a sudden
up pops this frog
musta come from the sewer
swimmin aroun an tryin ta
climb up the sida the bowl
so i goes ta flushm down

but sohelpmegod he starts talkin 10
bout a golden ball
an how i can be a princess
me a princess
well my mouth drops
all the way to the floor
an he says
kiss me just kiss me
once on the nose
well i screams
ya little green pervert 20
an i hitsm with my mop
an has ta flush
the toilet down three times
me
a princess

FOR ANALYSIS

1. How would you describe Hazel?

2. What does Hazel's language tell us about her?

3. Would the use of punctuation change the poem in any way?

WRITING TOPIC

Write an analysis of this poem's humor.

MAKING CONNECTIONS

1. Compare the endings of Sexton's "Cinderella" (p. 208) and Hacker's "Conte" (p. 212) to the ending of the original story, in terms of both events and **tone**. Is either happy?

2. Each of the original fairy tales on which the selections in this unit are based features royalty. How do the poems handle the element of royalty? What does royalty mean in the originals? What does it mean in these poems?

3. In what ways is each of these poems about the dream of a better life? What do the poems say about those dreams?

CONNECTING POEMS: VOICES OF EXPERIENCE

The poems in this unit explore the role parents, or parental figures, play in guiding children through the innocence of childhood into the world of experience. The poems also address the contradictions and inconsistencies inherent in this role and in the world of human experience. As you read, pay attention not only to the ways the experienced try to guide the innocent—and the difficulties they have doing it—but also to the texture of their voices. How have the poets personalized these voices? How does the way they speak relate to what they have to say? What do the innocent have to say about the advice they are being given, and how does the way the poets have them express their thoughts relate to how we hear them?

LANGSTON HUGHES   (1902–1967)

MOTHER TO SON   1926

Well, son, I'll tell you:
Life for me ain't been no crystal stair.
It's had tacks in it,
And splinters,
And boards torn up,
And places with no carpet on the floor—
Bare.
But all the time
I'se been a-climbin' on,
And reachin' landin's,   10
And turnin' corners,
And sometimes goin' in the dark
Where there ain't been no light.
So boy, don't you turn back.
Don't you set down on the steps
'Cause you finds it's kinder hard.
Don't you fall now—
For I'se still goin', honey,
I'se still climbin',
And life for me ain't been no crystal stair.   20

FOR ANALYSIS

1. What are the two kinds of stairs in this poem? What do they stand for?

2. Analyze the structure of the poem. What are the functions of the various instances of repetition?

WRITING TOPIC

Write a poem, "Son to Mother," in response to Hughes's poem. It should be about the same topic but have a different **point of view**, perhaps with a different **tone** or sense.

PETER MEINKE (B. 1932)

ADVICE TO MY SON 1965

—FOR TIM

The trick is, to live your days
as if each one may be your last
(for they go fast, and young men lose their lives
in strange and unimaginable ways)
but at the same time, plan long range
(for they go slow: if you survive
the shattered windshield and the bursting shell
you will arrive
at our approximation here below
of heaven or hell).   10

To be specific, between the peony and the rose
plant squash and spinach, turnips and tomatoes;
beauty is nectar
and nectar, in a desert, saves—
but the stomach craves stronger sustenance
than the honied vine.
Therefore, marry a pretty girl
after seeing her mother;
speak truth to one man,
work with another;   20
and always serve bread with your wine.

But, son,
always serve wine.

FOR ANALYSIS

1. Explain how the advice of lines 17–21 is logically related to the preceding lines.
2. What do the final two lines tell the reader about the speaker?

WRITING TOPIC

The advice of the first **stanza** seems contradictory. In what ways does the second
stanza attempt to resolve the contradiction or explain the "trick" (l. 1)? What do the
various plants and the bread and wine **symbolize**?

ROBERT MEZEY   (B. 1935)

MY MOTHER   1970

My mother writes from Trenton,
a comedian to the bone
but underneath, serious
and all heart. "Honey," she says,
"be a mensch[1] and Mary too,
it's no good to worry, you
are doing the best you can
your Dad and everyone
thinks you turned out very well
as long as you pay your bills   10
nobody can say a word
you can tell them to drop dead
so save a dollar it can't
hurt—remember Frank you went
to highschool with? he still lives
with his wife's mother, his wife
works while he writes his books and
did he ever sell a one
the four kids run around naked
36 and he's never had,   20
you'll forgive my expression
even a pot to piss in
or a window to throw it,
such a smart boy he couldn't
read the footprints on the wall
honey you think you know all
the answers you don't, please try
to put some money away
believe me it wouldn't hurt
artist shmartist life's too short   30
for that kind of, forgive me,
horseshit, I know what you want
better than you, all that counts
is to make a good living
and the best of everything,
as Sholem Aleichem[2] said
he was a great writer did

[1] A person of integrity and honor.
[2] Pen name of the Jewish author Sholem Naumovich Rabinovich.

you ever read his books dear,
you should make what he makes a year
anyway he says some place   40
Poverty is no disgrace
but it's no honor either
that's what I say,
              love,
                    Mother"

MOLLY PEACOCK   (B. 1947)

OUR ROOM   1984

I tell the children in school sometimes
why I hate alcoholics: my father was one.
"Alcohol" and "disease" I use, and shun
the word "drunk" or even "drinking," since one time
the kids burst out laughing when I told them.
I felt as though they were laughing at me.
I waited for them, wounded, remembering how I imagined they'd howl at me
when I was in grade 5. Acting drunk
is a guaranteed screamer, especially   10
for boys. I'm quiet when I sort the junk
of my childhood for them, quiet so we
will all be quiet, and they can ask what
questions they have to and tell about what
happened to them, too. The classroom becomes
oddly lonely when we talk about our homes.

FOR ANALYSIS

1. The implication of line 6 is that the children were laughing not at the speaker but
at something else. What might that have been?

2. Describe the speaker's attitude toward her classmates.

3. Explain the title.

WRITING TOPIC

Have you ever experienced shame about your family? Describe what caused the
shame, your feelings at the time, and your present feelings about it.

GARY SOTO (B. 1952)

BEHIND GRANDMA'S HOUSE   1985

At ten I wanted fame. I had a comb
And two Coke bottles, a tube of Bryl-creem.
I borrowed a dog, one with
Mismatched eyes and a happy tongue,
And wanted to prove I was tough
In the alley, kicking over trash cans,
A dull chime of tuna cans falling.
I hurled light bulbs like grenades
And men teachers held their heads,
Fingers of blood lengthening   10
On the ground. I flicked rocks at cats,
Their goofy faces spurred with foxtails.
I kicked fences. I shooed pigeons.
I broke a branch from a flowering peach
And frightened ants with a stream of piss.
I said "Shit," "Fuck you," and "No way
Daddy-O" to an imaginary priest
Until grandma came into the alley,
Her apron flapping in a breeze,
Her hair mussed, and said, "Let me help you,"   20
And punched me between the eyes.

FOR ANALYSIS

1. What word appears more than any other in this poem? What might it mean that it
appears so often?

2. Who gets "the last word" in this poem? Of what does this "last word" consist?

3. What is the actual last word in the poem? Is there a pun involved?

MAKING CONNECTIONS

1. Compare the **tone** of the advice given in Meinke's "Advice to My Son" (p. 216)
with that given in Mezey's "My Mother" (p. 217).

2. While only one of these poems is explicitly about school, all are in some way about
education. How is each of these about teaching and learning? Is there only one way to
teach?

3. The voices of experience in two of these poems are explicitly ethnic. What effects
do the poems get from quoting, directly or indirectly, the ethnic **dialects** of their
experienced voices?

WRITING TOPIC

Describe the effect of the poem's account of the speaker's actions. What feeling comes
across from the **rhythms** and sounds and **images**? What moral judgment do you make

of the actions they describe? Do these two sets of reactions go together? If not, what is the effect of their being seemingly mismatched?

CONNECTING POEMS:
HAPPY HOLIDAYS

For the most part, we think of holidays as times of celebration and reflection, as times to remind ourselves of what's important and to be thankful for what we have. While this aspect of holidays serves an important function, one of literature's important functions has been to make us think beyond the accepted, obvious meanings of the things we do and say—of the rituals, practices, and values of the groups and cultures to which we belong—and give us the opportunity to examine them and what they say about our lives more openly and critically. When reading these poems, pay attention to the ways in which they play on the tension between what's supposed to be happening and other things that take on importance or demand attention—yours or the speaker's.

W. S. MERWIN (B. 1927)

THANKS 1988

Listen
with the night falling we are saying thank you
we are stopping on the bridges to bow from the railings
we are running out of the glass rooms
with our mouths full of food to look at the sky
and say thank you
we are standing by the water thanking it
smiling by the windows looking out
in our directions

back from a series of hospitals back from a mugging   10
after funerals we are saying thank you
after the news of the dead
whether or not we knew them we are saying thank you

over telephones we are saying thank you
in doorways and in the backs of cars and in elevators
remembering wars and the police at the door
and the beatings on stairs we are saying thank you

in the banks we are saying thank you
in the faces of the officials and the rich
and of all who will never change   20
we go on saying thank you thank you

with the animals dying around us
our lost feelings we are saying thank you
with the forests falling faster than the minutes
of our lives we are saying thank you
with the words going out like cells of a brain
with the cities growing over us
we are saying thank you faster and faster
with nobody listening we are saying thank you
we are saying thank you and waving   30
dark though it is

FOR ANALYSIS

1. What types of things are "we" thankful for? What kind of people are "we" in this
poem?

2. What kinds of events are occurring in the background of the poem as thanks are
being given? How does the nature of these events change over the course of the poem?
To what effect?

3. What effect is saying "thank you" supposed to have here? Does it work?

WRITING TOPIC

Reflect on the act of giving thanks. Can we give thanks for other people's good fortune? Is the act of giving thanks for one's own good fortune selfish?

CARL DENNIS (B. 1939)

THANKSGIVING LETTER
FROM HARRY   2007

I guess I have to begin by admitting
I'm thankful today I don't reside in a country
My country has chosen to liberate,
That Bridgeport's my home, not Baghdad.
Thankful my chances are good, when I leave
For the Super Duper, that I'll be returning.
And I'm thankful my TV set is still broken.
No point in wasting energy feeling shame
For the havoc inflicted on others in my name
When I need all the strength I can muster   10

To teach my eighth-grade class in the low-rent district.
There, at least, I don't feel powerless.
There my choices can make some difference.

This month I'd like to believe I've widened
My students' choice of vocation, though the odds
My history lessons on working the land
Will inspire any of them to farm
Are almost as small as the odds
One will become a monk or nun
Trained in the Buddhist practice   20
We studied last month in the unit on India.
The point is to get them suspecting the world
They know first hand isn't the only world.

As for the calling of soldier, if it comes up in class,
It's not because I feel obliged to include it,
As you, as a writer, may feel obliged.
A student may happen to introduce it,
As a girl did yesterday when she read her essay
About her older brother, Ramon,
Listed as "missing in action" three years ago,   30
And about her dad, who won't agree with her mom
And the social worker on how small the odds are
That Ramon's alive, a prisoner in the mountains.

I didn't allow the discussion that followed
More time than I allowed for the other essays.
And I wouldn't take sides: not with the group
That thought the father, having grieved enough,
Ought to move on to the life still left him;
Not with the group that was glad he hadn't made do
With the next-to-nothing the world's provided,   40
That instead he's invested his trust in a story
That saves the world from shameful failure.

Let me know of any recent attempts on your part
To save our fellow-citizens from themselves.
In the meantime, if you want to borrow Ramon
For a narrative of your own, remember that any scene
Where he appears under guard in a mountain village
Should be confined to the realm of longing. There
His captors may leave him when they move on.
There his wounds may be healed,   50

His health restored. A total recovery
Except for a lingering fog of forgetfulness
A father dreams he can burn away.

SHEILA ORTIZ TAYLOR   (B. 1939)

THE WAY BACK   1989

FOR UNCLE JIM

They stand in this Christmas snapshot
poised like adagio dancers
facing each other
their arms draped around
their matching bones
brother and sister
while behind them
out of focus
the family
spins   10

Around these two
youngest of thirteen
held now for eternity
in this moment before their
twin feet slide them out
in a celestial tango
a silence gathers

We see their handsome faces
Indian bones in glinting cheeks
their raven hair, gray-streaked   20
their eyes as deep and dark as wells
holding a history of careless loss
land, lovers, mothers, maps

The way back is a land
more innocent than this
He joined the navy
She married a judge
They both baked bread in institutional ovens
He wrote long letters home
and sent his mother silk pillows   30
embroidered with military targets

He baked bread while
his eight brothers lost fingers
toes, knees, elbows
He could almost hear the bullets
thud into dough
and the sound made him rise
growing from uniform to uniform
until they had to declare peace

Home again   40
he folded away his whites
kissed his sisters
and told his brothers
he was going to become
a hairdresser
news that made their wounds ache
more than seemed possible
Finally he followed them to work at Lockheed
learned to drill holes in himself
discovered insomnia   50
married a beautician named Molly
whose hair he dyed green every Christmas

He loved all holidays
Life needed themes
spelled out in sparkles, sprinkles
cutouts, paste-ups
but most of all
in costume.

Halloweens found brother and sister
on their knees   60
before bolts of cloth
and wimpling tissue
pins in their mouths
blue chalk on their hands
for years
artists of the self

You can see it here
in this snapshot
white polyester pants belling out
around white cowboy boots   70

red western shirts
tailored close to the rib
Indian silver at the waist
twins in spirit
if not by birth
holding each other
in a light embrace
their grace
not lost

And yet   80
the way back is a land
more innocent than this
The time came round
when neighbors
preferring razor blades to invention
would not let their children
trick or treat
where a grown man
put costumes on.

That Christmas night   90
very late
he backed his throbbing
Continental
into the dark garage
that shut down tight behind him
crawled into the backseat
bearing a bottle of champagne
one glass
a photograph

FOR ANALYSIS

1. How would you characterize the poem's **tone**? Does it match the holiday setting of the photograph with which it opens?

2. How is the brother different than the other male children in the family? How does the world around him react to this difference? What feelings does the poem convey about this difference?

3. Compare this poem's use of the photograph to Sandra Castillo's in "Christmas, 1970" (p. 203). Is the speaker in "The Way Back" in the snapshot? Does it matter?

WRITING TOPIC

What do you think happens at the end of this poem? Write one more **stanza** that makes this explicit. Do you think your stanza improves on the poem?

JAMES WELCH (1940–2003)

CHRISTMAS COMES
TO MOCCASIN FLAT   1976

Christmas comes like this: Wise men
unhurried, candles bought on credit (poor price
for calves), warriors face down in wine sleep.
Winds cheat to pull heat from smoke.

Friends sit in chinked cabins, stare out
plastic windows and wait for commodities.
Charlie Blackbird, twenty miles from church
and bar, stabs his fire with flint.

When drunks drain radiators for love
or need, chiefs eat snow and talk of change,   10
an urge to laugh pounding their ribs.
Elk play games in high country.

Medicine Woman, clay pipe and twist tobacco,
calls each blizzard by name and predicts
five o'clock by spitting at her television.
Children lean into her breath to beg a story:

Something about honor and passion,
warriors back with meat and song,
a peculiar evening star, quick vision of birth.
Blackbird feeds his fire. Outside, a quick 30 below.   20

FOR ANALYSIS

1. What kind of place is Moccasin Flat?

2. Welch's poem relies heavily on **irony**. How does he use it? To what effect?

3. Compare this poem's invocation of Christmas to that in Sheila Ortiz Taylor's "The
Way Back" (p. 223). How does each use the association with the holiday?

WRITING TOPIC

Welch's poem refers to stereotypes of Native American life. Create a list of elements
or **images** in this poem that are other than you expect them to be. What is the effect of
all this unmet expectation?

MAGGIE NELSON (B. 1973)

THANKSGIVING 2008

Can beauty save us? Yesterday
I looked at the river and a sliver
of moon and knew the answer;

today I fell asleep in a spot of sun
behind a Vermont barn, woke to
darkness, a thin whistle of wind

and the answer changed. Inside the barn
the boys build bongs out of
copper piping, electrical tape, and

jars. All of the children here have   10
leaky brown eyes, and a certain precision
of gesture. Even the maple syrup

tastes like liquor. After dinner
I sit the cutest little boy on my knee
and read him a book about the history of cod

absentmindedly explaining overfishing,
the slave trade. People for rum? he asks,
incredulously. Yes, I nod. People for rum.

FOR ANALYSIS

1. What purpose does the little boy's incredulity serve at the end of the poem?

2. How is this a Thanksgiving poem? Aside from the speaker's story seeming to happen on the day, what is the connection of the poem to the day?

3. "Can beauty save us?" is a question that has been answered in the affirmative by a long line of poems throughout history. How does Nelson's evocation of that history work here?

WRITING TOPIC

Research the history of your favorite holiday and write a short account of a little-known or often overlooked historical aspect of it. Does this aspect make you think differently about the holiday?

DRAMA

HENRIK IBSEN   (1828–1906)

A DOLL'S HOUSE[1]   1879

CHARACTERS

Torvald Helmer, a lawyer
Nora, his wife
Dr. Rank
Mrs. Linde
Krogstad

The Helmers' three small
   children
Anne, the children's nurse
A Maid
A Porter

ACT I

Scene

A room furnished comfortably and tastefully, but not extravagantly. At the back, a door to the right leads to the entrance hall, another to the left leads to Helmer's study. Between the doors stands a piano. In the middle of the left-hand wall is a door, and beyond it a window. Near the window are a round table, armchairs and a small sofa. In the right-hand wall, at the farther end, another door; and on the same side, nearer the footlights, a stove, two easy chairs and a rocking-chair; between the stove and the door, a small table. Engravings on the walls; a cabinet with china and other small objects; a small bookcase with well-bound books. The floors are carpeted, and a fire burns in the stove. It is winter.

A bell rings in the hall; shortly afterwards the door is heard to open. Enter Nora, humming a tune and in high spirits. She is in outdoor dress and carries a number of parcels; these she lays on the table to the right. She leaves the outer door open after her, and through it is seen a Porter who is carrying a Christmas tree and a basket, which he gives to the Maid who has opened the door.

Nora. Hide the Christmas tree carefully, Helen. Be sure the children do not see it till this evening, when it is dressed. *(To the Porter, taking out her purse.)* How much?
Porter. Sixpence.

---

[1] Translated by R. Farquharson Sharp.

Nora. There is a shilling. No, keep the change. (*The Porter thanks her, and goes out. Nora shuts the door. She is laughing to herself, as she takes off her hat and coat. She takes a packet of macaroons from her pocket and eats one or two; then goes cautiously to her husband's door and listens.*) Yes, he is in.

(*Still humming, she goes to the table on the right.*)

Helmer (*calls out from his room*). Is that my little lark twittering out there?

Nora (*busy opening some of the parcels*). Yes, it is!

Helmer. Is it my little squirrel bustling about?

Nora. Yes!

Helmer. When did my squirrel come home?

Nora. Just now. (*Puts the bag of macaroons into her pocket and wipes her mouth.*) Come in here, Torvald, and see what I have bought.

Helmer. Don't disturb me. (*A little later, he opens the door and looks into the room, pen in hand.*) Bought, did you say? All these things? Has my little spendthrift been wasting money again?

Nora. Yes, but, Torvald, this year we really can let ourselves go a little. This is the first Christmas that we have not needed to economise.

Helmer. Still, you know, we can't spend money recklessly.

Nora. Yes, Torvald, we may be a wee bit more reckless now, mayn't we? Just a tiny wee bit! You are going to have a big salary and earn lots and lots of money.

Helmer. Yes, after the New Year; but then it will be a whole quarter before the salary is due.

Nora. Pooh! we can borrow till then.

Helmer. Nora! (*Goes up to her and takes her playfully by the ear.*) The same little featherhead! Suppose, now, that I borrowed fifty pounds to-day, and you spent it all in the Christmas week, and then on New Year's Eve a slate fell on my head and killed me, and——

Nora (*putting her hands over his mouth*). Oh! don't say such horrid things.

Helmer. Still, suppose that happened,—what then?

Nora. If that were to happen, I don't suppose I should care whether I owed money or not.

Helmer. Yes, but what about the people who had lent it?

Nora. They? Who would bother about them? I should not know who they were.

Helmer. That is like a woman! But seriously, Nora, you know what I think about that. No debt, no borrowing. There can be no freedom or beauty about a home life that depends on borrowing and debt. We two have kept bravely on the straight road so far, and we will go on the same way for the short time longer that there need be any struggle.

Nora (*moving towards the stove*). As you please, Torvald.

Helmer (*following her*). Come, come, my little skylark must not droop her wings. What is this! Is my little squirrel out of temper? (*Taking out his purse.*) Nora, what do you think I have got here?

Nora (*turning round quickly*). Money!

Helmer. There you are. *(Gives her some money.)* Do you think I don't know what a lot is wanted for house-keeping at Christmas-time?

Nora *(counting).* Ten shillings—a pound—two pounds! Thank you, thank you, Torvald; that will keep me going for a long time.

Helmer. Indeed it must.

Nora. Yes, yes, it will. But come here and let me show you what I have bought. And all so cheap! Look, here is a new suit for Ivar, and a sword; and a horse and a trumpet for Bob; and a doll and dolly's bedstead for Emmy,—they are very plain, but anyway she will soon break them in pieces. And here are dress-lengths and handkerchiefs for the maids; old Anne ought really to have something better.

Helmer. And what is in this parcel?

Nora *(crying out).* No, no! you mustn't see that till this evening.

Helmer. Very well. But now tell me something reasonable that you would particularly like to have.

Nora. No, I really can't think of anything—unless, Torvald——

Helmer. Well?

Nora *(playing with his coat buttons, and without raising her eyes to his).* If you really want to give me something, you might—you might——

Helmer. Well, out with it!

Nora *(speaking quickly).* You might give me money, Torvald. Only just as much as you can afford; and then one of these days I will buy something with it.

Helmer. But, Nora——

Nora. Oh, do! dear Torvald; please, please do! Then I will wrap it up in beautiful gilt paper and hang it on the Christmas tree. Wouldn't that be fun?

Helmer. What are little people called that are always wasting money?

Nora. Spendthrifts—I know. Let us do as you suggest, Torvald, and then I shall have time to think what I am most in want of. That is a very sensible plan, isn't it?

Helmer *(smiling).* Indeed it is—that is to say, if you were really to save out of the money I give you, and then really buy something for yourself. But if you spend it all on the housekeeping and any number of unnecessary things, then I merely have to pay up again.

Nora. Oh but, Torvald——

Helmer. You can't deny it, my dear little Nora. *(Puts his arm round her waist.)* It's a sweet little spendthrift, but she uses up a deal of money. One would hardly believe how expensive such little persons are!

Nora. It's a shame to say that. I do really save all I can.

Helmer *(laughing).* That's very true,—all you can. But you can't save anything!

Nora *(smiling quietly and happily).* You haven't any idea how many expenses we skylarks and squirrels have, Torvald.

Helmer. You are an odd little soul. Very like your father. You always find some new way of wheedling money out of me, and, as soon as you have got it, it seems to melt in your hands. You never know where it has gone. Still, one must take you as you are. It is in the blood; for indeed it is true that you can inherit these things, Nora.

Nora. Ah, I wish I had inherited many of papa's qualities.

Helmer. And I would not wish you to be anything but just what you are, my sweet little skylark. But, do you know, it strikes me that you are looking rather—what shall I say—rather uneasy to-day?

Nora. Do I?

Helmer. You do, really. Look straight at me.

Nora (*looks at him*). Well?

Helmer (*wagging his finger at her*). Hasn't Miss Sweet-Tooth been breaking rules in town to-day?

Nora. No; what makes you think that?

Helmer. Hasn't she paid a visit to the confectioner's?

Nora. No, I assure you, Torvald——

Helmer. Not been nibbling sweets?

Nora. No, certainly not.

Helmer. Not even taken a bite at a macaroon or two?

Nora. No, Torvald, I assure you really——

Helmer. There, there, of course I was only joking.

Nora (*going to the table on the right*). I should not think of going against your wishes.

Helmer. No, I am sure of that! Besides, you gave me your word——(*Going up to her.*) Keep your little Christmas secrets to yourself, my darling. They will all be revealed to-night when the Christmas tree is lit, no doubt.

Nora. Did you remember to invite Doctor Rank?

Helmer. No. But there is no need; as a matter of course he will come to dinner with us. However, I will ask him, when he comes in this morning. I have ordered some good wine. Nora, you can't think how I am looking forward to this evening.

Nora. So am I! And how the children will enjoy themselves, Torvald!

Helmer. It is splendid to feel that one has a perfectly safe appointment, and a big enough income. It's delightful to think of, isn't it?

Nora. It's wonderful!

Helmer. Do you remember last Christmas? For a full three weeks beforehand you shut yourself up every evening till long after midnight, making ornaments for the Christmas tree and all the other fine things that were to be a surprise to us. It was the dullest three weeks I ever spent!

Nora. I didn't find it dull.

Helmer (*smiling*). But there was precious little result, Nora.

Nora. Oh, you shouldn't tease me about that again. How could I help the cat's going in and tearing everything to pieces?

Helmer. Of course you couldn't, poor little girl. You had the best of intentions to please us all, and that's the main thing. But it is a good thing that our hard times are over.

Nora. Yes, it is really wonderful.

Helmer. This time I needn't sit here and be dull all alone, and you needn't ruin your dear eyes and your pretty little hands——

Nora (*clapping her hands*). No, Torvald, I needn't any longer, need I! It's wonderfully lovely to hear you say so! (*Taking his arm.*) Now I will tell you how I have been thinking we ought to arrange things, Torvald. As soon as Christmas is over——(*A bell rings in the hall.*) There's the bell. (*She tidies the room a little.*) There's someone at the door. What a nuisance!

Helmer. If it is a caller, remember I am not at home.

Maid (*in the doorway*). A lady to see you, ma'am,—a stranger.

Nora. Ask her to come in.

Maid (*to Helmer*). The doctor came at the same time, sir.

Helmer. Did he go straight into my room?

Maid. Yes, sir.

(*Helmer goes into his room. The Maid ushers in Mrs. Linde, who is in traveling dress, and shuts the door.*)

Mrs. Linde (*in a dejected and timid voice*). How do you do, Nora?

Nora (*doubtfully*). How do you do——

Mrs. Linde. You don't recognise me, I suppose.

Nora. No, I don't know—yes, to be sure, I seem to——(*Suddenly.*) Yes! Christine! Is it really you?

Mrs. Linde. Yes, it is I.

Nora. Christine! To think of my not recognising you! And yet how could I——(*In a gentle voice.*) How you have altered, Christine!

Mrs. Linde. Yes, I have indeed. In nine, ten long years——

Nora. Is it so long since we met? I suppose it is. The last eight years have been a happy time for me, I can tell you. And so now you have come into the town, and have taken this long journey in winter—that was plucky of you.

Mrs. Linde. I arrived by steamer this morning.

Nora. To have some fun at Christmas-time, of course. How delightful! We will have such fun together! But take off your things. You are not cold, I hope. (*Helps her.*) Now we will sit down by the stove, and be cosy. No, take this arm-chair; I will sit here in the rocking-chair. (*Takes her hands.*) Now you look like your old self again; it was only the first moment——You are a little paler, Christine, and perhaps a little thinner.

Mrs. Linde. And much, much older, Nora.

Nora. Perhaps a little older; very, very little; certainly not much. (*Stops suddenly and speaks seriously.*) What a thoughtless creature I am, chattering away like this. My poor, dear Christine, do forgive me.

Mrs. Linde. What do you mean, Nora?

Nora (*gently*). Poor Christine, you are a widow.

Mrs. Linde. Yes; it is three years ago now.

Nora. Yes, I knew; I saw it in the papers. I assure you, Christine, I meant ever so often to write to you at the time, but I always put it off and something always prevented me.

Mrs. Linde. I quite understand, dear.

Nora. It was very bad of me, Christine. Poor thing, how you must have suffered. And he left you nothing?

Mrs. Linde. No.

Nora. And no children?

Mrs. Linde. No.

Nora. Nothing at all, then?

Mrs. Linde. Not even any sorrow or grief to live upon.

Nora (*looking incredulously at her*). But, Christine, is that possible?

Mrs. Linde (*smiles sadly and strokes her hair*). It sometimes happens, Nora.

Nora. So you are quite alone. How dreadfully sad that must be. I have three lovely children. You can't see them just now, for they are out with their nurse. But now you must tell me all about it.

Mrs. Linde. No, no; I want to hear you.

Nora. No, you must begin. I mustn't be selfish to-day, to-day I must only think of your affairs. But there is one thing I must tell you. Do you know we have just had a great piece of good luck?

Mrs. Linde. No, what is it?

Nora. Just fancy, my husband has been made manager of the Bank!

Mrs. Linde. Your husband? What good luck!

Nora. Yes, tremendous! A barrister's profession is such an uncertain thing, especially if he won't undertake unsavoury cases; and naturally Torvald has never been willing to do that, and I quite agree with him. You may imagine how pleased we are! He is to take up his work in the Bank at the New Year, and then he will have a big salary and lots of commissions. For the future we can live quite differently—we can do just as we like. I feel so relieved and so happy, Christine! It will be splendid to have heaps of money and not need to have any anxiety, won't it?

Mrs. Linde. Yes, anyhow I think it would be delightful to have what one needs.

Nora. No, not only what one needs, but heaps and heaps of money.

Mrs. Linde (*smiling*). Nora, Nora, haven't you learnt sense yet? In our schooldays you were a great spendthrift.

Nora (*laughing*). Yes, that is what Torvald says now. (*Wags her finger at her.*) But "Nora, Nora" is not so silly as you think. We have not been in a position for me to waste money. We have both had to work.

Mrs. Linde. You too?

Nora. Yes; odds and ends, needlework, crochet-work, embroidery, and that kind of thing. (*Dropping her voice.*) And other things as well. You know Torvald left his office when we were married? There was no prospect of promotion there, and he had to try and earn more than before. But during the first year he overworked himself dreadfully. You see, he had to make money every way he could, and he worked early and late; but he couldn't stand it, and fell dreadfully ill, and the doctors said it was necessary for him to go south.

Mrs. Linde. You spent a whole year in Italy, didn't you?

Nora. Yes. It was no easy matter to get away, I can tell you. It was just after Ivar was born; but naturally we had to go. It was a wonderfully beautiful journey, and it saved Torvald's life. But it cost a tremendous lot of money, Christine.

Mrs. Linde. So I should think.

Nora. It cost about two hundred and fifty pounds. That's a lot, isn't it?

Mrs. Linde. Yes, and in emergencies like that it is lucky to have the money.

Nora. I ought to tell you that we had it from papa.

Mrs. Linde. Oh, I see. It was just about that time that he died, wasn't it?

Nora. Yes; and, just think of it, I couldn't go and nurse him. I was expecting little Ivar's birth every day and I had my poor sick Torvald to look after. My dear, kind father—I never saw him again, Christine. That was the saddest time I have known since our marriage.

Mrs. Linde. And your husband came back quite well?

Nora. As sound as a bell!

Mrs. Linde. But—the doctor?

Nora. What doctor?

Mrs. Linde. I thought your maid said the gentleman who arrived here just as I did was the doctor?

Nora. Yes, that was Doctor Rank, but he doesn't come here professionally. He is our greatest friend, and comes in at least once every day. No, Torvald has not had an hour's illness since then, and our children are strong and healthy and so am I. *(Jumps up and claps her hands.)* Christine! Christine! it's good to be alive and happy!—— But how horrid of me; I am talking of nothing but my own affairs. *(Sits on a stool near her, and rests her arms on her knees.)* You mustn't be angry with me. Tell me, is it really true that you did not love your husband? Why did you marry him?

Mrs. Linde. My mother was alive then, and was bedridden and helpless, and I had to provide for my two younger brothers; so I did not think I was justified in refusing his offer.

Nora. No, perhaps you were quite right. He was rich at that time, then?

Mrs. Linde. I believe he was quite well off. But his business was a precarious one; and, when he died, it all went to pieces and there was nothing left.

Nora. And then?——

Mrs. Linde. Well, I had to turn my hand to anything I could find—first a small shop, then a small school, and so on. The last three years have seemed like one long working-day, with no rest. Now it is at an end, Nora. My poor mother needs me no more, for she is gone; and the boys do not need me either; they have got situations and can shift for themselves.

Nora. What a relief you must feel it——

Mrs. Linde. No, indeed; I only feel my life unspeakably empty. No one to live for any more. *(Gets up restlessly.)* That was why I could not stand the life in my little backwater any longer. I hope it may be easier here to find something which will busy me and occupy my thoughts. If only I could have the good luck to get some regular work—office work of some kind——

Nora. But, Christine, that is so frightfully tiring, and you look tired out now. You had far better go away to some watering-place.

Mrs. Linde *(walking to the window).* I have no father to give me money for a journey, Nora.

Nora *(rising).* Oh, don't be angry with me.

Mrs. Linde *(going up to her).* It is you that must not be angry with me, dear. The worst of a position like mine is that it makes one so bitter. No one to work for, and yet obliged to be always on the look-out for chances. One must live, and so one becomes selfish. When you told me of the happy turn your fortunes have taken—you will hardly believe it—I was delighted not so much on your account as on my own.

Nora. How do you mean?—Oh, I understand. You mean that perhaps Torvald could get you something to do.

Mrs. Linde. Yes, that was what I was thinking of.

Nora. He must, Christine. Just leave it to me; I will broach the subject very cleverly—I will think of something that will please him very much. It will make me so happy to be of some use to you.

Mrs. Linde. How kind you are, Nora, to be so anxious to help me! It is doubly kind in you, for you know so little of the burdens and troubles of life.

Nora. I——? I know so little of them?

Mrs. Linde (*smiling*). My dear! Small household cares and that sort of thing!—You are a child, Nora.

Nora (*tosses her head and crosses the stage*). You ought not to be so superior.

Mrs. Linde. No?

Nora. You are just like the others. They all think that I am incapable of anything really serious——

Mrs. Linde. Come, come——

Nora. —that I have gone through nothing in this world of cares.

Mrs. Linde. But, my dear Nora, you have just told me all your troubles.

Nora. Pooh!—those were trifles. (*Lowering her voice.*) I have not told you the important thing.

Mrs. Linde. The important thing? What do you mean?

Nora. You look down upon me altogether, Christine—but you ought not to. You are proud, aren't you, of having worked so hard and so long for your mother?

Mrs. Linde. Indeed, I don't look down on any one. But it is true that I am both proud and glad to think that I was privileged to make the end of my mother's life almost free from care.

Nora. And you are proud to think of what you have done for your brothers.

Mrs. Linde. I think I have the right to be.

Nora. I think so, too. But now, listen to this; I too have something to be proud and glad of.

Mrs. Linde. I have no doubt you have. But what do you refer to?

Nora. Speak low. Suppose Torvald were to hear! He mustn't on any account—no one in the world must know, Christine, except you.

Mrs. Linde. But what is it?

Nora. Come here. (*Pulls her down on the sofa beside her.*) Now I will show you that I too have something to be proud and glad of. It was I who saved Torvald's life.

Mrs. Linde. "Saved"? How?

Nora. I told you about our trip to Italy. Torvald would never have recovered if he had not gone there——

Mrs. Linde. Yes, but your father gave you the necessary funds.

Nora (*smiling*). Yes, that is what Torvald and all the others think, but——

Mrs. Linde. But——

Nora. Papa didn't give us a shilling. It was I who procured the money.

Mrs. Linde. You? All that large sum?

Nora. Two hundred and fifty pounds. What do you think of that?

Mrs. Linde. But, Nora, how could you possibly do it? Did you win a prize in the Lottery?

Nora (*contemptuously*). In the Lottery? There would have been no credit in that.

Mrs. Linde. But where did you get it from, then?

Nora (*humming and smiling with an air of mystery*). Hm, hm! Aha!

Mrs. Linde. Because you couldn't have borrowed it.

Nora. Couldn't I? Why not?

Mrs. Linde. No, a wife cannot borrow without her husband's consent.

Nora (*tossing her head*). Oh, if it is a wife who has any head for business—a wife who has the wit to be a little bit clever——

Mrs. Linde. I don't understand it at all, Nora.

Nora. There is no need you should. I never said I had borrowed the money. I may have got it some other way. (*Lies back on the sofa.*) Perhaps I got it from some other admirer. When anyone is as attractive as I am——

Mrs. Linde. You are a mad creature.

Nora. Now, you know you're full of curiosity, Christine.

Mrs. Linde. Listen to me, Nora dear. Haven't you been a little bit imprudent?

Nora (*sits up straight*). Is it imprudent to save your husband's life?

Mrs. Linde. It seems to me imprudent, without his knowledge, to——

Nora. But it was absolutely necessary that he should not know! My goodness, can't you understand that? It was necessary he should have no idea what a dangerous condition he was in. It was to me that the doctors came and said that his life was in danger, and that the only thing to save him was to live in the south. Do you suppose I didn't try, first of all, to get what I wanted as if it were for myself? I told him how much I should love to travel abroad like other young wives; I tried tears and entreaties with him; I told him that he ought to remember the condition I was in, and that he ought to be kind and indulgent to me; I even hinted that he might raise a loan. That nearly made him angry, Christine. He said I was thoughtless, and that it was his duty as my husband not to indulge me in my whims and caprices—as I believe he called them. Very well I thought, you must be saved—and that was how I came to devise a way out of the difficulty——

Mrs. Linde. And did your husband never get to know from your father that the money had not come from him?

Nora. No, never. Papa died just at that time. I had meant to let him into the secret and beg him never to reveal it. But he was so ill then—alas, there never was any need to tell him.

Mrs. Linde. And since then have you never told your secret to your husband?

Nora. Good Heavens, no! How could you think so? A man who has such strong opinions about these things! And besides, how painful and humiliating it would be for Torvald, with his manly independence, to know that he owed me anything! It would upset our mutual relations altogether; our beautiful happy home would no longer be what it is now.

Mrs. Linde. Do you mean never to tell him about it?

Nora (*meditatively, and with a half smile*). Yes—some day, perhaps, after many years, when I am no longer as nice-looking as I am now. Don't laugh at me! I mean, of course, when Torvald is no longer as devoted to me as he is now; when my dancing and dressing-up and reciting have palled on him; then it may be a good thing to have something in reserve——(*Breaking off.*) What nonsense! That time will never come. Now, what do you think of my great secret, Christine? Do you still think I am of no use? I can tell you, too, that this affair has caused me a lot of worry. It has been by no means easy for me to meet my engagements punctually. I may tell you that there is something that is called, in business, quarterly interest, and another thing called payment in instalments, and it is always so dreadfully difficult to manage them. I have had to save a little here and there, where I could, you understand. I have not been able to put aside much from my housekeeping money, for Torvald must have a good table. I couldn't let my children be shabbily dressed; I have felt obliged to use up all he gave me for them, the sweet little darlings!

Mrs. Linde. So it has all had to come out of your own necessaries of life, poor Nora?

Nora. Of course. Besides, I was the one responsible for it. Whenever Torvald has given me money for new dresses and such things, I have never spent more than half of it; I have always bought the simplest and cheapest things. Thank Heaven, any clothes look well on me, and so Torvald has never noticed it. But it was often very hard on me, Christine—because it is delightful to be really well dressed, isn't it?

Mrs. Linde. Quite so.

Nora. Well, then I have found other ways of earning money. Last winter I was lucky enough to get a lot of copying to do; so I locked myself up and sat writing every evening until quite late at night. Many a time I was desperately tired; but all the same it was a tremendous pleasure to sit there working and earning money. It was like being a man.

Mrs. Linde. How much have you been able to pay off in that way?

Nora. I can't tell you exactly. You see, it is very difficult to keep an account of a business matter of that kind. I only know that I have paid every penny that I could scrape together. Many a time I was at my wits' end. (*Smiles.*) Then I used to sit here and imagine that a rich old gentleman had fallen in love with me——

Mrs. Linde. What! Who was it?

Nora. Be quiet!—that he had died; and that when his will was opened it contained, written in big letters, the instruction: "The lovely Mrs. Nora Helmer is to have all I possess paid over to her at once in cash."

Mrs. Linde. But, my dear Nora—who could the man be?

Nora. Good gracious, can't you understand? There was no old gentleman at all; it was only something that I used to sit here and imagine, when I couldn't think of any way of procuring money. But it's all the same now; the tiresome old person can stay where he is, as far as I am concerned; I don't care about him or his will either, for I am free from care now. (*Jumps up.*) My goodness, it's delightful to think of, Christine! Free from care! To be able to be free from care, quite free from care; to be able to play and romp with the children; to be able to keep the house beautifully and have everything just as Torvald likes it! And, think of it, soon the spring will come and the big blue sky! Perhaps we shall be able to take a little trip—perhaps I shall see the sea again! Oh, it's a wonderful thing to be alive and be happy. *(A bell is heard in the hall.)*

Mrs. Linde *(rising).* There is the bell; perhaps I had better go.

Nora. No, don't go; no one will come in here; it is sure to be for Torvald.

Servant *(at the hall door).* Excuse me, ma'am—there is a gentleman to see the master, and as the doctor is with him——

Nora. Who is it?

Krogstad *(at the door).* It is I, Mrs. Helmer. *(Mrs. Linde starts, trembles, and turns to the window.)*

Nora *(takes a step towards him, and speaks in a strained, low voice).* You? What is it? What do you want to see my husband about?

Krogstad. Bank business—in a way. I have a small post in the Bank, and I hear your husband is to be our chief now——

Nora. Then it is——

Krogstad. Nothing but dry business matters, Mrs. Helmer; absolutely nothing else.

Nora. Be so good as to go into the study, then. *(She bows indifferently to him and shuts the door into the hall; then comes back and makes up the fire in the stove.)*

Mrs. Linde. Nora—who was that man?

Nora. A lawyer, of the name of Krogstad.

Mrs. Linde. Then it really was he.

Nora. Do you know the man?

Mrs. Linde. I used to—many years ago. At one time he was a solicitor's clerk in our town.

Nora. Yes, he was.

Mrs. Linde. He is greatly altered.

Nora. He made a very unhappy marriage.

Mrs. Linde. He is a widower now, isn't he?

Nora. With several children. There now, it is burning up.

(Shuts the door of the stove and moves the rocking-chair aside.)

Mrs. Linde. They say he carries on various kinds of business.

Nora. Really! Perhaps he does; I don't know anything about it. But don't let us think of business; it is so tiresome.

Doctor Rank *(comes out of Helmer's study. Before he shuts the door he calls to him).* No, my dear fellow, I won't disturb you; I would rather go in to your wife for a little while. *(Shuts the door and sees Mrs. Linde.)* I beg your pardon; I am afraid I am disturbing you too.

Nora. No, not at all. *(Introducing him.)* Doctor Rank, Mrs. Linde.

Rank. I have often heard Mrs. Linde's name mentioned here. I think I passed you on the stairs when I arrived, Mrs. Linde?

Mrs. Linde. Yes, I go up very slowly; I can't manage stairs well.

Rank. Ah! some slight internal weakness?

Mrs. Linde. No, the fact is I have been overworking myself.

Rank. Nothing more than that? Then I suppose you have come to town to amuse yourself with our entertainments?

Mrs. Linde. I have come to look for work.

Rank. Is that a good cure for overwork?

Mrs. Linde. One must live, Doctor Rank.

Rank. Yes, the general opinion seems to be that it is necessary.

Nora. Look here, Doctor Rank—you know you want to live.

Rank. Certainly. However wretched I may feel, I want to prolong the agony as long as possible. All my patients are like that. And so are those who are morally diseased; one of them, and a bad case too, is at this very moment with Helmer——

Mrs. Linde (*sadly*). Ah!

Nora. Whom do you mean?

Rank. A lawyer of the name of Krogstad, a fellow you don't know at all. He suffers from a diseased moral character, Mrs. Helmer; but even he began talking of its being highly important that he should live.

Nora. Did he? What did he want to speak to Torvald about?

Rank. I have no idea; I only heard that it was something about the Bank.

Nora. I didn't know this—what's his name—Krogstad had anything to do with the Bank.

Rank. Yes, he has some sort of appointment there. (*To Mrs. Linde.*) I don't know whether you find also in your part of the world that there are certain people who go zealously snuffing about to smell out moral corruption, and, as soon as they have found some, put the person concerned into some lucrative position where they can keep their eye on him. Healthy natures are left out in the cold.

Mrs. Linde. Still I think the sick are those who most need taking care of.

Rank (*shrugging his shoulders*). Yes, there you are. That is the sentiment that is turning Society into a sickhouse.

(*Nora, who has been absorbed in her thoughts, breaks out into smothered laughter and claps her hands.*)

Rank. Why do you laugh at that? Have you any notion what Society really is?

Nora. What do I care about tiresome Society? I am laughing at something quite different, something extremely amusing. Tell me, Doctor Rank, are all the people who are employed in the Bank dependent on Torvald now?

Rank. Is that what you find so extremely amusing?

Nora (*smiling and humming*). That's my affair! (*Walking about the room.*) It's perfectly glorious to think that we have—that Torvald has so much power over so many people. (*Takes the packet from her pocket.*) Doctor Rank, what do you say to a macaroon?

Rank. What, macaroons? I thought they were forbidden here.

Nora. Yes, but these are some Christine gave me.

Mrs. Linde. What! I?—

Nora. Oh, well, don't be alarmed! You couldn't know that Torvald had forbidden them. I must tell you that he is afraid they will spoil my teeth. But, bah!—once in a way——That's so, isn't it, Doctor Rank? By your leave? *(Puts a macaroon into his mouth.)* You must have one too, Christine. And I shall have one, just a little one—or at most two. *(Walking about.)* I am tremendously happy. There is just one thing in the world now that I should dearly love to do.

Rank. Well, what is that?

Nora. It's something I should dearly love to say, if Torvald could hear me.

Rank. Well, why can't you say it?

Nora. No, I daren't; it's so shocking.

Mrs. Linde. Shocking?

Rank. Well, I should not advise you to say it. Still, with us you might. What is it you would so much like to say if Torvald could hear you?

Nora. I should just love to say—Well, I'm damned!

Rank. Are you mad?

Mrs. Linde. Nora, dear——!

Rank. Say it, here he is!

Nora *(hiding the packet).* Hush! Hush! Hush!

(Helmer comes out of his room, with his coat over his arm and his hat in his hand.)

Nora. Well, Torvald dear, have you got rid of him?

Helmer. Yes, he has just gone.

Nora. Let me introduce you—this is Christine, who has come to town.

Helmer. Christine——? Excuse me, but I don't know——

Nora. Mrs. Linde, dear; Christine Linde.

Helmer. Of course. A school friend of my wife's, I presume?

Mrs. Linde. Yes, we have known each other since then.

Nora. And just think, she has taken a long journey in order to see you.

Helmer. What do you mean?

Mrs. Linde. No, really, I——

Nora. Christine is tremendously clever at book-keeping, and she is frightfully anxious to work under some clever man, so as to perfect herself——

Helmer. Very sensible, Mrs. Linde.

Nora. And when she heard you had been appointed manager of the Bank—the news was telegraphed, you know—she travelled here as quick as she could. Torvald, I am sure you will be able to do something for Christine, for my sake, won't you?

Helmer. Well, it is not altogether impossible. I presume you are a widow, Mrs. Linde?

Mrs. Linde. Yes.

Helmer. And have had some experience of book-keeping?

Mrs. Linde. Yes, a fair amount.

Helmer. Ah! well, it's very likely I may be able to find something for you——

Nora (*clapping her hands*). What did I tell you? What did I tell you?

Helmer. You have just come at a fortunate moment, Mrs. Linde.

Mrs. Linde. How am I to thank you?

Helmer. There is no need. (*Puts on his coat.*) But to-day you must excuse me——

Rank. Wait a minute; I will come with you.

(*Brings his fur coat from the hall and warms it at the fire.*)

Nora. Don't be long away, Torvald dear.

Helmer. About an hour, not more.

Nora. Are you going too, Christine?

Mrs. Linde (*putting on her cloak*).   Yes, I must go and look for a room.

Helmer. Oh, well then, we can walk down the street together.

Nora (*helping her*). What a pity it is we are so short of space here; I am afraid it is impossible for us——

Mrs. Linde. Please don't think of it! Good-bye, Nora dear, and many thanks.

Nora. Good-bye for the present. Of course you will come back this evening. And you too, Dr. Rank. What do you say? If you are well enough? Oh, you must be! Wrap yourself up well.

(*They go to the door all talking together. Children's voices are heard on the staircase.*)

Nora. There they are. There they are! (*She runs to open the door. The Nurse comes in with the children.*) Come in! Come in! (*Stoops and kisses them.*) Oh, you sweet blessings! Look at them, Christine! Aren't they darlings?

Rank. Don't let us stand here in the draught.

Helmer. Come along, Mrs. Linde; the place will only be bearable for a mother now!

(*Rank, Helmer, and Mrs. Linde go downstairs. The Nurse comes forward with the children; Nora shuts the hall door.*)

Nora. How fresh and well you look! Such red cheeks!—like apples and roses. (*The children all talk at once while she speaks to them.*) Have you had great fun? That's splendid! What, you pulled both Emmy and Bob along on the sledge?— both at once?—that *was* good. You are a clever boy, Ivar. Let me take her for a little, Anne. My sweet little baby doll! (*Takes the baby from the Maid and dances it up and down.*) Yes, yes, mother will dance with Bob too. What! Have you been snowballing? I wish I had been there too! No, no, I will take their things off, Anne; please let me do it, it is such fun. Go in now, you look half frozen. There is some hot coffee for you on the stove.

(*The Nurse goes into the room on the left. Nora takes off the children's things and throws them about, while they all talk to her at once.*)

Nora. Really! Did a big dog run after you? But it didn't bite you? No, dogs don't bite nice little dolly children. You mustn't look at the parcels, Ivar. What are they? Ah, I daresay you would like to know. No, no—it's something nasty! Come, let us have a game! What shall we play at? Hide and Seek? Yes, we'll play Hide and Seek. Bob shall hide first. Must I hide? Very well, I'll hide first.

(She and the children laugh and shout, and romp in and out of the room; at last Nora hides under the table, the children rush in and look for her, but do not see her; they hear her smothered laughter, run to the table, lift up the cloth and find her. Shouts of laughter. She crawls forward and pretends to frighten them. Fresh laughter. Meanwhile there has been a knock at the hall door, but none of them has noticed it. The door is half opened, and Krogstad appears. He waits a little; the game goes on.)

Krogstad. Excuse me, Mrs. Helmer.

Nora *(with a stifled cry, turns round and gets up on to her knees).* Ah! what do you want?

Krogstad. Excuse me, the outer door was ajar; I suppose someone forgot to shut it.

Nora *(rising).* My husband is out, Mr. Krogstad.

Krogstad. I know that.

Nora. What do you want here, then?

Krogstad. A word with you.

Nora. With me?—*(to the children, gently.)* Go in to nurse. What? No, the strange man won't do mother any harm. When he has gone we will have another game. *(She takes the children into the room on the left, and shuts the door after them.)* You want to speak to me?

Krogstad. Yes, I do.

Nora. To-day? It is not the first of the month yet.

Krogstad. No, it is Christmas Eve, and it will depend on yourself what sort of a Christmas you will spend.

Nora. What do you want? To-day it is absolutely impossible for me——

Krogstad. We won't talk about that till later on. This is something different. I presume you can give me a moment?

Nora. Yes—yes, I can—although——

Krogstad. Good. I was in Olsen's Restaurant and saw your husband going down the street——

Nora. Yes?

Krogstad. With a lady.

Nora. What then?

Krogstad. May I make so bold as to ask if it was a Mrs. Linde?

Nora. It was.

Krogstad. Just arrived in town?

Nora. Yes, to-day.

Krogstad. She is a great friend of yours, isn't she?

Nora. She is. But I don't see——

Krogstad. I knew her too, once upon a time.

Nora. I am aware of that.

Krogstad. Are you? So you know all about it; I thought as much. Then I can ask you, without beating about the bush—is Mrs. Linde to have an appointment in the Bank?

Nora. What right have you to question me, Mr. Krogstad?—You, one of my husband's subordinates! But since you ask, you shall know. Yes, Mrs. Linde *is* to have an appointment. And it was I who pleaded her cause, Mr. Krogstad, let me tell you that.

Krogstad. I was right in what I thought, then.

Nora *(walking up and down the stage).* Sometimes one has a tiny little bit of influence, I should hope. Because one is a woman, it does not necessarily follow that——. When anyone is in a subordinate position, Mr. Krogstad, they should really be careful to avoid offending anyone who—who——

Krogstad. Who has influence?

Nora. Exactly.

Krogstad *(changing his tone).* Mrs. Helmer, you will be so good as to use your influence on my behalf.

Nora. What? What do you mean?

Krogstad. You will be so kind as to see that I am allowed to keep my subordinate position in the Bank.

Nora. What do you mean by that? Who proposes to take your post away from you?

Krogstad. Oh, there is no necessity to keep up the pretence of ignorance. I can quite understand that your friend is not very anxious to expose herself to the chance of rubbing shoulders with me; and I quite understand, too, whom I have to thank for being turned off.

Nora. But I assure you——

Krogstad. Very likely; but, to come to the point, the time has come when I should advise you to use your influence to prevent that.

Nora. But, Mr. Krogstad, I *have* no influence.

Krogstad. Haven't you? I thought you said yourself just now——

Nora. Naturally I did not mean you to put that construction on it. I! What should make you think I have any influence of that kind with my husband?

Krogstad. Oh, I have known your husband from our student days. I don't suppose he is any more unassailable than other husbands.

Nora. If you speak slightingly of my husband, I shall turn you out of the house.

Krogstad. You are bold, Mrs. Helmer.

Nora. I am not afraid of you any longer. As soon as the New Year comes, I shall in a very short time be free of the whole thing.

Krogstad *(controlling himself).* Listen to me, Mrs. Helmer. If necessary, I am prepared to fight for my small post in the Bank as if I were fighting for my life.

Nora. So it seems.

Krogstad. It is not only for the sake of the money; indeed, that weighs least with me in the matter. There is another reason—well, I may as well tell you. My position is this. I daresay you know, like everybody else, that once, many years ago, I was guilty of an indiscretion.

Nora. I think I have heard something of the kind.

Krogstad. The matter never came into court; but every way seemed to be closed to me after that. So I took to the business that you know of. I had to do something; and, honestly, I don't think I've been one of the worst. But now I must cut myself free from all that. My sons are growing up; for their sake I must try and win back as much respect as I can in the town. This post in the Bank was like the first step up for me—and now your husband is going to kick me downstairs again into the mud.

Nora. But you must believe me, Mr. Krogstad; it is not in my power to help you at all.

Krogstad. Then it is because you haven't the will; but I have means to compel you.

Nora. You don't mean that you will tell my husband that I owe you money?

Krogstad. Hm!—suppose I were to tell him?

Nora. It would be perfectly infamous of you. (*Sobbing.*) To think of his learning my secret, which has been my joy and pride, in such an ugly, clumsy way—that he should learn it from you! And it would put me in a horribly disagreeable position——

Krogstad. Only disagreeable?

Nora (*impetuously*). Well, do it, then!—and it will be the worse for you. My husband will see for himself what a blackguard you are, and you certainly won't keep your post then.

Krogstad. I asked you if it was only a disagreeable scene at home that you were afraid of?

Nora. If my husband does get to know of it, of course he will at once pay you what is still owing, and we shall have nothing more to do with you.

Krogstad (*coming a step nearer*). Listen to me, Mrs. Helmer. Either you have a very bad memory or you know very little of business. I shall be obliged to remind you of a few details.

Nora. What do you mean?

Krogstad. When your husband was ill, you came to me to borrow two hundred and fifty pounds.

Nora. I didn't know anyone else to go to.

Krogstad. I promised to get you that amount——

Nora. Yes, and you did so.

Krogstad. I promised to get you that amount, on certain conditions. Your mind was so taken up with your husband's illness, and you were so anxious to get the money for your journey, that you seem to have paid no attention to the conditions of our bargain. Therefore it will not be amiss if I remind you of them. Now, I promised to get the money on the security of a bond which I signed.

Nora. Yes, and which I signed.

Krogstad. Good. But below your signature there were a few lines constituting your father a surety for the money; those lines your father should have signed.

Nora. Should? He did sign them.

Krogstad. I had left the date blank; that is to say your father should himself have inserted the date on which he signed the paper. Do you remember that?

Nora. Yes, I think I remember——

Krogstad. Then I gave you the bond to send by post to your father. Is that not so?

Nora. Yes.

Krogstad. And you naturally did so at once, because five or six days afterwards you brought me the bond with your father's signature. And then I gave you the money.

Nora. Well, haven't I been paying it off regularly?

Krogstad. Fairly so, yes. But—to come back to the matter in hand—that must have been a very trying time for you, Mrs. Helmer?

Nora. It was, indeed.

Krogstad. Your father was very ill, wasn't he?

Nora. He was very near his end.

Krogstad. And died soon afterwards?

Nora. Yes.

Krogstad. Tell me, Mrs. Helmer, can you by any chance remember what day your father died?—on what day of the month, I mean.

Nora. Papa died on the 29th of September.

Krogstad. That is correct; I have ascertained it for myself. And, as that is so, there is a discrepancy *(taking a paper from his pocket)* which I cannot account for.

Nora. What discrepancy? I don't know——

Krogstad. The discrepancy consists, Mrs. Helmer, in the fact that your father signed this bond three days after his death.

Nora. What do you mean? I don't understand——

Krogstad. Your father died on the 29th of September. But, look here; your father has dated his signature the 2nd of October. It is a discrepancy, isn't it? *(Nora is silent.)* Can you explain it to me? *(Nora is still silent.)* It is a remarkable thing, too, that the words "2nd of October," as well as the year, are not written in your father's handwriting but in one that I think I know. Well, of course it can be explained; your father may have forgotten to date his signature, and someone else may have dated it haphazard before they knew of his death. There is no harm in that. It all depends on the signature of the name; and *that* is genuine, I suppose, Mrs. Helmer? It was your father himself who signed his name here?

Nora *(after a short pause, throws her head up and looks defiantly at him).* No, it was not. It was I that wrote papa's name.

Krogstad. Are you aware that is a dangerous confession?

Nora. In what way? You shall have your money soon.

Krogstad. Let me ask you a question; why did you not send the paper to your father?

Nora. It was impossible; papa was so ill. If I had asked him for his signature, I should have had to tell him what the money was to be used for; and when he was so ill himself I couldn't tell him that my husband's life was in danger—it was impossible.

Krogstad. It would have been better for you if you had given up your trip abroad.

Nora. No, that was impossible. That trip was to save my husband's life; I couldn't give that up.

Krogstad. But did it never occur to you that you were committing a fraud on me?

Nora. I couldn't take that into account; I didn't trouble myself about you at all. I couldn't bear you, because you put so many heartless difficulties in my way, although you knew what a dangerous condition my husband was in.

Krogstad. Mrs. Helmer, you evidently do not realise clearly what it is that you have been guilty of. But I can assure you that my one false step, which lost me all my reputation, was nothing more or nothing worse than what you have done.

Nora. You? Do you ask me to believe that you were brave enough to run a risk to save your wife's life?

Krogstad. The law cares nothing about motives.

Nora. Then it must be a very foolish law.

Krogstad. Foolish or not, it is the law by which you will be judged, if I produce this paper in court.

Nora. I don't believe it. Is a daughter not to be allowed to spare her dying father anxiety and care? Is a wife not to be allowed to save her husband's life? I don't know much about law; but I am certain that there must be laws permitting such things as that. Have you no knowledge of such laws—you who are a lawyer? You must be a very poor lawyer, Mr. Krogstad.

Krogstad. Maybe. But matters of business—such business as you and I have had together—do you think I don't understand that? Very well. Do as you please. But let me tell you this—if I lose my position a second time, you shall lose yours with me.

(He bows, and goes out through the hall.)

Nora *(appears buried in thought for a short time, then tosses her head).* Nonsense! Trying to frighten me like that—I am not so silly as he thinks. *(Begins to busy herself putting the children's things in order.)* And yet——? No, it's impossible! I did it for love's sake.

The Children *(in the doorway on the left).* Mother, the stranger man has gone out through the gate.

Nora. Yes, dears, I know. But don't tell anyone about the stranger man. Do you hear? Not even papa.

Children. No, mother; but will you come and play again?

Nora. No, no,—not now.

Children. But, mother, you promised us.

Nora. Yes, but I can't now. Run away in; I have such a lot to do. Run away in, my sweet little darlings. *(She gets them into the room by degrees and shuts the door on them; then sits down on the sofa, takes up a piece of needlework and sews a few stitches, but soon stops.)* No! *(Throws down the work, gets up, goes to the hall door and calls out.)* Helen! bring the tree in. *(Goes to the table on the left, opens a drawer, and stops again.)* No, no! it is quite impossible!

Maid *(coming in with the tree).* Where shall I put it, ma'am?

Nora. Here, in the middle of the floor.

Maid. Shall I get you anything else?

Nora. No, thank you. I have all I want.

(Exit Maid.)

Nora *(begins dressing the tree).* A candle here—and flowers here——. The horrible man! It's all nonsense—there's nothing wrong. The tree shall be splendid! I will do everything I can think of to please you, Torvald!—I will sing for you, dance for you—*(Helmer comes in with some papers under his arm.)* Oh! are you back already?

Helmer. Yes. Has anyone been here?

Nora. Here? No.

Helmer. That is strange. I saw Krogstad going out of the gate.

Nora. Did you? Oh yes, I forgot, Krogstad was here for a moment.

Helmer. Nora, I can see from your manner that he has been here begging you to say a good word for him.

Nora. Yes.

Helmer. And you were to appear to do it of your own accord; you were to conceal from me the fact of his having been here; didn't he beg that of you too?

Nora. Yes, Torvald, but——

Helmer. Nora, Nora, and you would be a party to that sort of thing? To have any talk with a man like that, and give him any sort of promise? And to tell me a lie into the bargain?

Nora. A lie——?

Helmer. Didn't you tell me no one had been here? *(Shakes his finger at her.)* My little song-bird must never do that again. A song-bird must have a clean beak to chirp with—no false notes! *(Puts his arm round her waist.)* That is so, isn't it? Yes, I am sure it is. *(Lets her go.)* We will say no more about it. *(Sits down by the stove.)* How warm and snug it is here!

(Turns over his papers.)

Nora *(after a short pause, during which she busies herself with the Christmas tree).* Torvald!

Helmer. Yes.

Nora. I am looking forward tremendously to the fancy dress ball at the Stenborgs' the day after to-morrow.

Helmer. And I am tremendously curious to see what you are going to surprise me with.

Nora. It was very silly of me to want to do that.

Helmer. What do you mean?

Nora. I can't hit upon anything that will do; everything I think of seems so silly and insignificant.

Helmer. Does my little Nora acknowledge that at last?

Nora *(standing behind his chair with her arms on the back of it).* Are you very busy, Torvald?

Helmer. Well——

Nora. What are all those papers?

Helmer. Bank business.

Nora. Already?

Helmer. I have got authority from the retiring manager to undertake the necessary changes in the staff and in the rearrangement of the work; and I must make use of the Christmas week for that, so as to have everything in order for the new year.

Nora. Then that was why this poor Krogstad——

Helmer. Hm!

Nora *(leans against the back of his chair and strokes his hair).* If you hadn't been so busy I should have asked you a tremendously big favour, Torvald.

Helmer. What is that? Tell me.

Nora. There is no one has such good taste as you. And I do so want to look nice at the fancy-dress ball. Torvald, couldn't you take me in hand and decide what I shall go as, and what sort of a dress I shall wear?

Helmer. Aha! so my obstinate little woman is obliged to get someone to come to her rescue?

Nora. Yes, Torvald, I can't get along a bit without your help.

Helmer. Very well, I will think it over, we shall manage to hit upon something.

Nora. That *is* nice of you. *(Goes to the Christmas tree. A short pause.)* How pretty the red flowers look——. But, tell me, was it really something very bad that this Krogstad was guilty of?

Helmer. He forged someone's name. Have you any idea what that means?

Nora. Isn't it possible that he was driven to do it by necessity?

Helmer. Yes; or, as in so many cases, by imprudence. I am not so heartless as to condemn a man altogether because of a single false step of that kind.

Nora. No you wouldn't, would you, Torvald?

Helmer. Many a man has been able to retrieve his character, if he has openly confessed his fault and taken his punishment.

Nora. Punishment——?

Helmer. But Krogstad did nothing of that sort; he got himself out of it by a cunning trick, and that is why he has gone under altogether.

Nora. But do you think it would——?

Helmer. Just think how a guilty man like that has to lie and play the hypocrite with everyone, how he has to wear a mask in the presence of those near and dear to him, even before his own wife and children. And about the children—that is the most terrible part of it all, Nora.

Nora. How?

Helmer. Because such an atmosphere of lies infects and poisons the whole life of a home. Each breath the children take in such a house is full of the germs of evil.

Nora *(coming nearer him).* Are you sure of that?

Helmer. My dear, I have often seen it in the course of my life as a lawyer. Almost everyone who has gone to the bad early in life has had a deceitful mother.

Nora. Why do you only say—mother?

Helmer. It seems most commonly to be the mother's influence, though naturally a bad father's would have the same result. Every lawyer is familiar with the fact. This Krogstad, now, has been persistently poisoning his own children with lies and dissimulation; that is why I say he has lost all moral character. (*Holds out his hands to her.*) That is why my sweet little Nora must promise me not to plead his cause. Give me your hand on it. Come, come, what is this? Give me your hand. There now, that's settled. I assure you it would be quite impossible for me to work with him; I literally feel physically ill when I am in the company of such people.

Nora (*takes her hand out of his and goes to the opposite side of the Christmas tree*). How hot it is in here; and I have such a lot to do.

Helmer (*getting up and putting his papers in order*). Yes, and I must try and read through some of these before dinner; and I must think about your costume, too. And it is just possible I may have something ready in gold paper to hang up on the tree. (*Puts his hand on her head.*) My precious little singing-bird!

(*He goes into his room and shuts the door after him.*)

Nora (*after a pause, whispers*). No, no—it isn't true. It's impossible; it must be impossible.

(*The Nurse opens the door on the left.*)

Nurse. The little ones are begging so hard to be allowed to come in to mamma.
Nora. No, no, no! Don't let them come in to me! You stay with them, Anne.
Nurse. Very well, ma'am.

(*Shuts the door.*)

Nora (*pale with terror*). Deprave my little children? Poison my home? (*A short pause. Then she tosses her head.*) It's not true. It can't possibly be true.

ACT II

The Same Scene

The Christmas tree is in the corner by the piano, stripped of its ornaments and with burnt-down candle-ends on its dishevelled branches. Nora's cloak and hat are lying on the sofa. She is alone in the room, walking about uneasily. She stops by the sofa and takes up her cloak.

Nora (*drops the cloak*). Someone is coming now! (*Goes to the door and listens.*) No—it is no one. Of course, no one will come to-day, Christmas Day—nor tomorrow either. But, perhaps—(*Opens the door and looks out*). No, nothing in the letter-box; it is quite empty. (*Comes forward.*) What rubbish! of course he can't be in earnest about it. Such a thing couldn't happen; it is impossible—I have three little children.

(*Enter the Nurse from the room on the left, carrying a big cardboard box.*)

Nurse. At last I have found the box with the fancy dress.

Nora. Thanks; put it on the table.

Nurse (*doing so*). But it is very much in want of mending.

Nora. I should like to tear it into a hundred thousand pieces.

Nurse. What an idea! It can easily be put in order—just a little patience.

Nora. Yes, I will go and get Mrs. Linde to come and help me with it.

Nurse. What, out again? In this horrible weather? You will catch cold, ma'am, and make yourself ill.

Nora. Well, worse than that might happen. How are the children?

Nurse. The poor little souls are playing with their Christmas presents, but——

Nora. Do they ask much for me?

Nurse. You see, they are so accustomed to have their mamma with them.

Nora. Yes, but, nurse, I shall not be able to be so much with them now as I was before.

Nurse. Oh well, young children easily get accustomed to anything.

Nora. Do you think so? Do you think they would forget their mother if she went away altogether?

Nurse. Good heavens!—went away altogether?

Nora. Nurse, I want you to tell me something I have often wondered about—how could you have the heart to put your own child out among strangers?

Nurse. I was obliged to, if I wanted to be little Nora's nurse.

Nora. Yes, but how could you be willing to do it?

Nurse. What, when I was going to get such a good place by it? A poor girl who has got into trouble should be glad to. Besides, that wicked man didn't do a single thing for me.

Nora. But I suppose your daughter has quite forgotten you.

Nurse. No, indeed she hasn't. She wrote to me when she was confirmed, and when she was married.

Nora (*putting her arms round her neck*). Dear old Anne, you were a good mother to me when I was little.

Nurse. Little Nora, poor dear, had no other mother but me.

Nora. And if my little ones had no other mother, I am sure you would——What nonsense I am talking! (*Opens the box.*) Go in to them. Now I must——. You will see to-morrow how charming I shall look.

Nurse. I am sure there will be no one at the ball so charming as you, ma'am.

(*Goes into the room on the left.*)

Nora (*begins to unpack the box, but soon pushes it away from her*). If only I dared go out. If only no one would come. If only I could be sure nothing would happen here in the meantime. Stuff and nonsense! No one will come. Only I mustn't think about it. I will brush my muff. What lovely, lovely gloves! Out of my thoughts, out of my thoughts! One, two, three, four, five, six——(*Screams.*) Ah! there is someone coming——

(Makes a movement towards the door, but stands irresolute. Enter Mrs. Linde from the hall, where she has taken off her cloak and hat.)

Nora. Oh, it's you, Christine. There is no one else out there, is there? How good of you to come!

Mrs. Linde. I heard you were up asking for me.

Nora. Yes, I was passing by. As a matter of fact, it is something you could help me with. Let us sit down here on the sofa. Look here. To-morrow evening there is to be a fancy-dress ball at the Stenborgs', who live above us; and Torvald wants me to go as a Neapolitan fisher-girl, and dance the Tarantella that I learnt at Capri.

Mrs. Linde. I see; you are going to keep up the character.

Nora. Yes, Torvald wants me to. Look, here is the dress; Torvald had it made for me there, but now it is all so torn, and I haven't any idea——

Mrs. Linde. We will easily put that right. It is only some of the trimming come unsewn here and there. Needle and thread? Now then, that's all we want.

Nora. It *is* nice of you.

Mrs. Linde *(sewing)*. So you are going to be dressed up to-morrow, Nora. I will tell you what—I shall come in for a moment and see you in your fine feathers. But I have completely forgotten to thank you for a delightful evening yesterday.

Nora *(gets up, and crosses the stage)*. Well I don't think yesterday was as pleasant as usual. You ought to have come to town a little earlier, Christine. Certainly Torvald does understand how to make a house dainty and attractive.

Mrs. Linde. And so do you, it seems to me; you are not your father's daughter for nothing. But tell me, is Doctor Rank always as depressed as he was yesterday?

Nora. No; yesterday it was very noticeable. I must tell you that he suffers from a very dangerous disease. He has consumption of the spine, poor creature. His father was a horrible man who committed all sorts of excesses; and that is why his son was sickly from childhood, do you understand?

Mrs. Linde *(dropping her sewing)*. But, my dearest Nora, how do you know anything about such things?

Nora *(walking about)*. Pooh! When you have three children, you get visits now and then from—from married women, who know something of medical matters, and they talk about one thing and another.

Mrs. Linde *(goes on sewing. A short silence)*. Does Doctor Rank come here every day?

Nora. Every day regularly. He is Torvald's most intimate friend, and a great friend of mine too. He is just like one of the family.

Mrs. Linde. But tell me this—is he perfectly sincere? I mean, isn't he the kind of man that is very anxious to make himself agreeable?

Nora. Not in the least. What makes you think that?

Mrs. Linde. When you introduced him to me yesterday, he declared he had often heard my name mentioned in this house; but afterwards I noticed that your husband hadn't the slightest idea who I was. So how could Doctor Rank——?

Nora. That is quite right, Christine. Torvald is so absurdly fond of me that he wants me absolutely to himself, as he says. At first he used to seem almost jealous if I mentioned any of the dear folk at home, so naturally I gave up doing so. But I often talk about such things with Doctor Rank, because he likes hearing about them.

Mrs. Linde. Listen to me, Nora. You are still very like a child in many things, and I am older than you in many ways and have a little more experience. Let me tell you this—you ought to make an end of it with Doctor Rank.

Nora. What ought I to make an end of?

Mrs. Linde. Of two things, I think. Yesterday you talked some nonsense about a rich admirer who was to leave you money——

Nora. An admirer who doesn't exist, unfortunately! But what then?

Mrs. Linde. Is Doctor Rank a man of means?

Nora. Yes, he is.

Mrs. Linde. And has no one to provide for?

Nora. No, no one; but——

Mrs. Linde. And comes here every day?

Nora. Yes, I told you so.

Mrs. Linde. But how can this well-bred man be so tactless?

Nora. I don't understand you at all.

Mrs. Linde. Don't prevaricate, Nora. Do you suppose I don't guess who lent you the two hundred and fifty pounds?

Nora. Are you out of your senses? How can you think of such a thing! A friend of ours, who comes here every day! Do you realise what a horribly painful position that would be?

Mrs. Linde. Then it really isn't he?

Nora. No, certainly not. It would never have entered into my head for a moment. Besides, he had no money to lend then; he came into his money afterwards.

Mrs. Linde. Well, I think that was lucky for you, my dear Nora.

Nora. No, it would never have come into my head to ask Doctor Rank. Although I am quite sure that if I had asked him——

Mrs. Linde. But of course you won't.

Nora. Of course not. I have no reason to think it could possibly be necessary. But I am quite sure that if I told Doctor Rank——

Mrs. Linde. Behind your husband's back?

Nora. I must make an end of it with the other one, and that will be behind his back too. I *must* make an end of it with him.

Mrs. Linde. Yes, that is what I told you yesterday, but——

Nora (*walking up and down*). A man can put a thing like that straight much easier than a woman——

Mrs. Linde. One's husband, yes.

Nora. Nonsense! (*Standing still.*) When you pay off a debt you get your bond back, don't you?

Mrs. Linde. Yes, as a matter of course.

Nora. And can tear it into a hundred thousand pieces, and burn it up—the nasty dirty paper!

Mrs. Linde *(looks hard at her, lays down her sewing and gets up slowly).* Nora, you are concealing something from me.

Nora. Do I look as if I were?

Mrs. Linde. Something has happened to you since yesterday morning. Nora, what is it?

Nora *(going nearer to her).* Christine! *(Listens.)* Hush! there's Torvald come home. Do you mind going in to the children for the present? Torvald can't bear to see dressmaking going on. Let Anne help you.

Mrs. Linde *(gathering some of the things together).* Certainly—but I am not going away from here till we have had it out with one another.

(She goes into the room on the left, as Helmer comes in from the hall.)

Nora *(going up to Helmer).* I have wanted you so much, Torvald dear.

Helmer. Was that the dressmaker?

Nora. No, it was Christine; she is helping me to put my dress in order. You will see I shall look quite smart.

Helmer. Wasn't that a happy thought of mine, now?

Nora. Splendid! But don't you think it is nice of me, too, to do as you wish?

Helmer. Nice?—because you do as your husband wishes? Well, well, you little rogue, I am sure you did not mean it in that way. But I am not going to disturb you; you will want to be trying on your dress, I expect.

Nora. I suppose you are going to work.

Helmer. Yes. *(Shows her a bundle of papers.)* Look at that. I have just been into the bank.

(Turns to go into his room.)

Nora. Torvald.

Helmer. Yes.

Nora. If your little squirrel were to ask you for something very, very prettily——?

Helmer. What then?

Nora. Would you do it?

Helmer. I should like to hear what it is, first.

Nora. Your squirrel would run about and do all her tricks if you would be nice, and do what she wants.

Helmer. Speak plainly.

Nora. Your skylark would chirp about in every room, with her song rising and falling——

Helmer. Well, my skylark does that anyhow.

Nora. I would play the fairy and dance for you in the moonlight, Torvald.

Helmer. Nora—you surely don't mean that request you made of me this morning?

Nora *(going near him).* Yes, Torvald, I beg you so earnestly——

Helmer. Have you really the courage to open up that question again?

Nora. Yes, dear, you *must* do as I ask; you *must* let Krogstad keep his post in the Bank.

Helmer. My dear Nora, it is his post that I have arranged Mrs. Linde shall have.

Nora. Yes, you have been awfully kind about that; but you could just as well dismiss some other clerk instead of Krogstad.

Helmer. This simply incredible obstinacy! Because you chose to give him a thoughtless promise that you would speak for him, I am expected to——

Nora. That isn't the reason, Torvald. It is for your own sake. This fellow writes in the most scurrilous newspapers; you have told me so yourself. He can do you an unspeakable amount of harm. I am frightened to death of him——

Helmer. Ah, I understand; it is recollections of the past that scare you.

Nora. What do you mean?

Helmer. Naturally you are thinking of your father.

Nora. Yes—yes, of course. Just recall to your mind what these malicious creatures wrote in the papers about papa, and how horribly they slandered him. I believe they would have procured his dismissal if the Department had not sent you over to inquire into it, and if you had not been so kindly disposed and helpful to him.

Helmer. My little Nora, there is an important difference between your father and me. Your father's reputation as a public official was not above suspicion. Mine is, and I hope it will continue to be so, as long as I hold my office.

Nora. You never can tell what mischief these men may contrive. We ought to be so well off, so snug and happy here in our peaceful home, and have no cares— you and I and the children, Torvald! That is why I beg of you so earnestly——

Helmer. And it is just by interceding for him that you make it impossible for me to keep him. It is already known at the Bank that I mean to dismiss Krogstad. Is it to get about now that the new manager has changed his mind at his wife's bidding——

Nora. And what if it did?

Helmer. Of course!—if only this obstinate little person can get her way! Do you suppose I am going to make myself ridiculous before my whole staff, to let people think that I am a man to be swayed by all sorts of outside influence? I should very soon feel the consequences of it, I can tell you! And besides, there is one thing that makes it quite impossible for me to have Krogstad in the Bank as long as I am manager.

Nora. Whatever is that?

Helmer. His moral failings I might perhaps have overlooked, if necessary——

Nora. Yes, you could—couldn't you?

Helmer. And I hear he is a good worker, too. But I knew him when we were boys. It was one of those rash friendships that so often prove an incubus in after life. I may as well tell you plainly, we were once on very intimate terms with one another. But this tactless fellow lays no restraint on himself when other people are present. On the contrary, he thinks it gives him the right to adopt a familiar tone with me, and every minute it is "I say, Helmer, old fellow!" and that sort of thing. I assure you it is extremely painful for me. He would make my position in the Bank intolerable.

Nora. Torvald, I don't believe you mean that.

Helmer. Don't you? Why not?

Nora. Because it is such a narrow-minded way of looking at things.

Helmer. What are you saying? Narrow-minded? Do you think I am narrow-minded?

Nora. No, just the opposite, dear—and it is exactly for that reason.

Helmer. It's the same thing. You say my point of view is narrow-minded, so I must be so too. Narrow-minded! Very well—I must put an end to this. *(Goes to the hall-door and calls.)* Helen!

Nora. What are you going to do?

Helmer *(looking among his papers).* Settle it. *(Enter Maid.)* Look here; take this letter and go downstairs with it at once. Find a messenger and tell him to deliver it, and be quick. The address is on it, and here is the money.

Maid. Very well, sir.   *(Exit with the letter.)*

Helmer *(putting his papers together).* Now then, little Miss Obstinate.

Nora *(breathlessly).* Torvald—what was that letter?

Helmer. Krogstad's dismissal.

Nora. Call her back, Torvald! There is still time. Oh Torvald, call her back! Do it for my sake—for your own sake—for the children's sake! Do you hear me, Torvald? Call her back! You don't know what that letter can bring upon us.

Helmer. It's too late.

Nora. Yes, it's too late.

Helmer. My dear Nora, I can forgive the anxiety you are in, although really it is an insult to me. It is, indeed. Isn't it an insult to think that I should be afraid of a starving quill-driver's vengeance? But I forgive you nevertheless, because it is such eloquent witness to your great love for me. *(Takes her in his arms.)* And that is as it should be, my darling Nora. Come what will, you may be sure I shall have both courage and strength if they be needed. You will see I am man enough to take everything upon myself.

Nora *(in a horror-stricken voice).* What do you mean by that?

Helmer. Everything, I say——

Nora *(recovering herself).* You will never have to do that.

Helmer. That's right. Well, we will share it, Nora, as man and wife should. That is how it shall be. *(Caressing her.)* Are you content now? There! there!—not these frightened dove's eyes! The whole thing is only the wildest fancy!—Now, you must go and play through the Tarantella and practise with your tambourine. I shall go into the inner office and shut the door, and I shall hear nothing; you can make as much noise as you please. *(Turns back at the door.)* And when Rank comes, tell him where he will find me.

(Nods to her, takes his papers and goes into his room, and shuts the door after him.)

Nora *(bewildered with anxiety, stands as if rooted to the spot, and whispers).* He was capable of doing it. He will do it. He will do it in spite of everything.—No, not that! Never, never! Anything rather than that! Oh, for some help, some way out of it! *(The door-bell rings.)* Doctor Rank! Anything rather than that—anything, whatever it is!

(She puts her hands over her face, pulls herself together, goes to the door and opens it. Rank is standing without, hanging up his coat. During the following dialogue it begins to grow dark.)

Nora. Good-day, Doctor Rank. I knew your ring. But you mustn't go in to Torvald now; I think he is busy with something.

Rank. And you?

Nora *(brings him in and shuts the door after him).* Oh, you know very well I always have time for you.

Rank. Thank you. I shall make use of as much of it as I can.

Nora. What do you mean by that? As much of it as you can?

Rank. Well, does that alarm you?

Nora. It was such a strange way of putting it. Is anything likely to happen?

Rank. Nothing but what I have long been prepared for. But certainly didn't expect it to happen so soon.

Nora *(gripping him by the arm).* What have you found out? Doctor Rank, you must tell me.

Rank *(sitting down by the stove).* It is all up with me. And it can't be helped.

Nora *(with a sigh of relief).* Is it about yourself?

Rank. Who else? It is no use lying to one's self. I am the most wretched of all my patients, Mrs. Helmer. Lately I have been taking stock of my internal economy. Bankrupt! Probably within a month I shall lie rotting in the churchyard.

Nora. What an ugly thing to say!

Rank. The thing itself is cursedly ugly, and the worst of it is that I shall have to face so much more that is ugly before that. I shall only make one more examination of myself; when I have done that, I shall know pretty certainly when it will be that the horrors of dissolution will begin. There is something I want to tell you. Helmer's refined nature gives him an unconquerable disgust at everything that is ugly; I won't have him in my sick-room.

Nora. Oh, but, Doctor Rank——

Rank. I won't have him there. Not on any account. I bar my door to him. As soon as I am quite certain that the worst has come, I shall send you my card with a black cross on it, and then you will know that the loathsome end has begun.

Nora. You are quite absurd to-day. And I wanted you so much to be in a really good humour.

Rank. With death stalking beside me?—To have to pay this penalty for another man's sin! Is there any justice in that? And in every single family, in one way or another, some such inexorable retribution is being exacted——

Nora *(putting her hands over her ears).* Rubbish! Do talk of something cheerful.

Rank. Oh, it's a mere laughing matter, the whole thing. My poor innocent spine has to suffer for my father's youthful amusements.

Nora *(sitting at the table on the left).* I suppose you mean that he was too partial to asparagus and pâté de foie gras, don't you.

Rank. Yes, and to truffles.

Nora. Truffles, yes. And oysters too, I suppose?

Rank. Oysters, of course, that goes without saying.

Nora. And heaps of port and champagne. It is sad that all these nice things should take their revenge on our bones.

Rank. Especially that they should revenge themselves on the unlucky bones of those who have not had the satisfaction of enjoying them.

Nora. Yes, that's the saddest part of it all.

Rank *(with a searching look at her).* Hm!——

Nora *(after a short pause).* Why did you smile?

Rank. No, it was you that laughed.

Nora. No, it was you that smiled, Doctor Rank!

Rank *(rising).* You are a greater rascal than I thought.

Nora. I am in a silly mood to-day.

Rank. So it seems.

Nora *(putting her hands on his shoulders).* Dear, dear Doctor Rank, death mustn't take you away from Torvald and me.

Rank. It is a loss you would easily recover from. Those who are gone are soon forgotten.

Nora *(looking at him anxiously).* Do you believe that?

Rank. People form new ties, and then——

Nora. Who will form new ties?

Rank. Both you and Helmer, when I am gone. You yourself are already on the high road to it, I think. What did that Mrs. Linde want here last night?

Nora. Oho!—you don't mean to say you are jealous of poor Christine?

Rank. Yes, I am. She will be my successor in this house. When I am done for, this woman will——

Nora. Hush! don't speak so loud. She is in that room.

Rank. To-day again. There, you see.

Nora. She has only come to sew my dress for me. Bless my soul, how unreasonable you are! *(Sits down on the sofa.)* Be nice now, Doctor Rank, and to-morrow you will see how beautifully I shall dance, and you can imagine I am doing it all for you—and for Torvald too, of course. *(Takes various things out of the box.)* Doctor Rank, come and sit down here, and I will show you something.

Rank *(sitting down).* What is it?

Nora. Just look at those!

Rank. Silk stockings.

Nora. Flesh-coloured. Aren't they lovely? It is so dark here now, but tomorrow——. No, no, no! you must only look at the feet. Oh well, you may have leave to look at the legs too.

Rank. Hm!——

Nora. Why are you looking so critical? Don't you think they will fit me?

Rank. I have no means of forming an opinion about that.

Nora *(looks at him for a moment).* For shame! *(Hits him lightly on the ear with the stockings.)* That's to punish you. *(Folds them up again.)*

Rank. And what other nice things am I to be allowed to see?

Nora. Not a single thing more, for being so naughty. *(She looks among the things, humming to herself.)*

Rank *(after a short silence).* When I am sitting here, talking to you as intimately as this, I cannot imagine for a moment what would have become of me if I had never come into this house.

Nora *(smiling).* I believe you do feel thoroughly at home with us.

Rank *(in a lower voice, looking straight in front of him).* And to be obliged to leave it all——

Nora. Nonsense, you are not going to leave it.

Rank *(as before).* And not be able to leave behind one the slightest token of one's gratitude, scarcely even a fleeting regret—nothing but an empty place which the first comer can fill as well as any other.

Nora. And if I asked you now for a—? No!

Rank. For what?

Nora. For a big proof of your friendship——

Rank. Yes, yes!

Nora. I mean a tremendously big favour——

Rank. Would you really make me so happy for once?

Nora. Ah, but you don't know what it is yet.

Rank. No—but tell me.

Nora. I really can't, Doctor Rank. It is something out of all reason; it means advice, and help, and a favour——

Rank. The bigger a thing it is the better. I can't conceive what it is you mean. Do tell me. Haven't I your confidence?

Nora. More than anyone else. I know you are my truest and best friend, and so I will tell you what it is. Well, Doctor Rank, it is something you must help me to prevent. You know how devotedly, how inexpressibly deeply Torvald loves me; he would never for a moment hesitate to give his life for me.

Rank *(leaning towards her).* Nora—do you think he is the only one——?

Nora *(with a slight start).* The only one——?

Rank. The only one who would gladly give his life for your sake.

Nora *(sadly).* Is that it?

Rank. I was determined you should know it before I went away, and there will never be a better opportunity than this. Now you know it, Nora. And now you know, too, that you can trust me as you would trust no one else.

Nora *(rises, deliberately and quietly).* Let me pass.

Rank *(makes room for her to pass him, but sits still).* Nora!

Nora *(at the hall door).* Helen, bring in the lamp. *(Goes over to the stove.)* Dear Doctor Rank, that was really horrid of you.

Rank. To have loved you as much as anyone else does? Was that horrid?

Nora. No, but to go and tell me so. There was really no need——

Rank. What do you mean? Did you know——? *(Maid enters with lamp, puts it down on the table, and goes out.)* Nora—Mrs. Helmer—tell me, had you any idea of this?

Nora. Oh, how do I know whether I had or whether I hadn't? I really can't tell you—— To think you could be so clumsy, Doctor Rank! We were getting on so nicely.

Rank. Well, at all events you know now that you can command me, body and soul. So won't you speak out?

Nora *(looking at him).* After what happened?

Rank. I beg you to let me know what it is.

Nora. I can't tell you anything now.

Rank. Yes, yes. You mustn't punish me in that way. Let me have permission to do for you whatever a man may do.

Nora. You can do nothing for me now. Besides, I really don't need any help at all. You will find that the whole thing is merely fancy on my part. It really is so——of course it is! *(Sits down in the rocking-chair, and looks at him with a smile.)* You are a nice sort of man, Doctor Rank!—don't you feel ashamed of yourself, now the lamp has come?

Rank. Not a bit. But perhaps I had better go—forever?

Nora. No, indeed, you shall not. Of course you must come here just as before. You know very well Torvald can't do without you.

Rank. Yes, but you?

Nora. Oh, I am always tremendously pleased when you come.

Rank. It is just that, that put me on the wrong track. You are a riddle to me. I have often thought that you would almost as soon be in my company as in Helmer's.

Nora. Yes—you see there are some people one loves best, and others whom one would almost always rather have as companions.

Rank. Yes, there is something in that.

Nora. When I was at home, of course I loved papa best. But I always thought it tremendous fun if I could steal down into the maids' room, because they never moralised at all, and talked to each other about such entertaining things.

Rank. I see—it is *their* place I have taken.

Nora *(jumping up and going to him).* Oh, dear, nice Doctor Rank, I never meant that at all. But surely you can understand that being with Torvald is a little like being with papa——

(Enter Maid from the hall.)

Maid. If you please, ma'am. *(Whispers and hands her a card.)*

Nora *(glancing at the card).* Oh! *(Puts it in her pocket.)*

Rank. Is there anything wrong?

Nora. No, no, not in the least. It is only something—it is my new dress——

Rank. What? Your dress is lying there.

Nora. Oh, yes, that one; but this is another. I ordered it. Torvald mustn't know about it——

Rank. Oho! Then that was the great secret.

Nora. Of course. Just go in to him; he is sitting in the inner room. Keep him as long as——

Rank. Make your mind easy; I won't let him escape. *(Goes into Helmer's room.)*

Nora *(to the Maid).* And he is standing waiting in the kitchen?

Maid. Yes; he came up the back stairs.

Nora. But didn't you tell him no one was in?

Maid. Yes, but it was no good.

Nora. He won't go away?

Maid. No; he says he won't until he has seen you, ma'am.

Nora. Well, let him come in—but quietly. Helen, you mustn't say anything about it to anyone. It is a surprise for my husband.

Maid. Yes ma'am, I quite understand. *(Exit.)*

Nora. This dreadful thing is going to happen! It will happen in spite of me! No, no, no, it can't happen—it shan't happen!

(She bolts the door of Helmer's room. The Maid opens the hall door for Krogstad and shuts it after him. He is wearing a fur coat, high boots, and a fur cap.)

Nora *(advancing towards him).* Speak low—my husband is at home.

Krogstad. No matter about that.

Nora. What do you want of me?

Krogstad. An explanation of something.

Nora. Make haste then. What is it?

Krogstad. You know, I suppose, that I have got my dismissal.

Nora. I couldn't prevent it, Mr. Krogstad. I fought as hard as I could on your side, but it was no good.

Krogstad. Does your husband love you so little, then? He knows what I can expose you to, and yet he ventures——

Nora. How can you suppose that he has any knowledge of the sort?

Krogstad. I didn't suppose so at all. It would not be the least like our dear Torvald Helmer to show so much courage—

Nora. Mr. Krogstad, a little respect for my husband, please.

Krogstad. Certainly—all the respect he deserves. But since you have kept the matter so carefully to yourself, I make bold to suppose that you have a little clearer idea, than you had yesterday, of what it actually is that you have done?

Nora. More than you could ever teach me.

Krogstad. Yes, such a bad lawyer as I am.

Nora. What is it you want of me?

Krogstad. Only to see how you were, Mrs. Helmer. I have been thinking about you all day long. A mere cashier, a quill-driver, a—well, a man like me—even he has a little of what is called feeling, you know.

Nora. Show it, then; think of my little children.

Krogstad. Have you and your husband thought of mine? But never mind about that. I only wanted to tell you that you need not take this matter too seriously. In the first place there will be no accusation made on my part.

Nora. No, of course not; I was sure of that.

Krogstad. The whole thing can be arranged amicably; there is no reason why anyone should know anything about it. It will remain a secret between us three.

Nora. My husband must never get to know anything about it.

Krogstad. How will you be able to prevent it? Am I to understand that you can pay the balance that is owing?

Nora. No, not just at present.

Krogstad. Or perhaps that you have some expedient for raising the money soon?

Nora. No expedient that I mean to make use of.

Krogstad. Well, in any case, it would have been of no use to you now. If you stood there with ever so much money in your hand, I would never part with your bond.

Nora. Tell me what purpose you mean to put it to.

Krogstad. I shall only preserve it—keep it in my possession. No one who is not concerned in the matter shall have the slightest hint of it. So that if the thought of it has driven you to any desperate resolution——

Nora. It has.

Krogstad. If you had it in your mind to run away from your home——

Nora. I had.

Krogstad. Or even something worse——

Nora. How could you know that?

Krogstad. Give up the idea.

Nora. How did you know I had thought of *that*?

Krogstad. Most of us think of that at first. I did, too—but I hadn't the courage.

Nora (*faintly*). No more had I.

Krogstad (*in a tone of relief*). No, that's it, isn't it—you hadn't the courage either?

Nora. No, I haven't—I haven't.

Krogstad. Besides, it would have been a great piece of folly. Once the first storm at home is over—. I have a letter for your husband in my pocket.

Nora. Telling him everything?

Krogstad. In as lenient a manner as I possibly could.

Nora (*quickly*). He mustn't get the letter. Tear it up. I will find some means of getting money.

Krogstad. Excuse me, Mrs. Helmer, but I think I told you just now——

Nora. I am not speaking of what I owe you. Tell me what sum you are asking my husband for, and I will get the money.

Krogstad. I am not asking your husband for a penny.

Nora. What do you want, then?

Krogstad. I will tell you. I want to rehabilitate myself, Mrs. Helmer; I want to get on; and in that your husband must help me. For the last year and a half I have not had a hand in anything dishonourable, and all that time I have been struggling in most restricted circumstances. I was content to work my way up step by step. Now I am turned out, and I am not going to be satisfied with merely being taken into favour again. I want to get on, I tell you. I want to get into the Bank again, in a higher position. Your husband must make a place for me——

Nora. That he will never do!

Krogstad. He will; I know him; he dare not protest. And as soon as I am in there again with him, then you will see! Within a year I shall be the manager's right hand. It will be Nils Krogstad and not Torvald Helmer who manages the Bank.

Nora. That's a thing you will never see!

Krogstad. Do you mean that you will——?

Nora. I have courage enough for it now.

Krogstad. Oh, you can't frighten me. A fine, spoilt lady like you——

Nora. You will see, you will see.

Krogstad. Under the ice, perhaps? Down into the cold, coal-black water? And then, in the spring, to float up to the surface, all horrible and unrecognisable, with your hair fallen out——

Nora. You can't frighten me.

Krogstad. Nor you me. People don't do such things, Mrs. Helmer. Besides, what use would it be? I should have him completely in my power all the same.

Nora. Afterwards? When I am no longer——

Krogstad. Have you forgotten that it is I who have the keeping of your reputation? (*Nora stands speechlessly looking at him.*) Well, now, I have warned you. Do not do anything foolish. When Helmer has had my letter, I shall expect a message from him. And be sure you remember that it is your husband himself who has forced me into such ways as this again. I will never forgive him for that. Good-bye, Mrs. Helmer.   (*Exit through the hall.*)

Nora (*goes to the hall door, opens it slightly and listens*). He is going. He is not putting the letter in the box. Oh no, no! that's impossible! (*Opens the door by degrees.*) He is going. He is standing outside. He is not going downstairs. Is he hesitating? Can he——

(*A letter drops into the box; then Krogstad's footsteps are heard, till they die away as he goes downstairs. Nora utters a stifled cry and runs across the room to the table by the sofa. A short pause.*)

Nora. In the letter-box. (*Steals across to the hall door.*) There it lies—Torvald, Torvald, there is no hope for us now!

(*Mrs. Linde comes in from the room on the left carrying the dress.*)

Mrs. Linde. There, I can't see anything more to mend now. Would you like to try it on——?

Nora (*in a hoarse whisper*). Christine, come here.

Mrs. Linde (*throwing the dress down on the sofa*). What is the matter with you? You look so agitated!

Nora. Come here. Do you see that letter? There look—you can see it through the glass in the letter-box.

Mrs. Linde. Yes, I see it.

Nora. That letter is from Krogstad.

Mrs. Linde. Nora—it was Krogstad who lent you the money!

Nora. Yes, and now Torvald will know all about it.

Mrs. Linde. Believe me, Nora, that's the best thing for both of you.

Nora. You don't know all. I forged a name.

Mrs. Linde. Good heavens——!

Nora. I only want to say this to you, Christine—you must be my witness.

Mrs. Linde. Your witness? What do you mean? What am I to—?

Nora. If I should go out of my mind—and it might easily happen——

Mrs. Linde. Nora!

Nora. Or if anything else should happen to me—anything, for instance, that might prevent my being here—

Mrs. Linde. Nora! Nora! you are quite out of your mind.

Nora. And if it should happen that there were someone who wanted to take all the responsibility, all the blame, you understand——

Mrs. Linde. Yes, yes—but how can you suppose—?

Nora. Then you must be my witness, that it is not true, Christine. I am not out of my mind at all; I am in my right senses now, and I tell you no one else has known anything about it; I, and I alone, did the whole thing. Remember that.

Mrs. Linde. I will, indeed. But I don't understand all this.

Nora. How should you understand it? A wonderful thing is going to happen.

Mrs. Linde. A wonderful thing?

Nora. Yes, a wonderful thing!—But it is so terrible, Christine; it *mustn't* happen, not for all the world.

Mrs. Linde. I will go at once and see Krogstad.

Nora. Don't go to him; he will do you some harm.

Mrs. Linde. There was a time when he would gladly do anything for my sake.

Nora. He?

Mrs. Linde. Where does he live?

Nora. How should I know—? Yes *(feeling in her pocket)* here is his card. But the letter, the letter——!

Helmer *(calls from his room, knocking at the door).* Nora!

Nora *(cries out anxiously).* Oh, what's that? What do you want?

Helmer. Don't be so frightened. We are not coming in; you have locked the door. Are you trying on your dress?

Nora. Yes, that's it. I look so nice, Torvald.

Mrs. Linde *(who has read the card).* I see he lives at the corner here.

Nora. Yes, but it's no use. It is hopeless. The letter is lying there in the box.

Mrs. Linde. And your husband keeps the key?

Nora. Yes, always.

Mrs. Linde. Krogstad must ask for his letter back unread, he must find some pretence——

Nora. But it is just at this time that Torvald generally——

Mrs. Linde. You must delay him. Go in to him in the meantime. I will come back as soon as I can.

(She goes out hurriedly through the hall door.)

Nora *(goes to Helmer's door, opens it and peeps in).* Torvald!

Helmer *(from the inner room).* Well? May I venture at last to come into my own room again? Come along, Rank, now you will see— *(Halting in the doorway.)* But what is this?

Nora. What is what, dear?

Helmer. Rank led me to expect a splendid transformation.

Rank *(in the doorway).* I understood so, but evidently I was mistaken.

Nora. Yes, nobody is to have the chance of admiring me in my dress until to-morrow.

Helmer. But, my dear Nora, you look so worn out. Have you been practising too much?

Nora. No, I have not practised at all.

Helmer. But you will need to—

Nora. Yes, indeed I shall, Torvald. But I can't get on a bit without you to help me; I have absolutely forgotten the whole thing.

Helmer. Oh, we will soon work it up again.

Nora. Yes, help me, Torvald. Promise that you will! I am so nervous about it—all the people—. You must give yourself up to me entirely this evening. Not the tiniest bit of business—you mustn't even take a pen in your hand. Will you promise, Torvald dear?

Helmer. I promise. This evening I will be wholly and absolutely at your service, you helpless little mortal. Ah, by the way, first of all I will just——

(Goes towards the hall door.)

Nora. What are you going to do there?

Helmer. Only see if any letters have come.

Nora. No, no! don't do that, Torvald!

Helmer. Why not?

Nora. Torvald, please don't. There is nothing there.

Helmer. Well, let me look. *(Turns to go to the letter-box. Nora at the piano, plays the first bars of the Tarantella. Helmer stops in the doorway.)* Aha!

Nora. I can't dance to-morrow if I don't practise with you.

Helmer *(going up to her).* Are you really so afraid of it, dear?

Nora. Yes, so dreadfully afraid of it. Let me practise at once; there is time now, before we go to dinner. Sit down and play for me, Torvald dear; criticise me, and correct me as you play.

Helmer. With great pleasure, if you wish me to.

(Sits down at the piano.)

Nora *(takes out of the box a tambourine and a long variegated shawl. She hastily drapes the shawl round her. Then she springs to the front of the stage and calls out).* Now play for me! I am going to dance!

(Helmer plays and Nora dances. Rank stands by the piano behind Helmer and looks on.)

Helmer *(as he plays).* Slower, slower!

Nora. I can't do it any other way.

Helmer. Not so violently, Nora!

Nora. This is the way.

Helmer *(stops playing).* No, no—that is not a bit right.

Nora *(laughing and swinging the tambourine).* Didn't I tell you so?

Rank. Let me play for her.

Helmer *(getting up).* Yes, do. I can correct her better then.

(Rank sits down at the piano and plays. Nora dances more and more wildly. Helmer has taken up a position beside the stove, and during her dance gives her frequent instructions. She does not seem to hear him; her hair comes down and falls over her shoulders; she pays no attention to it, but goes on dancing. Enter Mrs. Linde.)

Mrs. Linde *(standing as if spell-bound in the doorway).* Oh!——

Nora *(as she dances).* Such fun, Christine!

Helmer. My dear darling Nora, you are dancing as if your life depended on it.

Nora. So it does.

Helmer. Stop, Rank; this is sheer madness. Stop, I tell you! *(Rank stops playing, and Nora suddenly stands still. Helmer goes up to her.)* I could never have believed it. You have forgotten everything I taught you.

Nora *(throwing away the tambourine).* There, you see.

Helmer. You will want a lot of coaching.

Nora. Yes, you see how much I need it. You must coach me up to the last minute. Promise me that, Torvald!

Helmer. You can depend on me.

Nora. You must not think of anything but me, either to-day or to-morrow; you mustn't open a single letter—not even open the letter-box——

Helmer. Ah, you are still afraid of that fellow——

Nora. Yes, indeed I am.

Helmer. Nora, I can tell from your looks that there is a letter from him lying there.

Nora. I don't know; I think there is; but you must not read anything of that kind now. Nothing horrid must come between us till this is all over.

Rank *(whispers to Helmer).* You mustn't contradict her.

Helmer *(taking her in his arms).* The child shall have her way. But to-morrow night, after you have danced——

Nora. Then you will be free.

(The Maid appears in the doorway to the right.)

Maid. Dinner is served, ma'am.

Nora. We will have champagne, Helen.

Maid. Very good, ma'am. *(Exit.)*

Helmer. Hullo!—are we going to have a banquet?

Nora. Yes, a champagne banquet till the small hours. *(Calls out.)* And a few macaroons, Helen—lots, just for once!

Helmer. Come, come, don't be so wild and nervous. Be my own little skylark, as you used.

Nora. Yes, dear, I will. But go in now and you too, Doctor Rank. Christine, you must help me to do up my hair.

Rank *(whispers to Helmer as they go out)*. I suppose there is nothing—she is not expecting anything?

Helmer. Far from it, my dear fellow; it is simply nothing more than this childish nervousness I was telling you of.

(They go into the right-hand room.)

Nora. Well!

Mrs. Linde. Gone out of town.

Nora. I could tell from your face.

Mrs. Linde. He is coming home to-morrow evening. I wrote a note for him.

Nora. You should have let it alone; you must prevent nothing. After all, it is splendid to be waiting for a wonderful thing to happen.

Mrs. Linde. What is it that you are waiting for?

Nora. Oh, you wouldn't understand. Go in to them, I will come in a moment. *(Mrs. Linde goes into the dining-room. Nora stands still for a little while, as if to compose herself. Then she looks at her watch.)* Five o'clock. Seven hours till midnight. Then the Tarantella will be over. Twenty-four and seven? Thirty-one hours to live.

Helmer *(from the doorway on the right)*. Where's my little skylark?

Nora *(going to him with her arms outstretched)*. Here she is!

Act III

The Same Scene

The table has been placed in the middle of the stage, with chairs round it. A lamp is burning on the table. The door into the hall stands open. Dance music is heard in the room above. Mrs. Linde is sitting at the table idly turning over the leaves of a book; she tries to read, but does not seem able to collect her thoughts. Every now and then she listens intently for a sound at the outer door.

Mrs. Linde *(looking at her watch)*. Not yet—and the time is nearly up. If only he does not—. *(Listens again.)* Ah, there he is. *(Goes into the hall and opens the outer door carefully. Light footsteps are heard on the stairs. She whispers.)* Come in. There is no one here.

Krogstad *(in the doorway).* I found a note from you at home. What does this mean?

Mrs. Linde. It is absolutely necessary that I should have a talk with you.

Krogstad. Really? And is it absolutely necessary that it should be here?

Mrs. Linde. It is impossible where I live; there is no private entrance to my rooms. Come in; we are quite alone. The maid is asleep, and the Helmers are at the dance upstairs.

Krogstad *(coming into the room).* Are the Helmers really at a dance to-night?

Mrs. Linde. Yes, why not?

Krogstad. Certainly—why not?

Mrs. Linde. Now, Nils, let us have a talk.

Krogstad. Can we two have anything to talk about?

Mrs. Linde. We have a great deal to talk about.

Krogstad. I shouldn't have thought so.

Mrs. Linde. No, you have never properly understood me.

Krogstad. Was there anything else to understand except what was obvious to all the world—a heartless woman jilts a man when a more lucrative chance turns up?

Mrs. Linde. Do you believe I am as absolutely heartless as all that? And do you believe that I did it with a light heart?

Krogstad. Didn't you?

Mrs. Linde. Nils, did you really think that?

Krogstad. If it were as you say, why did you write to me as you did at the time?

Mrs. Linde. I could do nothing else. As I had to break with you, it was my duty also to put an end to all that you felt for me.

Krogstad *(wringing his hands).* So that was it. And all this—only for the sake of money!

Mrs. Linde. You must not forget that I had a helpless mother and two little brothers. We couldn't wait for you, Nils; your prospects seemed hopeless then.

Krogstad. That may be so, but you had no right to throw me over for anyone else's sake.

Mrs. Linde. Indeed I don't know. Many a time did I ask myself if I had the right to do it.

Krogstad *(more gently).* When I lost you, it was as if all the solid ground went from under my feet. Look at me now—I am a shipwrecked man clinging to a bit of wreckage.

Mrs. Linde. But help may be near.

Krogstad. It *was* near; but then you came and stood in my way.

Mrs. Linde. Unintentionally, Nils. It was only to-day that I learnt it was your place I was going to take in the Bank.

Krogstad. I believe you, if you say so. But now that you know it, are you not going to give it up to me?

Mrs. Linde. No, because that would not benefit you in the least.

Krogstad. Oh, benefit, benefit—I would have done it whether or no.

Mrs. Linde. I have learnt to act prudently. Life, and hard, bitter necessity have taught me that.

Krogstad. And life has taught me not to believe in fine speeches.

Mrs. Linde. Then life has taught you something very reasonable. But deeds you must believe in?

Krogstad. What do you mean by that?

Mrs. Linde. You said you were like a shipwrecked man clinging to some wreckage.

Krogstad. I had good reason to say so.

Mrs. Linde. Well, I am like a shipwrecked woman clinging to some wreckage—no one to mourn for, no one to care for.

Krogstad. It was your own choice.

Mrs. Linde. There was no other choice—then.

Krogstad. Well, what now?

Mrs. Linde. Nils, how would it be if we two shipwrecked people could join forces?

Krogstad. What are you saying?

Mrs. Linde. Two on the same piece of wreckage would stand a better chance than each on their own.

Krogstad. Christine!

Mrs. Linde. What do you suppose brought me to town?

Krogstad. Do you mean that you gave me a thought?

Mrs. Linde. I could not endure life without work. All my life, as long as I can remember, I have worked, and it has been my greatest and only pleasure. But now I am quite alone in the world—my life is so dreadfully empty and I feel so forsaken. There is not the least pleasure in working for one's self. Nils, give me someone and something to work for.

Krogstad. I don't trust that. It is nothing but a woman's overstrained sense of generosity that prompts you to make such an offer of yourself.

Mrs. Linde. Have you ever noticed anything of the sort in me?

Krogstad. Could you really do it? Tell me—do you know all about my past life?

Mrs. Linde. Yes.

Krogstad. And do you know what they think of me here?

Mrs. Linde. You seemed to me to imply that with me you might have been quite another man.

Krogstad. I am certain of it.

Mrs. Linde. Is it too late now?

Krogstad. Christine, are you saying this deliberately? Yes, I am sure you are. I see it in your face. Have you really the courage then—?

Mrs. Linde. I want to be a mother to someone, and your children need a mother. We two need each other. Nils, I have faith in your real character—I can dare anything together with you.

Krogstad (*grasps her hands*). Thanks, thanks, Christine! Now I shall find a way to clear myself in the eyes of the world. Ah, but I forgot——

Mrs. Linde (*listening*). Hush! The Tarantella! Go, go!

Krogstad. Why? What is it?

Mrs. Linde. Do you hear them up there? When that is over, we may expect them back.

Krogstad. Yes, yes—I will go. But it is all no use. Of course you are not aware what steps I have taken in the matter of the Helmers.

Mrs. Linde. Yes, I know all about that.

Krogstad. And in spite of that have you the courage to—?

Mrs. Linde. I understand very well to what lengths a man like you might be driven by despair.

Krogstad. If I could only undo what I have done!

Mrs. Linde. You cannot. Your letter is lying in the letter-box now.

Krogstad. Are you sure of that?

Mrs. Linde. Quite sure, but——

Krogstad (with a searching look at her). Is that what it all means?—that you want to save your friend at my cost? Tell me frankly. Is that it?

Mrs. Linde. Nils, a woman who has once sold herself for another's sake, doesn't do it a second time.

Krogstad. I will ask for my letter back.

Mrs. Linde. No, no.

Krogstad. Yes, of course I will. I will wait here till Helmer comes; I will tell him he must give me my letter back—that it only concerns my dismissal—that he is not to read it——

Mrs. Linde. No, Nils, you must not recall your letter.

Krogstad. But, tell me, wasn't it for that very purpose that you asked me to meet you here?

Mrs. Linde. In my first moment of fright, it was. But twenty-four hours have elapsed since then, and in that time I have witnessed incredible things in this house. Helmer must know all about it. This unhappy secret must be disclosed; they must have a complete understanding between them, which is impossible with all this concealment and falsehood going on.

Krogstad. Very well, if you will take the responsibility. But there is one thing I can do in any case, and I shall do it at once.

Mrs. Linde (listening). You must be quick and go! The dance is over; we are not safe a moment longer.

Krogstad. I will wait for you below.

Mrs. Linde. Yes, do. You must see me back to my door.

Krogstad. I have never had such an amazing piece of good fortune in my life.

(Goes out through the outer door. The door between the room and the hall remains open.)

Mrs. Linde (tidying up the room and laying her hat and cloak ready). What a difference! what a difference! Someone to work for and live for—a home to bring comfort into. That I will do, indeed. I wish they would be quick and come— (Listens.) Ah, there they are now. I must put on my things.

(Takes up her hat and cloak. Helmer's and Nora's voices are heard outside; a key is turned, and Helmer brings Nora almost by force into the hall. She is in an Italian *costume with a large black shawl round her; he is in evening dress and a black domino[2] which is flying open.)*

Nora *(hanging back in the doorway, and struggling with him).* No, no, no!—don't take me in. I want to go upstairs again; I don't want to leave so early.

Helmer. But, my dearest Nora——

Nora. Please, Torvald dear—please, *please*—only an hour more.

Helmer. Not a single minute, my sweet Nora. You know that was our agreement. Come along into the room; you are catching cold standing there.

(He brings her gently into the room, in spite of her resistance.)

Mrs. Linde. Good evening.

Nora. Christine!

Helmer. You here, so late, Mrs. Linde?

Mrs. Linde. Yes, you must excuse me; I was so anxious to see Nora in her dress.

Nora. Have you been sitting here waiting for me?

Mrs. Linde. Yes, unfortunately I came too late, you had already gone upstairs; and I thought I couldn't go away again without having seen you.

Helmer *(taking off Nora's shawl).* Yes, take a good look at her. I think she is worth looking at. Isn't she charming, Mrs. Linde?

Mrs. Linde. Yes, indeed she is.

Helmer. Doesn't she look remarkably pretty? Everyone thought so at the dance. But she is terribly self-willed, this sweet little person. What are we to do with her? You will hardly believe that I had almost to bring her away by force.

Nora. Torvald, you will repent not having let me stay, even if it were only for half an hour.

Helmer. Listen to her, Mrs. Linde! She had danced her Tarantella, and it had been a tremendous success, as it deserved—although possibly the performance was a trifle too realistic—a little more so, I mean, than was strictly compatible with the limitations of art. But never mind about that! The chief thing is, she had made a success—she had made a tremendous success. Do you think I was going to let her remain there after that, and spoil the effect? No indeed! I took my charming little Capri maiden—my capricious little Capri maiden, I should say—on my arm; took one quick turn round the room; a curtsey on either side, and, as they say in novels, the beautiful apparition disappeared. An exit ought always to be effective, Mrs. Linde; but that is what I cannot make Nora understand. Pooh! this room is hot. *(Throws his domino on a chair and opens the door of his room.)* Hullo! it's dark in here. Oh, of course—excuse me——.

(He goes in and lights some candles.)

---

[2] A long, loose, hooded cloak.

Nora *(in a hurried and breathless whisper)*. Well?

Mrs. Linde *(in a low voice)*. I have had a talk with him.

Nora. Yes, and——

Mrs. Linde. Nora, you must tell your husband all about it.

Nora *(in an expressionless voice)*. I knew it.

Mrs. Linde. You have nothing to be afraid of as far as Krogstad is concerned; but you must tell him.

Nora. I won't tell him.

Mrs. Linde. Then the letter will.

Nora. Thank you, Christine. Now I know what I must do. Hush——!

Helmer *(coming in again)*. Well, Mrs. Linde, have you admired her?

Mrs. Linde. Yes, and now I will say good-night.

Helmer. What, already? Is this yours, this knitting?

Mrs. Linde *(taking it)*. Yes, thank you, I have very nearly forgotten it.

Helmer. So you knit?

Mrs. Linde. Of course.

Helmer. Do you know, you ought to embroider.

Mrs. Linde. Really? Why?

Helmer. Yes, it's far more becoming. Let me show you. You hold the embroidery thus in your left hand, and use the needle with the right—like this—with a long, easy sweep. Do you see?

Mrs. Linde. Yes, perhaps——

Helmer. But in the case of knitting—that can never be anything but ungraceful; look here—the arms close together, the knitting-needles going up and down—it has a sort of Chinese effect—. That was really excellent champagne they gave us.

Mrs. Linde. Well,—good-night, Nora, and don't be self-willed any more.

Helmer. That's right, Mrs. Linde.

Mrs. Linde. Good-night, Mr. Helmer.

Helmer *(accompanying her to the door)*. Good-night, good-night. I hope you will get home all right. I should be very happy to—but you haven't any great distance to go. Good-night, good-night. *(She goes out; he shuts the door after her, and comes in again.)* Ah!—at last we have got rid of her. She is a frightful bore, that woman.

Nora. Aren't you very tired, Torvald?

Helmer. No, not in the least.

Nora. Nor sleepy?

Helmer. Not a bit. On the contrary, I feel extraordinarily lively. And you?—you really look both tired and sleepy.

Nora. Yes, I am very tired. I want to go to sleep at once.

Helmer. There, you see it was quite right of me not to let you stay there any longer.

Nora. Everything you do is quite right, Torvald.

Helmer *(kissing her on the forehead)*. Now my little skylark is speaking reasonably. Did you notice what good spirits Rank was in this evening?

Nora. Really? Was he? I didn't speak to him at all.

Helmer. And I very little, but I have not for a long time seen him in such good form. (*Looks for a while at her and then goes nearer to her.*) It is delightful to be at home by ourselves again, to be all alone with you—you fascinating, charming little darling!

Nora. Don't look at me like that, Torvald.

Helmer. Why shouldn't I look at my dearest treasure?—at all the beauty that is mine, all my very own?

Nora (*going to the other side of the table*). You mustn't say things like that to me to-night.

Helmer (*following her*). You have still got the Tarantella in your blood, I see. And it makes you more captivating than ever. Listen—the guests are beginning to go now. (*In a lower voice.*) Nora—soon the whole house will be quiet.

Nora. Yes, I hope so.

Helmer. Yes, my own darling Nora. Do you know, when I am out at a party with you like this, why I speak so little to you, keep away from you, and only send a stolen glance in your direction now and then?—do you know why I do that? It is because I make believe to myself that we are secretly in love, and you are my secretly promised bride, and that no one suspects there is anything between us.

Nora. Yes, yes—I know very well your thoughts are with me all the time.

Helmer. And when we are leaving, and I am putting the shawl over your beautiful young shoulders—on your lovely neck—then I imagine that you are my young bride and that we have just come from the wedding, and I am bringing you for the first time into our home—to be alone with you for the first time—quite alone with my shy little darling! All this evening I have longed for nothing but you. When I watched the seductive figures of the Tarantella, my blood was on fire; I could endure it no longer, and that was why I brought you down so early——

Nora. Go away, Torvald! You must let me go. I won't——

Helmer. What's that? You're joking, my little Nora! You won't—you won't? Am I not your husband—?

(*A knock is heard at the outer door.*)

Nora (*starting*). Did you hear——?

Helmer (*going into the hall*). Who is it?

Rank (*outside*). It is I. May I come in for a moment?

Helmer (*in a fretful whisper*). Oh, what does he want now? (*Aloud.*) Wait a minute? (*Unlocks the door.*) Come, that's kind of you not to pass by our door.

Rank. I thought I heard your voice, and felt as if I should like to look in. (*With a swift glance round.*) Ah, yes!—these dear familiar rooms. You are very happy and cosy in here, you two.

Helmer. It seems to me that you looked after yourself pretty well upstairs too.

Rank. Excellently. Why shouldn't I? Why shouldn't one enjoy everything in this world?—at any rate as much as one can, and as long as one can. The wine was capital——

Helmer. Especially the champagne.

Rank. So you noticed that too? It is almost incredible how much I managed to put away!

Nora. Torvald drank a great deal of champagne tonight, too.

Rank. Did he?

Nora. Yes, and he is always in such good spirits afterwards.

Rank. Well, why should one not enjoy a merry evening after a well-spent day?

Helmer. Well spent? I am afraid I can't take credit for that.

Rank (*clapping him on the back*). But I can, you know!

Nora. Doctor Rank, you must have been occupied with some scientific investigation to-day.

Rank. Exactly.

Helmer. Just listen—little Nora talking about scientific investigations!

Nora. And may I congratulate you on the result?

Rank. Indeed you may.

Nora. Was it favourable, then?

Rank. The best possible, for both doctor and patient—certainty.

Nora (*quickly and searchingly*). Certainty?

Rank. Absolute certainty. So wasn't I entitled to make a merry evening of it after that?

Nora. Yes, you certainly were, Doctor Rank.

Helmer. I think so too, so long as you don't have to pay for it in the morning.

Rank. Oh well, one can't have anything in this life without paying for it.

Nora. Doctor Rank—are you fond of fancy-dress balls?

Rank. Yes, if there is a fine lot of pretty costumes.

Nora. Tell me—what shall we two wear at the next?

Helmer. Little featherbrain!—are you thinking of the next already?

Rank. We two? Yes, I can tell you. You shall go as a good fairy——

Helmer. Yes, but what do you suggest as an appropriate costume for that?

Rank. Let your wife go dressed just as she is in everyday life.

Helmer. That was really very prettily turned. But can't you tell us what you will be?

Rank. Yes, my dear friend, I have quite made up my mind about that.

Helmer. Well?

Rank. At the next fancy dress ball I shall be invisible.

Helmer. That's a good joke!

Rank. There is a big black hat—have you never heard of hats that make you invisible? If you put one on, no one can see you.

Helmer (*suppressing a smile*). Yes, you are quite right.

Rank. But I am clean forgetting what I came for. Helmer, give me a cigar—one of the dark Havanas.

Helmer. With the greatest pleasure.

(*Offers him his case.*)

Rank (*takes a cigar and cuts off the end*). Thanks.

Nora (*striking a match*). Let me give you a light.

Rank. Thank you. *(She holds the match for him to light his cigar.)* And now good-bye!

Helmer. Good-bye, good-bye, dear old man!

Nora. Sleep well, Doctor Rank.

Rank. Thank you for that wish.

Nora. Wish me the same.

Rank. You? Well, if you want me to—sleep well! And thanks for the light.

(He nods to them both and goes out.)

Helmer *(in a subdued voice).* He has drunk more than he ought.

Nora *(absently).* Maybe. *(Helmer takes a bunch of keys out of his pocket and goes into the hall.)* Torvald! what are you going to do there?

Helmer. Empty the letter-box; it is quite full; there will be no room to put the newspaper in to-morrow morning.

Nora. Are you going to work to-night?

Helmer. You know quite well I'm not. What is this? Some one has been at the lock.

Nora. At the lock—?

Helmer. Yes, someone has. What can it mean? I should never have thought the maid—. Here is a broken hairpin. Nora, it is one of yours.

Nora *(quickly).* Then it must have been the children—

Helmer. Then you must get them out of those ways. There, at last I have got it open. *(Takes out the contents of the letter-box, and calls to the kitchen.)* Helen!—Helen, put out the light over the front door. *(Goes back into the room and shuts the door into the hall. He holds out his hand full of letters.)* Look at that—look what a heap of them there are. *(Turning them over.)* What on earth is that?

Nora *(at the window).* The letter—No! Torvald, no!

Helmer. Two cards—of Rank's.

Nora. Of Doctor Rank's?

Helmer *(looking at them).* Doctor Rank. They were on the top. He must have put them in when he went out.

Nora. Is there anything written on them?

Helmer. There is a black cross over the name. Look there—what an uncomfortable idea! It looks as if he were announcing his own death.

Nora. It is just what he is doing.

Helmer. What? Do you know anything about it? Has he said anything to you?

Nora. Yes. He told me that when the cards came it would be his leave-taking from us. He means to shut himself up and die.

Helmer. My poor old friend. Certainly I knew we should not have him very long with us. But so soon! And so he hides himself away like a wounded animal.

Nora. If it has to happen, it is best it should be without a word—don't you think so, Torvald?

Helmer *(walking up and down).* He had so grown into our lives. I can't think of him as having gone out of them. He, with his sufferings and his loneliness, was like a cloudy background to our sunlit happiness. Well, perhaps it is best so. For him, anyway. *(Standing still.)* And perhaps for us too, Nora. We two are thrown quite upon each other now. *(Puts his arms round her.)* My darling wife, I don't feel as if I could hold you tight enough. Do you know, Nora, I have often wished that you might be threatened by some great danger, so that I might risk my life's blood, and everything, for your sake.

Nora *(disengages herself, and says firmly and decidedly).* Now you must read your letters, Torvald.

Helmer. No, no; not to-night. I want to be with you, my darling wife.

Nora. With the thought of your friend's death——

Helmer. You are right, it has affected us both. Something ugly has come between us—the thought of the horrors of death. We must try and rid our minds of that. Until then—we will each go to our own room.

Nora *(hanging on his neck).* Good-night, Torvald—Good-night!

Helmer *(kissing her on the forehead).* Good-night, my little singing-bird. Sleep sound, Nora. Now I will read my letters through.

(He takes his letters and goes into his room, shutting the door after him.)

Nora *(gropes distractedly about, seizes Helmer's domino, throws it round her, while she says in quick, hoarse, spasmodic whispers).* Never to see him again. Never! Never! *(Puts her shawl over her head.)* Never to see my children again either— never again. Never! Never!—Ah! the icy, black water—the unfathomable depths—If only it were over! He has got it now—now he is reading it. Good-bye, Torvald and my children!

(She is about to rush out through the hall, when Helmer opens his door hurriedly and stands with an open letter in his hand.)

Helmer. Nora!

Nora. Ah!——

Helmer. What is this? Do you know what is in this letter?

Nora. Yes, I know. Let me go! Let me get out!

Helmer *(holding her back).* Where are you going?

Nora *(trying to get free).* You shan't save me, Torvald!

Helmer *(reeling).* True? Is this true, what I read here? Horrible! No, no—it is impossible that it can be true.

Nora. It is true. I have loved you above everything else in the world.

Helmer. Oh, don't let us have any silly excuses.

Nora *(taking a step towards him).* Torvald——!

Helmer. Miserable creature—what have you done?

Nora. Let me go. You shall not suffer for my sake. You shall not take it upon yourself.

Helmer. No tragedy airs, please. *(Locks the hall door.)* Here you shall stay and give me an explanation. Do you understand what you have done? Answer me! Do you understand what you have done?

Nora *(looks steadily at him and says with a growing look of coldness in her face).* Yes, now I am beginning to understand thoroughly.

Helmer *(walking about the room).* What a horrible awakening! All these eight years—she who was my joy and pride—a hypocrite, a liar—worse, worse—a criminal! The unutterable ugliness of it all! For shame! For shame! *(Nora is silent and looks steadily at him. He stops in front of her.)* I ought to have suspected that something of the sort would happen. I ought to have foreseen it. All your father's want of principle—be silent!—all your father's want of principle has come out in you. No religion, no morality, no sense of duty—. How I am punished for having winked at what he did! I did it for your sake, and this is how you repay me.

Nora. Yes, that's just it.

Helmer. Now you have destroyed all my happiness. You have ruined all my future. It is horrible to think of! I am in the power of an unscrupulous man; he can do what he likes with me, ask anything he likes of me, give me any orders he pleases—I dare not refuse. And I must sink to such miserable depths because of a thoughtless woman!

Nora. When I am out of the way, you will be free.

Helmer. No fine speeches, please. Your father had always plenty of those ready, too. What good would it be to me if you were out of the way, as you say? Not the slightest. He can make the affair known everywhere; and if he does, I may be falsely suspected of having been a party to your criminal action. Very likely people will think I was behind it all—that it was I who prompted you! And I have to thank you for all this—you whom I have cherished during the whole of our married life. Do you understand now what it is you have done for me?

Nora *(coldly and quietly).* Yes.

Helmer. It is so incredible that I can't take it in. But we must come to some understanding. Take off that shawl. Take it off, I tell you. I must try and appease him some way or another. The matter must be hushed up at any cost. And as for you and me, it must appear as if everything between us were just as before—but naturally only in the eyes of the world. You will still remain in my house, that is a matter of course. But I shall not allow you to bring up the children; I dare not trust them to you. To think that I should be obliged to say so to one whom I have loved so dearly, and whom I still——. No, that is all over. From this moment happiness is not the question; all that concerns us is to save the remains, the fragments, the appearance——

(A ring is heard at the front-door bell.)

Helmer *(with a start).* What is that? So late! Can the worst——? Can he——? Hide yourself, Nora. Say you are ill.

(Nora stands motionless. Helmer goes and unlocks the hall door.)

Maid *(half-dressed, comes to the door).* A letter for the mistress.

Helmer. Give it to me. *(Takes the letter, and shuts the door.)* Yes, it is from him. You shall not have it; I will read it myself.

Nora. Yes, read it.

Helmer *(standing by the lamp).* I scarcely have the courage to do it. It may mean ruin for both of us. No, I must know. *(Tears open the letter, runs his eye over a few lines, looks at a paper enclosed and gives a shout of joy.)* Nora! *(She looks at him questioningly.)* Nora!—No, I must read it once again——. Yes, it is true! I am saved! Nora, I am saved!

Nora. And I?

Helmer. You too, of course; we are both saved, both you and I. Look, he sends you your bond back. He says he regrets and repents—that a happy change in his life—never mind what he says! We are saved, Nora! No one can do anything to you. Oh, Nora, Nora!—no, first I must destroy these hateful things. Let me see——. *(Takes a look at the bond.)* No, no, I won't look at it. The whole thing shall be nothing but a bad dream to me. *(Tears up the bond and both letters, throws them all into the stove, and watches them burn.)* There—now it doesn't exist any longer. He says that since Christmas Eve you——. These must have been three dreadful days for you, Nora.

Nora. I have fought a hard fight these three days.

Helmer. And suffered agonies, and seen no way out but——. No, we won't call any of the horrors to mind. We will only shout with joy, and keep saying, "It's all over! It's all over!" Listen to me, Nora. You don't seem to realise that it is all over. What is this?—such a cold, set face! My poor little Nora, I quite understand; you don't feel as if you could believe that I have forgiven you. But it is true, Nora, I swear it; I have forgiven you everything. I know that what you did, you did out of love for me.

Nora. That is true.

Helmer. You have loved me as a wife ought to love her husband. Only you had not sufficient knowledge to judge of the means you used. But do you suppose you are any the less dear to me, because you don't understand how to act on your own responsibility? No, no; only lean on me; I will advise you and direct you. I should not be a man if this womanly helplessness did not just give you a double attractiveness in my eyes. You must not think any more about the hard things I said in my first moment of consternation, when I thought everything was going to overwhelm me. I have forgiven you, Nora; I swear to you I have forgiven you.

(She goes out through the door to the right.)

Helmer. No, don't go——. *(Looks in.)* What are you doing in there?

Nora *(from within).* Taking off my fancy dress.

Helmer *(standing at the open door).* Yes, do. Try and calm yourself, and make your mind easy again, my frightened little singing-bird. Be at rest, and feel secure; I have broad wings to shelter you under. *(Walks up and down by the door.)* How warm and cosy our home is, Nora. Here is shelter for you; here I will protect you like a hunted dove that I have saved from a hawk's claws. I will bring peace to your poor beating heart. It will come, little by little, Nora, believe me.

Tomorrow morning you will look upon it all quite differently; soon everything will be just as it was before. Very soon you won't need me to assure you that I have forgiven you; you will yourself feel the certainty that I have done so. Can you suppose I should ever think of such a thing as repudiating you, or even reproaching you? You have no idea what a true man's heart is like, Nora. There is something so indescribably sweet and satisfying, to a man, in the knowledge that he has forgiven his wife—forgiven her freely, and with all his heart. It seems as if that had made her, as it were, doubly his own; he has given her a new life, so to speak; and she has in a way become both wife and child to him. So you shall be for me after this, my little scared, helpless darling. Have no anxiety about anything, Nora; only be frank and open with me, and I will serve as will and conscience both to you———. What is this? Not gone to bed? Have you changed your things?

Nora (*in everyday dress*). Yes, Torvald, I have changed my things now.

Helmer. But what for?—so late as this.

Nora. I shall not sleep to-night.

Helmer. But, my dear Nora——

Nora (*looking at her watch*). It is not so very late. Sit down here, Torvald. You and I have much to say to one another.

(*She sits down at one side of the table.*)

Helmer. Nora—what is this?—this cold, set face?

Nora. Sit down. It will take some time; I have a lot to talk over with you.

Helmer (*sits down at the opposite side of the table*). You alarm me, Nora!—and I don't understand you.

Nora. No, that is just it. You don't understand me, and I have never understood you either—before to-night. No, you mustn't interrupt me. You must simply listen to what I say. Torvald, this is a settling of accounts.

Helmer. What do you mean by that?

Nora (*after a short silence*). Isn't there one thing that strikes you as strange in our sitting here like this?

Helmer. What is that?

Nora. We have been married now eight years. Does it not occur to you that this is the first time we two, you and I, husband and wife, have had a serious conversation?

Helmer. What do you mean by serious?

Nora. In all these eight years—longer than that—from the very beginning of our acquaintance, we have never exchanged a word on any serious subject.

Helmer. Was it likely that I would be continually and for ever telling you about worries that you could not help me to bear?

Nora. I am not speaking about business matters. I say that we have never sat down in earnest together to try and get at the bottom of anything.

Helmer. But, dearest Nora, would it have been any good to you?

Nora. That is just it; you have never understood me. I have been greatly wronged, Torvald—first by papa and then by you.

Helmer. What! By us two—by us two, who have loved you better than anyone else in the world?

Nora *(shaking her head)*. You have never loved me. You have only thought it pleasant to be in love with me.

Helmer. Nora, what do I hear you saying?

Nora. It is perfectly true, Torvald. When I was at home with papa, he told me his opinion about everything, and so I had the same opinions; and if I differed from him I concealed the fact, because he would not have liked it. He called me his doll-child, and he played with me just as I used to play with my dolls. And when I came to live with you——

Helmer. What sort of an expression is that to use about our marriage?

Nora *(undisturbed)*. I mean that I was simply transferred from papa's hands into yours. You arranged everything according to your own taste, and so I got the same tastes as you—or else I pretended to, I am really not quite sure which—I think sometimes the one and sometimes the other. When I look back on it, it seems to me as if I had been living here like a poor woman—just from hand to mouth. I have existed merely to perform tricks for you, Torvald. But you would have it so. You and papa have committed a great sin against me. It is your fault that I have made nothing of my life.

Helmer. How unreasonable and how ungrateful you are, Nora! Have you not been happy here?

Nora. No, I have never been happy. I thought I was, but it has never really been so.

Helmer. Not—not happy!

Nora. No, only merry. And you have always been so kind to me. But our home has been nothing but a playroom. I have been your doll-wife, just as at home I was papa's doll-child; and here the children have been my dolls. I thought it great fun when you played with me, just as they thought it great fun when I played with them. That is what our marriage has been, Torvald.

Helmer. There is some truth in what you say—exaggerated and strained as your view of it is. But for the future it shall be different. Playtime shall be over, and lesson-time shall begin.

Nora. Whose lessons? Mine, or the children's?

Helmer. Both your and the children's, my darling Nora.

Nora. Alas, Torvald, you are not the man to educate me into being a proper wife for you.

Helmer. And you can say that!

Nora. And I—how am I fitted to bring up the children?

Helmer. Nora!

Nora. Didn't you say so yourself a little while ago—that you dare not trust me to bring them up?

Helmer. In a moment of anger! Why do you pay any heed to that?

Nora. Indeed, you were perfectly right. I am not fit for the task. There is another task I must undertake first. I must try and educate myself—you are not the man to help me in that. I must do that for myself. And that is why I am going to leave you now.

Helmer (*springing up*). What do you say?

Nora. I must stand quite alone, if I am to understand myself and everything about me. It is for that reason that I cannot remain with you any longer.

Helmer. Nora! Nora!

Nora. I am going away from here now, at once. I am sure Christine will take me in for the night——

Helmer. You are out of your mind! I won't allow it! I forbid you!

Nora. It is no use forbidding me anything any longer. I will take with me what belongs to myself. I will take nothing from you, either now or later.

Helmer. What sort of madness is this!

Nora. To-morrow I shall go home—I mean, to my old home. It will be easiest for me to find something to do there.

Helmer. You blind, foolish woman!

Nora. I must try and get some sense, Torvald.

Helmer. To desert your home, your husband and your children! And you don't consider what people will say!

Nora. I cannot consider that at all. I only know that it is necessary for me.

Helmer. It's shocking. This is how you would neglect your most sacred duties.

Nora. What do you consider my most sacred duties?

Helmer. Do I need to tell you that? Are they not your duties to your husband and your children?

Nora. I have other duties just as sacred.

Helmer. That you have not. What duties could those be?

Nora. Duties to myself.

Helmer. Before all else, you are a wife and a mother.

Nora. I don't believe that any longer. I believe that before all else I am a reasonable human being, just as you are—or, at all events, that I must try and become one. I know quite well, Torvald, that most people would think you right, and that views of that kind are to be found in books; but I can no longer content myself with what most people say, or with what is found in books. I must think over things for myself and get to understand them.

Helmer. Can you not understand your place in your own home? Have you not a reliable guide in such matters as that?—have you no religion?

Nora. I am afraid, Torvald, I do not exactly know what religion is.

Helmer. What are you saying?

Nora. I know nothing but what the clergyman said, when I went to be confirmed. He told us that religion was this, and that, and the other. When I am away from all this, and am alone, I will look into that matter too. I will see if what the clergyman said is true, or at all events if it is true for me.

Helmer. This is unheard of in a girl of your age! But if religion cannot lead you aright, let me try and awaken your conscience. I suppose you have some moral sense? Or—answer me—am I to think you have none?

Nora. I assure you, Torvald, that is not an easy question to answer. I really don't know. The thing perplexes me altogether. I only know that you and I look at it in quite another light. I am learning, too, that the law is quite another thing from what I supposed; but I find it impossible to convince myself that the law is right. According to it a woman has no right to spare her old dying father, or to save her husband's life. I can't believe that.

Helmer. You talk like a child. You don't understand the conditions of the world in which you live.

Nora. No, I don't. But now I am going to try. I am going to see if I can make out who is right, the world or I.

Helmer. You are ill, Nora; you are delirious; I almost think you are out of your mind.

Nora. I have never felt my mind so clear and certain as to-night.

Helmer. And is it with a clear and certain mind that you forsake your husband and your children?

Nora. Yes, it is.

Helmer. Then there is only one possible explanation.

Nora. What is that?

Helmer. You do not love me any more.

Nora. No, that is just it.

Helmer. Nora!—and you can say that?

Nora. It gives me great pain, Torvald, for you have always been so kind to me, but I cannot help it. I do not love you any more.

Helmer (*regaining his composure*). Is that a clear and certain conviction too?

Nora. Yes, absolutely clear and certain. That is the reason why I will not stay here any longer.

Helmer. And can you tell me what I have done to forfeit your love?

Nora. Yes, indeed I can. It was to-night, when the wonderful thing did not happen; then I saw you were not the man I had thought you.

Helmer. Explain yourself better—I don't understand you.

Nora. I have waited so patiently for eight years; for, goodness knows, I knew very well that wonderful things don't happen every day. Then this horrible misfortune came upon me; and then I felt quite certain that the wonderful thing was going to happen at last. When Krogstad's letter was lying out there, never for a moment did I imagine that you would consent to accept this man's conditions. I was so absolutely certain that you would say to him: Publish the thing to the whole world. And when that was done——

Helmer. Yes, what then?—when I had exposed my wife to shame and disgrace?

Nora. When that was done, I was so absolutely certain, you would come forward and take everything upon yourself, and say: I am the guilty one.

Helmer. Nora——!

Nora. You mean that I would never have accepted such a sacrifice on your part? No, of course not. But what would my assurances have been worth against yours? That was the wonderful thing which I hoped for and feared; and it was to prevent that, that I wanted to kill myself.

Helmer. I would gladly work night and day for you, Nora—bear sorrow and want for your sake. But no man would sacrifice his honour for the one he loves.

Nora. It is a thing hundreds of thousands of women have done.

Helmer. Oh, you think and talk like a heedless child.

Nora. Maybe. But you neither think nor talk like the man I could bind myself to. As soon as your fear was over—and it was not fear for what threatened me, but for what might happen to you—when the whole thing was past, as far as you were concerned it was exactly as if nothing at all had happened. Exactly as before, I was your little skylark, your doll, which you would in future treat with doubly gentle care, because it was so brittle and fragile. *(Getting up.)* Torvald—it was then it dawned upon me that for eight years I had been living here with a strange man, and had borne him three children——. Oh, I can't bear to think of it! I could tear myself into little bits!

Helmer *(sadly).* I see, I see. An abyss has opened between us—there is no denying it. But, Nora, would it not be possible to fill it up?

Nora. As I am now, I am no wife for you.

Helmer. I have it in me to become a different man.

Nora. Perhaps—if your doll is taken away from you.

Helmer. But to part!—to part from you! No, no, Nora, I can't understand that idea.

Nora *(going out to the right).* That makes it all the more certain that it must be done.

(She comes back with her cloak and hat and a small bag which she puts on a chair by the table.)

Helmer. Nora, Nora, not now! Wait till to-morrow.

Nora *(putting on her cloak).* I cannot spend the night in a strange man's room.

Helmer. But can't we live here like brother and sister——?

Nora *(putting on her hat).* You know very well that would not last long. *(Puts the shawl round her.)* Good-bye, Torvald. I won't see the little ones. I know they are in better hands than mine. As I am now, I can be of no use to them.

Helmer. But some day, Nora—some day?

Nora. How can I tell? I have no idea what is going to become of me.

Helmer. But you are my wife, whatever becomes of you.

Nora. Listen, Torvald. I have heard that when a wife deserts her husband's house, as I am doing now, he is legally freed from all obligations towards her. In any case I set you free from all your obligations. You are not to feel yourself bound in the slightest way, any more than I shall. There must be perfect freedom on both sides. See here is your ring back. Give me mine.

Helmer. That too?

Nora. That too.

Helmer. Here it is.

Nora. That's right. Now it is all over. I have put the keys here. The maids know all about everything in the house—better than I do. To-morrow, after I have left her, Christine will come here and pack up my own things that I brought with me from home. I will have them sent after me.

Helmer. All over! All over!—Nora, shall you never think of me again?

Nora. I know I shall often think of you and the children and this house.

Helmer. May I write to you, Nora?

Nora. No—never. You must not do that.

Helmer. But at least let me send you——

Nora. Nothing—nothing——

Helmer. Let me help you if you are in want.

Nora. No. I can receive nothing from a stranger.

Helmer. Nora—can I never be anything more than a stranger to you?

Nora *(taking her bag)*. Ah, Torvald, the most wonderful thing of all would have to happen.

Helmer. Tell me what that would be!

Nora. Both you and I would have to be so changed that——. Oh, Torvald, I don't believe any longer in wonderful things happening.

Helmer. But I will believe in it. Tell me? So changed that——?

Nora. That our life together would be a real wedlock. Good-bye.

(She goes out through the hall.)

Helmer *(sinks down on a chair at the door and buries his face in his hands)*. Nora! Nora! *(Looks round, and rises.)* Empty. She is gone. *(A hope flashes across his mind.)* The most wonderful thing of all——?

(The sound of a door shutting is heard from below.)

FOR ANALYSIS

1. What evidence can you find to support the interpretation that this play is not only about the Helmers' marriage but also about the institution of marriage itself?

2. What does the first meeting between Nora and Mrs. Linde tell us about Nora's character?

3. On a number of occasions, Nora recalls her father. What relevance do these recollections have to the development of the **theme**?

4. Is Krogstad presented as a conventional villain, or are we meant to sympathize with him? Explain.

5. What function does Dr. Rank serve in the play?

6. Examine the stage directions at the beginning of each act. In what ways do they contribute to and reflect the developing action?

7. Acts I and II contain early **dialogues** between Nora and Torvald. What changes in Nora does a comparison between the two dialogues reveal?

8. At what point in the action does Nora begin to understand the truth of her situation and take responsibility for her life?

9. Summarize the various arguments Torvald uses in his attempt to persuade Nora not to leave.

10. Is the feminist theme of the play weakened by Ibsen's failure to suggest how Nora could conceivably make it on her own in such a patriarchal society? Explain.

MAKING CONNECTIONS

Compare the attitudes toward women revealed in this play with those in Susan Glaspell's *Trifles* (p. 1050) and Lorraine Hansberry's *A Raisin in the Sun* (p. 724).

WRITING TOPICS

1. Does the fact that Nora abandons her children undermine her otherwise heroic decision to walk out on a hollow marriage? For an 1880 German production, Ibsen— in response to public demand—provided an alternate ending in which Nora, after struggling with her conscience, decides that she cannot abandon her children. Do you think this is a better ending than the original one?

2. How does the **subplot** involving the relationship between Mrs. Linde and Krogstad add force to the main **plot** of *A Doll's House*?

3. When you were younger, did you ever defy social pressure because the cost of conforming was too high? Describe the source of the pressure, the issues at stake, and the consequences of your refusal. Since then, have you had second thoughts about your actions? Would you act the same way now that you are older?

4. Write a brief description of a marriage you are familiar with that endured only out of inertia, economic pressure, or fear.

SUZAN-LORI PARKS (B. 1963)

FATHER COMES HOME FROM THE WARS[1] 2006

FATHER COMES HOME FROM THE WARS (PART 1)

Father. Hi honey, Im home.
Mother. Yr home.
Father. Yes.
Mother. I wasnt expecting you. Ever.
Father. Should I go back out and come back in again?
Mother. Please.

He goes back out and comes back in again.

Mother. Once more.
Father. Yr kidding.
Mother. Please.

He goes back out and comes back in again.

Mother. Yr home.
Father. Yes.
Mother. Let me get a good look at you.
Father. I'll just turn around.
Mother. Please.

He turns around once. Counterclockwise,

Mother. They should of sent a letter. A letter saying you were coming home. Or at least a telephone call. That is the least they could do. Give a woman and her family and her friends and neighbors a chance to get ready. A chance to spruce things up. Put new ribbons in the hair of the dog. Get the oil changed. Have everything running. Smoothly. And bake a cake of course. Hang

Father. They sent a letter saying I was coming or at least they telephoned. Maybe you didnt open the letter. I dont blame you. It could have been bad news. I see yr unopened envelopes piled up. I dont blame you. I dont blame you at all. They called several times. Maybe you were out. Maybe you were screwing the yard man. If you had known I was coming you woulda put new ribbons

[1] The following twelve plays are from *365 Days/365 Plays* by Suzan-Lori Parks.

Mother (cont). streamers. Tell the yard man to—tidy up his act. Oh God. Long story. Oh God. Long story. Oh God. Long story. I woulda invited the neighbors over. Had everyone on the block jump out from their hiding places from behind the brand-new furniture with the plastic still on it and say—WHAT? Say: "Welcome Home" of course. And then after a few slices of cake and a few drinks theyd all get the nerve to say what theyre really thinking. For now itll stay unthought and unsaid. Well. You came home. All in one piece looks like. We're lucky. I guess. We're lucky, right? Hhhhh.

Father (cont). in the hair of the dog, got the oil changed, baked a cake and invited all the neighbors over so they could jump out of their various hiding places behind the brand-new furniture purchased with the blood of some people I used to know— and some blood of some people I used to kill. Oh God. Long story. Oh God. Long story. And theyd shout at me—WHAT? "Welcome Home" of course. And then after a few slices of cake and a few drinks theyd get the nerve to tell me what they really think: "Murderer, baby killer, racist, government pawn, ultimate patsy, stooge, fall guy, camp follower, dumbass, dope fiend, loser." Hhhhh.

Mother
Father

(Rest)

Mother. I cant understand a word yr saying.
Father. I dont speak English anymore.
Mother. I dont blame you. SIT DOWN, I'LL FIX YOU SOMETHING.

He sits. She takes a heavy frying pan and holds it over his head. Almost murder. She lowers the pan.

Mother
Father

(Rest)

He sits. Again she raises the frying pan and holds it over his head. Almost murder. She lowers the pan.

Father. Where are the children?
Mother. What children?

Sound of the wind and the rain.

FATHER COMES HOME FROM THE WARS (PART 2)

A Family (Mother, Father, Children) sitting. Neatly dressed. Theyre posing for a family portrait. Painter walks in.

Painter. Lets take up where we left off yesterday, shall we?
Mother. Thatll do nicely.

Painter paints. Children fidget. Mother eyes them or slaps them on their hands and they do their best to keep still. Painter paints. Soldier Man arrives, dressed in battle dress. It does not matter from what war; the Trojan war, WWI, American Civil, Iran-Iraq, Napoleonic, Spanish Civil, Crimean, Zulu, ANC against the Powers that Were, whatever, the Chinese-Tibetan conflict, the War of the Worlds, whatever, it does not matter. Soldier Man taps the Father of the Family on the shoulder, relieving him from duty. The Father was only a father figure, and, very graciously bows, clicks his heels and leaves. The Family does not flinch. The Painter continues to paint. After posing for awhile with his Family, Soldier Man wanders away. He puts on a record. Opera. A Puccini aria. He starts moving around.

Soldier Man. Lets have a sing-along, shall we?

He reaches out to the Family. They cringe and shrink from his touch. He can live with it. He dances around. Its clear that he's missing an eye, a leg, an arm—he sings and dances, quite beautifully, though, all the same. The Family watches him, with mounting horror, spoiling the portrait. The Painter turns to the audience:

Painter. Oh, this will never do!

The Family snaps back into polite alignment. The Painter continues painting. The Soldier Man's hearing is now gone too. He turns up the record player and continues singing and dancing as the Family, very bravely, you understand, holds very very still.

FATHER COMES HOME FROM THE WARS (PART 3)

Father, surrounded by his Soldiers, stands at the door. The Family is at dinner.

Father. Hi, honey, Im home.

The Family stares.

1st Soldier. When you hear the word "war" what comes to mind?
Father. Dont start that talk here. Im home.
2nd Soldier. You dont mind if we wait here do you?
Father. Do what you gotta do. Im home.

Father sits in his easy chair. His Soldiers wait.

Father. Come on, Junior. Lets watch some game shows.
Mother. Yr not hungry?
Sister. Mother and me made a welcome home pie for you. See the
　　writing: "Welcome home from the wars, Father!"
(Rest)
Yr not even looking.
Father. All I wanna do is watch some goddamn game shows.
Junior. All thats on is war movies.
Father. Fine.
Mother. Who are yr friends, honey?
Father. Turn up the volume, Junior.
Junior. Im gonna be a soldier just like yr a soldier, right, Pop?

Father
Father

Father. You betcha.

Junior turns up the volume and the Soldiers in the doorway make loud war sounds. Father leans back and relaxes.

FATHER COMES HOME FROM THE WARS (PART 4)

A man, the Father, comes in wearing army fatigues.

Father. Hello? Im home. Made it home in one piece! Anybody home?

He looks for the Family, finds no one. Even goes looking offstage. No one. He spies a note.

Father. "Gone to the store. Back soon. Love, Family."
(Rest)
Thats nice.
(Rest)
Gives me plenty of time to change.

He opens his pack. Changes into an army-issued business suit. Complete with army-issued shoes and socks, a necktie, and a pipe and tobacco.

Father. Army issue. Could be worse. Made in a country I cant even pronounce.
　　Could be worse. I got a full suit. Some guys just get the jacket or just the shoes.
　　Some guys dont got a need for the shoes, cause they dont got feet. There was a

guy I knew, he used to be 6′4″: Save that story. Dont tell the kids. Dont tell the missus. Not suitable. Tell the soldiers at the VA hospital when you go in for yr shots. Right. Some lost their feet or their arms. Or their minds. Or they house. Or they wife and kids. Put that in yr army-issue pipe and smoke it. Leave yr edge at the door. Think: "Peace." Think: "Lucky You." Think: "Same Old Same Old." Sit in my favorite chair. Watch my army-issue tv. All I need is an army-issue dog. "Gone to the store. Back soon." I'll wait.

(Rest)

Im a lucky man.

FATHER COMES HOME FROM THE WARS (PART 5)

Cocktails before dinner. Very stylish. The den of an early 1960s home. Sophisticated but not over-the-top. Joe and Lovey (husband and wife) are the center of attention.

Joe. Crawling. For miles.
Host. Yr exaggerating.
Hostess. Let him tell his story.
Host. Just as long as you dont exaggerate.
Hostess. He loves tales, he hates tall tales.

Joe gives Lovey's hand a squeeze. Too hard.

Lovey. Its not a tall tale. Its the facts.
Host. Miles?
Joe. Scout's honor.

After a beat. The girls laugh in a stylish upscale manner.

Next Door Neighbor. Crawling for miles in the dirt? Go on—
Joe. In the sand.
Host. Tall tale.
Lovey. Not at all. He had so much sand in his boots. There was barely any room for his feet!

More stylish laughter.

Joe. I had sand in my mouth too. And every other uniform I saw—
Next Door Neighbor. Had the enemy in it.
Lovey. Worse.
Joe. Had a dead man in it.

Joe
Joe

(Rest)

A Kitchen Servant appears and whispers to the Host.

Host. The cook is making yr favorite dish, Joe. He wants to know how you like yr meat.
Joe. Raw.
Host. You mean rare.
Joe. 1 mean raw. With the skin of the animal still on it. Right, Lovey?

He hugs Lovey too hard.

Lovey. Joe's such a kidder.

Host
Joe

Host. How about well-done, Joe?
Joe. How about well-done, Sam?
Lovey. Yr home now, Joe.
Hostess. How about well-done, Joe?
Joe. Well-done it is. Im home now. After all.
Host. 3 cheers for Joe.

They toast Joe.

FATHER COMES HOME FROM THE WARS (PART 6)

The same people—minus Joe. All are many years older.

Host. 3 cheers for Joe. Come on.

They toast Joe.

Lovey. They wanted me to testify against him.
Hostess. No!
Lovey. They wanted me to say he beat me.
Next Door Neighbor. And after all he's done for this country.

Lovey
Host
Hostess
Next Door Neighbor

(Rest)

Host. Good old Joe!

(Rest)

Next Door Neighbor. Lovey, how about I sit on the picnic bench and you do for me what you do for Joe? Whaddayathink?
Lovey. I dont think so, K?
Next Door Neighbor. Dont hurt to ask, does it?

(Rest)

Hostess. Does Joe like it better at the Front?
Host. Its where he can be himself with no pretense.
Lovey. He writes to me every day. I have a whole room full of letters and theyre all love letters. And sometimes, when he writes about something—Top Secret— you know something he knows but that he's not supposed to know, something he knows that he's not supposed to say he knows, the censors crop it out. And—

Lovey
Lovey

Hostess. Well at least he doesnt come home with blood on his clothes anymore.
Host. Thats something.
Lovey. He doesnt come home at all.

They raise their glasses and laugh politely.

MOTHER COMES HOME FROM THE WARS

A Man looks up at the sky. A Woman enters.

Man. Yr back.
Woman. I got in last night.
Man. I heard they freed you.
Woman. Ive been doing interviews nonstop. The National Publisher wants to buy rights to my story.
Man. The National Publisher?
Woman. That means big money.
Man. Wow.
Woman. There was a picture of me on the front page of the paper.
Man. I missed it.
Woman. Ive got a copy for you.
Man. Thanks.

Woman
Man

Woman. Hon?
Man. What.
Woman. What are you looking at?
Man. God.
Woman. Youll go blind.

The Man lowers his head—he wears black spectacles.

Woman. Yr blind already.
Man. Yep.

The Man lifts his glasses and smiles.

Man. Just kidding.
Woman. Yr such a joker. I could have you shot. I had a lot of men shot. They
   were all just like you. Just like you but—
Man. Foreign.
Woman. Just like you but foreign. Yes.

Man
Woman

Man. Welcome home, hon.

*They embrace. We can see that their embrace, while warm and passionate, causes
them both excruciating pain.*

PLAYING CHOPSTICKS (FATHER COMES
HOME FROM THE WARS, PART 7)

*A Soldier Dad in an army uniform, like he's just come in from jungle combat.
He's still got a camouflage suit on, and dark paint covers his face. Maybe even jungle
twigs and branches stick out of his helmet and clothing. He sits on a campstool, a
Kid sits with him. The Soldier Dad is teaching the Kid to use chopsticks. They are
moving a mountain of rice into another pile, far across the other side of the stage,
making another, hopefully identical mountain. The Soldier Dad is great with
chopsticks. The Kid is hopeless. Somewhere offstage someone plays the piano. Theyre
playing "Chopsticks" over and over.*

Soldier Dad. You wanted yr dad to bring you back something from over there. I
   brought you something, right?

Kid. Right.
(Rest)
Whats "gonorrhea"?

(Rest)

Soldier Dad. Thats something for adults, Kid. Lets stick to our chopsticks.
Kid. I heard Mom telling Grandmom that you brought her some "gonorrhea" home from the war.

Soldier Dad
Soldier Dad

Soldier Dad. I brought you something nice and yr acting like you dont like it, Kid. Here. Watch Dad do it.

Soldier Dad effortlessly picks up a piece of rice and walks over to the other side of the stage where he arranges it carefully on the pile.

Soldier Dad. The idea is to pick up the rice with the chopsticks, carry it over here and put the rice down. And put it down in such a way as we remake the rice mountain over here.
Kid. Right.
Soldier Dad. Its good practice.
Kid. For what?

Soldier Dad
Kid

Soldier Dad smacks Kid upside the head. The move comes so fast and seemingly out of nowhere. Like a flash flood. The Kid's head snaps horribly back, but then, just as quickly, the Soldier Dad's anger is spent. The Kid doesnt cry or anything.

Soldier Dad. Try it again. Go on. You gotta learn it.

The Kid tries moving the rice with the chopsticks again.

Soldier Dad. Not much better. Ok, a little better, but, watch.

Soldier Dad moves several pieces of rice, all one at a time, very quickly and with great fanfare, talking as he moves them.

Soldier Dad. Soldier Dad can move them quick. Soldier Dad can hold the chopsticks in his right hand and move rice, and he can hold them in his left hand too.

Makes no difference. Soldier Dad can hold the sticks behind his back, he doesnt have to look, its just that easy. And every piece of rice gets put in its place!

The Kid watches with mounting awe and mounting anger. Offstage the piano playing gets louder.

Soldier Dad *(Yelling to the offstage piano)*. CUT THAT OUT, HUH? HOW AM I SUPPOSED TO FUCKING THINK WITH YOU FUCKING, FUCKING THAT MUSIC UP??!!

The music stops.

Kid
Soldier Dad

Kid. You want me to try it again?
Soldier Dad. Yr mother used to be a concert pianist.
Kid. You want me to try it again?
Soldier Dad. Yeah. Go ahead.

The Kid tries moving the rice again. He's much better this time—like a miracle happened—and now he's actually pretty good.

Soldier Dad. Wow! Great job, Kid.
Kid. Thanks.
Soldier Dad. Chip off the old block after all. I was worried. I'd been away for so long and you—you couldnt do the rice thing.
(Rest)
It was the only thing I brought you back and you couldnt do it and I was worried. But you can do it. My Kid's my Kid! Good. So lets get to work, huh?

The music starts up again and the Kid and Soldier Dad get back to work. Each is amazing at moving the rice. And they are enjoying themselves. It is horrible to see them enjoying themselves doing such a pointless task. But they are building a monument together—and this monument will be a fortress against the future pain. And the music, playing all the while, seeps into the walls of the fortress, seeps in and holds it like stone.

FATHER COMES HOME FROM THE WARS (PART 8)

Mother stares out toward the audience into space. Father enters dragging an enormous bloody sword.

Father. Im home.
Mother. At last.

Father. Yes

(Rest)

Mother. Where were you?
Father. The wars.
Mother. And then?
Father. Lost.
Mother. Oh.
Father. Where are the children?
Mother. Grown up and moved away.
Father. Oh.

Sounds of the sea in the near distance

FATHER COMES HOME FROM THE WARS (PART 9)

Several Fathers, men in army suits or uniforms, are sitting in a row: a Soldier, a Sailor, a Janitor with a broom, a Security Guard with a badge and a gun, a Mechanic with an oily rag and a wrench, a Businessman with a suit and a briefcase, maybe an Astronaut even. They are all young-looking: fresh-faced, and firm-limbed; but very, very old-acting in the most typical of ways: forgetful, passive, paranoid, sad, weak, infirm, angry. The Mechanic wipes his head. The Security Guard peers worriedly at the audience. The Janitor sweeps. The Businessman opens his briefcase, realizes its empty, and closes it. The Soldier and Sailor are having a conversation:

Soldier. "Father's Home—Comes from the Wars."
Sailor. You got the title wrong.
Soldier. Did not.
Sailor. Did too.
Soldier. You got water in yr ears. You wanna step outside?
Sailor. You got the title wrong. Im just trying to—
Soldier. What the hell is it, then?
Sailor. I dont know. But "Father's Home—Comes from the Wars" it aint.

(Rest)

Janitor. They put me in the doghouse. Thats not a lie. Do you know how hard it was? A man my size, living in a house so small. And in the backyard.
Mechanic. Least they didnt put you on the junk pile. Thats where they put me. Cause I'd cost them an arm and a leg to fix. So they junked me. After that, I turned to junk. Drugs, you know. Thats what I did. Lots of drugs. What else could I do?

Security Guard. Look! The war!

They strain their necks downstage to get a better look.

Businessman. Its something, isnt it?
Soldier. Its bloody.
Businessman. Cant have a war without blood.
Janitor. Why have a war at all?
Businessman. Clean-up. Theres money in the clean-up.
Sailor. Its closer than it was yesterday. I can feel the heat from the fire on my face.

They all lean in their chairs slightly, like heliotropism, when flowers crane and strain and turn beautifully toward the sun. Theres the sound of a high-pitched whine underneath, like the barely audible (but sustained) screeching of fingernails on a blackboard. The lights grow very bright and then pop out.

SWEET (FATHER COMES HOME FROM THE WARS, PART 10)

A Man eats slowly, but like an animal. A Woman watches.

Woman. Yr home.
Man. I know.

His plate is empty. The Woman piles more food onto his plate.

Man. Im home but I still got the taste for killing, you know?
Woman. Lemmie put some sugar on. It tastes like shit without sugar.

She pours a lot of sugar on his food. He continues eating. At last his plate is empty. He puts his knife in its sheath.

Man. Im gonna go out for awhile.
Woman. Where to?
Man. Nowhere special. I'll just, you know—
Woman. Walk around.
Man. Yeah.

(Rest)

Woman. Just smell them before you cut them, ok?
Man. Have I ever killed one of our own?
Woman. No, but—

Man. Yr talking to me like I killed one of our own.
Woman. You never done nothing like that—its just—I worry.
Man. If you kept them in the house you wouldnt have no worries.
Woman. Theyre grown. And the house is small.
Man. So I'll get us a bigger house. WHEN I GET A BIGGER JOB!
(Rest)
In the meantime, I gotta go out.

Woman
Man

(Rest)

Man. Itll wear off in awhile. The taste for it.
Woman. Lets hope.

He goes. She frets, then cleans up the dishes. A Young Man enters.

Junior. Hey Mom. Wheres Pop?—
Woman. Out bowling—with his bowling buddies, Junior.
Junior. Sweet. Im history, K?
Woman. Oh no yr not.
Junior. Come on, I did my homework. And my chores.
Woman. One step out there and yr grounded, mister.
Junior. You cant ground me, Ive served my country.
(Rest)
Later, K, Mom?

He kisses her and goes. As soon as he has cleared the stage, Sister comes on.

Sister. Wheres Junior and Pop?
Woman. Out and about.
Sister. Im—
Woman. Dont—
Sister. Hey—
Woman. Sure. Yr history. I know. Whatever. Sweet.

Sister
Woman

*Sister goes. The Woman very meticulously cleans up the dishes and sits. Then she
quickly gets up, puts on a coat and hat and hurries out the door. The house is empty.
No foul play will happen to any of them, although, of course, they may cause foul
play to others, and, of course, none of them will ever ever return.*

FATHER COMES HOME FROM THE WARS (PART 11: HIS ETERNAL RETURN—A PLAY FOR MY FATHER)

During this play we hear a war news-in-brief soundtrack, laced with military band music thats played at a slower than normal speed. The action is as follows: A never-ending loop of action—Servicemen walk downstage together. All wear military uniforms from the same side of the same war, but not necessarily the same branch of Service. They stand upstage and walk very vibrantly and heroically downstage. Theyre returning home as heroes. As they reach centerstage, 5 women, their Service-wives, stand up from the audience, and run toward the men. Just as the Servicemen reach the downstage edge, the Servicewives meet them. The Servicemen pick up their Servicewives, twirling them around very joyfully. Before each Wife returns to the ground a Child comes onstage and, racing toward its respective Mother and Father, jumps for joy. This action repeats. New Servicemen walk downstage, new Wives leap up from the audience and rush into their arms, new Children run in to cheer. The action repeats eternally. Long after the audience has emptied of Women; long after the Men have grown out of the desire to be hugged and kissed and welcomed; long after the Children have become less cheerful and more sensible and have taken up trades, like accounting or teaching or real estate or politics; long after the Children's Children have outgrown joy and have all grown-up and moved away. Forever.

FOR ANALYSIS

1. Would you describe these short plays as realistic or unrealistic? How does their realism or irrealism serve their subject?

2. It is typical to think of soldiers who make it back from wars, and the families to whom they return, as lucky. Is that how these short plays present this situation? How else do they portray these soldiers and their families?

MAKING CONNECTIONS

1. Compare Parks's techniques for reflecting on war to those employed by Wilfred Owen in "Dulce et Decorum Est" (p. 462). Do they have similar things to say? How does the way they say them affect their meaning?

2. Compare the depictions of Father by Parks to one of the fathers in "Connecting Poems: Remembering Fathers" (p. 936) in "Love and Hate." Based on the settings, what are fathers "supposed" to be like? How, in these works, do they really behave?

WRITING TOPICS

1. Characterize the stance these different *Father Comes Home from the Wars* plays have toward war. Are they prowar? Antiwar? Prosoldier? Antisoldier? Explain your **characterization** with support from specific moments in the plays.

2. In *Father Comes Home from the Wars (Part 4)*, Father says, "Save that story. Dont tell the kids. Dont tell the missus. Not suitable" (p. 289). What kind of story is Father not telling? How does Parks herself do the same thing and to what effect?

NONFICTION

LANGSTON HUGHES (1902–1967)

SALVATION 1940

I was saved from sin when I was going on thirteen. But not really saved. It happened like this. There was a big revival at my Auntie Reed's church. Every night for weeks there had been much preaching, singing, praying, and shouting, and some very hardened sinners had been brought to Christ, and the membership of the church had grown by leaps and bounds. Then just before the revival ended, they held a special meeting for children, "to bring the young lambs to the fold." My aunt spoke of it for days ahead. That night I was escorted to the front row and placed on the mourners' bench with all the other young sinners, who had not yet been brought to Jesus.

My aunt told me that when you were saved you saw a light, and something happened to you inside! And Jesus came into your life! And God was with you from then on! She said you could see and hear and feel Jesus in your soul. I believed her. I had heard a great many old people say the same thing and it seemed to me they ought to know. So I sat there calmly in the hot, crowded church, waiting for Jesus to come to me.

The preacher preached a wonderful rhythmical sermon, all moans and shouts and lonely cries and dire pictures of hell, and then he sang a song about the ninety and nine safe in the fold, but one little lamb was left out in the cold. Then he said: "Won't you come? Won't you come to Jesus? Young lambs, won't you come?" And he held out his arms to all us young sinners there on the mourners' bench. And the little girls cried. And some of them jumped up and went to Jesus right away. But most of us just sat there.

A great many old people came and knelt around us and prayed, old women with jet-black faces and braided hair, old men with work-gnarled hands. And the church sang a song about the lower lights are burning, some poor sinners to be saved. And the whole building rocked with prayer and song.

Still I kept waiting to *see* Jesus.   5

Finally all the young people had gone to the altar and were saved, but one boy and me. He was a rounder's son named Westley. Westley and I were surrounded by sisters and deacons praying. It was very hot in the church, and getting late now. Finally Westley said to me in a whisper: "God damn! I'm tired o' sitting here. Let's get up and be saved." So he got up and was saved.

Then I was left all alone on the mourners' bench. My aunt came and knelt at my knees and cried, while prayers and song swirled all around me in the little church. The whole congregation prayed for me alone, in a mighty wail of moans and voices. And I kept waiting serenely for Jesus, waiting, waiting—but he didn't come. I wanted to see him, but nothing happened to me. Nothing! I wanted something to happen to me, but nothing happened.

I heard the songs and the minister saying: "Why don't you come? My dear child, why don't you come to Jesus? Jesus is waiting for you. He wants you. Why don't you come? Sister Reed, what is this child's name?"

"Langston," my aunt sobbed.

"Langston, why don't you come? Why don't you come and be saved? Oh, 10 Lamb of God! Why don't you come?"

Now it was really getting late. I began to be ashamed of myself, holding everything up so long. I began to wonder what God thought about Westley, who certainly hadn't seen Jesus either, but who was now sitting proudly on the platform, swinging his knickerbockered legs and grinning down at me, surrounded by deacons and old women on their knees praying. God had not struck Westley dead for taking his name in vain or for lying in the temple. So I decided that maybe to save further trouble, I'd better lie, too, and say that Jesus had come, and get up and be saved.

So I got up.

Suddenly the whole room broke into a sea of shouting, as they saw me rise. Waves of rejoicing swept the place. Women leaped in the air. My aunt threw her arms around me. The minister took me by the hand and led me to the platform.

When things quieted down, in a hushed silence, punctuated by a few ecstatic "Amens," all the new young lambs were blessed in the name of God. Then joyous singing filled the room.

That night, for the last time in my life but one—for I was a big boy twelve 15 years old—I cried. I cried, in bed alone, and couldn't stop. I buried my head under the quilts, but my aunt heard me. She woke up and told my uncle I was crying because the Holy Ghost had come into my life, and because I had seen Jesus. But I was really crying because I couldn't bear to tell her that I had lied, that I had deceived everybody in the church, that I hadn't seen Jesus, and that now I didn't believe there was a Jesus any more, since he didn't come to help me.

FOR ANALYSIS

1. Is the **tone** of this essay comic or serious or both? Explain.
2. What role does Westley (para. 6) play in the narrative?

3. Can the word *salvation* as Hughes uses it be construed in more than one way? Explain.

4. Discuss how the **point of view** of a **narrator** who looks back on a childhood experience helps define the meaning of the experience.

MAKING CONNECTIONS

1. Compare and contrast Hughes's loss of **innocence** with that of Sylvia in Bambara's "The Lesson" (p. 96).

2. Compare and contrast the **narrator's** attitude toward adult authority in this story with Sylvia's in Bambara's "The Lesson" (p. 96).

WRITING TOPIC

Describe an experience in which public pressure forced you either to express an opinion or a belief that you didn't really hold or to act in a way you otherwise would not have.

JUDITH ORTIZ COFER (B. 1952)

AMERICAN HISTORY 1993

I once read in a *Ripley's Believe It or Not* column that Paterson, New Jersey, is the place where the Straight and Narrow (streets) intersect. The Puerto Rican tenement known as El Building was one block up from Straight. It was, in fact, the corner of Straight and Market; not "at" the corner, but *the* corner. At almost any hour of the day, El Building was like a monstrous jukebox, blasting out *salsas* from open windows as the residents, mostly new immigrants just up from the island, tried to drown out whatever they were currently enduring with loud music. But the day President Kennedy was shot, there was a profound silence in El Building, even the abusive tongues of viragoes, the cursing of the unemployed, and the screeching of small children had been somehow muted. President Kennedy was a saint to these people. In fact, soon his photograph would be hung alongside the Sacred Heart and over the spiritist altars that many women kept in their apartments. He would become part of the hierarchy of martyrs they prayed to for favors that only one who had died for a cause would understand.

On the day that President Kennedy was shot, my ninth grade class had been out in the fenced playground of Public School Number 13. We had been given "free" exercise time and had been ordered by our P.E. teacher, Mr. DePalma, to "keep moving." That meant that the girls should jump rope and the boys toss basketballs through a hoop at the far end of the yard. He in the meantime would "keep an eye" on us from just inside the building.

It was a cold gray day in Paterson. The kind that warns of early snow. I was miserable, since I had forgotten my gloves and my knuckles were turning red and raw from the jump rope. I was also taking a lot of abuse from the black girls for not turning the rope hard and fast enough for them.

"Hey, Skinny Bones, pump it, girl. Ain't you got no energy today?" Gail, the biggest of the black girls who had the other end of the rope yelled, "Didn't you eat your rice and beans and pork chops for breakfast today?"

The other girls picked up the "pork chop" and made it into a refrain: "pork chop, pork chop, did you eat your pork chop?" They entered the double ropes in pairs and exited without tripping or missing a beat. I felt a burning on my cheeks, and then my glasses fogged up so that I could not manage to coordinate the jump rope with Gail. The chill was doing to me what it always did, entering my bones, making me cry, humiliating me. I hated the city, especially in winter. I hated Public School Number 13. I hated my skinny flat-chested body, and I envied the black girls who could jump rope so fast that their legs became a blur. They always seemed to be warm while I froze.

There was only one source of beauty and light for me that school year. The only thing I had anticipated at the start of the semester. That was seeing Eugene. In August, Eugene and his family had moved into the only house on the block that had a yard and trees. I could see his place from my window in El Building. In fact, if I sat on the fire escape I was literally suspended above Eugene's backyard. It was my favorite spot to read my library books in the summer. Until that August the house had been occupied by an old Jewish couple. Over the years I had become part of their family, without their knowing it, of course. I had a view of their kitchen and their backyard, and though I could not hear what they said, I knew when they were arguing, when one of them was sick, and many other things. I knew all this by watching them at mealtimes. I could see their kitchen table, the sink and the stove. During good times, he sat at the table and read his newspapers while she fixed the meals. If they argued, he would leave and the old woman would sit and stare at nothing for a long time. When one of them was sick, the other would come and get things from the kitchen and carry them out on a tray. The old man had died in June. The last week of school I had not seen him at the table at all. Then one day I saw that there was a crowd in the kitchen. The old woman had finally emerged from the house on the arm of a stocky middle-aged woman whom I had seen there a few times before, maybe her daughter. Then a man had carried out suitcases. The house had stood empty for weeks. I had had to resist the temptation to climb down into the yard and water the flowers the old lady had taken such good care of.

By the time Eugene's family moved in, the yard was a tangled mass of weeds. The father had spent several days mowing, and when he finished, I didn't see the red, yellow, and purple clusters that meant flowers to me from where I sat. I didn't see this family sit down at the kitchen table together. It was just the mother, a red-headed tall woman who wore a white uniform—a nurse's, I guessed it was; the father was gone before I got up in the morning and was never there at dinner time. I only saw him on weekends when they sometimes sat on lawn chairs under the oak tree, each hidden behind a section of the newspaper; and there was Eugene. He was tall and blond, and he wore glasses. I liked him right away because he sat at the kitchen table and read books for hours. That summer, before we had even spoken one word to each other, I kept him company on my fire escape.

Once school started I looked for him in all my classes, but P.S. 13 was a huge, overpopulated place and it took me days and many discreet questions to discover that Eugene was in honors classes for all his subjects; classes that were not open to me because English was not my first language, though I was a straight A student. After much maneuvering I managed "to run into him" in the hallway where his locker was—on the other side of the building from mine—and in study hall at the library, where he first seemed to notice me but did not speak; and finally, on the way home after school one day when I decided to approach him directly, though my stomach was doing somersaults.

I was ready for rejection, snobbery, the worst. But when I came up to him, practically panting in my nervousness, and blurted out: "You're Eugene. Right?" He smiled, pushed his glasses up on his nose, and nodded. I saw then that he was blushing deeply. Eugene liked me, but he was shy. I did most of the talking that day. He nodded and smiled a lot. In the weeks that followed, we walked home together. He would linger at the corner of El Building for a few minutes then walk down to his two-story house. It was not until Eugene moved into that house that I noticed that El Building blocked most of the sun and that the only spot that got a little sunlight during the day was the tiny square of earth the old woman had planted with flowers.

I did not tell Eugene that I could see inside his kitchen from my bedroom. I felt dishonest, but I liked my secret sharing of his evenings, especially now that I knew what he was reading, since we chose our books together at the school library.

One day my mother came into my room as I was sitting on the windowsill staring out. In her abrupt way she said: "Elena, you are acting 'moony.'" *Enamorada* was what she really said—that is, like a girl stupidly infatuated. Since I had turned fourteen and started menstruating my mother had been more vigilant than ever. She acted as if I was going to go crazy or explode or something if she didn't watch me and nag me all the time about being a señorita now. She kept talking about virtue, morality, and other subjects that did not interest me in the least. My mother was unhappy in Paterson, but my father had a good job at the blue jeans factory in Passaic, and soon, he kept assuring us, we would be moving to our own house there. Every Sunday we drove out to the suburbs of Paterson, Clifton, and Passaic, out to where people mowed grass on Sundays in the summer and where children made snowmen in the winter from pure white snow, not like the gray slush of Paterson, which seemed to fall from the sky in that hue. I had learned to listen to my parents' dreams, which were spoken in Spanish, as fairy tales, like the stories about life in the island paradise of Puerto Rico before I was born. I had been to the Island once as a little girl, to grandmother's funeral, and all I remembered was wailing women in black, my mother becoming hysterical and being given a pill that made her sleep two days, and me feeling lost in a crowd of strangers all claiming to be my aunts, uncles, and cousins. I had actually been glad to return to the city. We had not been back there since then, though my parents talked constantly about buying a house on the beach someday, retiring on the island—that was a common topic among the residents of El Building. As for me, I was going to go to college and become a teacher.

But after meeting Eugene I began to think of the present more than of the future. What I wanted now was to enter that house I had watched for so many years. I wanted to see the other rooms where the old people had lived and where the boy I liked spent his time. Most of all, I wanted to sit at the kitchen table with Eugene like two adults, like the old man and his wife had done, maybe drink some coffee and talk about books. I had started reading *Gone with the Wind*. I was enthralled by it, with the daring and the passion of the beautiful girl living in a mansion, and with her devoted parents and the slaves who did everything for them. I didn't believe such a world had ever really existed, and I wanted to ask Eugene some questions, since he and his parents, he had told me, had come up from Georgia, the same place where the novel was set. His father worked for a company that had transferred him to Paterson. His mother was very unhappy, Eugene said, in his beautiful voice that rose and fell over words in a strange, lilting way. The kids at school called him the Hick and made fun of the way he talked. I knew I was his only friend so far, and I liked that, though I felt sad for him sometimes. Skinny Bones and the Hick, was what they called us at school when we were seen together.

The day Mr. DePalma came out into the cold and asked us to line up in front of him was the day that President Kennedy was shot. Mr. DePalma, a short, muscular man with slicked-down black hair, was the science teacher, P.E. coach, and disciplinarian at P.S. 13. He was the teacher to whose homeroom you got assigned if you were a troublemaker, and the man called out to break up playground fights, and to escort violently angry teenagers to the office. And Mr. DePalma was the man who called your parents in for "a conference."

That day, he stood in front of two rows of mostly black and Puerto Rican kids, brittle from their efforts to "keep moving" on a November day that was turning bitter cold. Mr. DePalma, to our complete shock, was crying. Not just silent adult tears, but really sobbing. There were a few titters from the back of the line where I stood, shivering.

"Listen," Mr. DePalma raised his arms over his head as if he were about to 15 conduct an orchestra. His voice broke, and he covered his face with his hands. His barrel chest was heaving. Someone giggled behind me.

"Listen," he repeated, "something awful has happened." A strange gurgling came from his throat, and he turned around and spit on the cement behind him.

"Gross," someone said, and there was a lot of laughter.

"The president is dead, you idiots. I should have known that wouldn't mean anything to a bunch of losers like you kids. Go home." He was shrieking now. No one moved for a minute or two, but then a big girl let out a "yeah!" and ran to get her books piled up with the others against the brick wall of the school building. The others followed in a mad scramble to get to their things before somebody caught on. It was still an hour to the dismissal bell.

A little scared, I headed for El Building. There was an eerie feeling on the streets. I looked into Mario's drugstore, a favorite hangout for the high school crowd, but there were only a couple of old Jewish men at the soda bar, talking with the short order cook in tones that sounded almost angry, but they were keeping their voices low. Even the traffic on one of the busiest intersections in Paterson—Straight Street and Park Avenue—seemed to be moving slower. There were no horns blasting that day. At El Building, the usual little group of unemployed men were not hanging out on the front stoop, making it difficult for women to enter the front door. No music spilled out from open doors in the hallway. When I walked into our apartment, I found my mother sitting in front of the grainy picture of the television set.

She looked up at me with a tear-streaked face and just said: "Dios mío," 20 turning back to the set as if it were pulling at her eyes. I went into my room.

Though I wanted to feel the right thing about President Kennedy's death, I could not fight the feeling of elation that stirred in my chest. Today was the day I was to visit Eugene in his house. He had asked me to come over after school to study for an American history test with him. We had also planned to walk to the public library together. I looked down into his yard. The oak tree was bare of leaves, and the ground looked gray with ice. The light through the large kitchen window of his house told me that El Building blocked the sun to such an extent that they had to turn lights on in the middle of the day. I felt ashamed about it. But the white kitchen table with the lamp hanging just above it looked cozy and inviting. I would soon sit there, across from Eugene, and I would tell him about my perch just above his house. Maybe I would.

In the next thirty minutes I changed clothes, put on a little pink lipstick, and got my books together. Then I went in to tell my mother that I was going to a friend's house to study. I did not expect her reaction.

"You are going out *today*?" The way she said "today" sounded as if a storm warning had been issued. It was said in utter disbelief. Before I could answer, she came toward me and held my elbows as I clutched my books.

"*Hija*, the president has been killed. We must show respect. He was a great man. Come to church with me tonight."

She tried to embrace me, but my books were in the way. My first impulse 25 was to comfort her, she seemed so distraught, but I had to meet Eugene in fifteen minutes.

"I have a test to study for, Mama. I will be home by eight."

"You are forgetting who you are, *Niña*. I have seen you staring down at that boy's house. You are heading for humiliation and pain." My mother said this in Spanish and in a resigned tone that surprised me, as if she had no intention of stopping me from "heading for humiliation and pain." I started for the door. She sat in front of the TV, holding a white handkerchief to her face.

I walked out to the street and around the chain-link fence that separated El Building from Eugene's house. The yard was neatly edged around the little walk that led to the door. It always amazed me how Paterson, the inner core of the city, had no apparent logic to its architecture. Small, neat, single residences like this one could be found right next to huge, dilapidated apartment buildings like El Building. My guess was that the little houses had been there first, then the immigrants had come in droves, and the monstrosities had been raised for them—the Italians, the Irish, the Jews, and now us, the Puerto Ricans, and the blacks. The door was painted a deep green: *verde,* the color of hope. I had heard my mother say it: *Verde-Esperanza.*

I knocked softly. A few suspenseful moments later the door opened just a crack. The red, swollen face of a woman appeared. She had a halo of red hair floating over a delicate ivory face—the face of a doll—with freckles on the nose. Her smudged eye makeup made her look unreal to me, like a mannequin seen through a warped store window.

"What do you want?" Her voice was tiny and sweet-sounding, like a little 30 girl's, but her tone was not friendly.

"I'm Eugene's friend. He asked me over. To study." I thrust out my books, a silly gesture that embarrassed me almost immediately.

"You live there?" She pointed up to El Building, which looked particularly ugly, like a gray prison with its many dirty windows and rusty fire escapes. The woman had stepped halfway out, and I could see that she wore a white nurse's uniform with "St. Joseph's Hospital" on the name tag.

"Yes. I do."

She looked intently at me for a couple of heartbeats, then said as if to herself, "I don't know how you people do it." Then directly to me: "Listen. Honey. Eugene doesn't want to study with you. He is a smart boy. Doesn't need help. You understand me. I am truly sorry if he told you you could come over. He cannot study with you. It's nothing personal. You understand? We won't be in this place much longer, no need for him to get close to people—it'll just make it harder for him later. Run back home now."

I couldn't move. I just stood there in shock at hearing these things said to 35 me in such a honey-drenched voice. I had never heard an accent like hers except for Eugene's softer version. It was as if she were singing me a little song.

"What's wrong? Didn't you hear what I said?" She seemed very angry, and I finally snapped out of my trance. I turned away from the green door and heard her close it gently.

Our apartment was empty when I got home. My mother was in someone else's kitchen, seeking the solace she needed. Father would come in from his late shift at midnight. I would hear them talking softly in the kitchen for hours that night. They would not discuss their dreams for the future, or life in Puerto Rico, as they often did; that night they would talk sadly about the young widow and her two children, as if they were family. For the next few days, we would observe *luto* in our apartment; that is, we would practice restraint and silence—no loud music or laughter. Some of the women of El Building would wear black for weeks.

That night, I lay in my bed, trying to feel the right thing for our dead president. But the tears that came up from a deep source inside me were strictly for me. When my mother came to the door, I pretended to be sleeping. Sometime during the night, I saw from my bed the streetlight come on. It had a pink halo around it. I went to my window and pressed my face to the cool glass. Looking up at the light I could see the white snow falling like a lace veil over its face. I did not look down to see it turning gray as it touched the ground below.

FOR ANALYSIS

1. Suggest a reason why the **narrator** spies on the neighbors.

2. Why does Elena's mother warn her that "[y]ou are forgetting who you are" and that "[y]ou are heading for humiliation and pain" (para. 27)?

3. What does Eugene's mother reveal when she says, "I don't know how you people do it" (para. 34)? Why does she refuse to let Elena study with Eugene?

4. How would you describe the **tone** of this essay? Is it bitter? Belligerent? Argumentative? Accepting? Explain.

5. Discuss the implications of the essay's title.

WRITING TOPIC

Explain which event—President Kennedy's death or Eugene's mother's remarks—more significantly shapes the **narrator's** view of American history

BRIAN DOYLE (B. 1956)

POP ART 2001

In nine years I have been graced with three children and here is what I have learned about them. They are engines of incalculable joy and agonizing despair. They are comedy machines. Their language is their own and the order of their new halting words has never been heard before in the whole history of the world. They are headlong and hilarious. Their hearts are enormous and sensitive beyond calculation by man or machine. Their pride is vast. They are cruel, and move in herds and gaggles and mobs, and woe unto the silent one, the one who looks funny, the one who speaks awkwardly, the fat one, for she will be shouldered aside, he will never get the ball, she will never be asked to jump rope, he will not be invited to the pool party, she will weep with confusion and rage, he will lash out with sharp small fists. Yet they are endlessly kind, kind by nature, and among them there is often an artless democracy, a linking of arms against the vast puzzle of the long people. They search for rules and rank, for what is allowed and what is forbidden, and poke the rules to see which bends and which is steel, for they wish to know their place in the world, where they might walk, what they may wear, which shows are allowed, how far they can go, who they are. They rise early in excitement and return reluctantly to barracks at night for fear of missing a shred of the daily circus. They eat nothing to speak of but grow at stunning rates that produce mostly leg. They are absorbed by dogs and toast. Mud and jelly accrue to them. They are at war with wasps. They eat no green things. Once they learn sarcasm they use it with abandon, slashing here and there without control and wreaking havoc. When they weep they weep utterly from the marrows of their lonely bones. They will not speak of death but when it comes, a dark hooded hawk on the fence, they face it without fear. They are new creatures hourly, and what you think you know of them is already lost in the river. Their hearts are dense books no one can read. They speak many languages of the body. To them you are a stone who has always been and will always be. When they are ill they shrivel. To father them is not a brief noun but an endless verb that exhausts, enrages, edifies, elevates, educates; I am a thinner and grayer man than I was; and closer to joy. They frighten me, for they will make a new world on the bowed back of the one I love; but they delight me, for to have loved them is to have tasted the furious love the Maker has for what He made, and fathers still, and always will.

FOR ANALYSIS

1. Why do you think Doyle chose "Pop Art" as his title?
2. Describe the **tone** of "Pop Art." Does it have only one, or is it varied? Can you chart its changes? What effect do these changes have?

MAKING CONNECTIONS

1. In "Those Winter Sundays," Hayden writes, "What did I know, what did I know / of love's austere and lonely offices?" (p. 938). In what ways could "Pop Art" be seen as a response to Hayden's speaker's innocence of fathering?

2. Both "Pop Art" and Galway Kinnell's "After Making Love We Hear Footsteps" (p. 919) examine the relationship between parents and children in ways that move beyond the stereotypical and expected. How does each look at parenthood?

WRITING TOPICS

1. "Pop Art" first appeared in a creative nonfiction venue called *Brevity*. Write an essay in which you describe the effects "Pop Art" makes with its brevity. Can you imagine it longer? How would it change?

2. Write your own short piece, modeled on Doyle's, in which you list descriptions of something or someone in a way that adds up to more than a roster of characteristics and reveals the nature of the subject.

The college experience is a significant stage in the passage from adolescence to adulthood, from school to work, from dependence to independence, and from innocence to experience. College is also the place where students learn to think in new and different ways about the world in which they live. No matter what students learn, the college experience is part of the process through which they discover who they are and their place in the world. While you read the selections in this unit, pay attention to the ways the movement from teenage innocence to adult experience is connected with the education that college offers—not just about the world, but about the students themselves. Also look for the ways in which the essays reveal that the college experience is sometimes about learning that the world is a bigger, more complicated place than students thought it was. Finally, keep an eye out for the ways that the essays themselves acknowledge how the form on which they are based—the commencement address—is supposed to function, and what that function means.

DAVID SEDARIS (B. 1956)

WHAT I LEARNED
AND WHAT I SAID AT PRINCETON   2006

It's been interesting to walk around campus this afternoon, as when *I* went to Princeton things were completely different. This chapel, for instance—I remember when it was just a clearing, cordoned off with sharp sticks. Prayer was compulsory back then, and you couldn't just fake it by moving your lips; you had to know the words, and really mean them. I'm dating myself, but this was before Jesus Christ. We worshipped a God named Sashatiba, who had five eyes, including one right here, on the Adam's apple. None of us ever met him, but word had it that he might appear at any moment, so we were always at the ready. *Whatever you do, don't look at his neck*, I used to tell myself

It's funny now, but I thought about it a lot. Some people thought about it a little too much, and it really affected their academic performance. Again, I date myself, but back then we were on a pass-fail system. If you passed, you got to live, and if you failed you were burned alive on a pyre that's now the Transgender Studies Building. Following the first grading period, the air was so thick with smoke you could barely find your way across campus. There were those who said that it smelled like meat, no different from a barbecue, but I could tell the difference. I mean, really. Since when do you grill hair? Or those ugly, chunky shoes we all used to wear?

It kept you on your toes, though, I'll say that much. If I'd been burned alive because of bad grades, my parents would have killed me, especially my father, who meant well but was just a little too gung ho for my taste. He had the whole outfit: Princeton breastplate, Princeton nightcap; he even got the velvet cape with the tiger head hanging like a rucksack from between the shoulder blades. In those days, the mascot was a sabretooth, so you can imagine how silly it looked, and how painful it was to sit down. Then, there was his wagon, completely covered with decals and bumper stickers: "I hold my horses for Ivy league schools," "My son was accepted at the best university in the United States and all I got was a bill for a hundred and sixty-eight thousand dollars." On and on, which was just so . . . *wrong.*

One of the things they did back then was start you off with a modesty seminar, an eight-hour session that all the freshmen had to sit through. It might be different today, but in my time it took the form of a role-playing exercise, my classmates and I pretending to be graduates, and the teacher assuming the part of an average citizen: the soldier, the bloodletter, the whore with a heart of gold.

"Tell me, young man. Did you attend a university of higher learning?"   5

To anyone holding a tool or a weapon, we were trained to respond, "What? Me go to college?" If, on the other hand, the character held a degree, you were allowed to say, "Sort of," or, sometimes, "I think so."

"So where do you sort of think you went?"

And it was the next bit that you had to get just right. Inflection was everything, and it took the foreign students forever to master it.

"Where do you sort of think you went?"

And we'd say, "Umm, Princeton?"—as if it were an oral exam, and we   10 weren't quite sure that this was the correct answer.

"Princeton, my goodness," the teacher would say. "That must have been quite something!"

You had to let him get it out, but once he started in on how brilliant and committed you must be it was time to hold up your hands, saying, "Oh, it isn't that hard to get into."

Then he'd say, "Really? But I heard—"

"Wrong," you'd tell him. "You heard wrong. It's not that great of a school."

This was the way it had to be done— you had to play it down, which wasn't   15 easy when your dad was out there, reading your acceptance letter into a bullhorn.

I needed to temper my dad's enthusiasm a bit, and so I announced that I would be majoring in patricide. The Princeton program was very strong back then, the best in the country, but it wasn't the sort of thing your father could get too worked up about. Or, at least, most fathers wouldn't. Mine was over the moon. "Killed by a Princeton graduate!" he said. "And my own son, no less."

My mom was actually jealous. "So what's wrong with matricide?" she asked. "What, I'm not good enough to murder?"

They started bickering, so in order to make peace I promised to consider a double major.

"And how much more is that going to cost us?" they said.

Those last few months at home were pretty tough, but then I started my freshman year, and got caught up in the life of the mind. My idol-worship class was the best, but my dad didn't get it. "What the hell does that have to do with patricide?" he asked.

And I said, "Umm. *Everything*?"

He didn't understand that it's all connected, that one subject leads to another and forms a kind of chain that raises its head and nods like a cobra when you're sucking on a bong after three days of no sleep. On acid it's even wilder, and appears to eat things. But, not having gone to college, my dad had no concept of a well-rounded liberal-arts education. He thought that all my classes should be murder-related, with no lunch breaks or anything. Fortunately, it doesn't work that way.

In truth, I had no idea what I wanted to study, so for the first few years I took everything that came my way. I enjoyed pillaging and astrology, but the thing that ultimately stuck was comparative literature. There wasn't much of it to compare back then, no more than a handful of epic poems and one novel about a lady detective, but that's part of what I liked about it. The field was new, and full of possibilities, but try telling that to my parents.

"You mean you *won't* be killing us?" my mother said. "But I told everyone you were going for that double major."

Dad followed his "I'm so disappointed" speech with a lecture on career opportunities. "You're going to study literature and get a job doing *what*?" he said. "*Literaturizing*?"

We spent my entire vacation arguing; then, just before I went back to school, my father approached me in my bedroom. "Promise me you'll keep an open mind," he said. And, as he left, he slipped an engraved dagger into my book bag.

I had many fine teachers during my years at Princeton, but the one I think of most often was my fortune-telling professor—a complete hag with wild gray hair, warts the size of new potatoes, the whole nine yards. She taught us to forecast the weather up to two weeks in advance, but ask her for anything weightier and you were likely to be disappointed.

The alchemy majors wanted to know how much money they'd be making after graduation. "Just give us an approximate figure," they'd say, and the professor would shake her head and cover her crystal ball with a little cozy given to her by one of her previous classes. When it came to our futures, she drew the line, no matter how hard we begged—and, I mean, we really tried. I was as let down as the next guy, but, in retrospect, I can see that she acted in our best interests. Look at yourself on the day that you graduated from college, then look at yourself today. I did that recently, and it was, like, "What the hell happened?"

The answer, of course, is life. What the hag chose not to foretell—and what we, in our certainty, could not have fathomed—is that stuff comes up. Weird doors open. People fall into things. Maybe the engineering whiz will wind up brewing cider, not because he has to but because he finds it challenging. Who knows? Maybe the athlete will bring peace to all nations, or the class moron will go on to become the President of the United States—though that's more likely to happen at Harvard or Yale, schools that will pretty much let in anybody.

There were those who left Princeton and soared like arrows into the bosoms 30 of power and finance, but I was not one of them. My path was a winding one, with plenty of obstacles along the way. When school was finished, I went back home, an Ivy League graduate with four years' worth of dirty laundry and his whole life ahead of him. "What are you going to do now?" my parents asked.

And I said, "Well, I was thinking of washing some of these underpants."

That took six months. Then I moved on to the shirts.

"Now what?" my parents asked.

And, when I told them I didn't know, they lost what little patience they had left. "What kind of a community-college answer is that?" my mother said. "You went to the best school there is—how can you not know something?"

And I said, "I don't know." 35

In time, my father stopped wearing his Princeton gear. My mother stopped talking about my "potential," and she and my dad got themselves a brown-and-white puppy. In terms of intelligence, it was just average, but they couldn't see that at all. "Aren't you just the smartest dog in the world?" they'd ask, and the puppy would shake their hands just like I used to do.

My first alumni weekend cheered me up a bit. It was nice to know that I wasn't the only unemployed graduate in the world, but the warm feeling evaporated when I got back home and saw that my parents had given the dog my bedroom. In place of the Princeton pennant they'd bought for my first birthday was a banner reading, "Westminster or bust."

I could see which way the wind was blowing, and so I left, and moved to the city, where a former classmate, a philosophy major, got me a job on his rag-picking crew. When the industry moved overseas—this the doing of *another* former classmate—I stayed put, and eventually found work skinning hides for a ratcatcher, a thin, serious man with the longest beard I had ever seen.

At night, I read and reread the handful of books I'd taken with me when I left home, and eventually, out of boredom as much as anything else, I started to write myself. It wasn't much, at first: character sketches, accounts of my day, parodies of articles in the alumni newsletter. Then, in time, I became more ambitious, and began crafting little stories about my family. I read one of them out loud to the ratcatcher, who'd never laughed at anything but roared at the description of my mother and her puppy. "My mom was just the same," he said. "I graduated from Brown, and two weeks later she was raising falcons on my top bunk!" The story about my dad defecating in his neighbor's well pleased my boss so much that he asked for a copy, and sent it to his own father.

This gave me the confidence to continue, and in time I completed an entire book, which was subsequently published. I presented a first edition to my parents, who started with the story about our neighbor's well, and then got up to close the drapes. Fifty pages later, they were boarding up the door and looking for ways to disguise themselves. Other people had loved my writing, but these two didn't get it at all. "What's wrong?" I asked.

My father adjusted his makeshift turban, and sketched a mustache on my mother's upper lip. "What's wrong?" he said. "I'll tell you what's wrong: you're killing us."

"But I thought that's what you wanted?"

"We did," my mother wept, "but not this way."

It hadn't occurred to me until that moment, but I seemed to have come full circle. What started as a dodge had inadvertently become my life's work, an irony I never could have appreciated had my extraordinary parents not put me through Princeton.

FOR ANALYSIS

1. Do you think this essay was delivered at a real commencement? Why or why not?

2. Can you isolate serious moments among this essay's general silliness? How do they function? What do they say?

WRITING TOPIC

Pick a form of ceremonial address—a graduation address, a wedding toast, a retirement speech—and write a **parody** of it. Think about what the different aspects of the address are supposed to do and how each might be subverted not just to be funny but to make a point.

DAVID FOSTER WALLACE (1962–2008)

COMMENCEMENT SPEECH, KENYON COLLEGE[1] 2005

There are these two young fish swimming along, and they happen to meet an older fish swimming the other way, who nods at them and says, "Morning, boys, how's the water?" And the two young fish swim on for a bit, and then eventually one of them looks over at the other and goes, "What the hell is water?"

If at this moment, you're worried that I plan to present myself here as the wise old fish explaining what water is to you younger fish, please don't be. I am not the wise old fish. The immediate point of the fish story is that the most obvious, ubiquitous, important realities are often the ones that are the hardest

---

[1] Adapted from a commencement speech given by David Foster Wallace to the 2005 graduating class at Kenyon College.

to see and talk about. Stated as an English sentence, of course, this is just a banal platitude—but the fact is that, in the day-to-day trenches of adult existence, banal platitudes can have life-or-death importance. That may sound like hyperbole, or abstract nonsense.

A huge percentage of the stuff that I tend to be automatically certain of is, it turns out, totally wrong and deluded. Here's one example of the utter wrongness of something I tend to be automatically sure of: everything in my own immediate experience supports my deep belief that I am the absolute center of the universe, the realest, most vivid, and important person in existence. We rarely talk about this sort of natural, basic self-centeredness, because it's so socially repulsive, but it's pretty much the same for all of us, deep down. It is our default-setting, hard-wired into our boards at birth. Think about it: there is no experience you've had that you were not at the absolute center of. The world as you experience it is right there in front of you, or behind you, to the left or right of you, on your TV, or your monitor, or whatever. Other people's thoughts and feelings have to be communicated to you somehow, but your own are so immediate, urgent, *real*—you get the idea. But please don't worry that I'm getting ready to preach to you about compassion or other-directedness or the so-called virtues. This is not a matter of virtue—it's a matter of my choosing to do the work of somehow altering or getting free of my natural, hard-wired default-setting, which is to be deeply and literally self-centered, and to see and interpret everything through this lens of self.

People who can adjust their natural default-setting this way are often described as being "well adjusted," which I suggest to you is not an accidental term.

Given the triumphal academic setting here, an obvious question is how much of this work of adjusting our default-setting involves actual knowledge or intellect. This question gets tricky. Probably the most dangerous thing about college education, at least in my own case, is that it enables my tendency to over-intellectualize stuff, to get lost in abstract arguments inside my head instead of simply paying attention to what's going on right in front of me. Paying attention to what's going on inside me. As I'm sure you guys know by now, it is extremely difficult to stay alert and attentive instead of getting hypnotized by the constant monologue inside your own head. Twenty years after my own graduation, I have come gradually to understand that the liberal-arts cliché about "teaching you how to think" is actually shorthand for a much deeper, more serious idea: "learning how to think" really means learning how to exercise some control over how and what you think. It means being conscious and aware enough to choose what you pay attention to and to choose how you construct meaning from experience. Because if you cannot exercise this kind of choice in adult life, you will be totally hosed. Think of the old cliché about "the mind being an excellent servant but a terrible master." This, like many clichés, so lame and unexciting on the surface, actually expresses a great and terrible truth. It is not the least bit coincidental that adults who commit suicide with firearms almost always shoot themselves in the head. And the truth is that most of these suicides are actually dead long before they pull the trigger. And

I submit that this is what the real, no-bull-value of your liberal-arts education is supposed to be about: how to keep from going through your comfortable, prosperous, respectable adult life dead, unconscious, a slave to your head and to your natural default-setting of being uniquely, completely, imperially alone, day in and day out.

That may sound like hyperbole, or abstract nonsense. So let's get concrete. The plain fact is that you graduating seniors do not yet have any clue what "day in, day out" really means. There happen to be whole large parts of adult American life that nobody talks about in commencement speeches. One such part involves boredom, routine, and petty frustration. The parents and older folks here will know all too well what I'm talking about.

By way of example, let's say it's an average day, and you get up in the morning, go to your challenging job, and you work hard for nine or ten hours, and at the end of the day you're tired, and you're stressed out, and all you want is to go home and have a good supper and maybe unwind for a couple of hours and then hit the rack early because you have to get up the next day and do it all again. But then you remember there's no food at home—you haven't had time to shop this week, because of your challenging job—and so now after work you have to get in your car and drive to the supermarket. It's the end of the workday, and the traffic's very bad, so getting to the store takes way longer than it should, and when you finally get there the supermarket is very crowded, because of course it's the time of day when all the other people with jobs also try to squeeze in some grocery shopping, and the store's hideously, fluorescently lit, and infused with soul-killing Muzak or corporate pop, and it's pretty much the last place you want to be, but you can't just get in and quickly out: you have to wander all over the huge, overlit store's crowded aisles to find the stuff you want, and you have to maneuver your junky cart through all these other tired, hurried people with carts, and of course there are also the glacially slow old people and the spacey people and the ADHD kids who all block the aisle and you have to grit your teeth and try to be polite as you ask them to let you by, and eventually, finally, you get all your supper supplies, except now it turns out there aren't enough checkout lanes open even though it's the end-of-the-day-rush, so the checkout line is incredibly long, which is stupid and infuriating, but you can't take your fury out on the frantic lady working the register.

Anyway, you finally get to the checkout line's front, and pay for your food, and wait to get your check or card authenticated by a machine, and then get told to "Have a nice day" in a voice that is the absolute voice of *death*, and then you have to take your creepy flimsy plastic bags of groceries in your cart through the crowded, bumpy, littery parking lot, and try to load the bags in your car in such a way that everything doesn't fall out of the bags and roll around in the trunk on the way home, and then you have to drive all the way home through slow, heavy, SUV-intensive rush-hour traffic, etcetera, etcetera.

The point is that petty, frustrating crap like this is exactly where the work of choosing comes in. Because the traffic jams and crowded aisles and long checkout lines give me time to think, and if I don't make a conscious decision about how to think and what to pay attention to, I'm going to be pissed and miserable every time I have to food-shop, because my natural default-setting is the certainty that situations like this are really all about *me*, about my hungriness and my fatigue and my desire to just get home, and it's going to seem, for all the world, like everybody else is just *in my way,* and who are all these people in my way? And look at how repulsive most of them are and how stupid and cow-like and dead-eyed and nonhuman they seem here in the checkout line, or at how annoying and rude it is that people are talking loudly on cell phones in the middle of the line, and look at how deeply unfair this is: I've worked really hard all day and I'm starved and tired and I can't even get home to eat and unwind because of all these stupid g-d- *people.*

Or, of course, if I'm in a more socially conscious form of my default-setting, 10 I can spend time in the end-of-the-day traffic jam being angry and disgusted at all the huge, stupid, lane-blocking SUVs and Hummers and V-12 pickup trucks burning their wasteful, selfish, forty-gallon tanks of gas, and I can dwell on the fact that the patriotic or religious bumper stickers always seem to be on the biggest, most disgustingly selfish vehicles driven by the ugliest, most inconsiderate and aggressive drivers, who are usually talking on cell phones as they cut people off in order to get just twenty stupid feet ahead in a traffic jam, and I can think about how our children's children will despise us for wasting all the future's fuel and probably screwing up the climate, and how spoiled and stupid and disgusting we all are, and how it all just *sucks,* and so on and so forth. . . .

Look, if I choose to think this way, fine, lots of us do—except that thinking this way tends to be so easy and automatic it doesn't *have* to be a choice. Thinking this way is my natural default-setting. It's the automatic, unconscious way that I experience the boring, frustrating, crowded parts of adult life when I'm operating on the automatic, unconscious belief that I am the center of the world and that my immediate needs and feelings are what should determine the world's priorities. The thing is that there are obviously different ways to think about these kinds of situations. In this traffic, all these vehicles stuck and idling in my way: it's not impossible that some of these people in SUVs have been in horrible auto accidents in the past and now find driving so traumatic that their therapist has all but ordered them to get a huge, heavy SUV so they can feel safe enough to drive; or that the Hummer that just cut me off is maybe being driven by a father whose little child is hurt or sick in the seat next to him, and he's trying to rush to the hospital, and he's in a way bigger, more legitimate hurry than I am—it is actually *I* who am in *his* way. Or I can choose to force myself to consider the likelihood that everyone else in the supermarket's checkout line is just as bored and frustrated as I am, and that some of these people probably have much harder, more tedious or painful lives than I do, overall.

Again, please don't think that I'm giving you moral advice, or that I'm saying you're "supposed to" think this way, or that anyone expects you to just automatically do it, because it's hard, it takes will and mental effort, and if you're like me, some days you won't be able to do it, or you just flat-out won't want to.

But most days, if you're aware enough to give yourself a choice, you can choose to look differently at this fat, dead-eyed, over-made-lady who just screamed at her little child in the checkout line—maybe she's not usually like this; maybe she's been up three straight nights holding the hand of her husband who's dying of bone cancer, or maybe this very lady is the low-wage clerk at the Motor Vehicles Department, who just yesterday helped your spouse resolve a night-marish red-tape problem through some small act of bureaucratic kindness. Of course, none of this is likely, but it's also not impossible—it just depends on what you want to consider. If you're automatically sure that you know what reality is and who and what is really important—if you want to operate on your default-setting—then you, like me, will not consider possibilities that aren't pointless and annoying. But if you've really learned how to think, how to pay attention, then you will know you have other options. It will actually be within your power to experience a crowded, loud, slow, consumer-hell-type situa-tion as not only meaningful but sacred, on fire with the same force that lit the stars—compassion, love, the subsurface unity of all things. Not that that mysti-cal stuff's necessarily true: the only thing that's capital-T True is that you get to *decide* how you're going to try to see it. You get to consciously decide what has meaning and what doesn't. You get to decide what to worship. . . .

Because here's something else that's true. In the day-to-day trenches of adult life, there is actually no such thing as atheism. There is no such thing as not wor-shipping. Everybody worships. The only choice we get is *what* to worship. And an outstanding reason for choosing some sort of God or spiritual-type thing to worship—be it J.C. or Allah, be it Yahweh or the Wiccan mother-goddess or the Four Noble Truths or some infrangible set of ethical principles—is that pretty much anything else you worship will eat you alive. If you worship money and things—if they are where you tap real meaning in life—then you will never have enough. Never feel you have enough. It's the truth. Worship your own body and beauty and sexual allure and you will always feel ugly, and when time and age start showing, you will die a million deaths before they finally plant you. On one level, we all know this stuff already—it's been codified as myths, proverbs, clichés, bromides, epigrams, parables: the skeleton of every great story. The trick is keeping the truth up front in daily consciousness. Worship power—you will feel weak and afraid, and you will need ever more power over others to keep the fear at bay. Worship your intellect, being seen as smart—you will end up feeling stupid, a fraud, always on the verge of being found out. And so on.

Look, the insidious thing about these forms of worship is not that they're evil or sinful; it is that they are *unconscious.* They are default-settings. They're the kind of worship you just gradually slip into, day after day, getting more and more selective about what you see and how you measure value without ever being fully aware that that's what you're doing. And the world will not discourage you from operating on your default-settings, because the world of men and money and power hums along quite nicely on the fuel of fear and contempt and frustration and craving and the worship of self. Our own present culture has harnessed these forces in ways that have yielded extraordinary wealth and comfort and personal freedom. The freedom to be lords of our own tiny skull-sized kingdoms, alone at the center of all creation. This kind of freedom has much to recommend it. But of course there are all different kinds of freedom, and the kind that is most precious you will not hear much talked about in the great outside world of winning and achieving and displaying. The really important kind of freedom involves attention, and awareness, and discipline, and effort, and being able truly to care about other people and to sacrifice for them, over and over, in myriad petty little unsexy ways, every day. That is real freedom. The alternative is unconsciousness, the default-setting, the "rat race"—the constant gnawing sense of having had and lost some infinite thing.

I know that this stuff probably doesn't sound fun and breezy or grandly 15 inspirational. What it is, so far as I can see, is the truth with a whole lot of rhetorical bullshit pared away. Obviously, you can think of it whatever you wish. But please don't dismiss it as some finger-wagging Dr. Laura sermon. None of this is about morality, or religion, or dogma, or big fancy questions of life after death. The capital-T Truth is about life *before* death. It is about making it to thirty, or maybe fifty, without wanting to shoot yourself in the head. It is about simple awareness—awareness of what is so real and essential, so hidden in plain sight all around us, that we have to keep reminding ourselves, over and over: "This is water, this is water."

It is unimaginably hard to do this, to stay conscious and alive, day in and day out.

FOR ANALYSIS

1. What does Wallace mean when he says, "This is water" (para. 15)?

2. "That may sound like hyperbole, or abstract nonsense," Wallace comments on something he's said, "So let's get concrete" (para. 6). What are Wallace's **abstractions**? How does he use the **concrete** to anchor them?

MAKING CONNECTIONS

1. Wallace writes, "A huge percentage of the stuff that I tend to be automatically certain of is, it turns out, totally wrong and deluded" (para. 3). Education, especially higher education, is often thought of as the way people prepare themselves for careers by mastering particular thinking skills and bodies of knowledge. How do Wallace and Sedaris challenge this idea?

2. Which view of higher education appeals to you more? Why?

3. Compare Wallace's writing style to Sedaris's. Both have been praised as stylists, but they write very differently. How do they write? Think about different elements of writing—**diction,** sentence structure, voice—and different adjectives used to describe writing—flowery, spare, hard-edged, sophisticated, showy, smug, generous. Do you like one's **style** more? Why?

WRITING TOPIC

Write your own reflection on an everyday event, like Wallace's on the checkout line (or the traffic jam). Try to make a more general statement based on these reflections.

FURTHER QUESTIONS
FOR THINKING AND WRITING

1. How do the works in this section illustrate Thomas Gray's well-known observation that "where ignorance is bliss, / 'Tis folly to be wise"? **Writing Topic:** Use Gray's observation as the basis for an analysis of Toni Cade Bambara's "The Lesson" or Hanan Mikha'il 'Ashrawi's "From the Diary of an Almost-Four-Year-Old."

2. In poems such as William Blake's "The Garden of Love," Robert Frost's "Birches," and Stevie Smith's "To Carry the Child," growing up is seen as a growing away from a kind of truth and reality; in other poems, such as Gerard Manley Hopkins's "Spring and Fall," and Dylan Thomas's "Fern Hill," growing up is seen as growing into truth and reality. Do these two groups of poems embody contradictory and mutually exclusive conceptions of childhood? Explain. **Writing Topic:** Select one poem from each of these two groups, and contrast the conception of childhood embodied in each.

3. Eighteenth-century novelist Henry Fielding wrote: "Oh Innocence, how glorious and happy a portion art thou to the breast that possesses thee! Thou fearest neither the eyes nor the tongues of men. Truth, the most powerful of all things, is thy strongest friend; and the brighter the light is in which thou art displayed, the more it discovers thy transcendent beauties." Which works in this section support this assessment of innocence? Which works contradict it? How would you characterize the relationship between "truth" and "innocence" in the fiction, drama, and essays presented here? **Writing Topic:** Use this observation as the basis for an analysis of Nathaniel Hawthorne's "Young Goodman Brown" or Toni Cade Bambara's "The Lesson."

4. James Joyce's "Araby" and Rivka Galchen's "Wild Berry Blue" deal with some aspect of sexuality as a force that moves the **protagonist** from innocence toward experience. How does the recognition of sexuality function in each of the stories? **Writing Topic:** Discuss the relationship between sexuality and innocence in these stories.

5. Which poems in this section depend largely on **irony** for their force? Why do you think irony is a useful device in literature that portrays innocence and experience? **Writing Topic:** Analyze the function of irony in Blake's "The Garden of Love" and Hardy's "The Ruined Maid."

6. Some authors treat the passage from innocence to experience as **comedy**, while others treat it more seriously, even as **tragedy**. Do you find one or the other treatment more satisfying? Explain. **Writing Topic:** Select one short story, and show how the author achieves either a comic or a serious tone.

CONFORMITY
AND REBELLION

Untitled, 1985, by Keith Haring. © Keith Haring Foundation. Used by permission.

The works in this section, "Conformity and Rebellion," feature a clash between two well-articulated positions in which a rebel, on principle, confronts and struggles with established authority. Central in these works are powerful external forces—the state, the church, tradition—which sometimes can be obeyed only at the expense of conscience and humanity. At the most general level, these works confront the ages-old dilemma that the very organizations men and women establish to protect and nurture the individual often demand—on pain of economic ruin, social ostracism, even spiritual or physical death—that individuals violate their most deeply cherished beliefs. In these works, some individuals refuse such a demand and translate their awareness of a hostile social order into action against it. In "'Repent, Harlequin!' Said the Ticktockman," Everett C. Marm disrupts a system he doesn't believe in. On a different note, in Melville's "Bartleby, the Scrivener" the crisis arises out of the protagonist's passive refusal to conform to the expectations of society.

Many of the works in this section, particularly the poems, do not treat the theme of conformity and rebellion quite so explicitly and dramatically. Some, like Emily Dickinson's "She rose to His Requirement," reveal the painful injustice of certain traditional values; others, like W. H. Auden's "The Unknown Citizen," tell us that the price exacted for total conformity to the industrial superstate is spiritual death. In "Easter 1916," William Butler Yeats meditates on the awesome meaning of the lives and deaths of political revolutionaries, and in "Harlem," Langston Hughes warns that an inflexible and constricting social order will generate explosion.

While in many of the works the individual is caught up in a crisis that forces him or her into rebellion, in other works the focus may be on the individual's failure to move from awareness into action. For example, the portrait of Auden's unknown citizen affirms the necessity for rebellion by rendering so effectively the hollow life of mindless conformity.

Although diverse in treatment and technique, all the works in this section are about individuals struggling with complex sets of external forces that regulate and define their lives. As social beings, these individuals may recognize that they must be controlled for some larger good; yet they are aware that established social power is often abusive. The institution at its best can act as a conserving force, keeping in check the individual's disruptive impulse to abandon and destroy, without cause, old ways and ideas. At its worst, the power of social institutions is self-serving. It is up to the individual to judge whether power is being abused. Because the power of the individual is often negligible beside that of abusive social forces, it is not surprising that many artists find a fundamental human dignity in the resistance of the individual to organized society.

QUESTIONS FOR THINKING AND WRITING

Before you begin reading the selections in "Conformity and Rebellion," consider the following questions. Then write out your thoughts informally in a reading journal, if you are keeping one, as a way of preparing to respond to the selections. Or you may wish to make your response to one of these questions the basis for a formal essay.

1. How do you define *conformity*? What forms of rebellion are possible for a person in your situation? Do you perceive yourself as a conformist? A rebel? Some combination of the two? Explain.

2. How do you define *sanity*? Based on your definition, do you know an insane person? What form does that insanity take? Do you agree or disagree with Emily Dickinson's assertion that "Much Madness is divinest Sense"? Explain.

3. Discuss this proposition: governments routinely engage in behavior for which an individual would be imprisoned or institutionalized.

4. Freewrite an extended response to each of the following questions: Is war sane? Should one obey an "unjust" law? Should one be guided absolutely by religious principles?

FICTION

HERMAN MELVILLE (1819–1891)

BARTLEBY, THE SCRIVENER 1853

A STORY OF WALL STREET

I am a rather elderly man. The nature of my avocations, for the last thirty years, has brought me into more than ordinary contact with what would seem an interesting and somewhat singular set of men, of whom, as yet, nothing, that I know of, has ever been written—I mean, the law-copyists, or scriveners. I have known very many of them, professionally and privately, and, if I pleased, could relate divers histories, at which good-natured gentlemen might smile, and sentimental souls might weep. But I waive the biographies of all other scriveners, for a few passages in the life of Bartleby, who was a scrivener, the strangest I ever saw, or heard of. While, of other law-copyists, I might write the complete life, of Bartleby nothing of that sort can be done. I believe that no materials exist for a full and satisfactory biography of this man. It is an irreparable loss to literature. Bartleby was one of those beings of whom nothing is ascertainable, except from the original sources, and, in his case, those are very small. What my own astonished eyes saw of Bartleby, *that* is all I know of him, except, indeed, one vague report, which will appear in the sequel.

Ere introducing the scrivener, as he first appeared to me, it is fit I make some mention of myself, my employees, my business, my chambers, and general surroundings; because some such description is indispensable to an adequate understanding of the chief character about to be presented. Imprimis: I am a man who, from his youth upwards, has been filled with a profound conviction that the easiest way of life is the best. Hence, though I belong to a profession proverbially energetic and nervous, even to turbulence, at times, yet nothing of that sort have I ever suffered to invade my peace. I am one of those unambitious lawyers who never addresses a jury, or in any way draws down public applause; but, in the cool tranquillity of a snug retreat, do a snug business among rich men's bonds, and mortgages, and title-deeds. All who know me, consider me an eminently *safe* man. The late John Jacob Astor,[1] a personage little given to poetic enthusiasm, had no hesitation in pronouncing my first grand point to be prudence; my next, method. I do not speak it in vanity, but simply record the fact, that I was not unemployed in my profession by the late John Jacob Astor; a name which, I admit, I love to repeat; for it hath a rounded and orbicular sound to it, and rings like unto bullion. I will freely add, that I was not insensible to the late John Jacob Astor's good opinion.

Some time prior to the period at which this little history begins, my avocations had been largely increased. The good old office, now extinct in the State of New York, of a Master in Chancery,[2] had been conferred upon me. It was not a very arduous office, but very pleasantly remunerative. I seldom lose my temper; much more seldom indulge in dangerous indignation at wrongs and outrages; but, I must be permitted to be rash here, and declare that I consider the sudden and violent abrogation of the office of Master in Chancery, by the new Constitution, as a—premature act; inasmuch as I had counted upon a lifelease of the profits, whereas I only received those of a few short years. But this is by the way.

My chambers were up stairs, at No. ———— Wall Street. At one end, they looked upon the white wall of the interior of a spacious sky-light shaft, penetrating the building from top to bottom.

This view might have been considered rather tame than otherwise, deficient 5 in what landscape painters call "life." But, if so, the view from the other end of my chambers offered, at least, a contrast, if nothing more. In that direction, my windows commanded an unobstructed view of a lofty brick wall, black by age and everlasting shade; which wall required no spyglass to bring out its lurking beauties, but, for the benefit of all near-sighted spectators, was pushed up to within ten feet of my window panes. Owing to the great height of the surrounding buildings, and my chambers being on the second floor, the interval between this wall and mine not a little resembled a huge square cistern.

At the period just preceding the advent of Bartleby, I had two persons as copyists in my employment, and a promising lad as an office-boy. First, Turkey; second, Nippers; third, Ginger Nut. These may seem names, the like of which are not usually found in the Directory. In truth, they were nicknames, mutually conferred upon each other by my three clerks, and were deemed expressive of their respective persons or characters. Turkey was a short, pursy Englishman, of about my own age—that is, somewhere not far from sixty. In the morning, one might say, his face was of a fine florid hue, but after twelve o'clock, meridian—his dinner hour—it blazed like a grate full of Christmas coals; and continued blazing—but, as it were, with a gradual wane—till six o'clock P.M., or thereabouts; after which, I saw no more of the proprietor of the face, which, gaining its meridian with the sun, seemed to set with it, to rise, culminate, and decline the following day, with the like regularity and

---

[1] A poor immigrant from Germany who became one of the great business tycoons of the nineteenth century.

[2] Courts of Chancery often adjudicated business disputes.

undiminished glory. There are many singular coincidences I have known in the course of my life, not the least among which was the fact, that, exactly when Turkey displayed his fullest beams from his red and radiant countenance, just then, too, at that critical moment, began the daily period when I considered his business capacities as seriously disturbed for the remainder of the twenty-four hours. Not that he was absolutely idle, or averse to business, then; far from it. The difficulty was, he was apt to be altogether too energetic. There was a strange, inflamed, flurried, flighty recklessness of activity about him. He would be incautious in dipping his pen into his inkstand. All his blots upon my documents were dropped there after twelve o'clock meridian. Indeed, not only would he be reckless, and sadly given to making blots in the afternoon, but, some days, he went further, and was rather noisy. At such times, too, his face flamed with augmented blazonry, as if cannel coal had been heaped on anthracite. He made an unpleasant racket with his chair; spilled his sand-box; in mending his pens, impatiently split them all to pieces, and threw them on the floor in a sudden passion; stood up, and leaned over his table, boxing his papers about in a most indecorous manner, very sad to behold in an elderly man like him. Nevertheless, as he was in many ways a most valuable person to me, and all the time before twelve o'clock meridian, was the quickest, steadiest creature, too, accomplishing a great deal of work in a style not easily to be matched—for these reasons, I was willing to overlook his eccentricities, though, indeed, occasionally, I remonstrated with him. I did this very gently, however, because, though the civilest, nay, the blandest and most reverential of men in the morning, yet, in the afternoon, he was disposed, upon provocation, to be slightly rash with his tongue—in fact, insolent. Now, valuing his morning services as I did, and resolved not to lose them—yet, at the same time, made uncomfortable by his inflamed ways after twelve o'clock— and being a man of peace, unwilling by my admonitions to call forth unseemly retorts from him, I took upon me, one Saturday noon (he was always worse on Saturdays) to hint to him, very kindly, that, perhaps, now that he was growing old, it might be well to abridge his labors; in short, he need not come to my chambers after twelve o'clock, but, dinner over, had best go home to his lodgings, and rest himself till tea-time. But no; he insisted upon his afternoon devotions. His countenance became intolerably fervid, as he oratorically assured me—gesticulating with a long ruler at the other end of the room—that if his services in the morning were useful, how indispensable, then, in the afternoon?

"With submission, sir," said Turkey, on this occasion, "I consider myself your right-hand man. In the morning I but marshal and deploy my columns; but in the afternoon I put myself at their head, and gallantly charge the foe, thus"—and he made a violent thrust with the ruler.

"But the blots, Turkey," intimated I.

"True; but, with submission, sir, behold these hairs! I am getting old. Surely, sir, a blot or two of a warm afternoon is not to be severely urged against gray hairs. Old age—even if it blot the page—is honorable. With submission, sir, we *both* are getting old."

This appeal to my fellow-feeling was hardly to be resisted. At all events, 10
I saw that go he would not. So, I made up my mind to let him stay, resolving,
nevertheless, to see to it that, during the afternoon, he had to do with my less
important papers.

Nippers, the second on my list, was a whiskered, sallow, and, upon the
whole, rather piratical-looking young man, of about five and twenty. I always
deemed him the victim of two evil powers—ambition and indigestion. The
ambition was evinced by a certain impatience of the duties of a mere copyist, an unwarrantable usurpation of strictly professional affairs, such as the
original drawing up of legal documents. The indigestion seemed betokened in
an occasional nervous testiness and grinning irritability, causing the teeth to
audibly grind together over mistakes committed in copying; unnecessary maledictions, hissed, rather than spoken, in the heat of business; and especially by
a continual discontent with the height of the table where he worked. Though
of a very ingenious, mechanical turn, Nippers could never get this table to suit
him. He put chips under it, blocks of various sorts, bits of pasteboard, and at
last went so far as to attempt an exquisite adjustment, by final pieces of folded
blotting-paper. But no invention would answer. If, for the sake of easing his
back, he brought the table-lid at a sharp angle well up towards his chin, and
wrote there like a man using the steep roof of a Dutch house for his desk, then
he declared that it stopped the circulation in his arms. If now he lowered the
table to his waistbands, and stooped over it in writing, then there was a sore
aching in his back. In short, the truth of the matter was, Nippers knew not
what he wanted. Or, if he wanted anything, it was to be rid of a scrivener's
table altogether. Among the manifestations of his diseased ambition was a
fondness he had for receiving visits from certain ambiguous-looking fellows
in seedy coats, whom he called his clients. Indeed, I was aware that not only
was he, at times, considerable of a ward-politician, but he occasionally did a
little business at the Justices' courts, and was not unknown on the steps of
the Tombs.[3] I have good reason to believe, however, that one individual who
called upon him at my chambers, and who, with a grand air, he insisted was
his client, was no other than a dun, and the alleged title-deed, a bill. But, with
all his failings, and the annoyances he caused me, Nippers, like his compatriot
Turkey, was a very useful man to me; wrote a neat, swift hand; and, when he
chose, was not deficient in a gentlemanly sort of deportment. Added to this,
he always dressed in a gentlemanly sort of way; and so, incidentally, reflected
credit upon my chambers. Whereas, with respect to Turkey, I had much ado
to keep him from being a reproach to me. His clothes were apt to look oily,
and smell of eating houses. He wore his pantaloons very loose and baggy in
summer. His coats were execrable, his hat not to be handled. But while the
hat was a thing of indifference to me, inasmuch as his natural civility and
deference, as a dependent Englishman, always led him to doff it the moment
he entered the room, yet his coat was another matter. Concerning his coats,

[3] A prison in New York City.

I reasoned with him; but with no effect. The truth was, I suppose, that a man with so small an income could not afford to sport such a lustrous face and a lustrous coat at one and the same time. As Nippers once observed, Turkey's money went chiefly for red ink. One winter day, I presented Turkey with a highly respectable-looking coat of my own—a padded gray coat, of a most comfortable warmth, and which buttoned straight up from the knee to the neck. I thought Turkey would appreciate the favor, and abate his rashness and obstreperousness of afternoons. But no; I verily believe that buttoning himself up in so downy and blanket-like a coat had a pernicious effect upon him— upon the same principle that too much oats are bad for horses. In fact, precisely as a rash, restive horse is said to feel his oats, so Turkey felt his coat. It made him insolent. He was a man whom prosperity harmed.

Though, concerning the self-indulgent habits of Turkey, I had my own private surmises, yet, touching Nippers, I was well persuaded that, whatever might be his faults in other respects, he was, at least, a temperate young man. But, indeed, nature herself seemed to have been his vintner, and, at his birth, charged him so thoroughly with an irritable, brandy-like disposition, that all subsequent potations were needless. When I consider how, amid the stillness of my chambers, Nippers would sometimes impatiently rise from his seat, and stooping over his table, spread his arms wide apart, seize the whole desk, and move it, and jerk it, with a grim, grinding motion on the floor, as if the table were a perverse voluntary agent and vexing him, I plainly perceive that, for Nippers, brandy-and-water were altogether superfluous.

It was fortunate for me that, owing to its peculiar cause—indigestion—the irritability and consequent nervousness of Nippers were mainly observable in the morning, while in the afternoon he was comparatively mild. So that, Turkey's paroxysms only coming on about twelve o'clock, I never had to do with their eccentricities at one time. Their fits relieved each other, like guards. When Nippers's was on, Turkey's was off; and *vice versa*. This was a good natural arrangement, under the circumstances.

Ginger Nut, the third on my list, was a lad, some twelve years old. His father was a car-man, ambitious of seeing his son on the bench instead of a cart, before he died. So he sent him to my office, as student at law, errand-boy, cleaner and sweeper, at the rate of one dollar a week. He had a little desk to himself; but he did not use it much. Upon inspection, the drawer exhibited a great array of shells of various sorts of nuts. Indeed, to this quick-witted youth, the whole noble science of the law was contained in a nutshell. Not the least among the employments of Ginger Nut, as well as one which he discharged with the most alacrity, was his duty as cake and apple purveyor for Turkey and Nippers. Copying law-papers being proverbially a dry, husky sort of business, my two scriveners were fain to moisten their mouths very often with Spitzenbergs,[4] to be had at the numerous stalls nigh the Custom House and Post Office. Also, they sent Ginger Nut very frequently for that peculiar

---

[4] A variety of apple.

cake—small, flat, round, and very spicy—after which he had been named by them. Of a cold morning, when business was but dull, Turkey would gobble up scores of these cakes, as if they were mere wafers—indeed, they sell them at the rate of six or eight for a penny—the scrape of his pen blending with the crunching of the crisp particles in his mouth. Rashest of all the fiery after- noon blunders and flurried rashnesses of Turkey, was his once moistening a ginger-cake between his lips, and clapping it on to a mortgage, for a seal. I came within an ace of dismissing him then. But he mollified me by making an oriental bow, and saying—

"With submission, sir, it was generous of me to find you in stationery on my 15 own account."

Now my original business—that of a conveyancer and title hunter, and drawer-up of recondite documents of all sorts—was considerably increased by receiving the master's office. There was now great work for scriveners. Not only must I push the clerks already with me, but I must have additional help.

In answer to my advertisement, a motionless young man one morning stood upon my office threshold, the door being open, for it was summer. I can see that figure now—pallidly neat, pitiably respectable, incurably forlorn! It was Bartleby.

After a few words touching his qualifications, I engaged him, glad to have among my corps of copyists a man of so singularly sedate an aspect, which I thought might operate beneficially upon the flighty temper of Turkey, and the fiery one of Nippers.

I should have stated before that ground-glass folding-doors divided my premises into two parts, one of which was occupied by my scriveners, the other by myself. According to my humor, I threw open these doors, or closed them. I resolved to assign Bartleby a corner by the folding-doors, but on my side of them, so as to have this quiet man within easy call, in case any trifling thing was to be done. I placed his desk close up to a small side-window in that part of the room, a window which originally had afforded a lateral view of certain grimy backyards and bricks, but which, owing to subsequent erections, commanded at present no view at all, though it gave some light. Within three feet of the panes was a wall, and the light came down from far above, between two lofty buildings, as from a very small opening in a dome. Still further to a satisfactory arrangement, I procured a high green folding screen, which might entirely isolate Bartleby from my sight, though not remove him from my voice. And thus, in a manner, privacy and society were conjoined.

At first, Bartleby did an extraordinary quantity of writing. As if long famish- 20 ing for something to copy, he seemed to gorge himself on my documents. There was no pause for digestion. He ran a day and night line, copying by sun-light and by candle-light. I should have been quite delighted with his application, had he been cheerfully industrious. But he wrote on silently, palely, mechanically.

It is, of course, an indispensable part of a scrivener's business to verify the accuracy of his copy, word by word. Where there are two or more scriveners in an office, they assist each other in this examination, one reading from the copy, the other holding the original. It is a very dull, wearisome, and lethargic affair. I can readily imagine that, to some sanguine temperaments, it would be altogether intolerable. For example, I cannot credit that the mettlesome poet, Byron, would have contentedly sat down with Bartleby to examine a law document of, say five hundred pages, closely written in a crimpy hand.

Now and then, in the haste of business, it had been my habit to assist in comparing some brief document myself, calling Turkey or Nippers for this purpose. One object I had, in placing Bartleby so handy to me behind the screen, was to avail myself of his services on such trivial occasions. It was on the third day, I think, of his being with me, and before any necessity had arisen for having his own writing examined, that, being much hurried to complete a small affair I had in hand, I abruptly called to Bartleby. In my haste and natural expectancy of instant compliance, I sat with my head bent over the original on my desk, and my right hand sideways, and somewhat nervously extended with the copy, so that, immediately upon emerging from his retreat, Bartleby might snatch it and proceed to business without the least delay.

In this very attitude did I sit when I called to him, rapidly stating what it was I wanted him to do—namely, to examine a small paper with me. Imagine my surprise, nay, my consternation, when, without moving from his privacy, Bartleby, in a singularly mild, firm voice, replied, "I would prefer not to."

I sat awhile in perfect silence, rallying my stunned faculties. Immediately it occurred to me that my ears had deceived me, or Bartleby had entirely misunderstood my meaning. I repeated my request in the clearest tone I could assume; but in quite as clear a one came the previous reply, "I would prefer not to."

"Prefer not to," echoed I, rising in high excitement, and crossing the room 25 with a stride. "What do you mean? Are you moon-struck? I want you to help me compare this sheet here—take it," and I thrust it towards him.

"I would prefer not to," said he.

I looked at him steadfastly. His face was leanly composed; his gray eye dimly calm. Not a wrinkle of agitation rippled him. Had there been the least uneasiness, anger, impatience, or impertinence in his manner; in other words, had there been any thing ordinarily human about him, doubtless I should have violently dismissed him from the premises. But as it was, I should have as soon thought of turning my pale plaster-of-paris bust of Cicero out of doors. I stood gazing at him awhile, as he went on with his own writing, and then reseated myself at my desk. This is very strange, thought I. What had one best do? But my business hurried me. I concluded to forget the matter for the present, reserving it for my future leisure. So calling Nippers from the other room, the paper was speedily examined.

A few days after this, Bartleby concluded four lengthy documents, being quadruplicates of a week's testimony taken before me in my High Court of Chancery. It became necessary to examine them. It was an important suit, and great accuracy was imperative. Having all things arranged, I called Turkey, Nippers, and Ginger Nut from the next room, meaning to place the four copies in the hands of my four clerks, while I should read from the original. Accordingly,

Turkey, Nippers, and Ginger Nut had taken their seats in a row, each with his document in his hand, when I called to Bartleby to join this interesting group.

"Bartleby! quick, I am waiting."

I heard a slow scrape of his chair legs on the uncarpeted floor, and soon he 30 appeared standing at the entrance of his hermitage.

"What is wanted?" said he, mildly.

"The copies, the copies," said I, hurriedly. "We are going to examine them. There—" and I held towards him the fourth quadruplicate.

"I would prefer not to," he said, and gently disappeared behind the screen.

For a few moments I was turned into a pillar of salt, standing at the head of my seated column of clerks. Recovering myself, I advanced towards the screen, and demanded the reason for such extraordinary conduct.

"*Why* do you refuse?"   35

"I would prefer not to."

With any other man I should have flown outright into a dreadful passion, scorned all further words, and thrust him ignominiously from my presence. But there was something about Bartleby that not only strangely disarmed me, but in a wonderful manner, touched and disconcerted me. I began to reason with him.

"These are your own copies we are about to examine. It is labor saving to you, because one examination will answer for your four papers. It is common usage. Every copyist is bound to help examine his copy. Is it not so? Will you not speak? Answer!"

"I prefer not to," he replied in a flutelike tone. It seemed to me that, while I had been addressing him, he carefully revolved every statement that I made; fully comprehended the meaning; could not gainsay the irresistible conclusion; but, at the same time, some paramount consideration prevailed with him to reply as he did.

"You are decided, then, not to comply with my request—a request made 40 according to common usage and common sense?"

He briefly gave me to understand, that on that point my judgment was sound. Yes: his decision was irreversible.

It is not seldom the case that, when a man is browbeaten in some unprecedented and violently unreasonable way, he begins to stagger in his own plainest faith. He begins, as it were, vaguely to surmise that, wonderful as it may be, all the justice and all the reason is on the other side. Accordingly, if any disinterested persons are present, he turns to them for some reinforcement of his own faltering mind.

"Turkey," said I, "what do you think of this? Am I not right?"

"With submission, sir," said Turkey, in his blandest tone, "I think that you are."

"Nippers," said I, "what do *you* think of it?"   45

"I think I should kick him out of the office."

(The reader, of nice perceptions, will here perceive that, it being morning, Turkey's answer is couched in polite and tranquil terms, but Nippers replies in ill-tempered ones. Or, to repeat a previous sentence, Nippers's ugly mood was on duty, and Turkey's off.)

"Ginger Nut," said I, willing to enlist the smallest suffrage in my behalf, "what do *you* think of it?"

"I think, sir, he's a little *luny*," replied Ginger Nut, with a grin.

"You hear what they say," said I, turning towards the screen, "come forth   50 and do your duty."

But he vouchsafed no reply. I pondered a moment in sore perplexity. But once more business hurried me. I determined again to postpone the consideration of this dilemma to my future leisure. With a little trouble we made out to examine the papers without Bartleby, though at every page or two Turkey deferentially dropped his opinion, that this proceeding was quite out of the common; while Nippers, twitching in his chair with a dyspeptic nervousness, ground out, between his set teeth, occasional hissing maledictions against the stubborn oaf behind the screen. And for his (Nippers's) part, this was the first and the last time he would do another man's business without pay.

Meanwhile Bartleby sat in his hermitage, oblivious to everything but his own peculiar business there.

Some days passed, the scrivener being employed upon another lengthy work. His late remarkable conduct led me to regard his ways narrowly. I observed that he never went to dinner; indeed, that he never went anywhere. As yet I had never, of my personal knowledge, known him to be outside of my office. He was a perpetual sentry in the corner. At about eleven o'clock though, in the morning, I noticed that Ginger Nut would advance toward the opening in Bartleby's screen, as if silently beckoned thither by a gesture invisible to me where I sat. The boy would then leave the office, jingling a few pence, and reappear with a handful of ginger-nuts, which he delivered in the hermitage, receiving two of the cakes for his trouble.

He lives, then, on ginger-nuts, thought I; never eats a dinner, properly speaking; he must be a vegetarian, then; but no; he never eats even vegetables; he eats nothing but ginger-nuts. My mind then ran on in reveries concerning the probable effects upon the human constitution of living entirely on ginger-nuts. Ginger-nuts are so called, because they contain ginger as one of their peculiar constituents, and the final flavoring one. Now, what was ginger? A hot, spicy thing. Was Bartleby hot and spicy? Not at all. Ginger, then, had no effect upon Bartleby. Probably he preferred it should have none.

Nothing so aggravates an earnest person as a passive resistance. If the indi-   55 vidual so resisted be of a not inhumane temper, and the resisting one perfectly harmless in his passivity, then, in the better moods of the former, he will endeavor charitably to construe to his imagination what proves impossible to be solved by his judgment. Even so, for the most part, I regarded Bartleby and his ways. Poor fellow! thought I, he means no mischief; it is plain he intends no insolence; his aspect sufficiently evinces that his eccentricities are involuntary. He is useful to me. I can get along with him. If I turn him away, the chances are he will fall in with some less-indulgent employer, and then he will be rudely treated, and perhaps driven forth miserably to starve. Yes. Here I can cheaply purchase a delicious self-approval. To befriend Bartleby; to humor him in his strange willfulness, will cost me little or nothing, while I lay up in my soul what will eventually prove a sweet morsel for my conscience. But this mood was not invariable with me. The passiveness of Bartleby sometimes irritated me. I felt strangely goaded on to encounter him in new opposition—to elicit some angry spark from him answerable to my own. But, indeed, I might as well have essayed to strike fire with my knuckles against a bit of Windsor soap. But one afternoon the evil impulse in me mastered me, and the following little scene ensued:

"Bartleby," said I, "when those papers are all copied, I will compare them with you."

"I would prefer not to."

"How? Surely you do not mean to persist in that mulish vagary?"

No answer.

I threw open the folding-doors near by, and, turning upon Turkey and Nip- 60 pers, exclaimed:

"Bartleby a second time says, he won't examine his papers. What do you think of it, Turkey?"

It was afternoon, be it remembered. Turkey sat glowing like a brass boiler; his bald head steaming; his hands reeling among his blotted papers.

"Think of it?" roared Turkey; "I think I'll just step behind his screen, and black his eyes for him!"

So saying, Turkey rose to his feet and threw his arms into a pugilistic position. He was hurrying away to make good his promise, when I detained him, alarmed at the effect of incautiously rousing Turkey's combativeness after dinner.

"Sit down, Turkey," said I, "and hear what Nippers has to say. What do 65 you think of it, Nippers? Would I not be justified in immediately dismissing Bartleby?"

"Excuse me, that is for you to decide, sir. I think his conduct quite unusual, and, indeed, unjust, as regards Turkey and myself. But it may only be a passing whim."

"Ah," exclaimed I, "you have strangely changed your mind, then—you speak very gently of him now."

"All beer," cried Turkey; "gentleness is effects of beer—Nippers and I dined together to-day. You see how gentle *I* am, sir. Shall I go and black his eyes?"

"You refer to Bartleby, I suppose. No, not to-day, Turkey," I replied; "pray, put up your fists."

I closed the doors, and again advanced towards Bartleby. I felt additional 70 incentives tempting me to my fate. I burned to be rebelled against again. I remembered that Bartleby never left the office.

"Bartleby," said I, "Ginger Nut is away; just step around to the post office, won't you? (it was but a three minutes' walk), and see if there is anything for me."

"I would prefer not to."

"You *will* not?"

"I *prefer* not."

I staggered to my desk, and sat there in a deep study. My blind inveteracy 75
returned. Was there any other thing in which I could procure myself to be
ignominiously repulsed by this lean, penniless wight?—my hired clerk? What
added thing is there, perfectly reasonable, that he will be sure to refuse to do?
"Bartleby!"

No answer.

"Bartleby," in a louder tone.

No answer.

"Bartleby," I roared.

Like a very ghost, agreeably to the laws of magical invocation, at the third 80
summons, he appeared at the entrance of his hermitage.

"Go to the next room, and tell Nippers to come to me."

"I prefer not to," he respectfully and slowly said and mildly disappeared.

"Very good, Bartleby," said I, in a quiet sort of serenely-severe, self-possessed
tone, intimating the unalterable purpose of some terrible retribution very
close at hand. At the moment I half intended something of the kind. But upon
the whole, as it was drawing towards my dinner-hour, I thought it best to put
on my hat and walk home for the day, suffering much from perplexity and
distress of mind.

Shall I acknowledge it? The conclusion of this whole business was, that it
soon became a fixed fact of my chambers, that a pale young scrivener, by the
name of Bartleby, had a desk there; that he copied for me at the usual rate of
four cents a folio (one hundred words); but he was permanently exempt from
examining the work done by him, that duty being transferred to Turkey and
Nippers, out of compliment, doubtless, to their superior acuteness; moreover,
said Bartleby was never, on any account, to be dispatched on the most trivial
errand of any sort; and that even if entreated to take upon him such a matter,
it was generally understood that he would "prefer not to"—in other words, he
would refuse point blank.

As days passed on, I became considerably reconciled to Bartleby. His steadi- 85
ness, his freedom from all dissipation, his incessant industry (except when he
chose to throw himself into a standing revery behind his screen), his great stillness, his unalterableness of demeanor under all circumstances, made him a
valuable acquisition. One prime thing was this—*he was always there*—first in
the morning, continually through the day, and the last at night. I had a singular confidence in his honesty. I felt my most precious papers perfectly safe in
his hands. Sometimes, to be sure, I could not, for the very soul of me, avoid
falling into sudden spasmodic passions with him. For it was exceeding difficult
to bear in mind all the time those strange peculiarities, privileges, and unheard
of exemptions, forming the tacit stipulations on Bartleby's part under which
he remained in my office. Now and then, in the eagerness of dispatching pressing business, I would inadvertently summon Bartleby, in a short, rapid tone,
to put his finger, say, on the incipient tie of a bit of red tape with which I was

about compressing some papers. Of course, from behind the screen the usual answer, "I prefer not to," was sure to come; and then, how could a human creature, with the common infirmities of our nature, refrain from bitterly exclaiming upon such perverseness—such unreasonableness? However, every added repulse of this sort which I received only tended to lessen the probability of my repeating the inadvertence.

Here it must be said, that according to the custom of most legal gentlemen occupying chambers in densely-populated law buildings, there were several keys to my door. One was kept by a woman residing in the attic, which person weekly scrubbed and daily swept and dusted my apartments. Another was kept by Turkey for convenience sake. The third I sometimes carried in my own pocket. The fourth I knew not who had.

Now, one Sunday morning I happened to go to Trinity Church, to hear a celebrated preacher, and finding myself rather early on the ground I thought I would walk round to my chambers for a while. Luckily I had my key with me; but upon applying it to the lock, I found it resisted by something inserted from the inside. Quite surprised, I called out; when to my consternation a key was turned from within; and thrusting his lean visage at me, and holding the door ajar, the apparition of Bartleby appeared, in his shirt sleeves, and otherwise in a strangely tattered *déshabillé*, saying quietly that he was sorry, but he was deeply engaged just then, and—preferred not admitting me at present. In a brief word or two, he moreover added, that perhaps I had better walk around the block two or three times, and by that time he would probably have concluded his affairs.

Now, the utterly unsurmised appearance of Bartleby, tenanting my law-chambers of a Sunday morning, with his cadaverously gentlemanly *nonchalance*, yet withal firm and self-possessed, had such a strange effect upon me, that incontinently I slunk away from my own door, and did as desired. But not without sundry twinges of impotent rebellion against the mild effrontery of this unaccountable scrivener. Indeed, it was his wonderful mildness chiefly, which not only disarmed me, but unmanned me as it were. For I consider that one, for the time, is somehow unmanned when he tranquilly permits his hired clerk to dictate to him, and order him away from his own premises. Furthermore, I was full of uneasiness as to what Bartleby could possibly be doing in my office in his shirt sleeves, and in an otherwise dismantled condition of a Sunday morning. Was anything amiss going on? Nay, that was out of the question. It was not to be thought of for a moment that Bartleby was an immoral person. But what could he be doing there?—copying? Nay again, whatever might be his eccentricities, Bartleby was an eminently decorous person. He would be the last man to sit down to his desk in any state approaching to nudity. Besides, it was Sunday; and there was something about Bartleby that forbade the supposition that he would by any secular occupation violate the proprieties of the day.

Nevertheless, my mind was not pacified; and full of a restless curiosity, at last I returned to the door. Without hindrance I inserted my key, opened it, and entered. Bartleby was not to be seen. I looked round anxiously, peeped behind his screen; but it was very plain that he was gone. Upon more closely examining the place, I surmised that for an indefinite period Bartleby must have eaten, dressed, and slept in my office, and that, too, without plate, mirror, or bed. The cushioned seat of a rickety old sofa in one corner bore the faint impress of a lean, reclining form. Rolled away under his desk, I found a blanket; under the empty grate, a blacking box and brush; on a chair, a tin basin, with soap and a ragged towel; in a newspaper a few crumbs of ginger-nuts and a morsel of cheese. Yes, thought I, it is evident enough that Bartleby has been making his home here, keeping bachelor's hall all by himself. Immediately then the thought came sweeping across me, what miserable friendlessness and loneliness are here revealed! His poverty is great; but his solitude, how horrible! Think of it. Of a Sunday, Wall Street is deserted as Petra;[5] and every night of every day it is an emptiness. This building, too, which of week-days hums with industry and life, at nightfall echoes with sheer vacancy, and all through Sunday is forlorn. And here Bartleby makes his home; sole spectator of a solitude which he has seen all populous—a sort of innocent and transformed Marius brooding among the ruins of Carthage![6]

For the first time in my life a feeling of over-powering stinging melancholy   90 seized me. Before, I had never experienced aught but a not unpleasing sadness. The bond of a common humanity now drew me irresistibly to gloom. A fraternal melancholy! For both I and Bartleby were sons of Adam. I remembered the bright silks and sparkling faces I had seen that day, in gala trim, swan-like sailing down the Mississippi of Broadway; and I contrasted them with the pallid copyist, and thought to myself, Ah, happiness courts the light, so we deem the world is gay; but misery hides aloof, so we deem that misery there is none. These sad fancyings—chimeras, doubtless, of a sick and silly brain—led on to other and more special thoughts, concerning the eccentricities of Bartleby. Presentiments of strange discoveries hovered round me. The scrivener's pale form appeared to me laid out, among uncaring strangers, in its shivering winding sheet.

Suddenly I was attracted by Bartleby's closed desk, the key in open sight left in the lock.

I mean no mischief, seek the gratification of no heartless curiosity, thought I; besides, the desk is mine, and its contents, too, so I will make bold to look within. Everything was methodically arranged, the papers smoothly placed. The pigeon holes were deep, and removing the files of documents, I groped into their recesses. Presently I felt something there, and dragged it out. It was an old bandanna handkerchief, heavy and knotted. I opened it, and saw it was a saving's bank.

I now recalled all the quiet mysteries which I had noted in the man. I remembered that he never spoke but to answer; that, though at intervals he had considerable time to himself, yet I had never seen him reading—no, not even a newspaper; that for long periods he would stand looking out, at his pale

[5] A city in Palestine found by explorers in 1812. It had been deserted and lost for centuries.
[6] Gaius Marius (155–86 B.C.), a plebeian general who was forced to flee from Rome. Nineteenth-century democratic literature sometimes pictured him old and alone among the ruins of Carthage.

window behind the screen, upon the dead brick wall; I was quite sure he never visited any refectory or eating house; while his pale face clearly indicated that he never drank beer like Turkey; or tea and coffee even, like other men; that he never went anywhere in particular that I could learn; never went out for a walk, unless, indeed, that was the case at present; that he had declined telling who he was, or whence he came, or whether he had any relatives in the world; that though so thin and pale, he never complained of ill health. And more than all, I remembered a certain unconscious air of pallid—how shall I call it?—of pallid haughtiness, say, or rather an austere reserve about him, which had positively awed me into my tame compliance with his eccentricities, when I had feared to ask him to do the slightest incidental thing for me, even though I might know, from his long-continued motionlessness, that behind his screen he must be standing in one of those dead-wall reveries of his.

Revolving all these things, and coupling them with the recently discovered fact, that he made my office his constant abiding place and home, and not forgetful of his morbid moodiness; revolving all these things, a prudential feeling began to steal over me. My first emotions had been those of pure melancholy and sincerest pity; but just in proportion as the forlornness of Bartleby grew and grew to my imagination, did that same melancholy merge into fear, that pity into repulsion. So true it is, and so terrible, too, that up to a certain point the thought or sight of misery enlists our best affections; but, in certain special cases, beyond that point it does not. They err who would assert that invariably this is owing to the inherent selfishness of the human heart. It rather proceeds from a certain hopelessness of remedying excessive and organic ill. To a sensitive being, pity is not seldom pain. And when at last it is perceived that such pity cannot lead to effectual succor, common sense bids the soul be rid of it. What I saw that morning persuaded me that the scrivener was the victim of innate and incurable disorder. I might give alms to his body; but his body did not pain him; it was his soul that suffered, and his soul I could not reach.

I did not accomplish the purpose of going to Trinity Church that morning. 95 Somehow, the things I had seen disqualified me for the time from church-going. I walked homeward, thinking what I would do with Bartleby. Finally, I resolved upon this—I would put certain calm questions to him the next morning, touching his history, etc., and if he declined to answer them openly and unreservedly (and I supposed he would prefer not), then to give him a twenty dollar bill over and above whatever I might owe him, and tell him his services were no longer required; but that if in any other way I could assist him, I would be happy to do so, especially if he desired to return to his native place, wherever that might be, I would willingly help to defray the expenses. Moreover, if, after reaching home, he found himself at any time in want of aid, a letter from him would be sure of a reply.

The next morning came.

"Bartleby," said I, gently calling to him behind his screen.

No reply.

"Bartleby," said I, in a still gentler tone, "come here; I am not going to ask you to do anything you would prefer not to do—I simply wish to speak to you."

Upon this he noiselessly slid into view.   100

"Will you tell me, Bartleby, where you were born?"

"I would prefer not to."

"Will you tell me *anything* about yourself?"

"I would prefer not to."

"But what reasonable objection can you have to speak to me? I feel friendly   105
towards you."

He did not look at me while I spoke, but kept his glance fixed upon my bust of Cicero, which, as I then sat, was directly behind me, some six inches above my head.

"What is your answer, Bartleby," said I, after waiting a considerable time for a reply, during which his countenance remained immovable, only there was the faintest conceivable tremor of the white attenuated mouth.

"At present I prefer to give no answer," he said, and retired into his hermitage.

It was rather weak in me I confess, but his manner, on this occasion, nettled me. Not only did there seem to lurk in it a certain calm disdain, but his perverseness seemed ungrateful, considering the undeniable good usage and indulgence he had received from me.

Again I sat ruminating what I should do. Mortified as I was at his behavior,   110
and resolved as I had been to dismiss him when I entered my office, nevertheless I strangely felt something superstitious knocking at my heart, and forbidding me to carry out my purpose, and denouncing me for a villain if I dared to breathe one bitter word against this forlornest of mankind. At last, familiarly drawing my chair behind his screen, I sat down and said: "Bartleby, never mind, then, about revealing your history; but let me entreat you, as a friend, to comply as far as may be with the usages of this office. Say now, you will help to examine papers tomorrow or next day: in short, say now, that in a day or two you will begin to be a little reasonable—say so, Bartleby."

"At present I would prefer not to be a little reasonable," was his mildly cadaverous reply.

Just then the folding-doors opened, and Nippers approached. He seemed suffering from an unusually bad night's rest, induced by severer indigestion than common. He overheard those final words of Bartleby.

"*Prefer not,* eh?" gritted Nippers—"I'd *prefer* him, if I were you, sir," addressing me—"I'd *prefer* him; I'd give him preferences, the stubborn mule! What is it, sir, pray, that he *prefers* not to do now?"

Bartleby moved not a limb.

"Mr. Nippers," said I, "I'd prefer that you would withdraw for the present."   115

Somehow, of late, I had got into the way of involuntarily using this word "prefer" upon all sorts of not exactly suitable occasions. And I trembled to think that my contact with the scrivener had already and seriously affected me in a mental way. And what further and deeper aberration might it not yet produce? This apprehension had not been without efficacy in determining me to summary measures.

As Nippers, looking very sour and sulky, was departing, Turkey blandly and deferentially approached.

"With submission, sir," said he, "yesterday I was thinking about Bartleby here, and I think that if he would but prefer to take a quart of good ale every day, it would do much towards mending him, and enabling him to assist in examining his papers."

"So you have got the word, too," said I, slightly excited.

"With submission, what word, sir," asked Turkey, respectfully crowding himself into the contracted space behind the screen, and by so doing, making me jostle the scrivener. "What word, sir?" 120

"I would prefer to be left alone here," said Bartleby, as if offended at being mobbed in his privacy.

"That's the word, Turkey," said I—*"that's* it."

"Oh, *prefer?* oh yes—queer word. I never use it myself. But, sir, as I was saying, if he would but prefer—"

"Turkey," interrupted I, "you will please withdraw."

"Oh certainly, sir, if you prefer that I should." 125

As he opened the folding-door to retire, Nippers at his desk caught a glimpse of me, and asked whether I would prefer to have a certain paper copied on blue paper or white. He did not in the least roguishly accent the word prefer. It was plain that it involuntarily rolled from his tongue. I thought to myself, surely I must get rid of a demented man, who already has in some degree turned the tongues, if not the heads of myself and clerks. But I thought it prudent not to break the dismission at once.

The next day I noticed that Bartleby did nothing but stand at his window in his dead-wall revery. Upon asking him why he did not write, he said that he had decided upon doing no more writing.

"Why, how now? What next?" exclaimed I, "do no more writing?"

"No more."

"And what is the reason?" 130

"Do you not see the reason for yourself?" he indifferently replied.

I looked steadfastly at him, and perceived that his eyes looked dull and glazed. Instantly it occurred to me, that his unexampled diligence in copying by his dim window for the first few weeks of his stay with me might have temporarily impaired his vision.

I was touched. I said something in condolence with him. I hinted that of course he did wisely in abstaining from writing for a while; and urged him to embrace that opportunity of taking wholesome exercise in the open air. This, however, he did not do. A few days after this, my other clerks being absent, and being in a great hurry to dispatch certain letters by the mail, I thought that, having nothing else earthly to do, Bartleby would surely be less inflexible than usual, and carry these letters to the post office. But he blankly declined. So, much to my inconvenience, I went myself.

Still added days went by. Whether Bartleby's eyes improved or not, I could not say. To all appearance, I thought they did. But when I asked him if they did, he vouchsafed no answer. At all events, he would do no copying. At last, in reply to my urgings, he informed me that he had permanently given up copying.

"What!" exclaimed I; "suppose your eyes should get entirely well—better 135 than ever before—would you not copy then?"

"I have given up copying," he answered, and slid aside.

He remained as ever, a fixture in my chamber. Nay—if that were possible—he became still more of a fixture than before. What was to be done? He would do nothing in the office; why should he stay there? In plain fact, he had now become a millstone to me, not only useless as a necklace, but afflictive to bear. Yet I was sorry for him. I speak less than truth when I say that, on his own account, he occasioned me uneasiness. If he would but have named a single relative or friend, I would instantly have written, and urged their taking the poor fellow away to some convenient retreat. But he seemed alone, absolutely alone in the universe. A bit of wreck in the mid-Atlantic. At length, necessities connected with my business tyrannized over all other considerations. Decently as I could, I told Bartleby that in six days time he must unconditionally leave the office. I warned him to take measures, in the interval, for procuring some other abode. I offered to assist him in this endeavor, if he himself would but take the first step towards a removal. "And when you finally quit me, Bartleby," added I, "I shall see that you go not away entirely unprovided. Six days from this hour, remember."

At the expiration of that period, I peeped behind the screen, and lo! Bartleby was there.

I buttoned up my coat, balanced myself; advanced slowly towards him, touched his shoulder, and said, "The time has come; you must quit this place; I am sorry for you; here is money; but you must go."

"I would prefer not," he replied, with his back still towards me. 140

"You *must*."

He remained silent.

Now I had an unbounded confidence in this man's common honesty. He had frequently restored to me sixpences and shillings carelessly dropped upon the floor, for I am apt to be very reckless in such shirt-button affairs. The proceeding, then, which followed will not be deemed extraordinary.

"Bartleby," said I, "I owe you twelve dollars on account; here are thirty-two, the odd twenty are yours—Will you take it?" and I handed the bills towards him.

But he made no motion. 145

"I will leave them here, then," putting them under a weight on the table. Then taking my hat and cane and going to the door, I tranquilly turned and added—"After you have removed your things from these offices, Bartleby, you will of course lock the door—since every one is now gone for the day but you—and if you please, slip your key underneath the mat, so that I may have it in the morning. I shall not see you again; so good-by to you. If, hereafter, in your new place of abode, I can be of any service to you, do not fail to advise me by letter. Good-by, Bartleby, and fare you well."

But he answered not a word; like the last column of some ruined temple, he remained standing mute and solitary in the middle of the otherwise deserted room.

As I walked home in a pensive mood, my vanity got the better of my pity. I could not but highly plume myself on my masterly management in getting rid of Bartleby. Masterly I call it, and such it must appear to any dispassionate thinker. The beauty of my procedure seemed to consist in its perfect quietness. There was no vulgar bullying, no bravado of any sort, no choleric hectoring, and striding to and fro across the apartment, jerking out vehement commands for Bartleby to bundle himself off with his beggarly traps. Nothing of the kind. Without loudly bidding Bartleby depart—as an inferior genius might have done—I *assumed* the ground that depart he must; and upon that assumption built all I had to say. The more I thought over my procedure, the more I was charmed with it. Nevertheless, next morning, upon awakening, I had my doubts—I had somehow slept off the fumes of vanity. One of the coolest and wisest hours a man has, is just after he awakes in the morning. My procedure seemed as sagacious as ever—but only in theory. How it would prove in practice—there was the rub. It was truly a beautiful thought to have assumed Bartleby's departure; but, after all, that assumption was simply my own, and none of Bartleby's. The great point was, not whether I had assumed that he would quit me, but whether he would prefer to do so. He was more a man of preferences than assumptions.

After breakfast, I walked down town, arguing the probabilities *pro* and *con*. One moment I thought it would prove a miserable failure, and Bartleby would be found all alive at my office as usual; the next moment it seemed certain that I should find his chair empty. And so I kept veering about. At the corner of Broadway and Canal Street, I saw quite an excited group of people standing in earnest conversation.

"I'll take odds he doesn't," said a voice as I passed.   150

"Doesn't go?—done!" said I; "put up your money."

I was instinctively putting my hand in my pocket to produce my own, when I remembered that this was an election day. The words I had overheard bore no reference to Bartleby, but to the success or non-success of some candidate for the mayoralty. In my intent frame of mind, I had, as it were, imagined that all Broadway shared in my excitement, and were debating the same question with me. I passed on, very thankful that the uproar of the street screened my momentary absent-mindedness.

As I had intended, I was earlier than usual at my office door. I stood listening for a moment. All was still. He must be gone. I tried the knob. The door was locked. Yes, my procedure had worked to a charm; he indeed must be vanished. Yet a certain melancholy mixed with this: I was almost sorry for my brilliant success. I was fumbling under the door mat for the key, which Bartleby was to have left there for me, when accidentally my knee knocked against a panel, producing a summoning sound, and in response a voice came to me from within—"Not yet; I am occupied."

It was Bartleby.

I was thunderstruck. For an instant I stood like the man who, pipe in mouth,   155
was killed one cloudless afternoon long ago in Virginia, by summer lightning;
at his own warm open window he was killed, and remained leaning out there
upon the dreamy afternoon, till some one touched him, when he fell.

"Not gone!" I murmured at last. But again obeying that wondrous ascendancy which the inscrutable scrivener had over me, and from which ascendancy,
for all my chafing, I could not completely escape, I slowly went down stairs and
out into the street, and while walking round the block, considered what I should
next do in this unheard-of perplexity. Turn the man out by an actual thrusting
I could not; to drive him away by calling him hard names would not do; calling
in the police was an unpleasant idea; and yet, permit him to enjoy his cadaverous triumph over me—this, too, I could not think of. What was to be done? or,
if nothing could be done, was there anything further that I could *assume* in the
matter? Yes, as before I had prospectively assumed that Bartleby would depart,
so now I might retrospectively assume that departed he was. In the legitimate
carrying out of this assumption, I might enter my office in a great hurry, and
pretending not to see Bartleby at all, walk straight against him as if he were air.
Such a proceeding would in a singular degree have the appearance of a home-
thrust. It was hardly possible that Bartleby could withstand such an application
of the doctrine of assumption. But upon second thoughts the success of the plan
seemed rather dubious. I resolved to argue the matter over with him again.

"Bartleby," said I, entering the office, with a quietly severe expression, "I
am seriously displeased. I am pained, Bartleby. I had thought better of you.
I had imagined you of such a gentlemanly organization, that in any delicate
dilemma a slight hint would suffice—in short, an assumption. But it appears I
am deceived. Why," I added, unaffectedly starting, "you have not even touched
that money yet," pointing to it, just where I had left it the evening previous.

He answered nothing.

"Will you, or will you not, quit me?" I now demanded in a sudden passion,
advancing close to him.

"I would prefer *not* to quit you," he replied, gently emphasizing the *not*.   160

"What earthly right have you to stay here? Do you pay any rent? Do you pay
my taxes? Or is this property yours?"

He answered nothing.

"Are you ready to go on and write now? Are your eyes recovered? Could you
copy a small paper for me this morning? or help examine a few lines? or step
round to the post office? In a word, will you do anything at all, to give a coloring to your refusal to depart the premises?"

He silently retired into his hermitage.

I was now in such a state of nervous resentment that I thought it but pru-   165
dent to check myself at present from further demonstrations. Bartleby and I
were alone. I remembered the tragedy of the unfortunate Adams and the still
more unfortunate Colt in the solitary office of the latter; and how poor Colt,
being dreadfully incensed by Adams, and imprudently permitting himself to
get wildly excited, was at unawares hurried into his fatal act—an act which

certainly no man could possibly deplore more than the actor himself.[7] Often it had occurred to me in my ponderings upon the subject that had that altercation taken place in the public street, or at a private residence, it would not have terminated as it did. It was the circumstance of being alone in a solitary office, up stairs, of a building entirely unhallowed by humanizing domestic associations—an uncarpeted office, doubtless, of a dusty, haggard sort of appearance—this it must have been, which greatly helped to enhance the irritable desperation of the hapless Colt.

But when this old Adam of resentment rose in me and tempted me concerning Bartleby, I grappled him and threw him. How? Why, simply by recalling the divine injunction: "A new commandment give I unto you, that ye love one another." Yes, this it was that saved me. Aside from higher considerations, charity often operates as a vastly wise and prudent principle—a great safeguard to its possessor. Men have committed murder for jealousy's sake, and anger's sake, and hatred's sake, and selfishness' sake, and spiritual pride's sake; but no man, that ever I heard of, ever committed a diabolical murder for sweet charity's sake. Mere self-interest, then, if no better motive can be enlisted, should, especially with high-tempered men, prompt all beings to charity and philanthropy. At any rate, upon the occasion in question, I strove to drown my exasperated feelings towards the scrivener by benevolently construing his conduct. Poor fellow, poor fellow! thought I, he don't mean anything; and besides, he has seen hard times, and ought to be indulged.

I endeavored, also, immediately to occupy myself, and at the same time to comfort my despondency. I tried to fancy, that in the course of the morning, at such time as might prove agreeable to him, Bartleby, of his own free accord, would emerge from his hermitage and take up some decided line of march in the direction of the door. But no. Half-past twelve o'clock came; Turkey began to glow in the face, overturn his inkstand, and become generally obstreperous; Nippers abated down into quietude and courtesy; Ginger Nut munched his noon apple; and Bartleby remained standing at his window in one of his profoundest dead-wall reveries. Will it be credited? Ought I to acknowledge it? That afternoon I left the office without saying one further word to him.

Some days now passed, during which, at leisure intervals I looked a little into "Edwards on the Will," and "Priestley on Necessity."[8] Under the circumstances, those books induced a salutary feeling. Gradually I slid into the persuasion that these troubles of mine, touching the scrivener, had been all predestinated from eternity, and Bartleby was billeted upon me for some mysterious purpose of an all-wise Providence, which it was not for a mere mortal like me to fathom. Yes, Bartleby, stay there behind your screen, thought I; I shall persecute you no more; you are harmless and noiseless as any of these old chairs; in short, I never feel so private as when I know you are here. At last I see it, I feel it; I penetrate

---

[7] A sensational 1841 homicide case in which John C. Colt murdered printer Samuel Adams in a fit of passion.

[8] Jonathan Edwards (1703–1758), American theologian, and Joseph Priestley (1733–1804), English clergyman and chemist, both held that a person's life was predetermined.

to the predestinated purpose of my life. I am content. Others may have loftier parts to enact; but my mission in this world, Bartleby, is to furnish you with office-room for such period as you may see fit to remain.

I believe that this wise and blessed frame of mind would have continued with me, had it not been for the unsolicited and uncharitable remarks obtruded upon me by my professional friends who visited the rooms. But thus it often is, that the constant friction of illiberal minds wears out at last the best resolves of the more generous. Though to be sure, when I reflected upon it, it was not strange that people entering my office should be struck by the peculiar aspect of the unaccountable Bartleby, and so be tempted to throw out some sinister observations concerning him. Sometimes an attorney, having business with me, and calling at my office, and finding no one but the scrivener there, would undertake to obtain some sort of precise information from him touching my whereabouts; but without heeding his idle talk, Bartleby would remain standing immovable in the middle of the room. So after contemplating him in that position for a time, the attorney would depart, no wiser than he came.

Also, when a reference was going on, and the room full of lawyers and 170 witnesses, and business driving fast, some deeply-occupied legal gentleman present, seeing Bartleby wholly unemployed, would request him to run round to his (the legal gentleman's) office and fetch some papers for him. Thereupon, Bartleby would tranquilly decline, and yet remain idle as before. Then the lawyer would give a great stare, and turn to me. And what could I say? At last I was made aware that all through the circle of my professional acquaintance, a whisper of wonder was running round, having reference to the strange creature I kept at my office. This worried me very much. And as the idea came upon me of his possibly turning out a long-lived man, and keep occupying my chambers, and denying my authority; and perplexing my visitors; and scandalizing my professional reputation; and casting a general gloom over the premises; keeping soul and body together to the last upon his savings (for doubtless he spent but half a dime a day), and in the end perhaps outlive me, and claim possession of my office by right of his perpetual occupancy: as all these dark anticipations crowded upon me more and more, and my friends continually intruded their relentless remarks upon the apparition in my room; a great change was wrought in me. I resolved to gather all my faculties together, and forever rid me of this intolerable incubus.

Ere revolving any complicated project, however, adapted to this end, I first simply suggested to Bartleby the propriety of his permanent departure. In a calm and serious tone, I commended the idea to his careful and mature consideration. But, having taken three days to meditate upon it, he apprised me, that his original determination remained the same; in short, that he still preferred to abide with me.

What shall I do? I now said to myself, buttoning up my coat to the last button. What shall I do? what ought I to do? what does conscience say I *should* do with this man, or, rather, ghost. Rid myself of him, I must; go, he shall. But how? You will not thrust him, the poor, pale, passive mortal—you will not thrust such a helpless creature out of your door? you will not dishonor yourself by such cruelty? No, I will not, I cannot do that. Rather would I let him live and die here, and then mason up his remains in the wall. What, then, will you do? For all your coaxing, he will not budge. Bribes he leaves under your own paper-weight on your table; in short, it is quite plain that he prefers to cling to you.

Then something severe, something unusual must be done. What! surely you will not have him collared by a constable, and commit his innocent pallor to the common jail? And upon what ground could you procure such a thing to be done?—a vagrant, is he? What! he a vagrant, a wanderer, who refuses to budge? It is because he will *not* be a vagrant, then, that you seek to count him *as* a vagrant. That is too absurd. No visible means of support: there I have him. Wrong again: for indubitably he *does* support himself, and that is the only unanswerable proof that any man can show of his possessing the means so to do. No more, then. Since he will not quit me, I must quit him. I will change my offices; I will move elsewhere, and give him fair notice, that if I find him in my new premises I will then proceed against him as a common trespasser.

Acting accordingly, next day I thus addressed him: "I find these chambers too far from the City Hall; the air is unwholesome. In a word, I propose to remove my offices next week, and shall no longer require your services. I tell you this now, in order that you may seek another place."

He made no reply, and nothing more was said. 175

On the appointed day I engaged carts and men, proceeded to my chambers, and, having but little furniture, everything was removed in a few hours. Throughout, the scrivener remained standing behind the screen, which I directed to be removed the last thing. It was withdrawn; and, being folded up like a huge folio, left him the motionless occupant of a naked room. I stood in the entry watching him a moment, while something from within me upbraided me.

I re-entered, with my hand in my pocket—and—and my heart in my mouth.

"Good-by, Bartleby; I am going—good-by, and God some way bless you; and take that," slipping something in his hand. But it dropped upon the floor, and then—strange to say—I tore myself from him whom I had so longed to be rid of.

Established in my new quarters, for a day or two I kept the door locked, and started at every footfall in the passages. When I returned to my rooms, after any little absence, I would pause at the threshold for an instant, and attentively listen, ere applying my key. But these fears were needless. Bartleby never came nigh me.

I thought all was going well, when a perturbed-looking stranger visited 180 me, inquiring whether I was the person who had recently occupied rooms at No. ——— Wall Street.

Full of forebodings, I replied that I was.

"Then, sir," said the stranger, who proved a lawyer, "you are responsible for the man you left there. He refuses to do any copying; he refuses to do anything; he says he prefers not to; and he refuses to quit the premises."

"I am very sorry, sir," said I, with assumed tranquillity, but an inward tremor, "but, really, the man you allude to is nothing to me—he is no relation or apprentice of mine, that you should hold me responsible for him."

"In mercy's name, who is he?"

"I certainly cannot inform you. I know nothing about him. Formerly I 185 employed him as a copyist; but he has done nothing for me now for some time past."

"I shall settle him, then—good morning, sir."

Several days passed, and I heard nothing more; and, though I often felt a charitable prompting to call at the place and see poor Bartleby, yet a certain squeamishness, of I know not what, withheld me.

All is over with him, by this time, thought I, at last, when, through another week, no further intelligence reached me. But, coming to my room the day after, I found several persons waiting at my door in a high state of nervous excitement.

"That's the man—here he comes," cried the foremost one, whom I recognized as the lawyer who had previously called upon me alone.

"You must take him away, sir, at once," cried a portly person among them, 190 advancing upon me, and whom I knew to be the landlord of No. —— Wall Street. "These gentlemen, my tenants, cannot stand it any longer; Mr. B——," pointing to the lawyer, "has turned him out of his room, and he now persists in haunting the building generally, sitting upon the banisters of the stairs by day, and sleeping in the entry by night. Everybody is concerned; clients are leaving the offices; some fears are entertained of a mob; something you must do, and that without delay."

Aghast at this torrent, I fell back before it, and would fain have locked myself in my new quarters. In vain I persisted that Bartleby was nothing to me—no more than to any one else. In vain   I was the last person known to have anything to do with him, and they held me to the terrible account. Fearful, then, of being exposed in the papers (as one person present obscurely threatened), I considered the matter, and, at length, said, that if the lawyer would give me a confidential interview with the scrivener, in his (the lawyer's) own room, I would, that afternoon, strive my best to rid them of the nuisance they complained of.

Going up stairs to my old haunt, there was Bartleby silently sitting upon the banister at the landing.

"What are you doing here, Bartleby?" said I.

"Sitting upon the banister," he mildly replied.

I motioned him into the lawyer's room, who then left us.   195

"Bartleby," said I, "are you aware that you are the cause of great tribulation to me, by persisting in occupying the entry after being dismissed from the office?"

No answer.

"Now one of two things must take place. Either you must do something, or something must be done to you. Now what sort of business would you like to engage in? Would you like to re-engage in copying for some one?"

"No; I would prefer not to make any change."

"Would you like a clerkship in a dry-goods store?" 200

"There is too much confinement about that. No, I would not like a clerkship; but I am not particular."

"Too much confinement," I cried, "why, you keep yourself confined all the time!"

"I would prefer not to take a clerkship," he rejoined, as if to settle that little item at once.

"How would a bar-tender's business suit you? There is no trying of the eyesight in that."

"I would not like it at all; though, as I said before, I am not particular." 205

His unwonted wordiness inspirited me. I returned to the charge.

"Well, then, would you like to travel through the country collecting bills for the merchants? That would improve your health."

"No, I would prefer to be doing something else."

"How, then, would going as a companion to Europe, to entertain some young gentleman with your conversation—how would that suit you?"

"Not at all. It does not strike me that there is anything definite about that. I 210
like to be stationary. But I am not particular."

"Stationary you shall be, then," I cried, now losing all patience, and, for the first time in all my exasperating connection with him, fairly flying into a passion. "If you do not go away from these premises before night, I shall feel bound—indeed, I *am* bound—to—to—to quit the premises myself!" I rather absurdly concluded, knowing not with what possible threat to try to frighten his immobility into compliance. Despairing of all further efforts, I was precipitately leaving him, when a final thought occurred to me—one which had not been wholly unindulged before.

"Bartleby," said I, in the kindest tone I could assume under such exciting circumstances, "will you go home with me now—not to my office, but my dwelling—and remain there till we can conclude upon some convenient arrangement for you at our leisure? Come, let us start now, right away."

"No: at present I would prefer not to make any change at all."

I answered nothing; but, effectually dodging every one by the suddenness and rapidity of my flight, rushed from the building, ran up Wall Street towards Broadway, and, jumping into the first omnibus, was soon removed from pursuit. As soon as tranquillity returned, I distinctly perceived that I had now done all that I possibly could, both in respect to the demands of the landlord and his tenants, and with regard to my own desire and sense of duty, to benefit Bartleby, and shield him from rude persecution. I now strove to be entirely care-free and quiescent; and my conscience justified me in the attempt; though, indeed, it was not so successful as I could have wished. So fearful was I of being again hunted out by the incensed landlord and his exasperated tenants, that, surrendering my business to Nippers, for a few days, I drove about the upper part of the town and through the suburbs, in my rockaway; crossed over to Jersey City and Hoboken, and paid fugitive visits to Manhattanville and Astoria. In fact, I almost lived in my rockaway for the time.

When again I entered my office, lo, a note from the landlord lay upon the 215
desk. I opened it with trembling hands. It informed me that the writer had sent
to the police, and had Bartleby removed to the Tombs as a vagrant. Moreover,
since I knew more about him than any one else, he wished me to appear at
that place, and make a suitable statement of the facts. These tidings had a conflicting effect upon me. At first I was indignant; but, at last, almost approved.
The landlord's energetic, summary disposition, had led him to adopt a procedure which I do not think I would have decided upon myself; and yet, as a last
resort, under such peculiar circumstances, it seemed the only plan.

As I afterwards learned, the poor scrivener, when told that he must be
conducted to the Tombs, offered not the slightest obstacle, but, in his pale,
unmoving way, silently acquiesced.

Some of the compassionate and curious by-standers joined the party; and
headed by one of the constables arm in arm with Bartleby, the silent procession filed its way through all the noise, and heat, and joy of the roaring thor-
oughfares at noon.

The same day I received the note, I went to the Tombs, or, to speak more
properly, the Halls of Justice. Seeking the right officer, I stated the purpose of
my call, and was informed that the individual I described was, indeed, within.
I then assured the functionary that Bartleby was a perfectly honest man,
and greatly to be compassionated, however unaccountably eccentric. I narrated all I knew, and closed by suggesting the idea of letting him remain in as
indulgent confinement as possible, till something less harsh might be done—
though, indeed, I hardly knew what. At all events, if nothing else could be
decided upon, the alms-house must receive him. I then begged to have an
interview.

Being under no disgraceful charge, and quite serene and harmless in all his
ways, they had permitted him freely to wander about the prison, and, especially, in the inclosed grass-platted yards thereof. And so I found him there,
standing all alone in the quietest of the yards, his face towards a high wall,
while all around, from the narrow slits of the jail windows, I thought I saw
peering out upon him the eyes of murderers and thieves.

"Bartleby!" 220

"I know you," he said, without looking round—"and I want nothing to say
to you."

"It was not I that brought you here, Bartleby," said I, keenly pained at his
implied suspicion. "And to you, this should not be so vile a place. Nothing
reproachful attaches to you by being here. And see, it is not so sad a place as
one might think. Look, there is the sky, and here is the grass."

"I know where I am," he replied, but would say nothing more, and so I left
him.

As I entered the corridor again, a broad meat-like man, in an apron, accosted
me, and, jerking his thumb over his shoulder, said—"Is that your friend?"

"Yes." 225

"Does he want to starve? If he does, let him live on the prison fare, that's all."

"Who are you?" asked I, not knowing what to make of such an unofficially speaking person in such a place.

"I am the grub-man. Such gentlemen as have friends here, hire me to provide them with something good to eat."

"Is this so?" said I, turning to the turnkey.

He said it was. 230

"Well, then," said I, slipping some silver into the grub-man's hands (for so they called him), "I want you to give particular attention to my friend there; let him have the best dinner you can get. And you must be as polite to him as possible."

"Introduce me, will you?" said the grub-man, looking at me with an expression which seemed to say he was all impatience for an opportunity to give a specimen of his breeding.

Thinking it would prove of benefit to the scrivener, I acquiesced; and, asking the grub-man his name, went up with him to Bartleby.

"Bartleby, this is a friend; you will find him very useful to you."

"Your sarvant, sir, your sarvant," said the grub-man, making a low saluta- 235 tion behind his apron. "Hope you find it pleasant here, sir; nice grounds—cool apartments—hope you'll stay with us some time—try to make it agreeable. What will you have for dinner to-day?"

"I prefer not to dine to-day," said Bartleby, turning away. "It would disagree with me; I am unused to dinners." So saying, he slowly moved to the other side of the inclosure, and took up a position fronting the deadwall.

"How's this?" said the grub-man, addressing me with a stare of astonishment. "He's odd, ain't he?"

"I think he is a little deranged," said I, sadly.

"Deranged? deranged is it? Well, now, upon my word, I thought that friend of yourn was a gentleman forger; they are always pale and genteel-like, them forgers. I can't help pity 'em—can't help it, sir. Did you know Monroe Edwards?" he added, touchingly, and paused. Then, laying his hand piteously on my shoulder, sighed, "he died of consumption at Sing-Sing.[9] So you weren't acquainted with Monroe?"

"No, I was never socially acquainted with any forgers. But I cannot stop 240 longer. Look to my friend yonder. You will not lose by it. I will see you again."

Some few days after this, I again obtained admission to the Tombs, and went through the corridors in quest of Bartleby; but without finding him.

"I saw him coming from his cell not long ago," said a turnkey, "may be he's gone to loiter in the yards."

So I went in that direction.

"Are you looking for the silent man?" said another turnkey, passing me. "Yonder he lies—sleeping in the yard there. 'Tis not twenty minutes since I saw him lie down."

The yard was entirely quiet. It was not accessible to the common prisoners. 245 The surrounding walls of amazing thickness, kept off all sounds behind them.

---

[9] The state prison near Ossining, New York.

The Egyptian character of the masonry weighed upon me with its gloom. But a soft imprisoned turf grew under foot. The heart of the eternal pyramids, it seemed, wherein, by some strange magic, through the clefts, grass-seed, dropped by birds, had sprung.

Strangely huddled at the base of the wall, his knees drawn up, and lying on his side, his head touching the cold stones, I saw the wasted Bartleby. But nothing stirred. I paused; then went close up to him; stooped over, and saw that his dim eyes were open; otherwise he seemed profoundly sleeping. Something prompted me to touch him. I felt his hand, when a tingling shiver ran up my arm and down my spine to my feet.

The round face of the grub-man peered upon me now. "His dinner is ready. Won't he dine to-day, either? Or does he live without dining?"

"Lives without dining," said I, and closed the eyes.

"Eh!—He's asleep, ain't he?"

"With kings and counselors," murmured I.

250

There would seem little need for proceeding further in this history. Imagination will readily supply the meagre recital of poor Bartleby's interment. But, ere parting with the reader, let me say, that if this little narrative has sufficiently interested him, to awaken curiosity as to who Bartleby was, and what manner of life he led prior to the present narrator's making his acquaintance, I can only reply, that in such curiosity I fully share, but am wholly unable to gratify it. Yet here I hardly know whether I should divulge one little item of rumor, which came to my ear a few months after the scrivener's decease. Upon what basis it rested, I could never ascertain; and hence, how true it is I cannot now tell. But, inasmuch as this vague report has not been without a certain suggestive interest to me, however said, it may prove the same with some others; and so I will briefly mention it. The report was this: that Bartleby had been a subordinate clerk in the Dead Letter[10] Office at Washington, from which he had been suddenly removed by a change in the administration. When I think over this rumor, hardly can I express the emotions which seize me. Dead letters! does it not sound like dead men? Conceive a man by nature and misfortune prone to a pallid hopelessness, can any business seem more fitted to heighten it than that of continually handling these dead letters, and assorting them for the flames? For by the cart-load they are annually burned. Some times from out the folded paper the pale clerk takes a ring—the finger it was meant for, perhaps, moulders in the grave; a bank-note sent in swiftest charity—he whom it would relieve, nor eats nor hungers any more; pardon for those who died despairing; hope for those who died unhoping; good tidings for those who died stifled by unrelieved calamities. On errands of life, these letters speed to death.

Ah, Bartleby! Ah, humanity!

---

[10] A letter that is undeliverable and unreturnable.

FOR ANALYSIS

1. List a half dozen adjectives that describe the **narrator**. Would the narrator agree that these adjectives are accurate?

2. What is it about Bartleby that so intrigues and fascinates the narrator? Why does the narrator continue to feel a moral obligation to an employee who refuses to work and curtly rejects kind offers of help?

3. What thematic function do Turkey and Nippers serve?

4. As the narrator congratulates himself on the cleverness of his scheme to dismiss Bartleby, he becomes fascinated with his "assumptions" about how Bartleby will behave. Examine the passage (paras. 149–56), and show how it advances the narrator's growing awareness of what Bartleby represents.

5. Readers differ as to whether this is the story of Bartleby or the lawyer-narrator. What is your view?

6. Would it be fair to describe Bartleby as a rebel without a cause, as a young man who refuses to participate in a comfortable and well-ordered business world but fails to offer any alternative way of life? Write a paragraph or two explaining why or why not.

MAKING CONNECTIONS

Compare and contrast Bartleby's form of rebellion with the rebellion of those who leave Omelas in Le Guin's "The Ones Who Walk Away from Omelas" (p. 380)?

WRITING TOPICS

1. About midway through the story (paras. 87–94), the **narrator** discovers that Bartleby has been living in the law offices, and he is profoundly moved when his eyes fall on the scrivener's worldly possessions. Reread those paragraphs, and write an analysis showing how they describe the narrator's growing awareness of who Bartleby is.

2. With his final utterance, "Ah, Bartleby! Ah, humanity!" the narrator apparently penetrates the mystery of the silent scrivener. The comment suggests that the narrator sees Bartleby as a representative of humanity. In what sense might the narrator have come to see Bartleby in this light?

3. Why does Melville allow the narrator (and the reader) to discover so little about Bartleby and the causes of his behavior? All we learn of Bartleby's past is told in the next-to-last paragraph. What clues does this paragraph give us to the narrator's fascination with Bartleby?

FRANZ KAFKA   (1883–1924)

A HUNGER ARTIST[1]   1924

During these last decades the interest in professional fasting has markedly diminished. It used to pay very well to stage such great performances under one's own management, but today that is quite impossible. We live in a different world now. At one time the whole town took a lively interest in the hunger artist; from day to day of his fast the excitement mounted; everybody wanted to see him at least once a day; there were people who bought season tickets for the last few days and sat from morning till night in front of his small barred cage; even in the nighttime there were visiting hours, when the whole effect was heightened by torch flares; on fine days the cage was set out in the open air, and then it was the children's special treat to see the hunger artist; for their elders he was often just a joke that happened to be in fashion, but the children stood open-mouthed, holding each other's hands for greater security, marveling at him as he sat there pallid in black tights, with his ribs sticking out so prominently, not even on a seat but down among straw on the ground, sometimes giving a courteous nod, answering questions with a constrained smile, or perhaps stretching an arm through the bars so that one might feel how thin it was, and then again withdrawing deep into himself, paying no attention to anyone or anything, not even to the all-important striking of the clock that was the only piece of furniture in his cage, but merely staring into vacancy with half shut eyes, now and then taking a sip from a tiny glass of water to moisten his lips.

Besides casual onlookers there were also relays of permanent watchers selected by the public, usually butchers, strangely enough, and it was their task to watch the hunger artist day and night, three of them at a time, in case he should have some secret recourse to nourishment. This was nothing but a formality, instituted to reassure the masses, for the initiates knew well enough that during his fast the artist would never in any circumstances, not even under forcible compulsion, swallow the smallest morsel of food; the honor of his profession forbade it. Not every watcher, of course, was capable of understanding this; there were often groups of night watchers who were very lax in carrying out their duties and deliberately huddled together in a retired corner to play cards with great absorption, obviously intending to give the hunger artist the chance of a little refreshment, which they supposed he could draw from some private hoard. Nothing annoyed the artist more than such watchers; they made him miserable; they made his fast seem unendurable; sometimes he mastered his

[1] Translated by Edwin and Willa Muir.

feebleness sufficiently to sing during their watch for as long as he could keep going, to show them how unjust their suspicions were. But that was of little use; they only wondered at his cleverness in being able to fill his mouth even while singing. Much more to his taste were the watchers who sat close up to the bars, who were not content with the dim night lighting of the hall but focused him in the full glare of the electric pocket torch given them by the impresario. The harsh light did not trouble him at all, in any case he could never sleep properly, and he could always drowse a little, whatever the light, at any hour, even when the hall was thronged with noisy onlookers. He was quite happy at the prospect of spending a sleepless night with such watchers; he was ready to exchange jokes with them, to tell them stories out of his nomadic life, anything at all to keep them awake and demonstrate to them again that he had no eatables in his cage and that he was fasting as not one of them could fast. But his happiest moment was when the morning came and an enormous breakfast was brought them, at his expense, on which they flung themselves with the keen appetite of healthy men after a weary night of wakefulness. Of course there were people who argued that this breakfast was an unfair attempt to bribe the watchers, but that was going rather too far, and when they were invited to take on a night's vigil without a breakfast, merely for the sake of the cause, they made themselves scarce, although they stuck stubbornly to their suspicions.

Such suspicions, anyhow, were a necessary accompaniment to the profession of fasting. No one could possibly watch the hunger artist continuously, day and night, and so no one could produce first-hand evidence that the fast had really been rigorous and continuous; only the artist himself could know that, he was therefore bound to be the sole completely satisfied spectator of his own fast. Yet for other reasons he was never satisfied; it was not perhaps mere fasting that had brought him to such skeleton thinness that many people had regretfully to keep away from his exhibitions, because the sight of him was too much for them, perhaps it was dissatisfaction with himself that had worn him down. For he alone knew, what no other initiate knew, how easy it was to fast. It was the easiest thing in the world. He made no secret of this, yet people did not believe him, at the best they set him down as modest; most of them, however, thought he was out for publicity or else was some kind of cheat who found it easy to fast because he had discovered a way of making it easy, and then had the impudence to admit the fact, more or less. He had to put up with all that, and in the course of time had got used to it, but his inner dissatisfaction always rankled, and never yet, after any term of fasting—this must be granted to his credit—had he left the cage of his own free will. The longest period of fasting was fixed by his impresario at forty days, beyond that term he was not allowed to go, not even in great cities, and there was good reason for it, too. Experience had proved that for about forty days the interest of the public could be stimulated by a steadily increasing pressure of advertisement, but after that the town began to lose interest, sympathetic support began notably to fall off; there were of course local variations as between one town and another or one country and another, but as a general rule forty days marked the limit. So on the fortieth day the flower bedecked cage was opened, enthusiastic spectators filled the hall, a military band played, two doctors entered the cage to measure the results of the fast, which were announced through a megaphone, and finally two young ladies appeared, blissful at having been selected for the honor, to help the hunger artist down the few steps leading to a small table on which was spread a carefully chosen invalid repast. And at this very moment the artist always turned stubborn. True, he would entrust his bony arms to the outstretched helping hands of the ladies bending over him, but stand up he would not. Why stop fasting at this particular moment, after forty days of it? He had held out for a long time, an illimitably long time; why stop now, when he was in his best fasting form, or rather, not yet quite in his best fasting form? Why should he be cheated of the fame he would get for fasting longer, for being not only the record hunger artist of all time, which presumably he was already, but for beating his own record by a performance beyond human imagination, since he felt that there were no limits to his capacity for fasting? His public pretended to admire him so much, why should it have so little patience with him; if he could endure fasting longer, why shouldn't the public endure it? Besides, he was tired, he was comfortable sitting in the straw, and now he was supposed to lift himself to his full height and go down to a meal the very thought of which gave him a nausea that only the presence of the ladies kept him from betraying, and even that with an effort. And he looked up into the eyes of the ladies who were apparently so friendly and in reality so cruel, and shook his head, which felt too heavy on its strengthless neck. But then there happened yet again what always happened. The impresario came forward, without a word—for the band made speech impossible—lifted his arms in the air above the artist, as if inviting Heaven to look down upon its creature here in the straw, this suffering martyr, which indeed he was, although in quite another sense; grasped him round the emaciated waist, with exaggerated caution, so that the frail condition he was in might be appreciated; and committed him to the care of the blenching ladies, not without secretly giving him a shaking so that his legs and body tottered and swayed. The artist now submitted completely; his head lolled on his breast as if it had landed there by chance; his body was hollowed out; his legs in a spasm of self-preservation clung close to each other at the knees, yet scraped on the ground as if it were not really solid ground, as if they were only trying to find solid ground; and the whole weight of his body, a feather-weight after all, relapsed onto one of the ladies, who, looking round for help and panting a little—this post of honor was not at all what she had expected it to be—first stretched her neck as far as she could to keep her face at least free from contact with the artist, when finding this impossible, and her more fortunate companion not coming to her aid but merely holding extended on her own trembling hand the little bunch of knucklebones that was the artist's, to the great delight of the spectators burst into tears and had to be replaced by an attendant who had long been stationed in readiness. Then came the food, a little of which the impresario managed to get between the artist's lips, while he sat in a kind of half-fainting trance, to the accompaniment of cheerful patter designed to distract the public's attention from the artist's condition; after that a toast was drunk to the public, supposedly prompted by a whisper from the artist in the impresario's ear; the band confirmed it with a mighty flourish, the spectators melted away, and no one had any cause to be dissatisfied with the proceedings, no one except the hunger artist himself, he only, as always.

So he lived for many years, with small regular intervals of recuperation, in visible glory, honored by the world, yet in spite of that troubled in spirit, and all the more troubled because no one would take his trouble seriously. What comfort could he possibly need? What more could he possibly wish for? And if some good-natured person, feeling sorry for him, tried to console him by pointing out that his melancholy was probably caused by fasting; it could happen, especially when he had been fasting for some time, that he reacted with an outburst of fury and to the general alarm began to shake the bars of his cage like a wild animal. Yet the impresario had a way of punishing these outbreaks which he rather enjoyed putting into operation. He would apologize publicly for the artist's behavior, which was only to be excused, he admitted, because of the irritability caused by fasting; a condition hardly to be understood by well-fed people; then by natural transition he went on to mention the artist's equally incomprehensible boast that he could fast for much longer than he was doing; he praised the high ambition, the good will, the great self-denial undoubtedly implicit in such a statement; and then quite simply countered it by bringing out photographs, which were also on sale to the public, showing the artist on the fortieth day of a fast lying in bed almost dead from exhaustion. This perversion of the truth, familiar to the artist though it was, always unnerved him afresh and proved too much for him. What was a consequence of the premature ending of his fast was here presented as the cause of it! To fight against this lack of understanding, against a whole world of nonunderstanding, was impossible. Time and again in good faith he stood by the bars listening to the impresario, but as soon as the photographs appeared he always let go and sank with a groan back on to his straw, and the reassured public could once more come close and gaze at him.

A few years later when the witnesses of such scenes called them to mind, 5 they often failed to understand themselves at all. For meanwhile the aforementioned change in public interest had set in; it seemed to happen almost overnight; there may have been profound causes for it, but who was going to bother about that; at any rate the pampered hunger artist suddenly found himself deserted one fine day by the amusement seekers, who were streaming past him to other more favored attractions. For the last time the impresario hurried him over half Europe to discover whether the old interest might still survive here and there; all in vain; everywhere, as if by secret agreement, a positive revulsion from professional fasting was in evidence. Of course it could not really have sprung up so suddenly as all that, and many premonitory symptoms which had not been sufficiently remarked or suppressed during the rush and glitter of success now came retrospectively to mind, but it was now too late to take any countermeasures. Fasting would surely come into fashion again at some future date, yet that was no comfort for those living in the present. What, then, was the hunger artist to do? He had been applauded by thousands in his time and could hardly come down to showing himself in a street booth at village fairs, and as for adopting another profession, he was not only too old for that but too frantically devoted to fasting. So he took leave of the impresario, his partner in an unparalleled career, and hired himself to a large circus; in order to spare his own feelings he avoided reading the conditions of his contract.

A large circus with its enormous traffic in replacing and recruiting men, animals, and apparatus can always find a use for people at any time, even for a hunger artist, provided of course that he does not ask too much, and in this particular case anyhow it was not only the artist who was taken on but his famous and long-known name as well, indeed considering the peculiar nature of his performance, which was not impaired by advancing age, it could not be objected that there was an artist past his prime, no longer at the height of his professional skill, seeking a refuge in some quiet corner of a circus; on the contrary, the hunger artist averred that he could fast as well as ever, which was entirely credible; he even alleged that if he were allowed to fast as he liked, and this was at once promised him without more ado, he could astound the world by establishing a record never yet achieved, a statement which certainly provoked a smile among the other professionals, since it left out of account the change in public opinion, which the hunger artist in his zeal conveniently forgot.

He had not, however, actually lost his sense of the real situation and took it as a matter of course that he and his cage should be stationed, not in the middle of the ring as a main attraction, but outside, near the animal cages, on a site that was after all easily accessible. Large and gaily painted placards made a frame for the cage and announced what was to be seen inside it. When the public came thronging out in the intervals to see the animals, they could hardly avoid passing the hunger artist's cage and stopping there for a moment; perhaps they might even have stayed longer had not those pressing behind them in the narrow gangway, who did not understand why they should be held up on their way toward the excitements of the menagerie, made it impossible for anyone to stand gazing quietly for any length of time. And that was the reason why the hunger artist, who had of course been looking forward to these visiting hours as the main achievement of his life, began instead to shrink from them. At first he could hardly wait for the intervals; it was exhilarating to watch the crowds come streaming his way, until only too soon—not even the most obstinate self-deception, clung to almost consciously, could hold out against the fact—the conviction was borne in upon him that these people, most of them, to judge from their actions, again and again, without exception, were all on their way to the menagerie. And the first sight of them from the distance remained the best. For when they reached his cage he was at once deafened by the storm of shouting and abuse that arose from the two contending factions, which renewed themselves continuously, of those who wanted to stop and stare at him—he soon began to dislike them more than the others—not out of real interest but only out of obstinate self-assertiveness, and those who wanted to go straight on to the animals. When the first great rush was past, the stragglers came along, and these, whom nothing could have prevented from stopping to look at him as long as they had breath, raced past with long strides, hardly even glancing at him, in their haste to get to the menagerie in time. And all too rarely did it happen that he had a stroke of luck, when some father of a family fetched up before him with his children, pointed a finger at the hunger artist, and explained at length what the phenomenon meant, telling stories of earlier years when he himself had watched similar but much more thrilling performances, and the children, still rather uncomprehending, since neither inside nor outside school had they been sufficiently prepared for this lesson—what did they care about fasting?—yet showed by the brightness of their intent eyes that new and better times might be coming. Perhaps, said the hunger artist to himself many a time, things would be a little better if his cage were set not quite so near the menagerie. That made it too easy for people to make their choice, to say nothing of what he suffered from the stench of the menagerie, the animals' restlessness by night, the carrying past of raw lumps of flesh for the beasts of prey, the roaring at feeding times, which depressed him continually. But he did not dare to lodge a complaint with the management; after all, he had the animals to thank for the troops of people who passed his cage, among whom there might always be one here and there to take an interest in him, and who could tell where they might seclude him if he called attention to his existence and thereby to the fact that, strictly speaking, he was only an impediment on the way to the menagerie.

A small impediment, to be sure, one that grew steadily less. People grew familiar with the strange idea that they could be expected, in times like these, to take an interest in a hunger artist, and with this familiarity the verdict went out against him. He might fast as much as he could, and he did so; but nothing could save him now, people passed him by. Just try to explain to anyone the art of fasting! Anyone who has no feeling for it cannot be made to understand it. The fine placards grew dirty and illegible, they were torn down; the little notice board telling the number of fast days achieved, which at first was changed carefully every day, had long stayed at the same figure, for after the first few weeks even this small task seemed pointless to the staff; and so the artist simply fasted on and on, as he had once dreamed of doing, and it was no trouble to him, just as he had always foretold, but no one counted the days, no one, not even the artist himself, knew what records he was already breaking, and his heart grew heavy. And when once in a time some leisurely passerby stopped, made merry over the old figure on the board, and spoke of swindling, that was in its way the stupidest lie ever invented by indifference and inborn malice, since it was not the hunger artist who was cheating; he was working honestly, but the world was cheating him of his reward.

Many more days went by, however, and that too came to an end. An overseer's eye fell on the cage one day and asked the attendants why this perfectly good cage should be left standing there unused with dirty straw inside it; nobody knew, until one man, helped out by the notice board, remembered about the hunger artist. They poked into the straw with sticks and found him in it. "Are you still fasting?" asked the overseer. "When on earth do you mean to stop?" "Forgive me, everybody," whispered the hunger artist; only the overseer, who had his ear to the bars, understood him. "Of course," said the overseer, and tapped his forehead with a finger to let the attendants know what state the man was in, "we forgive you." "I always wanted you to admire my fasting," said the hunger artist. "We do admire it," said the overseer, affably. "But you shouldn't admire it," said the hunger artist. "Well, then we don't admire it," said the overseer, "but why shouldn't we admire it?" "Because I have to fast, I can't help it," said the hunger artist. "What a fellow you are," said the overseer, "and why can't you help it?" "Because," said the hunger artist, lifting his head a little and speaking, with his lips pursed, as if for a kiss, right into the overseer's ear, so that no syllable might be lost, "because I couldn't find the food I liked. If I had found it, believe me, I should have made no fuss and stuffed myself like you or anyone else." These were his last words, but in his dimming eyes remained the firm though no longer proud persuasion that he was still continuing to fast.

"Well, clear this out now!" said the overseer, and they buried the hunger 10 artist, straw and all. Into the cage they put a young panther. Even the most insensitive felt it refreshing to see this wild creature leaping around the cage that had so long been dreary. The panther was all right. The food he liked was brought him without hesitation by the attendants; he seemed not even to miss his freedom; his noble body, furnished almost to the bursting point with all that it needed, seemed to carry freedom around with it too; somewhere in his jaws it seemed to lurk; and the joy of life streamed with such ardent passion from his throat that for the onlookers it was not easy to stand the shock of it. But they braced themselves, crowded round the cage, and did not want ever to move away.

FOR ANALYSIS

1. Many readers interpret this story as a parable of the artist in the modern world, while others see it as a religious parable. What evidence do you find in the story to support either interpretation?

2. Suggest reasons for Kafka's selection of an expert in fasting (rather than a priest or a singer, for example) as the central figure in the story.

3. How does Kafka manage to achieve such a bizarre, dreamlike effect with dry and factual **prose**?

4. Since his greatest achievements involve inwardness and withdrawal, why does the hunger artist nevertheless seem to need an audience?

MAKING CONNECTIONS

1. Compare this story with Hawthorne's "Young Goodman Brown" (p. 79) and Melville's "Bartleby the Scrivener" (p. 325). What similarities do the central figures in the three stories share? What differences do you find? How does the alienation of each of the central figures contribute to each story's **theme**?

2. Describe feelings of isolation and alienation that you have experienced. What caused those feelings? How did you cope with them? How, finally, do you differ from the hunger artist?

WRITING TOPICS

1. Should the hunger artist be admired for his passionate and single-minded devotion to his art or condemned for his withdrawal from humanity and his sickness of will? Why? Be sure to discuss the significance of the panther put in the cage after the artist's death.

2. In an essay, compare the hunger artist with Melville's Bartleby. Discuss the origins, rationale, consequences, and significance of their behavior.

RALPH ELLISON (1914–1994)

BATTLE ROYAL 1952

It goes a long way back, some twenty years. All my life I had been looking for something, and everywhere I turned someone tried to tell me what it was. I accepted their answers too, though they were often in contradiction and even self-contradictory. I was naive. I was looking for myself and asking everyone except myself questions which I, and only I, could answer. It took me a long time and much painful boomeranging of my expectations to achieve a realization everyone else appears to have been born with: that I am nobody but myself. But first I had to discover that I am an invisible man!

And yet I am no freak of nature, nor of history. I was in the cards, other things having been equal (or unequal) eighty-five years ago. I am not ashamed of my grandparents for having been slaves. I am only ashamed of myself for having at one time been ashamed. About eighty-five years ago they were told that they were free, united with others of our country in everything pertaining to the common good, and, in everything social, separate like the fingers of the hand. And they believed it. They exulted in it. They stayed in their place, worked hard, and brought up my father to do the same. But my grandfather is the one. He was an odd old guy, my grandfather, and I am told I take after him. It was he who caused the trouble. On his deathbed he called my father to him and said, "Son, after I'm gone I want you to keep up the good fight. I never told you, but our life is a war and I have been a traitor all my born days, a spy in the enemy's country ever since I give up my gun back in the Reconstruction. Live with your head in the lion's mouth. I want you to overcome 'em with yeses, undermine 'em with grins, agree 'em to death and destruction, let 'em swoller you till they vomit or bust wide open." They thought the old man had gone out of his mind. He had been the meekest of men. The younger children were rushed from the room, the shades drawn, and the flame of the lamp turned so low that it sputtered on the wick like the old man's breathing. "Learn it to the younguns," he whispered fiercely; then he died.

But my folks were more alarmed over his last words than over his dying. It was as though he had not died at all, his words caused so much anxiety. I was warned emphatically to forget what he had said and, indeed, this is the first time it has been mentioned outside the family circle. It had a tremendous effect upon me, however. I could never be sure of what he meant. Grandfather had been a quiet old man who never made any trouble, yet on his deathbed he had called himself a traitor and a spy, and he had spoken of his meekness as a dangerous activity. It became a constant puzzle which lay unanswered in the back of my mind. And whenever things went well for me I remembered my

361

grandfather and felt guilty and uncomfortable. It was as though I was carrying out his advice in spite of myself. And to make it worse, everyone loved me for it. I was praised by the most lily-white men of the town. I was considered an example of desirable conduct—just as my grandfather had been. And what puzzled me was that the old man had defined it as *treachery*. When I was praised for my conduct I felt a guilt that in some way I was doing something that was really against the wishes of the white folks, that if they had understood they would have desired me to act just the opposite, that I should have been sulky and mean, and that that really would have been what they wanted, even though they were fooled and thought they wanted me to act as I did. It made me afraid that some day they would look upon me as a traitor and I would be lost. Still I was more afraid to act any other way because they didn't like that at all. The old man's words were like a curse. On my graduation day I delivered an oration in which I showed that humility was the secret, indeed, the very essence of progress. (Not that I believed this—how could I, remembering my grandfather?—I only believed that it worked.) It was a great success. Everyone praised me and I was invited to give the speech at a gathering of the town's leading white citizens. It was a triumph for our whole community.

It was in the main ballroom of the leading hotel. When I got there I discovered that it was on the occasion of a smoker, and I was told that since I was to be there anyway I might as well take part in the battle royal to be fought by some of my schoolmates as part of the entertainment. The battle royal came first.

All of the town's big shots were there in their tuxedoes, wolfing down the   5 buffet foods, drinking beer and whiskey and smoking black cigars. It was a large room with a high ceiling. Chairs were arranged in neat rows around three sides of a portable boxing ring. The fourth side was clear, revealing a gleaming space of polished floor. I had some misgivings over the battle royal, by the way. Not from a distaste for fighting, but because I didn't care too much for the other fellows who were to take part. They were tough guys who seemed to have no grandfather's curse worrying their minds. No one could mistake their toughness. And besides, I suspected that fighting a battle royal might detract from the dignity of my speech. In those pre-invisible days I visualized myself as a potential Booker T. Washington. But the other fellows didn't care too much for me either, and there were nine of them. I felt superior to them in my way, and I didn't like the manner in which we were all crowded together into the servants' elevator. Nor did they like my being there. In fact, as the warmly lighted floors flashed past the elevator we had words over the fact that I, by taking part in the fight, had knocked one of their friends out of a night's work.

We were led out of the elevator through a rococo hall into an anteroom and told to get into our fighting togs. Each of us was issued a pair of boxing gloves and ushered out into the big mirrored hall, which we entered looking cautiously about us and whispering, lest we might accidentally be heard above the noise of the room. It was foggy with cigar smoke. And already the whiskey was taking effect. I was shocked to see some of the most important men of the town quite tipsy. They were all there—bankers, lawyers, judges, doctors, fire chiefs, teachers, merchants. Even one of the more fashionable pastors. Something we could not see was going on up front. A clarinet was vibrating sensuously and the men were standing up and moving eagerly forward. We were a small tight group, clustered together, our bare upper bodies touching and shining with anticipatory sweat; while up front the big shots were becoming increasingly excited over something we still could not see. Suddenly I heard the school superintendent, who had told me to come, yell, "Bring up the shines, gentlemen! Bring up the little shines!"

We were rushed up to the front of the ballroom, where it smelled even more strongly of tobacco and whiskey. Then we were pushed into place. I almost wet my pants. A sea of faces, some hostile, some amused, ringed around us, and in the center, facing us, stood a magnificent blonde—stark naked. There was dead silence. I felt a blast of cold air chill me. I tried to back away, but they were behind me and around me. Some of the boys stood with lowered heads, trembling. I felt a wave of irrational guilt and fear. My teeth chattered, my skin turned to goose flesh, my knees knocked. Yet I was strongly attracted and looked in spite of myself. Had the price of looking been blindness, I would have looked. The hair was yellow like that of a circus kewpie doll, the face heavily powdered and rouged, as though to form an abstract mask, the eyes hollow and smeared a cool blue, the color of a baboon's butt. I felt a desire to spit upon her as my eyes brushed slowly over her body. Her breasts were firm and round as the domes of East Indian temples, and I stood so close as to see the fine skin texture and beads of pearly perspiration glistening like dew around the pink and erected buds of her nipples. I wanted at one and the same time to run from the room, to sink through the floor, or go to her and cover her from my eyes and the eyes of the others with my body; to feel the soft thighs, to caress her and destroy her, to love her and murder her, to hide from her, and yet to stroke where below the small American flag tattooed upon her belly her thighs formed a capital V. I had a notion that of all in the room she saw only me with her impersonal eyes.

And then she began to dance, a slow sensuous movement; the smoke of a hundred cigars clinging to her like the thinnest of veils. She seemed like a fair bird-girl girdled in veils calling to me from the angry surface of some gray and threatening sea. I was transported. Then I became aware of the clarinet playing and the big shots yelling at us. Some threatened us if we looked and others if we did not. On my right I saw one boy faint. And now a man grabbed a silver pitcher from a table and stepped close as he dashed ice water upon him and stood him up and forced two of us to support him as his head hung and moans issued from his thick bluish lips. Another boy began to plead to go home. He was the largest of the group, wearing dark red fighting trunks much too small to conceal the erection which projected from him as though in answer to the insinuating low-registered moaning of the clarinet. He tried to hide himself with his boxing gloves.

And all the while the blonde continued dancing, smiling faintly at the big shots who watched her with fascination, and faintly smiling at our fear.

I noticed a certain merchant who followed her hungrily, his lips loose and drooling. He was a large man who wore diamond studs in a shirtfront which swelled with the ample paunch underneath, and each time the blonde swayed her undulating hips he ran his hand through the thin hair of his bald head and, with his arms upheld, his posture clumsy like that of an intoxicated panda, wound his belly in a slow and obscene grind. This creature was completely hypnotized. The music had quickened. As the dancer flung herself about with a detached expression on her face, the men began reaching out to touch her. I could see their beefy fingers sink into her soft flesh. Some of the others tried to stop them and she began to move around the floor in graceful circles, as they gave chase, slipping and sliding over the polished floor. It was mad. Chairs went crashing, drinks were spilt, as they ran laughing and howling after her. They caught her just as she reached a door, raised her from the floor, and tossed her as college boys are tossed at a hazing, and above her red fixed-smiling lips I saw the terror and disgust in her eyes, almost like my own terror and that which I saw in some of the other boys. As I watched, they tossed her twice and her soft breasts seemed to flatten against the air and her legs flung wildly as she spun. Some of the more sober ones helped her to escape. And I started off the floor, heading for the anteroom with the rest of the boys.

Some were still crying and in hysteria. But as we tried to leave we were 10 stopped and ordered to get into the ring. There was nothing to do but what we were told. All ten of us climbed under the ropes and allowed ourselves to be blindfolded with broad bands of white cloth. One of the men seemed to feel a bit sympathetic and tried to cheer us up as we stood with our backs against the ropes. Some of us tried to grin. "See that boy over there?" one of the men said. "I want you to run across at the bell and give it to him right in the belly. If you don't get him, I'm going to get you. I don't like his looks." Each of us was told the same. The blindfolds were put on. Yet even then I had been going over my speech. In my mind each word was as bright as flame. I felt the cloth pressed into place, and frowned so that it would be loosened when I relaxed.

But now I felt a sudden fit of blind terror. I was unused to darkness. It was as though I had suddenly found myself in a dark room filled with poisonous cottonmouths. I could hear the bleary voices yelling insistently for the battle royal to begin.

"Get going in there!"

"Let me at that big nigger!"

I strained to pick up the school superintendent's voice, as though to squeeze some security out of that slightly more familiar sound.

"Let me at those black sonsabitches!" someone yelled. 15

"No, Jackson, no!" another voice yelled. "Here, somebody, help me hold Jack."

"I want to get at that ginger-colored nigger. Tear him limb from limb," the first voice yelled.

I stood against the ropes trembling. For in those days I was what they called ginger-colored, and he sounded as though he might crunch me between his teeth like a crisp ginger cookie.

Quite a struggle was going on. Chairs were being kicked about and I could hear voices grunting as with a terrific effort. I wanted to see, to see more desperately than ever before. But the blindfold was as tight as a thick skin-puckering scab and when I raised my gloved hands to push the layers of white aside a voice yelled, "Oh, no you don't, black bastard! Leave that alone!"

"Ring the bell before Jackson kills him a coon!" someone boomed in the 20 sudden silence. And I heard the bell clang and the sound of the feet scuffling forward.

A glove smacked against my head. I pivoted, striking out stiffly as someone went past, and felt the jar ripple along the length of my arm to my shoulder. Then it seemed as though all nine of the boys had turned upon me at once. Blows pounded me from all sides while I struck out as best I could. So many blows landed upon me that I wondered if I were not the only blindfolded fighter in the ring, or if the man called Jackson hadn't succeeded in getting me after all.

Blindfolded, I could no longer control my motions. I had no dignity. I stumbled about like a baby or a drunken man. The smoke had become thicker and with each new blow it seemed to sear and further restrict my lungs. My saliva became like hot bitter glue. A glove connected with my head, filling my mouth with warm blood. It was everywhere. I could not tell if the moisture I felt upon my body was sweat or blood. A blow landed hard against the nape of my neck. I felt myself going over, my head hitting the floor. Streaks of blue light filled the black world behind the blindfold. I lay prone, pretending that I was knocked out, but felt myself seized by hands and yanked to my feet. "Get going, black boy! Mix it up!" My arms were like lead, my head smarting from blows. I managed to feel my way to the ropes and held on, trying to catch my breath. A glove landed in my mid-section and I went over again, feeling as though the smoke had become a knife jabbed into my guts. Pushed this way and that by the legs milling around me, I finally pulled erect and discovered that I could see the black, sweat-washed forms weaving in the smoky-blue atmosphere like drunken dancers weaving to the rapid drum-like thuds of blows.

Everyone fought hysterically. It was complete anarchy. Everybody fought everybody else. No group fought together for long. Two, three, four, fought one, then turned to fight each other, were themselves attacked. Blows landed below the belt and in the kidney, with the gloves open as well as closed, and with my eye partly opened now there was not so much terror. I moved carefully, avoiding blows, although not too many to attract attention, fighting from group to group. The boys groped about like blind, cautious crabs crouching to protect their mid-sections, their heads pulled in short against their shoulders, their arms stretched nervously before them, with their fists testing the smoke-filled air like the knobbed feelers of hypersensitive snails. In one corner I glimpsed a boy violently punching the air and heard him scream in pain as he smashed his hand against a ring post. For a second I saw him bent over holding his hand, then going down as a blow caught his unprotected head. I played one group against the other, slipping in and throwing a punch then stepping out of range while pushing the others into the melee to take the blows blindly aimed at me. The smoke was agonizing and there were no rounds, no bells at three minute intervals to relieve our exhaustion. The room spun round me, a swirl of lights, smoke, sweating bodies surrounded by tense white faces. I bled from both nose and mouth, the blood spattering upon my chest.

The men kept yelling, "Slug him, black boy! Knock his guts out!"

"Uppercut him! Kill him! Kill that big boy!"   25

Taking a fake fall, I saw a boy going down heavily beside me as though we were felled by a single blow, saw a sneaker-clad foot shoot into his groin as the two who had knocked him down stumbled upon him. I rolled out of range, feeling a twinge of nausea.

The harder we fought the more threatening the men became. And yet, I had begun to worry about my speech again. How would it go? Would they recognize my ability? What would they give me?

I was fighting automatically and suddenly I noticed that one after another of the boys was leaving the ring. I was surprised, filled with panic, as though I had been left alone with an unknown danger. Then I understood. The boys had arranged it among themselves. It was the custom for the two men left in the ring to slug it out for the winner's prize. I discovered this too late. When the bell sounded two men in tuxedoes leaped into the ring and removed the blindfold. I found myself facing Tatlock, the biggest of the gang. I felt sick at my stomach. Hardly had the bell stopped ringing in my ears than it clanged again and I saw him moving swiftly toward me. Thinking of nothing else to do I hit him smash on the nose. He kept coming, bringing the rank sharp violence of stale sweat. His face was a black blank of a face, only his eyes alive—with hate of me and aglow with a feverish terror from what had happened to us all. I became anxious. I wanted to deliver my speech and he came at me as though he meant to beat it out of me. I smashed him again and again, taking his blows as they came. Then on a sudden impulse I struck him lightly and as we clinched, I whispered, "Fake like I knocked you out, you can have the prize."

"I'll break your behind," he whispered hoarsely.

"For *them*?"   30

"For *me*, sonofabitch!"

They were yelling for us to break it up and Tatlock spun me half around with a blow, and as a joggled camera sweeps in a reeling scene, I saw the howling red faces crouching tense beneath the cloud of blue-gray smoke. For a moment the world wavered, unraveled, flowed, then my head cleared and Tatlock bounced before me. That fluttering shadow before my eyes was his jabbing left hand. Then falling forward, my head against his damp shoulder, I whispered,

"I'll make it five dollars more."

"Go to hell!"

But his muscles relaxed a trifle beneath my pressure and I breathed, "Seven!"   35

"Give it to your ma," he said, ripping me beneath the heart.

And while I still held him I butted him and moved away. I felt myself bombarded with punches. I fought back with hopeless desperation. I wanted to deliver my speech more than anything else in the world, because I felt that only these men could judge truly my ability, and now this stupid clown was ruining my chances. I began fighting carefully now, moving in to punch him and out again with my greater speed. A lucky blow to his chin and I had him going too—until I heard a loud voice yell, "I got my money on the big boy."

Hearing this, I almost dropped my guard. I was confused: Should I try to win against the voice out there? Would not this go against my speech, and was not this a moment for humility, for nonresistance? A blow to my head as I danced about sent my right eye popping like a jack-in-the-box and settled my dilemma. The room went red as I fell. It was a dream fall, my body languid and fastidious as to where to land, until the floor became impatient and smashed up to meet me. A moment later I came to. An hypnotic voice said FIVE emphatically. And I lay there, hazily watching a dark red spot of my own blood shaping itself into a butterfly, glistening and soaking into the soiled gray world of the canvas.

When the voice drawled TEN I was lifted up and dragged to a chair. I sat dazed. My eye pained and swelled with each throb of my pounding heart and I wondered if now I would be allowed to speak. I was wringing wet, my mouth still bleeding. We were grouped along the wall now. The other boys ignored me as they congratulated Tatlock and speculated as to how much they would be paid. One boy whimpered over his smashed hand. Looking up front, I saw attendants in white jackets rolling the portable ring away and placing a small square rug in the vacant space surrounded by chairs. Perhaps, I thought, I will stand on the rug to deliver my speech.

Then the M.C. called to us, "Come on up here boys and get your money." 40

We ran forward to where the men laughed and talked in their chairs, waiting. Everyone seemed friendly now.

"There it is on the rug," the man said. I saw the rug covered with coins of all dimensions and a few crumpled bills. But what excited me, scattered here and there, were the gold pieces.

"Boys, it's all yours," the man said. "You get all you grab."

"That's right, Sambo," a blond man said, winking at me confidentially.

I trembled with excitement, forgetting my pain. I would get the gold and the 45 bills, I thought. I would use both hands. I would throw my body against the boys nearest me to block them from the gold.

"Get down around the rug now," the man commanded, "and don't anyone touch it until I give the signal."

"This ought to be good," I heard.

As told, we got around the square rug on our knees. Slowly the man raised his freckled hand as we followed it upward with our eyes.

I heard, "These niggers look like they're about to pray!"

Then, "Ready," the man said. "Go!" 50

I lunged for a yellow coin lying on the blue design of the carpet, touching it and sending a surprised shriek to join those rising around me. I tried frantically to remove my hand but could not let go. A hot, violent force tore through my body, shaking me like a wet rat. The rug was electrified. The hair bristled up on my head as I shook myself free. My muscles jumped, my nerves jangled, writhed. But I saw that this was not stopping the other boys. Laughing in fear and embarrassment, some were holding back and scooping up the coins knocked off by the painful contortions of the others. The men roared above us as we struggled.

"Pick it up, goddamnit, pick it up!" someone called like a bass-voiced parrot. "Go on, get it!"

I crawled rapidly around the floor, picking up the coins, trying to avoid the coppers and to get greenbacks and the gold. Ignoring the shock by laughing, as I brushed the coins off quickly, I discovered that I could contain the electricity—a contradiction, but it works. Then the men began to push us onto the rug. Laughing embarrassedly, we struggled out of their hands and kept after the coins. We were all wet and slippery and hard to hold. Suddenly I saw a boy lifted into the air, glistening with sweat like a circus seal, and dropped, his wet back landing flush upon the charged rug, heard him yell and saw him literally dance upon his back, his elbows beating a frenzied tatoo upon the floor, his muscles twitching like the flesh of a horse stung by many flies. When he finally rolled off, his face was gray and no one stopped him when he ran from the floor amid booming laughter.

"Get the money," the M.C. called. "That's good hard American cash!"

And we snatched and grabbed, snatched and grabbed. I was careful not to 55 come too close to the rug now, and when I felt the hot whiskey breath descend upon me like a cloud of foul air I reached out and grabbed the leg of a chair. It was occupied and I held on desperately.

"Leggo, nigger! Leggo!"

The huge face wavered down to mine as he tried to push me free. But my body was slippery and he was too drunk. It was Mr. Colcord, who owned a chain of movie houses and "entertainment palaces." Each time he grabbed me I slipped out of his hands. It became a real struggle. I feared the rug more than I did the drunk, so I held on, surprising myself for a moment by trying to topple *him* upon the rug. It was such an enormous idea that I found myself actually carrying it out. I tried not to be obvious, yet when I grabbed his leg, trying to tumble him out of the chair, he raised up roaring with laughter, and, looking at me with soberness dead in the eye, kicked me viciously in the chest. The chair leg flew out of my hand. I felt myself going and rolled. It was as though I had rolled through a bed of hot coals. It seemed a whole century would pass before I would roll free, a century in which I was seared through the deepest levels of my body to the fearful breath within me and the breath seared and heated to the point of explosion. It'll all be over in a flash, I thought as I rolled clear. It'll all be over in a flash.

But not yet, the men on the other side were waiting, red faces swollen as though from apoplexy as they bent forward in their chairs. Seeing their fingers coming toward me I rolled away as a fumbled football rolls off the receiver's fingertips, back into the coals. That time I luckily sent the rug sliding out of place and heard the coins ringing against the floor and the boys scuffling to pick them up and the M.C. calling, "All right, boys, that's all. Go get dressed and get your money."

I was limp as a dish rag. My back felt as though it had been beaten with wires.

When we had dressed the M.C. came in and gave us each five dollars, except 60 Tatlock, who got ten for being last in the ring. Then he told us to leave. I was not to get a chance to deliver my speech, I thought. I was going out into the dim alley in despair when I was stopped and told to go back. I returned to the ballroom, where the men were pushing back their chairs and gathering in groups to talk.

The M.C. knocked on a table for quiet. "Gentlemen," he said, "we almost forgot an important part of the program. A most serious part, gentlemen. This boy was brought here to deliver a speech which he made at his graduation yesterday...."

"Bravo!"

"I'm told that he is the smartest boy we've got out there in Greenwood. I'm told that he knows more big words than a pocket-sized dictionary."

Much applause and laughter.

"So now, gentlemen, I want you to give him your attention." 65

There was still laughter as I faced them, my mouth dry, my eye throbbing. I began slowly, but evidently my throat was tense, because they began shouting, "Louder! Louder!"

"We of the younger generation extol the wisdom of that great leader and educator," I shouted, "who first spoke these flaming words of wisdom: 'A ship lost at sea for many days suddenly sighted a friendly vessel. From the mast of the unfortunate vessel was seen a signal: "Water, water; we die of thirst!" The answer from the friendly vessel came back: "Cast down your bucket where you are." The captain of the distressed vessel, at last heeding the injunction, cast down his bucket, and it came up full of fresh sparkling water from the mouth of the Amazon River.' And like him I say, and in his words, 'To those of my race who depend upon bettering their condition in a foreign land, or who underestimate the importance of cultivating friendly relations with the Southern white man, who is his next-door neighbor, I would say: "Cast down your bucket where you are"—cast it down in making friends in every manly way of the people of all races by whom we are surrounded....'"

I spoke automatically and with such fervor that I did not realize that the men were still talking and laughing until my dry mouth, filling up with blood from the cut, almost strangled me. I coughed, wanting to stop and go to one of the tall brass, sand-filled spittoons to relieve myself, but a few of the men, especially the superintendent, were listening and I was afraid. So I gulped it down, blood, saliva, and all, and continued. (What powers of endurance I had during those days! What enthusiasm! What a belief in the rightness of things!) I spoke even louder in spite of the pain. But still they talked and still they laughed, as though deaf with cotton in dirty ears. So I spoke with greater emotional emphasis. I closed my ears and swallowed blood until I was nauseated.

The speech seemed a hundred times as long as before, but I could not leave out a single word. All had to be said, each memorized nuance considered, rendered. Nor was that all. Whenever I uttered a word of three or more syllables a group of voices would yell for me to repeat it. I used the phrase "social responsibility" and they yelled:

"What's the word you say, boy?"

"Social responsibility," I said.

"What?"

"Social . . ."

"Louder."

". . . responsibility."

"More!"

"Respon—"

"Repeat!"

"—sibility."

The room filled with the uproar of laughter until, no doubt, distracted by having to gulp down my blood, I made a mistake and yelled a phrase I had often seen denounced in newspaper editorials, heard debated in private.

"Social . . ."

"What?" they yelled.

". . . equality—"

The laughter hung smokelike in the sudden stillness. I opened my eyes, puzzled. Sounds of displeasure filled the room. The M.C. rushed forward. They shouted hostile phrases at me. But I did not understand.

A small dry mustached man in the front row blared out, "Say that slowly, son!"

"What sir?"

"What you just said!"

"Social responsibility, sir," I said.

"You weren't being smart, were you, boy?" he said, not unkindly.

"No, sir!"

"You sure that about 'equality' was a mistake?"

"Oh, yes, sir," I said. "I was swallowing blood."

"Well, you had better speak more slowly so we can understand. We mean to do right by you, but you've got to know your place at all times. All right, now, go on with your speech."

I was afraid. I wanted to leave but I wanted also to speak and I was afraid they'd snatch me down.

"Thank you, sir," I said, beginning where I had left off, and having them ignore me as before.

Yet when I finished there was a thunderous applause. I was surprised to see the superintendent come forth with a package wrapped in white tissue paper, and, gesturing for quiet, address the men.

"Gentlemen, you see that I did not overpraise this boy. He makes a good speech and some day he'll lead his people in the proper paths. And I don't have to tell you that that is important in these days and times. This is a good, smart boy, and so to encourage him in the right direction, in the name of the Board of Education I wish to present him a prize in the form of this . . ."

He paused, removing the tissue paper and revealing a gleaming calfskin brief case.

". . . in the form of this first-class article from Shad Whitmore's shop."

"Boy," he said, addressing me, "take this prize and keep it well. Consider it a badge of office. Prize it. Keep developing as you are and some day it will be filled with important papers that will help shape the destiny of your people."

I was so moved that I could hardly express my thanks. A rope of bloody 100 saliva forming a shape like an undiscovered continent drooled upon the leather and I wiped it quickly away. I felt an importance that I had never dreamed.

"Open it and see what's inside," I was told.

My fingers a-tremble, I complied, smelling the fresh leather and finding an official-looking document inside. It was a scholarship to the state college for Negroes. My eyes filled with tears and I ran awkwardly off the floor.

I was overjoyed; I did not even mind when I discovered that the gold pieces I had scrambled for were brass pocket tokens advertising a certain make of automobile.

When I reached home everyone was excited. Next day the neighbors came to congratulate me. I even felt safe from grandfather, whose deathbed curse usually spoiled my triumphs. I stood beneath his photograph with my brief case in hand and smiled triumphantly into his stolid black peasant's face. It was a face that fascinated me. The eyes seemed to follow everywhere I went.

That night I dreamed I was at a circus with him and that he refused to 105 laugh at the clowns no matter what they did. Then later he told me to open my brief case and read what was inside and I did, finding an official envelope stamped with the state seal; and inside the envelope I found another and another, endlessly, and I thought I would fall of weariness. "Them's years," he said. "Now open that one." And I did and in it I found an engraved document containing a short message in letters of gold. "Read it," my grandfather said. "Out loud."

"To Whom It May Concern," I intoned. "Keep This Nigger-Boy Running."

I awoke with the old man's laughter ringing in my ears.

(It was a dream I was to remember and dream again for many years after. But at the time I had no insight into its meaning. First I had to attend college.)

FOR ANALYSIS

1. What phrase does the **narrator** inadvertently utter, causing the room to go quiet? Why does it have such an effect?

2. Why is it significant that the naked woman in the story is white?

3. The meaning of the grandfather's last words, recounted at the story's opening, are ambiguous; the narrator even says, "I could never be sure of what he meant" (para. 3). Does the meaning become clearer by the end of the story? What do you think it is, and how is it revealed?

MAKING CONNECTIONS

1. There is much more action in "Battle Royal" than in Bambara's "The Lesson" (p. 96). It is more obvious, then, that Bambara's story is about what its main **character** sees and what she learns from it. How, in spite of Ellison's story's differences, is it like Bambara's? Does the main character learn a lesson? How? What is it?

2. Read "Battle Royal" in the context of the connections unit "Voices of Experience" (p. 214). What voices of experience speak in this story, including but not limited to the grandfather? What advice do they give? How is it taken? From which of the poems in "Voices of Experience" is "Battle Royal" most similar? To which is it most different?

WRITING TOPICS

1. Write about the **symbolism** in "Battle Royal." For what might the different objects and different activities stand? How do they fit together? Why do you think Ellison has his **protagonist** see and experience these symbolic things?

2. Write a reflective personal essay on invisibility. Possible topics for this essay include ways in which you are invisible, ways in which other people you know or see are invisible, and ways in which you are guilty of not seeing others.

SHIRLEY JACKSON   (1919–1965)

THE LOTTERY   1948

The morning of June 27th was clear and sunny, with the fresh warmth of a full-summer day; the flowers were blossoming profusely and the grass was richly green. The people of the village began to gather in the square, between the post office and the bank, around ten o'clock; in some towns there were so many people that the lottery took two days and had to be started on June 26th, but in this village, where there were only about three hundred people, the whole lottery took less than two hours, so it could begin at ten o'clock in the morning and still be through in time to allow the villagers to get home for noon dinner.

The children assembled first, of course. School was recently over for the summer, and the feeling of liberty sat uneasily on most of them; they tended to gather together quietly for a while before they broke into boisterous play, and their talk was still of the classroom and the teacher, of books and reprimands. Bobby Martin had already stuffed his pockets full of stones, and the other boys soon followed his example, selecting the smoothest and roundest stones; Bobby and Harry Jones and Dickie Delacroix—the villagers pronounced his name "Dellacroy"—eventually made a great pile of stones in one corner of the square and guarded it against the raids of the other boys. The girls stood aside, talking among themselves, looking over their shoulders at the boys, and the very small children rolled in the dust or clung to the hands of their older brothers or sisters.

Soon the men began to gather, surveying their own children, speaking of planting and rain, tractors and taxes. They stood together, away from the pile of stones in the corner, and their jokes were quiet and they smiled rather than laughed. The women, wearing faded house dresses and sweaters, came shortly after their menfolk. They greeted one another and exchanged bits of gossip as they went to join their husbands. Soon the women, standing by their husbands, began to call to their children, and the children came reluctantly, having to be called four or five times. Bobby Martin ducked under his mother's grasping hand and ran, laughingly, back to the pile of stones. His father spoke up sharply, and Bobby came quickly and took his place, between his father and his oldest brother.

The lottery was conducted—as were the square dances, the teenage club, the Halloween program—by Mr. Summers, who had time and energy to devote to civic activities. He was a round-faced, jovial man and he ran the coal business, and people were sorry for him, because he had no children and his wife was a scold. When he arrived in the square, carrying the black wooden box, there was a murmur of conversation among the villagers, and he waved and called

"Little late today, folks." The postmaster, Mr. Graves, followed him, carrying a three-legged stool, and the stool was put in the center of the square and Mr. Summers set the black box down on it. The villagers kept their distance, leaving a space between themselves and the stool, and when Mr. Summers said, "Some of you fellows want to give me a hand?" there was a hesitation before two men, Mr. Martin and his oldest son, Baxter, came forward to hold the box steady on the stool while Mr. Summers stirred up the papers inside it.

The original paraphernalia for the lottery had been lost long ago, and the $_5$ black box now resting on the stool had been put into use even before Old Man Warner, the oldest man in town, was born. Mr. Summers spoke frequently to the villagers about making a new box, but no one liked to upset even as much tradition as was represented by the black box. There was a story that the present box had been made with some pieces of the box that had preceded it, the one that had been constructed when the first people settled down to make a village here. Every year, after the lottery, Mr. Summers began talking about a new box, but every year the subject was allowed to fade off without anything's being done. The black box grew shabbier each year; by now it was no longer completely black but splintered badly along one side to show the original wood color, and in some places faded and stained.

Mr. Martin and his oldest son, Baxter, held the black box securely on the stool until Mr. Summers had stirred the papers thoroughly with his hand. Because so much of the ritual had been forgotten or discarded, Mr. Summers had been successful in having slips of paper substituted for the chips of wood that had been used for generations. Chips of wood, Mr. Summers had argued, had been all very well when the village was tiny, but now that the population was more than three hundred and likely to keep on growing, it was necessary to use something that would fit more easily into the black box. The night before the lottery, Mr. Summers and Mr. Graves made up the slips of paper and put them in the box, and it was then taken to the safe of Mr. Summers's coal company and locked up until Mr. Summers was ready to take it to the square the next morning. The rest of the year, the box was put away, sometimes one place, sometimes another; it had spent one year in Mr. Graves's barn and another year underfoot in the post office, and sometimes it was set on a shelf in the Martin grocery and left there.

There was a great deal of fussing to be done before Mr. Summers declared the lottery open. There were the lists to make up—of heads of families, heads of households in each family, members of each household in each family. There was the proper swearing-in of Mr. Summers by the postmaster, as the official of the lottery; at one time, some people remembered, there had been a recital of some sort, performed by the official of the lottery, a perfunctory, tuneless chant that had been rattled off duly each year; some people believed that the official of the lottery used to stand just so when he said or sang it, others believed that he was supposed to walk among the people, but years and years ago this part of the ritual had been allowed to lapse. There had been, also, a ritual salute, which the official of the lottery had had to use in addressing each person who came up to draw from the box, but this also had changed with time, until now it was felt necessary only for the official to speak to each person approaching. Mr. Summers was very good at all this; in his clean white shirt and blue jeans, with one hand resting carelessly on the black box, he seemed very proper and important as he talked interminably to Mr. Graves and the Martins.

Just as Mr. Summers finally left off talking and turned to the assembled villagers, Mrs. Hutchinson came hurriedly along the path to the square, her sweater thrown over her shoulders, and slid into place in the back of the crowd. "Clean forgot what day it was," she said to Mrs. Delacroix, who stood next to her, and they both laughed softly. "Thought my old man was out back stacking wood," Mrs. Hutchinson went on, "and then I looked out the window and the kids were gone, and then I remembered it was the twenty-seventh and came a-running." She dried her hands on her apron, and Mrs. Delacroix said, "You're in time, though. They're still talking away up there."

Mrs. Hutchinson craned her neck to see through the crowd and found her husband and children standing near the front. She tapped Mrs. Delacroix on the arm as a farewell and began to make her way through the crowd. The people separated good-humoredly to let her through; two or three people said, in voices just loud enough to be heard across the crowd, "Here comes your Missus, Hutchinson," and "Bill, she made it after all." Mrs. Hutchinson reached her husband, and Mr. Summers, who had been waiting, said cheerfully, "Thought we were going to have to get on without you, Tessie." Mrs. Hutchinson said, grinning, "Wouldn't have me leave m'dishes in the sink, now, would you, Joe?" and soft laughter ran through the crowd as the people stirred back into position after Mrs. Hutchinson's arrival.

"Well, now," Mr. Summers said soberly, "guess we better get started, get 10
this over with, so's we can go back to work. Anybody ain't here?"

"Dunbar," several people said. "Dunbar, Dunbar."

Mr. Summers consulted his list. "Clyde Dunbar," he said. "That's right. He's broke his leg, hasn't he? Who's drawing for him?"

"Me, I guess," a woman said, and Mr. Summers turned to look at her. "Wife draws for her husband," Mr. Summers said. "Don't you have a grown boy to do it for you, Janey?" Although Mr. Summers and everyone else in the village knew the answer perfectly well, it was the business of the official of the lottery to ask such questions formally. Mr. Summers waited with an expression of polite interest while Mrs. Dunbar answered.

"Horace's not but sixteen yet," Mrs. Dunbar said regretfully. "Guess I gotta fill in for the old man this year."

"Right," Mr. Summers said. He made a note on the list he was holding. 15
Then he asked, "Watson boy drawing this year?"

A tall boy in the crowd raised his hand. "Here," he said. "I'm drawing for m'mother and me." He blinked his eyes nervously and ducked his head as several voices in the crowd said things like "Good fellow, Jack," and "Glad to see your mother's got a man to do it."

"Well," Mr. Summers said, "guess that's everyone. Old Man Warner make it?"

"Here," a voice said, and Mr. Summers nodded.

A sudden hush fell on the crowd as Mr. Summers cleared his throat and looked at the list. "All ready?" he called. "Now, I'll read the names—heads of families first— and the men come up and take a paper out of the box. Keep the paper folded in your hand without looking at it until everyone has had a turn. Everything clear?"

The people had done it so many times that they only half listened to the directions; most of them were quiet, wetting their lips, not looking around. Then Mr. Summers raised one hand high and said, "Adams." A man disengaged himself from the crowd and came forward. "Hi, Steve," Mr. Summers said, and Mr. Adams said, "Hi, Joe." They grinned at one another humorlessly and nervously. Then Mr. Adams reached into the black box and took out a folded paper. He held it firmly by one corner as he turned and went hastily back to his place in the crowd, where he stood a little apart from his family, not looking down at his hand.

"Allen." Mr. Summers said. "Anderson. . . . Betham."

"Seems like there's no time at all between lotteries any more," Mrs. Delacroix said to Mrs. Graves in the back row. "Seems like we got through the last one only last week."

"Time sure goes fast," Mrs. Graves said.

"Clark. . . . Delacroix."

"There goes my old man," Mrs. Delacroix said. She held her breath while her husband went forward.

"Dunbar," Mr. Summers said, and Mrs. Dunbar went steadily to the box while one of the women said, "Go on, Janey," and another said, "There she goes."

"We're next," Mrs. Graves said. She watched while Mr. Graves came around from the side of the box, greeted Mr. Summers gravely, and selected a slip of paper from the box. By now, all through the crowd there were men holding the small folded papers in their large hands, turning them over and over nervously. Mrs. Dunbar and her two sons stood together, Mrs. Dunbar holding the slip of paper.

"Harburt. . . . Hutchinson."

"Get up there, Bill," Mrs. Hutchinson said, and the people near her laughed.

"Jones."

"They do say," Mr. Adams said to Old Man Warner, who stood next to him, "that over in the north village they're talking of giving up the lottery."

Old Man Warner snorted. "Pack of crazy fools," he said. "Listening to the young folks, nothing's good enough for *them*. Next thing you know, they'll be wanting to go back to living in caves, nobody work any more, live *that* way for a while. Used to be a saying about 'Lottery in June, corn be heavy soon.' First thing you know, we'd all be eating stewed chickweed and acorns. There's *always* been a lottery," he added petulantly. "Bad enough to see young Joe Summers up there joking with everybody."

"Some places have already quit lotteries," Mrs. Adams said.

"Nothing but trouble in *that*," Old Man Warner said stoutly. "Pack of young fools."

20
25
30

"Martin." And Bobby Martin watched his father go forward. "Overdyke. . . . 35 Percy."

"I wish they'd hurry," Mrs. Dunbar said to her older son. "I wish they'd hurry."

"They're almost through," her son said.

"You get ready to run tell Dad," Mrs. Dunbar said.

Mr. Summers called his own name and then stepped forward precisely and selected a slip from the box. Then he called, "Warner."

"Seventy-seventh year I been in the lottery," Old Man Warner said as he 40 went through the crowd. "Seventy-seventh time."

"Watson." The tall boy came awkwardly through the crowd. Someone said, "Don't be nervous, Jack," and Mr. Summers said, "Take your time, son."

"Zanini."

After that, there was a long pause, a breathless pause, until Mr. Summers, holding his slip of paper in the air, said, "All right fellows." For a minute, no one moved, and then all the slips of paper were opened. Suddenly, all the women began to speak at once, saying, "Who is it?" "Who's got it?" "Is it the Dunbars?" "Is it the Watsons?" Then the voices began to say, "It's Hutchinson. It's Bill," "Bill Hutchinson's got it."

"Go tell your father," Mrs. Dunbar said to her older son.

People began to look around to see the Hutchinsons. Bill Hutchinson 45 was standing quiet, staring down at the paper in his hand. Suddenly, Tessie Hutchinson shouted to Mr. Summers, "You didn't give him time enough to take any paper he wanted. I saw you. It wasn't fair!"

"Be a good sport, Tessie," Mrs. Delacroix called, and Mrs. Graves said, "All of us took the same chance."

"Shut up, Tessie," Bill Hutchinson said.

"Well, everyone," Mr. Summers said, "That was done pretty fast, and now we've got to be hurrying a little more to get it done in time." He consulted his next list. "Bill," he said, "you draw for the Hutchinson family. You got any other households in the Hutchinsons?"

"There's Don and Eva," Mrs. Hutchinson yelled. "Make *them* take their chance!"

"Daughters draw with their husbands' families, Tessie," Mr. Summers said 50 gently. "You know that as well as anyone else."

"It wasn't fair," Tessie said.

"I guess not, Joe," Bill Hutchinson said regretfully. "My daughter draws with her husband's family, that's only fair. And I've got no other family except the kids."

"Then, as far as drawing for families is concerned, it's you," Mr. Summers said in explanation, "and as far as drawing for households is concerned, that's you, too. Right?"

"Right," Bill Hutchinson said.

"How many kids, Bill?" Mr. Summers asked formally. 55

"Three," Bill Hutchinson said. "There's Bill, Jr., and Nancy, and little Dave. And Tessie and me."

"All right then," Mr. Summers said. "Harry, you got their tickets back?"

Mr. Graves nodded and held up the slips of paper. "Put them in the box, then," Mr. Summers directed. "Take Bill's and put it in."

"I think we ought to start over," Mrs. Hutchinson said, as quietly as she could. "I tell you it wasn't *fair*. You didn't give him time enough to choose. *Every*body saw that."

Mr. Graves had selected the five slips and put them in the box, and he dropped all the papers but those onto the ground, where the breeze caught them and lifted them off. 60

"Listen, everybody," Mrs. Hutchinson was saying to the people around her.

"Ready, Bill?" Mr. Summers asked, and Bill Hutchinson, with one quick glance around at his wife and children, nodded.

"Remember," Mr. Summers said, "take the slips and keep them folded until each person has taken one. Harry, you help little Dave." Mr. Graves took the hand of the little boy, who came willingly with him up to the box. "Take a paper out of the box, Davy," Mr. Summers said. Davy put his hand into the box and laughed. "Take just *one* paper," Mr. Summers said. "Harry, you hold it for him." Mr. Graves took the child's hand and removed the folded paper from the tight fist and held it while little Dave stood next to him and looked up at him wonderingly.

"Nancy next," Mr. Summers said. Nancy was twelve, and her school friends breathed heavily as she went forward, switching her skirt, and took a slip daintily from the box. "Bill, Jr.," Mr. Summers said, and Billy, his face red and his feet over-large, nearly knocked the box over as he got a paper out. "Tessie," Mr. Summers said. She hesitated for a minute, looking around defiantly, and then set her lips and went up to the box. She snatched a paper out and held it behind her.

"Bill," Mr. Summers said, and Bill Hutchinson reached into the box and felt around, bringing his hand out at last with the slip of paper in it. 65

The crowd was quiet. A girl whispered, "I hope it's not Nancy," and the sound of the whisper reached the edges of the crowd.

"It's not the way it used to be," Old Man Warner said clearly. "People ain't the way they used to be."

"All right," Mr. Summers said. "Open the papers. Harry, you open little Dave's."

Mr. Graves opened the slip of paper and there was a general sigh through the crowd as he held it up and everyone could see that it was blank. Nancy and Bill, Jr., opened theirs at the same time, and both beamed and laughed, turning around to the crowd and holding their slips of paper above their heads.

"Tessie," Mr. Summers said. There was a pause, and then Mr. Summers looked at Bill Hutchinson, and Bill unfolded his paper and showed it. It was blank. 70

"It's Tessie," Mr. Summers said, and his voice was hushed. "Show us her paper, Bill."

Bill Hutchinson went over to his wife and forced the slip of paper out of her hand. It had a black spot on it, the black spot Mr. Summers had made the night before with the heavy pencil in the coal-company office. Bill Hutchinson held it up, and there was a stir in the crowd.

"All right, folks," Mr. Summers said. "Let's finish quickly."

Although the villagers had forgotten the ritual and lost the original black box, they still remembered to use stones. The pile of stones the boys had made earlier was ready; there were stones on the ground with the blowing scraps of paper that had come out of the box. Mrs. Delacroix selected a stone so large she had to pick it up with both hands and turned to Mrs. Dunbar. "Come on," she said. "Hurry up."

Mrs. Dunbar had small stones in both hands, and she said, gasping for 75 breath, "I can't run at all. You'll have to go ahead and I'll catch up with you."

The children had stones already, and someone gave little Davy Hutchinson a few pebbles.

Tessie Hutchinson was in the center of a cleared space by now, and she held her hands out desperately as the villagers moved in on her. "It isn't fair," she said. A stone hit her on the side of the head.

Old Man Warner was saying, "Come on, come on, everyone." Steve Adams was in the front of the crowd of villagers, with Mrs. Graves beside him.

"It isn't fair, it isn't right," Mrs. Hutchinson screamed, and then they were upon her.

FOR ANALYSIS

1. What evidence in the story suggests that the lottery is a ritualistic ceremony?

2. Does the straightforward narrative **style** describing the holiday atmosphere diminish or intensify the horror of the story's conclusion? Explain.

3. Might the story be a comment on religious orthodoxy? Explain.

MAKING CONNECTIONS

Compare this story with Silko's "The Man to Send Rain Clouds" (p. 1173). What similarities do you find? What differences?

WRITING TOPICS

1. Explain the purpose of the lottery, and identify contemporary rituals that exhibit similar purposes.

2. Magic and religion differ because magicians can compel change whereas priests can only ask for change. Comment on this distinction. Can you identify magical elements in religion?

URSULA K. LE GUIN   (B. 1929)

THE ONES WHO WALK
AWAY FROM OMELAS   1974

With a clamor of bells that set the swallows soaring, the Festival of Summer came to the city Omelas, bright-towered by the sea. The rigging of the boats in harbor sparkled with flags. In the streets between houses with red roofs and painted walls, between old moss-grown gardens and under avenues of trees, past great parks and public buildings, processions moved. Some were decorous: old people in long stiff robes of mauve and grey, grave master work-men, quiet, merry women carrying their babies and chatting as they walked. In other streets the music beat faster, a shimmering of gong and tambourine, and the people went dancing, the procession was a dance. Children dodged in and out, their high calls rising like the swallows' crossing flights over the music and the singing. All the processions wound towards the north side of the city, where on the great water-meadow called the Green Fields boys and girls, naked in the bright air, with mud-stained feet and ankles and long, lithe arms, exercised their restive horses before the race. The horses wore no gear at all but a halter without bit. Their manes were braided with streamers of silver, gold, and green. They flared their nostrils and pranced and boasted to one another; they were vastly excited, the horse being the only animal who has adopted our ceremonies as his own. Far off to the north and west the mountains stood up half encircling Omelas on her bay. The air of morning was so clear that the snow still crowning the Eighteen Peaks burned with white-gold fire across the miles of sunlit air, under the dark blue of the sky. There was just enough wind to make the ban-ners that marked the racecourse snap and flutter now and then. In the silence of the broad green meadows one could hear the music winding through the city streets, farther and nearer and ever approaching, a cheerful faint sweetness of the air that from time to time trembled and gathered together and broke out into the great joyous clanging of the bells.

Joyous! How is one to tell about joy? How describe the citizens of Omelas?

They were not simple folk, you see, though they were happy. But we do not say the words of cheer much any more. All smiles have become archaic. Given a description such as this one tends to make certain assumptions. Given a description such as this one tends to look next for the King, mounted on a splendid stallion and surrounded by his noble knights, or perhaps in a golden litter borne by great-muscled slaves. But there was no king. They did not use swords, or keep slaves. They were not barbarians. I do not know the rules and laws of their society, but I suspect that they were singularly few. As they did without monarchy and slavery, so they also got on without the stock exchange, the advertisement, the secret police, and the bomb. Yet I repeat that these were not simple folk, not dulcet shepherds, noble savages, bland utopians. They were not less complex than us. The trouble is that we have a bad habit, encouraged by pedants and sophisticates, of considering happiness as something rather stupid. Only pain is intellectual, only evil interesting. This is the treason of the artist: a refusal to admit the banality of evil and the terrible boredom of pain. If you can't lick 'em, join 'em. If it hurts, repeat it. But to praise despair is to condemn delight, to embrace violence is to lose hold of everything else. We have almost lost hold; we can no longer describe a happy man, nor make any celebration of joy. How can I tell you about the people of Omelas? They were not naïve and happy children—though their children were, in fact, happy. They were mature, intelligent, passionate adults whose lives were not wretched. O miracle! but I wish I could describe it better. I wish I could convince you. Omelas sounds in my words like a city in a fairy tale, long ago and far away, once upon a time. Perhaps it would be best if you imagined it as your own fancy bids, assuming it will rise to the occasion, for certainly I cannot suit you all. For instance, how about technology? I think that there would be no cars or helicopters in and above the streets; this follows from the fact that the people of Omelas are happy people. Happiness is based on a just discrimination of what is necessary, what is neither necessary nor destructive, and what is destructive. In the middle category, however—that of the unnecessary but undestructive, that of comfort, luxury, exuberance, etc.—they could perfectly well have central heating, subway trains, washing machines, and all kinds of marvelous devices not yet invented here, floating light-sources, fuelless power, a cure for the common cold. Or they could have none of that: it doesn't matter. As you like it. I incline to think that people from towns up and down the coast have been coming in to Omelas during the last days before the Festival on very fast little trains and double-decker trams, and that the train station of Omelas is actually the handsomest building in town, though plainer than the magnificent Farmers' Market. But even granted trains, I fear that Omelas so far strikes some of you as goody-goody. Smiles, bells, parades, horses, bleh. If so, please add an orgy. If an orgy would help, don't hesitate. Let us not, however, have temples from which issue beautiful nude priests and priestesses already half in ecstasy and ready to copulate with any man or woman, lover or stranger, who desires union with the deep godhead of the blood, although that was my first idea. But really it would be better not to have any temples in Omelas—at least, not manned temples. Religion yes, clergy no. Surely the beautiful nudes can just wander about, offering themselves like divine soufflés to the hunger of the needy and the rapture of the flesh. Let them join the processions. Let tambourines be struck above the copulations, and the glory of desire be proclaimed upon the gongs, and (a not unimportant point) let the offspring of these delightful rituals be beloved and looked after by all. One thing I know there is none of in Omelas is guilt. But what else should there be? I thought at first there were no drugs, but that is puritanical. For those who like it, the faint insistent sweetness of *drooz* may perfume the ways of the city, *drooz* which first brings a great lightness and brilliance to the mind and limbs, and then after some hours a dreamy languor, and wonderful visions at last of the very arcana and inmost secrets of the Universe, as well as exciting the pleasure of sex beyond all belief; and it is not habit-forming. For more modest tastes I think there ought to be beer. What else, what else belongs in the joyous city? The sense of victory, surely, the celebration of courage. But as we did without clergy, let us do without soldiers. The joy built upon successful slaughter is not the right kind of joy; it will not do; it is fearful and it is trivial. A boundless and generous contentment, a magnanimous triumph felt not against some outer enemy but in communion with the finest and fairest in the souls of all men everywhere and the splendor of the world's summer: this is what swells the hearts of the people of Omelas, and the victory they celebrate is that of life. I really don't think many of them need to take *drooz*.

Most of the processions have reached the Green Fields by now. A marvelous smell of cooking goes forth from the red and blue tents of the provisioners. The faces of small children are amiably sticky; in the benign grey beard of a man a couple of crumbs of rich pastry are entangled. The youths and girls have mounted their horses and are beginning to group around the starting line of the course. An old woman, small, fat, and laughing, is passing out flowers from a basket, and tall young men wear her flowers in their shining hair. A child of nine or ten sits at the edge of the crowd, alone, playing on a wooden flute. People pause to listen, and they smile, but they do not speak to him, for he never ceases playing and never sees them, his dark eyes wholly rapt in the sweet, thin magic of the tune.

He finishes, and slowly lowers his hands holding the wooden flute. 5

As if that little private silence were the signal, all at once a trumpet sounds from the pavilion near the starting line: imperious, melancholy, piercing. The horses rear on their slender legs, and some of them neigh in answer. Sober-faced, the young riders stroke the horses' necks and soothe them, whispering, "Quiet, quiet, there my beauty, my hope. . . ." They begin to form in rank along the starting line. The crowds along the racecourse are like a field of grass and flowers in the wind. The Festival of Summer has begun.

Do you believe? Do you accept the festival, the city, the joy? No? Then let me describe one more thing.

In a basement under one of the beautiful public buildings of Omelas, or perhaps in the cellar of one of its spacious private homes, there is a room. It has one locked door, and no window. A little light seeps in dustily between cracks in the boards, secondhand from a cobwebbed window somewhere across the cellar. In one corner of the little room a couple of mops, with stiff, clotted, foul-smelling heads, stand near a rusty bucket. The floor is dirt, a little damp to the touch, as cellar dirt usually is. The room is about three paces long and two wide: a mere broom closet or disused tool room. In the room a child is sitting. It could be a boy or a girl. It looks about six, but actually is nearly ten. It is feeble-minded. Perhaps it was born defective, or perhaps it has become imbecile through fear, malnutrition, and neglect. It picks its nose and occasionally fumbles vaguely with its toes or genitals, as it sits hunched in the corner farthest from the bucket and the two mops. It is afraid of the mops. It finds them horrible. It shuts its eyes, but it knows the mops are still standing there; and the door is locked; and nobody will come. The door is always locked; and nobody ever comes, except that sometimes—the child has no understanding of time or interval—sometimes the door rattles terribly and opens, and a person, or several people, are there. One of them may come in and kick the child to make it stand up. The others never come close, but peer in at it with frightened, disgusted eyes. The food bowl and the water jug are hastily filled, the door is locked, the eyes disappear. The people at the door never say anything, but the child, who has not always lived in the tool room, and can remember sunlight and its mother's voice, sometimes speaks. "I will be good," it says. "Please let me out. I will be good!" They never answer. The child used to scream for help at night, and cry a good deal, but now it only makes a kind of whining, "eh-haa, eh-haa," and it speaks less and less often. It is so thin there are no calves to its legs; its belly protrudes; it lives on a half-bowl of corn meal and grease a day. It is naked. Its buttocks and thighs are a mass of festered sores, as it sits in its own excrement continually.

They all know it is there, all the people of Omelas. Some of them have come to see it, others are content merely to know it is there. They all know that it has to be there. Some of them understand why, and some do not, but all understand that their happiness, the beauty of their city, the tenderness of their friendships, the health of their children, the wisdom of their scholars, the skill of their makers, even the abundance of their harvest and the kindly weathers of their skies, depend wholly on this child's abominable misery.

This is usually explained to children when they are between eight and 10 twelve, whenever they seem capable of understanding; and most of those who come to see the child are young people, though often enough an adult comes, or comes back, to see the child. No matter how well the matter has been explained to them, these young spectators are always shocked and sickened at the sight. They feel disgust, which they had thought themselves superior to. They feel anger, outrage, impotence, despite all the explanations. They would like to do something for the child. But there is nothing they can do. If the child were brought up into the sunlight out of that vile place, if it were cleaned and fed and comforted, that would be a good thing, indeed; but if it were done, in that day and hour all the prosperity and beauty and delight of Omelas would wither and be destroyed. Those are the terms. To exchange all the goodness and grace of every life in Omelas for that single, small improvement: to throw away the happiness of thousands for the chance of the happiness of one: that would be to let guilt within the walls indeed.

The terms are strict and absolute; there may not even be a kind word spoken to the child.

Often the young people go home in tears, or in a tearless rage, when they have seen the child and faced this terrible paradox. They may brood over it for weeks or years. But as time goes on they begin to realize that even if the child could be released, it would not get much good of its freedom: a little vague pleasure of warmth and food, no doubt, but little more. It is too degraded and imbecile to know any real joy. It has been afraid too long ever to be free of fear. Its habits are too uncouth for it to respond to humane treatment. Indeed, after so long it would probably be wretched without walls about it to protect it, and darkness for its eyes, and its own excrement to sit in. Their tears at the bitter injustice dry when they begin to perceive the terrible justice of reality, and to accept it. Yet it is their tears and anger, the trying of their generosity and the acceptance of their helplessness, which are perhaps the true source of the splendor of their lives. Theirs is no vapid, irresponsible happiness. They know that they, like the child, are not free. They know compassion. It is the existence of the child, and their knowledge of its existence, that makes possible the nobility of their architecture, the poignancy of their music, the profundity of their science. It is because of the child that they are so gentle with children. They know that if the wretched one were not there snivelling in the dark, the other one, the flute-player, could make no joyful music as the young riders line up in their beauty for the race in the sunlight of the first morning of summer.

Now do you believe in them? Are they not more credible? But there is one more thing to tell, and this is quite incredible.

At times one of the adolescent girls or boys who go to see the child does not go home to weep or rage, does not, in fact, go home at all. Sometimes also a man or woman much older falls silent for a day or two, and then leaves home. These people go out into the street, and walk down the street alone. They keep walking, and walk straight out of the city of Omelas, through the beautiful gates. They keep walking across the farmlands of Omelas. Each one goes alone, youth or girl, man or woman. Night falls; the traveler must pass down village streets, between the houses with yellow-lit windows, and on out into the darkness of the fields. Each alone, they go west or north, towards the mountains. They go on. They leave Omelas, they walk ahead into the darkness, and they do not come back. The place they go towards is a place even less imaginable to most of us than the city of happiness. I cannot describe it at all. It is possible that it does not exist. But they seem to know where they are going, the ones who walk away from Omelas.

FOR ANALYSIS

1. Who is the **narrator**? What are her feelings about Omelas, particularly about the misery of the child on which the happiness of the city depends?

2. Does the narrator sympathize with those who walk away? Or with those who remain? Or is she ambivalent?

3. Is Omelas described in sufficient detail, or are there other things about the city you wish the author had included?

4. Look up the dictionary definition of *utopia*. Does Omelas fit that definition?

5. How would you describe the **conflict** in this story? Is there a **protagonist** and an **antagonist**? Who are they?

MAKING CONNECTIONS

1. This story, Hawthorne's "Young Goodman Brown" (p. 79), and Ellison's "'Repent, Harlequin!' Said the Ticktockman" (p. 401) all rely on fantasy. What advantages does the use of fantasy give the authors?

2. Compare the statement this story makes about the human spirit with that made by Ellison's "'Repent, Harlequin!' Said the Ticktockman" (p. 401). Do the ones who walk away from Omelas share any of the attributes of the Harlequin?

WRITING TOPICS

1. The narrator comments, "The trouble is that we have a bad habit, encouraged by pedants and sophisticates, of considering happiness as something rather stupid. Only pain is intellectual, only evil interesting. This is the treason of the artist: a refusal to admit the banality of evil and the terrible boredom of pain" (para. 3). Write an essay examining this statement. Are the **narrator's** claims persuasive?

2. Is Le Guin's story, first published in 1974, still relevant? Why or why not?

AMY TAN (B. 1952)

TWO KINDS   1989

M y mother believed you could be anything you wanted to be in America. You could open a restaurant. You could work for the government and get good retirement. You could buy a house with almost no money down. You could become rich. You could become instantly famous.

"Of course you can be prodigy, too," my mother told me when I was nine. "You can be best anything. What does Auntie Lindo know? Her daughter, she is only best tricky."

America was where all my mother's hopes lay. She had come here in 1949 after losing everything in China: her mother and father, her family home, her first husband, and two daughters, twin baby girls. But she never looked back with regret. There were so many ways for things to get better.

We didn't immediately pick the right kind of prodigy. At first my mother thought I could be a Chinese Shirley Temple. We'd watch Shirley's old movies on TV as though they were training films. My mother would poke my arm and say, "*Ni kan*"—You watch. And I would see Shirley tapping her feet, or singing a sailor song, or pursing her lips into a very round O while saying, "Oh my goodness."

"*Ni kan,*" said my mother as Shirley's eyes flooded with tears. "You already 5 know how. Don't need talent for crying!"

Soon after my mother got this idea about Shirley Temple, she took me to a beauty training school in the Mission district and put me in the hands of a student who could barely hold the scissors without shaking. Instead of getting big fat curls, I emerged with an uneven mass of crinkly black fuzz. My mother dragged me off to the bathroom and tried to wet down my hair.

"You look like Negro Chinese," she lamented, as if I had done this on purpose.

The instructor of the beauty training school had to lop off these soggy clumps to make my hair even again. "Peter Pan is very popular these days," the instructor assured my mother. I now had hair the length of a boy's, with straight-across bangs that hung at a slant two inches above my eyebrows. I liked the haircut and it made me actually look forward to my future fame.

In fact, in the beginning, I was just as excited as my mother, maybe even more so. I pictured this prodigy part of me as many different images, trying each one on for size. I was a dainty ballerina girl standing by the curtains, waiting to hear the right music that would send me floating on my tiptoes. I was like the Christ child lifted out of the straw manger, crying with holy indignity. I was Cinderella stepping from her pumpkin carriage with sparkly cartoon music filling the air.

In all of my imaginings, I was filled with a sense that I would soon become 10 *perfect*. My mother and father would adore me. I would be beyond reproach. I would never feel the need to sulk for anything.

But sometimes the prodigy in me became impatient. "If you don't hurry up and get me out of here, I'm disappearing for good," it warned. "And then you'll always be nothing."

Every night after dinner, my mother and I would sit at the Formica kitchen table. She would present new tests, taking her examples from stories of amazing children she had read in *Ripley's Believe It or Not*, or *Good Housekeeping, Reader's Digest*, and a dozen other magazines she kept in a pile in our bathroom. My mother got these magazines from people whose houses she cleaned. And since she cleaned many houses each week, we had a great assortment. She would look through them all, searching for stories about remarkable children.

The first night she brought out a story about a three-year-old boy who knew the capitals of all the states and even of most of the European countries. A teacher was quoted as saying the little boy could also pronounce the names of the foreign cities correctly.

"What's the capital of Finland?" my mother asked me, looking at the magazine story.

All I knew was the capital of California, because Sacramento was the name 15 of the street we lived on in Chinatown. "Nairobi!" I guessed, saying the most foreign word I could think of. She checked to see if that was possibly one way to pronounce "Helsinki" before showing me the answer.

The tests got harder—multiplying numbers in my head, finding the queen of hearts in a deck of cards, trying to stand on my head without using my hands, predicting the daily temperatures in Los Angeles, New York, and London.

One night I had to look at a page from the Bible for three minutes and then report everything I could remember. "Now Jehoshaphat had riches and honor in abundance and . . . that's all I remember, Ma," I said.

And after seeing my mother's disappointed face once again, something inside of me began to die. I hated the tests, the raised hopes and failed expectations. Before going to bed that night, I looked in the mirror above the bathroom sink and when I saw only my face staring back—and that it would always be this ordinary face—I began to cry. Such a sad, ugly girl! I made high-pitched noises like a crazed animal, trying to scratch out the face in the mirror.

And then I saw what seemed to be the prodigy side of me—because I had never seen that face before. I looked at my reflection, blinking so I could see more clearly. The girl staring back at me was angry, powerful. This girl and I were the same. I had new thoughts, willful thoughts, or rather thoughts filled with lots of won'ts. I won't let her change me, I promised myself. I won't be what I'm not.

So now on nights when my mother presented her tests, I performed listlessly, 20 my head propped on one arm. I pretended to be bored. And I was. I got so bored I started counting the bellows of the foghorns out on the bay while my mother drilled me in other areas. The sound was comforting and reminded me of the cow jumping over the moon. And the next day, I played a game with myself, seeing if my mother would give up on me before eight bellows. After a while I usually counted only one, maybe two bellows at most. At last she was beginning to give up hope.

Two or three months had gone by without any mention of my being a prodigy again. And then one day my mother was watching *The Ed Sullivan Show* on TV. The TV was old and the sound kept shorting out. Every time my mother got halfway up from the sofa to adjust the set, the sound would come back on and Ed would be talking. As soon as she sat down, Ed would go silent again. She got up, the TV broke into loud piano music. She sat down. Silence. Up and down, back and forth, quiet and loud. It was like a stiff embraceless dance between her and the TV set. Finally she stood by the set with her hand on the sound dial.

She seemed entranced by the music, a little frenzied piano piece with this mesmerizing quality, sort of quick passages and then teasing lilting ones before it returned to the quick playful parts.

"Ni kan," my mother said, calling me over with hurried hand gestures, "Look here."

I could see why my mother was fascinated by the music. It was being pounded out by a little Chinese girl, about nine years old, with a Peter Pan haircut. The girl had the sauciness of a Shirley Temple. She was proudly modest like a proper Chinese child. And she also did a fancy sweep of a curtsy, so that the fluffy skirt of her white dress cascaded slowly to the floor like the petals of a large carnation.

In spite of these warning signs, I wasn't worried. Our family had no piano 25 and we couldn't afford to buy one, let alone reams of sheet music and piano lessons. So I could be generous in my comments when my mother bad-mouthed the little girl on TV.

"Play note right, but doesn't sound good! No singing sound," complained my mother.

"What are you picking on her for?" I said carelessly. "She's pretty good. Maybe she's not the best, but she's trying hard." I knew almost immediately I would be sorry I said that.

"Just like you," she said. "Not the best. Because you not trying." She gave a little huff as she let go of the sound dial and sat down on the sofa.

The little Chinese girl sat down also to play an encore of "Anitra's Dance" by Grieg.[1] I remember the song, because later on I had to learn how to play it.

Three days after watching *The Ed Sullivan Show*, my mother told me what 30 my schedule would be for piano lessons and piano practice. She had talked to Mr. Chong, who lived on the first floor of our apartment building. Mr. Chong was a retired piano teacher, and my mother had traded housecleaning services

---

[1] From Edvard Grieg's (1843–1907) incidental music composed for Henrik Ibsen's play *Peer Gynt*.

for weekly lessons and a piano for me to practice on every day, two hours a day, from four until six.

When my mother told me this, I felt as though I had been sent to hell. I whined and then kicked my foot a little when I couldn't stand it anymore.

"Why don't you like me the way I am? I'm *not* a genius! I can't play the piano. And even if I could, I wouldn't go on TV if you paid me a million dollars!" I cried.

My mother slapped me. "Who ask you be genius?" she shouted. "Only ask you be your best. For you sake. You think I want you be genius? Hnnh! What for! Who ask you!"

"So ungrateful," I heard her mutter in Chinese. "If she had as much talent as she has temper, she would be famous now."

Mr. Chong, whom I secretly nicknamed Old Chong, was very strange, 35 always tapping his fingers to the silent music of an invisible orchestra. He looked ancient in my eyes. He had lost most of the hair on top of his head and he wore thick glasses and had eyes that always looked tired and sleepy. But he must have been younger than I thought, since he lived with his mother and was not yet married.

I met Old Lady Chong once and that was enough. She had this peculiar smell like a baby that had done something in its pants. And her fingers felt like a dead person's, like an old peach I once found in the back of the refrigerator; the skin just slid off the meat when I picked it up.

I soon found out why Old Chong had retired from teaching piano. He was deaf. "Like Beethoven!" he shouted to me. "We're both listening only in our head!" And he would start to conduct his frantic silent sonatas.

Our lessons went like this. He would open the book and point to different things, explaining their purpose: "Key! Treble! Bass! No sharps or flats! So this is C major! Listen now and play after me!"

And then he would play the C scale a few times, a simple chord, and then, as if inspired by an old unreachable itch, he would gradually add more notes and running trills and a pounding bass until the music was really something quite grand.

I would play after him, the simple scale, the simple chord, and then I just 40 played some nonsense that sounded like a cat running up and down on top of garbage cans. Old Chong smiled and applauded and then said, "Very good! But now you must learn to keep time!"

So that's how I discovered that Old Chong's eyes were too slow to keep up with the wrong notes I was playing. He went through the motions in half-time. To help me keep rhythm, he stood behind me, pushing down on my right shoulder for every beat. He balanced pennies on top of my wrists so I would keep them still as I slowly played scales and arpeggios. He had me curve my hand around an apple and keep that shape when playing chords. He marched stiffly to show me how to make each finger dance up and down, staccato like an obedient little soldier.

He taught me all these things, and that was how I also learned I could be lazy and get away with mistakes, lots of mistakes. If I hit the wrong notes because

I hadn't practiced enough, I never corrected myself. I just kept playing in rhythm. And Old Chong kept conducting his own private reverie.

So maybe I never really gave myself a fair chance. I did pick up the basics pretty quickly, and I might have become a good pianist at that young age. But I was so determined not to try, not to be anybody different that I learned to play only the most ear-splitting preludes, the most discordant hymns.

Over the next year, I practiced like this, dutifully in my own way. And then one day I heard my mother and her friend Lindo Jong both talking in a loud bragging tone of voice so others could hear. It was after church, and I was leaning against the brick wall wearing a dress with stiff white petticoats. Auntie Lindo's daughter, Waverly, who was about my age, was standing farther down the wall about five feet away. We had grown up together and shared all the closeness of two sisters squabbling over crayons and dolls. In other words, for the most part, we hated each other. I thought she was snotty. Waverly Jong had gained a certain amount of fame as "Chinatown's Littlest Chinese Chess Champion."

"She bring home too many trophy," lamented Auntie Lindo that Sunday. "All day she play chess. All day I have no time do nothing but dust off her winnings." She threw a scolding look at Waverly, who pretended not to see her. 45

"You lucky you don't have this problem," said Auntie Lindo with a sigh to my mother.

And my mother squared her shoulders and bragged: "Our problem worser than yours. If we ask Jing-mei wash dish, she hear nothing but music. It's like you can't stop this natural talent."

And right then I was determined to put a stop to her foolish pride.

A few weeks later, Old Chong and my mother conspired to have me play in a talent show which would be held in the church hall. By then, my parents had saved up enough to buy me a secondhand piano, a black Wurlitzer spinet with a scarred bench. It was the showpiece of our living room.

For the talent show, I was to play a piece called "Pleading Child" from 50 Schumann's *Scenes from Childhood*. It was a simple, moody piece that sounded more difficult than it was. I was supposed to memorize the whole thing, playing the repeat parts twice to make the piece sound longer. But I dawdled over it, playing a few bars and then cheating, looking up to see what notes followed. I never really listened to what I was playing. I daydreamed about being somewhere else, about being someone else.

The part I liked to practice best was the fancy curtsy: right foot out, touch the rose on the carpet with a pointed foot, sweep to the side, left leg bends, look up, and smile.

My parents invited all the couples from the Joy Luck Club to witness my debut. Auntie Lindo and Uncle Tin were there. Waverly and her two older brothers had also come. The first two rows were filled with children both younger and older than I was. The littlest ones got to go first. They recited simple nursery rhymes, squawked out tunes on miniature violins, twirled Hula Hoops, pranced in pink ballet tutus, and when they bowed or curtsied, the audience would sigh in unison, "Awww," and then clap enthusiastically.

When my turn came, I was very confident. I remember my childish excitement. It was as if I knew, without a doubt, that the prodigy side of me really did exist. I had no fear whatsoever, no nervousness. I remember thinking to myself, This is it! This is it! I looked out over the audience, at my mother's blank face, my father's yawn, Auntie Lindo's stiff-lipped smile, Waverly's sulky expression. I had on a white dress, layered with sheets of lace, and a pink bow in my Peter Pan haircut. As I sat down, I envisioned people jumping to their feet and Ed Sullivan rushing up to introduce me to everyone on TV.

And I started to play. It was so beautiful. I was so caught up in how lovely I looked that at first I didn't worry how I would sound. So it was a surprise to me when I hit the first wrong note and I realized something didn't sound quite right. And then I hit another and another followed that. A chill started at the top of my head and began to trickle down. Yet I couldn't stop playing, as though my hands were bewitched. I kept thinking my fingers would adjust themselves back, like a train switching to the right track. I played this strange jumble through two repeats, the sour notes staying with me all the way to the end.

When I stood up, I discovered my legs were shaking. Maybe I had just been   55
nervous and the audience, like Old Chong, had seen me go through the right motions and had not heard anything wrong at all. I swept my right foot out, went down on my knee, looked up and smiled. The room was quiet, except for Old Chong, who was beaming and shouting, "Bravo! Bravo! Well done!" But then I saw my mother's face, her stricken face. The audience clapped weakly, and as I walked back to my chair, with my whole face quivering as I tried not to cry, I heard a little boy whisper loudly to his mother, "That was awful," and the mother whispered, "Well, she certainly tried."

And now I realized how many people were in the audience, the whole world, it seemed. I was aware of eyes burning into my back. I felt the shame of my mother and father as they sat stiffly throughout the rest of the show.

We could have escaped during intermission. Pride and some strange sense of honor must have anchored my parents to their chairs. And so we watched it all: the eighteen-year-old boy with a fake moustache who did a magic show and juggled flaming hoops while riding a unicycle. The breasted girl with white makeup who sang an aria from *Madama Butterfly* and got an honorable mention. And the eleven-year-old boy who won first prize playing a tricky violin song that sounded like a busy bee.

After the show, the Hsus, the Jongs, and the St. Clairs from the Joy Luck Club came up to my mother and father.

"Lots of talented kids," Auntie Lindo said vaguely, smiling broadly.

"That was somethin' else," my father said, and I wondered if he was referring   60
to me in a humorous way, or whether he even remembered what I had done.

Waverly looked at me and shrugged her shoulders. "You aren't a genius like me," she said matter-of-factly. And if I hadn't felt so bad, I would have pulled her braids and punched her stomach.

But my mother's expression was what devastated me: a quiet, blank look that said she had lost everything. I felt the same way, and it seemed as if everybody were now coming up, like gawkers at the scene of an accident, to see what parts were actually missing. When we got on the bus to go home, my father was humming the busy-bee tune and my mother was silent. I kept thinking she wanted to wait until we got home before shouting at me. But when my father unlocked the door to our apartment, my mother walked in and then went to the back, into the bedroom. No accusations. No blame. And in a way, I felt disappointed. I had been waiting for her to start shouting, so I could shout back and cry and blame her for all my misery.

I assumed my talent-show fiasco meant I never had to play the piano again. But two days later, after school, my mother came out of the kitchen and saw me watching TV.

"Four clock," she reminded me as if it were any other day. I was stunned, as though she were asking me to go through the talent-show torture again. I wedged myself more tightly in front of the TV.

"Turn off TV," she called from the kitchen five minutes later. 65

I didn't budge. And then I decided. I didn't have to do what my mother said anymore. I wasn't her slave. This wasn't China. I had listened to her before, and look what happened. She was the stupid one.

She came out of the kitchen and stood in the arched entryway of the living room. "Four clock," she said once again, louder.

"I'm not going to play anymore," I said nonchalantly. "Why should I? I'm not a genius."

She stood in front of the TV. I saw her chest was heaving up and down in an angry way.

"No!" I said, and I now felt stronger, as if my true self had finally emerged. 70 So this was what had been inside me all along.

"No! I won't!" I screamed.

She yanked me by the arm, pulled me off the floor, snapped off the TV. She was frighteningly strong, half pulling, half carrying me toward the piano as I kicked the throw rugs under my feet. She lifted me up and onto the hard bench. I was sobbing by now, looking at her bitterly. Her chest was heaving even more and her mouth was open, smiling crazily as if she were pleased that I was crying.

"You want me to be someone that I'm not!" I sobbed. "I'll never be the kind of daughter you want me to be!"

"Only two kinds of daughters," she shouted in Chinese. "Those who are obedient and those who follow their own mind! Only one kind of daughter can live in this house. Obedient daughter!"

"Then I wish I weren't your daughter. I wish you weren't my mother," I 75 shouted. As I said these things I got scared. It felt like worms and toads and slimy things crawling out of my chest, but it also felt good, as if this awful side of me had surfaced, at last.

"Too late change this," said my mother shrilly.

And I could sense her anger rising to its breaking point. I wanted to see it spill over. And that's when I remembered the babies she had lost in China, the ones we never talked about. "Then I wish I'd never been born!" I shouted. "I wish I were dead! Like them."

It was as if I had said the magic words. Alakazam!—and her face went blank, her mouth closed, her arms went slack, and she backed out of the room, stunned, as if she were blowing away like a small brown leaf, thin, brittle, lifeless.

It was not the only disappointment my mother felt in me. In the years that followed, I failed her so many times, each time asserting my own will, my right to fall short of expectations. I didn't get straight As. I didn't become class president. I didn't get into Stanford. I dropped out of college.

For unlike my mother, I did not believe I could be anything I wanted to be. I 80
could only be me.

And for all those years, we never talked about the disaster at the recital or my terrible accusations afterward at the piano bench. All that remained unchecked, like a betrayal that was now unspeakable. So I never found a way to ask her why she had hoped for something so large that failure was inevitable.

And even worse, I never asked her about what frightened me the most: Why had she given up hope?

For after our struggle at the piano, she never mentioned my playing again. The lessons stopped. The lid to the piano was closed, shutting out the dust, my misery, and her dreams.

So she surprised me. A few years ago, she offered to give me the piano, for my thirtieth birthday. I had not played in all those years. I saw the offer as a sign of forgiveness, a tremendous burden removed.

"Are you sure?" I asked shyly. "I mean, won't you and Dad miss it?" 85

"No, this your piano," she said firmly. "Always your piano. You only one can play."

"Well, I probably can't play anymore," I said. "It's been years."

"You pick up fast," said my mother, as if she knew this was certain. "You have natural talent. You could been genius if you want to."

"No I couldn't."

"You just not trying," said my mother. And she was neither angry nor sad. She 90
said it as if to announce a fact that could never be disproved. "Take it," she said.

But I didn't at first. It was enough that she had offered it to me. And after that, every time I saw it in my parents' living room, standing in front of the bay windows, it made me feel proud, as if it were a shiny trophy that I had won back.

Last week I sent a tuner over to my parents' apartment and had the piano reconditioned, for purely sentimental reasons. My mother had died a few months before and I had been getting things in order for my father, a little bit at a time. I put the jewelry in special silk pouches. The sweaters she had knitted in yellow, pink, bright orange—all the colors I hated—I put those in moth-proof boxes. I found some old Chinese silk dresses, the kind with little slits up the sides. I rubbed the old silk against my skin, then wrapped them in tissue and decided to take them home with me.

After I had the piano tuned, I opened the lid and touched the keys. It sounded even richer than I remembered. Really, it was a very good piano. Inside the bench were the same exercise notes with handwritten scales, the same second-hand music books with their covers held together with yellow tape.

I opened up the Schumann book to the dark little piece I had played at the recital. It was on the left-hand page, "Pleading Child." It looked more difficult than I remembered. I played a few bars, surprised at how easily the notes came back to me.

And for the first time, or so it seemed, I noticed the piece on the right-hand side. It was called "Perfectly Contented." I tried to play this one as well. It had a lighter melody but the same flowing rhythm and turned out to be quite easy. "Pleading Child" was shorter but slower; "Perfectly Contented" was longer, but faster. And after I played them both a few times, I realized they were two halves of the same song. 95

FOR ANALYSIS

1. Do you think the **conflict** between the mother and daughter is unique to this family? To Asian American families? To any group of families? Why or why not?

2. What does the mother want for her daughter? What does the daughter want for herself?

3. What is the significance of the story's last paragraph?

MAKING CONNECTIONS

Several of the stories in "Conformity and Rebellion" are driven by tensions between parents and children. Compare "Two Kinds" with stories from elsewhere in this anthology, such as Faulkner's "A Rose for Emily" (p. 649) or Walker's "Everyday Use" (p. 589). Each of these stories deals with a different culture. What significant similarities do you find among them? What substantive differences?

WRITING TOPICS

1. Describe the similarities or the differences between the mother's attempt to influence her daughter's life and your own family's attempt to influence yours.

2. Defend or attack this proposition: children should be allowed to choose their own paths.

TIGER MENDING   2004

M y sister got the job. She's the overachiever, and she went to med school
for two years before she decided she wanted to be a gifted seamstress.
(What? they said, on the day she left. A surgeon! they told her. You could be
a tremendous surgeon! But she said she didn't like the late hours, she got too
tired around midnight.) She has small-motor skills better than a machine; she'll
fix your handkerchief so well you can't even see the stitches, like she became
one with the handkerchief. I once split my lip, jumping from the tree, and she
sewed it up, with ice and a needle she'd run through the fire. I never even had a
scar, just the thinnest white line.

So of course, when the two women came through the sewing school, they
spotted her first. She was working on her final exam, a lime-colored ball
gown with tiny diamonds sewn into the collar, and she was fully absorbed in
it, constructing infinitesimal loops, while they hovered with their severe hair
and heady tree smell—like bamboo, my sister said—watching her work. My
sister's so steady she didn't even flinch, but everyone else in class seized upon
the distraction, staring at the two Amazonian women, both six feet tall and
strikingly beautiful. When I met them later I felt like I'd landed straight inside
a magazine ad. At the time, I was working at Burger King, as a block manager
(there were two on the block), and I took any distraction offered me and used
it to the hilt. Once, a guy came in and ordered a Big Mac, and for two days I
told that story to every customer, and it's not a good story. There's so rarely
any intrigue in this shabberdash world of burger warming, you take what you
can get.

But my sister was born with supernatural focus, and the two women
watched her and her alone. Who can compete? My sister's won all the contests she's ever been in not because she's such an outrageous competitor, but
because she's so focused in this gentle way. Why not win? Sometimes it's all
you need to run the fastest, or to play the clearest piano, or to ace the stan-
dardized test, pausing at each question until it has slid through your mind to
exit as a penciled-in circle.

In low, sweet voices, the women asked my sister if she'd like to see Asia. She
finally looked up from her work. Is there a sewing job there? They nodded. She
said she'd love to see Asia, she'd never left America. They said, Well, it's a highly
unusual job. May I bring my sister? she asked. She's never traveled either.

The two women glanced at each other. What does your sister do?   5

She's the manager of the Burger King down on Fourth.

Their disapproval was faint but palpable, especially in the upper lip.

She would simply keep you company?

What we are offering you is a position of tremendous privilege. Aren't you interested in hearing about it first?

My sister nodded lightly. It sounds very interesting, she said. But I cannot travel without my sister. 10

This is true. My sister, the one with that incredible focus, has a terrible fear of airplanes. Terrible. Incapacitating. The only way she can relax on a flight is if I am there, because I am always, always having some kind of crisis, and she focuses in and fixes me and forgets her own concerns. I become her ripped hemline. In general, I call her every night, and we talk for an hour, which is forty-five minutes of me, and fifteen minutes of her stirring her tea, which she steeps with the kind of Zen patience that would make Buddhists sit up in envy, and then breathe through their envy, and then move past their envy. I'm really really lucky she's my sister. Otherwise, no one like her would give someone like me the time of day.

The two Amazonian women, lousy with confidence, with their ridiculous cheekbones, in these long yellow print dresses, said OK. They observed my sister's hands quiet in her lap.

Do you get along with animals? They asked and she said, Yes. She loved every animal. Do you have allergies to cats? they asked, and she said, No. She was allergic only to pine nuts. The slightly taller one reached into her dress pocket, a pocket so well hidden inside the fabric it was like she was reaching into the ether of space, and from it her hand returned with an airplane ticket.

We are very happy to have found you, they said. The additional ticket will arrive tomorrow.

My sister smiled. I know her; she was probably terrified to see that ticket, 15 and also she really wanted to return to the diamond loops. She probably wasn't even that curious about the new job yet. She was and is stubbornly, mind-numbingly, interested in the present moment.

When we were kids, I used to come home and she'd be at the living room window. It was the best window in the apartment, looking out, in the far distance, on the tip of a mountain. For years I tried to get her to play with me, but she was unplayable. She'd stare out that window, never moving, for hours. By night, when she'd returned, I'd usually injured myself in some way or other, and I'd ask her about it as she tended to me; she said the reason she could pay acute attention was because of the window. It empties me out, she'd said, which scared me. No, she'd said, to my frightened face, and she'd sat on the edge of my bed and ran a washcloth over my forehead. It's good, she'd said. It makes room for other things.

Me? I'd asked, with hope, and she'd nodded. You.

We had no parents, by that point. They'd died at the hands of surgeons, which is the real reason my sister stopped medical school.

That night, after she took the job, she called me up and told me to quit my job, which was what I'd been praying for for months—that somehow I'd get a magical phone call telling me to quit my job because I was going on an exciting vacation. I threw down my BK apron, packed, and prepared as long an account of my life complaints as I could. On the plane, I asked my sister what we were doing, what her job was, but she refolded her tray table and said nothing. Asia, I said. What country? She stared out the porthole. It was the pilot who told us, as we buckled our seat belts; we were heading to Kuala Lumpur, straight into the heart of Malaysia.

Wait, where's Malaysia again? I whispered, and my sister drew a map on the 20 napkin beneath her ginger ale.

During the flight, I drank Bloody Marys while my sister embroidered a doily. Even the other passengers seemed soothed by watching her work. I whispered all my problems into her ear and she returned them back to me in slow sentences that did the work of a lullaby. My eyes grew heavy. During the descent, she gave the doily to the man across the aisle, worried about his ailing son, and the needlework was so elegant it made him feel better just holding it. That's the thing with handmade items. They still have the person's mark on them, and when you hold them, you feel less alone. This is why everyone who eats a Whopper leaves a little more depressed than they were when they came in. Nobody cooked that burger.

When we arrived, a friendly driver took us to a cheerful green hotel, where we found a note on the bed telling my sister to be ready at 6 A.M. sharp. It didn't say I could come, but bright and early the next morning, scrubbed and fed, we faced the two Amazons in the lobby, who looked scornfully at me and my unsteady hands—I sort of pick at my hair a lot—and asked my sister why I was there. Can't she watch? She asked, and they said they weren't sure. She, they said, might be too anxious.

I swear I won't touch anything, I said.

This is a private operation, they said.

My sister breathed. I work best when she's nearby, she said. Please.   25

And like usual it was the way she said it. In that gentle voice that had a back to it. They opened the car door.

Thank you, my sister said.

They blindfolded us, for reasons of security, and we drove for more than an hour, down winding, screeching roads, parking finally in a place that smelled like garlic and fruit. In front of a stone mansion, two more women dressed in printed robes waved as we removed our blindfolds. These two were short. Delicate. Calm. They led us into the living room, and we hadn't been there for ten minutes when we heard the moaning.

A bad moaning sound. A real bad, real mournful moaning, coming from the north, outside, that reminded me of the worst loneliness, the worst long lonely night. The Amazonian with the short shining cap of hair nodded.

Those are the tigers, she said.   30

What tigers? I said.

Shh, she said. I will call her Sloane, for no other reason than it's a good name for an intimidating person.

Sloane said, Shh. Quiet now. She took my sister by the shoulders and led her to a wide window that looked out on the land. As if she knew, instinctively, how wise it was to place my sister at a window.

Watch, Sloane whispered.

I stood behind. The two women from the front walked into view and set- 35 tled on the ground near some clumps of ferns. They waited. They were very still-minded, like my sister, that stillness of mind. That ability I will never have, to sit still. That ability to have the hands forget they are hands. They closed their eyes, and the moaning I'd heard before got louder, and then in the distance, I mean waaaay off, the moaning grew even louder, almost unbearable to hear, and limping from the side lumbered two enormous tigers. Wailing as if they were dying. As they got closer, you could see that their backs were split open, sort of peeled, as if someone had torn them in two. The fur was matted, and the stripes hung loose, like packing tape, ripped off their bodies. The women did not seem to move, but two glittering needles worked their way out of their knuckles, climbing up out of their hands, and one of the tigers stepped closer. I thought I'd lose it; he was easily four times her size, and she was small, a tiger's snack, but he lumped over, in his giantness, and fell into her lap. Let his heavy striped head sink to the ground. She smoothed the stripe back over, and the moment she pierced his fur with the needle, those big cat eyes dripped over with tears.

It was very powerful. It brought me to tears, too. Those expert hands, as steady as if they were holding a pair of pants, while the tiger's enormous head hung to the ground. My sister didn't move, but I cried and cried, seeing those giant broken animals resting in the laps of the small precise women. It is so often surprising, who rescues you at your lowest moment. When our parents died in surgery, the jerk at the liquor store suddenly became the nicest man alive, and gave us free cranberry juice for a year.

What happened to them? I asked Sloane. Why are they like that?

She lifted her chin slightly. We do not know, but they emerge from the forests, peeling. More and more of them. Always torn at the central stripe.

Do they ever eat people?

Not so far, she said. But they do not respond well to fidgeting, she said, 40 watching me clear out my thumbnail with my other thumbnail.

Well, I'm not doing it.

You have not been asked.

They are so sad, said my sister.

Well, wouldn't you be? If you were a tiger, peeling? Sloane put a hand on my sister's shoulder. When mending was done, all four—women and beasts—sat in the sun for at least half an hour, tigers chests heaving, women's hands clutched in their fur. The day grew warm. In the distance, the moaning began again, and two more tigers limped up while the first two stretched out and slept. The women sewed the next two, and the next. One had a bloody rip across its white belly.

After a few hours of work, the women put their needles away, the tigers 45 raised themselves up, and without any lick or acknowledgment, walked off deep into that place where tigers live. The women returned to the house.

Inside, they smelled so deeply and earthily of cat that they were almost unrecognizable. They also seemed lighter, nearly giddy. It was lunchtime. They joined us at the table, where Sloane served an amazing soup of curry and prawns.

It is an honor, said Sloane, to mend the tigers.

I see, said my sister.

You will need very little training, since your skill level is already so high.

But my sister seemed frightened, in a way I hadn't seen before. She didn't eat much of her soup, and she returned her eyes to the window, to the tangles of fluttering leaves.

I would have to go find out, she said finally, when the chef entered with a tray of mango tartlets.

Find out what?

Why they peel, she said. She hung her head, as if she was ashamed of her interest.

You are a mender, said Sloane, gently. Not a zoologist.

I support my sister's interest in the source, I said.

Sloane flinched every time I opened my mouth.

The source, my sister echoed.

The world has changed, said Sloane, passing a mango tartlet to me, reluctantly, which I ate, pronto.

It was unlike my sister, to need the cause. She was fine, usually, with just how things were. But she whispered to me, as we roamed outside looking for clues, of which we found none; she whispered that she felt something dangerous in the peeling, and she felt she would have to know about it in order to sew the tigers suitably. I am not worried about the sewing, she said. I am worried about the gesture I place inside the thread.

I nodded. I am a good fighter, is all. I don't care about thread gestures, but I am willing to throw a punch at some tiger asshole if need be.

We spent the rest of the day outside, but there were no tigers to be seen— where they lived was somewhere far, far off, and the journey they took to arrive here must have been the worst time of their lives, ripped open like that, suddenly prey to vultures and other predators, when they were usually the ones to instill fear.

We spent that night at the mansion, in feather beds so soft I found them impossible to sleep in. Come morning, Sloane had my sister join the two women outside, and I cried again, watching the big tiger head at her feet while she sewed with her usual stillness. The three together were unusually productive, and sewn tigers piled up around them. But instead of that giddiness that showed up in the other women, my sister grew heavier that afternoon, and said she was sure she was doing something wrong. Oh no, said Sloane, serving us tea. You were remarkable.

I am missing something, said my sister. I am missing something important.

Sloane retired for a nap, but I snuck out. I had been warned, but really, they were treating me like shit anyway. I walked a long distance, but I'm a sturdy walker, and I trusted where my feet went, and I did not like the sight of my sister staring into her teacup. I did not like the feeling it gave me, of worrying. Before I left, I sat her in front of the window and told her to empty herself, and her eyes were grateful in a way I was used to feeling in my own face but was not accustomed to seeing in hers.

I walked for hours, and the wet air clung to my shirt and hair. I took a nap inside some ferns. The sun was setting, and I would've walked all night, but when I reached a cluster of trees something felt different. There was no wailing yet, but I could feel the stirring before the wailing, which is almost worse. I swear I could hear the dread. I climbed up a tree and waited.

I don't know what I expected—people, I guess. People with knives, cutting 65 in. I did not expect to see the tigers themselves, jumpy, agitated, yawning their mouths beyond wide, the wildness in their eyes, and finally the yawning so large and insistent that they split their own back in two. They all did it, one after the other—as if they wanted to peel the fur off their backs, and then, amazed at what they'd done, the wailing began.

One by one, they left the trees and began their slow journey to be mended. It left me with the oddest, most unsettled feeling.

I walked back when it was night, under a half-moon, and found my sister still at the window.

They do it to themselves, I whispered to her, and she took my hand. Her face lightened. Thank you, she said. She tried to hug me, but I pulled away. No, I said, and in the morning, I left for the airport.

FOR ANALYSIS

1. What words would you use to describe the **narrator**? Is she serious or sarcastic? Purposeful or scattered? How is she different from her sister?

2. What is bothering the narrator's sister at the end of the story? Why does the narrator's discovery in the forest make her sister feel better but cause the narrator to leave?

MAKING CONNECTIONS

"Tiger Mending" is about the desire not simply to experience the world but to find out why things are the way they are. Kincaid's "Girl" (p. 103) is about how the world is and how to behave in it. While "Girl" has no **characters** who show evidence of wanting to know why things are the way they are, it could be said that the story itself is curious in this way. Compare the two stories in terms of how they ask Why? and how (or whether) they answer this question.

WRITING TOPICS

1. At the end of the story the **narrator** says she is "left . . . with the oddest, most unsettled feeling" (para. 66). How do you feel at the end of the story? Like the narrator, or different? Describe the feeling the story leaves you with, and explain how you think the story achieves this effect.

2. Write a brief essay exploring the meaning of the tigers' stripes. Why do you think Bender chooses them as the thing that needs repairing?

CONNECTING STORIES:
SUPERANTIHEROES

The hero, a figure as old as mythology, embodies the ideals of cultures: their self-images, their hopes, and their fantasies. Superman, for instance, represented the immigrant American Dream with his arrival from another planet and his bulletproof invincibility. The power of heroes to embody ideals, however, can sometimes be undermined by the questioning of those same ideals in the wake of historical change. A man in patriotic-colored tights was perceived differently during the Vietnam War—or the war in Iraq—than he was at the height of World War II. As you read Harlan Ellison's and Jonathan Lethem's stories, think about the role of the hero—and the superhero—and think about the connections between what makes that role possible and what makes it impossible.

HARLAN ELLISON® (B. 1934)

"REPENT, HARLEQUIN!"
SAID THE TICKTOCKMAN   1965

There are always those who ask, what is it all about? For those who need to ask, for those who need points sharply made, who need to know "where it's at," this:

> The mass of men serve the state thus, not as men mainly, but as machines, with their bodies. They are the standing army, and the militia, jailors, constables, posse comitatus, etc. In most cases there is no free exercise whatever of the judgment or of the moral sense; but they put themselves on a level with wood and earth and stones; and wooden men can perhaps be manufactured that will serve the purpose as well. Such command no more respect than men of straw or a lump of dirt. They have the same sort of worth only as horses and dogs. Yet such as these even are commonly esteemed good citizens. Others—as most legislators, politicians, lawyers, ministers, and officeholders—serve the state chiefly with their heads; and, as they rarely make any moral distinctions, they are as likely to serve the Devil, without intending it, as God. A very few, as heroes, patriots, martyrs, reformers in the great sense, and men, serve the state with their consciences also, and so necessarily resist it for the most part; and they are commonly treated as enemies by it.

Henry David Thoreau
CIVIL DISOBEDIENCE

That is the heart of it. Now begin in the middle, and later learn the beginning; the end will take care of itself.

But because it was the very world it was, the very world they had allowed it to *become*, for months his activities did not come to the alarmed attention of The Ones Who Kept The Machine Functioning Smoothly, the ones who poured the very best butter over the cams and mainsprings of the culture. Not until it had become obvious that somehow, someway, he had become a notoriety, a celebrity, perhaps even a hero for (what Officialdom inescapably tagged) "an emotionally disturbed segment of the populace," did they turn it over to the Ticktockman and his legal machinery. But by then, because it was the very world it was, and they had no way to predict he would happen— possibly a strain of disease long-defunct, now, suddenly, reborn in a system where immunity had been forgotten, had lapsed—he had been allowed to become too real. Now he had form and substance.

He had become a *personality*, something they had filtered out of the system many decades before. But there it was, and there *he* was, a very definitely imposing personality. In certain circles—middle-class circles—it was thought disgusting. Vulgar ostentation. Anarchistic. Shameful. In others, there was only sniggering: those strata where thought is subjugated to form and ritual, niceties, proprieties. But down below, ah, down below, where the people always needed their saints and sinners, their bread and circuses, their heroes and villains, he was considered a Bolivar; a Napoleon; a Robin Hood; a Dick Bong (Ace of Aces); a Jesus; a Jomo Kenyatta.

And at the top—where, like socially-attuned Shipwreck Kellys, every tremor ⁵ and vibration threatening to dislodge the wealthy, powerful and titled from their flagpoles—he was considered a menace; a heretic; a rebel; a disgrace; a peril. He was known down the line, to the very heartmeat core, but the important reactions were high above and far below. At the very top, at the very bottom.

So his file was turned over, along with his time-card and his cardioplate, to the office of the Ticktockman.

The Ticktockman: very much over six feet tall, often silent, a soft purring man when things went timewise. The Ticktockman.

Even in the cubicles of the hierarchy, where fear was generated, seldom suffered, he was called the Ticktockman. But no one called him that to his mask.

You don't call a man a hated name, not when that man, behind his mask, is capable of revoking the minutes, the hours, the days and nights, the years of your life. He was called the Master Timekeeper to his mask. It was safer that way.

"This is *what* he is," said the Ticktockman with genuine softness, "but not ¹⁰ *who* he is. This time-card I'm holding in my left hand has a name on it, but it is the name of *what* he is, not *who* he is. The cardioplate here in my right hand is also named, but not *whom* named, merely *what* named. Before I can exercise proper revocation, I have to know *who* this *what* is."

To his staff, all the ferrets, all the loggers, all the finks, all the commex, even the mineez, he said, "Who is this Harlequin?"

He was not purring smoothly. Timewise, it was jangle.

However, it *was* the longest speech they had ever heard him utter at one time, the staff, the ferrets, the loggers, the finks, the commex, but not the mineez, who usually weren't around to know, in any case. But even they scurried to find out.

Who is the Harlequin?

High above the third level of the city, he crouched on the humming aluminum-frame platform of the air-boat (foof! air-boat, indeed! swizzleskid is what it was, with a tow-rack jerry-rigged) and he stared down at the neat Mondrian arrangement of the buildings.

Somewhere nearby, he could hear the metronomic left-right-left of the 2:47 PM shift, entering the Timkin roller-bearing plant in their sneakers. A minute later, precisely, he heard the softer right-left-right of the 5:00 AM formation, going home.

An elfin grin spread across his tanned features, and his dimples appeared for a moment. Then, scratching at his thatch of auburn hair, he shrugged within his motley, as though girding himself for what came next, and threw the joystick forward, and bent into the wind as the air-boat dropped. He skimmed over a slidewalk, purposely dropping a few feet to crease the tassels of the ladies of fashion, and—inserting thumbs in large ears—he stuck out his tongue, rolled his eyes, and went wugga-wugga-wugga. It was a minor diversion. One pedestrian skittered and tumbled, sending parcels every-whichway, another wet herself, a third keeled slantwise and the walk was stopped automatically by the servitors till she could be resuscitated. It was a minor diversion.

Then he swirled away on a vagrant breeze, and was gone. Hi-ho. As he rounded the cornice of the Time-Motion Study Building, he saw the shift, just boarding the slidewalk. With practiced motion and an absolute conservation of movement, they sidestepped up onto the slow-strip and (in a chorus line reminiscent of a Busby Berkeley film of the antediluvian 1930s) advanced across the strips ostrich-walking till they were lined up on the expresstrip.

Once more, in anticipation, the elfin grin spread, and there was a tooth missing back there on the left side. He dipped, skimmed, and swooped over them; and then, scrunching about on the air-boat, he released the holding pins that fastened shut the ends of the home-made pouring troughs that kept his cargo from dumping prematurely. And as he pulled the trough-pins, the air-boat slid over the factory workers and one hundred and fifty thousand dollars' worth of jelly beans cascaded down on the expresstrip.

Jelly beans! Millions and billions of purples and yellows and greens and lico-rice and grape and raspberry and mint and round and smooth and crunchy outside and soft-mealy inside and sugary and bouncing jouncing tumbling clittering clattering skittering fell on the heads and shoulders and hardhats and carapaces of the Timkin workers, tinkling on the slidewalk and bouncing away and rolling about underfoot and filling the sky on their way down with all the colors of joy and childhood and holidays, coming down in a steady rain, a solid wash, a torrent of color and sweetness out of the sky from above, and entering a universe of sanity and metronomic order with quite-mad coocoo newness. Jelly beans!

The shift workers howled and laughed and were pelted, and broke ranks, and the jelly beans managed to work their way into the mechanism of the slidewalks after which there was a hideous scraping as the sound of a million fingernails rasped down a quarter of a million blackboards, followed by a coughing and a sputtering, and then the slidewalks all stopped and everyone was dumped thisawayandthataway in a jackstraw tumble, still laughing and popping little jelly bean eggs of childish color into their mouths. It was a holiday, and a jollity, an absolute insanity, a giggle. But . . .

The shift was delayed seven minutes.

They did not get home for seven minutes.

The master schedule was thrown off by seven minutes.

Quotas were delayed by inoperative slidewalks for seven minutes.   25

He had tapped the first domino in the line, and one after another, like chik chik chik, the others had fallen.

The System had been seven minutes' worth of disrupted. It was a tiny matter, one hardly worthy of note, but in a society where the single driving force was order and unity and equality and promptness and clocklike precision and attention to the clock, reverence of the gods of the passage of time, it was a disaster of major importance.

So he was ordered to appear before the Ticktockman. It was broadcast across every channel of the communications web. He was ordered to be *there* at 7:00 dammit on time. And they waited, and they waited, but he didn't show up till almost ten-thirty, at which time he merely sang a little song about moonlight in a place no one had ever heard of, called Vermont, and vanished again. But they had all been waiting since seven, and it wrecked *hell* with their schedules. So the question remained: Who is the Harlequin?

But the *unasked* question (more important of the two) was: how did we get *into* this position, where a laughing, irresponsible japer of jabberwocky and jive could disrupt our entire economic and cultural life with a hundred and fifty thousand dollars' worth of jelly beans . . .

Jelly for God's sake *beans!* This is madness! Where did he get the money   30 to buy a hundred and fifty thousand dollars' worth of jelly beans? (They knew it would have cost that much, because they had a team of Situation Analysts pulled off another assignment, and rushed to the slidewalk scene to sweep up and count the candies, and produce findings, which disrupted *their* schedules and threw their entire branch at least a day behind.) Jelly beans! Jelly . . . *beans?* Now wait a second—a second accounted for—no one has manufactured jelly beans for over a hundred years. Where did he get jelly beans?

That's another good question. More than likely it will never be answered to your complete satisfaction. But then, how many questions ever are?

· · · ·

The middle you know. Here is the beginning. How it starts:

A DESK PAD. DAY FOR DAY, AND TURN EACH DAY. 9:00—OPEN THE MAIL. 9:45—APPOINTMENT WITH PLANNING COMMISSION BOARD. 10:30—DISCUSS INSTALLATION PROGRESS CHARTS WITH J.L. 11:45—PRAY FOR RAIN. 12:00—LUNCH. *AND SO IT GOES.*

"I'm sorry, Miss Grant, but the time for interviews was set at 2:30, and it's almost five now. I'm sorry you're late, but those are the rules. You'll have to wait till next year to submit application for this college again." *And so it goes.*

The 10:10 local stops at Cresthaven, Galesville, Tonawanda Junction, Selby, and 35 Farnhurst, but not at Indiana City, Lucasville and Colton, except on Sunday. The 10:35 express stops at Galesville, Selby, and Indiana City, except on Sundays & Holidays, at which time it stops at . . . *and so it goes.*

"I couldn't wait, Fred. I had to be at Pierre Cartain's by 3:00, and you said you'd meet me under the clock in the terminal at 2:45, and you weren't there, so I had to go on. You're always late, Fred. If you'd been there, we could have sewed it up together, but as it was, well, I took the order alone . . ." *And so it goes.*

Dear Mr. and Mrs. Atterley: In reference to your son Gerold's constant tardiness, I am afraid we will have to suspend him from school unless some more reliable method can be instituted guaranteeing he will arrive at his classes on time. Granted he is an exemplary student, and his marks are high, his constant flouting of the schedules of this school makes it impractical to maintain him in a system where the other children seem capable of getting where they are supposed to be on time *and so it goes.*

YOU CANNOT VOTE UNLESS YOU APPEAR AT 8:45 AM.

"I don't care if the script is *good*, I need it Thursday!"

CHECK-OUT TIME IS 2:00 PM.   40

"You got here late. The job's taken. Sorry."

YOUR SALARY HAS BEEN DOCKED FOR TWENTY MINUTES TIME LOST.

"God, what time is it, I've gotta run!"

And so it goes. And so it goes. And so it goes. And so it goes goes goes goes goes tick tock tick tock tick tock and one day we no longer let time serve us, we serve time and we are slaves of the schedule, worshippers of the sun's passing, bound into a life predicated on restrictions because the system will not function if we don't keep the schedule tight.

Until it becomes more than a minor inconvenience to be late. It becomes a   45
sin. Then a crime. Then a crime punishable by this:

> EFFECTIVE 15 JULY 2389 12:00:00 midnight, the office of the Master
> Timekeeper will require all citizens to submit their time-cards and cardi-
> oplates for processing. In accordance with Statute 555-7-SGH-999 gov-
> erning the revocation of time per capita, all cardioplates will be keyed to
> the individual holder and—

What they had done was devise a method of curtailing the amount of life a
person could have. If he was ten minutes late, he lost ten minutes of his life. An
hour was proportionately worth more revocation. If someone was consistently
tardy, he might find himself, on a Sunday night, receiving a communiqué from
the Master Timekeeper that his time had run out, and he would be "turned off"
at high noon on Monday, please straighten your affairs, sir, madame, or bisex.
   And so, by this simple scientific expedient (utilizing a scientific process held
dearly secret by the Ticktockman's office) the System was maintained. It was
the only expedient thing to do. It was, after all, patriotic. The schedules had to
be met. After all, there *was* a war on!
   But, wasn't there always?

"Now that is really disgusting," the Harlequin said, when Pretty Alice   50
showed him the wanted poster. "Disgusting and *highly* improbable. After all,
this isn't the Day of the Desperado. A *wanted* poster!"
   "You know," Pretty Alice noted, "you speak with a great deal of inflection."
   "I'm sorry," said the Harlequin, humbly.
   "No need to be sorry. You're always saying 'I'm sorry.' You have such massive guilt, Everett, it's really very sad."
   "I'm sorry," he said again, then pursed his lips so the dimples appeared
momentarily. He hadn't wanted to say that at all. "I have to go out again. I
have to *do* something."
   Pretty Alice slammed her coffee-bulb down on the counter. "Oh for God's   55
sake, Everett, can't you stay home just *one* night! Must you always be out in
that ghastly clown suit, running around an*noy*ing people?"
   "I'm—" He stopped, and clapped the jester's hat onto his auburn thatch
with a tiny tinkling of bells. He rose, rinsed out his coffee-bulb at the spray,
and put it into the dryer for a moment. "I have to go."
   She didn't answer. The faxbox was purring, and she pulled a sheet out,
read it, threw it toward him on the counter. "It's about you. Of course.
You're ridiculous."
   He read it quickly. It said the Ticktockman was trying to locate him. He
didn't care, he was going out to be late again. At the door, dredging for an exit
line, he hurled back petulantly, "Well, *you* speak with inflection, *too!*"
   Pretty Alice rolled her pretty eyes heavenward. "You're ridiculous."
   The Harlequin stalked out, slamming the door, which sighed shut softly,   60
and locked itself.

There was a gentle knock, and Pretty Alice got up with an exhalation of exasperated breath, and opened the door. He stood there. "I'll be back about ten-thirty, okay?"

She pulled a rueful face. "Why do you tell me that? Why? You *know* you'll be late! You *know* it! You're *always* late, so why do you tell me these dumb things?" She closed the door.

On the other side, the Harlequin nodded to himself. *She's right. She's always right. I'll be late. I'm always late. Why* do *I tell her these dumb things?*

He shrugged again, and went off to be late once more.

He had fired off the firecracker rockets that said: I will attend the 115th 65 annual International Medical Association Invocation at 8:00 PM precisely. I do hope you will all be able to join me.

The words had burned in the sky, and of course the authorities were there, lying in wait for him. They assumed, naturally, that he would be late. He arrived twenty minutes early, while they were setting up the spiderwebs to trap and hold him. Blowing a large bullhorn, he frightened and unnerved them so, their own moisturized encirclement webs sucked closed, and they were hauled up, kicking and shrieking, high above the amphitheater's floor. The Harlequin laughed and laughed, and apologized profusely. The physicians, gathered in solemn conclave, roared with laughter, and accepted the Harlequin's apologies with exaggerated bowing and posturing, and a merry time was had by all, who thought the Harlequin was a regular foofaraw in fancy pants; all, that is, but the authorities, who had been sent out by the office of the Ticktockman; they hung there like so much dockside cargo, hauled up above the floor of the amphitheater in a most unseemly fashion.

(In another part of the same city where the Harlequin carried on his "activities," totally unrelated in every way to what concerns us here, save that it illustrates the Ticktockman's power and import, a man named Marshall Delahanty received his turn-off notice from the Ticktockman's office. His wife received the notification from the gray-suited minee who delivered it, with the traditional "look of sorrow" plastered hideously across his face. She knew what it was, even without unsealing it. It was a billet-doux of immediate recognition to everyone these days. She gasped, and held it as though it were a glass slide tinged with botulism, and prayed it was not for her. Let it be for Marsh, she thought, brutally, realistically, or one of the kids, but not for me, please dear God, not for me. And then she opened it, and it *was* for Marsh, and she was at one and the same time horrified and relieved. The next trooper in the line had caught the bullet. "Marshall," she screamed, "Marshall! Termination, Marshall! OhmiGod, Marshall, whattl we do, whattl we do, Marshall omigodmarshall . . ." and in their home that night was the sound of tearing paper and fear, and the stink of madness went up the flue and there was nothing, absolutely nothing they could do about it.

(But Marshall Delahanty tried to run. And early the next day, when turn-off time came, he was deep in the Canadian forest two hundred miles away, and the office of the Ticktockman blanked his cardioplate, and Marshall

Delahanty keeled over, running, and his heart stopped, and the blood dried up on its way to his brain, and he was dead that's all. One light went out on the sector map in the office of the Master Timekeeper, while notification was entered for fax reproduction, and Georgette Delahanty's name was entered on the dole roles till she could remarry. Which is the end of the footnote, and all the point that need be made, except don't laugh, because that is what would happen to the Harlequin if ever the Ticktockman found out his real name. It isn't funny.)

The shopping level of the city was thronged with the Thursday-colors of the buyers. Women in canary yellow chitons and men in pseudo-Tyrolean outfits that were jade and leather and fit very tightly, save for the balloon pants.

When the Harlequin appeared on the still-being-constructed shell of the 70 new Efficiency Shopping Center, his bullhorn to his elfishly-laughing lips, everyone pointed and stared, and he berated them:

"Why let them order you about? Why let them tell you to hurry and scurry like ants or maggots? Take your time! Saunter a while! Enjoy the sunshine, enjoy the breeze, let life carry you at your own pace! Don't be slaves of time, it's a helluva way to die, slowly, by degrees . . . down with the Ticktockman!"

Who's the nut? most of the shoppers wanted to know. Who's the nut oh wow I'm gonna be late I gotta run . . .

And the construction gang on the Shopping Center received an urgent order from the office of the Master Timekeeper that the dangerous criminal known as the Harlequin was atop their spire, and their aid was urgently needed in apprehending him. The work crew said no, they would lose time on their construction schedule, but the Ticktockman managed to pull the proper threads of governmental webbing, and they were told to cease work and catch that nitwit up there on the spire; up there with the bullhorn. So a dozen and more burly workers began climbing into their construction platforms, releasing the a-grav plates, and rising toward the Harlequin.

After the debacle (in which, through the Harlequin's attention to personal safety, no one was seriously injured), the workers tried to reassemble, and assault him again, but it was too late. He had vanished. It had attracted quite a crowd, however, and the shopping cycle was thrown off by hours, simply hours. The purchasing needs of the system were therefore falling behind, and so measures were taken to accelerate the cycle for the rest of the day, but it got bogged down and speeded up and they sold too many float-valves and not nearly enough wegglers, which meant that the popli ratio was off, which made it necessary to rush cases and cases of spoiling Smash-O to stores that usually needed a case only every three or four hours. The shipments were bollixed, the transshipments were misrouted, and in the end, even the swizzleskid industries felt it.

"Don't come back till you have him!" the Ticktockman said, very quietly, 75 very sincerely, extremely dangerously.

They used dogs. They used probes. They used cardioplate crossoffs. They used teepers. They used bribery. They used stiktytes. They used intimidation. They used torment. They used torture. They used finks. They used cops. They used search&seizure. They used fallaron. They used betterment incentive. They used fingerprints. They used the Bertillon system. They used cunning. They used guile. They used treachery. They used Raoul Mitgong, but he didn't help much. They used applied physics. They used techniques of criminology.

And what the hell: they caught him.

After all, his name was Everett C. Marm, and he wasn't much to begin with, except a man who had no sense of time.

"Repent, Harlequin!" said the Ticktockman.

"Get stuffed!" the Harlequin replied, sneering.   80

"You've been late a total of sixty-three years, five months, three weeks, two days, twelve hours, forty-one minutes, fifty-nine seconds, point oh three six one one one microseconds. You've used up everything you can, and more. I'm going to turn you off."

"Scare someone else. I'd rather be dead than live in a dumb world with a bogeyman like you."

"It's my job."

"You're full of it. You're a tyrant. You have no right to order people around and kill them if they show up late."

"You can't adjust. You can't fit in."   85

"Unstrap me, and I'll fit my fist into your mouth."

"You're a nonconformist."

"That didn't used to be a felony."

"It is now. Live in the world around you."

"I hate it. It's a terrible world."   90

"Not everyone thinks so. Most people enjoy order."

"I don't, and most of the people I know don't."

"That's not true. How do you think we caught you?"

"I'm not interested."

"A girl named Pretty Alice told us who you were."   95

"That's a lie."

"It's true. You unnerve her. She wants to belong; she wants to conform; I'm going to turn you off."

"Then do it already, and stop arguing with me."

"I'm not going to turn you off."

"You're an idiot!"   100

"Repent, Harlequin!" said the Ticktockman.

"Get stuffed."

So they sent him to Coventry. And in Coventry they worked him over. It was just like what they did to Winston Smith in NINETEEN EIGHTY-FOUR, which was a book none of them knew about, but the techniques are really quite ancient, and so they did it to Everett C. Marm; and one day, quite a long time later, the Harlequin appeared on the communications web, appearing elfin and dimpled and bright-eyed, and not at all brainwashed, and he said he had been wrong, that it was a good, a very good thing indeed, to belong, to be right on time hip-ho and away we go, and everyone stared up at him on the public screens that covered an entire city block, and they said to themselves, well, you see, he was just a nut after all, and if that's the way the system is run, then let's do it that way, because it doesn't pay to fight city hall, or in this case, the Ticktockman. So Everett C. Marm was destroyed, which was a loss, because of what Thoreau said earlier, but you can't make an omelet without breaking a few eggs, and in every revolution a few die who shouldn't, but they have to, because that's the way it happens, and if you make only a little change, then it seems to be worthwhile. Or, to make the point lucidly:

"Uh, excuse me, sir, I, uh, don't know how to uh, to uh, tell you this, but you were three minutes late. The schedule is a little, uh, bit off."

He grinned sheepishly. 105

"That's ridiculous!" murmured the Ticktockman behind his mask. "Check your watch." And then he went into his office, going *mrmee, mrmee, mrmee, mrmee.*

FOR ANALYSIS

1. What are the **connotations** of the names *Harlequin* and *Everett C. Marm*? Is the contrast between the names similar to that between, say, *Superman* and *Clark Kent*?

2. What is it about his society that drives Everett C. Marm to rebel?

3. What is Pretty Alice's role in the story?

4. Explain the final section of the story (paras. 104–6). Has the Ticktockman triumphed?

MAKING CONNECTIONS

1. Compare the statement this story makes about the human spirit with that made in Le Guin's "The Ones Who Walk Away from Omelas" (p. 380). Does Everett C. Marm share any of the attributes of the ones who walk away from Omelas?

2. Compare Everett C. Marm and the **narrator** in Ellison's "Battle Royal" (p. 361) as rebels. Who is more successful as a rebel? As a conformist? Will the narrator of "Battle Royal" grow up to be like the Harlequin?

WRITING TOPICS

1. Carefully read the passage (para. 1) taken from Thoreau's "Civil Disobedience." Write an essay explaining why you do or do not agree (in whole or in part) with Thoreau's view of "the state" and with his classification of citizens as those who serve the state with their "bodies," those who serve it with their "heads," and those who serve it with their "consciences." Where would you place Everett C. Marm?

2. Characterize Pretty Alice. Why does she turn Everett in?

JONATHAN LETHEM (B. 1964)

SUPER GOAT MAN 2004

When Super Goat Man moved into the commune on our street, I was ten years old. Though I liked superheroes, I wasn't familiar with Super Goat Man. His presence didn't mean much to me or to the other kids in the neighborhood. For us, as we ran and screamed and played our secret games on the sidewalk, Super Goat Man was only another of the guys who sat on stoops in sleeveless undershirts on hot summer days, watching the slow progress of life on the block. The two little fleshy horns on his forehead didn't make him especially interesting. We weren't struck by his fall from grace, out of the world of comic-book heroes, among which he had been at best a minor star, to land here in Cobble Hill, Brooklyn, in a single room in what was basically a dorm for college dropouts, a hippie group shelter, any more than we were by the tufts of extra hair at his throat and behind his ears. We had eyes only for Spider-Man and Batman in those days, superheroes in two dimensions, with lunchboxes and television shows and theme songs. Super Goat Man had none of those.

It was our dads who cared. They were unmistakably drawn to the strange figure who'd moved to our block, as though for them he represented some lost possibility in their own lives. My father in particular seemed fascinated with Super Goat Man, though he disguised this interest by acting as though it was on my behalf. One day toward the end of that summer, he and I walked to Montague Street to visit the comics shop there. This was a tiny storefront filled with long white boxes packed with carefully archived comics, protected by plastic bags and cardboard backing. The boxes contained ancient runs of back issues of titles I'd heard of, as well as thousands of other comics featuring characters I'd never encountered. The shop was presided over by a nervous young pedant with long hair and a beard, a collector type himself, an old man in spirit who distrusted children in his store, as he ought to have. He helped my father to find what he sought, deep in the alphabetical archive: a five-issue run of *The Remarkable Super Goat Man*, from Electric Comics. These were the only comics in which Super Goat Man had appeared. There were just five issues because after five the title had been forever canceled. My father seemed satisfied with what he'd found. We paid for the five issues and left.

I didn't know how to explain to my father that Electric wasn't one of the major comics publishers. The stories the comics contained, when we inspected them together, were both ludicrous and boring. Super Goat Man's five issues showed him rescuing old ladies from swerving trucks and kittens from lightning-struck trees, and battling dull villains like Vest Man and False Dave. The drawings were amateurish, cut-rate, antiquated. I couldn't have articulated these judgments then, of course. I knew only that I disliked the comics, found them embarrassing, for myself, for Super Goat Man, and for my dad. They languished in my room, unread, and were eventually cleaned up—I mean, thrown out—by my mom.

411

For the next few years, Super Goat Man was less than a minor curiosity to me. I didn't waste thought on him. The younger men and women who lived in the commune took him for granted, as anyone should have, so far as I knew. We kids would see him in their company, moving furniture up the stoop and into the house—discarded dressers and couches and lamps they'd found on the street—or taping up posters on lampposts announcing demonstrations against nuclear power or in favor of day-care centers, or weeding in the commune's pathetic front yard, which was intended as a vegetable garden but was choked not only with uninvited growth but with ice-cream wrappers and soda bottles—we kids used the commune's yard as a dumping ground. It didn't occur to me that Super Goat Man was much older, really, than the commune's other occupants, that in fact they might be closer to my age than to his. However childish their behavior, the hippies all seemed as dull and remote as grown-ups to me.

It was the summer when I was thirteen that my parents allowed me to   5
accompany them to one of the commune's potluck dinners. The noise and vibrancy of that house's sporadic celebrations were impossible to ignore on our street, and I knew that my parents had attended a few earlier parties—warily, I imagined. The inhabitants of the commune were always trying to sweep their neighbors into dubious causes, and it might be a mistake to be seduced by frivolity into some sticky association. But my parents liked fun, too. And had too little of it. Their best running jokes concerned the dullness of their friends' dinner parties. This midsummer evening, they brought me along to see inside the life of the scandalous, anomalous house.

The house was already full, many of the guests bearded and jeweled and scruffy, reeking of patchouli and musk, others, like my parents, dressed in their hippest collarless shirts and paisley blouses, wearing their fattest beads and bracelets. The offerings, nearly all casseroles brimming with exotic gray proteins—beans and tofu and eggplant and more I couldn't name—were lined up on a long side table, mostly ignored. This was a version of cocktail hour, with beer drunk from the bottle and well-rolled marijuana cigarettes. I didn't see whether my parents indulged in the latter. My mother accepted a glass of orange juice, surely spiked. I meant not to pay them any attention, so I moved for the stairs. There were partyers leaning on the bannister at the first landing, and music was playing in upstairs rooms, so I didn't doubt that the whole house was open to wandering.

There was no music coming from the garden-facing room on the second floor, but the door was open and three figures were visible inside, seated on cushions on a mattress on the floor: a young couple and Super Goat Man. From his bare hairy feet on the mattress, I guessed that it was his room I'd entered. The walls were sparse apart from a low bookcase, on which I spotted, laid crosswise in the row of upright spines, Norman Mailer's *Armies of the Night,* Sergei Eisenstein's *Film Form/The Film Sense,* and Thomas Pynchon's *V.* The three titles stuck in my head; I would later attempt to read all three in college, succeeding only with the Mailer. Next to the bookcase was a desk heaped with papers, and behind it a few black-and-white postcards had been thumbtacked to the wall. One of the postcard images I recognized as Charlie Parker, clutching a saxophone with his meaty hands. The jazz-man was an idol of my father's, perhaps a symbol of his vanished youth.

The young man on the mattress was holding a book: *Memories, Dreams, Reflections*, by Carl Jung. Super Goat Man had evidently just pressed it on him, and had likely been extolling its virtues when I walked into the room.

"Hello," the young woman said, her voice warm. I must have been staring from my place in the middle of the room.

"You're Everett, aren't you?" Super Goat Man said, before I could speak.   10

"How'd you know my name?"

"You live on the block," Super Goat Man said. "I've seen you running around."

"I think we'll head down, Super Goat Man," the young man said abruptly, tucking the book under his arm as he got up from the mattress. "Get something to eat before it's too late."

"I want to hit the dance floor," the young woman said.

"See you down there," Super Goat Man said. With that, the young couple   15 were gone.

"You checking out the house?" Super Goat Man said once we were alone. "Casing the joint?"

"I'm looking for my friend," I lied.

"I think some kids are hanging out in the backyard."

"No, she went upstairs." I wanted him to think I had a girlfriend.

"O.K., cool," Super Goat Man said. He smiled. I suppose he was waiting for   20 me to leave, but he didn't give any sign that I was bothering him by staying.

"Why do you live here?" I asked.

"These are my friends," he said. "They helped me out when I lost my job."

"You're not a superhero anymore, are you?"

Super Goat Man shrugged. "Some people felt I was being too outspoken about the war. Anyway, I wanted to accomplish things on a more local level."

"Why don't you have a secret identity?"   25

"I wasn't that kind of superhero."

"But what was your name before?"

"Ralph Gersten."

"What did Ralph Gersten do?"

"He was a college teacher, for a couple of years."   30

"So why aren't you Ralph Gersten now?"

"Sometime around when they shot Kennedy I just realized that Ralph Gersten wasn't who I was. He was a part of an old life I was holding on to. So I became Super Goat Man. I've come to understand that this is who I am, for better or worse."

This was a bit much for me to assimilate, so I changed the subject. "Do you smoke pot?"

"Sometimes."

"Were Mr. and Mrs. Gersten sad when you gave up your secret identity?"   35
"Who?"
"Your parents."
Super Goat Man smiled. "They weren't my real parents. I was adopted."
Suddenly I was done. "I'm going downstairs, Super Goat Man."
"O.K., Everett," he said. "See you down there, probably."   40

I made my way downstairs to the commune's muddy and ill-lit backyard, milling with the other teenagers and children stranded there by the throngs of frolickers—for the party was now overflowing its bounds, and we were free to steal beers from the counter and carry on our own tentative party, our own fumbling flirtations. I had no girlfriend, but I did play spin the bottle that night, crouched on the ground beneath a fig tree.

Then, near midnight, I went back inside. The living room was jammed with bodies—dancers on a parquet floor that had been revealed when the vast braided rug was rolled up against the base of the mantelpiece. Colored Christmas lights were bunched in one corner, and some of them blinked to create a gently eerie strobe. I smelled sweat and smoke. Feeling perverse and thrilled by the kisses I'd exchanged in the mud beneath the tree, I meandered into the web of celebrants.

Super Goat Man was there. He was dancing with my mother. She was as I'd never seen her, braceleted wrists crossed above her head, swaying to the reggae—I think it was the sound track to *The Harder They Come*. Super Goat Man was more dressed up than he'd been in his room upstairs. He wore a felt brocade vest and striped pants. He danced in tiny little steps, as though losing and regaining his balance, his arms loose at his sides, fingers snapping. Mostly he moved his head to the beat, shaking it back and forth as if saying no-no-no, no-no-no. He shook his head at my mother's dancing, as if he couldn't approve of the way she was moving but couldn't quit paying attention, either.

My father? He was seated on the rolled-up rug, his back against the mantelpiece, elbows on his knees, dangling with forefinger and thumb a nearly empty paper cup of red wine. Like me, he was watching my mom and Super Goat Man. It didn't look as if it bothered him at all.

My junior year at Corcoran College, in Corcoran, New Hampshire, Super   45
Goat Man was brought in to fill the Walt Whitman Chair in the Humanities. This was 1981, the dawn of Reagan. The chair was required to teach one course; Super Goat Man's was listed in the catalog as "Dissidence and Desire: Marginal Heroics in American Life, 1955–1975." The reading list included Franz Fanon, Roland Barthes, and Timothy Leary. It was typical of Corcoran that it would choose that particular moment to recuperate a figure associated with sixties protest, to enshrine what had once been at the vigorous center of the culture in the harmless pantheon of academia. It was Super Goat Man's first teaching job since the fifties. The commune on our street had shut down at some point in my high-school years, and I don't know where Super Goat Man had been in the intervening time. I certainly hadn't thought about him since departing for college.

He'd gained a little weight, but was otherwise unchanged. I first spotted him moving across the Commons lawn on a September afternoon, the scent of fallen and fermenting crab apples on the breeze. It was one of those rare, sweet days on either side of the long New Hampshire winter, when the school year was either falsely fresh before its plunge into bleak December or exhausted and ready to give way to summer. Super Goat Man wore a forest-green corduroy suit and a wide salmon tie, but his feet were still bare. A couple of Corcoran girls trailed alongside him. He had a book open as he walked—perhaps he was reading them a poem.

The college had assigned Super Goat Man a dormitory apartment—a suite of rooms built into Sweeney House, one of the student residences. That is to say, he lived on the edge of the vast Commons lawn, and we students felt his watchful presence much as I had on our street in Brooklyn. I didn't take Super Goat Man's class, which was full of freshmen and those renegade history and rhetoric majors who'd been seduced by French strains of philosophy and literary theory. I fancied myself a classics scholar then—though I'd soon divert into a major in history—and wasn't curious about contemporary political theory; nor did I believe Super Goat Man to be a superior teacher. I wasn't certain that he had nothing to offer the Corcoran students, but whatever he did have to offer it wasn't summed up by the title of his class.

I did, however, participate in one of the late-night salons in the living room of Sweeney House. Super Goat Man had begun appearing there casually, showing up after a few students had occupied the couches and lit a fire or opened a bottle of red wine. Increasingly, his presence was relied upon; soon he was the center of an unnamed tradition. Though Corcoran College was then in the midst of a wave of glamorous eighties-style binge parties, and cocaine had begun to infiltrate our sanctum in the New Hampshire woods, the Sweeney House salons were a return to an earlier temperature of college socializing. Bearded art students who disdained dancing in favor of bull sessions, Woolfian-Plathian girls in long vintage dresses, and lonely gay virgins of both genders—these were the types who found their way to Sweeney to sit at Super Goat Man's feet. There were also, from what I observed, a handful of quiet superhero-comic-book fans who revered Super Goat Man in that capacity and were covertly basking in his aura, ashamed to ask the sorts of questions I'd peppered him with in his room in the communal house so long ago.

The evening I sat in, Super Goat Man had dragged his phonograph out from his apartment and set it up in the living room so that he could play Lenny Bruce records for his acolytes. He spoke intermittently, his voice unhurried and reflective, explaining the context of the famous comedian's arrests and courtroom battles before dropping the needle on a given track. After a while, conversation drifted to other subjects. Cross talk arose, though whenever Super Goat Man began to speak, in his undemonstrative way, all fell deferentially silent. Then Super Goat Man went into his apartment and brought out an Ornette Coleman LP.

"You know a bit about jazz, don't you, Everett?" It was the first time he'd 50 addressed me directly. I hadn't known he'd recognized me.

"A thing or two, I guess."

"Everett's father was the one who turned me on to Rahsaan Roland Kirk," Super Goat Man told a teenager I recognized, a bespectacled sophomore who'd impressively talked his way into a classics seminar that was meant for upperclassmen. "I always thought that stuff was too gimmicky, but I'd never really listened."

I tried to imagine when Super Goat Man and my dad had spent so much time together. It was almost impossible to picture, but Super Goat Man didn't have any reason to be lying about it. It was one of the first times I was forced to consider the possibility that my parents had social lives—that they had lives.

"Does your father write about jazz?" the sophomore asked me, wide-eyed. I suppose he'd misunderstood Super Goat Man's remark. There were plenty of famous—or at least interesting—fathers at Corcoran College, but mine wasn't one of them.

"My father works for New York State," I said. "Department of Housing and Urban Development. Well, he just lost his job, in fact." 55

"He's a good five-card-stud player, too," said Super Goat Man. "Cleaned me out a few times, I don't mind saying."

"Oh, yeah, my dad's a real supervillain," I said with the heaviest sarcasm I could muster. I was embarrassed to think of my father sucking up to Super Goat Man, as he surely had during their long evenings together, whoever had taken the bulk of the chips.

Then the squeaky jazz began playing, and Super Goat Man, though seated in one of the dormitory's ratty armchairs, closed his eyes and began shaking his head as if transported back to the commune's dance floor, or perhaps to some even earlier time. I studied his face. The tufts around his ears and throat were graying. I puzzled over his actual age. Had Super Goat Man once spent decades frozen in a block of ice, like Captain America? If Ralph Gersten had been a college teacher in the fifties, he was probably older than my dad.

Eight months later, the campus was green again. The term was almost finished, all of us nearly freed to summer, when it happened: the incident at the Campanile. A Saturday, late in a balmy night of revels, the Commons lawn full of small groups crossing from dorm to dorm, cruising the parties that flared like bonfires in the landscape of the campus. Many of us still owed papers, others would have to sit in a final class the following Monday, but the mood was one of expulsive release from our labors. It was nearly three in the morning when Rudy Krugerrand and Seth Brummell, two of the wealthiest and most widely reviled frat boys at Corcoran, scaled the Campanile and began bellowing.

I was among those awake and near enough by to be drawn by the commotion into the small crowd at the dark base of the Campanile tower. When I first gazed up at Rudy and Seth, I was confused by what I saw: were there four figures spotlit against the clock beneath the bells? And where were the campus authorities? It was as though this night had been officially ceded to some bacchanalian imperative. 60

That spring, a sculpture student had, as his thesis project, decorated the Commons with oversized office supplies—a stapler in the dimensions of a limousine, a log painted as a No. 2 pencil, and a pile of facsimile paper clips, each the height of a human being, fashioned out of plastic piping and silver paint. I suppose the work was derivative of Claes Oldenburg, but the result made an impressive spectacle. It was two of the paper-clip sculptures that Rudy Krugerrand and Seth Brummell had managed to attach to their belts like mannequin dance partners and drag with them out onto the ledge of the Campanile clock, where they stood now, six stories from the ground. Their faces uplit in the floodlights, Rudy and Seth were almost like players in the climax of some gothic silent-film drama, but they didn't have the poise or imagination to know it. They were only college pranksters, reeling drunk, Seth with a three-quarters-empty bottle of Jack Daniel's still in his hand, and at first it was hard to make out what they were shouting. We on the ground predictably shouted "Jump!" back at them, knowing that they loved themselves too dearly ever to consider it.

Then Rudy Krugerrand's slurred voice rose above the din—or perhaps it was only that I picked it out of the din for the first time. "Calling Super Goat Man! Calling Super Goat Man!" He shouted this until his voice broke hoarse. "This looks like a job for Super Goat Man! Come out, come out, wherever you are!"

"What's going on?" I asked a student beside me.

He shrugged. "I guess they're calling out Super Goat Man. They want to see if he can get them down from the ledge."

"What do you mean?" 65

"They want to see him use his powers."

From the clock tower, Seth Brummell screamed now, in a girlish falsetto, "Oh, Super Goat Man, where are you?"

A stirring had begun in the crowd, which had grown to a hundred or more. A murmuring. Under the guise of concern for Rudy and Seth, but certainly with a shiver of voyeuristic anticipation, some had begun to speak of going to the Sweeney House apartment to see if Super Goat Man could be found. There was a hint of outrage: Why wasn't he here already? What kind of Super Goat Man was he, anyway?

Now a group of fifteen or twenty broke out and streamed down the hill toward Sweeney House. Others trailed after them, myself included. I hid in the crowd, feeling like an observer, though I suppose I was as complicit as anyone. Were we only curious, or part of a mob? It seemed, anyway, that we were under the direction of Rudy and Seth.

"That's right," mocked Rudy. "Only Super Goat Man can save us now!" 70

Those who'd led the charge hammered on Super Goat Man's apartment door for a good few minutes before getting a result. Bold enough to have woken him, they inched backward at the sight of him on his threshold, dressed only in a flowery silk kimono, blinking groggily at the faces arrayed on the hill. Then someone stepped forward, took his arm, and pointed him toward the Campanile. Any conversation was drowned by the sound of sirens, as the campus police belatedly pulled up to the tower. Super Goat Man shook his head sorrowfully, but he began the trek up the hill toward the Campanile. We all fell in around and behind him, emboldened at marching to the beat of a superhero's step, feeling the pulse of the script that it now appeared would be played out, and ignoring the fact that it had been written by Rudy and Seth and Jack Daniel's. Super Goat Man's kimono fluttered slightly, not quite a cape. He tightened the sash, then strode, rubbing at his eyes with balled fists.

This success seemed only to enrage Rudy and Seth, who writhed and scorned from atop their perch. "Baaahh, baaahh, Super Goat Man!" they roared. "What's the matter with your goaty senses? Smoke too much dope tonight? Fuck you, Super Goat Man!" Seth lifted his giant paper clip above his head and shook it like a fake strongman's prop barbell.

The campus police had begun to herd the students away from the base of the tower, but our arriving throng pushed the opposite way. In the confusion, the young policemen seemed utterly helpless, and fell back. Straining on tiptoe to see over the heads of the crowd, I followed the progress of the lime-green kimono as Super Goat Man was thrust to the fore, not necessarily by his own efforts. Above, Seth was strumming air-guitar chords on his paper clip, then waggling it over our heads like an enormous phallus.

"Bite my crank, Super Goat Man!"

The crowd gasped as Super Goat Man shed his garb—for mobility, I suppose— 75 and started shimmying, almost scampering, up the face of the tower. His pelt was glossy in the moonlight, but nobody could have mistaken the wide streak of white above his dusky buttocks for sheen. Super Goat Man was aging. He scurried through the leaf-blobby shade that a tree branch cast against the side of the tower, then back into the light. Whether it was the pressure of expectation on a still sleepy mind or possibly a genuine call to heroics, a hope that he could do some good here, Super Goat Man had taken the bait. His limbs worked miraculously as he ascended the tower, yet one could only dread what would happen if he reached the idiot boys at the top, who were growing more agitated and furious with every inch he achieved. Rudy had lifted his own paper clip, to match Seth, and now he swung it out over us.

The plummet silenced us. It was over before we could swallow our words and form a cry to replace them. Six stories is no distance at all. Rudy's paper clip had overbalanced him. Super Goat Man had braced three limbs, and reached out with a fourth—some of us saw, others only imagined afterward— but he didn't come away with Rudy. Super Goat Man caught the paper clip in mid-flight with the prehensile toes of his left foot, and the sculpture was jerked free from Rudy as he fell. That's how firm was Super Goat Man's hold on the tower's third story: it was left for later to speculate whether he might have been able to halt a human body's fall. Rudy came to earth, shattering at the feet of the policemen there at the tower's base. Now the nude furry figure could only undertake a sober, methodical descent, paper clip tucked beneath one arm. At the clockface, Seth Brummell was mute, clinging to a post, waiting for the security men who would soon unlock the small door in the tower behind him and angrily yank him to safety.

Rudy Krugerrand survived his fall. It cost him the use of his legs, cost him all feeling below some point at his middle. Only a junior, he rather courageously reappeared in a motorized wheelchair the following September, resumed his studies, resumed drinking, too, though his temperament had mellowed. He'd be seen at parties dozing in the corner after the dance floor had filled—it took very little beer to knock his dwindled body out. If Rudy had died, or never returned, the incident likely would have been avidly discussed, etched into campus legend. Instead it was covered in a clumsy hush. The coexistence in the same small community of Rudy and Super Goat Man—who'd been offered a seat in the social sciences, and accepted—created a kind of odd, insoluble puzzle: Had the hero failed the crisis? Caused it, by some innate provocation? Or was the bogus crisis unworthy, and the outcome its own reward? Who'd shamed whom?

I contemplated this koan, or didn't, for just another year. My graduate studies took me to the University of California, Irvine, three thousand grateful miles from Corcoran. I didn't see Super Goat Man or think of him again for more than a decade.

The sweetest student I ever had was an Italian girl named Angela Verucci. Tall, bronze-skinned, with a quizzical, slightly humorless cast, dressed no matter the weather in neat pants suits or skirts with stockings, she wore heavy tortoiseshell eyeglasses and kept her blond hair knit in a tight, almost Japanese bun. She had an aura of seriousness and a Mediterranean lustre that outshone to near invisibility the blandly corn-fed and T-shirted students in whose midst she had materialized. Angela Verucci was not so much a girl, really: twenty-four years old, she'd studied at Oxford before winning the Reeves Fellowship that brought her to America. She spoke immaculate English, and though her accreditation was a mess, she was nearly as accomplished a medievalist as I was the day she appeared in my class. This was at Oregon State University, in Corvallis, where I'd been given a two-year postdoc after my six years at Irvine. Oregon State was the third stop in Angela Verucci's American tour—she'd spent a year at Columbia and, as it happened, a term at Corcoran.

What does a single thirty-year-old history professor do with the sweetest 80 student he's ever had? He waits until the end of the semester, then he asks her out. We were married two years later.

I was at Rutgers by then, on a second postdoc, and hungry for a tenure-track position. My job interviews weren't exactly unsuccessful: I was never summarily dismissed. Instead I was always called back for second and third visits, always asked to teach a sample class. Afterward, polite notes flew back and forth, candidate and committee reassuring each other of how fine the experience had been, how glad we both were to have met. Only I never got a job.

By the time I got the invitation to interview for a position at Corcoran, the New England pastures of my alma mater didn't look like such a poor fate. It was the week of Halloween, the weather glorious, so at the very least the day of the interview would be a nice jaunt. We left early, to roam a few New Hampshire back roads, then ate a picnic lunch beside Corcoran Pond before I checked in for an afternoon of meetings.

Corcoran looked implacable, though I knew it was changed. The school had been through financial shake-ups and tenure scandals that had, in turn, purged most of the administrators and faculty I'd known. But the grounds, the crab-apple trees and white clapboard, were as eternal as a country-store calendar. While Angela took a memory tour, heading for her old dorm, I showed up for my scheduled tribunal. There I was debriefed by peers, a couple of them younger than myself. The room was full of the usual tensions: some of these people had an investment in my candidacy, some had bets on other tables. No one was in the least sentimental about my status as an alumnus—that was reserved, I supposed, for the dinner that night, arranged in my honor at the President's House. After a final round of polite handclasps, I was ferried to the president's office for a private meeting. I figured this was a good sign.

The president asked how I felt about the interview; we made this and other small talk. She asked about my years at Corcoran, which I painted in rosy tones. Then she said, "Did you know Super Goat Man when you were a student here?"

"Sure," I said. "I mean, I never took a class with him." 85

"He surprised me by asking to join us at the dinner tonight—he doesn't usually bother with faculty socializing anymore."

"He's still here?" I was amazed that Super Goat Man, of all people, had threaded his way through so many personnel shake-ups.

"Yes, though he's reduced to a kind of honorary presence. He doesn't actually teach now. I don't know if he'd be capable of it. But he's beloved. The students joke that he can be spotted strolling across Commons lawn twice a semester. And that if you want to get any time with him you can join him on the stroll."

"He recognized my name?"

"He seemed to, yes. You should prepare yourself. He's quite infirm." 90

"How—how old is he?"

"Measured in years, I don't know. But there's been an accelerated aging process. You'll see."

Perhaps superheroism was a sort of toxin, like a steroid, one with a punitive cost to the body. I mused on this as I crossed the Commons and headed through the parking lot and downhill to find the bench beside Corcoran Creek, a favorite spot, where Angela had said she'd wait. I saw my wife before she saw me, her feet tucked up on the slats, abandoned shoes beneath, her body curled around a big hardback biography of Rousseau. In the distance, dying October light drew long saddle-shaped curves on the White Mountains of New Hampshire. Suddenly, I could picture us here for a long time, and picture it happily.

"How did it go?" she asked when she noticed me.

"Par: two friends, two enemies, one sleeper." 95

"And the president?"

"Nice, but she wasn't giving anything away."

She closed the book. "You seem distant," she said. "Memories?"

"Yes." In fact, I was thinking about Super Goat Man. I'd never before considered the sacrifice he'd made by enunciating his political views so long ago. Fruitlessly, it seemed to me. What had he gained in exchange for his iconic, trapped-in-amber status? Had Super Goat Man really accomplished much outside the parameters of his comics? However unglamorous the chores, didn't kittens need rescuing from trees? Didn't Vest Man require periodic defeating? Why jettison Ralph Gersten if in the end all you attained was the life of a campus mascot?

I wanted to convey some of this to Angela, but didn't know where to begin. 100 "When you were here," I said, "did you know Super Goat Man?"

I saw her stiffen. "Of course. Everybody knew him," she said.

"He's still here." I watched her as I spoke. Her gaze dipped to the ground.

"You saw him?"

"No, but we will at dinner tonight."

"How . . . unexpected." Now Angela was the one in fugue. 105

"Did you study with him?"

"He rarely taught. I attended a few talks."

"I thought you didn't like that stuff."

She shrugged. "I was curious."

I waited to understand. Crickets had begun a chorus in the grass. Soon we'd 110 need to visit our off-campus bed-and-breakfast, to change into fresh clothes for the dinner party. Ordinarily such gatherings were clumsy at best, with grudges incompletely smothered under the surface of the talk, among tenured faculty who knew one another far too well. Something in me now curdled at the prospect of this one. In fact, I'd begun to dread it.

"Everett." There was something Angela wanted to tell me.

I made a preemptive guess. "Did you have some sort of thing with Super Goat Man?" This was how she and I blundered through each other's past liaisons—we'd never been systematic.

"Just an—affair. Nothing."

"What's nothing?"

She shrugged, and flipped her fingers as though dispelling a small fog. "We 115 fooled around a few times. It was stupid."

I felt the poison of bitterness leach into my bloodstream. "I don't know why, but I find that totally disgusting."

"Oh, Everett." Angela raised her arms, moved to assuage me, knowing as she did my visceral possessiveness, the bolt of jealousy that shot through me when contemplating her real past, anytime it arose. Of course she couldn't understand my special history with Super Goat Man. How could she if I didn't? I'd never even mentioned him.

"I was a silly girl." She spoke gently. "And I didn't know you yet."

Unsatisfied, I wished her to declare that the encounter had been abusive, an ethical violation. Not that I had any ground to stand on. Anyway, she was Italian in this, as in all things. It was just an affair.

"Do you want to skip the dinner?" 120

She scowled. "That's unnecessary. He wouldn't even remember. And I don't care. It's really nothing, my darling. My love."

At the president's house, Super Goat Man was the last to arrive, so I was allowed briefly to fantasize that I'd been spared. The sight, when he did come in, was startling. He'd not only aged but shrunk—I doubted if he was even five feet tall. He was, as ever, barefoot, and he wore white muslin pajamas with purple piping. The knees of the pajama bottoms were smudged with mud. As he entered the room, creeping in amid us as we stood with our cocktail glasses, I quickly saw the reason for the smudges: as Super Goat Man's rickety steps faltered, he dropped briefly to all fours. There, on the ground, he shook himself, like a wet dog. Then he rose again, on palsied limbs.

No one took notice of this. The guests, the other faculty, were inured, polite. In this halting manner, Super Goat Man made his way past us to the dining room. Apparently he wasn't capable of mingling, or even necessarily of speech. He took a seat at the long table, his bunched face, his squinting eyes and wrinkled horns, nearly at the level of his place setting. We began drifting in behind him, almost guiltily. The president's husband showed us to our places, which had been carefully designated, though an accommodation was evidently being made for Super Goat Man, who'd plopped down where he liked and wasn't to be budged. I was at the right hand of the president, and the left of the chair of the hiring committee. Another good sign. Angela sat across from me, Super Goat Man many places away, at the other end of the table.

I actually managed to forget him for the duration of the meal. He was, so far as I could tell, silent at his feed, and the women on either side of him turned to their other partners or conversed across the width of the table. Toward the end, we were served Cognac and dessert, and the president's husband passed around cigars, which he bragged were Cuban. Some of the women fled their chairs to avoid the smoke; other guests rose and mingled in the corners of the room. It was in this interval of disarrangement that Super Goat Man pushed himself off his chair and made his way to the seat at my left, which the president had vacated. He had to collapse to his knees only once on the way, and he offered no evidence of sacrificed dignity as he rose from the floor.

Angela remained in her seat. Unlike any of the American women, she'd 125 accepted a cigar, and now leaned it into the flame of a lighter proffered by an older professor she'd been entertaining throughout the meal. Her eyes found mine as Super Goat Man approached. Her expression was curious, and not unsympathetic.

Super Goat Man prodded my arm with a finger. I turned and considered him. Black pupils gleamed behind a hedge of eyebrows. His resplendent tufts had thinned and spread—the hair of his face had been redistributed, to form a merciful gauze across his withered features.

"I . . . knew . . . your . . . father." His voice was mossy, sepulchral.

"Yes," I said simply, keeping my voice low. No one was paying any attention to us, yet, apart from Angela.

"You . . . remember . . . ?"

"Of course." 130

"We . . . love . . . jazz . . ."

I wondered whether he meant my father or, somehow, me. I had in fact over the years come around to my father's love of jazz, though my preference was not so much Ornette Coleman and Rahsaan Roland Kirk as Duke Ellington and Fletcher Henderson.

". . . poker . . ."

"He cleaned you out," I reminded him.

"Yezz . . . good times . . . beautiful women . . ." He struggled, swallowed 135 hard, blinked. "All this controversy . . . not worth it . . ."

"My father was never involved in any controversy," I heard myself say, though I knew Super Goat Man was speaking only of himself, his lost career.

"No . . . absolutely true . . . knew how to live . . ."

Angela had leaned back, pursing her lips to savor the cigar. I might have noticed that the room's gabble of conversation had dampened somewhat— might have noticed sooner, I mean.

"So . . . many . . . hangovers . . ."

"But you and I have something in common besides my father," I told Super 140 Goat Man.

"Yezz . . . yezz . . . ?"

"Of course we do," I began, and though I now understood that we had the attention of the entire room, that the novelty of Super Goat Man's reminiscences had drawn every ear, I found myself unable to quit before I finished the thought. Further, having gained their attention, I allowed my voice to rise to a garrulous, plummy tone, as if I were starring in dinner theater. Before the line was half out of my mouth, I knew that the words, by airing the sort of laundry so desperately repressed in a community as precious as Corcoran, damned my candidacy. But that was a prize I no longer sought. Broader repercussions I could only guess at. My wife's eyes were on me now, her cigar's blunt tip flaring. I'd answer to her later, if she gave me the chance.

It was the worst thing I could think to say. The impulse had formed in the grip of sexual jealousy, of course. But before it crossed my lips I knew that my loathing had its origins in an even deeper place, in the mind of a child wondering at his father's own susceptibility to the notion of a hero.

What I said was this: "I once saw you rescue a paper clip."

FOR ANALYSIS

1. Why is the connection between Everett's father and Super Goat Man so important? How does it relate to the former relationship between Super Goat Man and Angela?

2. What does it mean to Everett when Super Goat Man catches only the giant paper clip? Does the author relate the event in a manner that is sympathetic to the **narrator**? Are readers supposed to agree with Everett's feelings about the incident and about Super Goat Man?

MAKING CONNECTIONS

1. Compare Ellison's and Lethem's stories in terms of their realism. How does each use fantasy? Is one story more fantastic than the other and one more realistic? How does each writer use the improbable/impossible to tell his story?

2. Compare Everetts: How does each conform and/or rebel? How does each think about the status quo? What might Lethem's Everett think of Ellison's?

3. What do these stories' treatments of their heroes have to say about the world in which they are set—or written? Are these worlds in which heroism is still possible, no longer possible, or very difficult to achieve or recognize?

WRITING TOPICS

1. Write your own serious **parody** of a genre story—it can be a superhero story, a Western, a war story, or a sports story. Try to incorporate turns on your chosen genre similar to some Lethem makes on his. Then reflect on your parody: What does it say about the conventions of the genre, such as heroism, morality, or fairness?

2. Super Goat Man is very much the focus of another's gaze in this story—he is seen and described by someone else. Turn one scene of the story around and write it from his **point of view**. What changes?

POETRY

JOHN DONNE   (1572-1631)

HOLY SONNETS: "IF POISONOUS MINERALS, AND IF THAT TREE"   1609

If poisonous minerals, and if that tree
Whose fruit threw death on else immortal us,
If lecherous goats, if serpents envious
Cannot be damn'd, alas, why should I be?
Why should intent or reason, born in me,
Make sins, else equal, in me more heinous?
And mercy being easy, and glorious
To God, in his stern wrath why threatens he?
But who am I, that dare dispute with thee,
O God? Oh, of thine only worthy blood   10
And my tears, make a heavenly Lethean flood,
And drown in it my sins' black memory.
That thou remember them, some claim as debt;
I think it mercy, if thou wilt forget.

FOR ANALYSIS

1. What is a "Lethean flood"? What does the speaker want it to wash away?

2. Does this poem express one **mood**, or does it shift between moods? If it shifts, to what effect does it do so, and what it is it trying to express with this shift?

WRITING TOPIC

The ideas of damnation and mercy have motivated an endless number of poems. What makes this one stand out? What makes it seem so personal?

RICHARD CRASHAW   (1613–1649)

BUT MEN LOVED DARKNESS
RATHER THAN LIGHT   1646

The world's light shines, shine as it will,
The world will love its darkness still.
I doubt though when the world's in hell,
It will not love its darkness half so well.

FOR ANALYSIS

1. Would you characterize this poem as complicated or simple? Think in terms of
rhyme, **rhythm**, **diction**, and **imagery**. How does the complexity—or simplicity—of
its form relate to its subject and meaning?

2. What is the biblical **allusion** that Crashaw makes here? Use a search engine to find
it. Does knowing the lines to which the poem refers help you to better understand it?

WRITING TOPIC

While Crashaw was writing out of a specifically religious worldview, it's not hard to
imagine a way in which this poem could be read more broadly if the idea of hell is not
taken literally. To what other situations or phenomena or ideas could this poem apply?

PHILLIS WHEATLEY   (1753–1784)

ON BEING BROUGHT FROM
AFRICA TO AMERICA   1773

'Twas mercy brought me from my pagan land,
Taught my benighted soul to understand
That there's a God, that there's a Savior too:
Once I redemption neither sought nor knew.
Some view our sable race with scornful eye,
"Their color is a diabolic die."   dye
Remember, Christians, Negros, black as Cain,
May be refined, and join th' angelic train.

FOR ANALYSIS

1. Wheatley was brought from Senegal or Gambia to the United States and sold as a
slave to the Wheatley family in Boston when she was seven or eight years old. What is
your response to the poem's first three lines? Why?

2. Paraphrase "Negros, black as Cain, / May be refined, and join th' angelic train."

3. What historical conditions would perhaps account for the fame of the poet and the extraordinary contemporary wonder at her achievements?

4. Can you imagine an African American poet writing a similar poem in the twenty-first century? Explain.

WRITING TOPIC

First write a review of this poem based on your perception of eighteenth-century society in Massachusetts; then write a twenty-first-century review.

WILLIAM WORDSWORTH   (1770–1850)

THE WORLD IS
TOO MUCH WITH US   1807

The world is too much with us; late and soon,
Getting and spending, we lay waste our powers;
Little we see in Nature that is ours;
We have given our hearts away, a sordid boon!
This Sea that bares her bosom to the moon,
The winds that will be howling at all hours,
And are up-gathered now like sleeping flowers,
For this, for everything, we are out of tune;
It moves us not.—Great God! I'd rather be
A Pagan suckled in a creed outworn;   10
So might I, standing on this pleasant lea,
Have glimpses that would make me less forlorn;
Have sight of Proteus rising from the sea;
Or hear old Triton blow his wreathèd horn.[1]

FOR ANALYSIS

1. What does "world" mean in line 1?

2. What does Wordsworth complain of in the first four lines?

3. In lines 4–8 Wordsworth tells us what we have lost; in the concluding lines he suggests a remedy. What is that remedy? What do Proteus and Triton **symbolize**?

WRITING TOPIC

In what ways does Wordsworth's use of **images** both define what we have lost and suggest a remedy for this loss?

[1] Proteus and Triton are both figures from Greek mythology. Proteus had the power to assume different forms; Triton was often represented blowing on a conch shell.

ALFRED, LORD TENNYSON (1809–1892)

ULYSSES[1] 1833

It little profits that an idle king,
By this still hearth, among these barren crags,
Matched with an agéd wife, I mete and dole
Unequal laws unto a savage race,
That hoard, and sleep, and feed, and know not me.

    I cannot rest from travel; I will drink
Life to the lees. All times I have enjoyed
Greatly, have suffered greatly, both with those
That loved me, and alone; on shore, and when
Through scudding drifts the rainy Hyades[2]   10
Vexed the dim sea. I am become a name;
For always roaming with a hungry heart
Much have I seen and known—cities of men
And manners, climates, councils, governments,
Myself not least, but honored of them all—
And drunk delight of battle with my peers,
Far on the ringing plains of windy Troy.
I am a part of all that I have met;
Yet all experience is an arch wherethrough
Gleams that untraveled world whose margin fades   20
Forever and forever when I move.
How dull it is to pause, to make an end,
To rust unburnished, not to shine in use!
As though to breathe were life. Life piled on life
Were all too little, and of one to me
Little remains; but every hour is saved
From that eternal silence, something more,
A bringer of new things; and vile it were
For some three suns to store and hoard myself,
And this gray spirit yearning in desire   30
To follow knowledge like a sinking star,
Beyond the utmost bound of human thought.

    This is my son, mine own Telemachus,
To whom I leave the scepter and the isle—

---

[1] Ulysses, according to Greek legend, was the king of Ithaca and a hero of the Trojan War. Tennyson represents him as eager to resume the life of travel and adventure.

[2] A group of stars in the constellation Taurus. According to Greek mythology, the rising of these stars with the sun foretold rain.

Well-loved of me, discerning to fulfill
This labor, by slow prudence to make mild
A rugged people, and through soft degrees
Subdue them to the useful and the good.
Most blameless is he, centered in the sphere
Of common duties, decent not to fail   40
In offices of tenderness, and pay
Meet° adoration to my household gods,   proper
When I am gone. He works his work, I mine.

   There lies the port; the vessel puffs her sail;
There gloom the dark, broad seas. My mariners,
Souls that have toiled, and wrought, and thought with me—
That ever with a frolic welcome took
The thunder and the sunshine, and opposed
Free hearts, free foreheads—you and I are old;
Old age hath yet his honor and his toil.   50
Death closes all; but something ere the end,
Some work of noble note, may yet be done,
Not unbecoming men that strove with Gods.
The lights begin to twinkle from the rocks;
The long day wanes; the slow moon climbs; the deep
Moans round with many voices. Come, my friends,
'Tis not too late to seek a newer world.
Push off, and sitting well in order smite
The sounding furrows; for my purpose holds
To sail beyond the sunset, and the baths   60
Of all the western stars, until I die.
It may be that the gulfs will wash us down;
It may be we shall touch the Happy Isles,[3]
And see the great Achilles, whom we knew.
Though much is taken, much abides; and though
We are not now that strength which in old days
Moved earth and heaven, that which we are, we are—
One equal temper of heroic hearts,
Made weak by time and fate, but strong in will
To strive, to seek, to find, and not to yield.   70

For Analysis

1. Is Ulysses' desire to abdicate his duties as king irresponsible?

2. Contrast Ulysses with his son Telemachus (see ll. 33–43). Is Telemachus admirable?

3. At the conclusion of the poem, Ulysses is determined not to yield. Yield to what?

---

[3] The Islands of the Blessed (also Elysium), thought to be in the far western oceans, where those favored by the gods, such as Achilles, enjoyed life after death.

EMILY DICKINSON (1830–1886)

MUCH MADNESS IS
DIVINEST SENSE— 1862

Much Madness is divinest Sense—
To a discerning Eye—
Much Sense—the starkest Madness—
'Tis the Majority
In this, as All, prevail—
Assent—and you are sane—
Demur—you're straightway dangerous—
And handled with a Chain—

SHE ROSE TO HIS
REQUIREMENT CA. 1863

She rose to His Requirement—dropt
The Playthings of Her Life
To take the honorable Work
Of Woman, and of Wife—

If ought° She missed in Her new Day,   anything
Of Amplitude, or Awe—
Or first Prospective—Or the Gold
In using, wear away,

It lay unmentioned—as the Sea
Develope Pearl, and Weed,
But only to Himself—be known   10
The Fathoms they abide—

FOR ANALYSIS

1. What are the "Playthings" referred to in line 2?

2. Why does the poet refer to both "Woman" and "Wife" in line 4, since a wife is also a woman?

3. Look up the words *amplitude*, *awe*, and *prospective* in your dictionary, and consider how these words help you to understand the woman's losses.

4. What does "It" in the third **stanza** refer to?

5. Why is the sea **image** at the end of the poem appropriate? What does the contrast between "Pearl" and "Weed" suggest?

6. The last word of the poem, *abide*, has several meanings. Which of them are relevant to the meaning of the poem?

MAKING CONNECTIONS

Compare and contrast the attitudes toward marriage in this poem with those in Marilyn Hacker's "Conte" (p. 212).

WRITING TOPIC

Write an essay describing a woman you know who gave up an important part of herself to be a wife.

WILLIAM BUTLER YEATS   (1865–1939)

EASTER 1916[1]   1916

I have met them at close of day
Coming with vivid faces
From counter or desk among grey
Eighteenth-century houses.
I have passed with a nod of the head
Or polite meaningless words,
Or have lingered awhile and said
Polite meaningless words,
And thought before I had done
Of a mocking tale or a gibe   10
To please a companion
Around the fire at the club,
Being certain that they and I
But lived where motley is worn:
All changed, changed utterly:
A terrible beauty is born.

That woman's days were spent
In ignorant good-will,
Her nights in argument
Until her voice grew shrill.   20
What voice more sweet than hers
When, young and beautiful,

[1] On Easter Monday in 1916, a group of Irish nationalists seized key points in Ireland, including the Dublin Post Office, from which they proclaimed an independent Irish Republic. At first, most of the Irish were indifferent to the nationalists' futile yet heroic gesture, but as the rebellion was crushed and the leaders executed, they became heroes in the eyes of their fellow citizens. Some of those leaders are alluded to in the second stanza and are named in lines 75 and 76.

She rode to harriers?[2]
This man had kept a school
And rode our wingéd horse;[3]
This other his helper and friend
Was coming into his force;
He might have won fame in the end,
So sensitive his nature seemed,
So daring and sweet his thought.
This other man I had dreamed   30
A drunken, vainglorious lout.
He had done most bitter wrong
To some who are near my heart,
Yet I number him in the song;
He, too, has resigned his part
In the casual comedy;
He, too, has been changed in his turn,
Transformed utterly:
A terrible beauty is born.   40

Hearts with one purpose alone
Through summer and winter seem
Enchanted to a stone
To trouble the living stream.
The horse that comes from the road,
The rider, the birds that range
From cloud to tumbling cloud,
Minute by minute they change;
A shadow of cloud on the stream
Changes minute by minute;   50
A horse-hoof slides on the brim,
And a horse plashes within it;
The long-legged moor-hens dive,
And hens to moor-cocks call;
Minute by minute they live:
The stone's in the midst of all.

Too long a sacrifice
Can make a stone of the heart.
O when may it suffice?
That is Heaven's part, our part   60
To murmur name upon name,
As a mother names her child

---

[2] In the aristocratic sport of hare hunting, a "pack of harriers" refers to the hounds as well as the persons following the chase.

[3] In Greek mythology, a winged horse is associated with poetic inspiration.

When sleep at last has come
On limbs that had run wild.
What is it but nightfall?
No, no, not night but death;
Was it needless death after all?
For England may keep faith
For all that is done and said.
We know their dream; enough   70
To know they dreamed and are dead;
And what if excess of love
Bewildered them till they died?
I write it out in a verse—
MacDonagh and MacBride
And Connolly and Pearse[4]
Now and in time to be,
Wherever green is worn,
Are changed, changed utterly:
A terrible beauty is born.   80

FOR ANALYSIS

1. What is "changed utterly"? In what sense can beauty be "terrible" (ll. 15–16)?

2. Who or what does "they" in line 55 refer to? What does the "stone" in lines 43 and 56 **symbolize**? What is Yeats contrasting?

3. How does the poet answer the question he asks in line 67?

WRITING TOPIC

In the first **stanza**, the attitude of the poet toward the people he is describing is indifferent, even contemptuous. How is that attitude modified in the rest of the poem?

THE SECOND COMING[1]   1921

Turning and turning in the widening gyre°   spiral
The falcon cannot hear the falconer;
Things fall apart; the center cannot hold;
Mere anarchy is loosed upon the world,

Easter 1916
    [4] Thomas MacDonagh, John MacBride, James Connolly, and Patrick Pearse, shot by a firing squad at Kilmainham Jail in Dublin following the Easter Rising.

The Second Coming
    [1] The New Testament (Matthew 24:29–44) describes the Second Coming of Christ as following a period of tribulation to judge the living and the dead and to inaugurate the millennium.

The blood-dimmed tide is loosed, and everywhere
The ceremony of innocence is drowned;
The best lack all conviction, while the worst
Are full of passionate intensity.

Surely some revelation is at hand;
Surely the Second Coming is at hand;   10
The Second Coming! Hardly are those words out
When a vast image out of *Spiritus Mundi*[2]
Troubles my sight: somewhere in sands of the desert
A shape with lion body and the head of a man,
A gaze blank and pitiless as the sun,
Is moving its slow thighs, while all about it
Reel shadows of the indignant desert birds.
The darkness drops again; but now I know
That twenty centuries of stony sleep
Were vexed to nightmare by a rocking cradle,   20
And what rough beast, its hour come round at last,
Slouches towards Bethlehem to be born?

CARL SANDBURG   (1878–1967)

I AM THE PEOPLE, THE MOB   1916

I am the people—the mob—the crowd—the mass.
Do you know that all the great work of the world is done through me?
I am the workingman, the inventor, the maker of the world's food and clothes.
I am the audience that witnesses history. The Napoleons come from me
        and the Lincolns. They die. And then I send forth more Napoleons
        and Lincolns.
I am the seed ground. I am a prairie that will stand for much plowing.
        Terrible storms pass over me. I forget. The best of me is sucked
        out and wasted. I forget. Everything but Death comes to me and
        makes me work and give up what I have. And I forget.   10
Sometimes I growl, shake myself and spatter a few red drops for history to
        remember. Then—I forget.
When I, the People, learn to remember, when I, the People, use the lessons
        of yesterday and no longer forget who robbed me last year, who
        played me for a fool—then there will be no speaker in all the

The Second Coming
    [2] The Soul or Spirit of the Universe, which Yeats believed constituted a fund of racial images and
memories.

world say the name: "The People," with any fleck of a sneer in
   his voice or any far-off smile of derision.
The mob—the crowd—the mass—will arrive then.

FOR ANALYSIS

1. Describe the speaker in this poem. Who is speaking? What is the effect of having
this kind of speaker?

2. How does the poem change in the last of the lines that begins "I am"?

WRITING TOPIC

What political beliefs does this poem implicitly champion? Try to construct a **concrete**
political platform out of the more **abstract** ideas expressed here.

WALLACE STEVENS   (1879–1955)

SUNDAY MORNING   1923

I

Complacencies of the peignoir, and late
Coffee and oranges in a sunny chair,
And the green freedom of a cockatoo
Upon a rug mingle to dissipate
The holy hush of ancient sacrifice.
She dreams a little, and she feels the dark
Encroachment of that old catastrophe,
As a calm darkens among water-lights.
The pungent oranges and bright, green wings
Seem things in some procession of the dead,   10
Winding across wide water, without sound.
The day is like wide water, without sound,
Stilled for the passing of her dreaming feet
Over the seas, to silent Palestine,
Dominion of the blood and sepulchre.

II

Why should she give her bounty to the dead?
What is divinity if it can come
Only in silent shadows and in dreams?
Shall she not find in comforts of the sun,

In pungent fruit and bright, green wings, or else   20
In any balm or beauty of the earth,
Things to be cherished like the thought of heaven?
Divinity must live within herself:
Passions of rain, or moods in falling snow;
Grievings in loneliness, or unsubdued
Elations when the forest blooms; gusty
Emotions on wet roads on autumn nights;
All pleasures and all pains, remembering
The bough of summer and the winter branch.
These are the measures destined for her soul.   30

III

Jove in the clouds had his inhuman birth.[1]
No mother suckled him, no sweet land gave
Large-mannered motions to his mythy mind
He moved among us, as a muttering king,
Magnificent, would move among his hinds,°   farm servants
Until our blood, commingling, virginal,
With heaven, brought such requital to desire
The very hinds discerned it, in a star.
Shall our blood fail? Or shall it come to be
The blood of paradise? And shall the earth   40
Seem all of paradise that we shall know?
The sky will be much friendlier then than now,
A part of labor and a part of pain,
And next in glory to enduring love,
Not this dividing and indifferent blue.

IV

She says, "I am content when wakened birds,
Before they fly, test the reality
Of misty fields, by their sweet questionings;
But when the birds are gone, and their warm fields
Return no more, where, then, is paradise?"   50
There is not any haunt of prophecy,
Nor any old chimera[2] of the grave,
Neither the golden underground, nor isle

---

[1] Jove is Jupiter, the principal god of the Romans, who, unlike Jesus, had an "inhuman birth."
[2] A monster with a lion's head, a goat's body, and a serpent's tail. Here an emblem for the belief in other worlds described in the following lines.

Melodious, where spirits gat them home,
Nor visionary south, nor cloudy palm
Remote on heaven's hill, that has endured
As April's green endures; or will endure
Like her remembrance of awakened birds,
Or her desire for June and evening, tipped
By the consummation of the swallow's wings.   60

V

She says, "But in contentment I still feel
The need of some imperishable bliss."
Death is the mother of beauty; hence from her,
Alone, shall come fulfilment to our dreams
And our desires. Although she strews the leaves
Of sure obliteration on our paths,
The path sick sorrow took, the many paths
Where triumph rang its brassy phrase, or love
Whispered a little out of tenderness,
She makes the willow shiver in the sun   70
For maidens who were wont to sit and gaze
Upon the grass, relinquished to their feet.
She causes boys to pile new plums and pears
On disregarded plate. The maidens taste
And stray impassioned in the littering leaves.

VI

Is there no change of death in paradise?
Does ripe fruit never fall? Or do the boughs
Hang always heavy in that perfect sky,
Unchanging, yet so like our perishing earth,
With rivers like our own that seek for seas   80
They never find, the same receding shores
That never touch with inarticulate pang?
Why set the pear upon those river-banks
Or spice the shores with odors of the plum?
Alas, that they should wear our colors there,
The silken weavings of our afternoons,
And pick the strings of our insipid lutes!
Death is the mother of beauty, mystical,
Within whose burning bosom we devise
Our earthly mothers waiting, sleeplessly.   90

VII

Supple and turbulent, a ring of men
Shall chant in orgy on a summer morn
Their boisterous devotion to the sun,
Not as a god, but as a god might be,
Naked among them, like a savage source.
Their chant shall be a chant of paradise,
Out of their blood, returning to the sky;
And in their chant shall enter, voice by voice,
The windy lake wherein their lord delights,
The trees, like serafin,[3] and echoing hills,   100
That choir among themselves long afterward.
They shall know well the heavenly fellowship
Of men that perish and of summer morn.
And whence they came and whither they shall go
The dew upon their feet shall manifest.

VIII

She hears, upon that water without sound,
A voice that cries, "The tomb in Palestine
Is not the porch of spirits lingering.
It is the grave of Jesus, where he lay."
We live in an old chaos of the sun,   110
Or old dependency of day and night,
Or island solitude, unsponsored, free,
Of that wide water, inescapable.
Deer walk upon our mountains, and the quail
Whistle about us their spontaneous cries;
Sweet berries ripen in the wilderness;
And, in the isolation of the sky,
At evening, casual flocks of pigeons make
Ambiguous undulations as they sink,
Downward to darkness, on extended wings.   120

FOR ANALYSIS

1. In the opening **stanza**, the woman's enjoyment of a late Sunday morning breakfast in a relaxed and sensuous atmosphere is troubled by thoughts of what Sunday morning *should* mean to her. What are the thoughts that disturb her complacency?

2. What does the speaker mean when he says, "Death is the mother of beauty" (ll. 63 and 88)?

---

[3] The plural form of *seraph*, an angel.

3. In stanza VI, what is the speaker's attitude toward the conventional concept of paradise?

4. Stanza VII presents the speaker's vision of an alternative religion. How does it differ from the paradise of stanza VI?

5. In what ways does the cry of the voice in the final stanza (ll. 107–9) state the woman's dilemma? How do the lines about the pigeons at the end of the poem sum up the speaker's belief?

WRITING TOPIC

This poem is, in a sense, a commentary by the speaker on the woman's desire for truth and certainty more enduring than the physical world can provide. Is the speaker sympathetic to her quest?

ANNA AKHMATOVA   (1889–1966)

FROM REQUIEM   1963

Translated by Judith Hemschemeyer

No, not under the vault of alien skies,
And not under the shelter of alien wings—
I was with my people then,
There, where my people, unfortunately, were.

Instead of a Preface

In the terrible years of the Yezhov terror,[1] I spent seventeen months in the prison lines of Leningrad. Once, someone "recognized" me. Then a woman with bluish lips standing behind me, who, of course, had never heard me called by name before, woke up from the stupor to which everyone had succumbed and whispered in my ear (everyone spoke in whispers there):
"Can you describe this?"   10
And I answered: "Yes, I can."
Then something that looked like a smile passed over what had once been her face.

Dedication

Mountains bow down to this grief,
Mighty rivers cease to flow,
But the prison gates hold firm,
And behind them are the "prisoners' burrows"

---

[1] Nikolai Yezhov was chief of secret police under Josef Stalin during the Soviet Union's Great Purge of 1936–1938.

And mortal woe.
For someone a fresh breeze blows,
For someone the sunset luxuriates—   20
We wouldn't know, we are those who everywhere
Hear only the rasp of the hateful key
And the soldiers' heavy tread.
We rose as if for an early service,
Trudged through the savaged capital
And met there, more lifeless than the dead;
The sun is lower and the Neva[2] mistier,
But hope keeps singing from afar.
The verdict . . . And her tears gush forth,
Already she is cut off from the rest,   30
As if they painfully wrenched life from her heart,
As if they brutally knocked her flat,
But she goes on . . . Staggering . . . Alone . . .
Where now are my chance friends
Of those two diabolical years?
What do they imagine is in Siberia's storms,
What appears to them dimly in the circle of the moon?
I am sending my farewell greeting to them.

Prologue

That was when the ones who smiled
Were the dead, glad to be at rest.   40
And like a useless appendage, Leningrad
Swung from its prisons.
And when, senseless from torment,
Regiments of convicts marched,
And the short songs of farewell
Were sung by locomotive whistles.
The stars of death stood above us
And innocent Russia writhed
Under bloody boots
And under the tires of the Black Marias.[3]   50

. . . .

Epilogue I

I learned how faces fall,
How terror darts from under eyelids,

---

[2] River that flows through Leningrad.
[3] Paddywagons, or cars used to transport prisoners.

How suffering traces lines
Of stiff cuneiform on cheeks,
How locks of ashen-blonde or black
Turn silver suddenly,
Smiles fade on submissive lips
And fear trembles in a dry laugh.
And I pray not for myself alone,
But for all those who stood there with me   60
In cruel cold, and in July's heat,
At that blind, red wall.

Epilogue II

Once more the day of remembrance[4] draws near.
I see, I hear, I feel you:

The one they almost had to drag at the end,
And the one who tramps her native land no more,

And the one who, tossing her beautiful head,
Said: "Coming here's like coming home."

I'd like to name them all by name,
But the list has been confiscated and is nowhere to be found.   70

I have woven a wide mantle for them
From their meager, overheard words.

I will remember them always and everywhere,
I will never forget them no matter what comes.

And if they gag my exhausted mouth
Through which a hundred million scream,

Then may the people remember me
On the eve of my remembrance day.

And if ever in this country
They decide to erect a monument to me,   80

I consent to that honor
Under these conditions—that it stand

---

[4] Literally, Remembrance Day, the first anniversary of someone's death and the day on which the Russian Orthodox Church holds a memorial service for the deceased.

Neither by the sea, where I was born:
My last tie with the sea is broken,

Nor in the tsar's garden near the cherished pine stump,[5]
Where an inconsolable shade looks for me,

But here, where I stood for three hundred hours,
And where they never unbolted the doors for me

This, lest in blissful death
I forget the rumbling of the Black Marias,   90

Forget how that detested door slammed shut
And an old woman howled like a wounded animal.

And may the melting snow stream like tears
From my motionless lids of bronze,

And a prison dove coo in the distance,
And the ships of the Neva sail calmly on.

CLAUDE MCKAY   (1890-1948)

IF WE MUST DIE   1922

If we must die, let it not be like hogs
Hunted and penned in an inglorious spot,
While round us bark the mad and hungry dogs,
Making their mock at our accursèd lot.
If we must die, O let us nobly die,
So that our precious blood may not be shed
In vain; then even the monsters we defy
Shall be constrained to honor us though dead!
O kinsmen! we must meet the common foe!
Though far outnumbered let us show us brave,   10
And for their thousand blows deal one deathblow!
What though before us lies the open grave?
Like men we'll face the murderous, cowardly pack,
Pressed to the wall, dying, but fighting back!

From Requiem
[5] Old imperial estate south of Leningrad.

LANGSTON HUGHES (1902–1967)

HARLEM 1951

What happens to a dream deferred?

  Does it dry up
  like a raisin in the sun?
  Or fester like a sore—
  And then run?
  Does it stink like rotten meat?
  Or crust and sugar over—
  like a syrupy sweet?

  Maybe it just sags
  like a heavy load.   10

  Or does it explode?

W. H. AUDEN (1907–1973)

THE UNKNOWN CITIZEN 1940

(To JS/07/M/378

This Marble Monument

Is Erected by the State)

He was found by the Bureau of Statistics to be
One against whom there was no official complaint,
And all the reports on his conduct agree
That, in the modern sense of an old-fashioned word, he was a saint,
For in everything he did he served the Greater Community.
Except for the War till the day he retired
He worked in a factory and never got fired,
But satisfied his employers, Fudge Motors Inc.
Yet he wasn't a scab or odd in his views,
For his Union reports that he paid his dues,   10
(Our report on his Union shows it was sound)
And our Social Psychology workers found
That he was popular with his mates and liked a drink.
The Press are convinced that he bought a paper every day
And that his reactions to advertisements were normal in every way.
Policies taken out in his name prove that he was fully insured,

443

And his Health-card shows he was once in hospital but left it cured.
Both Producers Research and High-Grade Living declare
He was fully sensible to the advantages of the Installment Plan
And had everything necessary to the Modern Man,   20
A phonograph, radio, a car and a frigidaire.
Our researchers into Public Opinion are content
That he held the proper opinions for the time of year;
When there was peace, he was for peace; when there was war, he went.
He was married and added five children to the population,
Which our Eugenist says was the right number for a parent of his generation,
And our teachers report that he never interfered with their education.
Was he free? Was he happy? The question is absurd:
Had anything been wrong, we should certainly have heard.

DUDLEY RANDALL   (1914–2000)

BALLAD OF BIRMINGHAM   1969

(ON THE BOMBING OF A CHURCH IN
BIRMINGHAM, ALABAMA, 1963)[1]

"Mother dear, may I go downtown
Instead of out to play,
And march the streets of Birmingham
In a Freedom March today?"

"No, baby, no, you may not go,
For the dogs are fierce and wild,
And clubs and hoses, guns and jails
Aren't good for a little child."

"But, mother, I won't be alone.
Other children will go with me,   10
And march the streets of Birmingham
To make our country free."

"No, baby, no, you may not go,
For I fear those guns will fire.
But you may go to church instead
And sing in the children's choir."

Ballad of Birmingham
[1] This poem commemorates the murder of four young African American girls when a bomb was thrown into the Sixteenth Street Baptist Church in 1963, one of the early and most traumatic events in the modern civil rights movement.

She has combed and brushed her night-dark hair,
And bathed rose petal sweet.
And drawn white gloves on her small brown hands,
And white shoes on her feet.   20

The mother smiled to know her child
Was in the sacred place,
But that smile was the last smile
To come upon her face.

For when she heard the explosion,
Her eyes grew wet and wild.
She raced through the streets of Birmingham
Calling for her child.

She clawed through bits of glass and brick,
Then lifted out a shoe.   30
"Oh, here's the shoe my baby wore,
But, baby, where are you?"

HENRY REED   (1914–1986)

NAMING OF PARTS   1946

Today we have naming of parts. Yesterday,
We had daily cleaning. And tomorrow morning
We shall have what to do after firing. But today,
Today we have naming of parts. Japonica
Glistens like coral in all of the neighboring gardens,
    And today we have naming of parts.

This is the lower sling swivel. And this
Is the upper sling swivel, whose use you will see,
When you are given your slings. And this is the piling swivel,
Which in your case you have not got. The branches   10
Hold in the gardens their silent, eloquent gestures,
    Which in our case we have not got.

This is the safety-catch, which is always released
With an easy flick of the thumb. And please do not let me
See anyone using his finger. You can do it quite easy
If you have any strength in your thumb. The blossoms
Are fragile and motionless, never letting anyone see
    Any of them using their finger.

And this you can see is the bolt. The purpose of this
Is to open the breech, as you see. We can slide it   20
Rapidly backwards and forwards: we call this
Easing the spring. And rapidly backwards and forwards
The early bees are assaulting and fumbling the flowers:
    They call it easing the Spring.

They call it easing the Spring: it is perfectly easy
If you have any strength in your thumb: like the bolt,
And the breech, and the cocking-piece, and the point of balance,
Which in our case we have not got; and the almond-blossom
Silent in all of the gardens and the bees going backwards and forwards,
    For today we have naming of parts.   30

FOR ANALYSIS

1. The poem has two speakers. Identify their voices, and describe the speakers.

2. The last line of each **stanza** repeats a phrase from within the stanza. What is the effect of the repetition?

WRITING TOPIC

This poem incorporates a subtle underlying sexuality. Trace the language that generates it. What function does this sexuality serve in the poem?

GWENDOLYN BROOKS   (1917–2000)

WE REAL COOL   1959

THE POOL PLAYERS
SEVEN AT THE GOLDEN SHOVEL.

We real cool. We
Left school. We

Lurk late. We
Strike straight. We

Sing sin. We
Thin gin. We

Jazz June. We
Die soon.

DONALD DAVIE   (1922–1995)

THE NONCONFORMIST   1985

X, whom society's most mild command,
For instance evening dress, infuriates,
In art is seen confusingly to stand
For disciplined conformity, with Yeats.

Taxed to explain what this resentment is
He feels for small proprieties, it comes,
He likes to think, from old enormities
And keeps the faith with famous martyrdoms.

Yet it is likely, if indeed the crimes
His fathers suffered rankle in his blood,   10
That he find least excusable the times
When they acceded, not when they withstood.

How else explain this bloody-minded bent
To kick against the prickings of the norm;
When to conform is easy, to dissent;
And when it is most difficult, conform?

FOR ANALYSIS

1. Reread the poem's final two lines. What is noteworthy about the word order in this sentence? How does it affect you as you read it? How does it relate to the lines' meaning?

2. What is the speaker's attitude toward X?

3. How would you characterize the range of conformities that are resisted in this poem?

WRITING TOPIC

How do you feel about dissent? Do you think American society is hostile or hospitable to it? Discuss with concrete contemporary and/or historical examples.

PHILIP LEVINE   (B. 1928)

WHAT WORK IS   1991

We stand in the rain in a long line
waiting at Ford Highland Park. For work.
You know what work is—if you're

old enough to read this you know what
work is, although you may not do it.
Forget you. This is about waiting,
shifting from one foot to another.
Feeling the light rain falling like mist
into your hair, blurring your vision
until you think you see your own brother   10
ahead of you, maybe ten places.
You rub your glasses with your fingers,
and of course it's someone else's brother,
narrower across the shoulders than
yours but with the same sad slouch, the grin
that does not hide the stubbornness,
the sad refusal to give in to
rain, to the hours wasted waiting,
to the knowledge that somewhere ahead
a man is waiting who will say, "No,   20
we're not hiring today," for any
reason he wants. You love your brother,
now suddenly you can hardly stand
the love flooding you for your brother,
who's not beside you or behind or
ahead because he's home trying to
sleep off a miserable night shift
at Cadillac so he can get up
before noon to study his German.
Works eight hours a night so he can sing   30
Wagner, the opera you hate most,
the worst music ever invented.
How long has it been since you told him
you loved him, held his wide shoulders,
opened your eyes wide and said those words,
and maybe kissed his cheek? You've never
done something so simple, so obvious,
not because you're too young or too dumb,
not because you're jealous or even mean
or incapable of crying in   40
the presence of another man, no,
just because you don't know what work is.

FOR ANALYSIS

1. What is the poem's **tone**? Is it simple or complicated? Does it evoke one feeling or many?

2. Does the poem supply the definition it promises in its title?

WRITING TOPICS

1. Who is the "you" addressed in this poem? What is the speaker's attitude toward this "you"? Write an essay in which you analyze Levine's use of the second-person **point of view** in this poem. What are the effects of this choice?

2. Write a poem that at first seems to be about a sibling (or another close family member or a friend) but is really as much about you as it is about them.

MARVIN KLOTZ (B. 1930)

GOD: THE VILLANELLE 2010

The formal villanelle is really odd.
It forces climaxes before the end—
Reveals too soon the human horror: god.

Imagination pushes, gleams, and prods
While humans struggle, swirl, attempt to fend.
The formal villanelle is really odd—

But odder still, that we inflamed our sod
With gross divinity—foul mythos penned—
Created the dread horror of man's gods.

Compassion tinted us and we outlawed
Fierce pain—except for infidels condemned.
The formal villanelle is really odd.   10

We burn, behead, ruin, rack, pursue jihad
Against the wretches who refuse to bend—
Reveal eternal horrors of our gods.

Of all ideas we humans shaped, hurrahed,
Not one can rival, subtly portend
The villanelle's construction (beyond odd),
Nor match the horror of invented gods.

MARGE PIERCY (B. 1936)

THE MARKET ECONOMY 1973

Suppose some peddler offered
you can have a color TV
but your baby will be
born with a crooked spine;
you can have polyvinyl cups
and wash and wear
suits but it will cost
you your left lung
rotted with cancer; suppose
somebody offered you   10
a frozen precooked dinner
every night for ten years
but at the end
your colon dies
and then you do,
slowly and with much pain.
You get a house in the suburbs
but you work in a new plastics
factory and die at fifty-one
when your kidneys turn off.   20
But where else will you
work? where else can
you rent but Smog City?
The only houses for sale
are under the yellow sky.
You've been out of work for
a year and they're hiring
at the plastics factory.
Don't read the fine
print, there isn't any.   30

FOR ANALYSIS

1. Characterize the **tone** of this poem.

2. Would this still be a poem if it were printed as a paragraph? Compare this poem
with Forché's "The Colonel" (p. 452), which is written as a paragraph. Which do you
find more "poetic"? Explain.

3. What is meant by the last two lines of the poem?

Richard Garcia (B. 1941)

Why I Left the Church 1993

Maybe it was
because the only time
I hit a baseball
it smashed the neon cross
on the church across
the street. Even
twenty-five years later
when I saw Father Harris
I would wonder
if he knew it was me.   10
Maybe it was the demon-stoked
rotisseries of purgatory
where we would roast
hundreds of years
for the smallest of sins.
Or was it the day
I wore my space helmet
to catechism? Clear plastic
with a red-and-white
inflatable rim.   20
Sister Mary Bernadette
pointed toward the door
and said, "Out! Come back
when you're ready."
I rose from my chair
and kept rising
toward the ceiling
while the children
screamed and Sister
kept crossing herself.   30
The last she saw of me
was my shoes disappearing
through cracked plaster.
I rose into the sky and beyond.
It is a good thing
I am wearing my helmet,
I thought as I floated
and turned in the blackness
and brightness of outer space,
my body cold on one side and hot   40
on the other. It would

451

have been very quiet
if my blood had not been
rumbling in my ears so loud.
I remember thinking,
Maybe I will come back
when I'm ready.
But I won't tell
the other children
what it was like.   50
I'll have to make something up.

FOR ANALYSIS

1. What are the meanings of the third word in the title? Why does Garcia have the poem's **persona** imagine leaving the church this way? Or does he actually do it—is the "something" he says he'll have to "make up" (l. 51) something other than this exit by ceiling? Is the poem's meaning affected by your answer?

2. What is the answer to the poem's title? Do you think the speaker will be going back?

WRITING TOPIC

Write a short poem, set in a real place you often find yourself, in which something fantastic happens to you. What kind of poetic/intellectual effects can such an occurrence have? How can it make you see that place, yourself, or especially yourself in that place differently?

CAROLYN FORCHÉ   (B. 1950)

THE COLONEL   1981

What you have heard is true. I was in his house. His wife carried a tray of coffee and sugar. His daughter filed her nails, his son went out for the night. There were daily papers, pet dogs, a pistol on the cushion beside him. The moon swung bare on its black cord over the house. On the television was a cop show. It was in English. Broken bottles were embedded in the walls round the house to scoop the kneecaps from a man's legs or cut his hands to lace. On the windows there were gratings like those in liquor stores. We had dinner, rack of lamb, good wine, a gold bell was on the table for calling the maid. The maid brought green mangoes, salt, a type of bread. I was asked how I enjoyed the country. There was a brief commercial in Spanish. His wife took everything 10
away. There was some talk then of how difficult it had become to govern. The parrot said hello on the terrace. The colonel told it to shut up, and pushed himself from the table. My friend said to me with his eyes: say nothing. The colonel

returned with a sack used to bring groceries home. He spilled many human ears on the table. They were like dried peach halves. There is no other way to say this. He took one of them in his hands, shook it in our faces, dropped it into a water glass. It came alive there. I am tired of fooling around he said. As for the rights of anyone, tell your people they can go fuck themselves. He swept the ears to the floor with his arm and held the last of his wine in the air. Something for your poetry, no? he said. Some of the ears on the floor caught this scrap of 20 his voice. Some of the ears on the floor were pressed to the ground.

FOR ANALYSIS

1. What is the occasion of this poem? Where is it set? How would you characterize the colonel's family?

2. In line 11 the speaker recounts, "There was some talk then of how difficult it had become to govern." Can you suggest why it had become difficult to govern? How does the colonel respond to these difficulties?

3. What does the last sentence suggest?

4. This piece is printed as if it were **prose**. Does it have any of the formal characteristics of a poem?

NATASHA TRETHEWEY (B. 1966)

FLOUNDER 2000

Here, she said, *put this on your head.*
She handed me a hat.
You 'bout as white as your dad,
and you gone stay like that.

Aunt Sugar rolled her nylons down
around each bony ankle,
and I rolled down my white knee socks
letting my thin legs dangle,

circling them just above water
and silver backs of minnows   10
flitting here then there between
the sun spots and the shadows.

This is how you hold the pole
to cast the line out straight.
Now put that worm on your hook,
throw it out and wait.

She sat spitting tobacco juice
into a coffee cup.
Hunkered down when she felt the bite,
jerked the pole straight up   20

reeling and tugging hard at the fish
that wriggled and tried to fight back.
A flounder, she said, and *you can tell
'cause one of its sides is black.*

The other side is white, she said.
It landed with a thump.
I stood there watching that fish flip-flop,
switch sides with every jump.

FOR ANALYSIS

1. Why does Aunt Sugar want the speaker to put a hat on? Why is it important to her?

2. What is the most important physical characteristic of the flounder? What is the most important action it takes?

3. What kind of sentence does Aunt Sugar address the speaker with in lines 1, 15, and 16? Why might that be important for the poem's depiction of their relationship and of what the aunt has to say to the speaker?

WRITING TOPIC

Animals are used in literature for as many different reasons as there are different kinds of animals on the planet. Most animal appearances in stories and poems are motivated by something other than a desire to focus on the animals themselves; more often, they are there in the service of a **plot** or as **metaphorical** illustrations about people. Do you think the way we use animals in imaginative literature is significant? What does it mean to you about our relation to the nonhuman animal world?

CONNECTING POEMS: REVOLUTIONARY THINKING

"Hurrah for revolution and more cannon-shot!" So begins William Butler Yeats's "The Great Day." In this beginning line—and the title—we hear both the anger some poets have felt about revolution and the energy it can take to oppose popular support of the idea. Throughout history, there has been a romantic attraction to revolution, as there has been to armed struggle. In Yeats's mock cheer, and ironic "Great," readers encounter a poet challenging that romantic attitude. As you read the poems in this unit, think about the different things revolutions can do, the different ways they can end, and especially the different things they can mean—to revolutionaries, to those in power, and to those who engage in revolutionary thinking.

WILLIAM BUTLER YEATS (1865–1939)

THE GREAT DAY 1939

Hurrah for revolution and more cannon-shot!
A beggar upon horseback lashes a beggar on foot.
Hurrah for revolution and cannon come again!
The beggars have changed places, but the lash goes on.

ROBERT FROST (1874–1963)

A SEMI-REVOLUTION 1942

I advocate a semi-revolution.
The trouble with a total revolution
(Ask any reputable Rosicrucian)[1]
Is that it brings the same class up on top.
Executives of skillful execution
Will therefore plan to go half-way and stop.
Yes, revolutions are the only salves,
But they're one thing that should be done by halves.

OSCAR WILLIAMS (1900–1964)

A TOTAL REVOLUTION 1952

(AN ANSWER FOR ROBERT FROST)

I advocate a total revolution.
The trouble with a semi-revolution,
It's likely to be slow as evolution.
Who wants to spend the ages in collusion
With Compromise, Complacence and Confusion?

A Semi-Revolution
[1] Rosicrucians are members of a society professing mystic religious principles and a belief in occult knowledge and powers. William Butler Yeats was a member of this group (see his poem "The Great Day" at the top of this page).

As for the same class coming up on top
That's wholecloth from the propaganda shop;
The old saw says there's loads of room on top,
That's where the poor should really plan to stop.
And speaking of those people called the "haves,"　　　　　　　10
Who own the whole cow and must have the calves
(And plant the wounds so they can sell the salves)
They won't be stopped by doing things by halves.

NIKKI GIOVANNI　(B. 1943)

DREAMS　1968

i used to dream militant
dreams of taking
over america to show
these white folks how it should be
done
i used to dream radical dreams
of blowing everyone away with my perceptive powers
of correct analysis
i even used to think i'd be the one
to stop the riot and negotiate the peace　　　　　　　10
then i awoke and dug
that if i dreamed natural
dreams of being a natural
woman doing what a woman
does when she's natural
i would have a revolution

MAKING CONNECTIONS

1. Ten years after Frost's "A Semi-Revolution" appeared, Williams's "A Total Revolution" answered it with thoughts on the topic. How does Williams answer Frost? Do you find one of the poems more convincing or true? Which one? Why?

2. All of these poems make skillful use of **tone**, often hiding **irony** not too far beneath what seem at first straightforward statements. In what ways do these different poems manipulate tone, and to what effect?

3. When we think of revolutions, we often think of action—of warfare—but, as the unit title suggests, these poems instead focus on thinking *about* revolutions. Why is thinking—or to use Giovanni's phrase "militant dream[ing]" (above)—so important to revolutions? What kind of revolution is Giovanni imagining in her poem?

The poems in this section are all about America the nation and America the idea. None of them celebrates the nation—in its present or in its past—in an uncritical way, but neither do any of them condemn it wholesale. As you read these poems, written in a number of different places and times, pay attention to how they are in some ways quite similar and how in others they diverge in what they have to say about the American present, the American past, and American identity—and in the way they say those things. Also look for connections between what they have to say and how that message is presented through form.

WALT WHITMAN (1819–1892)

ONE SONG, AMERICA, BEFORE I GO   1872

One song, America, before I go,
I'd sing, o'er all the rest, with trumpet sound,
For thee—the Future.

I'd sow a seed for thee of endless Nationality;
I'd fashion thy Ensemble, including Body and Soul;
I'd show, away ahead, thy real Union, and how it may be accomplish'd.

(The paths to the House I seek to make,
But leave to those to come, the House itself.)

Belief I sing—and Preparation;
As Life and Nature are not great with reference to the Present only,   10
But greater still from what is yet to come,
Out of that formula for Thee I sing.

FOR ANALYSIS

1. In his poem "America," Whitman **parodies** the patriotic song "My Country 'Tis of Thee" to draw attention to some less positive aspects of American history. What kind of song of America does Whitman sing here?

2. Why is the future important here? What is Whitman saying about the present and past of America?

LANGSTON HUGHES   (1902–1967)

I, TOO   1926

I, too, sing America.

I am the darker brother.
They send me to eat in the kitchen
When company comes,
But I laugh,
And eat well,
And grow strong.

Tomorrow,
I'll be at the table
When company comes.   10
Nobody'll dare
Say to me,
"Eat in the kitchen,"
Then.

Besides,
They'll see how beautiful I am
And be ashamed—

I, too, am America.

FOR ANALYSIS

1. The title "I, Too" alludes to Walt Whitman's "I Hear America Singing" (you may find it helpful to look at Whitman's poem online). Why does Hughes add the word "too"? How does it respond to the Whitman poem to which it **alludes**?

2. How does this poem's last line relate to the first? What does the difference express?

ALLEN GINSBERG   (1926–1997)

A SUPERMARKET IN CALIFORNIA   1955

   What thoughts I have of you tonight, Walt Whitman, for I walked
down the sidestreets under the trees with a headache self-conscious looking
at the full moon.
   In my hungry fatigue, and shopping for images, I went into the neon
fruit supermarket, dreaming of your enumerations!

What peaches and what penumbras! Whole families shopping at
night! Aisles full of husbands! Wives in the avocados, babies in the tomatoes!
—and you, Garcia Lorca, what were you doing down by the watermelons?

I saw you, Walt Whitman, childless, lonely old grubber, poking
among the meats in the refrigerator and eyeing the grocery boys.   10
I heard you asking questions of each: Who killed the pork chops?
What price bananas? Are you my Angel?
I wandered in and out of the brilliant stacks of cans following you,
and followed in my imagination by the store detective.
We strode down the open corridors together in our solitary fancy
tasting artichokes, possessing every frozen delicacy, and never passing the
cashier.

Where are we going, Walt Whitman? The doors close in a hour.
Which way does your beard point tonight?
(I touch your book and dream of our odyssey in the supermarket and   20
feel absurd.)
Will we walk all night through solitary streets? The trees add shade
to shade, lights out in the houses, we'll both be lonely.
Will we stroll dreaming of the lost America of love past blue automobiles
in driveways, home to our silent cottage?
Ah, dear father, graybeard, lonely old courage-teacher, what America
did you have when Charon quit poling his ferry and you got out on a
smoking bank and stood watching the boat disappear on the black waters of
Lethe?

FOR ANALYSIS

1. Why does the speaker address Whitman? What is the poem's relation to him?

2. How does the speaker feel about contemporary America? How does he feel about
the America of the past?

SHIRLEY GEOK-LIN LIM   (B. 1944)

LEARNING TO LOVE AMERICA   1998

because it has no pure products

because the Pacific Ocean sweeps along the coastline
because the water of the ocean is cold
and because land is better than ocean

because I say we rather than they

because I live in California
I have eaten fresh artichokes
and jacaranda bloom in April and May

because my senses have caught up with my body
my breath with the air it swallows   10
my hunger with my mouth

because I walk barefoot in my house

because I have nursed my son at my breast
because he is a strong American boy
because I have seen his eyes redden when he is asked who he is
because he answers I don't know

because to have a son is to have a country
because my son will bury me here
because countries are in our blood and we bleed them

because it is late and too late to change my mind   20
because it is time.

FOR ANALYSIS

1. The first line of William Carlos Williams's "To Elsie" refers to "The pure products of America." What about this line might have made Lim want to invoke it in the first line of her poem?

2. What do the words that follow the repeated "because" explain? Of what are they the cause?

MAKING CONNECTIONS

1. Each of the poems in this section refers to other, earlier creative works. Are there any parallels in the way they make these references? Why do you think they make them? What's the connection between poetic **allusion** and the way these poems view America?

2. Many of these poems reflect on America not simply in general but in relation to personal identity. What are the connections between them in regard to the way national identity takes shape? What kinds of identity are implicitly and explicitly considered?

3. What role does love play in these poems? What kinds of love are represented? How are they treated? How does their treatment relate to their poem's **themes**?

4. Each of these poems is in some way about process—about being in the middle of something happening, becoming, or being undertaken. Why is this shared trait significant? How are these poems about a process or processes?

War is many things to many people; however, it is rarely described as "quaint and curious," as the speaker in Hardy's "The Man He Killed" (below) says it is. Hardy's speaker arrives at this conclusion as he confronts the realization, after shooting someone, that his victim was probably just a regular guy like he is, someone he'd loan a little money to or buy a drink for. As you read the poems in this unit, think about the different voices in them and the different realizations they have about war and the people who fight and die in them. Think also about the times and places these poets wrote from—England before and after the Great War (what we now call World War I), the Middle East in the late 1980s, the United States during the Iraq War—and about what changes and what stays the same, across place and time, in these war poems.

THOMAS HARDY   (1840–1928)

THE MAN HE KILLED   1902

"Had he and I but met
By some old ancient inn,
We should have sat us down to wet
Right many a nipperkin!

"But ranged as infantry,
And staring face to face,
I shot at him as he at me,
And killed him in his place.

"I shot him dead because—
Because he was my foe,
Just so: my foe of course he was:
That's clear enough; although   10

"He thought he'd 'list, perhaps,
Off-hand-like—just as I—
Was out of work—had sold his traps—
No other reason why.

"Yes; quaint and curious war is!
You shoot a fellow down
You'd treat, if met where any bar is,
Or help to half-a-crown."   20

WILFRED OWEN   (1893–1918)

DULCE ET DECORUM EST   1920

Bent double, like old beggars under sacks,
Knock-kneed, coughing like hags, we cursed through sludge,
Till on the haunting flares we turned our backs,
And towards our distant rest began to trudge.
Men marched asleep. Many had lost their boots,
But limped on, blood-shod. All went lame, all blind;
Drunk with fatigue; deaf even to the hoots
Of gas-shells dropping softly behind.

Gas! GAS! Quick, boys!—An ecstasy of fumbling,
Fitting the clumsy helmets just in time,   10
But someone still was yelling out and stumbling
And flound'ring like a man in fire or lime.—
Dim through the misty panes and thick green light,
As under a green sea, I saw him drowning.
In all my dreams before my helpless sight
He plunges at me, guttering, choking, drowning.

If in some smothering dreams, you too could pace
Behind the wagon that we flung him in,
And watch the white eyes writhing in his face,
His hanging face, like a devil's sick of sin,   20
If you could hear, at every jolt, the blood
Come gargling from the froth-corrupted lungs
Bitter as the cud
Of vile, incurable sores on innocent tongues,—
My friend, you would not tell with such high zest
To children ardent for some desperate glory,
The old lie: *Dulce et decorum est
Pro patria mori.*[1]

---

[1] A quotation from the Latin poet Horace, "It is sweet and fitting to die for one's country."

Hanan Mikha'il 'Ashrawi (B. 1946)

Night Patrol 1988

(An Israeli Soldier on the West Bank)

It's not the sudden hail
of stones, nor the mocking of
their jeers, but this deliberate
quiet in their eyes that
threatens to wipe itself
around my well-armed uniformed
presence and drag me into
depths of confrontation I
never dared to probe.

Their stares bounce off stone,   10
walls and amateur barricades, and
I'm forced to listen
to the echo of my own
gun fire and tear gas
grenades in the midst of
a deafening silence which
I could almost touch, almost
But not quite.
I refuse to be made
into a figment of my   20
own imagination. I catch
myself, at times, glimpsing
glimpsing the child I
was in one of them. That
same old recklessness, a daredevil
stance, a secret wisdom only
youth can impart as it hurtles
towards adulthood. Then I
begin to take substance before
my very eyes, and   30
shrink back in terror—as
an organism on its long
evolutionary trek recoils at the
touch of a human hand.

If I should once, just
once, grasp the elusive
end of the thread which

ties my being here with
their being there, I
could unravel the beginning . . . no,   40
no, it was not an act
of will that brought me
here, and I shall wrap myself in
fabric woven by hands
other than mine, perhaps
lie down and take a nap.

Should I admit then into
my hapless dreams a thousand
eyes, a thousand hands, and allow
unknowingly the night's   50
silence to conceal me, I
would have done no
more or less than what
thousands have done before, turning
over in sleep clutching my
cocoon of army issue blankets,
and hope for a different posting
in the morning.

FOR ANALYSIS

1. Why do the children from the West Bank hurl stones at the soldier?

2. This Palestinian poet speaks with the voice of an Israeli soldier. In the first **stanza**, how would "this deliberate / quiet in their eyes" drag the soldier into "depths of confrontation I / never dared to probe"? How does this confrontation differ from the "hail of stones"? How would you characterize the "depths of confrontation"? Why had the speaker "never dared to probe" such a confrontation?

3. In the second stanza, what is the consequence for the speaker when he perceives himself "glimpsing the child I / was in one of them"?

4. Why does the speaker "hope for a different posting / in the morning"?

WRITING TOPIC

Evaluate the character of the Israeli soldier on night patrol. Is he a good person or an evil one? A true patriot or a troubled one? What human and moral imperatives embody his consciousness?

STEVE EARLE   (B. 1955)

RICH MAN'S WAR   2004

Jimmy joined the army 'cause he had no place to go
There ain't nobody hirin'
'round here since all the jobs went
down to Mexico
Reckoned that he'd learn himself a trade maybe see the world
Move to the city someday and marry a black-haired girl
Somebody somewhere had another plan
Now he's got a rifle in his hand
Rollin' into Baghdad wonderin' how he got this far
Just another poor boy off to fight a rich man's war   10

Bobby had an eagle and a flag tattooed on his arm
Red white and blue to the bone when he landed in Kandahar[1]
Left behind a pretty young wife and a baby girl
A stack of overdue bills and went off to save the world
Been a year now and he's still there
Chasin' ghosts in the thin dry air
Meanwhile back at home the finance company took his car
Just another poor boy off to fight a rich man's war

When will we ever learn
When will we ever see   20
We stand up and take our turn
And keep tellin' ourselves we're free

Ali was the second son of a second son
Grew up in Gaza throwing bottles and rocks when the tanks would come
Ain't nothin' else to do around here just a game children play
Somethin' 'bout livin' in fear all your life makes you hard that way

He answered when he got the call
Wrapped himself in death and praised Allah
A fat man in a new Mercedes drove him to the door
Just another poor boy off to fight a rich man's war   30

FOR ANALYSIS

1. Do the words of this song attack war in general, or only the Israeli-Palestinian,
Afghanistan, and Iraq conflicts? Explain.

---

[1] A southern Afghanistan city, bombed by U.S. forces in late 2001 to punish the Taliban for
harboring Al Qaeda militants responsible for the September 11, 2001, attacks on the United States.

2. What purpose does a protest song such as Earle's serve? Can such songs affect people's behavior? Explain.

3. Explain lines 19–22. What is it that "we" need to learn?

WRITING TOPIC

Describe the differences and the similarities between Bobby and Ali as they relate to the **theme** of Earle's **lyric**.

KEVIN C. POWERS   (B. ?)

LETTER COMPOSED DURING A LULL IN THE FIGHTING   2009

I tell her I love her like not killing
or ten minutes of sleep
beneath the low rooftop wall
on which my rifle rests.

I tell her in a letter that will stink,
when she opens it,
of bolt oil and burned powder
and the things it says.

I tell her how Pvt. Bartle says, offhand,
that war is just us
making little pieces of metal
pass through each other.

FOR ANALYSIS

1. List the **images** in this poem, then list the **metaphors**. How do they interact? Does one kind of element illuminate the other? What is the effect of the intermingling of the two?

2. What things do you think the letter says?

MAKING CONNECTIONS

1. Compare the different effects achieved by the choice of **persona** in these poems. Hardy's, for example, is entirely within quotation marks, a speech delivered by someone—the "He" of the title—while Owen's poem ranges from first-person plural to first-person singular to second-person **point of view**. How do these choices help shape the effects of these poems?

2. What do these poems have to say about the reasons for war? Which seem unconcerned with this question or seem to think it doesn't matter? Which seem more concerned with the reasons why individuals become soldiers than the reasons why nations enter armed conflict? Do you think poetry may be more suited to exploring the former concern? Why?

3. None of these poems seems interested in defending the old idea that, to paraphrase Owen quoting Horace, it is sweet and proper to die for one's country. Are there any voices within the poems who say that, or who might say that? Are there voices who actually believe it or might say it without believing it?

DRAMA

SOPHOCLES   (496?–406 B.C.)

ANTIGONÊ[1]   CA. 441 B.C.

CHARACTERS

Antigonê	Teiresias
Ismenê	A Sentry
Eurydicê	A Messenger
Creon	Chorus
Haimon	

Scene

Before the Palace of Creon, King of Thebes. A central double door, and two lateral doors. A platform extends the length of the facade, and from this platform three steps lead down into the "orchestra," or chorus-ground.

Time

Dawn of the day after the repulse of the Argive army from the assault on Thebes.

PROLOGUE

(Antigonê and Ismenê enter from the central door of the Palace.)

Antigonê. Ismenê, dear sister,
  You would think that we had already suffered enough
  For the curse on Oedipus:[2]

---

[1] An English version by Dudley Fitts and Robert Fitzgerald.   [2] Oedipus, a former king of Thebes, unwittingly killed his father and married his own mother, Iocastê. By her he had four children, the sisters Antigonê and Ismenê and the brothers Polyneicês and Eteoclês. When Oedipus realized what he had done, he blinded himself and left Thebes. Eteoclês drove Polyneicês out of Thebes after a quarrel, but Polyneicês returned with an army and laid siege to Thebes. In the ensuing struggle, the brothers killed each other. Creon became king and, as a punishment, decreed that Polyneicês be denied the rites of burial.

I cannot imagine any grief
That you and I have not gone through. And now—
Have they told you of the new decree of our King Creon?
Ismenê. I have heard nothing: I know
That two sisters lost two brothers, a double death
In a single hour; and I know that the Argive army
Fled in the night; but beyond this, nothing.   10
Antigonê. I thought so. And that is why I wanted you
To come out here with me. There is something we must do.
Ismenê. Why do you speak so strangely?
Antigonê. Listen, Ismenê:
Creon buried our brother Eteoclês
With military honors, gave him a soldier's funeral,
And it was right that he should; but Polyneicês,
Who fought as bravely and died as miserably,—
They say that Creon has sworn
No one shall bury him, no one mourn for him,   20
But his body must lie in the fields, a sweet treasure
For carrion birds to find as they search for food.
That is what they say, and our good Creon is coming here
To announce it publicly; and the penalty—
Stoning to death in the public square.
                         There it is,
And now you can prove what you are:
A true sister, or a traitor to your family.
Ismenê. Antigonê, you are mad! What could I possibly do?
Antigonê. You must decide whether you will help me or not.
Ismenê. I do not understand you. Help you in what?   30
Antigonê. Ismenê, I am going to bury him. Will you come?
Ismenê. Bury him! You have just said the new law forbids it.
Antigonê. He is my brother. And he is your brother, too.
Ismenê. But think of the danger! Think what Creon will do!
Antigonê. Creon is not strong enough to stand in my way.
Ismenê. Ah sister!
Oedipus died, everyone hating him
For what his own search brought to light, his eyes
Ripped out by his own hand; and Iocastê died,
His mother and wife at once: she twisted the cords   40
That strangled her life; and our two brothers died,
Each killed by the other's sword. And we are left:
But oh, Antigonê,
Think how much more terrible than these
Our own death would be if we should go against Creon
And do what he has forbidden! We are only women,
We cannot fight with men, Antigonê!

The law is strong, we must give in to the law
In this thing, and in worse. I beg the Dead
To forgive me, but I am helpless: I must yield   50
To those in authority. And I think it is dangerous business
To be always meddling.

Antigonê.   If that is what you think,
I should not want you, even if you asked to come.
You have made your choice, you can be what you want to be.
But I will bury him; and if I must die,
I say that this crime is holy: I shall lie down
With him in death, and I shall be as dear
To him as he to me.
                          It is the dead,
Not the living, who make the longest demands:
We die for ever . . .
                          You may do as you like,   60
Since apparently the laws of the gods mean nothing to you.

Ismenê. They mean a great deal to me; but I have no strength
To break laws that were made for the public good.

Antigonê. That must be your excuse, I suppose. But as for me,
I will bury the brother I love.

Ismenê.   Antigonê,
I am so afraid for you!

Antigonê.   You need not be:
You have yourself to consider, after all.

Ismenê. But no one must hear of this, you must tell no one!
I will keep it a secret, I promise!

Antigonê.   Oh tell it! Tell everyone!
Think how they'll hate you when it all comes out   70
If they learn that you knew about it all the time!

Ismenê. So fiery! You should be cold with fear.

Antigonê. Perhaps. But I am doing only what I must.

Ismenê. But can you do it? I say that you cannot.

Antigonê. Very well: when my strength gives out, I shall do no more.

Ismenê. Impossible things should not be tried at all.

Antigonê. Go away, Ismenê:
I shall be hating you soon, and the dead will too,
For your words are hateful. Leave me my foolish plan:
I am not afraid of the danger; if it means death,   80
It will not be the worst of deaths—death without honor.

Ismenê. Go then, if you feel you must.
You are unwise,
But a loyal friend indeed to those who love you.

(Exit into the Palace. Antigonê goes off, L. Enter the Chorus.)

PÁRODOS[3]

Chorus. Now the long blade of the sun, lying   *(Strophe 1)*
   Level east to west, touches with glory
   Thebes of the Seven Gates. Open, unlidded
   Eye of golden day! O marching light
   Across the eddy and rush of Dircê's stream,[4]
   Striking the white shields of the enemy
   Thrown headlong backward from the blaze of morning!
Choragos.[5] Polyneicês their commander
   Roused them with windy phrases,
   He the wild eagle screaming   10
   Insults above our land,
   His wings their shields of snow,
   His crest their marshalled helms.

Chorus. Against our seven gates in a yawning ring   *(Antistrophe 1)*
   The famished spears came onward in the night;
   But before his jaws were sated with our blood,
   Or pinefire took the garland of our towers,
   He was thrown back; and as he turned, great Thebes—
   No tender victim for his noisy power—
   Rose like a dragon behind him, shouting war.   20
Choragos. For God hates utterly
   The bray of bragging tongues;
   And when he beheld their smiling,
   Their swagger of golden helms,
   The frown of his thunder blasted
   Their first man from our walls.

Chorus. We heard his shout of triumph high in the air   *(Strophe 2)*
   Turn to a scream; far out in a flaming arc
   He fell with his windy torch, and the earth struck him.
   And others storming in fury no less than his   30
   Found shock of death in the dusty joy of battle.
Choragos. Seven captains at seven gates
   Yielded their clanging arms to the god
   That bends the battle-line and breaks it.
   These two only, brothers in blood,
   Face to face in matchless rage,
   Mirroring each the other's death,

---

[3] The Párodos is the *ode* sung by the Chorus as it entered the theater and moved down the aisles to the playing area. The *strophe*, in Greek tragedy, is the unit of verse the Chorus chanted as it moved to the left in a dance rhythm. The Chorus sang the *antistrophe* as it moved to the right, and the *epode* while standing still.   [4] A stream near Thebes.   [5] Choragos is the leader of the Chorus.

Clashed in long combat.

Chorus. But now in the beautiful morning of victory   *(Antistrophe 2)*
  Let Thebes of the many chariots sing for joy!   40
  With hearts for dancing we'll take leave of war:
  Our temples shall be sweet with hymns of praise,
  And the long night shall echo with our chorus.

SCENE 1

Choragos. But now at last our new King is coming:
  Creon of Thebes, Menoikeus' son.
  In this auspicious dawn of his reign
  What are the new complexities
  That shifting Fate has woven for him?
  What is his counsel? Why has he summoned
  The old men to hear him?

(Enter Creon from the Palace, C. He addresses the Chorus from the top step.)

Creon. Gentlemen: I have the honor to inform you that our Ship of State, which recent storms have threatened to destroy, has come safely to harbor at last, guided by the merciful wisdom of Heaven. I have summoned you   10
here this morning because I know that I can depend upon you: your devotion to King Laïos was absolute; you never hesitated in your duty to our late ruler Oedipus; and when Oedipus died, your loyalty was transferred to his children. Unfortunately, as you know, his two sons, the princes Eteoclês and Polyneicês, have killed each other in battle; and I, as the next in blood, have succeeded to the full power of the throne.

I am aware, of course, that no Ruler can expect complete loyalty from his subjects until he has been tested in office. Nevertheless, I say to you at the very outset that I have nothing but contempt for the kind of Governor who is afraid, for whatever reason, to follow the course that he knows is best for   20
the State; and as for the man who sets private friendship above the public welfare,—I have no use for him, either. I call God to witness that if I saw my country headed for ruin, I should not be afraid to speak out plainly; and I need hardly remind you that I would never have any dealings with an enemy of the people. No one values friendship more highly than I; but we must remember that friends made at the risk of wrecking our Ship are not real friends at all.

These are my principles, at any rate, and that is why I have made the following decision concerning the sons of Oedipus: Eteoclês, who died as a man should die, fighting for his country, is to be buried with full military honors, with all the ceremony that is usual when the greatest heroes die; but his   30 brother Polyneicês, who broke his exile to come back with fire and sword against his native city and the shrines of his fathers' gods, whose one idea was to spill the blood of his blood and sell his own people into slavery— Polyneicês, I say, is to have no burial: no man is to touch him or say the least prayer for him; he shall lie on the plain, unburied; and the birds and the scavenging dogs can do with him whatever they like.

This is my command, and you can see the wisdom behind it. As long as I am King, no traitor is going to be honored with the loyal man. But whoever shows by word and deed that he is on the side of the State,—he shall have   40 my respect while he is living and my reverence when he is dead.

Choragos. If that is your will, Creon, son of Menoikeus,
You have the right to enforce it: we are yours.

Creon. That is my will. Take care that you do your part.

Choragos. We are old men: let the younger ones carry it out.

Creon. I do not mean that: the sentries have been appointed.

Choragos. Then what is it that you would have us do?

Creon. You will give no support to whoever breaks this law.

Choragos. Only a crazy man is in love with death!

Creon. And death it is; yet money talks, and the wisest   50
Have sometimes been known to count a few coins too many.

(Enter Sentry from L.)

Sentry. I'll not say that I'm out of breath from running, King, because every time I stopped to think about what I have to tell you, I felt like going back. And all the time a voice kept saying, "You fool, don't you know you're walking straight into trouble?"; and then another voice: "Yes, but if you let somebody else get the news to Creon first, it will be even worse than that for you!" But good sense won out, at least I hope it was good sense, and here I am with a story that makes no sense at all; but I'll tell it anyhow, because, as they say, what's going to happen's going to happen, and—   60

Creon. Come to the point. What have you to say?

Sentry. I did not do it. I did not see who did it. You must not punish me for what someone else has done.

Creon. A comprehensive defense! More effective, perhaps,
If I knew its purpose. Come: what is it?

Sentry. A dreadful thing . . . I don't know how to put it—

Creon. Out with it!

Sentry.   Well, then;
The dead man—
                    Polyneicês—

(Pause. The Sentry is overcome, fumbles for words. Creon waits impassively.)

out there—

someone,—

New dust on the slimy flesh!

(Pause. No sign from Creon.)

Someone has given it burial that way, and   70
Gone . . .

(Long pause. Creon finally speaks with deadly control.)

Creon. And the man who dared do this?
Sentry.   I swear I
Do not know! You must believe me!

Listen:

The ground was dry, not a sign of digging, no,
Not a wheel track in the dust, no trace of anyone.
It was when they relieved us this morning: and one of them,
The corporal, pointed to it.

There it was,

The strangest—

Look:

The body, just mounded over with light dust: you see?
Not buried really, but as if they'd covered it   80
Just enough for the ghost's peace. And no sign
Of dogs or any wild animal that had been there.

And then what a scene there was! Every man of us
Accusing the other: we all proved the other man did it,
We all had proof that we could not have done it.
We were ready to take hot iron in our hands,
Walk through fire, swear by all the gods,
It was not I!
I do not know who it was, but it was not I!

*(Creon's rage has been mounting steadily, but the Sentry is too intent upon his story
to notice it.)*

And then, when this came to nothing, someone said   90
A thing that silenced us and made us stare
Down at the ground: you had to be told the news,
And one of us had to do it! We threw the dice,
And the bad luck fell to me. So here I am,
No happier to be here than you are to have me:
Nobody likes the man who brings bad news.

Choragos. I have been wondering, King: can it be that the gods have done this?

Creon (*furiously*). Stop!

    Must you doddering wrecks

    Go out of your heads entirely? "The gods!"   100

    Intolerable!

    The gods favor this corpse? Why? How had he served them?

    Tried to loot their temples, burn their images,

    Yes, and the whole State, and its laws with it!

    Is it your senile opinion that the gods love to honor bad men?

    A pious thought—

                No, from the very beginning

    There have been those who have whispered together,

    Stiff-necked anarchists, putting their heads together,

    Scheming against me in alleys. These are the men,

    And they have bribed my own guard to do this thing.   110

    (*Sententiously.*) Money!

    There's nothing in the world so demoralizing as money.

    Down go your cities,

    Homes gone, men gone, honest hearts corrupted,

    Crookedness of all kinds, and all for money!

    (*To Sentry.*)   But you—!

    I swear by God and by the throne of God,

    The man who has done this thing shall pay for it!

    Find that man, bring him here to me, or your death

    Will be the least of your problems: I'll string you up

    Alive, and there will be certain ways to make you   120

    Discover your employer before you die;

    And the process may teach you a lesson you seem to have missed:

    The dearest profit is sometimes all too dear:

    That depends on the source. Do you understand me?

    A fortune won is often misfortune.

Sentry. King, may I speak?

Creon.   Your very voice distresses me.

Sentry. Are you sure that it is my voice, and not your conscience?

Creon. By God, he wants to analyze me now!

Sentry. It is not what I say, but what has been done, that hurts you.

Creon. You talk too much.

Sentry.   Maybe; but I've done nothing.   130

Creon. Sold your soul for some silver: that's all you've done.

Sentry. How dreadful it is when the right judge judges wrong!

Creon. Your figures of speech

    May entertain you now; but unless you bring me the man,

    You will get little profit from them in the end.

(*Exit Creon into the Palace.*)

Sentry. "Bring me the man"—!
   I'd like nothing better than bringing him the man!
   But bring him or not, you have seen the last of me here.
   At any rate, I am safe!

(Exit Sentry.)

ODE I

Chorus. Numberless are the world's wonders, but none   *(Strophe 1)*
   More wonderful than man; the stormgray sea
   Yields to his prows, the huge crests bear him high;
   Earth, holy and inexhaustible, is graven
   With shining furrows where his plows have gone
   Year after year, the timeless labor of stallions.

   The lightboned birds and beasts that cling to cover,   *(Antistrophe 1)*
   The lithe fish lighting their reaches of dim water,
   All are taken, tamed in the net of his mind;
   The lion on the hill, the wild horse windy-maned,   10
   Resign to him; and his blunt yoke has broken
   The sultry shoulders of the mountain bull.

   Words also, and thought as rapid as air,   *(Strophe 2)*
   He fashions to his good use; statecraft is his,
   And his the skill that deflects the arrows of snow,
   The spears of winter rain: from every wind
   He has made himself secure—from all but one:
   In the late wind of death he cannot stand.

   O clear intelligence, force beyond all measure!   *(Antistrophe 2)*
   O fate of man, working both good and evil!   20
   When the laws are kept, how proudly his city stands!
   When the laws are broken, what of his city then?
   Never may the anarchic man find rest at my hearth,
   Never be it said that my thoughts are his thoughts.

SCENE 2

(Re-enter Sentry leading Antigonê.)

Choragos. What does this mean? Surely this captive woman
   Is the Princess, Antigonê. Why should she be taken?

Sentry. Here is the one who did it! We caught her
  In the very act of burying him.—Where is Creon?
Choragos. Just coming from the house.

(Enter Creon, C.)

Creon.   What has happened?
  Why have you come back so soon?
Sentry *(expansively)*.   O King,
  A man should never be too sure of anything:
  I would have sworn
  That you'd not see me here again: your anger
  Frightened me so, and the things you threatened me with;   10
  But how could I tell then
  That I'd be able to solve the case so soon?
  No dice-throwing this time: I was only too glad to come!

  Here is this woman. She is the guilty one:
  We found her trying to bury him.
  Take her, then; question her; judge her as you will.
  I am through with the whole thing now, and glad of it.
Creon. But this is Antigonê! Why have you brought her here?
Sentry. She was burying him, I tell you!
Creon *(severely)*.   Is this the truth?
Sentry. I saw her with my own eyes. Can I say more?   20
Creon. The details: come, tell me quickly!
Sentry.   It was like this:
  After those terrible threats of yours, King,
  We went back and brushed the dust away from the body.
  The flesh was soft by now, and stinking,
  So we sat on a hill to windward and kept guard.
  No napping this time! We kept each other awake.
  But nothing happened until the white round sun
  Whirled in the center of the round sky over us:
  Then, suddenly,
  A storm of dust roared up from the earth, and the sky   30
  Went out, the plain vanished with all its trees
  In the stinging dark. We closed our eyes and endured it.
  The whirlwind lasted a long time, but it passed;
  And then we looked, and there was Antigonê!
  I have seen ,
  A mother bird come back to a stripped nest, heard
  Her crying bitterly a broken note or two
  For the young ones stolen. Just so, when this girl
  Found the bare corpse, and all her love's work wasted,

She wept, and cried on heaven to damn the hands 40
That had done this thing.
                              And then she brought more dust
And sprinkled wine three times for her brother's ghost.
We ran and took her at once. She was not afraid,
Not even when we charged her with what she had done.
She denied nothing.
                              And this was a comfort to me,
And some uneasiness: for it is a good thing
To escape from death, but it is no great pleasure
To bring death to a friend.
                              Yet I always say
There is nothing so comfortable as your own safe skin!
Creon (*slowly, dangerously*). And you, Antigonê, 50
You with your head hanging,—do you confess this thing?
Antigonê. I do. I deny nothing.
Creon (*to Sentry*).   You may go.

(*Exit Sentry.*)

(*To Antigonê.*) Tell me, tell me briefly:
Had you heard my proclamation touching this matter?
Antigonê. It was public. Could I help hearing it?
Creon. And yet you dared defy the law.
Antigonê.   I dared.
It was not God's proclamation. That final Justice
That rules the world below makes no such laws.

Your edict, King, was strong,
But all your strength is weakness itself against 60
The immortal unrecorded laws of God.
They are not merely now: they were, and shall be,
Operative for ever, beyond man utterly.

I knew I must die, even without your decree:
I am only mortal. And if I must die
Now, before it is my time to die,
Surely this is no hardship: can anyone
Living, as I live, with evil all about me,
Think Death less than a friend? This death of mine
Is of no importance; but if I had left my brother 70
Lying in death unburied, I should have suffered.
Now I do not.
              You smile at me. Ah Creon,

Think me a fool, if you like; but it may well be
That a fool convicts me of folly.

Choragos. Like father, like daughter: both headstrong, deaf to reason!
She has never learned to yield.

Creon.   She has much to learn.
The inflexible heart breaks first, the toughest iron
Cracks first, and the wildest horses bend their necks
At the pull of the smallest curb.

                                        Pride? In a slave?
This girl is guilty of a double insolence,   80
Breaking the given laws and boasting of it.
Who is the man here,
She or I, if this crime goes unpunished?
Sister's child, or more than sister's child,
Or closer yet in blood—she and her sister
Win bitter death for this!
(To servants.)   Go, some of you,
Arrest Ismenê. I accuse her equally.
Bring her: you will find her sniffling in the house there.

Her mind's a traitor: crimes kept in the dark
Cry for light, and the guardian brain shudders;   90
But how much worse than this
Is brazen boasting of barefaced anarchy!

Antigonê. Creon, what more do you want than my death?

Creon.   Nothing.
That gives me everything.

Antigonê.   Then I beg you: kill me.
This talking is a great weariness: your words
Are distasteful to me, and I am sure that mine
Seem so to you. And yet they should not seem so:
I should have praise and honor for what I have done.
All these men here would praise me
Were their lips not frozen shut with fear of you.   100
(Bitterly.) Ah the good fortune of kings,
Licensed to say and do whatever they please!

Creon. You are alone here in that opinion.

Antigonê. No, they are with me. But they keep their tongues in leash.

Creon. Maybe. But you are guilty, and they are not.

Antigonê. There is no guilt in reverence for the dead.

Creon. But Eteoclês—was he not your brother too?

Antigonê. My brother too.

Creon.   And you insult his memory?

Antigonê *(softly).* The dead man would not say that I insult it.

Creon. He would: for you honor a traitor as much as him. 110

Antigonê. His own brother, traitor or not, and equal in blood.

Creon. He made war on his country. Eteoclês defended it.

Antigonê. Nevertheless, there are honors due all the dead.

Creon. But not the same for the wicked as for the just.

Antigonê. Ah Creon, Creon,
Which of us can say what the gods hold wicked?

Creon. An enemy is an enemy, even dead.

Antigonê. It is my nature to join in love, not hate.

Creon *(finally losing patience).* Go join them, then; if you must have your
love,
Find it in hell! 120

Choragos. But see, Ismenê comes:

(Enter Ismenê, guarded.)

Those tears are sisterly, the cloud
That shadows her eyes rains down gentle sorrow.

Creon. You too, Ismenê,
Snake in my ordered house, sucking my blood
Stealthily—and all the time I never knew
That these two sisters were aiming at my throne!
                                                   Ismenê,
Do you confess your share in this crime, or deny it?
Answer me.

Ismenê. Yes, if she will let me say so. I am guilty. 130

Antigonê *(coldly).* No, Ismenê. You have no right to say so.
You would not help me, and I will not have you help me.

Ismenê. But now I know what you meant; and I am here
To join you, to take my share of punishment.

Antigonê. The dead man and the gods who rule the dead
Know whose act this was. Words are not friends.

Ismenê. Do you refuse me, Antigonê? I want to die with you:
I too have a duty that I must discharge to the dead.

Antigonê. You shall not lessen my death by sharing it.

Ismenê. What do I care for life when you are dead? 140

Antigonê. Ask Creon. You're always hanging on his opinions.

Ismenê. You are laughing at me. Why, Antigonê?

Antigonê. It's a joyless laughter, Ismenê.

Ismenê.   But can I do nothing?

Antigonê. Yes. Save yourself. I shall not envy you.
There are those who will praise you; I shall have honor, too.

Ismenê. But we are equally guilty!

Antigonê.   No more, Ismenê.
You are alive, but I belong to Death.

Creon (*to the Chorus*). Gentlemen, I beg you to observe these girls:
  One has just now lost her mind; the other,
  It seems, has never had a mind at all.   150
Ismenê. Grief teaches the steadiest minds to waver, King.
Creon. Yours certainly did, when you assumed guilt with the guilty!
Ismenê. But how could I go on living without her?
Creon.   You are.
  She is already dead.
Ismenê.   But your own son's bride!
Creon. There are places enough for him to push his plow.
  I want no wicked women for my sons!
Ismenê. O dearest Haimon, how your father wrongs you!
Creon. I've had enough of your childish talk of marriage!
Choragos. Do you really intend to steal this girl from your son?
Creon. No; Death will do that for me.
Choragos.   Then she must die?   160
Creon (*ironically*). You dazzle me.
                        —But enough of this talk!
  (*To Guards.*) You there, take them away and guard them well:
  For they are but women, and even brave men run
  When they see Death coming.

(*Exeunt Ismenê, Antigonê, and Guards.*)

ODE II

Chorus. Fortunate is the man who has never tasted   (*Strophe 1*)
    God's vengeance!
  Where once the anger of heaven has struck, that house is shaken
  For ever: damnation rises behind each child
  Like a wave cresting out of the black northeast,
  When the long darkness under sea roars up
  And bursts drumming death upon the windwhipped sand.

  I have seen this gathering sorrow from time long past   (*Antistrophe I*)
  Loom upon Oedipus' children: generation from generation
  Takes the compulsive rage of the enemy god.
  So lately this last flower of Oedipus' line   10
  Drank the sunlight! but now a passionate word
  And a handful of dust have closed up all its beauty.

    What mortal arrogance   (*Strophe 2*)
    Transcends the wrath of Zeus?
  Sleep cannot lull him, nor the effortless long months

Of the timeless gods: but he is young for ever,
And his house is the shining day of high Olympos.
    And that is and shall be,
    And all the past, is his.
No pride on earth is free of the curse of heaven,   20

    The straying dreams of men   *(Antistrophe 2)*
    May bring them ghosts of joy:
But as they drowse, the waking embers burn them;
Or they walk with fixed eyes, as blind men walk.
But the ancient wisdom speaks for our own time:
    Fate works most for woe
    With Folly's fairest show.
Man's little pleasure is the spring of sorrow.

SCENE 3

Choragos. But here is Haimon, King, the last of all your sons.
    Is it grief for Antigonê that brings him here,
    And bitterness at being robbed of his bride?

(Enter Haimon.)

Creon. We shall soon see, and no need of diviners,
                            —Son,
    You have heard my final judgment on that girl:
    Have you come here hating me, or have you come
    With deference and with love, whatever I do?
Haimon. I am your son, father. You are my guide.
    You make things clear for me, and I obey you.
    No marriage means more to me than your continuing wisdom.   10
Creon. Good. That is the way to behave: subordinate
    Everything else, my son, to your father's will.
    This is what a man prays for, that he may get
    Sons attentive and dutiful in his house,
    Each one hating his father's enemies,
    Honoring his father's friends. But if his sons
    Fail him, if they turn out unprofitably,
    What has he fathered but trouble for himself
    And amusement for the malicious?
                      So you are right
    Not to lose your head over this woman.   20
    Your pleasure with her would soon grow cold, Haimon,

And then you'd have a hellcat in bed and elsewhere.
Let her find her husband in Hell!
Of all the people in this city, only she
Has had contempt for my law and broken it.

Do you want me to show myself weak before the people?
Or to break my sworn word? No, and I will not.
The woman dies.
I suppose she'll plead "family ties." Well, let her.
If I permit my own family to rebel,   30
How shall I earn the world's obedience?
Show me the man who keeps his house in hand,
He's fit for public authority.
                              I'll have no dealings
With law-breakers, critics of the government:
Whoever is chosen to govern should be obeyed—
Must be obeyed, in all things, great and small,
Just and unjust! O Haimon,
The man who knows how to obey, and that man only,
Knows how to give commands when the time comes.
You can depend on him, no matter how fast   40
The spears come: he's a good soldier, he'll stick it out.
Anarchy, anarchy! Show me a greater evil!
This is why cities tumble and the great houses rain down,
This is what scatters armies!

No, no: good lives are made so by discipline.
We keep the laws then, and the lawmakers,
And no woman shall seduce us. If we must lose,
Let's lose to a man, at least! Is a woman stronger than we?

Choragos. Unless time has rusted my wits,
What you say, King, is said with point and dignity.   50

Haimon *(boyishly earnest).* Father:
Reason is God's crowning gift to man, and you are right
To warn me against losing mine. I cannot say—
I hope that I shall never want to say!—that you
Have reasoned badly. Yet there are other men
Who can reason, too; and their opinions might be helpful.
You are not in a position to know everything
That people say or do, or what they feel:
Your temper terrifies them—everyone
Will tell you only what you like to hear.   60
But I, at any rate, can listen; and I have heard them
Muttering and whispering in the dark about this girl.

They say no woman has ever, so unreasonably,
Died so shameful a death for a generous act:
"She covered her brother's body. Is this indecent?
She kept him from dogs and vultures. Is this a crime?
Death?—She should have all the honor that we can give her!"

This is the way they talk out there in the city.

You must believe me:
Nothing is closer to me than your happiness.   70
What could be closer? Must not any son
Value his father's fortune as his father does his?
I beg you, do not be unchangeable:
Do not believe that you alone can be right.
The man who thinks that,
The man who maintains that only he has the power
To reason correctly, the gift to speak, the soul—
A man like that, when you know him, turns out empty.
It is not reason never to yield to reason!

In flood time you can see how some trees bend   80
And because they bend, even their twigs are safe,
While stubborn trees are torn up, roots and all.
And the same thing happens in sailing:
Make your sheet fast, never slacken—and over you go,
Head over heels and under: and there's your voyage.
Forget you are angry! Let yourself be moved!
I know I am young; but please let me say this:
The ideal condition
Would be, I admit, that men should be right by instinct;
But since we are all too likely to go astray,   90
The reasonable thing is to learn from those who can teach.
Choragos. You will do well to listen to him, King,
    If what he says is sensible. And you, Haimon,
    Must listen to your father.—Both speak well.
Creon. You consider it right for a man of my years and experience
    To go to school to a boy?
Haimon.   It is not right
    If I am wrong. But if I am young, and right,
    What does my age matter?
Creon. You think it right to stand up for an anarchist?
Haimon. Not at all. I pay no respect to criminals.   100
Creon. Then she is not a criminal?
Haimon. The City would deny it, to a man.
Creon. And the City proposes to teach me how to rule?

Haimon. Ah. Who is it that's talking like a boy now?
Creon. My voice is the one voice giving orders in this City!
Haimon. It is no City if it takes orders from one voice.
Creon. The State is the King!
Haimon.   Yes, if the State is a desert.

(Pause.)

Creon. This boy, it seems, has sold out to a woman.
Haimon. If you are a woman: my concern is only for you.
Creon. So? Your "concern"! In a public brawl with your father!   110
Haimon. How about you, in a public brawl with justice?
Creon. With justice, when all that I do is within my rights?
Haimon. You have no right to trample on God's right.
Creon *(completely out of control).*   Fool, adolescent fool! Taken in by a
    woman!
Haimon. You'll never see me taken in by anything vile.
Creon. Every word you say is for her!
Haimon *(quietly, darkly).*   And for you.
    And for me. And for the gods under the earth.
Creon. You'll never marry her while she lives.
Haimon. Then she must die.—But her death will cause another.
Creon. Another?   120
    Have you lost your senses? Is this an open threat?
Haimon. There is no threat in speaking to emptiness.
Creon. I swear you'll regret this superior tone of yours!
    You are the empty one!
Haimon.   If you were not my father,
    I'd say you were perverse.
Creon. You girlstruck fool, don't play at words with me!
Haimon. I am sorry. You prefer silence.
Creon.   Now, by God—!
    I swear, by all the gods in heaven above us,
    You'll watch it, I swear you shall!
    (To the servants.)   Bring her out!
    Bring the woman out! Let her die before his eyes!   130
    Here, this instant, with her bridegroom beside her!
Haimon. Not here, no; she will not die here, King.
    And you will never see my face again.
    Go on raving as long as you've a friend to endure you.

(Exit Haimon.)

Choragos. Gone, gone.
    Creon, a young man in a rage is dangerous!

Creon. Let him do, or dream to do, more than a man can.
  He shall not save these girls from death.
Choragos.   These girls?
  You have sentenced them both?
Creon.   No, you are right.
  I will not kill the one whose hands are clean.   140
Choragos. But Antigonê?
Creon (*somberly*). I will carry her far away
  Out there in the wilderness, and lock her
  Living in a vault of stone. She shall have food,
  As the custom is, to absolve the State of her death.
  And there let her pray to the gods of hell:
  They are her only gods:
  Perhaps they will show her an escape from death,
  Or she may learn
                though late,
  That piety shown the dead is pity in vain.   150

(*Exit Creon.*)

ODE III

Chorus. Love, unconquerable   (*Strophe*)
  Waster of rich men, keeper
  Of warm lights and all-night vigil
  In the soft face of a girl:
  Sea-wanderer, forest-visitor!
  Even the pure Immortals cannot escape you,
  And mortal man, in his one day's dusk,
  Trembles before your glory.

  Surely you swerve upon ruin   (*Antistrophe*)
  The just man's consenting heart,   10
  As here you have made bright anger
  Strike between father and son—
  And none had conquered but Love!
  A girl's glance working the will of heaven:
  Pleasure to her alone who mocks us,
  Merciless Aphroditê.[6]

---

[6] Aphroditê is the goddess of love.

SCENE 4

Choragos *(as Antigonê enters guarded).* But I can no longer stand in awe
   of this,
   Nor, seeing what I see, keep back my tears.
   Here is Antigonê, passing to that chamber
   Where all find sleep at last.

Antigonê. Look upon me, friends, and pity me   *(Strophe 1)*
   Turning back at the night's edge to say
   Good-by to the sun that shines for me no longer;
   Now sleepy Death
   Summons me down to Acheron,[7] that cold shore:
   There is no bridesong there, nor any music.   10
Chorus. Yet not unpraised, not without a kind of honor,
   You walk at last into the underworld;
   Untouched by sickness, broken by no sword.
   What woman has ever found your way to death?
Antigonê. How often I have heard the story of Niobê,[8]   *(Antistrophe 1)*
   Tantalos' wretched daughter, how the stone
   Clung fast about her, ivy-close: and they say
   The rain falls endlessly
   And sifting soft snow; her tears are never done.
   I feel the loneliness of her death in mine.   20
Chorus. But she was born of heaven, and you
   Are woman, woman-born. If her death is yours,
   A mortal woman's, is this not for you
   Glory in our world and in the world beyond?

Antigonê. You laugh at me. Ah, friends, friends,   *(Strophe 2)*
   Can you not wait until I am dead? O Thebes,
   O men many-charioted, in love with Fortune,
   Dear springs of Dircê, sacred Theban grove,
   Be witnesses for me, denied all pity,
   Unjustly judged! and think a word of love   30
   For her whose path turns
   Under dark earth, where there are no more tears.
Chorus. You have passed beyond human daring and come at last
   Into a place of stone where Justice sits.
   I cannot tell
   What shape of your father's guilt appears in this.

---

[7] A river of Hades.   [8] Niobê married an ancestor of Oedipus named Amphion. Her fourteen
children were killed by Apollo and Artemis after Niobê boasted to their mother, Leto, that her
children were superior to them. She wept incessantly and was finally transformed into a rock on
Mt. Sipylos, whose streams are her tears.

Antigonê. You have touched it at last: that bridal bed   *(Antistrophe 2)*
    Unspeakable, horror of son and mother mingling:
    Their crime, infection of all our family!
    O Oedipus, father and brother!   40
    Your marriage strikes from the grave to murder mine.
    I have been a stranger here in my own land:
    All my life
    The blasphemy of my birth has followed me.
Chorus. Reverence is a virtue, but strength
    Lives in established law: that must prevail.
    You have made your choice,
    Your death is the doing of your conscious hand.

Antigonê. Then let me go, since all your words are bitter,   *(Epode)*
    And the very light of the sun is cold to me.   50
    Lead me to my vigil, where I must have
    Neither love nor lamentation; no song, but silence.

(Creon interrupts impatiently.)

Creon. If dirges and planned lamentations could put off death,
    Men would be singing for ever.
    (To the servants.)   Take her, go!
    You know your orders: take her to the vault
    And leave her alone there. And if she lives or dies,
    That's her affair, not ours: our hands are clean.
Antigonê. O tomb, vaulted bride-bed in eternal rock,
    Soon I shall be with my own again
    Where Persephonê[9] welcomes the thin ghosts underground: 60
    And I shall see my father again, and you, mother,
    And dearest Polyneicês—
                      dearest indeed
    To me, since it was my hand
    That washed him clean and poured the ritual wine:
    And my reward is death before my time!

    And yet, as men's hearts know, I have done no wrong,
    I have not sinned before God. Or if I have,
    I shall know the truth in death. But if the guilt
    Lies upon Creon who judged me, then, I pray,
    May his punishment equal my own.
Choragos.   O passionate heart,   70
    Unyielding, tormented still by the same winds!
Creon. Her guards shall have good cause to regret their delaying.

    [9] Queen of Hades.

Antigonê. Ah! That voice is like the voice of death!

Creon. I can give you no reason to think you are mistaken.

Antigonê. Thebes, and you my fathers' gods,
And rulers of Thebes, you see me now, the last
Unhappy daughter of a line of kings,
Your kings, led away to death. You will remember
What things I suffer, and at what men's hands,
Because I would not transgress the laws of heaven.   80
(To the guards, simply.) Come: let us wait no longer.

(Exit Antigonê, L., guarded.)

ODE IV

Chorus. All Danaê's[10] beauty was locked away   *(Strophe 1)*
In a brazen cell where the sunlight could not come:
A small room, still as any grave, enclosed her.
Yet she was a princess too,
And Zeus in a rain of gold poured love upon her.
O child, child,
No power in wealth or war
Or tough sea-blackened ships
Can prevail against untiring Destiny!

And Dryas' son[11] also, that furious king,   *(Antistrophe 1)*   10
Bore the god's prisoning anger for his pride:
Sealed up by Dionysos in deaf stone,
His madness died among echoes.
So at the last he learned what dreadful power
His tongue had mocked:
For he had profaned the revels,
And fired the wrath of the nine
Implacable Sisters[12] that love the sound of the flute.

And old men tell a half-remembered tale   *(Strophe 2)*
Of horror where a dark ledge splits the sea   20
And a double surf beats on the gray shores:
How a king's new woman,[13] sick

---

[10] Though Danaê, a beautiful princess of Argos, was confined by her father, Zeus visited her
in the form of a shower of gold, and she gave birth to Perseus as a result.   [11] Lycurgus, king of
Thrace, who was driven mad by Dionysos, the god of wine.   [12] The Muses.   [13] The ode alludes
to a story indicating the uselessness of high birth against implacable fate. The king's new woman
is Eidothea, the second wife of King Phineus. Though Cleopatra, his first wife, was the daughter of
Boreas, the north wind, and Phineus himself was descended from kings, Eidothea, out of hatred for
Cleopatra, blinded her two sons.

With hatred for the queen he had imprisoned,
Ripped out his two sons' eyes with her bloody hands
While grinning Arês[14] watched the shuttle plunge
Four times: four blind wounds crying for revenge,

Crying, tears and blood mingled.—Piteously born,   *(Antistrophe 2)*
Those sons whose mother was of heavenly birth!
Her father was the god of the North Wind
And she was cradled by gales,   30
She raced with young colts on the glittering hills
And walked untrammeled in the open light:
But in her marriage deathless Fate found means
To build a tomb like yours for all her joy.

SCENE 5

(Enter blind Teiresias, led by a boy. The opening speeches of Teiresias should be in singsong contrast to the realistic lines of Creon.)

Teiresias. This is the way the blind man comes, Princes, Princes,
     Lock-step, two heads lit by the eyes of one.
Creon. What new thing have you to tell us, old Teiresias?
Teiresias. I have much to tell you: listen to the prophet, Creon.
Creon. I am not aware that I have ever failed to listen.
Teiresias. Then you have done wisely, King, and ruled well.
Creon. I admit my debt to you. But what have you to say?
Teiresias. This, Creon: you stand once more on the edge of fate.
Creon. What do you mean? Your words are a kind of dread.
Teiresias. Listen, Creon: 10
     I was sitting in my chair of augury, at the place
     Where the birds gather about me. They were all a-chatter,
     As is their habit, when suddenly I heard
     A strange note in their jangling, a scream, a
     Whirring fury; I knew that they were fighting,
     Tearing each other, dying
     In a whirlwind of wings clashing. And I was afraid.
     I began the rites of burnt-offering at the altar,
     But Hephaistos[15] failed me: instead of bright flame,
     There was only the sputtering slime of the fat thigh-flesh   20
     Melting: the entrails dissolved in gray smoke;
     The bare bone burst from the welter. And no blaze!

---

[14] The god of war.   [15] The god of fire.

This was a sign from heaven. My boy described it,
Seeing for me as I see for others.

I tell you, Creon, you yourself have brought
This new calamity upon us. Our hearths and altars
Are stained with the corruption of dogs and carrion birds
That glut themselves on the corpse of Oedipus' son.
The gods are deaf when we pray to them, their fire
Recoils from our offering, their birds of omen   30
Have no cry of comfort, for they are gorged
With the thick blood of the dead.
                             O my son,
These are no trifles! Think: all men make mistakes,
But a good man yields when he knows his course is wrong,
And repairs the evil. The only crime is pride.

Give in to the dead man, then: do not fight with a corpse—
What glory is it to kill a man who is dead?
Think, I beg you:
It is for your own good that I speak as I do.
You should be able to yield for your own good.   40

Creon. It seems that prophets have made me their especial province.
All my life long
I have been a kind of butt for the dull arrows
Of doddering fortune-tellers!
                             No, Teiresias:
If your birds—if the great eagles of God himself
Should carry him stinking bit by bit to heaven,
I would not yield. I am not afraid of pollution:
No man can defile the gods.
                             Do what you will,
Go into business, make money, speculate
In India gold or that synthetic gold from Sardis,   50
Get rich otherwise than by my consent to bury him.
Teiresias, it is a sorry thing when a wise man
Sells his wisdom, lets out his words for hire!

Teiresias. Ah Creon! Is there no man left in the world—

Creon. To do what?—Come, let's have the aphorism!

Teiresias. No man who knows that wisdom outweighs any wealth?

Creon. As surely as bribes are baser than any baseness.

Teiresias. You are sick, Creon! You are deathly sick!

Creon. As you say: it is not my place to challenge a prophet.

Teiresias. Yet you have said my prophecy is for sale.   60

Creon. The generation of prophets has always loved gold.

Teiresias. The generation of kings has always loved brass.

Creon. You forget yourself! You are speaking to your King.

Teiresias. I know it. You are a king because of me.

Creon. You have a certain skill; but you have sold out.

Teiresias. King, you will drive me to words that—

Creon.   Say them, say them!
    Only remember: I will not pay you for them.

Teiresias. No, you will find them too costly.

Creon.   No doubt. Speak:
    Whatever you say, you will not change my will.

Teiresias. Then take this, and take it to heart!   70
    The time is not far off when you shall pay back
    Corpse for corpse, flesh of your own flesh.
    You have thrust the child of this world into living night,
    You have kept from the gods below the child that is theirs:
    The one in a grave before her death, the other,
    Dead, denied the grave. This is your crime:
    And the Furies and the dark gods of Hell
    Are swift with terrible punishment for you.

    Do you want to buy me now, Creon?
                       Not many days,
    And your house will be full of men and women weeping,   80
    And curses will be hurled at you from far
    Cities grieving for sons unburied, left to rot
    Before the walls of Thebes.
    These are my arrows, Creon: they are all for you.

    (To boy.) But come, child: lead me home.
    Let him waste his fine anger upon younger men.
    Maybe he will learn at last
    To control a wiser tongue in a better head.

(Exit Teiresias.)

Choragos. The old man has gone, King, but his words
    Remain to plague us. I am old, too,   90
    But I cannot remember that he was ever false.

Creon. That is true. . . . It troubles me.
    Oh it is hard to give in! but it is worse
    To risk everything for stubborn pride.

Choragos. Creon: take my advice.

Creon.   What shall I do?

Choragos. Go quickly: free Antigonê from her vault
    And build a tomb for the body of Polyneicês.

Creon. You would have me do this?

Choragos. Creon, yes!
And it must be done at once: God moves 100
Swiftly to cancel the folly of stubborn men.
Creon. It is hard to deny the heart! But I
Will do it: I will not fight with destiny.
Choragos. You must go yourself, you cannot leave it to others.
Creon. I will go
　　　　　—Bring axes, servants:
Come with me to the tomb. I buried her, I
Will set her free.
　　　　　Oh quickly!
My mind misgives—
The laws of the gods are mighty, and a man must serve them
To the last days of his life!

(Exit Creon.)

PAEAN[16]

Choragos. God of many names　　　　　　　　　　*(Strophe 1)*
Chorus.　　　　　　　　　O Iacchos[17]
　　　　　　　　　　　　Son
of Kadmeian Sémelê
　　　　　　O born of the Thunder!
Guardian of the West
　　　　　　　　Regent
of Eleusis's plain
　　　　　　　O Prince of maenad Thebes
and the Dragon Field by rippling Ismenos:[18]

Choragos. God of many names　　　　　　　　　　*(Antistrophe 1)*
Chorus.　　　　　　　　the flame of torches
flares on our hills
　　　　　　　the nymphs of Iacchos
dance at the spring of Castalia:[19]
from the vine-close mountain
　　　　　　　　　come ah come in ivy:
Evohé evohé! sings through the streets of Thebes 10

---

[16] A hymn.　[17] Iacchos is a name for Dionysos. His mother was Sémelê, daughter of Kadmos, the founder of Thebes. His father was Zeus. The Maenads were priestesses of Dionysos who cry "evohé evohé." 　[18] A river of Thebes, sacred to Apollo. Dragon Field refers to the legend that the ancestors of Thebes sprang from the dragon's teeth sown by Kadmos.　[19] A spring on Mt. Parnasos.

Choragos. God of many names   *(Strophe 2)*
Chorus.   Iacchos of Thebes
  heavenly Child
               of Sémelê bride of the Thunderer!
  The shadow of plague is upon us:
                                        come
  with clement feet;
                         oh come from Parnasos
    down the long slopes
                    across the lamenting water

Choragos. Iô Fire! Chorister of the throbbing stars!   *(Antistrophe 2)*
  O purest among the voices of the night!
  Thou son of God, blaze for us!
Chorus. Come with choric rapture of circling Maenads
  Who cry Iô Iacche!
                God of many names!   20

EXODOS

(Enter Messenger, L.)

Messenger. Men of the line of Kadmos, you who live
  Near Amphion's[20] citadel:
                        I cannot say
  Of any condition of human life "This is fixed,
  This is clearly good, or bad." Fate raises up,
  And Fate casts down the happy and unhappy alike:
  No man can foretell his Fate.
                        Take the case of Creon:
  Creon was happy once, as I count happiness:
  Victorious in battle, sole governor of the land,
  Fortunate father of children nobly born.
  And now it has all gone from him! Who can say   10
  That a man is still alive when his life's joy fails?
  He is a walking dead man. Grant him rich,
  Let him live like a king in his great house:
  If his pleasure is gone, I would not give
  So much as the shadow of smoke for all he owns.
Choragos. Your words hint at sorrow: what is your news for us?
Messenger. They are dead. The living are guilty of their death.

---

[20] A child of Zeus and Antiope. He is noted for building the walls of Thebes by charming the stones into place with a lyre.

Choragos. Who is guilty? Who is dead? Speak!
Messenger.   Haimon.
  Haimon is dead; and the hand that killed him
  Is his own hand.   20
Choragos. His father's? or his own?
Messenger. His own, driven mad by the murder his father had done.
Choragos. Teiresias, Teiresias, how clearly you saw it all!
Messenger. This is my news: you must draw what conclusions you can from it.
Choragos. But look: Eurydicê, our Queen:
  Has she overheard us?

(Enter Eurydicê from the Palace, C.)

Eurydicê. I have heard something, friends:
  As I was unlocking the gate of Pallas'[21] shrine,
  For I needed her help today, I heard a voice
  Telling of some new sorrow. And I fainted   30
  There at the temple with all my maidens about me.
  But speak again: whatever it is, I can bear it:
  Grief and I are no strangers.
Messenger.   Dearest lady,
  I will tell you plainly all that I have seen.
  I shall not try to comfort you: what is the use,
  Since comfort could lie only in what is not true?
  The truth is always best.
                                      I went with Creon
  To the outer plain where Polyneicês was lying,
  No friend to pity him, his body shredded by dogs.
  We made our prayers in that place to Hecatê[22]   40
  And Pluto,[23] that they would be merciful. And we bathed
  The corpse with holy water, and we brought
  Fresh-broken branches to burn what was left of it,
  And upon the urn we heaped up a towering barrow
  Of the earth of his own land.
                                      When we were done, we ran
  To the vault where Antigonê lay on her couch of stone.
  One of the servants had gone ahead,
  And while he was yet far off he heard a voice
  Grieving within the chamber, and he came back
  And told Creon. And as the King went closer,   50
  The air was full of wailing, the words lost,

---

[21] Pallas Athene, goddess of wisdom.   [22] Hecatê is often identified with Persephone, a goddess of Hades; generally Hecatê is a goddess of sorcery and witchcraft.   [23] King of Hades and brother of Zeus and Poseidon.

And he begged us to make all haste. "Am I a prophet?"
He said, weeping, "And must I walk this road,
The saddest of all that I have gone before?
My son's voice calls me on. Oh quickly, quickly!
Look through the crevice there, and tell me
If it Haimon, or some deception of the gods!"

We obeyed; and in the cavern's farthest corner
We saw her lying:
She had made a noose of her fine linen veil   60
And hanged herself. Haimon lay beside her,
His arms about her waist, lamenting her,
His love lost under ground, crying out
That his father had stolen her away from him.

When Creon saw him the tears rushed to his eyes
And he called to him: "What have you done, child? Speak to me.
What are you thinking that makes your eyes so strange?
O my son, my son, I come to you on my knees!"
But Haimon spat in his face. He said not a word,
Staring—
                    And suddenly drew his sword   70
And lunged. Creon shrank back, the blade missed; and the boy,
Desperate against himself, drove it half its length
Into his own side, and fell. And as he died
He gathered Antigonê close in his arms again,
Choking, his blood bright red on her white cheek.
And now he lies dead with the dead, and she is his
At last, his bride in the houses of the dead.

(Exit Eurydicê into the Palace.)

Choragos. She has left us without a word. What can this mean?
Messenger. It troubles me, too; yet she knows what is best,
Her grief is too great for public lamentation,   80
And doubtless she has gone to her chamber to weep
For her dead son, leading her maidens in his dirge.
Choragos. It may be so: but I fear this deep silence.

(Pause.)

Messenger. I will see what she is doing. I will go in.

(Exit Messenger into the Palace.)
(Enter Creon with attendants, bearing Haimon's body.)

Choragos. But here is the King himself: oh look at him,
    Bearing his own damnation in his arms.
Creon. Nothing you say can touch me any more.
    My own blind heart has brought me
    From darkness to final darkness. Here you see   90
    The father murdering, the murdered son—
    And all my civic wisdom!
    Haimon my son, so young to die,
    I was the fool, not you; and you died for me.
Choragos. That is the truth; but you were late in learning it.
Creon. This truth is hard to bear. Surely a god
    Has crushed me beneath the hugest weight of heaven,
    And driven me headlong a barbaric way
    To trample out the thing I held most dear.

    The pains that men will take to come to pain!

(Enter Messenger from the Palace.)

Messenger. The burden you carry in your hands is heavy,   100
    But it is not all: you will find more in your house.
Creon. What burden worse than this shall I find there?
Messenger. The Queen is dead.
Creon. O port of death, deaf world,
    Is there no pity for me? And you, Angel of evil,
    I was dead, and your words are death again.
    Is it true, boy? Can it be true?
    Is my wife dead? Has death bred death?
Messenger. You can see for yourself.

(The doors are opened, and the body of Eurydicê is disclosed within.)

Creon. Oh pity!   110
    All true, all true, and more than I can bear!
    O my wife, my son!
Messenger. She stood before the altar, and her heart
    Welcomed the knife her own hand guided,
    And a great cry burst from her lips for Megareus[24] dead,
    And for Haimon dead, her sons; and her last breath
    Was a curse for their father, the murderer of her sons,
    And she fell, and the dark flowed in through her closing eyes.
Creon. O God, I am sick with fear.
    Are there no swords here? Has no one a blow for me?   120

[24] Son of Creon who was killed in the attack on Thebes.

Messenger. Her curse is upon you for the deaths of both.
Creon. It is right that it should be. I alone am guilty.
  I know it, and I say it. Lead me in,
  Quickly, friends.
  I have neither life nor substance. Lead me in.
Choragos. You are right, if there can be right in so much wrong.
  The briefest way is best in a world of sorrow.
Creon. Let it come,
  Let death come quickly, and be kind to me.   130
  I would not ever see the sun again.
Choragos. All that will come when it will; but we, meanwhile,
  Have much to do. Leave the future to itself.
Creon. All my heart was in that prayer!
Choragos. Then do not pray any more: the sky is deaf.
Creon. Lead me away. I have been rash and foolish.
  I have killed my son and my wife.
  I look for comfort; my comfort lies here dead.
  Whatever my hands have touched has come to nothing.
  Fate has brought all my pride to a thought of dust.

(As Creon is being led into the house, the Choragos advances and speaks directly to the audience.)

Choragos. There is no happiness where there is no wisdom;   140
  No wisdom but in submission to the gods.
  Big words are always punished,
  And proud men in old age learn to be wise.

FOR ANALYSIS

1. Critics are divided over the question of whether Antigonê or Creon is the **protagonist** of the play. How does the answer to this question affect one's interpretation of the play?

2. Show how the Prologue establishes the **mood** and **theme** of the play. What does it reveal about the characters of the two sisters?

3. What evidence is there that Creon would treat Antigonê differently if she were a man?

4. Does the character of Antigonê change in the course of the play?

5. Does the action of the play prepare us for Creon's sudden realization that he has been wrong?

6. Is there any justification for Antigonê's cold refusal to allow Ismenê to share her martyrdom?

7. Speculate on why Sophocles never brings Haimon and Antigonê together.

8. How does the **chorus** contribute to the dramatic development and tension of the play?

9. Analyze the use of **dramatic irony** in the play.

MAKING CONNECTIONS

What arguments used by Martin Luther King Jr. in "Letter from Birmingham Jail" (p. 533) echo Antigonê's arguments and actions?

WRITING TOPICS

1. In a brief paragraph, summarize the **theme** of this play.

2. Write a one-page essay using this play and Susan Glaspell's *Trifles* (p. 1050) as the basis for defining poetic drama on the one hand and realistic drama on the other.

NONFICTION

JONATHAN SWIFT (1667–1745)

A MODEST PROPOSAL 1729

It is a melancholy object to those who walk through this great town[1] or travel in the country, when they see the streets, the roads, and cabin doors, crowded with beggars of the female sex, followed by three, four, or six children, all in rags and importuning every passenger for an alms. These mothers, instead of being able to work for their honest livelihood, are forced to employ all their time in strolling to beg sustenance for their helpless infants, who, as they grow up, either turn thieves for want of work, or leave their dear native country to fight for the Pretender in Spain, or sell themselves to the Barbados.[2]

I think it is agreed by all parties that this prodigious number of children in the arms, or on the backs, or at the heels of their mothers, and frequently of their fathers, is in the present deplorable state of the kingdom a very great additional grievance; and therefore whoever could find out a fair, cheap, and easy method of making these children sound, useful members of the commonwealth would deserve so well of the public as to have his statue set up for a preserver of the nation.

But my intention is very far from being confined to provide only for the children of professed beggars; it is of a much greater extent, and shall take in the whole number of infants at a certain age who are born of parents in effect as little able to support them as those who demand our charity in the streets.

As to my own part, having turned my thoughts for many years upon this important subject, and maturely weighed the several schemes of other projectors,[3] I have always found them grossly mistaken in their computation. It is

---

[1] Dublin.

[2] Many Irish men joined the army of the exiled James Stuart (1688–1766), who laid claim to the British throne. Others exchanged their labor for passage to the British colony of Barbados, in the Caribbean.

[3] People with projects.

true, a child just dropped from its dam may be supported by her milk for a solar year, with little other nourishment; at most not above the value of two shillings,[4] which the mother may certainly get, or the value in scraps, by her lawful occupation of begging; and it is exactly at one year that I propose to provide for them in such a manner as instead of being a charge upon their parents or the parish, or wanting food and raiment for the rest of their lives, they shall on the contrary contribute to the feeding, and partly to the clothing, of many thousands.

There is likewise another great advantage in my scheme, that it will prevent those voluntary abortions, and that horrid practice of women murdering their bastard children, alas, too frequent among us, sacrificing the poor innocent babes, I doubt, more to avoid the expense than the shame, which would move tears and pity in the most savage and inhuman breast.

The number of souls in this kingdom being usually reckoned one million and a half, of these I calculate there may be about two hundred thousand couples whose wives are breeders; from which number I subtract thirty thousand couples who are able to maintain their own children, although I apprehend there cannot be so many under the present distress of the kingdom; but this being granted, there will remain an hundred and seventy thousand breeders. I again subtract fifty thousand for those women who miscarry, or whose children die by accident or disease within the year. There only remain an hundred and twenty thousand children of poor parents annually born. The question therefore is, how this number shall be reared and provided for, which, as I have already said, under the present situation of affairs, is utterly impossible by all the methods hitherto proposed. For we can neither employ them in handicraft or agriculture; we neither build houses (I mean in the country) nor cultivate land. They can very seldom pick up a livelihood by stealing till they arrive at six years old except where they are of towardly parts;[5] although I confess they learn the rudiments much earlier, during which time they can however be looked upon only as probationers, as I have been informed by a principal gentleman in the country of Cavan, who protested to me that he never knew above one or two instances under the age of six, even in a part of the kingdom so renowned for the quickest proficiency in that art.

I am assured by our merchants that a boy or a girl before twelve years old is no salable commodity; and even when they come to this age they will not yield above three pounds, or three pounds and half a crown at most on the Exchange;[6] which cannot turn to account either to the parents or the kingdom, the charge of nutriment and rags having been at least four times that value.

I shall now therefore humbly propose my own thoughts, which I hope will not be liable to the least objection.

I have been assured by a very knowing American of my acquaintance in London, that a young healthy child well nursed is at a year old a most delicious,

4 A shilling was worth about twenty-five cents.
5 Able and eager to learn.
6 A pound was twenty shillings; a crown, five shillings.

nourishing, and wholesome food, whether stewed, roasted, baked, or boiled; and I make no doubt that it will equally serve in a fricassee or a ragout.

I do therefore humbly offer it to public consideration that of the hundred 10 and twenty thousand children, already computed, twenty thousand may be reserved for breed, whereof only one fourth part to be males, which is more than we allow to sheep, black cattle, or swine; and my reason is that these children are seldom the fruits of marriage, a circumstance not much regarded by our savages, therefore one male will be sufficient to serve four females. That the remaining hundred thousand may at a year old be offered in sale to the persons of quality and fortune through the kingdom, always advising the mother to let them suck plentifully in the last month, so as to render them plump and fat for a good table. A child will make two dishes at an entertainment for friends; and when the family dines alone, the fore or hind quarter will make a reasonable dish, and seasoned with a little pepper or salt will be very good boiled on the fourth day, especially in winter.

I have reckoned upon a medium that a child just born will weigh twelve pounds, and in a solar year if tolerably nursed increaseth to twenty-eight pounds.

I grant this food will be somewhat dear, and therefore very proper for landlords, who, as they have already devoured most of the parents, seem to have the best title to the children.

Infant's flesh will be in season throughout the year, but more plentiful in March, and a little before and after. For we are told by a grave author, an eminent French physician,[7] that fish being a prolific diet, there are more children born in Roman Catholic countries about nine months after Lent than at any other season; therefore, reckoning a year after Lent, the markets will be more glutted than usual, because the number of popish infants is at least three to one in this kingdom; and therefore it will have one other collateral advantage, by lessening the number of Papists among us.

I have already computed the charge of nursing a beggar's child (in which list I reckon all cottagers, laborers, and four-fifths of the farmers) to be about two shillings per annum, rags included; and I believe no gentleman would repine to give ten shillings for the carcass of a good fat child, which, as I have said, will make four dishes of excellent nutritive meat, when he hath only some particular friend or his own family to dine with him. Thus the squire will learn to be a good landlord, and grow popular among the tenants; the mother will have eight shillings net profit, and be fit for work till she produces another child.

Those who are more thrifty (as I must confess the times require) may flay 15 the carcass; the skin of which artificially[8] dressed will make admirable gloves for ladies, and summer boots for fine gentlemen.

As to our city of Dublin, shambles[9] may be appointed for this purpose in the most convenient parts of it, and butchers we may be assured will not be wanting;

---

[7] François Rabelais, sixteenth-century French comic writer.
[8] Skillfully.
[9] Slaughterhouses.

although I rather recommend buying the children alive, and dressing them hot from the knife as we do roasting pigs.

A very worthy person, a true lover of his country, and whose virtues I highly esteem, was lately pleased in discoursing on this matter to offer a refinement upon my scheme. He said that many gentlemen of his kingdom, having of late destroyed their deer, he conceived that the want of venison might be well supplied by the bodies of young lads and maidens, not exceeding fourteen years of age nor under twelve, so great a number of both sexes in every country being now ready to starve for want of work or service; and these to be disposed of by their parents, if alive, or otherwise by their nearest relations. But with due deference to so excellent a friend and so deserving a patriot, I cannot be altogether in his sentiments; for as to the males, my American acquaintance assured me from frequent experience that their flesh was generally tough and lean, like that of our schoolboys, by continual exercise, and their taste disagreeable; and to fatten them would not answer the charge. Then as to the females; it would, I think with humble submission, be a loss to the public, because they soon would become breeders themselves; and besides, it is not improbable that some scrupulous people might be apt to censure such a practice (although indeed very unjustly) as a little bordering upon cruelty; which, I confess, hath always been with me the strongest objection against any project, how well soever intended.

But in order to justify my friend, he confessed that this expedient was put into his head by the famous Psalmanazar,[10] a native of the island Formosa, who came from thence to London above twenty years ago, and in conversation told my friend that in his country when any young person happened to be put to death, the executioner sold the carcass to persons of quality as a prime dainty; and that in his time the body of a plump girl of fifteen, who was crucified for an attempt to poison the emperor, was sold to his Imperial Majesty's prime minister of state, and other great mandarins of the court, in joints from the gibbet, at four hundred crowns. Neither indeed can I deny that if the same use were made of several plump young girls in this town, who without one single groat[11] to their fortunes cannot stir abroad without a chair,[12] and appear at the playhouse and assemblies in foreign fineries which they never will pay for, the kingdom would not be the worse.

Some persons of a desponding spirit are in great concern about the vast number of poor people who are aged, diseased, or maimed, and I have been desired to employ my thoughts what course may be taken to ease the nation of so grievous an encumberance. But I am not in the least pain upon the matter, because it is very well known that they are every day dying and rotting by cold and famine, and filth and vermin, as fast as can be reasonably expected. And as

---

[10] George Psalmanazar was a Frenchman who passed himself off as a native of Formosa (the former name for Taiwan).

[11] A coin worth about four cents.

[12] A sedan chair, an enclosed chair carried by poles on the front and back.

to the younger laborers, they are now in almost as hopeful a condition. They cannot get work, and consequently pine away for want of nourishment to a degree that if any time they are accidently hired to common labor, they have not the strength to perform it; and thus the country and themselves are happily delivered from the evils to come.

I have too long digressed, and therefore I shall return to my subject. I think 20 the advantages by the proposal which I have made are obvious and many, as well as of the highest importance.

For first, I have already observed, it would greatly lessen the number of Papists, with whom we are yearly overrun, being the principal breeders of the nation as well as our most dangerous enemies; and who stay at home on purpose to deliver the kingdom to the Pretender, hoping to take their advantage by the absence of so many good Protestants, who have chose rather to leave their country than to stay at home and pay tithes against their conscience to an Episcopal curate.

Secondly, the poorer tenants will have something valuable of their own, which by law may be made liable to distress,[13] and help to pay their landlord's rent, their corn and cattle being already seized and money a thing unknown.

Thirdly, whereas the maintenance of a hundred thousand children, from two years old and upwards, cannot be computed at less than ten shillings a piece per annum, the nation's stock will be thereby increased fifty thousand pounds per annum, besides the profit of a new dish introduced to the tables of all gentlemen of fortune in the kingdom who have any refinement in taste. And all the money will circulate among ourselves, the goods being entirely of our own growth and manufacture.

Fourthly, the constant breeders, besides the gain of eight shillings sterling per annum by the sale of their children, will be rid of the charge of maintaining them after the first year.

Fifthly, this food would likewise bring great custom to taverns, where the 25 vintners will certainly be so prudent as to procure the best receipts[14] for dressing it to perfection, and consequently have their houses frequented by all the fine gentlemen, who justly value themselves upon their knowledge in good eating; and a skillful cook, who understands how to oblige his guests, will contrive to make it as expensive as they please.

Sixthly, this would be a great inducement to marriage, which all wise nations have either encouraged by rewards or enforced by laws and penalties. It would increase the care and tenderness of mothers towards their children, when they were sure of a settlement for life to the poor babes, provided in some sort by the public, to their annual profit instead of expense. We should see an honest emulation among the married women, which of them could bring the fattest child to the market. Men would become as fond of their wives during the time of their pregnancy as they are now of their mares in foal, their cows in calf, or

---

[13] Seizure for payment of debts.
[14] Recipes.

sows when they are ready to farrow; nor offer to beat or kick them (as is too frequent a practice) for fear of a miscarriage.

Many other advantages might be enumerated. For instance, the addition of some thousand carcasses in our exportation of barreled beef, the propagation of swine's flesh, and improvements in the art of making good bacon, so much wanted among us by the great destruction of pigs, too frequent at our tables, which are no way comparable in taste or magnificence to a well-grown, fat, yearling child, which roasted whole will make a considerable figure at a lord mayor's feast or any other public entertainment. But this and many others I omit, being studious of brevity.

Supposing that one thousand families in this city would be constant customers for infants' flesh, besides others who might have it at merry meetings, particularly weddings and christenings, I compute that Dublin would take off annually about twenty thousand carcasses, and the rest of the kingdom (where probably they will be sold somewhat cheaper) the remaining eighty thousand.

I can think of no one objection that will possibly be raised against this proposal unless it should be urged that the number of people will be thereby much lessened in the kingdom. This I freely own, and it was indeed one principal design in offering it to the world. I desire the reader will observe, that I calculate my remedy for this one individual kingdom of Ireland and for no other that ever was, is, or I think ever can be upon earth. Therefore let no man talk to me of other expedients: of taxing our absentees at five shillings a pound: of using neither clothes nor household furniture except what is of our own growth and manufacture: of utterly rejecting the materials and instruments that promote foreign luxury: of curing the expensiveness of pride, vanity, idleness, and gaming in our women: of introducing a vein of parsimony, prudence, and temperance: of learning to love our country, in the want of which we differ even from Laplanders and the inhabitants of Topinamboo:[15] of quitting our animosities and factions, nor acting any longer like the Jews, who were murdering one another at the very moment their city was taken:[16] of being a little cautious not to sell our country and conscience for nothing: of teaching landlords to have at least one degree of mercy toward their tenants: lastly, of putting a spirit of honesty, industry, and skill into our shopkeepers; who, if a resolution could now be taken to buy only our native goods, would immediately unite to cheat and exact upon us in the price, the measure, and the goodness, nor could ever yet be brought to make one fair proposal of just dealing, though often and earnestly invited to it.

Therefore, I repeat, let no man talk to me of these and the like expedients, till he hath at least some glimpse of hope that there will be some hearty and sincere attempt to put them in practice.

---

[15] A district in Brazil, inhabited in Swift's day by primitive tribes.
[16] While the Roman emperor Titus laid siege to Jerusalem in A.D. 70, bloody fighting erupted among factions within the city.

But as to myself, having been wearied out for many years of offering vain, idle, visionary thoughts, and at length utterly despairing of success, I fortunately fell upon this proposal, which, as it is wholly new, so it hath something solid and real, of no expense and little trouble, full in our own power, and whereby we can incur no danger in disobliging England. For this kind of commodity will not bear exportation, the flesh being of too tender a consistence to admit a long continuance in salt, although perhaps I could name a country[17] which would be glad to eat up our whole nation without it.

After all, I am not so violently bent upon my own opinion as to reject any offer proposed by wise men, which shall be found equally innocent, cheap, easy, and effectual. But before something of that kind shall be advanced in contradiction to my scheme, and offering a better, I desire the author or authors will be pleased maturely to consider two points. First, as things now stand, how they will be able to find food and raiment for an hundred thousand useless mouths and backs. And secondly, there being a round million of creatures in human figure throughout this kingdom, whose sole subsistence put into a common stock would leave them in debt two millions of pounds sterling, adding those who are beggars by profession to the bulk of farmers, cottagers, and laborers, with their wives and children who are beggars in effect; I desire those politicians who dislike my overture, and may perhaps be so bold to attempt to answer, that they will first ask the parents of these mortals whether they would not at this day think it a great happiness to have been sold for food at a year old in this manner I prescribe, and thereby have avoided such a perpetual scene of misfortunes as they have since gone through by the oppression of landlords, the impossibility of paying rent without money or trade, the want of common sustenance, with neither house nor clothes to cover them from the inclemencies of the weather, and the most inevitable prospect of entailing the like or greater miseries upon their breed forever.

I profess, in the sincerity of my heart, that I have not the least personal interest in endeavoring to promote this necessary work, having no other motive than the public good of my country, by advancing our trade, providing for infants, relieving the poor, and giving some pleasure to the rich. I have no children by which I can propose to get a single penny; the youngest being nine years old, and my wife past childbearing.

FOR ANALYSIS

1. What kind of person is the speaker? What does his tone of voice reveal about who he is? Is his voice direct and transparent, or does it seem deliberately created to achieve a specific effect?

2. In what sense is the proposal "modest"?

3. Where are the major divisions of the essay? What function does each serve?

---

[17] England.

4. What function does paragraph 29 serve?

5. Explain what Swift means when he says in paragraph 20, "I have too long digressed."

6. Whom is Swift addressing in this essay?

MAKING CONNECTIONS

Some other works in this anthology that use **satire** include e. e. cummings, "the Cambridge ladies who live in furnished souls" (p. 679); W. H. Auden, "The Unknown Citizen" (p. 443) and Harlan Ellison, "'Repent, Harlequin!' Said the Ticktockman" (p. 401). Compare and contrast the use of satire in one of these works with Swift's use of satire.

WRITING TOPICS

1. Some background information on Swift's life, as well as familiarity with his other works, would make it clear that in this essay he is being satiric. Without that background—that is, on the basis of this essay alone—would you conclude that Swift is writing **satire**? Explain.

2. In one brief paragraph, paraphrase the major arguments Swift uses to support his plan.

JAMAICA KINCAID (B. 1949)

ON SEEING ENGLAND
FOR THE FIRST TIME   1991

When I saw England for the first time, I was a child in school sitting at a desk. The England I was looking at was laid out on a map gently, beautifully, delicately, a very special jewel; it lay on a bed of sky blue—the background of the map—its yellow form mysterious, because though it looked like a leg of mutton, it could not really look like anything so familiar as a leg of mutton because it was England—with shadings of pink and green, unlike any shadings of pink and green I had seen before, squiggly veins of red running in every direction. England was a special jewel all right, and only special people got to wear it. The people who got to wear England were English people. They wore it well and they wore it everywhere: in jungles, in deserts, on plains, on top of the highest mountains, on all the oceans, on all the seas, in places where they were not welcome, in places they should not have been. When my teacher had pinned this map up on the blackboard, she said, "This is England"—and she said it with authority, seriousness, and adoration, and we all sat up. It was as if she had said, "This is Jerusalem, the place you will go to when you die but only if you have been good." We understood then—we were meant to understand then—that England was to be our source of myth and the source from which we got our sense of reality, our sense of what was meaningful, our sense of what was meaningless—and much about our own lives and much about the very idea of us headed that last list.

At the time I was a child sitting at my desk seeing England for the first time, I was already very familiar with the greatness of it. Each morning before I left for school, I ate a breakfast of half a grapefruit, an egg, bread and butter and a slice of cheese, and a cup of cocoa; or half a grapefruit, a bowl of oat porridge, bread and butter and a slice of cheese, and a cup of cocoa. The can of cocoa was often left on the table in front of me. It had written on it the name of the company, the year the company was established, and the words "Made in England." Those words, "Made in England," were written on the box the oats came in too. They would also have been written on the box the shoes I was wearing came in; a bolt of gray linen cloth lying on the shelf of a store from which my mother had bought three yards to make the uniform that I was wearing had written along its edge those three words. The shoes I wore were made in England; so were my socks and cotton undergarments and the satin ribbons I wore tied at the end of two plaits of my hair. My father, who might have sat next to me at breakfast, was a carpenter and cabinet maker. The shoes he wore to work would have been made in England, as were his khaki shirt and trousers, his underpants and undershirt, his socks and brown felt hat. Felt was not the proper material from which a hat that was expected to provide shade from the hot sun should be made, but my father must have seen and admired a picture of an Englishman wearing such a hat in England, and this picture that he saw must have been so compelling that it caused him to wear the wrong hat for a hot climate most of his long life. And this hat—a brown felt hat—became so central to his character that it was the first thing he put on in the morning as he stepped out of bed and the last thing he took off before he stepped back into bed at night. As we sat at breakfast a car might go by. The car, a Hillman or a Zephyr, was made in England. The very idea of the meal itself, breakfast, and its substantial quality and quantity was an idea from England; we somehow knew that in England they began the day with this meal called breakfast and a proper breakfast was a big breakfast. No one I knew liked eating so much food so early in the day; it made us feel sleepy, tired. But this breakfast business was Made in England like almost everything else that surrounded us, the exceptions being the sea, the sky, and the air we breathed.

At the time I saw this map—seeing England for the first time—I did not say to myself, "Ah, so that's what it looks like," because there was no longing in me to put a shape to those three words that ran through every part of my life, no matter how small; for me to have had such a longing would have meant that I lived in a certain atmosphere, an atmosphere in which those three words were felt as a burden. But I did not live in such an atmosphere. My father's brown felt hat would develop a hole in its crown, the lining would separate from the hat itself, and six weeks before he thought that he could not be seen wearing it—he was a very vain man—he would order another hat from England. And my mother taught me to eat my food in the English way: the knife in the right hand, the fork in the left, my elbows held still close to my side, the food carefully balanced on my fork and then brought up to my mouth. When I had finally mastered it, I overheard her saying to a friend, "Did you see how nicely she can eat?" But I knew then that I enjoyed my food more when I ate it with my bare hands, and I continued to do so when she wasn't looking. And when my teacher showed us the map, she asked us to study it carefully, because no test we would ever take would be complete without this statement: "Draw a map of England."

I did not know then that the statement "Draw a map of England" was something far worse than a declaration of war, for in fact a flat-out declaration of war would have put me on alert, and again in fact, there was no need for war—I had long ago been conquered. I did not know then that this statement was part of a process that would result in my erasure, not my physical erasure, but my erasure all the same. I did not know then that this statement was meant to make me feel in awe and small whenever I heard the word "England": awe at its existence, small because I was not from it. I did not know very much of anything then—certainly not what a blessing it was that I was unable to draw a map of England correctly.

After that there were many times of seeing England for the first time. I saw ₅ England in history. I knew the names of all the kings of England. I knew the names of their children, their wives, their disappointments, their triumphs, the names of people who betrayed them, I knew the dates on which they were born and the dates they died. I knew their conquests and was made to feel glad if I figured in them; I knew their defeats. I knew the details of the year 1066 (the Battle of Hastings, the end of the reign of the Anglo-Saxon kings) before I knew the details of the year 1832 (the year slavery was abolished). It wasn't as bad as I make it sound now; it was worse. I did like so much hearing again and again how Alfred the Great, traveling in disguise, had been left to watch cakes, and because he wasn't used to this the cakes got burned, and Alfred burned his hands pulling them out of the fire, and the woman who had left him to watch the cakes screamed at him. I loved King Alfred. My grandfather was named after him; his son, my uncle, was named after King Alfred; my brother is named after King Alfred. And so there are three people in my family named after a man they have never met, a man who died over ten centuries ago. The first view I got of England then was not unlike the first view received by the person who named my grandfather.

This view, though—the naming of the kings, their deeds, their disappointments—was the vivid view, the forceful view. There were other views, subtler ones, softer, almost not there—but these were the ones that made the most lasting impression on me, these were the ones that made me really feel like nothing. "When morning touched the sky" was one phrase, for no morning touched the sky where I lived. The mornings where I lived came on abruptly, with a shock of heat and loud noises. "Evening approaches" was another, but the evenings where I lived did not approach; in fact, I had no evening—I had night and I had day and they came and went in a mechanical way: on, off; on, off. And then there were gentle mountains and low blue skies and moors over which people took walks for nothing but pleasure, when where I lived a walk was an act of labor, a burden, something only death or the automobile could relieve. And there were things that a small turn of a head could convey—entire worlds, whole lives would depend on this thing, a certain turn of a head. Everyday life could be quite tiring, more tiring than anything I was told not to do. I was told not to gossip, but they did that all the time. And they ate so much food, violating another of those rules they taught me: do not indulge in gluttony. And the foods they ate actually: if only sometime I could eat cold cuts after theater, cold cuts of lamb and mint sauce, and Yorkshire pudding and scones, and clotted cream, and sausages that came from upcountry (imagine, "up-country"). And having troubling thoughts at twilight, a good time to have troubling thoughts, apparently; and servants who stole and left in the middle of a crisis, who were born with a limp or some other kind of deformity, not nourished properly in their mother's womb (that last part I figured out for myself; the point was, oh to have an untrustworthy servant); and wonderful cobbled streets onto which solid front doors opened; and people whose eyes were blue and who had fair skins and who smelled only of lavender, or sometimes sweet pea or primrose. And those flowers with those names: delphiniums, foxgloves, tulips, daffodils, floribunda, peonies; in bloom, a striking display, being cut and placed in large glass bowls, crystal, decorating rooms so large twenty families the size of mine could fit in comfortably but used only for passing through. And the weather was so remarkable because the rain fell gently always, only occasionally in deep gusts, and it colored the air various shades of gray, each an appealing shade for a dress to be worn when a portrait was being painted; and when it rained at twilight, wonderful things happened: people bumped into each other unexpectedly and that would lead to all sorts of turns of events—a plot, the mere weather caused plots. I saw that people rushed: they rushed to catch trains, they rushed toward each other and away from each other; they rushed and rushed and rushed. That word: rushed! I did not know what it was to do that. It was too hot to do that, and so I came to envy people who would rush, even though it had no meaning to me to do such a thing. But there they are again. They loved their children; their children were sent to their own rooms as a punishment, rooms larger than my entire house. They were special, everything about them said so, even their clothes; their clothes rustled, swished, soothed. The world was theirs, not mine; everything told me so.

If now as I speak of all this I give the impression of someone on the outside looking in, nose pressed up against a glass window, that is wrong. My nose was pressed up against a glass window all right, but there was an iron vise at the back of my neck forcing my head to stay in place. To avert my gaze was to fall back into something from which I had been rescued, a hole filled with nothing, and that was the word for everything about me, nothing. The reality of my life was conquests, subjugation, humiliation, enforced amnesia. I was forced to forget. Just for instance, this: I lived in a part of St. John's, Antigua, called Ovals. Ovals was made up of five streets, each of them named after a famous English seaman—to be quite frank, an officially sanctioned criminal: Rodney Street (after George Rodney), Nelson Street (after Horatio Nelson), Drake Street (after Francis Drake), Hood Street, and Hawkins Street (after John Hawkins). But John Hawkins was knighted after a trip he made to Africa, opening up a new trade, the slave trade. He was then entitled to wear as his crest a Negro bound with a cord. Every single person living on Hawkins Street was descended from a slave. John Hawkins's ship, the one in which he transported the people he had bought and kidnapped, was called *The Jesus*. He later became the treasurer of the Royal Navy and rear admiral.

Again, the reality of my life, the life I led at the time I was being shown these views of England for the first time, for the second time, for the one-hundred-millionth time, was this: the sun shone with what sometimes seemed to be a deliberate cruelty; we must have done something to deserve that. My dresses did not rustle in the evening air as I strolled to the theater (I had no evening, I had no theater; my dresses were made of a cheap cotton, the weave of which would give way after not too many washings). I got up in the morning, I did my chores (fetched water from the public pipe for my mother, swept the yard).

I washed myself, I went to a woman to have my hair combed freshly every day (because before we were allowed into our classroom our teachers would inspect us, and children who had not bathed that day, or had dirt under their fingernails, or whose hair had not been combed anew that day, might not be allowed to attend class). I ate that breakfast. I walked to school. At school we gathered in an auditorium and sang a hymn, "All Things Bright and Beautiful," and looking down on us as we sang were portraits of the Queen of England and her husband; they wore jewels and medals and they smiled. I was a Brownie. At each meeting we would form a little group around a flagpole, and after raising the Union Jack, we would say, "I promise to do my best, to do my duty to God and the Queen, to help other people every day and obey the scouts' law."

Who were these people and why had I never seen them, I mean really seen them, in the place where they lived? I had never been to England. No one I knew had ever been to England, or I should say, no one I knew had ever been and returned to tell me about it. All the people I knew who had gone to England had stayed there. Sometimes they left behind them their small children, never to see them again. England! I had seen England's representatives. I had seen the governor general at the public grounds at a ceremony celebrating the Queen's birthday. I had seen an old princess and I had seen a young princess. They had both been extremely not beautiful, but who of us would have told them that? I had never seen England, really seen it, I had only met a representative, seen a picture, read books, memorized its history. I had never set foot, my own foot, in it.

The space between the idea of something and its reality is always wide and deep and dark. The longer they are kept apart—idea of thing, reality of thing—the wider the width, the deeper the depth, the thicker and darker the darkness. This space starts out empty, there is nothing in it, but it rapidly becomes filled up with obsession or desire or hatred or love—sometimes all of these things, sometimes some of these things, sometimes only one of these things. The existence of the world as I came to know it was a result of this: idea of thing over here, reality of thing way, way over there. There was Christopher Columbus, an unlikable man, an unpleasant man, a liar (and so, of course, a thief) surrounded by maps and schemes and plans, and there was the reality on the other side of that width, that depth, that darkness. He became obsessed, he became filled with desire, the hatred came later, love was never a part of it. Eventually, his idea met the longed-for reality. That the idea of something and its reality are often two completely different things is something no one ever remembers; and so when they meet and find that they are not compatible, the weaker of the two, idea or reality, dies. That idea Christopher Columbus had was more powerful than the reality he met, and so the reality he met died.

And so finally, when I was a grown-up woman, the mother of two children, the wife of someone, a person who resides in a powerful country that takes up more than its fair share of a continent, the owner of a house with many rooms in it and of two automobiles, with the desire and will (which I very much act upon) to take from the world more than I give back to it, more than I deserve, more than I need, finally then, I saw England, the real England, not a picture, not a painting, not through a story in a book, but England, for the first time. In me, the space between the idea of it and its reality had become filled with hatred, and so when at last I saw it I wanted to take it into my hands and tear it into little pieces and then crumble it up as if it were clay, child's clay. That was impossible, and so I could only indulge in not-favorable opinions.

There were monuments everywhere; they commemorated victories, battles fought between them and the people who lived across the sea from them, all vile people, fought over which of them would have dominion over the people who looked like me. The monuments were useless to them now, people sat on them and ate their lunch. They were like markers on an old useless trail, like a piece of old string tied to a finger to jog the memory, like old decoration in an old house, dirty, useless, in the way. Their skins were so pale, it made them look so fragile, so weak, so ugly. What if I had the power to simply banish them from their land, send boat after boatload of them on a voyage that in fact had no destination, force them to live in a place where the sun's presence was a constant? This would rid them of their pale complexion and make them look more like me, make them look more like the people I love and treasure and hold dear, and more like the people who occupy the near and far reaches of my imagination, my history, my geography, and reduce them and everything they have ever known to figurines as evidence that I was in divine favor, what if all this was in my power? Could I resist it? No one ever has.

And they were rude, they were rude to each other. They didn't like each other very much. They didn't like each other in the way they didn't like me, and it occurred to me that their dislike for me was one of the few things they agreed on.

I was on a train in England with a friend, an English woman. Before we were in England she liked me very much. In England she didn't like me at all. She didn't like the claim I said I had on England, she didn't like the views I had of England. I didn't like England, she didn't like England, but she didn't like me not liking it too. She said, "I want to show you my England, I want to show you the England that I know and love." I had told her many times before that I knew England and I didn't want to love it anyway. She no longer lived in England; it was her own country, but it had not been kind to her, so she left. On the train, the conductor was rude to her; she asked something, and he responded in a rude way. She became ashamed. She was ashamed at the way he treated her; she was ashamed at the way he behaved. "This is the new England," she said. But I liked the conductor being rude; his behavior seemed quite appropriate. Earlier this had happened: we had gone to a store to buy a shirt for my husband; it was meant to be a special present, a special shirt to wear on special occasions. This was a store where the Prince of Wales has his shirts made, but the shirts sold in this store are beautiful all the same. I found a shirt I thought my husband would like and I wanted to buy him a tie to go with it. When I couldn't decide which one to choose, the salesman showed me a new set. He was very pleased with these, he said, because they bore the crest of the Prince of Wales, and the Prince of Wales had never allowed his crest to decorate an article of clothing before. There was something in the way he said it; his tone was slavish, reverential, awed. It made me feel angry; I wanted to hit him. I didn't do that. I said, my husband and I hate princes, my husband would never wear anything that had a prince's anything on it. My friend stiffened. The salesman stiffened. They both drew themselves in, away from me. My friend told me that the prince was a symbol of her Englishness, and I could see that I had caused offense. I looked at her. She was an English person, the sort of English person I used to know at home, the sort who was nobody in England but somebody when they came to live among the people like me. There were many people I could have seen England with; that I was seeing it with this particular person, a person who reminded me of the people who showed me England long ago as I sat in church or at my desk, made me feel silent and afraid, for I wondered if, all these years of our friendship, I had had a friend or had been in the thrall of a racial memory.

I went to Bath—we, my friend and I, did this, but though we were together, 15 I was no longer with her. The landscape was almost as familiar as my own hand, but I had never been in this place before, so how could that be again? And the streets of Bath were familiar, too, but I had never walked on them before. It was all those years of reading, starting with Roman Britain. Why did I have to know about Roman Britain? It was of no real use to me, a person living on a hot, drought-ridden island, and it is of no use to me now, and yet my head is filled with this nonsense, Roman Britain. In Bath, I drank tea in a room I had read about in a novel written in the eighteenth century. In this very same room, young women wearing those dresses that rustled and so on danced and flirted and sometimes disgraced themselves with young men, soldiers, sailors, who were on their way to Bristol or someplace like that, so many places like that where so many adventures, the outcome of which was not good for me, began. Bristol, England. A sentence that began "That night the ship sailed from Bristol, England" would end not so good for me. And then I was driving through the countryside in an English motorcar, on narrow winding roads, and they were so familiar, though I had never been on them before; and through little villages the names of which I somehow knew so well though I had never been there before. And the countryside did have all those hedges and hedges, fields hedged in. I was marveling at all the toil of it, the planting of the hedges to begin with and then the care of it, all that clipping, year after year of clipping, and I wondered at the lives of the people who would have to do this, because wherever I see and feel the hands that hold up the world, I see and feel myself and all the people who look like me. And I said, "Those hedges" and my friend said that someone, a woman named Mrs. Rothchild, worried that the hedges weren't being taken care of properly; the farmers couldn't afford or find the help to keep up the hedges, and often they replaced them with wire fencing. I might have said to that, well if Mrs. Rothchild doesn't like the wire fencing, why doesn't she take care of the hedges herself, but I didn't. And then in those fields that were now hemmed in by wire fencing that a privileged woman didn't like was planted a vile yellow flowering bush that produced an oil, and my friend said that Mrs. Rothchild didn't like this either; it ruined the English countryside, it ruined the traditional look of the English countryside.

It was not at that moment that I wished every sentence, everything I knew, that began with England would end with "and then it all died; we don't know how, it just all died." At that moment, I was thinking, who are these people who forced me to think of them all the time, who forced me to think that the world I knew was incomplete, or without substance, or did not measure up because it was not England; that I was incomplete, or without substance, and did not measure up because I was not English. Who were these people? The person sitting next to me couldn't give me a clue; no one person could. In any case, if I had said to her, I find England ugly, I hate England; the weather is like a jail sentence, the English are a very ugly people, the food in England is like a jail sentence, the hair of English people is so straight, so dead looking, the English have an unbearable smell so different from the smell of people I know, real people of course, she would have said that I was a person full of prejudice. Apart from the fact that it is I—that is, the people who look like me— who made her aware of the unpleasantness of such a thing, the idea of such a thing, prejudice, she would have been only partly right, sort of right: I may be capable of prejudice, but my prejudices have no weight to them, my prejudices have no force behind them, my prejudices remain opinions, my prejudices remain my personal opinion. And a great feeling of rage and disappointment came over me as I looked at England, my head full of personal opinions that could not have public, my public, approval. The people I come from are powerless to do evil on grand scale.

The moment I wished every sentence, everything I knew, that began with England would end with "and then it all died, we don't know how, it just all died" was when I saw the white cliffs of Dover. I had sung hymns and recited poems that were about a longing to see the white cliffs of Dover again. At the time I sang the hymns and recited the poems, I could really long to see them again because I had never seen them at all, nor had anyone around me at the time. But there we were, groups of people longing for something we had never seen. And so there they were, the white cliffs, but they were not that pearly majestic thing I used to sing about, that thing that created such a feeling in these people that when they died in the place where I lived they had themselves buried facing a direction that would allow them to see the white cliffs of Dover when they were resurrected, as surely they would be. The white cliffs of Dover, when finally I saw them, were cliffs, but they were not white; you would only call them that if the word "white" meant something special to you; they were dirty and they were steep; they were so steep, the correct height from which all my views of England, starting with the map before me in my classroom and ending with the trip I had just taken, should jump and die and disappear forever.

FOR ANALYSIS

1. How does the England that Kincaid reads about as a schoolgirl contrast to the Jamaica she lived in?

2. Why does England, never seen by Kincaid until her adulthood, inspire such strong feelings in her? How does her essay convey the depth of these feelings?

3. Kincaid writes, "The space between the idea of something and its reality is always wide and deep and dark" (para. 10). How does the essay dramatize this idea? What figures of speech or other techniques does Kincaid use that represent the gap between the real and the idea of it?

MAKING CONNECTIONS

1. Compare any of the poems in "Connecting Poems: Revising America" (p. 457) to "On Seeing England for the First Time." How is Kincaid's essay similarly interested in rethinking an **image** of a nation? How is it different in the object of its scrutiny not being the place where its author lives?

2. Compare Kincaid's use of the recalled-from-adulthood child's **point of view** to Hanan Ashrawi's use of the point of view of the child in the moment in "Night Patrol" (p. 463). What is gained or lost in terms of knowledge and immediacy in each case?

WRITING TOPIC

Name a place that you had a strong sense of without having visited it. If you have since been there, how was it similar or different? If not, how do you think it might be similar or different?

CONNECTING NONFICTION: WEIGHING BELIEF

For much of human history, religious belief has been an inextricable and unexamined part of culture—it was unthinkable for individuals to doubt their culture's singular story of creation and divine involvement in daily life. In the modern world, it is much more possible to weigh belief—to choose to believe or not to believe, to adhere to one or a number of available religions, or to choose to disbelieve in any theological explanation whatsoever of existence.

The world has recently seen an upsurge in fundamentalism, in styles of religious belief that offer a return to the time before doubt. The two essays in this unit deal with this phenomenon in different ways, but both speak from outside fundamentalist religious belief, examining it in itself and in its (to them) unavoidable historical and social contexts. As you read Rushdie's and Doctorow's thoughts, "imagine" discussions of religious belief that avoid these framing issues. Is it possible to critically examine religion, or any system of belief or ostensible knowledge, without taking into account other, ever-changing elements of human experience?

E. L. DOCTOROW   (B. 1931)

WHY WE ARE INFIDELS   2003

We have lately been called infidels. Yet we are perhaps the most prayerful nation in the world. Both Tocqueville and Dickens[1] when they came over here to have a look at us were astonished at how much God there was in American society. True, the infidel is not necessarily a nonbeliever; he may also be a believer of the wrong stripe. But I think, given the variety of religious practice in our country, including that of Islam, that the term *infidel* as it has lately been applied to us probably does not refer to any particular religion we may as a nation subscribe to, but to the fact that we subscribe, within our population of three hundred million, to all of them.

Of course most of our religions, including Christianity, Judaism, Islam, Buddhism, landed here at different times from other parts of the world. They have been vulnerable as religions usually are to such denominational fracture as to offer a potential parishioner a virtual supermarket of spiritual choice. Some of our religions, Mormonism, Christian Science, Native American Anthropomorphism, were invented, or revealed, right here. And if we think even casually of

---

[1] Alexis de Tocqueville (1805–1859), an eminent French statesman who traveled to the United States in 1831 to study its prison system. His general observations on democratic government were recorded in *Democracy in America* (1835). The popular English novelist Charles Dickens (1812–1870) recorded his views of American life gathered during a trip in 1842.

the parade of creative and influential religionists on our shores[2]—from the colonists Anne Hutchinson and Roger Williams, George Fox, Jonathan Edwards, and Cotton Mather to our citizen evangelicals Aimee Semple McPherson, Billy Sunday, Father Divine, and Billy Graham, we notice immediately that we have left out the Adventists, the Millerites, the Shakers, Swedenborgians, and Perfectionists of the nineteenth century, to say nothing of the stadium-filling brides and grooms of the Reverend Moon's Unification Church, or the suicidal cultists of Jim Jones, or the unfortunate Branch Davidians of Waco, Texas, or the Heaven's Gate believers who castrated themselves and took their own lives in order to board the Hale-Bopp comet when it flew past in 1997.

One of the less scintillating debates among theologians is on the distinction between a religion and a cult. But all together, our religions or religious cults testify to the deeply serious American thirst for celestial connection. We want a spiritual release from the society we have made out of secular humanism.

That our God-soaked country is, as political science, secular, may be indicated by the fact that the word for the state of being of an infidel, *infidelity*, brings to our minds not a violation of faith in the true God but a violation of the marriage contract between ordinary mortals. Philandering husbands and adulterous wives may be viewed as immoral and looked upon with contempt or pity, but they are not usually regarded as infidels. The term however may be justly applied to all of us, including the most pious and monogamous among us, because of a major national sin committed over two hundred years ago when religion and the American state were rent asunder and all worship was consigned to private life. It was Jefferson who said, "Our civil rights have no dependence on our religious opinions, any more than our opinions in physics or geometry." And while it is precisely because of this principle of religious freedom that we enjoy such a continuous national uproar of praying and singing and studying and fasting and confessing and atoning and praising and preaching and dancing and dunking and vowing and quaking and shaking and abstaining and ordaining, a paradox arises from this expression of our religious democracy: if you have extracted the basic ethics of religious invention and found the mechanism for installing them in the statutes of the secular civil order, as we have with our Constitution and our Bill of Rights, but have consigned all the doctrine and rite and ritual, all the symbols and traditional practices to the precincts of private life, you are saying there is no one proven path to salvation, there are only traditions. If you relegate the old stories to the personal choices of private worship, you admit the ineffable[3] is ineffable, and in terms of a possible theological triumphalism everything is up for grabs.

Our pluralism has to be a profound offense to the fundamentalist who by 5 definition is an absolutist intolerant of all forms of belief but his own, all stories but his own. In our raucous democracy fundamentalist religious belief has

---

[2] Doctorow alludes to a number of persons and religious constructs in paragraph 2. Use a search engine to find information on those unfamiliar to you.
[3] Indescribable; too awesome to be spoken.

organized itself with political acumen to promulgate law that would undermine just those secular humanist principles that encourage it to flourish in freedom. Of course there has rarely been a period in our history when God has not been called upon to march. The abolitionists decried slavery as a sin against God. The South claimed biblical authority for its slaveholding. The civil disobedience of Dr. Martin Luther King Jr.'s civil rights movement drew its strength from prayer and the examples of Christian fortitude, while the Ku Klux Klan and other white supremacy groups invoked Jesus as a sponsor of their racism. But there is a crucial difference of emphasis between these traditional invocations and the politically astute and well-funded actions in recent years of the leaders of the movement known as the Christian Right, who do not call upon their faith to certify their politics as much as they call for a country that certifies their faith.

Fundamentalism really cannot help itself—it is absolutist and can compromise with nothing, not even democracy. It is not surprising that immediately after the Islamic fundamentalist attack on the World Trade Center and the Pentagon two prominent Christian fundamentalists were reported to have accounted it as justifiable punishment by God for our secularism, our civil libertarianism, our feminists, our gay and lesbian citizens, our abortion providers, and everything and everyone else which their fundamentalist belief condemns. In thus honoring the foreign killers of over three thousand Americans as agents of God's justice, they established their own consanguinity with the principle of righteous warfare in the name of all that is holy, and gave their pledge of allegiance to the theocratic ideal of government of whatever sacred text.

Not just on other shores are we considered a nation of infidels.

FOR ANALYSIS

1. In religious terms, what is an infidel?

2. What are religious fundamentalists? How would they respond to the presumptions of a religion different from their own?

3. What is the official relationship between religion and government in the United States? Do you approve or disapprove of that relationship? Explain.

4. Two American religious leaders asserted that the Islamic attackers who killed over 3,000 people on September 11, 2001, were used by God to punish the country for allowing behavior "which their fundamentalist belief condemns." How does Doctorow characterize this argument? How do you?

5. On what issues does the conflict between civil government and religious conviction often center? Describe the positions that animate such disagreements.

WRITING TOPICS

1. If a majority of Americans voted to abolish the separation between church and state embedded in the Constitution, should the United States amend the Constitution to reflect that position and become a Protestant Christian theocratic state? Upon what assumptions does your position rest?

2. America's justification for its presence in the Middle East is that it wishes to bring "freedom and democracy" to Afghanistan, Iraq, and the entire region; what do you believe should be the response of the United States if one or more of these nations, in a fair and open election, chooses to have a theocratic authoritarian government?

3. Discuss Doctorow's view of the relationship between religion and politics in the modern world.

SALMAN RUSHDIE   (B. 1947)

"IMAGINE THERE'S NO HEAVEN"[1]   1997

A LETTER TO THE SIX BILLIONTH WORLD CITIZEN

[Written for a UN-backed anthology of such letters]

Dear little Six Billionth Living Person,

As the newest member of a notoriously inquisitive species, you'll probably soon be asking the two sixty-four-thousand-dollar questions with which the other 5,999,999,999 of us have been wrestling for some time: How did we get here? And, now that we are here, how shall we live?

Oddly—as if six billion of us weren't enough to be going on with—it will almost certainly be suggested to you that the answer to the question of origins requires you to believe in the existence of a further, invisible, ineffable Being "somewhere up there," an omnipotent creator whom we poor limited creatures are unable even to perceive, much less to understand. That is, you will be strongly encouraged to imagine a heaven, with at least one god in residence. This sky-god, it's said, made the universe by churning its matter in a giant pot. Or, he danced. Or, he vomited Creation out of himself. Or, he simply called it into being, and lo, it Was. In some of the more interesting creation stories, the single mighty sky-god is subdivided into many lesser forces—junior deities, avatars, gigantic metamorphic "ancestors" whose adventures create the landscape, or the whimsical, wanton, meddling, cruel pantheons of the great polytheisms, whose wild doings will convince you that the real engine of creation was lust: for infinite power, for too easily broken human bodies, for clouds of glory. But it's only fair to add that there are also stories which offer the message that the primary creative impulse was, and is, love.

Many of these stories will strike you as extremely beautiful, and therefore seductive. Unfortunately, however, you will not be required to make a purely literary response to them. Only the stories of "dead" religions can be

---

[1] Rushdie takes his title from the first line of "Imagine," a song by John Lennon (1940–1980).

appreciated for their beauty. Living religions require much more of you. So you will be told that belief in "your" stories, and adherence to the rituals of worship that have grown up around them, must become a vital part of your life in the crowded world. They will be called the heart of your culture, even of your individual identity. It is possible that they may at some point come to feel inescapable, not in the way that the truth is inescapable but in the way that a jail is. They may at some point cease to feel like the texts in which human beings have tried to solve a great mystery and feel, instead, like the pretexts for other, properly anointed human beings to order you around. And it's time that human history is full of the public oppression wrought by the charioteers of the gods. In the opinion of religious people, however, the private comfort that religion brings more than compensates for the evil done in its name.

As human knowledge has grown, it has also become plain that every religious story ever told about how we got here is quite simply wrong. This, finally, is what all religions have in common. They didn't get it right. There was no celestial churning, no maker's dance, no vomiting of galaxies, no snake or kangaroo ancestors, no Valhalla, no Olympus, no six-day conjuring trick followed by a day of rest. Wrong, wrong, wrong. But here's something genuinely odd. The wrongness of the sacred tales hasn't lessened the zeal of the devout in the least. If anything, the sheer out-of-step zaniness of religion leads the religious to insist ever more stridently on the importance of blind faith.

As a result of this faith, by the way, it has proved impossible, in many parts ⁵ of the world, to prevent the human race's numbers from swelling alarmingly. Blame the overcrowded planet at least partly on the misguidedness of the race's spiritual guides. In your own lifetime, you may well witness the arrival of the nine billionth world citizen. If you're Indian (and there's a one in six chance that you are) you will be alive when, thanks to the failure of family-planning schemes in that poor, God-ridden land, its population surges past China's. And if too many people are being born as a result, in part, of religious strictures against birth control, then too many people are also dying because religious culture, by refusing to face the facts of human sexuality, also refuses to fight against the spread of sexually transmitted diseases.

There are those who say that the great wars of the new century will once again be wars of religion, jihads and crusades, as they were in the Middle Ages. I don't believe them, or not in the way they mean it. Take a look at the Muslim world, or rather the *Islamist* world, to use the word coined to describe Islam's present-day "political arm." The divisions between its great powers (Afghanistan versus Iran versus Iraq versus Saudi Arabia versus Syria versus Egypt) are what strike you most forcefully. There's very little resembling a common purpose. Even after the non-Islamic NATO fought a war for the Muslim Kosovar Albanians, the Muslim world was slow in coming forward with much-needed humanitarian aid.

The real wars of religion are the wars religions unleash against ordinary citizens within their "spheres of influence." They are wars of the godly against the largely defenseless—American fundamentalists against pro-choice doctors, Iranian mullahs against their country's Jewish minority, the Taliban against the people of Afghanistan, Hindu fundamentalists in Bombay against that city's increasingly fearful Muslims.

The victors in that war must not be the closed-minded, marching into battle with, as ever, God on their side. To choose unbelief is to choose mind over dogma, to trust in our humanity instead of all these dangerous divinities. So, how did we get here? Don't look for the answer in storybooks. Imperfect human knowledge may be a bumpy, potholed street, but it's the only road to wisdom worth taking. Virgil, who believed that the apiarist Aristaeus could spontaneously generate new bees from the rotting carcass of a cow, was closer to a truth about origins than all the revered old books.

The ancient wisdoms are modern nonsenses. Live in your own time, use what we know, and as you grow up, perhaps the human race will finally grow up with you and put aside childish things.

As the song says, "It's easy if you try."   10

As for morality, the second great question—how to live? What is right action, and what wrong?—it comes down to your willingness to think for yourself. Only you can decide if you want to be handed down the law by priests, and accept that good and evil are somehow external to ourselves. To my mind religion, even at its most sophisticated, essentially infantilizes our ethical selves by setting infallible moral Arbiters and irredeemably immoral Tempters above us; the eternal parents, good and bad, light and dark, of the supernatural realm.

How, then, are we to make ethical choices without a divine rulebook or judge? Is unbelief just the first step on the long slide into the brain-death of cultural relativism,[2] according to which many unbearable things—female circumcision, to name just one—can be excused on culturally specific grounds, and the universality of human rights, too, can be ignored? (This last piece of moral unmaking finds supporters in some of the world's most authoritarian regimes and also, unnervingly, on the op-ed pages of *The Daily Telegraph.*)

Well, no, it isn't, but the reasons for saying so aren't clear-cut. Only hardline ideology is clear-cut. Freedom, which is the word I use for the secular-ethical position, is inevitably fuzzier. Yes, freedom is that space in which contradiction can reign, it is a never-ending debate. It is not in itself the answer to the question of morals but the conversation about that question.

And it is much more than mere relativism, because it is not merely a never-ending talk-shop, but a place in which choices are made, values defined and defended. Intellectual freedom, in European history, has mostly meant freedom from the restraints of the Church, not the State. This is the battle Voltaire[3] was fighting, and it's also what all six billion of us could do

---

[2] The view that truth is relative and may differ depending on the believer's situation, and that all beliefs are equally valid. Cultural relativism developed in the late nineteenth century as a backlash against the Western tendency to perceive culture as advancing from ignorant savagery to enlightened civilization.

[3] The pen name of François-Marie Arouet (1694–1778), author of *Candide* and a major antiecclesiastical writer of his time.

for ourselves, the revolution in which each of us could play our small, six-billionth part: once and for all we could refuse to allow priests, and the fictions on whose behalf they claim to speak, to be the policemen of our liberties and behavior. Once and for all we could put the stories back into the books, put the books back on the shelves, and see the world undogmatized and plain.

Imagine there's no heaven, my dear Six Billionth, and at once the sky's the limit. 15

FOR ANALYSIS

1. Rushdie argues from the **point of view** of a "secular-ethical" humanist. How do his arguments differ from those a religious leader might put forward?

2. Using a search engine, try to identify the sources of the "creation stories" that Rushdie enumerates in paragraph 2.

3. At the end of paragraph 4, Rushdie speaks of "blind faith." How does blind faith differ from faith?

4. In paragraph 5, Rushdie argues that overpopulation and certain diseases are the direct result of religious strictures. Do you agree or disagree? Explain.

5. Since this essay was written in 1997, much has changed in the "Islamist world." Do you find Rushdie's assertions about the struggle among Islamic nations (paras. 6–7) convincing or misguided? Explain.

6. In Rushdie's world without religion, what will determine "right action" (para. 11)? Do you find Rushdie's position valid or foolish? Explain.

7. In paragraph 12, Rushdie alludes to the "brain-death of cultural relativism." What is cultural relativism? Why would the author characterize it as "brain-death"?

8. Rushdie promotes "freedom" (paras. 13–14) as the appropriate source of ethical choices and behavior. Do you find his argument convincing? Explain.

MAKING CONNECTIONS

1. Compare and contrast Rushdie's and Doctorow's essays. Which do you find more stirring? More persuasive? Do they both advocate the same principles?

2. While both of these essays take a negative stance toward their shared subject, they adopt a variety of **tones** over the course of their arguments. Describe the tones adopted in each essay. How do Rushdie and Doctorow each use shifts in tone to help get across their messages?

3. If you do not agree with one or both of these essays, what would you say in defense of the thing they attack? Are Rushdie and Doctorow unreasonably harsh about religious belief? How so? What might you say, if writing your own essay, to counter their arguments?

WRITING TOPICS

1. The essay embodies this seminal assertion: "To choose unbelief is to choose mind over dogma, to trust in our humanity instead of all these dangerous divinities." Defend or rebut this assertion.

2. Distinguish between what Rushdie calls "cultural relativism" and "freedom."

3. Defend or rebut Rushdie's argument by examining the significance of religious principles as the source of rules that make social organization possible.

4. Hinduism, Jainism, Buddhism, Judaism, Christianity, Islam, Taoism, Shinto-ism, animism, Bahaism—these "great" religions—exist side by side throughout the world. And these religious structures are complicated by internal divisions. There are Reform, Conservative, and Orthodox Jews; Catholic and Protestant Christians; Orthodox Catholics (Russian, Greek, and others) and Roman Catholics. Protestants include Baptists, Methodists, Lutherans, Anglicans, Seventh-Day Adventists, and many other churches. Buddhism includes many competing congregations. Islam is divided (bitterly in some regions) into Sunni and Shiite congregations, with further prominent divisions within each group. In an essay, (1) suggest the conditions under which these disparate and competing systems might peacefully coexist, or (2) describe the likely outcome of the ultimate collision between such disparate worldviews.

CASE STUDY

"LETTER FROM BIRMINGHAM JAIL" IN HISTORICAL CONTEXT

During the 1950s and 1960s, black citizens of the American South engaged in a great struggle to win the civil rights accorded to other U.S. citizens as a matter of course. That struggle nurtured many leaders, but none as charismatic and eloquent as Martin Luther King Jr., who wrote, from his Birmingham jail cell, the essay at the center of this investigation of one interaction between literature and history. The documents collected here reveal that the seeds of the conflict were planted at the very founding of the Republic. Article I, Section 2, of the U.S. Constitution defined a slave as three-fifths of a person when it established the rules that governed the congressional House of Representatives. The Supreme Court, in 1856, found in the Constitution the grounds for denying Dred Scott, a slave who had been taken by his owner into a free territory, the dignity of his own humanity, as is delineated in the excerpted transcript from that case. After the Civil War, the Fourteenth Amendment to the Constitution (1868) redefined the idea of citizenship to include "all persons born or naturalized in the United States," but the resistance of the defeated Confederate states led to the formulation of the so-called Jim Crow laws—named after an African American character in minstrel shows—that endured well past the middle of the twentieth century. Examples of these laws are included in this section.

When the freedom riders came into the Deep South in the 1960s to organize black citizens, conduct voter registration drives, and demonstrate against unfair laws as well as unfair treatment under the law, many white communities responded fiercely and violently. On Good Friday, April 12, 1963, Martin Luther King Jr. was arrested for participating in a peaceful protest parade that was held without a permit. On April 13, a group of "liberal" white clergymen published a letter—included here, in an article reprinted from the *Birmingham News*—urging restraint, cautioning against "outsiders," and advising the local African American community to turn to the courts for redress of their grievances. King's famous reply appeared on April 16. After a week of negotiations between protest leaders and representatives of the city of Birmingham, the Birmingham Truce Agreement was drafted (May 10, 1963). As can be seen from reading this agreement, included at the end of this section, the terms were very modest; however, it was several years before the city implemented the conditions of the agreement.

Before examining these documents, read the brief biography of Martin Luther King Jr. (p. 1362). Note that the U.S. Constitution and Supreme Court decisions can be found at several Web sites. We downloaded the sample list of Jim Crow laws from http://www.nps.gov/malu/forteachers/jim_crow_laws.htm.

FROM THE U.S. CONSTITUTION, ARTICLE I, SECTION 2 1787

Representatives and direct Taxes shall be apportioned among the several States which may be included within this Union, according to their respective Numbers, which shall be determined by adding to the whole Number of free Persons, including those bound to Service for a Term of Years, and excluding Indians not taxed, three-fifths of all other Persons. The actual Enumeration shall be made within three Years after the first Meeting of the Congress of the United States, and within every subsequent Term of ten Years, in such Manner as they shall by Law direct. The Number of Representatives shall not exceed one for every thirty Thousand, but each State shall have at Least one Representative; and until such enumeration shall be made, the State of New-Hampshire shall be entitled to chuse three, Massachusetts eight, Rhode-Island and Providence Plantations one, Connecticut five, New-York six, New-Jersey four, Pennsylvania eight, Delaware one, Maryland six, Virginia ten, North-Carolina five, South-Carolina five, and Georgia three.

MAKING CONNECTIONS

A class of persons called "indentured servants" were counted as part of a state's population to determine the number of representatives the state could send to Congress, but the Constitution excludes Native Americans from such a count. Can you suggest a reason for that exclusion? A slave was counted as three-fifths of a person. Can you suggest a reason?

FROM DRED SCOTT V. SANDFORD 1856

4. A free negro of the African race, whose ancestors were brought to this country and sold as slaves, is not a "citizen" within the meaning of the Constitution of the United States.

5. When the Constitution was adopted, they were not regarded in any of the States as members of the community which constituted the State, and were not numbered among its "people or citizens." Consequently, the special rights and immunities guaranteed to citizens do not apply to them. And not being "citizens" within the meaning of the Constitution, they are not entitled to sue in that character in a court of the United States, and the Circuit Court has not jurisdiction in such a suit.

6. The only two clauses in the Constitution which point to this race, treat them as persons whom it was morally lawful to deal in as articles of property and to hold as slaves.

7. Since the adoption of the Constitution of the United States, no State can by any subsequent law make a foreigner or any other description of persons citizens of the United States, nor entitle them to the rights and privileges secured to citizens by that instrument.

8. A State, by its laws passed since the adoption of the Constitution, may put a foreigner or any other description of persons upon a footing with its own citizens, as to all the rights and privileges enjoyed by them within its dominion and by its laws. But that will not make him a citizen of the United States, nor entitle him to sue in its courts, nor to any of the privileges and immunities of a citizen in another State.

9. The change in public opinion and feeling in relation to the African race, which has taken place since the adoption of the Constitution, cannot change its construction and meaning, and it must be construed and administered now according to its true meaning and intention when it was formed and adopted.

10. The plaintiff having admitted, by his demurrer to the plea in abatement, that his ancestors were imported from Africa and sold as slaves, he is not a citizen of the State of Missouri according to the Constitution of the United States, and was not entitled to sue in that character in the Circuit Court.

11. This being the case, the judgment of the court below, in favor of the plaintiff on the plea in abatement, was erroneous.

MAKING CONNECTIONS

1. In 1857, could a person be a "citizen" of a state but not a "citizen" of the United States? Explain.

2. Is such a distinction possible now?

3. Do you find a contradiction between the statements in number 5 and Article I, Section 2, of the Constitution? Explain.

4. Research the consequences of the *Dred Scott* decision, either at the library or on the Internet. In an essay, describe the immediate consequences of the decision and its impact on constitutional amendments in the mid-nineteenth century.

JIM CROW LAWS   CA. 1880S–1960S

From the 1880s into the 1960s, a majority of American states enforced segregation through Jim Crow laws, which often imposed legal punishments on people for consorting with members of another race.

Here is a sampling of laws from various states:

Nurses No person or corporation shall require any white female nurse to nurse in wards or rooms in hospitals, either public or private, in which negro men are placed. *Alabama*

Buses All passenger stations in this state operated by any motor transportation company shall have separate waiting rooms or space and separate ticket windows for the white and colored races. *Alabama*

Railroads The conductor of each passenger train is authorized and required to assign each passenger to the car or the division of the car, when it is divided by a partition, designated for the race to which such passenger belongs. *Alabama*

Restaurants   It shall be unlawful to conduct a restaurant or other place for the serving of food in the city, at which white and colored people are served in the same room, unless such white and colored persons are effectually separated by a solid partition extending from the floor upward to a distance of seven feet or higher, and unless a separate entrance from the street is provided for each compartment. *Alabama*

Pool and Billiard Rooms   It shall be unlawful for a negro and white person to play together or in company with each other at any game of pool or billiards. *Alabama*

Toilet Facilities, Male   Every employer of white or negro males shall provide for such white or negro males reasonably accessible and separate toilet facilities. *Alabama*

Intermarriage   The marriage of a person of Caucasian blood with a Negro, Mongolian, Malay, or Hindu shall be null and void. *Arizona*

Intermarriage   All marriages between a white person and a negro, or between a white person and a person of negro descent to the fourth generation inclusive, are hereby forever prohibited. *Florida*

Cohabitation   Any negro man and white woman, or any white man and negro woman, who are not married to each other, who shall habitually live in and occupy in the nighttime the same room, shall each be punished by imprisonment not exceeding twelve (12) months, or by fine not exceeding five hundred ($500.00) dollars. *Florida*

Education   The schools for white children and the schools for negro children shall be conducted separately. *Florida*

Juvenile Delinquents   There shall be separate buildings, not nearer than one-fourth mile to each other, one for white boys and one for negro boys. White boys and negro boys shall not, in any manner, be associated together or worked together. *Florida*

Intermarriage   It shall be unlawful for a white person to marry anyone except a white person. Any marriage in violation of this section shall be void. *Georgia*

Burial   The officer in charge shall not bury, or allow to be buried, any colored persons upon ground set apart or used for the burial of white persons. *Georgia*

Amateur Baseball　It shall be unlawful for any amateur white baseball team to play baseball on any vacant lot or baseball diamond within two blocks of a playground devoted to the Negro race, and it shall be unlawful for any amateur colored baseball team to play baseball in any vacant lot or baseball diamond within two blocks of any playground devoted to the white race. *Georgia*

Parks　It shall be unlawful for colored people to frequent any park owned or maintained by the city for the benefit, use, and enjoyment of white persons . . . and unlawful for any white person to frequent any park owned or maintained by the city for the use and benefit of colored persons. *Georgia*

Wine and Beer　All persons licensed to conduct the business of selling beer or wine shall serve either white people exclusively or colored people exclusively and shall not sell to the two races within the same room at any time. *Georgia*

Circus Tickets　All circuses, shows, and tent exhibitions, to which the attendance of more than one race is invited or expected to attend, shall provide for the convenience of its patrons not less than two ticket offices with individual ticket sellers, and not less than two entrances to the said performance, with individual ticket takers and receivers, and in the case of outside or tent performances, the said ticket offices shall not be less than twenty-five (25) feet apart. *Louisiana*

Promotion of Equality　Any person . . . who shall be guilty of printing, publishing, or circulating printed, typewritten, or written matter urging or presenting for public acceptance or general information, arguments or suggestions in favor of social equality or of intermarriage between whites and negroes, shall be guilty of a misdemeanor and subject to fine not exceeding five hundred ($500.00) dollars or imprisonment not exceeding six (6) months or both. *Mississippi*

Prisons　The warden shall see that the white convicts shall have separate apartments for both eating and sleeping from the negro convicts. *Mississippi*

Child Custody　It shall be unlawful for any parent, relative, or other white person in this State, having the control or custody of any white child, by right of guardianship, natural or acquired, or otherwise, to dispose of, give, or surrender such white child permanently into the custody, control, maintenance, or support of a negro. *South Carolina*

Libraries　Any white person of such county may use the county free library under the rules and regulations prescribed by the commissioners court and may be entitled to all the privileges thereof. Said court shall make proper provision for the negroes of said county to be served through a separate branch

or branches of the county free library, which shall be administered by [a] custodian of the negro race under the supervision of the county librarian. *Texas*

Education [The County Board of Education] shall provide schools of two
kinds, those for white children and those for colored children. *Texas*

MAKING CONNECTIONS

1. Research the term *Jim Crow*. Where does it come from, and what does it mean?

2. Jim Crow laws began to appear in the 1880s. Why do you suppose they did not
appear earlier?

3. Note that the grassroots activities for which Martin Luther King Jr. was imprisoned occurred in 1963. Why did the African American community and its allies
believe it was necessary to break local laws?

4. Place yourself in the position of an African American southerner in 1950. How
would you react to the limitations imposed on you by the Jim Crow laws?

A CALL FOR UNITY FROM
ALABAMA CLERGYMEN[1]   1963

Leading Protestant, Catholic, and Jewish clerics Friday called on local Negro
citizens to withdraw support of racial demonstrations and unite for a peaceful
Birmingham.

In a prepared statement, the clergy praised the manner in which the 10 days
of demonstrations have been handled by the Birmingham Police Department.

The same clergy were among others who recently issued "An Appeal for
Law and Order and Common Sense" in dealing with the racial problems in
Alabama.

Saturday's statement was signed by C.C.J. Carpenter, Episcopal Bishop
of Alabama; Joseph A. Durick, auxiliary bishop, Catholic Diocese of
Mobile-Birmingham; Rabbi Milton Grafman, Temple Emanu-El; Bishop Paul
Hardin, Bishop of the Alabama–West Florida Conference of the Methodist
Church; Bishop Nolan B. Harmon, Bishop of the North Alabama Conference
of the Methodist Church; George M. Murray, Bishop Coadjutor, Episcopal
Diocese of Alabama; Edward V. Ramage, moderator, Synod of the Alabama
Presbyterian Church in the United States, and the Reverend Earl Stallings,
pastor, First Baptist Church of Birmingham.

The text of the statement follows: 5

"We, the undersigned clergymen are among those who in January issued
'An Appeal for Law and Order and Common Sense' in dealing with the racial

---

[1] The article appeared in the *Birmingham News* on Saturday, April 13, 1963, under the headline
"White Clergymen Urge Local Negroes to Withdraw from Demonstrations."

problems in Alabama. We expressed understanding that honest convictions in racial matters could properly be pursued in the courts, but urged that decisions of these courts should in the meantime be peacefully obeyed.

"Since that time there had been some evidence of increased forbearance and a willingness to face facts. Responsible citizens have undertaken to work on various problems which cause racial friction and unrest.

"In Birmingham recent public events have given indication that we all have opportunity for a new constructive and realistic approach to racial problems.

"However, we are now confronted by a series of demonstrations by some of our Negro citizens directed and led in part by outsiders. We recognize the natural impatience of people who feel their hopes are slow in being realized. But we are convinced that these demonstrations are unwise and untimely.

"We agree rather with certain local Negro leadership which has called for 10
honest and open negotiation of racial issues in our area.

"And we believe this kind of facing issues can best be accomplished by citizens of our own metropolitan area, white and Negro, meeting with their knowledge and experience of the local situation. All of us need to face that responsibility and find proper channels for its accomplishment.

"Just as we formerly pointed out that 'hatred and violence have no sanction in our religious and political traditions,' we also point out that such actions as incite hatred and violence, however technically peaceful those actions may be, have not contributed to the resolution of our local problems.

"We do not believe that these days of new hope are days when extreme measures are justified in Birmingham.

"We commend the community as a whole, and the local news media and law enforcement officials in particular, on the calm manner in which these demonstrations have been handled.

"We urge the public to continue to show restraint should the demonstra- 15
tions continue, and the law enforcement officials to remain calm and continue to protect our city from violence.

"We further strongly urge our own Negro community to withdraw support from these demonstrations, and to unite locally in working peacefully for a better Birmingham.

"When rights are consistently denied, a cause should be pressed in the courts and negotiations among local leaders, and not in the streets.

"We appeal to both our white and Negro citizenry to observe the principles of law and order and common sense."

MAKING CONNECTIONS

1. Do you agree with the Alabama clergymen that "honest convictions in racial matters could properly be pursued in the courts" (para. 6)? Explain.

2. If the courts do not provide a means to redress grievances, what are the alternatives?

3. What were the "racial matters" the clergymen were speaking of?

4. Do you find their views on "outsiders" persuasive? Explain.

5. The clergymen say that "extreme measures" are not justified (para. 13). What do you suppose they mean by "extreme measures"? Are there any circumstances that would justify extreme measures? Explain.

THE BIRMINGHAM TRUCE AGREEMENT   1963

1. Within 3 days after close of demonstrations, fitting rooms will be desegregated.

2. Within 30 days after the city government is established by court order, signs on wash rooms, rest rooms and drinking fountains will be removed.

3. Within 60 days after the city government is established by court order, a program of lunchroom counter desegregation will be commenced.

4. When the city government is established by court order, a program of upgrading Negro employment will be continued and there will be meetings with responsible local leadership to consider further steps.

Within 60 days from the court order determining Birmingham's city government, the employment program will include at least one sales person or cashier.

Within 15 days from the cessation of demonstrations, a Committee on Racial Problems and Employment composed of members of the Senior Citizens' Committee will be established, with a membership made public and the publicly announced purpose of establishing liaison with members of the Negro community to carry out a program of up-grading and improving employment opportunities with the Negro citizens of the Birmingham community.

MAKING CONNECTIONS

1. Do you feel that the Birmingham Truce Agreement represented total victory for the demonstrators? Explain.

2. Research the behavior of the Birmingham city government after May 10, 1963 (the date this agreement was reached). Did the government meet the terms of the truce agreement? Explain.

MARTIN LUTHER KING JR. (1929–1968)

LETTER FROM BIRMINGHAM JAIL[1] 1963

My Dear Fellow Clergymen:

While confined here in the Birmingham city jail, I came across your recent statement calling my present activities "unwise and untimely." Seldom do I pause to answer criticism of my work and ideas. If I sought to answer all the criticisms that cross my desk, my secretaries would have little time for anything other than such correspondence in the course of the day, and I would have no time for constructive work. But since I feel that you are men of genuine good will and that your criticisms are sincerely set forth, I want to try to answer your statement in what I hope will be patient and reasonable terms.

I think I should indicate why I am here in Birmingham, since you have been influenced by the view which argues against "outsiders coming in." I have the honor of serving as president of the Southern Christian Leadership Conference, an organization operating in every southern state, with headquarters in Atlanta, Georgia. We have some eighty-five affiliated organizations across the South, and one of them is the Alabama Christian Movement for Human Rights. Frequently we share staff, educational, and financial resources with our affiliates. Several months ago the affiliate here in Birmingham asked us to be on call to engage in a nonviolent direct-action program if such were deemed necessary. We readily consented, and when the hour came we lived up to our promise. So I, along with several members of my staff, am here because I was invited here. I am here because I have organizational ties here.

But more basically, I am in Birmingham because injustice is here. Just as the prophets of the eighth century B.C. left their villages and carried their "thus saith the Lord" far beyond the boundaries of their home towns, and just as the Apostle Paul left his village of Tarsus[2] and carried the gospel of Jesus Christ to the far corners of the Greco-Roman world, so am I compelled to carry the gospel of freedom beyond my own home town. Like Paul, I must constantly respond to the Macedonian call for aid.[3]

Moreover, I am cognizant of the interrelatedness of all communities and states. I cannot sit idly by in Atlanta and not be concerned about what happens in Birmingham. Injustice anywhere is a threat to justice everywhere. We

---

[1] This response to a published statement by eight fellow clergymen from Alabama (Bishop C. C. J. Carpenter, Bishop Joseph A. Durick, Rabbi Milton L. Grafman, Bishop Paul Hardin, Bishop Nolan B. Harmon, the Reverend George M. Murray, the Reverend Edward V. Ramage, and the Reverend Earl Stallings) was composed under somewhat constricting circumstances. Begun on the margins of the newspaper in which the statement appeared while I was in jail, the letter was continued on scraps of writing paper supplied by a friendly Negro trusty, and concluded on a pad my attorneys were eventually permitted to leave me. Although the text remains in substance unaltered, I have indulged in the author's prerogative of polishing it for publication. [King's note]

[2] Birthplace of St. Paul, in present-day Turkey.

[3] St. Paul was frequently called upon to aid the Christian community in Macedonia.

are caught in an inescapable network of mutuality, tied in a single garment of destiny. Whatever affects one directly, affects all indirectly. Never again can we afford to live with the narrow, provincial "outside agitator" idea. Anyone who lives inside the United States can never be considered an outsider anywhere within its bounds.

You deplore the demonstrations taking place in Birmingham. But your   5 statement, I am sorry to say, fails to express a similar concern for the conditions that brought about the demonstrations. I am sure that none of you would want to rest content with the superficial kind of social analysis that deals merely with effects and does not grapple with the underlying causes. It is unfortunate that demonstrations are taking place in Birmingham, but it is even more unfortunate that the city's white power structure left the Negro community with no alternative.

In any nonviolent campaign there are four basic steps: collection of the facts to determine whether injustices exist; negotiation; self-purification; and direct action. We have gone through all these steps in Birmingham. There can be no gainsaying the fact that racial injustice engulfs this community. Birmingham is probably the most thoroughly segregated city in the United States. Its ugly record of brutality is widely known. Negroes have experienced grossly unjust treatment in the courts. There have been more unsolved bombings of Negro homes and churches in Birmingham than in any other city in the nation. These are the hard, brutal facts of the case. On the basis of these conditions, Negro leaders sought to negotiate with the city fathers. But the latter consistently refused to engage in good-faith negotiation.

Then, last September, came the opportunity to talk with leaders of Birmingham's economic community. In the course of the negotiations, certain promises were made by the merchants—for example, to remove the stores' humiliating racial signs. On the basis of these promises, the Reverend Fred Shuttlesworth and the leaders of the Alabama Christian Movement for Human Rights agreed to a moratorium on all demonstrations. As the weeks and months went by, we realized that we were the victims of a broken promise. A few signs, briefly removed, returned; the others remained.

As in so many past experiences, our hopes had been blasted, and the shadow of deep disappointment settled upon us. We had no alternative except to prepare for direct action, whereby we would present our very bodies as a means of laying our case before the conscience of the local and the national community. Mindful of the difficulties involved, we decided to undertake a process of self-purification. We began a series of workshops on nonviolence, and we repeatedly asked ourselves: "Are you able to accept blows without retaliating?" "Are you able to endure the ordeal of jail?" We decided to schedule our direct-action program for the Easter season, realizing that except for Christmas, this is the main shopping period of the year. Knowing that a strong economic-withdrawal program would be the by-product of direct action, we felt that this would be the best time to bring pressure to bear on the merchants for the needed change.

Then it occurred to us that Birmingham's mayoral election was coming up in March, and we speedily decided to postpone action until after election day. When we discovered that the Commissioner of Public Safety, Eugene "Bull" Connor, had piled up enough votes to be in the run-off, we decided again to postpone action until the day after the run-off so that the demonstrations could not be used to cloud the issues. Like many others, we waited to see Mr. Connor defeated, and to this end we endured postponement after postponement. Having aided in this community need, we felt that our direct-action program could be delayed no longer.

You may well ask, "Why direct action? Why sit-ins, marches, and so forth? 10 Isn't negotiation a better path?" You are quite right in calling for negotiation. Indeed, this is the very purpose of direct action. Nonviolent direct action seeks to create such a crisis and foster such a tension that a community which has constantly refused to negotiate is forced to confront the issue. It seeks so to dramatize the issue that it can no longer be ignored. My citing the creation of tension as part of the work of the nonviolent-resister may sound rather shocking. But I must confess that I am not afraid of the word "tension." I have earnestly opposed violent tension, but there is a type of constructive, nonviolent tension which is necessary for growth. Just as Socrates[4] felt that it was necessary to create a tension in the mind so that individuals could rise from the bondage of myths and half-truths to the unfettered realm of creative analysis and objective appraisal, so must we see the need for nonviolent gadflies to create the kind of tension in society that will help men rise from the dark depths of prejudice and racism to the majestic heights of understanding and brotherhood.

The purpose of our direct-action program is to create a situation so crisis-packed that it will inevitably open the door to negotiation. I therefore concur with you in your call for negotiation. Too long has our beloved Southland been bogged down in a tragic effort to live in monologue rather than dialogue.

One of the basic points in your statement is that the action that I and my associates have taken in Birmingham is untimely. Some have asked: "Why didn't you give the new city administration time to act?" The only answer that I can give to this query is that the new Birmingham administration must be prodded about as much as the outgoing one, before it will act. We are sadly mistaken if we feel that the election of Albert Boutwell as mayor will bring the millennium to Birmingham. While Mr. Boutwell is a much more gentle person than Mr. Connor, they are both segregationists, dedicated to maintenance of the status quo. I have hoped that Mr. Boutwell will be reasonable enough to see the futility of massive resistance to desegregation. But he will not see this without pressure from devotees of civil rights. My friends, I must say to you that we have not made a single gain in civil rights without determined legal and nonviolent pressure. Lamentably, it is an historical fact that privileged groups seldom give up their privileges voluntarily. Individuals may see

---

[4] Socrates (469–399 B.C.), a Greek philosopher who often pretended ignorance in arguments to expose the errors in his opponent's reasoning.

the moral light and voluntarily give up their unjust posture; but, as Reinhold Niebuhr[5] has reminded us, groups tend to be more immoral than individuals.

We know through painful experience that freedom is never voluntarily given by the oppressor; it must be demanded by the oppressed. Frankly, I have yet to engage in a direct-action campaign that was "well timed" in the view of those who have not suffered unduly from the disease of segregation. For years now I have heard the word "Wait!" It rings in the ear of every Negro with piercing familiarity. This "Wait" has almost always meant "Never." We must come to see, with one of our distinguished jurists, that "justice too long delayed is justice denied."

We have waited for more than 340 years for our constitutional and God-given rights. The nations of Asia and Africa are moving with jetlike speed toward gaining political independence, but we still creep at horse-and-buggy pace toward gaining a cup of coffee at a lunch counter. Perhaps it is easy for those who have never felt the stinging darts of segregation to say, "Wait." But when you have seen vicious mobs lynch your mothers and fathers at will and drown your sisters and brothers at whim; when you have seen hate-filled policemen curse, kick, and even kill your black brothers and sisters; when you see the vast majority of your twenty million Negro brothers smothering in an airtight cage of poverty in the midst of an affluent society; when you suddenly find your tongue twisted and your speech stammering as you seek to explain to your six-year-old daughter why she can't go to the public amusement park that has just been advertised on television, and see tears welling up in her eyes when she is told that Funtown is closed to colored children, and see ominous clouds of inferiority beginning to form in her little mental sky, and see her beginning to distort her personality by developing an unconscious bitterness toward white people; when you have to concoct an answer for a five-year-old son who is asking, "Daddy, why do white people treat colored people so mean?"; when you take a cross-country drive and find it necessary to sleep night after night in the uncomfortable corners of your automobile because no motel will accept you; when you are humiliated day in and day out by nagging signs reading "white" and "colored"; when your first name becomes "nigger," your middle name becomes "boy" (however old you are) and your last name becomes "John," and your wife and mother are never given the respected title "Mrs."; when you are harried by day and haunted by night by the fact that you are a Negro, living constantly at tiptoe stance, never quite knowing what to expect next, and are plagued with inner fears and outer resentments; when you are forever fighting a degenerating sense of "nobodiness"—then you will understand why we find it difficult to wait. There comes a time when the cup of endurance runs over, and men are no longer willing to be plunged into the abyss of despair. I hope, sirs, you can understand our legitimate and unavoidable impatience.

---

[5] Reinhold Niebuhr (1892–1971), American philosopher and theologian.

You express a great deal of anxiety over our willingness to break laws. This 15 is certainly a legitimate concern. Since we so diligently urge people to obey the Supreme Court's decision of 1954 outlawing segregation in the public schools, at first glance it may seem rather paradoxical for us consciously to break laws. One may well ask: "How can you advocate breaking some laws and obeying others?" The answer lies in the fact that there are two types of laws: just and unjust. I would be the first to advocate obeying just laws. One has not only a legal but a moral responsibility to obey just laws. Conversely, one has a moral responsibility to disobey unjust laws. I would agree with St. Augustine that "an unjust law is no law at all."

Now, what is the difference between the two? How does one determine whether a law is just or unjust? A just law is a man-made code that squares with the moral law or the law of God. An unjust law is a code that is out of harmony with the moral law. To put it in the terms of St. Thomas Aquinas: an unjust law is a human law that is not rooted in eternal law and natural law. Any law that uplifts human personality is just. Any law that degrades human personality is unjust. All segregation statutes are unjust because segregation distorts the soul and damages the personality. It gives the segregator a false sense of superiority and the segregated a false sense of inferiority. Segregation, to use the terminology of the Jewish philosopher Martin Buber, substitutes an "I-it" relationship for an "I-thou" relationship and ends up relegating persons to the status of things. Hence segregation is not only politically, economically, and sociologically unsound, it is morally wrong and sinful. Paul Tillich has said that sin is separation. Is not segregation an existential expression of man's tragic separation, his awful estrangement, his terrible sinfulness? Thus it is that I can urge men to obey the 1954 decision of the Supreme Court, for it is morally right; and I can urge them to disobey segregation ordinances, for they are morally wrong.

Let us consider a more concrete example of just and unjust laws. An unjust law is a code that a numerical or power majority group compels a minority group to obey but does not make binding on itself. This is *difference* made legal. By the same token, a just law is a code that a majority compels a minority to follow and that it is willing to follow itself. This is *sameness* made legal.

Let me give another explanation. A law is unjust if it is inflicted on a minority that, as a result of being denied the right to vote, had no part in enacting or devising the law. Who can say that the legislature of Alabama which set up that state's segregation laws was democratically elected? Throughout Alabama all sorts of devious methods are used to prevent Negroes from becoming registered voters, and there are some counties in which, even though Negroes constitute a majority of the population, not a single Negro is registered. Can any law enacted under such circumstances be considered democratically structured?

Sometimes a law is just on its face and unjust in its application. For instance, I have been arrested on a charge of parading without a permit. Now, there is nothing wrong in having an ordinance which requires a permit for a parade. But such an ordinance becomes unjust when it is used to maintain segregation and to deny citizens the First-Amendment privilege of peaceful assembly and protest.

I hope you are able to see the distinction I am trying to point out. In no sense 20 do I advocate evading or defying the law, as would the rabid segregationist. That would lead to anarchy. One who breaks an unjust law must do so openly, lovingly, and with a willingness to accept the penalty. I submit that an individual who breaks a law that conscience tells him is unjust, and who willingly accepts the penalty of imprisonment in order to arouse the conscience of the community over its injustice, is in reality expressing the highest respect for law.

Of course, there is nothing new about this kind of civil disobedience. It was evidenced sublimely in the refusal of Shadrach, Meshach, and Abednego to obey the laws of Nebuchadnezzar, on the ground that a higher moral law was at stake.[6] It was practiced superbly by the early Christians, who were willing to face hungry lions and the excruciating pain of chopping blocks rather than submit to certain unjust laws of the Roman Empire. To a degree, academic freedom is a reality today because Socrates practiced civil disobedience. In our own nation, the Boston Tea Party represented a massive act of civil disobedience.

We should never forget that everything Adolf Hitler did in Germany was "legal" and everything the Hungarian freedom fighters did in Hungary was "illegal." It was "illegal" to aid and comfort a Jew in Hitler's Germany. Even so, I am sure that, had I lived in Germany at the time, I would have aided and comforted my Jewish brothers. If today I lived in a Communist country where certain principles dear to the Christian faith are suppressed, I would openly advocate disobeying that country's anti-religious laws.

I must make two honest confessions to you, my Christian and Jewish brothers. First, I must confess that over the past few years I have been gravely disappointed with the white moderate. I have almost reached the regrettable conclusion that the Negro's great stumbling block in his stride toward freedom is not the white Citizen's Counciler[7] or the Ku Klux Klanner, but the white moderate, who is more devoted to "order" than to justice; who prefers a negative peace which is the absence of tension to a positive peace which is the presence of justice; who constantly says, "I agree with you in the goal you seek, but I cannot agree with your methods of direct action"; who paternalistically believes he can set the timetable for another man's freedom; who lives by a mythical concept of time and who constantly advises the Negro to wait for a "more convenient season." Shallow understanding from people of good will is more frustrating than absolute misunderstanding from people of ill will. Lukewarm acceptance is much more bewildering than outright rejection.

I had hoped that the white moderate would understand that law and order exist for the purpose of establishing justice and that when they fail in this purpose they become the dangerously structured dams that block the flow of social progress. I had hoped that the white moderate would understand that the present tension in the South is a necessary phase of the transition from an

---

[6] See Daniel 1:7–3:30.

[7] White Citizen's Councils sprang up in the South after 1954 (the year the Supreme Court declared segregated education unconstitutional) to fight against desegregation.

obnoxious negative peace, in which the Negro passively accepted his unjust plight, to a substantive and positive peace, in which all men will respect the dignity and worth of human personality. Actually, we who engage in nonviolent direct action are not the creators of tension. We merely bring to the surface the hidden tension that is already alive. We bring it out in the open, where it can be seen and dealt with. Like a boil that can never be cured so long as it is covered up but must be opened with all its ugliness to the natural medicines of air and light, injustice must be exposed, with all the tension its exposure creates, to the light of human conscience and the air of national opinion, before it can be cured.

In your statement you assert that our actions, even though peaceful, must be condemned because they precipitate violence. But is this a logical assertion? Isn't this like condemning a robbed man because his possession of money precipitated the evil act of robbery? Isn't this like condemning Socrates because his unswerving commitment to truth and his philosophical inquiries precipitated the act by the misguided populace in which they made him drink hemlock? Isn't this like condemning Jesus because his unique God-consciousness and never-ceasing devotion to God's will precipitated the evil act of crucifixion? We must come to see that, as the federal courts have consistently affirmed, it is wrong to urge an individual to cease his efforts to gain his basic constitutional rights because the quest may precipitate violence. Society must protect the robbed and punish the robber. 25

I had also hoped that the white moderate would reject the myth concerning time in relation to the struggle for freedom. I have just received a letter from a white brother in Texas. He writes: "All Christians know that the colored people will receive greater equal rights eventually, but it is possible that you are in too great a religious hurry. It has taken Christianity almost two thousand years to accomplish what it has. The teachings of Christ take time to come to earth." Such an attitude stems from a tragic misconception of time, from the strangely irrational notion that there is something in the very flow of time that will inevitably cure all ills. Actually, time itself is neutral; it can be used either destructively or constructively. More and more I feel that the people of ill will have used time much more effectively than have the people of good will. We will have to repent in this generation not merely for the hateful words and actions of the bad people, but for the appalling silence of the good people. Human progress never rolls in on wheels of inevitability; it comes through the tireless efforts of men willing to be co-workers with God, and without this hard work, time itself becomes an ally of the forces of social stagnation. We must use time creatively, in the knowledge that the time is always ripe to do right. Now is the time to make real the promise of democracy and transform our pending national elegy into a creative psalm of brotherhood. Now is the time to lift our national policy from the quicksand of racial injustice to the solid rock of human dignity.

You speak of our activity in Birmingham as extreme. At first I was rather disappointed that fellow clergymen would see my nonviolent efforts as those of an extremist. I began thinking about the fact that I stand in the middle of two opposing forces in the Negro community. One is a force of complacency, made up in part of Negroes, who, as a result of long years of oppression, are so drained of self-respect and a sense of "somebodiness" that they have adjusted to segregation; and in part of a few middle-class Negroes who, because of a degree of academic and economic security and because in some ways they profit by segregation, have become insensitive to the problems of the masses. The other force is one of bitterness and hatred, and it comes perilously close to advocating violence. It is expressed in the various black nationalist groups that are springing up across the nation, the largest and best-known being Elijah Muhammad's Muslim movement.[8] Nourished by the Negro's frustration over the continued existence of racial discrimination, this movement is made up of people who have lost faith in America, who have absolutely repudiated Christianity, and who have concluded that the white man is an incorrigible "devil."

I have tried to stand between these two forces, saying that we need emulate neither the "do-nothingism" of the complacent nor the hatred and despair of the black nationalist. For there is the more excellent way of love and nonviolent protest. I am grateful to God that, through the influence of the Negro church, the way of nonviolence became an integral part of our struggle.

If this philosophy had not emerged, by now many streets of the South would, I am convinced, be flowing with blood. And I am further convinced that if our white brothers dismiss as "rabble-rousers" and "outside agitators" those of us who employ nonviolent direct action, and if they refuse to support our nonviolent efforts, millions of Negroes will, out of frustration and despair, seek solace and security in black-nationalist ideologies—a development that would inevitably lead to a frightening racial nightmare.

Oppressed people cannot remain oppressed forever. The yearning for freedom eventually manifests itself, and that is what has happened to the American Negro. Something within has reminded him of his birthright of freedom, and something without has reminded him that it can be gained. Consciously or unconsciously, he has been caught up by the *Zeitgeist*,[9] and with his black brothers of Africa and his brown and yellow brothers of Asia, South America, and the Caribbean, the United States Negro is moving with a sense of great urgency toward the promised land of racial justice. If one recognizes this vital urge that has engulfed the Negro community, one should readily understand why public demonstrations are taking place. The Negro has many pent-up resentments and latent frustrations, and he must release them. So let him march; let him make prayer pilgrimages to the city hall; let him go on freedom rides[10]—and try to

30

---

[8] Elijah Muhammad (1897–1975), leader of the Nation of Islam, a black Muslim religious group that rejected integration and called upon blacks to fight to establish their own nation.

[9] The spirit of the time.

[10] In 1961, hundreds of blacks and whites, under the direction of the Congress of Racial Equality (CORE), deliberately violated laws in southern states that required segregation in buses and bus terminals.

understand why he must do so. If his repressed emotions are not released in nonviolent ways, they will seek expression through violence; this is not a threat but a fact of history. So I have not said to my people, "Get rid of your discontent." Rather, I have tried to say that this normal and healthy discontent can be channeled into the creative outlet of nonviolent direct action. And now this approach is being termed extremist.

But though I was initially disappointed at being categorized as an extremist, as I continued to think about the matter I gradually gained a measure of satisfaction from the label. Was not Jesus an extremist for love: "Love your enemies, bless them that curse you, do good to them that hate you, and pray for them that despitefully use you, and persecute you." Was not Amos an extremist for justice: "Let justice roll down like waters and righteousness like an ever-flowing stream." Was not Paul an extremist for the Christian gospel: "I bear in my body the marks of the Lord Jesus." Was not Martin Luther an extremist: "Here I stand; I cannot do otherwise, so help me God." And John Bunyan: "I will stay in jail to the end of my days before I make a butchery of my conscience." And Abraham Lincoln: "This nation cannot survive half slave and half free." And Thomas Jefferson: "We hold these truths to be self-evident, that all men are created equal. . . ." So the question is not whether we will be extremists, but what kind of extremists we will be. Will we be extremists for the preservation of injustice or for the extension of justice? In that dramatic scene on Calvary's hill three men were crucified. We must never forget that all three were crucified for the same crime—the crime of extremism. Two were extremists for immorality, and thus fell below their environment. The other, Jesus Christ, was an extremist for love, truth, and goodness, and thereby rose above his environment. Perhaps the South, the nation, and the world are in dire need of creative extremists.

I had hoped that the white moderate would see this need. Perhaps I was too optimistic; perhaps I expected too much. I suppose I should have realized that few members of the oppressor race can understand the deep groans and passionate yearnings of the oppressed race, and still fewer have the vision to see that injustice must be rooted out by strong, persistent, and determined action. I am thankful, however, that some of our white brothers in the South have grasped the meaning of this social revolution and committed themselves to it. They are still all too few in quantity, but they are big in quality. Some—such as Ralph McGill, Lillian Smith, Harry Golden, James McBride Dabbs, Ann Braden, and Sarah Patton Boyle—have written about our struggle in eloquent and prophetic terms. Others have marched with us down nameless streets of the South. They have languished in filthy, roach-infested jails, suffering the abuse and brutality of policemen who view them as "dirty nigger-lovers." Unlike so many of their moderate brothers and sisters, they have recognized the urgency of the moment and sensed the need for powerful "action" antidotes to combat the disease of segregation.

Let me take note of my other major disappointment. I have been so greatly disappointed with the white church and its leadership. Of course, there are some notable exceptions. I am not unmindful of the fact that each of you has taken some significant stands on this issue. I commend you, Reverend Stallings, for your Christian stand on this past Sunday, in welcoming Negroes to your worship service on a nonsegregated basis. I commend the Catholic leaders of this state for integrating Spring Hill College several years ago.

But despite these notable exceptions, I must honestly reiterate that I have been disappointed with the church. I do not say this as one of those negative critics who can always find something wrong with the church. I say this as a minister of the gospel, who loves the church; who was nurtured in its bosom; who has been sustained by its spiritual blessings and who will remain true to it as long as the cord of life shall lengthen.

When I was suddenly catapulted into the leadership of the bus protest in 35 Montgomery, Alabama, a few years ago, I felt we would be supported by the white church. I felt that the white ministers, priests, and rabbis of the South would be among our strongest allies. Instead, some have been outright opponents, refusing to understand the freedom movement and misrepresenting its leaders; all too many others have been more cautious than courageous and have remained silent behind the anesthetizing security of stained-glass windows.

In spite of my shattered dreams, I came to Birmingham with the hope that the white religious leadership of this community would see the justice of our cause and, with deep moral concern, would serve as the channel through which our just grievances could reach the power structure. I had hoped that each of you would understand. But again I have been disappointed.

I have heard numerous southern religious leaders admonish their worshipers to comply with a desegregation decision because it is the law, but I have longed to hear white ministers declare: "Follow this decree because integration is morally right and because the Negro is your brother." In the midst of blatant injustices inflicted upon the Negro, I have watched white churchmen stand on the sideline and mouth pious irrelevancies and sanctimonious trivialities. In the midst of a mighty struggle to rid our nation of racial and economic injustice, I have heard many ministers say: "Those are social issues, with which the gospel has no real concern." And I have watched many churches commit themselves to a completely otherworldly religion which makes a strange, unBiblical distinction between body and soul, between the sacred and the secular.

I have traveled the length and breadth of Alabama, Mississippi, and all the other southern states. On sweltering summer days and crisp autumn mornings I have looked at the South's beautiful churches with their lofty spires pointing heavenward. I have beheld the impressive outlines of her massive religious-education buildings. Over and over I have found myself asking: "What kind of people worship here? Who is their God? Where were their voices when the lips of Governor Barnett dripped with words of interposition and nullification? Where were they when Governor Wallace gave a clarion call for defiance and hatred? Where were their voices of support when bruised and weary Negro men and women decided to rise from the dark dungeons of complacency to the bright hills of creative protest?"

Yes, these questions are still in mind. In deep disappointment I have wept over the laxity of the church. But be assured that my tears have been tears of love. There can be no deep disappointment where there is not deep love. Yes, I love the church. How could I do otherwise? I am in the rather unique position of being the son, the grandson, and the great-grandson of preachers. Yes, I see the church as the body of Christ. But, oh! How we have blemished and scarred the body through social neglect and through fear of being nonconformists.

There was a time when the church was very powerful—in the time when 40 the early Christians rejoiced at being deemed worthy to suffer for what they believed. In those days the church was not merely a thermometer that transformed the mores of society. Whenever the early Christians entered a town, the people in power became disturbed and immediately sought to convict the Christians for being "disturbers of the peace" and "outside agitators." But the Christians pressed on, in the conviction that they were "a colony of heaven," called to obey God rather than man. Small in number, they were big in commitment. They were too God-intoxicated to be "astronomically intimidated." By their effort and example they brought an end to such ancient evils as infanticide and gladiatorial contests.

Things are different now. So often the contemporary church is a weak, ineffectual voice with an uncertain sound. So often it is an archdefender of the status quo. Far from being disturbed by the presence of the church, the power structure of the average community is consoled by the church's silent—and often even vocal—sanction of things as they are.

But the judgment of God is upon the church as never before. If today's church does not recapture the sacrificial spirit of the early church, it will lose its authenticity, forfeit the loyalty of millions, and be dismissed as an irrelevant social club with no meaning for the twentieth century. Every day I meet young people whose disappointment with the church has turned into outright disgust.

Perhaps I have once again been too optimistic. Is organized religion too inextricably bound to the status quo to save our nation and the world? Perhaps I must turn my faith to the inner spiritual church, the church within the church, as the true *ekklesia*[11] and the hope of the world. But again I am thankful to God that some noble souls from the ranks of organized religion have broken loose from the paralyzing chains of conformity and joined us as active partners in the struggle for freedom. They have left their secure congregations and walked the streets of Albany, Georgia, with us. They have gone down the highways of the South on tortuous rides for freedom. Yes, they have gone to jail with us. Some have been dismissed from their churches, have lost the support of their bishops and fellow ministers. But they have acted in the faith that right defeated is stronger than evil triumphant. Their witness has been the spiritual salt that has preserved the true meaning of the gospel in these troubled times. They have carved a tunnel of hope through the dark mountain of disappointment.

---

[11] The Greek New Testament word for the early Christian church.

I hope that the church as a whole will meet the challenge of this decisive hour. But even if the church does not come to the aid of justice, I have no despair about the future. I have no fear about the outcome of our struggle in Birmingham, even if our motives are at present misunderstood. We will reach the goal of freedom in Birmingham and all over the nation, because the goal of America is freedom. Abused and scorned though we may be, our destiny is tied up with America's destiny. Before the pilgrims landed at Plymouth, we were here. Before the pen of Jefferson etched the majestic words of the Declaration of Independence across the pages of history, we were here. For more than two centuries our forebears labored in this country without wages; they made cotton king; they built the homes of their masters while suffering gross injustice and shameful humiliation—and yet out of a bottomless vitality they continued to thrive and develop. If the inexpressible cruelties of slavery could not stop us, the opposition we now face will surely fail. We will win our freedom because the sacred heritage of our nation and the eternal will of God are embodied in our echoing demands.

Before closing I feel impelled to mention one other point in your statement that has troubled me profoundly. You warmly commended the Birmingham police force for keeping "order" and "preventing violence." I doubt that you would have so warmly commended the police force if you had seen its dogs sinking their teeth into unarmed, nonviolent Negroes. I doubt that you would so quickly commend the policemen if you were to observe their ugly and inhumane treatment of Negroes here in the city jail; if you were to watch them push and curse old Negro women and young Negro girls; if you were to see them slap and kick old Negro men and young boys; if you were to observe them, as they did on two occasions, refuse to give us food because we wanted to sing our grace together. I cannot join you in your praise of the Birmingham police department.

It is true that the police have exercised a degree of discipline in handling the demonstrators. In this sense they have conducted themselves rather "nonviolently" in public. But for what purpose? To preserve the evil system of segregation. Over the past few years I have consistently preached that nonviolence demands that the means we use must be as pure as the ends we seek. I have tried to make clear that it is wrong to use immoral means to attain moral ends. But now I must affirm that it is just as wrong, or perhaps even more so, to use moral means to preserve immoral ends. Perhaps Mr. Connor and his policemen have been rather nonviolent in public, as was Chief Pritchett in Albany, Georgia, but they have used the moral means of nonviolence to maintain the immoral end of racial injustice. As T. S. Eliot[12] has said, "The last temptation is the greatest treason: To do the right deed for the wrong reason."

I wish you had commended the Negro sit-inners and demonstrators of Birmingham for their sublime courage, their willingness to suffer, and their amazing discipline in the midst of great provocation. One day the South will

45

---

[12] Thomas Stearns Eliot (1888–1965), American-born poet.

recognize its real heroes. They will be the James Merediths,[13] with the noble sense of purpose that enables them to face jeering and hostile mobs, and with the agonizing loneliness that characterizes the life of the pioneer. They will be old, oppressed, battered Negro women, symbolized in a seventy-two-year-old woman in Montgomery, Alabama, who rose up with a sense of dignity and with her people decided not to ride segregated buses, and who responded with ungrammatical profundity to one who inquired about her weariness: "My feets is tired, but my soul is at rest." They will be the young high school and college students, the young ministers of the gospel and a host of their elders, courageously and nonviolently sitting in at lunch counters and willingly going to jail for conscience' sake. One day the South will know that when these dis-inherited children of God sat down at lunch counters, they were in reality standing up for what is best in the American dream and for the most sacred values in our Judaeo-Christian heritage, thereby bringing our nation back to those great wells of democracy which were dug deep by the founding fathers in their formulation of the Constitution and the Declaration of Independence.

Never before have I written so long a letter. I'm afraid it is much too long to take your precious time. I can assure you that it would have been much shorter if I had been writing from a comfortable desk, but what else can one do when he is alone in a narrow jail cell, other than write long letters, think long thoughts, and pray long prayers?

If I have said anything in this letter that overstates the truth and indicates an unreasonable impatience, I beg you to forgive me. If I have said anything that understates the truth and indicates my having a patience that allows me to settle for anything less than brotherhood, I beg God to forgive me.

I hope this letter finds you strong in the faith. I hope that circumstances will soon make it possible for me to meet each of you, not as an integrationist or a civil-rights leader but as a fellow clergyman and a Christian brother. Let us all hope that the dark clouds of a racial prejudice will soon pass away and the deep fog of misunderstanding will be lifted from our fear-drenched communities, and in some not too distant tomorrow the radiant stars of love and brotherhood will shine over our great nation with all their scintillating beauty.

> Yours for the cause of Peace and Brotherhood,
> Martin Luther King Jr.

FOR ANALYSIS

1. What is King's definition of "civil disobedience"?

2. Summarize and explain the argument King makes in paragraph 46 about "means" and "ends."

3. Those opposed to civil disobedience frequently argue that in a democratic society, change should be pursued through legislation and the courts because if people are

---

[13] James Meredith was the first black to be admitted as a student to the University of Mississippi.

allowed to disobey laws with which they disagree, there will be chaos and violence. How does King seek to allay those fears?

4. How does King deal with the charge that he is an outsider meddling in the affairs of others?

5. What are the "four basic steps" (para. 6) in a nonviolent campaign, according to King?

6. What is King's answer to his critics who urge negotiation instead of direct action?

MAKING CONNECTIONS

Swift uses **satire** in "A Modest Proposal" (p. 500) to protest the injustice of British rule in Ireland. King adopts a direct personal **tone** to convey his position. How are these contrasting approaches appropriate for each author's purpose?

WRITING TOPICS

1. King offers a philosophical justification for civil disobedience (paras. 15–22), at the heart of which is his distinction between a just and an unjust law. Do you agree with that distinction? Explain.

2. In your opinion, has the history of race relations in the United States since King's assassination in 1968 strengthened or weakened his arguments on the necessity and value of civil disobedience?

FURTHER QUESTIONS
FOR THINKING AND WRITING

1. What support do the works in this section offer for Emily Dickinson's assertion that "Much Madness is divinest Sense"? **Writing Topic:** The central characters in Herman Melville's "Bartleby the Scrivener" and Harlan Ellison's "'Repent, Harlequin!' Said the Ticktockman" are viewed by society as mad. How might it be argued that they exhibit "divinest sense"?

2. In a number of these works, a single individual rebels against society and suffers defeat or death. Are these works therefore pessimistic and despairing? If not, what is the purpose of the rebellions, and why do the authors choose to bring their characters to such ends? **Writing Topic:** Compare two works from this section that offer support for the idea that a single individual can have a decisive effect on society.

3. Examine some of the representatives of established order—the lawyer in "Bartleby the Scrivener," the Ticktockman—and discuss what attitudes they share and how effectively they function as spokespeople for law and order. **Writing Topic:** Compare and evaluate the kinds of order that each represents.

4. William Butler Yeats's "Easter 1916," Lawrence Ferlinghetti's "In Goya's Greatest Scenes," and Carolyn Forché's "The Colonel" are poems about political struggle against oppressive rulers. In what ways are the poems similar? In what ways are they different? **Writing Topic:** Select the poem that makes the most powerful and effective case on behalf of the oppressed, and write an argument defending your choice.

5. Most of us live out our lives in the ordinary and humdrum world that is rejected in poems such as William Wordsworth's "The World Is Too Much with Us" and W. H. Auden's "The Unknown Citizen." Can these poems be said to be calls to social irresponsibility? **Writing Topic:** Consider whether "we" in Wordsworth's poem and the unknown citizen are simply objects of scorn or whether they deserve sympathy and perhaps even respect.

6. Characters in several of the works in this section—the Harlequin in "'Repent, Harlequin!' Said the Ticktockman" and Bartleby in "Bartleby the Scrivener"—are rebels. What similarities do you find among these rebels? **Writing Topic:** Explain how the attitudes and actions of these characters constitute an attack on the status quo.

7. Many works in this section deal explicitly with the relationship between individuals and religion. What similarities do you find among them? What differences? **Writing Topic:** Compare and contrast the way that relationship is perceived in Shirley Jackson's "The Lottery," and Salman Rushdie's "Imagine There's No Heaven."

CULTURE AND IDENTITY

This Is Harlem (detail), 1943, by Jacob Lawrence.

Historically, a group of people bound together by kinship and geography will form a society that exhibits a *culture*—common language, behavioral rules, traditions, skills, mores, religion, and art that define the civilization of that group. Literary works, including folklore and myth, are inseparable from the particular human society from which they emerge.

Until relatively recently, with the invention of trains, automobiles, and airplanes, travel over long distances was difficult. Instant communication—the telephone, the computer network—is an innovation of our time. Originally, information about other societies could be heard only as far away as a human could shout. Letters helped transmit ideas and cultural values over time and distance, but no more quickly than a horse could gallop or a ship could sail. For thousands of years cultures lived in relative isolation from each other, and hence they tended to develop distinctive traits and values. Within China, for instance, there are numerous well-defined cultures: the Uighurs of the northwest, the coastal Chinese of Shanghai, the Tibetan mountain people, the Szechuanese of the southwest. They eat different foods; they practice different religions; they speak different dialects.

Though technological advances have made the world seem smaller and, generally, have ended the geographical isolation of various cultures, these advances have not diminished the powerful cultural distinctions that mark societies all over the world. In fact, modern communication and transport have sometimes served to bring cultures into conflict. The works in this section, varied as they are, share a preoccupation with the connection between culture and identity. Some, such as George Orwell's "Shooting an Elephant," examine the devastating consequences of cultural imperialism. Others, such as Zora Neale Hurston's "How It Feels to Be Colored Me," focus on the way dominant cultural stereotypes distort and undermine the sense of self of those who are different.

The works in this section demonstrate how powerfully culture shapes identity. They reveal the tension generated by interacting cultures, and offer insight into the conflicts that usually emerge. But these works also provide an opportunity for us to step outside the bounds and bonds of our own culture and to experience just how complex, diverse, and interesting the human condition can be.

QUESTIONS FOR THINKING AND WRITING

As you read the selections in this section, consider the questions that follow. You may want to write out your thoughts informally—in a journal, if you are keeping one—as a way of preparing to respond to the selections. Or you may wish to make one of these questions the basis for a formal essay.

1. What cultural tradition(s) do you come from? Describe this tradition as fully as you can. Do you feel that you live in or out of the cultural mainstream? Explain.

2. Except for Native Americans, the people of the United States descended from or arrived as citizens of foreign cultures. Is there, nonetheless, an American culture? Explain. The United States was once called a *cultural melting pot.* Now it is sometimes called a *cultural mosaic.* Which **metaphor** strikes you as more apt? Explain.

3. Do economic considerations affect culture? Aside from their wealth, are the rich different from the poor? Explain. Does education strengthen or weaken traditional culture? Explain.

4. What are some of the positive and negative associations you have with the values of the cultural tradition(s) you come from? Is the preservation of these values a good thing or a bad thing? Explain.

FICTION

CHARLOTTE PERKINS GILMAN   (1860–1935)

THE YELLOW WALLPAPER   1892

It is very seldom that mere ordinary people like John and myself secure ancestral halls for the summer.

A colonial mansion, a hereditary estate, I would say a haunted house and reach the height of romantic felicity—but that would be asking too much of fate!

Still I will proudly declare that there is something queer about it.

Else, why should it be let so cheaply? And why have stood so long untenanted?

John laughs at me, of course, but one expects that.   5

John is practical in the extreme. He has no patience with faith, an intense horror of superstition, and he scoffs openly at any talk of things not to be felt and seen and put down in figures.

John is a physician, and *perhaps*—(I would not say it to a living soul, of course, but this is dead paper and a great relief to my mind)—*perhaps* that is one reason I do not get well faster.

You see, he does not believe I am sick! And what can one do?

If a physician of high standing, and one's own husband, assures friends and relatives that there is really nothing the matter with one but temporary nervous depression—a slight hysterical tendency—what is one to do?

My brother is also a physician, and also of high standing, and he says the   10 same thing.

So I take phosphates or phosphites—whichever it is, and tonics, and air and exercise, and journeys, and am absolutely forbidden to "work" until I am well again.

Personally, I disagree with their ideas.

Personally, I believe that congenial work, with excitement and change, would do me good.

But what is one to do?

I did write for a while in spite of them; but it *does* exhaust me a good deal—   15 having to be so sly about it, or else meet with heavy opposition.

I sometimes fancy that in my condition if I had less opposition and more society and stimulus—but John says the very worst thing I can do is to think about my condition, and I confess it always makes me feel bad.

So I will let it alone and talk about the house.

The most beautiful place! It is quite alone, standing well back from the road, quite three miles from the village. It makes me think of English places that you read about, for there are hedges and walls and gates that lock, and lots of separate little houses for the gardeners and people.

There is a *delicious* garden! I never saw such a garden—large and shady, full of box-bordered paths, and lined with long grape-covered arbors with seats under them.

There were greenhouses, too, but they are all broken now. 20

There was some legal trouble, I believe, something about the heirs and co-heirs; anyhow, the place has been empty for years.

That spoils my ghostliness, I am afraid, but I don't care—there is something strange about the house—I can feel it.

I even said so to John one moonlight evening, but he said what I felt was a draught, and shut the window.

I get unreasonably angry with John sometimes. I'm sure I never used to be so sensitive. I think it is due to this nervous condition.

But John says if I feel so I shall neglect proper self-control; so I take pains to 25 control myself—before him, at least, and that makes me very tired.

I don't like our room a bit. I wanted one downstairs that opened onto the piazza and had roses all over the window, and such pretty old-fashioned chintz hangings! But John would not hear of it.

He said there was only one window and not room for two beds, and no near room for him if he took another.

He is very careful and loving, and hardly lets me stir without special direction.

I have a schedule prescription for each hour in the day; he takes all care from me, and so I feel basely ungrateful not to value it more.

He said we came here solely on my account, that I was to have perfect rest 30 and all the air I could get. "Your exercise depends on your strength, my dear," said he, "and your food somewhat on your appetite; but air you can absorb all the time." So we took the nursery at the top of the house.

It is a big, airy room, the whole floor nearly, with windows that look all ways, and air and sunshine galore. It was a nursery first, and then playroom and gymnasium, I should judge, for the windows are barred for little children, and there are rings and things in the walls.

The paint and paper look as if a boys' school had used it. It is stripped off—the paper—in great patches all around the head of my bed, about as far as I can reach, and in a great place on the other side of the room low down. I never saw a worse paper in my life. One of those sprawling, flamboyant patterns committing every artistic sin.

It is dull enough to confuse the eye in following, pronounced enough constantly to irritate and provoke study, and when you follow the lame uncertain curves for a little distance they suddenly commit suicide—plunge off at outrageous angles, destroy themselves in unheard-of contradictions.

The color is repellent, almost revolting; a smouldering unclean yellow, strangely faded by the slow-turning sunlight. It is a dull yet lurid orange in some places, a sickly sulphur tint in others.

No wonder the children hated it! I should hate it myself if I had to live in 35 this room long.

There comes John, and I must put this away—he hates to have me write a word.

We have been here two weeks, and I haven't felt like writing before, since that first day.

I am sitting by the window now, up in this atrocious nursery, and there is nothing to hinder my writing as much as I please, save lack of strength.

John is away all day, and even some nights when his cases are serious.

I'm glad my case is not serious! 40

But these nervous troubles are dreadfully depressing.

John does not know how much I really suffer. He knows there is no reason to suffer, and that satisfies him.

Of course it is only nervousness. It does weigh on me so not to do my duty in any way!

I meant to be such a help to John, such a real rest and comfort, and here I am a comparative burden already!

Nobody would believe what an effort it is to do what little I am able—to 45 dress and entertain, and order things.

It is fortunate Mary is so good with the baby. Such a dear baby!

And yet I *cannot* be with him, it makes me so nervous.

I suppose John never was nervous in his life. He laughs at me so about this wallpaper!

At first he meant to repaper the room, but afterward he said that I was letting it get the better of me, and that nothing was worse for a nervous patient than to give way to such fancies.

He said that after the wallpaper was changed it would be the heavy bedstead, 50 and then the barred windows, and then that gate at the head of the stairs, and so on.

"You know the place is doing you good," he said, "and really, dear, I don't care to renovate the house just for a three months' rental."

"Then do let us go downstairs," I said. "There are such pretty rooms there."

Then he took me in his arms and called me a blessed little goose, and said he would go down to the cellar, if I wished, and have it whitewashed into the bargain.

But he is right enough about the beds and windows and things.

It is as airy and comfortable a room as anyone need wish, and, of course, 55 I would not be so silly as to make him uncomfortable just for a whim.

I'm really getting quite fond of the big room, all but that horrid paper.

Out of one window I can see the garden—those mysterious deep-shaded arbors, the riotous old-fashioned flowers, and bushes and gnarly trees.

Out of another I get a lovely view of the bay and a little private wharf belonging to the estate. There is a beautiful shaded lane that runs down there from the house. I always fancy I see people walking in these numerous paths and arbors, but John has cautioned me not to give way to fancy in the least. He says that with my imaginative power and habit of story-making, a nervous weakness like mine is sure to lead to all manner of excited fancies, and that I ought to use my will and good sense to check the tendency. So I try.

I think sometimes that if I were only well enough to write a little it would relieve the press of ideas and rest me.

But I find I get pretty tired when I try.   60

It is so discouraging not to have any advice and companionship about my work. When I get really well, John says we will ask Cousin Henry and Julia down for a long visit; but he says he would as soon put fireworks in my pillow-case as to let me have those stimulating people about now.

I wish I could get well faster.

But I must not think about that. This paper looks to me as if it *knew* what a vicious influence it had!

There is a recurrent spot where the pattern lolls like a broken neck and two bulbous eyes stare at you upside down.

I get positively angry with the impertinence of it and the everlastingness.   65 Up and down and sideways they crawl, and those absurd, unblinking eyes are everywhere. There is one place where two breadths didn't match, and the eyes go all up and down the line, one a little higher than the other.

I never saw so much expression in an inanimate thing before, and we all know how much expression they have! I used to lie awake as a child and get more entertainment and terror out of blank walls and plain furniture than most children could find in a toy-store.

I remember what a kindly wink the knobs of our big old bureau used to have, and there was one chair that always seemed like a strong friend.

I used to feel that if any of the other things looked too fierce I could always hop into that chair and be safe.

The furniture in this room is no worse than inharmonious, however, for we had to bring it all from downstairs. I suppose when this was used as a play-room they had to take the nursery things out, and no wonder! I never saw such ravages as the children have made here.

The wallpaper, as I said before, is torn off in spots, and it sticketh closer than   70 a brother—they must have had perseverance as well as hatred.

Then the floor is scratched and gouged and splintered, the plaster itself is dug out here and there, and this great heavy bed, which is all we found in the room, looks as if it had been through the wars.

But I don't mind it a bit—only the paper.

There comes John's sister. Such a dear girl as she is, and so careful of me! I must not let her find me writing.

She is a perfect and enthusiastic housekeeper, and hopes for no better profession. I verily believe she thinks it is the writing which made me sick!

But I can write when she is out, and see her a long way off from these windows. 75

There is one that commands the road, a lovely shaded winding road, and one that just looks off over the country. A lovely country, too, full of great elms and velvet meadows.

This wallpaper has a kind of sub-pattern in a different shade, a particularly irritating one, for you can only see it in certain lights, and not clearly then.

But in the places where it isn't faded and where the sun is just so—I can see a strange, provoking, formless sort of figure that seems to skulk about behind that silly and conspicuous front design.

There's sister on the stairs!

Well, the Fourth of July is over! The people are all gone and I am tired out. 80 John thought it might do me good to see a little company, so we just had Mother and Nellie and the children down for a week.

Of course I didn't do a thing. Jennie sees to everything now.

But it tired me all the same.

John says if I don't pick up faster he shall send me to Weir Mitchell in the fall.

But I don't want to go there at all. I had a friend who was in his hands once, and she says he is just like John and my brother, only more so!

Besides, it is such an undertaking to go so far.   85

I don't feel as if it was worthwhile to turn my hand over for anything, and I'm getting dreadfully fretful and querulous.

I cry at nothing, and cry most of the time.

Of course I don't when John is here, or anybody else, but when I am alone.

And I am alone a good deal just now. John is kept in town very often by serious cases, and Jennie is good and lets me alone when I want her to.

So I walk a little in the garden or down that lovely lane, sit on the porch 90 under the roses, and lie down up here a good deal.

I'm getting really fond of the room in spite of the wallpaper. Perhaps *because* of the wallpaper.

It dwells in my mind so!

I lie here on this great immovable bed—it is nailed down, I believe—and follow that pattern about by the hour. It is as good as gymnastics, I assure you. I start, we'll say, at the bottom, down in the corner over there where it has not been touched, and I determine for the thousandth time that I *will* follow that pointless pattern to some sort of a conclusion.

I know a little of the principle of design, and I know this thing was not arranged on any laws of radiation, or alternation, or repetition, or symmetry, or anything else that I ever heard of.

It is repeated, of course, by the breadths, but not otherwise.   95

Looked at in one way, each breadth stands alone; the bloated curves and flourishes—a kind of "debased Romanesque" with delirium tremens—go waddling up and down in isolated columns of fatuity.

But, on the other hand, they connect diagonally, and the sprawling outlines run off in great slanting waves of optic horror, like a lot of wallowing seaweeds in full chase.

The whole thing goes horizontally, too, at least it seems so, and I exhaust myself in trying to distinguish the order of its going in that direction.

They have used a horizontal breadth for a frieze, and that adds wonderfully to the confusion.

There is one end of the room where it is almost intact, and there, when the 100 crosslights fade and the low sun shines directly upon it, I can almost fancy radiation after all,—the interminable grotesque seems to form around a common center and rush off in headlong plunges of equal distraction.

It makes me tired to follow it. I will take a nap, I guess.

I don't know why I should write this.

I don't want to.

I don't feel able.

And I know John would think it absurd. But I *must* say what I feel and think 105 in some way—it is such a relief!

But the effort is getting to be greater than the relief.

Half the time now I am awfully lazy, and lie down ever so much. John says I musn't lose my strength, and has me take cod liver oil and lots of tonics and things, to say nothing of ale and wine and rare meat.

Dear John! He loves me very dearly, and hates to have me sick. I tried to have a real earnest reasonable talk with him the other day, and tell him how I wish he would let me go and make a visit to Cousin Henry and Julia.

But he said I wasn't able to go, nor able to stand it after I got there; and I did not make out a very good case for myself, for I was crying before I had finished.

It is getting to be a great effort for me to think straight. Just this nervous 110 weakness, I suppose.

And dear John gathered me up in his arms, and just carried me upstairs and laid me on the bed, and sat by me and read to me till it tired my head.

He said I was his darling and his comfort and all he had, and that I must take care of myself for his sake, and keep well.

He says no one but myself can help me out of it, that I must use my will and self-control and not let any silly fancies run away with me.

There's one comfort—the baby is well and happy, and does not have to occupy this nursery with the horrid wallpaper.

If we had not used it, that blessed child would have! What a fortunate 115 escape! Why, I wouldn't have a child of mine, an impressionable little thing, live in such a room for worlds.

I never thought of it before, but it is lucky that John kept me here after all; I can stand it so much easier than a baby, you see.

Of course I never mention it to them any more—I am too wise—but I keep watch of it all the same.

There are things in that wallpaper that nobody knows but me, or ever will.

Behind that outside pattern the dim shapes get clearer every day.

It is always the same shape, only very numerous.   120

And it is like a woman stooping down and creeping about behind that pattern. I don't like it a bit. I wonder—I begin to think—I wish John would take me away from here!

It is so hard to talk with John about my case, because he is so wise, and because he loves me so.

But I tried it last night.

It was moonlight. The moon shines in all around just as the sun does.

I hate to see it sometimes, it creeps so slowly, and always comes in by one   125
window or another.

John was asleep and I hated to waken him, so I kept still and watched the moonlight on that undulating wallpaper till I felt creepy.

The faint figure behind seemed to shake the pattern, just as if she wanted to get out.

I got up softly and went to feel and see if the paper *did* move, and when I came back John was awake.

"What is it, little girl?" he said. "Don't go walking about like that—you'll get cold."

I thought it was a good time to talk, so I told him that I really was not gain-   130
ing here, and that I wished he would take me away.

"Why, darling!" said he, "Our lease will be up in three weeks, and I can't see how to leave before.

"The repairs are not done at home, and I cannot possibly leave town just now. Of course if you were in any danger, I could and would, but you really are better, dear, whether you can see it or not. I am a doctor, dear, and I know. You are gaining flesh and color, your appetite is better, I feel really much easier about you."

"I don't weigh a bit more," said I, "nor as much; and my appetite may be better in the evening when you are here but it is worse in the morning when you are away!"

"Bless her little heart!" said he with a big hug, "She shall be as sick as she pleases! But now let's improve the shining hours by going to sleep, and talk about it in the morning!"

"And you won't go away?" I asked gloomily.   135

"Why, how can I, dear? It is only three weeks more and then we will take a nice little trip of a few days while Jennie is getting the house ready. Really, dear, you are better!"

"Better in body perhaps—" I began, and stopped short, for he sat up straight and looked at me with such a stern, reproachful look that I could not say another word.

"My darling," said he, "I beg of you, for my sake and for our child's sake, as well as for your own, that you will never for one instant let that idea enter your mind! There is nothing so dangerous, so fascinating, to a temperament like yours. It is a false and foolish fancy. Can you trust me as a physician when I tell you so?"

So of course I said no more on that score, and we went to sleep before long. He thought I was asleep first, but I wasn't, and lay there for hours trying to decide whether that front pattern and the back pattern really did move together or separately.

On a pattern like this, by daylight, there is a lack of sequence, a defiance of law, that is a constant irritant to a normal mind. 140

The color is hideous enough, and unreliable enough, and infuriating enough, but the pattern is torturing.

You think you have mastered it, but just as you get well under way in following, it turns a back-somersault and there you are. It slaps you in the face, knocks you down, and tramples upon you. It is like a bad dream.

The outside pattern is a florid arabesque, reminding one of a fungus. If you can imagine a toadstool in joints, an interminable string of toadstools, budding and sprouting in endless convolutions—why, that is something like it.

That is, sometimes!

There is one marked peculiarity about this paper, a thing nobody seems to notice but myself, and that is that it changes as the light changes. 145

When the sun shoots in through the east window—I always watch for that first long, straight ray—it changes so quickly that I never can quite believe it.

That is why I watch it always.

By moonlight—the moon shines in all night when there is a moon—I wouldn't know it was the same paper.

At night in any kind of light, in twilight, candlelight, lamplight, and worst of all by moonlight, it becomes bars! The outside pattern, I mean, and the woman behind it is as plain as can be.

I didn't realize for a long time what the thing was that showed behind, that dim sub-pattern, but now I am quite sure it is a woman. 150

By daylight she is subdued, quiet. I fancy it is the pattern that keeps her so still. It is so puzzling. It keeps me quiet by the hour.

I lie down ever so much now. John says it is good for me, and to sleep all I can.

Indeed he started the habit by making me lie down for an hour after each meal.

It is a very bad habit, I am convinced, for you see, I don't sleep.

And that cultivates deceit, for I don't tell them I'm awake—oh, no! 155

The fact is I am getting a little afraid of John.

He seems very queer sometimes, and even Jennie has an inexplicable look.

It strikes me occasionally, just as a scientific hypothesis, that perhaps it is the paper!

I have watched John when he did not know I was looking, and come into the room suddenly on the most innocent excuses, and I've caught him several times *looking at the paper!* And Jennie too. I caught Jennie with her hand on it once.

She didn't know I was in the room, and when I asked her in a quiet, a very quiet voice, with the most restrained manner possible, what she was doing 160 with the paper—she turned around as if she had been caught stealing, and looked quite angry—asked me why I should frighten her so!

Then she said that the paper stained everything it touched, that she had found yellow smooches on all my clothes and John's and she wished we would be more careful!

Did not that sound innocent? But I know she was studying that pattern, and I am determined that nobody shall find it out but myself!

Life is very much more exciting now than it used to be. You see, I have something more to expect, to look forward to, to watch. I really do eat better, and am more quiet than I was.

John is so pleased to see me improve! He laughed a little the other day, and said I seemed to be flourishing in spite of my wallpaper.

I turned it off with a laugh. I had no intention of telling him it was *because* of 165
the wallpaper—he would make fun of me. He might even want to take me away.

I don't want to leave now until I have found it out. There is a week more, and I think that will be enough.

I'm feeling so much better!

I don't sleep much at night, for it is so interesting to watch developments; but I sleep a good deal in the daytime.

In the daytime it is tiresome and perplexing.

There are always new shoots on the fungus, and new shades of yellow all 170
over it. I cannot keep count of them, though I have tried conscientiously.

It is the strangest yellow, that wallpaper! It makes me think of all the yellow things I ever saw—not beautiful ones like buttercups, but old, foul, bad yellow things.

But there is something else about that paper—the smell! I noticed it the moment we came into the room, but with so much air and sun it was not bad. Now we have had a week of fog and rain, and whether the windows are open or not, the smell is here.

It creeps all over the house.

I find it hovering in the dining-room, skulking in the parlor, hiding in the hall, lying in wait for me on the stairs.

It gets into my hair. 175

Even when I go to ride, if I turn my head suddenly and surprise it—there is that smell!

Such a peculiar odor, too! I have spent hours in trying to analyze it, to find what it smelled like.

It is not bad—at first—and very gentle, but quite the subtlest, most enduring odor I ever met.

In this damp weather it is awful. I wake up in the night and find it hanging over me.

It used to disturb me at first. I thought seriously of burning the house—to 180
reach the smell.

But now I am used to it. The only thing I can think of that it is like is the *color* of the paper! A yellow smell.

There is a very funny mark on this wall, low down, near the mopboard. A streak that runs round the room. It goes behind every piece of furniture, except the bed, a long, straight, even *smooch*, as if it had been rubbed over and over.

I wonder how it was done and who did it, and what they did it for. Round and round and round—round and round and round—it makes me dizzy!

I really have discovered something at last.

Through watching so much at night, when it changes so, I have finally found out.

The front pattern *does* move—and no wonder! The woman behind shakes it!

Sometimes I think there are a great many women behind, and sometimes only one, and she crawls around fast, and her crawling shakes it all over.

Then in the very bright spots she keeps still, and in the very shady spots she just takes hold of the bars and shakes them hard.

And she is all the time trying to climb through. But nobody could climb through that pattern—it strangles so; I think that is why it has so many heads.

They get through, and then the pattern strangles them off and turns them upside down and makes their eyes white!

If those heads were covered or taken off it would not be half so bad.

I think that woman gets out in the daytime!

And I'll tell you why—privately—I've seen her!

I can see her out of every one of my windows!

It is the same woman, I know, for she is always creeping, and most women do not creep by daylight.

I see her in that long shaded lane, creeping up and down. I see her in those dark grape arbors, creeping all around the garden.

I see her on that long road under the trees, creeping along, and when a carriage comes she hides under the blackberry vines.

I don't blame her a bit. It must be very humiliating to be caught creeping by daylight!

I always lock the door when I creep by daylight. I can't do it at night, for I know John would suspect something at once.

And John is so queer now that I don't want to irritate him. I wish he would take another room! Besides, I don't want anybody to get that woman out at night but myself.

I often wonder if I could see her out of all the windows at once.

But, turn as fast as I can, I can only see out of one at one time.

And though I always see her, she *may* be able to creep faster than I can turn! I have watched her sometimes away off in the open country, creeping as fast as a cloud shadow in a high wind.

If only that top pattern could be gotten off from the under one! I mean to try it, little by little.

I have found out another funny thing, but I shan't tell it this time! It does 205 not do to trust people too much.

There are only two more days to get this paper off, and I believe John is beginning to notice. I don't like the look in his eyes.

And I hear him ask Jennie a lot of professional questions about me. She had a very good report to give.

She said I slept a good deal in the daytime.

John knows I don't sleep very well at night, for all I'm so quiet!

He asked me all sorts of questions, too, and pretended to be very loving and 210 kind.

As if I couldn't see through him!

Still, I don't wonder he acts so, sleeping under this paper for three months.

It only interests me, but I feel sure John and Jennie are secretly affected by it.

Hurrah! This is the last day, but it is enough. John is to stay in town over night, and won't be out until this evening.

Jennie wanted to sleep with me—the sly thing; but I told her I should 215 undoubtedly rest better for a night all alone.

That was clever, for really I wasn't alone a bit! As soon as it was moonlight and that poor thing began to crawl and shake the pattern, I got up and ran to help her.

I pulled and she shook. I shook and she pulled, and before morning we had peeled off yards of that paper.

A strip about as high as my head and half around the room.

And then when the sun came and that awful pattern began to laugh at me, I declared I would finish it to-day!

We go away to-morrow, and they are moving all my furniture down again 220 to leave things as they were before.

Jennie looked at the wall in amazement, but I told her merrily that I did it out of pure spite at the vicious thing.

She laughed and said she wouldn't mind doing it herself, but I must not get tired.

How she betrayed herself that time!

But I am here, and no person touches this paper but Me—not *alive!*

She tried to get me out of the room—it was too patent! But I said it was so 225 quiet and empty and clean now that I believed I would lie down again and sleep all I could, and not to wake me even for dinner—I would call when I woke.

So now she is gone, and the servants are gone, and the things are gone, and there is nothing left but that great bedstead nailed down, with the canvas mattress we found on it.

We shall sleep downstairs to-night, and take the boat home to-morrow.

I quite enjoy the room, now it is bare again.

How those children did tear about here!

This bedstead is fairly gnawed!   230

But I must get to work.

I have locked the door and thrown the key down into the front path.

I don't want to go out, and I don't want to have anybody come in, till John comes.

I want to astonish him.

I've got a rope up here that even Jennie did not find. If that woman does get 235 out, and tries to get away, I can tie her!

But I forgot I could not reach far without anything to stand on!

This bed will *not* move!

I tried to lift and push it until I was lame, and then I got so angry I bit off a little piece at one corner—but it hurt my teeth.

Then I peeled off all the paper I could reach standing on the floor. It sticks horribly and the pattern just enjoys it! All those strangled heads and bulbous eyes and waddling fungus growths just shriek with derision!

I am getting angry enough to do something desperate. To jump out of the 240 window would be admirable exercise, but the bars are too strong even to try.

Besides I wouldn't do it. Of course not. I know well enough that a step like that is improper and might be misconstrued.

I don't like to *look* out of the windows even—there are so many of those creeping women, and they creep so fast.

I wonder if they all come out of that wallpaper as I did?

But I am securely fastened now by my well-hidden rope—you don't get *me* out in the road there!

I suppose I shall have to get back behind the pattern when it comes night, 245 and that is hard!

It is so pleasant to be out in this great room and creep around as I please!

I don't want to go outside. I won't, even if Jennie asks me to.

For outside you have to creep on the ground, and everything is green instead of yellow.

But here I can creep smoothly on the floor, and my shoulder just fits in that long smooch around the wall, so I cannot lose my way.

Why, there's John at the door! 250

It is no use, young man, you can't open it!

How he does call and pound!

Now he's crying to Jennie for an axe.

It would be a shame to break down that beautiful door!

"John, dear!" said I in the gentlest voice, "The key is down by the front steps, 255 under a plantain leaf!"

That silenced him for a few moments.

Then he said—very quietly indeed, "Open the door, my darling!"

"I can't," said I. "The key is down by the front door under a plantain leaf!" And then I said it again, several times, very gently and slowly, and said it so often that he had to go and see, and he got it of course, and came in. He stopped short by the door.

"What is the matter?" he cried. "For God's sake, what are you doing!"

I kept on creeping just the same, but I looked at him over my shoulder. 260

"I've got out at last," said I, "in spite of you and Jane. And I've pulled off most of the paper, so you can't put me back!"

Now why should that man have fainted? But he did, and right across my path by the wall, so that I had to creep over him every time!

FOR ANALYSIS

1. Why have the **narrator** and her husband John rented the mansion?

2. In the opening paragraphs, what **tone** does the narrator's description of the mansion establish?

3. Describe the **character** of John. Does the narrator's view of him change in the course of the story? Explain.

4. After telling us that her husband John is a physician, the narrator adds that "*perhaps that is one reason I do not get well faster*" (para. 7). What does she mean by this comment?

5. How does the narrator's description of what she sees in the outside world reflect her inner state?

6. Who is Jennie? What is her function in the story?

7. The narrator both accepts her husband's control over her and disobeys him by secretly continuing to write. What effect does writing have on her? Is her husband correct in his judgment that writing will hinder her recovery?

8. What evidence does the story provide to explain the narrator's present state?

9. Can it be argued that, on some level, the narrator refuses to recover? Explain.

10. In what ways does the wallpaper embody the **theme** of the story?

MAKING CONNECTIONS

1. Compare the marriage relationship in this story with the marriage in Ibsen's play *A Doll's House* (p. 228).

2. Compare and contrast the **narrator** in this story with Emily Grierson in William Faulkner's story "A Rose for Emily" (p. 649) as examples of women wounded by a patriarchal society.

3. Compare the wallpaper in this story with the birdcage in Susan Glaspell's play *Trifles* (p. 1050) as **symbols**. In what ways are they similar? In what ways different? Which do you find more effective? Explain.

4. Considered as a horror story, in what ways is Gilman's narrative similar to Edgar Allan Poe's "The Cask of Amontillado" (p. 1108)? In what ways is it different?

WRITING TOPICS

1. Analyze the way **irony** is used in this story.

2. Write an essay in which you imaginatively reconstruct the early life of the **narrator**, including her marriage, to explain her illness.

3. Write an essay describing the aptness of wallpaper as a **symbol** for the life of the narrator.

4. In a paragraph, explain why we never learn the narrator's name.

JAMES BALDWIN   (1924–1987)

SONNY'S BLUES   1957

I read about it in the paper, in the subway, on my way to work. I read it, and I couldn't believe it, and I read it again. Then perhaps I just stared at it, at the newsprint spelling out his name, spelling out the story. I stared at it in the swinging lights of the subway car, and in the faces and bodies of the people, and in my own face, trapped in the darkness which roared outside.

It was not to be believed and I kept telling myself that, as I walked from the subway station to the high school. And at the same time I couldn't doubt it. I was scared, scared for Sonny. He became real to me again. A great block of ice got settled in my belly and kept melting there slowly all day long, while I taught my classes algebra. It was a special kind of ice. It kept melting, sending trickles of ice water all up and down my veins, but it never got less. Sometimes it hardened and seemed to expand until I felt my guts were going to come spilling out or that I was going to choke or scream. This would always be at a moment when I was remembering some specific thing Sonny had once said or done.

When he was about as old as the boys in my classes his face had been bright and open, there was a lot of copper in it; and he'd had wonderfully direct brown eyes, and great gentleness and privacy. I wondered what he looked like now. He had been picked up, the evening before, in a raid on an apartment downtown, for peddling and using heroin.

I couldn't believe it: but what I mean by that is that I couldn't find any room for it anywhere inside me. I had kept it outside me for a long time. I hadn't wanted to know. I had had suspicions, but I didn't name them, I kept putting them away. I told myself that Sonny was wild, but he wasn't crazy. And he'd always been a good boy, he hadn't ever turned hard or evil or disrespectful, the way kids can, so quick, so quick, especially in Harlem. I didn't want to believe that I'd ever see my brother going down, coming to nothing, all that light in his face gone out, in the condition I'd already seen so many others. Yet it had happened and here I was, talking about algebra to a lot of boys who might, every one of them for all I knew, be popping off needles every time they went to the head. Maybe it did more for them than algebra could.

I was sure that the first time Sonny had ever had horse,[1] he couldn't have 5 been much older than these boys were now. These boys, now, were living as we'd been living then, they were growing up with a rush and their heads bumped abruptly against the low ceiling of their actual possibilities. They were filled with rage. All they really knew were two darknesses, the darkness

[1] Heroin.

564

of their lives, which was now closing in on them, and the darkness of the movies, which had blinded them to that other darkness, and in which they now, vindictively, dreamed, at once more together than they were at any other time, and more alone.

When the last bell rang, the last class ended, I let out my breath. It seemed I'd been holding it for all that time. My clothes were wet—I may have looked as though I'd been sitting in a steam bath, all dressed up, all afternoon. I sat alone in the classroom a long time. I listened to the boys outside, downstairs, shouting and cursing and laughing. Their laughter struck me for perhaps the first time. It was not the joyous laughter which—God knows why—one associates with children. It was mocking and insular, its intent to denigrate. It was disenchanted, and in this, also, lay the authority of their curses. Perhaps I was listening to them because I was thinking about my brother and in them I heard my brother. And myself.

One boy was whistling a tune, at once very complicated and very simple, it seemed to be pouring out of him as though he were a bird, and it sounded very cool and moving through all that harsh, bright air, only just holding its own through all those other sounds.

I stood up and walked over to the window and looked down into the courtyard. It was the beginning of the spring and the sap was rising in the boys. A teacher passed through them every now and again, quickly, as though he or she couldn't wait to get out of that courtyard, to get those boys out of their sight and off their minds. I started collecting my stuff. I thought I'd better get home and talk to Isabel.

The courtyard was almost deserted by the time I got downstairs. I saw this boy standing in the shadow of a doorway, looking just like Sonny. I almost called his name. Then I saw that it wasn't Sonny, but somebody we used to know, a boy from around our block. He'd been Sonny's friend. He'd never been mine, having been too young for me, and, anyway, I'd never liked him. And now, even though he was a grown-up man, he still hung around that block, still spent hours on the street corners, was always high and raggy. I used to run into him from time to time and he'd often work around to asking me for a quarter or fifty cents. He always had some real good excuse, too, and I always gave it to him. I don't know why.

But now, abruptly, I hated him. I couldn't stand the way he looked at me, 10 partly like a dog, partly like a cunning child. I wanted to ask him what the hell he was doing in the school courtyard.

He sort of shuffled over to me, and he said, "I see you got the papers. So you already know about it."

"You mean about Sonny? Yes, I already know about it. How come they didn't get you?"

He grinned. It made him repulsive and it also brought to mind what he'd looked like as a kid. "I wasn't there. I stay away from them people."

"Good for you." I offered him a cigarette and I watched him through the smoke. "You come all the way down here just to tell me about Sonny?"

"That's right." He was sort of shaking his head and his eyes looked strange,   15
as though they were about to cross. The bright sun deadened his damp dark
brown skin and it made his eyes look yellow and showed up the dirt in his
kinked hair. He smelled funky. I moved a little away from him and I said,
"Well, thanks. But I already know about it and I got to get home."

"I'll walk you a little ways," he said. We started walking. There were a couple
of kids still loitering in the courtyard and one of them said goodnight to me
and looked strangely at the boy beside me.

"What're you going to do?" he asked me. "I mean, about Sonny?"

"Look. I haven't seen Sonny for over a year, I'm not sure I'm going to do
anything. Anyway, what the hell *can* I do?"

"That's right," he said quickly, "ain't nothing you can do. Can't much help
old Sonny no more, I guess."

It was what I was thinking and so it seemed to me he had no right to say it.   20

"I'm surprised at Sonny, though," he went on—he had a funny way of talking, he looked straight ahead as though he were talking to himself—"I thought
Sonny was a smart boy, I thought he was too smart to get hung."

"I guess he thought so too," I said sharply, "and that's how he got hung. And
how about you? You're pretty goddamn smart, I bet."

Then he looked directly at me, just for a minute. "I ain't smart," he said. "If
I was smart, I'd have reached for a pistol a long time ago."

"Look. Don't tell *me* your sad story, if it was up to me, I'd give you one."
Then I felt guilty—guilty, probably, for never having supposed that the poor
bastard *had* a story of his own, much less a sad one, and I asked, quickly,
"What's going to happen to him now?"

He didn't answer this. He was off by himself some place.   25

"Funny thing," he said, and from his tone we might have been discussing
the quickest way to get to Brooklyn, "when I saw the papers this morning,
the first thing I asked myself was if I had anything to do with it. I felt sort of
responsible."

I began to listen more carefully. The subway station was on the corner, just
before us, and I stopped. He stopped, too. We were in front of a bar and he
ducked slightly, peering in, but whoever he was looking for didn't seem to be
there. The juke box was blasting away with something black and bouncy and I
half watched the barmaid as she danced her way from the juke box to her place
behind the bar. And I watched her face as she laughingly responded to something someone said to her, still keeping time to the music. When she smiled
one saw the little girl, one sensed the doomed, still-struggling woman beneath
the battered face of the semi-whore.

"I never *give* Sonny nothing," the boy said finally, "but a long time ago I
come to school high and Sonny asked me how it felt." He paused, I couldn't
bear to watch him, I watched the barmaid, and I listened to the music which
seemed to be causing the pavement to shake. "I told him it felt great." The
music stopped, the barmaid paused and watched the juke box until the music
began again. "It did."

All this was carrying me some place I didn't want to go. I certainly didn't want to know how it felt. It filled everything, the people, the houses, the music, the dark, quicksilver barmaid, with menace; and this menace was their reality.

"What's going to happen to him now?" I asked again.   30

"They'll send him away some place and they'll try to cure him." He shook his head. "Maybe he'll even think he's kicked the habit. Then they'll let him loose"—he gestured, throwing his cigarette into the gutter. "That's all."

"What do you mean, that's *all*?"

But I knew what he meant.

"I *mean,* that's *all.*" He turned his head and looked at me, pulling down the corners of his mouth. "Don't you know what I mean?" he asked, softly.

"How the hell *would* I know what you mean?" I almost whispered it, I don't   35 know why.

"That's right," he said to the air, "how would *he* know what I mean?" He turned toward me again, patient and calm, and yet I somehow felt him shaking, shaking as though he were going to fall apart. I felt that ice in my guts again, the dread I'd felt all afternoon; and again I watched the barmaid, moving about the bar, washing glasses, and singing. "Listen. They'll let him out and then it'll just start all over again. That's what I mean."

"You mean—they'll let him out. And then he'll just start working his way back in again. You mean he'll never kick the habit. Is that what you mean?"

"That's right," he said, cheerfully. "*You* see what I mean."

"Tell me," I said at last, "why does he want to die? He must want to die, he's killing himself, why does he want to die?"

He looked at me in surprise. He licked his lips. "He don't want to die. He   40 wants to live. Don't nobody want to die, ever."

Then I wanted to ask him—too many things He could not have answered, or if he had, I could not have borne the answers. I started walking. "Well, I guess it's none of my business."

"It's going to be rough on old Sonny," he said. We reached the subway station. "This is your station?" he asked. I nodded. I took one step down. "Damn!" he said, suddenly. I looked up at him. He grinned again. "Damn it if I didn't leave all my money home. You ain't got a dollar on you, have you? Just for a couple of days, is all."

All at once something inside gave and threatened to come pouring out of me. I didn't hate him any more. I felt that in another moment I'd start crying like a child.

"Sure," I said. "Don't sweat." I looked in my wallet and didn't have a dollar, I only had a five. "Here," I said. "That hold you?"

He didn't look at it—he didn't want to look at it. A terrible, closed look   45 came over his face, as though he were keeping the number on the bill a secret from him and me. "Thanks," he said, and now he was dying to see me go. "Don't worry about Sonny. Maybe I'll write him or something."

"Sure," I said. "You do that. So long."

"Be seeing you," he said. I went on down the steps.

And I didn't write Sonny or send him anything for a long time. When I finally did, it was just after my little girl died, and he wrote me back a letter which made me feel like a bastard.

Here's what he said:

> Dear brother,
>
> You don't know how much I needed to hear from you. I wanted to write you many a time but I dug how much I must have hurt you and so I didn't write. But now I feel like a man who's been trying to climb up out of some deep, real deep and funky hole and just saw the sun up there, outside. I got to get outside.
>
> I can't tell you much about how I got here. I mean I don't know how to tell you. I guess I was afraid of something or I was trying to escape from something and you know I have never been very strong in the head (smile). I'm glad Mama and Daddy are dead and can't see what's happened to their son and I swear if I'd known what I was doing I would never have hurt you so, you and a lot of other fine people who were nice to me and who believed in me.
>
> I don't want you to think it had anything to do with me being a musician. It's more than that. Or maybe less than that. I can't get anything straight in my head down here and I try not to think about what's going to happen to me when I get outside again. Sometime I think I'm going to flip and never get outside and sometime I think I'll come straight back. I tell you one thing, though, I'd rather blow my brains out than go through this again. But that's what they all say, so they tell me. If I tell you when I'm coming to New York and if you could meet me, I sure would appreciate it. Give my love to Isabel and the kids and I was sure sorry to hear about little Gracie. I wish I could be like Mama and say the Lord's will be done, but I don't know it seems to me that trouble is the one thing that never does get stopped and I don't know what good it does to blame it on the Lord. But maybe it does some good if you believe it.
>
> Your brother,
> Sonny

Then I kept in constant touch with him and I sent him whatever I could and 50 I went to meet him when he came back to New York. When I saw him many things I thought I had forgotten came flooding back to me. This was because I had begun, finally, to wonder about Sonny, about the life that Sonny lived inside. This life, whatever it was, had made him older and thinner and it had deepened the distant stillness in which he had always moved. He looked very unlike my baby brother. Yet, when he smiled, when we shook hands, the baby brother I'd never known looked out from the depths of his private life, like an animal waiting to be coaxed into the light.

"How you been keeping?" he asked me.

"All right. And you?"

"Just fine." He was smiling all over his face. "It's good to see you again."

"It's good to see you."

The seven years' difference in our ages lay between us like a chasm: I won- 55 dered if these years would ever operate between us as a bridge. I was remembering, and it made it hard to catch my breath, that I had been there when he was born; and I had heard the first words he had ever spoken. When he started to walk, he walked from our mother straight to me. I caught him just before he fell when he took the first steps he ever took in this world.

"How's Isabel?"

"Just fine. She's dying to see you."

"And the boys?"

"They're fine, too. They're anxious to see their uncle."

"Oh, come on. You know they don't remember me." 60

"Are you kidding? Of course they remember you."

He grinned again. We got into a taxi. We had a lot to say to each other, far too much to know how to begin.

As the taxi began to move, I asked, "You still want to go to India?"

He laughed. "You still remember that. Hell, no. This place is Indian enough for me."

"It used to belong to them," I said. 65

And he laughed again. "They damn sure knew what they were doing when they got rid of it."

Years ago, when he was around fourteen, he'd been all hipped on the idea of going to India. He read books about people sitting on rocks, naked, in all kinds of weather, but mostly bad, naturally, and walking barefoot through hot coals and arriving at wisdom. I used to say that it sounded to me as though they were getting away from wisdom as fast as they could. I think he sort of looked down on me for that.

"Do you mind," he asked, "if we have the driver drive alongside the park? On the west side—I haven't seen the city in so long."

"Of course not," I said. I was afraid that I might sound as though I were humoring him, but I hoped he wouldn't take it that way.

So we drove along, between the green of the park and the stony, lifeless 70 elegance of hotels and apartment buildings, toward the vivid, killing streets of our childhood. These streets hadn't changed, though housing projects jutted up out of them now like rocks in the middle of a boiling sea. Most of the houses in which we had grown up had vanished, as had the stores from which we had stolen, the basements in which we had first tried sex, the rooftops from which we had hurled tin cans and bricks. But houses exactly like the houses of our past yet dominated the landscape, boys exactly like the boys we once had been found themselves smothering in these houses, came down into the streets for light and air and found themselves encircled by disaster. Some escaped the trap, most didn't. Those who got out always left something of themselves behind, as some animals amputate a leg and leave it in the trap. It might be said, perhaps, that I had escaped, after all, I was a school teacher; or that Sonny had, he hadn't lived in Harlem for years. Yet, as the cab moved uptown through streets which seemed, with a rush, to darken with dark people, and as

I covertly studied Sonny's face, it came to me that what we both were seeking through our separate cab windows was that part of ourselves which had been left behind. It's always at the hour of trouble and confrontation that the missing member aches.

We hit 110th Street and started rolling up Lenox Avenue. And I'd known this avenue all my life, but it seemed to me again, as it had seemed on the day I'd first heard about Sonny's trouble, filled with a hidden menace which was its very breath of life.

"We almost there," said Sonny.

"Almost." We were both too nervous to say anything more.

We live in a housing project. It hasn't been up long. A few days after it was up it seemed uninhabitably new, now, of course, it's already rundown. It looks like a parody of the good, clean, faceless life—God knows the people who live in it do their best to make it a parody. The beat-looking grass lying around isn't enough to make their lives green, the hedges will never hold out the streets, and they know it. The big windows fool no one, they aren't big enough to make space out of no space. They don't bother with the windows, they watch the TV screen instead. The playground is most popular with the children who don't play at jacks, or skip rope, or roller skate, or swing, and they can be found in it after dark. We moved in partly because it's not too far from where I teach, and partly for the kids; but it's really just like the houses in which Sonny and I grew up. The same things happen, they'll have the same things to remember. The moment Sonny and I started into the house I had the feeling that I was simply bringing him back into the danger he had almost died trying to escape.

Sonny has never been talkative. So I don't know why I was sure he'd be dying to talk to me when supper was over the first night. Everything went fine, the oldest boy remembered him, and the youngest boy liked him, and Sonny had remembered to bring something for each of them; and Isabel, who is really much nicer than I am, more open and giving, had gone to a lot of trouble about dinner and was genuinely glad to see him. And she's always been able to tease Sonny in a way that I haven't. It was nice to see her face so vivid again and to hear her laugh and watch her make Sonny laugh. She wasn't, or, anyway, she didn't seem to be, at all uneasy or embarrassed. She chatted as though there were no subject which had to be avoided and she got Sonny past his first, faint stiffness. And thank God she was there, for I was filled with that icy dread again. Everything I did seemed awkward to me, and everything I said sounded freighted with hidden meaning. I was trying to remember everything I'd heard about dope addiction and I couldn't help watching Sonny for signs. I wasn't doing it out of malice. I was trying to find out something about my brother. I was dying to hear him tell me he was safe. 75

"Safe!" my father grunted, whenever Mama suggested trying to move to a neighborhood which might be safer for children. "Safe, hell! Ain't no place safe for kids, nor nobody."

He always went on like this, but he wasn't, ever, really as bad as he sounded, not even on weekends, when he got drunk. As a matter of fact, he was always on the lookout for "something a little better," but he died before he found it. He died suddenly, during a drunken weekend in the middle of the war, when Sonny was fifteen. He and Sonny hadn't ever got on too well. And this was partly because Sonny was the apple of his father's eye. It was because he loved Sonny so much and was frightened for him, that he was always fighting with him. It doesn't do any good to fight with Sonny. Sonny just moves back, inside himself, where he can't be reached. But the principal reason that they never hit it off is that they were so much alike. Daddy was big and rough and loud-talking, just the opposite of Sonny, but they both had—that same privacy.

Mama tried to tell me something about this, just after Daddy died. I was home on leave from the army.

This was the last time I ever saw my mother alive. Just the same, this picture gets all mixed up in my mind with pictures I had of her when she was younger. The way I always see her is the way she used to be on a Sunday afternoon, say, when the old folks were talking after the big Sunday dinner. I always see her wearing pale blue. She'd be sitting on the sofa. And my father would be sitting in the easy chair, not far from her. And the living room would be full of church folks and relatives. There they sit, in chairs all around the living room, and the night is creeping up outside, but nobody knows it yet. You can see the darkness growing against the windowpanes and you hear the street noises every now and again, or maybe the jangling beat of a tambourine from one of the churches close by, but it's real quiet in the room. For a moment nobody's talking, but every face looks darkening, like the sky outside. And my mother rocks a little from the waist, and my father's eyes are closed. Everyone is looking at something a child can't see. For a minute they've forgotten the children. Maybe a kid is lying on the rug, half asleep. Maybe somebody's got a kid in his lap and is absent-mindedly stroking the kid's head. Maybe there's a kid, quiet and big-eyed, curled up in a big chair in the corner. The silence, the darkness coming, and the darkness in the faces frighten the child obscurely. He hopes that the hand which strokes his forehead will never stop—will never die. He hopes that there will never come a time when the old folks won't be sitting around the living room, talking about where they've come from, and what they've seen, and what's happened to them and their kinfolk.

But something deep and watchful in the child knows that this is bound 80 to end, is already ending. In a moment someone will get up and turn on the light. Then the old folks will remember the children and they won't talk any more that day. And when light fills the room, the child is filled with darkness. He knows that every time this happens he's moved just a little closer to that darkness outside. The darkness outside is what the old folks have been talking about. It's what they've come from. It's what they endure. The child knows that they won't talk any more because if he knows too much about what's happened to *them,* he'll know too much too soon, about what's going to happen to *him.*

The last time I talked to my mother, I remember I was restless. I wanted to get out and see Isabel. We weren't married then and we had a lot to straighten out between us.

There Mama sat, in black, by the window. She was humming an old church song, *Lord, you brought me from a long ways off.* Sonny was out somewhere. Mama kept watching the streets.

"I don't know," she said, "if I'll ever see you again, after you go off from here. But I hope you'll remember the things I tried to teach you."

"Don't talk like that," I said, and smiled. "You'll be here a long time yet."

She smiled, too, but she said nothing. She was quiet for a long time. And 85 I said, "Mama, don't you worry about nothing. I'll be writing all the time, and you be getting the checks. . . ."

"I want to talk to you about your brother," she said, suddenly. "If anything happens to me he ain't going to have nobody to look out for him."

"Mama," I said, "ain't nothing going to happen to you *or* Sonny. Sonny's all right. He's a good boy and he's got good sense."

"It ain't a question of his being a good boy," Mama said, "nor of his having good sense. It ain't only the bad ones, nor yet the dumb ones that gets sucked under." She stopped, looking at me. "Your Daddy once had a brother," she said, and she smiled in a way that made me feel she was in pain. "You didn't never know that, did you?"

"No," I said, "I never knew that," and I watched her face.

"Oh, yes," she said, "your Daddy had a brother." She looked out of the win- 90 dow again. "I know you never saw your Daddy cry. But *I* did—many a time, through all these years."

I asked her, "What happened to his brother? How come nobody's ever talked about him?"

This was the first time I ever saw my mother look old.

"His brother got killed," she said, "when he was just a little younger than you are now. I knew him. He was a fine boy. He was maybe a little full of the devil, but he didn't mean nobody no harm."

Then she stopped and the room was silent, exactly as it had sometimes been on those Sunday afternoons. Mama kept looking out into the streets.

"He used to have a job in the mill," she said, "and, like all young folks, he 95 just liked to perform on Saturday nights. Saturday nights, him and your father would drift around to different places, go to dances and things like that, or just sit around with people they knew, and your father's brother would sing, he had a fine voice, and play along with himself on his guitar. Well, this particular Saturday night, him and your father was coming home from some place, and they were both a little drunk and there was a moon that night, it was bright like day. Your father's brother was feeling kind of good, and he was whistling to himself, and he had his guitar slung over his shoulder. They was coming down a hill and beneath them was a road that turned off from the highway. Well, your father's brother, being always kind of frisky, decided to run down this hill, and he did, with that guitar banging and clanging behind him, and he ran across the road, and he was making water behind a tree. And your father was sort of amused at him and he was still coming down the hill, kind of slow. Then he heard a car motor and that same minute his brother stepped from behind the tree, into the road, in the moonlight. And he started to cross the road. And your father started to run down the hill, he says he don't know why. This car was full of white men. They was all drunk, and when they seen your father's brother they let out a great whoop and holler and they aimed the car straight at him. They was having fun, they just wanted to scare him, the way they do sometimes, you know. But they was drunk. And I guess the boy, being drunk, too, and scared, kind of lost his head. By the time he jumped it was too late. Your father says he heard his brother scream when the car rolled over him, and he heard the wood of that guitar when it give, and he heard them strings go flying, and he heard them white men shouting, and the car kept on a-going and it ain't stopped till this day. And, time your father got down the hill, his brother weren't nothing but blood and pulp."

Tears were gleaming on my mother's face. There wasn't anything I could say.

"He never mentioned it," she said, "because I never let him mention it before you children. Your Daddy was like a crazy man that night and for many a night thereafter. He says he never in his life seen anything as dark as that road after the lights of that car had gone away. Weren't nothing, weren't nobody on that road, just your Daddy and his brother and that busted guitar. Oh, yes. Your Daddy never did really get right again. Till the day he died he weren't sure but that every white man he saw was the man that killed his brother."

She stopped and took out her handkerchief and dried her eyes and looked at me.

"I ain't telling you all this," she said, "to make you scared or bitter or to make you hate nobody. I'm telling you this because you got a brother. And the world ain't changed."

I guess I didn't want to believe this. I guess she saw this in my face. She turned away from me, toward the window again, searching those streets.   100

"But I praise my Redeemer," she said at last, "that He called your Daddy home before me. I ain't saying it to throw no flowers at myself, but, I declare, it keeps me from feeling too cast down to know I helped your father get safely through this world. Your father always acted like he was the roughest, strongest man on earth. And everybody took him to be like that. But if he hadn't had me there—to see his tears!"

She was crying again. Still, I couldn't move. I said, "Lord, Lord, Mama, I didn't know it was like that."

"Oh, honey," she said, "there's a lot that you don't know. But you are going to find out." She stood up from the window and came over to me. "You got to hold on to your brother," she said, "and don't let him fall, no matter what it looks like is happening to him and no matter how evil you gets with him. You going to be evil with him many a time. But don't you forget what I told you, you hear?"

"I won't forget," I said. "Don't you worry, I won't forget. I won't let nothing happen to Sonny."

My mother smiled as though she was amused at something she saw in my 105
face. Then, "You may not be able to stop nothing from happening. But you
got to let him know you's *there*."

Two days later I was married, and then I was gone. And I had a lot of things
on my mind and I pretty well forgot my promise to Mama until I got shipped
home on a special furlough for her funeral.

And, after the funeral, with just Sonny and me alone in the empty kitchen, I
tried to find out something about him.

"What do you want to do?" I asked him.

"I'm going to be a musician," he said.

For he had graduated, in the time I had been away, from dancing to the juke 110
box to finding out who was playing what, and what they were doing with it,
and he had bought himself a set of drums.

"You mean, you want to be a drummer?" I somehow had the feeling that
being a drummer might be all right for other people but not for my brother
Sonny.

"I don't think," he said, looking at me very gravely, "that I'll ever be a good
drummer. But I think I can play a piano."

I frowned. I'd never played the role of the oldest brother quite so seriously
before, had scarcely ever, in fact, *asked* Sonny a damn thing. I sensed myself in
the presence of something I didn't really know how to handle, didn't understand. So I made my frown a little deeper as I asked: "What kind of musician
do you want to be?"

He grinned. "How many kinds do you think there are?"

"Be *serious*," I said. 115

He laughed, throwing his head back, and then looked at me. "I *am* serious."

"Well, then, for Christ's sake, stop kidding around and answer a serious
question. I mean, do you want to be a concert pianist, you want to play classical music and all that, or—or what?" Long before I finished he was laughing
again. "For Christ's *sake*, Sonny!"

He sobered, but with difficulty. "I'm sorry. But you sound so—*scared!*" and
he was off again.

"Well, you may think it's funny now, baby, but it's not going to be so funny
when you have to make your living at it, let me tell you *that*." I was furious
because I knew he was laughing at me and I didn't know why.

"No," he said, very sober now, and afraid, perhaps, that he'd hurt me, "I 120
don't want to be a classical pianist. That isn't what interests me. I mean"—he
paused, looking hard at me, as though his eyes would help me to understand,
and then gestured helplessly, as though perhaps his hand would help—"I
mean, I'll have a lot of studying to do, and I'll have to study *everything*, but, I
mean, I want to play *with*—jazz musicians." He stopped. "I want to play jazz,"
he said.

Well, the word had never before sounded as heavy, as real, as it sounded that
afternoon in Sonny's mouth. I just looked at him and I was probably frowning a real frown by this time. I simply couldn't see why on earth he'd want to

spend his time hanging around nightclubs, clowning around on bandstands, while people pushed each other around a dance floor. It seemed—beneath him, somehow. I had never thought about it before, had never been forced to, but I suppose I had always put jazz musicians in a class with what Daddy called "good-time people."

"Are you *serious*?"

"Hell, *yes*, I'm serious."

He looked more helpless than ever, and annoyed, and deeply hurt.

I suggested, helpfully: "You mean—like Louis Armstrong?"[2]   125

His face closed as though I'd struck him. "No. I'm not talking about none of that old-time, down home crap."

"Well, look, Sonny, I'm sorry, don't get mad. I just don't altogether get it, that's all. Name somebody—you know, a jazz musician you admire."

"Bird."

"Who?"

"Bird! Charlie Parker![3] Don't they teach you nothing in the goddamn army?"   130

I lit a cigarette. I was surprised and then a little amused to discover that I was trembling. "I've been out of touch," I said. "You'll have to be patient with me. Now. Who's this Parker character?"

"He's just one of the greatest jazz musicians alive," said Sonny, sullenly, his hands in his pockets, his back to me. "Maybe *the* greatest," he added, bitterly, "that's probably why *you* never heard of him."

"All right," I said, "I'm ignorant. I'm sorry. I'll go out and buy all the cat's records right away, all right?"

"It don't," said Sonny, with dignity, "make any difference to me. I don't care what you listen to. Don't do me no favors."

I was beginning to realize that I'd never seen him so upset before. With   135
another part of my mind I was thinking that this would probably turn out to be one of those things kids go through and that I shouldn't make it seem important by pushing it too hard. Still, I didn't think it would do any harm to ask: "Doesn't all this take a lot of time? Can you make a living at it?"

He turned back to me and half leaned, half sat, on the kitchen table. "Everything takes time," he said, "and—well, yes, sure, I can make a living at it. But what I don't seem to be able to make you understand is that it's the only thing I want to do."

"Well, Sonny," I said, gently, "you know people can't always do exactly what they *want* to do—"

"*No,* I don't know that," said Sonny, surprising me. "I think people *ought* to do what they want to do, what else are they alive for?"

"You getting to be a big boy," I said desperately, "it's time you started thinking about your future."

---

[2] Louis "Satchmo" Armstrong (1901–1971) played the trumpet and was one of the most innovative and influential figures in the history of jazz.
[3] Charlie "Bird" Parker (1920–1955), a seminal saxophonist, was one of the originators of the bebop style of jazz. Parker was also a heroin addict.

"I'm thinking about my future," said Sonny, grimly. "I think about it all the time." 140

I gave up. I decided, if he didn't change his mind, that we could always talk about it later. "In the meantime," I said, "you got to finish school." We had already decided that he'd have to move in with Isabel and her folks. I knew this wasn't the ideal arrangement because Isabel's folks are inclined to be dicty[4] and they hadn't especially wanted Isabel to marry me. But I didn't know what else to do. "And we have to get you fixed up at Isabel's."

There was a long silence. He moved from the kitchen table to the window. "That's a terrible idea. You know it yourself."

"Do you have a *better* idea?"

He just walked up and down the kitchen for a minute. He was as tall as I was. He had started to shave. I suddenly had the feeling that I didn't know him at all.

He stopped at the kitchen table and picked up my cigarettes. Looking at me 145 with a kind of mocking, amused defiance, he put one between his lips. "You mind?"

"You smoking already?"

He lit the cigarette and nodded, watching me through the smoke. "I just wanted to see if I'd have the courage to smoke in front of you." He grinned and blew a great cloud of smoke to the ceiling. "It was easy." He looked at my face. "Come on, now. I bet you was smoking at my age, tell the truth."

I didn't say anything but the truth was on my face, and he laughed. But now there was something very strained in his laugh. "Sure. And I bet that ain't all you was doing."

He was frightening me a little. "Cut the crap," I said. "We already decided that you was going to go and live at Isabel's. Now what's got into you all of a sudden?"

"*You* decided it," he pointed out. "*I* didn't decide nothing." He stopped in 150 front of me, leaning against the stove, arms loosely folded. "Look, brother. I don't want to stay in Harlem no more, I really don't." He was very earnest. He looked at me, then over toward the kitchen window. There was something in his eyes I'd never seen before, some thoughtfulness, some worry all his own. He rubbed the muscle of one arm. "It's time I was getting out of here."

"Where do you want to *go*, Sonny?"

"I want to join the army. Or the navy, I don't care. If I say I'm old enough, they'll believe me."

Then I got mad. It was because I was so scared. "You must be crazy. You goddamn fool, what the hell do you want to go and join the *army* for?"

"I just told you. To get out of Harlem."

"Sonny, you haven't even finished *school*. And if you really want to be a 155 musician, how do you expect to study if you're in the *army*?"

He looked at me, trapped, and in anguish. "There's ways. I might be able to work out some kind of deal. Anyway, I'll have the G.I. Bill when I come out."

---

[4] Snobbish.

"*If* you come out." We stared at each other. "Sonny, please. Be reasonable. I know the setup is far from perfect. But we got to do the best wc can."

"I ain't learning nothing in school," he said. "Even when I go." He turned away from me and opened the window and threw his cigarette out into the narrow alley. I watched his back. "At least, I ain't learning nothing you'd want me to learn." He slammed the window so hard I thought the glass would fly out, and turned back to me. "And I'm sick of the stink of these garbage cans!"

"Sonny," I said, "I know how you feel. But if you don't finish school now, you're going to be sorry later that you didn't." I grabbed him by the shoulders. "And you only got another year. It ain't so bad. And I'll come back and I swear I'll help you do *whatever* you want to do. Just try to put up with it till I come back. Will you please do that? For me?"

He didn't answer and he wouldn't look at me. 160

"Sonny. You hear me?"

He pulled away. "I hear you. But you never hear anything *I* say."

I didn't know what to say to that. He looked out of the window and then back at me. "OK," he said, and sighed. "I'll try."

Then I said, trying to cheer him up a little, "They got a piano at Isabel's. You can practice on it."

And as a matter of fact, it did cheer him up for a minute. "That's right," 165 he said to himself. "I forgot that." His face relaxed a little. But the worry, the thoughtfulness, played on it still, the way shadows play on a face which is staring into the fire.

But I thought I'd never hear the end of that piano. At first, Isabel would write me, saying how nice it was that Sonny was so serious about his music and how, as soon as he came in from school, or wherever hc had been when he was supposed to be at school, he went straight to that piano and stayed there until suppertime. And, after supper, he went back to that piano and stayed there until everybody went to bed. He was at the piano all day Saturday and all day Sunday. Then he bought a record player and started playing records. He'd play one record over and over again, all day long sometimes, and he'd improvise along with it on the piano. Or he'd play one section of the record, one chord, one change, one progression, then he'd do it on the piano. Then back to the record. Then back to the piano.

Well, I really don't know how they stood it. Isabel finally confessed that it wasn't like living with a person at all, it was like living with sound. And the sound didn't make any sense to her, didn't make any sense to any of them— naturally. They began, in a way, to be afflicted by this presence that was living in their home. It was as though Sonny were some sort of god, or monster. He moved in an atmosphere which wasn't like theirs at all. They fed him and he ate, he washed himself, he walked in and out of their door; he certainly wasn't nasty or unpleasant or rude, Sonny isn't any of those things; but it was as though he were all wrapped up in some cloud, some fire, some vision all his own; and there wasn't any way to reach him.

At the same time, he wasn't really a man yet, he was still a child, and they had to watch out for him in all kinds of ways. They certainly couldn't throw him out. Neither did they dare to make a great scene about that piano because even they dimly sensed, as I sensed, from so many thousands of miles away, that Sonny was at that piano playing for his life.

But he hadn't been going to school. One day a letter came from the school board and Isabel's mother got it—there had, apparently, been other letters but Sonny had torn them up. This day, when Sonny came in, Isabel's mother showed him the letter and asked where he'd been spending his time. And she finally got it out of him that he'd been down in Greenwich Village, with musicians and other characters, in a white girl's apartment. And this scared her and she started to scream at him and what came up, once she began—though she denies it to this day—was what sacrifices they were making to give Sonny a decent home and how little he appreciated it.

Sonny didn't play the piano that day. By evening, Isabel's mother had   170 calmed down but then there was the old man to deal with, and Isabel herself. Isabel says she did her best to be calm but she broke down and started crying. She says she just watched Sonny's face. She could tell, by watching him, what was happening with him. And what was happening was that they penetrated his cloud, they had reached him. Even if their fingers had been a thousand times more gentle than human fingers ever are, he could hardly help feeling that they had stripped him naked and were spitting on that nakedness. For he also had to see that his presence, that music, which was life or death to him, had been torture for them and that they had endured it, not at all for his sake, but only for mine. And Sonny couldn't take that. He can take it a little better today than he could then but he's still not very good at it and, frankly, I don't know anybody who is.

The silence of the next few days must have been louder than the sound of all the music ever played since time began. One morning, before she went to work, Isabel was in his room for something and she suddenly realized that all of his records were gone. And she knew for certain that he was gone. And he was. He went as far as the navy would carry him. He finally sent me a postcard from some place in Greece and that was the first I knew that Sonny was still alive. I didn't see him any more until we were both back in New York and the war had long been over.

He was a man by then, of course, but I wasn't willing to see it. He came by the house from time to time, but we fought almost every time we met. I didn't like the way he carried himself, loose and dreamlike all the time, and I didn't like his friends, and his music seemed to be merely an excuse for the life he led. It sounded just that weird and disordered.

Then we had a fight, a pretty awful fight, and I didn't see him for months. By and by I looked him up, where he was living, in a furnished room in the Village, and I tried to make it up. But there were lots of other people in the room and Sonny just lay on his bed, and he wouldn't come downstairs with me, and he treated these other people as though they were his family and

I weren't. So I got mad and then he got mad, and then I told him that he might just as well be dead as live the way he was living. Then he stood up and he told me not to worry about him any more in life, that he *was* dead as far as I was concerned. Then he pushed me to the door and the other people looked on as though nothing were happening, and he slammed the door behind me. I stood in the hallway, staring at the door. I heard somebody laugh in the room and then the tears came to my eyes. I started down the steps, whistling to keep from crying, I kept whistling to myself, *You going to need me, baby, one of these cold, rainy days.*

I read about Sonny's trouble in the spring. Little Grace died in the fall. She was a beautiful little girl. But she only lived a little over two years. She died of polio and she suffered. She had a slight fever for a couple of days, but it didn't seem like anything and we just kept her in bed. And we would certainly have called the doctor, but the fever dropped, she seemed to be all right. So we thought it had just been a cold. Then, one day, she was up, playing, Isabel was in the kitchen fixing lunch for the two boys when they'd come in from school, and she heard Grace fall down in the living room. When you have a lot of children you don't always start running when one of them falls, unless they start screaming or something. And, this time, Gracie was quiet. Yet, Isabel says that when she heard that *thump* and then that silence, something happened to her to make her afraid. And she ran to the living room and there was little Grace on the floor, all twisted up, and the reason she hadn't screamed was that she couldn't get her breath. And when she did scream, it was the worst sound, Isabel says, that she'd ever heard in all her life, and she still hears it sometimes in her dreams. Isabel will sometimes wake me up with a low, moaning, strangling sound and I have to be quick to awaken her and hold her to me and where Isabel is weeping against me seems a mortal wound.

I think I may have written Sonny the very day that little Grace was buried. I 175 was sitting in the living room in the dark, by myself, and I suddenly thought of Sonny. My trouble made his real.

One Saturday afternoon, when Sonny had been living with us, or, anyway, been in our house, for nearly two weeks, I found myself wandering aimlessly about the living room, drinking from a can of beer, and trying to work up courage to search Sonny's room. He was out, he was usually out whenever I was home, and Isabel had taken the children to see their grandparents. Suddenly I was standing still in front of the living room window, watching Seventh Avenue. The idea of searching Sonny's room made me still. I scarcely dared to admit to myself what I'd be searching for. I didn't know what I'd do if I found it. Or if I didn't.

On the sidewalk across from me, near the entrance to a barbecue joint, some people were holding an old-fashioned revival meeting. The barbecue cook, wearing a dirty white apron, his conked[5] hair reddish and metallic in

---

[5] Straightened and greased.

the pale sun, and a cigarette between his lips, stood in the doorway, watching them. Kids and older people paused in their errands and stood there, along with some older men and a couple of very tough-looking women who watched everything that happened on the avenue, as though they owned it, or were maybe owned by it. Well, they were watching this, too. The revival was being carried on by three sisters in black, and a brother. All they had were their voices and their Bibles and a tambourine. The brother was testifying and while he testified two of the sisters stood together, seeming to say, amen, and the third sister walked around with the tambourine outstretched and a couple of people dropped coins into it. Then the brother's testimony ended and the sister who had been taking up the collection dumped the coins into her palm and transferred them to the pocket of her long black robe. Then she raised both hands, striking the tambourine against the air, and then against one hand, and she started to sing. And the two other sisters and the brother joined in.

It was strange, suddenly, to watch, though I had been seeing these meetings all my life. So, of course, had everybody else down there. Yet, they paused and watched and listened and I stood still at the window. "*'Tis the old ship of Zion*," they sang, and the sister with the tambourine kept a steady, jangling beat, "*it has rescued many a thousand!*" Not a soul under the sound of their voices was hearing this song for the first time, not one of them had been rescued. Nor had they seen much in the way of rescue work being done around them. Neither did they especially believe in the holiness of the three sisters and the brother, they knew too much about them, knew where they lived, and how. The woman with the tambourine, whose voice dominated the air, whose face was bright with joy, was divided by very little from the woman who stood watching her, a cigarette between her heavy, chapped lips, her hair a cuckoo's nest, her face scarred and swollen from many beatings, and her black eyes glittering like coal. Perhaps they both knew this, which was why, when, as rarely, they addressed each other, they addressed each other as Sister. As the singing filled the air the watching, listening faces underwent a change, the eyes focusing on something within; the music seemed to soothe a poison out of them; and time seemed, nearly, to fall away from the sullen, belligerent, battered faces, as though they were fleeing back to their first condition, while dreaming of their last. The barbecue cook half shook his head and smiled, and dropped his cigarette and disappeared into his joint. A man fumbled in his pockets for change and stood holding it in his hand impatiently, as though he had just remembered a pressing appointment further up the avenue. He looked furious. Then I saw Sonny, standing on the edge of the crowd. He was carrying a wide, flat notebook with a green cover, and it made him look, from where I was standing, almost like a schoolboy. The coppery sun brought out the copper in his skin, he was very faintly smiling, standing very still. Then the singing stopped, the tambourine turned into a collection plate again. The furious man dropped in his coins and vanished, so did a couple of the women, and Sonny dropped some change in the plate, looking directly at the woman with a little smile. He started across the avenue, toward the house. He has a slow, loping walk, something like the

way Harlem hipsters walk, only he's imposed on this his own half-beat. I had
never really noticed it before.

I stayed at the window, both relieved and apprehensive. As Sonny disappeared from my sight, they began singing again. And they were still singing
when his key turned in the lock.

"Hey," he said.   180

"Hey, yourself. You want some beer?"

"No. Well, maybe." But he came up to the window and stood beside me,
looking out. "What a warm voice," he said.

They were singing *If I could only hear my mother pray again!*

"Yes," I said, "and she can sure beat that tambourine."

"But what a terrible song," he said, and laughed. He dropped his notebook   185
on the sofa and disappeared into the kitchen. "Where's Isabel and the kids?"

"I think they went to see their grandparents. You hungry?"

"No." He came back into the living room with his can of beer. "You want to
come some place with me tonight?"

I sensed, I don't know how, that I couldn't possibly say no. "Sure. Where?"

He sat down on the sofa and picked up his notebook and started leafing
through it. "I'm going to sit in with some fellows in a joint in the Village."

"You mean, you're going to play, tonight?"   190

"That's right." He took a swallow of his beer and moved back to the window.
He gave me a sidelong look. "If you can stand it."

"I'll try," I said.

He smiled to himself and we both watched as the meeting across the way
broke up. The three sisters and the brother, heads bowed, were singing *God be
with you till we meet again.* The faces around them were very quiet. Then the
song ended. The small crowd dispersed. We watched the three women and the
lone man walk slowly up the avenue.

"When she was singing before," said Sonny, abruptly, "her voice reminded
me for a minute of what heroin feels like sometimes—when it's in your veins.
It makes you feel sort of warm and cool at the same time. And distant. And—
and sure." He sipped his beer, very deliberately not looking at me. I watched
his face. "It makes you feel—in control. Sometimes you've got to have that
feeling."

"Do you?" I sat down slowly in the easy chair.   195

"Sometimes." He went to the sofa and picked up his notebook again. "Some
people do."

"In order," I asked, "to play?" And my voice was very ugly, full of contempt
and anger.

"Well"—he looked at me with great, troubled eyes, as though, in fact, he
hoped his eyes would tell me things he could never otherwise say—"they *think*
so. And *if* they think so—!"

"And what do *you* think?" I asked.

He sat on the sofa and put his can of beer on the floor. "I don't know," he   200
said, and I couldn't be sure if he were answering my question or pursuing his

thoughts. His face didn't tell me. "It's not so much to *play*. It's to *stand* it, to be able to make it at all. On any level." He frowned and smiled: "In order to keep from shaking to pieces."

"But these friends of yours," I said, "they seem to shake themselves to pieces pretty goddamn fast."

"Maybe." He played with the notebook. And something told me that I should curb my tongue, that Sonny was doing his best to talk, that I should listen. "But of course you only know the ones that've gone to pieces. Some don't—or at least they haven't *yet* and that's just about all *any* of us can say." He paused. "And then there are some who just live, really, in hell, and they know it and they see what's happening and they go right on. I don't know." He sighed, dropped the notebook, folded his arms. "Some guys, you can tell from the way they play, they on something *all* the time. And you can see that, well, it makes something real for them. But of course," he picked up his beer from the floor and sipped it and put the can down again, "they *want* to, too, you've got to see that. Even some of them that say they don't—*some*, not all."

"And what about you?" I asked—I couldn't help it. "What about you? Do *you* want to?"

He stood up and walked to the window and remained silent for a long time. Then he sighed. "Me," he said. Then: "While I was downstairs before, on my way here, listening to that woman sing, it struck me all of a sudden how much suffering she must have had to go through—to sing like that. It's *repulsive* to think you have to suffer that much."

I said: "But there's no way not to suffer—is there, Sonny?"   205

"I believe not," he said and smiled, "but that's never stopped anyone from trying." He looked at me. "Has it?" I realized, with this mocking look, that there stood between us, forever, beyond the power of time or forgiveness, the fact that I had held silence—so long!—when he had needed human speech to help him. He turned back to the window. "No, there's no way not to suffer. But you try all kinds of ways to keep from drowning in it, to keep on top of it, and to make it seem—well, like *you*. Like you did something, all right, and now you're suffering for it. You know?" I said nothing. "Well you know," he said, impatiently, "why *do* people suffer? Maybe it's better to do something to give it a reason, *any* reason."

"But we just agreed," I said, "that there's no way not to suffer. Isn't it better, then, just to—take it?"

"But nobody just takes it," Sonny cried, "that's what I'm telling you! *Everybody* tries not to. You're just hung up on the *way* some people try—it's not *your* way!"

The hair on my face began to itch, my face felt wet. "That's not true," I said, "that's not true. I don't give a damn what other people do, I don't even care how they suffer. I just care how *you* suffer." And he looked at me. "Please believe me," I said, "I don't want to see you—die—trying not to suffer."

"I won't," he said, flatly, "die trying not to suffer. At least, not any faster   210 than anybody else."

"But there's no need," I said, trying to laugh, "is there? in killing yourself."

I wanted to say more, but I couldn't. I wanted to talk about will power and how life could be—well, beautiful. I wanted to say that it was all within; but was it? or, rather, wasn't that exactly the trouble? And I wanted to promise that I would never fail him again. But it would all have sounded—empty words and lies.

So I made the promise to myself and prayed that I would keep it.

"It's terrible sometimes, inside," he said, "that's what's the trouble. You walk these streets, black and funky and cold, and there's not really a living ass to talk to, and there's nothing shaking, and there's no way of getting it out—that storm inside. You can't talk it and you can't make love with it, and when you finally try to get with it and play it, you realize *nobody's* listening. So *you've* got to listen. You got to find a way to listen."

And then he walked away from the window and sat on the sofa again, as 215 though all the wind had suddenly been knocked out of him. "Sometimes you'll do *anything* to play, even cut your mother's throat." He laughed and looked at me. "Or your brother's." Then he sobered. "Or your own." Then: "Don't worry. I'm all right now and I think I'll *be* all right. But I can't forget—where I've been. I don't mean just the physical place I've been, I mean where I've *been*. And *what* I've been."

"What have you been, Sonny?" I asked.

He smiled—but sat sideways on the sofa, his elbow resting on the back, his fingers playing with his mouth and chin, not looking at me. "I've been something I didn't recognize, didn't know I could be. Didn't know anybody could be." He stopped, looking inward, looking helplessly young, looking old. "I'm not talking about it now because I feel *guilty* or anything like that—maybe it would be better if I did, I don't know. Anyway, I can't really talk about it. Not to you, not to anybody," and now he turned and faced me. "Sometimes, you know, and it was actually when I was most *out* of the world, I felt that I was in it, that I was *with* it, really, and I could play or I didn't really have to *play*, it just came out of me, it was there. And I don't know how I played, thinking about it now, but I know I did awful things, those times, sometimes, to people. Or it wasn't that I *did* anything to them—it was that they weren't real." He picked up the beer can; it was empty; he rolled it between his palms: "And other times—well, I needed a fix, I needed to find a place to lean, I needed to clear a space to *listen*—and I couldn't find it, and I—went crazy, I did terrible things to *me*, I was terrible *for* me." He began pressing the beer can between his hands, I watched the metal begin to give. It glittered, as he played with it like a knife, and I was afraid he would cut himself, but I said nothing. "Oh well. I can never tell you. I was all by myself at the bottom of something, stinking and sweating and crying and shaking, and I smelled it, you know? *my* stink, and I thought I'd die if I couldn't get away from it and yet, all the same, I knew that everything I was doing was just locking me in with it. And I didn't know," he paused, still flattening the beer can, "I didn't know, I still *don't* know, something kept telling me that maybe it was good to smell your own stink, but

I didn't think that *that* was what I'd been trying to do—and—who can stand it?" and he abruptly dropped the ruined beer can, looking at me with a small, still smile, and then rose, walking to the window as though it were the lodestone rock. I watched his face, he watched the avenue. "I couldn't tell you when Mama died—but the reason I wanted to leave Harlem so bad was to get away from drugs. And then, when I ran away, that's what I was running from—really. When I came back, nothing had changed, *I* hadn't changed, I was just—older." And he stopped, drumming with his fingers on the windowpane. The sun had vanished, soon darkness would fall. I watched his face. "It can come again," he said, almost as though speaking to himself. Then he turned to me. "It can come again," he repeated. "I just want you to know that."

"All right," I said, at last. "So it can come again. All right."

He smiled, but the smile was sorrowful. "I had to try to tell you," he said.

"Yes," I said. "I understand that."   220

"You're my brother," he said, looking straight at me, and not smiling at all.

"Yes," I repeated, "yes. I understand that."

He turned back to the window, looking out. "All that hatred down there," he said, "all that hatred and misery and love. It's a wonder it doesn't blow the avenue apart."

We went to the only nightclub on a short, dark street, downtown. We squeezed through the narrow, chattering, jampacked bar to the entrance of the big room, where the bandstand was. And we stood there for a moment, for the lights were very dim in this room and we couldn't see. Then, "Hello, boy," said the voice and an enormous black man, much older than Sonny or myself, erupted out of all that atmospheric lighting and put an arm around Sonny's shoulder. "I been sitting right here," he said, "waiting for you."

He had a big voice, too, and heads in the darkness turned toward us.   225

Sonny grinned and pulled a little away, and said, "Creole, this is my brother. I told you about him."

Creole shook my hand. "I'm glad to meet you, son," he said, and it was clear that he was glad to meet me *there,* for Sonny's sake. And he smiled, "You got a real musician in *your* family," and he took his arm from Sonny's shoulder and slapped him, lightly, affectionately, with the back of his hand.

"Well. Now I've heard it all," said a voice behind us. This was another musician, and a friend of Sonny's, a coal-black, cheerful-looking man, built close to the ground. He immediately began confiding to me, at the top of his lungs, the most terrible things about Sonny, his teeth gleaming like a lighthouse and his laugh coming up out of him like the beginning of an earthquake. And it turned out that everyone at the bar knew Sonny, or almost everyone; some were musicians, working there, or nearby, or not working, some were simply hangers-on, and some were there to hear Sonny play. I was introduced to all of them and they were all very polite to me. Yet, it was clear that, for them, I was only Sonny's brother. Here, I was in Sonny's world. Or, rather: his kingdom. Here, it was not even a question that his veins bore royal blood.

They were going to play soon and Creole installed me, by myself, at a table in a dark corner. Then I watched them, Creole, and the little black man, and Sonny, and the others, while they horsed around, standing just below the bandstand. The light from the bandstand spilled just a little short of them and, watching them laughing and gesturing and moving about, I had the feeling that they, nevertheless, were being most careful not to step into that circle of light too suddenly; that if they moved into the light too suddenly, without thinking, they would perish in flame. Then, while I watched, one of them, the small, black man, moved into the light and crossed the bandstand and started fooling around with his drums. Then—being funny and being, also, extremely ceremonious—Creole took Sonny by the arm and led him to the piano. A woman's voice called Sonny's name and a few hands started clapping. And Sonny, also being funny and being ceremonious, and so touched, I think, that he could have cried, but neither hiding it nor showing it, riding it like a man, grinned, and put both hands to his heart and bowed from the waist.

Creole then went to the bass fiddle and a lean, very bright-skinned brown 230 man jumped up on the bandstand and picked up his horn. So there they were, and the atmosphere on the bandstand and in the room began to change and tighten. Someone stepped up to the microphone and announced them. Then there were all kinds of murmurs. Some people at the bar shushed others. The waitress ran around, frantically getting in the last orders, guys and chicks got closer to each other, and the lights on the bandstand, on the quartet, turned to a kind of indigo. Then they all looked different there. Creole looked about him for the last time, as though he were making certain that all his chickens were in the coop, and then he—jumped and struck the fiddle. And there they were.

All I know about music is that not many people ever really hear it. And even then, on the rare occasions when something opens within, and the music enters, what we mainly hear, or hear corroborated, are personal, private, vanishing evocations. But the man who creates the music is hearing something else, is dealing with the roar rising from the void and imposing order on it as it hits the air. What is evoked in him, then, is of another order, more terrible because it has no words, and triumphant, too, for that same reason. And his triumph, when he triumphs, is ours. I just watched Sonny's face. His face was troubled, he was working hard, but he wasn't with it. And I had the feeling that, in a way, everyone on the bandstand was waiting for him, both waiting for him and pushing him along. But as I began to watch Creole, I realized that it was Creole who held them all back. He had them on a short rein. Up there, keeping the beat with his whole body, wailing on the fiddle, with his eyes half closed, he was listening to everything, but he was listening to Sonny. He was having a dialogue with Sonny. He wanted Sonny to leave the shoreline and strike out for the deep water. He was Sonny's witness that deep water and drowning were not the same thing—he had been there, and he knew. And he wanted Sonny to know. He was waiting for Sonny to do the things on the keys which would let Creole know that Sonny was in the water.

And, while Creole listened, Sonny moved, deep within, exactly like someone in torment. I had never before thought of how awful the relationship must
be between the musician and his instrument. He has to fill it, this instrument,
with the breath of life, his own. He has to make it do what he wants it to do.
And a piano is just a piano. It's made out of so much wood and wires and little
hammers and big ones, and ivory. While there's only so much you can do with
it, the only way to find this out is to try; to try and make it do everything.

And Sonny hadn't been near a piano for over a year. And he wasn't on much
better terms with his life, not the life that stretched before him now. He and
the piano stammered, started one way, got scared, stopped; started another
way, panicked, marked time, started again; then seemed to have found a direction, panicked again, got stuck. And the face I saw on Sonny I'd never seen
before. Everything had been burned out of it, and, at the same time, things
usually hidden were being burned in, by the fire and fury of the battle which
was occurring in him up there.

Yet, watching Creole's face as they neared the end of the first set, I had the
feeling that something had happened, something I hadn't heard. Then they
finished, there was scattered applause, and then, without an instant's warning, Creole started into something else, it was almost sardonic, it was *Am I
Blue.*[6] And, as though he commanded, Sonny began to play. Something began
to happen. And Creole let out the reins. The dry, low, black man said something awful on the drums, Creole answered, and the drums talked back. Then
the horn insisted, sweet and high, slightly detached perhaps, and Creole listened, commenting now and then, dry, and driving, beautiful and calm and
old. Then they all came together again, and Sonny was part of the family again.
I could tell this from his face. He seemed to have found, right there beneath his
fingers, a damn brand-new piano. It seemed that he couldn't get over it. Then,
for a while, just being happy with Sonny, they seemed to be agreeing with him
that brand-new pianos certainly were a gas.

Then Creole stepped forward to remind them that what they were playing   235
was the blues. He hit something in all of them, he hit something in me, myself,
and the music tightened and deepened, apprehension began to beat the air.
Creole began to tell us what the blues were all about. They were not about
anything very new. He and his boys up there were keeping it new, at the risk of
ruin, destruction, madness, and death, in order to find new ways to make us
listen. For, while the tale of how we suffer, and how we are delighted, and how
we may triumph is never new, it always must be heard. There isn't any other
tale to tell, it's the only light we've got in all this darkness.

And this tale, according to that face, that body, those strong hands on those
strings, has another aspect in every country, and a new depth in every generation. Listen, Creole seemed to be saying, listen. Now these are Sonny's blues.
He made the little black man on the drums know it, and the bright, brown

[6] One of the standard tunes in the jazz/blues repertoire.

man on the horn. Creole wasn't trying any longer to get Sonny in the water. He was wishing him Godspeed. Then he stepped back, very slowly, filling the air with the immense suggestion that Sonny speak for himself.

Then they all gathered around Sonny and Sonny played. Every now and again one of them seemed to say, amen. Sonny's fingers filled the air with life, his life. But that life contained so many others. And Sonny went all the way back, he really began with the spare, flat statement of the opening phrase of the song. Then he began to make it his. It was very beautiful because it wasn't hurried and it was no longer a lament. I seemed to hear with what burning he had made it his, and what burning we had yet to make it ours, how we could cease lamenting. Freedom lurked around us and I understood, at last, that he could help us to be free if we would listen, that he would never be free until we did. Yet, there was no battle in his face now, I heard what he had gone through, and would continue to go through until he came to rest in earth. He had made it his: that long line, of which we knew only Mama and Daddy. And he was giving it back, as everything must be given back, so that, passing through death, it can live forever. I saw my mother's face again, and felt, for the first time, how the stones of the road she had walked on must have bruised her feet. I saw the moonlit road where my father's brother died. And it brought something else back to me, and carried me past it, I saw my little girl again and felt Isabel's tears again, and I felt my own tears begin to rise. And I was yet aware that this was only a moment, that the world waited outside, as hungry as a tiger, and that trouble stretched above us, longer than the sky.

Then it was over. Creole and Sonny let out their breath, both soaking wet, and grinning. There was a lot of applause and some of it was real. In the dark, the girl came by and I asked her to take drinks to the bandstand. There was a long pause, while they talked up there in the indigo light and after awhile I saw the girl put a Scotch and milk on top of the piano for Sonny. He didn't seem to notice it, but just before they started playing again, he sipped from it and looked toward me, and nodded. Then he put it back on top of the piano. For me, then, as they began to play again, it glowed and shook above my brother's head like the very cup of trembling.[7]

For Analysis

1. Explain the title.

2. What is the relation between the opening events and the end of the story?

3. What function does the **narrator's** encounter with Sonny's friend at the beginning of the story (paras. 9–47) serve?

---

[7] See the Old Testament, Isaiah 51:17, 22–23: "Awake, awake, stand up, O Jerusalem, which hast drunk at the hand of the Lord the cup of his fury; thou hast drunken the dregs of the cup of trembling, and wrung them out. . . . Behold, I have taken out of thine hand the cup of trembling, even the dregs of the cup of my fury; thou shalt no more drink it again: But I will put it into the hand of them that afflict thee."

4. Does the story offer any explanation for Sonny's addiction? Explain.

5. What adjectives would you use to describe the narrator? Does he change in the course of the story? Explain.

6. What effects does Baldwin achieve by rearranging the order of events?

7. What does the final sentence mean?

MAKING CONNECTIONS

1. Compare and contrast the way racism is portrayed in this story with its portrayal in Bambara's "The Lesson" (p. 96).

2. Kafka's "A Hunger Artist" (p. 353) is also about an artist and the process of artistic creation. What similarities or differences do you find between Kafka's story and Baldwin's?

WRITING TOPICS

1. What does this story have to say about the sources of creativity?

2. Discuss the significance of the **narrator's** observations on the revival meeting (paras. 177–78) to the **theme** of the story.

ALICE WALKER (B. 1944)

EVERYDAY USE   1973

FOR YOUR GRANDMAMA

I will wait for her in the yard that Maggie and I made so clean and wavy yesterday afternoon. A yard like this is more comfortable than most people know. It is not just a yard. It is like an extended living room. When the hard clay is swept clean as a floor and the fine sand around the edges lined with tiny, irregular grooves anyone can come and sit and look up into the elm tree and wait for the breezes that never come inside the house.

Maggie will be nervous until after her sister goes: she will stand hopelessly in corners homely and ashamed of the burn scars down her arms and legs, eyeing her sister with a mixture of envy and awe. She thinks her sister has held life always in the palm of one hand, that "no" is a word the world never learned to say to her.

You've no doubt seen those TV shows where the child who has "made it" is confronted, as a surprise, by her own mother and father, tottering in weakly from backstage. (A pleasant surprise, of course: What would they do if parent and child came on the show only to curse out and insult each other?) On TV mother and child embrace and smile into each other's faces. Sometimes the mother and father weep, the child wraps them in her arms and leans across the table to tell how she would not have made it without their help. I have seen these programs.

Sometimes I dream a dream in which Dee and I are suddenly brought together on a TV program of this sort. Out of a dark and soft-seated limousine I am ushered into a bright room filled with many people. There I meet a smiling, gray, sporty man like Johnny Carson who shakes my hand and tells me what a fine girl I have. Then we are on the stage and Dee is embracing me with tears in her eyes. She pins on my dress a large orchid, even though she has told me once that she thinks orchids are tacky flowers.

In real life I am a large, big-boned woman with rough, man-working hands. 5 In the winter I wear flannel nightgowns to bed and overalls during the day. I can kill and clean a hog as mercilessly as a man. My fat keeps me hot in zero weather. I can work outside all day, breaking ice to get water for washing. I can eat pork liver cooked over the open fire minutes after it comes steaming from the hog. One winter I knocked a bull calf straight in the brain between the eyes with a sledge hammer and had the meat hung up to chill before nightfall. But of course all this does not show on television. I am the way my daughter would want me to be: a hundred pounds lighter, my skin like an uncooked barley pancake. My hair glistens in the hot bright lights. Johnny Carson has much to do to keep up with my quick and witty tongue.

But that is a mistake. I know even before I wake up. Who ever knew a Johnson with a quick tongue? Who can even imagine me looking a strange white man in the eye? It seems to me I have talked to them always with one foot raised in flight, with my head turned in whichever way is farthest from them. Dee, though. She would always look anyone in the eye. Hesitation was no part of her nature.

"How do I look, Mama?" Maggie says, showing just enough of her thin body enveloped in pink skirt and red blouse for me to know she's there, almost hidden by the door.

"Come out into the yard," I say.

Have you ever seen a lame animal, perhaps a dog run over by some careless person rich enough to own a car, sidle up to someone who is ignorant enough to be kind to him? That is the way my Maggie walks. She has been like this, chin on chest, eyes on ground, feet in shuffle, ever since the fire that burned the other house to the ground.

Dee is lighter than Maggie, with nicer hair and a fuller figure. She's a woman 10 now, though sometimes I forget. How long ago was it that the other house burned? Ten, twelve years? Sometimes I can still hear the flames and feel Maggie's arms sticking to me, her hair smoking and her dress falling off her in little black papery flakes. Her eyes seemed stretched open, blazed open by the flames reflected in them. And Dee. I see her standing off under the sweet gum tree she used to dig gum out of; a look of concentration on her face as she watched the last dingy gray board of the house fall in toward the red-hot brick chimney. Why don't you do a dance around the ashes? I'd wanted to ask her. She had hated the house that much.

I used to think she hated Maggie, too. But that was before we raised the money, the church and me, to send her to Augusta to school. She used to read to us without pity; forcing words, lies, other folks' habits, whole lives upon us two, sitting trapped and ignorant underneath her voice. She washed us in a river of make-believe, burned us with a lot of knowledge we didn't necessarily need to know. Pressed us to her with the serious way she read, to shove us away at just the moment, like dimwits, we seemed about to understand.

Dee wanted nice things. A yellow organdy dress to wear to her graduation from high school; black pumps to match a green suit she'd made from an old suit somebody gave me. She was determined to stare down any disaster in her efforts. Her eyelids would not flicker for minutes at a time. Often I fought off the temptation to shake her. At sixteen she had a style of her own: and knew what style was.

I never had an education myself. After second grade the school was closed down. Don't ask me why: in 1927 colored asked fewer questions than they do now. Sometimes Maggie reads to me. She stumbles along good-naturedly but can't see well. She knows she is not bright. Like good looks and money, quickness passed her by. She will marry John Thomas (who has mossy teeth in an earnest face) and then I'll be free to sit here and I guess just sing church songs to myself. Although I never was a good singer. Never could carry a tune. I was always better at a man's job. I used to love to milk till I was hoofed in the side in '49. Cows are soothing and slow and don't bother you, unless you try to milk them the wrong way.

I have deliberately turned my back on the house. It is three rooms, just like the one that burned, except the roof is tin; they don't make shingle roofs any more. There are no real windows, just some holes cut in the sides, like the portholes in a ship, but not round and not square, with rawhide holding the shutters up on the outside. This house is in a pasture, too, like the other one. No doubt when Dee sees it she will want to tear it down. She wrote me once that no matter where we "choose" to live, she will manage to come see us. But she will never bring her friends. Maggie and I thought about this and Maggie asked me, "Mama, when did Dee ever *have* any friends?"

She had a few. Furtive boys in pink shirts hanging about on washday after 15 school. Nervous girls who never laughed. Impressed with her they worshiped the well-turned phrase, the cute shape, the scalding humor that erupted like bubbles in lye. She read to them.

When she was courting Jimmy T she didn't have much time to pay to us, but turned all her faultfinding power on him. He *flew* to marry a cheap gal from a family of ignorant flashy people. She hardly had time to recompose herself.

When she comes I will meet—but there they are!

Maggie attempts to make a dash for the house, in her shuffling way, but I stay her with my hand. "Come back here," I say. And she stops and tries to dig a well in the sand with her toe.

It is hard to see them clearly through the strong sun. But even the first glimpse of leg out of the car tells me it is Dee. Her feet were always neat-looking, as if God himself had shaped them with a certain style. From the other side of the car comes a short, stocky man. Hair is all over his head a foot long and hanging from his chin like a kinky mule tail. I hear Maggie suck in her breath. "Uhnnnh," is what it sounds like. Like when you see the wriggling end of a snake just in front of your foot on the road. "Uhnnnh."

Dee next. A dress down to the ground, in this hot weather. A dress so loud 20 it hurts my eyes. There are yellows and oranges enough to throw back the light of the sun. I feel my whole face warming from the heat waves it throws out. Earrings, too, gold and hanging down to her shoulders. Bracelets dangling and making noises when she moves her arm up to shake the folds of the dress out of her armpits. The dress is loose and flows, and as she walks closer, I like it. I hear Maggie go "Uhnnnh" again. It is her sister's hair. It stands straight up like the wool on a sheep. It is black as night and around the edges are two long pigtails that rope about like small lizards disappearing behind her ears.

"Wa-su-zo-Tean-o!" she says, coming on in that gliding way the dress makes her move. The short stocky fellow with the hair to his navel is all grinning and he follows up with "Asalamalakim, my mother and sister!" He moves to hug

Maggie but she falls back, right up against the back of my chair. I feel her trembling there and when I look up I see the perspiration falling off her chin.

"Don't get up," says Dee. Since I am stout it takes something of a push. You can see me trying to move a second or two before I make it. She turns, showing white heels through her sandals, and goes back to the car. Out she peeks next with a Polaroid. She stoops down quickly and lines up picture after picture of me sitting there in front of the house with Maggie cowering behind me. She never takes a shot without making sure the house is included. When a cow comes nibbling around the edge of the yard she snaps it and me and Maggie *and* the house. Then she puts the Polaroid in the back seat of the car, and comes up and kisses me on the forehead.

Meanwhile Asalamalakim is going through motions with Maggie's hand. Maggie's hand is as limp as a fish, and probably as cold, despite the sweat, and she keeps trying to pull it back. It looks like Asalamalakim wants to shake hands but wants to do it fancy. Or maybe he don't know how people shake hands. Anyhow, he soon gives up on Maggie.

"Well," I say. "Dee."

"No, Mama," she says. "Not 'Dee,' Wangero Leewanika Kemanjo!" 25

"What happened to 'Dee'?" I wanted to know.

"She's dead," Wangero said. "I couldn't bear it any longer being named after the people who oppress me."

"You know as well as me you was named after your aunt Dicie," I said. Dicie is my sister. She named Dee. We called her "Big Dee" after Dee was born.

"But who was *she* named after?" asked Wangero.

"I guess after Grandma Dee," I said. 30

"And who was she named after?" asked Wangero.

"Her mother," I said, and saw Wangero was getting tired. "That's about as far back as I can trace it," I said. Though, in fact, I probably could have carried it back beyond the Civil War through the branches.

"Well," said Asalamalakim, "there you are."

"Uhnnnh," I heard Maggie say.

"There I was not," I said, "before 'Dicie' cropped up in our family, so why 35 should I try to trace it that far back?"

He just stood there grinning, looking down on me like somebody inspecting a Model A car. Every once in a while he and Wangero sent eye signals over my head.

"How do you pronounce this name?" I asked.

"You don't have to call me by it if you don't want to," said Wangero.

"Why shouldn't I?" I asked. "If that's what you want us to call you, we'll call you."

"I know it might sound awkward at first," said Wangero. 40

"I'll get used to it," I said. "Ream it out again."

Well, soon we got the name out of the way. Asalamalakim had a name twice as long and three times as hard. After I tripped over it two or three times he told me to just call him Hakim-a-barber. I wanted to ask him was he a barber, but I didn't really think he was, so I didn't ask.

"You must belong to those beef-cattle peoples down the road," I said. They said "Asalamalakim" when they met you, too, but they didn't shake hands. Always too busy: feeding the cattle, fixing the fences, putting up salt-lick shelters, throwing down hay. When the white folks poisoned some of the herd the men stayed up all night with rifles in their hands. I walked a mile and a half just to see the sight.

Hakim-a-barber said, "I accept some of their doctrines, but farming and raising cattle is not my style." (They didn't tell me, and I didn't ask, whether Wangero [Dee] had really gone and married him.)

We sat down to eat and right away he said he didn't eat collards and pork was unclean. Wangero, though, went on through the chitlins and corn bread, the greens and everything else. She talked a blue streak over the sweet potatoes. Everything delighted her. Even the fact that we still used the benches her daddy made for the table when we couldn't afford to buy chairs.

"Oh, Mama!" she cried. Then turned to Hakim-a-barber. "I never knew how lovely these benches are. You can feel the rump prints," she said, running her hands underneath her and along the bench. Then she gave a sigh and her hand closed over Grandma Dee's butter dish. "That's it!" she said. "I knew there was something I wanted to ask you if I could have." She jumped up from the table and went over in the corner where the churn stood, the milk in its clabber by now. She looked at the churn and looked at it.

"This churn top is what I need," she said. "Didn't Uncle Buddy whittle it out of a tree you all used to have?"

"Yes," I said.

"Uh huh," she said happily. "And I want the dasher, too."

"Uncle Buddy whittle that, too?" asked the barber.

Dee (Wangero) looked up at me.

"Aunt Dee's first husband whittled the dash," said Maggie so low you almost couldn't hear her. "His name was Henry, but they called him Stash."

"Maggie's brain is like an elephant's," Wangero said, laughing. "I can use the churn top as a centerpiece for the alcove table," she said, sliding a plate over the churn, "and I'll think of something artistic to do with the dasher."

When she finished wrapping the dasher the handle stuck out. I took it for a moment in my hands. You didn't even have to look close to see where hands pushing the dasher up and down to make butter had left a kind of sink in the wood. In fact, there were a lot of small sinks; you could see where thumbs and fingers had sunk into the wood. It was beautiful light yellow wood, from a tree that grew in the yard where Big Dee and Stash had lived.

After dinner Dee (Wangero) went to the trunk at the foot of my bed and started rifling through it. Maggie hung back in the kitchen over the dishpan. Out came Wangero with two quilts. They had been pieced by Grandma Dee and then Big Dee and me had hung them on the quilt frames on the front porch and quilted them. One was in the Lone Star pattern. The other was Walk Around the Mountain. In both of them were scraps of dresses Grandma Dee had worn fifty and more years ago. Bits and pieces of Grandpa Jarrell's Paisley shirts. And one teeny faded blue piece, about the size of a penny matchbox, that was from Great Grandpa Ezra's uniform that he wore in the Civil War.

"Mama," Wangero said sweet as a bird. "Can I have these old quilts?"

I heard something fall in the kitchen, and a minute later the kitchen door slammed.

"Why don't you take one or two of the others?" I asked. "These old things was just done by me and Big Dee from some tops your grandma pieced before she died."

"No," said Wangero. "I don't want those. They are stitched around the borders by machine."

"That'll make them last better," I said.   60

"That's not the point," said Wangero. "These are all pieces of dresses Grandma used to wear. She did all this stitching by hand. Imagine!" She held the quilts securely in her arms, stroking them.

"Some of the pieces, like those lavender ones, come from old clothes her mother handed down to her," I said, moving up to touch the quilts. Dee (Wangero) moved back just enough so that I couldn't reach the quilts. They already belonged to her.

"Imagine!" she breathed again, clutching them closely to her bosom.

"The truth is," I said, "I promised to give them quilts to Maggie, for when she marries John Thomas."

She gasped like a bee had stung her.   65

"Maggie can't appreciate these quilts!" she said. "She'd probably be backward enough to put them to everyday use."

"I reckon she would," I said. "God knows I been saving 'em for long enough with nobody using 'em. I hope she will!" I didn't want to bring up how I had offered Dee (Wangero) a quilt when she went away to college. Then she had told me they were old-fashioned, out of style.

"But they're *priceless!*" she was saying now, furiously; for she has a temper. "Maggie would put them on the bed and in five years they'd be in rags. Less than that!"

"She can always make some more," I said. "Maggie knows how to quilt."

Dee (Wangero) looked at me with hatred. "You just will not understand.   70 The point is these quilts, *these* quilts!"

"Well," I said, stumped. "What would *you* do with them?"

"Hang them," she said. As if that was the only thing you *could* do with quilts.

Maggie by now was standing in the door. I could almost hear the sound her feet made as they scraped over each other.

"She can have them, Mama," she said, like somebody used to never winning anything, or having anything reserved for her. "I can 'member Grandma Dee without the quilts."

I looked at her hard. She had filled her bottom lip with checkerberry snuff 75 and it gave her face a kind of dopey, hangdog look. It was Grandma Dee and Big Dee who taught her how to quilt herself. She stood there with her scarred hands hidden in the folds of her skirt. She looked at her sister with something like fear but she wasn't mad at her. This was Maggie's portion. This was the way she knew God to work.

When I looked at her like that something hit me in the top of my head and ran down to the soles of my feet. Just like when I'm in church and the spirit of God touches me and I get happy and shout. I did something I never had done before: hugged Maggie to me, then dragged her on into the room, snatched the quilts out of Miss Wangero's hands and dumped them into Maggie's lap. Maggie just sat there on my bed with her mouth open.

"Take one or two of the others," I said to Dee.

But she turned without a word and went out to Hakim-a-barber.

"You just don't understand," she said, as Maggie and I came out to the car.

"What don't I understand?" I wanted to know.

"Your heritage," she said. And then she turned to Maggie, kissed her, and said, "You ought to try to make something of yourself, too, Maggie. It's really a new day for us. But from the way you and Mama still live you'd never know it."

She put on some sunglasses that hid everything above the tip of her nose and her chin.

Maggie smiled; maybe at the sunglasses. But a real smile, not scared. After we watched the car dust settle I asked Maggie to bring me a dip of snuff. And then the two of us sat there just enjoying, until it was time to go in the house and go to bed.

FOR ANALYSIS

1. What are the **narrator's** outstanding traits, her weaknesses, and her strengths?

2. How would you describe the narrator's feelings about her daughter Dee? About her daughter Maggie?

3. How would you describe the narrator's descriptions of herself? Are her actions consistent with the kind of person she says she is? Explain.

4. Why does the narrator recall the burning of the house? How does this event from the past help the reader understand the present action?

5. What are the sources of the story's humor?

6. What does Dee's boyfriend, Asalamalakim, represent?

7. Why does the narrator give the quilts to Maggie?

8. Explain the title. What is the meaning of the subtitle, "For Your Grandmama"?

MAKING CONNECTIONS

Compare Dee in this story and Miss Moore in Bambara's "The Lesson" (p. 96) as characters whose intellectual and educational superiority enables them to unsettle the tranquillity of those around them.

WRITING TOPICS

1. Analyze the opening two paragraphs of the story, showing how they set the **tone** and establish the tension of the story.

2. Write an essay analyzing the **conflict** in the story and the way it is resolved. Is the resolution satisfying? Explain.

DAGOBERTO GILB (B. 1950)

UNCLE ROCK 2010

In the morning, at his favorite restaurant, Erick got to order his favorite American food, sausage and eggs and hash-brown *papitas* fried crunchy on top. He'd be sitting there, eating with his mother, not bothering anybody, and life was good, when a man started changing it all. Most of the time it was just a man staring too much—but then one would come over. Friendly, he'd put his thick hands on the table as if he were touching water, and squat low, so that he was at sitting level, as though he were being so polite, and he'd smile, with coffee-and-tobacco-stained teeth. He might wear a bolo tie and speak in a drawl. Or he might have a tan uniform on, a company logo on the back, an oval name patch on the front. Or he'd be in a nothing-special work shirt, white or striped, with a couple of pens clipped onto the left side pocket, tucked into a pair of jeans or chinos that were morning-clean still, with a pair of scuffed work boots that laced up higher than regular shoes. He'd say something about her earrings, or her bracelet, or her hair, or her eyes, and if she had on her white uniform how nice it looked on her. Or he'd come right out with it and tell her how pretty she was, how he couldn't keep himself from walking up, speaking to her directly, and could they talk again? Then he'd wink at Erick. Such a fine-looking boy! How old is he, eight or nine? Erick wasn't even small for an eleven-year-old. He tightened his jaw then, slanted his eyes up from his plate at his mom and not the man, definitely not this man he did not care for. Erick drove a fork into a goopy American egg yolk and bled it into his American potatoes. She wouldn't offer the man Erick's correct age, either, saying only that he was growing too fast.

She almost always gave the man her number if he was wearing a suit. Not a sports coat but a buttoned suit with a starched white shirt and a pinned tie meant something to her. Once in a while, Erick saw one of these men again at the front door of the apartment in Silverlake. The man winked at Erick as if they were buddies. Grabbed his shoulder or arm, squeezed the muscle against the bone. What did Erick want to be when he grew up? A cop, a jet-airplane mechanic, a travel agent, a court reporter? A dog groomer? Erick stood there, because his mom said that he shouldn't be impolite. His mom's date said he wanted to take Erick along with them sometime. The three of them. What kind of places did Erick think were fun? Erick said nothing. He never said anything when the men were around, and not because of his English, even if that was the excuse his mother gave for his silence. He didn't talk to any of the men and he didn't talk much to his mom, either. Finally they took off, and Erick's night was his alone. He raced to the grocery store and bought half a gallon of chocolate ice cream. When he got back, he turned on the TV, scooted up real close, as close as he could, and ate his dinner with a soup spoon. He was away from all the men. Even though a man had given the TV to them. He was a salesman in an appliance store who'd bragged that a rich customer had given it to him and so why shouldn't he give it to Erick's mom, who couldn't afford such a good TV otherwise?

When his mom was working as a restaurant hostess, and was going to marry the owner, Erick ate hot-fudge sundaes and drank chocolate shakes. When she worked at a trucking company, the owner of all the trucks told her he was getting a divorce. Erick climbed into the rigs, with their rooms full of dials and levers in the sky. Then she started working in an engineer's office. There was no food or fun there, but even he could see the money. He was not supposed to touch anything, but what was there to touch—the tubes full of paper? He and his mom were invited to the engineer's house, where he had two horses and a stable, a swimming pool, and two convertible sports cars. The engineer's family was there: his grown children, his gray-haired parents. They all sat down for dinner in a dining room that seemed bigger than Erick's apartment, with three candelabras on the table, and a tablecloth and cloth napkins. Erick's mom took him aside to tell him to be well mannered at the table and polite to everyone. Erick hadn't said anything. He never spoke anyway, so how could he have said anything wrong? She leaned into his ear and said that she wanted them to know that he spoke English. That whole dinner he was silent, chewing quietly, taking the smallest bites, because he didn't want them to think he liked their food.

When she got upset about days like that, she told Erick that she wished they could just go back home. She was tired of worrying. "Back," for Erick, meant mostly the stories he'd heard from her, which never sounded so good to him: She'd had to share a room with her brothers and sisters. They didn't have toilets. They didn't have electricity. Sometimes they didn't have enough food. He saw this Mexico as if it were the backdrop of a movie on afternoon TV, where children walked around barefoot in the dirt or on broken sidewalks and small men wore wide-brimmed straw hats and baggy white shirts and pants. The women went to church all the time and prayed to alcoved saints and, heads down, fearful, counted rosary beads. There were rocks everywhere, and scorpions and tarantulas and rattlesnakes, and vultures and no trees and not much water, and skinny dogs and donkeys, and ugly bad guys with guns and bullet vests who rode laughing into town to drink and shoot off their pistols and rifles, as if it were the Fourth of July, driving their horses all over town like dirt bikes on desert dunes. When they spoke English, they had stupid accents—his mom didn't have an accent like theirs. It didn't make sense to him that Mexico would only be like that, but what if it was close? He lived on paved, lighted city streets, and a bicycle ride away were the Asian drugstore and the Armenian grocery store and the corner where black Cubans drank coffee and talked Dodgers baseball.

When he was in bed, where he sometimes prayed, he thanked God for his 5
mom, who he loved, and he apologized to Him for not talking to her, or to
anyone, really, except his friend Albert, and he apologized for her never going
to church and for his never taking Holy Communion, as Albert did—though
only to God would he admit that he wanted to because Albert did. He prayed
for good to come, for his mom and for him, since God was like magic, and
happiness might come the way of early morning, in the trees and bushes full of
sparrows next to his open window, louder and louder when he listened hard,
eyes closed.

The engineer wouldn't have mattered if Erick hadn't told Albert that he was
his dad. Albert had just moved into the apartment next door and lived with
both his mother and his father, and since Albert's mother already didn't like
Erick's mom, Erick told him that his new dad was an engineer. Erick actually believed it, too, and thought that he might even get his own horse. When
that didn't happen, and his mom was lying on her bed in the middle of the
day, blowing her nose, because she didn't have the job anymore, that was
when Roque came around again. Roque was nobody—or he was anybody. He
wasn't special, he wasn't not. He tried to speak English to Erick, thinking that
was the reason Erick didn't say anything when he was there. And Erick had to
tell Albert that Roque was his uncle, because the engineer was supposed to be
his new dad any minute. Uncle Rock, Erick said. His mom's brother, he told
Albert. Roque worked at night and was around during the day, and one day
he offered Erick and Albert a ride. When his mom got in the car, she scooted
all the way over to Roque on the bench seat. Who was supposed to be her
brother, Erick's Uncle Rock. Albert didn't say anything, but he saw what had
happened, and that was it for Erick. Albert had parents, grandparents, and a
brother and a sister, and he'd hang out only when one of his cousins wasn't
coming by. Erick didn't need a friend like him.

What if she married Roque, his mom asked him one day soon afterward.
She told Erick that they would move away from the apartment in Silverlake
to a better neighborhood. He did want to move, but he wished that it weren't
because of Uncle Rock. It wasn't just because Roque didn't have a swimming
pool or horses or a big ranch house. There wasn't much to criticize except that
he was always too willing and nice, too considerate, too generous. He wore
nothing flashy or expensive, just ordinary clothes that were clean and ironed,
and shoes he kept shined. He combed and parted his hair neatly. He didn't have
a buzzcut like the men who didn't like kids. He moved slow, he talked slow, as
quiet as night. He only ever said yes to Erick's mom. How could she not like
him for that? He loved her so much—anybody could see his pride when he
was with her. He signed checks and gave her cash. He knocked on their door
carrying cans and fruit and meat. He was there when she asked, gone when she
asked, back whenever, grateful. He took her out to restaurants on Sunset, to the
movies in Hollywood, or on drives to the beach in rich Santa Monica.

Roque knew that Erick loved baseball. Did Roque like baseball? It was doubtful that he cared even a little bit— he didn't listen to games on the radio or TV, and he never looked at a newspaper. He loved boxing, though. He knew the names of all the Mexican fighters as if they lived here, as if they were Dodgers players, like Steve Sax or Steve Yeager, Dusty Baker, Kenny Landreaux or Mike Marshall, Pedro Guerrero. Roque did know about Fernando Valenzuela, as everyone did, even his mom, which is why she agreed to let Roque take them to a game. What Mexican didn't love Fernando? Dodger Stadium was close to their apartment. He'd been there once with Albert and his family—well, outside it, on a nearby hill, to see the fireworks for Fourth of July. His mom decided that all three of them would go on a Saturday afternoon, since Saturday night, Erick thought, she might want to go somewhere else, even with somebody else.

Roque, of course, didn't know who the Phillies were. He knew nothing about the strikeouts by Steve Carlton or the home runs by Mike Schmidt. He'd never heard of Pete Rose. It wasn't that Erick knew very much, either, but there was nothing that Roque could talk to him about, if they were to talk.

If Erick showed his excitement when they drove up to Dodger Stadium and 10 parked, his mom and Roque didn't really notice it. They sat in the bleachers, and for him the green of the field was a magic light; the stadium decks surrounding them seemed as far away as Rome. His body was somewhere it had never been before. The fifth inning? That's how late they were. Or were they right on time, because they weren't even sure they were sitting in the right seats yet when he heard the crack of the ball, saw the crowd around them rising as it came at them. Erick saw the ball. He had to stand and move and stretch his arms and want that ball until it hit his bare hands and stayed there. Everybody saw him catch it with no bobble. He felt all the eyes and voices around him as if they were every set of eyes and every voice in the stadium. His mom was saying something, and Roque, too, and then, finally, it was just him and that ball and his stinging hands. He wasn't even sure if it had been hit by Pete Guerrero. He thought for sure it had been, but he didn't ask. He didn't watch the game then—he couldn't. He didn't care who won. He stared at his official National League ball, reimagining what had happened. He ate a hot dog and drank a soda and he sucked the salted peanuts and the wooden spoon from his chocolate-malt ice cream. He rubbed the bumpy seams of his home-run ball.

Game over, they were the last to leave. People were hanging around, not going straight to their cars. Roque didn't want to leave. He didn't want to end it so quickly, Erick thought, while he still had her with him. Then one of the Phillies came out of the stadium door and people swarmed—boys mostly, but also men and some women and girls—and they got autographs before the player climbed onto the team's bus. Joe Morgan, they said. Then Garry Maddox appeared. Erick clutched the ball but he didn't have a pen. He just watched, his back to the gray bus the Phillies were getting into.

Then a window slid open. *Hey, big man,* a voice said. Erick really wasn't sure. *Gimme the ball, la Pelota,* the face in the bus said. *I'll have it signed, compren-des? Échalo, just toss it to me.* Erick obeyed. He tossed it up to the hand that was reaching out. The window closed. The ball was gone a while, so long that his mom came up to him, worried that he'd lost it. The window slid open again and the voice spoke to her. *We got the ball, Mom. It's not lost, just a few more.* When the window opened once more, this time the ball was there. *Catch.* There were all kinds of signatures on it, though none that he could really recognize except for Joe Morgan and Pete Rose.

Then the voice offered more, and the hand threw something at him. *For your mom, O.K.? Comprendes?* Erick stared at the asphalt lot where the object lay, as if he'd never seen a folded-up piece of paper before. *Para tu mamâ, bueno?* He picked it up, and he started to walk over to his mom and Roque, who were so busy talking they hadn't noticed anything. Then he stopped. He opened the note himself. No one had said he couldn't read it. It said, *I'd like to get to know you. You are muy linda. Very beautiful and sexy. I don't speak Spanish very good, may be you speak better English, pero No Importa. Would you come by tonite and let me buy you a drink?* There was a phone number and a hotel-room number. A name, too. A name that came at him the way that the home run had.

Erick couldn't hear. He could see only his mom ahead of him. She was talking to Roque, Roque was talking to her. Roque was the proudest man, full of joy because he was with her. It wasn't his fault he wasn't an engineer. Now Erick could hear again. Like sparrows hunting seed, boys gathered round the bus, calling out, while the voice in the bus was yelling at him, *Hey, big guy! Give it to her!* Erick had the ball in one hand and the note in the other. By the time he reached his mom and Roque, the note was already somewhere on the asphalt parking lot. *Look,* he said in a full voice. *They all signed the ball.*

FOR ANALYSIS

1. What is Gilb telling us when he has Erick note his mother's higher success rate with men wearing suits?

2. When Erick is described as imagining Mexico as like something he saw on television, what do we learn about his sense of his cultural identity? How does he compare the Mexico of his imagination to the U.S. neighborhoods within bike-riding distance?

3. Even before Erick decides how he feels about Roque, we see Roque through Erick's eyes. How is he described? How does Gilb let us understand how Erick feels about Roque through the details of those descriptions?

4. Do you feel the ending of this story is a happy one? Why or why not?

MAKING CONNECTIONS

Consider "Uncle Rock" against Sandra Castillo's "Christmas, 1970" (p. 203). How does each present the place from which its main **character** comes?

WRITING TOPICS

1. When Erick goes to Dodger Stadium, the moment is described oddly—"His body was somewhere it had never been before"—and the physical details of the experience are noted minutely, especially after he catches the ball. Write a description of a time when you went someplace that made you feel as if a whole new world were opening up for you, noting the details as best you can. Was it about geography or something else? Did it make you feel differently about yourself?

2. Erick lies to his friend Albert about the men who visit his mother. Write an account of a time from your childhood when you lied to your friends. Why did you do it? How did it make you feel? What does it tell you about yourself now, looking back on it?

SHERMAN ALEXIE   (B. 1966)

WAR DANCES   2009

MY KAFKA BAGGAGE

A few years ago, after I returned home to Seattle from a trip to Los Angeles, I unpacked my bag and found a dead cockroach, shrouded by a dirty sock, in a corner. Shit, I thought. We're being invaded. So I threw the clothes, books, shoes, and toiletries back into the suitcase, carried it out to the driveway, and dumped the contents onto the pavement, ready to stomp on any other cockroach stowaways. But there was only the one cockroach, dead and stiff. As he lay on the pavement, I leaned closer to him. His legs were curled under his body. His head was tilted at a sad angle. Sad? Yes, sad. For who is lonelier than the cockroach without his tribe? I laughed at myself. I was feeling empathy for a dead cockroach. I wondered about its story. How had it got into my bag? And where? At the hotel in Los Angeles? In the airport baggage system? It hadn't originated in our house. We've kept those tiny bastards from our place for fifteen years. So where had this little vermin come from? Had he smelled something delicious in my bag—my musky deodorant or some crumb from a chocolate Power Bar—and climbed inside, only to be crushed by the shifts of fate and garment bags? As he died, did he feel fear? Isolation? Existential dread?

SYMPTOMS

Last summer, in reaction to various allergies I was suffering from, defensive mucus flooded my inner right ear and confused, frightened, and unmoored me. My allergies had never been this severe. I could barely hear a fucking thing with that side, so I had to turn my head in order to understand what my two sons, ages eight and ten, were saying.

"We're hungry," they said. "We keep telling you."

I was embarrassed.

"Mom would have fed us by now," they said.

Their mother had left for Italy with her mother two days before. My sons and I were going to enjoy a boys' week, filled with unwashed socks, REI rock-wall climbing, and ridiculous heaps of pasta.

"What are you going to cook?" my sons asked. "Why haven't you cooked yet?"

I'd been lying on the couch reading a book while they played and I hadn't realized that I'd gone partially deaf. So, for just, a moment, I could only weakly blame my allergies.

Then I recalled the man who went to the emergency room because he'd woken having lost most, if not all, of his hearing. The doctor peered into one ear, saw an obstruction, reached in with small tweezers, and pulled out a cock-roach, then reached into the other ear and extracted a much larger cockroach. Did you know that ear wax is a delicacy for roaches?

I cooked dinner for my sons—overfed them out of guilt—and cleaned the hell out of our home. Then I walked into the bathroom and stood before the mirror. I turned my head and body at weird angles and tried to see deeply into my congested ear; I sang hymns and prayed that I'd see a small angel trapped in the canal. I would free the poor thing, and she'd unfurl and pat dry her tiny wings, then fly to my lips and give me a sweet kiss for sheltering her metamorphosis.

When I woke at 3 A.M., completely deaf in my right ear, and positive that a damn swarm of locusts was wedged inside, I left a message for my doctor, and told him that I would be sitting outside his office when he reported for work.

This would be the first time I had been inside a health-care facility since my father's last surgery.

BLANKETS

After the surgeon had cut off my father's right foot—no, half of my father's right foot—and three toes from the left, I sat with him in the recovery room. It was more like a recovery hallway. There was no privacy, not even a thin cur-tain. I supposed this made it easier for the nurses to monitor the post-surgical patients, but, still, my father was exposed—his decades of poor health and worse decisions were illuminated—on white sheets in a white hallway under white lights.

"Are you O.K.?" I asked. It was a stupid question. Who could be O.K. after such a thing? Yesterday, my father had walked into the hospital. Yes, he'd shuffled while balancing on two canes, but that was still called walking. A few hours ago, my father still had both of his feet. They were black with rot and disease, but they were still, technically speaking, feet and toes. And, most important, those feet had belonged to my father. Now they were gone, sliced off. Where were they? What had the hospital done with the right foot and the toes from the left foot? Had they been thrown into the incinerator? Were their ashes already floating over the city?

"Doctor, I'm cold," my father said.

"Dad, it's me," I said.

"I know who you are. You're my son." But, given the blankness in my father's eyes, I assumed he was just guessing.

"Dad, you're in the hospital. You just had surgery."

"I know where I am. I'm cold."

"Do you want another blanket?" Stupid question. Of course, he wanted another blanket. He probably wanted me to build a fucking campfire or drag in one of those giant heat blasters that N.F.L. football teams use on the sidelines.

I walked down the hallway—the recovery hallway—to the nurses' station. There were three women nurses there, two white and one black. I am Native American—Spokane and Coeur d'Alene Indian—and I thought my darker pigment might give me an edge with the black nurse, so I addressed her directly.

"My father is cold," I said. "Can I get another blanket?"

The nurse glanced up from her paperwork and regarded me. Her expression was neither compassionate nor callous.

"How can I help you, sir?" she asked.

"I'd like another blanket for my father. He's cold."   25

"I'll be with you in a moment, sir."

She looked back down at her paperwork. She made a few notes. Not knowing what else to do, I stood there and waited.

"Sir," the nurse said, "I'll be with you in a moment."

She was irritated. I understood. After all, how many thousands of times had she been asked for an extra blanket? She was a nurse, an educated woman, not a damn housekeeper. And it was never really about an extra blanket, was it? No, when people asked for an extra blanket they were asking for a time machine. My father, an alcoholic, diabetic Indian with terminally damaged kidneys, had just endured an incredibly expensive surgery for what? So that he could ride his motorized wheelchair to the bar and win bets by showing off his disfigured foot? Yes, she was a health-care worker and she didn't want to be cruel, but she believed that there came a point when doctors should stop rescuing people from their own self-destructive impulses. And I couldn't disagree with her, but I could ask for the most basic of comforts, couldn't I?

"My father," I said. "An extra blanket, please."   30

"Fine," she said. She got up and walked back to a linen closet, grabbed a white blanket, and handed it to me. "If you need anything else—"

I didn't wait around for the end of her sentence. With the blanket in hand, I walked back to my father. It was a thin blanket, laundered and sterilized a hundred times. In fact, it was too thin. It wasn't really a blanket. It was more like a large beach towel. Hell, it wasn't even good enough for that. It was more like the world's biggest coffee filter. Jesus, had health care finally come to this? Everybody was uninsured and unblanketed.

"Dad, I'm back."

He looked so small and pale lying in that hospital bed. How had this happened? For the first sixty-seven years of his life, my father had been a large and dark man. Now he was just another pale, sick drone in a hallway of pale, sick drones. A hive, I thought. This place is like a beehive with colony-collapse disorder.

"Dad, it's me."   35

"I'm cold."

"I have a blanket."

As 1 draped it over my father and tucked it around his body, I felt the first sting of grief. I'd read the hospital literature about this moment. There would come a time when roles would reverse and the adult child would become the caretaker of the ill parent. The circle of life. Such poetic bullshit.

"I can't get warm," my father said. "I'm freezing."

"I brought you a blanket, Dad. I put it on you."   40

"Get me another one. Please. I'm so cold. I need another blanket."

I knew that ten more of these cheap blankets wouldn't be enough. My father needed a real blanket, a good blanket.

I walked out of the recovery hallway and made my way through various doorways and other hallways, peering into rooms, looking at the patients and their families, searching for a particular kind of patient and family.

I walked through the E.R., through the cancer, heart and vascular, neuroscience, orthopedic, women's health, pediatric, and surgical wards. Nobody stopped me. My expression and posture were those of a man with a sick father, and so I belonged.

And then I saw him, another Native man, leaning against a wall near the   45
gift shop. Well, maybe he was Asian—lots of those in Seattle. He was a small man, pale brown, with muscular arms and a soft belly. Maybe he was Mexican, which is really a kind of Indian, too, but not the kind that I needed. It's hard to tell sometimes what people are. Even brown people guess at the identity of other brown people.

"Hey," I said.

"Hey," the other man said.

"You Indian?" I asked.

"Yeah."

"What tribe?"   50

"Lummi."

"I'm Spokane."

"My first wife was Spokane. I hated her."

"My first wife was Lummi. She hated me."

We laughed at the new jokes that instantly sounded old.   55

"Why are you in here?" I asked.

"My sister is having a baby," he said. "But don't worry, it's not mine."

"Ayyyyyy," I said and laughed.

"I don't even want to be here," the other Indian said. "But my dad started, like, this new Indian tradition. He says it's a thousand years old. But that's bullshit. He just made it up to impress himself. And the whole family goes along with it, even when we know it's bullshit. He's in the delivery room waving eagle feathers around. Jesus."

"What's the tradition?"   60

"Oh, he does a naming ceremony right in the hospital. It's supposed to protect the baby from all the technology and shit. Like hospitals are the big problem. You know how many babies died before we had good hospitals?"

"I don't know."

"Most of them. Well, shit, a lot of them, at least."

This guy was talking out of his ass. I liked him immediately.

"I mean," the guy said. "You should see my dad right now. He's pretending 65 to go into this, like, fucking trance, dancing around my sister in the bed, and he says he's trying to, you know, see into her womb, to see who the baby is, to see its true nature, so he can give it a name—a protective name—before it's born."

The guy laughed and threw his head back, banging it on the wall.

"I mean, come on, I'm a loser," he said and rubbed his sore skull. "My whole family is filled with losers."

The Indian world is filled with charlatans, men and women who pretend— hell, who might have come to believe—that they are holy. The year before, I went to a lecture at the University of Washington. An elderly Indian woman, a scholar, had come to orate on Indian sovereignty and literature. She kept arguing for some kind of separate indigenous literary identity, which was ironic considering that she was speaking English to a room full of white professors. But I wasn't angry with the woman, or even bored. No, I felt sorry for her. I realized that she was dying of nostalgia. She had taken nostalgia as her false idol—her thin blanket—and it was murdering her.

"Nostalgia," I said.

"What?" 70

"Your dad, he sounds like he's got a bad case of nostalgia."

"Yeah, I hear you catch that from fucking old high-school girlfriends," the man said. "What the hell you doing here, anyway?"

"My dad just got his feet cut off," I said.

"Diabetes?"

"And vodka." 75

"Vodka straight up or with a nostalgia chaser?"

"Both."

"Natural causes for an Indian."

"Yep."

There wasn't much to say after that. 80

"Well, I better get back," the man said. "Otherwise, my dad might wave an eagle feather and change my name."

"Hey, wait," I said.

"Yeah?"

"Can I ask you a favor?"

"What?" 85

"My dad, he's in the recovery room," I said. "Well, it's more like a hallway, and he's freezing, and they've only got these shitty little blankets, and I came looking for Indians in the hospital because I figured—well, I guessed if I found any Indians they might have some good blankets."

"So you want to borrow a blanket from us?" the man asked.

"Yeah."

"Because you thought Indians would just happen to have some extra blankets lying around?"

"Yeah." 90

"That's fucking ridiculous."

"I know."

"And it's racist."

"I know."

"You're stereotyping your own damn people." 95

"I know."

"But damn if we don't have a room full of Pendleton blankets. New ones. Jesus, you'd think my sister was having, like, a dozen babies."

Five minutes later, carrying a Pendleton Star blanket, the Indian man walked out of his sister's hospital room, accompanied by his father, who wore Levi's, a black T-shirt, and eagle feathers in his gray braids.

"We want to give your father this blanket," the old man said. "It was meant for my grandson, but I think it will be good for your father, too."

"Thank you." 100

"Let me bless it. I will sing a healing song for the blanket. And for your father."

I flinched. This old man wanted to sing a song? That was dangerous. The song could take two minutes or two hours. It was impossible to know. Hell, considering how desperate the old man was to be seen as holy, he might sing for a week. I couldn't let him begin his song without issuing a caveat.

"My dad," I said. "I really need to get back to him. He's really sick."

"Don't worry," the old man said, winking. "I'll sing one of my short ones."

Jesus, who'd ever heard of a self-aware fundamentalist? The son, perhaps 105 not the unbeliever he'd pretended to be, sang backup as his father launched into a radio-friendly honor song, just three and a half minutes, like any Top Forty rock song of the past fifty years. But here's the funny thing: the old man couldn't sing very well. If you had the balls to sing healing songs in hospital hallways, then you should have a great voice, right? But, no, this guy couldn't keep the tune; his voice cracked and wavered. Does a holy song lose its power if the singer is untalented?

"That is your father's song," the old man said when he finished. "I give it to him. I will never sing it again. It belongs to your father now."

Behind his back, the old man's son rolled his eyes and walked into his sister's room.

"O.K., thank you," I said. I felt like an ass, accepting the blanket and the old man's good wishes, and silently mocking them at the same time. But maybe the old man did have some power, some real medicine, because he peeked into my brain.

"It doesn't matter if you believe in the healing song," he said. "It only matters that the blanket heard."

"Where have you been?" my father asked when I returned. "I'm cold." 110

"I know, I know," I said. "I found you a blanket. A good one. It will keep you warm."

I draped the Star blanket over my father. He pulled the thick wool up to his chin. And then he began to sing. It was a healing song, not the same song that

I had just heard but a healing song nonetheless. My father could sing beautifully. I wondered if it was proper for a man to sing a healing song for himself.
I wondered if my father needed help with the song. I hadn't sung for many
years, not like that, but I joined him. I knew that this song would not bring
back my father's feet. This song would not repair my father's bladder, kidneys, lungs, and heart. This song would not prevent my father from drinking a bottle of vodka as soon as he could sit up in bed. This song would not
defeat death. No, I thought, this song is temporary, but right now temporary
is good enough. And it was a good song. Our voices filled the recovery hallway. The sick and the healthy stopped to listen. The nurses, even the remote
black one, unconsciously took a few steps toward us. She sighed and smiled.
I smiled back. I knew what she was thinking. Sometimes, even after all these
years, she could still be surprised by her work. She still marvelled at the infinite
and ridiculous faith of other people.

DOCTOR'S OFFICE

I took my kids with me to my doctor, a handsome man—a reservist—who'd
served in both Iraq wars. I told him that I couldn't hear because of my allergies. He said he would likely have to clear wax and mucus out of my ear, but
when he scoped inside he discovered nothing.

"Nope, it's all dry in there," he said.

He led my sons and me to the audiologist in the other half of the building.   115
I was scared, but I wanted my children to remain calm, so I tried to stay measured. More than anything, I wanted my wife to materialize.

During the hearing test, I heard only thirty per cent of the clicks, bells, and
words—I apparently had nerve- and bone-conductive deafness. My inner ear
thumped and thumped.

How many cockroaches were in my head?

My doctor said, "We need an MRI of your ear and brain, and maybe we'll
find out what's going on."

"Maybe"? That word terrified me.

What the fuck was wrong with my fucking head? Had my hydrocephalus   120
come back? Had my levees burst? Was I going to flood?

HYDROCEPHALUS

Merriam-Webster's dictionary defines "hydrocephalus" as "an abnormal
increase in the amount of cerebrospinal fluid within the cranial cavity that is
accompanied by expansion of the cerebral ventricles, enlargement of the skull
and especially the forehead, and atrophy of the brain." I define "hydrocephalus" as "the obese, imperialistic water demon that nearly killed me when I was
a baby."

In order to save my life, and stop the water demon, I had brain surgery in 1967, when I was six months old. I was supposed to die. Obviously, I didn't. I was supposed to be severely mentally disabled. I have only minor to moderate brain damage. I was supposed to have epileptic seizures. Those I did have, until I was seven years old. I was on phenobarbital, a major-league anti-seizure medication, for six years.

The side effects of phenobarbital—all of which I suffered to some degree or another as a child—are sleepwalking, agitation, confusion, depression, nightmares, hallucinations, insomnia, apnea, vomiting, constipation, dermatitis, fever, liver and bladder dysfunction, and psychiatric disturbance.

How do you like them cockroaches?

Now, as an adult, thirty-three years removed from phenobarbital, I still 125 suffer—to some degree or another—from sleepwalking, agitation, confusion, depression, nightmares, hallucinations, insomnia, bladder dysfunction, apnea, and dermatitis.

Is there such a disease as post-phenobarbital traumatic stress disorder?

Most hydrocephalics are shunted. A shunt is essentially brain plumbing that drains away excess cerebrospinal fluid. The shunts often fuck up and stop working. I know hydrocephalics who've had a hundred or more shunt revisions and repairs. That's more than a hundred brain surgeries. There are ten fingers on any surgeon's hands. There are two or three surgeons involved in any particular brain operation. That means that some hydrocephalics have had their brains fondled by three thousand fingers.

I'm lucky. I was shunted only temporarily. And I hadn't suffered any hydrocephalic symptoms since I was seven years old.

Until July, 2008, when, at the age of forty-one, I went deaf in my right ear.

CONVERSATION

Sitting in my car in the hospital parking garage, I called my brother-in-law, 130 who was babysitting my sons.

"Hey, it's me. I just got done with the MRI on my head."

My brother-in-law said something unintelligible. I realized that I was holding my cell to my bad ear, and I switched it to the good ear.

"The MRI dude didn't look happy," I said.

"That's not good," my brother-in-law said.

"No, it's not. But he's just a tech guy, right? He's not an expert on brains or 135 anything. He's just the photographer, really. And he doesn't know anything about ears or deafness or anything, I don't think. Ah, hell, I don't know what he knows. I just didn't like the look on his face when I was done."

"Maybe he just didn't like you."

"Well, I got worried when I told him I had hydrocephalus when I was a baby and he didn't seem to know what that was."

"Nobody knows what that is."

"That's the truth. Have you fed the boys dinner?'

"Yeah, but I was scrounging. There's not much here." 140

"I better go shopping."

"Are you sure? I can do it if you need me to. I can shop the shit out of Trader Joe's."

"No, it'll be good for me. I feel good. I fell asleep during the MRI. And I kept twitching, so we had to do it twice. Otherwise, I would've been done earlier."

"That's O.K. I'm O.K. The boys are O.K."

"You know, before you go in the MRI tube they ask you what kind of music 145 you want to listen to—jazz, classical, rock, or country—and I remembered how my dad spent a lot of time in MRI tubes near the end of his life. So I was wondering what kind of music he chose. I mean, he couldn't hear shit anyway by that time, but he still must have chosen something. And I wanted to choose the same thing he chose. So I picked country."

"Was it good country?"

"It was fucking Shania Twain and Faith Hill shit. I was hoping for George Jones or Loretta Lynn, or even some George Strait. Hell, I would've cried if they'd played Charley Pride or Freddy Fender."

"You wanted to hear the Alcoholic Indian Father Jukebox."

"Hey, that's my line. You can't quote me to me."

"Why not? You're always quoting you to you." 150

"Kiss my ass. So, hey, I'm O.K., I think. And I'm going to the store. I'll see you in a bit. You want anything?"

"Ah, man, I love Trader Joe's. But you know what's bad about them? You fall in love with something they have—they stock it for a year—and then it just disappears. They had those wontons I loved, and now they don't. I was willing to shop for you and the boys, but I don't want anything for me. I'm on a one-man hunger strike against them."

WORLD PHONE CONVERSATION, 3 A.M.

After I got home with yogurt and turkey dogs and Cinnamon Toast Crunch and my brother-in-law left, I watched George Romero's "Diary of the Dead," and laughed at myself for choosing a movie that featured dozens of zombies getting shot in the head.

When the movie was over, I called my wife, nine hours ahead in Italy.

"I should come home," she said. 155

"No, I'm O.K.," I said. "Come on, you're in Rome. What are you seeing today?"

"The Vatican."

"You can't leave now. You have to go and steal something. It will be revenge for every Indian. Or maybe you can plant an eagle feather and claim that you just discovered Italy."

"I'm worried."

"Yeah, Catholicism has always worried me."   160

"Stop being funny. I should see if I can get Mom and me on a flight tonight."

"No, no, listen, your mom is old. This might be her last adventure. It might be your last adventure with her. Stay there. Say hi to the Pope for me. Tell him I like his shoes."

That night, my sons climbed into bed with me. We all slept curled around one another like sled dogs in a snowstorm. I woke, hour by hour, and touched my head and neck to see if they had changed shape—to feel if antennae were growing. Some insects hear with their antennae. Maybe that was what was happening to me.

VALEDICTION

My father, a part-time blue-collar construction worker, died of full-time alcoholism in March, 2003. On his deathbed, he said to me, "Turn down that light, please."

"Which light?" I asked.   165

"The light on the ceiling."

"Dad, there's no light."

"It burns my skin, son. It's too bright. It hurts my eyes."

"Dad, I promise you there's no light."

"Don't lie to me, son. It's God passing judgment on earth."   170

"Dad, you've been an atheist since '79. Come on, you're just remembering your birth. On your last day, you're going back to your first."

"No, son, it's God telling me I'm doomed. He's using the brightest lights in the universe to show me the way to my flame-filled tomb."

"No, Dad, those lights were in your delivery room."

"If that's true, son, then turn down my mother's womb."

We buried my father in the tiny Catholic cemetery on our reservation.   175
Since I am named after him, I had to stare at a tombstone with my name on it.

BATTLE FATIGUE

Two months after my father's death, I began research on a book about our family's history with war. I had a cousin who served as a cook in the Gulf War, in 1990; I had another cousin who served in the Vietnam War as a cook; and my father's father, Adolph, served in the Second World War and was killed in action on Okinawa, on April 5, 1945.

During my research, I interviewed thirteen men who'd served with my cousin in Vietnam but could find only one surviving man who'd served with my grandfather. This is a partial transcript of that interview, recorded with a microphone and an iPod on January 14, 2008:

Me: Ah, yes, hello. I'm here in Livonia, Michigan, to interview—well, perhaps you should introduce yourself, please?

Leonard Elmore: What?

Me: Um, oh, I'm sorry, I was asking if you could perhaps introduce yourself. 180

L.E.: You're going to have to speak up. I think my hearing aid is going low on power or something.

Me: That is a fancy thing in your ear.

L.E.: Yeah, let me mess with it a bit. I got a remote control for it. I can listen to the TV, the stereo, and the telephone with this thing. It's fancy. It's one of them Bluetooth hearing aids. My grandson bought it for me. Wait, O.K., there we go. I can hear now. So, what were you asking?

Me: I was hoping you could introduce yourself into my recorder here.

L.E.: Sure, my name is Leonard Elmore. 185

Me: How old are you?

L.E.: I'm eighty-five and a half years old (*laughter*). My great-grandkids are always saying they're seven and a half or nine and a half or whatever. It just cracks me up to say the same thing at my age.

Me: So, that's funny, um, but I'm here to ask you some questions about my grandfather—

L.E.: Adolph. It's hard to forget a name like that. An Indian named Adolph, and there was that Nazi bastard named Adolph. Your grandfather caught plenty of grief over that. But we mostly called him Chief. Did you know that?

Me: I could have guessed. 190

L.E.: Yeah, nowadays I suppose it isn't a good thing to call an Indian Chief, but back then it was what we did. I served with a few Indians. They didn't segregate them Indians, you know, not like the black boys. I know you aren't supposed to call them boys anymore, but they were boys. All of us were boys, I guess. But the thing is, those Indian boys lived and slept and ate with us white boys. They were right there with us. But, anyway, we called all them Indians Chief. I bet you've been called Chief a few times yourself.

Me: Just once.

L.E.: Were you all right with it?

Me: I threw a basketball in the guy's face.

L.E. (*laughs*). 195

Me: We live in different times.

L.E.: Yes, we do. Yes, we do.

Me: So, perhaps you could, uh, tell me something about my grandfather.

L.E.: I can tell you how he died.

Me: Really? 200

L.E.: Yeah, it was on Okinawa, and we hit the beach, and, well, it's hard to talk about it. It was the worst thing—it was hell. No, that's not even a good way to describe it. I'm not a writer like you, I'm not a poet, so I don't have the word, but just think of it this way. That beach, that island, was filled with sons and fathers, men who loved and were loved, American and Japanese and Okinawan, and all of us were dying, were being killed by other sons and fathers who also loved and were loved.

Me: That sounds like poetry to me—tragic poetry.

L.E.: Well, anyway, it was like that. Fire everywhere. And two of our boys, Jonesy and O'Neal, went down, were wounded and in the open on the sand. And your grandfather—who was just this little man, barely over five feet tall and maybe a hundred and thirty pounds—he just ran out there and picked up those two guys, one on each shoulder, and carried them to cover. Hey, are you O.K., son?

Me: Yes, I'm sorry. But, well, the thing is, I knew my grandfather was a war hero—he won twelve medals—but I could never find out what he did to win the medals.

L.E.: I didn't know about any medals. I just know what I saw. Your grand- 205 father saved those two boys, but he got shot in the back doing it. And he lay there in the sand—I was lying right beside him—and he died.

Me: Did he say anything before he died?

L.E.: Hold on. I need to—

Me: Are you O.K.?

L.E.: It's just—I can't—

Me: I'm sorry. Is there something wrong? 210

L.E.: No, it's just—with your book and everything, I know you want something big here. I know you want something big from your grandfather. I know you're hoping he said something huge and poetic, and, honestly, I was thinking about lying to you. I was thinking about making up something as beautiful as I could. Something about love and forgiveness and courage and all that. But I couldn't think of anything good enough. And I didn't want to lie to you. So I have to be honest and say that your grandfather didn't say anything. He just died there in the sand. In silence.

ORPHANS

I could not sleep. I was scared that I would die if I slept. And I didn't want my sons to become orphans—partial orphans—as they slept. So I stayed awake and waited for dawn. Then, at 3 A.M., the phone rang.

"It's me," my wife said. "I don't care what you say. I'll be home in sixteen hours."

"Thank you," I said.

COFFEE-SHOP NEWS

While I waited for the results of the MRI, I asked my brother-in-law to watch 215 the boys again because I didn't want to get bad news in front of them.

Alone and haunted, I wandered the mall, tried on clothes, and waited for my cell phone to ring.

Two hours later, I wanted to murder everything, so I drove south to a coffee joint, a spotless place called Dirty Joe's. Yes, I was silly enough to think that I'd be calmer with a caffeinated drink.

As I sat outside in a wooden chair and sipped my coffee, I cursed the vague, rumbling, ringing noise in my ear. And yet when my cell phone rang I again held it to my deaf ear.

"Hello. Hello," I said and wondered if it was a prank call, then remembered and switched the phone to my left ear.

"Hello," my doctor said. "Are you there?   220

"Yes," I said. "So what's going on?"

"There are irregularities in your head."

"My head's always been irregular."

"It's good to have a sense of humor," the doctor said. "You have a small tumor that is called a meningioma. They grow in the meninges membranes that lie between your brain and your skull."

"Shit," I said. "I have cancer."   225

"Well," he said. "These kinds of tumors are usually non-cancerous. And they grow very slowly, so in six months or so we'll do another MRI. Don't worry. You're going to be O.K."

"What about my hearing?" I asked.

"We don't know what is causing the hearing loss, but you should start a course of prednisone, a steroid, just to go with the odds. Your deafness might lessen if left alone, but we've had success with the steroids in bringing back hearing. There are side effects, like insomnia, weight gain, night sweats, and depression."

"Oh, boy," I said. "Those side effects might make up most of my personality already. Will the 'roids also make me quick to pass judgment? And I've always wished I had a dozen more skin tags and moles."

The doctor chuckled. "You're a funny man."   230

I wanted to throw my phone into a wall, but I said goodbye instead and glared at the tumorless people and their pretty tumorless heads.

MENINGIOMA

Mayoclinic.com gave this definition of "meningioma": "a tumor that arises from the meninges—the membranes that surround your brain and spinal cord. The majority of meningioma cases are noncancerous (benign), though rarely a meningioma can be cancerous (malignant)."

It was a scary and yet strangely positive description. No one ever wants to read the word "malignant" unless you're reading a Charles Dickens novel about an evil landlord, but "benign" and "majority" are two words that go well together.

From the University of Washington Medical School Web site I learned that meningioma tumors "are usually benign, slow growing and do not spread into normal brain tissue. Typically, a meningioma grows inward causing pressure on the brain or spinal cord. It may grow outward toward the skull, causing it to thicken."

So, wait, what the fuck? A meningioma can cause pressure on the brain, and 235
spinal fluid? Oh, you mean just like fucking hydrocephalus? Just like the water
demon that once tried to crush my brain and kill me? Armed with this new
information—with these new questions—I called my doctor.

"Hey, you're O.K.," he said. "We're going to closely monitor you. And your
meningioma is very small."

"O.K., but I just read—"

"Did you go on the Internet?"

"Yes."

"Which sites?"   240

"Mayo Clinic and the University of Washington."

"O.K., those are pretty good sites. Let me look at them."

I listened to my doctor type.

"O.K., those are accurate," he said.

"What do you mean by accurate?" I asked. "I mean, the whole pressure-on-   245
the-brain thing—that sounds like hydrocephalus."

"Well, there were some irregularities in your MRI that were the burr holes
from your surgery, and there seems to be some scarring and perhaps you had
an old concussion. But other than that it all looks fine."

"But what about me going deaf? Can't these tumors make you lose hearing?"

"Yes, but only if they're located near an auditory nerve. And your tumor is
not."

"Can this tumor cause pressure on my brain?"

"It could, but yours is too small for that."   250

"So I'm supposed to trust you on the tumor thing when you can't figure out
the hearing thing?"

"There is no physical correlation between your deafness and the tumor. Do
the twenty-day treatment of prednisone, and the audiologist and I will examine your ear and your hearing then. If there's no improvement, we'll figure out
other ways of treating you."

"But you won't be treating the tumor?"

"Like I said, we'll scan you again in six to nine months—"

"You said six before."   255

"O.K., in six months we'll take another MRI, and if it has grown significantly—or has changed shape or location or anything dramatic—then we'll
talk about treatment options. But if you look on the Internet—and I know
you're going to spend a lot of time obsessing about this, so I'll tell you what
you'll find. About two per cent of the population live their whole lives with
undetected meningiomas. The tumors can become quite large, without any
side effects, and are found only at autopsies conducted for other reasons
of death. Even when these kinds of tumors become invasive or dangerous,
they are still rarely fatal. And your tumor, even if it grows fairly quickly, will
not likely become an issue for many years, decades. So that's what I can tell
you right now. How are you feeling?"

"Freaked and fucked,"

I wanted to feel reassured, but I had a brain tumor. How can one feel any optimism about being diagnosed with a brain tumor? Even if that brain tumor is neither cancerous nor interested in crushing one's brain?

DRUGSTORE INDIAN

In Bartell Drugs, I gave the pharmacist my prescription for prednisone.

"Is this your first fill with us?" she asked.   260

"No," I said. "And it won't be my last."

I felt like an ass, but she looked bored.

"It'll take thirty minutes," she said. "More or less. We'll page you over the speakers."

I don't think I'd ever felt weaker. Or more vulnerable. Or more absurd. I was the weak antelope in the herd—yeah, the mangy fucker with the big limp and a sign that read, "Eat Me! I'm a Gimp!"

So for thirty minutes I walked the store and found myself shoving more   265 and more useful shit into my shopping basket, as if I were filling my casket with things I'd need in the afterlife. I grabbed toothpaste, a Swiss Army knife, moisturizer, mouthwash, nonstick Band-Aids, antacid, protein bars, and extra razor blades. I grabbed pen and paper. And I also grabbed an ice scraper and sunscreen. Who can predict what kind of weather awaits us in Heaven?

This random shopping made me feel better for a few minutes, but then I stopped and walked to the toy aisle. My boys needed gifts, Lego cars or something, for a lift, a shot of capitalist joy. But the selection of proper toys is both an art and a science. I have been wrong as often as right and have heard the sad song of a disappointed son.

Shit, I knew that if I died my sons would survive, even thrive, because of their graceful mother.

I thought of my father's life. He had been just six when his father was killed in the Second World War. Then his mother, ill with tuberculosis, had died a few months later. Six years old and my father was cratered. In most ways, he never stopped being six. There was no religion, no magic, and no song or dance that could have helped my father.

I needed a drink of water, so I found the fountain and drank and drank until the pharmacist called my name.

"Have you taken these before?" she asked.   270

I said, "No, but they're going to kick my ass, aren't they?"

That made the pharmacist smile, so I felt sadly and briefly worthwhile. But another customer, some nosy hag, said, "You've got a lot of sleepless nights ahead of you."

I was shocked. I stammered, glared at her, and said, "Miss, how is this any of your business? Please, just fuck all the way off, O.K.?"

She had no idea what to say, so she just turned and walked away, and I pulled out my credit card and paid far too much for my goddam steroids, and forgot to bring the toys home to my boys.

EXIT INTERVIEW FOR MY FATHER

• True or False: When a reservation-raised Native American dies of alcohol- 275
ism, it should be considered death by natural causes.

• Do you understand the term "wanderlust," and, if you do, can you please
tell us, in twenty-five words or less, what place made you wanderlust the most?

• Did you, when drunk, ever get behind the tattered wheel of a '76 Ford
three-speed van and somehow drive your family a thousand miles on an
empty tank of gas?

• Is it true that the only literary term that has any real meaning in the Native
American world is "road movie"?

• How many times, during any of your road trips, did your children ask
you, "Are we there yet?"

• In twenty-five words or less, please define "there."   280

• Sir, in your thirty-nine years as a parent you broke your children's hearts,
collectively and individually, six hundred and twelve times, and you did this
without ever striking any human being in anger. Does this absence of physical
violence make you a better man than you might otherwise have been?

• Without using the words "man" or "good," can you please define what it
means to be a good man?

• Do you think you will see angels before you die? Do you think angels will
come to escort you to Heaven? As the angels are carrying you to Heaven, how
many times will you ask, "Are we there yet?"

• Your son distinctly remembers stopping once or twice a month at that
grocery store in Freeman, Washington, where you would buy him a red-
white-and-blue rocket Popsicle and purchase for yourself a pickled pig foot.
Your son distinctly remembers that the feet still had their toenails and little
tufts of pig fur. Could this be true? Did you actually eat such horrendous food?

• Your son has often made the joke that you were the only Indian of your   285
generation who went to Catholic school on purpose. This is, of course, a tasteless joke that makes light of the forced incarceration and subsequent physical,
spiritual, cultural, and sexual abuse of tens of thousands of Native American
children in Catholic and Protestant boarding schools. In consideration of your
son's questionable judgment in telling jokes, do you think there should be any
moral limits placed on comedy?

• Your other son and your two daughters, all over thirty-six years of age,
still live in your house. Do you think that this is a lovely expression of tribal
culture? Or is it a symptom of extreme familial co-dependency? Or is it both
things at the same time?

• F. Scott Fitzgerald wrote that the sign of a superior mind "is the ability to
hold two opposing ideas at the same time." Do you believe this to be true? And
is it also true that you once said, "The only time white people tell the truth is
when they keep their mouths shut"?

• A poet once wrote, "Pain is never added to pain. It multiplies." Can you
tell us, in twenty-five words or less, exactly how much we all hate mathematical blackmail?

• Your son wrote this poem to explain one of the most significant nights in his life:

Mutually Assured Destruction

When I was nine, my father sliced his knee
With a chainsaw. But he let himself bleed
And finished cutting down one more tree
Before his boss drove him to EMERGENCY.

Late that night, stoned on morphine and beer,
My father needed my help to steer
His pickup into the woods. "Watch for deer,"
My father said. "Those things just appear

Like magic." It was an Indian summer
And we drove through warm rain and thunder,
Until we found that chainsaw, lying under
The fallen pine. Then I watched, with wonder,

As my father, shotgun-rich and impulse-poor,
Blasted that chainsaw dead. "What was that for?"
I asked. "Son," my father said. "Here's the score.
Once a thing tastes blood, it will come for more."

• Well, first of all, as you know, you did cut your knee with a chainsaw, but 290 in direct contradiction to your son's poem:

(a) You immediately went to the emergency room.

(b) Your boss called your wife, who drove you to the emergency room.

(c) You were given morphine, but even you were not stupid enough to drink alcohol while on serious narcotics.

(d) You and your son did not get into the pickup that night.

(e) And, even if you had driven the pickup, you were not injured seriously 295 enough to need your son's help with the pedals and/or the steering wheel.

(f) You never in your life used the word "appear," and you certainly never used the phrase "like magic."

(g) You think that "Indian summer" is a questionable seasonal reference for an Indian poet to use.

(h) What the fuck is "warm rain and thunder"? Well, everybody knows what "warm rain" is, but what the fuck is "warm thunder"?

(i) You never went looking for that chainsaw, because it belonged to the Spokane Tribe of Indians, and what kind of freak would want to reclaim the chainsaw that had just cut the shit out of his knee?

(j) You also agree that the entire third stanza of this poem sounds like a 300 Bruce Springsteen song, and not necessarily one of the great ones.

(k) And yet "shotgun-rich and impulse-poor" is one of the greatest descriptions your son has ever written and probably redeems the entire poem.

(l) You never owned a shotgun. You did own a few rifles in your youth, but did not own so much as a pellet gun during the last thirty years of your life.

(m) You never said, in any context, "Once a thing tastes blood, it will come for more."

(n) But, as you read it, you know that is absolutely true and does indeed sound suspiciously like your entire life philosophy.

(o) Other summations of your life philosophy include: "It's all wasted days 305 and wasted nights."

(p) And: "If God really loved Indians, he would have made us white people."

(q) And: "Oscar Robertson should be the man on the N.B.A. logo. They only put Jerry West on there because he's a white guy."

(r) And: "A peanut-butter sandwich with onions—damn, that's the way to go."

(s) And: "Why eat a pomegranate when you can eat a plain old apple. Or a carrot. When it comes to fruit and vegetables, eat only the simple stuff."

(t) And: "If you really want a woman to love you, then you have to dance. 310 And if you don't want to dance, then you're going to have to work extra hard to make a woman love you forever, and you will always run the risk that she will leave you at any second for a man who knows how to tango."

(u) And: "I really miss those cafeterias they used to have at Kmart. I don't know why they stopped having those. If there is a Heaven, I firmly believe it's a Kmart cafeteria."

(v) And: "A father always knows what his sons are doing. For instance, boys, I knew you were sneaking that *Hustler* magazine out of my bedroom. You remember that one. Where actors who looked like Captain Kirk and Lieutenant Uhura were screwing on the bridge of the Enterprise. Yeah, that one. I know you kept borrowing it. I let you borrow it. Remember this: men and pornography are like plants and sunshine. To me, porn is photosynthesis."

(w) And: "Your mother is a better man than me. Mothers are almost always better men than men are."

REUNION

After she returned from Italy, my wife climbed into bed with me. I felt as if I hadn't slept comfortably in years.

I said, "There was a rumor that I'd grown a tumor, but I killed it with 315 humor."

"How long have you been waiting to tell me that one?" she asked.

"Oh, probably since the first time some doctor put his fingers in my brain."

We made love. We fell asleep. But, agitated by the steroids, I woke at 2, 3, 4, and 5 A.M. The bed was killing my back, so I lay flat on the floor. I wasn't going to die anytime soon, at least not because of my little friend Tumor, but that didn't make me feel any more comfortable or comforted. I felt distant from the world—from my wife and my sons, from my mother and my siblings, from all my friends. I felt closest to those who'd always had fingers in their brains.

I didn't feel any closer to the world six months later, when another MRI revealed that my meningioma had not grown in size or changed its shape.

"You're looking good," my doctor said. "How's your hearing?" 320

"I think I've got about ninety per cent of it back."

"Well, then, the steroids worked. Good."

And I didn't feel any more intimate with the world nine months after that, when one more MRI made my doctor hypothesize that my meningioma might only be more scar tissue from the hydrocephalus.

"Frankly," he said, "your brain is beautiful."

"Thank you," I said, though it was the oddest compliment I'd ever received. 325

I wanted to call my father and tell him that a white man thought my brain was beautiful. But I couldn't tell him anything. He was dead. I told my wife and my sons that I was O.K. I told my mother and my siblings. I told my friends. But none of them laughed as hard about my beautiful brain as I knew my father—the drunk bastard—would have.

FOR ANALYSIS

1. Why do you think Alexie calls the first section of his story "My Kafka Baggage"?

2. Can you identify the main **plot** of this story? If so, what is it? If not, why?

3. When (in terms of events, not the calendar) does the main action in the story take place? Identify the other plotlines and describe their chronological relation to it.

4. What is the significance to the story of the ceremony that takes place in the hospital? How would you describe the **narrator's** reaction to it?

5. Why might it be important that three generations of the narrator's family are present in the story? How is this story not only about the narrator's relationship with his father but also about his relationship with his children?

6. What role does humor play in this story? Do you expect humor in a story about a subject such as this? What effects does it have on you as you read?

7. How does the narrator feel about his Native American heritage? Is there a simple answer to this question? Why or why not?

8. Reread the story's last sentence. What about the entire story does it capture?

MAKING CONNECTIONS

Compare this story's orientation in time to that of Jonathan Lethem's "Super Goat Man" (p. 411). Alexie's story uses flashbacks, while Lethem's, also told from the present, uses a different strategy. How does each work? Do they seem the right choices for the stories they tell?

WRITING TOPICS

1. The penultimate section of the story is titled "Exit Interview for My Father." Write your own "exit interview" for either yourself or someone else—for example, a person you are close to, a public figure, or someone you see around town. Following this interview, reflect on what it means to look back on a life after its end, and also to do it by asking questions of the deceased.

2. The first question in the "Exit Interview" section reads: "True or False: When a reservation-raised Native American dies of alcoholism, it should be considered death by natural causes." Write a response to this "question." What is it arguing? On the evidence of the rest of the story, how do you think the **narrator** would answer it? How would his father?

JHUMPA LAHIRI   (B. 1967)

HELL-HEAVEN   2004

Pranab Chakraborty wasn't technically my father's younger brother. He was a fellow-Bengali from Calcutta who had washed up on the barren shores of my parents' social life in the early seventies, when they lived in a rented apartment in Central Square and could number their acquaintances on one hand. But I had no real uncles in America, and so I was taught to call him Pranab Kaku. Accordingly, he called my father Shyamal Da, always addressing him in the polite form, and he called my mother Boudi, which is how Bengalis are supposed to address an older brother's wife, instead of using her first name, Aparna. After Pranab Kaku was befriended by my parents, he confessed that on the day we first met him he had followed my mother and me for the better part of an afternoon around the streets of Cambridge, where she and I tended to roam after I got out of school. He had trailed behind us along Massachusetts Avenue, and in and out of the Harvard Coop, where my mother liked to look at discounted housewares. He wandered with us into Harvard Yard, where my mother often sat on the grass on pleasant days and watched the stream of students and professors filing busily along the paths, until, finally, as we were climbing the steps to Widener Library so that I could use the bathroom, he tapped my mother on the shoulder and inquired, in English, if she might be a Bengali. The answer to his question was clear, given that my mother was wearing the red and white bangles unique to Bengali married women, and a common Tangail sari, and had a thick stem of vermillion powder in the center parting of her hair, and the full round face and large dark eyes that are so typical of Bengali women. He noticed the two or three safety pins she wore fastened to the thin gold bangles that were behind the red and white ones, which she would use to replace a missing hook on a blouse or to draw a string through a petticoat at a moment's notice, a practice he associated strictly with his mother and sisters and aunts in Calcutta. Moreover, Pranab Kaku had overheard my mother speaking to me in Bengali, telling me that I couldn't buy an issue of *Archie* at the Coop. But back then, he also confessed, he was so new to America that he took nothing for granted, and doubted even the obvious.

My parents and I had lived in Central Square for three years prior to that day; before that, we had lived in Berlin, where I was born and where my father had finished his training in microbiology before accepting a position as a researcher at Mass General, and before Berlin my mother and father had lived in India, where they had been strangers to each other, and where their marriage had been arranged. Central Square is the first place I can recall living, and in my memories of our apartment, in a dark-brown shingled house on Ashburton Place, Pranab Kaku is always there. According to the story he liked to recall often, my mother invited him to accompany us back to our apartment that very afternoon, and prepared tea for the two of them; then, after learning that he had not had a proper Bengali meal in more than three months, she served him the leftover curried mackerel and rice that we had eaten for dinner the night before. He remained into the evening, for a second dinner, after my father got home, and after that he showed up for dinner almost every night, occupying the fourth chair at our square Formica kitchen table, and becoming a part of our family in practice as well as in name.

He was from a wealthy family in Calcutta and had never had to do so much as pour himself a glass of water before moving to America, to study engineering at M.I.T. Life as a graduate student in Boston was a cruel shock, and in his first month he lost nearly twenty pounds. He had arrived in January, in the middle of a snowstorm, and at the end of a week he had packed his bags and gone to Logan, prepared to abandon the opportunity he'd worked toward all his life, only to change his mind at the last minute. He was living on Trowbridge Street in the home of a divorced woman with two young children who were always screaming and crying. He rented a room in the attic and was permitted to use the kitchen only at specified times of the day, and instructed always to wipe down the stove with Windex and a sponge. My parents agreed that it was a terrible situation, and if they'd had a bedroom to spare they would have offered it to him. Instead, they welcomed him to our meals, and opened up our apartment to him at any time, and soon it was there he went between classes and on his days off, always leaving behind some vestige of himself: a nearly finished pack of cigarettes, a newspaper, a piece of mail he had not bothered to open, a sweater he had taken off and forgotten in the course of his stay.

I remember vividly the sound of his exuberant laughter and the sight of his lanky body slouched or sprawled on the dull, mismatched furniture that had come with our apartment. He had a striking face, with a high forehead and a thick mustache, and overgrown, untamed hair that my mother said made him look like the American hippies who were everywhere in those days. His long legs jiggled rapidly up and down wherever he sat, and his elegant hands trembled when he held a cigarette between his fingers, tapping the ashes into a teacup that my mother began to set aside for this exclusive purpose. Though he was a scientist by training, there was nothing rigid or predictable or orderly about him. He always seemed to be starving, walking through the door and announcing that he hadn't had lunch, and then he would eat ravenously, reaching behind my mother to steal cutlets as she was frying them, before she had a chance to set them properly on a plate with red-onion salad. In private, my parents remarked that he was a brilliant student, a star at Jadavpur who had come to M.I.T. with an impressive assistantship, but Pranab Kaku was cavalier about his classes, skipping them with frequency. "These Americans are learning equations I knew at Usha's age," he would complain. He was stunned that my second-grade teacher didn't assign any homework, and that at the age of seven I hadn't yet been taught square roots or the concept of pi.

He appeared without warning, never phoning beforehand but simply 5 knocking on the door the way people did in Calcutta and calling out "Boudi!" as he waited for my mother to let him in. Before we met him, I would return from school and find my mother with her purse in her lap and her trench-coat on, desperate to escape the apartment where she had spent the day alone. But now I would find her in the kitchen, rolling out dough for *luchis*, which she normally made only on Sundays for my father and me, or putting up new curtains she'd bought at Woolworth's. I did not know, back then, that Pranab Kaku's visits were what my mother looked forward to all day, that she changed into a new sari and combed her hair in anticipation of his arrival, and that she planned, days in advance, the snacks she would serve him with such noncha-lance. That she lived for the moment she heard him call out "Boudi!" from the porch, and that she was in a foul humor on the days he didn't materialize.

It must have pleased her that I looked forward to his visits as well. He showed me card tricks and an optical illusion in which he appeared to be sev-ering his own thumb with enormous struggle and strength, and taught me to memorize multiplication tables well before I had to learn them in school. His hobby was photography. He owned an expensive camera that required thought before you pressed the shutter, and I quickly became his favorite sub-ject, round-faced, missing teeth, my thick bangs in need of a trim. They are still the pictures of myself I like best, for they convey that confidence of youth I no longer possess, especially in front of a camera. I remember having to run back and forth in Harvard Yard as he stood with the camera, trying to capture me in motion, or posing on the steps of university buildings and on the street and against the trunks of trees. There is only one photograph in which my mother appears; she is holding me as I sit straddling her lap, her head tilted toward me, her hands pressed to my ears as if to prevent me from hearing something. In that picture, Pranab Kaku's shadow, his two arms raised at angles to hold the camera to his face, hovers in the corner of the frame, his darkened, featureless shape superimposed on one side of my mother's body. It was always the three of us. I was always there when he visited. It would have been inappropriate for my mother to receive him in the apartment alone; this was something that went without saying.

They had in common all the things she and my father did not: a love of music, film, leftist politics, poetry. They were from the same neighborhood in North Calcutta, their family homes within walking distance, the façades familiar to them once the exact locations were described. They knew the same shops, the same bus and tram routes, the same holes-in-the-wall for the best *jelabis* and *moghlai parathas*. My father, on the other hand, came from a sub-urb twenty miles outside Calcutta, an area that my mother considered the wil-derness, and even in her bleakest hours of homesickness she was grateful that my father had at least spared her a life in the stern house of her in-laws, where she would have had to keep her head covered with the end of her sari at all times and use an outhouse that was nothing but a raised platform with a hole, and where, in the rooms, there was not a single painting hanging on the walls. Within a few weeks, Pranab Kaku had brought his reel-to-reel over to our apartment, and he played for my mother medley after medley of songs from the Hindi films of their youth. They were cheerful songs of courtship, which transformed the quiet life in our apartment and transported my mother back to the world she'd left behind in order to marry my father. She and Pranab Kaku would try to recall which scene in which movie the songs were from, who the actors were and what they were wearing. My mother would describe Raj Kapoor and Nargis singing under umbrellas in the rain, or Dev Anand strumming a guitar on the beach in Goa. She and Pranab Kaku would argue passionately about these matters, raising their voices in playful combat, confronting each other in a way she and my father never did.

Because he played the part of a younger brother, she felt free to call him Pranab, whereas she never called my father by his first name. My father was thirty-seven then, nine years older than my mother. Pranab Kaku was twenty-five. My father was monkish by nature, a lover of silence and solitude. He had married my mother to placate his parents; they were willing to accept his desertion as long as he had a wife. He was wedded to his work, his research, and he existed in a shell that neither my mother nor I could penetrate. Conversation was a chore for him; it required an effort he preferred to expend at the lab. He disliked excess in anything, voiced no cravings or needs apart from the frugal elements of his daily routine: cereal and tea in the mornings, a cup of tea after he got home, and two different vegetable dishes every night with dinner. He did not eat with the reckless appetite of Pranab Kaku. My father had a survivor's mentality. From time to time, he liked to remark, in mixed company and often with no relevant provocation, that starving Russians under Stalin had resorted to eating the glue off the back of their wallpaper. One might think that he would have felt slightly jealous, or at the very least suspicious, about the regularity of Pranab Kaku's visits and the effect they had on my mother's behavior and mood. But my guess is that my father was grateful to Pranab Kaku for the companionship he provided, freed from the sense of responsibility he must have felt for forcing her to leave India, and relieved, perhaps, to see her happy for a change.

In the summer, Pranab Kaku bought a navy-blue Volkswagen Beetle, and began to take my mother and me for drives through Boston and Cambridge, and soon outside the city, flying down the highway. He would take us to India Tea and Spices in Watertown, and one time he drove us all the way to New Hampshire to look at the mountains. As the weather grew hotter, we started going, once or twice a week, to Walden Pond. My mother always prepared a picnic of hard-boiled eggs and cucumber sandwiches, and talked fondly about the winter picnics of her youth, grand expeditions with fifty of her relatives, all taking the train into the West Bengal countryside. Pranab Kaku listened to these stories with interest, absorbing the vanishing details of her past. He did not turn a deaf ear to her nostalgia, like my father, or listen uncomprehending, like me. At Walden Pond, Pranab Kaku would coax my mother through the woods, and lead her down the steep slope to the water's edge. She would unpack the picnic things and sit and watch us as we swam. His chest was matted with thick dark hair, all the way to his waist. He was an odd sight, with his pole-thin legs and a small, flaccid belly, like an otherwise svelte woman who has had a baby and not bothered to tone her abdomen. "You're making me fat, Boudi," he would complain after gorging himself on my mother's cooking. He swam noisily, clumsily, his head always above the water; he didn't know how to blow bubbles or hold his breath, as I had learned in swimming class. Wherever we went, any stranger would have naturally assumed that Pranab Kaku was my father, that my mother was his wife.

It is clear to me now that my mother was in love with him. He wooed her 10 as no other man had, with the innocent affection of a brother-in-law. In my mind, he was just a family member, a cross between an uncle and a much older brother, for in certain respects my parents sheltered and cared for him in much the same way they cared for me. He was respectful of my father, always seeking his advice about making a life in the West, about setting up a bank account and getting a job, and deferring to his opinions about Kissinger and Watergate. Occasionally, my mother would tease him about women, asking about female Indian students at M.I.T., or showing him pictures of her younger cousins in India. "What do you think of her?" she would ask. "Isn't she pretty?" She knew that she could never have Pranab Kaku for herself, and I suppose it was her attempt to keep him in the family. But, most important, in the beginning he was totally dependent on her, needing her for those months in a way my father never did in the whole history of their marriage. He brought to my mother the first and, I suspect, the only pure happiness she ever felt. I don't think even my birth made her as happy. I was evidence of her marriage to my father, an assumed consequence of the life she had been raised to lead. But Pranab Kaku was different. He was the one totally unanticipated pleasure in her life.

In the fall of 1974, Pranab Kaku met a student at Radcliffe named Deborah, an American, and she began to accompany him to our house. I called Deborah by her first name, as my parents did, but Pranab Kaku taught her to call my father Shyamal Da and my mother Boudi, something with which Deborah gladly complied. Before they came to dinner for the first time, I asked my mother, as she was straightening up the living room, if I ought to address her as Deborah Kakima, turning her into an aunt as I had turned Pranab into an uncle. "What's the point?" my mother said, looking back at me sharply. "In a few weeks, the fun will be over and she'll leave him." And yet Deborah remained by his side, attending the weekend parties that Pranab Kaku and my parents were becoming more involved with, gatherings that were exclusively Bengali with the exception of her. Deborah was very tall, taller than both my parents and nearly as tall as Pranab Kaku. She wore her long brass-colored hair center-parted, as my mother did, but it was gathered into a low ponytail instead of a braid, or it spilled messily over her shoulders and down her back in a way that my mother considered indecent. She wore small silver spectacles and not a trace of makeup, and she studied philosophy. I found her utterly beautiful, but according to my mother she had spots on her face, and her hips were too small.

For a while, Pranab Kaku still showed up once a week for dinner on his own, mostly asking my mother what she thought of Deborah. He sought her approval, telling her that Deborah was the daughter of professors at Boston College, that her father published poetry, and that both her parents had Ph.D.s. When he wasn't around, my mother complained about Deborah's visits, about having to make the food less spicy even though Deborah said she liked spicy food, and feeling embarrassed to put a fried fish head in the dal. Pranab Kaku taught Deborah to say *khub bhalo* and *aacha* and to pick up certain foods with her fingers instead of with a fork. Sometimes they ended up feeding each other, allowing their fingers to linger in each other's mouth, causing my parents to look down at their plates and wait for the moment to pass. At larger gatherings, they kissed and held hands in front of everyone, and when they were out of earshot my mother would talk to the other Bengali women. "He used to be so different. I don't understand how a person can change so suddenly. It's just hell-heaven, the difference," she would say, always using the English words for her self-concocted, backward metaphor.

The more my mother began to resent Deborah's visits, the more I began to anticipate them. I fell in love with Deborah, the way young girls often fall in love with women who are not their mothers. I loved her serene gray eyes, the ponchos and denim wrap skirts and sandals she wore, her straight hair that she let me manipulate into all sorts of silly styles. I longed for her casual appearance; my mother insisted whenever there was a gathering that I wear one of my ankle-length, faintly Victorian dresses, which she referred to as maxis, and have party hair, which meant taking a strand from either side of my head and joining them with a barrette at the back. At parties, Deborah would, eventually, politely slip away, much to the relief of the Bengali women with whom she was expected to carry on a conversation, and she would play with me. I was older than all my parents' friends' children, but with Deborah I had a companion. She knew all about the books I read, about Pippi Longstocking and Anne of Green Gables. She gave me the sorts of gifts my parents had neither the money nor the inspiration to buy: a large book of Grimms' fairy tales with watercolor illustrations on thick, silken pages, wooden puppets with hair fashioned from yarn. She told me about her family, three older sisters and two brothers, the youngest of whom was closer to my age than to hers. Once, after visiting her parents, she brought back three Nancy Drews, her name written in a girlish hand at the top of the first page, and an old toy she'd had, a small paper theatre set with interchangeable backdrops, the exterior of a castle and a ballroom and an open field. Deborah and I spoke freely in English, a language in which, by that age, I expressed myself more easily than Bengali, which I was required to speak at home. Sometimes she asked me how to say this or that in Bengali; once, she asked me what *asobbho* meant. I hesitated, then told her it was what my mother called me if I had done something extremely naughty, and Deborah's face clouded. I felt protective of her, aware that she was unwanted, that she was resented, aware of the nasty things people said.

Outings in the Volkswagen now involved the four of us, Deborah in the front, her hand over Pranab Kaku's while it rested on the gearshift, my mother and I in the back. Soon, my mother began coming up with reasons to excuse herself, headaches and incipient colds, and so I became part of a new triangle. To my surprise, my mother allowed me to go with them, to the Museum of Fine Arts and the Public Garden and the aquarium. She was waiting for the affair to end, for Deborah to break Pranab Kaku's heart and for him to return to us, scarred and penitent. I saw no sign of their relationship foundering. Their open affection for each other, their easily expressed happiness, was a new and romantic thing to me. Having me in the back seat allowed Pranab Kaku and Deborah to practice for the future, to try on the idea of a family of their own. Countless photographs were taken of me and Deborah, of me sitting on Deborah's lap, holding her hand, kissing her on the cheek. We exchanged what I believed were secret smiles, and in those moments I felt that she understood me better than anyone else in the world. Anyone would have said that Deborah would make an excellent mother one day. But my mother refused to acknowledge such a thing. I did not know at the time that my mother allowed me to go off with Pranab Kaku and Deborah because she was pregnant for the fifth time since my birth, and was so sick and exhausted and fearful of losing another baby that she slept most of the day. After ten weeks, she miscarried once again, and was advised by her doctor to stop trying.

By summer, there was a diamond on Deborah's left hand, something   15 my mother had never been given. Because his own family lived so far away, Pranab Kaku came to the house alone one day, to ask for my parents' blessing before giving her the ring. He showed us the box, opening it and taking out the diamond nestled inside. "I want to see how it looks on someone," he said, urging my mother to try it on, but she refused. I was the one who stuck out my hand, feeling the weight of the ring suspended at the base of my finger. Then he asked for a second thing: he wanted my parents to write to his parents, saying that they had met Deborah and that they thought highly of her. He was nervous, naturally, about telling his family that he intended to marry an American girl. He had told his parents all about us, and at one point my parents had received a letter from them, expressing appreciation for taking such good care of their son and for giving him a proper home in America. "It needn't be long," Pranab Kaku said. "Just a few lines. They'll accept it more easily if it comes from you." My father thought neither ill nor well of Deborah, never commenting or criticizing as my mother did, but he assured Pranab Kaku that a letter of endorsement would be on its way to Calcutta by the end of the week. My mother nodded her assent, but the following day I saw the teacup Pranab Kaku had used all this time as an ashtray in the kitchen garbage can, in pieces, and three Band-Aids taped to my mother's hand.

Pranab Kaku's parents were horrified by the thought of their only son marrying an American woman, and a few weeks later our telephone rang in the middle of the night: it was Mr. Chakraborty telling my father that they could not possibly bless such a marriage, that it was out of the question, that if Pranab Kaku dared to marry Deborah he would no longer acknowledge him as a son. Then his wife got on the phone, asking to speak to my mother, and attacked her as if they were intimate, blaming my mother for allowing the affair to develop. She said that they had already chosen a wife for him in Calcutta, that he'd left for America with the understanding that he'd go back after he had finished his studies, and marry this girl. They had bought the neighboring flat in their building for Pranab and his betrothed, and it was sitting empty, waiting for his return. "We thought we could trust you, and yet you have betrayed us so deeply," his mother said, taking out her anger on a stranger in a way she could not with her son. "Is this what happens to people in America?" For Pranab Kaku's sake, my mother defended the engagement, telling his mother that Deborah was a polite girl from a decent family. Pranab Kaku's parents pleaded with mine to talk him out of the engagement, but my father refused, deciding that it was not their place to get embroiled in a situation that had nothing to do with them. "We are not his parents," he told my mother. "We can tell him they don't approve but nothing more." And so my parents told Pranab Kaku nothing about how his parents had berated them, and blamed them, and threatened to disown Pranab Kaku, only that they had refused to give him their blessing. In the face of this refusal, Pranab Kaku shrugged. "I don't care. Not everyone can be as open-minded as you," he told my parents. "Your blessing is blessing enough."

After the engagement, Pranab Kaku and Deborah began drifting out of our lives. They moved in together, to an apartment in Boston, in the South End, a part of the city my parents considered unsafe. We moved as well, to a house in Natick. Though my parents had bought the house, they occupied it as if they were still tenants, touching up scuff marks with leftover paint and reluctant to put holes in the walls, and every afternoon when the sun shone through the living-room window my mother closed the blinds so that our new furniture would not fade. A few weeks before the wedding, my parents invited Pranab Kaku to the house alone, and my mother prepared a special meal to mark the end of his bachelorhood. It would be the only Bengali aspect of the wedding; the rest of it would be strictly American, with a cake and a minister and Deborah in a long white dress and veil. There is a photograph of the dinner, taken by my father, the only picture, to my knowledge, in which my mother and Pranab Kaku appear together. The picture is slightly blurry; I remember Pranab Kaku explaining to my father how to work the camera, and so he is captured looking up from the kitchen table and the elaborate array of food my mother had prepared in his honor, his mouth open, his long arm outstretched and his finger pointing, instructing my father how to read the light meter or some such thing. My mother stands beside him, one hand placed on top of his head in a gesture of blessing, the first and last time she was to touch him in her life. "She will leave him," my mother told her friends afterward. "He is throwing his life away."

The wedding was at a church in Ipswich, with a reception at a country club. It was going to be a small ceremony, which my parents took to mean one or two hundred people as opposed to three or four hundred. My mother was shocked that fewer than thirty people had been invited, and she was more perplexed than honored that, of all the Bengalis Pranab Kaku knew by then, we were the only ones on the list. At the wedding, we sat, like the other guests, first on the hard wooden pews of the church and then at a long table that had been set up for lunch. Though we were the closest thing Pranab Kaku had to a family that day, we were not included in the group photographs that were taken on the grounds of the country club, with Deborah's parents and grandparents and her many siblings, and neither my mother nor my father got up to make a toast. My mother did not appreciate the fact that Deborah had made sure that my parents, who did not eat beef, were given fish instead of filet mignon like everyone else. She kept speaking in Bengali, complaining about the formality of the proceedings, and the fact that Pranab Kaku, wearing a tuxedo, barely said a word to us because he was too busy leaning over the shoulders of his new American in-laws as he circled the table. As usual, my father said nothing in response to my mother's commentary, quietly and methodically working though his meal, his fork and knife occasionally squeaking against the surface of the china, because he was accustomed to eating with his hands. He cleared his plate and then my mother's, for she had pronounced the food inedible, and then he announced that he had overeaten and had a stomach ache. The only time my mother forced a smile was when Deborah appeared behind her chair, kissing her on the cheek and asking if we were enjoying ourselves. When the dancing started, my parents remained at the table, drinking tea, and after two or three songs they decided that it was time for us to go home, my mother shooting me looks to that effect across the room, where I was dancing in a circle with Pranab Kaku and Deborah and the other children at the wedding. I wanted to stay, and when, reluctantly, I walked over to where my parents sat Deborah followed me. "Boudi, let Usha stay. She's having such a good time," she said to my mother. "Lots of people will be heading back your way, someone can drop her off in a little while." But my mother said no, I had had plenty of fun already, and forced me to put on my coat over my long puff-sleeved dress. As we drove home from the wedding I told my mother, for the first but not the last time in my life, that I hated her.

The following year, we received a birth announcement from the Chakrabortys, a picture of twin girls, which my mother did not paste into an album or display on the refrigerator door. The girls were named Srabani and Sabitri, but were called Bonny and Sara. Apart from a thank-you card for our wedding gift, it was their only communication; we were not invited to the new house in Marblehead, bought after Pranab Kaku got a high-paying job at Stone & Webster. For a while, my parents and their friends continued to invite the Chakrabortys to gatherings, but because they never came, or left after staying only an hour, the invitations stopped. Their absences were attributed, by my parents and their circle, to Deborah, and it was universally agreed that she had stripped Pranab Kaku not only of his origins but of his independence. She was the enemy, he was her prey, and their example was invoked as a warning, and as vindication, that mixed marriages were a doomed enterprise. Occasionally, they surprised everyone, appearing at a *pujo* for a few hours with their two identical little girls who barely looked Bengali and spoke only English and were being raised so differently from me and most of the other children. They were not taken to Calcutta every summer, they did not have parents who were clinging to another way of life and exhorting their children to do the same. Because of Deborah, they were exempt from all that, and for this reason I envied them. "Usha, look at you, all grown up and so pretty," Deborah would say whenever she saw me, rekindling, if only for a minute, our bond of years before. She had cut off her beautiful long hair by then, and had a bob. "I bet you'll be old enough to babysit soon," she would say. "I'll call you—the girls would love that." But she never did.

I began to grow out of my girlhood, entering middle school and developing 20 crushes on the American boys in my class. The crushes amounted to nothing; in spite of Deborah's compliments, I was always overlooked at that age. But my mother must have picked up on something, for she forbade me to attend the dances that were held the last Friday of every month in the school cafeteria, and it was an unspoken law that I was not allowed to date. "Don't think you'll get away with marrying an American, the way Pranab Kaku did," she would say from time to time. I was thirteen, the thought of marriage irrelevant to my life. Still, her words upset me, and I felt her grip on me tighten. She would fly into a rage when I told her I wanted to start wearing a bra, or if I wanted to go to Harvard Square with a friend. In the middle of our arguments, she often conjured Deborah as her antithesis, the sort of woman she refused to be. "If *she* were your mother, she would let you do whatever you wanted, because she wouldn't care. Is that what you want, Usha, a mother who doesn't care?" When I began menstruating, the summer before I started ninth grade, my mother gave me a speech, telling me that I was to let no boy touch me, and then she asked if I knew how a woman became pregnant. I told her what I had been taught in science, about the sperm fertilizing the egg, and then she asked if I knew how, exactly, that happened. I saw the terror in her eyes and so, though I knew that aspect of procreation as well, I lied, and told her it hadn't been explained to us.

I began keeping other secrets from her, evading her with the aid of my friends. I told her I was sleeping over at a friend's when really I went to parties, drinking beer and allowing boys to kiss me and fondle my breasts and press their erections against my hip as we lay groping on a sofa or the back seat of a car. I began to pity my mother; the older I got, the more I saw what a desolate life she led. She had never worked, and during the day she watched soap operas to pass the time. Her only job, every day, was to clean and cook for my father and me. We rarely went to restaurants, my father always pointing out, even in cheap ones, how expensive they were compared with eating at home. When my mother complained to him about how much she hated life in the suburbs and how lonely she felt, he said nothing to placate her. "If you are so unhappy, go back to Calcutta," he would offer, making it clear that their separation would not affect him one way or the other. I began to take my cues from my father in dealing with her, isolating her doubly. When she screamed at me for talking too long on the telephone, or for staying too long in my room, I learned to scream back, telling her that she was pathetic, that she knew nothing about me, and it was clear to us both that I had stopped needing her, definitively and abruptly, just as Pranab Kaku had.

Then, the year before I went off to college, my parents and I were invited to the Chakrabortys' home for Thanksgiving. We were not the only guests from my parents' old Cambridge crowd; it turned out that Pranab Kaku and Deborah wanted to have a sort of reunion of all the people they had been friendly with back then. Normally, my parents did not celebrate Thanksgiving; the ritual of a large sit-down dinner and the foods that one was supposed to eat was lost on them. They treated it as if it were Memorial Day or Veterans Day—just another holiday in the American year. But we drove out to Marblehead, to an impressive stone-faced house with a semicircular gravel driveway clogged with cars. The house was a short walk from the ocean; on our way, we had driven by the harbor overlooking the cold, glittering Atlantic, and when we stepped out of the car we were greeted by the sound of gulls and waves. Most of the living-room furniture had been moved to the basement, and extra tables joined to the main one to form a giant U. They were covered with tablecloths, set with white plates and silverware, and had centerpieces of gourds. I was struck by the toys and dolls that were everywhere, dogs that shed long yellow hairs on everything, all the photographs of Bonny and Sara and Deborah decorating the walls, still more plastering the refrigerator door. Food was being prepared when we arrived, something my mother always frowned upon, the kitchen a chaos of people and smells and enormous dirtied bowls.

Deborah's family, whom we remembered dimly from the wedding, was there, her parents and her brothers and sisters and their husbands and wives and boyfriends and babies. Her sisters were in their thirties, but, like Deborah, they could have been mistaken for college students, wearing jeans and clogs and fisherman sweaters, and her brother Matty, with whom I had danced in a circle at the wedding, was now a freshman at Amherst, with wide-set green eyes and wispy brown hair and a complexion that reddened easily. As soon as I saw Deborah's siblings, joking with one another as they chopped and stirred things in the kitchen, I was furious with my mother for making a scene before we left the house and forcing me to wear a shalwar kameez. I knew they assumed, from my clothing, that I had more in common with the other Bengalis than with them. But Deborah insisted on including me, setting me to work peeling apples with Matty, and out of my parents' sight I was given beer to drink. When the meal was ready, we were told where to sit, in an alternating boy-girl formation that made the Bengalis uncomfortable. Bottles of wine were lined up on the table. Two turkeys were brought out, one stuffed with sausage and one without. My mouth watered at the food, but I knew that afterward, on our way home, my mother would complain that it was all tasteless and bland. "Impossible," my mother said, shaking her hand over the top of her glass when someone tried to pour her a little wine.

Deborah's father, Gene, got up to say grace, and asked everyone at the table to join hands. He bowed his head and closed his eyes. "Dear Lord, we thank you today for the food we are about to receive," he began. My parents were seated next to each other, and I was stunned to see that they complied, that my father's brown fingers lightly clasped my mother's pale ones. I noticed Matty seated on the other side of the room, and saw him glancing at me as his father spoke. After the chorus of amens, Gene raised his glass and said, "Forgive me, but I never thought I'd have the opportunity to say this: Here's to Thanksgiving with the Indians." Only a few people laughed at the joke.

Then Pranab Kaku stood up and thanked everyone for coming. He was relaxed 25 from alcohol, his once wiry body beginning to thicken. He started to talk sentimentally about his early days in Cambridge, and then suddenly he recounted the story of meeting me and my mother for the first time, telling the guests about how he had followed us that afternoon. The people who did not know us laughed, amused by the description of the encounter, and by Pranab Kaku's desperation. He walked around the room to where my mother was sitting and draped a lanky arm around her shoulder, forcing her, for a brief moment, to stand up. "This woman," he declared, pulling her close to his side, "this woman hosted my first real Thanksgiving in America. It might have been an afternoon in May, but that first meal at Boudi's table was Thanksgiving to me. If it weren't for that meal, I would have gone back to Calcutta." My mother looked away, embarrassed. She was thirty-eight, already going gray, and she looked closer to my father's age than to Pranab Kaku's; regardless of his waistline, he retained his handsome, carefree looks. Pranab Kaku went back to his place at the head of the table, next to Deborah, and concluded, "And if that had been the case I'd have never met you, my darling," and he kissed her on the mouth in front of everyone, to much applause, as if it were their wedding day all over again.

After the turkey, smaller forks were distributed and orders were taken for three different kinds of pie, written on small pads by Deborah's sisters, as if they were waitresses. After dessert, the dogs needed to go out, and Pranab Kaku volunteered to take them. "How about a walk on the beach?" he suggested, and Deborah's side of the family agreed that that was an excellent idea. None of the Bengalis wanted to go, preferring to sit with their tea and cluster together, at last, at one end of the room, speaking freely after the forced chitchat with the Americans during the meal. Matty came over and sat in the chair beside me that was now empty, encouraging me to join the walk. When I hesitated, pointing to my inappropriate clothes and shoes but also aware of my mother's silent fury at the sight of us together, he said, "I'm sure Deb can lend you something." So I went upstairs, where Deborah gave me a pair of her jeans and a thick sweater and some sneakers, so that I looked like her and her sisters.

She sat on the edge of her bed, watching me change, as if we were girlfriends, and she asked if I had a boyfriend. When I told her no, she said, "Matty thinks you're cute."

"He told you?"

"No, but I can tell."

As I walked back downstairs, emboldened by this information, in the jeans   30
I'd had to roll up and in which I felt finally like myself, I noticed my mother lift
her eyes from her teacup and stare at me, but she said nothing, and off I went,
with Pranab Kaku and his dogs and his in-laws, along a road and then down
some steep wooden steps to the water. Deborah and one of her sisters stayed
behind, to begin the cleanup and see to the needs of those who remained. Initially, we all walked together, in a single row across the sand, but then I noticed
Matty hanging back, and so the two of us trailed behind, the distance between
us and the others increasing. We began flirting, talking of things I no longer
remember, and eventually we wandered into a rocky inlet and Matty fished a
joint out of his pocket. We turned our backs to the wind and smoked it, our
cold fingers touching in the process, our lips pressed to the same damp section
of the rolling paper. At first I didn't feel any effect, but then, listening to him
talk about the band he was in, I was aware that his voice sounded miles away,
and that I had the urge to laugh, even though what he was saying was not terribly funny. It felt as if we were apart from the group for hours, but when we
wandered back to the sand we could still see them, walking out onto a rocky
promontory to watch the sun set. It was dark by the time we all headed back to
the house, and I dreaded seeing my parents while I was still high. But when we
got there Deborah told me that my parents, feeling tired, had left, agreeing to
let someone drive me home later. A fire had been lit and I was told to relax and
have more pie as the leftovers were put away and the living room slowly put
back in order. Of course, it was Matty who drove me home, and sitting in my
parents' driveway I kissed him, at once thrilled and terrified that my mother
might walk onto the lawn in her nightgown and discover us. I gave Matty my
phone number, and for a few weeks I thought of him constantly, and hoped
foolishly that he would call.

In the end, my mother was right, and fourteen years after that Thanksgiving, after twenty-three years of marriage, Pranab Kaku and Deborah got
divorced. It was he who had strayed, falling in love with a married Bengali woman, destroying two families in the process. The other woman was
someone my parents knew, though not very well. Deborah was in her forties by then, Bonny and Sara away at college. In her shock and grief, it was
my mother whom Deborah turned to, calling and weeping into the phone.
Somehow, through all the years, she had continued to regard us as quasi in-
laws, sending flowers when my grandparents died, and giving me a compact
edition of the O.E.D. as a college-graduation present. "You knew him so well.
How could he do something like this?" Deborah asked my mother. And then,
"Did you know anything about it?" My mother answered truthfully that she
did not. Their hearts had been broken by the same man, only my mother's
had long ago mended, and in an odd way, as my parents approached their
old age, she and my father had grown fond of each other, out of habit if

nothing else. I believe my absence from the house, once I left for college, had something to do with this, because over the years, when I visited, I noticed a warmth between my parents that had not been there before, a quiet teasing, a solidarity, a concern when one of them fell ill. My mother and I had also made peace; she had accepted the fact that I was not only her daughter but a child of America as well. Slowly, she accepted that I dated one American man, and then another, and then yet another, that I slept with them, and even that I lived with one though we were not married. She welcomed my boyfriends into our home and when things didn't work out she told me I would find someone better. After years of being idle, she decided, when she turned fifty, to get a degree in library science at a nearby university.

On the phone, Deborah admitted something that surprised my mother: that all these years she had felt hopelessly shut out of a part of Pranab Kaku's life. "I was so horribly jealous of you back then, for knowing him, understanding him in a way I never could. He turned his back on his family, on all of you, really, but I still felt threatened. I could never get over that." She told my mother that she had tried, for years, to get Pranab Kaku to reconcile with his parents, and that she had also encouraged him to maintain ties with other Bengalis, but he had resisted. It had been Deborah's idea to invite us to their Thanksgiving; ironically, the other woman had been there, too. "I hope you don't blame me for taking him away from your lives, Boudi. I always worried that you did."

My mother assured Deborah that she blamed her for nothing. She confessed nothing to Deborah about her own jealousy of decades before, only that she was sorry for what had happened, that it was a sad and terrible thing for their family. She did not tell Deborah that a few weeks after Pranab Kaku's wedding, while I was at a Girl Scout meeting and my father was at work, she had gone through the house, gathering up all the safety pins that lurked in drawers and tins, and adding them to the few fastened to her bracelets. When she'd found enough, she pinned them to her sari one by one, attaching the front piece to the layer of material underneath, so that no one would be able to pull the garment off her body. Then she took a can of lighter fluid and a box of kitchen matches and stepped outside, into our chilly back yard, which was full of leaves needing to be raked. Over her sari she was wearing a knee-length lilac trenchcoat, and to any neighbor she must have looked as though she'd simply stepped out for some fresh air. She opened up the coat and removed the tip from the can of lighter fluid and doused herself, then buttoned and belted the coat. She walked over to the garbage barrel behind our house and disposed of the fluid, then returned to the middle of the yard with the box of matches in her coat pocket. For nearly an hour she stood there, looking at our house, trying to work up the courage to strike a match. It was not I who saved her, or my father, but our next-door neighbor, Mrs. Holcomb, with whom my mother had never been particularly friendly. She came out to rake the leaves in her yard, calling out to my mother and remarking how beautiful the sunset was. "I see you've been admiring it for a while now," she said. My mother agreed, and then she went back into the house. By the time my father and

I came home in the early evening, she was in the kitchen boiling rice for our dinner, as if it were any other day.

My mother told Deborah none of this. It was to me that she confessed, after my own heart was broken by a man I'd hoped to marry.

FOR ANALYSIS

1. Who is this story about? The **narrator**? Her mother? Both of them?

2. When the narrator changes out of traditional Indian dress and into some American-style clothing for a walk on the beach, she says that "I felt finally like myself" (para. 30). In this story, who determines who the narrator's self is?

3. At the end of "Hell-Heaven," Lahiri makes two unusual choices: she tells of the most shocking event of the story—the mother's near suicide, years after it happens—almost as an afterthought, and she only mentions (rather than presents as a scene) the important moment when the mother tells the daughter about it. What effect do these choices have? Why do you think Lahiri made them?

MAKING CONNECTIONS

Compare the **narrator's** mother in Lahiri's story and the main character in Charlotte Perkins Gilman's "The Yellow Wallpaper" (p. 551). Though their stories are very different, can you think of similarities between the two in terms of their lives and their reactions to them? How are they different on these same terms?

WRITING TOPICS

1. Clothes and food are two ways immigrants are distinguished, or distinguish themselves, from natives. Make a list of all the moments in the story when these details are included, and see if you can discern any patterns. Are they distributed evenly or randomly or do they cluster around significant moments?

2. Imagine this story with the mother as **narrator**. How would it be different? Why do you think Lahiri chose to tell the story the way she did?

The Science of Flight   2010

At lunch, Zichen told her two co-workers that she was considering going to a new place for her vacation. Feeling more adventurous this year? Ted said. Since Zichen had begun to work with Henry and Ted, thirteen years earlier, she had taken two weeks off every November to visit China—her hibernation retreat, as Ted called it. England, she said now when he asked, and she wondered which would be more adventurous in her colleagues' opinion, England or China.

Henry had been sent to Vietnam at eighteen, and had returned to Iowa six months later with ruptured intestines; at nineteen, barely recovered, he had married his high-school sweetheart. Every summer he and Caroline spent three weeks in a lakeside cabin in Wisconsin with their children and grandchildren. The farthest place Ted had travelled to was Chicago. A few years earlier, he had accompanied his daughter there for a high-school volleyball tournament; her team had lost in the final match, and with his daughter now a senior at the state university Ted still held Chicago responsible for the disappointment.

What's there to see in England in November? Ted asked. Zichen did not answer, because anything she said would fall short of his expectations. In previous years, he had wondered belligerently what there was to see in China, and Henry had been the one to shush Ted. Like Zichen's other acquaintances in America, they had been led to believe that in China she had a pair of parents, and that, like many, she had wedged some distance between herself and her parents, reducing her filial duty to an annual two-week visit.

What about China? Henry asked, laying out his lunch—a sandwich, a thermos of soup, and a banana—on a paper napkin. His time in the Army must have taught him to keep the contents of his life in good order. Henry was a neat man, his lab coat clean, what remained of his hair combed and parted precisely; he was quiet, but said enough not to seem sullen.

Her parents were taking a tour to Thailand with a group of retired people, 5 Zichen said. Why couldn't she meet them in Thailand? Ted demanded, and predicted that she would see nothing in England but rain and coldness and people who were too polite to ask her to repeat her name.

There was a reason to visit a place where one's name was unpronounceable, Zichen thought, just as there was a reason that her parents continued to share a life in their daughter's mind. A month from now, rather than telling Henry and Ted about England, Zichen knew she would be relating tales of her parents' trip to Thailand: the crowded marketplace after nightfall, the cabaret show that they disliked but felt obliged to enjoy because it was said to be the highlight of their tour, the hotel bed that was too hard, or perhaps too soft. There were other moments, also imagined, though these she would keep to herself: her father's insistence on splitting a dish in a restaurant because he was unwilling to pay for two, her mother eying a grain of rice on her father's sleeve without pointing it out. They would've been one of those couples who had married young, and had, over the years, developed their separate ways to live with the mistake, he with his tyranny, she with her wordless contempt.

Henry, Ted, and Zichen worked in an animal-care center, in a two-story brick building next to a research facility that a hundred years ago had been an infirmary for tuberculosis patients. Because they were on the edge of a university town—the facility, a satellite site that housed some projects from the medical school, was in the middle of cornfields—the three of them had over the years become a more or less autonomous unit. Janice, their supervisor, a tall and angular woman who took pride in her extreme fairness and efficiency, came for a routine inspection once a week; Dr. Wilson, the attending veterinarian, a genial and absent-minded man, was about to retire any day now. The only crisis since Zichen had begun to work there—if one did not count the time the water was contaminated and fifty cages of mice contracted hepatitis, or the occasions when breeding went wrong, and the due date passed without a litter, or worse, with a disturbed mother mouse feeding on her own babies—was when a group of animal-rights activists had tried to break into the building on the eve of the new millennium. They had given up when the alarm went off, and instead liberated cages of minks from a farm thirty miles west on the country road. The farmer and his family had recovered less than a third of their loss, the local paper had reported. The rest of the minks, the farmer had told the *Gazette*, would not survive the Midwest winter and their many predators.

Zichen had been reading the newspaper in the office, pondering the fate of the homeless minks, when Henry, looking over her shoulder, said that he and the farmer had gone to the same high school. She was about to express her sympathy for his old classmate when Henry mentioned that the guy had once pursued Caroline when he was in Vietnam. She was glad that Caroline had not married the mink farmer, Zichen said, and Henry said he was, too, though come to think about it, perhaps Caroline wouldn't have minded a mink coat. Ted, entering the office with a stack of yellow death slips to file and overhearing the conversation, reminded Henry that a mink farmer's wife does not wear mink, just as cobblers' children have no shoes. What does that mean? Zichen asked. When the expression was explained to her, she thought of the way her grandmother used to clip her hair shorter than a boy's, in summer or winter, but this would not make a good office tale.

Zichen had grown up in her grandmother's hair salon—a small shack really, at the entrance of an apartment complex, with a wooden plank propped up by two stacks of bricks that served as a bench for the waiting customers, a folding chair in front of a mirror that hung from a low beam, and a makeshift washstand, next to which a kettle of water was kept warm on a coal stove. On the curtain that separated the salon from the bed shared by Zichen and her grandmother, there were prints of bunnies, white on a green-and-yellow background. There was no window in the shack, and a fluorescent light was turned on the moment her grandmother opened up the shop and continued buzzing until the end of the day, giving everything a perpetual bluish-white hue.

That her grandmother could have had an easier life in her old age was 10 made clear to Zichen from her first years: Zichen's two uncles—her mother's elder brothers—would have dutifully taken in their mother, and between the two families they would have seen to it that she had a decent retirement. But how could you burden your own sons with a child like that? her grandmother used to ask her customers, as though the time Zichen had spent in the shop learning to sit up and then to walk, and later to assist her grandmother, handing her warm towels or cleaning the ashtrays—two blue-and-white china bowls placed at either end of the bench, the rims chipped, filled with smoldering cigarette ends and streaks of ash—had never softened the shock of the child's existence. It would have been a different story had she been an orphan, her grandmother would say; it would have been sensible for any uncle to take in an orphan, a statement her audience readily agreed with. Indeed, a woman who had run away with a man against her family's wish, who had given birth to a baby out of wedlock, and had then been abandoned by the man—that mother would have done her baby more of a favor had she died during childbirth.

It hadn't taken long for Zichen to piece together her own story from the parts alluded to by her grandmother and uncles and customers and neighbors: that her grandmother had agreed to raise her on the condition that her mother sever all connections with the family; that a couple had once come to the shop to look her over, but then decided not to adopt her; that she owed her life not only to her grandmother, who had to toil at an age when other women could rest, but also to the patrons of the shop, who remained loyal to her grandmother because of the responsibility they felt toward her.

Sitting on a bamboo stool in a corner and listening to her own luck, both good and bad, discussed, Zichen would clandestinely move her feet and make piles of hair according to a system known only to her. Inevitably the game would be interrupted by the strokes of her grandmother's broom, but even that did not disturb Zichen, as the disassembling of the small hills of hair could also be part of her scheme. Quit grinning like an idiot, her grandmother would sometimes tell Zichen, turning from her clipping, and Zichen would straighten her face, but when her grandmother turned back to her customer she smiled again at the back of a man's half-shaved head, or at the shoelaces of someone waiting on the bench. Where on earth did the girl get that smile? her grandmother complained to the customers. One would think a child like that should know how to make people forget her for a moment.

Hydrangea House, a sixteenth-century timber-framed house, had served as a family home for generations before it was turned into a B. and B.; Zichen wondered, reading the information provided on its Web site, how such a change had come about. Perhaps the owners would tell her when she asked—if not the whole story, then bits and pieces that would nevertheless delight her.

On the Web site, there were no photographs of the kind that other places, with more business-minded management, displayed: blooming flowers in a garden or soft-colored curtains lifted by unseen wind. Instead, a small sketch of the house, made in ink or perhaps pencil, showed little except a white-washed front wall and four rectangular windows. It was said to be "never a grand house"; two rooms, the Rose Room and the Lilac Room, were available upstairs.

The modest, almost apologetic way that Hydrangea House advertised itself 15 made it easy for Zichen to choose it. The trip to England, despite Henry's baf-flement and Ted's disapproval, was becoming a certainty in her mind. Tomor-row she would buy the plane ticket; next week she would call and reserve a room.

Contrary to Henry and Ted's beliefs, Zichen was neither an experienced nor a willing traveller. The summer she had begun to work at the animal-care center, Ted had invited her, along, with Caroline and Henry, to a picnic on the Fourth of July. She had apologized and said that she needed to go to the East Coast to visit her husband, who had finished graduate school earlier that year and moved away for a job.

Before the holiday weekend, she had purchased more food than she could consume, and for four days she had hidden herself in her apartment and worked slowly through a Latin reader of Cicero's speeches. She had picked up the book from the library not for any grand ideas she might glean from the text; sometimes she forgot a sentence the moment she figured out its meaning. But the effort of making sense out of something that was at first glance indeci-pherable satisfied her, as did the slowness of the activity: an hour or two would pass as she made her way through one passage on a war; a day that would have otherwise been long was shortened.

Her interest in a dead language had been one of the things her husband had held against her when he asked for the divorce, which to Zichen had come neither as a surprise nor as a disappointment. There was a practical order of things for an immigrant couple like them, he had once explained to her. They would start a family when they had finally made it, he'd said comfortingly when the baby that Zichen so desired, who must have sensed itself unwanted by its father, miscarried. He'd had plans for her to go to graduate school to become a statistician, or an accountant, or a nurse, part of that order of things that would help them make it in the new country; he was finishing a Ph.D. in mathematics, and had a goal of working on Wall Street. Zichen, never argu-ing, for arguing was not in her nature, nevertheless dismissed his blueprint for her career with unconcealed resistance. There was no use in her copying Latin vocabulary onto flashcards, he had yelled at her—only once, as yelling was not in his nature, either—when she had outraged him by missing the G.R.E. test he had registered her to take, wasting more than a hundred dollars, half a month's rent.

The marriage had ended shortly before he moved away, but Zichen had used him to excuse herself from two years of social life. The cheek of it. When she lied to Henry and Ted, she could hear her grandmother's words, those she would say after Zichen had read her report card aloud in the shop. Unable to concentrate, the teachers commented every year; a lack of interest in both studying and participating in school activities. Her grades were meagre, barely good enough for her to proceed to the next level. What will you do with your life if you don't catch up with your schoolwork? her grandmother's customers ceaselessly asked her; not knowing the answer, she would smile as though she did not understand the question, and it was her smile more than her grades that had marked her as beyond teachable.

Zichen had given Henry and Ted a skeletal account of her divorce the third   20 year into her work, as it had not felt right to continue to lie about a marriage that no longer existed. But an ex-husband was easy to be done with and never mentioned again, while a pair of parents, even if they lived on another continent, needed careful maintenance: an annual trip; phone calls that brought news from China; presents to take home—Wisconsin ginseng for her father, anti-aging cream for her mother.

She could easily take the usual trip back to China this year, a routine unbroken, thus causing little concern or suspense, but the truth was the shack that had housed her grandmother's shop had been demolished, her grandmother reduced to an urn of ashes. Her grandmother had lived in the shop until a month before her death, at ninety-three, and Zichen knew that for as long as her grandmother had lived there the shop door was opened every morning, the fluorescent light kept on till closing time, as it was during her annual visits. The news of the death had reached Zichen after the funeral; she had not been invited to it, as she knew her mother had not been. Together they, rather than an early widowhood, were blamed for her grandmother's harsh life; together they had been the old woman's disappointments, a daughter who had brought humiliation to the family, a granddaughter who had rashly married a man she had met twice and had then been unable to stay married for longer than three years.

The B. and B. was in a village called Neville Hill, some distance from Brighton, but to simplify the matter Zichen told Ted and Henry that Brighton was her final destination. They were eating lunch together, savoring one of the last warm autumn days before a cold front set in. She described the places she wanted to see: the promenade, the beach, the English Channel.

"Now, explain two things to me," Ted said, and for a moment Zichen thought Henry looked relieved that someone was going to confront her as he would never do. "First, why do you want to go to the beach in the winter?"

November was not winter yet, Zichen argued, and Ted merely nodded at her with a triumphant smile as though he had cornered a runaway rat that Zichen wasn't able to catch. It was rare that a mouse or a rat slipped through her grip, and when it did happen—a few times over the years—Ted would talk about it for days afterward with a childlike glee. When you touch an animal, it can tell right away if you are nervous or if you are the master, Henry had explained to Zichen when he trained her. Ted, during the first weeks, had liked to seek her out and tell her gruesome tales; his favorite one concerned a home-made rat guillotine that he and Henry had once built for a neurologist's study. But to her co-workers' surprise Zichen had never been jittery. She had applied for the opening because she had no other profitable skills, but in retrospect she wondered if she had found the right job out of blind luck. From the beginning, she had clipped a mouse's ear or prepped a rat for a skin graft as deftly as if she had always worked with animals. Even the bigger mammals had not distressed her: the monkeys that clamored in the cages and made faces at her when she came in with feed or a hose, the forlorn-looking dogs that rarely barked. After her training, Henry had told her that he and Ted would split the care of big-ger mammals because they thought her too small, for instance, to dispose of a thirty-pound carcass by herself. The Rodent Queen—on her thirtieth birth-day, they had left a toy crown on her desk, the words scrawled on with perma-nent marker.

"Now, winter or not winter," Ted said. "Why do you want to go to England all by yourself?" 25

People travelled alone all the time, Zichen said, and there was nothing wrong with that.

"But what are you going to do in a place where you don't know anyone?"

"How do you know I don't know anyone there?" Zichen said, but the moment the words came out she regretted them. Over the years she had become accustomed to who she was in other people's eyes: she knew she would be considered a loser by her Chinese acquaintances in America, a divorced woman toiling her life away in an animal-care facility, someone who had failed to make it; in her landlord's and neighbors' eyes she was the quiet, good-mannered foreigner who paid her rent on time, who every Halloween put out a couple of pumpkins, uncarved but with drawn-on eyes and mouths, and who had no visitors on weekends or holidays, so there was no conflict regarding the guest parking; for her grandmother and her aging customers, who spent their days in the shack for conversation and companionship more than for the care of their thinning hair or balding heads, she was—despite being a baby who should have remained unborn, a child with little merit and an unnerving man-ner, and a young woman who had no respect for marriage or her own future—a proof, in the end, of the ultimate mercy of life. She had been able to build a life out of her failures, to wire dollars to her grandmother, to return every year like a loyal homing pigeon and sit with the old customers, still with that unnerving smile on her face although they no longer cared; simply sitting with them and listening to them had absolved Zichen of all possible sins.

But it was who she was in the eyes of Henry and Ted that she cherished the most: sure-handed and efficient at her job, quiet yet at times chatty, uncomplicated. That she had memorized passages from "Winnie-the-Pooh," that she had read its Latin translation before reading the English text, she did not share with them, because that would make her an eccentric in their eyes. The things that gave her pleasure—the pile of wood shavings meant for the animals' bedding, which she assembled into small hills; the time she spent imagining her ex-husband in a pale-blue suburban house in New Jersey, his two sons growing up and looking more like him each year, his new wife unaging; the marriage she had given her father, whom she had never known, and her mother, whom she had met only once, in a small one-bedroom apartment in an older neighborhood in Beijing—these she did not share with Henry and Ted, because they would have made her a person with a history, in this or that time, this or that place,

"So, you are meeting someone in England?" Ted said.   30

"No," Zichen said. "Why should I?"

The unusual confrontational tone in her reply made Ted flinch, as though he had trespassed. He shrugged and, with a theatrical gesture, threw a half-eaten sandwich to a squirrel. Years earlier, Molly, Ted's wife, had asked Zichen if she wanted to meet someone she knew who was available; Henry's wife, Caroline, had mentioned once or twice her Chinese dentist, divorced, according to his office manager. When Zichen had not followed up on either lead, the women had not pressed her. Henry and Ted had never asked about her personal life. The ease into which the three of them had settled left her life outside work irrelevant, and she liked to imagine that for them it was as natural for her to cease to exist the moment she left work as it was natural that she could handle the animals with confidence and calm. The only time they had experienced discomfort was when Henry first trained her to breed the mice—he had asked Ted to be present when he showed her how to detect vaginal plugs, the evidence of successful copulation. Beet red, Henry had grabbed a few females to display their private parts to Zichen, then explained that sometimes the plugs did not guarantee pregnancy. Ted, rearranging the charts on the cages with a look of concentration, had remained uncharacteristically quiet on a subject that he might otherwise have joked about with Henry.

Had Ted been offended by her abruptness, Zichen wondered, but she could not find the words to soften the tension as he continued to whistle to the squirrel, which was ignoring his generosity. She had unwisely opened a door and then clumsily slammed it shut, but perhaps some harm had already been done.

"You'll do just fine," Henry said when it was apparent that Ted would not fill the rest of the lunch break with one of his favorite topics, the upcoming basketball game or a wrestling match. "When you think about it, I've seen my share of pictures of China but never any of England."

Zichen took pictures when she travelled to China, of things she imagined   35
Henry might like to see, or of strange sights that would offer Ted an opportunity

to criticize. Yes, she agreed. England would be a good change. She then dusted off the crumbs from the picnic table so that they would not find ants crawling over their space the next day. Before she had joined them, Henry and Ted used to eat in the office, the door open to the hallway with its constant odor of bleach and rodent pellets and damp bedding and dead animals; they did not seem to be bothered by this, but when Henry noticed that Zichen often sat on the steps in front of the building to eat her lunch, he had requested a picnic table as an improvement for their work environment.

Josephina, the proprietress of Hydrangea House, had been easy to talk with on the phone. If she had felt curious as to why a woman from America with an unpronounceable Chinese name would want to spend two weeks in Neville Hill she had not shown it. Zichen wondered, after the phone call, whether the thought would be shared with Josephina's husband; she wondered if they would decide that such a question did not matter in a bed-and-breakfast business.

When she got to Neville Hill, Zichen would explain to the owners that she had come in memory of an elderly woman who had befriended her when she first moved to America. Margaret was the woman's name. She had spent her childhood in Neville Hill before marrying an American pastor, John Hubor, and had lived in the States for fifty-three years. Would the couple at Hydrangea House try to locate a girl in the village's past, one who had left, taken away by a marriage after the war? Perhaps they had heard of a girl named Margaret, or perhaps they would apologize for having no such recollection. The truth was, the name Neville Hill had never been mentioned in any of Zichen's conversations with Margaret, yet it was Neville Hill that Zichen had decided to go to, her research fitting the village to an old woman's descriptions: the school trips to Seaford taken on foot; the car rides to Brighton for special family occasions.

It was in the spring of 1994 when Zichen had met Margaret and John, in a supermarket; the autumn of 1995 when Margaret had been buried in a hillside cemetery. In the aisle between shelves of sugar, flour, and cooking utensils, Margaret had mistaken Zichen for a Chinese student she knew, who had recently graduated and moved to California; John had invited Zichen to become their friend, as the woman before her must have been invited, whose name Margaret had used for Zichen for as long as she had visited their house.

She would describe Margaret to the couple at Hydrangea House, and tell them how Margaret had tutored her in English when she first arrived in America because she had wanted Zichen, a young woman who had left her country for marriage, to have a friendship.

Growing up, Zichen had never had a close friend. A bastard was what some 40 of the children at school had called her, the word learned from older siblings. Once, when Zichen was ten, and tired of being teased by her schoolmates, she had pointed to a neighbor who was passing by on the street and said that he was her real father. The man, overhearing Zichen's claim, had paled but said nothing—he had recently divorced, and his twin daughters had moved away with their mother.

The cheek of it; her grandmother would have been shocked by her shamelessness. The man Zichen had appointed as her father, a week later, asked her if she would like to see a butterfly exhibit that he perhaps imagined his own daughters would enjoy. Across the street from the park was the Friendship Hotel, and after the exhibit the man took her to the hotel entrance. It was one of only two hotels where foreigners were allowed to stay in Beijing, he explained; once, when he and his daughters were there, an American had given each of the girls a chocolate. It was ridiculous to stand in front of a hotel for the prospect of a chocolate; still, Zichen smiled at the two armed guards, and, later, at a pair of foreigners walking out of the hotel. The couple, both with pale skin and straw-colored hair, must have assumed that the man and Zichen were father and daughter, for they signalled and made it understood that they would take a picture of them. It was the first Polaroid Zichen had seen. The man had offered it to her, but she had refused to take it, the unspoken agreement being that their lives would go on as though the outing had never happened.

As a teen-ager she was one of the girls no one wanted to be close to; she was too strange and unpredictable to be a confidante, too inconspicuous to be a subject of any confidences. At that age, friendship had to offer drama or ease; she had been unable to provide either, and later, as a young woman, had been unable to provide either to attract a boy.

Yet it was ease she had offered in Margaret's brightly lit sunroom, giving the old woman the impression that she was tutoring Zichen, although the language they were studying was not English but Latin. Margaret's mind by then had been tangled, and Zichen, working by herself through "Wheelock's Latin," nonetheless allowed the old woman the luxury of repetitions: farmer, farmer, of the farmer, to the farmer, by the farmer, O farmer. Repeated, too, were the memories of Margaret's childhood village, which she must have known by then she would not be able to visit again: the trail that led to a secret pond, the couple in the red-roofed farmhouse giving birth to a baby who had six fingers on one hand. Every spring saw a batch of new chicks in the yard; in the summer the fluffy clouds sometimes stayed motionless for hours; any month could be called a rainy season, and the rain seemed to keep their house perpetually damp and chilly.

It was kind of Zichen to come and sit with Margaret, John had said the first time he drove her home at the end of the afternoon, apologizing for Margaret's confusions. She had come from a seaman's family, he had told Zichen on another ride home, as if that explained the fact that Margaret had picked up fourteen languages, when all of them, other than Latin and French and English, had been learned during her decades of marriage in America. Toward the summer of her last year, Margaret had shown signs of the approaching end, her words sometimes ungraspable even for John. Out of the blue one day she had produced a copy of "Winnie Ille Pu," the first edition of the Latin translation, for Zichen as a present; the translator, like Margaret and Zichen, was a man who had left home and settled in a foreign land, but that fact Zichen discovered only later.

No, she had not heard of "Winnie-the-Pooh," she had told John in the car 45 that day. She had not had any children's books when she was growing up. It must have been the gentle sadness in John's eyes that had made her tell him other things, of being called a bastard when young, of having miscarried a baby, of not loving her husband. John, a careful driver, had removed a hand from the steering wheel and held hers for the rest of the drive. Had that been a moment of deception? Zichen wondered sometimes; had she betrayed Margaret's friendship?—not because Margaret had ever learned of the moment from Zichen or from John but because Zichen had relived it now and again, long after Margaret had been buried and John had moved away to Sioux City, to be close to his children and eventually, as he had explained to Zichen after Margaret's funeral, to be placed in a nursing home.

Once a year in December, Henry took Ted and Zichen out for a drink in a nearby village called Tiffin, since none of them liked the places in the university town, where the music was too loud, and the college students made heartless noises. The bar was on a country road and was never full. The men there were older; some of them, the more talkative ones, had once played in a paintball league with Henry; others remained reticent. The bartender, a former wrestler who had been a state champion in high school, liked to tease Ted; every year, he asked him what color underwear he had on that day, for Ted, being Ted, had once bragged that he bought only two kinds: black-and-gold for the university's colors, and red-and-white for his high school, which was also his wife's and his daughter's alma mater. The men at the bar had always been courteous toward Zichen, but as the years went by they had grown more relaxed, raising their glasses to her when she arrived, calling her the Rodent Queen.

A mail-order bride she was, she had told the bartender one year, when she had drunk more than she should have. It was not true, for there had not been any business transaction in her marriage: she and her ex-husband had agreed to marry after meeting twice in a teahouse near her grandmother's shop, he choosing her because she had grown up in a harsh environment, which would make her a good companion in America, she choosing him because of America.

It had made her feel happy for a moment, voicing the words "mail-order bride" and watching the bartender take in the information with an acknowledgment that felt neither aloof nor unnecessarily concerned. It would make her happy, too, she knew, when she told the story in Hydrangea House about Margaret and reading "Winnie-the-Pooh" in Latin, about how she herself, inexperienced with the language, had let the poor bear's head thump and thump again on the stairs.

"Your father and I did what we could for you," Zichen's mother had said, the only time they had met, perhaps the only time, too, since giving birth to Zichen that she had put herself and Zichen's father in the same sentence. Zichen did not know why her mother had agreed to see her before her departure for America, but she had recognized, at the first sight of her mother, the sternness and the stubbornness she had grown used to in her grandmother's face. One's parents could do only so much, her mother had explained, and a child was responsible for her own life. Her mother had not told her anything about her father, saying only that they had long since lost contact; she had not said anything about her new family, either, even though Zichen had known there was one, with a husband and two children. That Zichen's grandmother had kept her in order to spite her rebellious and humiliated daughter Zichen had always known; that her mother had given birth to her in order to spite her father had become evident when they met.

Every year, on the drive back from the out-of-town bar, Zichen sat in the back of the car and quietly wept. Henry drove cautiously, both hands gripping the steering wheel, as he always did after a drink, while Ted, in the passenger seat, talked with expert knowledge about a coming basketball game. She blamed the alcohol for her tears—that, and the cold moon in the winter sky. 50

One year when Ted had asked to be dropped off first, to attend a wrestling; match, she had told Henry that she had grown up without knowing her parents' love for each other. Through the windshield she watched the frozen rain rushing toward them, and when the sound of the windshield wipers seemed too loud she said that her parents had stayed in the marriage because of her, and they had learned to tolerate each other for her sake. It was as close to the truth as she could get—she wished she could tell Henry about the man in front of the Friendship Hotel, or John's hand holding hers, but those stories would make her a different person in Henry's eyes—and afterward he patted her on the back as he walked her to her door, saying it was all right, because that was all he could say.

In Hydrangea House, perhaps she would tell the owners about her grandmother and her mother, the two women in her life whose blind passions had sustained them through the blows of fate, but even as she imagined that she knew she wouldn't. There was no way to leave herself out of their battle stories, and she knew that in all stories she must be left out—the life she had made for herself was a life of flight, of discarding the inessential and the essential alike, making use of the stolen pieces and memories, retreating to the lost moments of other people's lives.

FOR ANALYSIS

1. Why does Zichen's grandmother say of her, "One would think a child like that should know how to make people forget her for a moment" (para. 12)?

2. Why does Zichen lie to her coworkers?

3. Is there any significance to the fact that Zichen works where she does?

4. How do you think Li wants us to feel about Zichen? Is there a simple answer to this question? If not, why not?

MAKING CONNECTIONS

Both "The Science of Flight" and Dagoberto Gilb's "Uncle Rock" (p. 596) pair the experience of immigration with that of growing up with one or both parents absent. What about these two phenomena makes them an intriguing combination?

WRITING TOPICS

1. One of the remarkable aspects of "The Science of Flight" is Zichen's imagination. Imagine alternate realities for yourself and your family that you could present to your friends or coworkers. What would they entail? What might these stories say about you?

2. Imagine a different life for Zichen, though one that has the same unfortunate beginning. What other kinds of responses might this **character** have had to her circumstances? Are you able to imagine a happier ending for Zichen? Does your ablity to do so (or not do so) say something about your understanding of the power of a person's past to determine his or her future?

William Faulkner's "A Rose for Emily" is a classic example of a story depicting the tension between the community and the individual—a conflict that animates so much fiction. Ha Jin's "The Bridegroom" is a contemporary example, one that equals Faulkner's in addressing the more universal question of the fate of the individual in a world organized by groups. As you read these two stories, think about how the manner of their telling implicates not just the characters on whom the stories focus but also the tellers themselves. Think also about the endings of these stories, which reveal much about the character of the people, the complex social issues of the settings, and the larger difficulties of the human experience.

WILLIAM FAULKNER (1897–1962)

A ROSE FOR EMILY 1931

I

When Miss Emily Grierson died, our whole town went to her funeral: the men through a sort of respectful affection for a fallen monument, the women mostly out of curiosity to see the inside of her house, which no one save an old manservant—a combined gardener and cook—had seen in at least ten years.

It was a big, squarish frame house that had once been white, decorated with cupolas and spires and scrolled balconies in the heavily lightsome style of the seventies, set on what had once been our most select street. But garages and cotton gins had encroached and obliterated even the august names of that neighborhood; only Miss Emily's house was left, lifting its stubborn and coquettish decay above the cotton wagons and the gasoline pumps—an eyesore among eyesores. And now Miss Emily had gone to join the representatives of those august names where they lay in the cedar-bemused cemetery among the ranked and anonymous graves of Union and Confederate soldiers who fell at the battle of Jefferson.

Alive, Miss Emily had been a tradition, a duty, and a care; a sort of hereditary obligation upon the town, dating from that day in 1894 when Colonel Sartoris, the mayor—he who fathered the edict that no Negro woman should appear on the streets without an apron—remitted her taxes, the dispensation dating from the death of her father on into perpetuity. Not that Miss Emily would have accepted charity. Colonel Sartoris invented an involved tale to the effect that Miss Emily's father had loaned money to the town, which the town, as a matter of business, preferred this way of repaying. Only a man of Colonel

Sartoris' generation and thought could have invented it, and only a woman could have believed it.

When the next generation, with its more modern ideas, became mayors and aldermen, this arrangement created some little dissatisfaction. On the first of the year they mailed her a tax notice. February came, and there was no reply. They wrote her a formal letter, asking her to call at the sheriff's office at her convenience. A week later the mayor wrote her himself, offering to call or to send his car for her, and received in reply a note on paper of an archaic shape, in a thin, flowing calligraphy in faded ink, to the effect that she no longer went out at all. The tax notice was also enclosed, without comment.

They called a special meeting of the Board of Aldermen. A deputation 5 waited upon her, knocked at the door through which no visitor had passed since she ceased giving china-painting lessons eight or ten years earlier. They were admitted by the old Negro into a dim hall from which a stairway mounted into still more shadow. It smelled of dust and disuse—a close, dank smell. The Negro led them into the parlor. It was furnished in heavy, leather-covered furniture. When the Negro opened the blinds of one window, they could see that the leather was cracked; and when they sat down, a faint dust rose sluggishly about their thighs, spinning with slow motions in the single sun-ray. On a tarnished gilt easel before the fireplace stood a crayon portrait of Miss Emily's father.

They rose when she entered—a small, fat woman in black, with a thin gold chain descending to her waist and vanishing into her belt, leaning on an ebony cane with a tarnished gold head. Her skeleton was small and spare; perhaps that was why what would have been merely plumpness in another was obesity in her. She looked bloated, like a body long submerged in motionless water, and of that pallid hue. Her eyes, lost in the fatty ridges of her face, looked like two small pieces of coal pressed into a lump of dough as they moved from one face to another while the visitors stated their errand.

She did not ask them to sit. She just stood in the door and listened quietly until the spokesman came to a stumbling halt. Then they could hear the invisible watch ticking at the end of the gold chain.

Her voice was dry and cold. "I have no taxes in Jefferson. Colonel Sartoris explained it to me. Perhaps one of you can gain access to the city records and satisfy yourselves."

"But we have. We are the city authorities, Miss Emily. Didn't you get a notice from the sheriff, signed by him?"

"I received a paper, yes," Miss Emily said. "Perhaps he considers himself the 10 sheriff . . . I have no taxes in Jefferson."

"But there is nothing on the books to show that, you see. We must go by the—"

"See Colonel Sartoris." (Colonel Sartoris had been dead almost ten years.) "I have no taxes in Jefferson. Tobe!" The Negro appeared. "Show these gentlemen out."

II

So she vanquished them, horse and foot, just as she had vanquished their fathers thirty years before about the smell. That was two years after her father's death and a short time after her sweetheart—the one we believed would marry her—had deserted her. After her father's death she went out very little; after her sweetheart went away, people hardly saw her at all. A few of the ladies had the temerity to call, but were not received, and the only sign of life about the place was the Negro man—a young man then—going in and out with a market basket.

"Just as if a man—any man—could keep a kitchen properly," the ladies said; so they were not surprised when the smell developed. It was another link between the gross, teeming world and the high and mighty Griersons.

A neighbor, a woman, complained to the mayor, Judge Stevens, eighty years old. 15

"But what will you have me do about it, madam?" he said.

"Why, send her word to stop it," the woman said. "Isn't there a law?"

"I'm sure that won't be necessary," Judge Stevens said. "It's probably just a snake or a rat that nigger of hers killed in the yard. I'll speak to him about it."

The next day he received two more complaints, one from a man who came in diffident deprecation. "We really must do something about it, Judge. I'd be the last one in the world to bother Miss Emily, but we've got to do something." That night the Board of Aldermen met—three graybeards and one younger man, a member of the rising generation.

"It's simple enough," he said. "Send her word to have her place cleaned up. 20
Give her a certain time to do it in, and if she don't . . ."

"Dammit, sir," Judge Stevens said, "will you accuse a lady to her face of smelling bad?"

So the next night, after midnight, four men crossed Miss Emily's lawn and slunk about the house like burglars, sniffing along the base of the brickwork and at the cellar openings while one of them performed a regular sowing motion with his hand out of a sack slung from his shoulder. They broke open the cellar door and sprinkled lime there, and in all the outbuildings. As they recrossed the lawn, a window that had been dark was lighted and Miss Emily sat in it, the light behind her, and her upright torso motionless as that of an idol. They crept quietly across the lawn and into the shadow of the locusts that lined the street. After a week or two the smell went away.

That was when people had begun to feel really sorry for her. People in our town, remembering how old lady Wyatt, her great-aunt, had gone completely crazy at last, believed that the Griersons held themselves a little too high for what they really were. None of the young men were quite good enough for Miss Emily and such. We had long thought of them as a tableau, Miss Emily a slender figure in white in the background, her father a spraddled silhouette in the foreground, his back to her and clutching a horsewhip, the two of them framed by the back-flung front door. So when she got to be thirty and was still single, we were not pleased exactly, but vindicated; even with insanity in the family she wouldn't have turned down all of her chances if they had really materialized.

When her father died, it got about that the house was all that was left to her; and in a way, people were glad. At last they could pity Miss Emily. Being left alone, and a pauper, she had become humanized. Now she too would know the old thrill and the old despair of a penny more or less.

The day after his death all the ladies prepared to call at the house and offer   25 condolence and aid, as is our custom. Miss Emily met them at the door, dressed as usual and with no trace of grief on her face. She told them that her father was not dead. She did that for three days, with the ministers calling on her, and the doctors, trying to persuade her to let them dispose of the body. Just as they were about to resort to law and force, she broke down, and they buried her father quickly.

We did not say she was crazy then. We believed she had to do that. We remembered all the young men her father had driven away, and we knew that with nothing left, she would have to cling to that which had robbed her, as people will.

III

She was sick for a long time. When we saw her again, her hair was cut short, making her look like a girl, with a vague resemblance to those angels in colored church windows—sort of tragic and serene.

The town had just let the contracts for paving the sidewalks, and in the summer after her father's death they began the work. The construction company came with niggers and mules and machinery, and a foreman named Homer Barron, a Yankee—a big, dark, ready man, with a big voice and eyes lighter than his face. The little boys would follow in groups to hear him cuss the niggers, and the niggers singing in time to the rise and fall of picks. Pretty soon he knew everybody in town. Whenever you heard a lot of laughing anywhere about the square, Homer Barron would be in the center of the group. Presently we began to see him and Miss Emily on Sunday afternoons driving in the yellow-wheeled buggy and the matched team of bays from the livery stable.

At first we were glad that Miss Emily would have an interest, because the ladies all said, "Of course a Grierson would not think seriously of a Northerner, a day laborer." But there were still others, older people, who said that even grief could not cause a real lady to forget *noblesse oblige*—without calling it *noblesse oblige*. They just said, "Poor Emily. Her kinsfolk should come to her." She had some kin in Alabama; but years ago her father had fallen out with them over the estate of old lady Wyatt, the crazy woman, and there was no communication between the two families. They had not even been represented at the funeral.

And as soon as the old people said, "Poor Emily," the whispering began.   30 "Do you suppose it's really so?" they said to one another. "Of course it is.

What else could . . ." This behind their hands; rustling of craned silk and satin behind jalousies closed upon the sun of Sunday afternoon as the thin, swift clop-clop-clop of the matched team passed: "Poor Emily."

She carried her head high enough—even when we believed that she was fallen. It was as if she demanded more than ever the recognition of her dignity as the last Grierson; as if it had wanted that touch of earthiness to reaffirm her imperviousness. Like when she bought the rat poison, the arsenic. That was over a year after they had begun to say "Poor Emily," and while the two female cousins were visiting her.

"I want some poison," she said to the druggist. She was over thirty then, still a slight woman, though thinner than usual, with cold, haughty black eyes in a face the flesh of which was strained across the temples and about the eye-sockets as you imagine a lighthouse-keeper's face ought to look. "I want some poison," she said.

"Yes, Miss Emily. What kind? For rats and such? I'd recom—"

"I want the best you have. I don't care what kind."

The druggist named several. "They'll kill anything up to an elephant. But 35 what you want is—"

"Arsenic," Miss Emily said. "Is that a good one?"

"Is . . . arsenic? Yes, ma'am. But what you want—"

"I want arsenic."

The druggist looked down at her. She looked back at him, erect, her face like a strained flag. "Why, of course," the druggist said. "If that's what you want. But the law requires you to tell what you are going to use it for."

Miss Emily just stared at him, her head tilted back in order to look him eye 40 for eye, until he looked away and went and got the arsenic and wrapped it up. The Negro delivery boy brought her package; the druggist didn't come back. When she opened the package at home there was written on the box, under the skull and bones: "For rats."

IV

So the next day we all said, "She will kill herself"; and we said it would be the best thing. When she had first begun to be seen with Homer Barron, we had said, "She will marry him." Then we said, "She will persuade him yet," because Homer himself had remarked—he liked men, and it was known that he drank with the younger men in the Elks' Club—that he was not a marrying man. Later we said, "Poor Emily" behind the jalousies as they passed on Sunday afternoon in the glittering buggy, Miss Emily with her head high and Homer Barron with his hat cocked and a cigar in his teeth, reins and whip in a yellow glove.

Then some of the ladies began to say that it was a disgrace to the town and a bad example to the young people. The men did not want to interfere, but at last the ladies forced the Baptist minister—Miss Emily's people were Episcopal—to call upon her. He would never divulge what happened during that interview, but he refused to go back again. The next Sunday they again drove about the streets, and the following day the minister's wife wrote to Miss Emily's relations in Alabama.

So she had blood-kin under her roof again and we sat back to watch developments. At first nothing happened. Then we were sure that they were to be married. We learned that Miss Emily had been to the jeweler's and ordered a man's toilet set in silver, with the letters H.B. on each piece. Two days later we learned that she had bought a complete outfit of men's clothing, including a nightshirt, and we said, "They are married." We were really glad. We were glad because the two female cousins were even more Grierson than Miss Emily had ever been.

So we were not surprised when Homer Barron—the streets had been finished some time since—was gone. We were a little disappointed that there was not a public blowing-off, but we believed that he had gone on to prepare for Miss Emily's coming, or to give her a chance to get rid of the cousins. (By that time it was a cabal, and we were all Miss Emily's allies to help circumvent the cousins.) Sure enough, after another week they departed. And, as we had expected all along, within three days Homer Barron was back in town. A neighbor saw the Negro man admit him at the kitchen door at dusk one evening.

And that was the last we saw of Homer Barron. And of Miss Emily for some 45 time. The Negro man went in and out with the market basket, but the front door remained closed. Now and then we would see her at the window for a moment, as the men did that night when they sprinkled the lime, but for almost six months she did not appear on the streets. Then we knew that this was to be expected too; as if that quality of her father which had thwarted her woman's life so many times had been too virulent and too furious to die.

When we next saw Miss Emily, she had grown fat and her hair was turning gray. During the next few years it grew grayer and grayer until it attained an even pepper-and-salt iron-gray, when it ceased turning. Up to the day of her death at seventy-four it was still that vigorous iron-gray, like the hair of an active man.

From that time on her front door remained closed, save during a period of six or seven years, when she was about forty, during which she gave lessons in china-painting. She fitted up a studio in one of the downstairs rooms, where the daughters and granddaughters of Colonel Sartoris' contemporaries were sent to her with the same regularity and in the same spirit that they were sent to church on Sundays with a twenty-five-cent piece for the collection plate. Meanwhile her taxes had been remitted.

Then the newer generation became the backbone and the spirit of the town, and the painting pupils grew up and fell away and did not send their children to her with boxes of color and tedious brushes and pictures cut from the ladies' magazines. The front door closed upon the last one and remained closed for good. When the town got free postal delivery, Miss Emily alone refused to let them fasten the metal numbers above her door and attach a mailbox to it. She would not listen to them.

Daily, monthly, yearly we watched the Negro grow grayer and more stooped, going in and out with the market basket. Each December we sent her a tax notice, which would be returned by the post office a week later, unclaimed. Now and then we would see her in one of the downstairs windows—she had evidently shut up the top floor of the house—like the carven torso of an idol in a niche, looking or not looking at us, we could never tell which. Thus she passed from generation to generation—dear, inescapable, impervious, tranquil, and perverse.

And so she died. Fell ill in the house filled with dust and shadows, with only 50 a doddering Negro man to wait on her. We did not even know she was sick; we had long since given up trying to get any information from the Negro. He talked to no one, probably not even to her, for his voice had grown harsh and rusty, as if from disuse.

She died in one of the downstairs rooms, in a heavy walnut bed with a curtain, her gray head propped on a pillow yellow and moldy with age and lack of sunlight.

V

The Negro met the first of the ladies at the front door and let them in, with their hushed, sibilant voices and their quick, curious glances, and then he disappeared. He walked right through the house and out the back and was not seen again.

The two female cousins came at once. They held the funeral on the second day, with the town coming to look at Miss Emily beneath a mass of bought flowers, with the crayon face of her father musing profoundly above the bier and the ladies sibilant and macabre; and the very old men—some in their brushed Confederate uniforms—on the porch and the lawn, talking of Miss Emily as if she had been a contemporary of theirs, believing they had danced with her and courted her perhaps, confusing time with its mathematical progression, as the old do, to whom all the past is not a diminishing road but, instead, a huge meadow which no winter ever quite touches, divided from them now by the narrow bottle-neck of the most recent decade of years.

Already we knew that there was one room in that region above stairs which no one had seen in forty years, and which would have to be forced. They waited until Miss Emily was decently in the ground before they opened it.

The violence of breaking down the door seemed to fill this room with per- 55 vading dust. A thin, acrid pall as of the tomb seemed to lie everywhere upon this room decked and furnished as for a bridal: upon the valance curtains of faded rose color, upon the rose-shaded lights, upon the dressing table, upon the delicate array of crystal and the man's toilet things backed with tarnished silver, silver so tarnished that the monogram was obscured. Among them lay a collar and tie, as if they had just been removed, which, lifted, left upon the surface a pale crescent in the dust. Upon a chair hung the suit, carefully folded; beneath it the two mute shoes and the discarded socks.

The man himself lay in the bed.

For a long while we just stood there, looking down at the profound and fleshless grin. The body had apparently once lain in the attitude of an embrace, but now the long sleep that outlasts love, that conquers even the grimace of love, had cuckolded him. What was left of him, rotted beneath what was left of the nightshirt, had become inextricable from the bed in which he lay; and upon him and upon the pillow beside him lay that even coating of the patient and biding dust.

Then we noticed that in the second pillow was the indentation of a head. One of us lifted something from it, and leaning forward, that faint and invisible dust dry and acrid in the nostrils, we saw a long strand of iron-gray hair.

FOR ANALYSIS

1. Why does Faulkner title the narrative "A Rose for Emily"?

2. At the end of section II, the **narrator** says, "We remembered all the young men her father had driven away." What is the significance of this statement? How would you characterize Emily's relationship with her father? Her father's relationship with the town?

3. In section III, we learn that "the ladies all said, 'Of course a Grierson would not think seriously of a Northerner, a day laborer.' " Why not? What are Emily's alternatives?

4. What is the effect of the final paragraph?

5. Why does the narrator use the pronoun *we*? The narrator often speaks of "the town." What does "the town" signify?

6. Reread the description of Emily's house in paragraph 2. What does this description suggest?

7. What does the author accomplish by not presenting the story in chronological order?

WRITING TOPICS

1. Write a brief essay discussing the role of time in this story. How does the town's response to the Griersons in general, and Emily in particular, change as time passes?

2. Write an essay arguing for or against the assertion that Emily's father determined the course of her life.

HA JIN (B. 1956)

THE BRIDEGROOM 1999

Before Beina's father died, I promised him that I'd take care of his daughter. He and I had been close friends for twenty years. He left his only child with me because my wife and I had no children of our own. It was easy to keep my word when Beina was still a teenager. As she grew older, it became more difficult, not because she was willful or troublesome but because no man was interested in her, a short, homely girl. When she turned twenty-three and still had no boyfriend,

I began to worry. Where could I find her a husband? Timid and quiet, she didn't know how to get close to a man. I was afraid she'd become an old maid.

Then out of the blue Baowen Huang proposed to her. I found myself at a loss, because they'd hardly known each other. How could he be serious about his offer? I feared he might make a fool of Beina, so I insisted they get engaged if he meant business. He came to my home with two trussed-up capons, four cartons of Ginseng cigarettes, two bottles of Five Grains' Sap, and one tall tin of oolong tea. I was pleased, though not very impressed by his gifts.

Two months later they got married. My colleagues congratulated me, saying, "That was fast, Old Cheng."

What a relief to me. But to many young women in our sewing-machine factory, Beina's marriage was a slap in the face. They'd say, "A hen cooped up a peacock." Or, "A fool always lands in the arms of fortune." True, Baowen had been one of the most handsome unmarried men in the factory, and nobody had expected that Beina, stocky and stout, would win him. What's more, Baowen was good-natured and well educated—a middle-school graduate—and he didn't smoke or drink or gamble. He had fine manners and often smiled politely, showing his bright, straight teeth. In a way he resembled a woman, delicate, clear-skinned, and soft-spoken; he even could knit things out of wool. But no men dared bully him because he was skilled at martial arts. Three times in a row he had won the first prize for kung fu at our factory's annual sports meet. He was very good at the long sword and freestyle boxing. When he was in middle school, bigger boys had often picked on him, so his stepfather had sent him to the martial arts school in their hometown. A year later nobody would ever bug him again.

Sometimes I couldn't help wondering why Baowen had chosen Beina. 5 What in her had caught his heart? Did he really like her fleshy face, which often reminded me of a globefish? Although we had our doubts, my wife and I couldn't say anything negative about the marriage. Our only concern was that Baowen might be too good for our nominal daughter. Whenever I heard that somebody had divorced, I'd feel a sudden flutter of panic.

As the head of the Security Section in the factory, I had some pull and did what I could to help the young couple. Soon after their wedding I secured them a brand-new two-bedroom apartment, which angered some people waiting in line for housing. I wasn't daunted by their criticism. I'd do almost anything to make Beina's marriage stable, because I believed that if it survived the first two years, it might last decades—once Baowen became a father, it would be difficult for him to break loose.

But after they'd been married for eight months, Beina still wasn't pregnant. I was afraid that Baowen would soon grow tired of her and run after another woman, since many young women in the factory were still attracted to him. A brazen one even declared that she'd leave her door open for him all night long. Some of them frequently offered him movie tickets and meat coupons. It seemed that they were determined to wreck Beina's marriage. I hated them, and just the thought of them would give me an earache or a sour stomach.

Fortunately, Baowen hadn't yet done anything outside the bounds of a decent husband.

One morning in early November, Beina stepped into my office. "Uncle," she said in a tearful voice, "Baowen didn't come home last night."

I tried to remain calm, though my head began to swim. "Do you know where he's been?" I asked.

"I don't know. I looked for him everywhere." She licked her cracked lips 10 and took off her green work cap, her hair in a huge bun.

"When did you see him last?"

"At dinner yesterday evening. He said he was going to see somebody. He has lots of buddies in town."

"Is that so?" I didn't know he had many friends. "Don't worry. Go back to your workshop and don't tell anybody about this. I'll call around and find him."

She dragged herself out of my office. She must have gained at least a dozen pounds since the wedding. Her blue dungarees had become so tight that they seemed about to burst. Viewed from behind, she looked like a giant turnip.

I called the Rainbow Movie Theater, Victory Park, and a few restaurants 15 in town. They all said they had not seen anyone matching Baowen's description. Before I could phone the city library, where Baowen sometimes spent his weekends, a call came in. It was from the city's Public Security Bureau. The man on the phone said they'd detained a worker of ours named Baowen Huang. He wouldn't tell me what had happened. He just said, "Indecent activity. Come as soon as you can."

It was a cold day. As I cycled toward downtown, the shrill north wind kept flipping up the front ends of my overcoat. My knees were sore, and I couldn't help shivering. Soon my asthma tightened my throat and I began moaning. I couldn't stop cursing Baowen. "I knew it. I just knew it," I said to myself. I had sensed that sooner or later he'd seek pleasure with another woman. Now he was in the police's hands, and the whole factory would talk about him. How could Beina take this blow?

At the Public Security Bureau I was surprised to see that about a dozen officials from other factories, schools, and companies were already there. I knew most of them, who were in charge of security affairs at their workplaces. A policewoman conducted us into a conference room upstairs, where green silk curtains hung in the windows. We sat down around a long mahogany table and waited to be briefed about the case. The glass tabletop was brand new, its edge still sharp. I saw worry and confusion on the other men's faces. I figured Baowen must have been involved in an organized crime—either an orgy or a gang rape. On second thought I felt he couldn't have been a rapist; by nature he was kindhearted, very gentle. I hoped this was not a political case, which would be absolutely unpardonable. Six or seven years ago a half-wit and a high school graduate had started an association in our city, named the China Liberation Party, which had later recruited nine members. Although the sparrow is small it has a complete set of organs—their party elected a chairman, a secretary, and even a prime minister. But before they could print their manifesto, which expressed their intention to overthrow the government, the police rounded them up. Two of the top leaders were executed, and the rest of the members were jailed.

As I was wondering about the nature of Baowen's crime, a middle-aged man came in. He had a solemn face, and his eyes were half closed. He took off his dark blue tunic, hung it on the back of a chair, and sat down at the end of the table. I recognized him; he was Chief Miao of the Investigation Department. Wearing a sheepskin jerkin, he somehow reminded me of Genghis Khan, thick-boned and round-faced. His hooded eyes were shrewd, though they looked sleepy. Without any opening remarks he declared that we had a case of homosexuality on our hands. At that, the room turned noisy. We'd heard of the term but didn't know what it meant exactly. Seeing many of us puzzled, Chief Miao explained, "It's a social disease, like gambling, or prostitution, or syphilis." He kept on squirming as if itchy with hemorrhoids.

A young man from the city's Fifth Middle School raised his hand. He asked, "What do homosexuals do?"

Miao smiled and his eyes almost disappeared. He said, "People of the same   20
sex have a sexual relationship."

"Sodomy!" cried someone.

The room turned quiet for at least ten seconds. Then somebody asked what kind of crime this was.

Chief Miao explained, "Homosexuality originated from Western capitalism and bourgeois lifestyle. According to our law it's dealt with as a kind of hooliganism. Therefore, every one of the men we arrested will serve a sentence, from six months to five years, depending on the severity of his crime and his attitude toward it."

A truck blew its horn on the street and made my heart twinge. If Baowen went to prison, Beina would live like a widow, unless she divorced him. Why had he married her to begin with? Why did he ruin her this way?

What had happened was that a group of men, mostly clerks, artists, and   25
schoolteachers, had formed a club called Men's World, a salon of sorts. Every Thursday evening they'd met in a large room on the third floor of the office building of the Forestry Institute. Since the club admitted only men, the police suspected that it might be a secret association with a leaning toward violence, so they assigned two detectives to mix with the group. True, some of the men appeared to be intimate with each other in the club, but most of the time they talked about movies, books, and current events. Occasionally music was played, and they danced together. According to the detectives' account, it was a bizarre, emotional scene. A few men appeared in pairs, unashamed of necking and cuddling in the presence of others, and some would say with tears, "At last we men have a place for ourselves." A middle-aged painter wearing earrings exclaimed, "Now I feel alive! Only in here can I stop living in hypocrisy." Every week two or three new faces would show up. When the club grew close to the size of thirty men, the police took action and arrested them all.

After Chief Miao's briefing, we were allowed to meet with the criminals for fifteen minutes. A policeman led me into a small room in the basement and let me read Baowen's confession while he went to fetch him. I glanced through the four pages of interrogation notes, which stated that Baowen had been new to the club and that he'd joined them only twice, mainly because he was interested in their talks. Yet he didn't deny that he was a homosexual.

The room smelled of urine, since it was next to a bathroom. The policeman took Baowen in and ordered him to sit opposite me at the table. Baowen, in handcuffs, avoided looking at me. His face was bloated, covered with bruises. A broad welt left by a baton, about four inches long, slanted across his forehead. The collar of his jacket was torn open. Yet he didn't appear frightened. His calm manner angered me, though I felt sorry for him.

I kept a hard face, and said, "Baowen, do you know you committed a crime?"

"I didn't do anything. I just went there to listen to them talk."

"You mean you didn't do that thing with any man?" I wanted to make sure 30 so that I could help him.

He looked at me, then lowered his eyes, saying, "I might've done something, to be honest, but I didn't."

What's that supposed to mean?

"I—liked a man in the club, a lot. If he'd asked me, I might've agreed." His lips curled upward as if he prided himself on what he had said.

"You're sick!" I struck the table with my knuckles.

To my surprise, he said, "So? I'm a sick man. You think I don't know that?" 35

I was bewildered. He went on, "Years ago I tried everything to cure myself. I took a lot of herbs and boluses, and even ate baked scorpions, lizards, and toads. Nothing helped me. Still I'm fond of men. I don't know why I'm not interested in women. Whenever I'm with a woman my heart is as calm as a stone."

Outraged by his confession, I asked, "Then why did you marry my Beina? To make fun of her, eh? To throw mud in my face?"

"How could I be that mean? Before we got married, I told her I didn't like women and might not give her a baby."

"She believed you?"

"Yes. She said she wouldn't mind. She just wanted a husband." 40

"She's an idiot!" I unfolded my hanky and blew my clogged nose into it, then asked, "Why did you choose her if you had no feelings for her at all?"

"What was the difference? For me she was similar to other women."

"You're a scoundrel!"

"If I didn't marry her, who would? The marriage helped us both, covering me and saving face for her. Besides, we could have a good apartment—a home. You see, I tried living like a normal man. I've never been mean to Beina."

"But the marriage is a fake! You lied to your mother too, didn't you?" 45

"She wanted me to marry."

The policeman signaled that our meeting was over. In spite of my anger, I told Baowen that I'd see what I could do, and that he'd better cooperate with the police and show a sincere attitude.

What should I do? I was sick of him, but he belonged to my family, at least in name, and I was obligated to help him.

On the way home I pedaled slowly, my mind heavy with thoughts. Gradually I realized that I might be able to do something to prevent him from going to jail. There were two steps I could take: first, I would maintain that he had done nothing in the club, so as to isolate him from those real criminals; second, I would present him as a sick man, so that he might receive medical treatment instead of a prison term. Once he became a criminal, he'd be marked forever as an enemy of society, no longer redeemable. Even his children might suffer. I ought to save him.

Fortunately both the party secretary and the director of our factory were willing to accept Baowen as a sick man, particularly Secretary Zhu, who liked Baowen's kung-fu style and had once let him teach his youngest son how to use a three-section cudgel. Zhu suggested we make an effort to rescue Baowen from the police. He said to me in the men's room inside our office building, "Old Cheng, we must not let Baowen end up in prison." I was grateful for his words. 50

All of a sudden homosexuality became a popular topic in the factory. A few old workers said that some actors of the Beijing opera had slept together as lovers in the old days, because no women were allowed to perform in any troupe and the actors could spend time with men only. Secretary Zhu, who was well read, said that some emperors in the Han Dynasty had owned male lovers in addition to their large harems. Director Liu had heard that the last emperor, Puyi, had often ordered his eunuchs to suck his penis and caress his testicles. Someone even claimed that homosexuality was an upper-class thing, not something for ordinary people. All the talk sickened me. I felt ashamed of my nominal son-in-law. I wouldn't join them in talking and just listened, pretending I wasn't bothered.

As I expected, rumors went wild in the factory, especially in the foundry shop. Some people said Baowen was impotent. Some believed he was a hermaphrodite, otherwise his wife would've been pregnant long ago.

To console Beina, I went to see her one evening. She had a pleasant home, in which everything was in order. Two bookcases, filled with industrial manuals, biographies, novels, and medical books, stood against the whitewashed wall, on either side of the window. In one corner of the living room was a coat tree on which hung the red feather parka Baowen had bought her before their wedding, and in another corner sat a floor lamp. At the opposite end of the room two pots of blooming flowers, one of cyclamens and the other of Bengal roses, were placed on a pair of low stools kept at an equal distance from each other and from the walls on both sides. Near the inner wall, beside a yellow enamel spittoon, was a large sofa upholstered in orange imitation leather. A black-and-white TV perched on an oak chest against the outer wall.

I was impressed, especially by the floor inlaid with bricks and coated with bright red paint. Even my wife couldn't keep a home so neat. No doubt it was Baowen's work, because Beina couldn't be so tidy. Already the room showed the trace of her sloppy habits—in a corner were scattered an empty flour sack and a pile of soiled laundry. Sipping the tea she had poured me, I said, "Beina, I'm sorry about Baowen. I didn't know he was so bad."

"No, he's a good man." Her round eyes looked at me with a steady light.   55

"Why do you say that?"

"He's been good to me."

"But he can't be a good husband, can he?"

"What do you mean?"

I said bluntly, "He didn't go to bed with you very often, did he?"   60

"Oh, he can't do that because he practices kung fu. He said if he slept with a woman, all his many years' work would be gone. From the very beginning his master told him to avoid women."

"So you don't mind?" I was puzzled, saying to myself, What a stupid girl.

"Not really."

"But you two must've shared the bed a couple of times, haven't you?"

"No, we haven't."   65

"Really? Not even once?"

"No." She blushed a little and looked away, twisting her earlobe with her fingertips.

My head was reeling. After eight months' marriage she was still a virgin! And she didn't mind! I lifted the cup and took a large gulp of the jasmine tea.

A lull settled in. We both turned to watch the evening news; my numb mind couldn't take in what the anchorwoman said about a border skirmish between Vietnamese and Chinese troops.

A moment later I told Beina, "I'm sorry he has such a problem. If only we   70 had known."

"Don't feel so bad, Uncle. In fact he's better than a normal man."

"How so?"

"Most men can't stay away from pretty women, but Baowen just likes to have a few buddies. What's wrong with that? It's better this way, 'cause I don't have to worry about those shameless bitches in our factory. He won't bother to give them a look. He'll never have a lifestyle problem."

I almost laughed, wondering how I should explain to her that he could have a sexual relationship with a man and that he'd been detained precisely because of a lifestyle problem. On second thought I realized it might be better for her to continue to think that way. She didn't need more stress at the moment.

Then we talked about how to help Baowen. I told her to write a report,   75 emphasizing what a good, considerate husband he'd been. Of course she must not mention his celibacy in their marriage. Also, from now on, however vicious her fellow workers' remarks were, she should ignore them and never talk back, as if she'd heard nothing.

That night when I told my wife about Beina's silly notions, she smiled, saying, "Compared with most men, Baowen isn't too bad. Beina's not a fool."

I begged Chief Miao and a high-ranking officer to treat Baowen leniently and even gave each of them two bottles of brandy and a coupon for a Butterfly sewing machine. They seemed willing to help but wouldn't promise me anything. For days I was so anxious that my wife was afraid my ulcer might recur.

One morning the Public Security Bureau called, saying they had accepted our factory's proposal and would have Baowen transferred to the mental hospital in a western suburb, provided our factory agreed to pay for his hospitalization. I accepted the offer readily, feeling relieved. Later, I learned that there wasn't enough space in the city's prison for twenty-seven gay men, who couldn't be mixed with other inmates and had to be put in solitary cells. So only four of them were jailed; the rest were either hospitalized (if their work units agreed to pay for the medical expenses) or sent to some labor farms to be reformed. The two party members among them didn't go to jail, though they were expelled from the party, a very severe punishment that ended their political lives.

The moment I put down the phone, I hurried to the assembly shop and found Beina. She broke into tears at the good news. She ran back home and filled a duffel bag with Baowen's clothes. We met at my office, then together set out for the Public Security Bureau. I rode my bicycle while she sat behind me, embracing the duffel as if it were a baby. With a strong tailwind, the cycling was easy and fast, so we arrived before Baowen left for the hospital. He was waiting for a van in front of the police station, accompanied by two policemen.

The bruises on his face had healed, so he looked handsome again. He smiled 80 at us, and said rather secretively, "I want to ask you a favor." He rolled his eyes as the dark green van rounded the street corner, coming toward us.

"What?" I said.

"Don't let my mother know the truth. She's too old to take it. Don't tell her, please!"

"What should we say to her, then?" I asked.

"Just say I have a temporary mental disorder."

Beina couldn't hold back her tears anymore, saying loudly, "Don't worry. 85 We won't let her know. Take care of yourself and come back soon." She handed him the duffel, which he took without a word.

I nodded to assure him that I wouldn't reveal the truth. He smiled at her, then at me. For some reason his face turned rather sweet—charming and enticing, as though it were a mysterious female face. I blinked my eyes and wondered if he was really a man. It flashed through my mind that if he were a woman he could've been a beauty—tall, slim, muscular, and slightly languid.

My thoughts were cut short by a metallic screech as the van stopped in front of us. Baowen climbed into it; so did the policemen. I walked around the van, and shook his hand, saying that I'd visit him the next week and that meanwhile, if he needed anything, just to give me a ring.

We waved good-bye as the van drew away, its tire chains clattering and flinging up bits of snow. After a blasting toot, it turned left and disappeared from the icy street. I got on my bicycle as a gust of wind blew up and almost threw me down. Beina followed me for about twenty yards, then leaped on the carrier, and together we headed home. She was so heavy. Thank heaven, I was riding a Great Golden Deer, one of the sturdiest makes.

During the following week I heard from Baowen once. He said on the phone that he felt better now and less agitated. Indeed his voice sounded calm and smooth. He asked me to bring him a few books when I came, specifically his *Dictionary of Universal Knowledge,* which was a hefty, rare book translated from the Russian in the late fifties. I had no idea how he had come by it.

I went to see him on Thursday morning. The hospital was on a mountain, 90 six miles southwest of Muji City. As I was cycling on the asphalt road, a few tall smokestacks fumed lazily beyond the larch woods in the west. To my right the power lines along the roadside curved, heavy with fluffy snow, which would drop in little chunks whenever the wind blew across them. Now and then I overtook a horse cart loaded with earless sheaves of wheat, followed by one or two foals. After I pedaled across a stone bridge and turned into the mouth of a valley, a group of brick buildings emerged on a gentle slope, connected with one another by straight cement paths. Farther up the hill, past the buildings, there was a cow pen, in which about two dozen milk cows were grazing on dry grass while a few others huddled together to keep warm.

It was so peaceful here that if you hadn't known this was a mental hospital, you might have imagined it was a sanatorium for ranking officials. Entering Building 9, I was stopped by a guard, who then took me to Baowen's room on the ground floor. It happened that the doctor on duty, a tall fortyish man with tapering fingers, was making the morning rounds and examining Baowen. He shook hands with me and said that my son-in-law was doing fine. His surname was Mai; his whiskered face looked very intelligent. When he turned to give a male nurse instructions about Baowen's treatment, I noticed an enormous wart in his ear almost blocking the ear hole like a hearing aid. In a way he looked like a foreigner. I wondered if he had some Mongolian or Tibetan blood.

"We give him the electric bath," Doctor Mai said to me a moment later.

"What?" I asked, wincing.

"We treat him with the electric bath."

I turned to Baowen. "How is it?"   95

"It's good, really soothing." He smiled, but there was a churlish look in his eyes, and his mouth tightened.

The nurse was ready to take him for the treatment. Never having heard of such a bath, I asked Doctor Mai, "Can I see how it works?"

"All right, you may go with them."

Together we climbed the stairs to the second floor. There was another reason for me to join them. I wanted to find out whether Baowen was a normal man. The rumors in our factory had gotten on my nerves, particularly the one that said he had no penis—that was why he had always avoided bathing in the workers' bathhouse.

After taking off our shoes and putting on plastic slippers, we entered a 100 small room that had pea green walls and a parquet floor. At its center lay a porcelain bathtub, as ghastly as an apparatus of torture. Affixed along the interior wall of the tub were rectangles of black perforated metal. Three thick rubber cords connected them to a tall machine standing by the wall. A control board full of buttons, gauges, and switches slanted atop the machine. The young nurse, burly and square-faced, turned on the faucet; steaming water began to tumble into the tub. Then he went over to operate the machine. He seemed good-natured; his name was Fuhai Dong. He said he came from the countryside, apparently of peasant stock, and had graduated from Jilin Nursing School.

Baowen smiled at me while unbuttoning his zebra-striped hospital robe. He looked fine now—all the bruises had disappeared from his face, which had become pinkish and smooth. I was scared by the tub. It seemed suitable for electrocuting a criminal. However sick I was, I wouldn't lie in it with my back resting against that metal groove. What if there was an electricity leak?

"Does it hurt?" I asked Baowen.

"No."

He went behind a khaki screen in a corner and began taking off his clothes. When the water half filled the tub, the nurse took a small bag of white powder out of a drawer, cut it open with scissors, and poured the stuff into the water. It must have been salt. He tucked up his shirtsleeves and bent double to agitate the solution with both hands, which were large and sinewy.

To my dismay, Baowen came out in a clean pair of shorts. Without hesita- 105
tion he got into the tub and lay down, just as one would enter a lukewarm bathing pool. I was amazed. "Have you given him electricity yet?" I asked Nurse Dong.

"Yes, a little. I'll increase it by and by." He turned to the machine and adjusted a few buttons.

"You know," he said to me, "your son-in-law is a very good patient, always cooperative."

"He should be."

"That's why we give him the bath. Other patients get electric cuffs around their limbs or electric rods on their bodies. Some of them scream like animals every time. We have to tie them up."

"When will he be cured?" 110

"I'm not sure."

Baowen was noiseless in the electrified water, with his eyes shut and his head resting on a black rubber pad at the end of the tub. He looked fine, rather relaxed.

I drew up a chair and sat down. Baowen seemed reluctant to talk, concentrating on the treatment, so I remained silent, observing him. His body was wiry, his legs hairless, and the front of his shorts bulged quite a bit. He looked all right physically. Once in a while he breathed a feeble sigh.

As the nurse increased the electric current, Baowen began to squirm in the tub as if smarting from something. "Are you all right?" I asked, and dared not touch him.

"Yeah." 115

He kept his eyes shut. Glistening beads of sweat gathered on his forehead. He looked pale, his lips curling now and again as though he were thirsty.

Then the nurse gave him more electricity. Baowen began writhing and moaning a little. Obviously he was suffering. This bath couldn't be as soothing as he'd claimed. With a white towel Nurse Dong wiped the sweat off Baowen's face, and whispered, "I'll turn it down in a few minutes."

"No, give me more!" Baowen said resolutely without opening his eyes, his face twisted.

I felt as though he was ashamed of himself. Perhaps my presence made this section of the treatment more uncomfortable to him. His hands gripped the rim of the tub, the arched wrists trembling. For a good three minutes nobody said a word; the room was so quiet that its walls seemed to be ringing.

As the nurse gradually reduced the electricity, Baowen calmed down. His   120
toes stopped wiggling.

Not wanting to bother him further with my presence, I went out to look for Doctor Mai, to thank him and find out when Baowen could be cured. The doctor was not in his office, so I walked out of the building for a breath of air. The sun was high and the snow blazingly white. Once outside, I had to close my eyes for a minute to adjust them. I then sat down on a bench and lit a cigarette. A young woman in an ermine hat and army mittens passed by, holding an empty milk pail and humming the song "Comrade, Please Have a Cup of Tea." She looked handsome, and her crisp voice pleased me. I gazed at the pair of thick braids behind her, which swayed a little in the wind.

My heart was full of pity for Baowen. He was such a fine young man that he ought to be able to love a woman, have a family, and enjoy a normal life.

Twenty minutes later I rejoined him in his room. He looked tired, still shivering a little. He told me that as the electric currents increased, his skin had begun prickling as though stung by hundreds of mosquitoes. That was why he couldn't stay in the tub for longer than half an hour.

I felt for him, and said, "I'll tell our leaders how sincere your attitude is and how cooperative you are."

"Oh sure." He tilted his damp head. "Thanks for bringing the books."   125
"Do you need something else?"
"No." He sounded sad.
"Baowen, I hope you can come home before the New Year. Beina needs you."
"I know. I don't want to be locked up here forever."

I told him that Beina had written to his mother, saying he'd been away on   130
a business trip. Then the bell for lunch rang in the building, and outside the loudspeaker began broadcasting the fiery music of "March of the Volunteers." Nurse Dong walked in with a pair of chopsticks and a plate containing two corn buns. He said cheerily to Baowen, "I'll bring you the dish in a minute. We have tofu stewed with sauerkraut today, also bean sprout soup."

I stood up and took my leave.

When I reported Baowen's condition to the factory leaders, they seemed impressed. The term "electric bath" must have given their imagination free rein. Secretary Zhu kept shaking his head, and said, "I'm sorry Baowen has to go through such a thing."

I didn't explain that the electric bath was a treatment less severe than the other kinds, nor did I describe what the bath was like. I just said, "They steep him in electrified water every day." Let the terror seize their brains, I thought, so that they might be more sympathetic to Baowen when he is discharged from the hospital.

It was mid-December, and Baowen had been in the hospital for a month already. For days Beina went on saying that she wanted to see how her husband was doing; she was eager to take him home before the New Year. Among her fellow workers rumors persisted. One said the electric bath had blistered Baowen; another claimed that his genitals had been shriveled up by the treatment; another added that he had become a vegetarian, nauseated at the mere sight of meat. The young woman who had once declared she'd leave her door open for him had just married and proudly told everybody she was pregnant. People began to be kind and considerate to Beina, treating her like an abused wife. The leaders of the assembly shop assigned her only the daytime shift. I was pleased that Finance still paid Baowen his wages as though he were on sick leave. Perhaps they did this because they didn't want to upset me.

On Saturday Beina and I went to the mental hospital. She couldn't pedal, 135 and it was too far for me to carry her on my bicycle, so we took the bus. She had been there by herself two weeks ago to deliver some socks and a pair of woolen pajamas she'd knitted for Baowen.

We arrived at the hospital early in the afternoon. Baowen looked healthy, in good spirits. It seemed that the bath had helped him. He was happy to see Beina and even cuddled her in my presence. He gave her two toffees; knowing I disliked candies, he didn't give me one. He poured a large mug of malted milk for both of us, since there was only one mug in the room. I didn't touch the milk, unsure whether homosexuality was communicable. I was glad to see that he treated his wife well. He took a genuine interest in what she said about their comrades in our factory, and now and then laughed heartily. What a wonderful husband he could have been if he were not sick.

Having sat with the couple for a few minutes, I left so that they could be alone. I went to the nurses' office upstairs and found Fuhai Dong writing at a desk. The door was open, and I knocked on its frame. Startled, he closed his brown notebook and stood up.

"I didn't mean to scare you," I said.

"No, Uncle, I just didn't expect anyone to come up here."

I took a carton of Peony cigarettes out of my bag and put it on the desk, 140 saying, "I won't take too much of your time, young man. Please keep this as a token of my regards." I didn't mean to bribe him. I was sincerely grateful to him for treating Baowen well.

"Oh, don't give me this, please."

"You don't smoke?"

"I do. Tell you what, give it to Doctor Mai. He'll help Baowen more."

I was puzzled. Why didn't he want the top-quality cigarettes if he smoked? Seeing that I was confused, he went on, "I'll be nice to Baowen without any gift from you. He's a good man. It's the doctor's wheels that you should grease."

"I have another carton for him." 145

"One carton's nothing here. You should give him at least two."

I was moved by his words, thanked him, and said good-bye.

Doctor Mai happened to be in his office. When I walked in, he was reading the current issue of *Women's Life,* whose back cover carried a large photo of Madame Mao on trial—she wore black and stood, handcuffed, between two young policewomen. Doctor Mai put the magazine aside and asked me to sit down. In the room, tall shelves, loaded with books and files, lined the walls. A smell of rotten fruit hung in there. He seemed pleased to see me.

After we exchanged a few words, I took out both cartons of cigarettes and handed them to him. "This is just a small token of my gratitude, for the New Year," I said.

He took the cigarettes and put them away under his desk. "Thanks a lot," he 150 whispered.

"Doctor Mai, do you think Baowen will be cured before the holiday?" I asked.

"What did you say? Cured?" He looked surprised.

"Yes."

He shook his head slowly, then turned to check that the door was shut. He motioned me to move closer. I pulled the chair forward a little and rested my forearms on the edge of his Bakelite desktop.

"To be honest, there's no cure," he said. 155

"What?"

"Homosexuality isn't an illness, so it has no cure. Don't tell anyone I said this."

"Then why torture Baowen like that?"

"The police sent him here and we couldn't refuse. Besides, we ought to make him feel better and hopeful."

"So it isn't a disease?" 160

"Unfortunately no. Let me say this again: there's no cure for your son-in-law, Old Cheng. It's not a disease. It's just a sexual preference; it may be congenital, like being left-handed. Got it?"

"Then why give him the electric bath?" Still I wasn't convinced.

"Electrotherapy is prescribed by the book—a standard treatment required by the Department of Public Health. I have no choice but to follow the regulations. That's why I didn't give him any of those harsher treatments. The bath is very mild by comparison. You see, I've done everything in my power to help him. Let me tell you another fact: according to the statistics, so far electrotherapy has cured only one out of a thousand homosexuals. I bet cod liver oil, or chocolate, or fried pork, anything, could produce a better result. All right, enough of this. I've talked too much."

At last his words sank in. For a good while I sat there motionless with a numb mind. A flock of sparrows were flitting about in the naked branches outside the window, chasing the one that held a tiny ear of millet in its bill. Another of them dragged a yellow string tied around its leg, unable to fly as nimbly as the others. I rose to my feet and thanked the doctor for his candid words. He stubbed out his cigarette in the ashtray on the windowsill, and said, "I'll take special care of your son-in-law. Don't worry."

I rejoined Beina downstairs. Baowen looked quite cheerful, and it seemed   165
they'd had a good time. He said to me, "If I can't come home soon, don't try too hard to get me out. They won't keep me here forever."

"I'll see what I can do."

In my heart I was exasperated, because if Doctor Mai's words were true, there'd be little I could do for Baowen. If homosexuality wasn't a disease, why had he felt sick and tried to have himself cured? Had he been shamming? It was unlikely.

Beina had been busy cleaning their home since her last visit to the hospital. She bought two young drakes and planned to make drunk duck, a dish she said Baowen liked best. My heart was heavy. On the one hand, I'd have loved to have him back for the holiday; on the other hand, I was unsure what would happen if his condition hadn't improved. I dared not reveal my thoughts to anybody, not even to my wife, who had a big mouth. Because of her, the whole factory knew that Beina was still a virgin, and some people called her the Virgin Bride.

For days I pondered what to do. I was confused. Everybody thought homosexuality was a disease except for Doctor Mai, whose opinion I dared not mention to others. The factory leaders would be mad at me if they knew there was no cure for homosexuality. We had already spent over three thousand yuan on Baowen. I kept questioning in my mind, If homosexuality is a natural thing, then why are there men and women? Why can't two men get married and make a baby? Why didn't nature give men another hole? I was beset by doubts. If only I could have seen a trustworthy doctor for a second opinion. If only there were a knowledgeable, honest friend I could have talked with.

I hadn't yet made up my mind about what to do when Chief Miao called   170
from the Public Security Bureau five days before the holiday. He informed me that Baowen had repeated his crime, so the police had taken him out of the hospital and sent him to the prison in Tangyuan County. "This time he did it," said the chief.

"Impossible!" I cried.

"We have evidence and witnesses. He doesn't deny it himself."

"Oh." I didn't know how to continue.

"He has to be incarcerated now."

"Are you sure he's not a hermaphrodite?" I mentioned that as a last resort.   175

Miao chuckled dryly. "No, he's not. We had him checked. Physically he's a man, healthy and normal. Obviously it's a mental, moral disease, like an addiction to opium."

Putting down the phone, I felt dizzy, cursing Baowen for having totally ruined himself. What had happened was that he and Fuhai Dong had developed a relationship secretly. The nurse often gave him a double amount of meat or fish at dinner. Baowen, in return, unraveled his woolen pajamas and knitted Dong a pullover with the wool. One evening when they were lying in each other's arms in the nurses' office, an old cleaner passed by in the corridor and coughed. Fuhai Dong was terrified and convinced that the man had seen what they had been doing. For days, however hard Baowen tried to talk him out of his conviction, Dong wouldn't change his mind, blaming Baowen for having misled him. He said that the old cleaner often smiled at him meaningfully and would definitely turn them in. Finally Fuhai Dong went to the hospital leaders and confessed everything. So, unlike Baowen, who got three and a half years in jail, Nurse Dong was merely put on probation; if he worked harder and criticized himself well, he might keep his current job.

That evening I went to tell Beina about the new development. As I was talking, she sobbed continually. Although she'd been cleaning the apartment for several days, her home was in shambles, most of the flowers half-dead, and dishes and pots piled in the sink. Mopping her face with a pink towel, she asked me, "What should I tell my mother-in-law?"

"Tell her the truth."

She made no response. I said again, "You should consider a divorce." 180

"No!" Her sobbing turned into wailing. "He—he's my husband and I'm his wife. If I die my soul belongs to him. We've sworn never to leave each other. Let others say whatever they want, I know he's a good man."

"Then why did he go to bed with a guy?"

"He just wanted to have a good time. That was all. It's nothing like adultery or bigamy, is it?"

"But it's a crime that got him into jail," I said. Although in my heart I admitted that Baowen in every way was a good fellow except for his fondness for men, I had to be adamant about my position. I was in charge of security for our factory; if I had a criminal son-in-law, who would listen to me? Wouldn't I be removed from my office soon? If I lost my job, who could protect Beina? Sooner or later she would be laid off, since a criminal's wife was not supposed to have the same opportunities for employment as others. Beina remained silent; I asked again, "What are you going to do?"

"Wait for him." 185

I took a few spiced pumpkin seeds from a bowl, stood up, and went over to the window. Under the sill the radiator was hissing softly with a tiny steam leak. Outside, in the distance, firecrackers one after another scattered clusters of sparks into the indigo dusk. I turned around, and said, "He's not worth waiting for. You must divorce him."

"No, I won't," she moaned.

"Well, it's impossible for me to have a criminal as my son-in-law. I've been humiliated enough. If you want to wait for him, don't come to see me again."

I put the pumpkin seeds back into the bowl, picked up my fur hat, and dragged myself out the door.

FOR ANALYSIS

1. Toward the end of the story, the **narrator** asks himself of Baowen, "If homosexuality wasn't a disease, why had he felt sick and tried to have himself cured?" (para. 167). What do you think is the story's answer to this question?

2. Why does the doctor continue Baowen's treatment if he knows homosexuality is not a disease that can be cured?

3. While this story is about a small number of **characters,** it is also about an entire society. What do the events in this story imply about life in China? Consider both the actions taken by and against Baowen and the actions taken by his wife and father-in-law. Consider also the attitudes and behaviors of "the people" generally, such as those of the factory workers and the bureaucrats.

MAKING CONNECTIONS

1. In spite of the very different **settings** and situations in "A Rose for Emily" (p. 649) and "The Bridegroom," what makes Miss Emily and Baowen similar?

2. At the center of both stories is the relation of the main characters to their societies. This is true beyond the title **characters**; for example, the relationship of the narrator of "The Bridegroom" to his society is very important to the story. Is there an analogous figure in "A Rose for Emily"?

3. Both stories feature judgmental narrating figures. Do the stories (or the authors) seem to agree entirely with these **narrators'** opinions? Do the stories present these judgments straight, or is there some **ironic** distance between what the narrators say and what you think the stories themselves say?

WRITING TOPICS

1. While the story is called "The Bridegroom," it is really as much about the **narrator** as it is about Baowen. What kind of man is the narrator? How do you feel about him? Do your feelings about him change over the course of the story? How about at the end?

2. How would this story be different if it were narrated by Baowen? What would be gained, in terms of understanding the situation and the events? What would be lost?

POETRY

EMILY DICKINSON   (1830–1886)

I'M NOBODY! WHO ARE YOU?   c.1861, 1891

I'm Nobody! Who are you?
Are you—Nobody—Too?
Then there's a pair of us!
Don't tell! they'd advertise—you know!

How dreary—to be—Somebody!
How public—like a Frog—
To tell one's name—the livelong June—
To an admiring Bog!

JAMES WELDON JOHNSON   (1871–1938)

A POET TO HIS BABY SON   1935

Tiny bit of humanity,
Blessed with your mother's face,
And cursed with your father's mind.

I say cursed with your father's mind,
Because you can lie so long and so quietly on your back,
Playing with the dimpled big toe of your left foot,
And looking away,
Through the ceiling of the room, and beyond.
Can it be that already you are thinking of being a poet?

Why don't you kick and howl,   10
And make the neighbors talk about
"That damned baby next door,"
And make up your mind forthwith

To grow up and be a banker
Or a politician or some other sort of go-getter
Or—?—whatever you decide upon,
Rid yourself of these incipient thoughts
About being a poet.

For poets no longer are makers of songs,
Chanters of the gold and purple harvest,   20
Sayers of the glories of earth and sky,
Of the sweet pain of love
And the keen joy of living;
No longer dreamers of the essential dreams,
And interpreters of the eternal truth,
Through the eternal beauty.
Poets these days are unfortunate fellows.
Baffled in trying to say old things in a new way
Or new things in an old language,
They talk abracadabra   30
In an unknown tongue,
Each one fashioning for himself
A wordy world of shadow problems,
And as a self-imagined Atlas,
Struggling under it with puny legs and arms,
Groaning out incoherent complaints at his load.

My son, this is no time nor place for a poet;
Grow up and join the big, busy crowd
That scrambles for what it thinks it wants
Out of this old world which is—as it is—   40
And, probably, always will be.

Take the advice of a father who knows:
You cannot begin too young
Not to be a poet.

FOR ANALYSIS

1. What is this poem's **tone**? Does it have more than one?

2. What did you expect the poem to be like based on the poem's title and opening lines? How did it meet or not meet your expectations?

3. Why does the speaker think his son shouldn't grow up to be a poet?

WRITING TOPICS

1. Many poems are in part about poetry itself. What does this poem have to say specifically about poetry? Paraphrase its thoughts about the state of the genre.

2. "A Poet to His Baby Son" would not be what it is without the skillful use of **irony.** List the different ways and moments in which Johnson uses irony. What is the effect on you as you read? How is that effect different than it might be if Johnson's sentiments were expressed more directly?

PAUL LAURENCE DUNBAR   (1872–1906)

WE WEAR THE MASK   1896

We wear the mask that grins and lies,
It hides our cheeks and shades our eyes—
This debt we pay to human guile;
With torn and bleeding hearts we smile,
And mouth with myriad subtleties.

Why should the world be over-wise,
In counting all our tears and sighs?
Nay, let them only see us, while
    We wear the mask.

We smile, but, O great Christ, our cries   10
To thee from tortured souls arise.
We sing, but oh the clay is vile
Beneath our feet, and long the mile;
But let the world dream otherwise,
    We wear the mask!

GEORGIA DOUGLAS JOHNSON   (1880–1966)

OLD BLACK MEN   1922

They have dreamed as young men dream
    Of glory, love and power;
They have hoped as youth will hope
    Of life's sun-minted hour.

They have seen as other saw
    Their bubbles burst in air,
And they have learned to live it down
    As though they did not care.

T. S. ELIOT (1888–1965)

THE LOVE SONG OF
J. ALFRED PRUFROCK 1917

*S'io credessi che mia risposta fosse
a persona che mai tornasse al mondo,
questa fiamma staria senza più scosse.
Ma per ciò che giammai di questo fondo
non tornò vivo alcun, s'i'odo il vero,
senza tema d'infamia ti rispondo.*[1]

Let us go then, you and I,
When the evening is spread out against the sky
Like a patient etherized upon a table;
Let us go, through certain half-deserted streets,
The muttering retreats
Of restless nights in one-night cheap hotels
And sawdust restaurants with oyster shells:
Streets that follow like a tedious argument
Of insidious intent
To lead you to an overwhelming question . . .   10
Oh, do not ask, "What is it?"
Let us go and make our visit.

In the room the women come and go
Talking of Michelangelo.

The yellow fog that rubs its back upon the windowpanes,
The yellow smoke that rubs its muzzle on the windowpanes
Licked its tongue into the corners of the evening,
Lingered upon the pools that stand in drains,
Let fall upon its back the soot that falls from chimneys,
Slipped by the terrace, made a sudden leap,   20
And seeing that it was a soft October night,
Curled once about the house, and fell asleep.

And indeed there will be time
For the yellow smoke that slides along the street,
Rubbing its back upon the windowpanes;

---

[1] From Dante, *Inferno*, XXVII, 61–66. The speaker is Guido da Montefeltro, who is imprisoned in a flame in the level of hell reserved for false counselors. He tells Dante and Virgil, "If I thought my answer were given to one who might return to the world, this flame would stay without further movement. But since from this depth none has ever returned alive, if what I hear is true, I answer you without fear of infamy."

675

There will be time, there will be time
To prepare a face to meet the faces that you meet;
There will be time to murder and create,
And time for all the works and days of hands
That lift and drop a question on your plate;   30
Time for you and time for me,
And time yet for a hundred indecisions,
And for a hundred visions and revisions,
Before the taking of a toast and tea.

In the room the women come and go
Talking of Michelangelo.

And indeed there will be time
To wonder, "Do I dare?" and, "Do I dare?"
Time to turn back and descend the stair,
With a bald spot in the middle of my hair—   40
(They will say: "How his hair is growing thin!")
My morning coat, my collar mounting firmly to the chin,
My necktie rich and modest, but asserted by a simple pin—
(They will say: "But how his arms and legs are thin!")
Do I dare
Disturb the universe?
In a minute there is time
For decisions and revisions which a minute will reverse.

For I have known them all already, known them all—
Have known the evenings, mornings, afternoons,   50
I have measured out my life with coffee spoons;
I know the voices dying with a dying fall
Beneath the music from a farther room.
      So how should I presume?

And I have known the eyes already, known them all—
The eyes that fix you in a formulated phrase,
And when I am formulated, sprawling on a pin,
When I am pinned and wriggling on the wall,
Then how should I begin
To spit out all the butt-ends of my days and ways?   60
      And how should I presume?

And I have known the arms already, known them all—
Arms that are braceleted and white and bare
(But in the lamplight, downed with light brown hair!)
Is it perfume from a dress

That makes me so digress?
Arms that lie along a table, or wrap about a shawl.
    And should I then presume?
    And how should I begin?

. . . . . .

Shall I say, I have gone at dusk through narrow streets   70
And watched the smoke that rises from the pipes
Of lonely men in shirt-sleeves, leaning out of windows? . . .

I should have been a pair of ragged claws
Scuttling across the floors of silent seas.

. . . . . .

And the afternoon, the evening, sleeps so peacefully!
Smoothed by long fingers,
Asleep . . . tired . . . or it malingers,
Stretched on the floor, here beside you and me.
Should I, after tea and cakes and ices,
Have the strength to force the moment to its crisis?   80
But though I have wept and fasted, wept and prayed,
Though I have seen my head (grown slightly bald) brought in upon a platter,[2]
I am no prophet—and here's no great matter;
I have seen the moment of my greatness flicker,
And I have seen the eternal Footman hold my coat, and snicker,
And in short, I was afraid.

And would it have been worth it, after all,
After the cups, the marmalade, the tea,
Among the porcelain, among some talk of you and me,
Would it have been worth while,   90
To have bitten off the matter with a smile,
To have squeezed the universe into a ball
To roll it toward some overwhelming question,
To say: "I am Lazarus,[3] come from the dead,
Come back to tell you all, I shall tell you all"—
If one, settling a pillow by her head,
    Should say: "That is not what I meant at all.
    That is not it, at all."

And would it have been worth it, after all,
Would it have been worth while,   100

---

[2] Like the head of John the Baptist. See Matthew 14:3–12.
[3] See John 11:1–14 and Luke 16:19–26.

After the sunsets and the dooryards and the sprinkled streets,
After the novels, after the teacups, after the skirts that trail along the floor—
And this, and so much more?—
It is impossible to say just what I mean!
But as if a magic lantern threw the nerves in patterns on a screen:
Would it have been worth while
If one, settling a pillow or throwing off a shawl,
And turning toward the window, should say:
  "That is not it at all,
  That is not what I meant, at all."   110

· · · ·

No! I am not Prince Hamlet, nor was meant to be;
Am an attendant lord, one that will do
To swell a progress,° start a scene or two,   state journey
Advise the prince; no doubt, an easy tool,
Deferential, glad to be of use,
Politic, cautious, and meticulous;
Full of high sentence,° but a bit obtuse;   sententiousness
At times, indeed, almost ridiculous—
Almost, at times, the Fool.

I grow old . . . I grow old . . .   120
I shall wear the bottoms of my trousers rolled.°   cuffed

Shall I part my hair behind? Do I dare to eat a peach?
I shall wear white flannel trousers, and walk upon the beach.
I have heard the mermaids singing, each to each.

I do not think that they will sing to me.

I have seen them riding seaward on the waves
Combing the white hair of the waves blown back
When the wind blows the water white and black.

We have lingered in the chambers of the sea
By sea-girls wreathed with seaweed red and brown   130
Till human voices wake us, and we drown.

FOR ANALYSIS

1. This poem may be understood as a **stream of consciousness** passing through
the mind of Prufrock. The "you and I" of line 1 may be different aspects of his
personality. Or perhaps the "you and I" is parallel to Guido da Montefeltro, who
speaks the epigraph, and Dante, to whom he tells the story that resulted in his

damnation—hence, "you" is the reader and "I" is Prufrock. The poem is disjointed because it proceeds by psychological rather than logical stages. To what social class does Prufrock belong? How does Prufrock respond to the attitudes and values of his class? Does he change in the course of the poem?

2. Line 92 provides a good example of literary **allusion** (see the last stanza of Marvell's "To His Coy Mistress," p. 944). How does an awareness of the allusion contribute to your response?

3. What might the song of the mermaids (l. 124) signify, and why does Prufrock think they will not sing to him (l. 125)?

4. T. S. Eliot once said that some poetry "can communicate without being understood." Is this such a poem?

WRITING TOPIC

What sort of man is J. Alfred Prufrock? How does the poet establish his characteristics?

E. E. CUMMINGS   (1894–1962)

THE CAMBRIDGE LADIES WHO LIVE IN FURNISHED SOULS   1923

the Cambridge ladies who live in furnished souls
are unbeautiful and have comfortable minds
(also, with the church's protestant blessings
daughters, unscented shapeless spirited)
they believe in Christ and Longfellow, both dead,
are invariably interested in so many things—
at the present writing one still finds
delighted fingers knitting for the is it Poles?
perhaps. While permanent faces coyly bandy
scandal of Mrs. N. and Professor D.   10
. . . the Cambridge ladies do not care, above
Cambridge if sometimes in its box of
sky lavender and cornerless, the
moon rattles like a fragment of angry candy

FOR ANALYSIS

1. What **images** does the poet use to describe "the Cambridge ladies"? What do the images suggest?

2. What is the effect of the interruption "is it" in line 8?

3. In the final lines, the moon seems to protest against the superficiality of these women. What is the effect of comparing the moon to a fragment of candy?

WRITING TOPICS

1. Compare this poem with Dickinson's "What Soft—Cherubic Creatures—" (p. 715).

2. This poem **satirizes** the behavior of the Cambridge ladies. Does it imply how they *should* behave?

ETHERIDGE KNIGHT   (1931–1991)

HARD ROCK RETURNS TO PRISON
FROM THE HOSPITAL
FOR THE CRIMINAL INSANE   1968

Hard Rock was "known not to take no shit
From nobody," and he had the scars to prove it:
Split purple lips, lumped ears, welts above
His yellow eyes, and one long scar that cut
Across his temple and plowed through a thick
Canopy of kinky hair.

The WORD was that Hard Rock wasn't a mean nigger
Anymore, that the doctors had bored a hole in his head,
Cut out part of his brain, and shot electricity
Through the rest. When they brought Hard Rock back,   10
Handcuffed and chained, he was turned loose,
Like a freshly gelded stallion, to try his new status.
And we all waited and watched, like Indians at a corral,
To see if the WORD was true.

As we waited we wrapped ourselves in the cloak
Of his exploits: "Man, the last time, it took eight
Screws to put him in the Hole." "Yeah, remember when he
Smacked the captain with his dinner tray?" "He set
The record for time in the Hole—67 straight days!"
"Ol Hard Rock! man, that's one crazy nigger."   20
And then the jewel of a myth that Hard Rock had once bit
A screw on the thumb and poisoned him with syphilitic spit.

The testing came, to see if Hard Rock was really tame.
A hillbilly called him a black son of a bitch
And didn't lose his teeth, a screw who knew Hard Rock
From before shook him down and barked in his face.
And Hard Rock did nothing. Just grinned and looked silly,
His eyes empty like knot holes in a fence.

And even after we discovered that it took Hard Rock
Exactly 3 minutes to tell you his first name,   30
We told ourselves that he had just wised up,
Was being cool; but we could not fool ourselves for long,
And we turned away, our eyes on the ground. Crushed.

He had been our Destroyer, the doer of things
We dreamed of doing but could not bring ourselves to do,
The fears of years, like a biting whip,
Had cut grooves too deeply across our backs.

YEVGENY YEVTUSHENKO (B. 1933)

I WOULD LIKE   TRANS. 1962

I would like
       to be born
              in every country,
have a passport
           for them all,
to throw
       all foreign offices
               into panic,
be every fish
           in every ocean   10
and every dog
           along the path.
I don't want to bow down
               before any idols
or play at being
           an Orthodox church hippy,
but I would like to plunge
               deep into Lake Baikal[1]
and surface snorting
           somewhere,   20
              why not in the Mississippi?
In my beloved universe
           I would like
to be a lonely weed,
           but not a delicate Narcissus[2]

---

[1] A large lake in Siberia, just north of Mongolia.
[2] In Greek myth, a beautiful youth who pines away for love of his own reflection and is changed into a flower.

kissing his own mug
                    in the mirror.
I would like to be
                    any of God's creatures
right down to the last mangy hyena—
but never a tyrant
                    or even the cat of a tyrant.
I would like to be
                    reincarnated as a man
                                        in any circumstance:
a victim of Paraguayan prison tortures,
a homeless child in the slums of Hong Kong,
a living skeleton in Bangladesh,
a holy beggar in Tibet,
a black in Cape Town,
but never
            in the image of Rambo
The only people whom I hate
                        are the hypocrites—
pickled hyenas
            in heavy syrup.
I would like to lie
                    under the knives of all the surgeons in the world,
be hunchbacked, blind,
                        suffer all kinds of diseases,
                                        wounds and scars,
be a victim of war,
                    or a sweeper of cigarette butts,
just so a filthy microbe of superiority
                            doesn't creep inside.
I would not like to be in the elite,
nor of course,
            in the cowardly herd,
nor be a guard-dog of that herd,
nor a shepherd,
                    sheltered by that herd.
And I would like happiness,
                        but not at the expense of the unhappy,
and I would like freedom,
                        but not at the expense of the unfree.
I would like to love
                    all the women in the world,
and I would like to be a woman, too—
                            just once. . . .

Men have been diminished
by Mother Nature.
Suppose she'd given motherhood
to men?
If an innocent child
stirred
below his heart,
man would probably
not be so cruel.
I would like to be man's daily bread—
say,
a cup of rice
for a Vietnamese woman in mourning,
cheap wine
in a Neapolitan workers' trattoria,[3]
or a tiny tube of cheese
in orbit round the moon:
let them eat me,
let them drink me,
only let my death
be of some use.
I would like to belong to all times,
shock all history so much
that it would be amazed
what a smart aleck I was.
I would like to bring Nefertiti
to Pushkin in a troika.[4]
I would like to increase
the space of a moment
a hundredfold,
so that in the same moment
I could drink vodka with fishermen in Siberia
and sit together with Homer,
Dante,
Shakespeare,
and Tolstoy,
drinking anything,
except of course,
Coca-Cola,
—dance to the tom-toms in the Congo,

---

[3] A type of small, inexpensive restaurant in Italy.

[4] Nefertiti was a famously beautiful fourteenth-century B.C. queen of Egypt. Aleksandr Sergeyevich Pushkin (1799–1837) was perhaps the greatest Russian writer and poet of his time. A troika is a Russian vehicle drawn by a team of three horses.

—strike at Renault, 110
—chase a ball with Brazilian boys
                              at Copacabana Beach.
I would like
        to know every language,
                              the secret waters under the earth,
and do all kinds of work at once.
                              I would make sure
that one Yevtushenko was merely a poet,
                    the second—an underground fighter,
                                          somewhere, 120
I couldn't say where
                    for security reasons,
the third—a student at Berkeley,
                              the fourth—a jolly Georgian[5] drinker,
and the fifth—
                maybe a teacher of Eskimo children in Alaska,
the sixth—
        a young president,
                    somewhere, say even in Sierra Leone,
the seventh— 130
                would still be shaking a rattle in his stroller,
and the tenth . . .
                the hundredth . . .
                              the millionth . . .
For me it's not enough to be myself,
                        let me be everyone!
Every creature
                usually has a double,
but God was stingy
                    with the carbon paper,
and in his Paradise Publishing Company
                              made a unique copy of me. 140
But I shall muddle up
                all God's cards—
                              I shall confound God!
I shall be in a thousand copies
                        to the end of my days,
so that the earth buzzes with me,
                        and computers go berserk
in the world census of me. 150
I would like to fight on all your barricades,
                        humanity,

[5] Georgia is one of the republics that made up the former Soviet Union. It lies along the east coast of the Black Sea.

dying each night
        an exhausted moon,
and being resurrected each morning
                like a newborn sun,
with an immortal soft spot
            on my skull.
And when I die,
        a smart-aleck Siberian François Villon,[6]   160
do not lay me in the earth
          of France
             or Italy,
but in our Russian, Siberian earth,
                on a still green hill,
where I first felt
      that I was
          everyone.

FOR ANALYSIS

1. The poet declares that he would like to be a certain kind of person. What kind of person? What specific **images** lead you to your judgment?

2. What kind of person does he *not* wish to be? What images support your conclusion?

3. Discuss the images that address chronological time. Discuss those that address geographical distance. Discuss those that address a sort of chain of being among creatures, moving from "low" to "high." How does Yevtushenko use these images to define his social and political views?

WRITING TOPIC

In an essay, describe the poet's notion of an ideal person, and speculate on how that person would get along in the real world. Do you accept, or would you modify, Yevtushenko's ideal? Explain.

WOLE SOYINKA   (B. 1934)

TELEPHONE CONVERSATION   1960

The price seemed reasonable, location
Indifferent. The landlady swore she lived
Off premises. Nothing remained
But self-confession. "Madam," I warned,

I Would Like
   [6] A French balladeer, born in 1431, who was often in trouble with the law.

"I hate a wasted journey—I am African."
Silence. Silenced transmission of
Pressurized good-breeding. Voice, when it came,
Lipstick coated, long gold-rolled
Cigarette-holder pipped. Caught I was, foully.
"HOW DARK?" . . . I had not misheard. . . . "ARE YOU LIGHT   10
OR VERY DARK?" Button B. Button A. Stench
Of rancid breath of public hide-and-speak.
Red booth.¹ Red pillar-box.² Red double-tiered
Omnibus squelching tar. It *was* real! Shamed
By ill-mannered silence, surrender
Pushed dumbfoundment to beg simplification.
Considerate she was, varying the emphasis—
"ARE YOU DARK? OR VERY LIGHT?" Revelation came.
"You mean—like plain or milk chocolate?"
Her assent was clinical, crushing in its light   20
Impersonality. Rapidly, wave-length adjusted.
I chose. "West African sepia"—and as afterthought,
"Down in my passport." Silence for spectroscopic
Flight of fancy, till truthfulness clanged her accent
Hard on the mouthpiece. "WHAT'S THAT?" conceding
"DON'T KNOW WHAT THAT IS." "Like brunette."
"THAT'S DARK, ISN'T IT?" "Not altogether.
Facially, I am brunette, but madam, you should see
The rest of me. Palm of my hand, soles of my feet
Are a peroxide blonde. Friction, caused—   30
Foolishly madam—by sitting down, has turned
My bottom raven black—One moment madam!"—sensing
Her receiver rearing on the thunderclap
About my ears—"Madam," I pleaded, "wouldn't you rather
See for yourself?"

FOR ANALYSIS

1. Aware of the racism of the culture in which he lives, the speaker volunteers to the landlady that he is African in order to avoid "a wasted journey" (l. 5). Why, then, is he so taken aback when she asks him how dark he is?

2. Describe the meaning and **tone** of the speaker's comment, "Caught I was, foully" (l. 9).

3. Explain the pun in line 12.

4. What does "It" in line 14 refer to?

Telephone Conversation
    ¹ Older British public phones, whose booths were painted red, had one button that had to be depressed when a connection was made, and a second one that allowed the caller to disconnect.
    ² A public mailbox.

WRITING TOPIC

How would the landlady have answered the speaker's question at the end of the poem, and how might she have justified her response?

KAY RYAN (B. 1945)

ALL SHALL BE RESTORED 1996

The grains shall be collected
from the thousand shores
to which they found their way,
and the boulder restored,
and the boulder itself replaced
in the cliff, and likewise
the cliff shall rise
or subside until the plate of earth
is without fissure. Restoration
knows no half measure. It will   10
not stop when the treasured and lost
bronze horse remounts the steps.
Even this horse will founder backward
to coin, cannon, and domestic pots,
which themselves shall bubble and
drain back to green veins in stone.
And every word written shall lift off
letter by letter, the backward text
read ever briefer, ever more antic
in its effort to insist that nothing   20
shall be lost.

FOR ANALYSIS

1. What process is being reversed in lines 1–9? In lines 10–16? What kind of processes are these? Are they actually reversible?

2. What does the last sentence add to the poem's meaning? How is the last clause—"nothing shall be lost"—related to the poem's title?

3. Describe the **style** of the poem. What kind of voice does Ryan create? How does she do it?

WRITING TOPIC

One of the most important facts of human experience is that it ends—at least in the case of individual life. Many different aspects of human culture can be seen, in part, to be dealing with this eventuality: either accepting this natural process or working against it. What does "All Shall Be Restored" say about the way people deal with death?

JUAN FELIPE HERRERA (B. 1948)

187 REASONS MEXICANOS CAN'T CROSS THE BORDER (REMIX) 1994

—Abutebaris modo subjunctivo denuo.[1]

Because Lou Dobbs has been misusing the subjunctive again
Because our suitcases are made with biodegradable maguey fibers
Because we still resemble La Malinche
Because multiplication is our favorite sport
Because we'll dig a tunnel to Seattle
Because Mexico needs us to keep the peso from sinking
Because the Berlin Wall is on the way through Veracruz
Because we just learned we are Huichol
Because someone made our IDs out of corn
Because our border thirst is insatiable   10
Because we're on peyote & Coca-Cola & Banamex
Because it's Indian land stolen from our mothers
Because we're too emotional when it comes to our mothers
Because we've been doing it for over five hundred years already
Because it's too easy to say "I am from here"
Because Latin American petrochemical juice flows first
Because what would we do in El Norte
Because Nahuatl, Mayan & Chicano will spread to Canada
Because Zedillo & Salinas & Fox are still on vacation
Because the World Bank needs our abuelita's account   20
Because the CIA trains better with brown targets
Because our accent is unable to hide U.S. colonialism
Because what will the Hispanik MBAs do
Because our voice resembles La Llorona's
Because we are still voting
Because the North is really South
Because we can read about it in an ethnic prison
Because Frida beat us to it
Because U.S. & European Corporations would rather visit us first
Because environmental U.S. industrial pollution suits our color   30
Because of a new form of Overnight Mayan Anarchy
Because there are enough farmworkers in California already
Because we're meant to usher a postmodern gloom into Mexico
Because Nabisco, Exxon, & Union Carbide gave us Mal de Ojo
Because every nacho chip can morph into a Mexican Wrestler

[1] You've been misusing the subjunctive again.

688

Because it's better to be rootless, unconscious, & rapeable
Because we're destined to have the "Go Back to Mexico" Blues
Because of Pancho Villa's hidden treasure in Chihuahua
Because of Bogart's hidden treasure in the Sierra Madre
Because we need more murals honoring our Indian Past   40
Because we are really dark French Creoles in a Cantínflas costume
Because of this Aztec reflex to sacrifice ourselves
Because we couldn't clean up hurricane Katrina
Because of this Spanish penchant to be polite and aggressive
Because we had a vision of Sor Juana in drag
Because we smell of tamales soaked in Tequila
Because we got hooked listening to Indian Jazz in Chiapas
Because we're still waiting to be cosmic
Because our passport says we're out of date
Because our organ donor got lost in a Bingo game   50
Because we got to learn English first & get in line & pay a little fee
Because we're understanding & appreciative of our Capitalist neighbors
Because our 500-year penance was not severe enough
Because we're still running from La Migra
Because we're still kissing the Pope's hand
Because we're still practicing to be Franciscan priests
Because they told us to sit & meditate & chant "Nosotros los Pobres"
Because of the word "Revolución" & the words "Viva Zapata"
Because we rely more on brujas than lawyers
Because we never finished our Ph.D. in Total United Service   60
Because our identity got mixed up with passion
Because we have visions instead of televisions
Because our huaraches are made with Goodyear & Uniroyal
Because the pesticides on our skin are still glowing
Because it's too easy to say "American Citizen" in cholo
Because you can't shrink-wrap enchiladas
Because a Spy in Spanish sounds too much like "Es Pie" in English
Because our comadres are an International Political Party
Because we believe in The Big Chingazo Theory of the Universe
Because we're still holding our breath in the Presidential Palace in   70
     Mexico City
Because every Mexican is a Living Theatre of Rebellion
Because Hollywood needs its subject matter in proper folkloric costume
Because the Grammys & iTunes are finally out in Spanish
Because the Right is writing an epic poem of apology for our proper edification
Because the Alamo really is pronounced "Alamadre"
Because the Mayan concept of zero means "U.S. Out of Mexico"
Because the oldest ceiba in Yucatán is prophetic
Because England is making plans
Because we can have Nicaragua, Honduras, & Panama anyway

Because 125 million Mexicans can be wrong   80
Because we'll smuggle an earthquake into New York
Because we'll organize like the Vietnamese in San José
Because we'll organize like the Mixtecos in Fresno
Because East L.A. is sinking
Because the Christian Coalition doesn't cater at César Chávez Parque
Because you can't make mace out of beans
Because the computers can't pronounce our names
Because the National Border Police are addicted to us
Because Africa will follow
Because we're still dressed in black rebozos   90
Because we might sing a corrido at any moment
Because our land grants are still up for grabs
Because our tattoos are indecipherable
Because people are hanging milagros on the 2,000 miles of border wire
Because we're locked into Magical Realism
Because Mexican dependence is a form of higher learning
Because making chilaquiles leads to plastic explosives
Because a simple Spanish Fly can mutate into a raging Bird Flu
Because we eat too many carbohydrates
Because we gave enough blood at the Smithfield, Inc., slaughterhouse in   100
     Tar Heel, North Carolina
Because a quinceañera will ruin the concept of American virginity
Because huevos rancheros are now being served at Taco Bell as Wavoritos
Because every Mexican grito undermines English intonation
Because the President has a Mexican maid
Because the Vice President has a Mexican maid
Because it's Rosa López's fault O.J. Simpson was guilty
Because Banda music will take over the White House
Because Aztec sexual aberrations are still in practice
Because our starvation & squalor isn't as glamorous as Somalia's
Because agribusiness will whack us anyway   110
Because the information superhighway is not for Chevys & Impalas
Because white men are paranoid of Frida's mustache
Because the term "mariachi" comes from the word "cucarachi"
Because picking grapes is not a British tradition
Because they are still showing Zoot Suit in prisons
Because Richie Valens is alive in West Liberty, Iowa
Because ? & the Mysterians cried 97 tears not 96
Because Hoosgow, Riata and Rodeo are Juzgado, Riata and Rodeo
Because Jackson Hole, Wyoming, will blow as soon as we hit Oceanside
Because U.S. narco-business needs us in Nogales   120
Because the term "Mexican" comes from "Mexicanto"
Because Mexican queers crossed already
Because Mexican lesbians wear Ben Davis pants & sombreros de palma to work

Because VFW halls aren't built to serve cabeza con tripas
Because the National Guard are going international
Because we still bury our feria in the backyard
Because we don't have international broncas for profit
Because we are in love with our sister Rigoberta Menchú
Because California is on the verge of becoming California
Because the PRI is a family affair   130
Because we may start a television series called *No Chingues Conmigo*
Because we are too sweet & obedient & confused & (still) full of rage
Because the CIA needs us in a Third World State of mind
Because brown is the color of the future
Because we turned Welfare into El Huero Fèlix
Because we know what the Jews have been through
Because we know what the Blacks have been through
Because the Irish became the San Patricio Corps at the Battle of Churubusco
Because of our taste for Yiddish gospel raps & tardeadas & salsa limericks
Because El Sistema Nos La Pela   140
Because you can take the boy outta Mexico but not outta the Boycott
Because the Truckers, Arkies and Okies enjoy our telenovelas
Because we'd rather shop at the flea market than Macy's
Because pan dulce feels sexual, especially conchas & the elotes
Because we'll Xerox tamales in order to survive
Because we'll export salsa to Russia & call it "Pikushki"
Because cilantro aromas follow us wherever we go
Because we'll unionize & sing *De Colores*
Because A Day Without a Mexican is a day away
Because we're in touch with our Boricua camaradas   150
Because we are the continental majority
Because we'll build a sweat lodge in front of Bank of America
Because we should wait for further instructions from Televisa
Because 125 million Mexicanos are potential Chicanos
Because we'll take over the Organic Foods business with a
        molcajete
Because 2,000 miles of maquiladoras want to promote us
Because the next Olympics will commemorate the Mexico City
        massacre of 1968
Because there is an Aztec temple beneath our Nopales
Because we know how to pronounce all the Japanese corporations
Because the Comadre network is more accurate than CNN   160
Because the Death Squads are having a hard time with Caló
Because the mayor of San Diego likes salsa medium-picante
Because the Navy, Army, Marines like us topless in Tijuana
Because when we see red, white & blue we just see red
Because when we see the numbers 187 we still see red
Because we need to pay a little extra fee to the Border

Because Mexican Human Rights sounds too Mexican
Because Chrysler is putting out a lowrider
Because they found a lost Chicano tribe in Utah
Because harina white flour bag suits don't cut it at graduation   170
Because we'll switch from AT&T & MCI to Y-que, y-que
Because our hand signs aren't registered
Because Freddy Fender wasn't Baldomar Huerta's real name
Because "lotto" is another Chicano word for "pronto"
Because we won't nationalize a State of Immigrant Paranoia
Because the depression of the '30s was our fault
Because "xenophobia" is a politically correct term
Because we shoulda learned from the Chinese Exclusion Act of 1882
Because we shoulda listened to the Federal Immigration Laws of
          1917, '21, '24 & '30
Because we lack a Nordic/Teutonic approach   180
Because Executive Order 9066 of 1942 shudda had us too
Because Operation Wetback took care of us in the '50s
Because Operation Clean Sweep picked up the loose ends in the '70s
Because one more operation will finish us off anyway
Because you can't deport 12 million migrantes in a Greyhound bus
Because we got this thing about walking out of everything
Because we have a heart that sings rancheras and feet that polka

FOR ANALYSIS

1. In 1994, California voters passed a ballot initiative called Proposition 187 that sought to deny "illegal aliens" a variety of social services guaranteed to legal residents, claiming that such services placed an undue financial burden on the state. The measure was later overturned by federal courts. Why do you think Herrera chose 187 for his title? How many lines are in the poem?

2. Repetition of a word or phrase at the beginning of a sentence, clause, or line of poetry is called *anaphora*. How does Herrera use anaphora, and to what effect?

MAKING CONNECTIONS

Compare the ways in which Erdrich's "Dear John Wayne" (p. 696) and "187 Reasons Mexicanos Can't Cross the Border" are concerned not just with how minorities are seen by the majority culture but also how minorities see themselves.

WRITING TOPICS

1. Write a "because" list poem about some issue of interest to you and in which you dispute reasons or motivations.

2. Describe the complicated use of **irony** in "187 Reasons Mexicanos Can't Cross the Border."

MAGGIE ANDERSON   (B. 1948)

LONG STORY   1992

To speak in a flat voice
Is all that I can do
—James Wright, "Speak"

I need to tell you that I live in a small town
in West Virginia you would not know about.
It is one of the places I think of as home.
When I go for a walk, I take my basset hound
whose sad eyes and ungainliness always draw
a crowd of children. She tolerates anything
that seems to be affection, so she lets the kids
put scarves and ski caps on her head
until she starts to resemble the women who have to dress
from rummage sales in poverty's mismatched polyester.   10

The dog and I trail the creek bank with the kids,
past clapboard row houses with Christmas seals
pasted to the windows as a decoration.
Inside, television glows around the vinyl chairs
and curled linoleum, and we watch someone old
perambulating to the kitchen on a shiny walker.
Up the hill in town, two stores have been
boarded up beside the youth center and miners
with amputated limbs are loitering outside
the Heart and Hand. They wear Cat diesel caps   20
and spit into the street. The wind
carries on, whining through the alleys,
rustling down the sidewalks, agitating
leaves, and circling the courthouse steps
past the toothless Field sisters who lean
against the flagpole holding paper bags
of chestnuts they bring to town to sell.

History is one long story of what happened to us,
and its rhythms are local dialect and anecdote.
In West Virginia a good story takes awhile,   30
and if it has people in it, you have to swear
that it is true. I tell the kids the one about
my Uncle Craig who saw the mountain move
so quickly and so certainly it made the sun
stand in a different aspect to his little town

until it rearranged itself and settled down again.
This was his favorite story. When he got old,
he mixed it up with baseball games, his shift boss
pushing scabs through a picket line, the Masons
in white aprons at a funeral, but he remembered   40
everything that ever happened, and he knew how far
he lived from anywhere you would have heard of.

Anything that happens here has a lot of versions,
how to get from here to Logan twenty different ways.
The kids tell me convoluted country stories
full of snuff and bracken, about how long
they sat quiet in the deer blind with their fathers
waiting for the ten-point buck that got away.
They like to talk about the weather,
how the wind we're walking in means rain,   50
how the flood pushed cattle fifteen miles downriver.

These kids know mines like they know hound dogs
and how the sirens blow when something's wrong.
They know the blast, and the stories, how
the grown-ups drop whatever they are doing
to get out there. Story is shaped
by sound, and it structures what we know.
They told me this, and three of them
swore it was true, so I'll tell you
even though I know you do not know   60
this place, or how tight and dark the hills
pull in around the river and the railroad.

I'll say it as the children spoke it,
in the flat voice of my people:
down in Boone County, they sealed up
forty miners in a fire. The men who had come
to help tried and tried to get down to them,
but it was a big fire and there was danger,
so they had to turn around
and shovel them back in. All night long   70
they stood outside with useless picks and axes
in their hands, just staring at the drift mouth.
Here's the thing: what the sound must have been,
all those fire trucks and ambulances, the sirens,
and the women crying and screaming out
the names of their buried ones, who must have

called back up to them from deep inside
the burning mountain, right up to the end.

FOR ANALYSIS

1. The speaker says her uncle "knew how far / he lived from anywhere you would
have heard of" (ll. 44–45). What does this fact mean to him, and to the speaker? How
does the poem give a sense of this place, which most of the poem's readers will not
know?

2. Do you think the voice the speaker uses in this poem remains uniform throughout? If not, when and how does it change, and why do you think the poet chose to
have it change?

WRITING TOPICS

1. Describe the feeling of the poem's last line and how Anderson achieves it.

2. List examples of ways in which Anderson creates the "flat voice" referred to at the
beginning of the poem and again in line 67. What makes it flat? How would a different voice have changed the poem's effects?

JUDITH ORTIZ COFER   (B. 1952)

LATIN WOMEN PRAY   1987

Latin women pray
In incense sweet churches
They pray in Spanish to an Anglo God
With a Jewish heritage.

And this Great White Father
Imperturbable in his marble pedestal
Looks down upon his brown daughters
Votive candles shining like lust
In his all seeing eyes
Unmoved by their persistent prayers.   10

Yet year after year
Before his image they kneel
Margarita Josefina Maria and Isabel
All fervently hoping
That if not omnipotent
At least he be bilingual.

LOUISE ERDRICH   (B. 1954)

DEAR JOHN WAYNE   1984

August and the drive-in picture is packed.
We lounge on the hood of the Pontiac
surrounded by the slow-burning spirals they sell
at the window, to vanquish the hordes of mosquitoes.
Nothing works. They break through the smoke screen for blood.

Always the lookout spots the Indians first,
spread north to south, barring progress.
The Sioux or some other Plains bunch
in spectacular columns, ICBM missiles,
feathers bristling in the meaningful sunset.   10

The drum breaks. There will be no parlance.
Only the arrows whining, a death-cloud of nerves
swarming down on the settlers
who die beautifully, tumbling like dust weeds
into the history that brought us all here
together: this wide screen beneath the sign of the bear.

The sky fills, acres of blue squint and eye
that the crowd cheers. His face moves over us,
a thick cloud of vengeance, pitted
like the land that was once flesh. Each rut,   20
each scar makes a promise: *It is
not over, this fight, not as long as you resist.*

Everything we see belongs to us.

A few laughing Indians fall over the hood
slipping in the hot spilled butter.
The eye sees a lot, John, but the heart is so blind.
Death makes us owners of nothing.
He smiles, a horizon of teeth
the credits reel over, and then the white fields
again blowing in the true-to-life dark.   30
The dark films over everything.
We get into the car
scratching our mosquito bites, speechless and small
as people are when the movie is done.
We are back in our skins.

696

How can we help but keep hearing his voice,
the flip side of the sound track, still playing:
Come on, boys, we got them
where we want them, drunk, running.
They'll give us what we want, what we need.   40
Even his disease was the idea of taking everything.
Those cells, burning, doubling, splitting out of their skins.

FOR ANALYSIS

1. Part of the power of "Dear John Wayne" lies in the difference between its two **settings,** or places. What are they? What are their differences, and why are they significant?

2. Describing the "Indians" in the movie, Erdrich calls them "The Sioux, or some other Plains bunch" (l. 8). What **ironic** effect is intended by this last phrase? Note other places where Erdrich is being ironic. What are the effects there?

3. From its very title onward, Erdrich's poem is concerned with the question of audience. Who are the different audiences implied in this poem, intended and actual? Who are the different speakers? As a reader, which audience are you?

WRITING TOPICS

1. Address the issue of this poem's complicated **tone.** What are its various **moods** and attitudes toward its subjects? When and how do they shift, and to what effect?

2. Draw a line down the middle of a piece of paper. In the left column, write down everything the white men in the poem see. In the right column, write down everything the Native Americans in the poem see. Compare the two columns in an essay that discusses the issue of power in seeing and being seen.

MARILYN CHIN   (B. 1955)

HOW I GOT THAT NAME   1994

AN ESSAY ON ASSIMILATION

I am Marilyn Mei Ling Chin.
Oh, how I love the resoluteness
of that first person singular
followed by that stalwart indicative
of "be," without the uncertain i-n-g
of "becoming." Of course,
the name had been changed
somewhere between Angel Island and the sea,
when my father the paperson

in the late 1950s   10
obsessed with a bombshell blonde
transliterated "Mei Ling" to "Marilyn."
And nobody dared question
his initial impulse—for we all know
lust drove men to greatness,
not goodness, not decency.
And there I was, a wayward pink baby,
named after some tragic white woman
swollen with gin and Nembutal.
My mother couldn't pronounce the "r."   20
She dubbed me "Numba one female offshoot"
for brevity: henceforth, she will live and die
in sublime ignorance, flanked
by loving children and the "kitchen deity."
While my father dithers,
a tomcat in Hong Kong trash—
a gambler, a petty thug,
who bought a chain of chopsuey joints
in Piss River, Oregon,
with bootlegged Gucci cash.   30
Nobody dared question his integrity given
his nice, devout daughters
and his bright, industrious sons
as if filial piety were the standard
by which all earthly men were measured.

Oh, how trustworthy our daughters,
how thrifty our sons!
How we've managed to fool the experts
in education, statistics and demography—
We're not very creative but not adverse to rote-learning.   40
Indeed, they can *use* us.
But the "Model Minority" is a tease.
We know you are watching now,
so we refuse to give you any!
Oh, bamboo shoots, bamboo shoots!
The further west we go, we'll hit east;
the deeper down we dig, we'll find China.
History has turned its stomach
on a black polluted beach—
where life doesn't hinge   50
on that red, red wheelbarrow,
but whether or not our new lover
in the final episode of "Santa Barbara"

will lean over a scented candle
and call us a "bitch."
Oh God, where have we gone wrong?
We have no inner resources!

Then, one redolent spring morning
the Great Patriarch Chin
peered down from his kiosk in heaven   60
and saw that his descendants were ugly.
One had a squarish head and a nose without a bridge.
Another's profile—long and knobbed as a gourd.
A third, the sad, brutish one
may never, never marry.
And I, his least favorite—
"not quite boiled, not quite cooked,"
a plump pomfret simmering in my juices—
too listless to fight for my people's destiny.
"To kill without resistance is not slaughter"   70
says the proverb. So, I wait for imminent death.
The fact that this death is also metaphorical
is testament to my lethargy.

So here lies Marilyn Mei Ling Chin,
married once, twice to so-and-so, a Lee and a Wong,
granddaughter of Jack "the patriarch"
and the brooding Suilin Fong,
daughter of the virtuous Yuet Kuen Wong
and G. G. Chin the infamous,
sister of a dozen, cousin of a million,   80
survived by everybody and forgotten by all.
She was neither black nor white,
neither cherished nor vanquished,
just another squatter in her own bamboo grove
minding her poetry—
when one day heaven was unmerciful,
and a chasm opened where she stood.
Like the jowls of a mighty white whale,
or the jaws of a metaphysical Godzilla,
it swallowed her whole.   90
She did not flinch nor writhe,
nor fret about the afterlife,
but stayed! Solid as wood, happily
a little gnawed, tattered, mesmerized
by all that was lavished upon her
and all that was taken away!

FOR ANALYSIS

1. Why does the speaker "love the resoluteness / of that first person singular / followed by that stalwart indicative / of 'be' " (ll. 2–5)?

2. Why is how the poet/**persona** got her name so important?

3. What is wrong, in the speaker's eyes, with being a "Model Minority" (l. 42)?

WRITING TOPICS

1. How is this poem, as its subtitle claims, "An essay on assimilation"? What was "lavished upon her" (l. 95) and what was "taken away" (l. 96)?

2. *Assimilation* is usually meant to indicate what happens to immigrants in a new land. Write about a situation in your life when you had to assimilate in a different sense—not as an international immigrant or a child of immigrants but as a person in a new place. What impact did the experience have on your sense of self?

JOSHUA CLOVER   (B. 1962)

THE NEVADA GLASSWORKS   1997

Ka-Boom! They're making glass in Nevada!
Figure August, 1953,
mom's 13, it's hot as a simile.
Ker-Pow! Transmutation in Nevada!
Imagine mom: pre-postModern new teen,
innocent for Elvis, ditto "Korean
conflict," John Paul George Ringo Viet Nam.
Mom's 1 state west of the glassworks, she's
in a tree/K*I*S*S*I*N*G,
lurid cartoon-colored kisses. Ka-Blam!   10
They're blowing peacock-tinted New World glass
in southern Nevada, the alchemists
& architects of mom's duck-&-cover
adolescence, they're making Las Vegas
turn to gold—real neon gold—in the blast
furnace heat that reaches clear to Clover
Ranch in dry Central Valley: O the dust—
It is the Golden State! O the landscape—
dreaming of James Dean! O mom in a tree
close-range kissing as in Nevada just   20
now they're making crazy ground-zero shapes
of radiant see-through geography.
What timing! What kisses! What a fever

this day's become, humming hundred-degree
California afternoon that she's
sure she could never duplicate, *never,*
she feels transparent, gone—isn't this heat
suffocating—no, she forgot to breathe
for a flash while in the Nevada flats
factory glassblowers exhale . . . exhale . . .   30
a philosopher's stone, a crystal ball,
a spectacular machine. Hooray! Hats
off—they're making a window in the sand!
Mom's in the tree—picture this—all alone!
Unforgettable kisses, comic-book
mnemonic kisses. O something's coming
out of the ranch road heat mirage: That drone—
an engine? Mom quits practice & looks
east, cups an ear to the beloved humming,
the hazy gold dust kicked wildly west   40
ahead of something almost . . . in . . . sight. Vroom!
It's the Future, hot like nothing else, dressed
as sonic-boom Cadillac. O mom!
This land *is* your land/This land Amnesia—
they're dropping some new science out there,
a picture-perfect hole blown clear to Asia:
everything in the desert—Shazam!—turns
to glass, gold glass, a picture-window where
the bomb-dead kids are burned & burn & burn

For Analysis

1. What exactly is happening in Nevada to make glass? What is the "new science" (l. 45)?

2. When Clover writes, "What timing!" (l. 23), to what is he referring? Why does the poem cut back and forth between Nevada and "1 state west" (l. 8)?

3. Identify Clover's **tone**. What is his attitude toward his subject? Is it directly stated? If not, how do you know what it is?

Writing Topic

Clover mixes various kinds of language and **imagery**. Catalog examples of one element—kinds of words, kind of images (remembering that images aren't necessarily only visual)—and group them into different types (for example, long complicated words and simple words). In an essay, consider how and why Clover uses the kinds of elements he does.

KEVIN YOUNG (B. 1970)

NEGATIVE   2005

Wake to find everything black
what was white, all the vice
versa   white maids on TV, black

sitcoms that star white dwarfs
cute as pearl buttons, Black Presidents,
Black Houses, White Horse

candidates. All bleach burns
clothes black. Drive roads
white as you are, white songs

on the radio stolen by black bands   10
like secret pancake recipes, white back-up
singers, ball-players & boxers all

white as tar. Feathers on chickens
dark as everything, boiling in the pot
that called the kettle honky. Even

whites of the eye turn dark, pupils
clear & changing as a cat's.
Is this what we've wanted

& waited for? to see snow
covering everything black   20
as Christmas, dark pages written

white upon? All our eclipses bright,
dark stars shooting across pale
sky, glowing like ash in fire, shower

every skin. Only money keeps
green, still grows & burns like grass
under dark daylight.

TERRANCE HAYES   (B. 1971)

ROOT   2006

My parents would have had me believe
there was no such thing as race
there in the wild backyard, our knees black
with store-bought grass and dirt,
black as the soil of pastures or of orchards
grown above graves. We clawed free
the stones and filled their beds with soil
and covered the soil with sod
as if we owned the earth.
We worked into the edge of darkness   10
and rose in the edge of darkness
until everything came from the dirt.
We clawed free the moss and brambles,
the colonies of crab-weed, the thorns
patrolling stems and I liked it then:
the mute duty that tightened my parents'
backs as if they meant to work
the devil from his den. Rock and spore
and scraps of leaf; wild bouquets withered
in bags by the road, cast from the ground   20
we broke. We scrubbed the patio,
we raked the cross hatch of pine needles,
we soaked the ant-cathedrals in gas.
I found an axe blade beneath an untamed hedge,
its edge too dull to sever vine and half expected
to find a jawbone scabbed with mud,
because no one told me what happened
to the whites who'd owned the house.
No one spoke of the color that curled
around our tools or of the neighbors   30
who knew our name before we knew theirs.
Sometimes they were almost visible,
clean as fence posts in porch light;
their houses burning with wonder,
their hammocks drunk with wind.
When I dreamed, I dreamed of them
and believed they dreamed of us
and believed we were made of dirt or shadows:
something not held or given, irredeemable, inexact,
all of us asking what it means to be black . . .   40

I have never wanted another life, but I know the story
of pursuit: the dream of a gate standing open,
a grill and folding chairs, a new yard boxed in light.

FOR ANALYSIS

1. Does the speaker believe what his parents wanted him to believe? How do you
know?

2. Who is "them" in line 36? Who is "us" in line 37? What is the nature of their
relationship?

3. Describe the main action in this poem. Does its significance lie in what it is or
in what it stands for? If the latter, why do you think Hayes chooses to dramatize his
subject in this way?

WRITING TOPIC

Imaginative literature often works by indirection—by finding hidden, obscured, or
circuitous routes to ideas rather than following well-worn, straight paths to the thing or
idea or feeling it wants to represent. From the first line, "Root" works in this way. Write
a description of the ways in which Hayes says things in ways other than straight out.

ALEXANDRA TEAGUE   (B. 1974)

ADJECTIVES OF ORDER   2007

That summer, she had a student who was obsessed
with the order of adjectives. A soldier in the South
Vietnamese army, he had been taken prisoner when

Saigon fell. He wanted to know why the order
could not be altered. The sweltering city streets shook
with rockets and helicopters. The city sweltering

streets. On the dusty brown field of the chalkboard,
she wrote: *The mother took warm homemade bread
from the oven. City* is essential to *streets* as *homemade*

is essential to *bread.* He copied this down, but   10
he wanted to know if his brothers were *lost* before
older, if he worked security at a twenty-story modern

downtown bank or downtown twenty-story modern.
When he first arrived, he did not know enough English
to order a sandwich. He asked her to explain each part

of *Lovely big rectangular old red English Catholic*
leather Bible. Evaluation before size. Age before color.
Nationality before religion. Time before length. Adding

and, one could determine if two adjectives were equal.
After Saigon fell, he had survived nine long years   20
of torture. Nine *and* long. He knew no other way to say this.

CONNECTING POEMS: POETIC IDENTITIES

The poems in this unit are about the "self," but not just any self: They are about
the selves of poets. Because of this, they are about poetry and the writing of poetry,
of course, but they are also in some measure about the identities of people who
lived in particular places at particular times and dealt with the possibilities and
challenges presented by their circumstances, as all people do. As you read their
reflections on those circumstances and the ways in which these poets lived
within them, thought about them, and challenged them, note the different ways
in which each poet also reflects on how those external circumstances interact
with the singular circumstance of being someone who writes poetry.

WALT WHITMAN   (1819–1892)

FROM SONG OF MYSELF   1855

1

I celebrate myself, and sing myself,
And what I assume you shall assume,
For every atom belonging to me as good belongs to you.

I loafe and invite my soul,
I lean and loafe at my ease observing a spear of summer grass.

My tongue, every atom of my blood, form'd from this soil, this air,
Born here of parents born here from parents the same, and their parents
        the same,
I, now thirty-seven years old in perfect health begin,
Hoping to cease not till death.

Creeds and schools in abeyance,   10
Retiring back a while sufficed at what they are, but never forgotten,
I harbor for good or bad, I permit to speak at every hazard,
Nature without check with original energy.

6

A child said *What is the grass?* fetching it to me with full hands;
How could I answer the child? I do not know what it is any more than he.

I guess it must be the flag of my disposition, out of hopeful green stuff woven.

Or I guess it is the handkerchief of the Lord,
A scented gift and remembrancer designedly dropt,
Bearing the owner's name someway in the corners, that we may see and
remark, and say *Whose?*

Or I guess the grass is itself a child, the produced babe of the vegetation.   20

Or I guess it is a uniform hieroglyphic,
And it means, Sprouting alike in broad zones and narrow zones,
Growing among black folks as among white,
Kanuck, Tuckahoe, Congressman, Cuff, I give them the same, I receive them the
same.

And now it seems to me the beautiful uncut hair of graves.

Tenderly will I use you curling grass,
It may be you transpire from the breasts of young men,
It may be if I had known them I would have loved them,
It may be you are from old people, or from offspring taken soon out of
their mothers' laps,
And here you are the mothers' laps.   30

This grass is very dark to be from the white heads of old mothers,
Darker than the colorless beards of old men,
Dark to come from under the faint red roofs of mouths.

O I perceive after all so many uttering tongues,
And I perceive they do not come from the roofs of mouths for nothing.

I wish I could translate the hints about the dead young men and women,
And the hints about old men and mothers, and the offspring taken soon out
of their laps.

What do you think has become of the young and old men?
And what do you think has become of the women and children?

They are alive and well somewhere,   40
The smallest sprout shows there is really no death,

And if ever there was it led forward life, and does not wait at the end to arrest it,
And ceas'd the moment life appear'd.

All goes onward and outward, nothing collapses,
And to die is different from what anyone supposed, and luckier.

50

There is that in me—I do not know what it is—but I know it is in me.

Wrench'd and sweaty—calm and cool then my body becomes,
I sleep—I sleep long.

I do not know it—it is without name—it is a word unsaid,
It is not in any dictionary, utterance, symbol.   50

Sometimes it swings on more than the earth I swing on,
To it the creation is the friend whose embracing awakes me.

Perhaps I might tell more. Outlines! I plead for my brothers and sisters.

Do you see O my brothers and sisters?
It is not chaos or death—it is form, union, plan—it is eternal life—it is
        Happiness.

51

The past and present wilt—I have fill'd them, emptied them.
And proceed to fill my next fold of the future.

Listener up there! what have you to confide to me?
Look in my face while I snuff the sidle of evening,
(Talk honestly, no one else hears you, and I stay only a minute longer.)   60

Do I contradict myself?
Very well then I contradict myself.
(I am large, I contain multitudes.)

I concentrate toward them that are nigh, I wait on the door-slab.

Who has done his day's work? who will soonest be through with his supper?
Who wishes to walk with me?

Will you speak before I am gone? will you prove already too late?

52

The spotted hawk swoops by and accuses me, he complains of my gab
     and my loitering.

I too am not a bit tamed, I too am untranslatable,
I sound my barbaric yawp over the roofs of the world.   70

The last scud of day holds back for me,
It flings my likeness after the rest and true as any on the shadowed wilds,
It coaxes me to the vapor and the dusk.

I depart as air, I shake my white locks at the runaway sun,
I effuse my flesh in eddies, and drift it in lacy jags.

I bequeath myself to the dirt to grow from the grass I love,
If you want me again look for me under your boot-soles.

You will hardly know who I am or what I mean,
But I shall be good health to you nevertheless,
And filter and fibre your blood.   80

Failing to fetch me at first keep encouraged,
Missing me one place search another,
I stop somewhere waiting for you.

FOR ANALYSIS

1. Who or what is the speaker of this poem? List the lines in which he seems to be an individual speaker. Then make a list of the lines in which he seems to be something more.

2. The poem from which these excerpts are drawn is part of a book, *Leaves of Grass*. Why does this poem pay so much attention to grass? What does it mean?

3. How does this poem "contain multitudes" (l. 63)?

WRITING TOPICS

1. Whitman writes, "You will hardly know who I am or what I mean, / But I shall be good health to you nevertheless" (ll. 78–79). How might this poem be intended to be "good" for its readers?

2. "Song of Myself" achieves strong and varied effects. Reread the poem, and keep a log of your reactions—your emotional, intellectual, and hard-to-categorize responses— as you encounter the different parts of the poem. Then write a reflection on this log. Do you see any patterns? As you moved again through "Song of Myself," what did you notice about how it works as a poem and on you as a reader?

FRANK O'HARA   (1926–1966)

MY HEART   1970

I'm not going to cry all the time
nor shall I laugh all the time,
I don't prefer one "strain" to another.
I'd have the immediacy of a bad movie,
not just a sleeper, but also the big,
overproduced first-run kind. I want to be
at least as alive as the vulgar. And if
some aficionado of my mess says "That's
not like Frank!", all to the good! I
don't wear brown and grey suits all the time,   10
do I? No. I wear workshirts to the opera,
often. I want my feet to be bare,
I want my face to be shaven, and my heart—
you can't plan on the heart, but
the better part of it, my poetry, is open.

FOR ANALYSIS

1. What is this poem about—a person or his poetry? Why is it necessary to ask this question? What is the effect of O'Hara's writing the poem in such a way that the reader has to ask it?

2. How would you characterize the voice in this poem? What kinds of words and sentences does the speaker use? What are the effects?

3. What stands out about line 11? Why does it stand out? What effect does it have on you as you read?

WRITING TOPIC

List the different things the speaker wants. Can you divide the list up into categories? What does the divisibility of the list and the nature of the categories say about the poem?

BILLY COLLINS   (B. 1941)

MONDAY   2005

The birds are in their trees,
the toast is in the toaster,
and the poets are at their windows.

They are at their windows
in every section of the tangerine of earth—

the Chinese poets looking up at the moon,
the American poets gazing out
at the pink and blue ribbons of sunrise.

The clerks are at their desks,
the miners are down in their mines,   10
and the poets are looking out their windows
maybe with a cigarette, a cup of tea,
and maybe a flannel shirt or bathrobe is involved.

The proofreaders are playing the ping-pong
game of proofreading,
glancing back and forth from page to page,
the chefs are dicing celery and potatoes,
and the poets are at their windows
because it is their job for which
they are paid nothing every Friday afternoon.   20

Which window it hardly seems to matter
though many have a favorite,
for there is always something to see—
a bird grasping a thin branch,
the headlights of a taxi rounding a corner,
those two boys in wool caps angling across the street.

The fishermen bob in their boats,
the linemen climb their round poles,
the barbers wait by their mirrors and chairs,
and the poets continue to stare   30
at the cracked birdbath or a limb knocked down by the wind.

By now, it should go without saying
that what the oven is to the baker
and the berry-stained blouse to the dry cleaner,
so the window is to the poet.

Just think—
before the invention of the window,
the poets would have had to put on a jacket
and a winter hat to go outside
or remain indoors with only a wall to stare at.   40

And when I say a wall,
I do not mean a wall with striped wallpaper
and a sketch of a cow in a frame.

I mean a cold wall of fieldstones,
the wall of the medieval sonnet,
the original woman's heart of stone,
the stone caught in the throat of her poet-lover.

FOR ANALYSIS

1. Who or what is the speaker of this poem? List the lines in which he seems to be an individual speaker. Then list the lines in which he seems to be something more.

2. What does this poem have to say about poetry writing as work? In what ways is it like the other kinds of occupations mentioned in the poem? In what ways is it unlike them?

3. How does the last **stanza** differ from those that precede it? What is the effect? Why do you think Collins chose to write the ending this way?

WRITING TOPIC

Make an argument for why you think Collins chose the title he did. Use textual evidence.

CARL PHILLIPS (B. 1959)

BLUE 1992

As through marble or the lining of
certain fish split open and scooped
clean, this is the blue vein
that rides, where the flesh is even
whiter than the rest of her, the splayed
thighs mother forgets, busy struggling
for command over bones: her own,
those of the chaise longue, all
equally uncooperative, and there's
the wind, too. This is her hair, gone   10
from white to blue in the air.

This is the black, shot with blue, of my dark
daddy's knuckles, that do not change, ever.
Which is to say they are no more pale
in anger than at rest, or when, as
I imagine them now, they follow
the same two fingers he has always used
to make the rim of every empty blue
glass in the house sing.
Always, the same   20

blue-to-black sorrow
no black surface can entirely hide.

Under the night, somewhere
between the white that is nothing so much as
blue, and the black that is, finally; nothing,
I am the man neither of you remembers.
Shielding, in the half-dark,
the blue eyes I sometimes forget
I don't have. Pulling my own stoop-
shouldered kind of blues across paper.   30
Apparently misinformed about the rumored
stuff of dreams: everywhere I inquired,
I was told look for blue.

FOR ANALYSIS

1. This poem is filled with **concrete** visual detail. Why is that appropriate for this poem?

2. Colors lend detail to **imagery** in poems, but they also connote a range of
meanings. What are the dominant colors in this poem? What are their different
connotations?

3. What is the **setting** of this poem in terms of the speaker's life? What time or times
is he writing about? What time in his life is he writing from? What is the relation
between these times, and what is the effect of putting them together in one poem?

MAKING CONNECTIONS

1. Many of these poems feature the **first-person** "I." What do these "I"s have in
common? How do they differ?

2. These poems all address identity; many do so in part with references to the past.
What roles does the past play in these poems? How do the poets connect the past to
their present identities?

3. These poems are about not just personal identity, but the personal identity of
poets. In this way, they are different from poems that are just about poetry; the poems
in this unit are about poetry too, of course, but they also pay attention to the makers of poems. What different things do these poems say about poetic identity? Which
seem similar, and which are more in contrast?

WRITING TOPIC

In what way is this poem a blues poem? (If you are unfamiliar with the blues as a
musical genre, do a few minutes of research on it.) Think in terms of sounds and
rhythm as well as content.

TIMOTHY YU   (B. 1974)

CHINESE SILENCE NO. 22   2011

AFTER BILLY COLLINS, "MONDAY"

The Italians are making their pasta,
the French are making things French,
and the Chinese cultivate their silence.

They cultivate silence
in every Chinatown on the persimmon of earth—
mute below the towers of Toronto,
silently sweeping the streets of Singapore
clear of noisy self-expression.

The Americans are in their sport utility vehicles,
the Canadians are behaving reasonably,   10
but the Chinese remain silent
maybe with a cup of tea or an opium pipe
and maybe a finger puzzle or water torture is involved.

Or maybe the Chinese are playing the Chinese
game of ping-pong,
the pock-pock of the ball against their tight-lipped mouths
as their chefs dice scallions and bean curd.
The Chinese are silent
because it is their job for which
I pay them what they got for building the railroads.   20

Which silence it is hardly seems to matter
though many have a favorite
out of the 100 different kinds—
the Silence of the Well-Adjusted Minority,
the Girlish Silence of Reluctant Acquiescence,
the Silence that by No Means Should Be Mistaken for Bitterness.

By now, it should go without saying
that what Crocodile Dundee is to the Australian
and Mel Gibson is to the Scot,
so is silence to the Chinese.   30

Just think—
before I invented the 100 Chinese silences,

the Chinese would have had to stay indoors
and gabble about civil war and revolution
or go outside and build a really loud wall.

And when I say a wall,
I do not mean a wall of thousands of miles
that is visible from the moon.

I mean a noisy wall of language
that dwarfs my medieval battlements   40
and paves the Pacific to lap
California's shores with its brick-hard words.

FOR ANALYSIS

1. What principle of selection governed Yu's choices for things he has "the Chinese" doing in this poem? What is the poem's attitude toward these things and toward the thing that unites them?

2. What does the "after" in the poem's subtitle mean? What is the relationship between Yu's poem and Collins's?

3. This poem is one of a series of 100 "Chinese Silence" poems. When Yu alludes to the series in the poem, what does he reveal about his view of himself as a poet?

4. How would you characterize the poem's voice? Is it straightforward, or **ironic**? Detached, or full of feeling?

WRITING TOPIC

While we often think of poems as simply things to be studied, enjoyed quietly, or maybe shared—especially when we encounter them in class—"Chinese Silence No. 22" considers poetry as something with power in the real world. Reflect on how you think of poetry. Is it something that lives only on pages between covers, or is it something that can make real things happen?

CONNECTING POEMS:
FASHIONING SELVES

Each of the poems in this unit addresses the pressures women feel to conform to social expectations. From Emily Dickinson's nineteenth-century New England to Taslima Nasrin's contemporary India, women have received, subtly and not so subtly, instructions about what they are supposed to be, what they are supposed to want, and how they are supposed to feel. As you read, note how these poems choose to not simply observe from the outside but instead get inside the heads of women feeling and acting on these pressures—perhaps unknown to themselves—and how they use **irony** to critique a world in which such pressures exist.

EMILY DICKINSON (1830-1886)

WHAT SOFT—
CHERUBIC CREATURES— CA. 1862

What Soft—Cherubic Creatures—
These Gentlewomen are—
One would as soon assault a Plush—
Or violate a Star—

Such Dimity Convictions—
A Horror so refined
Of freckled Human Nature—
Of Deity—ashamed—

It's such a common—Glory—
A Fisherman's—Degree— 10
Redemption—Brittle Lady—
Be so—ashamed of Thee—

FOR ANALYSIS

1. How can human nature be seen as "freckled" (l. 7)?
2. What is the poem's **tone**? Does the speaker really think the women are "cherubic"?
3. What is the effect of the use of violence in the third and fourth lines?

JUNE JORDAN (1936-2002)

MEMO: 1980

When I hear some woman say she
has finally decided you can spend time with
other women, I wonder what she means: Her
mother? My mother?
I've always despised my woman friends. Even
if they introduced me to a man I found
attractive I have never let them become
what you could call my intimates. Why
should I? Men are the ones with the money and
the big way with waiters and the passkey 10
to excitement in strange places of real
danger and the power to make things happen
like babies or war and all these great ideas
about mass magazines for members of the weaker sex

715 .

who need permission
to eat potatoes or a doctor's opinion on orgasm after death
or the latest word on what the female
executive should do, after hours, wearing
what. They must be morons: women!
Don't you think?   20
I guess you could say
I'm stuck in my ways
as
That Cosmopolitan Girl.

FOR ANALYSIS

1. Explain the title.

2. What do the first three lines mean? Why would a woman feel she *can't* spend time with other women?

3. Does this poem accurately describe the power relations in our society? Explain.

4. Describe the **tone** of this poem.

WRITING TOPIC

Examine a few issues of *Cosmopolitan* magazine, and write an essay imagining how it inspired this poem.

MARGE PIERCY   (B. 1936)

BARBIE DOLL   1973

This girlchild was born as usual
and presented dolls that did pee-pee
and miniature GE stoves and irons
and wee lipsticks the color of cherry candy.
Then in the magic of puberty, a classmate said:
You have a great big nose and fat legs.

She was healthy, tested intelligent,
possessed strong arms and back,
abundant sexual drive and manual dexterity.
She went to and fro apologizing.   10
Everyone saw a fat nose on thick legs.

She was advised to play coy,
exhorted to come on hearty,
exercise, diet, smile and wheedle.

Her good nature wore out
like a fan belt.
So she cut off her nose and her legs
and offered them up.

In the casket displayed on satin she lay
with the undertaker's cosmetics painted on,   20
a turned-up putty nose,
dressed in a pink and white nightie.
Doesn't she look pretty? everyone said.
Consummation at last.
To every woman a happy ending.

FOR ANALYSIS

1. In what way does this poem have a "happy ending" (l. 25)? Is it really happy?

2. List the characteristics attributed to the girl in the poem. Which are judged by others to be important? Which are judged unimportant? Why?

3. Why does the girl apologize? Should she?

WRITING TOPICS

1. People have long argued over what makes boys and girls conform to society's expectations. Some argue that the differences are genetic: that boys and girls are intrinsically different. Others argue that gendered behavior is socialized: that differences come not from nature but from nurture. Where does Piercy's poem fall on the nature-nurture question? Where do you fall? Why?

2. Reflect on the turn in line 17. Why is this an unusual moment? What are its effects? Why do you think Piercy chooses to have something like this happen?

TASLIMA NASRIN   (B. 1962)

THINGS CHEAPLY HAD[1]   1991

In the market nothing can be had as cheap as women.
If they get a small bottle of *alta*[2] for their feet
            they spend three nights sleepless for sheer joy.
If they get a few bars of soap to scrub their skin
            and some scented oil for their hair

Things Cheaply Had

[1] Translated from the Bengali by Carolyne Wright with Mohammad Nurul Huda and the author.

[2] *Alta*, or lac-dye, is a red liquid with which South Asian women decorate the borders of their feet on ceremonial occasions, such as weddings and dance performances. *Alta* is more in vogue among Hindus, but Bangladeshi women also use it, and it can be seen on the feet of Muslim heroines and harem women in Moghul miniature paintings. [Translator's note.]

they become so submissive that they scoop out
        chunks of their flesh
to be sold in the flea market twice a week.
If they get a jewel for their nose
        they lick feet for seventy days or so,   10
a full three and a half months
        if it's a single striped sari.[3]

Even the mangy cur of the house barks now and then,
and over the mouths of women cheaply had
        there's a lock
a golden lock.

FOR ANALYSIS

1. Why is the lock in the final line of the poem "golden"?

2. What are the "things" of the title? Do they include more than the items the women "get"?

MAKING CONNECTIONS

1. How does each of these poems use **irony**? Why is irony an effective tool for poems about this shared subject?

2. Though men are not mentioned in all of these poems, they play a role in each of them. What are those roles, and how are they implicitly or explicitly brought into the poems?

3. Only one of these poems features an explicitly female **persona**, yet all could be said to explore female consciousness. How does each do so, and to what effect?

CONNECTING POEMS: WORKING MOTHERS

The kind of work people do is often partly determined by their gender. Particular jobs are often restricted to or almost always filled by either men or women, and particular kinds of uncompensated tasks, like housework, are too. The poems in this unit address work from the viewpoint of the women who do it or the daughters who watch them do it. As you read, notice the shared **point of view** but also the different situations in which these women find themselves. How does lifestyle—social class, typical experiences—help shape what these women see when they look at work?

Things Cheaply Had
  [3] An outer garment worn chiefly by women of India and Pakistan, consisting of a length of cloth wrapped around the waist at one end and draped over the shoulder or head at the other.

TESS GALLAGHER (B. 1943)

I STOP WRITING THE POEM 1992

to fold the clothes. No matter who lives
or who dies, I'm still a woman.
I'll always have plenty to do.
I bring the arms of his shirt
together. Nothing can stop
our tenderness. I'll get back
to the poem. I'll get back to being
a woman. But for now
there's a shirt, a giant shirt
in my hands, and somewhere a small girl   10
standing next to her mother
watching to see how it's done.

FOR ANALYSIS

1. Does the speaker stop writing the poem? Does the continuation of the title into the
first line help answer this question?

2. How does the **enjambment**, or continuation, of the first and second lines help
signal an important context for the poem's situation?

3. If the speaker is not being a poet or a woman at the end of the poem, what is she
being?

WRITING TOPICS

1. Especially for a self-conscious poem, "I Stop Writing the Poem" is simple, relatively devoid of poetic devices. Reflect on why Gallagher chose to write the poem in
this spare style.

2. The "it" in the last line refers to more than shirt folding; the poem is about more
than poetry or laundry, and, though it alludes to a context, it does not explore it. Tell
the story that you think lays behind this poem, and explain what the "it" of the last
line might be.

JULIA ALVAREZ (B. 1950)

WOMAN'S WORK 1996

Who says a woman's work isn't high art?
She'd challenge as she scrubbed the bathroom tiles.
Keep house as if the address were your heart.

We'd clean the whole upstairs before we'd start
downstairs, I'd sigh, hearing my friends outside.
Doing her woman's work was a hard art

to practice when the summer sun would bar
the floor I swept till she was satisfied.
She kept me prisoner in her housebound heart.

She'd shine the tines of forks, the wheels of carts,   10
cut lacy lattices for all her pies.
Her woman's work was nothing less than art.

And I, her masterpiece since I was smart,
was primed, praised, polished, scolded and advised
to keep a house much better than my heart.

I did not want to be her counterpart!
I struck out . . . but became my mother's child:
a woman working at home on her art,
housekeeping paper as if it were her heart.

FOR ANALYSIS

1. How is the speaker her mother's "masterpiece" (l. 13)?

2. To what does "housekeeping paper" (l. 19) refer?

3. Answer the first line's question as if it weren't rhetorical.

WRITING TOPICS

1. Write an account of Alvarez's use of repetition and **rhyme** in "Woman's Work."
What effects does Alvarez achieve?

2. Tone in this poem is complicated and nuanced. Make a list of words that seem to
have positive **connotations**. Then make a list of words that seem to have negative connotations. How do these words express how the speaker feels about the various subjects?

RITA DOVE (B. 1952)

MY MOTHER ENTERS THE WORK FORCE 2000

The path to ABC Business School
was paid for by a lucky sign:
Alterations, Qualified Seamstress Inquire Within.
Tested on Sleeves, hers

never puckered—puffed or sleek,
Leg o' or Raglan—
they barely needed the damp cloth
to steam them perfect.

Those were the afternoons. Evenings
she took in piecework, the treadle machine   10
with its locomotive whir
traveling the lit path of the needle
through quicksand taffeta
or velvet deep as a forest.
And now and now sang the treadle,
I know, I know . . . .

And then it was day again, all morning
at the office machines, their clack and chatter
another journey—rougher,
that would go on forever   20
until she could break a hundred words
with no errors—ah, and then

no more postponed groceries,
and that blue pair of shoes!

FOR ANALYSIS

1. Dove's poem describes the mother's sewing work in great detail. What does the specific nature of this detail express about the daughter-speaker's attitude toward her mother's work?

2. How would you characterize the poem's **tone** overall? What about it informs the tone?

3. What is the treadle saying, and to whom?

WRITING TOPICS

1. Although the poem speaks very little about it, this mother and daughter are not as comfortable economically as they might be. How do we know this? What is the poem's attitude toward this situation?

2. Write a poem about work you have done, or work a parent or another relative or a friend has done. Describe that work in a way that reveals, without being explicit, your (or his or her) feelings about it.

DEBORAH GARRISON   (B. 1965)

SESTINA FOR THE WORKING MOTHER   2007

No time for a sestina for the working mother.
Who has so much to do, from first thing in the morning
When she has to get herself dressed and the children
Too, when they tumble in the pillow pile rather than listening
To her exhortations about brushing teeth, making ready for the day;
They clamor with "up" hugs when she struggles out the door.

Every time, as if shot from a cannon when she shuts the door.
She stomps down the street in her city boots, slipping from mother
Mode into commuter trance, trees swaying at the corner of a new day
Nearly turned, her familiar bus stop cool and welcoming in the morning.   10
She hears her own heart here, though no one else is listening,
And if the bus is late she hears down the block the voices of her children

Bobbing under their oversized backpacks to greet other children
At their own bus stop. They too have come flying from the door,
Brave for the journey, and everyone is talking and no one is listening
As they head off to school. The noisy children of the working mother,
Waiting with their sitter for the bus, are healthy and happy this morning.
And that's the best way, the mother knows, for a day

To begin. The apprehension of what kind of day
It will be in the world of work, blissful without children,   20
Trembles in the anxious and pleasurable pulse of the morning;
It has tamped her down tight and lit her out the door
And away from what she might have been as a mother
At home, perhaps drinking coffee and listening

To NPR, what rapt and intelligent listening
She'd do at home. And volunteering, she thinks, for part of the day
At their school—she'd be a playground monitor, a PTA mother!
She'd see them straggle into the sunshine, her children
Bright in the slipstream, and she a gracious shadow at the school door;
She would not be separated from them for long by the morning.   30

But she has chosen her flight from them, on this and every morning.
She's now so far away she trusts someone else is listening
To their raised voices, applying a Band-Aid, opening the door
For them when the sunshine calls them out into the day.
At certain moments, head bent at her desk, she can see her children,
And feels the quick stab. She hasn't forgotten that she is their mother.

722

Every weekday morning, every working day,
She listens to her heart and the voices of her children.
Goodbye! they shout, and the door closes behind the working mother.

FOR ANALYSIS

1. *Sestina* is a highly structured traditional form of poetry. Can you guess what the "rules" are for a sestina by figuring out the structure of this one?

2. What is the effect of reading a sestina, or at least this sestina? Considering these effects, why do you think Garrison chose the sestina form for this poem? What about her poem's **themes** might be expressed by its form?

3. Is the speaker happy to be a working mother? Sad? Both?

MAKING CONNECTIONS

1. Three of the four poems in this unit feature a speaker who might be understood to be a poet. How does each of these poems relate poetry to the other things—work, motherhood, and so on—that these poems are about? Is poetry work? Is it more or less than work?

2. All of these poems reflect on issues surrounding women working, sometimes explicitly. Though the first concern is often about social expectations—what work is "appropriate" for women and what isn't—in the background is the question of economics. Which of these poems makes economics a central concern? Which of these does not? Can you read the economics behind one or more that don't foreground it?

3. Address the role housework plays in these poems. Is it drudgery or an art? A necessity or a way to teach work habits?

WRITING TOPICS

1. What function do lines 23–30 serve? How do they fit into the larger poem? What about the opening of the sixth stanza helps you understand its function and its fit?

2. The final stanza in a sestina, the *envoi*, is often used to comment on the rest of the poem. How does the envoi in "Sestina for the Working Mother" comment on the rest of it?

DRAMA

LORRAINE HANSBERRY (1930–1965)

A RAISIN IN THE SUN 1959

CHARACTERS (in order of appearance)

Ruth Younger

Walter Lee Younger, brother

Lena Younger, Mama

George Murchison

Karl Lindner

Moving Men

Travis Younger

Beneatha Younger

Joseph Asagai

Mrs. Johnson

Bobo

The action of the play is set in Chicago's Southside, sometime between World War II and the present.

ACT I

Scene 1.   *(Friday morning.)*

The Younger living room would be a comfortable and well-ordered room if it were not for a number of indestructible contradictions to this state of being. Its furnishings are typical and undistinguished and their primary feature now is that they have clearly had to accommodate the living of too many people for too many years—and they are tired. Still, we can see that at some time, a time probably no longer remembered by the family (except perhaps for Mama), the furnishings of this room were actually selected with care and love and even hope—and brought to this apartment and arranged with taste and pride.

That was a long time ago. Now the once loved pattern of the couch upholstery has to fight to show itself from under acres of crocheted doilies and couch covers which have themselves finally come to be more important than the upholstery. And here a table or a chair has been moved to disguise the worn places in the carpet; but the carpet has fought back by showing its weariness, with depressing uniformity, elsewhere on its surface.

Weariness has, in fact, won in this room. Everything has been polished, washed, sat on, used, scrubbed too often. All pretenses but living itself have long since vanished from the very atmosphere of this room.

Moreover, a section of this room, for it is not really a room unto itself, though the landlord's lease would make it seem so, slopes backward to provide a small kitchen area, where the family prepares the meals that are eaten in the living room proper, which must also serve as dining room. The single window that has been provided for these "two" rooms is located in this kitchen area. The sole natural light the family may enjoy in the course of a day is only that which fights its way through this little window.

At left, a door leads to a bedroom which is shared by Mama and her daughter, Beneatha. At right, opposite, is a second room (which in the beginning of the life of this apartment was probably a breakfast room) which serves as a bedroom for Walter and his wife, Ruth.

Time: Sometime between World War II and the present.

Place: Chicago's Southside.

At Rise: It is morning dark in the living room. Travis is asleep on the make-down bed at center. An alarm clock sounds from within the bedroom at right, and presently Ruth enters from that room and closes the door behind her. She crosses sleepily toward the window. As she passes her sleeping son she reaches down and shakes him a little. At the window she raises the shade and a dusky Southside morning light comes in feebly. She fills a pot with water and puts it on to boil. She calls to the boy, between yawns, in a slightly muffled voice.

Ruth is about thirty. We can see that she was a pretty girl, even exceptionally so, but now it is apparent that life has been little that she expected, and disappointment has already begun to hang in her face. In a few years, before thirty-five even, she will be known among her people as a "settled woman."

She crosses to her son and gives him a good, final, rousing shake.

Ruth. Come on now, boy, it's seven thirty! *(Her son sits up at last, in a stupor of sleepiness.)* I say hurry up, Travis! You ain't the only person in the world got to use a bathroom! *(The child, a sturdy, handsome little boy of ten or eleven, drags himself out of the bed and almost blindly takes his towels and "today's clothes" from drawers and a closet and goes out to the bathroom, which is in an outside hall and which is shared by another family or families on the same floor. Ruth crosses to the bedroom door at right and opens it and calls in to her husband.)* Walter Lee! . . . It's after seven thirty! Lemme see you do some waking up in there now! *(She waits.)* You better get up from there, man! It's after seven thirty I tell you. *(She waits again.)* All right, you just go ahead and lay there and next thing you know Travis be finished and Mr. Johnson'll be in there and you'll be fussing and cussing round here like a madman! And be late too! *(She waits, at the end of patience.)* Walter Lee—it's time for you to GET UP!

She waits another second and then starts to go into the bedroom, but is apparently satisfied that her husband has begun to get up. She stops, pulls the door to, and returns to the kitchen area. She wipes her face with a moist cloth and runs her fingers through her sleep-disheveled hair in a vain effort and ties an apron around her housecoat. The bedroom door at right opens and her husband stands in the doorway in his pajamas, which are rumpled and mismated. He is a lean, intense young man in his middle thirties, inclined to quick nervous movements and erratic speech habits—and always in his voice there is a quality of indictment.

Walter. Is he out yet?

Ruth. What you mean *out?* He ain't hardly got in there good yet.

Walter *(wandering in, still more oriented to sleep than to a new day).* Well, what was you doing all that yelling for if I can't even get in there yet? *(Stopping and thinking.)* Check coming today?

Ruth. They *said* Saturday and this is just Friday and I hopes to God you ain't going to get up here first thing this morning and start talking to me 'bout no money—'cause I 'bout don't want to hear it.

Walter. Something the matter with you this morning?

Ruth. No—I'm just sleepy as the devil. What kind of eggs you want?

Walter. Not scrambled. *(Ruth starts to scramble eggs.)* Paper come? *(Ruth points impatiently to the rolled up* Tribune *on the table, and he gets it and spreads it out and vaguely reads the front page.)* Set off another bomb yesterday.

Ruth *(maximum indifference).* Did they?

Walter *(looking up).* What's the matter with you?

Ruth. Ain't nothing the matter with me. And don't keep asking me that this morning.

Walter. Ain't nobody bothering you. *(Reading the news of the day absently again.)* Say Colonel McCormick is sick.

Ruth *(affecting tea-party interest).* Is he now? Poor thing.

Walter (sighing and looking at his watch). Oh, me. (He waits.) Now what is that boy doing in that bathroom all this time? He just going to have to start getting up earlier. I can't be being late to work on account of him fooling around in there.

Ruth *(turning on him).* Oh, no he ain't going to be getting up no earlier no such thing! It ain't his fault that he can't get to bed no earlier nights 'cause he got a bunch of crazy good-for-nothing clowns sitting up running their mouths in what is supposed to be his bedroom after ten o'clock at night . . .

Walter. That's what you mad about, ain't it? The things I want to talk about with my friends just couldn't be important in your mind, could they?

He rises and finds a cigarette in her handbag on the table and crosses to the little window and looks out, smoking and deeply enjoying this first one.

Ruth *(almost matter of factly, a complaint too automatic to deserve emphasis).* Why you always got to smoke before you eat in the morning?

Walter *(at the window).* Just look at 'em down there . . . Running and racing to work . . . *(He turns and faces his wife and watches her a moment at the stove, and then, suddenly.)* You look young this morning, baby.

Ruth *(indifferently).* Yeah?

Walter. Just for a second—stirring them eggs. Just for a second it was—you looked real young again. *(He reaches for her; she crosses away. Then, drily.)* It's gone now—you look like yourself again!

Ruth. Man, if you don't shut up and leave me alone.

Walter (*looking out to the street again*). First thing a man ought to learn in life is not to make love to no colored woman first thing in the morning. You all some eeeevil people at eight o'clock in the morning.

Travis appears in the hall doorway, almost fully dressed and quite wide awake now, his towels and pajamas across his shoulders. He opens the door and signals for his father to make the bathroom in a hurry.

Travis (*watching the bathroom*). Daddy, come on!

Walter gets his bathroom utensils and flies out to the bathroom.

Ruth. Sit down and have your breakfast, Travis.

Travis. Mama, this is Friday. (*Gleefully.*) Check coming tomorrow, huh?

Ruth. You get your mind off money and eat your breakfast.

Travis (*eating*). This is the morning we supposed to bring the fifty cents to school.

Ruth. Well, I ain't got no fifty cents this morning.

Travis. Teacher say we have to.

Ruth. I don't care what teacher say. I ain't got it. Eat your breakfast, Travis.

Travis. I *am* eating.

Ruth. Hush up now and just eat!

The boy gives her an exasperated look for her lack of understanding, and eats grudgingly.

Travis. You think Grandmama would have it?

Ruth. No! And I want you to stop asking your grandmother for money, you hear me?

Travis (*outraged*). Gaaaleee! I don't ask her, she just gimme it sometimes!

Ruth. Travis Willard Younger—I got too much on me this morning to be—

Travis. Maybe Daddy—

Ruth. *Travis!*

The boy hushes abruptly. They are both quiet and tense for several seconds.

Travis (*presently*). Could I maybe go carry some groceries in front of the supermarket for a little while after school then?

Ruth. Just hush, I said. (*Travis jabs his spoon into his cereal bowl viciously, and rests his head in anger upon his fists.*) If you through eating, you can get over there and make up your bed.

The boy obeys stiffly and crosses the room, almost mechanically, to the bed and more or less folds the bedding into a heap, then angrily gets his books and cap.

Travis (*sulking and standing apart from her unnaturally*). I'm gone.

Ruth (*looking up from the stove to inspect him automatically*). Come here. (*He crosses to her and she studies his head.*) If you don't take this comb and fix this here head, you better! (*Travis puts down his books with a great sigh of oppression, and crosses to the mirror. His mother mutters under her breath about his "slubbornness."*) 'Bout to march out of here with that head looking just like chickens slept in it! I just don't know where you get your slubborn ways . . . And get your jacket, too. Looks chilly out this morning.

Travis (*with conspicuously brushed hair and jacket*). I'm gone.

Ruth. Get carfare and milk money—(*Waving one finger.*)—and not a single penny for no caps, you hear me?

Travis (*with sullen politeness*). Yes'm.

He turns in outrage to leave. His mother watches after him as in his frustration he approaches the door almost comically. When she speaks to him, her voice has become a very gentle tease.

Ruth (*mocking; as she thinks he would say it*). Oh, Mama makes me so mad sometimes, I don't know what to do! (*She waits and continues to his back as he stands stock-still in front of the door.*) I wouldn't kiss that woman good-bye for nothing in this world this morning! (*The boy finally turns around and rolls his eyes at her, knowing the mood has changed and he is vindicated; he does not, however, move toward her yet.*) Not for nothing in this world! (*She finally laughs aloud at him and holds out her arms to him and we see that it is a way between them, very old and practiced. He crosses to her and allows her to embrace him warmly but keeps his face fixed with masculine rigidity. She holds him back from her presently and looks at him and runs her fingers over the features of his face. With utter gentleness—.*) Now—whose little old angry man are you?

Travis (*the masculinity and gruffness start to fade at last*). Aw gaalee—Mama . . .

Ruth (*mimicking*). Aw—gaaaaalleeeee, Mama! (*She pushes him, with rough playfulness and finality, toward the door.*) Get on out of here or you going to be late.

Travis (*in the face of love, new aggressiveness*). Mama, could I *please* go carry groceries?

Ruth. Honey, it's starting to get so cold evenings.

Walter (*coming in from the bathroom and drawing a make-believe gun from a make-believe holster and shooting at his son*). What is it he wants to do?

Ruth. Go carry groceries after school at the supermarket.

Walter. Well, let him go . . .

Travis (*quickly, to the ally*). I *have* to—she won't gimme the fifty cents . . .

Walter (*to his wife only*). Why not?

Ruth (*simply, and with flavor*). 'Cause we don't have it.

Walter (*to Ruth only*). What you tell the boy things like that for? (*Reaching down into his pants with a rather important gesture.*) Here, son—

He hands the boy the coin, but his eyes are directed to his wife's. Travis takes the money happily.

Travis. Thanks, Daddy.

He starts out. Ruth watches both of them with murder in her eyes. Walter stands and stares back at her with defiance, and suddenly reaches into his pocket again on an afterthought.

Walter *(without even looking at his son, still staring hard at his wife).* In fact, here's another fifty cents . . . Buy yourself some fruit today—or take a taxicab to school or something!

Travis. Whoopee—

He leaps up and clasps his father around the middle with his legs, and they face each other in mutual appreciation; slowly Walter Lee peeks around the boy to catch the violent rays from his wife's eyes and draws his head back as if shot.

Walter. You better get down now—and get to school, man.

Travis *(at the door).* O.K. Good-bye.

He exits.

Walter *(after him, pointing with pride).* That's *my* boy. *(She looks at him in disgust and turns back to her work.)* You know what I was thinking 'bout in the bathroom this morning?

Ruth. No.

Walter. How come you always try to be so pleasant!

Ruth. What is there to be pleasant 'bout!

Walter. You want to know what I was thinking 'bout in the bathroom or not!

Ruth. I know what you thinking 'bout.

Walter *(ignoring her).* 'Bout what me and Willy Harris was talking about last night.

Ruth *(immediately—a refrain).* Willy Harris is a good-for-nothing loudmouth.

Walter. Anybody who talks to me has got to be a good-for-nothing loudmouth, ain't he? And what you know about who is just a good-for-nothing loudmouth? Charlie Atkins was just a "good-for-nothing loudmouth" too, wasn't he! When he wanted me to go in the dry-cleaning business with him. And now—he's grossing a hundred thousand a year. A hundred thousand dollars a year! You still call *him* a loudmouth!

Ruth *(bitterly).* Oh, Walter Lee . . .

She folds her head on her arms over the table.

Walter *(rising and coming to her and standing over her).* You tired, ain't you? Tired of everything. Me, the boy, the way we live—this beat-up hole—everything. Ain't you? *(She doesn't look up, doesn't answer.)* So tired—moaning and groaning all the time, but you wouldn't do nothing to help, would you? You couldn't be on my side that long for nothing, could you?

Ruth. Walter, please leave me alone.

Walter. A man needs for a woman to back him up . . .

Ruth. Walter—

Walter. Mama would listen to you. You know she listen to you more than she do me and Bennie. She think more of you. All you have to do is just sit down with her when you drinking your coffee one morning and talking 'bout things like you do and—*(He sits down beside her and demonstrates graphically what he thinks her methods and tone should be.)*—you just sip your coffee, see, and say easy like that you been thinking 'bout that deal Walter Lee is so interested in, 'bout the store and all, and sip some more coffee, like what you saying ain't really that important to you—And the next thing you know, she be listening good and asking you questions and when I come home—I can tell her the details. This ain't no fly-by-night proposition, baby. I mean we figured it out, me and Willy and Bobo.

Ruth *(with a frown).* Bobo?

Walter. Yeah. You see, this little liquor store we got in mind cost seventy-five thousand and we figured the initial investment on the place be 'bout thirty thousand, see. That be ten thousand each. Course, there's a couple of hundred you got to pay so's you don't spend your life just waiting for them clowns to let your license get approved—

Ruth. You mean graft?

Walter *(frowning impatiently).* Don't call it that. See there, that just goes to show you what women understand about the world. Baby, don't *nothing* happen for you in the world 'less you pay *somebody* off!

Ruth. Walter, leave me alone! *(She raises her head and stares at him vigorously— then says, more quietly.)* Eat your eggs, they gonna be cold.

Walter *(straightening up from her and looking off).* That's it. There you are. Man say to his woman: I got me a dream. His woman say: Eat your eggs. *(Sadly, but gaining in power.)* Man say: I got to take hold of this here world, baby! And a woman will say: Eat your eggs and go to work. *(Passionately now.)* Man say: I got to change my life, I'm choking to death, baby! And his woman say— *(In utter anguish as he brings his fists down on his thighs.)*—Your eggs is getting cold!

Ruth *(softly).* Walter, that ain't none of our money.

Walter *(not listening at all or even looking at her).* This morning, I was lookin' in the mirror and thinking about it . . . I'm thirty-five years old; I been married eleven years and I got a boy who sleeps in the living room—*(Very, very quietly.)*—and all I got to give him is stories about how rich white people live . . .

Ruth. Eat your eggs, Walter.

Walter *(slams the table and jumps up).* —DAMN MY EGGS—DAMN ALL THE EGGS THAT EVER WAS!

Ruth. Then go to work.

Walter *(looking up at her).* See—I'm trying to talk to you 'bout myself—*(Shaking his head with the repetition.)*—and all you can say is eat them eggs and go to work.

Ruth *(wearily).* Honey, you never say nothing new. I listen to you every day, every night and every morning, and you never say nothing new. *(Shrugging.)* So you would rather *be* Mr. Arnold than be his chauffeur. So—I would *rather* be living in Buckingham Palace.

Walter. That is just what is wrong with the colored woman in this world . . . Don't understand about building their men up and making 'em feel like they somebody. Like they can do something.

Ruth *(drily, but to hurt).* There *are* colored men who do things.

Walter. No thanks to the colored woman.

Ruth. Well, being a colored woman, I guess I can't help myself none.

She rises and gets the ironing board and sets it up and attacks a huge pile of rough-dried clothes, sprinkling them in preparation for the ironing and then rolling them into tight fat balls.

Walter *(mumbling).* We one group of men tied to a race of women with small minds!

His sister Beneatha enters. She is about twenty, as slim and intense as her brother. She is not as pretty as her sister-in-law, but her lean, almost intellectual face has a handsomeness of its own. She wears a bright-red flannel nightie, and her thick hair stands wildly about her head. Her speech is a mixture of many things; it is different from the rest of the family's insofar as education has permeated her sense of English—and perhaps the Midwest rather than the South has finally—at last—won out in her inflection; but not altogether, because over all of it is a soft slurring and transformed use of vowels which is the decided influence of the Southside. She passes through the room without looking at either Ruth or Walter and goes to the outside door and looks, a little blindly, out to the bathroom. She sees that it has been lost to the Johnsons. She closes the door with a sleepy vengeance and crosses to the table and sits down a little defeated.

Beneatha. I am going to start timing those people.

Walter. You should get up earlier.

Beneatha *(her face in her hands. She is still fighting the urge to go back to bed).* Really—would you suggest dawn? Where's the paper?

Walter *(pushing the paper across the table to her as he studies her almost clinically, as though he has never seen her before).* You a horrible-looking chick at this hour.

Beneatha *(drily).* Good morning, everybody.

Walter *(senselessly).* How is school coming?

Beneatha *(in the same spirit).* Lovely. Lovely. And you know, biology is the greatest. *(Looking up at him.)* I dissected something that looked just like you yesterday.

Walter. I just wondered if you've made up your mind and everything.

Beneatha *(gaining in sharpness and impatience).* And what did I answer yesterday morning—and the day before that?

Ruth *(from the ironing board, like someone disinterested and old).* Don't be so nasty, Bennie.

Beneatha (*still to her brother*). And the day before that and the day before that!

Walter (*defensively*). I'm interested in you. Something wrong with that? Ain't many girls who decide—

Walter and Beneatha (*in unison*). —"to be a doctor."

Silence.

Walter. Have we figured out yet just exactly how much medical school is going to cost?

Ruth. Walter Lee, why don't you leave that girl alone and get out of here to work?

Beneatha (*exits to the bathroom and bangs on the door*). Come on out of there, please!

She comes back into the room.

Walter (*looking at his sister intently*). You know the check is coming tomorrow.

Beneatha (*turning on him with a sharpness all her own*). That money belongs to Mama, Walter, and it's for her to decide how she wants to use it. I don't care if she wants to buy a house or a rocket ship or just nail it up somewhere and look at it. It's hers. Not ours—*hers*.

Walter (*bitterly*). Now ain't that fine! You just got your mother's interest at heart, ain't you, girl? You such a nice girl—but if Mama got that money she can always take a few thousand and help you through school too—can't she?

Beneatha. I have never asked anyone around here to do anything for me!

Walter. No! And the line between asking and just accepting when the time comes is big and wide—ain't it!

Beneatha (*with fury*). What do you want from me, Brother—that I quit school or just drop dead, which!

Walter. I don't want nothing but for you to stop acting holy 'round here. Me and Ruth done made some sacrifices for you—why can't you do something for the family?

Ruth. Walter, don't be dragging me in it.

Walter. You are in it—Don't you get up and go work in somebody's kitchen for the last three years to help put clothes on her back?

Ruth. Oh, Walter—that's not fair . . .

Walter. It ain't that nobody expects you to get on your knees and say thank you, Brother; thank you, Ruth; thank you, Mama—and thank you, Travis, for wearing the same pair of shoes for two semesters—

Beneatha (*dropping to her knees*). Well—I *do*—all right?—thank everybody! And forgive me for ever wanting to be anything at all! (*Pursuing him on her knees across the floor.*) FORGIVE ME, FORGIVE ME, FORGIVE ME!

Ruth. Please stop it! Your mama'll hear you.

Walter. Who the hell told you you had to be a doctor? If you so crazy 'bout messing 'round with sick people—then go be a nurse like other women—or just get married and be quiet . . .

Beneatha. Well—you finally got it said . . . It took you three years but you finally got it said. Walter, give up; leave me alone—it's Mama's money.

Walter. *He was my father, too!*

Beneatha. So what? He was mine, too—and Travis's grandfather—but the insurance money belongs to Mama. Picking on me is not going to make her give it to you to invest in any liquor stores—*(Under breath, dropping into a chair.)*—and I for one say, God bless Mama for that!

Walter *(to Ruth).* See—did you hear? Did you hear!

Ruth. Honey, please go to work.

Walter. Nobody in this house is ever going to understand me.

Beneatha. Because you're a nut.

Walter. Who's a nut?

Beneatha. You—you are a nut. Thee is mad, boy.

Walter *(looking at his wife and his sister from the door, very sadly).* The world's most backward race of people, and that's a fact.

Beneatha *(turning slowly in her chair).* And then there are all those prophets who would lead us out of the wilderness—*(Walter slams out of the house.)*—into the swamps!

Ruth. Bennie, why you always gotta be pickin' on your brother? Can't you be a little sweeter sometimes? *(Door opens. Walter walks in. He fumbles with his cap, starts to speak, clears throat, looks everywhere but at Ruth. Finally:)*

Walter *(to Ruth).* I need some money for carfare.

Ruth *(looks at him, then warms; teasing, but tenderly).* Fifty cents? *(She goes to her bag and gets money.)* Here—take a taxi!

Walter exits. Mama enters. She is a woman in her early sixties, full-bodied and strong. She is one of those women of a certain grace and beauty who wear it so unobtrusively that it takes a while to notice. Her dark-brown face is surrounded by the total white-ness of her hair, and, being a woman who has adjusted to many things in life and overcome many more, her face is full of strength. She has, we can see, wit and faith of a kind that keep her eyes lit and full of interest and expectancy. She is, in a word, a beautiful woman. Her bearing is perhaps most like the noble bearing of the women of the Hereros of Southwest Africa—rather as if she imagines that as she walks she still bears a basket or a vessel upon her head. Her speech, on the other hand, is as careless as her carriage is precise—she is inclined to slur everything—but her voice is perhaps not so much quiet as simply soft.

Mama. Who that 'round here slamming doors at this hour?

She crosses through the room, goes to the window, opens it, and brings in a feeble little plant growing doggedly in a small pot on the window sill. She feels the dirt and puts it back out.

Ruth. That was Walter Lee. He and Bennie was at it again.

Mama. My children and they tempers. Lord, if this little old plant don't get more sun than it's been getting it ain't never going to see spring again. *(She turns from* *the window.)* What's the matter with you this morning, Ruth? You looks right peaked. You aiming to iron all them things? Leave some for me. I'll get to 'em this afternoon. Bennie honey, it's too drafty for you to be sitting 'round half dressed. Where's your robe?

Beneatha. In the cleaners.

Mama. Well, go get mine and put it on.

Beneatha. I'm not cold, Mama, honest.

Mama. I know—but you so thin . . .

Beneatha *(irritably).* Mama, I'm not cold.

Mama *(seeing the make-down bed as Travis has left it).* Lord have mercy, look at that poor bed. Bless his heart—he tries, don't he?

She moves to the bed Travis has sloppily made up.

Ruth. No—he don't half try at all 'cause he knows you going to come along behind him and fix everything. That's just how come he don't know how to do nothing right now—you done spoiled that boy so.

Mama *(folding bedding).* Well—he's a little boy. Ain't supposed to know 'bout housekeeping. My baby, that's what he is. What you fix for his breakfast this morning?

Ruth *(angrily).* I feed my son, Lena!

Mama. I ain't meddling—*(Under breath; busy-bodyish.)* I just noticed all last week he had cold cereal, and when it starts getting this chilly in the fall a child ought to have some hot grits or something when he goes out in the cold—

Ruth *(furious).* I gave him hot oats—is that all right!

Mama. I ain't meddling. *(Pause.)* Put a lot of nice butter on it? *(Ruth shoots her an angry look and does not reply.)* He likes lots of butter.

Ruth *(exasperated).* Lena—

Mama *(to Beneatha. Mama is inclined to wander conversationally sometimes).* What was you and your brother fussing 'bout this morning?

Beneatha. It's not important, Mama.

She gets up and goes to look out at the bathroom, which is apparently free, and she picks up her towels and rushes out.

Mama. What was they fighting about?

Ruth. Now you know as well as I do.

Mama *(shaking her head).* Brother still worrying hisself sick about that money?

Ruth. You know he is.

Mama. You had breakfast?

Ruth. Some coffee.

Mama. Girl, you better start eating and looking after yourself better. You almost thin as Travis.

Ruth. Lena—

Mama. Un-hunh?

Ruth. What are you going to do with it?

Mama. Now don't you start, child. It's too early in the morning to be talking about money. It ain't Christian.

Ruth. It's just that he got his heart set on that store—

Mama. You mean that liquor store that Willy Harris want him to invest in?

Ruth. Yes—

Mama. We ain't no business people, Ruth. We just plain working folks.

Ruth. Ain't nobody business people till they go into business. Walter Lee say colored people ain't never going to start getting ahead till they start gambling on some different kinds of things in the world—investments and things.

Mama. What done got into you, girl? Walter Lee done finally sold you on investing.

Ruth. No. Mama, something is happening between Walter and me. I don't know what it is—but he needs something—something I can't give him any more. He needs this chance, Lena.

Mama *(frowning deeply).* But liquor, honey—

Ruth. Well—like Walter say—I spec people going to always be drinking themselves some liquor.

Mama. Well—whether they drinks it or not ain't none of my business. But whether I go into business selling it to 'em *is,* and I don't want that on my ledger this late in life. *(Stopping suddenly and studying her daughter-in-law.)* Ruth Younger, what's the matter with you today? You look like you could fall over right there.

Ruth. I'm tired.

Mama. Then you better stay home from work today.

Ruth. I can't stay home. She'd be calling up the agency and screaming at them, "My girl didn't come in today—send me somebody! My girl didn't come in!" Oh, she just have a fit . . .

Mama. Well, let her have it. I'll just call her up and say you got the flu—

Ruth *(laughing).* Why the flu?

Mama. 'Cause it sounds respectable to 'em. Something white people get, too. They know 'bout the flu. Otherwise they think you been cut up or something when you tell 'em you sick.

Ruth. I got to go in. We need the money.

Mama. Somebody would of thought my children done all but starved to death the way they talk about money here late. Child, we got a great big old check coming tomorrow.

Ruth *(sincerely, but also self-righteously).* Now that's your money. It ain't got nothing to do with me. We all feel like that—Walter and Bennie and me—even Travis.

Mama *(thoughtfully, and suddenly very far away).* Ten thousand dollars—

Ruth. Sure is wonderful.

Mama. Ten thousand dollars.

Ruth. You know what you should do, Miss Lena? You should take yourself a trip somewhere. To Europe or South America or someplace—

Mama *(throwing up her hands at the thought).* Oh, child!

Ruth. I'm serious. Just pack up and leave! Go on away and enjoy yourself some. Forget about the family and have yourself a ball for once in your life—

Mama *(drily).* You sound like I'm just about ready to die. Who'd go with me? What I look like wandering 'round Europe by myself?

Ruth. Shoot—these here rich white women do it all the time. They don't think nothing of packing up they suitcases and piling on one of them big steamships and swoosh!—they gone, child.

Mama. Something always told me I wasn't no rich white woman.

Ruth. Well—what are you going to do with it then?

Mama. I ain't rightly decided. *(Thinking. She speaks now with emphasis.)* Some of it got to be put away for Beneatha and her schoolin'—and ain't nothing going to touch that part of it. Nothing. *(She waits several seconds, trying to make up her mind about something, and looks at Ruth a little tentatively before going on.)* Been thinking that we maybe could meet the notes on a little old two-story somewhere, with a yard where Travis could play in the summertime, if we use part of the insurance for a down payment and everybody kind of pitch in. I could maybe take on a little day work again, few days a week—

Ruth *(studying her mother-in-law furtively and concentrating on her ironing, anxious to encourage without seeming to).* Well, Lord knows, we've put enough rent into this here rat trap to pay for four houses by now . . .

Mama *(looking up at the words "rat trap" and then looking around and leaning back and sighing—in a suddenly reflective mood—).* "Rat trap"—yes, that's all it is. *(Smiling.)* I remember just as well the day me and Big Walter moved in here. Hadn't been married but two weeks and wasn't planning on living here no more than a year. *(She shakes her head at the dissolved dream.)* We was going to set away, little by little, don't you know, and buy a little place out in Morgan Park. We had even picked out the house. *(Chuckling a little.)* Looks right dumpy today. But Lord, child, you should know all the dreams I had 'bout buying that house and fixing it up and making me a little garden in the back—*(She waits and stops smiling.)* And didn't none of it happen.

Dropping her hands in a futile gesture.

Ruth *(keeps her head down, ironing).* Yes, life can be a barrel of disappointments, sometimes.

Mama. Honey, Big Walter would come in here some nights back then and slump down on that couch there and just look at the rug, and look at me and look at the rug and then back at me—and I'd know he was down then . . . really down. *(After a second very long and thoughtful pause; she is seeing back to times that only she can see.)* And then, Lord, when I lost that baby—little Claude—I almost thought I was going to lose Big Walter too. Oh, that man grieved hisself! He was one man to love his children.

Ruth. Ain't nothin' can tear at you like losin' your baby.

Mama. I guess that's how come that man finally worked hisself to death like he done. Like he was fighting his own war with this here world that took his baby from him.

Ruth. He sure was a fine man, all right. I always liked Mr. Younger.

Mama. Crazy 'bout his children! God knows there was plenty wrong with Walter Younger—hard-headed, mean, kind of wild with women—plenty wrong with him. But he sure loved his children. Always wanted them to have something—be something. That's where Brother gets all these notions, I reckon. Big Walter used to say, he'd get right wet in the eyes sometimes, lean his head back with the water standing in his eyes and say, "Seem like God didn't see fit to give the black man nothing but dreams—but He did give us children to make them dreams seem worthwhile." *(She smiles.)* He could talk like that, don't you know.

Ruth. Yes, he sure could. He was a good man, Mr. Younger.

Mama. Yes, a fine man—just couldn't never catch up with his dreams, that's all.

Beneatha comes in, brushing her hair and looking up to the ceiling, where the sound of a vacuum cleaner has started up.

Beneatha. What could be so dirty on that woman's rugs that she has to vacuum them every single day?

Ruth. I wish certain young women 'round here who I could name would take inspiration about certain rugs in a certain apartment I could also mention.

Beneatha *(shrugging).* How much cleaning can a house need, for Christ's sakes.

Mama *(not liking the Lord's name used thus).* Bennie!

Ruth. Just listen to her—just listen!

Beneatha. Oh, God!

Mama. If you use the Lord's name just one more time—

Beneatha *(a bit of a whine).* Oh, Mama—

Ruth. Fresh—just fresh as salt, this girl!

Beneatha *(drily).* Well—if the salt loses its savor—

Mama. Now that will do. I just ain't going to have you 'round here reciting the scriptures in vain—you hear me?

Beneatha. How did I manage to get on everybody's wrong side by just walking into a room?

Ruth. If you weren't so fresh—

Beneatha. Ruth, I'm twenty years old.

Mama. What time you be home from school today?

Beneatha. Kind of late. *(With enthusiasm.)* Madeline is going to start my guitar lessons today.

Mama and Ruth look up with the same expression.

Mama. Your *what* kind of lessons?

Beneatha. Guitar.

Ruth. Oh, Father!

Mama. How come you done taken it in your mind to learn to play the guitar?

Beneatha. I just want to, that's all.

Mama *(smiling).* Lord, child, don't you know what to do with yourself? How long it going to be before you get tired of this now—like you got tired of that little play-acting group you joined last year? *(Looking at Ruth.)* And what was it the year before that?

Ruth. The horseback-riding club for which she bought that fifty-five-dollar riding habit that's been hanging in the closet ever since!

Mama *(to Beneatha).* Why you got to flit so from one thing to another, baby?

Beneatha *(sharply).* I just want to learn to play the guitar. Is there anything wrong with that?

Mama. Ain't nobody trying to stop you. I just wonders sometimes why you has to flit so from one thing to another all the time. You ain't never done nothing with all that camera equipment you brought home—

Beneatha. I don't flit! I—I experiment with different forms of expression—

Ruth. Like riding a horse?

Beneatha. —People have to express themselves one way or another.

Mama. What is it you want to express?

Beneatha *(angrily).* Me! *(Mama and Ruth look at each other and burst into raucous laughter.)* Don't worry—I don't expect you to understand.

Mama *(to change the subject).* Who you going out with tomorrow night?

Beneatha *(with displeasure).* George Murchison again.

Mama *(pleased).* Oh—you getting a little sweet on him?

Ruth. You ask me, this child ain't sweet on nobody but herself—*(Under breath.)* Express herself!

They laugh.

Beneatha. Oh—I like George all right, Mama. I mean I like him enough to go out with him and stuff, but—

Ruth *(for devilment).* What does *and stuff* mean?

Beneatha. Mind your own business.

Mama. Stop picking at her now, Ruth. *(She chuckles—then a suspicious sudden look at her daughter as she turns in her chair for emphasis.)* What DOES it mean?

Beneatha *(wearily).* Oh, I just mean I couldn't ever really be serious about George. He's—he's so shallow.

Ruth. Shallow—what do you mean he's shallow? He's *rich!*

Mama. Hush, Ruth.

Beneatha. I know he's rich. He knows he's rich, too.

Ruth. Well—what other qualities a man got to have to satisfy you, little girl?

Beneatha. You wouldn't even begin to understand. Anybody who married Walter could not possibly understand.

Mama *(outraged).* What kind of way is that to talk about your brother?

Beneatha. Brother is a flip—let's face it.

Mama *(to Ruth, helplessly).* What's a flip?

Ruth *(glad to add kindling).* She's saying he's crazy.

Beneatha. Not crazy. Brother isn't really crazy yet—he—he's an elaborate neurotic.

Mama. Hush your mouth!

Beneatha. As for George. Well. George looks good—he's got a beautiful car and he takes me to nice places and, as my sister-in-law says, he is probably the richest boy I will ever get to know and I even like him sometimes—but if the Youngers are sitting around waiting to see if their little Bennie is going to tie up the family with the Murchisons, they are wasting their time.

Ruth. You mean you wouldn't marry George Murchison if he asked you someday? That pretty, rich thing? Honey, I knew you was odd—

Beneatha. No I would not marry him if all I felt for him was what I feel now. Besides, George's family wouldn't really like it.

Mama. Why not?

Beneatha. Oh, Mama—The Murchisons are honest-to-God-real-*live*-rich colored people, and the only people in the world who are more snobbish than rich white people are rich colored people. I thought everybody knew that. I've met Mrs. Murchison. She's a scene!

Mama. You must not dislike people 'cause they well off, honey.

Beneatha. Why not? It makes just as much sense as disliking people 'cause they are poor, and lots of people do that.

Ruth (*a wisdom-of-the-ages manner. To Mama*). Well, she'll get over some of this—

Beneatha. Get over it? What are you talking about, Ruth? Listen, I'm going to be a doctor. I'm not worried about who I'm going to marry yet—if I ever get married.

Mama and Ruth. *If!*

Mama. Now, Bennie—

Beneatha. Oh, I probably will . . . but first I'm going to be a doctor, and George, for one, still thinks that's pretty funny. I couldn't be bothered with that. I am going to be a doctor and everybody around here better understand that!

Mama (*kindly*). 'Course you going to be a doctor, honey, God willing.

Beneatha (*drily*). God hasn't got a thing to do with it.

Mama. Beneatha—that just wasn't necessary.

Beneatha. Well—neither is God. I get sick of hearing about God.

Mama. Beneatha!

Beneatha. I mean it! I'm just tired of hearing about God all the time. What has He got to do with anything? Does He pay tuition?

Mama. You 'bout to get your fresh little jaw slapped!

Ruth. That's just what she needs, all right!

Beneatha. Why? Why can't I say what I want to around here, like everybody else?

Mama. It don't sound nice for a young girl to say things like that—you wasn't brought up that way. Me and your father went to trouble to get you and Brother to church every Sunday.

Beneatha. Mama, you don't understand. It's all a matter of ideas, and God is just one idea I don't accept. It's not important. I am not going out and be immoral or commit crimes because I don't believe in God. I don't even think about it. It's just that I get tired of Him getting credit for all the things the human race achieves through its own stubborn effort. There simply is no blasted God—there is only man and it is He who makes miracles!

Mama absorbs this speech, studies her daughter, and rises slowly and crosses to Beneatha and slaps her powerfully across the face. After, there is only silence and the daughter drops her eyes from her mother's face, and Mama is very tall before her.

Mama. Now—you say after me, in my mother's house there is still God. *(There is a long pause and Beneatha stares at the floor wordlessly. Mama repeats the phrase with precision and cool emotion.)* In my mother's house there is still God.
Beneatha. In my mother's house there is still God.

A long pause.

Mama *(walking away from Beneatha, too disturbed for triumphant posture. Stopping and turning back to her daughter).* There are some ideas we ain't going to have in this house. Not long as I am at the head of this family.
Beneatha. Yes, ma'am.

Mama walks out of the room.

Ruth *(almost gently, with profound understanding).* You think you a woman, Bennie—but you still a little girl. What you did was childish—so you got treated like a child.
Beneatha. I see. *(Quietly.)* I also see that everybody thinks it's all right for Mama to be a tyrant. But all the tyranny in the world will never put a God in the heavens!

She picks up her books and goes out. Pause.

Ruth *(goes to Mama's door).* She said she was sorry.
Mama *(coming out, going to her plant).* They frightens me, Ruth. My children.
Ruth. You got good children, Lena. They just a little off sometimes—but they're good.
Mama. No—there's something come down between me and them that don't let us understand each other and I don't know what it is. One done almost lost his mind thinking 'bout money all the time and the other done commence to talk about things I can't seem to understand in no form or fashion. What is it that's changing, Ruth?
Ruth *(soothingly, older than her years).* Now . . . you taking it all too seriously. You just got strong-willed children and it takes a strong woman like you to keep 'em in hand.
Mama *(looking at her plant and sprinkling a little water on it).* They spirited all right, my children. Got to admit they got spirit—Bennie and Walter. Like this

little old plant that ain't never had enough sunshine or nothing—and look at it . . .

She has her back to Ruth, who has had to stop ironing and lean against something and put the back of her hand to her forehead.

Ruth *(trying to keep Mama from noticing).* You . . . sure . . . loves that little old thing, don't you? . . .

Mama. Well, I always wanted me a garden like I used to see sometimes at the back of the houses down home. This plant is close as I ever got to having one. *(She looks out of the window as she replaces the plant.)* Lord, ain't nothing as dreary as the view from this window on a dreary day, is there? Why ain't you singing this morning, Ruth? Sing that "No Ways Tired." That song always lifts me up so—*(She turns at last to see that Ruth has slipped quietly to the floor, in a state of semiconsciousness.)* Ruth! Ruth honey— what's the matter with you . . . Ruth!

Curtain.

Scene 2.   *(The following morning.)*

It is the following morning; a Saturday morning, and house cleaning is in progress at the Youngers'. Furniture has been shoved hither and yon and Mama is giving the kitchen-area walls a washing down. Beneatha, in dungarees, with a handkerchief tied around her face, is spraying insecticide into the cracks in the walls. As they work, the radio is on and a Southside disk-jockey program is inappropriately filling the house with a rather exotic saxophone blues. Travis, the sole idle one, is leaning on his arms, looking out of the window.

Travis. Grandmama, that stuff Bennie is using smells awful. Can I go downstairs, please?

Mama. Did you get all them chores done already? I ain't seen you doing much.

Travis. Yes'm—finished early. Where did Mama go this morning?

Mama *(looking at Beneatha).* She had to go on a little errand.

The phone rings. Beneatha runs to answer it and reaches it before Walter, who has entered from bedroom.

Travis. Where?

Mama. To tend to her business.

Beneatha. Haylo . . . *(Disappointed.)* Yes, he is. *(She tosses the phone to Walter, who barely catches it.)* It's Willie Harris again.

Walter *(as privately as possible under Mama's gaze).* Hello, Willie. Did you get the papers from the lawyer? . . . No, not yet. I told you the mailman doesn't get here till ten-thirty . . . No, I'll come there . . . Yeah! Right away. *(He hangs up and goes for his coat.)*

Beneatha. Brother, where did Ruth go?

Walter *(as he exits).* How should I know!

Travis. Aw come on, Grandma. Can I go outside?

Mama. Oh, I guess so. You stay right in front of the house, though, and keep a good lookout for the postman.

Travis. Yes'm. *(He darts into bedroom for stickball and bat, reenters, and sees Beneatha on her knees spraying under sofa with behind upraised. He edges closer to the target, takes aim, and lets her have it. She screams.)* Leave them poor little cockroaches alone, they ain't bothering you none! *(He runs as she swings the spraygun at him viciously and playfully.)* Grandma! Grandma!

Mama. Look out there, girl, before you be spilling some of that stuff on that child!

Travis *(safely behind the bastion of Mama).* That's right—look out, now! *(He exits.)*

Beneatha *(drily).* I can't imagine that it would hurt him—it has never hurt the roaches.

Mama. Well, little boys' hides ain't as tough as Southside roaches. You better get over there behind the bureau. I seen one marching out of there like Napoleon yesterday.

Beneatha. There's really only one way to get rid of them, Mama—

Mama. How?

Beneatha. Set fire to this building! Mama, where did Ruth go?

Mama *(looking at her with meaning).* To the doctor, I think.

Beneatha. The doctor? What's the matter? *(They exchange glances.)* You don't think—

Mama *(with her sense of drama).* Now I ain't saying what I think. But I ain't never been wrong 'bout a woman neither.

The phone rings.

Beneatha *(at the phone).* Hay-lo . . . *(Pause, and a moment of recognition.)* Well—when did you get back! . . . And how was it? . . . Of course I've missed you—in my way . . . This morning? No . . . house cleaning and all that and Mama hates it if I let people come over when the house is like this . . . You *have?* Well, that's different . . . What is it—Oh, what the hell, come on over . . . Right, see you then. *Arrivederci.*

She hangs up.

Mama *(who has listened vigorously, as is her habit).* Who is that you inviting over here with this house looking like this? You ain't got the pride you was born with!

Beneatha. Asagai doesn't care how houses look, Mama—he's an intellectual.

Mama. *Who?*

Beneatha. Asagai—Joseph Asagai. He's an African boy I met on campus. He's been studying in Canada all summer.

Mama. What's his name?

Beneatha. Asagai, Joseph. Ah-sah-guy . . . He's from Nigeria.

Mama. Oh, that's the little country that was founded by slaves way back . . .

Beneatha. No, Mama—that's Liberia.

Mama. I don't think I never met no African before.

Beneatha. Well, do me a favor and don't ask him a whole lot of ignorant questions about Africans. I mean, do they wear clothes and all that—

Mama. Well, now, I guess if you think we so ignorant 'round here maybe you shouldn't bring your friends here—

Beneatha. It's just that people ask such crazy things. All anyone seems to know about when it comes to Africa is Tarzan—

Mama *(indignantly)*. Why should I know anything about Africa?

Beneatha. Why do you give money at church for the missionary work?

Mama. Well, that's to help save people.

Beneatha. You mean save them from *heathenism*—

Mama *(innocently)*. Yes.

Beneatha. I'm afraid they need more salvation from the British and the French.

Ruth comes in forlornly and pulls off her coat with dejection. They both turn to look at her.

Ruth *(dispiritedly)*. Well, I guess from all the happy faces—everybody knows.

Beneatha. You pregnant?

Mama. Lord have mercy, I sure hope it's a little old girl. Travis ought to have a sister.

Beneatha and Ruth give her a hopeless look for this grandmotherly enthusiasm.

Beneatha. How far along are you?

Ruth. Two months.

Beneatha. Did you mean to? I mean did you plan it or was it an accident?

Mama. What do you know about planning or not planning?

Beneatha. Oh, Mama.

Ruth *(wearily)*. She's twenty years old, Lena.

Beneatha. Did you plan it, Ruth?

Ruth. Mind your own business.

Beneatha. It is my business—where is he going to live, on the *roof*? *(There is silence following the remark as the three women react to the sense of it.)* Gee—I didn't mean that, Ruth, honest. Gee, I don't feel like that at all. I—I think it is wonderful.

Ruth *(dully)*. Wonderful.

Beneatha. Yes—really.

Mama *(looking at Ruth, worried)*. Doctor say everything going to be all right?

Ruth *(far away)*. Yes—she says everything is going to be fine . . .

Mama *(immediately suspicious)*. "She"—What doctor you went to?

Ruth folds over, near hysteria.

Mama *(worriedly hovering over Ruth).* Ruth honey—what's the matter with you—you sick?

Ruth has her fists clenched on her thighs and is fighting hard to suppress a scream that seems to be rising in her.

Beneatha. What's the matter with her, Mama?

Mama *(working her fingers in Ruth's shoulders to relax her).* She be all right. Women gets right depressed sometimes when they get her way. *(Speaking softly, expertly, rapidly.)* Now you just relax. That's right . . . just lean back, don't think 'bout nothing at all . . . nothing at all—

Ruth. I'm all right . . .

The glassy-eyed look melts and then she collapses into a fit of heavy sobbing. The bell rings.

Beneatha. Oh, my God—that must be Asagai.

Mama *(to Ruth).* Come on now, honey. You need to lie down and rest awhile . . . then have some nice hot food.

They exit, Ruth's weight on her mother-in-law. Beneatha, herself profoundly disturbed, opens the door to admit a rather dramatic-looking young man with a large package.

Asagai. Hello, Alaiyo—

Beneatha *(holding the door open and regarding him with pleasure).* Hello . . . *(Long pause.)* Well—come in. And please excuse everything. My mother was very upset about my letting anyone come here with the place like this.

Asagai *(coming into the room).* You look disturbed too . . . Is something wrong?

Beneatha *(still at the door, absently).* Yes . . . we've all got acute ghetto-itus. *(She smiles and comes toward him, finding a cigarette and sitting.)* So—sit down! No! Wait! *(She whips the spraygun off sofa where she had left it and puts the cushions back. At last perches on arm of sofa. He sits.)* So, how was Canada?

Asagai *(a sophisticate).* Canadian.

Beneatha *(looking at him).* Asagai, I'm very glad you are back.

Asagai *(looking back at her in turn).* Are you really?

Beneatha. Yes—very.

Asagai. Why?—you were quite glad when I went away. What happened?

Beneatha. You went away.

Asagai. Ahhhhhhhh.

Beneatha. Before—you wanted to be so serious before there was time.

Asagai. How much time must there be before one knows what one feels?

Beneatha *(stalling this particular conversation. Her hands pressed together, in a deliberately childish gesture).* What did you bring me?

Asagai *(handing her the package).* Open it and see.

Beneatha *(eagerly opening the package and drawing out some records and the colorful robes of a Nigerian woman).* Oh Asagai! . . . You got them for me! . . . How beautiful . . . and the records too! *(She lifts out the robes and runs to the mirror with them and holds the drapery up in front of herself.)*

Asagai *(coming to her at the mirror).* I shall have to teach you how to drape it properly. *(He flings the material about her for the moment and stands back to look at her.)* Ah—Oh-pay-gay-day, oh-gbah-mu-shay. *(A Yoruba exclamation for admiration.)* You wear it well . . . very well . . . mutilated hair and all.

Beneatha *(turning suddenly).* My hair—what's wrong with my hair?

Asagai *(shrugging).* Were you born with it like that?

Beneatha *(reaching up to touch it).* No . . . of course not.

She looks back to the mirror, disturbed.

Asagai *(smiling).* How then?

Beneatha. You know perfectly well how . . . as crinkly as yours . . . that's how.

Asagai. And it is ugly to you that way?

Beneatha *(quickly).* Oh, no—not ugly . . . *(More slowly, apologetically.)* But it's so hard to manage when it's, well—raw.

Asagai. And so to accommodate that—you mutilate it every week?

Beneatha. It's not mutilation!

Asagai *(laughing aloud at her seriousness).* Oh . . . please! I am only teasing you because you are so very serious about these things. *(He stands back from her and folds his arms across his chest as he watches her pulling at her hair and frowning in the mirror.)* Do you remember the first time you met me at school? . . . *(He laughs.)* You came up to me and you said—and I thought you were the most serious little thing I had ever seen—you said: *(He imitates her.)* "Mr. Asagai—I want very much to talk with you. About Africa. You see, Mr. Asagai, I am looking for my *identity!*"

He laughs.

Beneatha *(turning to him, not laughing).* Yes—

Her face is quizzical, profoundly disturbed.

Asagai *(still teasing and reaching out and taking her face in his hands and turning her profile to him).* Well . . . it is true that this is not so much a profile of a Hollywood queen as perhaps a queen of the Nile—*(A mock dismissal of the importance of the question.)* But what does it matter? Assimilationism is so popular in your country.

Beneatha *(wheeling, passionately, sharply).* I am not an assimilationist!

Asagai *(the protest hangs in the room for a moment and Asagai studies her, his laughter fading).* Such a serious one. *(There is a pause.)* So—you like the robes? You must take excellent care of them—they are from my sister's personal wardrobe.

Beneatha *(with incredulity).* You—you sent all the way home—for me?

Asagai *(with charm).* For you—I would do much more . . . Well, that is what I came for. I must go.

Beneatha. Will you call me Monday?

Asagai. Yes . . . We have a great deal to talk about. I mean about identity and time and all that.

Beneatha. Time?

Asagai. Yes. About how much time one needs to know what one feels.

Beneatha. You see! You never understood that there is more than one kind of feeling which can exist between a man and a woman—or, at least, there should be.

Asagai *(shaking his head negatively but gently).* No. Between a man and a woman there need be only one kind of feeling. I have that for you . . . Now even . . . right this moment . . .

Beneatha. I know—and by itself—it won't do. I can find that anywhere.

Asagai. For a woman it should be enough.

Beneatha. I know—because that's what it says in all the novels that men write. But it isn't. Go ahead and laugh—but I'm not interested in being someone's little episode in America or—*(With feminine vengeance.)*—one of them! *(Asagai has burst into laughter again.)* That's funny as hell, huh!

Asagai. It's just that every American girl I have known has said that to me. White—black—in this you are all the same. And the same speech, too!

Beneatha *(angrily).* Yuk, yuk, yuk!

Asagai. It's how you can be sure that the world's most liberated women are not liberated at all. You all talk about it too much!

Mama enters and is immediately all social charm because of the presence of a guest.

Beneatha. Oh—Mama—this is Mr. Asagai.

Mama. How do you do?

Asagai *(total politeness to an elder).* How do you do, Mrs. Younger. Please forgive me for coming at such an outrageous hour on a Saturday.

Mama. Well, you are quite welcome. I just hope you understand that our house don't always look like this. *(Chatterish.)* You must come again. I would love to hear all about—*(Not sure of the name.)*—your country. I think it's so sad the way our American Negroes don't know nothing about Africa 'cept Tarzan and all that. And all that money they pour into these churches when they ought to be helping you people over there drive out them French and Englishmen done taken away your land.

The mother flashes a slightly superior look at her daughter upon completion of the recitation.

Asagai *(taken aback by this sudden and acutely unrelated expression of sympathy).* Yes . . . yes . . .

Mama *(smiling at him suddenly and relaxing and looking him over).* How many miles is it from here to where you come from?

Asagai. Many thousands.

Mama *(looking at him as she would Walter).* I bet you don't half look after yourself, being away from your mama either. I spec you better come 'round here from time to time to get yourself some decent homecooked meals . . .

Asagai *(moved).* Thank you. Thank you very much. *(They are all quiet, then—)* Well . . . I must go. I will call you Monday, Alaiyo.

Mama. What's that he call you?

Asagai. Oh—"Alaiyo." I hope you don't mind. It is what you would call a nickname, I think. It is a Yoruba word. I am a Yoruba.

Mama *(looking at Beneatha).* I—I thought he was from—*(Uncertain.)*

Asagai *(understanding).* Nigeria is my country. Yoruba is my tribal origin—

Beneatha. You didn't tell us what Alaiyo means . . . for all I know, you might be calling me Little Idiot or something . . .

Asagai. Well . . . let me see . . . I do not know how just to explain it . . . The sense of a thing can be so different when it changes languages.

Beneatha. You're evading.

Asagai. No—really it is difficult . . . *(Thinking.)* It means . . . it means One for Whom Bread—Food—Is Not Enough. *(He looks at her.)* Is that all right?

Beneatha *(understanding, softly).* Thank you.

Mama *(looking from one to the other and not understanding any of it).* Well . . . that's nice . . . You must come see us again—Mr.—

Asagai. Ah-sah-guy . . .

Mama. Yes . . . Do come again.

Asagai. Good-bye.

He exits.

Mama *(after him).* Lord, that's a pretty thing just went out here! *(Insinuatingly, to her daughter.)* Yes, I guess I see why we done commence to get so interested in Africa 'round here. Missionaries my aunt Jenny!

She exits.

Beneatha. Oh, Mama! . . .

She picks up the Nigerian dress and holds it up to her in front of the mirror again. She sets the headdress on haphazardly and then notices her hair again and clutches at it and then replaces the headdress and frowns at herself. Then she starts to wriggle in front of the mirror as she thinks a Nigerian woman might. Travis enters and stands regarding her.

Travis. What's the matter, girl, you cracking up?
Beneatha. Shut up.

She pulls the headdress off and looks at herself in the mirror and clutches at her hair again and squinches her eyes as if trying to imagine something. Then, suddenly, she gets her raincoat and kerchief and hurriedly prepares for going out.

Mama *(coming back into the room).* She's resting now. Travis, baby, run next door and ask Miss Johnson to please let me have a little kitchen cleanser. This here can is empty as Jacob's kettle.
Travis. I just came in.
Mama. Do as you told. *(He exits and she looks at her daughter.)* Where you going?
Beneatha *(halting at the door).* To become a queen of the Nile!

She exits in a breathless blaze of glory. Ruth appears in the bedroom doorway.

Mama. Who told you to get up?
Ruth. Ain't nothing wrong with me to be lying in no bed for. Where did Bennie go?
Mama *(drumming her fingers).* Far as I could make out—to Egypt. *(Ruth just looks at her.)* What time is it getting to?
Ruth. Ten twenty. And the mailman going to ring that bell this morning just like he done every morning for the last umpteen years.

Travis comes in with the cleanser can.

Travis. She say to tell you that she don't have much.
Mama *(angrily).* Lord, some people I could name sure is tight-fisted! *(Directing her grandson.)* Mark two cans of cleanser on the list there. If she that hard up for kitchen cleanser, I sure don't want to forget to get her none!
Ruth. Lena—maybe the woman is just short on cleanser—
Mama *(not listening).* —Much baking powder as she done borrowed from me all these years, she could of done gone into the baking business!

The bell sounds suddenly and sharply and all three are stunned—serious and silent— midspeech. In spite of all the other conversations and distractions of the morning, this is what they have been waiting for, even Travis, who looks helplessly from his mother to his grandmother. Ruth is the first to come to life again.

Ruth *(to Travis).* Get down them steps, boy!

Travis snaps to life and flies out to get the mail.

Mama (*her eyes wide, her hand to her breast*). You mean it done really come?

Ruth (*excited*). Oh, Miss Lena!

Mama (*collecting herself*). Well . . . I don't know what we all so excited about 'round here for. We known it was coming for months.

Ruth. That's a whole lot different from having it come and being able to hold it in your hands . . . a piece of paper worth ten thousand dollars . . . (*Travis bursts back into the room. He holds the envelope high above his head, like a little dancer, his face is radiant and he is breathless. He moves to his grandmother with sudden slow ceremony and puts the envelope into her hands. She accepts it, and then merely holds it and looks at it.*) Come on! Open it . . . Lord have mercy, I wish Walter Lee was here!

Travis. Open it, Grandmama!

Mama (*staring at it*). Now you all be quiet. It's just a check.

Ruth. Open it . . .

Mama (*still staring at it*). Now don't act silly . . . We ain't never been no people to act silly 'bout no money—

Ruth (*swiftly*). We ain't never had none before—OPEN IT!

Mama finally makes a good strong tear and pulls out the thin blue slice of paper and inspects it closely. The boy and his mother study it raptly over Mama's shoulders.

Mama. Travis! (*She is counting off with doubt.*) Is that the right number of zeros?

Travis. Yes'm . . . ten thousand dollars. Gaalee, Grandmama, you rich.

Mama (*She holds the check away from her, still looking at it. Slowly her face sobers into a mask of unhappiness*). Ten thousand dollars. (*She hands it to Ruth.*) Put it away somewhere, Ruth. (*She does not look at Ruth; her eyes seem to be seeing something somewhere very far off.*) Ten thousand dollars they give you. Ten thousand dollars.

Travis (*to his mother, sincerely*). What's the matter with Grandmama—don't she want to be rich?

Ruth (*distractedly*). You go on out and play now, baby. (*Travis exits. Mama starts wiping dishes absently, humming intently to herself. Ruth turns to her, with kind exasperation.*) You've gone and got yourself upset.

Mama (*not looking at her*). I spec if it wasn't for you all . . . I would just put that money away or give it to the church or something.

Ruth. Now what kind of talk is that. Mr. Younger would just be plain mad if he could hear you talking foolish like that.

Mama (*stopping and staring off*). Yes . . . he sure would. (*Sighing.*) We got enough to do with that money, all right. (*She halts then, and turns and looks at her daughter-in-law hard; Ruth avoids her eyes and Mama wipes her hands with finality and starts to speak firmly to Ruth.*) Where did you go today, girl?

Ruth. To the doctor.

Mama (*impatiently*). Now, Ruth . . . you know better than that. Old Doctor Jones is strange enough in his way but there ain't nothing 'bout him make somebody slip and call him "she"—like you done this morning.

Ruth. Well, that's what happened—my tongue slipped.

Mama. You went to see that woman, didn't you?

Ruth *(defensively, giving herself away).* What woman you talking about?

Mama *(angrily).* That woman who—

Walter enters in great excitement.

Walter. Did it come?

Mama *(quietly).* Can't you give people a Christian greeting before you start asking about money?

Walter *(to Ruth).* Did it come? *(Ruth unfolds the check and lays it quietly before him, watching him intently with thoughts of her own. Walter sits down and grasps it close and counts off the zeros.)* Ten thousand dollars—*(He turns suddenly, frantically to his mother and draws some papers out of his breast pocket.)* Mama— look. Old Willy Harris put everything on paper—

Mama. Son—I think you ought to talk to your wife . . . I'll go on out and leave you alone if you want—

Walter. I can talk to her later—Mama, look—

Mama. Son—

Walter. WILL SOMEBODY PLEASE LISTEN TO ME TODAY!

Mama *(quietly).* I don't 'low no yellin' in this house, Walter Lee, and you know it—*(Walter stares at them in frustration and starts to speak several times.)* And there ain't going to be no investing in no liquor stores.

Walter. But, Mama, you ain't even looked at it.

Mama. I don't aim to have to speak on that again.

A long pause.

Walter. You ain't looked at it and you don't aim to have to speak on that again? You ain't even looked at it and *you* have decided—*(Crumpling his papers.)* Well, *you* tell that to my boy tonight when you put him to sleep on the living-room couch . . . *(Turning to Mama and speaking directly to her.)* Yeah—and tell it to my wife, Mama, tomorrow when she has to go out of here to look after somebody else's kids. And tell it to *me*, Mama, every time we need a new pair of curtains and I have to watch *you* go out and work in somebody's kitchen. Yeah, you tell me then!

Walter starts out.

Ruth. Where you going?

Walter. I'm going out!

Ruth. Where?

Walter. Just out of this house somewhere—

Ruth *(getting her coat).* I'll come too.

Walter. I don't want you to come!

Ruth. I got something to talk to you about, Walter.

Walter. That's too bad.

Mama *(still quietly).* Walter Lee—*(She waits and he finally turns and looks at her.)* Sit down.

Walter. I'm a grown man, Mama.

Mama. Ain't nobody said you wasn't grown. But you still in my house and my presence. And as long as you are—you'll talk to your wife civil. Now sit down.

Ruth *(suddenly).* Oh, let him go on out and drink himself to death! He makes me sick to my stomach! *(She flings her coat against him and exits to bedroom.)*

Walter *(violently flinging the coat after her).* And you turn mine too, baby! *(The door slams behind her.)* That was my biggest mistake—

Mama *(still quietly).* Walter, what is the matter with you?

Walter. Matter with me? Ain't nothing the matter with *me!*

Mama. Yes there is. Something eating you up like a crazy man. Something more than me not giving you this money. The past few years I been watching it happen to you. You get all nervous acting and kind of wild in the eyes—*(Walter jumps up impatiently at her words.)* I said sit there now, I'm talking to you!

Walter. Mama—I don't need no nagging at me today.

Mama. Seem like you getting to a place where you always tied up in some kind of knot about something. But if anybody ask you 'bout it you just yell at 'em and bust out the house and go out and drink somewheres. Walter Lee, people can't live with that. Ruth's a good, patient girl in her way—but you getting to be too much. Boy, don't make the mistake of driving that girl away from you.

Walter. Why—what she do for me?

Mama. She loves you.

Walter. Mama—I'm going out. I want to go off somewhere and be by myself for a while.

Mama. I'm sorry 'bout your liquor store, son. It just wasn't the thing for us to do. That's what I want to tell you about—

Walter. I got to go out, Mama—

He rises.

Mama. It's dangerous, son.

Walter. What's dangerous?

Mama. When a man goes outside his home to look for peace.

Walter *(beseechingly).* Then why can't there never be no peace in this house then?

Mama. You done found it in some other house?

Walter. No—there ain't no woman! Why do women always think there's a woman somewhere when a man gets restless. *(Picks up the check.)* Do you know what this money means to me? Do you know what this money can do for us? *(Puts it back.)* Mama—Mama—I want so many things . . .

Mama. Yes, son—

Walter. I want so many things that they are driving me kind of crazy . . . Mama— look at me.

Mama. I'm looking at you. You a good-looking boy. You got a job, a nice wife, a fine boy, and—

Walter. A job. *(Looks at her.)* Mama, a job? I open and close car doors all day long. I drive a man around in his limousine and I say, "Yes, sir; no, sir; very good, sir; shall I take the Drive, sir?" Mama, that ain't no kind of job . . . that ain't nothing at all. *(Very quietly.)* Mama, I don't know if I can make you understand.

Mama. Understand what, baby?

Walter *(quietly).* Sometimes it's like I can see the future stretched out in front of me—just plain as day. The future, Mama. Hanging over there at the edge of my days. Just waiting for me—a big, looming blank space—full of *nothing.* Just waiting for *me.* But it don't have to be. *(Pause. Kneeling beside her chair.)* Mama— sometimes when I'm downtown and I pass them cool, quiet-looking restaurants where them white boys are sitting back and talking 'bout things . . . sitting there turning deals worth millions of dollars . . . sometimes I see guys don't look much older than me—

Mama. Son—how come you talk so much 'bout money?

Walter *(with immense passion).* Because it is life, Mama!

Mama *(quietly).* Oh—*(Very quietly.)* So now it's life. Money is life. Once upon a time freedom used to be life—now it's money. I guess the world really do change . . .

Walter. No—it was always money, Mama. We just didn't know about it.

Mama. No . . . something has changed. *(She looks at him.)* You something new, boy. In my time we was worried about not being lynched and getting to the North if we could and how to stay alive and still have a pinch of dignity too . . . Now here come you and Beneatha—talking 'bout things we ain't never even thought about hardly, me and your daddy. You ain't satisfied or proud of nothing we done. I mean that you had a home; that we kept you out of trouble till you was grown; that you don't have to ride to work on the back of nobody's streetcar—You my children—but how different we done become.

Walter *(a long beat. He pats her hand and gets up).* You just don't understand, Mama, you just don't understand.

Mama. Son—do you know your wife is expecting another baby? *(Walter stands, stunned, and absorbs what his mother has said.)* That's what she wanted to talk to you about. *(Walter sinks down into a chair.)* This ain't for me to be telling—but you ought to know. *(She waits.)* I think Ruth is thinking 'bout getting rid of that child.

Walter *(slowly understanding).* —No—no—Ruth wouldn't do that.

Mama. When the world gets ugly enough—a woman will do anything for her family. *The part that's already living.*

Walter. You don't know Ruth, Mama, if you think she would do that.

Ruth opens the bedroom door and stands there a little limp.

Ruth *(beaten).* Yes I would too, Walter. *(Pause.)* I gave her a five-dollar down payment.

There is total silence as the man stares at his wife and the mother stares at her son.

Mama *(presently).* Well—*(Tightly.)* Well—son, I'm waiting to hear you say something . . . *(She waits.)* I'm waiting to hear how you be your father's son. Be the man he was . . . *(Pause. The silence shouts.)* Your wife say she going to destroy your child. And I'm waiting to hear you talk like him and say we a people who give children life, not who destroys them—*(She rises.)* I'm waiting to see you stand up and look like your daddy and say we done give up one baby to poverty and that we ain't going to give up nary another one . . . I'm waiting.

Walter. Ruth—*(He can say nothing.)*

Mama. If you a son of mine, tell her! *(Walter picks up his keys and his coat and walks out. She continues, bitterly.)* You . . . you are a disgrace to your father's memory. Somebody get me my hat!

Curtain.

ACT II

Scene 1.

Time: Later the same day.

At rise: Ruth is ironing again. She has the radio going. Presently Beneatha's bedroom door opens and Ruth's mouth falls and she puts down the iron in fascination.

Ruth. What have we got on tonight!

Beneatha *(emerging grandly from the doorway so that we can see her thoroughly robed in the costume Asagai brought).* You are looking at what a well-dressed Nigerian woman wears—*(She parades for Ruth, her hair completely hidden by the headdress; she is coquettishly fanning herself with an ornate oriental fan, mistakenly more like Butterfly than any Nigerian that ever was.)* Isn't it beautiful? *(She promenades to the radio and, with an arrogant flourish, turns off the good loud blues that is playing.)* Enough of this assimilationist junk! *(Ruth follows her with her eyes as she goes to the phonograph and puts on a record and turns and waits ceremoniously for the music to come up. Then, with a shout—)* OCOMOGOSIAY!

Ruth jumps. The music comes up, a lovely Nigerian melody. Beneatha listens, enraptured, her eyes far way—"back to the past." She begins to dance. Ruth is dumbfounded.

Ruth. What kind of dance is that?

Beneatha. A folk dance.

Ruth *(Pearl Bailey).* What kind of folks do that, honey?

Beneatha. It's from Nigeria. It's a dance of welcome.

Ruth. Who you welcoming?

Beneatha. The men back to the village.

Ruth. Where they been?

Beneatha. How should I know—out hunting or something. Anyway, they are coming back now . . .

Ruth. Well, that's good.

Beneatha (*with the record*)

Alundi, alundi
Alundi alunya
Jop pu a jeepua
Ang gu soooooooooo
Ai yai yae . . .
Ayehaye—alundi . . .

Walter comes in during this performance; he has obviously been drinking. He leans against the door heavily and watches his sister, at first with distaste. Then his eyes look off—"back to the past"—as he lifts both his fists to the roof, screaming.

Walter. YEAH . . . AND ETHIOPIA STRETCH FORTH HER HANDS AGAIN! . . .

Ruth (*drily, looking at him*). Yes—and Africa sure is claiming her own tonight. (*She gives them both up and starts ironing again.*)

Walter (*all in a drunken, dramatic shout*). Shut up! . . . I'm diggin them drums . . . them drums move me! . . . (*He makes his weaving way to his wife's face and leans in close to her.*) In my heart of hearts—(*He thumps his chest.*)—I am much warrior!

Ruth (*without even looking up*). In your heart of hearts you are much drunkard.

Walter (*coming away from her and starting to wander around the room, shouting*). Me and Jomo . . . (*Intently, in his sister's face. She has stopped dancing to watch him in this unknown mood.*) That's my man, Kenyatta. (*Shouting and thumping his chest.*) FLAMING SPEAR! HOT DAMN! (*He is suddenly in possession of an imaginary spear and actively spearing enemies all over the room.*) OCOMO-GOSIAY . . .

Beneatha (*to encourage Walter, thoroughly caught up with this side of him*). OCOMOGOSIAY, FLAMING SPEAR!

Walter. THE LION IS WAKING . . . OWIMOWEH!

He pulls his shirt open and leaps up on the table and gestures with his spear.

Beneatha. OWIMOWEH!

Walter (*on the table, very far gone, his eyes pure glass sheets. He sees what we cannot, that he is a leader of his people, a great chief, a descendant of Chaka, and that the hour to march has come*). Listen, my black brothers—

Beneatha. OCOMOGOSIAY!

Walter. —Do you hear the waters rushing against the shores of the coastlands—
Beneatha. OCOMOGOSIAY!
Walter. —Do you hear the screeching of the cocks in yonder hills beyond where
   the chiefs meet in council for the coming of the mighty war—
Beneatha. OCOMOGOSIAY!

*And now the lighting shifts subtly to suggest the world of Walter's imagination, and
the mood shifts from pure comedy. It is the inner Walter speaking: the Southside
chauffeur has assumed an unexpected majesty.*

Walter. —Do you hear the beating of the wings of the birds flying low over the
   mountains and the low places of our land—
Beneatha. OCOMOGOSIAY!
Walter. —Do you hear the singing of the women, singing the war songs of our
   fathers to the babies in the great houses? Singing the sweet war songs! (*The
   doorbell rings.*) OH, DO YOU HEAR, MY *BLACK* BROTHERS!
Beneatha (*completely gone*). We hear you, Flaming Spear—

Ruth shuts off the phonograph and opens the door. George Murchison enters.

Walter. Telling us to prepare for the GREATNESS OF THE TIME! (*Lights back to
   normal. He turns and sees George.*) Black Brother!

He extends his hand for the fraternal clasp.

George. Black Brother, hell!
Ruth (*having had enough, and embarrassed for the family*). Beneatha, you got
   company—what's the matter with you? Walter Lee Younger, get down off that
   table and stop acting like a fool . . .

Walter comes down off the table suddenly and makes a quick exit to the bathroom.

Ruth. He's had a little to drink . . . I don't know what her excuse is.
George (*to Beneatha*). Look honey, we're going to the theater—we're not going to
   be *in* it . . . so go change, huh?

*Beneatha looks at him and slowly, ceremoniously, lifts her hands and pulls off the
headdress. Her hair is close-cropped and unstraightened. George freezes mid-sentence
and Ruth's eyes all but fall out of her head.*

George. What in the name of—
Ruth (*touching Beneatha's hair*). Girl, you done lost your natural mind? Look at
   your head!
George. What have you done to your head—I mean your hair!
Beneatha. Nothing—except cut it off.

Ruth. Now that's the truth—it's what ain't been done to it! You expect this boy to go out with you with your head all nappy like that?

Beneatha *(looking at George).* That's up to George. If he's ashamed of his heritage—

George. Oh, don't be so proud of yourself, Bennie—just because you look eccentric.

Beneatha. How can something that's natural be eccentric?

George. That's what being eccentric means   being natural. Get dressed.

Beneatha. I don't like that, George.

Ruth. Why must you and your brother make an argument out of everything people say?

Beneatha. Because I hate assimilationist Negroes!

Ruth. Will somebody please tell me what assimila-whoever means!

George. Oh, it's just a college girl's way of calling people Uncle Toms—but that isn't what it means at all.

Ruth. Well, what does it mean?

Beneatha *(cutting George off and staring at him as she replies to Ruth).* It means someone who is willing to give up his own culture and submerge himself completely in the dominant, and in this case *oppressive* culture!

George. Oh, dear, dear, dear! Here we go! A lecture on the African past! On our Great West African Heritage! In one second we will hear all about the great Ashanti empires; the great Songhay civilizations; and the great sculpture of Bénin—and then some poetry in the Bantu—and the whole monologue will end with the word *heritage! (Nastily.)* Let's face it, baby, your heritage is nothing but a bunch of raggedy-assed spirituals and some grass huts!

Beneatha. GRASS HUTS! *(Ruth crosses to her and forcibly pushes her toward the bedroom.)* See there . . . you are standing there in your splendid ignorance talking about people who were the first to smelt iron on the face of the earth! *(Ruth is pushing her through the door.)* The Ashanti were performing surgical operations when the English—*(Ruth pulls the door to, with Beneatha on the other side, and smiles graciously at George. Beneatha opens the door and shouts the end of the sentence defiantly at George.)*—were still tattooing themselves with blue dragons! *(She goes back inside.)*

Ruth. Have a seat, George. *(They both sit. Ruth folds her hands rather primly on her lap, determined to demonstrate the civilization of the family.)* Warm, ain't it? I mean for September. *(Pause.)* Just like they always say about Chicago weather: if it's too hot or cold for you, just wait a minute and it'll change. *(She smiles happily at this cliché of clichés.)* Everybody say it's got to do with them bombs and things they keep setting off. *(Pause.)* Would you like a nice cold beer?

George. No, thank you. I don't care for beer. *(He looks at his watch.)* I hope she hurries up.

Ruth. What time is the show?

George. It's an eight-thirty curtain. That's just Chicago, though. In New York standard curtain time is eight–forty.

He is rather proud of this knowledge.

Ruth (*properly appreciating it*). You get to New York a lot?
George (*offhand*). Few times a year.
Ruth. Oh—that's nice. I've never been to New York.

Walter enters. We feel he has relieved himself, but the edge of unreality is still with him.

Walter. New York ain't got nothing Chicago ain't. Just a bunch of hustling people all squeezed up together—being "Eastern."

He turns his face into a screw of displeasure.

George. Oh—you've been?
Walter. *Plenty* of times.
Ruth (*shocked at the lie*). Walter Lee Younger!
Walter (*staring her down*). Plenty! (*Pause.*) What we got to drink in this house? Why don't you offer this man some refreshment. (*To George.*) They don't know how to entertain people in this house, man.
George. Thank you—I don't really care for anything.
Walter (*feeling his head; sobriety coming*). Where's Mama?
Ruth. She ain't come back yet.
Walter (*looking Murchison over from head to toe, scrutinizing his carefully casual tweed sports jacket over cashmere V-neck sweater over soft eyelet shirt and tie, and soft slacks, finished off with white buckskin shoes*). Why all you college boys wear them faggoty-looking white shoes?
Ruth. Walter Lee!

George Murchison ignores the remark.

Walter (*to Ruth*). Well, they look crazy as hell—white shoes, cold as it is.
Ruth (*crushed*). You have to excuse him—
Walter. No he don't! Excuse me for what? What you always excusing me for! I'll excuse myself when I needs to be excused! (*A pause.*) They look as funny as them black knee socks Beneatha wears out of here all the time.
Ruth. It's the college *style,* Walter.
Walter. Style, hell. She looks like she got burnt legs or something!
Ruth. Oh, Walter—
Walter (*an irritable mimic*). Oh, Walter! Oh, Walter! (*To Murchison.*) How's your old man making out? I understand you all going to buy that big hotel on the Drive? (*He finds a beer in the refrigerator, wanders over to Murchison, sipping and wiping his lips with the back of his hand, and straddling a chair backwards to talk to the other man.*) Shrewd move. Your old man is all right, man. (*Tapping his head and half winking for emphasis.*) I mean he knows how

to operate. I mean he thinks *big*, you know what I mean, I mean for a *home*, you know? But I think he's kind of running out of ideas now. I'd like to talk to him. Listen, man, I got some plans that could turn this city upside down. I mean think like he does. *Big*. Invest big, gamble big, hell, lose *big* if you have to, you know what I mean. It's hard to find a man on this whole Southside who understands my kind of thinking—you dig? *(He scrutinizes Murchison again, drinks his beer, squints his eyes and leans in close, confidential, man to man.)* Me and you ought to sit down and talk sometimes, man. Man, I got me some ideas . . .

Murchison *(with boredom).* Yeah—sometimes we'll have to do that, Walter.

Walter *(understanding the indifference, and offended).* Yeah—well, when you get the time, man. I know you a busy little boy.

Ruth. Walter, please—

Walter *(bitterly, hurt).* I know ain't nothing in this world as busy as you colored college boys with your fraternity pins and white shoes . . .

Ruth *(covering her face with humiliation).* Oh, Walter Lee—

Walter. I see you all all the time—with the books tucked under your arms—going to your *(British A—a mimic.)* "clahsses." And for what! What the hell you learning over there? Filling up your heads—*(Counting off on his fingers.)*—with the sociology and the psychology—but they teaching you how to be a man? How to take over and run the world? They teaching you how to run a rubber plantation or a steel mill? Naw—just to talk proper and read books and wear them faggoty-looking white shoes . . .

George *(looking at him with distaste, a little above it all).* You're all wacked up with bitterness, man.

Walter *(intently, almost quietly, between the teeth, glaring at the boy).* And you—ain't you bitter, man? Ain't you just about had it yet? Don't you see no stars gleaming that you can't reach out and grab? You happy?—You contented son-of-a-bitch—you happy? You got it made? Bitter? Man, I'm a volcano. Bitter? Here I am a giant—surrounded by ants! Ants who can't even understand what it is the giant is talking about.

Ruth *(passionately and suddenly).* Oh, Walter—ain't you with nobody!

Walter *(violently).* No! 'Cause ain't nobody with me! Not even my own mother!

Ruth. Walter, that's a terrible thing to say!

Beneatha enters, dressed for the evening in a cocktail dress and earrings, hair natural.

George. Well—hey—*(Crosses to Beneatha; thoughtful, with emphasis, since this is a reversal.)* You look great!

Walter *(seeing his sister's hair for the first time).* What's the matter with your head?

Beneatha *(tired of the jokes now).* I cut it off, Brother.

Walter *(coming close to inspect it and walking around her).* Well, I'll be damned. So that's what they mean by the African bush . . .

Beneatha. Ha ha. Let's go, George.

George *(looking at her)*. You know something? I like it. It's sharp. I mean it really is. *(Helps her into her wrap.)*

Ruth. Yes—I think so, too. *(She goes to the mirror and starts to clutch at her hair.)*

Walter. Oh no! You leave yours alone, baby. You might turn out to have a pin-shaped head or something!

Beneatha. See you all later.

Ruth. Have a nice time.

George. Thanks. Good night. *(Half out the door, he reopens it. To Walter.)* Good night, Prometheus!

Beneatha and George exit.

Walter *(to Ruth)*. Who is Prometheus?

Ruth. I don't know. Don't worry about it.

Walter *(in fury, pointing after George)*. See there—they get to a point where they can't insult you man to man—they got to go talk about something ain't nobody never heard of!

Ruth. How do you know it was an insult? *(To humor him.)* Maybe Prometheus is a nice fellow.

Walter. Prometheus! I bet there ain't even no such thing! I bet that simpleminded clown—

Ruth. Walter—

She stops what she is doing and looks at him.

Walter *(yelling)*. Don't start!

Ruth. Start what?

Walter. Your nagging! Where was I? Who was I with? How much money did I spend?

Ruth *(plaintively)*. Walter Lee—why don't we just try to talk about it . . .

Walter *(not listening)*. I been out talking with people who understand me. People who care about the things I got on my mind.

Ruth *(wearily)*. I guess that means people like Willy Harris.

Walter. Yes, people like Willy Harris.

Ruth *(with a sudden flash of impatience)*. Why don't you all just hurry up and go into the banking business and stop talking about it!

Walter. Why? You want to know why? 'Cause we all tied up in a race of people that don't know how to do nothing but moan, pray, and have babies!

The line is too bitter even for him and he looks at her and sits down.

Ruth. Oh, Walter . . . *(Softly.)* Honey, why can't you stop fighting me?

Walter *(without thinking)*. Who's fighting you? Who even cares about you?

This line begins the retardation of his mood.

Ruth. Well—*(She waits a long time, and then with resignation starts to put away her things.)* I guess I might as well go on to bed . . . *(More or less to herself.)* I don't know where we lost it . . . but we have . . . *(Then, to him.)* I—I'm sorry about this new baby, Walter. I guess maybe I better go on and do what I started . . . I guess I just didn't realize how bad things was with us . . . I guess I just didn't really realize—*(She starts out to the bedroom and stops.)* You want some hot milk?

Walter. Hot milk?

Ruth. Yes—hot milk.

Walter. Why hot milk?

Ruth. 'Cause after all that liquor you come home with you ought to have something hot in your stomach.

Walter. I don't want no milk.

Ruth. You want some coffee then?

Walter. No, I don't want no coffee. I don't want nothing hot to drink. *(Almost plaintively.)* Why you always trying to give me something to eat?

Ruth *(standing and looking at him helplessly).* What *else* can I give you, Walter Lee Younger?

She stands and looks at him and presently turns to go out again. He lifts his head and watches her going away from him in a new mood which began to emerge when he asked her "Who cares about you?"

Walter. It's been rough, ain't it, baby? *(She hears and stops but does not turn around and he continues to her back.)* I guess between two people there ain't never as much understood as folks generally thinks there is. I mean like between me and you—*(She turns to face him.)* How we gets to the place where we scared to talk softness to each other. *(He waits, thinking hard himself.)* Why you think it got to be like that? *(He is thoughtful, almost as a child would be.)* Ruth, what is it gets into people ought to be close?

Ruth. I don't know, honey. I think about it a lot.

Walter. On account of you and me, you mean? The way things are with us. The way something done come down between us.

Ruth. There ain't so much between us, Walter . . . Not when you come to me and try to talk to me. Try to be with me . . . a little even.

Walter *(total honesty).* Sometimes . . . sometimes . . . I don't even know how to try.

Ruth. Walter—

Walter. Yes?

Ruth *(coming to him, gently and with misgiving, but coming to him).* Honey . . . life don't have to be like this. I mean sometimes people can do things so that things are better . . . You remember how we used to talk when Travis was born . . .

about the way we were going to live . . . the kind of house . . . (*She is stroking his head.*) Well, it's all starting to slip away from us . . .

He turns her to him and they look at each other and kiss, tenderly and hungrily. The door opens and Mama enters—Walter breaks away and jumps up. A beat.

Walter. Mama, where have you been?

Mama. My—them steps is longer than they used to be. Whew! (*She sits down and ignores him.*) How you feeling this evening, Ruth?

Ruth shrugs, disturbed at having been interrupted and watching her husband knowingly.

Walter. Mama, where have you been all day?

Mama (*still ignoring him and leaning on the table and changing to more comfortable shoes*). Where's Travis?

Ruth. I let him go out earlier and he ain't come back yet. Boy, is he going to get it!

Walter. Mama!

Mama (*as if she has heard him for the first time*). Yes, son?

Walter. Where did you go this afternoon?

Mama. I went downtown to tend to some business that I had to tend to.

Walter. What kind of business?

Mama. You know better than to question me like a child, Brother.

Walter (*rising and bending over the table*). Where were you, Mama? (*Bringing his fists down and shouting.*) Mama, you didn't go do something with that insurance money, something crazy?

The front door opens slowly, interrupting him, and Travis peeks his head in, less than hopefully.

Travis (*to his mother*). Mama, I—

Ruth. "Mama I" nothing! You're going to get it, boy! Get on in that bedroom and get yourself ready!

Travis. But I—

Mama. Why don't you all never let the child explain hisself.

Ruth. Keep out of it now, Lena.

Mama clamps her lips together, and Ruth advances toward her son menacingly.

Ruth. A thousand times I have told you not to go off like that—

Mama (*holding out her arms to her grandson*). Well—at least let me tell him something. I want him to be the first one to hear . . . Come here, Travis. (*The boy obeys, gladly.*) Travis—(*She takes him by the shoulder and looks into his face.*)— you know that money we got in the mail this morning?

Travis. Yes'm—

Mama. Well—what you think your grandmama gone and done with that money?

Travis. I don't know, Grandmama.

Mama *(putting her finger on his nose for emphasis).* She went out and she bought you a house! *(The explosion comes from Walter at the end of the revelation and he jumps up and turns away from all of them in a fury. Mama continues, to Travis.)* You glad about the house? It's going to be yours when you get to be a man.

Travis. Yeah—I always wanted to live in a house.

Mama. All right, gimme some sugar then—*(Travis puts his arms around her neck as she watches her son over the boy's shoulder. Then, to Travis, after the embrace.)* Now when you say your prayers tonight, you thank God and your grandfather—'cause it was him who give you the house—in his way.

Ruth *(taking the boy from Mama and pushing him toward the bedroom).* Now you get out of here and get ready for your beating.

Travis. Aw, Mama—

Ruth. Get on in there—*(Closing the door behind him and turning radiantly to her mother-in-law.)* So you went and did it!

Mama *(quietly, looking at her son with pain).* Yes, I did.

Ruth *(raising both arms classically).* PRAISE GOD! *(Looks at Walter a moment, who says nothing. She crosses rapidly to her husband.)* Please, honey—let me be glad . . . you be glad too. *(She has laid her hands on his shoulders, but he shakes himself free of her roughly, without turning to face her.)* Oh, Walter . . . a home . . . a home. *(She comes back to Mama.)* Well—where is it? How big is it? How much it going to cost?

Mama. Well—

Ruth. When we moving?

Mama *(smiling at her).* First of the month.

Ruth *(throwing back her head with jubilance).* Praise God!

Mama *(tentatively, still looking at her son's back turned against her and Ruth).* It's—it's a nice house too . . . *(She cannot help speaking directly to him. An imploring quality in her voice, her manner, makes her almost like a girl now.)* Three bedrooms—nice big one for you and Ruth . . . Me and Beneatha still have to share our room, but Travis have one of his own—and *(With difficulty.)* I figure if the—new baby—is a boy, we could get one of them double-decker outfits . . . And there's a yard with a little patch of dirt where I could maybe get to grow me a few flowers . . . And a nice big basement . . .

Ruth. Walter honey, be glad—

Mama *(still to his back, fingering things on the table).* 'Course I don't want to make it sound fancier than it is . . . It's just a plain little old house—but it's made good and solid—and it will be *ours.* Walter Lee—it makes a difference in a man when he can walk on floors that belong to *him* . . .

Ruth. Where is it?

Mama *(frightened at this telling).* Well—well—it's out there in Clybourne Park—

Ruth's radiance fades abruptly, and Walter finally turns slowly to face his mother with incredulity and hostility.

Ruth. Where?

Mama *(matter-of-factly)*. Four o six Clybourne Street, Clybourne Park.

Ruth. Clybourne Park? Mama, there ain't no colored people living in Clybourne Park.

Mama *(almost idiotically)*. Well, I guess there's going to be some now.

Walter *(bitterly)*. So that's the peace and comfort you went out and bought for us today!

Mama *(raising her eyes to meet his finally)*. Son—I just tried to find the nicest place for the least amount of money for my family.

Ruth *(trying to recover from the shock)*. Well—well—'course I ain't one never been 'fraid of no crackers, mind you—but—well, wasn't there no other houses nowhere?

Mama. Them houses they put up for colored in them areas way out all seem to cost twice as much as other houses. I did the best I could.

Ruth *(struck senseless with the news, in its various degrees of goodness and trouble, she sits a moment, her fists propping her chin in thought, and then she starts to rise, bringing her fists down with vigor, the radiance spreading from cheek to cheek again)*. Well—well—All I can say is—if this is my time in life—MY TIME— to say good-bye—*(And she builds with momentum as she starts to circle the room with an exuberant, almost tearfully happy release.)*—to these Goddamned cracking walls!—*(She pounds the walls.)*—and these marching roaches!—*(She wipes at an imaginary army of marching roaches.)*—and this cramped little closet which ain't now or never was no kitchen! . . . then I say it loud and good, HALLELUJAH! AND GOOD-BYE MISERY . . . I DON'T NEVER WANT TO SEE YOUR UGLY FACE AGAIN! *(She laughs joyously, having practically destroyed the apartment, and flings her arms up and lets them come down happily, slowly, reflectively, over her abdomen, aware for the first time perhaps that the life therein pulses with happiness and not despair.)* Lena?

Mama *(moved, watching her happiness)*. Yes, honey?

Ruth *(looking off)*. Is there—is there a whole lot of sunlight?

Mama *(understanding)*. Yes, child, there's a whole lot of sunlight.

Long pause.

Ruth *(collecting herself and going to the door of the room Travis is in)*. Well—I guess I better see 'bout Travis. *(To Mama.)* Lord, I sure don't feel like whipping nobody today!

She exits.

Mama *(the mother and son are left alone now and the mother waits a long time, considering deeply, before she speaks)*. Son—you—you understand what I done, don't you? *(Walter is silent and sullen.)* I—I just seen my family falling apart today . . . just falling to pieces in front of my eyes . . . We couldn't of gone on like we was today. We was going backwards 'stead of forwards—talking 'bout killing babies and wishing each other was dead . . . When it gets like that in life— you just got to do something different, push on out and do something bigger . . . *(She waits.)* I wish you say something, son . . . I wish you'd say how deep inside you you think I done the right thing—

Walter *(crossing slowly to his bedroom door and finally turning there and speaking measuredly).* What you need me to say you done right for? *You* the head of this family. You run our lives like you want to. It was your money and you did what you wanted with it. So what you need for me to say it was all right for? *(Bitterly, to hurt her as deeply as he knows is possible.)* So you butchered up a dream of mine—you—who always talking 'bout your children's dreams . . .

Mama. Walter Lee—

He just closes the door behind him. Mama sits alone, thinking heavily.

Curtain.

Scene 2.

Time: Friday night, a few weeks later.

At rise: Packing crates mark the intention of the family to move. Beneatha and George come in, presumably from an evening out again.

George. O.K. . . . O.K., whatever you say . . . *(They both sit on the couch. He tries to kiss her. She moves away.)* Look, we've had a nice evening; let's not spoil it, huh? . . .

He again turns her head and tries to nuzzle in and she turns away from him, not with distaste but with momentary lack of interest; in a mood to pursue what they were talking about.

Beneatha. I'm *trying* to talk to you.

George. We always talk.

Beneatha. Yes—and I love to talk.

George *(exasperated; rising).* I know it and I don't mind it sometimes . . . I want you to cut it out, see—The moody stuff, I mean. I don't like it. You're a nice-looking girl . . . all over. That's all you need, honey, forget the atmosphere. Guys aren't going to go for the atmosphere—they're going to go for what they see. Be glad for that. Drop the Garbo routine. It doesn't go with you. As for myself, I want a nice—*(Groping.)*—simple *(Thoughtfully.)*—sophisticated girl . . . not a poet—O.K.?

He starts to kiss her, she rebuffs him again and he jumps up.

Beneatha. Why are you angry, George?

George. Because this is stupid! I don't go out with you to discuss the nature of "quiet desperation" or to hear all about your thoughts—because the world will go on thinking what it thinks regardless—

Beneatha. Then why read books? Why go to school?

George *(with artificial patience, counting on his fingers)*. It's simple. You read books—to learn facts—to get grades—to pass the course—to get a degree. That's all—it has nothing to do with thoughts.

A long pause.

Beneatha. I see. *(He starts to sit.)* Good night, George.

George looks at her a little oddly, and starts to exit. He meets Mama coming in.

George. Oh—hello, Mrs. Younger.

Mama. Hello, George, how you feeling?

George. Fine—fine, how are you?

Mama. Oh, a little tired. You know them steps can get you after a day's work. You all have a nice time tonight?

George. Yes—a fine time. A fine time.

Mama. Well, good night.

George. Good night. *(He exits. Mama closes the door behind her.)*

Mama. Hello, honey. What you sitting like that for?

Beneatha. I'm just sitting.

Mama. Didn't you have a nice time?

Beneatha. No.

Mama. No? What's the matter?

Beneatha. Mama, George is a fool—honest. *(She rises.)*

Mama *(hustling around unloading the packages she has entered with. She stops)*. Is he, baby?

Beneatha. Yes.

Beneatha makes up Travis's bed as she talks.

Mama. You sure?

Beneatha. Yes.

Mama. Well—I guess you better not waste your time with no fools.

Beneatha looks up at her mother, watching her put groceries in the refrigerator. Finally she gathers up her things and starts into the bedroom. At the door she stops and looks back at her mother.

Beneatha. Mama—
Mama. Yes, baby—
Beneatha. Thank you.
Mama. For what?
Beneatha. For understanding me this time.

She exits quickly and the mother stands, smiling a little, looking at the place where Beneatha just stood. Ruth enters.

Ruth. Now don't you fool with any of this stuff, Lena—
Mama. Oh, I just thought I'd sort a few things out. Is Brother here?
Ruth. Yes.
Mama (*with concern*). Is he—
Ruth (*reading her eyes*). Yes.

Mama is silent and someone knocks on the door. Mama and Ruth exchange weary and knowing glances and Ruth opens it to admit the neighbor, Mrs. Johnson,[1] *who is a rather squeaky wide-eyed lady of no particular age, with a newspaper under her arm.*

Mama (*changing her expression to acute delight and a ringing cheerful greeting*). Oh—hello there, Johnson.
Johnson (*this is a woman who decided long ago to be enthusiastic about EVERY-THING in life and she is inclined to wave her wrist vigorously at the height of her exclamatory comments*). Hello there, yourself! H'you this evening, Ruth?
Ruth (*not much of a deceptive type*). Fine, Mis' Johnson, h'you?
Johnson. Fine. (*Reaching out quickly, playfully, and patting Ruth's stomach.*) Ain't you starting to poke out none yet! (*She mugs with delight at the over familiar remark and her eyes dart around looking at the crates and packing preparation; Mama's face is a cold sheet of endurance.*) Oh, ain't we getting ready round here, though! Yessir! Lookathere! I'm telling you the Youngers is really getting ready to "move on up a little higher!"—Bless God!
Mama (*a little drily, doubting the total sincerity of the Blesser*). Bless God.
Johnson. He's good, ain't He?
Mama. Oh yes, He's good.
Johnson. I mean sometimes He works in mysterious ways . . . but He works, don't He!
Mama (*the same*). Yes, He does.
Johnson. I'm just soooooo happy for y'all. And this here child—(*About Ruth.*) looks like she could just pop open with happiness, don't she. Where's all the rest of the family?
Mama. Bennie's gone to bed—

[1] This character and the scene of her visit were cut from the original production and early editions of the play.

Johnson. Ain't no . . . *(The implication is pregnancy.)* sickness done hit you—I hope . . . ?

Mama. No—she just tired. She was out this evening.

Johnson *(all is a coo, an emphatic coo)*. Aw—ain't that lovely. She still going out with the little Murchison boy?

Mama *(drily)*. Ummmm huh.

Johnson. That's lovely. You sure got lovely children, Younger. Me and Isaiah talks all the time 'bout what fine children you was blessed with. We sure do.

Mama. Ruth, give Mis' Johnson a piece of sweet potato pie and some milk.

Johnson. Oh honey, I can't stay hardly a minute—I just dropped in to see if there was anything I could do. *(Accepting the food easily.)* I guess y'all seen the news what's all over the colored paper this week . . .

Mama. No—didn't get mine yet this week.

Johnson *(lifting her head and blinking with the spirit of catastrophe)*. You mean you ain't read 'bout them colored people that was bombed out their place out there?

Ruth straightens with concern and takes the paper and reads it. Johnson notices her and feeds commentary.

Johnson. Ain't it something how bad these here white folks is getting here in Chicago! Lord, getting so you think you right down in Mississippi! *(With a tremendous and rather insincere sense of melodrama.)* 'Course I thinks it's wonderful how our folk keeps on pushing out. You hear some of these Negroes round here talking 'bout how they don't go where they ain't wanted and all that—but not me, honey! *(This is a lie.)* Wilhemenia Othella Johnson goes anywhere, any time she feels like it! *(With head movement for emphasis.)* Yes I do! Why if we left it up to these here crackers, the poor niggers wouldn't have nothing—*(She clasps her hand over her mouth.)* Oh, I always forgets you don't 'low that word in your house.

Mama *(quietly, looking at her)*. No—I don't 'low it.

Johnson *(vigorously again)*. Me neither! I was just telling Isaiah yesterday when he come using it in front of me—I said, "Isaiah, it's just like Mis' Younger says all the time—"

Mama. Don't you want some more pie?

Johnson. No—no thank you; this was lovely. I got to get on over home and have my midnight coffee. I hear some people say it don't let them sleep but I finds I can't close my eyes right lessen I done had that laaaast cup of coffee . . . *(She waits. A beat. Undaunted.)* My Goodnight coffee, I calls it!

Mama *(with much eye-rolling and communication between herself and Ruth)*. Ruth, why don't you give Mis' Johnson some coffee.

Ruth gives Mama an unpleasant look for her kindness.

Johnson *(accepting the coffee)*. Where's Brother tonight?

Mama. He's lying down.

Johnson. Mmmmmmm, he sure gets his beauty rest, don't he? Good-looking man. Sure is a good-looking man! *(Reaching out to pat Ruth's stomach again.)* I guess that's how come we keep on having babies around here. *(She winks at Mama.)* One thing 'bout Brother, he always know how to have a *good* time. And soooooo ambitious! I bet it was his idea y'all moving out to Clybourne Park. Lord—I bet this time next month y'all's names will have been in the papers plenty—*(Holding up her hands to mark off each word of the headline she can see in front of her.)* "NEGROES INVADE CLYBOURNE PARK—BOMBED!"

Mama *(she and Ruth look at the woman in amazement).* We ain't exactly moving out there to get bombed.

Johnson. Oh honey—you know I'm praying to God every day that don't nothing like that happen! But you have to think of life like it is—and these here Chicago peckerwoods is some baaaad peckerwoods.

Mama *(wearily).* We done thought about all that Mis' Johnson.

Beneatha comes out of the bedroom in her robe and passes through to the bathroom. Mrs. Johnson turns.

Johnson. Hello there, Bennie!

Beneatha *(crisply).* Hello, Mrs. Johnson.

Johnson. How is school?

Beneatha *(crisply).* Fine, thank you. *(She goes out.)*

Johnson *(insulted).* Getting so she don't have much to say to nobody.

Mama. The child was on her way to the bathroom.

Johnson. I know—but sometimes she act like ain't got time to pass the time of day with nobody ain't been to college. Oh—I ain't criticizing her none. It's just—you know how some of our young people gets when they get a little education. *(Mama and Ruth say nothing, just look at her.)* Yes—well. Well, I guess I better get on home. *(Unmoving.)* 'Course I can understand how she must be proud and everything—being the only one in the family to make something of herself. I know just being a chauffeur ain't never satisfied Brother none. He shouldn't feel like that, though. Ain't nothing wrong with being a chauffeur.

Mama. There's plenty wrong with it.

Johnson. What?

Mama. Plenty. My husband always said being any kind of a servant wasn't a fit thing for a man to have to be. He always said a man's hands was made to make things, or to turn the earth with—not to drive nobody's car for 'em—or—*(She looks at her own hands.)* carry they slop jars. And my boy is just like him—he wasn't meant to wait on nobody.

Johnson *(rising, somewhat offended).* Mmmmmmmmm. The Youngers is too much for me! *(She looks around.)* You sure one proud-acting bunch of colored folks. Well—I always thinks like Booker T. Washington said that time— "Education has spoiled many a good plow hand"—

Mama. Is that what old Booker T. said?

Johnson. He sure did.

Mama. Well, it sounds just like him. The fool.

Johnson (*indignantly*). Well—he was one of our great men.

Mama. Who said so?

Johnson (*nonplussed*). You know, me and you ain't never agreed about some things, Lena Younger. I guess I better be going—

Ruth (*quickly*). Good night.

Johnson. Good night. Oh—(*Thrusting it at her.*) You can keep the paper! (*With a trill.*) 'Night.

Mama. Good night, Mis' Johnson.

Mrs. Johnson exits.

Ruth. If ignorance was gold . . .

Mama. Shush. Don't talk about folks behind their backs.

Ruth. You do.

Mama. I'm old and corrupted. (*Beneatha enters.*) You was rude to Mis' Johnson, Beneatha, and I don't like it at all.

Beneatha (*at her door*). Mama, if there are two things we, as a people, have got to overcome, one is the Ku Klux Klan—and the other is Mrs. Johnson. (*She exits.*)

Mama. Smart aleck.

The phone rings.

Ruth. I'll get it.

Mama. Lord, ain't this a popular place tonight.

Ruth (*at the phone*). Hello—Just a minute. (*Goes to door.*) Walter, it's Mrs. Arnold. (*Waits. Goes back to the phone. Tense.*) Hello. Yes, this is his wife speaking . . . He's lying down now. Yes . . . well, he'll be in tomorrow. He's been very sick. Yes—I know we should have called, but we were so sure he'd be able to come in today. Yes—yes, I'm very sorry. Yes . . . Thank you very much. (*She hangs up. Walter is standing in the doorway of the bedroom behind her.*) That was Mrs. Arnold.

Walter (*indifferently*). Was it?

Ruth. She said if you don't come in tomorrow that they are getting a new man . . .

Walter. Ain't that sad—ain't that crying sad.

Ruth. She said Mr. Arnold has had to take a cab for three days . . . Walter, you ain't been to work for three days! (*This is a revelation to her.*) Where you been, Walter Lee Younger? (*Walter looks at her and starts to laugh.*) You're going to lose your job.

Walter. That's right . . . (*He turns on the radio.*)

Ruth. Oh, Walter, and with your mother working like a dog every day—

A steamy, deep blues pours into the room.

Walter. That's sad too—Everything is sad.

Mama. What you been doing for these three days, son?

Walter. Mama—you don't know all the things a man what got leisure can find to do in this city . . . What's this—Friday night? Well—Wednesday I borrowed Willy Harris's car and I went for a drive . . . just me and myself and I drove and drove . . . Way out . . . way past South Chicago, and I parked the car and I sat and looked at the steel mills all day long. I just sat in the car and looked at them big black chimneys for hours. Then I drove back and I went to the Green Hat. *(Pause.)* And Thursday—Thursday I borrowed the car again and I got in it and I pointed it the other way and I drove the other way—for hours—way, way up to Wisconsin, and I looked at the farms. I just drove and looked at the farms. Then I drove back and I went to the Green Hat. *(Pause.)* And today—today I didn't get the car. Today I just walked. All over the Southside. And I looked at the Negroes and they looked at me and finally I just sat down on the curb at Thirty-ninth and South Parkway and I just sat there and watched the Negroes go by. And then I went to the Green Hat. You all sad? You all depressed? And you know where I am going right now—

Ruth goes out quietly.

Mama. Oh, Big Walter, is this the harvest of our days?

Walter. You know what I like about the Green Hat? I like this little cat they got there who blows a sax . . . He blows. He talks to me. He ain't but 'bout five feet tall and he's got a conked head and his eyes is always closed and he's all music—

Mama *(rising and getting some papers out of her handbag).* Walter—

Walter. And there's this other guy who plays the piano . . . and they got a sound. I mean they can work on some music . . . They got the best little combo in the world in the Green Hat . . . You can just sit there and drink and listen to them three men play and you realize that don't nothing matter worth a damn, but just being there—

Mama. I've helped do it to you, haven't I, son? Walter I been wrong.

Walter. Naw—you ain't never been wrong about nothing, Mama.

Mama. Listen to me, now. I say I been wrong, son. That I been doing to you what the rest of the world been doing to you. *(She turns off the radio.)* Walter—*(She stops and he looks up slowly at her and she meets his eyes pleadingly.)* What you ain't never understood is that I ain't got nothing, don't own nothing, ain't never really wanted nothing that wasn't for you. There ain't nothing as precious to me . . . There ain't nothing worth holding on to, money, dreams, nothing else—if it means—if it means it's going to destroy my boy. *(She takes an envelope out of her handbag and puts it in front of him and he watches her without speaking or moving.)* I paid the man thirty-five hundred dollars down on the house. That leaves sixty-five hundred dollars. Monday morning I want you to take this money and take three thousand dollars and put it in a savings account for Beneatha's medical schooling. The rest you put in a checking account—with your name on it. And from now on any penny that come out of it or that go in it is for you to look after. For you to decide. *(She drops her hands a little helplessly.)* It ain't much, but it's all I got in the world and I'm putting it in your hands. I'm telling you to be the head of this family from now on like you supposed to be.

Walter *(stares at the money).* You trust me like that, Mama?

Mama. I ain't never stop trusting you. Like I ain't never stop loving you.

She goes out, and Walter sits looking at the money on the table. Finally, in a decisive gesture, he gets up, and, in mingled joy and desperation, picks up the money. At the same moment, Travis enters for bed.

Travis. What's the matter, Daddy? You drunk?

Walter *(sweetly, more sweetly than we have ever known him).* No, Daddy ain't drunk. Daddy ain't going to never be drunk again . . .

Travis. Well, good night, Daddy.

The father has come from behind the couch and leans over, embracing his son.

Walter. Son, I feel like talking to you tonight.

Travis. About what?

Walter. Oh, about a lot of things. About you and what kind of man you going to be when you grow up . . . Son—son, what do you want to be when you grow up?

Travis. A bus driver.

Walter *(laughing a little).* A what? Man, that ain't nothing to want to be!

Travis. Why not?

Walter. 'Cause, man—it ain't big enough—you know what I mean.

Travis. I don't know then. I can't make up my mind. Sometimes Mama asks me that too. And sometimes when I tell her I just want to be like you—she says she don't want me to be like that and sometimes she says she does. . . .

Walter *(gathering him up in his arms).* You know what, Travis? In seven years you going to be seventeen years old. And things is going to be very different with us in seven years, Travis. . . . One day when you are seventeen I'll come home— home from my office downtown somewhere—

Travis. You don't work in no office, Daddy.

Walter. No—but after tonight. After what your daddy gonna do tonight, there's going to be offices—a whole lot of offices. . . .

Travis. What you gonna do tonight, Daddy?

Walter. You wouldn't understand yet, son, but your daddy's gonna make a transaction . . . a business transaction that's going to change our lives. . . . That's how come one day when you 'bout seventeen years old I'll come home and I'll be pretty tired, you know what I mean, after a day of conferences and secretaries getting things wrong the way they do . . . 'cause an executive's life is hell, man—*(The more he talks the farther away he gets.)* And I'll pull the car up on the driveway . . . just a plain black Chrysler, I think, with white walls—

no—black tires. More elegant. Rich people don't have to be flashy . . . though I'll have to get something a little sportier for Ruth—maybe a Cadillac convertible to do her shopping in. . . . And I'll come up the steps to the house and the gardener will be clipping away at the hedges and he'll say, "Good evening, Mr. Younger." And I'll say, "Hello, Jefferson, how are you this evening?" And I'll go inside and Ruth will come downstairs and meet me at the door and we'll kiss each other and she'll take my arm and we'll go up to your room to see you sitting on the floor with the catalogues of all the great schools in America around you. . . . All the great schools in the world! And—and I'll say, all right son—it's your seventeenth birthday, what is it you've decided? . . . Just tell me where you want to go to school and you'll *go*. Just tell me, what it is you want to be—and you'll *be* it. . . . Whatever you want to be—Yessir! *(He holds his arms open for Travis.)* You just name it, son . . . *(Travis leaps into them.)* and I hand you the world!

Walter's voice has risen in pitch and hysterical promise and on the last line he lifts Travis high.

Blackout.

Scene 3.

Time. Saturday, moving day, one week later.

Before the curtain rises, Ruth's voice, a strident, dramatic church alto, cuts through the silence.

It is, in the darkness, a triumphant surge, a penetrating statement of expectation: "Oh, Lord, I don't feel no ways tired! Children, oh, glory hallelujah!"

As the curtain rises we see that Ruth is alone in the living room, finishing up the family's packing. It is moving day. She is nailing crates and tying cartons. Beneatha enters, carrying a guitar case, and watches her exuberant sister-in-law.

Ruth. Hey!

Beneatha *(putting away the case).* Hi.

Ruth *(pointing at a package).* Honey—look in that package there and see what I found on sale this morning at the South Center. *(Ruth gets up and moves to the package and draws out some curtains.)* Lookahere—hand-turned hems!

Beneatha. How do you know the window size out there?

Ruth *(who hadn't thought of that).* Oh—Well, they bound to fit something in the whole house. Anyhow, they was too good a bargain to pass up. *(Ruth slaps her head, suddenly remembering something.)* Oh, Bennie—I meant to put a special note on that carton over there. That's your mama's good china and she wants 'em to be very careful with it.

Beneatha. I'll do it.

Beneatha finds a piece of paper and starts to draw large letters on it.

Ruth. You know what I'm going to do soon as I get in that new house?

Beneatha. What?

Ruth. Honey—I'm going to run me a tub of water up to here . . . *(With her fingers practically up to her nostrils.)* And I'm going to get in it—and I am going to sit . . . and sit . . . and sit in that hot water and the first person who knocks to tell *me* to hurry up and come out—

Beneatha. Gets shot at sunrise.

Ruth *(laughing happily)*. You said it, sister! *(Noticing how large Beneatha is absent-mindedly making the note)*: Honey, they ain't going to read that from no airplane.

Beneatha *(laughing herself)*. I guess I always think things have more emphasis if they are big, somehow.

Ruth *(looking up at her and smiling)*. You and your brother seem to have that as a philosophy of life. Lord, that man—done changed so 'round here. You know—you know what we did last night? Me and Walter Lee?

Beneatha. What?

Ruth *(smiling to herself)*. We went to the movies. *(Looking at Beneatha to see if she understands.)* We went to the movies. You know the last time me and Walter went to the movies together?

Beneatha. No.

Ruth. Me neither. That's how long it been. *(Smiling again.)* But we went last night. The picture wasn't much good, but that didn't seem to matter. We went—and we held hands.

Beneatha. Oh, Lord!

Ruth. We held hands—and you know what?

Beneatha. What?

Ruth. When we come out of the show it was late and dark and all the stores and things was closed up . . . and it was kind of chilly and there wasn't many people on the streets . . . and we was still holding hands, me and Walter.

Beneatha. You're killing me.

Walter enters with a large package. His happiness is deep in him; he cannot keep still with his newfound exuberance. He is singing and wiggling and snapping his fingers. He puts his package in a corner and puts a phonograph record, which he has brought in with him, on the record player. As the music, soulful and sensuous, comes up he dances over to Ruth and tries to get her to dance with him. She gives in at last to his raunchiness and in a fit of giggling allows herself to be drawn into his mood. They dip and she melts into his arms in a classic, body-melting "slow drag."

Beneatha *(regarding them a long time as they dance, then drawing in her breath for a deeply exaggerated comment which she does not particularly mean)*. Talk about—olddddddddddd-fashioneddddddddd—Negroes!

Walter *(stopping momentarily)*. What kind of Negroes?

He says this in fun. He is not angry with her today, nor with anyone. He starts to dance with his wife again.

Beneatha. Old-fashioned.

Walter *(as he dances with Ruth).* You know, when these *New Negroes* have their convention—*(Pointing at his sister.)*—that is going to be the chairman of the Committee on Unending Agitation. *(He goes on dancing, then stops.)* Race, race, race! ... Girl, I do believe you are the first person in the history of the entire human race to successfully brainwash yourself. *(Beneatha breaks up and he goes on dancing. He stops again, enjoying his tease.)* Damn, even the N double A C P takes a holiday sometimes! *(Beneatha and Ruth laugh. He dances with Ruth some more and starts to laugh and stops and pantomimes someone over an operating table.)* I can just see that chick someday looking down at some poor cat on an operating table and before she starts to slice him, she says ... *(Pulling his sleeves back maliciously.)* "By the way, what are your views on civil rights down there? ...."

He laughs at her again and starts to dance happily. The bell sounds.

Beneatha. Sticks and stones may break my bones but ... words will never hurt me!

Beneatha goes to the door and opens it as Walter and Ruth go on with the clowning. Beneatha is somewhat surprised to see a quiet-looking middle-aged white man in a business suit holding his hat and a briefcase in his hand and consulting a small piece of paper.

Man. Uh—how do you do, miss. I am looking for a Mrs.—*(He looks at the slip of paper.)* Mrs. Lena Younger? *(He stops short, struck dumb at the sight of the oblivious Walter and Ruth.)*

Beneatha *(smoothing her hair with slight embarrassment).* Oh—yes, that's my mother. Excuse me. *(She closes the door and turns to quiet the other two.)* Ruth! Brother! *(Enunciating precisely but soundlessly: "There's a white man at the door!" They stop dancing, Ruth cuts off the phonograph, Beneatha opens the door. The man casts a curious quick glance at all of them.)* Uh—come in please.

Man *(coming in).* Thank you.

Beneatha. My mother isn't here just now. Is it business?

Man. Yes ... well, of a sort.

Walter *(freely, the Man of the House).* Have a seat. I'm Mrs. Younger's son. I look after most of her business matters.

Ruth and Beneatha exchange amused glances.

Man *(regarding Walter, and sitting).* Well—My name is Karl Lindner ...

Walter *(stretching out his hand).* Walter Younger. This is my wife—*(Ruth nods politely.)*—and my sister.

Lindner. How do you do.

Walter *(amiably, as he sits himself easily on a chair, leaning forward on his knees with interest and looking expectantly into the newcomer's face).* What can we do for you, Mr. Lindner!

Lindner *(some minor shuffling of the hat and briefcase on his knees).* Well—I am a representative of the Clybourne Park Improvement Association—

Walter *(pointing).* Why don't you sit your things on the floor?

Lindner. Oh—yes. Thank you. *(He slides the briefcase and hat under the chair.)* And as I was saying—I am from the Clybourne Park Improvement Association and we have had it brought to our attention at the last meeting that you people—or at least your mother—has bought a piece of residential property at—*(He digs for the slip of paper again.)*—four o six Clybourne Street . . .

Walter. That's right. Care for something to drink? Ruth, get Mr. Lindner a beer.

Lindner *(upset for some reason).* Oh—no, really. I mean thank you very much, but no thank you.

Ruth *(innocently).* Some coffee?

Lindner. Thank you, nothing at all.

Beneatha is watching the man carefully.

Lindner. Well, I don't know how much you folks know about our organization. *(He is a gentle man; thoughtful and somewhat labored in his manner.)* It is one of these community organizations set up to look after—oh, you know, things like block upkeep and special projects and we also have what we call our New Neighbors Orientation Committee . . .

Beneatha *(drily).* Yes—and what do they do?

Lindner *(turning a little to her and then returning the main force to Walter).* Well— it's what you might call a sort of welcoming committee, I guess. I mean they, we—I'm the chairman of the committee—go around and see the new people who move into the neighborhood and sort of give them the lowdown on the way we do things out in Clybourne Park.

Beneatha *(with appreciation of the two meanings, which escape Ruth and Walter).* Un-huh.

Lindner. And we also have the category of what the association calls—*(He looks elsewhere.)*—uh—special community problems . . .

Beneatha. Yes—and what are some of those?

Walter. Girl, let the man talk.

Lindner *(with understated relief).* Thank you. I would sort of like to explain this thing in my own way. I mean I want to explain to you in a certain way.

Walter. Go ahead.

Lindner. Yes. Well. I'm going to try to get right to the point. I'm sure we'll all appreciate that in the long run.

Beneatha. Yes.

Walter. Be still now!

Lindner. Well—

Ruth *(still innocently).* Would you like another chair—you don't look comfortable.

Lindner *(more frustrated than annoyed).* No, thank you very much. Please. Well— to get right to the point, I—*(A great breath, and he is off at last.)* I am sure you people must be aware of some of the incidents which have happened in various parts of the city when colored people have moved into certain areas—*(Beneatha exhales heavily and starts tossing a piece of fruit up and down in the air.)* Well— because we have what I think is going to be a unique type of organization in American community life—not only do we deplore that kind of thing—but we are trying to do something about it. *(Beneatha stops tossing and turns with a new and quizzical interest to the man.)* We feel—*(gaining confidence in his mission because of the interest in the faces of the people he is talking to.)*—we feel that most of the trouble in this world, when you come right down to it—*(He hits his knee for emphasis.)*—most of the trouble exists because people just don't sit down and talk to each other.

Ruth *(nodding as she might in church, pleased with the remark).* You can say that again, mister.

Lindner *(more encouraged by such affirmation).* That we don't try hard enough in this world to understand the other fellow's problem. The other guy's point of view.

Ruth. Now that's right.

Beneatha and Walter merely watch and listen with genuine interest.

Lindner. Yes—that's the way we feel out in Clybourne Park. And that's why I was elected to come here this afternoon and talk to you people. Friendly like, you know, the way people should talk to each other and see if we couldn't find some way to work this thing out. As I say, the whole business is a matter of *caring* about the other fellow. Anybody can see that you are a nice family of folks, hard working and honest I'm sure. *(Beneatha frowns slightly, quizzically, her head tilted regarding him.)* Today everybody knows what it means to be on the outside of *something.* And of course, there is always somebody who is out to take advantage of people who don't always understand.

Walter. What do you mean?

Lindner. Well—you see our community is made up of people who've worked hard as the dickens for years to build up that little community. They're not rich and fancy people; just hard-working, honest people who don't really have much but those little homes and a dream of the kind of community they want to raise their children in. Now, I don't say we are perfect and there is a lot wrong in some of the things they want. But you've got to admit that a man, right or wrong, has the right to want to have the neighborhood he lives in a certain kind of way. And at the moment the overwhelming majority of our people out there feel that people get along better, take more of a common interest in the life of the community, when they share a common background. I want you to believe me when I tell you that race prejudice simply doesn't enter into it. It is a matter of the people of Clybourne Park believing, rightly or wrongly, as I say, that for the happiness of all concerned that our Negro families are happier when they live in their *own* communities.

Beneatha *(with a grand and bitter gesture).* This, friends, is the Welcoming Committee!

Walter (*dumfounded, looking at Lindner*). Is this what you came marching all the way over here to tell us?

Lindner. Well, now we've been having a fine conversation. I hope you'll hear me all the way through.

Walter (*tightly*). Go ahead, man.

Lindner. You see—in the face of all the things I have said, we are prepared to make your family a very generous offer . . .

Beneatha. Thirty pieces and not a coin less!

Walter. Yeah?

Lindner (*putting on his glasses drawing a form out of the briefcase*). Our association is prepared, through the collective effort of our people, to buy the house from you at a financial gain to your family.

Ruth. Lord have mercy, ain't this the living gall!

Walter. All right, you through?

Lindner. Well, I want to give you the exact terms of the financial arrangement—

Walter. We don't want to hear no exact terms of no arrangements. I want to know if you got any more to tell us 'bout getting together?

Lindner (*taking off his glasses*). Well—I don't suppose that you feel . . .

Walter. Never mind how I feel—you got any more to say 'bout how people ought to sit down and talk to each other? . . . Get out of my house, man.

He turns his back and walks to the door.

Lindner (*looking around at the hostile faces and reaching and assembling his hat and briefcase*). Well—I don't understand why you people are reacting this way. What do you think you are going to gain by moving into a neighborhood where you just aren't wanted and where some elements—well—people can get awful worked up when they feel that their whole way of life and everything they've ever worked for is threatened.

Walter. Get out.

Lindner (*at the door, holding a small card*). Well—I'm sorry it went like this.

Walter. Get out.

Lindner (*almost sadly regarding Walter*). You just can't force people to change their hearts, son.

He turns and puts his card on a table and exits. Walter pushes the door to with stinging hatred, and stands looking at it. Ruth just sits and Beneatha just stands. They say nothing. Mama and Travis enter.

Mama. Well—this all the packing got done since I left out of here this morning. I testify before God that my children got all the energy of the *dead!* What time the moving men due?

Beneatha. Four o'clock. You had a caller, Mama.

She is smiling, teasingly.

Mama. Sure enough—who?

Beneatha *(her arms folded saucily).* The Welcoming Committee.

Walter and Ruth giggle.

Mama *(innocently).* Who?

Beneatha. The Welcoming Committee. They said they're sure going to be glad to see you when you get there.

Walter *(devilishly).* Yeah, they said they can't hardly wait to see your face.

Laughter.

Mama *(sensing their facetiousness).* What's the matter with you all?

Walter. Ain't nothing the matter with us. We just telling you 'bout the gentleman who came to see you this afternoon. From the Clybourne Park Improvement Association.

Mama. What he want?

Ruth *(in the same mood as Beneatha and Walter).* To welcome you, honey.

Walter. He said they can't hardly wait. He said the one thing they don't have, that they just *dying* to have out there is a fine family of fine colored people! *(To Ruth and Beneatha.)* Ain't that right!

Ruth *(mockingly).* Yeah! He left his card—

Beneatha *(handing card to Mama).* In case.

Mama reads and throws it on the floor—understanding and looking off as she draws her chair up to the table on which she has put her plant and some sticks and some cord.

Mama. Father, give us strength. *(Knowingly—and without fun.)* Did he threaten us?

Beneatha. Oh—Mama—they don't do it like that any more. He talked Brother-hood. He said everybody ought to learn how to sit down and hate each other with good Christian fellowship.

She and Walter shake hands to ridicule the remark.

Mama *(sadly).* Lord, protect us . . .

Ruth. You should hear the money those folks raised to buy the house from us. All we paid and then some.

Beneatha. What they think we going to do—eat 'em?

Ruth. No, honey, marry 'em.

Mama *(shaking her head).* Lord, Lord, Lord . . .

Ruth. Well—that's the way the crackers crumble. *(A beat.)* Joke.

Beneatha *(laughingly noticing what her mother is doing).* Mama, what are you doing?

Mama. Fixing my plant so it won't get hurt none on the way . . .
Beneatha. Mama, you going to take *that* to the new house?
Mama. Un-huh—
Beneatha. That raggedy-looking old thing?
Mama (*stopping and looking at her*). It expresses ME!
Ruth (*with delight, to Beneatha*). So there, Miss Thing!

Walter comes to Mama suddenly and bends down behind her and squeezes her in his arms with all his strength. She is overwhelmed by the suddenness of it and, though delighted, her manner is like that of Ruth and Travis.

Mama. Look out now, boy! You make me mess up my thing here!
Walter (*his face lit, he slips down on his knees beside her, his arms still about her*).
    Mama . . . you know what it means to climb up in the chariot?
Mama (*gruffly, very happy*). Get on away from me now . . .
Ruth (*near the gift-wrapped package, trying to catch Walter's eye*). Psst—
Walter. What the old song say, Mama . . .
Ruth. Walter—Now?

She is pointing at the package.

Walter (*speaking the lines, sweetly, playfully, in his mother's face*).

    I got wings . . . you got wings . . .
    All God's Children got wings . . .

Mama. Boy—get out of my face and do some work . . .
Walter.

    When I get to heaven gonna put on my wings,
    Gonna fly all over God's heaven . . .

Beneatha (*teasingly, from across the room*). Everybody talking 'bout heaven ain't going there!
Walter (*to Ruth, who is carrying the box across to them*). I don't know, you think we ought to give her that . . . Seems to me she ain't been very appreciative around here.
Mama (*eying the box, which is obviously a gift*). What is that?
Walter (*taking it from Ruth and putting it on the table in front of Mama*). Well— what you all think? Should we give it to her?
Ruth. Oh—she was pretty good today.
Mama. I'll good you—

She turns her eyes to the box again.

Beneatha. Open it, Mama.

She stands up, looks at it, turns and looks at all of them, and then presses her hands together and does not open the package.

Walter *(sweetly)*. Open it, Mama. It's for you. *(Mama looks in his eyes. It is the first present in her life without its being Christmas. Slowly she opens her package and lifts out, one by one, a brand-new sparkling set of gardening tools. Walter continues, prodding.)* Ruth made up the note—read it . . .

Mama *(picking up the card and adjusting her glasses)*. "To our own Mrs. Miniver—Love from Brother, Ruth, and Beneatha." Ain't that lovely . . .

Travis *(tugging at his father's sleeve)*. Daddy, can I give her mine now?

Walter. All right, son. *(Travis flies to get his gift.)*

Mama. Now I don't have to use my knives and forks no more . . .

Walter. Travis didn't want to go in with the rest of us, Mama. He got his own. *(Somewhat amused.)* We don't know what it is . . .

Travis *(racing back in the room with a large hatbox and putting it in front of his grandmother)*. Here!

Mama. Lord have mercy, baby. You done gone and bought your grandmother a hat?

Travis *(very proud)*. Open it!

She does and lifts out an elaborate, but very elaborate, wide gardening hat, and all the adults break up at the sight of it.

Ruth. Travis, honey, what is that?

Travis *(who thinks it is beautiful and appropriate)*. It's a gardening hat! Like the ladies always have on in the magazines when they work in their gardens.

Beneatha *(giggling fiercely)*. Travis—we were trying to make Mama Mrs. Miniver—not Scarlett O'Hara!

Mama *(indignantly)*. What's the matter with you all! This here is a beautiful hat! *(Absurdly.)* I always wanted me one just like it!

She pops it on her head to prove it to her grandson, and the hat is ludicrous and considerably oversized.

Ruth. Hot dog! Go, Mama!

Walter *(doubled over with laughter)*. I'm sorry, Mama—but you look like you ready to go out and chop you some cotton sure enough!

They all laugh except Mama, out of deference to Travis's feelings.

Mama *(gathering the boy up to her)*. Bless your heart—this is the prettiest hat I ever owned—*(Walter, Ruth, and Beneatha chime in—noisily, festively, and insincerely congratulating Travis on his gift.)* What are we all standing around here for? We ain't finished packin' yet. Bennie, you ain't packed one book.

The bell rings.

Beneatha. That couldn't be the movers . . . it's not hardly two good yet—

Beneatha goes into her room. Mama starts for door.

Walter *(turning, stiffening).* Wait—wait—I'll get it.

He stands and looks at the door.

Mama. You expecting company, son?
Walter *(just looking at the door).* Yeah—yeah . . .

Mama looks at Ruth, and they exchange innocent and unfrightened glances.

Mama *(not understanding).* Well, let them in, son.
Beneatha *(from her room).* We need some more string.
Mama. Travis—you run to the hardware and get me some string cord.

Mama goes out and Walter turns and looks at Ruth. Travis goes to a dish for money.

Ruth. Why don't you answer the door, man?
Walter *(suddenly bounding across the floor to embrace her).* 'Cause sometimes it
   hard to let the future begin! *(Stooping down in her face.)*

   I got wings! You got wings!
   All God's children got wings!

*He crosses to the door and throws it open. Standing there is a very slight little man in
a not-too-prosperous business suit and with haunted frightened eyes and a hat pulled
down tightly, brim up, around his forehead. Travis passes between the men and exits.
Walter leans deep in the man's face, still in his jubilance.*

   When I get to heaven gonna put on my wings,
   Gonna fly all over God's heaven . . .

The little man just stares at him.

   Heaven—

Suddenly he stops and looks past the little man into the empty hallway.

   Where's Willy, man?
Bobo. He ain't with me.
Walter *(not disturbed).* Oh—come on in. You know my wife.

Bobo *(dumbly, taking off his hat).* Yes—h'you, Miss Ruth.

Ruth *(quietly, a mood apart from her husband already, seeing Bobo).* Hello, Bobo.

Walter. You right on time today . . . Right on time. That's the way! *(He slaps Bobo on his back.)* Sit down . . . lemme hear.

Ruth stands stiffly and quietly in back of them, as though somehow she senses death, her eyes fixed on her husband.

Bobo *(his frightened eyes on the floor, his hat in his hands).* Could I please get a drink of water, before I tell you about it, Walter Lee?

Walter does not take his eyes off the man. Ruth goes blindly to the tap and gets a glass of water and brings it to Bobo.

Walter. There ain't nothing wrong, is there?

Bobo. Lemme tell you—

Walter. Man—didn't nothing go wrong?

Bobo. Lemme tell you—Walter Lee. *(Looking at Ruth and talking to her more than to Walter.)* You know how it was. I got to tell you how it was. I mean first I got to tell you how it was all the way . . . I mean about the money I put in, Walter Lee . . .

Walter *(with taut agitation now).* What about the money you put in?

Bobo. Well—it wasn't much as we told you—me and Willy—*(He stops.)* I'm sorry, Walter. I got a bad feeling about it. I got a real bad feeling about it . . .

Walter. Man, what you telling me about all this for? . . . Tell me what happened in Springfield . . .

Bobo. Springfield.

Ruth *(like a dead woman).* What was supposed to happen in Springfield?

Bobo *(to her).* This deal that me and Walter went into with Willy—Me and Willy was going to go down to Springfield and spread some money 'round so's we wouldn't have to wait so long for the liquor license . . . That's what we were going to do. Everybody said that was the way you had to do, you understand, Miss Ruth?

Walter. Man—what happened down there?

Bobo *(a pitiful man, near tears).* I'm trying to tell you, Walter.

Walter *(screaming at him suddenly).* THEN TELL ME, GODDAMMIT . . . WHAT'S THE MATTER WITH YOU?

Bobo. Man . . . I didn't go to no Springfield, yesterday.

Walter *(halted, life hanging in the moment).* Why not?

Bobo *(the long way, the hard way to tell).* 'Cause I didn't have no reasons to . . .

Walter. Man, what are you talking about!

Bobo. I'm talking about the fact that when I got to the train station yesterday morning—eight o'clock like we planned . . . Man—*Willy didn't never show up.*

Walter. Why . . . where was he . . . where is he?

Bobo. That's what I'm trying to tell you . . . I don't know . . . I waited six hours . . . I called his house . . . and I waited . . . six hours . . . I waited in that train station six hours . . . (*Breaking into tears.*) That was all the extra money I had in the world . . . (*Looking up at Walter with the tears running down his face.*) Man, *Willy is gone.*

Walter. Gone, what you mean Willy is gone? Gone where? You mean he went by himself. You mean he went off to Springfield by himself—to take care of getting the license—(*Turns and looks anxiously at Ruth.*) You mean maybe he didn't want too many people in on the business down there? (*Looks to Ruth again, as before.*) You know Willy got his own ways. (*Looks back to Bobo.*) Maybe you was late yesterday and he just went on down there without you. Maybe—maybe—he's been callin' you at home tryin' to tell you what happened or something. Maybe—maybe—he just got sick. He's somewhere—he's got to be somewhere. We just got to find him   me and you got to find him. (*Grabs Bobo senselessly by the collar and starts to shake him.*) We got to!

Bobo (*in sudden angry, frightened agony*). What's the matter with you, Walter! *When a cat take off with your money he don't leave you no road maps!*

Walter (*turning madly, as though he is looking for Willy in the very room*). Willy! . . . Willy . . . don't do it . . . Please don't do it . . . Man, not with that money . . . Man, please, not with that money . . . Oh, God . . . Don't let it be true . . . (*He is wandering around, crying out for Willy and looking for him or perhaps for help from God.*) Man . . . I trusted you . . . Man, I put my life in your hands . . . (*He starts to crumple down on the floor as Ruth just covers her face in horror. Mama opens the door and comes into the room, with Beneatha behind her.*) Man . . . (*He starts to pound the floor with his fists, sobbing wildly.*) THAT MONEY IS MADE OUT OF MY FATHER'S FLESH—

Bobo (standing over him helplessly). I'm sorry, Walter . . . (*only Walter's sobs reply. Bobo puts on his hat.*) I had my life staked on this deal, too . . .

He exits.

Mama (*to Walter*). Son—(*She goes to him, bends down to him, talks to his bent head.*) Son . . . Is it gone? Son, I gave you sixty-five hundred dollars. Is it gone? All of it? Beneatha's money too?

Walter (*lifting his head slowly*). Mama . . . I never . . . went to the bank at all . . .

Mama (*not wanting to believe him*). You mean . . . your sister's school money . . . you used that too . . . Walter? . . .

Walter. Yessss! All of it . . . It's all gone . . .

There is total silence. Ruth stands with her face covered with her hands; Beneatha leans forlornly against a wall, fingering a piece of red ribbon from the mother's gift. Mama stops and looks at her son without recognition and then, quite without thinking about it, starts to beat him senselessly in the face. Beneatha goes to them and stops it.

Beneatha. Mama!

Mama stops and looks at both of her children and rises slowly and wanders vaguely, aimlessly away from them.

Mama. I seen ... him ... night after night ... come in ... and look at that rug ... and then look at me ... the red showing in his eyes ... the veins moving in his head ... I seen him grow thin and old before he was forty ... working and working and working like somebody's old horse ... killing himself ... and you—you give it all away in a day—*(She raises her arms to strike him again.)*

Beneatha. Mama—

Mama. Oh, God ... *(She looks up to Him.)* Look down here—and show me the strength.

Beneatha. Mama—

Mama *(folding over).* Strength ...

Beneatha *(plaintively).* Mama ...

Mama. Strength!

Curtain.

ACT III

Time: An hour later.

 At curtain, there is a sullen light of gloom in the living room, gray light not unlike that which began the first scene of Act I. At left we can see Walter within his room, alone with himself. He is stretched out on the bed, his shirt out and open, his arms under his head. He does not smoke, he does not cry out, he merely lies there, looking up at the ceiling, much as if he were alone in the world.

 In the living room Beneatha sits at the table, still surrounded by the now almost ominous packing crates. She sits looking off. We feel that this is a mood struck perhaps an hour before, and it lingers now, full of the empty sound of profound disappointment. We see on a line from her brother's bedroom the sameness of their attitudes. Presently the bell rings and Beneatha rises without ambition or interest in answering. It is Asagai, smiling broadly, striding into the room with energy and happy expectation and conversation.

Asagai. I came over ... I had some free time. I thought I might help with the packing. Ah, I like the look of packing crates! A household in preparation for a journey! It depresses some people ... but for me ... it is another feeling. Something full of the flow of life, do you understand? Movement, progress ... It makes me think of Africa.

Beneatha. Africa!

Asagai. What kind of a mood is this? Have I told you how deeply you move me?

Beneatha. He gave away the money, Asagai ...

Asagai. Who gave away what money?

Beneatha. The insurance money. My brother gave it away.

Asagai. Gave it away?

Beneatha. He made an investment! With a man even Travis wouldn't have trusted with his most worn-out marbles.

Asagai. And it's gone?

Beneatha. Gone!

Asagai. I'm very sorry . . . And you, now?

Beneatha. Me? . . . Me? . . . Me, I'm nothing . . . Me. When I was very small . . . we used to take our sleds out in the wintertime and the only hills we had were the ice-covered stone steps of some houses down the street. And we used to fill them in with snow and make them smooth and slide down them all day . . . and it was very dangerous, you know . . . far too steep . . . and sure enough one day a kid named Rufus came down too fast and hit the sidewalk and we saw his face just split open right there in front of us . . . And I remember standing there looking at his bloody open face thinking that was the end of Rufus. But the ambulance came and they took him to the hospital and they fixed the broken bones and they sewed it all up . . . and the next time I saw Rufus he just had a little line down the middle of his face . . . I never got over that . . .

Asagai. What?

Beneatha. That that was what one person could do for another, fix him up—sew up the problem, make him all right again. That was the most marvelous thing in the world . . . I wanted to do that. I always thought it was the one concrete thing in the world that a human being could do. Fix up the sick, you know—and make them whole again. This was truly being God . . .

Asagai. You wanted to be God?

Beneatha. No—I wanted to cure. It used to be so important to me. I wanted to cure. It used to matter. I used to care. I mean about people and how their bodies hurt . . .

Asagai. And you've stopped caring?

Beneatha. Yes—I think so.

Asagai. Why?

Beneatha (*bitterly*). Because it doesn't seem deep enough, close enough to what ails mankind! It was a child's way of seeing things—or an idealist's.

Asagai. Children see things very well sometimes—and idealists even better.

Beneatha. I know that's what you think. Because you are still where I left off. You with all your talk and dreams about Africa! You still think you can patch up the world. Cure the Great Sore of Colonialism—(*Loftily, mocking it.*) with the Penicillin of Independence—!

Asagai. Yes!

Beneatha. Independence *and then what?* What about all the crooks and thieves and just plain idiots who will come into power and steal and plunder the same as before—only now they will be black and do it in the name of the new Independence—WHAT ABOUT THEM?!

Asagai. That will be the problem for another time. First we must get there.

Beneatha. And where does it end?

Asagai. End? Who even spoke of an end? To life? To living?

Beneatha. An end to misery! To stupidity! Don't you see there isn't any real progress, Asagai, there is only one large circle that we march in, around and around, each of us with our own little picture in front of us—our own little mirage that we think is the future.

Asagai. That is the mistake.

Beneatha. What?

Asagai. What you just said—about the circle. It isn't a circle—it is simply a long line—as in geometry, you know, one that reaches into infinity. And because we cannot see the end—we also cannot see how it changes. And it is very odd but those who see the changes—who dream, who will not give up—are called idealists . . . and those who see only the circle—we call *them* the "realists"!

Beneatha. Asagai, while I was sleeping in that bed in there, people went out and took the future right out of my hands! And nobody asked me, nobody consulted me—they just went out and changed my life!

Asagai. Was it your money?

Beneatha. What?

Asagai. Was it your money he gave away?

Beneatha. It belonged to all of us.

Asagai. But did you earn it? Would you have had it at all if your father had not died?

Beneatha. No.

Asagai. Then isn't there something wrong in a house—in a world—where all dreams, good or bad, must depend on the death of a man? I never thought to see *you* like this, Alaiyo. You! Your brother made a mistake and you are grateful to him so that now you can give up the ailing human race on account of it! You talk about what good is struggle, what good is anything! Where are we all going and why are we bothering!

Beneatha. AND YOU CANNOT ANSWER IT!

Asagai (*shouting over her*). *I LIVE THE ANSWER!* (*Pause.*) In my village at home it is the exceptional man who can even read a newspaper . . . or who ever sees a book at all. I will go home and much of what I will have to say will seem strange to the people of my village. But I will teach and work and things will happen, slowly and swiftly. At times it will seem that nothing changes at all . . . and then again the sudden dramatic events which make history leap into the future. And then quiet again. Retrogression even. Guns, murder, revolution. And I even will have moments when I wonder if the quiet was not better than all that death and hatred. But I will look about my village at the illiteracy and disease and ignorance and I will not wonder long. And perhaps . . . perhaps I will be a great man . . . I mean perhaps I will hold on to the substance of truth and find my way always with the right course . . . and perhaps for it I will be butchered in my bed some night by the servants of empire . . .

Beneatha. *The martyr!*

Asagai (*he smiles*). . . . or perhaps I shall live to be a very old man, respected and esteemed in my new nation . . . And perhaps I shall hold office and this is what I'm trying to tell you, Alaiyo: perhaps the things I believe now for my country will be wrong and outmoded, and I will not understand and do terrible things to have things my way or merely to keep my power. Don't you see that there will be young men and women—not British soldiers then, but my own black countrymen—to step out of the shadows some evening and slit my then useless throat? Don't you see they have always been there . . . that they always will be. And that such a thing as my own death will be an advance? They who might kill me even . . . actually replenish all that I was.

Beneatha. Oh, Asagai, I know all that.

Asagai. Good! Then stop moaning and groaning and tell me what you plan to do.

Beneatha. Do?

Asagai. I have a bit of a suggestion.

Beneatha. What?

Asagai (*rather quietly for him*). That when it is all over—that you come home with me—

Beneatha (*staring at him and crossing away with exasperation*). Oh—Asagai—at this moment you decide to be romantic!

Asagai (*quickly understanding the misunderstanding*). My dear, young creature of the New World—I do not mean across the city—I mean across the ocean: home—to Africa.

Beneatha (*slowly understanding and turning to him with murmured amazement*). To Africa?

Asagai. Yes! . . . (*smiling and lifting his arms playfully.*) Three hundred years later the African Prince rose up out of the seas and swept the maiden back across the middle passage over which her ancestors had come—

Beneatha (*unable to play*). To—to Nigeria?

Asagai. Nigeria. Home. (*Coming to her with genuine romantic flippancy.*) I will show you our mountains and our stars; and give you cool drinks from gourds and teach you the old songs and the ways of our people—and, in time, we will pretend that—(*Very softly.*)—you have only been away for a day. Say that you'll come—(*He swings her around and takes her full in his arms in a kiss which proceeds to passion.*)

Beneatha (*pulling away suddenly*). You're getting me all mixed up—

Asagai. Why?

Beneatha. Too many things—too many things have happened today. I must sit down and think. I don't know what I feel about anything right this minute.

She promptly sits down and props her chin on her fist.

Asagai (*charmed*). All right, I shall leave you. No—don't get up. (*Touching her, gently, sweetly.*) Just sit awhile and think . . . Never be afraid to sit awhile and think. (*He goes to door and looks at her.*) How often I have looked at you and said, "Ah—so this is what the New World hath finally wrought . . ."

He exits. Beneatha sits on alone. Presently Walter enters from his room and starts to rummage through things, feverishly looking for something. She looks up and turns in her seat.

Beneatha *(hissingly).* Yes—just look at what the New World hath wrought! . . . Just look! *(She gestures with bitter disgust.)* There he is! *Monsieur le petit bourgeois noir*[2]—himself! There he is—Symbol of a Rising Class! Entrepreneur! Titan of the system! *(Walter ignores her completely and continues frantically and destructively looking for something and hurling things to floor and tearing things out of their place in his search. Beneatha ignores the eccentricity of his actions and goes on with the monologue of insult.)* Did you dream of yachts on Lake Michigan, Brother? Did you see yourself on that Great Day sitting down at the Conference Table, surrounded by all the mighty bald-headed men in America? All halted, waiting, breathless, waiting for your pronouncements on industry? Waiting for you—Chairman of the Board! *(Walter finds what he is looking for—a small piece of white paper—and pushes it in his pocket and puts on his coat and rushes out without ever having looked at her. She shouts after him.)* I look at you and I see the final triumph of stupidity in the world!

The door slams and she returns to just sitting again. Ruth comes quickly out of Mama's room.

Ruth. Who was that?

Beneatha. Your husband.

Ruth. Where did he go?

Beneatha. Who knows—maybe he has an appointment at U.S. Steel.

Ruth *(anxiously, with frightened eyes).* You didn't say nothing bad to him, did you?

Beneatha. Bad? Say anything bad to him? No—I told him he was a sweet boy and full of dreams and everything is strictly peachy keen, as the ofay kids say!

Mama enters from her bedroom. She is lost, vague, trying to catch hold, to make some sense of her former command of the world, but it still eludes her. A sense of waste overwhelms her gait; a measure of apology rides on her shoulders. She goes to her plant, which has remained on the table, looks at it, picks it up and takes it to the window sill and sits it outside, and she stands and looks at it a long moment. Then she closes the window, straightens her body with effort and turns around to her children.

Mama. Well—ain't it a mess in here, though? *(A false cheerfulness, a beginning of something.)* I guess we all better stop moping around and get some work done. All this unpacking and everything we got to do. *(Ruth raises her head slowly in response to the sense of the line; and Beneatha in similar manner turns very slowly to look at her mother.)* One of you all better call the moving people and tell 'em not to come.

Ruth. Tell 'em not to come?

Mama. Of course, baby. Ain't no need in 'em coming all the way here and having to go back. They charges for that too. *(She sits down, fingers to her brow, thinking.)* Lord, ever since I was a little girl, I always remembers people saying, "Lena—Lena Eggleston, you aims too high all the time. You needs to slow down

[2] Mr. Black Bourgeoisie.

and see life a little more like it is. Just slow down some." That's what they always used to say down home—"Lord, that Lena Eggleston is a high-minded thing. She'll get her due one day!"

Ruth. No, Lena . . .

Mama. Me and Big Walter just didn't never learn right.

Ruth. Lena, no! We gotta go. Bennie—tell her . . .

She rises and crosses to Beneatha with her arms outstretched. Beneatha doesn't respond.

Tell her we can still move . . . the notes ain't but a hundred and twenty-five a month. We got four grown people in this house—we can work . . .

Mama *(to herself)*. Just aimed too high all the time—

Ruth *(turning and going to Mama fast—the words pouring out with urgency and desperation)*. Lena—I'll work . . . I'll work twenty hours a day in all the kitchens in Chicago . . . I'll strap my baby on my back if I have to and scrub all the floors in America and wash all the sheets in America if I have to—but we got to MOVE! We got to get OUT OF HERE!!

Mama reaches out absently and pats Ruth's hand.

Mama. No—I sees things differently now. Been thinking 'bout some of the things we could do to fix this place up some. I seen a second-hand bureau over on Maxwell Street just the other day that could fit right there. *(She points to where the new furniture might go. Ruth wanders away from her.)* Would need some new handles on it and then a little varnish and it look like something brand-new. And—we can put up them new curtains in the kitchen . . . Why this place be looking fine. Cheer us all up so that we forget trouble ever come . . . *(To Ruth.)* And you could get some nice screens to put up in your room round the baby's bassinet . . . *(She looks at both of them pleadingly.)* Sometimes you just got to know when to give up some things . . . and hold on to what you got . . .

Walter enters from the outside, looking spent and leaning against the door, his coat hanging from him.

Mama. Where you been, son?

Walter *(breathing hard)*. Made a call.

Mama. To who, son?

Walter. To The Man. *(He heads for his room.)*

Mama. What man, baby?

Walter *(stops in the door)*. The Man, Mama. Don't you know who The Man is?

Ruth. Walter Lee?

Walter. *The Man.* Like the guys in the streets say—The Man. Captain Boss—Mistuh Charley . . . Old Cap'n Please Mr. Bossman . . .

Beneatha *(suddenly)*. Lindner!

Walter. That's right! That's good. I told him to come right over.

Beneatha *(fiercely, understanding).* For what? What do you want to see him for!

Walter *(looking at his sister).* We going to do business with him.

Mama. What you talking 'bout, son?

Walter. Talking 'bout life, Mama. You all always telling me to see life like it is. Well— I laid in there on my back today . . . and I figured it out. Life just like it is. Who gets and who don't get. *(He sits down with his coat on and laughs.)* Mama, you know it's all divided up. Life is. Sure enough. Between the takers and the "tooken." *(He laughs.)* I've figured it out finally. *(He looks around at them.)* Yeah. Some of us always getting "tooken." *(He laughs.)* People like Willy Harris, they don't never get "tooken." And you know why the rest of us do? 'Cause we all mixed up. Mixed up bad. We get to looking 'round for the right and the wrong; and we worry about it and cry about it and stay up nights trying to figure out 'bout the wrong and the right of things all the time . . . And all the time, man, them takers is out there operating, just taking and taking. Willy Harris? Shoot—Willy Harris don't even count. He don't even count in the big scheme of things. But I'll say one thing for old Willy Harris . . . he's taught me something. He's taught me to keep my eye on what counts in this world. Yeah—*(Shouting out a little.)* Thanks, Willy!

Ruth. What did you call that man for, Walter Lee?

Walter. Called him to tell him to come on over to the show. Gonna put on a show for the man. Just what he wants to see. You see, Mama, the man came here today and he told us that them people out there where you want us to move—well they so upset they willing to pay us *not* to move! *(He laughs again.)* And—and oh, Mama—you would of been proud of the way me and Ruth and Bennie acted. We told him to get out . . . Lord have mercy! We told the man to get out! Oh, we was some proud folks this afternoon, yeah. *(He lights a cigarette.)* We were still full of that old-time stuff . . .

Ruth *(coming toward him slowly).* You talking 'bout taking them people's money to keep us from moving in that house?

Walter. I ain't just talking 'bout it, baby—I'm telling you that's what's going to happen!

Beneatha. Oh, God! Where is the bottom! Where is the real honest-to-God bottom so he can't go any farther!

Walter. See—that's the old stuff. You and that boy that was here today. You all want everybody to carry a flag and a spear and sing some marching songs, huh? You wanna spend your life looking into things and trying to find the right and the wrong part, huh? Yeah. You know what's going to happen to that boy someday—he'll find himself sitting in a dungeon, locked in forever—and the takers will have the key! Forget it, baby! There ain't no causes—there ain't nothing but taking in this world, and he who takes most is smartest—and it don't make a damn bit of difference *how*.

Mama. You making something inside me cry, son. Some awful pain inside me.

Walter. Don't cry, Mama. Understand. That white man is going to walk in that door able to write checks for more money than we ever had. It's important to him and I'm going to help him . . . I'm going to put on the show, Mama.

Mama. Son—I come from five generations of people who was slaves and share-croppers—but ain't nobody in my family never let nobody pay 'em no money that was a way of telling us we wasn't fit to walk the earth. We ain't never been that poor. *(Raising her eyes and looking at him.)* We ain't never been that—dead inside.

Beneatha. Well—we are dead now. All the talk about dreams and sunlight that goes on in this house. It's all dead now.

Walter. What's the matter with you all! I didn't make this world! It was give to me this way! Hell, yes, I want me some yachts someday! Yes, I want to hang some real pearls 'round my wife's neck. Ain't she supposed to wear no pearls? Some-body tell me—tell me, who decides which women is suppose to wear pearls in this world. I tell you I am a *man*—and I think my wife should wear some pearls in this world!

This last line hangs a good while and Walter begins to move about the room. The word "Man" has penetrated his consciousness; he mumbles it to himself repeatedly between strange agitated pauses as he moves about.

Mama. Baby, how you going to feel on the inside?

Walter. Fine! . . . Going to feel fine . . . a man . . .

Mama. You won't have nothing left then, Walter Lee.

Walter *(coming to her).* I'm going to feel fine, Mama. I'm going to look that son-of-a-bitch in the eyes and say—*(He falters.)*—and say, "All right, Mr. Lindner—*(He falters even more.)*—that's *your* neighborhood out there! You got the right to keep it like you want! You got the right to have it like you want! Just write the check and—the house is yours." And—and I am going to say—*(His voice almost breaks.)* "And you—you people just put the money in my hand and you won't have to live next to this bunch of stinking niggers! . . ." *(He straightens up and moves away from his mother, walking around the room.)* And maybe—maybe I'll just get down on my black knees . . . *(He does so; Ruth and Bennie and Mama watch him in frozen horror.)* "Captain, Mistuh, Bossman—(Groveling and grin-ning and wringing his hands in profoundly anguished imitation of the slow-witted movie stereotype.) A-hee-hee-hee! Oh, yassuh boss! Yasssssuh! Great white—(Voice breaking, he forces himself to go on.)—Father, just gi' ussen de money, fo' God's sake, and we's—we's ain't gwine come out deh and dirty up yo' white folks neighborhood . . ." (He breaks down completely.)* And I'll feel fine! Fine! FINE! *(He gets up and goes into the bedroom.)*

Beneatha. That is not a man. That is nothing but a toothless rat.

Mama. Yes—death done come in this here house. *(She is nodding, slowly, reflec-tively.)* Done come walking in my house on the lips of my children. You what supposed to be my beginning again. You—what supposed to be my harvest. *(To Beneatha.)* You—you mourning your brother?

Beneatha. He's no brother of mine.

Mama. What you say?

Beneatha. I said that that individual in that room is no brother of mine.

Mama. That's what I thought you said. You feeling like you better than he is today? *(Beneatha does not answer.)* Yes? What you tell him a minute ago? That he wasn't a man? Yes? You give him up for me? You done wrote his epitaph too—like the rest of the world? Well, who give you the privilege?

Beneatha. Be on my side for once! You saw what he just did, Mama! You saw him—down on his knees. Wasn't it you who taught me to despise any man who would do that? Do what he's going to do?

Mama. Yes—I taught you that. Me and your daddy. But I thought I taught you something else too . . . I thought I taught you to love him.

Beneatha. Love him? There is nothing left to love.

Mama. There is *always* something left to love. And if you ain't learned that, you ain't learned nothing. *(Looking at her.)* Have you cried for that boy today? I don't mean for yourself and for the family 'cause we lost the money. I mean for him: what he been through and what it done to him. Child, when do you think is the time to love somebody the most? When they done good and made things easy for everybody? Well then, you ain't through learning—because that ain't the time at all. It's when he's at his lowest and can't believe in hisself 'cause the world done whipped him so! When you starts measuring somebody, measure him right, child, measure him right. Make sure you done taken into account what hills and valleys he come through before he got to wherever he is.

Travis bursts into the room at the end of the speech, leaving the door open.

Travis. Grandmama—the moving men are downstairs! The truck just pulled up.

Mama *(turning and looking at him).* Are they, baby? They downstairs?

She sighs and sits. Lindner appears in the doorway. He peers in and knocks lightly, to gain attention, and comes in. All turn to look at him.

Lindner *(hat and briefcase in hand).* Uh—hello . . .

Ruth crosses mechanically to the bedroom door and opens it and lets it swing open freely and slowly as the lights come up on Walter within, still in his coat, sitting at the far corner of the room. He looks up and out through the room to Lindner.

Ruth. He's here.

A long minute passes and Walter slowly gets up.

Lindner *(coming to the table with efficiency, putting his briefcase on the table and starting to unfold papers and unscrew fountain pens).* Well, I certainly was glad to hear from you people. *(Walter has begun the trek out of the room, slowly and awkwardly, rather like a small boy, passing the back of his sleeve across his mouth* *from time to time.)* Life can really be so much simpler than people let it be most of the time. Well—with whom do I negotiate? You, Mrs. Younger, or your son here? *(Mama sits with her hands folded on her lap and her eyes closed as Walter advances. Travis goes closer to Lindner and looks at the papers curiously.)* Just some official papers, sonny.

Ruth. Travis, you go downstairs—

Mama *(opening her eyes and looking into Walter's).* No. Travis, you stay right here. And you make him understand what you doing, Walter Lee. You teach him good. Like Willy Harris taught you. You show where our five generations done come to. *(Walter looks from her to the boy, who grins at him innocently.)* Go ahead, son—*(She folds her hands and closes her eyes.)* Go ahead.

Walter *(at last crosses to Lindner, who is reviewing the contract).* Well, Mr. Lindner. *(Beneatha turns away.)* We called you—*(There is a profound, simple groping quality in his speech.)*—because, well, me and my family *(He looks around and shifts from one foot to the other.)* Well—we are very plain people . . .

Lindner. Yes—

Walter. I mean—I have worked as a chauffeur most of my life—and my wife here, she does domestic work in people's kitchens. So does my mother. I mean—we are plain people . . .

Lindner. Yes, Mr. Younger—

Walter *(really like a small boy, looking down at his shoes and then up at the man).* And—uh—well, my father, well, he was a laborer most of his life. . . .

Lindner *(absolutely confused).* Uh, yes—yes, I understand. *(He turns back to the contract.)*

Walter *(a beat; staring at him).* And my father—*(With sudden intensity.)* My father almost *beat a man to death* once because this man called him a bad name or something, you know what I mean?

Lindner *(looking up, frozen).* No, no, I'm afraid I don't—

Walter *(a beat. The tension hangs; then Walter steps back from it).* Yeah. Well—what I mean is that we come from people who had a lot of *pride*. I mean—we are very proud people. And that's my sister over there and she's going to be a doctor—and we are very proud—

Lindner. Well—I am sure that is very nice, but—

Walter. What I am telling you is that we called you over here to tell you that we are very proud and that this—*(Signaling to Travis.)* Travis, come here. *(Travis crosses and Walter draws him before him facing the man.)* This is my son, and he makes the sixth generation our family in this country. And we have all thought about your offer—

Lindner. Well, good . . . good—

Walter. And we have decided to move into our house because my father—my father—he earned it for us brick by brick. *(Mama has her eyes closed and is rocking back and forth as though she were in church, with her head nodding the Amen yes.)* We don't want to make no trouble for nobody or fight no causes, and we will try to be good neighbors. And that's *all* we got to say about that. *(He looks* *the man absolutely in the eyes.)* We don't want your money. *(He turns and walks away.)*

Lindner *(looking around at all of them).* I take it then—that you have decided to occupy . . .

Beneatha. That's what the man said.

Lindner *(to Mama in her reverie).* Then I would like to appeal to you, Mrs. Younger. You are older and wiser and understand things better I am sure . . .

Mama. I am afraid you don't understand. My son said we was going to move and there ain't nothing left for me to say. *(Briskly.)* You know how these young folks is nowadays, mister. Can't do a thing with 'em! *(As he opens his mouth, she rises.)* Good-bye.

Lindner *(folding up his materials).* Well—if you are that final about it . . . there is nothing left for me to say. *(He finishes, almost ignored by the family, who are concentrating on Walter Lee. At the door Lindner halts and looks around.)* I sure hope you people know what you're getting into.

He shakes his head and exits.

Ruth *(looking around and coming to life).* Well, for God's sake—if the moving men are here—LET'S GET THE HELL OUT OF HERE!

Mama *(into action).* Ain't it the truth! Look at all this here mess. Ruth, put Travis's good jacket on him . . . Walter Lee, fix your tie and tuck your shirt in, you look like somebody's hoodlum! Lord have mercy, where is my plant? *(She flies to get it amid the general bustling of the family, who are deliberately trying to ignore the nobility of the past moment.)* You all start on down . . . Travis child, don't go empty-handed . . . Ruth, where did I put that box with my skillets in it? I want to be in charge of it myself . . . I'm going to make us the biggest dinner we ever ate tonight . . . Beneatha, what's the matter with them stockings? Pull them things up, girl . . .

The family starts to file out as two moving men appear and begin to carry out the heavier pieces of furniture, bumping into the family as they move about.

Beneatha. Mama, Asagai asked me to marry him today and go to Africa—

Mama *(in the middle of her getting-ready activity).* He did? You ain't old enough to marry nobody—*(Seeing the moving men lifting one of her chairs precariously.)* Darling, that ain't no bale of cotton, please handle it so we can sit in it again! I had that chair twenty-five years . . .

The movers sigh with exasperation and go on with their work.

Beneatha *(girlishly and unreasonably trying to pursue the conversation).* To go to Africa, Mama—be a doctor in Africa . . .

Mama *(distracted).* Yes, baby—

Walter. *Africa!* What he want you to go to Africa for?

Beneatha. To practice there . . .

Walter. Girl, if you don't get all them silly ideas out your head! You better marry yourself a man with some loot . . .

Beneatha *(angrily, precisely as in the first scene of the play).* What have you got to do with who I marry!

Walter. Plenty. Now I think George Murchison—

Beneatha. *George Murchison!* I wouldn't marry him if he was Adam and I was Eve!

Walter and Beneatha go out yelling at each other vigorously and the anger is loud and real till their voices diminish. Ruth stands at the door and turns to Mama and smiles knowingly.

Mama *(fixing her hat at last).* Yeah—they something all right, my children . . .

Ruth. Yeah—they're something. Let's go, Lena.

Mama *(stalling, starting to look around at the house).* Yes—I'm coming. Ruth—

Ruth. Yes?

Mama *(quietly, woman to woman).* He finally come into his manhood today, didn't he? Kind of like a rainbow after the rain . . .

Ruth *(biting her lip lest her own pride explode in front of Mama).* Yes, Lena.

Walter's voice calls for them raucously.

Walter *(off stage).* Y'all come on! These people charges by the hour, you know!

Mama *(waving Ruth out vaguely).* All right, honey—go on down. I be down directly.

Ruth hesitates, then exits. Mama stands, at last alone in the living room, her plant on the table before her as the lights start to come down. She looks around at all the walls and ceilings and suddenly, despite herself, while the children call below, a great heaving thing rises in her and she puts her fist to her mouth to stifle it, takes a final desperate look, pulls her coat about her, pats her hat, and goes out. The lights dim down. The door opens and she comes back in, grabs her plant, and goes out for the last time.

Curtain.

FOR ANALYSIS

1. In what ways does the opening **dialogue** between Ruth and Walter establish the major **themes** of the play?

2. Describe the shared values and dreams that give the family its cohesiveness.

3. Describe Walter's view of women. Is his view validated by the actions of the women? Explain.

4. Describe the contrast between Beneatha's two suitors, George Murchison and Joseph Asagai, and explain how it contributes to the theme of the play.

5. What is the significance of Mama's plant?

6. In what ways does the dialogue between Beneatha and Asagai that opens act III advance the theme of the play and prepare us for the ending?

7. Karl Lindner asserts that "the overwhelming majority of our people out there feel that people get along better, take more of a common interest in the life of the community, when they share a common background" (act II, scene 3). Is this a reasonable argument? Or is Lindner a racist? Explain.

8. In what sense is this play a celebration of African American life and culture?

9. Describe the speech patterns of the main **characters**. What function do the differences in **diction** serve? Is there any relationship between a character's diction and his or her moral standing in the play? Explain.

10. Even though he is dead, Big Walter is an important presence in the play. Examine the ways in which his presence is created, and explain what he represents.

MAKING CONNECTIONS

Compare and contrast the dynamics of family life in this play with those of the family in Walker's "Everyday Use" (p. 589). Which family do you think is more successful in coping with its problems? Explain.

WRITING TOPICS

1. Argue for or against the proposition that this play, written in 1959, is dated in its portrayal of black life and race relations.

2. Read Hughes's poem "Harlem" (p. 443), from which the title of the play is taken, and write an essay describing why you think Hansberry found the line appropriate as the title for her play.

3. Describe the significance of money in the play.

4. Write an essay in which you speculate on what happens to the members of the Younger family once they have moved into their new home.

DAVID HENRY HWANG (B. 1957)

TRYING TO FIND CHINATOWN 1996

CHARACTERS

Benjamin, Caucasian male, early twenties.
Ronnie, Asian American male, mid-twenties.

Time and Place

A street corner on the Lower East Side, New York City. The present.

Note on Music

Obviously, it would be foolish to require that the actor portraying Ronnie perform the specified violin music live. The score of this play can be played on tape over the house speakers, and the actor can feign playing the violin using a bow treated with soap. However, in order to effect a convincing illusion, it is desirable that the actor possess some familiarity with the violin or another stringed instrument.

Darkness. Over the house speakers, sound fades in: Hendrix-like virtuoso rock 'n' roll riffs—heavy feedback, distortion, phase shifting, wah-wah—amplified over a tiny Fender pug-nose.

Lights fade up to reveal that the music's being played over a solid-body electric violin by Ronnie, a Chinese American male in his mid-twenties; he is dressed in retro-'60s clothing and has a few requisite '90s body mutilations. He's playing on a sidewalk for money, his violin case open before him; change and a few stray bills have been left by previous passersby.

Benjamin enters; he's in his early twenties, blond, blue-eyed, a midwestern tourist in the big city. He holds a scrap of paper in his hands, scanning street signs for an address. He pauses before Ronnie, listens for a while. With a truly bravura run, Ronnie concludes the number and falls to his knees, gasping. Benjamin applauds.

Benjamin. Good. That was really great. *(Pause)* I didn't . . . I mean, a fiddle . . . I mean, I'd heard them at square dances, on country stations and all, but I never . . . wow, this must really be New York City!

(Benjamin applauds, starts to walk on. Still on his knees, Ronnie clears his throat loudly.)

Oh, I . . . you're not just doing this for your health, right?

(Benjamin reaches in his pocket, pulls out a couple of coins. Ronnie clears his throat again.)

Look, I'm not a millionaire, I'm just . . .

(Benjamin pulls out his wallet, removes a dollar bill. Ronnie nods his head and gestures toward the violin case as he takes out a pack of cigarettes, lights one.)

Ronnie. And don't call it a "fiddle," OK?

Benjamin. Oh. Well, I didn't mean to—

Ronnie. You sound like a wuss. A hick. A dipshit.

Benjamin. It just slipped out. I didn't really—

Ronnie. If this was a fiddle, I'd be sitting here with a cob pipe, stomping my cow-boy boots and kicking up hay. Then I'd go home and fuck my cousin.

Benjamin. Oh! Well, I don't really think—

Ronnie. Do you see a cob pipe? Am I fucking my cousin?

Benjamin. Well, no, not at the moment, but—

Ronnie. All right. Then this is a violin, now you give me your money, and I ignore the insult. Herein endeth the lesson.

(Pause.)

Benjamin. Look, a dollar's more than I've ever given to a . . . to someone ask-ing for money.

Ronnie. Yeah, well, this is New York. Welcome to the cost of living.

Benjamin. What I mean is, maybe in exchange, you could help me—?

Ronnie. Jesus Christ! Do you see a sign around my neck reading "Big Apple Fucking Tourist Bureau"?

Benjamin. I'm just looking for an address, I don't think it's far from here, maybe you could . . . ?

(Benjamin holds out his scrap of paper, Ronnie snatches it away.)

Ronnie. You're lucky I'm such a goddamn softy. *(He looks at the paper)* Oh, fuck you. Just suck my dick, you and the cousin you rode in on.

Benjamin. I don't get it! What are you—?

Ronnie. Eat me. You know exactly what I—

Benjamin. I'm just asking for a little—

Ronnie. "13 Doyers Street"? Like you don't know where that is?

Benjamin. Of course I don't know! That's why I'm asking—

Ronnie. C'mon, you trailer-park refugee. You don't know that's Chinatown?

Benjamin. Sure I know that's Chinatown.

Ronnie. I know you know that's Chinatown.

Benjamin. So? That doesn't mean I know where Chinatown—

Ronnie. So why is it that you picked *me*, of all the street musicians in the city—to point you in the direction of Chinatown? Lemme guess—is it the earring? No, I don't think so. The Hendrix riffs? Guess again, you fucking moron.

Benjamin. Now, wait a minute. I see what you're—

Ronnie. What are you gonna ask me next? Where you can find the best dim sum in the city? Whether I can direct you to a genuine opium den? Or do I happen to know how you can meet Miss Saigon for a night of nookie-nookie followed by a good old-fashioned ritual suicide? Now, get your white ass off my sidewalk.

One dollar doesn't even begin to make up for all this aggravation. Why don't you go back home and race bullfrogs, or whatever it is you do for—?

Benjamin. Brother, I can absolutely relate to your anger. Righteous rage, I suppose, would be a more appropriate term. To be marginalized, as we are, by a white racist patriarchy, to the point where the accomplishments of our people are obliterated from the history books, this is cultural genocide of the first order, leading to the fact that you must do battle with all of Euro-America's emasculating and brutal stereotypes of Asians—the opium den, the sexual objectification of the Asian female, the exoticized image of a tourist's Chinatown which ignores the exploitation of workers, the failure to unionize, the high rate of mental illness and tuberculosis—against these, each day, you rage, no, not as a victim, but as a survivor, yes, brother, a glorious warrior survivor!

(Silence.)

Ronnie. Say what?

Benjamin. So, I hope you can see that my request is not—

Ronnie. Wait, wait.

Benjamin. —motivated by the sorts of racist assumptions—

Ronnie. But, but where . . . how did you learn all that?

Benjamin. All what?

Ronnie. All that—you know—oppression stuff—tuberculosis . . .

Benjamin. It's statistically irrefutable. TB occurs in the community at a rate—

Ronnie. Where did *you* learn it?

Benjamin. I took Asian American studies. In college.

Ronnie. Where did you go to college?

Benjamin. University of Wisconsin. Madison.

Ronnie. Madison, Wisconsin?

Benjamin. That's not where the bridges are, by the way.

Ronnie. Huh? Oh, right . . .

Benjamin. You wouldn't believe the number of people who—

Ronnie. They have Asian American studies in Madison, Wisconsin? Since when?

Benjamin. Since the last Third World Unity hunger strike. *(Pause)* Why do you look so surprised? We're down.

Ronnie. I dunno. It just never occurred to me, the idea of Asian students in the Midwest going on a hunger strike.

Benjamin. Well, a lot of them had midterms that week, so they fasted in shifts. *(Pause)* The administration never figured it out. The Asian students put that "They all look alike" stereotype to good use.

Ronnie. OK, so they got Asian American studies. That still doesn't explain—

Benjamin. What?

Ronnie. Well . . . what *you* were doing taking it?

Benjamin. Just like everyone else. I wanted to explore my roots. And, you know, the history of oppression which is my legacy. After a lifetime of assimilation, I wanted to find out who I really am.

(Pause.)

Ronnie. And did you?

Benjamin. Sure. I learned to take pride in my ancestors who built the railroads, my Popo who would make me a hot bowl of jok with thousand-day-old eggs when the white kids chased me home yelling, "Gook! Chink! Slant-eyes!"

Ronnie. OK, OK, that's enough!

Benjamin. Painful to listen to, isn't it?

Ronnie. I don't know what kind of bullshit ethnic studies program they're running over in Wuss-consin, but did they bother to teach you that in order to find your Asian "roots," it's a good idea to first be Asian?

(Pause.)

Benjamin. Are you speaking metaphorically?

Ronnie. No! Literally! Look at your skin!

Benjamin. You know, it's very stereotypical to think that all Asian skin tones conform to a single hue.

Ronnie. You're white! Is this some kind of redneck joke or something? Am I the first person in the world to tell you this?

Benjamin. Oh! Oh! Oh!

Ronnie. I know real Asians are scarce in the Midwest, but . . . Jesus!

Benjamin. No, of course, I . . . I see where your misunderstanding arises.

Ronnie. Yeah. It's called, "You white."

Benjamin. It's just that—in my hometown of Tribune, Kansas, and then at school—see, everyone knows me—so this sort of thing never comes up. *(He offers his hand)* Benjamin Wong. I forget that a society wedded to racial constructs constantly forces me to explain my very existence.

Ronnie. Ronnie Chang. Otherwise known as "The Bow Man."

Benjamin. You see, I was adopted by Chinese American parents at birth. So, clearly, I'm an Asian American—

Ronnie. Even though you're blond and blue-eyed.

Benjamin. Well, you can't judge my race by my genetic heritage alone.

Ronnie. If genes don't determine race, what does?

Benjamin. Perhaps you'd prefer that I continue in denial, masquerading as a white man?

Ronnie. You can't just wake up and say, "Gee, I *feel* black today."

Benjamin. Brother, I'm just trying to find what you've already got.

Ronnie. What do I got?

Benjamin. A home. With your people. Picketing with the laundry workers. Taking refuge from the daily slights against your masculinity in the noble image of Gwan Gung.

Ronnie. Gwan who?

Benjamin. C'mon—the Chinese god of warriors and—what do you take me for? There're altars to him up all over the community.

Ronnie. I dunno what community you're talking about, but it's sure as hell not mine.

(Pause.)

Benjamin. What do you mean?

Ronnie. I mean, if you wanna call Chinatown *your* community, OK, knock yourself out, learn to use chopsticks, big deal. Go ahead, try and find your "roots" in some dim sum parlor with headless ducks hanging in the window. Those places don't tell you a thing about who *I* am.

Benjamin. Oh, I get it.

Ronnie. You get what?

Benjamin. You're one of those self-hating, *assimilated* Chinese Americans, aren't you?

Ronnie. Oh, Jesus.

Benjamin. You probably call yourself "Oriental," huh? Look, maybe I can help you. I have some books I can—

Ronnie. Hey, I read all those Asian identity books when you were still slathering on industrial-strength sunblock. *(Pause)* Sure, I'm Chinese. But folks like you act like that means something. Like, all of a sudden, you know who I am. You think identity's that simple? That you can wrap it all up in a neat package and say, "I have ethnicity, therefore I am"? All you fucking ethnic fundamentalists. Always settling for easy answers. You say you're looking for identity, but you can't begin to face the real mysteries of the search. So instead, you go skin-deep, and call it a day. *(Pause. He turns away from Benjamin and starts to play his violin—slow and bluesy.)*

Benjamin. So what are you? "Just a human being"? That's like saying you *have* no identity. If you asked me to describe my dog, I'd say more than, "He's just a dog."

Ronnie. What—you think if I deny the importance of my race, I'm nobody? There're worlds out there, worlds you haven't even begun to understand. Open your eyes. Hear with your ears.

(Ronnie holds his violin at chest level, but does not attempt to play during the following monologue. As he speaks, rock and jazz violin tracks fade in and out over the house speakers, bringing to life the styles of music he describes.)

I concede—it was called a fiddle long ago—but that was even before the birth of jazz. When the hollering in the fields, the rank injustice of human bondage, the struggle of God's children against the plagues of the devil's white man, when all these boiled up into that bittersweet brew, called by later generations, the blues. That's when fiddlers like Son Sims held their chin rests at their chests, and sawed away like the hillbillies still do today. And with the coming of ragtime appeared the pioneer Stuff Smith, who sang as he stroked the catgut, with his raspy, Louis Armstrong–voice—gruff and sweet like the timber of horsehair riding south below the fingerboard—and who finally sailed for Europe to find ears that would hear. Europe—where Stephane Grappelli initiated a magical French violin, to be passed from generation to generation—first he, to Jean-Luc Ponty, then Ponty to Didier Lockwood. Listening to Grappelli play "A Nightingale Sang in Berkeley Square" is to understand not only the song of birds, but also how they learn to fly, fall in love on the wing, and finally falter one day, to wait for darkness beneath a London street lamp. And Ponty—he showed how the modern violin man can accompany the shadow of his own lead lines, which cascade, one over another, into some nether world beyond the range of human hearing. Joe Venuti. Noel Pointer. Sven Asmussen. Even the Kronos Quartet, with their arrangement of "Purple Haze." Now, tell me, could any legacy be more rich, more crowded with mythology and heroes to inspire pride? What can I say if the banging of a gong or the clinking of a pickax on the Transcontinental Railroad fails to move me even as much as one note, played through a violin MIDI controller by Michael Urbaniak? *(He puts his violin to his chin, begins to play a jazz composition of his own invention)* Does it have to sound like Chinese opera before people like you decide I know who I am?

(Benjamin stands for a long moment, listening to Ronnie play. Then, he drops his dollar into the case, turns and exits right. Ronnie continues to play a long moment. Then Benjamin enters downstage left, illuminated in his own spotlight. He sits on the floor of the stage, his feet dangling off the lip. As he speaks, Ronnie continues playing his tune, which becomes underscoring for Benjamin's monologue. As the music continues, does it slowly begin to reflect the influence of Chinese music?)

Benjamin. When I finally found Doyers Street, I scanned the buildings for Number 13. Walking down an alley where the scent of freshly steamed char siu bao lingered in the air, I felt immediately that I had entered a world where all things were finally familiar. *(Pause)* An old woman bumped me with her shopping bag—screaming to her friend in Cantonese, though they walked no more than a few inches apart. Another man—shouting to a vendor in Sze-Yup. A youth, in white undershirt, perhaps a recent newcomer, bargaining with a grocer in Hokkien. I walked through this ocean of dialects, breathing in the richness with deep gulps, exhilarated by the energy this symphony brought to my step. And when I finally saw the number 13, I nearly wept at my good fortune. An old tenement, paint peeling, inside walls no doubt thick with a century of grease and broken dreams—and yet, to me, a temple—the house where my father was born. I suddenly saw it all: Gung Gung, coming home from his sixteen-hour days pressing shirts he could never afford to own, bringing with him candies for my father, each sweet wrapped in the hope of a better life. When my father left the ghetto, he swore he would never return. But he had, this day, in the thoughts and memories of his son, just six months after his death. And as I sat on the stoop, I pulled a hua-moi from my pocket, sucked on it, and felt his spirit returning. To this place where his ghost, and the dutiful hearts of all his descendants, would always call home. *(He listens for a long moment)* And I felt an ache in my heart for all those lost souls, denied this most important of revelations: to know who they truly are.

(Benjamin sucks his salted plum and listens to the sounds around him. Ronnie continues to play. The two remain oblivious of one another. Lights fade slowly to black.)

End of play

FOR ANALYSIS

1. Two things about Benjamin are revealed in his first big speech (p. 799). What are they? What two different sets of stereotypes make them surprising?

2. Why does Benjamin consider himself Chinese? Why does Ronnie disagree?

3. The second-to-last stage direction (not counting "End of play") ends: "As the music continues, does it slowly begin to reflect the influence of Chinese music?" (p. 802). Why might Hwang have written this stage direction? What comment might it be making about the discussion the two **characters** have been having?

MAKING CONNECTIONS

1. Compare this play to Chin's poem "How I Got That Name" (p. 696). How does each work relate Chinese identity to mainstream "white" American identity?

2. Compare Ronnie's attitudes about Asian stereotypes to the responses about gender stereotypes by the speakers in "Connecting Poems: Working Mothers" (p. 718). How are these responses—and the issues they concern—similar? How are they different?

WRITING TOPICS

1. Hwang writes **dialogue** in a very particular way for each character. Describe the **style** of each character's lines, and compare them. What does the way in which each talks say about him as a person? What do the similarities and differences between the ways they talk say about the similarities and differences between them as people?

2. Ronnie and Benjamin disagree about the importance of ethnic heritage to identity. Do you agree more with one than the other? In a brief essay, explain why.

NONFICTION

VIRGINIA WOOLF   (1882–1941)

WHAT IF SHAKESPEARE HAD HAD A SISTER?[1]   1929

It was disappointing not to have brought back in the evening some important statement, some authentic fact. Women are poorer than men because—this or that. Perhaps now it would be better to give up seeking for the truth, and receiving on one's head an avalanche of opinion hot as lava, discoloured as dish-water. It would be better to draw the curtains; to shut out distractions; to light the lamp; to narrow the enquiry and to ask the historian, who records not opinions but facts, to describe under what conditions women lived, not throughout the ages, but in England, say in the time of Elizabeth.

For it is a perennial puzzle why no woman wrote a word of that extraordinary literature when every other man, it seemed, was capable of song or sonnet. What were the conditions in which women lived, I asked myself; for fiction, imaginative work that is, is not dropped like a pebble upon the ground, as science may be; fiction is like a spider's web, attached ever so lightly perhaps, but still attached to life at all four corners. Often the attachment is scarcely perceptible; Shakespeare's plays, for instance, seem to hang there complete by themselves. But when the web is pulled askew, hooked up at the edge, torn in the middle, one remembers that these webs are not spun in midair by incorporeal creatures, but are the work of suffering human beings, and are attached to grossly material things, like health and money and the houses we live in.

I went, therefore, to the shelf where the histories stand and took down one of the latest, Professor Trevelyan's *History of England*. Once more I looked up

---

[1] *A Room of One's Own*, from which this essay is taken, is based on two lectures Woolf delivered on women and literature at Newnham College and Girton College, Cambridge University. In the opening chapter, Woolf declares that without "money and a room of her own," a woman cannot write fiction. In the following chapter, she recounts her unsuccessful attempt to turn up information at the British Library on the lives of women. This essay is from Chapter 3, from which a few passages are omitted. The essay ends with the concluding paragraph of the book.

Women, found "position of," and turned to the pages indicated. "Wife-beating," I read, "was a recognized right of man, and was practiced without shame by high as well as low. . . . Similarly," the historian goes on, "the daughter who refused to marry the gentleman of her parents' choice was liable to be locked up, beaten and flung about the room, without any shock being inflicted on public opinion. Marriage was not an affair of personal affection, but of family avarice, particularly in the 'chivalrous' upper classes. . . . Betrothal often took place while one or both of the parties was in the cradle, and marriage when they were scarcely out of the nurses' charge." That was about 1470, soon after Chaucer's time. The next reference to the position of women is some two hundred years later, in the time of the Stuarts. "It was still the exception for women of the upper and middle class to choose their own husbands, and when the husband had been assigned, he was lord and master, so far at least as law and custom could make him. Yet even so," Professor Trevelyan concludes, "neither Shakespeare's women nor those of authentic seventeenth-century memoirs, like the Verneys and the Hutchinsons, seem wanting in personality and character." Certainly, if we consider it, Cleopatra must have had a way with her; Lady Macbeth, one would suppose, had a will of her own; Rosalind, one might conclude, was an attractive girl. Professor Trevelyan is speaking no more than the truth when he remarks that Shakespeare's women do not seem wanting in personality and character. Not being a historian, one might go even further and say that women have burnt like beacons in all the works of all the poets from the beginning of time—Clytemnestra, Antigone, Cleopatra, Lady Macbeth, Phèdre, Cressida, Rosalind, Desdemona, the Duchess of Malfi, among the dramatists; then among the prose writers: Millamant, Clarissa, Becky Sharp, Anna Karenina, Emma Bovary, Madame de Guermantes[2]—the names flock to mind, nor do they recall women "lacking in personality and character." Indeed, if woman had no existence save in the fiction written by men, one would imagine her a person of the utmost importance; very various; heroic and mean; splendid and sordid; infinitely beautiful and hideous in the extreme; as great as a man, some think even greater. But this is woman in fiction. In fact, as Professor Trevelyan points out, she was locked up, beaten and flung about the room.

A very queer, composite being thus emerges. Imaginatively she is of the highest importance; practically she is completely insignificant. She pervades poetry from cover to cover; she is all but absent from history. She dominates the lives of kings and conquerors in fiction; in fact she was the slave of any boy whose parents forced a ring upon her finger. Some of the most inspired words, some of the most profound thoughts in literature fell from her lips; in real life she could hardly read, could scarcely spell, and was the property of her husband.

It was certainly an odd monster that one made up by reading the historians 5 first and the poets afterwards—a worm winged like an eagle; the spirit of life and beauty in a kitchen chopping up suet. But these monsters, however amusing to the imagination, have no existence in fact. What one must do to bring her to

[2] Female characters from great works of literature.

life was to think poetically and prosaically at one and the same moment, thus keeping in touch with fact—that she is Mrs. Martin, aged thirty-six, dressed in blue, wearing a black hat and brown shoes; but not losing sight of fiction either—that she is a vessel in which all sorts of spirits and forces are coursing and flashing perpetually. The moment, however, that one tries this method with the Elizabethan woman, one branch of illumination fails; one is held up by the scarcity of facts. One knows nothing detailed, nothing perfectly true and substantial about her. History scarcely mentions her. And I turned to Professor Trevelyan again to see what history meant to him. I found by looking at his chapter headings that it meant—

"The Manor Court and the Methods of Open-field Agriculture . . . The Cistercians and Sheep-farming . . . The Crusades . . . The University . . . The House of Commons . . . The Hundred Years' War . . . The Wars of the Roses . . . The Renaissance Scholars . . . The Dissolution of the Monasteries . . . Agrarian and Religious Strife . . . The Origin of English Seapower . . . The Armada . . ." and so on. Occasionally an individual woman is mentioned, an Elizabeth, or a Mary; a queen or a great lady. But by no possible means could middle-class women with nothing but brains and character at their command have taken part in any one of the great movements which, brought together, constitute the historian's view of the past. Nor shall we find her in any collection of anecdotes. Aubrey hardly mentions her.[3] She never writes her own life and scarcely keeps a diary; there are only a handful of her letters in existence. She left no plays or poems by which we can judge her . . . Here am I asking why women did not write poetry in the Elizabethan age, and I am not sure how they were educated; whether they were taught to write; whether they had sitting-rooms to themselves; how many women had children before they were twenty-one; what, in short, they did from eight in the morning till eight at night. They had no money evidently; according to Professor Trevelyan they were married whether they liked it or not before they were out of the nursery, at fifteen or sixteen very likely. It would have been extremely odd, even upon this showing, had one of them suddenly written the plays of Shakespeare, I concluded, and I thought of that old gentleman, who is dead now, but was a bishop, I think, who declared that it was impossible for any woman, past, present, or to come, to have the genius of Shakespeare. He wrote to the papers about it. He also told a lady who applied to him for information that cats do not as a matter of fact go to heaven, though they have, he added, souls of a sort. How much thinking those old gentlemen used to save one! How the borders of ignorance shrank back at their approach! Cats do not go to heaven. Women cannot write the plays of Shakespeare.

Be that as it may, I could not help thinking, as I looked at the works of Shakespeare on the shelf, that the bishop was right at least in this; it would have been impossible, completely and entirely, for any woman to have written the plays of Shakespeare in the age of Shakespeare. Let me imagine, since facts are so hard to come by, what would have happened had Shakespeare had

---

[3] John Aubrey (1626–1697), author of *Brief Lives*, a biographical work.

a wonderfully gifted sister, called Judith, let us say. Shakespeare himself went, very probably—his mother was an heiress—to the grammar school, where he may have learnt Latin—Ovid, Virgil and Horace—and the elements of grammar and logic. He was, it is well known, a wild boy who poached rabbits, perhaps shot a deer, and had, rather sooner than he should have done, to marry a woman in the neighbourhood, who bore him a child rather quicker than was right. That escapade sent him to seek his fortune in London. He had, it seemed, a taste for the theatre; he began by holding horses at the stage door. Very soon he got work in the theatre, became a successful actor, and lived in the hub of the universe, meeting everybody, knowing everybody, practising his art on the boards, exercising his wits in the streets, and even getting access to the palace of the queen. Meanwhile his extraordinarily gifted sister, let us suppose, remained at home. She was as adventurous, as imaginative, as agog to see the world as he was. But she was not sent to school. She had no chance of learning grammar and logic, let alone of reading Horace and Virgil. She picked up a book now and then, one of her brother's perhaps, and read a few pages. But then her parents came in and told her to mend the stockings or mind the stew and not moon about with books and papers. They would have spoken sharply but kindly, for they were substantial people who knew the conditions of life for a woman and loved their daughter—indeed, more likely than not she was the apple of her father's eye. Perhaps she scribbled some pages up in an apple loft on the sly, but was careful to hide them or set fire to them. Soon, however, before she was out of her teens, she was to be betrothed to the son of a neighbouring wool-stapler. She cried out that marriage was hateful to her, and for that she was severely beaten by her father. Then he ceased to scold her. He begged her instead not to hurt him, not to shame him in this matter of her marriage. He would give her a chain of beads or a fine petticoat, he said; and there were tears in his eyes. How could she disobey him? How could she break his heart? The force of her own gift alone drove her to it. She made up a small parcel of her belongings, let herself down by a rope one summer's night and took the road to London. She was not seventeen. The birds that sang in the hedge were not more musical than she was. She had the quickest fancy, a gift like her brother's, for the tune of words. Like him, she had a taste for the theatre. She stood at the stage door; she wanted to act, she said. Men laughed in her face. The manager—a fat, loose-lipped man—guffawed. He bellowed something about poodles dancing and women acting—no woman, he said, could possibly be an actress.[4] He hinted—you can imagine what. She could get no training in her craft. Could she even seek her dinner in a tavern or roam the streets at midnight? Yet her genius was for fiction and lusted to feed abundantly upon the lives of men and women and the study of their ways. At last—for she was very young, oddly like Shakespeare the poet in her face, with the same grey eyes and rounded brows—at last Nick Greene the actor-manager took pity on her; she found herself with

---

[4] In Shakespeare's day, women's roles were played by males.

child by that gentleman and so—who shall measure the heat and violence of the poet's heart when caught and tangled in a woman's body?—killed herself one winter's night and lies buried at some cross-roads where the omnibuses now stop outside the Elephant and Castle.[5]

That, more or less, is how the story would run, I think, if a woman in Shakespeare's day had had Shakespeare's genius. But for my part, I agree with the deceased bishop, if such he was—it is unthinkable that any woman in Shakespeare's day should have had Shakespeare's genius. For genius like Shakespeare's is not born among labouring, uneducated, servile people. It was not born in England among the Saxons and the Britons. It is not born today among the working classes. How, then, could it have been born among women whose work began, according to Professor Trevelyan, almost before they were out of the nursery, who were forced to it by their parents and held to it by all the power of law and custom? Yet genius of a sort must have existed among women as it must have existed among the working classes. Now and again an Emily Brontë or a Robert Burns blazes out and proves its presence.[6] But certainly it never got itself on to paper. When, however, one reads of a witch being ducked, of a woman possessed by devils, of a wise woman selling herbs, or even of a very remarkable man who had a mother, then I think we are on the track of a lost novelist, a suppressed poet, of some mute and inglorious[7] Jane Austen, some Emily Brontë who dashed her brains out on the moor or moped and mowed about the highways crazed with the torture that her gift had put her to. Indeed, I would venture to guess that Anon, who wrote so many poems without signing them, was often a woman. It was a woman Edward Fitzgerald,[8] I think, suggested who made the ballads and the folk-songs, crooning them to her children, beguiling her spinning with them, or the length of the winter's night.

This may be true or it may be false—who can say?—but what is true in it, so it seemed to me, reviewing the story of Shakespeare's sister as I had made it, is that any woman born with a great gift in the sixteenth century would certainly have gone crazed, shot herself, or ended her days in some lonely cottage outside the village, half witch, half wizard, feared and mocked at. For it needs little skill in psychology to be sure that a highly gifted girl who had tried to use her gift for poetry would have been so thwarted and hindered by other people, so tortured and pulled asunder by her own contrary instincts, that she must have lost her health and sanity to a certainty. No girl could have walked to London and stood at a stage door and forced her way into the presence of actor-managers without doing herself a violence and suffering an anguish which may have been irrational—for chastity may be a fetish invented by certain societies for unknown reasons—but were none the less inevitable. Chastity had then, it has even now, a religious importance in a woman's life, and has so

---

[5] A tavern.

[6] Emily Brontë (1818–1848), English novelist, and Robert Burns (1759–1796), Scottish poet.

[7] Thomas Gray's description in "Elegy Written in a Country Churchyard" of a peasant whose underdeveloped poetic genius might be as powerful as the great John Milton's.

[8] Edward FitzGerald (1809–1883), translator and poet.

wrapped itself round with nerves and instincts that to cut it free and bring it to the light of day demands courage of the rarest. To have lived a free life in London in the sixteenth century would have meant for a woman who was poet and playwright a nervous stress and dilemma which might well have killed her. Had she survived, whatever she had written would have been twisted and deformed, issuing from a strained and morbid imagination. And undoubtedly, I thought, looking at the shelf where there are no plays by women, her work would have gone unsigned. That refuge she would have sought certainly. It was the relic of the sense of chastity that dictated anonymity to women even so late as the nineteenth century. Currer Bell, George Eliot, George Sand,[9] all the victims of inner strife as their writings prove, sought ineffectively to veil themselves by using the name of a man. Thus they did homage to the convention, which if not implanted by the other sex was liberally encouraged by them (the chief glory of a woman is not to be talked of, said Pericles,[10] himself a much-talked-of man), that publicity in women is detestable. . . .

That woman, then, who was born with a gift of poetry in the sixteenth cen-   10
tury, was an unhappy woman, a woman at strife against herself. All the conditions of her life, all her own instincts, were hostile to the state of mind which is needed to set free whatever is in the brain. But what is the state of mind that is most propitious to the act of creation, I asked? Can one come by any notion of the state that furthers and makes possible that strange activity? Here I opened the volume containing the Tragedies of Shakespeare. What was Shakespeare's state of mind, for instance, when he wrote *Lear* and *Antony and Cleopatra*? It was certainly the state of mind most favourable to poetry that there has ever existed. But Shakespeare himself said nothing about it. We only know casually and by chance that he "never blotted a line."[11] Nothing indeed was ever said by the artist himself about his state of mind until the eighteenth century perhaps. Rousseau[12] perhaps began it. At any rate, by the nineteenth century self-consciousness had developed so far that it was the habit for men of letters to describe their minds in confessions and autobiographies. Their lives also were written, and their letters were printed after their deaths. Thus, though we do not know what Shakespeare went through when he wrote *Lear*, we do know what Carlyle went through when he wrote the *French Revolution*; what Flaubert went through when he wrote *Madame Bovary*; what Keats was going through when he tried to write poetry against the coming of death and the indifference of the world.

And one gathers from this enormous modern literature of confession and self-analysis that to write a work of genius is almost always a feat of prodigious difficulty. Everything is against the likelihood that it will come from the writer's mind whole and entire. Generally material circumstances are against it. Dogs

---

[9] The pseudonyms of Charlotte Brontë (1816–1855) and Mary Ann Evans (1819–1880), English novelists, and Amandine-Aurore-Lucie Dupin (1804–1876), French novelist.

[10] Pericles (ca. 495–429 B.C.), Athenian statesman and general.

[11] According to Ben Jonson, Shakespeare's contemporary.

[12] Jean-Jacques Rousseau (1712–1778), French philosopher, author of *The Confessions of Jean-Jacques Rousseau*.

will bark; people will interrupt; money must be made; health will break down. Further, accentuating all these difficulties and making them harder to bear is the world's notorious indifference. It does not ask people to write poems and novels and histories; it does not need them. It does not care whether Flaubert finds the right word or whether Carlyle scrupulously verifies this or that fact. Naturally, it will not pay for what it does not want. And so the writer, Keats, Flaubert, Carlyle, suffers, especially in the creative years of youth, every form of distraction and discouragement. A curse, a cry of agony, rises from those books of analysis and confession. "Mighty poets in their misery dead"[13]—that is the burden of their song. If anything comes through in spite of this, it is a miracle, and probably no book is born entire and uncrippled as it was conceived.

But for women, I thought, looking at the empty shelves, these difficulties were infinitely more formidable. In the first place, to have a room of her own, let alone a quiet room or a sound-proof room, was out of the question, unless her parents were exceptionally rich or very noble, even up to the beginning of the nineteenth century. Since her pin money, which depended on the good will of her father, was only enough to keep her clothed, she was debarred from such alleviations as came even to Keats or Tennyson or Carlyle, all poor men, from a walking tour, a little journey to France, from the separate lodging which, even if it were miserable enough, sheltered them from the claims and tyrannies of their families. Such material difficulties were formidable; but much worse were the immaterial. The indifference of the world which Keats and Flaubert and other men of genius have found so hard to bear was in her case not indifference but hostility. The world did not say to her as it said to them, Write if you choose; it makes no difference to me. The world said with a guffaw, Write? What's the good of your writing? . . .

I told you in the course of this paper that Shakespeare had a sister; but do not look for her in Sir Sidney Lee's life of the poet. She died young—alas, she never wrote a word. She lies buried where the omnibuses now stop, opposite the Elephant and Castle. Now my belief is that this poet who never wrote a word and was buried at the cross-roads still lives. She lives in you and me, and in many other women who are not here tonight, for they are washing up the dishes and putting the children to bed. But she lives; for great poets do not die; they are continuing presences; they need only the opportunity to walk among us in the flesh. This opportunity, as I think, it is now coming within your power to give her. For my belief is that if we live another century or so—I am talking of the common life which is the real life and not of the little separate lives which we live as individuals—and have five hundred a year each of us and rooms of our own; if we have the habit of freedom and the courage to write exactly what we think; if we escape a little from the common sitting-room and see human beings not always in their relation to each other but in relation to reality; and

---

[13] From William Wordsworth's poem "Resolution and Independence."

the sky, too, and the trees or whatever it may be in themselves; if we look past Milton's bogey, for no human being should shut out the view; if we face the fact, for it is a fact, that there is no arm to cling to, but that we go alone and that our relation is to the world of reality and not only to the world of men and women, then the opportunity will come and the dead poet who was Shakespeare's sister will put on the body which she has so often laid down. Drawing her life from the lives of the unknown who were her forerunners, as her brother did before her, she will be born. As for her coming without that preparation, without that effort on our part, without that determination that when she is born again she shall find it possible to live and write her poetry, that we cannot expect, for that would be impossible. But I maintain that she would come if we worked for her, and that so to work, even in poverty and obscurity, is worth while.

FOR ANALYSIS

1. How does Woolf explain the contrast between the women of fact and women as they have been portrayed in fiction?

2. What answers do historians provide to the "perennial puzzle" Woolf mentions in the first sentence of paragraph 2? What generalizations might we make about the meaning of "history" on the basis of Woolf's research into the status of women?

3. Analyze the effect of Woolf's concluding remarks about the bishop (para. 6): "Cats do not go to heaven. Women cannot write the plays of Shakespeare." Then consider her later comment (para. 8), "I agree with the deceased bishop, if such he was—it is unthinkable that any woman in Shakespeare's day should have had Shakespeare's genius." Does this contradict what she has been saying?

4. Explain the link Woolf makes between chastity and the problem of the gifted woman writer (para. 9).

5. In what ways does the first part of Woolf's essay prepare the reader to accept her imagined life of Shakespeare's sister?

MAKING CONNECTIONS

1. Among the women who "have burnt like beacons" (para. 3) in the works of great male writers, Woolf cites Desdemona in Shakespeare's *Othello* (p. 947). Do you agree with her assessment? Might Woolf have included Nora in Ibsen's *A Doll's House* (p. 228) and Mama in Hansberry's *A Raisin in the Sun* (p. 724)? Explain.

2. What do you think Woolf would think of Mrs. Peters and Mrs. Hale in Glaspell's *Trifles* (p. 1050) and Calixta in Kate Chopin's "The Storm" (p. 835)?

WRITING TOPICS

1. Do you believe that our culture has changed so significantly in its attitudes toward women that Woolf's arguments have lost their relevance? Write an essay explaining why or why not.

2. Speculate on why, while being as economically dependent on men as servants were throughout much of Western history, women were sometimes portrayed in fiction as being "as great as a man, some think even greater" (para. 3)?

Zora Neale Hurston   (1891–1960)

How It Feels to Be
Colored Me   1928

I am colored but I offer nothing in the way of extenuating circumstances except the fact that I am the only Negro in the United States whose grandfather on the mother's side was *not* an Indian chief.

I remember the very day that I became colored. Up to my thirteenth year I lived in the little Negro town of Eatonville, Florida. It is exclusively a colored town. The only white people I knew passed through the town going to or coming from Orlando. The native whites rode dusty horses, the Northern tourists chugged down the sandy village road in automobiles. The town knew the Southerners and never stopped cane chewing when they passed. But the Northerners were something else again. They were peered at cautiously from behind the curtains by the timid. The more venturesome would come out on the porch to watch them go past and got just as much pleasure out of the tourists as the tourists got out of the village.

The front porch might seem a daring place for the rest of the town, but it was a gallery seat for me. My favorite place was atop the gate-post. Proscenium box[1] for a born first-nighter. Not only did I enjoy the show, but I didn't mind the actors knowing that I liked it. I usually spoke to them in passing. I'd wave at them and when they returned my salute, I would say something like this: "Howdy-do-well-I-thank-you-where-you-goin'?" Usually automobile or the horse paused at this, and after a queer exchange of compliments, I would probably "go a piece of the way" with them, as we say in farthest Florida. If one of my family happened to come to the front in time to see me, of course negotiations would be rudely broken off. But even so, it is clear that I was the first "welcome-to-our-state" Floridian, and I hope the Miami Chamber of Commerce will please take notice.

During this period, white people differed from colored to me only in that they rode through town and never lived there. They liked to hear me "speak pieces" and sing and wanted to see me dance the parse-me-la, and gave me generously of their small silver for doing these things, which seemed strange to me for I wanted to do them so much that I needed bribing to stop. Only they didn't know it. The colored people gave no dimes. They deplored any joyful tendencies in me, but I was their Zora nevertheless. I belonged to them, to the nearby hotels, to the county—everybody's Zora.

---

[1] A box seat close to the stage.

But changes came in the family when I was thirteen, and I was sent to school 5
in Jacksonville. I left Eatonville, the town of the oleanders, as Zora. When I
disembarked from the river-boat at Jacksonville, she was no more. It seemed
that I had suffered a sea change. I was not Zora of Orange County any more, I
was now a little colored girl. I found it out in certain ways. In my heart as well
as in the mirror, I became a fast brown—warranted not to rub nor run.

But I am not tragically colored. There is no great sorrow dammed up in
my soul, nor lurking behind my eyes. I do not mind at all. I do not belong to
the sobbing school of Negrohood who hold that nature somehow has given
them a lowdown dirty deal and whose feelings are all hurt about it. Even in
the helter-skelter skirmish that is my life, I have seen that the world is to the
strong regardless of a little pigmentation more or less. No, I do not weep at the
world—I am too busy sharpening my oyster knife.

Someone is always at my elbow reminding me that I am the granddaughter
of slaves. It fails to register depression with me. Slavery is sixty years in the
past. The operation was successful and the patient is doing well, thank you.
The terrible struggle that made me an American out of a potential slave said
"On the line!" The Reconstruction said "Get set!"; and the generation before
said "Go!" I am off to a flying start and I must not halt in the stretch to look
behind and weep. Slavery is the price I paid for civilization, and the choice was
not with me. It is a bully adventure and worth all that I have paid through my
ancestors for it. No one on earth ever had a greater chance for glory. The world
to be won and nothing to be lost. It is thrilling to think—to know that for any
act of mine, I shall get twice as much praise or twice as much blame. It is quite
exciting to hold the center of the national stage, with the spectators not knowing whether to laugh or to weep.

The position of my white neighbor is much more difficult. No brown specter
pulls up a chair beside me when I sit down to eat. No dark ghost thrusts its leg
against mine in bed. The game of keeping what one has is never so exciting as
the game of getting.

I do not always feel colored. Even now I often achieve the unconscious Zora
of Eatonville before the Hegira.[2] I feel most colored when I am thrown against
a sharp white background.

For instance at Barnard. "Beside the waters of the Hudson" I feel my race. 10
Among the thousand white persons, I am a dark rock surged upon, and over-
swept, but through it all, I remain myself. When covered by the waters, I am;
and the ebb but reveals me again.

Sometimes it is the other way around. A white person is set down in our
midst, but the contrast is just as sharp for me. For instance, when I sit in the
drafty basement that is The New World Cabaret[3] with a white person, my

[2] A flight or journey to a better place.
[3] A Harlem nightclub popular in the 1920s.

color comes. We enter chatting about any little nothing that we have in common and are seated by the jazz waiters. In the abrupt way that jazz orchestras have, this one plunges into a number. It loses no time in circumlocutions, but gets right down to business. It constricts the thorax and splits the heart with its tempo and narcotic harmonies. This orchestra grows rambunctious, rears on its hind legs and attacks the tonal veil with primitive fury, rending it, clawing it until it breaks through to the jungle beyond. I follow those heathen—follow them exultingly. I dance wildly inside myself; I yell within, I whoop; I shake my assegai[4] above my head, I hurl it true to the mark *yeeeeooww!* I am in the jungle and living in the jungle way. My face is painted red and yellow and my body is painted blue. My pulse is throbbing like a war drum. I want to slaughter something—give pain, give death to what, I do not know. But the piece ends. The men of the orchestra wipe their lips and rest their fingers. I creep back slowly to the veneer we call civilization with the last tone and find the white friend sitting motionless in his seat—smoking calmly.

"Good music they have here," he remarks, drumming the table with his fingertips.

Music. The great blobs of purple and red emotion have not touched him. He has only heard what I felt. He is far away and I see him but dimly across the ocean and the continent that have fallen between us. He is so pale with his whiteness then and I am *so* colored.

At certain times I have no race, I am *me*. When I set my hat at a certain angle and saunter down Seventh Avenue, Harlem City, feeling as snooty as the lions in front of the Forty-Second Street Library, for instance. So far as my feelings are concerned, Peggy Hopkins Joyce on the Boule Mich[5] with her gorgeous raiment, stately carriage, knees knocking together in a most aristocratic manner, has nothing on me. The cosmic Zora emerges. I belong to no race nor time. I am the eternal feminine with its string of beads.

I have no separate feeling about being an American citizen and colored. I 15 am merely a fragment of the Great Soul that surges within the boundaries. My country, right or wrong.

Sometimes, I feel discriminated against, but it does not make me angry. It merely astonishes me. How *can* any deny themselves the pleasure of my company? It's beyond me.

But in the main, I feel like a brown bag of miscellany propped against a wall. Against a wall in company with other bags, white, red, and yellow. Pour out the contents, and there is discovered a jumble of small things priceless and worthless. A first-water diamond, an empty spool, bits of broken glass, lengths of string, a key to a door long since crumbled away, a rusty knife-blade, old shoes saved for a road that never was and never will be, a nail bent under the weight

[4] An iron-tipped spear used by the Bantu peoples of Africa.

[5] Peggy Hopkins Joyce (1893–1957) was a media icon of her day, celebrated for her beauty and succession of rich husbands. Boule Mich, short for Boulevard St-Michel, is a famous street on the Left Bank in Paris.

of things too heavy for any nail, a dried flower or two still a little fragrant. In your hand is the brown bag. On the ground before you is the jumble it held— so much like the jumble in the bags, could they be emptied, that all might be dumped in a single heap and the bags refilled without altering the content of any greatly. A bit of colored glass more or less would not matter. Perhaps that is how the Great Stuffer of Bags filled them in the first place—who knows?

FOR ANALYSIS

1. Describe the **tone** established in the opening paragraph. Is that tone maintained throughout? Explain.

2. What does Hurston mean by the first sentence of paragraph 6?

3. Describe Hurston's feelings about her African ancestry.

4. What does Hurston mean in paragraph 7 when she says, "Slavery is the price I paid for civilization"?

5. Is Hurston's argument in paragraph 7 convincing? Explain.

6. How do the four sections of the essay relate to one another?

MAKING CONNECTIONS

1. Compare Hurston's feelings about the connection between her racial/cultural identity and who she is with those of Kincaid in "Girl" (p. 103).

2. Compare the meaning of jazz music in this essay with its meaning in Baldwin's "Sonny's Blues" (p. 564).

WRITING TOPICS

1. Describe Hurston's sense of what it means to be black.

2. Write an essay either supporting or taking issue with the validity of Hurston's declaration that "At certain times I have no race, I am *me*" (para. 14).

3. Use the following passage from W. E. B. Du Bois's book *The Souls of Black Folk* (1903) as the basis for an analysis of Hurston's essay.

> It is a peculiar sensation, this double-consciousness, this sense of always looking at one's self through the eyes of others, of measuring one's soul by the tape of a world that looks on in amused contempt and pity. One ever feels his two-ness—an American, a Negro; two souls, two thoughts, two unreconciled strivings; two warring ideals in one dark body, whose dogged strength alone keeps it from being torn asunder.

GEORGE ORWELL   (1903–1950)

SHOOTING AN ELEPHANT   1936

In Moulmein, in lower Burma, I was hated by large numbers of people—the only time in my life that I have been important enough for this to happen to me. I was sub-divisional police officer of the town, and in an aimless, petty kind of way anti-European feeling was very bitter. No one had the guts to raise a riot, but if a European woman went through the bazaars alone somebody would probably spit betel juice over her dress. As a police officer I was an obvious target and was baited whenever it seemed safe to do so. When a nimble Burman tripped me up on the football field and the referee (another Burman) looked the other way, the crowd yelled with hideous laughter. This happened more than once. In the end the sneering yellow faces of young men that met me everywhere, the insults hooted after me when I was at a safe distance, got badly on my nerves. The young Buddhist priests were the worst of all. There were several thousands of them in the town and none of them seemed to have anything to do except stand on street corners and jeer at Europeans.

All this was perplexing and upsetting. For at that time I had already made up my mind that imperialism was an evil thing and the sooner I chucked up my job and got out of it the better. Theoretically—and secretly, of course—I was all for the Burmese and all against their oppressors, the British. As for the job I was doing, I hated it more bitterly than I can perhaps make clear. In a job like that you see the dirty work of Empire at close quarters. The wretched prisoners huddling in the stinking cages of the lock-ups, the grey, cowed faces of the long-term convicts, the scarred buttocks of the men who had been flogged with bamboos—all these oppressed me with an intolerable sense of guilt. But I could get nothing into perspective. I was young and ill-educated and I had had to think out my problems in the utter silence that is imposed on every Englishman in the East. I did not even know that the British Empire is dying, still less did I know that it is a great deal better than the younger empires that are going to supplant it. All I knew was that I was stuck between my hatred of the empire I served and my rage against the evil-spirited little beasts who tried to make my job impossible. With one part of my mind I thought of the British[1] as an unbreakable tyranny, as something clamped down, *in saecula saeculorum,*[2] upon the will of prostrate peoples; with another part I thought that the greatest joy in the world would be to drive a bayonet into a Buddhist priest's guts. Feelings like these are the normal by-products of imperialism; ask any Anglo-Indian official, if you can catch him off duty.

[1] The imperial British government of India and Burma.
[2] For eternity.

One day something happened which in a roundabout way was enlightening. It was a tiny incident in itself, but it gave me a better glimpse than I had had before of the real nature of imperialism—the real motive for which despotic governments act. Early one morning the sub-inspector at a police station the other end of the town rang me up on the 'phone and said that an elephant was ravaging the bazaar. Would I please come and do something about it? I did not know what I could do, but I wanted to see what was happening and I got on to a pony and started out. I took my rifle, an old .44 Winchester and much too small to kill an elephant, but I thought the noise might be useful *in terrorem*. Various Burmans stopped me on the way and told me about the elephant's doings. It was not, of course, a wild elephant, but a tame one which had gone "must." It had been chained up, as tame elephants always are when their attack of "must" is due, but on the previous night it had broken its chain and escaped. Its mahout,[3] the only person who could manage it when it was in that state, had set out in pursuit, but had taken the wrong direction and was now twelve hours' journey away, and in the morning the elephant had suddenly reappeared in the town. The Burmese population had no weapons and were quite helpless against it. It had already destroyed somebody's bamboo hut, killed a cow and raided some fruit-stalls and devoured the stock; also it had met the municipal rubbish van and, when the driver jumped out and took to his heels, had turned the van over and inflicted violences upon it.

The Burmese sub-inspector and some Indian constables were waiting for me in the quarter where the elephant had been seen. It was a very poor quarter, a labyrinth of squalid bamboo huts, thatched with palm-leaf, winding all over a steep hillside. I remember that it was a cloudy, stuffy morning at the beginning of the rains. We began questioning the people as to where the elephant had gone and, as usual, failed to get any definite information. That is invariably the case in the East; a story always sounds clear enough at a distance, but the nearer you get to the scene of events the vaguer it becomes. Some of the people said that the elephant had gone in one direction, some said that he had gone in another, some professed not even to have heard of any elephant. I had almost made up my mind that the whole story was a pack of lies, when we heard yells a little distance away. There was a loud, scandalized cry of "Go away, child! Go away this instant!" and an old woman with a switch in her hand came round the corner of a hut, violently shooing away a crowd of naked children. Some more women followed, clicking their tongues and exclaiming; evidently there was something that the children ought not to have seen. I rounded the hut and saw a man's dead body sprawling in the mud. He was an Indian, a black Dravidian coolie, almost naked, and he could not have been dead many minutes. The people said that the elephant had come suddenly upon him round the corner of the hut, caught him with its trunk, put its foot on his back and ground him into the earth. This was the rainy season and the ground was

---

[3] The keeper and driver of an elephant.

soft, and his face had scored a trench a foot deep and a couple of yards long. He was lying on his belly with arms crucified and head sharply twisted to one side. His face was coated with mud, the eyes wide open, the teeth bared and grinning with an expression of unendurable agony. (Never tell me, by the way, that the dead look peaceful. Most of the corpses I have seen look devilish.) The friction of the great beast's foot had stripped the skin from his back as neatly as one skins a rabbit. As soon as I saw the dead man I sent an orderly to a friend's house nearby to borrow an elephant rifle. I had already sent back the pony, not wanting it to go mad with fright and throw me if it smelt the elephant.

The orderly came back in a few minutes with a rifle and five cartridges, and 5 meanwhile some Burmans had arrived and told us that the elephant was in the paddy fields below, only a few hundred yards away. As I started forward practically the whole population of the quarter flocked out of the houses and followed me. They had seen the rifle and were all shouting excitedly that I was going to shoot the elephant. They had not shown much interest in the elephant when he was merely ravaging their homes, but it was different now that he was going to be shot. It was a bit of fun to them, as it would be to an English crowd; besides they wanted the meat. It made me vaguely uneasy. I had no intention of shooting the elephant—I had merely sent for the rifle to defend myself if necessary—and it is always unnerving to have a crowd following you. I marched down the hill, looking and feeling a fool, with the rifle over my shoulders and an ever-growing army of people jostling at my heels. At the bottom, when you got away from the huts, there was a metalled road and beyond that a miry waste of paddy fields a thousand yards across, not yet ploughed but soggy from the first rains and dotted with coarse grass. The elephant was standing eight yards from the road, his left side towards us. He took not the slightest notice of the crowd's approach. He was tearing up branches of grass, beating them against his knees to clean them and stuffing them into his mouth.

I had halted on the road. As soon as I saw the elephant I knew with perfect certainty that I ought not to shoot him. It is a serious matter to shoot a working elephant—it is comparable to destroying a huge and costly piece of machinery—and obviously one ought not to do it if it can possibly be avoided. And at that distance, peacefully eating, the elephant looked no more dangerous than a cow. I thought then and I think now that his attack of "must" was already passing off; in which case he would merely wander harmlessly about until the mahout came back and caught him. Moreover, I did not in the least want to shoot him. I decided that I would watch him for a little while to make sure that he did not turn savage again, and then go home.

But at that moment I glanced round at the crowd that had followed me. It was an immense crowd, two thousand at the least and growing every minute. It blocked the road for a long distance on either side. I looked at the sea of yellow faces above the garish clothes—faces all happy and excited over this bit of fun, all certain that the elephant was going to be shot. They were watching me as they would watch a conjurer about to perform a trick. They did not like me, but with the magical rifle in my hands I was momentarily worth watching. And suddenly I realized that I should have to shoot the elephant after all. The people expected it of me and I had got to do it; I could feel their two thousand wills pressing me forward, irresistibly. And it was at this moment, as I stood there with the rifle in my hands, that I first grasped the hollowness, the futility of the white man's dominion in the East. Here was I, the white man with his gun, standing in front of the unarmed native crowd—seemingly the leading actor of the piece; but in reality I was only an absurd puppet pushed to and fro by the will of those yellow faces behind. I perceived in this moment that when the white man turns tyrant it is his own freedoms that he destroys. He becomes a sort of hollow, posing dummy, the conventionalized figure of a sahib. For it is the condition of his rule that he shall spend his life in trying to impress the "natives," and so in every crisis he has got to do what the "natives" expect of him. He wears a mask, and his face grows to fit it. I had got to shoot the elephant. I had committed myself to doing it when I sent for the rifle. A sahib has got to act like a sahib; he has got to appear resolute, to know his own mind and do definite things. To come all that way, rifle in hand, with two thousand people marching at my heels, and then to trail feebly away, having done nothing—no, that was impossible. The crowd would laugh at me. And my whole life, every white man's life in the East, was one long struggle not to be laughed at.

But I did not want to shoot the elephant. I watched him beating his bunch of grass against his knees, with that preoccupied grandmotherly air that elephants have. It seemed to me that it would be murder to shoot him. At that age I was not squeamish about killing animals, but I had never shot an elephant and never wanted to. (Somehow it always seems worse to kill a *large* animal.) Besides, there was the beast's owner to be considered. Alive, the elephant was worth at least a hundred pounds; dead, he would only be worth the value of his tusks, five pounds, possibly. But I had to act quickly. I turned to some experienced-looking Burmans who had been there when we arrived, and asked them how the elephant had been behaving. They all said the same thing: he took no notice of you if you left him alone, but he might charge if you went too close to him.

It was perfectly clear to me what I ought to do. I ought to walk up to within, say, twenty-five yards of the elephant and test his behavior. If he charged, I could shoot; if he took no notice of me, it would be safe to leave him until the mahout came back. But also I knew that I was going to do no such thing. I was a poor shot with a rifle and the ground was soft mud into which one would sink at every step. If the elephant charged and I missed him, I should have about as much chance as a toad under a steam-roller. But even then I was not thinking particularly of my own skin, only of the watchful yellow faces behind. For at that moment, with the crowd watching me, I was not afraid in the ordinary sense, as I would have been if I had been alone. A white man mustn't be frightened in front of "natives"; and so, in general, he isn't frightened. The sole thought in my mind was that if anything went wrong those two thousand Burmans would see me pursued, caught, trampled on and reduced to a grinning corpse like that Indian up the hill. And if that happened it was quite probable that some of them would laugh. That would never do. There was only one alternative. I shoved the cartridges into the magazine and lay down on the road to get a better aim.

The crowd grew very still, and a deep, low, happy sigh, as of people who 10 see the theatre curtain go up at last, breathed from innumerable throats. They were going to have their bit of fun after all. The rifle was a beautiful German thing with cross-hair sights. I did not then know that in shooting an elephant one would shoot to cut an imaginary bar running from ear-hole to ear-hole. I ought, therefore, as the elephant was sideways on, to have aimed straight at his ear-hole; actually I aimed several inches in front of this, thinking the brain would be further forward.

When I pulled the trigger I did not hear the bang or feel the kick—one never does when a shot goes home—but I heard the devilish roar of glee that went up from the crowd. In that instant, in too short a time, one would have thought, even for the bullet to get there, a mysterious, terrible change had come over the elephant. He neither stirred nor fell, but every line of his body had altered. He looked suddenly stricken, shrunken, immensely old, as though the frightful impact of the bullet had paralysed him without knocking him down. At last, after what seemed a long time—it might have been five seconds, I dare say— he sagged flabbily to his knees. His mouth slobbered. An enormous senility seemed to have settled upon him. One could have imagined him thousands of years old. I fired again into the same spot. At the second shot he did not collapse but climbed with desperate slowness to his feet and stood weakly upright, with legs sagging and head drooping. I fired a third time. That was the shot that did for him. You could see the agony of it jolt his whole body and knock the last remnant of strength from his legs. But in falling he seemed for a moment to rise, for as his hind legs collapsed beneath him he seemed to tower upward like a huge rock toppling, his trunk reaching skywards like a tree. He trumpeted, for the first and only time. And then down he came, his belly towards me, with a crash that seemed to shake the ground even where I lay.

I got up. The Burmans were already racing past me across the mud. It was obvious that the elephant would never rise again, but he was not dead. He was breathing very rhythmically with long rattling gasps, his great mound of a side painfully rising and falling. His mouth was wide open—I could see far down into caverns of pale pink throat. I waited a long time for him to die, but his breathing did not weaken. Finally I fired my two remaining shots into the spot where I thought his heart must be. The thick blood welled out of him like red velvet, but still he did not die. His body did not even jerk when the shots hit him, the tortured breathing continued without a pause. He was dying, very slowly and in great agony, but in some world remote from me where not even a bullet could damage him further. I felt that I had got to put an end to that dreadful noise. It seemed dreadful to see the great beast lying there, powerless to move and yet powerless to die, and not even to be able to finish him. I sent back for my small rifle and poured shot after shot into his heart and down his throat. They seemed to make no impression. The tortured gasps continued as steadily as the ticking of a clock.

In the end I could not stand it any longer and went away. I heard later that it took him half an hour to die. Burmans were bringing dahs[4] and baskets even before I left, and I was told they had stripped his body almost to the bones by the afternoon.

Afterwards, of course, there were endless discussions about the shooting of the elephant. The owner was furious, but he was only an Indian and could do nothing. Besides, legally I had done the right thing, for a mad elephant has to be killed, like a mad dog, if its owner fails to control it. Among the Europeans opinion was divided. The older men said I was right, the younger men said it was a damn shame to shoot an elephant for killing a coolie, because an elephant was worth more than any damn Coringhee coolie. And afterwards I was very glad that the coolie had been killed; it put me legally in the right and it gave me a sufficient pretext for shooting the elephant. I often wondered whether any of the others grasped that I had done it solely to avoid looking a fool.

FOR ANALYSIS

1. Examine carefully paragraphs 11 and 12, in which Orwell describes the death of the elephant. Is the reader meant to take the passage only literally, or can a case be made that the elephant's death is imbued with **symbolic** meaning? Explain.

2. Orwell tells us repeatedly that his sympathies are with the Burmese. Yet he describes them as "evil-spirited little beasts" (para. 2). Explain this ambivalence.

3. What does the experience described in paragraph 7 teach Orwell?

4. Do you agree with Orwell's rationalization that under the circumstances he had no choice but "to shoot the elephant" (para. 7)?

5. What is your reaction to Orwell's final comment: "I was very glad that the coolie had been killed; it put me legally in the right and it gave me a sufficient pretext for shooting the elephant. I often wondered whether any of the others grasped that I had done it solely to avoid looking a fool"?

6. Midway through the essay (para. 7), Orwell discloses the significance the event had for him. Why does he disclose it then rather than save it for the conclusion?

MAKING CONNECTIONS

1. Compare the techniques and arguments used in this essay to attack imperialism with those used in Swift's "A Modest Proposal" (p. 500).

2. While they are dissimilar in subject matter, this story and Bambara's "The Lesson" (p. 96) culminate in climactic events that change the **protagonists**. Compare those events and their effect on the two protagonists.

---

[4] Knives.

WRITING TOPICS

1. In a brief paragraph, summarize the lesson Orwell learned from his experience.

2. What does Orwell conclude about the position of foreign authorities in a hostile country?

3. Describe a situation in which you were required to behave in an official capacity in a way that contradicted your personal beliefs.

CONNECTING NONFICTION: FITTING IN

There are different ways to feel alien to or excluded from a culture. Many people tend to think of immigrants this way: that they often experience a dislocation that is more than geographical, as their cultural environment changes while individual identity lags behind. But there are also ways in which native-born people can feel as if they do not belong. Sometimes this exclusion is felt as a result of racial or ethnic identity in places where the mainstream culture is defined partly by these things, but it can also be the result of differences in social class. All of these "outsider" positions can give writers a unique vantage point. As you read these essays, think about what the experiences of these authors allow them to see. Do they see things in America that native-born people, or people born to the dominant or majority ethnicity or class, may not? Do they see themselves differently, too?

BHARATI MUKHERJEE (B. 1940)

TWO WAYS TO BELONG IN AMERICA 1996

This is a tale of two sisters from Calcutta, Mira and Bharati, who have lived in the United States for some thirty-five years, but who find themselves on different sides in the current debate over the status of immigrants.

I am an American citizen and she is not. I am moved that thousands of long-term residents are finally taking the oath of citizenship. She is not.

Mira arrived in Detroit in 1960 to study child psychology and preschool education. I followed her a year later to study creative writing at the University of Iowa. When we left India, we were almost identical in appearance and attitude. We dressed alike, in saris; we expressed identical views on politics, social issues, love, and marriage in the same Calcutta convent-school accent. We would endure our two years in America, secure our degrees, then return to India to marry the grooms of our father's choosing.

Instead, Mira married an Indian student in 1962 who was getting his business administration degree at Wayne State University. They soon acquired the labor certifications necessary for the green card of hassle-free residence and employment.

Mira still lives in Detroit, works in the Southfield, Michigan, school system, 5
and has become nationally recognized for her contributions in the fields of preschool education and parent-teacher relationships. After thirty-six years as a legal immigrant in this country, she clings passionately to her Indian citizenship and hopes to go home to India when she retires.

In Iowa City in 1963, I married a fellow student, an American of Canadian parentage. Because of the accident of his North Dakota birth, I bypassed labor-certification requirements and the race-related "quota" system that favored the applicant's country of origin over his or her merit. I was prepared for (and even welcomed) the emotional strain that came with marrying outside my ethnic community. In thirty-three years of marriage, we have lived in every part of North America. By choosing a husband who was not my father's selection, I was opting for fluidity, self-invention, blue jeans and T-shirts, and renouncing three thousand years (at least) of caste-observant, "pure culture" marriage in the Mukherjee family. My books have often been read as unapologetic (and in some quarters overenthusiastic) texts for cultural and psychological "mongrelization." It's a word I celebrate.

Mira and I have stayed sisterly close by phone. In our regular Sunday morning conversations, we are unguardedly affectionate. I am her only blood relative on this continent. We expect to see each other through the looming crises of aging and ill health without being asked. Long before Vice President Gore's "Citizenship U.S.A." drive, we'd had our polite arguments over the ethics of retaining an overseas citizenship while expecting the permanent protection and economic benefits that come with living and working in America.

Like well-raised sisters, we never said what was really on our minds, but we probably pitied one another. She, for the lack of structure in my life, the erasure of Indianness, the absence of an unvarying daily core. I, for the narrowness of her perspective, her uninvolvement with the mythic depths or the superficial pop culture of this society. But, now, with the scapegoating of "aliens" (documented or illegal) on the increase, and the targeting of long-term legal immigrants like Mira for new scrutiny and new self-consciousness, she and I find ourselves unable to maintain the same polite discretion. We were always unacknowledged adversaries, and we are now, more than ever, sisters.

"I feel used," Mira raged on the phone the other night. "I feel manipulated and discarded. This is such an unfair way to treat a person who was invited to stay and work here because of her talent. My employer went to the I.N.S. and petitioned for the labor certification. For over thirty years, I've invested my creativity and professional skills into the improvement of this country's preschool system. I've obeyed all the rules, I've paid my taxes, I love my work, I love my students, I love the friends I've made. How dare America now change its rules in midstream? If America wants to make new rules curtailing benefits of legal immigrants, they should apply only to immigrants who arrive after those rules are already in place." To my ears, it sounded like the description of a long-enduring, comfortable yet loveless marriage, without risk or recklessness. Have we the right to demand, and to expect, that we be loved? (That, to me, is the subtext of the arguments by immigration advocates.) My sister is an expatriate, professionally generous and creative, socially courteous and gracious, and that's as far as her Americanization can go. She is here to maintain an identity, not to transform it.

I asked her if she would follow the example of others who have decided to become citizens because of the anti-immigration bills in Congress. And here, she 10 surprised me. "If America wants to play the manipulative game, I'll play it too," she snapped. "I'll become a U.S. citizen for now, then change back to Indian when I'm ready to go home. I feel some kind of irrational attachment to India that I don't to America. Until all this hysteria against legal immigrants, I was totally happy. Having my green card meant I could visit any place in the world I wanted to and then come back to a job that's satisfying and that I do very well."

In one family, from two sisters alike as peas in a pod, there could not be a wider divergence of immigrant experience. America spoke to me—I married it—I embraced the demotion from expatriate aristocrat to immigrant nobody, surrendering those thousands of years of "pure culture," the saris, the delightfully accented English. She retained them all. Which of us is the freak?

Mira's voice, I realize, is the voice not just of the immigrant South Asian community but of an immigrant community of the millions who have stayed rooted in one job, one city, one house, one ancestral culture, one cuisine, for the entirety of their productive years. She speaks for greater numbers than I possibly can. Only the fluency of her English and the anger, rather than fear, born of confidence from her education, differentiate her from the seamstresses, the domestics, the technicians, the shop owners, the millions of hardworking but effectively silenced documented immigrants as well as their less fortunate "illegal" brothers and sisters.

Nearly twenty years ago, when I was living in my husband's ancestral homeland of Canada, I was always well employed but never allowed to feel part of the local Quebec or larger Canadian society. Then, through a Green Paper that invited a national referendum on the unwanted side effects of "nontraditional" immigration, the government officially turned against its immigrant communities, particularly those from South Asia.

I felt then the same sense of betrayal that Mira feels now.

I will never forget the pain of that sudden turning, and the casual racist out- 15 bursts the Green Paper elicited. That sense of betrayal had its desired effect and drove me, and thousands like me, from the country.

Mira and I differ, however, in the ways in which we hope to interact with the country that we have chosen to live in. She is happier to live in America as expatriate Indian than as an immigrant American. I need to feel like a part of the community I have adopted (as I tried to feel in Canada as well). I need to put roots down, to vote and make the difference that I can. The price that the immigrant willingly pays, and that the exile avoids, is the trauma of self-transformation.

FOR ANALYSIS

1. What does Mukherjee mean by "mongrelization" (para. 6)?

2. What is the "trauma of self-transformation" (para. 16)? Are there traumas felt by those who choose to remain faithful to their original identity?

3. What are Mukherjee's feelings about the culture she left behind? What does she value? To what does she object?

WRITING TOPICS

1. Mukherjee's sister describes her attachment to India as "irrational" (para. 10), yet she maintains it. Does Mukherjee agree with her sister? Is she similarly attached to her nation, only her new one rather than her old one? Do you think feeling a deep connection to a nation and culture is irrational?

2. Immigration is a controversial political issue. Where do you stand on it? Should the United States make it easier or harder for immigrants to enter the country, to gain access to social services, to stay without becoming citizens, or to become citizens?

LACY M. JOHNSON (B. 1978)

WHITE TRASH PRIMER 2009

You live with your mama and daddy, your two sisters, three dogs, two horses and exactly twelve cats on a farm so far from town you barely see the street lights' bright white tossed over the horizon. Your mama grows a garden of fresh green vegetables right outside your back door and you and your sisters pick peas and tomatoes in the afternoon while mama hangs clean white sheets on the clothesline and the hot sun freckles your shoulders with small brown spots. When your daddy comes up to the house all sweating and covered in hayseed you set the table and make sure the silverware's in all the right places or you have to drink water with your dinner instead of tea.

You attend second service every Sunday since the day you are born and Brother Dan or Brother Darrell preach about the glory and grace of Jesus Christ and you accept Him as your Lord and Savior or you burn in hell and this is why you've been baptized twice and saved exactly twenty-seven times. Every week your mama and you and your sisters get real dressed up in the pretty cotton dresses she makes special for wearing to church. Your mama's always made all your clothes special with her own two hands and you are grateful for each hem until the rich kids in your Sunday School don't look at you even when you sit right next to them. Your daddy says vanity's an expensive sin but sometimes your mama drives you and your sisters to Wal-Mart anyway and she buys you underwear and socks and a pair of Lee jeans that are exactly two inches shorter than your legs and she presses her lips real tight together the whole time. One day she stops making pretty cotton dresses but the rich kids still don't look at you. They never look at you.

You and your sisters have always got on real good together. On hot summer days you pack peanut-butter sandwiches in a napkin your sister ties to your belt loop and you spend all day wandering the woods along the farm. Your daddy cuts a path with the brush hog and builds a square fort with sixteen knotty black logs instead of dragging them up to the house for firewood. You stop there every day to eat your lunch and you go skinny dipping in the creek and splash your little sister with the cold cold water and sometimes she tells your daddy and all three of you get spanked. Sometimes at night your sister comes to sleep in your bed and you stay up late talking real soft together with your heads under the covers like two peas in a pod and your daddy has to get on you for staying up past your bedtime. One night after mama and daddy are in bed your sister tells you she's moving to an APARTMENT above the Five and Dime downtown and you pull the covers back to see her face in the dark and she says you can come to her place to see her anytime you like. The next day she takes all of her clothes out of her closet and packs them up in a big black trash bag and carries them over her shoulder out the door. Your mama and daddy holler real loud when they find out your sister is living in sin with a black man and you don't get to see her for some time.

Your daddy lets you drive his pickup truck on the gravel road to your house when he's real tired even if you're not old enough because he says it's something you need to know how to do. When you're driving he turns on the radio and listens to Paul Harvey. Sometimes he disagrees with Paul Harvey and explains to you why he is right instead of resting. Sometimes he listens with his eyes closed and his head leaned back against the window. You know he's worrying over money because when your daddy worries over money his forehead gets to looking like tilled soil, mounded in rows like the creek bottom. He works real hard on the farm but the soybeans aren't selling and neither is the corn and the fence needs repairs and the plow's all busted so you take the truck into town without asking and you apply for a job at the fancy Wal-Mart but they don't call you to come in for an INTERVIEW. You apply six times and when they do call you pack peanut-butter sandwiches every day for lunch and every time you get a paycheck you put it in your daddy's bank and sometimes his eyes get to watering and you think he might be going soft. You save every penny you earn, but disappointment's what you get for dreaming because every penny ain't enough. Your daddy's a proud man and his eyes water the hardest you've ever seen when he signs the papers that sell the farm but this time you don't think it's cause he's soft.

You move into a white house with blue shutters and a yard with exactly 5 thirteen trees on a paved street in town and your daddy tears down all the walls and puts up new ones cause black mold spreads where you can't see. He works at the power plant and drops his yellow hard hat by the front door and your mama waits on rich folks at the restaurant and gets real dressed up for work every night and you don't have to set the table anymore cause you and your sister eat peanut-butter sandwiches for dinner and watch cable television before you go to bed. Sometimes you cut the sandwiches into circles with the mouth of a glass and sometimes you add pink and white candy sprinkles mama keeps in the cupboard for cupcakes and you tell your sister you've made her a SURPRISE. You walk to high school every day and you smoke cigarettes and cough down the peach schnapps your mama keeps hidden in the very back of the highest kitchen cabinet and even though it burns your stomach like hell fire you follow the kids to the one-block downtown and drive your truck in circles cause it's the only thing to do. You make friends with a girl your same age and she lets you spend the night at her place sometimes and you sleep real soundly in the AIR CONDITIONING. Sometimes she sneaks her boyfriend in and they have sex in the bed right next to you. One night he brings his friend over and he kisses you and claws your clothes off and you just want to sleep but his breath is stale and sweet like the beer your daddy drinks and when you try to push him off and tell him to stop he puts a pillow over your face and jams himself right up inside you and you can hardly breathe it burns so bad but there is nothing God will do.

You try real hard to get good grades in college cause you know exactly how much it cost but you work forty hours a week at Wal-Mart and sometimes you're so damn tired you can't read the PSYCHOLOGY open in front of you. Sometimes you don't know the words in front of you but you don't have a dictionary and if you fake it your teachers always know that you are faking. Your mama calls and asks how you're doing and you tell her you're doing great, mama, just great and one day she calls to tell you she has CANCER. Your hands sweat and your knees tremble together with sixteen of your cousins and your aunts and uncles and grandparents on both sides and both of your sisters in your mama's hospital room holding hands around her bed while your daddy asks the good Lord for STRENGTH. You don't even breathe until she's waking up from surgery with her mouth pawing open and each time you look she is weaker and smaller and closer to dying and each time your daddy palms his forehead he leaves tracks like the old creek bottom, but now you know it's not just money he worries over, so you tell him you'll drop out of school just till she's better but you don't plan to go back for some time.

You ask your mama how she feels when she picks you up from your apartment to take you to TACO BELL and she pushes you into the bathroom to show you where her breast used to be and hands you the silicon fist she keeps in her bra. You hold it with both hands. You order food. You sit down and when she's half-way through with her second SOFT TACO SUPREME you show her the pink flower tattoo your older sister bought you for your eighteenth birthday. Your mama doesn't say anything but her lips pressed real tight together tell you she is mad. Before she walks out the door and drives away she meets your eyes with hers and you know exactly what she means.

You hide that you are poor. You save up for a pair of LEVI'S jeans and put shirts on layaway. You take furniture from your neighbor's dumpster and thank your luck that they are wasteful. You fog your apartment for roaches and clean with bleach so they don't come out when you have company. You wash your car in the driveway with a hose and dishsoap. Your sister comes to visit and colors your hair NICE AND EASY 98 LIGHTEST BLONDE and paints your fingernails and toenails FIRE ENGINE RED. You make friends with a girl at work who is the same size as you and she gives you things she doesn't like anymore: a blue dress from the mall, a pair of black pumps, a pretty barrette with fake red crystals for your hair. She sets you up on dates with men and at dinner you order steaks and alcoholic drinks even if you're not old enough to drink. Sometimes you let them take you back to the fancy places where they live and if you have sex with them they take you shopping or to Springfield for the weekend and you thank your luck that they are gullible.

You act real tough but you've got a weak spot for HARLEY DAVIDSON motorcycles and a tall man in a leather coat with a broad chest and long black hair makes you want to ride. He takes you down a blacktop road clear out into nowhere and the whole time you've got that great big machine growling right under you, you're reeling in the smell of pine trees and wide green fields. So your fingers tighten on his arm. And your blond hair blows from underneath your helmet and all you can think about with the wind keeping your eyes closed tight is going and staying gone. When he stops his bike on the side of the road and turns around to hold your face real gentle between his hands you let him kiss you. And he takes you home without asking you for anything.

Your mama puts your picture in the paper when you go back to school. 10 You take classes with black folks and brown folks and yellow folks and make friends with who you like. Your parents take you out to dinner with your sisters and when your daddy is half-way through with his second beer and his cheeks are glowing with the red blood rushing to his face he lifts his glass and says that he is proud of you. When he finishes his third beer he goes out to sleep in the car and your mama gives you three brand new black pens and a pad of PostIts from her purse. You study real damn hard this time cause you know this is your last earthly chance to make something of yourself and you buy a dictionary at a yard sale and think you might learn every word if you have DETERMINATION and RESOLVE. When Wal-Mart doesn't let you off to study for a test you tell them to kiss your poor white ass and you apply for student loans and when they give out credit cards on campus you accept exactly three. Your English professor says you have POTENTIAL and you hold this real close to your heart when you're walking up to get your diploma and sixteen of your cousins and your aunts and uncles and grandparents on both sides and your two sisters are hooting and hollering from the stands and your mama blows an air horn and your daddy yells your name so loud and true it's like he's calling you to come up from the creek bottom. And you hear him calling for some time.

FOR ANALYSIS

1. What significance does the title have? What does Johnson mean by "white trash"? What is a "primer"?

2. How would you characterize the **style** of the **prose** with which Johnson writes "White Trash Primer"?

3. What **point of view** is this essay written in? What effect does it have on you as you read?

MAKING CONNECTIONS

1. Both of these essays are in part about what Mukherjee calls "the trauma of self-transformation." What is the nature of Johnson's transformation? How does Johnson present it? Is it traumatic?

2. Mukherjee's essay is about immigration, while Johnson's is not. Yet both are about different ways to be in America—different ways to live, different ways to see yourself and be seen by others. Compare the situations the two essays take as their subjects and the ways the two treat those situations.

3. Imagine a conversation between Mukherjee and Johnson on the subject of culture. What might each of them mean by the term? How might their definitions be similar, and how might they be different?

WRITING TOPICS

1. Johnson's essay closes on an emotional note. Going back through the essay, note the different **tones** she creates, and reflect on how she prepares her readers for the feelings evoked by the end of the essay.

2. Reflect on how you relate to the use of "you" in "White Trash Primer." How does it make you feel? Do you feel included by it or excluded by it? Why?

FURTHER QUESTIONS
FOR THINKING AND WRITING

1. Explain how Woolf's observations in "What If Shakespeare Had Had a Sister?" illuminate Emily's situation in Faulkner's "A Rose for Emily." **Writing Topic:** In an essay, argue for or against the proposition that women have achieved absolute equality in the United States.

2. Cummings's "the Cambridge ladies who live in furnished souls" and Dickinson's "What Soft—Cherubic Creatures—" both address certain culturally determined behavior patterns among women. Describe the behavior depicted in these poems. How do the authors feel about the behavior? What devices reveal the authors' attitudes? **Writing Topic:** Define the social tradition that produced the women in these poems. Either defend that tradition as crucial to the social order, or offer a cultural variation that would give women a different social role.

3. The speakers in Yevtushenko's "I Would Like" and Eliot's "The Love Song of J. Alfred Prufrock" exhibit quite different attitudes about their identities. Describe each speaker's attitude toward his identity, and identify which aspects of the poems define those attitudes. In what sense are the speakers' identities culturally determined? **Writing Topic:** In an imaginative essay, describe each speaker's early life, and suggest what cultural forces shaped him.

4. Some of the works in this section focus on intergenerational tensions within a culture. Compare such tensions among parents and offspring in Walker's "Everyday Use" and Alexie's "War Dances."

5. The struggle of women to achieve equality is the subject of many works in this section. **Writing Topic:** Examine some of the feminist works in this section. What, if any, common threads do you find running through them, either in content or in the use of literary devices?

6. Homer in Faulkner's "A Rose for Emily" and Prufrock in Eliot's "The Love Song of J. Alfred Prufrock" are both, in some sense, cultural outsiders. **Writing Topic:** Compare their positions in the dominant culture, the resulting conflicts or tensions, and the strategies they employ in dealing with their status.

LOVE AND HATE

Two Lovers, 1630, by Riza 'Abbasi.

Love and death, it is often noted, are the two great themes of literature. Many of the literary works we have placed in the sections "Innocence and Experience," "Conformity and Rebellion," and "Culture and Identity" speak of love and death as well. But in those works, other thematic interests dominate. In this section, we gather a number of works in which love and hate are thematically central.

The rosy conception of love presented in many popular and sentimental stories does not prepare us for the complicated reality we face. We know that the course of true love never runs smoothly, but in those popular stories the obstacles that hinder the lovers are simple and external. If the young lover can land the high-paying job or convince the beloved's parents that he or she is worthy despite social differences, all will be well. But love in life is rarely that simple. The external obstacles may be insuperable, or the obstacles may lie deep within the personality. The major obstacle may well be an individual's difficult and painful effort to understand that he or she has been deceived by an immature or sentimental conception of love.

In this age of psychological awareness, the claims of the flesh are well recognized. But psychology teaches us, as well, to recognize the aggressive aspect of the human condition. The omnipresent selfishness that civilization attempts to check may be aggressively violent as well as lustful. Thus, on one hand, we have the simple eroticism of Kate Chopin's "The Storm" and, on the other, the more complicated, dangerous attraction of Joyce Carol Oates's "Where Are You Going, Where Have You Been?" And Matthew Arnold in "Dover Beach" finds love the only refuge from a chaotic world in which "ignorant armies clash by night."

The cliché has it that love and hate are closely related, and much evidence supports this proposition. But why should love and hate, seeming opposites, lie so close together in the emotional lives of men and women? We are all egos, separate from each other. And as separate individuals, we develop elaborate behavior mechanisms that defend us from each other. But the erotic love relationship differs from other relationships in that it may be defined as a rejection of separateness. The common metaphor speaks of two lovers as joining, as merging into one. That surrender of the "me" to join in an "us" leaves lovers uniquely vulnerable to psychic injury. In short, the defenses are down, and the self-esteem of each of the lovers depends importantly on the behavior of the other. If the lover is betrayed by the beloved, the emotional consequences are uniquely disastrous—hence the peculiarly close relationship between passionate hatred and erotic love.

Words like *love* and *hate* are so general that poets rarely use them except as one term in a metaphor designed to project sharply some aspect of emotional life. The simple sexuality in poems such as Andrew Marvell's "To His Coy Mistress" and Christopher Marlowe's "The Passionate Shepherd to His Love" may be juxtaposed with the hatred and violence generated in *Othello* by sexual jealousy or with the quick reprisal of the slighted Barbara Allan. And Sharon Olds's description of lust in "Sex without Love" notes an aspect of love quite overlooked by Robert Burns in "A Red, Red Rose."

Perhaps more than anything, the works in this section celebrate the elemental impulses of men and women that run counter to those rational formulations by which we govern our lives. We pursue Othello's love for Desdemona and Iago's hate for Othello and arrive at an irreducible mystery, for neither Othello's love nor Iago's hate yields satisfactorily to rational explanation. Reason does not tell us why Othello and Desdemona love one another or why Iago hates rather than honors Othello.

Love is an act of faith springing from our deep-seated need to join with another human being not only in physical nakedness but in emotional and spiritual nakedness as well. While hate is a denial of that faith and therefore a retreat into spiritual isolation, love is an attempt to break out of the isolation.

QUESTIONS FOR THINKING AND WRITING

As you read the selections in this section, consider the following questions. You may want to write out your thoughts informally in a journal or notebook as a way of preparing to respond to the selections, or you may wish to make one of these questions the basis for a formal essay.

1. What is love? What is the source of your definition (literature, personal observation, discussions with those you trust)? Have you ever been in love? How did you know? Do you know someone who is in love? How has it changed that person?

2. Have you ever truly hated someone or something? Describe the circumstances, and characterize your hatred.

3. Do you believe that love and hate are closely related? Have you experienced a change from love to hatred, or do you know someone who has? Explain.

4. There are different kinds of love—love of family, of humankind, of a cause. Describe several different kinds of love, and examine your own motives and behavior in different love relationships. Is it possible that certain kinds of love necessarily generate certain hatreds? Explain.

FICTION

KATE CHOPIN   (1851–1904)

THE STORM   1898

I

The leaves were so still that even Bibi thought it was going to rain. Bobinôt, who was accustomed to converse on terms of perfect equality with his little son, called the child's attention to certain sombre clouds that were rolling with sinister intention from the west, accompanied by a sullen, threatening roar. They were at Friedheimer's store and decided to remain there till the storm had passed. They sat within the door on two empty kegs. Bibi was four years old and looked very wise.

"Mama'll be 'fraid, yes," he suggested with blinking eyes.

"She'll shut the house. Maybe she got Sylvie helpin' her this evenin'," Bobinôt responded reassuringly.

"No; she ent got Sylvie. Sylvie was helpin' her yistiday," piped Bibi.

Bobinôt arose and going across to the counter purchased a can of shrimps, 5 of which Calixta was very fond. Then he returned to his perch on the keg and sat stolidly holding the can of shrimps while the storm burst. It shook the wooden store and seemed to be ripping great furrows in the distant field. Bibi laid his little hand on his father's knee and was not afraid.

II

Calixta, at home, felt no uneasiness for their safety. She sat at a side window sewing furiously on a sewing machine. She was greatly occupied and did not notice the approaching storm. But she felt very warm and often stopped to mop her face on which the perspiration gathered in beads. She unfastened her white sacque at the throat. It began to grow dark, and suddenly realizing the situation she got up hurriedly and went about closing windows and doors.

Out on the small front gallery she had hung Bobinôt's Sunday clothes to air and she hastened out to gather them before the rain fell. As she stepped outside,

Alcée Laballière rode in at the gate. She had not seen him very often since her marriage, and never alone. She stood there with Bobinôt's coat in her hands, and the big rain drops began to fall. Alcée rode his horse under the shelter of a side projection where the chickens had huddled and there were plows and a harrow piled up in the corner.

"May I come and wait on your gallery till the storm is over, Calixta?" he asked.

"Come 'long in, M'sieu Alcée."

His voice and her own startled her as if from a trance, and she seized Bobinôt's 10 vest. Alcée, mounting to the porch, grabbed the trousers and snatched Bibi's braided jacket that was about to be carried away by a sudden gust of wind. He expressed an intention to remain outside, but it was soon apparent that he might as well have been out in the open: the water beat in upon the boards in driving sheets, and he went inside, closing the door after him. It was even necessary to put something beneath the door to keep the water out.

"My! what a rain! It's good two years since it rain' like that," exclaimed Calixta as she rolled up a piece of bagging and Alcée helped her to thrust it beneath the crack.

She was a little fuller of figure than five years before when she married; but she had lost nothing of her vivacity. Her blue eyes still retained their melting quality; and her yellow hair, dishevelled by the wind and rain, kinked more stubbornly than ever about her ears and temples.

The rain beat upon the low, shingled roof with a force and clatter that threatened to break an entrance and deluge them there. They were in the dining room—the sitting room—the general utility room. Adjoining was her bed room, with Bibi's couch along side her own. The door stood open, and the room with its white, monumental bed, its closed shutters, looked dim and mysterious.

Alcée flung himself into a rocker and Calixta nervously began to gather up from the floor the lengths of a cotton sheet which she had been sewing.

"If this keeps up, *Dieu sait*[1] if the levees goin' to stan' it!" she exclaimed.   15

"What have you got to do with the levees?"

"I got enough to do! An' there's Bobinôt with Bibi out in that storm—if he only didn' left Friedheimer's!"

"Let us hope, Calixta, that Bobinôt's got sense enough to come in out of a cyclone."

She went and stood at the window with a greatly disturbed look on her face. She wiped the frame that was clouded with moisture. It was stiflingly hot. Alcée got up and joined her at the window, looking over her shoulder. The rain was coming down in sheets obscuring the view of far-off cabins and enveloping the distant wood in a gray mist. The playing of the lightning was incessant. A bolt struck a tall chinaberry tree at the edge of the field. It filled all visible space with a blinding glare and the crash seemed to invade the very boards they stood upon.

[1] God knows.

Calixta put her hands to her eyes, and with a cry, staggered backward. 20
Alcée's arm encircled her, and for an instant he drew her close and spasmodically to him.

"*Bonté!*"[2] she cried, releasing herself from his encircling arm and retreating from the window, "the house'll go next! If I only knew w'ere Bibi was!" She would not compose herself; she would not be seated. Alcée clasped her shoulders and looked into her face. The contact of her warm, palpitating body when he had unthinkingly drawn her into his arms, had aroused all the old-time infatuation and desire for her flesh.

"Calixta," he said, "don't be frightened. Nothing can happen. The house is too low to be struck, with so many tall trees standing about. There! aren't you going to be quiet? say, aren't you?" He pushed her hair back from her face that was warm and steaming. Her lips were as red and moist as pomegranate seed. Her white neck and a glimpse of her full, firm bosom disturbed him powerfully. As she glanced up at him the fear in her liquid blue eyes had given place to a drowsy gleam that unconsciously betrayed a sensuous desire. He looked down into her eyes and there was nothing for him to do but to gather her lips in a kiss. It reminded him of Assumption.[3]

"Do you remember—in Assumption, Calixta?" he asked in a low voice broken by passion. Oh! she remembered; for in Assumption he had kissed her and kissed and kissed her; until his senses would well nigh fail, and to save her he would resort to a desperate flight. If she was not an immaculate dove in those days, she was still inviolate; a passionate creature whose very defenselessness had made her defense, against which his honor forbade him to prevail. Now— well, now—her lips seemed in a manner free to be tasted, as well as her round, white throat and her whiter breasts.

They did not heed the crashing torrents, and the roar of the elements made her laugh as she lay in his arms. She was a revelation in that dim, mysterious chamber; as white as the couch she lay upon. Her firm, elastic flesh that was knowing for the first time its birthright, was like a creamy lily that the sun invites to contribute its breath and perfume to the undying life of the world.

The generous abundance of her passion, without guile or trickery, was like a 25 white flame which penetrated and found response in depths of his own sensuous nature that had never yet been reached.

When he touched her breasts they gave themselves up in quivering ecstasy, inviting his lips. Her mouth was a fountain of delight. And when he possessed her, they seemed to swoon together at the very borderland of life's mystery.

He stayed cushioned upon her, breathless, dazed, enervated, with his heart beating like a hammer upon her. With one hand she clasped his head, her lips lightly touching his forehead. The other hand stroked with a soothing rhythm his muscular shoulders.

---

[2] An exclamation: Goodness!
[3] A holiday commemorating the ascent of the Virgin Mary to heaven. Assumption is also the name of a Louisiana parish (county) where Calixta and Alcée had a rendezvous in an earlier story.

The growl of the thunder was distant and passing away. The rain beat softly upon the shingles, inviting them to drowsiness and sleep. But they dared not yield.

The rain was over; and the sun was turning the glistening green world into a palace of gems. Calixta, on the gallery, watched Alcée ride away. He turned and smiled at her with a beaming face; and she lifted her pretty chin in the air and laughed aloud.

III

Bobinôt and Bibi, trudging home, stopped without at the cistern to make themselves presentable. 30

"My! Bibi, w'at will yo' mama say! You ought to be ashame'. You oughtn' put on those good pants. Look at 'em! An' that mud on yo' collar! How you got that mud on yo' collar, Bibi? I never saw such a boy!" Bibi was the picture of pathetic resignation. Bobinôt was the embodiment of serious solicitude as he strove to remove from his own person and his son's the signs of their tramp over heavy roads and through wet fields. He scraped the mud off Bibi's bare legs and feet with a stick and carefully removed all traces from his heavy brogans. Then, prepared for the worst—the meeting with an over-scrupulous housewife, they entered cautiously at the back door.

Calixta was preparing supper. She had set the table and was dripping coffee at the hearth. She sprang up as they came in.

"Oh, Bobinôt! You back! My! but I was uneasy. W'ere you been during the rain? An' Bibi? he ain't wet? he ain't hurt?" She had clasped Bibi and was kissing him effusively. Bobinôt's explanations and apologies which he had been composing all along the way, died on his lips as Calixta felt him to see if he were dry, and seemed to express nothing but satisfaction at their safe return.

"I brought you some shrimps, Calixta," offered Bobinôt, hauling the can from his ample side pocket and laying it on the table.

"Shrimps! Oh, Bobinôt! you too good fo' anything!" and she gave him a smacking kiss on the cheek that resounded. "*J'vous réponds,*[4] we'll have a feas' 35 to night! umph-umph!"

Bobinôt and Bibi began to relax and enjoy themselves, and when the three seated themselves at table they laughed much and so loud that anyone might have heard them as far away as Laballière's.

IV

Alcée Laballière wrote to his wife, Clarisse, that night. It was a loving letter, full of tender solicitude. He told her not to hurry back, but if she and the babies liked it at Biloxi, to stay a month longer. He was getting on nicely; and though

---

[4] I'm telling you.

he missed them, he was willing to bear the separation a while longer—realizing that their health and pleasure were the first things to be considered.

V

As for Clarisse, she was charmed upon receiving her husband's letter. She and the babies were doing well. The society was agreeable; many of her old friends and acquaintances were at the bay. And the first free breath since her marriage seemed to restore the pleasant liberty of her maiden days. Devoted as she was to her husband, their intimate conjugal life was something which she was more than willing to forego for a while.

So the storm passed and everyone was happy.

FOR ANALYSIS

1. Aside from the child Bibi, there are four characters in this story—two married couples. How did you respond to each of these characters? What are the sources for your reactions?

2. How do the characters in the story feel about themselves? About each other? On what evidence in the story do you base your response?

3. Discuss the title of the story.

4. During the second half of the nineteenth century, certain American writers, including Kate Chopin, evoked a sense of region in their work. What region of the United States provides the **setting** for this story? How do you know?

5. What aspects of this story's **style** contribute to its realism?

MAKING CONNECTIONS

Read this story against Kinnell's "After Making Love We Hear Footsteps" (p. 919). How do the children function in relation to the sex in each work? What does the boy's presence after the act mean in each selection?

WRITING TOPICS

1. Write an essay on modern marriage, using this story to support your analysis.

2. Comment on the story's final line. Is "the storm" literal or symbolic? If everyone is "happy," do you believe they have the right to be? Or is such a question irrelevant? Explain.

ZORA NEALE HURSTON (1891–1960)

SWEAT   1926

I

It was eleven o'clock of a Spring night in Florida. It was Sunday. Any other night, Delia Jones would have been in bed for two hours by this time. But she was a washwoman, and Monday morning meant a great deal to her. So she collected the soiled clothes on Saturday when she returned the clean things. Sunday night after church, she sorted and put the white things to soak. It saved her almost a half-day's start. A great hamper in the bedroom held the clothes that she brought home. It was so much neater than a number of bundles lying around.

She squatted on the kitchen floor beside the great pile of clothes, sorting them into small heaps according to color, and humming a song in a mournful key, but wondering through it all where Sykes, her husband, had gone with her horse and buckboard.

Just then something long, round, limp, and black fell upon her shoulders and slithered to the floor beside her. A great terror took hold of her. It softened her knees and dried her mouth so that it was a full minute before she could cry out or move. Then she saw that it was the big bull whip her husband liked to carry when he drove.

She lifted her eyes to the door and saw him standing there bent over with laughter at her fright. She screamed at him.

"Sykes, what you throw dat whip on me like dat? You know it would skeer 5 me—looks just like a snake, an' you knows how skeered Ah is of snakes."

"Course Ah knowed it! That's how come Ah done it." He slapped his leg with his hand and almost rolled on the ground in his mirth. "If you such a big fool dat you got to have a fit over a earth worm or a string, Ah don't keer how bad Ah skeer you."

"You ain't got no business doing it. Gawd knows it's a sin. Some day Ah'm gointuh drop dead from some of yo' foolishness. 'Nother thing, where you been wid mah rig? Ah feeds dat pony. He ain't fuh you to be drivin' wid no bull whip."

"You sho' is one aggravatin' nigger woman!" he declared and stepped into the room. She resumed her work and did not answer him at once. "Ah done tole you time and again to keep them white folks' clothes outa dis house."

He picked up the whip and glared at her. Delia went on with her work. She went out into the yard and returned with a galvanized tub and set it on the wash-bench. She saw that Sykes had kicked all of the clothes together again, and now stood in her way truculently, his whole manner hoping, *praying*, for an argument. But she walked calmly around him and commenced to re-sort the things.

"Next time, Ah'm gointer kick 'em outdoors," he threatened as he struck a 10 match along the leg of his corduroy breeches.

Delia never looked up from her work, and her thin, stooped shoulders sagged further.

"Ah ain't for no fuss t'night, Sykes. Ah just come from taking sacrament at the church house."

He snorted scornfully. "Yeah, you just come from de church house on a Sunday night, but heah you is gone to work on them clothes. You ain't nothing but a hypocrite. One of them amen-corner Christians—sing, whoop, and shout, then come home and wash white folks' clothes on the Sabbath."

He stepped roughly upon the whitest pile of things, kicking them helter-skelter as he crossed the room. His wife gave a little scream of dismay, and quickly gathered them together again.

"Sykes, you quit grindin' dirt into these clothes! How can Ah git through by 15 Sat'day if Ah don't start on Sunday?"

"Ah don't keer if you never git through. Anyhow, Ah done promised Gawd and a couple of other men, Ah ain't gointer have it in mah house. Don't gimme no lip neither, else Ah'll throw 'em out and put mah fist up side yo' head to boot."

Delia's habitual meekness seemed to slip from her shoulders like a blown scarf. She was on her feet; her poor little body, her bare knuckly hands bravely defying the strapping hulk before her.

"Looka heah, Sykes, you done gone too fur. Ah been married to you fur fifteen years, and Ah been takin' in washin' fur fifteen years. Sweat, sweat, sweat! Work and sweat, cry and sweat, pray and sweat!"

"What's that got to do with me?" he asked brutally.

"What's it got to do with you, Sykes? Mah tub of suds is filled yo' belly with 20 vittles more times than yo' hands is filled it. Mah sweat is done paid for this house and Ah reckon Ah kin keep on sweatin' in it."

She seized the iron skillet from the stove and struck a defensive pose, which act surprised him greatly, coming from her. It cowed him and he did not strike her as he usually did.

"Naw you won't," she panted, "that ole snaggle-toothed black woman you runnin' with ain't comin' heah to pile up on *mah* sweat and blood. You ain't paid for nothin' on this place, and Ah'm gointer stay right heah till Ah'm toted out foot foremost."

"Well, you better quit gittin' me riled up, else they'll be totin' you out sooner than you expect. Ah'm so tired of you Ah don't know whut to do. Gawd! How Ah hates skinny wimmen!"

A little awed by this new Delia, he sidled out of the door and slammed the back gate after him. He did not say where he had gone, but she knew too well. She knew very well that he would not return until nearly daybreak also. Her work over, she went on to bed but not to sleep at once. Things had come to a pretty pass!

She lay awake, gazing upon the debris that cluttered their matrimonial 25
trail. Not an image left standing along the way. Anything like flowers had long
ago been drowned in the salty stream that had been pressed from her heart.
Her tears, her sweat, her blood. She had brought love to the union and he
had brought a longing after the flesh. Two months after the wedding, he had
given her the first brutal beating. She had the memory of his numerous trips
to Orlando with all of his wages when he had returned to her penniless, even
before the first year had passed. She was young and soft then, but now she
thought of her knotty, muscled limbs, her harsh knuckly hands, and drew herself up into an unhappy little ball in the middle of the big feather bed. Too late
now to hope for love, even if it were not Bertha it would be someone else. This
case differed from the others only in that she was bolder than the others. Too
late for everything except her little home. She had built it for her old days, and
planted one by one the trees and flowers there. It was lovely to her, lovely.

Somehow, before sleep came, she found herself saying aloud: "Oh well,
whatever goes over the Devil's back, is got to come under his belly. Sometime
or ruther, Sykes, like everybody else, is gointer reap his sowing." After that she
was able to build a spiritual earthworks against her husband. His shells could
no longer reach her. AMEN. She went to sleep and slept until he announced his
presence in bed by kicking her feet and rudely snatching the covers away.

"Gimme some kivah heah, an' git yo' damn foots over on yo' own side! Ah
oughter mash you in yo' mouf fuh drawing dat skillet on me."

Delia went clear to the rail without answering him. A triumphant indifference to all that he was or did.

II

The week was full of work for Delia as all other weeks, and Saturday found her
behind her little pony, collecting and delivering clothes.

It was a hot, hot day near the end of July. The village men on Joe Clarke's 30
porch even chewed cane listlessly. They did not hurl the cane-knots as usual.
They let them dribble over the edge of the porch. Even conversation had collapsed under the heat.

"Heah come Delia Jones," Jim Merchant said, as the shaggy pony came
'round the bend of the road toward them. The rusty buckboard was heaped
with baskets of crisp, clean laundry.

"Yep," Joe Lindsay agreed. "Hot or col', rain or shine, jes'ez reg'lar ez de
weeks roll roun' Delia carries 'em an' fetches 'em on Sat'day."

"She better if she wanter eat," said Moss. "Syke Jones ain't wuth de shot an'
powder hit would tek tuh kill 'em. Not to *huh* he ain't."

"He sho' ain't," Walter Thomas chimed in. "It's too bad, too, cause she wuz
a right pretty li'l trick when he got huh. Ah'd uh mah'ied huh mahself if he
hadnter beat me to it."

Delia nodded briefly at the men as she drove past. 35

"Too much knockin' will ruin *any* 'oman. He done beat huh 'nough tuh kill three women, let 'lone change they looks," said Elijah Moseley. "How Syke kin stommuck dat big black greasy Mogul he's layin' roun' wid, gits me. Ah swear dat eight-rock couldn't kiss a sardine can Ah done thowed out de back do' 'way las' yeah."

"Aw, she's fat, thass how come. He's allus been crazy 'bout fat women," put in Merchant. "He'd a' been tied up wid one long time ago if he could a' found one tuh have him. Did Ah tell yuh 'bout him come sidlin' roun' *mah* wife— bringin' her a basket uh peecans outa his yard fuh a present? Yessir, mah wife! She tol' him tuh take 'em right straight back home, 'cause Delia works so hard ovah dat washtub she reckon everything on de place taste lak sweat an' soapsuds. Ah jus' wisht Ah'd a' caught 'im roun' dere! Ah'd a' made his hips ketch on fiah down dat shell road."

"Ah know he done it, too. Ah sees 'im grinnin' at every 'oman dat passes," Walter Thomas said. "But even so, he useter eat some mighty big hunks uh humble pie tuh git dat li'l 'oman he got. She wuz ez pritty ez a speckled pup! Dat wuz fifteen years ago. He useter be so skeered uh losin' huh, she could make him do some parts of a husband's duty. Dey never wuz de same in de mind."

"There oughter be a law about him," said Lindsay. "He ain't fit tuh carry guts tuh a bear."

Clarke spoke for the first time. "Tain't no law on earth dat kin make a man 40 be decent if it ain't in 'im. There's plenty men dat takes a wife lak dey do a joint uh sugar-cane. It's round, juicy, an' sweet when dey gits it. But dey squeeze an' grind, squeeze an' grind an' wring tell dey wring every drop uh pleasure dat's in 'em out. When dey's satisfied dat dey is wrung dry, dey treats 'em jes' lak dey do a cane-chew. Dey thows 'em away. Dey knows whut dey is doin' while dey is at it, an' hates theirselves fuh it but they keeps on hangin' after huh tell she's empty. Den dey hates huh fuh bein' a cane-chew an' in de way."

"We oughter take Syke an' dat stray 'oman uh his'n down in Lake Howell swamp an' lay on de rawhide till they cain't say Lawd a' mussy. He allus wuz uh ovahbearin niggah, but since dat white 'oman from up north done teached 'im how to run a automobile, he done got too beggety to live—an' we oughter kill 'im," Old Man Anderson advised.

A grunt of approval went around the porch. But the heat was melting their civic virtue and Elijah Moseley began to bait Joe Clarke.

"Come on, Joe, git a melon outa dere an' slice it up for yo' customers. We'se all sufferin' wid de heat. De bear's done got *me!*"

"Thass right, Joe, a watermelon is jes' whut Ah needs tuh cure de eppizudicks," Walter Thomas joined forces with Moseley. "Come on dere, Joe. We all is steady customers an' you ain't set us up in a long time. Ah chooses dat long, bowlegged Floridy favorite."

"A god, an' be dough. You all gimme twenty cents and slice away," Clarke 45 retorted. "Ah needs a col' slice m'self. Heah, everybody chip in. Ah'll lend y'all mah meat knife."

The money was all quickly subscribed and the huge melon brought forth. At that moment, Sykes and Bertha arrived. A determined silence fell on the porch and the melon was put away again.

Merchant snapped down the blade of his jacknife and moved toward the store door.

"Come on in, Joe, an' gimme a slab uh sow belly an' uh pound uh coffee— almost fuhgot 'twas Sat'day. Got to git on home." Most of the men left also.

Just then Delia drove past on her way home, as Sykes was ordering magnificently for Bertha. It pleased him for Delia to see.

"Git whutsoever yo' heart desires, Honey. Wait a minute, Joe. Give huh two 50 bottles uh strawberry soda-water, uh quart parched ground-peas, an' a block uh chewin' gum."

With all this they left the store, with Sykes reminding Bertha that this was his town and she could have it if she wanted it.

The men returned soon after they left, and held their watermelon feast.

"Where did Syke Jones git da 'oman from nohow?" Lindsay asked.

"Ovah Apopka. Guess dey musta been cleanin' out de town when she lef'. She don't look lak a thing but a hunk uh liver wid hair on it."

"Well, she sho' kin squall," Dave Carter contributed. "When she gits ready 55 tuh laff, she jes' opens huh mouf an' latches it back tuh de las' notch. No ole granpa alligator down in Lake Bell ain't got nothin' on huh."

III

Bertha had been in town three months now. Sykes was still paying her room-rent at Della Lewis'—the only house in town that would have taken her in. Sykes took her frequently to Winter Park to "stomps." He still assured her that he was the swellest man in the state.

"Sho' you kin have dat li'l ole house soon's Ah git dat 'oman outa dere. Everything b'longs tuh me an' you sho' kin have it. Ah sho' 'bominates uh skinny 'oman. Lawdy, you sho' is got one portly shape on you! You kin git *anything* you wants. Dis is *mah* town an' you sho' kin have it."

Delia's work-worn knees crawled over the earth in Gethsemane[1] and up the rocks of Calvary many, many times during these months. She avoided the villagers and meeting places in her efforts to be blind and deaf. But Bertha nullified this to a degree, by coming to Delia's house to call Sykes out to her at the gate.

Delia and Sykes fought all the time now with no peaceful interludes. They slept and ate in silence. Two or three times Delia had attempted a timid friendliness, but she was repulsed each time. It was plain that the breaches must remain agape.

The sun had burned July to August. The heat streamed down like a million 60 hot arrows, smiting all things living upon the earth. Grass withered, leaves

---

[1] Gethsemane is the garden where, according to the Bible, Jesus and his disciples prayed the night before Jesus was crucified on Calvary (which is also known as Golgotha, "the place of the skull").

browned, snakes went blind in shedding, and men and dogs went mad. Dog days!

Delia came home one day and found Sykes there before her. She wondered, but started to go on into the house without speaking, even though he was standing in the kitchen door and she must either stoop under his arm or ask him to move. He made no room for her. She noticed a soap box beside the steps, but paid no particular attention to it, knowing that he must have brought it there. As she was stooping to pass under his outstretched arm, he suddenly pushed her backward, laughingly.

"Look in de box dere Delia, Ah done brung yuh somethin'!"

She nearly fell upon the box in her stumbling, and when she saw what it held, she all but fainted outright.

"Syke! Syke, mah Gawd! You take dat rattlesnake 'way from heah! You *gottuh*. Oh, Jesus, have mussy!"

"Ah ain't got tuh do nuthin' uh de kin'—fact is Ah ain't got tuh do nothin' 65 but die. Tain't no use uh you puttin' on airs makin' out lak you skeered uh dat snake—he's gointer stay right heah tell he die. He wouldn't bite me cause Ah knows how tuh handle 'im. Nohow he wouldn't risk breakin' out his fangs 'gin *yo* skinny laigs."

"Naw, now Syke, don't keep dat thing 'round tryin' tuh skeer me tuh death. You knows Ah'm even feared uh earth worms. Thass de biggest snake Ah evah did se. Kill 'im Syke, please."

"Doan ast me tuh do nothin' fuh yuh. Goin' 'round tryin' tuh be so damn asterperious. Naw, Ah ain't gonna kill it. Ah think uh damn sight mo' uh him dan you! Dat's a nice snake an' anybody doan lak 'im kin jes' hit de grit."

The village soon heard that Sykes had the snake, and came to see and ask questions.

"How de hen-fire did you ketch dat six-foot rattler, Syke?" Thomas asked.

"He's full uh frogs so he cain't hardly move, thass how Ah eased up on 'im. 70 But Ah'm a snake charmer an' knows how tuh handle 'em. Shux, dat ain't nothin'. Ah could ketch one eve'y day if Ah so wanted tuh."

"Whut he needs is a heavy hick'ry club leaned real heavy on his head. Dat's de bes' way tuh charm a rattlesnake."

"Naw, Walt, y'all jes' don't understand dese diamon' backs lak Ah do," said Sykes in a superior tone of voice.

The village agreed with Walter, but the snake stayed on. His box remained by the kitchen door with its screen wire covering. Two or three days later it had digested its meal of frogs and literally came to life. It rattled at every movement in the kitchen or the yard. One day as Delia came down the kitchen steps she saw his chalky-white fangs curved like scimitars hung in the wire meshes. This time she did not run away with averted eyes as usual. She stood for a long time in the doorway in a red fury that grew bloodier for every second that she regarded the creature that was her torment.

That night she broached the subject as soon as Sykes sat down to the table.

"Syke, Ah wants you tuh take dat snake 'way fum heah. You done starved 75 me an' Ah put up widcher, you done beat me an Ah took dat, but you don kilt all mah insides bringin' dat varmint heah."

Sykes poured out a saucer full of coffee and drank it deliberately before he answered her.

"A whole lot Ah keer 'bout how you feels inside uh out. Dat snake ain't goin' no damn wheah till Ah gits ready fuh 'im tuh go. So fur as beatin' is concerned, yuh ain't took near all dat you gointer take ef yuh stay 'round *me*."

Delia pushed back her plate and got up from the table. "Ah hates you, Sykes," she said calmly. "Ah hates you tuh de same degree dat Ah useter love yuh. Ah done took an' took till mah belly is full up tuh mah neck. Dat's de reason Ah got mah letter fum de church an' moved mah membership tuh Woodbridge—so Ah don't haftuh take no sacrament wid yuh. Ah don't wan-tuh see yuh 'round me atall. Lay 'round wid dat 'oman all yuh wants tuh, but gwan 'way from me an' mah house. Ah hates yuh lak uh suck-egg dog."

Sykes almost let the huge wad of corn bread and collard greens he was chew-ing fall out of his mouth in amazement. He had a hard time whipping himself up to the proper fury to try to answer Delia.

"Well, Ah'm glad you does hate me. Ah'm sho' tiahed uh you hangin' ontuh 80 me. Ah don't want yuh. Look at yuh stringey ole neck! Yo' rawbony laigs an' arms is enough tuh cut uh man tuh death. You looks jes' lak de devvul's doll-baby tuh *me*. You cain't hate me no worse dan Ah hates you. Ah been hatin' *you* fuh years."

"Yo' ole black hide don't look lak nothin' tuh me, but uh passle uh wrinkled up rubber, wid yo' big ole yeahs flappin' on each side lak uh paih uh buzzard wings. Don't think Ah'm gointuh be run 'way fum mah house neither. Ah'm goin' tuh de white folks 'bout *you*, mah young man, de very nex' time you lay yo' han's on me. Mah cup is done run ovah." Delia said this with no signs of fear and Sykes departed from the house, threatening her, but made not the slightest move to carry out any of them.

That night he did not return at all, and the next day being Sunday, Delia was glad she did not have to quarrel before she hitched up her pony and drove the four miles to Woodbridge.

She stayed to the night service—"love feast"—which was very warm and full of spirit. In the emotional winds her domestic trials were borne far and wide so that she sang as she drove homeward,

Jurden water, black an' col
Chills de body, not de soul
An'Ah wantah cross Jurden in uh calm time.

She came from the barn to the kitchen door and stopped.

"Whut's de mattah, ol' Satan, you ain't kicken' up yo' racket?" She addressed the snake's box. Complete silence. She went on into the house with a new hope in its birth struggles. Perhaps her threat to go to the white folks had frightened Sykes! Perhaps he was sorry! Fifteen years of misery and suppression had brought Delia to the place where she would hope *anything* that looked towards a way over or through her wall of inhibitions.

She felt in the match-safe behind the stove at once for a match. There was 85 only one there.

"Dat niggah wouldn't fetch nothin' heah tuh save his rotten neck, but he kin run thew whut Ah brings quick enough. Now he done toted off nigh on tuh haff uh box uh matches. He done had dat 'oman heah in mah house, too."

Nobody but a woman could tell how she knew this even before she struck the match. But she did and it put her into a new fury.

Presently she brought in the tubs to put the white things to soak. This time she decided she need not bring the hamper out of the bedroom; she would go in there and do the sorting. She picked up the pot-bellied lamp and went in. The room was small and the hamper stood hard by the foot of the white iron bed. She could sit and reach through the bedposts—resting as she worked.

"Ah wantah cross Jurden in uh calm time." She was singing again. The mood of the "love feast," had returned. She threw back the lid of the basket almost gaily. Then, moved by both horror and terror, she sprang back toward the door. *There lay the snake in the basket!* He moved sluggishly at first, but even as she turned round and round, jumped up and down in an insanity of fear, he began to stir vigorously. She saw him pouring his awful beauty from the basket upon the bed, then she seized the lamp and ran as fast as she could to the kitchen. The wind from the open door blew out the light and the darkness added to her terror. She sped to the darkness of the yard, slamming the door after her before she thought to set down the lamp. She did not feel safe even on the ground, so she climbed up in the hay barn.

There for an hour or more she lay sprawled upon the hay a gibbering wreck. 90

Finally she grew quiet, and after that came coherent thought. With this stalked through her a cold, bloody rage. Hours of this. A period of introspection, a space of retrospection, then a mixture of both. Out of this an awful calm.

"Well, Ah done de bes' Ah could. If things ain't right, Gawd knows tain't mah fault."

She went to sleep—a twitch sleep—and woke up to a faint gray sky. There was a loud hollow sound below. She peered out. Sykes was at the woodpile, demolishing a wire-covered box.

He hurried to the kitchen door, but hung outside there some minutes before he entered, and stood some minutes more inside before he closed it after him.

The gray in the sky was spreading. Delia descended without fear now, and 95 crouched beneath the low bedroom window. The drawn shade shut out the dawn, shut in the night. But the thin walls held back no sound.

"Dat ol' scratch is woke up now!" She mused at the tremendous whirr inside, which every woodsman knows, is one of the sound illusions. The rattler is a ventriloquist. His whirr sounds to the right, to the left, straight ahead, behind, close under foot—everywhere but where it is. Woe to him who guesses wrong unless he is prepared to hold up his end of the argument! Sometimes he strikes without rattling at all.

Inside, Sykes heard nothing until he knocked a pot lid off the stove while trying to reach the match-safe in the dark. He had emptied his pockets at Bertha's.

The snake seemed to wake up under the stove and Sykes made a quick leap into the bedroom. In spite of the gin he had had, his head was clearing now.

"Mah Gawd!" he chattered, "ef Ah could on'y strack uh light!"

The rattling ceased for a moment as he stood paralyzed. He waited. It 100 seemed that the snake waited also.

"Oh, fuh de light! Ah thought he'd be too sick"—Sykes was muttering to himself when the whirr began again, closer, right underfoot this time. Long before this, Sykes' ability to think had been flattened down to primitive instinct and he leaped—onto the bed.

Outside Delia heard a cry that might have come from a maddened chimpanzee, a stricken gorilla. All the terror, all the horror, all the rage that man possibly could express, without a recognizable human sound.

A tremendous stir inside there, another series of animal screams, the intermittent whirr of the reptile. The shade torn violently down from the window, letting in the red dawn, a huge brown hand seizing the window stick, great dull blows upon the wooden floor punctuating the gibberish of sound long after the rattle of the snake had abruptly subsided. All this Delia could see and hear from her place beneath the window, and it made her ill. She crept over to the four o'clocks and stretched herself on the cool earth to recover.

She lay there. "Delia, Delia!" She could hear Sykes calling in a most despairing tone as one who expected no answer. The sun crept on up, and he called. Delia could not move—her legs had gone flabby. She never moved, he called, and the sun kept rising.

"Mah Gawd!" She heard him moan, "Mah Gawd fum Heben!" She heard 105 him stumbling about and got up from her flower-bed. The sun was growing warm. As she approached the door she heard him call out hopefully, "Delia, is dat you Ah heah?"

She saw him on his hands and knees as soon as she reached the door. He crept an inch or two toward her—all that he was able, and she saw his horribly swollen neck and his one open eye shining with hope. A surge of pity too strong to support bore her away from that eye that must, could not, fail to see the tubs. He would see the lamp. Orlando with its doctors was too far. She could scarcely reach the chinaberry tree, where she waited in the growing heat while inside she knew the cold river was creeping up and up to extinguish that eye which must know by now that she knew.

FOR ANALYSIS

1. What purpose do the men on the porch serve in the story? How are we supposed to take their opinions on Delia and Sykes?

2. While this story is about an unfortunate situation, the **tone** is not uniformly grave. How does Hurston manipulate tone? What are the effects of her choice to mix it up?

3. How do you feel about Delia's actions at the end of the story? Do you blame her? Has her love turned to hate, or does she still hope for love?

MAKING CONNECTIONS

Think about this story in connection to a very different story, Flannery O'Connor's "A Good Man Is Hard to Find" (p. 138). Both stories feature religious belief prominently, though in very different ways. How does belief inform each story? How do the characters relate to it?

WRITING TOPICS

1. One of the men on the porch says, "Tain't no law on earth dat kin make a man be decent if it ain't in 'im" (para. 40). Reflect on the nature of decentness, with special attention to its source. Do you think people are inherently decent or not? Or do you think the circumstances of their lives play a part in shaping their characters?

2. Stories are seldom written using **dialect** anymore. Why do you think that is? What do you think of Hurston's use of dialect?

RAYMOND CARVER (1938–1988)

WHAT WE TALK ABOUT
WHEN WE TALK ABOUT LOVE 1981

My friend Mel McGinnis was talking. Mel McGinnis is a cardiologist, and sometimes that gives him the right.

The four of us were sitting around his kitchen table drinking gin. Sunlight filled the kitchen from the big window behind the sink. There were Mel and me and his second wife, Teresa—Terri, we called her—and my wife, Laura. We lived in Albuquerque then. But we were all from somewhere else.

There was an ice bucket on the table. The gin and the tonic water kept going around, and we somehow got on the subject of love. Mel thought real love was nothing less than spiritual love. He said he'd spent five years in a seminary before quitting to go to medical school. He said he still looked back on those years in the seminary as the most important years in his life.

Terri said the man she lived with before she lived with Mel loved her so much he tried to kill her. Then Terri said, "He beat me up one night. He dragged me around the living room by my ankles. He kept saying, 'I love you, I love you, you bitch.' He went on dragging me around the living room. My head kept knocking on things." Terri looked around the table. "What do you do with love like that?"

She was a bone-thin woman with a pretty face, dark eyes, and brown hair 5 that hung down her back. She liked necklaces made of turquoise, and long pendant earrings.

"My God, don't be silly. That's not love, and you know it," Mel said. "I don't know what you'd call it, but I sure know you wouldn't call it love."

"Say what you want to, but I know it was," Terri said. "It may sound crazy to you, but it's true just the same. People are different, Mel. Sure, sometimes he may have acted crazy. Okay. But he loved me. In his own way maybe, but he loved me. There was love there, Mel. Don't say there wasn't."

Mel let out his breath. He held his glass and turned to Laura and me. "The man threatened to kill me," Mel said. He finished his drink and reached for the gin bottle. "Terri's a romantic. Terri's of the kick-me-so-I'll-know-you-love-me school. Terri, hon, don't look that way." Mel reached across the table and touched Terri's cheek with his fingers. He grinned at her.

"Now he wants to make up," Terri said.

"Make up what?" Mel said. "What is there to make up? I know what I know. 10 That's all."

"How'd we get started on this subject, anyway?" Terri said. She raised her glass and drank from it. "Mel always has love on his mind," she said. "Don't you, honey?" She smiled, and I thought that was the last of it.

"I just wouldn't call Ed's behavior love. That's all I'm saying, honey," Mel said. "What about you guys?" Mel said to Laura and me. "Does that sound like love to you?"

"I'm the wrong person to ask," I said. "I didn't even know the man. I've only heard his name mentioned in passing. I wouldn't know. You'd have to know the particulars. But I think what you're saying is that love is an absolute."

Mel said, "The kind of love I'm talking about is. The kind of love I'm talking about, you don't try to kill people."

Laura said, "I don't know anything about Ed, or anything about the situa- 15 tion. But who can judge anyone else's situation?"

I touched the back of Laura's hand. She gave me a quick smile. I picked up Laura's hand. It was warm, the nails polished, perfectly manicured. I encircled the broad wrist with my fingers, and I held her.

"When I left, he drank rat poison," Terri said. She clasped her arms with her hands. "They took him to the hospital in Sante Fe. That's where we lived then, about ten miles out. They saved his life. But his gums went crazy from it. I mean they pulled away from his teeth. After that, his teeth stood out like fangs. My God," Terri said. She waited a minute, then let go of her arms and picked up her glass.

"What people won't do!" Laura said.

"He's out of the action now," Mel said. "He's dead."

Mel handed me the saucer of limes. I took a section, squeezed it over my 20 drink, and stirred the ice cubes with my finger.

"It gets worse," Terri said. "He shot himself in the mouth. But he bungled that too. Poor Ed," she said. Terri shook her head.

"Poor Ed nothing," Mel said. "He was dangerous."

Mel was forty-five years old. He was tall and rangy with curly soft hair. His face and arms were brown from the tennis he played. When he was sober, his gestures, all his movements, were precise, very careful.

"He did love me though, Mel. Grant me that," Terri said. "That's all I'm asking. He didn't love me the way you love me. I'm not saying that. But he loved me. You can grant me that, can't you?"

"What do you mean, he bungled it?" I said. 25

Laura leaned forward with her glass. She put her elbows on the table and held her glass in both hands. She glanced from Mel to Terri and waited with a look of bewilderment on her open face, as if amazed that such things happened to people you were friendly with.

"How'd he bungle it when he killed himself?" I said.

"I'll tell you what happened," Mel said. "He took this twenty-two pistol he'd bought to threaten Terri and me with. Oh, I'm serious, the man was always threatening. You should have seen the way we lived in those days. Like fugitives. I even bought a gun myself. Can you believe it? A guy like me? But I did. I bought one for self-defense and carried it in the glove compartment. Sometimes I'd have to leave the apartment in the middle of the night. To go to the hospital, you know? Terri and I weren't married then, and my first wife had the house and kids, the dog, everything, and Terri and I were living in this apartment here. Sometimes, as I say, I'd get a call in the middle of the night and have to go in to the hospital at two or three in the morning. It'd be dark out there in the parking lot, and I'd break into a sweat before I could even get to my car. I never knew if he was going to come up out of the shrubbery or from behind a car and start shooting. I mean, the man was crazy. He was capable of wiring a bomb, anything. He used to call my service at all hours and say he needed to talk to the doctor, and when I'd return the call, he'd say, 'Son of a bitch, your days are numbered.' Little things like that. It was scary, I'm telling you."

"I still feel sorry for him," Terri said.

"It sounds like a nightmare," Laura said. "But what exactly happened after 30 he shot himself?"

Laura is a legal secretary. We'd met in a professional capacity. Before we knew it, it was a courtship. She's thirty-five, three years younger than I am. In addition to being in love, we like each other and enjoy one another's company. She's easy to be with.

"What happened?" Laura said.

Mel said, "He shot himself in the mouth in his room. Someone heard the shot and told the manager. They came in with a passkey, saw what had happened, and called an ambulance. I happened to be there when they brought him in, alive but past recall. The man lived for three days. His head swelled up to twice the size of a normal head. I'd never seen anything like it, and I hope I never do again. Terri wanted to go in and sit with him when she found out about it. We had a fight over it. I didn't think she should see him like that. I didn't think she should see him, and I still don't."

"Who won the fight?" Laura said.

"I was in the room with him when he died," Terri said. "He never came up 35 out of it. But I sat with him. He didn't have anyone else."

"He was dangerous," Mel said. "If you call that love, you can have it."

"It was love," Terri said. "Sure, it's abnormal in most people's eyes. But he was willing to die for it. He did die for it."

"I sure as hell wouldn't call it love," Mel said. "I mean, no one knows what he did it for. I've seen a lot of suicides, and I couldn't say anyone ever knew what they did it for."

Mel put his hands behind his neck and tilted his chair back. "I'm not interested in that kind of love," he said. "If that's love, you can have it."

Terri said, "We were afraid. Mel even made a will out and wrote to his 40 brother in California who used to be a Green Beret. Mel told him who to look for if something happened to him."

Terri drank from her glass. She said, "But Mel's right—we lived like fugitives. We were afraid. Mel was, weren't you, honey? I even called the police at one point, but they were no help. They said they couldn't do anything until Ed actually did something. Isn't that a laugh?" Terri said.

She poured the last of the gin into her glass and waggled the bottle. Mel got up from the table and went to the cupboard. He took down another bottle.

"Well, Nick and I know what love is," Laura said. "For us, I mean," Laura said. She bumped my knee with her knee. "You're supposed to say something now," Laura said, and turned her smile on me.

For an answer, I took Laura's hand and raised it to my lips. I made a big production out of kissing her hand. Everyone was amused.

"We're lucky," I said.

"You guys," Terri said. "Stop that now. You're making me sick. You're still on the honeymoon, for God's sake. You're still gaga, for crying out loud. Just wait. How long have you been together now? How long has it been? A year? Longer than a year?"

"Going on a year and a half," Laura said, flushed and smiling.

"Oh, now," Terri said. "Wait a while."

She held her drink and gazed at Laura.

"I'm only kidding," Terri said.

Mel opened the gin and went around the table with the bottle.

"Here, you guys," he said. "Let's have a toast. I want to propose a toast. A toast to love. To true love," Mel said.

We touched glasses.

"To love," we said.

Outside in the backyard, one of the dogs began to bark. The leaves of the aspen that leaned past the window ticked against the glass. The afternoon sun was like a presence in this room, the spacious light of ease and generosity. We could have been anywhere, somewhere enchanted. We raised our glasses again and grinned at each other like children who had agreed on something forbidden.

"I'll tell you what real love is," Mel said. "I mean, I'll give you a good example. And then you can draw your own conclusions." He poured more gin into his glass. He added an ice cube and a sliver of lime. We waited and sipped our drinks. Laura and I touched knees again. I put a hand on her warm thigh and left it there.

"What do any of us really know about love?" Mel said. "It seems to me we're just beginners at love. We say we love each other and we do, I don't doubt it. I love Terri and Terri loves me, and you guys love each other too. You know the kind of love I'm talking about now. Physical love, that impulse that drives you to someone special, as well as love of the other person's being, his or her essence, as it were. Carnal love and, well, call it sentimental love, the day-to-day caring about the other person. But sometimes I have a hard time accounting for the fact that I must have loved my first wife too. But I did, I know I did. So I suppose I am like Terri in that regard. Terri and Ed." He thought about it and then he went on. "There was a time when I thought I loved my first wife more than life itself. But now I hate her guts. I do. How do you explain that? What happened to that love? What happened to it, is what I'd like to know. I wish someone could tell me. Then there's Ed. Okay, we're back to Ed. He loves Terri so much he tries to kill her and he winds up killing himself." Mel stopped talking and swallowed from his glass. "You guys have been together eighteen months and you love each other. It shows all over you. You glow with it. But you both loved other people before you met each other. You've both been married before, just like us. And you probably loved other people before that too, even. Terri and I have been together five years, been married for four. And the terrible thing, the terrible thing is, but the good thing too, the saving grace, you might say, is that if something happened to one of us—excuse me for saying this—but if something happened to one of us tomorrow I think the other one, the other person, would grieve for a while, you know, but then the surviving party would go out and love again, have someone else soon enough. All this, all of this love we're talking about, it would just be a memory. Maybe not even a memory. Am I wrong? Am I way off base? Because I want you to set me straight if you think I'm wrong. I want to know. I mean, I don't know anything, and I'm the first one to admit it."

"Mel, for God's sake," Terri said. She reached out and took hold of his wrist. "Are you getting drunk? Honey? Are you drunk?"

"Honey, I'm just talking," Mel said. "All right? I don't have to be drunk to say what I think. I mean, we're all just talking, right?" Mel said. He fixed his eyes on her.

"Sweetie, I'm not criticizing," Terri said.   60

She picked up her glass.

"I'm not on call today," Mel said. "Let me remind you of that. I am not on call," he said.

"Mel, we love you," Laura said.

Mel looked at Laura. He looked at her as if he could not place her, as if she was not the woman she was.

"Love you too, Laura," Mel said. "And you, Nick, love you too. You know   65 something?" Mel said. "You guys are our pals," Mel said.

He picked up his glass.

Mel said, "I was going to tell you about something. I mean, I was going to prove a point. You see, this happened a few months ago, but it's still going on right now, and it ought to make us feel ashamed when we talk like we know what we're talking about when we talk above love."

"Come on now," Terri said. "Don't talk like you're drunk if you're not drunk."

"Just shut up for once in your life," Mel said very quietly. "Will you do me a favor and do that for a minute? So as I was saying, there's this old couple who had this car wreck out on the interstate. A kid hit them and they were all torn to shit and nobody was giving them much chance to pull through."

Terri looked at us and then back at Mel. She seemed anxious, or maybe 70
that's too strong a word.

Mel was handing the bottle around the table.

"I was on call that night," Mel said. "It was May or maybe it was June. Terri
and I had just sat down to dinner when the hospital called. There'd been this
thing out on the interstate. Drunk kid, teenager, plowed his dad's pickup into
this camper with this old couple in it. They were up in their mid-seventies, that
couple. The kid—eighteen, nineteen, something—he was DOA. Taken the steering wheel through his sternum. The old couple, they were alive, you understand.
I mean, just barely. But they had everything. Multiple fractures, internal injuries,
hemorrhaging, contusions, lacerations, the works, and they each of them had
themselves concussions. They were in a bad way, believe me. And, of course, their
age was two strikes against them. I'd say she was worse off than he was. Ruptured
spleen along with everything else. Both kneecaps broken. But they'd been wearing their seatbelts and, God knows, that's what saved them for the time being."

"Folks, this is an advertisement for the National Safety Council," Terri said.
"This is your spokesman, Dr. Melvin R. McGinnis, talking." Terri laughed.
"Mel," she said, "sometimes you're just too much. But I love you, hon," she said.

"Honey, I love you," Mel said.

He leaned across the table. Terri met him halfway. They kissed. 75

"Terri's right," Mel said as he settled himself again. "Get those seatbelts on.
But seriously, they were in some shape, those oldsters. By the time I got down
there, the kid was dead, as I said. He was off in a corner, laid out on a gurney. I
took one look at the old couple and told the ER nurse to get me a neurologist
and an orthopedic man and a couple of surgeons down there right away."

He drank from his glass. "I'll try to keep this short," he said. "So we took
the two of them up to the OR and worked like fuck on them most of the night.
They had these incredible reserves, those two. You see that once in a while. So
we did everything that could be done, and toward morning we're giving them
a fifty-fifty chance, maybe less than that for her. So here they are, still alive the
next morning. So, okay, we move them into the ICU, which is where they both
kept plugging away at it for two weeks, hitting it better and better on all the
scopes. So we transfer them out to their own room."

Mel stopped talking. "Here," he said, "let's drink this cheapo gin the hell up.
Then we're going to dinner, right? Terri and I know a new place. That's where
we'll go, to this new place we know about. But we're not going until we finish
up this cut-rate, lousy gin."

Terri said, "We haven't actually eaten there yet. But it looks good. From the
outside, you know."

"I like food," Mel said. "If I had it to do all over again, I'd be a chef, you 80
know? Right, Terri?" Mel said.

He laughed. He fingered the ice in his glass.

"Terri knows," he said. "Terri can tell you. But let me say this. If I could come
back again in a different life, a different time and all, you know what? I'd like

to come back as a knight. You were pretty safe wearing all that armor. It was all right being a knight until gunpowder and muskets and pistols came along."

"Mel would like to ride a horse and carry a lance," Terri said.

"Carry a woman's scarf with you everywhere," Laura said.

"Or just a woman," Mel said.   85

"Shame on you," Laura said.

Terri said, "Suppose you came back as a serf. The serfs didn't have it so good in those days," Terri said.

"The serfs never had it good," Mel said. "But I guess even the knights were vessels to someone. Isn't that the way it worked? But then everyone is always a vessel to someone. Isn't that right? Terri? But what I liked about knights, besides their ladies, was that they had that suit of armor, you know, and they couldn't get hurt very easy. No cars in those days, you know? No drunk teenagers to tear into your ass."

"Vassals," Terri said.

"What?" Mel said.   90

"Vassals," Terri said. "They were called vassals, not vessels."

"Vassals, vessels," Mel said, "what the fuck's the difference? You knew what I meant anyway. All right," Mel said. "So I'm not educated. I learned my stuff. I'm a heart surgeon, sure, but I'm just a mechanic. I go in and I fuck around and I fix things. Shit," Mel said.

"Modesty doesn't become you," Terri said.

"He's just a humble sawbones," I said. "But sometimes they suffocated in all that armor, Mel. They'd even have heart attacks if it got too hot and they were too tired and worn out. I read somewhere that they'd fall off their horses and not be able to get up because they were too tired to stand with all that armor on them. They got trampled by their own horses sometimes."

"That's terrible," Mel said. "That's a terrible thing, Nicky. I guess they'd just   95
lay there and wait until somebody came along and made a shish kebab out of them."

"Some other vessel," Terri said.

"That's right," Mel said. "Some vassal would come along and spear the bastard in the name of love. Or whatever the fuck it was they fought over in those days."

"Same things we fight over these days," Terri said.

Laura said, "Nothing's changed."

The color was still high in Laura's cheeks. Her eyes were bright. She brought   100
her glass to her lips.

Mel poured himself another drink. He looked at the label closely as if studying a long row of numbers. Then he slowly put the bottle down on the table and slowly reached for the tonic water.

"What about the old couple?" Laura said. "You didn't finish that story you started."

Laura was having a hard time lighting her cigarette. Her matches kept going out.

The sunshine inside the room was different now, changing, getting thinner. But the leaves outside the window were still shimmering, and I stared at the pattern they made on the panes and on the Formica counter. They weren't the same patterns, of course.

"What about the old couple?" I said.   105

"Older but wiser," Terri said.

Mel stared at her.

Terri said, "Go on with your story, hon. I was only kidding. Then what happened?"

"Terri, sometimes," Mel said.

"Please, Mel," Terri said. "Don't always be so serious, sweetie. Can't you   110 take a joke?"

"Where's the joke?" Mel said.

He held his glass and gazed steadily at his wife.

"What happened?" Laura said.

Mel fastened his eyes on Laura. He said, "Laura, if I didn't have Terri and if I didn't love her so much, and if Nick wasn't my best friend, I'd fall in love with you, I'd carry you off, honey," he said.

"Tell your story," Terri said. "Then we'll go to that new place, okay?"   115

"Okay," Mel said. "Where was I?" he said. He stared at the table and then he began again.

"I dropped in to see each of them every day, sometimes twice a day if I was up doing other calls anyway. Casts and bandages, head to foot, the both of them. You know, you've seen it in the movies. That's just the way they looked, just like in the movies. Little eye-holes and nose-holes and mouth-holes. And she had to have her legs slung up on top of it. Well, the husband was very depressed for the longest while. Even after he found out that his wife was going to pull through, he was still very depressed. Not about the accident, though. I mean, the accident was one thing, but it wasn't everything. I'd get up to his mouth-hole, you know, and he'd say no, it wasn't the accident exactly but it was because he couldn't see her through his eye-holes. He said that was what was making him feel so bad. Can you imagine? I'm telling you, the man's heart was breaking because he couldn't turn his goddamn head and *see* his goddamn wife."

Mel looked around the table and shook his head at what he was going to say.

"I mean, it was killing the old fart just because he couldn't *look* at the fucking woman."

We all looked at Mel.   120

"Do you see what I'm saying?" he said.

Maybe we were a little drunk by then. I know it was hard keeping things in focus. The light was draining out of the room, going back through the window where it had come from. Yet nobody made a move to get up from the table to turn on the overhead light.

"Listen," Mel said. "Let's finish this fucking gin. There's about enough left here for one shooter all around. Then let's go eat. Let's go to the new place."

"He's depressed," Terri said. "Mel, why don't you take a pill?"

Mel shook his head. "I've taken everything there is."   125

"We all need a pill now and then," I said.

"Some people are born needing them," Terri said.

She was using her finger to rub at something on the table. Then she stopped rubbing.

"I think I want to call my kids," Mel said. "Is that all right with everybody? I'll call my kids," he said.

Terri said, "What if Marjorie answers the phone? You guys, you've heard us 130
on the subject of Marjorie? Honey, you know you don't want to talk to Marjorie. It'll make you feel even worse."

"I don't want to talk to Marjorie," Mel said. "But I want to talk to my kids."

"There isn't a day goes by that Mel doesn't say he wishes she'd get married again. Or else die," Terri said. "For one thing," Terri said, "she's bankrupting us. Mel says it's just to spite him that she won't get married again. She has a boyfriend who lives with her and the kids, so Mel is supporting the boyfriend too."

"She's allergic to bees," Mel said. "If I'm not praying she'll get married again, I'm praying she'll get herself stung to death by a swarm of fucking bees."

"Shame on you," Laura said.

"Bzzzzzzz," Mel said, turning his fingers into bees and buzzing them at Ter- 135
ri's throat. Then he let his hands drop all the way to his sides.

"She's vicious," Mel said. "Sometimes I think I'll go up there dressed like a beekeeper. You know, that hat that's like a helmet with the plate that comes down over your face, the big gloves, and the padded coat? I'll knock on the door and let loose a hive of bees in the house. But first I'd make sure the kids were out, of course."

He crossed one leg over the other. It seemed to take him a lot of time to do it. Then he put both feet on the floor and leaned forward, elbows on the table, his chin cupped in his hands.

"Maybe I won't call the kids, after all. Maybe it isn't such a hot idea. Maybe we'll just go eat. How does that sound?"

"Sounds fine to me," I said. "Eat or not eat. Or keep drinking. I could head right on out into the sunset."

"What does that mean, honey?" Laura said.   140

"It just means what I said," I said. "It means I could just keep going. That's all it means."

"I could eat something myself," Laura said. "I don't think I've ever been so hungry in my life. Is there something to nibble on?"

"I'll put out some cheese and crackers," Terri said.

But Terri just sat there. She did not get up to get anything.

Mel turned his glass over. He spilled it out on the table.   145

"Gin's gone," Mel said.

Terri said, "Now what?"

I could hear my heart beating. I could hear everyone's heart. I could hear the human noise we sat there making, not one of us moving, not even when the room went dark.

FOR ANALYSIS

1. What is your reaction to Mel? Is he likable? What does his profession—a scientist and a cardiologist—represent?

2. What is the significance of Mel's account of the old couple injured in the car accident?

3. Do Mel's feelings about his ex-wife parallel Ed's feelings about Terri? Explain.

MAKING CONNECTIONS

Compare the marriages in this story, past and present, to the relationship between Sykes and Delia in Zora Neale Hurston's "Sweat" (p. 840). Think in terms of not only love and hate but also any other terms you can imagine. Are there some that are better or worse? What do "better" and "worse" mean to you, in this context?

WRITING TOPIC

In an essay, examine the various relationships in the story: Nick and Laura, Mel and Terri, Terri and Ed, Mel and his ex-wife Marjorie, and the injured old couple. How are they similar, and how are they different? Do they all have anything in common? Conclude your essay with a comment on "what we talk about when we talk about love."

JOYCE CAROL OATES (B. 1938)

WHERE ARE YOU GOING, WHERE HAVE YOU BEEN? 1970

FOR BOB DYLAN[1]

Her name was Connie. She was fifteen and she had a quick nervous giggling habit of craning her neck to glance into mirrors, or checking other people's faces to make sure her own was all right. Her mother, who noticed everything and knew everything and who hadn't much reason any longer to look at her own face, always scolded Connie about it. "Stop gawking at yourself, who are you? You think you're so pretty?" she would say. Connie would raise her eyebrows at these familiar complaints and look right through her mother, into a shadowy vision of herself as she was right at that moment: she knew she was pretty and that was everything. Her mother had been pretty once too, if you could believe those old snapshots in the album, but now her looks were gone and that was why she was always after Connie.

"Why don't you keep your room clean like your sister? How've you got your hair fixed—what the hell stinks? Hair spray? You don't see your sister using that junk."

Her sister June was twenty-four and still lived at home. She was a secretary in the high school Connie attended, and if that wasn't bad enough—with her in the same building—she was so plain and chunky and steady that Connie had to hear her praised all the time by her mother and her mother's sisters. June did this, June did that, she saved money and helped clean the house and cooked and Connie couldn't do a thing, her mind was all filled with trashy daydreams. Their father was away at work most of the time and when he came home he wanted supper and he read the newspaper at supper and after supper he went to bed. He didn't bother talking much to them, but around his bent head Connie's mother kept picking at her until Connie wished her mother was dead and she herself was dead and it was all over. "She makes me want to throw up sometimes," she complained to her friends. She had a high, breathless, amused voice which made everything she said sound a little forced, whether it was sincere or not.

There was one good thing: June went places with girl friends of hers, girls who were just as plain and steady as she, and so when Connie wanted to do that her mother had no objections. The father of Connie's best girl friend drove the girls the three miles to town and left them off at a shopping plaza, so

---

[1] Bob Dylan (b. 1941) is an influential folk-rock musician and songwriter. Oates has commented that she had in mind Dylan's song "It's All Over Now, Baby Blue" when she wrote this story.

that they could walk through the stores or go to a movie, and when he came to pick them up again at eleven he never bothered to ask what they had done.

They must have been familiar sights, walking around that shopping plaza 5 in their shorts and flat ballerina slippers that always scuffed the sidewalk, with charm bracelets jingling on their thin wrists; they would lean together to whisper and laugh secretly if someone passed by who amused or interested them. Connie had long dark blond hair that drew anyone's eye to it, and she wore part of it pulled up on her head and puffed out and the rest of it she let fall down her back. She wore a pull-over jersey blouse that looked one way when she was at home and another way when she was away from home. Everything about her had two sides to it, one for home and one for anywhere that was not home: her walk that could be childlike and bobbing, or languid enough to make anyone think she was hearing music in her head, her mouth which was pale and smirking most of the time, but bright and pink on these evenings out, her laugh which was cynical and drawling at home—"Ha, ha, very funny"—but high-pitched and nervous anywhere else, like the jingling of the charms on her bracelet.

Sometimes they did go shopping or to a movie, but sometimes they went across the highway, ducking fast across the busy road, to a drive-in restaurant where older kids hung out. The restaurant was shaped like a big bottle, though squatter than a real bottle, and on its cap was a revolving figure of a grinning boy who held a hamburger aloft. One night in mid-summer they ran across, breathless with daring, and right away someone leaned out a car window and invited them over, but it was just a boy from high school they didn't like. It made them feel good to be able to ignore him. They went up through the maze of parked and cruising cars to the bright-lit, fly-infested restaurant, their faces pleased and expectant as if they were entering a sacred building that loomed out of the night to give them what haven and what blessing they yearned for. They sat at the counter and crossed their legs at the ankles, their thin shoulders rigid with excitement, and listened to the music that made everything so good: the music was always in the background like music at a church service, it was something to depend upon.

A boy named Eddie came in to talk with them. He sat backwards on his stool, turning himself jerkily around in semi-circles and then stopping and turning again, and after a while he asked Connie if she would like something to eat. She said she did and so she tapped her friend's arm on her way out—her friend pulled her face up into a brave droll look—and Connie said she would meet her at eleven, across the way. "I just hate to leave her like that," Connie said earnestly, but the boy said that she wouldn't be alone for long. So they went out to his car and on the way Connie couldn't help but let her eyes wander over the windshields and faces all around her, her face gleaming with a joy that had nothing to do with Eddie or even this place; it might have been the music. She drew her shoulders up and sucked in her breath with the pure pleasure of being alive, and just at that moment she happened to glance at a face just a few feet from hers. It was a boy with shaggy black hair, in a convertible jalopy painted gold. He stared at her and then his lips widened into a grin. Connie slit her eyes at him and turned away, but she couldn't help glancing back and there he was still watching her. He wagged a finger and laughed and said, "Gonna get you, baby," and Connie turned away without Eddie noticing anything.

She spent three hours with him, at the restaurant where they ate hamburgers and drank Cokes in wax cups that were always sweating, and then down an alley a mile or so away, and when he left her off at five to eleven only the movie house was still open at the plaza. Her girl friend was there, talking with a boy. When Connie came up the two girls smiled at each other and Connie said, "How was the movie?" and the girl said, "*You* should know." They rode off with the girl's father, sleepy and pleased, and Connie couldn't help but look at the darkened shopping plaza with its big empty parking lot and its signs that were faded and ghostly now, and over at the drive-in restaurant where cars were still circling tirelessly. She couldn't hear the music at this distance.

Next morning June asked her how the movie was and Connie said, "So-so."

She and that girl and occasionally another girl went several times a week 10 that way, and the rest of the time Connie spent around the house—it was summer vacation—getting in her mother's way and thinking, dreaming, about the boys she met. But all the boys fell back and dissolved into a single face that was not even a face, but an idea, a feeling, mixed up with the urgent insistent pounding of the music and the humid night air of July. Connie's mother kept dragging her back to the daylight by finding things for her to do or saying, suddenly, "What's this about the Pettinger girl?"

And Connie would say nervously, "Oh, her. That dope." She always drew thick clear lines between herself and such girls, and her mother was simple and kindly enough to believe her. Her mother was so simple, Connie thought, that it was maybe cruel to fool her so much. Her mother went scuffling around the house in old bedroom slippers and complained over the telephone to one sister about the other, then the other called up and the two of them complained about the third one. If June's name was mentioned her mother's tone was approving, and if Connie's name was mentioned it was disapproving. This did not really mean she disliked Connie and actually Connie thought that her mother preferred her to June because she was prettier, but the two of them kept up a pretense of exasperation, a sense that they were tugging and struggling over something of little value to either of them. Sometimes, over coffee, they were almost friends, but something would come up—some vexation that was like a fly buzzing suddenly around their heads—and their faces went hard with contempt.

One Sunday Connie got up at eleven—none of them bothered with church—and washed her hair so that it could dry all day long, in the sun. Her parents and sister were going to a barbecue at an aunt's house and Connie said no, she wasn't interested, rolling her eyes to let her mother know just what she thought of it. "Stay home alone then," her mother said sharply. Connie sat out back in a lawn chair and watched them drive away, her father quiet and bald, hunched around so that he could back the car out, her mother with a look that was still angry and not at all softened through the windshield, and in the back seat poor old June all dressed up as if she didn't know what a barbecue was, with all the running yelling kids and the flies. Connie sat with her eyes closed in the sun, dreaming and dazed with the warmth about her as if this were a kind of love, the caresses of love, and her mind slipped over onto thoughts of the boy she had been with the night before and how nice he had been, how sweet it always was, not the way someone like June would suppose but sweet, gentle, the way it was in movies and promised in songs; and when she opened her eyes she hardly knew where she was, the back yard ran off into weeds and a fence-line of trees and behind it the sky was perfectly blue and still. The asbestos "ranch house" that was now three years old still startled her—it looked small. She shook her head as if to get awake.

It was too hot. She went inside the house and turned on the radio to drown out the quiet. She sat on the edge of her bed, barefoot, and listened for an hour and a half to a program called XYZ Sunday Jamboree, record after record of hard, fast, shrieking songs she sang along with, interspersed by exclamations from "Bobby King": "An' look here you girls at Napoleon's—Son and Charley want you to pay real close attention to this song coming up!"

And Connie paid close attention herself, bathed in a glow of slow-pulsed joy that seemed to rise mysteriously out of the music itself and lay languidly about the airless little room, breathed in and breathed out with each gentle rise and fall of her chest.

After a while she heard a car coming up the drive. She sat up at once, 15 startled, because it couldn't be her father so soon. The gravel kept crunching all the way in from the road—the driveway was long—and Connie ran to the window. It was a car she didn't know. It was an open jalopy, painted a bright gold that caught the sunlight opaquely. Her heart began to pound and her fingers snatched at her hair, checking it, and she whispered "Christ. Christ," wondering how bad she looked. The car came to a stop at the side door and the horn sounded four short taps as if this were a signal Connie knew.

She went into the kitchen and approached the door slowly, then hung out the screen door, her bare toes curling down off the step. There were two boys in the car and now she recognized the driver: he had shaggy, shabby black hair that looked crazy as a wig and he was grinning at her.

"I ain't late, am I?" he said.

"Who the hell do you think you are?" Connie said.

"Toldja I'd be out, didn't I?"

"I don't even know who you are." 20

She spoke sullenly, careful to show no interest or pleasure, and he spoke in a fast bright monotone. Connie looked past him to the other boy, taking her time. He had fair brown hair, with a lock that fell onto his forehead. His sideburns gave him a fierce, embarrassed look, but so far he hadn't even bothered to glance at her. Both boys wore sunglasses. The driver's glasses were metallic and mirrored everything in miniature.

"You wanta come for a ride?" he said.

Connie smirked and let her hair fall loose over one shoulder.

"Don'tcha like my car? New paint job," he said. "Hey."

"What?" 25

"You're cute."

She pretended to fidget, chasing flies away from the door.

"Don'tcha believe me, or what?" he said.

"Look, I don't even know who you are," Connie said in disgust.

"Hey, Ellie's got a radio, see. Mine's broke down." He lifted his friend's arm 30 and showed her the little transistor the boy was holding, and now Connie began to hear the music. It was the same program that was playing inside the house.

"Bobby King?" she said.

"I listen to him all the time. I think he's great."

"He's kind of great," Connie said reluctantly.

"Listen, that guy's *great*. He knows where the action is."

Connie blushed a little, because the glasses made it impossible for her to see 35 just what this boy was looking at. She couldn't decide if she liked him or if he was just a jerk, and so she dawdled in the doorway and wouldn't come down or go back inside. She said, "What's all that stuff painted on your car?"

"Can'tcha read it?" He opened the door very carefully, as if he was afraid it might fall off. He slid out just as carefully, planting his feet firmly on the ground, the tiny metallic world in his glasses slowing down like gelatine hardening and in the midst of it Connie's bright green blouse. "This here is my name, to begin with," he said. ARNOLD FRIEND was written in tarlike black letters on the side, with a drawing of a round grinning face that reminded Connie of a pumpkin, except it wore sunglasses. "I wanta introduce myself, I'm Arnold Friend and that's my real name and I'm gonna be your friend, honey, and inside the car's Ellie Oscar, he's kinda shy." Ellie brought his transistor radio up to his shoulder and balanced it there. "Now these numbers are a secret code, honey," Arnold Friend explained. He read off the numbers 33, 19, 17 and raised his eyebrows at her to see what she thought of that, but she didn't think much of it. The left rear fender had been smashed and around it was written on the gleaming gold background: DONE BY CRAZY WOMAN DRIVER. Connie had to laugh at that. Arnold Friend was pleased at her laughter and looked up at her. "Around the other side's a lot more—you wanta come and see them?"

"No."

"Why not?"

"Why should I?"

"Don'tcha wanta see what's on the car? Don'tcha wanta go for a ride?" 40

"I don't know."

"Why not?"

"I got things to do."

"Like what?"

"Things." 45

He laughed as if she had said something funny. He slapped his thighs. He was standing in a strange way, leaning back against the car as if he were balancing himself. He wasn't tall, only an inch or so taller than she would be if she came down to him. Connie liked the way he was dressed, which was the way all of them dressed: tight faded jeans stuffed into black, scuffed boots, a belt that pulled his waist in and showed how lean he was, and a white pull-over shirt that was a little soiled and showed the hard small muscles of his arms and shoulders. He looked as if he possibly did hard work, lifting and carrying things. Even his neck looked muscular. And his face was a familiar face, some-how: the jaw and chin and cheeks slightly darkened, because he hadn't shaved for a day or two, and the nose long and hawk-like, sniffing as if she were a treat he was going to gobble up and it was all a joke.

"Connie, you ain't telling the truth. This is your day set aside for a ride with me and you know it," he said, still laughing. The way he straightened and recovered from his fit of laughing showed that it had been all fake.

"How do you know what my name is?" she said suspiciously.

"It's Connie."

"Maybe and maybe not."   50

"I know my Connie," he said, wagging his finger. Now she remembered him even better, back at the restaurant, and her cheeks warmed at the thought of how she sucked in her breath just at the moment she passed him—how she must have looked to him. And he had remembered her. "Ellie and I came out here especially for you," he said. "Ellie can sit in back. How about it?"

"Where?"

"Where what?"

"Where're we going?"

He looked at her. He took off the sunglasses and she saw how pale the skin   55
around his eyes was, like holes that were not in shadow but instead in light. His eyes were chips of broken glass that catch the light in an amiable way. He smiled. It was as if the idea of going for a ride somewhere, to some place, was a new idea to him.

"Just for a ride, Connie sweetheart."

"I never said my name was Connie," she said.

"But I know what it is. I know your name and all about you, lots of things," Arnold Friend said. He had not moved yet but stood still leaning back against the side of his jalopy. "I took a special interest in you, such a pretty girl, and found out all about you like I know your parents and sister are gone somewheres and I know where and how long they're going to be gone, and I know who you were with last night, and your best girl friend's name is Betty. Right?"

He spoke in a simple lilting voice, exactly as if he were reciting the words to a song. His smile assured her that everything was fine. In the car, Ellie turned up the volume on his radio and did not bother to look around at them.

"Ellie can sit in the back seat," Arnold Friend said. He indicated his friend   60
with a casual jerk of his chin, as if Ellie did not count and she should not bother with him.

"How'd you find out all that stuff?" Connie said.

"Listen: Betty Schultz and Tony Fitch and Jimmy Pettinger and Nancy Pettinger," he said, in a chant. "Raymond Stanley and Bob Hutter—"

"Do you know all those kids?"

"I know everybody."

"Look, you're kidding. You're not from around here."   65

"Sure."

"But—how come we never saw you before?"

"Sure you saw me before," he said. He looked down at his boots, as if he were a little offended. "You just don't remember."

"I guess I'd remember you," Connie said.

"Yeah?" He looked up at this, beaming. He was pleased. He began to mark   70
time with the music from Ellie's radio, tapping his fists lightly together. Connie looked away from his smile to the car, which was painted so bright it almost hurt her eyes to look at it. She looked at that name, ARNOLD FRIEND. And up at the front fender was an expression that was familiar—MAN THE FLYING SAUCERS. It was an expression kids had used the year before, but didn't use this year. She looked at it for a while as if the words meant something to her that she did not yet know.

"What're you thinking about? Huh?" Arnold Friend demanded. "Not worried about your hair blowing around in the car, are you?"

"No."

"Think I maybe can't drive good?"

"How do I know?"

"You're a hard girl to handle. How come?" he said. "Don't you know I'm   75
your friend? Didn't you see me put my sign in the air when you walked by?"

"What sign?"

"My sign." And he drew an X in the air, leaning out toward her. They were maybe ten feet apart. After his hand fell back to his side, the X was still in the air, almost visible. Connie let the screen door close and stood perfectly still inside it, listening to the music from her radio and the boy's blend together. She stared at Arnold Friend. He stood there so stiffly relaxed, pretending to be relaxed, with one hand idly on the door handle as if he were keeping himself up that way and had no intention of ever moving again. She recognized most things about him, the tight jeans that showed his thighs and buttocks and the greasy leather boots and the tight shirt, and even that slippery friendly smile of his, that sleepy dreamy smile that all the boys used to get across ideas they didn't want to put into words. She recognized all this and also the singsong way he talked, slightly mocking, kidding, but serious and a little melancholy, and she recognized the way he tapped one fist against the other in homage to the perpetual music behind him. But all these things did not come together.

She said suddenly, "Hey, how old are you?"

His smile faded. She could see then that he wasn't a kid, he was much older—thirty, maybe more. At this knowledge her heart began to pound faster.

"That's a crazy thing to ask. Can'tcha see I'm your own age?"   80

"Like hell you are."

"Or maybe a couple years older, I'm eighteen."

"Eighteen?" she said doubtfully.

He grinned to reassure her and lines appeared at the corners of his mouth. His teeth were big and white. He grinned so broadly his eyes became slits and she saw how thick the lashes were, thick and black as if painted with a black tarlike material. Then he seemed to become embarrassed, abruptly, and looked over his shoulder at Ellie. "*Him*, he's crazy," he said. "Ain't he a riot, he's a nut, a real character." Ellie was still listening to the music. His sunglasses told nothing about what he was thinking. He wore a bright orange shirt unbuttoned halfway to show his chest, which was a pale, bluish chest and not muscular like Arnold Friend's. His shirt collar was turned up all around and the very tips of the collar pointed out past his chin as if they were protecting him. He was pressing the transistor radio up against his ear and sat there in a kind of daze, right in the sun.

"He's kinda strange," Connie said.   85

"Hey, she says you're kinda strange! Kinda strange!" Arnold Friend cried. He pounded on the car to get Ellie's attention. Ellie turned for the first time and Connie saw with shock that he wasn't a kid either—he had a fair, hairless face, cheeks reddened slightly as if the veins grew too close to the surface of his skin, the face of a forty-year-old baby. Connie felt a wave of dizziness rise in her at this sight and she stared at him as if waiting for something to change the shock of the moment, make it all right again. Ellie's lips kept shaping words, mumbling along, with the words blasting in his ear.

"Maybe you two better go away," Connie said faintly.

"What? How come?" Arnold Friend cried. "We come out here to take you for a ride. It's Sunday." He had the voice of the man on the radio now. It was the same voice, Connie thought. "Don'tcha know it's Sunday all day and honey, no matter who you were with last night today you're with Arnold Friend and don't you forget it!—Maybe you better step out here," he said, and this last was in a different voice. It was a little flatter, as if the heat was finally getting to him.

"No. I got things to do."   90

"Hey."

"You two better leave."

"We ain't leaving until you come with us."

"Like hell I am—"

"Connie, don't fool around with me. I mean, I mean, don't fool *around*," he said, shaking his head. He laughed incredulously. He placed his sunglasses on top of his head, carefully, as if he were indeed wearing a wig, and brought the stems down behind his ears. Connie stared at him, another wave of dizziness and fear rising in her so that for a moment he wasn't even in focus but was just a blur, standing there against his gold car, and she had the idea that he had driven up the driveway all right but had come from nowhere before that and belonged nowhere and that everything about him and even about the music that was so familiar to her was only half real.

"If my father comes and sees you—"

"He ain't coming. He's at the barbecue."   95

"How do you know that?"

"Aunt Tillie's. Right now they're—uh—they're drinking. Sitting around," he said vaguely, squinting as if he were staring all the way to town and over to Aunt Tillie's backyard. Then the vision seemed to get clear and he nodded energetically. "Yeah. Sitting around. There's your sister in a blue dress, huh? And high heels, the poor sad bitch—nothing like you, sweetheart! And your mother's helping some fat woman with the corn, they're cleaning the corn—husking the corn—"

"What fat woman?" Connie cried.

"How do I know what fat woman. I don't know every goddam fat woman in 100 the world!" Arnold Friend laughed.

"Oh, that's Mrs. Hornby. . . . Who invited her?" Connie said. She felt a little light-headed. Her breath was coming quickly.

"She's too fat. I don't like them fat. I like them the way you are, honey," he said, smiling sleepily at her. They stared at each other for awhile, through the screen door. He said softly, "Now what you're going to do is this: you're going to come out that door. You're going to sit up front with me and Ellie's going to sit in the back, the hell with Ellie, right? This isn't Ellie's date. You're my date. I'm your lover, honey."

"What? You're crazy—"

"Yes, I'm your lover. You don't know what that is but you will," he said. "I know that too. I know all about you. But look: it's real nice and you couldn't ask for nobody better than me, or more polite. I always keep my word. I'll tell you how it is, I'm always nice at first, the first time. I'll hold you so tight you won't think you have to try to get away or pretend anything because you'll know you can't. And I'll come inside you where it's all secret and you'll give in to me and you'll love me—"

"Shut up! You're crazy!" Connie said. She backed away from the door. She 105 put her hands against her ears as if she'd heard something terrible, something not meant for her. "People don't talk like that, you're crazy," she muttered. Her heart was almost too big now for her chest and its pumping made sweat break out all over her. She looked out to see Arnold Friend pause and then take a step toward the porch lurching. He almost fell. But, like a clever drunken man, he managed to catch his balance. He wobbled in high boots and grabbed hold of one of the porch posts.

"Honey?" he said. "You still listening?"

"Get the hell out of here!"

"Be nice, honey. Listen."

"I'm going to call the police—"

He wobbled again and out of the side of his mouth came a fast spat curse, 110 an aside not meant for her to hear. But even this "Christ!" sounded forced. Then he began to smile again. She watched this smile come, awkward as if he were smiling from inside a mask. His whole face was a mask, she thought wildly, tanned down onto his throat but then running out as if he had plastered make-up on his face but had forgotten about his throat.

"Honey—? Listen, here's how it is. I always tell the truth and I promise you this: I ain't coming in the house after you."

"You better not! I'm going to call the police if you—if you don't—"

"Honey," he said, talking right through her voice, "honey, I'm not coming in there but you are coming out here. You know why?"

She was panting. The kitchen looked like a place she had never seen before, some room she had run inside but which wasn't good enough, wasn't going to help her. The kitchen window had never had a curtain, after three years, and there were dishes in the sink for her to do—probably—and if you ran your hand across the table you'd probably feel something sticky there.

"You listening, honey? Hey?"   115

"— going to call the police—"

"Soon as you touch the phone I don't need to keep my promise and can come inside. You won't want that."

She rushed forward and tried to lock the door. Her fingers were shaking. "But why lock it," Arnold Friend said gently, talking right into her face. "It's just a screen door. It's just nothing." One of his boots was at a strange angle, as if his foot wasn't in it. It pointed out to the left, bent at the ankle. "I mean, anybody can break through a screen door and glass and wood and iron or anything else he needs to, anybody at all and specially Arnold Friend. If the place got lit up with a fire honey you'd come running out into my arms, right into my arms and safe at home—like you knew I was your lover and'd stopped fooling around. I don't mind a nice shy girl but I don't like no fooling around." Part of those words were spoken with a slight rhythmic lilt, and Connie some-how recognized them—the echo of a song from last year, about a girl rushing into her boy friend's arms and coming home again—

Connie stood barefoot on the linoleum floor, staring at him. "What do you want?" she whispered.

"I want you," he said.   120

"What?"

"Seen you that night and thought, that's the one, yes sir. I never needed to look any more."

"But my father's coming back. He's coming to get me. I had to wash my hair first—" She spoke in a dry, rapid voice, hardly raising it for him to hear.

"No, your daddy is not coming and yes, you had to wash your hair and you washed it for me. It's nice and shining and all for me, I thank you, sweetheart," he said, with a mock bow, but again he almost lost his balance. He had to bend and adjust his boots. Evidently his feet did not go all the way down; the boots must have been stuffed with something so that he would seem taller. Connie stared out at him and behind him Ellie in the car, who seemed to be looking off toward Con-nie's right, into nothing. This Ellie said, pulling the words out of the air one after another as if he were just discovering them, "You want me to pull out the phone?"

"Shut your mouth and keep it shut," Arnold Friend said, his face red from   125
bending over or maybe from embarrassment because Connie had seen his boots. "This ain't none of your business."

"What—what are you doing? What do you want?" Connie said. "If I call the police they'll get you, they'll arrest you—"

"Promise was not to come in unless you touch that phone, and I'll keep that promise," he said. He resumed his erect position and tried to force his shoulders back. He sounded like a hero in a movie, declaring something important. He spoke too loudly and it was as if he were speaking to someone behind Connie. "I ain't made plans for coming in that house where I don't belong but just for you to come out to me, the way you should. Don't you know who I am?"

"You're crazy," she whispered. She backed away from the door but did not want to go into another part of the house, as if this would give him permission to come through the door. "What do you . . . You're crazy, you . . ."

"Huh? What're you saying, honey?"

Her eyes darted everywhere in the kitchen. She could not remember what it   130
was, this room.

"This is how it is, honey: you come out and we'll drive away, have a nice ride. But if you don't come out we're gonna wait till your people come home and then they're all going to get it."

"You want that telephone pulled out?" Ellie said. He held the radio away from his ear and grimaced, as if without the radio the air was too much for him.

"I toldja shut up, Ellie," Arnold Friend said, "you're deaf, get a hearing aid, right? Fix yourself up. This little girl's no trouble and's gonna be nice to me, so Ellie keep to yourself, this ain't your date—right? Don't hem in on me. Don't hog. Don't crush. Don't bird dog. Don't trail me," he said in a rapid meaningless voice, as if he were running through all the expressions he'd learned but was no longer sure which one of them was in style, then rushing on to new ones, making them up with his eyes closed, "Don't crawl under my fence, don't squeeze in my chipmunk hole, don't sniff my glue, suck my popsicle, keep your own greasy fingers on yourself!" He shaded his eyes and peered in at Connie, who was backed against the kitchen table. "Don't mind him honey he's just a creep. He's a dope. Right? I'm the boy for you and like I said you come out here nice like a lady and give me your hand, and nobody else gets hurt, I mean, your nice old bald-headed daddy and your mummy and your sister in her high heels. Because listen: why bring them in this?"

"Leave me alone," Connie whispered.

"Hey, you know that old woman down the road, the one with the chickens   135
and stuff—you know her?"

"She's dead!"

"Dead? What? You know her?" Arnold Friend said.

"She's dead—"

"Don't you like her?"

"She's dead—she's—she isn't here any more—"   140

"But don't you like her, I mean, you got something against her? Some grudge or something?" Then his voice dipped as if he were conscious of a rudeness. He touched the sunglasses perched on top of his head as if to make sure they were still there. "Now you be a good girl."

"What are you going to do?"

"Just two things, or maybe three," Arnold Friend said. "But I promise it won't last long and you'll like me that way you get to like people you're close to. You will. It's all over for you here, so come on out. You don't want your people in any trouble, do you?"

She turned and bumped against a chair or something, hurting her leg, but she ran into the back room and picked up the telephone. Something roared in her ear, a tiny roaring, and she was so sick with fear that she could do nothing but listen to it—the telephone was clammy and very heavy and her fingers groped down to the dial but were too weak to touch it. She began to scream into the phone, into the roaring. She cried out, she cried for her mother, she felt her breath start jerking back and forth in her lungs as if it were something Arnold Friend were stabbing her with again and again with no tenderness. A noisy sorrowful wailing rose all about her and she was locked inside it the way she was locked inside that house.

After a while she could hear again. She was sitting on the floor with her wet 145
back against the wall.

Arnold Friend was saying from the door, "That's a good girl. Put the phone back."

She kicked the phone away from her.

"No, honey. Pick it up. Put it back right."

She picked it up and put it back. The dial tone stopped.

"That's a good girl. Now come outside." 150

She was hollow with what had been fear, but what was now just an emptiness. All that screaming had blasted it out of her. She sat, one leg cramped under her, and deep inside her brain was something like a pinpoint of light that kept going and would not let her relax. She thought, I'm not going to see my mother again. She thought, I'm not going to sleep in my bed again. Her bright green blouse was all wet.

Arnold Friend said, in a gentle-loud voice that was like a stage voice, "The place where you came from ain't there any more, and where you had in mind to go is cancelled out. This place you are now—inside your daddy's house—is nothing but a cardboard box I can knock down any time. You know that and always did know it. You hear me?"

She thought, I have got to think. I have to know what to do.

"We'll go out to a nice field, out in the country here where it smells so nice and it's sunny," Arnold Friend said. "I'll have my arms around you so you won't need to try to get away and I'll show you what love is like, what it does. The hell with this house! It looks solid all right," he said. He ran a fingernail down the screen and the noise did not make Connie shiver, as it would have the day before. "Now put your hand on your heart, honey. Feel that? That feels solid too but we know better, be nice to me, be sweet like you can because what else is there for a girl like you but to be sweet and pretty and give in?— and get away before her people come back?"

She felt her pounding heart. Her hand seemed to enclose it. She thought 155 for the first time in her life that it was nothing that was hers, that belonged to her, but just a pounding, living thing inside this body that wasn't really hers either.

"You don't want them to get hurt," Arnold Friend went on. "Now get up, honey. Get up all by yourself."

She stood up.

"Now turn this way. That's right. Come over here to me—Ellie, put that away, didn't I tell you? You dope. You miserable creepy dope," Arnold said. His words were not angry but only part of an incantation. The incantation was kindly. "Now come out through the kitchen to me honey and let's see a smile, try it, you're a brave sweet little girl and now they're eating corn and hotdogs cooked to bursting over an outdoor fire, and they don't know one thing about you and never did and honey, you're better than them because not a one of them would have done this for you."

Connie felt the linoleum under her feet; it was cool. She brushed her hair back out of her eyes. Arnold Friend let go of the post tentatively and opened his arms for her, his elbows pointing in toward each other and his wrists limp, to show that this was an embarrassed embrace and a little mocking, he didn't want to make her self-conscious.

She put out her hand against the screen. She watched herself push the door 160 slowly open as if she were safe back somewhere in the other doorway, watching this body and this head of long hair moving out into the sunlight where Arnold Friend waited.

"My sweet little blue-eyed girl," he said, in a half-sung sigh that had nothing to do with her brown eyes but was taken up just the same by the vast sunlit reaches of the land behind him and on all sides of him, so much land that Connie had never seen before and did not recognize except to know that she was going to it.

FOR ANALYSIS

1. Describe Connie in your own words. What are the sources of her values? What sort of love experience does she imagine?

2. When she agrees to go with Eddie, what do you suppose they did in the "alley a mile or so away" (para. 8)?

3. How does Arnold Friend differ from Eddie?

4. Why is attention paid in the story to Arnold's boots?

5. How does Ellie's repeated proposal that Arnold pull out the phone affect your understanding of Arnold and Ellie's motives?

6. Does Connie go to Arnold simply to protect her family from his threats? Explain.

7. What is going to happen to Connie? Why?

8. The story is told by a **third-person narrator**—yet it is limited, essentially, to Connie's viewpoint. Would multiple viewpoints—her mother's, June's, Eddie's, her friend's, Arnold's—enhance or impair the story's impact?

MAKING CONNECTIONS

Compare the situation in this story to that in Rivka Galchen's "Wild Berry Blue" (p. 127). Both situations are in some ways dangerous; both are in some ways about innocence. How are they similar in these regards? How are they different?

WRITING TOPICS

1. In your experience, do some women find dangerous and unstable men more attractive than gentle and kind men? Support your arguments with **allusions** to Oates's story and other stories you have read.

2. Using evidence from the story, argue that Arnold Friend is an incarnation of the devil or some fairy-tale villain.

CHIMAMANDA NGOZI ADICHIE (B. 1977)

BIRDSONG 2010

The woman, a stranger, was looking at me. In the glare of the hot afternoon, in the swirl of motorcycles and hawkers, she was looking down at me from the back seat of her jeep. Her stare was too direct, not sufficiently vacant. She was not merely resting her eyes on the car next to hers, as people often do in Lagos traffic; she was *looking* at me. At first, I glanced away, but then I stared back, at the haughty silkiness of the weave that fell to her shoulders in loose curls, the kind of extension called Brazilian Hair and paid for in dollars at Victoria Island hair salons; at her fair skin, which had the plastic sheen that comes from expensive creams; and at her hand, forefinger bejewelled, which she raised to wave a magazine hawker away, with the ease of a person used to waving people away. She was beautiful, or perhaps she was just so unusual-looking, with wide-set eyes sunk deep in her face, that "beautiful" was the easiest way of describing her. She was the kind of woman I imagined my lover's wife was, a woman for whom things were done.

My lover. It sounds a little melodramatic, but I never knew how to refer to him. "Boyfriend" seemed wrong for an urbane man of forty-five who carefully slipped off his wedding ring before he touched me. Chikwado called him "your man," with a faintly sneering smile, as though we were both in on the joke: he was not, of course, mine. "Ah, you are always rushing to leave because of this your man," she would say, leaning back in her chair and smacking her head with her hand, over and over. Her scalp was itchy beneath her weave, and this was the only way she could come close to scratching it. "Have fun oh, as long as your spirit accepts it, but as for me, I cannot spread my legs for a married man." She said this often, with a clear-eyed moral superiority, as I packed my files and shut down my computer for the day.

We were friends out of necessity, because we had both graduated from Enugu Campus and ended up working for Celnet Telecom, in Lagos, as the only females in the community-relations unit. Otherwise, we would not have been friends. I was irritated by how full of simplified certainties she was, and I knew that she thought I behaved like an irresponsible, vaguely foreign teenager: wearing my hair in a natural low-cut, smoking cigarettes right in front of the building, where everyone could see, and refusing to join in the prayer sessions our boss led after Monday meetings. I would not have told her about my lover—I did not tell her about my personal life—but she was there when he first walked into our office, a lean, dark man with a purple tie and a money-eyed manner. He was full of the glossy self-regard of men who shrugged off their importance in a way that only emphasized it. Our boss shook his hand with both hands and said, "Welcome, sir, it is good to see you, sir, how are you doing, sir, please come and sit down, sir." Chikwado was there when he looked at me and I looked at him and then he smiled, of all things, a warm, open smile. She heard when he said to our boss, "My family lives in America," a little too loudly, for my benefit, with that generic foreign accent of the worldly Nigerian, which, I would discover later, disappeared when he became truly animated about something. She saw him walk over and give me his business card. She was there, a few days later, when his driver come to deliver a gift bag. Because she had seen, and because I was swamped with emotions that I could not name for a man I knew was wrong for me, I showed her the perfume and the card that said, "I am thinking of you."

"*Na wa!* Look at how your eyes are shining because of a married man. You need deliverance prayers," Chikwado said, half joking. She went to night-vigil services often, at different churches, but all with the theme Finding Your God-Given Mate; she would come to work the next morning sleepy, the whites of her eyes flecked with red, but already planning to attend another service. She was thirty-two and tottering under the weight of her desire: to settle down. It was all she talked about. It was all our female co-workers talked about when we had lunch at the cafeteria. *Yewande is wasting her time with that man—he is not ready to settle down. Please ask him oh, if he does not see marriage in the future then you better look elsewhere; nobody is getting any younger. Ekaete is lucky, just six months and she is already engaged.* While they talked, I would look out the window, high up above Lagos, at the acres of rusted roofs, at the rise and fall of hope in this city full of tarnished angels.

Even my lover spoke of this desire. "You'll want to settle down soon," he 5 said. "I just want you to know I'm not going to stand in your way." We were naked in bed; it was our first time. A feather from the pillow was stuck in his hair, and I had just picked it out and showed it to him. I could not believe, in the aftermath of what had just happened, both of us still flush from each other's warmth, how easily the words rolled out of his mouth. "I'm not like other men, who think they can dominate your life and not let you move forward," he continued, propping himself up on his elbow to look at me. He was telling me that he played the game better than others, while I had not yet conceived of the game itself. From the moment I met him, I had had the sensation of possibility, but for him the path was already closed, had indeed never been open; there was no room for things to sweep in and disrupt.

"You're very thoughtful," I said, with the kind of overdone mockery that masks damage. He nodded, as though he agreed with me. I pulled the covers up to my chin. I should have got dressed, gone back to my flat in Surulere, and deleted his number from my phone. But I stayed. I stayed for thirteen months and eight days, mostly in his house in Victoria Island—a faded-white house, with its quiet grandeur and airy spaces, which was built during British colonial rule and sat in a compound full of fruit trees, the enclosing wall wreathed in creeping bougainvillea. He had told me he was taking me to a Lebanese friend's guesthouse, where he was staying while his home in Ikoyi was being refurbished. When I stepped out of the car, I felt as though I had stumbled into a secret garden. A dense mass of periwinkles, white and pink, bordered the walkway to the house. The air was clean here, even fragrant, and there was something about it all that made me think of renewal. He was watching me; I could sense how much he wanted me to like it.

"This is your house, isn't it?" I said. "It doesn't belong to your Lebanese friend."

He moved closer to me, surprised. "Please don't misunderstand. I was going to tell you. I just didn't want you to think it was some kind of . . ." He paused and took my hand. "I know what other men do, and I am not like that. I don't bring women here. I bought it last year to knock it down and build an apartment block, but it was so beautiful. My friends think I'm mad for keeping it. You know nobody respects old things in this country. I work from here most days now, instead of going to my office."

We were standing by sliding glass doors that led to a veranda, over which a large flame tree spread its branches. Wilted red flowers had fallen on the cane chairs. "I like to sit there and watch birds," he said, pointing.

He liked birds. Birds had always been just birds to me, but with him 10 I became someone else: I became a person who liked birds. The following Sunday morning, on our first weekend together, as we passed sections of *Next* to each other in the quiet of that veranda, he looked up at the sky and said, "There's a magpie. They like shiny things." I imagined putting his wedding ring on the cane table so that the bird would swoop down and carry it away forever.

"I knew you were different!" he said, thrilled, when he noticed that I read the business and sports sections, as though my being different reflected his good taste. And so we talked eagerly about newspapers, and about the newscasts on AIT and CNN, marvelling at how similar our opinions were. We never discussed my staying. It was not safe to drive back to Surulere late, and he kept saying, "Why don't you bring your things tomorrow so you can go to work from here?" until most of my clothes were in the wardrobe and my moisturizers were on the bathroom ledge. He left me money on the table, in brown envelopes on which he wrote "For your fuel," as if I could possibly spend fifty thousand naira on petrol. Sometimes, he asked if I needed privacy to change, as if he had not seen me naked many times.

We did not talk about his wife or his children or my personal life or when I would want to settle down so that he could avoid standing in my way. Perhaps it was all the things we left unsaid that made me watch him. His skin was so dark that I teased him about being from Gambia; if he were a woman, I told him, he would never find a face powder that matched his tone. I watched as he carefully unwrapped scented moist tissues to clean his glasses, or cut the chicken on his plate, or tied his towel round his waist in a knot that seemed too elaborate for a mere towel, just below the embossed scar by his navel. I memorized him, because I did not know him. He was courtly, his life lived in well-oiled sequences, his cufflinks always tasteful.

His three cell phones rang often; I knew when it was his wife, because he would go to the toilet or out to the veranda, and I knew when it was a government official, because he would say afterward, "Why won't these governors leave somebody alone?" But it was clear that he liked the governors' calls, and the restaurant manager who came to our table to say, "We are so happy to see you, sah." He searched the Sunday-magazine pullouts for pictures of himself, and when he found one he said in a mildly complaining tone, "Look at this, why should they turn businessmen into celebrities?" Yet he would not wear the same suit to two events because of the newspaper photographers. He had a glowing ego, like a globe, round and large and in constant need of polishing. He did things for people. He gave them money, introduced them to contacts, helped their relatives get jobs, and when the gratitude and praise came—he showed me text messages thanking him; I remember one that read "History will immortalize you as a great man"—his eyes would glaze over, and I could almost hear him purr.

One day he told me, while we were watching two kingfishers do a mating dance on a guava tree, that most birds did not have penises. I had never thought about the penises of birds.

"My mother had chickens in the yard when I was growing up, and I used to   15 watch them mating," I said.

"Of course they mate, but not with penises," he said. "Did you ever see a cock with a dick?"

I laughed, and he, only just realizing the joke, laughed, too. It became our endearment. "Cock with a dick," I would whisper, hugging him in greeting, and we would burst out laughing. He sent me texts signed "CwithaD." And each time I turned off the potholed road in Victoria Island and into that compound full of birdsong I felt as though I were home.

The woman was still looking at me. Traffic was at a standstill, unusual this early in the afternoon. A tanker must have fallen across the road—tankers were always falling across the roads—or a bus had broken down, or cars had formed a line outside a petrol station, blocking the road. My fuel gauge was close to empty. I switched off the ignition and rolled down the window, wondering if the woman would roll down hers as well and say something to me. I stared back at her, and yet she did not waver, her eyes remaining firm, until I looked away. There were many more hawkers now, holding out magazines, phone cards, plantain chips, newspapers, cans of Coke and Amstel Malta dipped in water to make them look cold. The driver in front of me was buying a phone card. The hawker, a boy in a red Arsenal shirt, scratched the card with his fingernail, and then waited for the driver to enter the numbers in his phone to make sure the card was not fake.

I turned again to look at the woman. I was reminded of what Chikwado had said about my lover the first day that he came to our office: "His face is full of overseas." The woman, too, had a face full of overseas, the face of a person whose life was a blur of comforts. There was something in the set of her lips, which were lined with cocoa lip pencil, that suggested an unsatisfying triumph, as though she had won a battle but hated having had to fight in the first place. Perhaps she was indeed my lover's wife and she had come back to Lagos and just found out about me, and then, as though in a bad farce, ended up next to me in traffic. But his wife could not possibly know; he had been so careful.

"I wish I could," he always said, when I asked him to spend Saturday after- 20 noon with me at Jazz Hole, or when I suggested we go to a play at Terra Kulture on Sunday, or when I asked if we could try dinner at a different restaurant. We only ever went to one on a dark street off Awolowo Road, a place with expensive wines and no sign on the gate. He said "I wish I could" as though some great and ineluctable act of nature made it impossible for him to be seen publicly with me. And impossible for him to keep my text messages. I wanted to ask how he could so efficiently delete my texts as soon as he read them, why he felt no urge to keep them on his phone, even if only for a few hours, even if only for a day. There were reams of questions unasked, gathering like rough pebbles in my throat. It was a strange thing to feel so close to a man—to tell him about my resentment of my parents, to lie supine for him with an abandon that was unfamiliar to me—and yet be unable to ask him questions, bound as I was by insecurity and unnamed longings.

The first time we quarrelled, he said to me accusingly, "You don't cry." I realized that his wife cried, that he could handle tears but not my cold defiance.

The fight was about his driver, Emmanuel, an elderly man who might have looked wise if his features were not so snarled with dissatisfaction. It was a Saturday afternoon. I had been at work that morning. My boss had called an emergency meeting that I thought unnecessary: we all knew that His Royal Highness, the Oba of the town near the lagoon, was causing trouble, saying that Celnet Telecom had made him look bad in front of his people. He had sent many messages asking how we could build a big base station on his ancestral land and yet donate only a small borehole to his people. That morning, his guards had blocked off our building site, shoved some of our engineers around, and punctured the tires of their van. My boss was furious, and he slammed his hand on the table as he spoke at the meeting. I, too, slammed my hand on the cane table as I imitated him later, while my lover laughed. "That is the problem with these godless, demon-worshipping traditional rulers," my boss said. "The man is a crook. A common crook! What happened to the one million naira we gave him? Should we also bring bags of rice and beans for all his people before we put up our base station? Does he want a supply of meat pies every day? Nonsense!"

"Meat pies" had made Chikwado and me laugh, even though our boss was not being funny. "Why not something more ordinary, like bread?" Chikwado whispered to me, and then promptly raised her hand when our boss asked for volunteers to go see the Oba right away. I never volunteered. I disliked those visits—villagers watching us with awed eyes, young men asking for free phone cards, even free phones—because it all made me feel helplessly powerful.

"Why meat pies?" my lover asked, still laughing.

"I have no idea."   25

"Actually, I would like to have a meat pie right now."

"Me, too."

We were laughing, and with the sun shining, the sound of birds above, the slight flutter of the curtains against the sliding door, I was already thinking of future Saturdays that we would spend together, laughing at funny stories about my boss. My lover summoned Emmanuel and asked him to take me to the supermarket to buy the meat pies. When I got into the car, Emmanuel did not greet me. He simply stared straight ahead. It was the first time that he had driven me without my lover. The silence was tense. Perhaps he was thinking that all his children were older than me.

"Well done, Emmanuel!" I said finally, greeting him with forced brightness. "Do you know the supermarket on Kofo Abayomi Street?"

He said nothing and started the car. When we arrived, he stopped at the   30 gate. "Come out here, let me go and park," he said.

"Please drop me at the entrance," I said. Every other driver did that, before looking for a parking space.

"Come out here." He still did not look at me. Rage rose under my skin, making me feel detached and bloodless, suspended in air; I could not sense the ground under my feet as I climbed out. After I had selected some meat pies from the display case, I called my lover and told him that Emmanuel had been rude and that I would be taking a taxi back.

"Emmanuel said the road was bad," my lover said when I got back, his tone conciliatory.

"The man insulted me," I said.

"No, he's not like that. Maybe he didn't understand you."   35

Emmanuel had shown me the power of my lover's wife; he would not have been so rude if he feared he might be reprimanded. I wanted to fling the bag of meat pies through the window.

"Is this what you do, have your driver remind your girlfriends of their place?" I was shrill and I disliked myself for it. Worse, I was horrified to notice that my eyes were watering. My lover gently wrapped his arms around me, as though I were an irrational child, and asked whether I would give him a meat pie.

"You've brought other women here, haven't you?" I asked, not entirely sure how this had become about other women.

He shook his head. "No, I have not. No more of this talk. Let's eat the meat pies and watch a film."

I let myself be mollified, be held, be caressed. Later, he said, "You know, I   40 have had only two affairs since I got married. I'm not like other men."

"You sound as if you think you deserve a prize," I said.

He was smiling. "Both of them were like you." He paused to search for a word, and when he found it he said it with enjoyment. "Feisty. They were feisty like you."

I looked at him. How could he not see that there were things he should not say to me, and that there were things I longed to have with him? It was a willed blindness; it had to be. He chose not to see. "You are such a bastard," I said.

"What?"

I repeated myself.

He looked as though he had just been stung by an insect. "Get out. Leave this house right now," he said, and then muttered, "This is unacceptable."

I had never before been thrown out of a house. Emmanuel sat in a chair in the shade of the garage and watched stone-faced as I hurried to my car. My lover did not call me for five days, and I did not call him. When he finally called, his first words were "There are two pigeons on the flame tree. I'd like you to see them."

"You are acting as if nothing happened."

"I called *you*," he said, as though the call itself were an apology. Later, he told me that if I had cried instead of calling him a bastard he would have behaved better. I should not have gone back—I knew that even then.

The woman, still staring at me, was talking on her cell phone. Her jeep was black and silver and miraculously free of scratches. How was that possible in this city where okada after okada sped through the narrow slices of space between cars in traffic as though motorcycles could shrink to fit any gap? Perhaps whenever her car was hit a mechanic descended from the sky and made the dent disappear. The car in front of me had a gash on its tail-light; it looked like one of the many cars that dripped oil, turning the roads into a slick sheet when the rains came. My own car was full of wounds. The biggest, a mangled bumper, was from a taxi that rammed into me at a red light on Kingsway Road a month before. The driver had jumped out with his shirt unbuttoned, all sweaty bravado, and screamed at me.

"Stupid girl! You are a common nuisance. Why did you stop like that? Nonsense!"

I stared at him, stunned, until he drove away, and then I began to think of what I could have said, what I could have shouted back.

"If you were wearing a wedding ring, he would not have shouted at you like that," Chikwado said when I told her, as she punched the redial button on her desk phone. At the cafeteria, she told our co-workers about it. *Ah, ah, stupid man! Of course he was shouting because he knew he was wrong—that is the Lagos way. So he thinks he can speak big English. Where did he even learn the word "nuisance"?* They sucked their teeth, telling their own stories about taxi-drivers, and then their outrage fizzled and they began to talk, voices lowered and excited, about a fertility biscuit that the new pastor at Redemption Church was giving women.

"It worked for my sister oh. First she did a dry fast for two days, then the pastor did a special deliverance prayer for her before she ate the biscuit. She had to eat it at exactly midnight. The next month, the very next month, she missed her period, I'm telling you," one of them, a contract staffer who was doing a master's degree part time at Ibadan, said.

"Is it an actual biscuit?" another asked.   55

"Yes now. But they bless the ingredients before they make the biscuits. God can work through anything, *sha*. I heard about a pastor that uses handkerchiefs."

I looked away and wondered what my lover would make of this story. He was visiting his family in America for two weeks. That evening, he sent me a text. "At a concert with my wife. Beautiful music. Will call you in ten minutes and leave phone on so you can listen in. CwithaD." I read it twice and then, even though I had saved all his other texts, I deleted it, as though my doing so would mean that it had never been sent. When he called, I let my phone ring and ring. I imagined them at the concert, his wife reaching out to hold his hand, because I could not bear the thought that it might be he who would reach out. I knew then that he could not possibly see me, the inconvenient reality of me; instead, all he saw was himself in an exciting game.

He came back from his trip wearing shoes I did not recognize, made of rich brown leather and much more tapered than his other shoes, almost comically pointy. He was in high spirits, twirling me around when we hugged, caressing the tightly coiled hair at the nape of my neck and saying, "So soft." He wanted to go out to dinner, he said, because he had a surprise for me, and when he went into the bathroom one of his phones rang. I took it and looked at his text messages. It was something I had never thought of doing before, and yet I suddenly felt compelled to do it. Text after text in his "sent" box were to Baby. The most recent said he had arrived safely. What struck me was not how often he texted his wife, or how short the texts were—"stuck in traffic," "missing you," "almost there"—but that all of them were signed "CwithaD." Inside me, something sagged. Had he choreographed a conversation with her, nimbly made the joke about a "cock with a dick" and then found a way to turn it into a shared endearment for the two of them? I thought of the effort it would take to do that. I put the phone down and glanced at the mirror, half expecting to see myself morphing into a slack, stringless marionette.

In the car, he asked, "Is something wrong? Are you feeling well?"

"I can't believe you called me so that I could listen to the music you and   60
your wife were listening to."

"I did that because I missed you so much," he said. "I really wanted to be there with you."

"But you *weren't* there with me."

"You're in a bad mood."

"Don't you see? You weren't there with *me*."

He reached over and took my hand, rubbing his thumb on my palm.   65
I looked out at the dimly lit street. We were on our way to our usual hidden

restaurant, where I had eaten everything on the menu a hundred times. A mosquito, now sluggish with my blood, had got in the car. I slapped myself as I tried to hit it.

"Good evening, sah," the waiter said when we were seated. "You are welcome, sah."

"Have you noticed that they never greet me?" I asked my lover.

"Well . . ." he said, and adjusted his glasses.

The waiter came back, a sober-faced man with a gentle demeanor, and I waited until he had opened the bottle of red wine before I asked, "Why don't you greet me?"

The waiter glanced at my lover, as though seeking guidance, and this infuri- 70 ated me even more. "Am I invisible? I am the one who asked you a question. Why do all of you waiters and gatemen and drivers in this Lagos refuse to greet me? Do you not see me?"

"Come back in ten minutes," my lover said to the waiter in his courteous, deep-voiced way. "You need to calm down," he told me. "Do you want us to go?"

"Why don't they greet me?" I asked, and gulped down half my glass of wine.

"I have a surprise for you. I've bought you a new car."

I looked at him blankly.   75

"Did you hear me?" he asked.

"I heard you." I was supposed to get up and hug him and tell him that history would remember him as a great man. A new car. I drank more wine.

"Did I tell you about my first bus ride when I arrived in Lagos, six years ago?" I asked. "When I got on the bus, a boy was screaming in shock because a stranger had found his lost wallet and given it back to him. The boy looked like me, a green, eager job seeker, and he, too, must have come from his home town armed with warnings. You know all the things they tell you: don't give to street beggars because they are only pretending to be lame; look through tomato pyramids for the rotten ones the hawkers hide underneath; don't help people whose cars have broken down, because they are really armed robbers. And then somebody found his wallet and gave it back to him."

My lover looked puzzled.

"Rituals of distrust," I said. "That is how we relate to one another here, 80 through rituals of distrust. Do you know how carefully I watch the fuel gauge when I buy petrol just to make sure the attendant hasn't tampered with it? We know the rules and we follow them, and we never make room for things we might not have imagined. We close the door too soon." I felt a little silly, saying things I knew he did not understand and did not want to understand, and also a little cowardly, saying them the way I did. He was resting his elbows on the table, watching me, and I knew that all he wanted was my excitement, my gratitude, my questions about when I could see the new car. I began to cry, and he came around and cradled me against his waist. My nose was running and my eyes itched as I dabbed them with my napkin. I never cried elegantly, and I imagined that his wife did; she was probably one of those women who could just have the tears trail down her cheeks, leaving her makeup intact, her nose dry.

The traffic had started to move a little. I saw an okada in my side mirror, coming too fast, swerving and honking, and I waited to hear the crunch as it hit my car. But it didn't. The driver was wearing a helmet, while his passenger merely held hers over her head—the smelly foam inside would have ruined her hair—close enough so that she could slip it on as soon as she saw a LASTMA official ahead. My lover once called it fatalism. He had given free helmets to all his staff, but most of them still got on an okada without one. The day before, an okada, the driver bareheaded and blindly speeding, had hit me as I turned onto Ogunlana Drive; the driver stuck his finger into his mouth and ran it over the scratch on the side of my car. "Auntie, sorry oh! Nothing happen to the car," he said, and continued his journey.

I laughed. I had not laughed in the three weeks since I had left work at lunchtime and driven to my lover's house. I had packed all my clothes, my books, and my toiletries and gone back to my flat, consumed as I went by how relentlessly unpretty Lagos was, with houses sprouting up unplanned like weeds.

During those three weeks, I had said little at work. Our office was suddenly very uncomfortable, the air-conditioning always too cold. His Royal Highness, the Oba of the town near the lagoon, was asking for more money; his town council had written a letter saying that the borehole was spewing blackish water. My boss was calling too many meetings.

"Let us give thanks," he said after one of the meetings.

"Why should we be praying in the workplace?" I asked. "Why must you 85 assume that we are all Christians?"

He looked startled. He knew that I never joined in, never said "Amen," but I had never been vocal about it.

"It is not by force to participate in thanking the Lord," he said, and then in the same breath continued, "In Jesus' name!"

"Amen!" the others chorused.

I turned to leave the meeting room.

"Don't go," my co-worker Gerald whispered to me. "Akin brought his 90 birthday cake."

I stood outside the meeting room until the prayer ended, and then we sang "Happy Birthday" to Akin. His cake looked like the unpretentious kind I liked, probably from Sweet Sensation, the kind that sometimes had bits of forgotten eggshells in it. Our boss asked him to give me or Chikwado the cake to serve.

"Why do we always have to serve the cake?" I asked. "Every time somebody brings in a cake, it is either Chikwado serves it or I serve it. You, Gerald, serve the cake. Or you, Emeka, since you are the most junior."

They stared at me. Chikwado got up hurriedly and began to slice the cake. "Please, don't mind her," she said to everyone, but her eyes were on our boss. "She is behaving like this because she did not take her madness medicine today."

Later, she said to me, "Why have you been behaving somehow? What's the problem? Did something happen with your man?"

For a moment, I wanted to tell her how I felt: as though bits of my skin had 95 warped and cracked and peeled off, leaving patches of raw flesh so agonizingly painful I did not know what to do. I wanted to tell her how often I stared at my phone, even though he had sent two feeble texts saying he did not understand why I'd left and then nothing else; and how I remembered clearly, too clearly, the scent of the moist tissues he used to clean his glasses. I didn't tell her, because I was sure she would deliver one of her petty wisdoms, like "If you see fire and you put your hand in fire, then fire will burn you." Still, there was a softness in her expression, something like sympathy, when I looked up from my computer screen and saw her watching me while her hand went slap, slap, slap on her head. Her weave was a new style, too long and too wiggy, with reddish highlights that brought to mind the hair of cheap plastic dolls. Yet there was an honesty about it; Chikwado owned it in a way that the woman in the jeep did not own her Brazilian hair.

A young boy approached my car, armed with a spray bottle of soapy water and a rag. I turned on my wipers to discourage him, but he still squirted my windscreen. I increased the wiper speed. The boy glared at me and moved on to the car behind me. I was seized with a sudden urge to step out and slap him. For a moment, my vision blurred. It was really the woman I wanted to slap. I turned to her jeep and, because she had looked away, I pressed my horn. I leaned out of my window.

"What is your problem? Why have you been staring at me? Do I owe you?" I shouted.

The traffic began to move. I thought she would roll down her window, too. She made as if to lean toward it, then turned away, the slightest of smiles on her face, her head held high, and I watched the jeep pick up speed and head to the bridge.

FOR ANALYSIS

1. How does the **narrator** feel about herself? How does having her lover make her feel?

2. How does the story present the narrator's lover? How does she feel about him? How do we feel about him?

3. The story of the narrator's relationship is framed by a scene in which she sits in her car in traffic. What is the relationship between these two stories?

4. This story is about a romantic relationship, but it is also about a historical moment. What moment is that? What is happening in the world in which the narrator and her lover meet? What are the connections between their story and the larger story that goes on around them?

5. Consider the story's title. What is the significance of the singing birds?

MAKING CONNECTIONS

Adichie's "Birdsong" features a woman ultimately unhappy in love in a culturally unsettled situation. Compare "Birdsong" to Jhumpa Lahiri's "Hell-Heaven" (p. 622). How are the **settings** similar and different in terms of nation and ethnicity? How do the romantic situations compare? Does reading "Birdsong" against "Hell-Heaven" help you see either story in a new light?

WRITING TOPICS

1. Adichie writes of what the **narrator** calls "rituals of distrust" in Lagos. Can you think of anything comparable in your own environment? Write about your home's "rituals of distrust" or, if you can't think of any, your home's lack of such things. How do these rituals make you feel?

2. Imagine this story from another **point of view**—that of the lover, his wife, or one of their children. (You could even write this version.) How would the story be related in a different way? How would its underlying reflections on culture be different?

The two stories in this cluster deal with a difficult subject (one that we want you to discover as you read). While it has become a difficult political subject over the years, it is treated in these stories as a difficult personal subject, one that touches the root of romantic and sexual relationships, and tests them. As you read these two stories, think about this subject's ramifications for the individuals involved and for the way they understand their own values and priorities.

ERNEST HEMINGWAY   (1899–1961)

HILLS LIKE WHITE ELEPHANTS   1927

The hills across the valley of the Ebro were long and white. On this side there was no shade and no trees and the station was between two lines of rails in the sun. Close against the side of the station there was the warm shadow of the building and a curtain, made of strings of bamboo beads, hung across the open door into the bar, to keep out flies. The American and the girl with him sat at a table in the shade, outside the building. It was very hot and the express from Barcelona would come in forty minutes. It stopped at this junction for two minutes and went on to Madrid.

"What should we drink?" the girl asked. She had taken off her hat and put it on the table.

"It's pretty hot," the man said.

"Let's drink beer."

"*Dos cervezas*," the man said into the curtain.   5

"Big ones?" a woman asked from the doorway.

"Yes. Two big ones."

The woman brought two glasses of beer and two felt pads. She put the felt pads and the beer glasses on the table and looked at the man and the girl. The girl was looking off at the line of hills. They were white in the sun and the country was brown and dry.

"They look like white elephants," she said.

"I've never seen one," the man drank his beer.   10

"No, you wouldn't have."

"I might have," the man said. "Just because you say I wouldn't have doesn't prove anything."

The girl looked at the bead curtain. "They've painted something on it," she said. "What does it say?"

"Anis del Toro. It's a drink."

"Could we try it?"

The man called "Listen" through the curtain. The woman came out from the bar.

"Four reales."

"We want two Anis del Toro."

"With water?"

"Do you want it with water?"

"I don't know," the girl said. "Is it good with water?"

"It's all right."

"You want them with water?" asked the woman.

"Yes, with water."

"It tastes like licorice," the girl said and put the glass down.

"That's the way with everything."

"Yes," said the girl. "Everything tastes of licorice. Especially all the things you've waited so long for, like absinthe."

"Oh, cut it out."

"You started it," the girl said. "I was being amused. I was having a fine time."

"Well, let's try and have a fine time."

"All right. I was trying. I said the mountains looked like white elephants. Wasn't that bright?"

"That was bright."

"I wanted to try this new drink: that's all we do, isn't it—look at things and try new drinks?"

"I guess so."

The girl looked across at the hills.

"They're lovely hills," she said. "They don't really look like white elephants. I just meant the coloring of their skin through the trees."

"Should we have another drink?"

"All right."

The warm wind blew the bead curtain against the table.

"The beer's nice and cool," the man said.

"It's lovely," the girl said.

"It's really an awfully simple operation, Jig," the man said. "It's not really an operation at all."

The girl looked at the ground the table legs rested on.

"I know you wouldn't mind it, Jig. It's really not anything. It's just to let the air in."

The girl did not say anything.

"I'll go with you and I'll stay with you all the time. They just let the air in and then it's all perfectly natural."

"Then what will we do afterward?"

"We'll be fine afterward. Just like we were before."

"What makes you think so?"

"That's the only thing that bothers us. It's the only thing that's made us unhappy."

The girl looked at the bead curtain, put her hand out, and took hold of two of the strings of beads.

"And you think then we'll be all right and be happy."

"I know we will. You don't have to be afraid. I've known lots of people that have done it."

"So have I," said the girl. "And afterward they were all so happy."

"Well," the man said, "if you don't want to you don't have to. I wouldn't 55 have you do it if you didn't want to. But I know it's perfectly simple."

"And you really want to?"

"I think it's the best thing to do. But I don't want you to do it if you don't really want to."

"And if I do it you'll be happy and things will be like they were and you'll love me?"

"I love you now. You know I love you."

"I know. But if I do it, then it will be nice again if I say things are like white 60 elephants, and you'll like it?"

"I'll love it. I love it now but I just can't think about it. You know how I get when I worry."

"If I do it you won't ever worry?"

"I won't worry about that because it's perfectly simple."

"Then I'll do it. Because I don't care about me."

"What do you mean?" 65

"I don't care about me."

"Well, I care about you."

"Oh, yes. But I don't care about me. And I'll do it and then everything will be fine."

"I don't want you to do it if you feel that way."

The girl stood up and walked to the end of the station. Across, on the other 70 side, were fields of grain and trees along the banks of the Ebro. Far away, beyond the river, were mountains. The shadow of a cloud moved across the field of grain and she saw the river through the trees.

"And we could have all this," she said. "And we could have everything and every day we make it more impossible."

"What did you say?"

"I said we could have everything."

"We can have everything."

"No, we can't." 75

"We can have the whole world."

"No, we can't."

"We can go everywhere."

"No, we can't. It isn't ours any more."

"It's ours." 80

"No, it isn't. And once they take it away, you never get it back."

"But they haven't taken it away."

"We'll wait and see."

"Come on back in the shade," he said. "You mustn't feel that way."

"I don't feel any way," the girl said. "I just know things." 85

"I don't want you to do anything that you don't want to do——"

"Nor that isn't good for me," she said. "I know. Could we have another beer?"

"All right. But you've got to realize——"

"I realize," the girl said. "Can't we maybe stop talking?"

They sat down at the table and the girl looked across at the hills on the dry 90 side of the valley and the man looked at her and at the table.

"You've got to realize," he said, "that I don't want you to do it if you don't want to. I'm perfectly willing to go through with it if it means anything to you."

"Doesn't it mean anything to you? We could get along."

"Of course it does. But I don't want anybody but you. I don't want any one else. And I know it's perfectly simple."

"Yes, you know it's perfectly simple."

"It's all right for you to say that, but I do know it." 95

"Would you do something for me now?"

"I'd do anything for you."

"Would you please please please please please please please stop talking?"

He did not say anything but looked at the bags against the wall of the station. There were labels on them from all the hotels where they had spent nights.

"But I don't want you to," he said, "I don't care anything about it." 100

"I'll scream," the girl said.

The woman came out through the curtains with two glasses of beer and put them down on the damp felt pads. "The train comes in five minutes," she said.

"What did she say?" asked the girl.

"That the train is coming in five minutes."

The girl smiled brightly at the woman, to thank her. 105

"I'd better take the bags over to the other side of the station," the man said. She smiled at him.

"All right. Then come back and we'll finish the beer."

He picked up the two heavy bags and carried them around the station to the other tracks. He looked up the tracks but could not see the train. Coming back, he walked through the barroom, where people waiting for the train were drinking. He drank an Anis at the bar and looked at the people. They were all waiting reasonably for the train. He went out through the bead curtain. She was sitting at the table and smiled at him.

"Do you feel better?" he asked.

"I feel fine," she said. "There's nothing wrong with me. I feel fine." 110

FOR ANALYSIS

1. What is a "white elephant"?

2. What do you think the couple is arguing about? Is it more than one thing?

3. How do you think their story will turn out? Is there a happy ending in store for this couple?

WRITING TOPICS

1. How would you characterize Hemingway's **style**? Focus on what he includes and what he leaves out. What are the effects of his stylistic choices?

2. Much attention is paid in the story to **setting**—to where the main characters are sitting in relation to the things around them. Write an analysis of setting in this story. What might the relations of the characters to their surroundings mean? How might it reinforce certain ideas about their situation?

DAVID FOSTER WALLACE (1962-2008)

GOOD PEOPLE   2007

They were up on a picnic table at that park by the lake, by the edge of the lake, with part of a downed tree in the shallows half hidden by the bank. Lane A. Dean, Jr., and his girlfriend, both in bluejeans and button-up shirts. They sat up on the table's top portion and had their shoes on the bench part that people sat on to picnic or fellowship together in carefree times. They'd gone to different high schools but the same junior college, where they had met in campus ministries. It was springtime, and the park's grass was very green and the air suffused with honeysuckle and lilacs both, which was almost too much. There were bees, and the angle of the sun made the water of the shallows look dark. There had been more storms that week, with some downed trees and the sound of chainsaws all up and down his parents' street. Their postures on the picnic table were both the same forward kind with their shoulders rounded and elbows on their knees. In this position the girl rocked slightly and once put her face in her hands, but she was not crying. Lane was very still and immobile and looking past the bank at the downed tree in the shallows and its ball of exposed roots going all directions and the tree's cloud of branches all half in the water. The only other individual nearby was a dozen spaced tables away, by himself, standing upright. Looking at the torn-up hole in the ground there where the tree had gone over. It was still early yet and all the shadows wheeling right and shortening. The girl wore a thin old checked cotton shirt with pearl-colored snaps with the long sleeves down and always smelled very good and clean, like someone you could trust and care about even if you weren't in love. Lane Dean had liked the smell of her right away. His mother called her *down to earth* and liked her, thought she was good people, you could tell—she made this evident in little ways. The shallows lapped from different directions at the tree as if almost teething on it. Sometimes when alone and thinking or struggling to turn a matter over to Jesus Christ in prayer, he would find himself putting his fist in his palm and turning it slightly as if still playing and pounding his glove to stay sharp and alert in center. He did not do this now; it would be cruel and indecent to do this now. The older individual stood beside his picnic table—he was at it but not sitting—and looked also out of place in a suit coat or jacket and the kind of men's hat Lane's grandfather wore in photos as a young insurance man. He appeared to be looking across the lake. If he moved, Lane didn't see it. He looked more like a picture than a man. There were not any ducks in view.

One thing Lane Dean did was reassure her again that he'd go with her and be there with her. It was one of the few safe or decent things he could really say. The second time he said it again now she shook her head and laughed in an unhappy way that was more just air out her nose. Her real laugh was different. Where he'd be was the waiting room, she said. That he'd be thinking about her and feeling bad for her, she knew, but he couldn't be in there with her. This was so obviously true that he felt like a ninny that he'd kept on about it and now knew what she had thought every time he went and said it—it hadn't brought her comfort or eased the burden at all. The worse he felt, the stiller he sat. The whole thing felt balanced on a knife or wire; if he moved to put his arm up or touch her the whole thing could tip over. He hated himself for sitting so frozen. He could almost visualize himself tiptoeing past something explosive. A big stupid-looking tiptoe, like in a cartoon. The whole last black week had been this way and it was wrong. He knew it was wrong, knew something was required of him that was not this terrible frozen care and caution, but he pretended to himself he did not know what it was that was required. He pretended it had no name. He pretended that not saying aloud what he knew to be right and true was for her sake, was for the sake of her needs and feelings. He also worked dock and routing at UPS, on top of school, but had traded to get the day off after they'd decided together. Two days before, he had awakened very early and tried to pray but could not. He was freezing more and more solid, he felt like, but he had not thought of his father or the blank frozenness of his father, even in church, which had once filled him with such pity. This was the truth. Lane Dean, Jr., felt sun on one arm as he pictured in his mind an image of himself on a train, waving mechanically to something that got smaller and smaller as the train pulled away. His father and his mother's father had the same birthday, a Cancer. Sheri's hair was colored an almost corn blond, very clean, the skin through her central part pink in the sunlight. They'd sat here long enough that only their right side was shaded now. He could look at her head, but not at her. Different parts of him felt unconnected to each other. She was smarter than him and they both knew it. It wasn't just school—Lane Dean was in accounting and business and did all right; he was hanging in there. She was a year older, twenty, but it was also more—she had always seemed to Lane to be on good terms with her life in a way that age could not account for. His mother had put it that she *knew what it is she wanted*, which was nursing and not an easy program at Peoria Junior College, and plus she worked hostessing at the Embers and had bought her own car. She was serious in a way Lane liked. She had a cousin that died when she was thirteen, fourteen, that she'd loved and been close with. She only talked about it that once. He liked her smell and her downy arms and the way she exclaimed when something made her laugh. He had liked just being with her and talking to her. She was serious in her faith and values in a way that Lane had liked and now, sitting here with her on the table, found himself afraid of. This was an awful thing. He was starting to believe that he might not be serious in his faith. He might be somewhat of a hypocrite, like the Assyrians in Isaiah, which would be a far graver sin than the appointment—he had decided he believed this. He was desperate to be good people, to still be able to feel he was good. He rarely before now had thought of damnation and Hell—that part of it didn't speak to his spirit—and in worship services he more just tuned himself out and tolerated Hell when it came up, the same way you tolerate the job you've got to have to save up for what it is you want. Her tennis shoes had little things doodled on them from sitting in her class lectures. She stayed looking down like that. Little notes or reading assignments in Bic in her neat round hand on the rubber elements around the sneaker's rim. Lane A. Dean, looking now at her inclined head's side's barrettes in the shape of blue ladybugs. The appointment was for afternoon, but when the doorbell had rung so early and his mother'd called to him up the stairs, he had known, and a terrible kind of blankness had commenced falling through him.

He told her that he did not know what to do. That he knew if he was the salesman of it and forced it upon her that was awful and wrong. But he was trying to understand—they'd prayed on it and talked it through from every different angle. Lane said how sorry she knew he was, and that if he was wrong in believing they'd truly decided together when they decided to make the appointment she should please tell him, because he thought he knew how she must have felt as it got closer and closer and how she must be so scared, but that what he couldn't tell was if it was more than that. He was totally still except for moving his mouth, it felt like. She did not reply. That if they needed to pray on it more and talk it through, then he was here, he was ready, he said. The appointment could get moved back; if she just said the word they could call and push it back to take more time to be sure in the decision. It was still so early in it—they both knew that, he said. This was true, that he felt this way, and yet he also knew he was also trying to say things that would get her to open up and say enough back that he could see her and read her heart and know what to say to get her to go through with it. He knew this without admitting to himself that this was what he wanted, for it would make him a hypocrite and liar. He knew, in some locked-up little part of him, why it was that he'd gone to no one to open up and seek their life counsel, not Pastor Steve or the prayer partners at campus ministries, not his UPS friends or the spiritual counselling available through his parents' old church. But he did not know why Sheri herself had not gone to Pastor Steve—he could not read her heart. She was blank and hidden. He so fervently wished it never happened. He felt like he knew now why it was a true sin and not just a leftover rule from past society.

He felt like he had been brought low by it and humbled and now did believe that the rules were there for a reason. That the rules were concerned with him personally, as an individual. He promised God he had learned his lesson. But what if that, too, was a hollow promise, from a hypocrite who repented only after, who promised submission but really only wanted a reprieve? He might not even know his own heart or be able to read and know himself. He kept thinking also of 1 Timothy and the hypocrite therein who *disputeth over words*. He felt a terrible inner resistance but could not feel what it was that it resisted. This was the truth. All the different angles and ways they had come at the decision together did not ever include it—the word—for had he once said it, avowed that he did love her, loved Sheri Fisher, then it all would have been transformed. It would not be a different stance or angle, but a difference in the very thing they were praying and deciding on together. Sometimes they had prayed together over the phone, in a kind of half code in case anybody accidentally picked up the extension. She continued to sit as if thinking, in the pose of thinking, like that one statue. They were right up next to each other on the table. He was looking over past her at the tree in the water. But he could not say he did: it was not true.

But neither did he ever open up and tell her straight out he did not love her. This might be his *lie by omission*. This might be the frozen resistance—were he to look right at her and tell her he didn't, she would keep the appointment and go. He knew this. Something in him, though, some terrible weakness or lack of values, could not tell her. It felt like a muscle he did not have. He didn't know why; he just could not do it, or even pray to do it. She believed he was good, serious in his values. Part of him seemed willing to more or less just about lie to someone with that kind of faith and trust, and what did that make him? How could such a type of individual even pray? What it really felt like was a taste of the reality of what might be meant by Hell. Lane Dean had never believed in Hell as a lake of fire or a loving God consigning folks to a burning lake of fire—he knew in his heart this was not true. What he believed in was a living God of compassion and love and the possibility of a personal relationship with Jesus Christ through whom this love was enacted in human time. But sitting here beside this girl as unknown to him now as outer space, waiting for whatever she might say to unfreeze him, now he felt like he could see the edge or outline of what a real vision of Hell might be. It was of two great and terrible armies within himself, opposed and facing each other, silent. There would be battle but no victor. Or never a battle—the armies would stay like that, motionless, looking across at each other, and seeing therein something so different and alien from themselves that they could not understand, could not hear each other's speech as even words or read anything from what their face looked like, frozen like that, opposed and uncomprehending, for all human time. Two-hearted, a hypocrite to yourself either way.

When he moved his head, a part of the lake further out flashed with sun— 5 the water up close wasn't black now, and you could see into the shallows and see that all the water was moving but gently, this way and that—and in this same way he besought to return to himself as Sheri moved her leg and started to turn beside him. He could see the man in the suit and gray hat standing motionless now at the lake's rim, holding something under one arm and looking across at the opposite side where a row of little forms on camp chairs sat in a way that meant they had lines in the water for crappie—which mostly only your blacks from the East Side ever did—and the little white shape at the row's end a Styrofoam creel. In his moment or time at the lake now just to come, Lane Dean first felt he could take this all in whole: everything seemed distinctly lit, for the circle of the pin oak's shade had rotated off all the way, and they sat now in sun with their shadow a two-headed thing in the grass before them. He was looking or gazing again at where the downed tree's branches seemed to all bend so sharply just under the shallows' surface when he was given to know that through all this frozen silence he'd despised he had, in truth, been praying, or some little part of his heart he could not hear had, for he was answered now with a type of vision, what he would later call within his own mind a vision or *moment of grace.* He was not a hypocrite, just broken and split off like all men. Later on, he believed that what happened was he'd had a moment of almost seeing them both as Jesus saw them—as blind but groping, wanting to please God despite their inborn fallen nature. For in that same given moment he saw, quick as light, into Sheri's heart, and was made to know what would occur here as she finished turning to him and the man in the hat watched the fishing and the downed elm shed cells into the water. This down-to-earth girl that smelled good and wanted to be a nurse would take and hold one of his hands in both of hers to unfreeze him and make him look at her, and she would say that she cannot do it. That she is sorry she did not know this sooner, that she hadn't meant to lie—she agreed because she'd wanted to believe that she could, but she cannot. That she will carry this and have it; she has to. With her gaze clear and steady. That all night last night she prayed and searched inside herself and decided this is what love commands of her. That Lane should please please sweetie let her finish. That listen—this is her own decision and obliges him to nothing. That she knows he does not love her, not that way, has known it all this time, and that it's all right. That it is as it is and it's all right. She will carry this, and have it, and love it and make no claim on Lane except his good wishes and respecting what she has to do. That she releases him, all claim, and hopes he finishes up at P.J.C. and does so good in his life and has all joy and good things. Her voice will be clear and steady, and she will be lying, for Lane has been given to read her heart. To see through her. One of the opposite side's blacks raises his arm in what may be greeting, or waving off a bee. There is a mower cutting grass someplace off behind them. It will be a terrible, last-ditch gamble born out of the desperation in Sheri Fisher's soul, the knowledge that she can neither do this thing today nor carry a child alone and shame her family. Her values blocked the way either way, Lane could see, and she has no other options or choice—this lie is not a sin. Galatians 4:16, *Have I then become your enemy?* She is gambling that he is good. There on the table, neither frozen nor yet moving, Lane Dean, Jr., sees all this, and is moved with pity, and also with something more, something without any name he knows, that is given to him in the form of a question that never once in all the long week's thinking and division had even so much as occurred—why is he so sure he doesn't love her? Why is one kind of love any different? What if he has no earthly idea what love is? What would even Jesus do? For it was just now he felt her two small strong soft hands on his, to turn him. What if he was just afraid, if the truth was no more than this, and if what to pray for was not even love but simple courage, to meet both her eyes as she says it and trust his heart?

FOR ANALYSIS

1. What truths does Lane feel unable to confront?

2. There are many biblical references in "Good People," and Lane often frames his thoughts in religious terms. How does the story present his faith, and faith in general?

3. How would you describe the **style** in which this story is written? How does the style serve the story's treatment of its subject and characters?

4. The **protagonist** is said to think that "He was desperate to be good people, to still be able to feel he was good" (para. 2). How does what happens at the end of the story affect this desire?

MAKING CONNECTIONS

1. Is it possible to read "Good People" as being consciously written in the shadow of "Hills Like White Elephants"? In what ways could it be seen to echo the earlier story? In what ways could it be seen to diverge? Do you think Wallace might even be offering a commentary on Hemingway's story?

2. In what way are both of these stories about characters wanting to have it all? What does "having it all" entail in each story? Is it possible in either?

3. Compare the two stories' treatment of abortion. How does each bring it up? How does each talk about it—directly or indirectly? How do the characters feel about it? How, as far as you can tell, do the authors themselves feel about it?

WRITING TOPICS

1. List appearances of **images** of division, doubleness, halfness, and dichotomy in the story. Reflect on your list: Why do you think there are so many of these instances? Is the story ultimately about division, or is it about its opposite—wholeness or union? How so?

2. What kind of note do you think the story ends on? Does it imply a happy future for the two characters, or do more difficulties lie ahead? What happens next? Write the next part of their story.

POETRY

SAPPHO   (CA. 610–CA. 580 B.C.)

WITH HIS VENOM[1]

With his venom

Irresistible
and bittersweet

that loosener
of limbs, Love

reptile-like
strikes me down

CATULLUS   (CA. 84–CA. 54 B.C.)

85

I hate and love. Why I do so, perhaps you ask.
I know not, but I feel it, and I am in torment.

FOR ANALYSIS

1. In the original Latin, the first sentence of the poem is *Odi et amo*, I hate and I love. It illustrates something general about the poem, which is the absence of adjectives and, for the most part, nouns. What is the effect of this choice on the reader?

2. This poem is one of twenty-six that Catullus wrote about a woman with whom he was in love. Many are not entirely happy poems, taking as their subjects infidelity, quarrels, and other topics not usually thought of as the stuff of love poetry. Is this a love poem?

With His Venom
   [1] Translated by Mary Barnard.

WRITING TOPIC

Write a love/hate poem, and afterward reflect on your poetic choices. What kinds of **imagery**, language, and figures of speech did you choose? Do you think they are generally good choices for this kind of poem? If so, what makes them so? If not, why not?

ANONYMOUS

BONNY BARBARA ALLAN

It was in and about the Martinmas[1] time,
    When the green leaves were a falling,
That Sir John Graeme, in the West Country,
    Fell in love with Barbara Allan.

He sent his man down through the town,
    To the place where she was dwelling:
"O haste and come to my master dear,
    Gin° ye be Barbara Allan."   if

O hooly,° hooly rose she up,   slowly
    To the place where he was lying,   10
And when she drew the curtain by:
    "Young man, I think you're dying."

"O it's I'm sick, and very, very sick,
    And 'tis a' for Barbara Allan."
"O the better for me ye s'° never be,   ye shall
    Tho your heart's blood were a-spilling."

"O dinna° ye mind,° young man," said she,   don't/remember
    "When ye was in the tavern a drinking,
That ye made the healths gae° round and round,   go
    And slighted Barbara Allan?"   20

He turned his face unto the wall,
    And death was with him dealing:
"Adieu, adieu, my dear friends all,
    And be kind to Barbara Allan."

[1] November 11.

And slowly, slowly raise she up,
   And slowly, slowly left him,
And sighing said she could not stay,
   Since death of life had reft him.

She had not gane a mile but twa,
   When she heard the dead-bell ringing,   30
And every jow° that the dead-bell geid,°   stroke/gave
   It cried, "Woe to Barbara Allan!"

"O mother, mother, make my bed!
   O make it saft and narrow!
Since my love died for me to-day,
   I'll die for him to-morrow."

WILLIAM SHAKESPEARE   (1564–1616)

SONNETS 1609

18

Shall I compare thee to a summer's day?
Thou art more lovely and more temperate:
Rough winds do shake the darling buds of May,
And summer's lease hath all too short a date:
Sometime too hot the eye of heaven shines,
And often is his gold complexion dimmed;
And every fair from fair sometimes declines,
By chance or nature's changing course untrimmed;
But thy eternal summer shall not fade,
Nor lose possession of that fair thou ow'st,°   owns 10
Nor shall death brag thou wander'st in his shade,
When in eternal lines to time thou grow'st:
   So long as men can breathe, or eyes can see,
   So long lives this, and this gives life to thee.

FOR ANALYSIS

1. Why does the speaker in the poem argue that "a summer's day" is an inappropriate **metaphor** for his beloved?

2. What is "this" in line 14?

29

When, in disgrace with fortune and men's eyes,
I all alone beweep my outcast state
And trouble deaf heaven with my bootless cries
And look upon myself and curse my fate,
Wishing me like to one more rich in hope,
Featured like him, like him with friends possessed,
Desiring this man's art and that man's scope,
With what I most enjoy contented least;
Yet in these thoughts myself almost despising,
Haply I think on thee, and then my state,   10
Like to the lark at break of day arising
From sullen earth, sings hymns at heaven's gate;
    For thy sweet love remembered such wealth brings
    That then I scorn to change my state with kings.

64

When I have seen by Time's fell hand defac'd
The rich-proud cost of outworn buried age;
When sometime lofty towers I see down-raz'd,
And brass eternal slave to mortal rage;
When I have seen the hungry ocean gain
Advantage on the kingdom of the shore,
And the firm soil win of the watery main,
Increasing store with loss, and loss with store;
When I have seen such interchange of state,
Or state itself confounded to decay;   10
Ruin hath taught me thus to ruminate—
That Time will come and take my love away.
    This thought is as a death, which cannot choose
    But weep to have that which it fears to lose.

FOR ANALYSIS

1. Why does the **narrator** "weep" in the final line? Does he or she mourn the actual death of a loved one? If not death, then what causes the weeping?

2. This poem could have been included in this book's final chapter on Life and Death. Why do you think it was included in this chapter? Is it simply a poem about death? If not, what does it have to say about love beyond the fear of a loved one's death?

116

Let me not to the marriage of true minds
Admit impediments. Love is not love
Which alters when it alteration finds,
Or bends with the remover to remove:
Oh, no! it is an ever-fixèd mark,
That looks on tempests and is never shaken;
It is the star to every wandering bark,
Whose worth's unknown, although his height be taken.
Love's not Time's fool, though rosy lips and cheeks
Within his bending sickle's compass come;   10
Love alters not with his brief hours and weeks,
But bears it out even to the edge of doom.
    If this be error and upon me proved,
    I never writ, nor no man ever loved.

130

My mistress' eyes are nothing like the sun;
Coral is far more red than her lips' red;
If snow be white, why then her breasts are dun;
If hairs be wires, black wires grow on her head.
I have seen roses damasked,° red and white,   variegated
But no such roses see I in her cheeks;
And in some perfumes is there more delight
Than in the breath that from my mistress reeks.
I love to hear her speak, yet well I know
That music hath a far more pleasing sound;   10
I grant I never saw a goddess go;
My mistress, when she walks, treads on the ground.
    And yet, by heaven, I think my love as rare
    As any she belied with false compare.[1]

FOR ANALYSIS

1. It seems at first like the speaker might be insulting his "mistress." Is he? What
evidence supports your answer?

2. Annotate the poem so that the **sonnet's rhyme** scheme is clear. Where does the
scheme change—that is, where does the pattern of alternating pairs of lines whose
last words rhyme (for example, in lines 1–4 "sun," "red," "dun," "head," or ABAB)
shift to a different pattern? How does the poem take advantage of this shift to make
meaning?

3. How do the last two lines echo the first line?

---

[1] I.e., as any woman misrepresented with false comparisons.

WRITING TOPIC

This poem plays off the tradition of Petrarchan love poetry, whose conventions include the worshipful idealization of the woman who is the subject of the poem. How does Shakespeare's poem **satirize** this kind of love poetry?

JOHN DONNE (1572–1631)

THE FLEA 1633

Mark but this flea, and mark in this,
How little that which thou deniest me is;
It sucked me first, and now sucks thee,
And in this flea our two bloods mingled be;
Thou know'st that this cannot be said
A sin, nor shame, nor loss of maidenhead,
    Yet this enjoys before it woo,
    And pampered swells with one blood made of two,
    And this, alas, is more than we would do.

Oh stay, three lives in one flea spare,   10
Where we almost, yea more than married, are.
This flea is you and I, and this
Our marriage bed and marriage temple is;
Though parents grudge, and you, we are met,
And cloistered in these living walls of jet,
    Though use° make you apt to kill me   custom
    Let not to that, self-murder added be,
    And sacrilege, three sins in killing three.

Cruel and sudden, hast thou since
Purpled thy nail, in blood of innocence?   20
Wherein could this flea guilty be,
Except in that drop which it sucked from thee?
Yet thou triumph'st, and say'st that thou
Find'st not thy self nor me the weaker now;
    'Tis true, then learn how false fears be;
    Just so much honor, when thou yield'st to me,
    Will waste, as this flea's death took life from thee.

FOR ANALYSIS

1. What does the woman addressed in this poem deny the poet (l. 2)?

2. What is the woman about to do at the beginning of the second **stanza**? What argument does the poet use to save the flea?

3. How does the poet turn the flea's life and death to his own purposes?

WRITING TOPIC

In a paragraph, discuss your response to Donne's use of a flea to animate a seduction poem.

THE PROHIBITION   1633

Take heed of loving mee,
At least remember, I forbade it thee;
Not that I shall repaire my'unthrifty wast
Of Breath and Blood, upon thy sighes, and teares,
By being to thee then what to me thou wast;
But, so great Joy, our life at once outweares,
Then, least thy love, by my death, frustrate bee,
If thou love mee, take heed of loving mee.

Take heed of hating mee,
Or too much triumph in the Victorie.   10
Not that I shall be mine owne officer,
And hate with hate againe retaliate;
But thou wilt lose the stile of conquerour,
If I, thy conquest, perish by thy hate.
Then, least my being nothing lessen thee,
If thou hate mee, take heed of hating mee.

Yet, love and hate mee too,
So, these extreames shall neithers office doe;
Love mee, that I may die the gentler way;
Hate mee, because thy love is too great for mee;   20
Or let these two, themselves, not me decay;
So shall I, live, thy Stage, not triumph bee;
Lest thou thy love and hate and mee undoe,
To let mee live, O love and hate mee too.

A VALEDICTION: FORBIDDING MOURNING   1633

As virtuous men pass mildly away,
    And whisper to their souls to go,
Whilst some of their sad friends do say
    The breath goes now, and some say, No;

So let us melt, and make no noise,
    No tear-floods, nor sigh-tempests move,
'Twere profanation of our joys
    To tell the laity our love.

Moving of th' earth° brings harms and fears,   earthquake
    Men reckon what it did and meant;   10
But trepidation of the spheres,
    Though greater far, is innocent.[1]

Dull sublunary° lovers' love   under the moon
    (Whose soul is sense) cannot admit
Absence, because it doth remove
    Those things which elemented it.

But we by a love so much refined
    That our selves know not what it is,
Inter-assuréd of the mind,
    Care less, eyes, lips, and hands to miss.   20

Our two souls therefore, which are one,
    Though I must go, endure not yet
A breach, but an expansion,
    Like gold to airy thinness beat.

If they be two, they are two so
    As stiff twin compasses are two;
Thy soul, the fixed foot, makes no show
    To move, but doth, if th' other do.

And though it in the center sit,
    Yet when the other far doth roam,   30
It leans and harkens after it,
    And grows erect, as that comes home.

Such wilt thou be to me, who must
    Like th' other foot, obliquely run;
Thy firmness makes my circle just,
    And makes me end where I begun.

---

[1] The movement of the heavenly spheres is harmless.

FOR ANALYSIS

1. Two kinds of love are described in this poem: spiritual and physical. How does the **simile** drawn in the first two **stanzas** help define the differences between them?

2. How does the contrast between earthquakes and the movement of the spheres in stanza 3 further develop the contrast between the two types of love?

3. Explain the comparison between a drawing compass and the lovers in the last three stanzas.

BEN JONSON   (1572–1637)

SONG, TO CELIA[1]   1616

Drink to me only with thine eyes,
    And I will pledge with mine;
Or leave a kiss but in the cup,
    And I'll not look for wine.
The thirst that from the soul doth rise
    Doth ask a drink divine;
But might I of Jove's nectar sup,
    I would not change for thine.
I sent thee late a rosy wreath,
    Not so much honoring thee   10
As giving it a hope, that there
    It could not withered be.
But thou thereon didst only breathe,
    And sent'st it back to me;
Since when it grows, and smells, I swear,
    Not of itself but thee.

LADY MARY WROTH   (CA. 1587–CA. 1651)

AM I THUS CONQUERED?   1621

Am I thus conquered? Have I lost the powers,
    That° to withstand, which joyes° to ruin me?   (love)/delights
    Must I be still while it my strength devours,
    And captive leads me prisoner bound, unfree?

Song, To Celia
[1] A widely recorded song.

Love first shall leave men's fant'sies to them free,
    Desire shall quench love's flames, spring hate sweet showers,
    Love shall loose all his darts, have sight, and see
    His shame, and wishings hinder happy hours.
Why should we not love's purblind° charms resist?   completely blind
    Must we be servile, doing what he list?°   pleases 10
    No, seek some host to harbor thee: I fly
Thy babish° tricks, and freedom do profess   childish
    But O my hurt makes my lost heart confess
    I love, and must: so farewell liberty.

ROBERT HERRICK   (1591–1674)

TO THE VIRGINS, TO MAKE
MUCH OF TIME[1]   1648

Gather ye rosebuds while ye may,
    Old Time is still a-flying;
And this same flower that smiles today,
    Tomorrow will be dying.

The glorious lamp of heaven, the sun,
    The higher he's a-getting,
The sooner will his race be run,
    And nearer he's to setting.

That age is best which is the first,
    When youth and blood are warmer;
But being spent, the worse, and worst   10
    Times still succeed the former.

Then be not coy, but use your time;
    And while ye may, go marry:
For having lost but once your prime,
    You may for ever tarry.

To the Virgins, to Make Much of Time
  [1] Available on CD, *In Praise of Woman* (Hyperion, 1994), composed by Madeleine Dring with Graham
Johnson and Anthony Rolfe-Johnson.

ANNE BRADSTREET (CA. 1612–1672)

TO MY DEAR AND LOVING HUSBAND   1678

If ever two were one, then surely we.
If ever man were loved by wife, then thee;
If ever wife was happy in a man,
Compare with me ye women if you can.
I prize thy love more than whole mines of gold
Or all the riches that the East doth hold.
My love is such that rivers cannot quench,
Nor ought but love from thee give recompense.
Thy love is such I can no way repay;
The heavens reward thee manifold, I pray.   10
Then while we live, in love let's so persever,
That when we live no more we may live ever.

KATHERINE PHILIPS (1631–1664)

FRIENDSHIP'S MYSTERY,
TO MY DEAREST LUCASIA   1667

1

Come, my *Lucasia*, since we see
    That Miracles Mens faith do move,
By wonder and by prodigy
    To the dull angry world let's prove
    There's a Religion in our Love.

2

For though we were design'd t' agree,
    That Fate no liberty destroyes,
But our Election is as free
    As Angels, who with greedy choice
    Are yet determin'd to their joyes.   10

3

Our hearts are doubled by the loss,
    Here Mixture is Addition grown;
We both diffuse, and both ingross:
    And we whose minds are so much one,
    Never, yet ever are alone.

906

4

We court our own Captivity
    Than Thrones more great and innocent:
'Twere banishment to be set free,
    Since we wear fetters whose intent
    Not Bondage is, but Ornament.   20

5

Divided joyes are tedious found,
    And griefs united easier grow:
We are our selves but by rebound,
    And all our Titles shuffled so,
    Both Princes, and both Subjects too.

6

Our Hearts are mutual Victims laid,
    While they (such power in Friendship lies)
Are Altars, Priests, and Off'rings made:
    And each Heart which thus kindly dies,
    Grows deathless by the Sacrifice.   30

"EPHELIA" (FL. CA. 1679)

TO MY RIVAL   1679

Since you dare Brave me, with a Rivals Name,
You shall prevail, and I will quite my Claime:
For know, proud Maid, I Scorn to call him mine,
Whom thou durst ever hope to have made thine:
Yet I confess, I lov'd him once so well,
His presence was my Heav'n, his absence Hell:
With gen'rous excellence I fill'd his Brest,
And in sweet Beauteous Forms his Person drest;
For him I did heaven, and its Pow'r despise,
And onely lived by th'Influence of his Eyes: 10
I fear'd not Rivals, for I thought that he
That was possess'd of such a Prize as me,
All meaner Objects wou'd Contemn, and Slight,
Nor let an abject thing Usurpe my Right:
But when I heard he was so wretched Base
To pay devotion to thy wrinkled Face
I Banish't him my sight, and told the Slave,
He had not Worth, but what my Fancy gave:

'Twas I that rais'd him to this Glorious State,
And can as easily Annihilate: 20
But let him live, Branded with Guilt and Shame,
And Shrink into the Shade from whence he came;
His Punishment shall be, the Loss of Me,
And be Augumented, by his gaining Thee.

FOR ANALYSIS

1. How has the speaker reacted to the apparent loss of this man to her rival? At whom does she direct her anger?

2. How would you characterize the speaker's **tone**? Does she express anything other than anger? If so, what, and how?

WRITING TOPIC

Love poetry often focuses on the beloved or the loss of the beloved, but it is less common to see poems expressing the change from love to hate. Why do you think this is? Write a short essay about love poetry and love-to-hate poetry (consider popular music lyrics if you think it might help).

WILLIAM BLAKE   (1757–1827)

A POISON TREE   1794

I was angry with my friend:
I told my wrath, my wrath did end.
I was angry with my foe:
I told it not, my wrath did grow.

And I watered it in fears,
Night & morning with my tears;
And I sunnéd it with smiles,
And with soft deceitful wiles.

And it grew both day and night,
Till it bore an apple bright.   10
And my foe beheld its shine,
And he knew that it was mine,

And into my garden stole,
When the night had veil'd the pole;
In the morning glad I see
My foe outstretched beneath the tree.

FOR ANALYSIS

1. Is anything gained from the parallel readers might draw between this tree and the tree in the Garden of Eden? Explain.

2. Explain what the "poison" is.

3. Does your own experience verify the first **stanza** of the poem?

ROBERT BURNS   (1759-1796)

A RED, RED ROSE   1796

O My Luve's like a red, red rose,
    That's newly sprung in June;
O My Luve's like a melodie
    That's sweetly played in tune.

As fair art thou, my bonnie lass,
    So deep in luve am I;
And I will luve thee still, my dear,
    Til a' the seas gang dry.

Till a' the seas gang dry, my dear,
    And the rocks melt wi' the sun: 10
O I will love thee still, my dear,
    While the sands o' life shall run.

And fare thee weel, my only luve,
    And fare thee weel awhile!
And I will come again, my luve,
    Though it were ten thousand mile.

MATTHEW ARNOLD   (1822-1888)

DOVER BEACH   1867

The sea is calm tonight.
The tide is full, the moon lies fair
Upon the straits; on the French coast the light
Gleams and is gone; the cliffs of England stand,
Glimmering and vast, out in the tranquil bay.
Come to the window, sweet is the night-air!
Only, from the long line of spray

Where the sea meets the moon-blanched land,
Listen! you hear the grating roar
Of pebbles which the waves draw back, and fling,　　　　　10
At their return, up the high strand,
Begin, and cease, and then again begin,
With tremulous cadence slow, and bring
The eternal note of sadness in.

Sophocles long ago
Heard it on the Aegean, and it brought
Into his mind the turbid ebb and flow
Of human misery; we
Find also in the sound a thought,
Hearing it by this distant northern sea.　　　　　20

The Sea of Faith
Was once, too, at the full, and round earth's shore
Lay like the folds of a bright girdle furled.
But now I only hear
Its melancholy, long, withdrawing roar,
Retreating, to the breath
Of the night-wind, down the vast edges drear
And naked shingles° of the world.　　　　　　　　pebble beaches

Ah, love, let us be true
To one another! for the world, which seems　　　　　30
To lie before us like a land of dreams,
So various, so beautiful, so new,
Hath really neither joy, nor love, nor light,
Nor certitude, nor peace, nor help for pain;
And we are here as on a darkling plain
Swept with confused alarms of struggle and flight,
Where ignorant armies clash by night.

ROBERT FROST　(1874–1963)

FIRE AND ICE　1923

Some say the world will end in fire,
Some say in ice,
From what I've tasted of desire
I hold with those who favor fire.

But if it had to perish twice,
I think I know enough of hate
To say that for destruction ice
Is also great
And would suffice.

DOROTHY PARKER   (1893–1967)

ONE PERFECT ROSE   1926

A single flow'r he sent me, since we met.
   All tenderly his messenger he chose;
Deep-hearted, pure, with scented dew still wet—
   One perfect rose.

I knew the language of the floweret;
   "My fragile leaves," it said, "his heart enclose."
Love long has taken for his amulet
   One perfect rose.

Why is it no one ever sent me yet
   One perfect limousine, do you suppose?   10
Ah no, it's always just my luck to get
   One perfect rose.

E. E. CUMMINGS   (1894–1962)

SHE BEING BRAND   1926

she being Brand

-new;and you
know consequently a
little stiff i was
careful of her and(having

thoroughly oiled the universal
joint tested my gas felt of
her radiator made sure her springs were O.

K.)i went right to it flooded-the-carburetor cranked her

up, slipped the
clutch(and then somehow got into reverse she
kicked what
the hell)next
minute i was back in neutral tried and

again slo-wly;bare,ly nudg. ing (my

lev-er Right-
oh and her gears being in
A 1 shape passed
from low through
second-in-to-high like
greasedlightning)just as we turned the corner of Divinity

avenue i touched the accelerator and give

her the juice, good

                    (it

was the first ride and believe i we was
happy to see how nice she acted right up to
the last minute coming back down by the Public
Gardens i slammed on

the
internalexpanding
&
externalcontracting
brakes Bothatonce and

brought allofher tremB
-ling
to a:dead.

stand-
;Still)

FOR ANALYSIS

1. People often use female gendered language when referring to cars and boats. How does Cummings take advantage of this convention? What **conceit** in the poem depends on it?

2. What is unusual about the way Cummings places words on the page? What effects does it achieve?

3. Describe the poem's tempo. Where does it speed up? Where does it slow down? If you were to draw a line or an arc depicting its speed, what would it look like? What other phenomenon or phenomena might such a drawing describe?

WRITING TOPICS

1. Automobiles began to be mass-produced at the beginning of the 1920s. How might "she being Brand" be a response to the new widespread availability of cars?

2. Write a poem in which you describe one experience or activity in language suggestive of another. Try to make the connection clear but not explicit.

THEODORE ROETHKE (1908–1963)

I KNEW A WOMAN 1958

I knew a woman, lovely in her bones,
When small birds sighed, she would sigh back at them;
Ah, when she moved, she moved more ways than one:
The shapes a bright container can contain!
Of her choice virtues only gods should speak,
Or English poets who grew up on Greek
(I'd have them sing in chorus, cheek to cheek).

How well her wishes went! She stroked my chin,
She taught me Turn, and Counter-turn, and Stand;
She taught me Touch, that undulant white skin;   10
I nibbled meekly from her proffered hand;
She was the sickle; I, poor I, the rake,
Coming behind her for her pretty sake
(But what prodigious mowing we did make).

Love likes a gander, and adores a goose:
Her full lips pursed, the errant note to seize;
She played it quick, she played it light and loose;
My eyes, they dazzled at her flowing knees;
Her several parts could keep a pure repose,
Or one hip quiver with a mobile nose   20
(She moved in circles, and those circles moved).

Let seed be grass, and grass turn into hay:
I'm martyr to a motion not my own;

What's freedom for? To know eternity.
I swear she cast a shadow white as stone.
But who would count eternity in days?
These old bones live to learn her wanton ways:
(I measure time by how a body sways).

FOR ANALYSIS

1. What is the **rhyme** scheme of this poem?
2. What does line 3 mean?
3. Describe the two principal images in the second **stanza**.

WRITING TOPIC

In an essay, describe the role of motion in this celebration of a woman's beauty.

ELIZABETH BISHOP   (1911–1979)

ONE ART   1976

The art of losing isn't hard to master;
so many things seem filled with the intent
to be lost that their loss is no disaster.

Lose something every day. Accept the fluster
of lost door keys, the hour badly spent.
The art of losing isn't hard to master.

Then practice losing farther, losing faster:
places, and names, and where it was you meant
to travel. None of these will bring disaster.

I lost my mother's watch. And look! my last, or   10
next-to-last, of three loved houses went.
The art of losing isn't hard to master.

I lost two cities, lovely ones. And, vaster,
some realms I owned, two rivers, a continent.
I miss them, but it wasn't a disaster.

—Even losing you (the joking voice, a gesture
I love) I shan't have lied. It's evident
the art of losing's not too hard to master
though it may look like (*Write* it!) like disaster.

JOHN FREDERICK NIMS (1913–1999)

LOVE POEM 1947

My clumbsiest dear, whose hands shipwreck vases,
At whose quick touch all glasses chip and ring,
Whose palms are bulls in china, burrs in linen,
And have no cunning with any soft thing

Except all ill at ease fidgeting people:
The refugee uncertain at the door
You make at home; deftly you steady
The drunk clambering on his undulant floor.

Unpredictable dear, the taxi drivers' terror,
Shrinking from far headlights pale as a dime   10
Yet leaping before red apoplectic streetcars—
Misfit in any space. And never on time.

A wrench in clocks and the solar system. Only
With words and people and love you move at ease.
In traffic of wit expertly maneuver
And keep us, all devotion, at your knees.

Forgeting your coffee spreading on our flannel,
Your lipstick grinning on our coat,
So gayly in love's unbreakable heaven
Our souls on glory of spilt bourbon float.   20

Be with me darling early and late. Smash glasses—
I will study wry music for your sake.
For should your hands drop white and empty
All the toys of the world would break.

WISLAWA SZYMBORSKA (1923–2012)

A HAPPY LOVE 1981

A happy love. Is it normal,
is it serious, is it profitable—
what use to the world are two people
who have no eyes for the world?

Elevated each for each, for no apparent merit,
by sheer chance singled out of a million, yet convinced
it had to be so—as reward for what? for nothing,
the light shines from nowhere—
why just on them, and not on others?
Is this an offense to justice? Yes.   10
Does it violate time-honored principles, does it cast
any moral down from the heights? It violates and casts down.

Look at the happy couple:
if they'd at least dissemble a bit,
feign depression and thereby cheer their friends!
Hear how they laugh—offensively.
And the language they speak—it only seems to make sense.
And all those ceremonials, ceremonies,
those elaborate obligations toward each other—
it all looks like a plot behind mankind's back!   20

It's even hard to foresee how far things might go,
if their example could be followed.
What could religions and poetries rely on,
what would be remembered, what abandoned,
who would want to keep within the bounds.

A happy love. Is it necessary?
Tact and common sense advise us to say no more of it
than of a scandal in Life's upper ranks.
Little cherubs get born without its help.
Never, ever could it populate the earth,   30
for it happens so seldom.

Let people who know naught of happy love
assert that nowhere is there a happy love.

With such faith, they would find it easier to live and to die.

LISEL MUELLER   (B. 1924)

HAPPY AND UNHAPPY FAMILIES I   1996

If all happy families are alike,[1]
then so are the unhappy families,
whose lives we celebrate

Happy and Unhappy Families I
[1] An allusion to the celebrated opening line of Leo Tolstoy's novel *Anna Karenina* (1873–1876).

because they are motion and heat,
because they are what we think of as *life*.
Someone is lying and someone else
is being lied to. Someone is beaten
and someone else is doing the beating.
Someone is praying, or weeps
because she does not know how to pray.   10
Someone drinks all night;
someone cowers in corners;
someone threatens and someone pleads.
Bitter words at the table,
bitter sobs in the bedroom;
reprisal breathed on the bathroom mirror.
The house crackles with secrets;
everyone draws up a plan of escape.
Somebody shatters without a sound.
Sometimes one of them leaves the house   20
on a stretcher, in terrible silence.
How much energy suffering takes!
It is like a fire that burns and burns
but cannot burn down to extinction.
Unhappy families are never idle;
they are where the action is,
unlike the others, the happy ones,
who never raise their voices
and spit no blood, who do nothing
to deserve their happiness.   30

FOR ANALYSIS

1. How does the speaker describe unhappy families? What do you think are the characteristics of happy families?

2. Describe the **images** used to identify the sources of unhappiness.

3. Describe the conditions that generate happy families (ll. 27–30). Do you agree with the speaker? Explain.

4. In line 22, the speaker laments, "How much energy suffering takes!" Do you agree? How much energy does happiness take?

WRITING TOPIC

Argue for or against the proposition that all happy (or unhappy) families are alike. On what assumptions do you base your argument?

CAROLYN KIZER   (B. 1925)

BITCH   1984

Now, when he and I meet, after all these years,
I say to the bitch inside me, don't start growling.
He isn't a trespasser anymore,
Just an old acquaintance tipping his hat.
My voice says, "Nice to see you,"
As the bitch starts to bark hysterically.
He isn't an enemy now,
Where are your manners, I say, as I say,
"How are the children? They must be growing up."
At a kind word from him, a look like the old days,   10
The bitch changes her tone: she begins to whimper.
She wants to snuggle up to him, to cringe.
Down, girl! Keep your distance
Or I'll give you a taste of the choke-chain.
"Fine, I'm just fine," I tell him.
She slobbers and grovels.
After all, I am her mistress. She is basically loyal.
It's just that she remembers how she came running
Each evening, when she heard his step;
How she lay at his feet and looked up adoringly   20
Though he was absorbed in his paper;
Or, bored with her devotion, ordered her to the kitchen
Until he was ready to play.
But the small careless kindnesses
When he'd had a good day, or a couple of drinks,
Come back to her now, seem more important
Than the casual cruelties, the ultimate dismissal.
"It's nice to know you are doing so well," I say.
He couldn't have taken you with him;
You were too demonstrative, too clumsy,   30
Not like the well-groomed pets of his new friends.
"Give my regards to your wife," I say. You gag
As I drag you off by the scruff,
Saying, "Goodbye! Goodbye! Nice to have seen you again."

FOR ANALYSIS

1. Who is being addressed in lines 13 and 14?

2. In what ways does the title suit the poem? In answering this question, consider the
tone of "Bitch," as well as the many **connotations** of the word.

3. What is "the ultimate dismissal" referred to in line 27?

4. How would you describe the speaker's present feelings about her former relationship?

GALWAY KINNELL   (B. 1927)

AFTER MAKING LOVE WE
HEAR FOOTSTEPS   1980

For I can snore like a bullhorn
or play loud music
or sit up talking with any reasonably sober Irishman
and Fergus will only sink deeper
into his dreamless sleep, which goes by all in one flash,
but let there be that heavy breathing
or a stifled come-cry anywhere in the house
and he will wrench himself awake
and make for it on the run—as now, we lie together,
after making love, quiet, touching along the length of our bodies,   10
familiar touch of the long-married,
and he appears—in his baseball pajamas, it happens,
the neck opening so small
he has to screw them on, which one day may make him wonder
about the mental capacity of baseball players—
and says, "Are you loving and snuggling? May I join?"
He flops down between us and hugs us and snuggles himself to sleep,
his face gleaming with satisfaction at being this very child.

In the half darkness we look at each other
and smile   20
and touch arms across his little, startlingly muscled body—
this one whom habit of memory propels to the ground of his making,
sleeper only the mortal sounds can sing awake,
this blessing love gives again into our arms.

FOR ANALYSIS

1. What two things appear in this poem that rarely appear together in poems? What is it like to read about them together? Why?

2. What expectation is set up by the event related in lines 6–9? Is it met? Does the speaker have the reaction to this event that we expect?

3. What function might lines 12–15 serve? How do they stand apart from the rest of the poem, and how do they fit in?

WRITING TOPICS

1. Do you believe the explanation in line 22? Do you have to for the poem to work?

2. Though it is not explicitly expressed, what might the speaker be said to be discovering in this poem?

ADRIENNE RICH   (1929–2012)

LIVING IN SIN   1955

She had thought the studio would keep itself;
no dust upon the furniture of love.
Half heresy, to wish the taps less vocal,
the panes relieved of grime. A plate of pears,
a piano with a Persian shawl, a cat
stalking the picturesque amusing mouse
had risen at his urging.
Not that at five each separate stair would writhe
under the milkman's tramp; that morning light
so coldly would delineate the scraps   10
of last night's cheese and three sepulchral bottles;
that on the kitchen shelf among the saucers
a pair of beetle-eyes would fix her own—
Envoy from some village in the moldings . . .
Meanwhile, he, with a yawn,
sounded a dozen notes upon the keyboard,
declared it out of tune, shrugged at the mirror,
rubbed at his beard, went out for cigarettes;
while she, jeered by the minor demons,
pulled back the sheets and made the bed and found   20
a towel to dust the table-top,
and let the coffee-pot boil over on the stove.
By evening she was back in love again,
though not so wholly but throughout the night
she woke sometimes to feel the daylight coming
like a relentless milkman up the stairs.

SYLVIA PLATH   (1932–1963)

DADDY   1965

You do not do, you do not do
Any more, black shoe
In which I have lived like a foot

For thirty years, poor and white,
Barely daring to breathe or Achoo.

Daddy, I have had to kill you,
You died before I had time—
Marble-heavy, a bag full of God,
Ghastly statue with one gray toe
Big as a Frisco seal   10

And a head in the freakish Atlantic
Where it pours bean green over blue
In the waters off beautiful Nauset.
I used to pray to recover you.
Ach, du.[1]

In the German tongue, in the Polish town
Scraped flat by the roller
Of wars, wars, wars.
But the name of the town is common.
My Polack friend   20

Says there are a dozen or two.
So I never could tell where you
Put your foot, your root,
I never could talk to you.
The tongue stuck in my jaw.

It stuck in a barb wire snare.
Ich, ich, ich, ich,[2]
I could hardly speak.
I thought every German was you.
And the language obscene   30

An engine, an engine
Chuffing me off like a Jew.
A Jew to Dachau, Auschwitz, Belsen.
I began to talk like a Jew.
I think I may well be a Jew.

The snows of the Tyrol, the clear beer of Vienna
Are not very pure or true.
With my gypsy ancestress and my weird luck

[1] German for "Oh, you."
[2] German for "I, I, I, I."

And my Taroc pack and my Taroc pack
I may be a bit of a Jew.   40

I have always been scared of *you*,
With your Luftwaffe,[3] your gobbledygoo.
And your neat mustache
And your Aryan eye, bright blue.
Panzer-man,[4] panzer-man, O You—

Not God but a swastika
So black no sky could squeak through.
Every woman adores a Fascist,
The boot in the face, the brute
Brute heart of a brute like you.   50

You stand at the blackboard, daddy,
In the picture I have of you,
A cleft in your chin instead of your foot
But no less a devil for that, no not
Any less the black man who

Bit my pretty red heart in two.
I was ten when they buried you.
At twenty I tried to die
And get back, back, back to you.
I thought even the bones would do   60

But they pulled me out of the sack,
And they stuck me together with glue.
And then I knew what to do.
I made a model of you,
A man in black with a Meinkampf[5] look

And a love of the rack and the screw.
And I said I do, I do.
So daddy, I'm finally through.
The black telephone's off at the root,
The voices just can't worm through.   70

If I've killed one man, I've killed two—
The vampire who said he was you
And drank my blood for a year,

---

[3] Name of the German air force during World War II.
[4] *Panzer* refers to German armored divisions during World War II.
[5] *My Struggle*, the title of Adolf Hitler's autobiography.

Seven years, if you want to know.
Daddy, you can lie back now.

There's a stake in your fat black heart
And the villagers never liked you.
They are dancing and stamping on you.
They always *knew* it was you.
Daddy, daddy, you bastard, I'm through.   80

FOR ANALYSIS

1. How do the **allusions** to Nazism function in the poem?

2. Does the poem exhibit the speaker's love for her father or her hatred of him? Explain.

3. What type of man does the speaker marry (see ll. 61–70)?

4. How does the speaker **characterize** her husband and her father in the last two **stanzas**? Might the "Daddy" of the last line of the poem refer to something more than the speaker's father? Explain.

WRITING TOPICS

1. What is the effect of the peculiar structure, idiosyncratic **rhyme**, unusual words (such as *achoo, gobbledygoo*), and repetitions in the poem?

2. What emotional associations does the title "Daddy" possess? Are those associations reinforced or contradicted by the poem?

LUCILLE CLIFTON   (B. 1936)

THERE IS A GIRL INSIDE   1977

there is a girl inside.
she is randy as a wolf.
she will not walk away
and leave these bones
to an old woman.

she is a green tree
in a forest of kindling.
she is a green girl
in a used poet.

she has waited   10
patient as a nun
for the second coming,

when she can break through gray hairs
into blossom

and her lovers will harvest
honey and thyme
and the woods will be wild
with the damn wonder of it.

FOR ANALYSIS

1. Who is the "girl" of this poem? What is she "inside" of?

2. What are the "bones" of the first **stanza**? What does the speaker's statement that she will not defer to an old woman tell us about her?

3. Describe the prevailing **metaphor** of the poem.

WRITING TOPIC

In an essay, discuss the appropriateness of the **images** Clifton uses to make her point.

SEAMUS HEANEY   (B. 1939)

VALEDICTION   1966

Lady with the frilled blouse
And simple tartan skirt,
Since you have left the house
Its emptiness has hurt
All thought. In your presence
Time rode easy, anchored
On a smile; but absence
Rocked love's balance, unmoored
The days. They buck and bound
Across the calendar   10
Pitched from the quiet sound
Of your flower-tender
Voice. Need breaks on my strand;
You've gone, I am at sea.
Until you resume command
Self is in mutiny.

FOR ANALYSIS

1. What is the central figure of speech (beginning in the middle of line 5) that animates this poem?

2. How are *time*, *love's balance*, and *the days* affected by the "lady's" behavior?

3. What sort of voice would a "flower-tender / Voice" (ll. 12–13) be?

WRITING TOPIC

Write an essay or a poem, serious or humorous, in which you use an extended **metaphor** to describe a fundamental emotion or experience—for example, how falling in love is like racing a car, or how the anguish of separation is like a visit to a dentist, or how attending classes is like a long hike through a desert.

BILLY COLLINS (B. 1941)

SONNET 1999

All we need is fourteen lines, well, thirteen now,
and after this one just a dozen
to launch a little ship on love's storm-tossed seas,
then only ten more left like rows of beans.
How easily it goes unless you get Elizabethan[1]
and insist the iambic bongos must be played
and rhymes positioned at the ends of lines,
one for every station of the cross.
But hang on here while we make the turn
into the final six where all will be resolved,   10
where longing and heartache will find an end,
where Laura will tell Petrarch[2] to put down his pen,
take off those crazy medieval tights,
blow out the lights, and come at last to bed.

ROBERT HASS (B. 1941)

MEDITATION AT LAGUNITAS 1979

All the new thinking is about loss.
In this it resembles all the old thinking.
The idea, for example, that each particular erases
the luminous clarity of a general idea. That the clown-
faced woodpecker probing the dead sculpted trunk
of that black birch is, by his presence,

Sonnet
   [1] The entry for **sonnet** in the "Glossary of Literary Terms" (p. 1401) distinguishes between the Elizabethan and the Italian, or Petrarchan, sonnet.
   [2] Francesco Petrarca (1304–1374), who employed the sonnet form named for him. Laura was the idealized woman he celebrated in his sonnets.

some tragic falling off from a first world
of undivided light. Or the other notion that,
because there is in this world no one thing
to which the bramble of *blackberry* corresponds,   10
a word is elegy to what it signifies.
We talked about it late last night and in the voice
of my friend, there was a thin wire of grief, a tone
almost querulous. After a while I understood that,
talking this way, everything dissolves: *justice,*
pine, hair, woman, you and I. There was a woman
I made love to and I remembered how, holding
her small shoulders in my hands sometimes,
I felt a violent wonder at her presence
like a thirst for salt, for my childhood river   20
with its island willows, silly music from the pleasure boat,
muddy places where we caught the little orange-silver fish
called *pumpkinseed.* It hardly had to do with her.
Longing, we say, because desire is full
of endless distances. I must have been the same to her.
But I remember so much, the way her hands dismantled bread,
the thing her father said that hurt her, what
she dreamed. There are moments when the body is as numinous
as words, days that are the good flesh continuing.
Such tenderness, those afternoons and evenings,   30
saying *blackberry, blackberry, blackberry.*

FOR ANALYSIS

1. The poem begins with an **allusion** to a fairly sophisticated idea—"the old
thinking" (l. 2)—that goes back to Plato, which holds that there are ideal forms
and that the particular instances of those forms that we see in our daily lives are
somehow less perfect than the ideal forms themselves. How does Hass convey that
idea poetically? What more mundane version of loss is he also concerned with in
this poem?

2. What is an **elegy**? What does it mean to say "A word is elegy to what it signifies"
(l. 11)? What other things might this poem be elegy to?

SHARON OLDS   (B. 1942)

SEX WITHOUT LOVE   1984

How do they do it, the ones who make love
without love? Beautiful as dancers,
gliding over each other like ice skaters

over the ice, fingers hooked
inside each other's bodies, faces
red as steak, wine, wet as the
children at birth whose mothers are going to
give them away. How do they come to the
come to the   come to the   God   come to the
still waters, and not love   10
the one who came there with them, light
rising slowly as steam off their joined
skin? These are the true religious,
the purists, the pros, the ones who will not
accept a false Messiah, love the
priest instead of the God. They do not
mistake the lover for their own pleasure,
they are like great runners: they know they are alone
with the road surface, the cold, the wind,
the fit of their shoes, their over-all cardio-
vascular health—just factors, like the partner   20
in the bed, and not the truth, which is the
single body alone in the universe
against its own best time.

FOR ANALYSIS

1. Describe the speaker's attitude toward "the ones who make love / without love" (ll. 1–2).

2. Who are the "These" of line 13?

3. What is the effect of the repetitions in lines 8 and 9?

4. What does "factors" of line 21 refer to?

5. Put into your own words the "truth" referred to in the final three lines. Does the speaker use the word straightforwardly or **ironically**? Explain.

DEBORAH POPE   (B. ?)

GETTING THROUGH   1995

Like a car stuck in gear,
a chicken too stupid to tell
its head is gone,
or sound ratcheting on
long after the film
has jumped the reel,
or a phone

ringing and ringing
in the house they have all
moved away from,   10
through rooms where dust
is a deepening skin,
and the locks unneeded,
so I go on loving you,
my heart blundering on,
a muscle spilling out
what is no longer wanted,
and my words hurtling past,
like a train off its track,
toward a boarded-up station,   20
closed for years,
like some last speaker
of a beautiful language
no one else can hear.

WYATT PRUNTY   (B. 1947)

LEARNING THE BICYCLE   2000

FOR HEATHER

The older children pedal past
Stable as little gyros, spinning hard
To supper, bath, and bed, until at last
We also quit, silent and tired
Beside the darkening yard where trees
Now shadow up instead of down.
Their predictable lengths can only tease
Her as, head lowered, she walks her bike alone
Somewhere between her wanting to ride
And her certainty she will always fall.   10

Tomorrow, though I will run behind,
Arms out to catch her, she'll tilt then balance wide
Of my reach, till distance makes her small,
Smaller, beyond the place I stop and know
That to teach her I had to follow
And when she learned to let her go.

FOR ANALYSIS

1. Describe the form and **rhyme** scheme of this poem. How does it differ from a **sonnet?**

2. What does the speaker learn from the experience of teaching his daughter to ride a bicycle?

WRITING TOPIC

Write an analysis of the poem's formal structure, noting how the poem shifts somewhat at lines 5, 9, and 11. How does the poem's organization and rhyme scheme mimic a typical sonnet?

ADRIAN BLEVINS   (B. 1964)

CASE AGAINST APRIL   2003

For a long time I was absolutely idiotic,
by which I mean I lashed and pulsed
like the cosmos of tissue at present on fire
inside the bodies of my students—
it being springtime, it being the season
of being naked under the cherry trees.
I'm not saying dig a hole and fall in it;

I'm not saying buy a cabin and a nanny goat
and walk around re-naming the forget-me-nots
after the lovers who said they'd slay you   10
and, well, *did*—for who ever heard
of a plant named Greg? Nevertheless,
sex is laughable; it's ultimately ridiculous;
it's what God invented since he couldn't have

Comedy Central. And still the young people
who aren't pushing their tongues
against the tongues of others
are weeping like babies
being prodded with thermometers
for the lack of good tongues   20
to lean their own tongues against.

I hear them complaining
about their would-be boyfriends and girlfriends,
and it's like they are all about to die,

like their hearts have spontaneously combusted
and little cell splinters are poking their lungs
and they're losing their balance,
falling like hail

or like meteors with pretty faces,
which is why when I say *up*, they look down.   30
And though I'm all for biology,
for the divine plan of multiplication
that calls for the pink of bodies
being bodies with other bodies
in beds and in bushes,
I'm sorry for all the time I wasted
being dramatic over the boys and their mustaches.
Maybe the heart, it gets colder.
But maybe the heart,
it learns a little self-preservation   40
and pulls the shades down
one window at a time. And it's not dark
in here. Really, there's a kind of light
between the marrow and the bone,
and sweet patches of grass to lie down on,
and muskrats and pied pipers
if that's the way you like to see the world,
if to get your kicks you choose to be delirious.
I mean, if you happen to be romantic

and don't mind splitting apart with longing   50
like a child in a toy store
with everywhere these primary colors
seeming to want to open what could be mouths
and seeming to want to sing what could be songs
if only you could catch your breath—
if only your heart would just stop seizing.

FOR ANALYSIS

1. What does April stand for here? Against what is the speaker making her case?

2. Where does the speaker come down on the issues of romance and love and sex? Is this poem's stance as simple as the title makes it seem?

WRITING TOPIC

The title's mention of April alludes to a long history of references to that month in poetry. Spend a few minutes of research on other famous poetic Aprils. While they all refer to the same month, do they all do so in exactly the same way? What are the variations? How does this new knowledge affect your reading of the poem?

DAISY FRIED (B. 1967)

ECONO MOTEL, OCEAN CITY 2010

Korean monster movie on the SyFy channel,
lurid *Dora the Explorer* blanket draped tentlike
over Baby's portacrib to shield us from unearned
innocence. The monster slings its carapace
in reverse swan dive up the embankment, triple-jointed bug legs
clattering, bathroom door ajar, exhaust roaring,
both of us naked, monster chomps
fast food stands, all that quilted aluminum, eats through streams
of running people, the promiscuously cheerful guilty American
scientist dies horribly. Grease-dusted ceiling fan   10
paddles erratically, two spars missing. Sheets whirled
to the polluted rug. I reach under the bed, fish out
somebody else's crunched beer can, my forearm comes out
dirty. Monster brachiates from bridge girders like a gibbon
looping round and around uneven bars, those are your fingers
in my tangles or my fingers, my head hangs
half off the king-size, monster takes tiny child actor
to its bone stash. Pillow's wet. The warped ceiling mirror
makes us look like fat porno dwarfs
in centripetal silver nitrate ripples. My glasses on the side table   20
tipped onto scratchproof lenses, earpieces sticking up
like arms out of disaster rubble. Your feet hooked over my feet. What miasma
lays gold dander down on forms of temporary
survivors wandering the promenade? You pull Dora
back over us—Baby's dead to the world—intrude
your propagandistic intimacy jokes,
unforgiving. "What, in a motel room?" I say.
Purple clouds roll back to reveal Armageddon
a dream in bad digital unreality. Explosions repeat patterns like
fake flames dance on fake fireplace logs. Sad Armageddon   30
of marriage: how pretty much nice
we meant to be, and couldn't make a difference.

931

CONNECTING POEMS:
LOOKING BACK ON LOVE

The four poems in this cluster tap into two of the most widely represented aspects of poetry: the act of looking back, and the subject of love. Recollecting, recreating, and reflecting on the past is one of the things writers do most; loving others is one of the things people do most. As you read these poems, think about how each of these writers confronts these fundamental acts and how the most basic parts of each of these phenomena relate—how looking back so often entails remembering love, and how loving is so much about loss.

SIR THOMAS WYATT   (1503-1542)

THEY FLEE FROM ME   1557

They flee from me that sometime did me seek
With naked foot, stalking in my chamber.
I have seen them gentle, tame, and meek,
That now are wild and do not remember
That sometime they put themself in danger
To take bread at my hand; and now they range,
Busily seeking with a continual change.

Thanked be fortune it hath been otherwise
Twenty times better; but once in special,
In thin array after a pleasant guise,   10
When her loose gown from her shoulders did fall,
And she me caught in her arms long and small;
Therewithall sweetly did me kiss
And softly said, "Dear heart, how like you this?"

It was no dream: I lay broad waking.
But all is turned thorough my gentleness
Into a strange fashion of forsaking;
And I have leave to go of her goodness,
And she also, to use newfangleness.
But since that I so kindly am served   20
I would fain know what she hath deserved.

FOR ANALYSIS

1. What picture of himself does the speaker paint in the first **stanza**? How does he relate to women? How does that change by the third stanza?

2. What is this poem's **conceit**? If unsure, consider the pun in line 14 ("heart" for "hart"). How does Wyatt use this conceit?

3. Do you think lines 18 and 20 are intended to be read straight or **ironically**? What's the difference for your understanding of the poem?

WRITING TOPIC

Newfangleness is a word Wyatt borrowed from fourteenth-century poet Geoffrey Chaucer. Look it up. What is its significance to the poem? What other words are key in the poem?

LADY MARY WROTH   (CA. 1587–CA. 1651)

"COME DARKEST NIGHT, BECOMING SORROW BEST"   1621

Come darkest night, becoming sorrow best;
    Light; leave thy light; fitt for a lightsome soule;
    Darknes doth truly sure with mee oprest
    Whom absence power doth from mirthe controle:

The very trees with hanging heads condole
    Sweet sommers parting, and of leaves distrest
    In dying coulers make a griefe-full role;
    Soe much (alas) to sorrow are they prest,

Thus of dead leaves her farewell carpett's made:
    Theyr fall, theyr branches, all theyr mournings prove;   10
    With leavles, naked bodies, whose huese vade
    From hopefull greene, to wither in theyr love,

If trees, and leaves for absence, mourners bee
Noe mervaile that I grieve, who like want see.

FOR ANALYSIS

1. What is this poem's **mood**? How does Wroth achieve it?

2. How does the speaker feel about her feelings? Does she try to fight them off? Does she accept them? Does she welcome them?

WRITING TOPIC

The sentimental or pathetic fallacy is the name given by critics to the practice of assigning human-like feelings and actions to inanimate objects, often natural ones. "Pathetic" here is not negative (nor is "fallacy"); instead, it has to do with *pathos*, or feeling. List Wroth's use of the pathetic fallacy in this poem. Do you think there is anything fallacious or false about it?

SHARON OLDS   (B. 1942)

MY FATHER'S DIARY   1998

I get into bed with it, and spring
the scarab legs of its locks. Inside,
the stacked, shy wealth of his print
he could not write in script, so the pages
are sturdy with the beamwork of printedness,
WENT TO LOOK AT A CAR, DAD
IN A GOOD MOOD AT DINNER, WENT
TO TRY OUT SOME NEW TENNIS RACQUETS,
LUNCH WITH MOM, life of ease—
except when he spun his father's DeSoto on the   10
ice, and a young tree whirled up to the
hood, throwing up her arms—until
LOIS. PLAYED TENNIS, WITH LOIS,
LUNCH WITH MOM AND LOIS, LOIS
LIKED THE CAR, DRIVING WITH LOIS,
LONG DRIVE WITH LOIS. And then,
LOIS! I CAN'T BELIEVE IT! SHE IS SO
GOOD, SO SWEET, SO GENEROUS, I HAVE
NEVER, WHAT HAVE I EVER DONE
TO DESERVE SUCH A GIRL? Between the dark   20
legs of the capitals, moonlight, soft
tines of the printed letter gentled
apart, nectar drawn from serif, the
self of the grown boy pouring
out, the heart's charge, the fresh
man kneeling in pine-needle weave,
worshipping her. It was my father
good, it was my father grateful,
it was my father dead, who had left me
these small structures of his young brain—   30
he wanted me to know him, he wanted
someone to know him.

FOR ANALYSIS

1. This poem is about the speaker's father as a boy, so retrospect—literally, looking back—is built into the situation. How does Olds set the stage for this situation in the poem's opening?

2. What does the speaker discover about her father? How does she feel about what she discovers?

WRITING TOPIC

There seems to be a lot left out of this poem, a great deal left unsaid about the father and the daughter's relationship with or her feelings about him. Drawing on the textual evidence in this poem and on your own imagination, write a short **prose** description of the man and his relationship with his daughter.

DEAN YOUNG (B. 1955)

WINGED PURPOSES 2009

Fly from me does all I would have stay,
the blossoms did not stay, stayed not the frost
in the yellow grass. Every leash snapped,
every contract void, and flying in the crows
lingers but a moment in the graveyard oaks
yet inside me it never stops so I can't tell
who is chasing, who chased, I can sleep
into afternoon and still wake soaring.
So out come the bats, down spiral swifts
into the chimneys, Hey, I'm real, say the dream-   10
figments then are gone like breath-prints
on a window, handwriting in snow. Whatever
I hold however flies apart, the children skip
into the park come out middle-aged
with children of their own. Your laugh
over the phone, will it ever answer me again?
Too much flying, photons perforating us,
voices hurtling into outer space, Whitman
out past Neptune, Dickinson retreating
yet getting brighter. Remember running   20
barefoot across hot sand into the sea's
hovering, remember my hand as we darted
against the holiday Broadway throng,
catching your train just as it was leaving?
Hey, it's real, your face like a comet,
horses coming from the field for morning
oats, insects hitting a screen, the message
nearly impossible to read, obscured by light
because carried by Mercury: I love you,
I'm coming. Sure, what fluttered is now gone,   30
maybe a smudge left, maybe a delicate under-
feather only then that too, yes, rained away.
And when the flying is flown and the heart's

a useless sliver in a glacier and the gown
hangs still as meat in a locker and eyesight
is dashed-down glass and the mouth rust-
stoppered, will some twinge still pass between us,
still some fledgling pledge?

FOR ANALYSIS

1. What does the speaker wish would stay that does not? How does he feel about these things?

2. While this poem is about memory and loss, would you say the **tone** is uniformly dark? Why or why not?

MAKING CONNECTIONS

1. All of these poems are in some way about looking back on love. How does each look back? In anger? Wistfully? How does the nature of their looking back help to shape the poems?

2. Compare Sir Thomas Wyatt's "They Flee From Me" (p. 932) to Dean Young's "Winged Purposes." While both are about things going away from the speaker, they take very different approaches to the topic. Wyatt pursues a single **conceit** throughout the poem; comparing Young's poem to Wyatt's, would you say he follows the same path? If not, what does he do differently? What is the effect of his choice?

3. Love and its loss is surely one of the oldest **themes** in literature. Compare the two twentieth-century poems in this cluster to those from the sixteenth and seventeenth centuries. What are the differences? Are they superficial or more profound?

WRITING TOPIC

Write a short description of Young's **style**. Is the language spare or flowery, intimate or oratorical? Is the **imagery** focused or encyclopedic? Why do the choices you think Young made in writing this poem fit the ideas and feelings he's trying to express?

CONNECTING POEMS: REMEMBERING FATHERS

No relationship is more primary to the human experience than that between parent and child. The relationship of mother or father to baby is one of complete responsibility and complete dependence, but this changes as both grow older and the emotional terrain becomes more tricky and harder to read. The poems in this unit express just a few of the very different kinds of emotions fathers and their children feel for each other, in the context of some of the many difficulties people encounter in life. As you read, take note of how the poems address the ways in which parents' and children's expectations of each other are or are not met and the ways in which feelings are or are not expressed.

THEODORE ROETHKE   (1908–1963)

MY PAPA'S WALTZ   1948

The whiskey on your breath
Could make a small boy dizzy;
But I hung on like death:
Such waltzing was not easy.

We romped until the pans
Slid from the kitchen shelf;
My mother's countenance
Could not unfrown itself.

The hand that held my wrist
Was battered on one knuckle;
At every step you missed
My right ear scraped a buckle.   10

You beat time on my head
With a palm caked hard by dirt,
Then waltzed me off to bed
Still clinging to your shirt.

FOR ANALYSIS

1. Why is **iambic trimeter** an appropriate **meter** for this poem?
2. What details reveal the kind of person the father is?
3. How would you describe the boy's feelings about his father? The father's about the boy?

WRITING TOPIC

Describe this poem's tone. What in the way it describes the events, from the title to
the **conceit**, expresses this tone?

ROBERT HAYDEN   (1913–1980)

THOSE WINTER SUNDAYS   1975

Sundays too my father got up early
and put his clothes on in the blueblack cold,
then with cracked hands that ached
from labor in the weekday weather made
banked fires blaze. No one ever thanked him.

I'd wake and hear the cold splintering, breaking.
When the rooms were warm, he'd call,
and slowly I would rise and dress,
fearing the chronic angers of that house,

Speaking indifferently to him,   10
who had driven out the cold
and polished my good shoes as well.
What did I know, what did I know
of love's austere and lonely offices?

FOR ANALYSIS

1. Why Sundays "too" (l. 1)?

2. What does *offices* mean (l. 14) in this poem? Why do you think Hayden chooses this word?

3. From when in his life does the speaker describe those winter Sundays? How does his relation to the event color his description?

WRITING TOPICS

1. In the last line of the second **stanza**, the speaker refers to "the chronic angers of that house." How does the anger the speaker fears relate to the "love" of the poem's last line?

2. Has there been a time in your life when you neglected to thank someone you should have or to appreciate something you should have? How does the recollection make you feel?

MOLLY PEACOCK   (B. 1947)

SAY YOU LOVE ME   1989

What happened earlier I'm not sure of.
Of course he was drunk, but often he was.
His face looked like a ham on a hook above

me—I was pinned to the chair because
he'd hunkered over me with arms like jaws
pried open by the chair arms. "Do you love

me?" he began to sob. "Say you love me!"
I held out. I was probably fifteen.
What had happened? Had my mother—had she

said or done something? Or had he just been 10
drinking too long after work? "He'll get *mean*,"
my sister hissed, "just *tell* him." I brought my knee

up to kick him, but was too scared. Nothing
could have got the words out of me then. Rage
shut me up, yet "DO YOU?" was beginning

to peel, as of live layers of skin, age
from age from age from him until he gazed
through hysteria as a wet baby thing

repeating, "Do you love me? Say you do,"
in baby chokes, only loud, for they came 20
from a man. There wouldn't be a rescue

from my mother, still at work. The same
choking sobs said, "Love me, love me," and my game
was breaking down because I couldn't do

anything, not escape into my own
refusal, *I won't, I won't*, not fantasize
a kind, rich father, not fill the narrowed zone,

empty except for confusion until the size
of my fear ballooned as I saw his eyes,
blurred, taurean°—my sister screamed—unknown,   bull-like 30

unknown to me, a voice rose and leveled
off, "I love you," I said. "*Say 'I love you,
Dad!*' " "I love you, Dad," I whispered, leveled

by defeat into a cardboard image, untrue,
unbending. I was surprised I could move
as I did to get up, but he stayed, burled

onto the chair—my monstrous fear—she screamed,
my sister, "Dad, the phone! Go answer it!"
The phone wasn't ringing, yet he seemed

to move toward it, and I ran. He had a fit— 40
"*It's not ringing!*"—but I was at the edge of it
as he collapsed into the chair and blamed

both of us at a distance. No, the phone
was not ringing. There was no world out there,
so there we remained, completely alone.

FOR ANALYSIS

1. Is the speaker a child or an adult? Explain.

2. How do the **images** of lines 16–18 capture the speaker's feelings?

3. When the speaker finally capitulates to her father's demand, she describes herself
in lines 33–35 as "leveled / by defeat into a cardboard image, untrue, / unbending."
What does she mean?

4. Explain what the speaker means by "my game" (l. 23).

WRITING TOPIC

What would motivate a parent, even a drunken one, to make the kind of demand the
father makes on his daughter?

LI-YOUNG LEE (B. 1957)

EATING ALONE 1986

I've pulled the last of the year's young onions.
The garden is bare now. The ground is cold,
brown and old. What is left of the day flames
in the maples at the corner of my
eye. I turn, a cardinal vanishes.
By the cellar door, I wash the onions,
then drink from the icy metal spigot.

Once, years back, I walked beside my father
among the windfall pears. I can't recall
our words. We may have strolled in silence. But
I still see him bend that way—left hand braced
on knee, creaky—to lift and hold to my
eye a rotten pear. In it, a hornet
spun crazily, glazed in slow, glistening juice.

It was my father I saw this morning
waving to me from the trees. I almost
called to him, until I came close enough
to see the shovel, leaning where I had
left it, in the flickering, deep green shade.

10

White rice steaming, almost done. Sweet green peas   20
fried in onions. Shrimp braised in sesame
oil and garlic. And my own loneliness.
What more could I, a young man, want.

FOR ANALYSIS

1. Why is the speaker eating alone?

2. How do the repeated references to youth and age, things being finished or almost done, function in the poem?

3. Why do you think the poet might have chosen to include the **image** of the hornet?

MAKING CONNECTIONS

1. Violence—actual or possible—is a presence in many of these poems. How do these poems express violence, explicitly and implicitly? Why is it such a presence?

2. In these poems, love is expressed in funny ways or goes unexpressed even when it is felt. What are some of the different ways in which these poems represent or hint at love?

3. With the modern advent of the nuclear family—consisting of only one set of parents and their unmarried children living together—families could be said to have become more isolated than they were previously. How does what Molly Peacock calls the "world out there" (l. 44) in "Say You Love Me" (p. 938) enter into these poems?

WRITING TOPICS

1. Read the last **stanza** closely. What is the effect of the **imagery**? What kind of question is asked in the last line? What do you think Lee was trying to do at the end of his poem?

2. Why do you think the poet chooses to write about a son remembering his father through the preparation of a meal? What is the significance of eating?

CONNECTING POEMS: PROPOSALS AND REPLIES

The four poems in this unit concern romantic proposals. Paired—the two original proposal poems, by Christopher Marlowe and Andrew Marvell, grouped with the responses they inspire, by Sir Walter Raleigh and Annie Finch—they can be read as statements on the assumptions and expectations encoded in romance, on their gendered nature, and on the use of poetry to talk about love. As you read these poetic conversations, try to take them in not just as individual works but as part of a long tradition of love poetry and a nearly as long tradition of sometimes angry, sometimes funny responses.

SIR WALTER RALEIGH (1554–1618)

THE NYMPH'S REPLY
TO THE SHEPHERD[1]   1600

If all the world and love were young,
And truth in every shepherd's tongue,
These pretty pleasures might me move
To live with thee and be thy love.

Time drives the flocks from field to fold,
When rivers rage and rocks grow cold,
And Philomel° becometh dumb;   the nightingale
The rest complains of cares to come.

The flowers do fade, and wanton fields
To wayward winter reckoning yields;   10
A honey tongue, a heart of gall,
Is fancy's spring, but sorrow's fall.

Thy gowns, thy shoes, thy beds of roses,
Thy cap, thy kirtle, and thy posies
Soon break, soon wither, soon forgotten—
In folly ripe, in reason rotten.

Thy belt of straw and ivy buds,
Thy coral clasps and amber studs,
All these in me no means can move
To come to thee and be thy love.   20

But could youth last and love still breed,
Had joys no date° nor age no need,   end
Then these delights my mind might move
To live with thee and be thy love.

FOR ANALYSIS

1. How does the poet use the natural **setting** to create the poem's **tone**?
2. What seasons are featured in the poem?
3. To what natural/physical phenomena does the speaker connect love's frailty?

---

[1] Available on CD, *Voices from the Lost Realms* (Albany Records, 1994), composed by William Mayer, performed by New Calliope Singers, conducted by Peter Schubert.

WRITING TOPIC

Raleigh's poem was written as a response to Marlowe's "The Passionate Shepherd to His Love" (below). Write a response in return from the Shepherd to the Nymph.

CHRISTOPHER MARLOWE   (1564–1593)

THE PASSIONATE SHEPHERD
TO HIS LOVE[1]   1600

Come live with me and be my love,
And we will all the pleasures prove
That valleys, groves, hills, and fields,
Woods, or steepy mountain yields.

And we will sit upon the rocks,
Seeing the shepherds feed their flocks,
By shallow rivers to whose falls
Melodious birds sing madrigals.

And I will make thee beds of roses
And a thousand fragrant posies,   10
A cap of flowers, and a kirtle°   skirt
Embroidered all with leaves of myrtle;

A gown made of the finest wool
Which from our pretty lambs we pull;
Fair lined slippers for the cold,
With buckles of the purest gold;

A belt of straw and ivy buds,
With coral clasps and amber studs:
And if these pleasures may thee move,
Come live with me, and be my love.   20

The shepherds' swains shall dance and sing
For thy delight each May morning:
If these delights thy mind may move,
Then live with me and be my love.

---

[1] The melody for Marlowe's song was published as early as 1603.

FOR ANALYSIS

1. How would you characterize the poem's **setting**? How does the poem use it to create its **mood**?

2. Which season or seasons are the setting for the speaker's pleas? Which are not? Why?

3. What aspects of the natural world are absent from this poem?

WRITING TOPIC

What kind of relationship does the shepherd envision? Does the poem go into much depth describing this hypothetical future? Why or why not?

ANDREW MARVELL   (1621–1678)

TO HIS COY MISTRESS   1681

Had we but world enough, and time,
This coyness, lady, were no crime.
We would sit down, and think which way
To walk, and pass our long love's day.
Thou by the Indian Ganges' side
Shouldst rubies find; I by the tide
Of Humber would complain. I would
Love you ten years before the flood,
And you should, if you please, refuse
Til the conversion of the Jews.   10
My vegetable love should grow
Vaster than empires and more slow;
An hundred years should go to praise
Thine eyes, and on thy forehead gaze;
Two hundred to adore each breast,
But thirty thousand to the rest;
An age at least to every part,
And the last age should show your heart.
For, lady, you deserve this state,
Nor would I love at lower rate.   20
    But at my back I always hear
Time's wingéd chariot hurrying near;
And yonder all before us lie
Deserts of vast eternity.
Thy beauty shall no more be found,
Nor, in thy marble vault, shall sound

My echoing song; then worms shall try
That long-preserved virginity,
And your quaint honor turn to dust,
And into ashes all my lust: 30
The grave's a fine and private place,
But none, I think, do there embrace.
   Now therefore, while the youthful hue
Sits on thy skin like morning dew,
And while thy willing soul transpires
At every pore with instant fires,
Now let us sport us while we may,
And now, like amorous birds of prey,
Rather at once our time devour
Than languish in his slow-chapped° power.   slow-jawed 40
Let us roll our strength and all
Our sweetness up into one ball,
And tear our pleasures with rough strife
Thorough° the iron gates of life: through
Thus, though we cannot make our sun
Stand still, yet we will make him run.

FOR ANALYSIS

1. State the argument of the poem (see ll. 1–2, 21–22, 33–34).

2. Compare the figures of speech in lines 1–20 with those in lines 33–46. How do
they differ?

3. Describe the attitude toward life recommended by the poet.

ANNIE FINCH   (B. 1956)

COY MISTRESS   1997

(IN ANSWER TO THE POEM BY ANDREW MARVELL)

Sir, I am not a bird of prey:
a Lady does not seize the day.
I trust that brief Time will unfold
our youth, before he makes us old.
How could we two write lines of rhyme
were we not fond of numbered Time
and grateful to the vast and sweet
trials his days will make us meet:
The Grave's not just the body's curse;

no skeleton can pen a verse!   10
So while this numbered World we see,
let's sweeten Time with poetry,
and Time, in turn, may sweeten Love
and give us time our love to prove.
You've praised my eyes, forehead, breast:
you've all our lives to praise the rest.

FOR ANALYSIS

1. What word appears more than any other in this poem? Why?

2. What is the poem's **tone**? How is it created?

3. What is the thing most valued in this poem?

MAKING CONNECTIONS

1. How does Marlowe use the **pastoral** to press his case? How does Marvell use time? Compare and contrast these authors' dependence on natural phenomena in their arguments.

2. Compare Raleigh's and Finch's responses. How do they counter Marlowe and Marvell?

3. The Marlowe and Marvell poems make great use of **style**. How do the Raleigh and Finch poems respond in their own use of style? That is, how do they write back to the earlier poems, not in terms of argument, but in terms of style?

WRITING TOPIC

Finch's poem is a response to Marvell's "To His Coy Mistress" (p. 944). Imagine a different response to Marvell's poem. What else could be said in reply? Who else could say it?

LOVE AND HATE

DRAMA

CASE STUDY

CULTURAL CONTEXTS FOR OTHELLO

William Shakespeare's *Othello* has remained popular during the four centuries since its composition and first performances in part because it explores timeless themes such as love, jealousy, race, and gender, which meet in a toxic combination with issues of power and class. But we know of course that these issues, though they persist across many centuries and parts of the world, aren't exactly timeless, nor are they placeless. They exist in very particular ways in their historical contexts. This case study brings together short accounts of how many members of the audience of Shakespeare's play (as well as its author, perhaps) thought about these issues in their particular time and place in Renaissance Europe. The impact on their thinking of European adventures abroad, of philosophical and pseudoscientific beliefs about the nature of the human animal, and of the constraints of the structures of social life was great, and considering the play in light of these facts can help illuminate it—without in any way diminishing the poetry and power of Shakespeare's vision.

WILLIAM SHAKESPEARE (1564-1616)

OTHELLO CA. 1604

CHARACTERS

Duke of Venice
Brabantio, a Senator
Senators
Gratiano, Brother to Brabantio
Lodovico, Kinsman to Brabantio
Othello, a noble Moor; in the service of the Venetian State
Cassio, his Lieutenant
Iago, his Ancient
Roderigo, a Venetian Gentleman

Montano, Othello's predecessor in the Government of Cyprus
Clown, Servant to Othello
Desdemona, Daughter to Brabantio, and Wife to Othello
Emilia, Wife to Iago
Bianca, Mistress to Cassio
Sailor, Officers, Gentlemen, Messengers, Musicians, Heralds, Attendants

Scene

For the first Act, in Venice; during the rest of the Play, at a Sea-port in Cyprus

ACT I

Scene 1.   Venice. A Street.

(Enter Roderigo and Iago.)

Roderigo. Tush! Never tell me; I take it much unkindly
That thou, Iago, who has had my purse
As if the strings were thine, shouldst know of this.[1]
Iago. 'Sblood,[2] but you will not hear me:
If ever I did dream of such a matter,
Abhor me.
Roderigo. Thou told'st me thou didst hold him[3] in thy hate.
Iago. Despise me if I do not. Three great ones of the city,
In personal suit to make me his lieutenant,
Off-capp'd[4] to him; and, by the faith of man,
I know my price, I am worth no worse a place;   10
But he, as loving his own pride and purposes,
Evades them, with a bombast circumstance[5]
Horribly stuff'd with epithets of war;
And, in conclusion,
Nonsuits[6] my mediators;[7] for, 'Certes,'[8] says he,
'I have already chosen my officer.'
And what was he?
Forsooth, a great arithmetician,
One Michael Cassio, a Florentine,
A fellow almost damn'd in a fair wife;[9]   20
That never set a squadron in the field,
Nor the division of a battle knows
More than a spinster; unless[10] the bookish theoric,[11]
Wherein the togèd consuls can propose
As masterly as he: mere prattle, without practice,
Is all his soldiership. But he, sir, had the election;
And I—of whom his eyes had seen the proof
At Rhodes, at Cyprus, and on other grounds

---

[1] I.e., Othello's successful courtship of Desdemona.   [2] By God's blood.   [3] I.e., Othello.   [4] Took off their caps.   [5] Pompous wordiness, circumlocution.   [6] Turns down.   [7] Spokesmen.   [8] In truth.
[9] A much debated phrase. In the Italian source the Captain (i.e., Cassio) was married, and it may be that Shakespeare originally intended Bianca to be Cassio's wife but later changed his mind and failed to alter the phrase here accordingly. Or perhaps Iago simply sneers at Cassio as a notorious ladies' man.   [10] Except.
[11] Theory.

Christian and heathen—must be be-lee'd[12] and calm'd
By debitor and creditor; this counter-caster,[13]   30
He, in good time, must his lieutenant be,
And I—God bless the mark!—his Moorship's ancient.[14]

Roderigo. By heaven, I rather would have been his hangman.

Iago. Why, there's no remedy: 'tis the curse of service,
Preferment goes by letter and affection,
Not by the old gradation,[15] where each second
Stood heir to the first. Now, sir, be judge yourself,
Whe'r[16] I in any just term am affin'd[17]
To love the Moor.

Roderigo.   I would not follow him then.

Iago. O! sir, content you;   40
I follow him to serve my turn upon him;
We cannot all be masters, nor all masters
Cannot be truly follow'd. You shall mark
Many a duteous and knee-crooking knave,
That, doting on his own obsequious bondage,
Wears out his time, much like his master's ass,
For nought but provender, and when he's old, cashier'd;
Whip me such honest knaves. Others there are
Who, trimm'd in forms and visages of duty,
Keep yet their hearts attending on themselves,   50
And, throwing but shows of service on their lords,
Do well thrive by them, and when they have lin'd their coats
Do themselves homage: these fellows have some soul;
And such a one do I profess myself. For, sir,
It is as sure as you are Roderigo,
Were I the Moor, I would not be Iago:
In following him, I follow but myself;
Heaven is my judge, not I for love and duty,
But seeming so, for my peculiar end:
For when my outward action doth demonstrate   60
The native act and figure of my heart
In compliment extern,[18] 'tis not long after
But I will wear my heart upon my sleeve
For daws to peck at: I am not what I am.

Roderigo. What a full fortune does the thick-lips owe,[19]
If he can carry 't thus!

Iago.   Call up her father;
Rouse him, make after him, poison his delight,
Proclaim him in the streets, incense her kinsmen,

---

[12] Left without wind for my sails.   [13] Bookkeeper (cf. "arithmetician" above).   [14] Ensign (but Iago's position in the play seems to be that of Othello's aide-de-camp).   [15] Seniority.   [16] Whether.   [17] Obliged.   [18] External show.   [19] Own.

And, though he in a fertile climate dwell,[20]
Plague him with flies; though that his joy be joy,   70
Yet throw such changes of vexation on 't
As it may lose some colour.

Roderigo. Here is her father's house; I'll call aloud.

Iago. Do; with like timorous[21] accent and dire yell
As when, by night and negligence, the fire
Is spied in populous cities.

Roderigo. What, ho! Brabantio: Signior Brabantio, ho!

Iago. Awake! what, ho! Brabantio! thieves! thieves! thieves!
Look to your house, your daughter, and your bags!
Thieves! thieves!   80

(Enter Brabantio, above, at a window.)

Brabantio. What is the reason of this terrible summons?
What is the matter there?

Roderigo. Signior, is all your family within?

Iago. Are your doors lock'd?

Brabantio.   Why? wherefore ask you this?

Iago. 'Zounds![22] sir, you're robb'd; for shame, put on your gown;
Your heart is burst, you have lost half your soul;
Even now, now, very now, an old black ram
Is tupping[23] your white ewe. Arise, arise!
Awake the snorting[24] citizens with the bell,
Or else the devil will make a grandsire of you.   90
Arise, I say.

Brabantio. What! have you lost your wits?

Roderigo. Most reverend signior, do you know my voice?

Brabantio. Not I, what are you?

Roderigo. My name is Roderigo.

Brabantio.   The worser welcome:
I have charg'd thee not to haunt about my doors:
In honest plainness thou hast heard me say
My daughter is not for thee; and now, in madness,
Being full of supper and distempering draughts,
Upon malicious knavery dost thou come
To start my quiet.   100

Roderigo. Sir, sir, sir!

Brabantio.   But thou must needs be sure
My spirit and my place[25] have in them power
To make this bitter to thee.

---

[20] I.e., is fortunate.   [21] Frightening.   [22] By God's wounds.   [23] Copulating.   [24] Snoring.
[25] Position.

Roderigo.   Patience, good sir.

Brabantio. What tell'st thou me of robbing? this is Venice;
   My house is not a grange.[26]

Roderigo.   Most grave Brabantio,
   In simple and pure soul I come to you.

Iago. 'Zounds! sir, you are one of those that will not serve God if the devil bid
   you. Because we come to do you service and you think we are ruffians, you'll
   have your daughter covered with a Barbary horse; you'll have your nephews
   neigh to you; you'll have coursers for cousins and gennets[27] for germans.[28]   110

Brabantio. What profane wretch art thou?

Iago. I am one, sir, that comes to tell you, your daughter and the Moor are now
   making the beast with two backs.

Brabantio. Thou art a villain.

Iago.   You are—a senator.

Brabantio. This thou shalt answer; I know thee, Roderigo.

Roderigo. Sir, I will answer any thing. But, I beseech you,
   If 't be your pleasure and most wise consent,—
   As partly, I find, it is,—that your fair daughter,
   At this odd-even[29] and dull watch o' the night,
   Transported with no worse nor better guard   120
   But with a knave of common hire, a gondolier,
   To the gross clasps of a lascivious Moor,—
   If this be known to you, and your allowance,[30]
   We then have done you bold and saucy wrongs;
   But if you know not this, my manners tell me
   We have your wrong rebuke. Do not believe
   That, from[31] the sense of all civility,
   I thus would play and trifle with your reverence:
   Your daughter, if you have not given her leave,
   I say again, hath made a gross revolt;   130
   Tying her duty, beauty, wit and fortunes
   In[32] an extravagant[33] and wheeling stranger
   Of here and every where. Straight satisfy yourself:
   If she be in her chamber or your house,
   Let loose on me the justice of the state
   For thus deluding you.

Brabantio.   Strike on the tinder, ho!
   Give me a taper! call up all my people!
   This accident[34] is not unlike my dream;
   Belief of it oppresses me already.
   Light, I say! light!   *(Exit, from above.)*

Iago.   Farewell, for I must leave you: 140
   It seems not meet nor wholesome to my place

---

[26] Isolated farmhouse.   [27] Spanish horses.   [28] Blood relations.   [29] Between night and morning.
[30] By your approval.   [31] Away from.   [32] To.   [33] Expatriate.   [34] Happening.

To be produc'd,[35] as, if I stay, I shall,
Against the Moor; for I do know the state,
However this may gall him with some check,[36]
Cannot with safety cast him; for he's embark'd
With such loud reason to the Cyprus wars,—
Which even now stand in act,—that, for their souls,
Another of his fathom[37] they have none,
To lead their business; in which regard,
Though I do hate him as I do hell-pains,   150
Yet, for necessity of present life,
I must show out a flag and sign of love,
Which is indeed but sign. That you shall surely find him,
Lead to the Sagittary[38] the raised search;
And there will I be with him. So, farewell.   *(Exit.)*

(Enter below, Brabantio, and servants with torches.)

Brabantio. It is too true an evil: gone she is,
   And what's to come of my despised time
   Is nought but bitterness. Now, Roderigo,
   Where didst thou see her? O, unhappy girl!
   With the Moor, sayst thou? Who would be a father!   160
   How didst thou know 'twas she? O, she deceives me
   Past thought. What said she to you? Get more tapers!
   Raise all my kindred! Are they married, think you?
Roderigo. Truly, I think they are.
Brabantio. O heaven! How got she out? O treason of the blood:
   Fathers, from hence trust not your daughters' minds
   By what you see them act. Are there not charms
   By which the property of youth and maidhood
   May be abus'd? Have you not read, Roderigo,
   Of some such thing?
Roderigo.   Yes, sir, I have indeed.   170
Brabantio. Call up my brother. O! that you had had her.
   Some one way, some another! Do you know
   Where we may apprehend her and the Moor?
Roderigo. I think I can discover him, if you please
   To get good guard and go along with me.
Brabantio. Pray you, lead on. At every house I'll call;
   I may command at most. Get weapons, ho!
   And raise some special officers of night.
   On, good Roderigo; I'll deserve[39] your pains.   *(Exeunt.)*

---

[35] I.e., as a witness.   [36] Restraining adversity.   [37] Caliber, ability.   [38] The name of an inn (?).
[39] I.e., reward.

Scene 2. Another Street.

(Enter Othello, Iago, and Attendants, with torches.)

Iago. Though in the trade of war I have slain men,
Yet do I hold it very stuff o' the conscience
To do no contriv'd murder: I lack iniquity
Sometimes to do me service. Nine or ten times
I had thought to have yerk'd[40] him here under the ribs.
Othello. 'Tis better as it is.
Iago.   Nay, but he prated,
And spoke such scurvy and provoking terms
Against your honour
That, with the little godliness I have,
I did full hard forbear him. But, I pray, sir,   10
Are you fast married? Be assur'd of this,
That the magnifico[41] is much belov'd,
And hath in his effect a voice potential
As double[42] as the duke's; he will divorce you,
Or put upon you what restraint and grievance
The law—with all his might to enforce it on—
Will give him cable.[43]
Othello.   Let him do his spite:
My services which I have done the signiory[44]
Shall out-tongue his complaints. 'Tis yet to know,[45]
Which when I know that boasting is an honour   20
I shall promulgate, I fetch my life and being
From men of royal siege, and my demerits[46]
May speak unbonneted[47] to as proud a fortune
As this[48] that I have reach'd; for know, Iago,
But that I love the gentle Desdemona,
I would not my unhoused[49] free condition
Put into circumscription and confine
For the sea's worth. But, look! what lights come yond?
Iago. Those are the raised[50] father and his friends:
You were best[51] go in.
Othello.   Not I; I must be found: 30
My parts, my title, and my perfect[52] soul
Shall manifest me rightly. Is it they?
Iago. By Janus,[53] I think no.

---

[40] Stabbed.   [41] One of the grandees, or rulers, of Venice; here, Brabantio.   [42] Iago means that Brabantio's influence equals that of the Doge's with his double vote.   [43] I.e., scope.   [44] The Venetian government.   [45] I.e., the signiory does not as yet know.   [46] Merits.   [47] I.e., as equals.   [48] I.e., that of Desdemona's family.   [49] Unconfined.   [50] Aroused.   [51] Had better.   [52] Untroubled by a bad conscience.   [53] The two-faced Roman god of portals and doors and (hence) of beginnings and ends.

(Enter Cassio and certain Officers, with torches.)

Othello. The servants of the duke, and my lieutenant.
  The goodness of the night upon you, friends!
  What is the news?
Cassio.   The duke does greet you, general,
  And he requires your haste-post-haste appearance,
  Even on the instant.
Othello.   What is the matter, think you?
Cassio. Something from Cyprus, as I may divine.
  It is a business of some heat;[54] the galleys   40
  Have sent a dozen sequent[55] messengers
  This very night at one another's heels,
  And many of the consuls,[56] rais'd and met,
  Are at the duke's already. You have been hotly call'd for;
  When, being not at your lodging to be found,
  The senate hath sent about three several[57] quests
  To search you out.
Othello.   'Tis well I am found by you.
  I will but spend a word here in the house,
  And go with you.   *(Exit.)*
Cassio.   Ancient, what makes he here?
Iago. Faith, he to-night hath boarded a land carrack;[58]   50
  If it prove lawful prize, he's made for ever.
Cassio. I do not understand.
Iago.   He's married.
Cassio.   To who?

(Re-enter Othello.)

Iago. Marry,[59] to—Come, captain, will you go?
Othello.   Have with you.
Cassio. Here comes another troop to seek for you.
Iago. It is Brabantio. General, be advis'd;
  He comes to bad intent.

(Enter Brabantio, Roderigo, and Officers, with torches and weapons.)

Othello.   Holla! stand there!
Roderigo. Signior, it is the Moor.
Brabantio.   Down with him, thief!

(They draw on both sides.)

---

[54] Urgency.   [55] Following one another.   [56] I.e., senators.   [57] Separate.   [58] Treasure ship.   [59] By the Virgin Mary.

Iago. You, Roderigo! Come, sir, I am for you.[60]
Othello. Keep up your bright swords, for the dew will rust them.
    Good signior, you shall more command with years   60
    Than with your weapons.
Brabantio. O thou foul thief! where hast thou stow'd my daughter?
    Damn'd as thou art, thou hast enchanted her;
    For I'll refer me to all things of sense,
    If she in chains of magic were not bound,
    Whether a maid so tender, fair, and happy,
    So opposite to marriage that she shunn'd
    The wealthy curled darlings of our nation,
    Would ever have, to incur a general mock,
    Run from her guardage to the sooty bosom   70
    Of such a thing as thou; to fear, not to delight.
    Judge me the world, if 'tis not gross in sense[61]
    That thou hast practis'd on her with foul charms,
    Abus'd her delicate youth with drugs or minerals
    That weaken motion:[62] I'll have 't disputed on;
    'Tis probable, and palpable to thinking.
    I therefore apprehend and do attach[63] thee
    For an abuser of the world, a practiser
    Of arts inhibited and out of warrant.[64]
    Lay hold upon him: if he do resist,   80
    Subdue him at his peril.
Othello.   Hold your hands,
    Both you of my inclining,[65] and the rest:
    Were it my cue to fight, I should have known it
    Without a prompter. Where will you that I go
    To answer this your charge?
Brabantio.   To prison; till fit time
    Of law and course of direct session[66]
    Call thee to answer.
Othello.   What if I do obey?
    How may the duke be therewith satisfied,
    Whose messengers are here about my side,
    Upon some present[67] business of the state   90
    To bring me to him?
Officer.   'Tis true, most worthy signior;
    The duke's in council, and your noble self,
    I am sure, is sent for.
Brabantio.   How! the duke in council!
    In this time of the night! Bring him away.
    Mine's not an idle cause: the duke himself,

---

[60] Let you and me fight.   [61] Obvious.   [62] Normal reactions.   [63] Arrest.   [64] Prohibited and illegal.
[65] Party.   [66] Normal process of law.   [67] Immediate, pressing.

Or any of my brothers of the state,[68]
Cannot but feel this wrong as 'twere their own;
For if such actions may have passage free,
Bond-slaves and pagans shall our statesmen be.   (*Exeunt.*)

Scene 3. A Council Chamber.

(*The Duke and Senators sitting at a table. Officers attending.*)

Duke. There is no composition[69] in these news
    That gives them credit.
First Senator.   Indeed, they are disproportion'd;
    My letters say a hundred and seven galleys.
Duke. And mine, a hundred and forty.
Second Senator.   And mine, two hundred:
    But though they jump[70] not on a just[71] account,—
    As in these cases, where the aim[72] reports,
    'Tis oft with difference,—yet do they all confirm
    A Turkish fleet, and bearing up to Cyprus.
Duke. Nay, it is possible enough to judgment:
    I do not so secure me in[73] the error,   10
    But the main article[74] I do approve[75]
    In fearful sense.
Sailor (*within*).   What, ho! what, ho! what, ho!
Officer. A messenger from the galleys.

(*Enter a Sailor.*)

Duke.   Now, what's the business?
Sailor.   The Turkish preparation makes for Rhodes;
    So was I bid report here to the state
    By Signior Angelo.
Duke. How say you by this change?
First Senator.   This cannot be
    By no[76] assay[77] of reason; 'tis a pageant[78]
    To keep us in false gaze.[79] When we consider
    The importancy of Cyprus to the Turk,   20
    And let ourselves again but understand,
    That as it more concerns the Turk than Rhodes,
    So may he with more facile question bear[80] it,
    For that it stands not in such warlike brace,[81]
    But altogether lacks the abilities

---

[68] Fellow senators.   [69] Consistency, agreement.   [70] Coincide.   [71] Exact.   [72] Conjecture.   [73] Draw comfort from.   [74] Substance.   [75] Believe.   [76] Any.   [77] Test.   [78] (Deceptive) show.   [79] Looking in the wrong direction.   [80] More easily capture.   [81] State of defense.

That Rhodes is dress'd in: if we make thought of this,
We must not think the Turk is so unskilful
To leave that latest which concerns him first,
Neglecting an attempt of ease and gain,
To wake and wage a danger profitless.   30
Duke. Nay, in all confidence, he's not for Rhodes.
Officer. Here is more news.

(Enter a Messenger.)

Messenger. The Ottomites,[82] reverend and gracious,
Steering with due course toward the isle of Rhodes,
Have there injointed[83] them with an after fleet.[84]
First Senator. Ay, so I thought. How many, as you guess?
Messenger. Of thirty sail; and now they do re-stem[85]
Their backward course, bearing with frank appearance
Their purposes toward Cyprus. Signior Montano,
Your trusty and most valiant servitor,   40
With his free duty[86] recommends[87] you thus,
And prays you to believe him.
Duke. 'Tis certain then, for Cyprus.
Marcus Luccicos, is not he in town?
First Senator. He's now in Florence.
Duke. Write from us to him; post-post-haste dispatch.
First Senator. Here comes Brabantio and the valiant Moor.

(Enter Brabantio, Othello, Iago, Roderigo, and Officers.)

Duke. Valiant Othello, we must straight employ you
Against the general enemy Ottoman.
(To Brabantio.) I did not see you; welcome, gentle signior;   50
We lack'd your counsel and your help to-night.
Brabantio. So did I yours. Good your Grace, pardon me;
Neither my place nor aught I heard of business
Hath rais'd me from my bed, nor doth the general care
Take hold of me, for my particular grief
Is of so flood-gate[88] and o'erbearing nature
That it engluts and swallows other sorrows
And it is still itself.
Duke.   Why, what's the matter?
Brabantio. My daughter! O! my daughter.

---

[82] Turks.   [83] Joined.   [84] Fleet that followed after.   [85] Steer again.   [86] Unqualified expressions of respect.   [87] Informs.   [88] Torrential.

Duke. }
Senators. } Dead?

Brabantio.   Ay, to me;
    She is abus'd, stol'n from me, and corrupted   60
    By spells and medicines bought of mountebanks;
    For nature so preposterously to err,
    Being not deficient, blind, or lame of sense,
    Sans[89] witchcraft could not.

Duke. Whoe'er he be that in this foul proceeding
    Hath thus beguil'd your daughter of herself
    And you of her, the bloody book of law
    You shall yourself read in the bitter letter
    After your own sense; yea, though our proper[90] son
    Stood[91] in your action.[92]

Brabantio.   Humbly I thank your Grace.   70
    Here is the man, this Moor; whom now, it seems,
    Your special mandate for the state affairs
    Hath hither brought.

Duke. }
Senators. } We are very sorry for it.

Duke (to Othello). What, in your own part, can you say to this?

Brabantio. Nothing, but this is so.

Othello. Most potent, grave, and reverend signiors,
    My very noble and approv'd[93] good masters,
    That I have ta'en away this old man's daughter,
    It is most true; true, I have married her:
    The very head and front of my offending   80
    Hath this extent, no more. Rude am I in my speech,
    And little bless'd with the soft phrase of peace;
    For since these arms of mine had seven years' pith,[94]
    Till now some nine moons wasted,[95] they have us'd
    Their dearest action in the tented field;
    And little of this great world can I speak,
    More than pertains to feats of broil and battle;
    And therefore little shall I grace my cause
    In speaking for myself. Yet, by your gracious patience,
    I will a round[96] unvarnish'd tale deliver   90
    Of my whole course of love; what drugs, what charms,
    What conjuration, and what mighty magic,
    For such proceeding I am charg'd withal,
    I won his daughter.

Brabantio.   A maiden never bold;
    Of spirit so still and quiet, that her motion

---

[89] Without.   [90] Own.   [91] Were accused.   [92] Suit.   [93] Tested (by past experience).   [94] Strength.
[95] Past.   [96] Blunt.

Blush'd at herself;[97] and she, in spite of nature,
Of years, of country, credit, every thing,
To fall in love with what she fear'd to look on!
It is a judgment maim'd and most imperfect
That will confess[98] perfection so could err   100
Against all rules of nature, and must be driven
To find out practices of cunning hell,
Why this should be. I therefore vouch again
That with some mixtures powerful o'er the blood,
Or with some dram conjur'd to this effect,
He wrought upon her.

Duke.   To vouch this, is no proof,
Without more certain and more overt test
Than these thin habits[99] and poor likelihoods
Of modern[100] seeming do prefer against him.

First Senator. But, Othello, speak: 110
Did you by indirect and forced courses
Subdue and poison this young maid's affections;
Or came it by request and such fair question[101]
As soul to soul affordeth?

Othello.   I do beseech you;
Send for the lady to the Sagittary,
And let her speak of me before her father:
If you do find me foul in her report,
The trust, the office I do hold of you,
Not only take away, but let your sentence
Even fall upon my life.

Duke.   Fetch Desdemona hither.   120

Othello. Ancient, conduct them; you best know the place.

(Exeunt Iago and Attendants.)

And, till she come, as truly as to heaven
I do confess the vices of my blood,
So justly to your grave ears I'll present
How I did thrive in this fair lady's love,
And she in mine.

Duke. Say it, Othello.

Othello. Her father lov'd me; oft invited me;
Still[102] question'd me the story of my life
From year to year, the battles, sieges, fortunes   130
That I have pass'd.

---

[97] I.e. (her modesty was such that) she blushed at her own emotions; or: she could not move without
blushing.   [98] Assert.   [99] Weak appearances.   [100] Commonplace.   [101] Conversation.   [102] Always,
regularly.

I ran it through, even from my boyish days
To the very moment that he bade me tell it;
Wherein I spake of most disastrous chances,
Of moving accidents by flood and field,
Of hair-breadth 'scapes i' the imminent deadly breach,
Of being taken by the insolent foe
And sold to slavery, of my redemption thence
And portance[103] in my travel's history;
Wherein of antres[104] vast and deserts idle,[105]   140
Rough quarries, rocks, and hills whose heads touch heaven,
It was my hint[106] to speak, such was the process;
And of the Cannibals that each other eat,
The Anthropophagi,[107] and men whose heads
Do grow beneath their shoulders. This to hear
Would Desdemona seriously incline;
But still the house-affairs would draw her thence;
Which ever as she could with haste dispatch,
She'd come again, and with a greedy ear
Devour up my discourse. Which I observing,   150
Took once a pliant[108] hour, and found good means
To draw from her a prayer of earnest heart
That I would all my pilgrimage dilate,[109]
Whereof by parcels[110] she had something heard,
But not intentively:[111] I did consent;
And often did beguile her of her tears,
When I did speak of some distressful stroke
That my youth suffer'd. My story being done,
She gave me for my pains a world of sighs:
She swore, in faith, 'twas strange, 'twas passing[112] strange;   160
'Twas pitiful, 'twas wondrous pitiful:
She wish'd she had not heard it, yet she wish'd
That heaven had made her[113] such a man; she thank'd me,
And bade me, if I had a friend that lov'd her,
I should but teach him how to tell my story,
And that would woo her. Upon this hint I spake.
She lov'd me for the dangers I had pass'd,
And I lov'd her that she did pity them.
This only is the witchcraft I have us'd:
Here comes the lady; let her witness it.   170

(Enter Desdemona, Iago, and Attendants.)

---

[103] Behavior.　　[104] Caves.　　[105] Empty, sterile.　　[106] Opportunity.　　[107] Man-eaters.　　[108] Suitable.
[109] Relate in full.　　[110] Piecemeal.　　[111] In sequence.　　[112] Surpassing.　　[113] Direct object; not "for her."

Duke. I think this tale would win my daughter too.
  Good Brabantio,
  Take up this mangled matter at the best;
  Men do their broken weapons rather use
  Than their bare hands.

Brabantio.   I pray you, hear her speak:
  If she confess that she was half the wooer,
  Destruction on my head, if my bad blame
  Light on the man! Come hither, gentle mistress:
  Do you perceive in all this noble company
  Where most you owe obedience?

Desdemona.   My noble father,   180
  I do perceive here a divided duty:
  To you I am bound for life and education;
  My life and education both do learn[114] me
  How to respect you; you are the lord of duty,
  I am hitherto your daughter: but here's my husband;
  And so much duty as my mother show'd
  To you, preferring you before her father,
  So much I challenge[115] that I may profess
  Due to the Moor my lord.

Brabantio.   God be with you! I have done.
  Please it your Grace, on to the state affairs;   190
  I had rather to adopt a child than get it.
  Come hither, Moor:
  I here do give thee that with all my heart
  Which, but thou hast[116] already, with all my heart
  I would keep from thee. For your sake,[117] jewel,
  I am glad at soul I have no other child;
  For thy escape would teach me tyranny,
  To hang clogs on them. I have done, my lord.

Duke. Let me speak like yourself and lay a sentence,[118]
  Which as a grize[119] or step, may help these lovers   200
  Into your favour.
  When remedies are past, the griefs are ended
  By seeing the worst, which[120] late on hopes depended.
  To mourn a mischief that is past and gone
  Is the next way to draw new mischief on.
  What cannot be preserv'd when Fortune takes,
  Patience her injury a mockery makes.[121]
  The robb'd that smiles steals something from the thief;
  He robs himself that spends a bootless grief.

---

[114] Teach.   [115] Claim as right.   [116] Didn't you have it.   [117] Because of you.   [118] Provide a maxim.   [119] Step.   [120] The antecedent is "griefs."   [121] To suffer an irreparable loss patiently is to make light of injury (i.e., to triumph over adversity).

Brabantio. So let the Turk of Cyprus us beguile;   210
  We lose it not so long as we can smile.
  He bears the sentence[122] well that nothing bears
  But the free comfort which from thence he hears;
  But he bears both the sentence and the sorrow
  That, to pay grief, must of poor patience borrow.
  These sentences, to sugar, or to gall,
  Being strong on both sides, are equivocal:[123]
  But words are words: I never yet did hear
  That the bruis'd heart was pierced[124] through the ear.
  I humbly beseech you, proceed to the affairs of state.   220

Duke. The Turk with a most mighty preparation makes for Cyprus. Othello, the fortitude[125] of the place is best known to you; and though we have there a substitute of most allowed sufficiency,[126] yet opinion, a sovereign mistress of effects, throws a more safer voice on you:[127] you must therefore be content to slubber[128] the gloss of your new fortunes with this more stubborn[129] and boisterous expedition.

Othello. The tyrant custom, most grave senators,
  Hath made the flinty and steel couch of war
  My thrice-driven[130] bed of down: I do agnize[131]
  A natural and prompt alacrity   230
  I find in hardness, and do undertake
  These present wars against the Ottomites.
  Most humbly therefore bending to your state,[132]
  I crave fit disposition[133] for my wife,
  Due reference of place and exhibition,[134]
  With such accommodation and besort[135]
  As levels with[136] her breeding.

Duke.   If you please,
  Be 't at her father's.

Brabantio.   I'll not have it so.

Othello. Nor I.

Desdemona. Nor I; I would not there reside,   240
  To put my father in impatient thoughts
  By being in his eye. Most gracious duke,
  To my unfolding[137] lend your gracious ear;
  And let me find a charter[138] in your voice
  To assist my simpleness.

Duke. What would you, Desdemona?

Desdemona. That I did love the Moor to live with him,

---

[122] (1) Verdict, (2) Maxim. [123] Sententious comfort (like the Duke's trite maxims) can hurt as well as soothe. [124] (1) Lanced (i.e., cured), (2) Wounded. [125] Strength. [126] Admitted competence. [127] General opinion, which mainly determines action, thinks Cyprus safer with you in command. [128] Besmear. [129] Rough. [130] Made as soft as possible. [131] Recognize. [132] Submitting to your authority. [133] Disposal. [134] Provision. [135] Fitness. [136] Is proper to. [137] Explanation. [138] Permission.

My downright violence and storm of fortunes
May trumpet to the world; my heart's subdu'd
Even to the very quality of my lord;[139]   250
I saw Othello's visage in his mind,
And to his honours and his valiant parts
Did I my soul and fortunes consecrate.
So that, dear lords, if I be left behind,
A moth of peace, and he go to the war,
The rites[140] for which I love him are bereft me,
And I a heavy interim shall support[141]
By his dear[142] absence. Let me go with him.

Othello.   Let her have your voices.
Vouch with me, heaven, I therefore beg it not   260
To please the palate of my appetite,
Nor to comply with heat,—the young affects[143]
In me defunct,—and proper satisfaction,
But to be free and bounteous to her mind;
And heaven defend[144] your good souls that you think
I will your serious and great business scant
For[145] she is with me. No, when light-wing'd toys
Of feather'd Cupid seel[146] with wanton dulness
My speculative and offic'd instruments,[147]
That[148] my disports corrupt and taint my business,   270
Let housewives make a skillet of my helm,
And all indign[149] and base adversities
Make head against my estimation![150]

Duke.   Be it as you shall privately determine,
Either for her stay or going. The affair cries haste,
And speed must answer it.

First Senator.   You must away to-night.

Othello.   With all my heart.

Duke.   At nine i' the morning here we'll meet again.
Othello, leave some officer behind,
And he shall our commission bring to you;   280
With such things else of quality and respect
As doth import you.[151]

Othello.   So please your Grace, my ancient;
A man he is of honesty and trust:
To his conveyance I assign my wife,
With what else needful your good grace shall think
To be sent after me.

---

[139] I.e., I have become a soldier, like Othello.   [140] I.e., of marriage, or of war, or of both.   [141] Endure.
[142] Closely concerning (i.e., Desdemona).   [143] The passions of youth (hence, here, *immoderate* sexual
passion).   [144] Forbid.   [145] Because.   [146] Blind (v.) by sewing up the eyelids (a term from falconry).
[147] Reflective and executive faculties and organs.   [148] So that.   [149] Shameful.   [150] Reputation.   [151] Concern.

Duke.   Let it be so.
 Good-night to every one. *(To Brabantio.)* And, noble signior,
 If virtue no delighted[152] beauty lack,
 Your son-in-law is far more fair than black.

First Senator. Adieu, brave Moor! use Desdemona well.   290

Brabantio. Look to her, Moor, if thou hast eyes to see:
 She has deceiv'd her father, and may thee.

                                    (Exeunt Duke, Senators, Officers, &c.)

Othello. My life upon her faith! Honest Iago,
 My Desdemona must I leave to thee:
 I prithee, let thy wife attend on her;
 And bring them after in the best advantage.[153]
 Come, Desdemona; I have but an hour
 Of love, of worldly matters and direction,
 To spend with thee: we must obey the time.

                                    (Exeunt Othello and Desdemona.)

Roderigo. Iago!   300

Iago. What sayst thou, noble heart?

Roderigo. What will I do, think'st thou?

Iago. Why, go to bed, and sleep.

Roderigo. I will incontinently[154] drown myself.

Iago. Well, if thou dost, I shall never love thee after.
 Why, thou silly gentleman!

Roderigo. It is silliness to live when to live is torment; and then have we a prescription
 to die when death is our physician.

Iago. O! villainous; I have looked upon the world for four times seven years, and
 since I could distinguish betwixt a benefit and an injury, I never found man that
 knew how to love himself. Ere I would say, I would drown myself for the love of
 a guinea-hen, I would change my humanity with a baboon.   312

Roderigo. What should I do? I confess it is my shame to be so fond;[155] but it is not
 in my virtue[156] to amend it.

Iago. Virtue! a fig! 'tis in ourselves that we are thus, or thus. Our bodies are our
 gardens, to the which our wills are gardeners; so that if we will plant nettles or
 sow lettuce, set hyssop and weed up thyme, supply it with one gender[157] of herbs
 or distract it with many, either to have it sterile with idleness or manured with
 industry, why, the power and corrigible[158] authority of this lies in our wills.
 If the balance of our lives had not one scale of reason to poise another of
 sensuality, the blood and baseness of our natures would conduct us to most

---

[152] Delightful.   [153] Opportunity.   [154] Forthwith.   [155] Infatuated.   [156] Strength.   [157] Kind.
[158] Corrective.

preposterous conclusions; but we have reason to cool our raging motions, our carnal stings, our unbitted[159] lusts, whereof I take this that you call love to be a sect or scion.[160]   324

Roderigo. It cannot be.

Iago. It is merely a lust of the blood and a permission of the will. Come, be a man. Drown thyself! drown cats and blind puppies. I have professed me thy friend, and I confess me knit to thy deserving with cables of perdurable toughness; I could never better stead thee than now. Put money in thy purse; follow these wars; defeat thy favour[161] with a usurped[162] beard; I say, put money in thy purse. It cannot be that Desdemona should long continue her love to the Moor,—put money in thy purse,—nor he his to her. It was a violent commencement in her, and thou shalt see an answerable sequestration;[163] put but money in thy purse. These Moors are changeable in their wills;—fill thy purse with money:—the food that to him now is as luscious as locusts,[164] shall be to him shortly as bitter as coloquintida.[165] She must change for youth: when she is sated with his body, she will find the error of her choice. She must have change, she must: therefore put money in thy purse. If thou wilt needs damn thyself, do it a more delicate way than drowning. Make all the money thou canst. If sanctimony and a frail vow betwixt an erring[166] barbarian and a supersubtle[167] Venetian be not too hard for my wits and all the tribe of hell, thou shalt enjoy her; therefore make money. A pox of drowning thyself! it is clean out of the way: seek thou rather to be hanged in compassing thy joy than to be drowned and go without her.   344

Roderigo. Wilt thou be fast to my hopes, if I depend on the issue?[168]

Iago. Thou art sure of me: go, make money. I have told thee often, and I retell thee again and again, I hate the Moor; my cause is hearted; thine hath no less reason. Let us be conjunctive[169] in our revenge against him; if thou canst cuckold him, thou dost thyself a pleasure, me a sport. There are many events in the womb of time which will be delivered. Traverse;[170] go: provide thy money. We will have more of this to-morrow. Adieu.   351

Roderigo. Where shall we meet i' the morning?

Iago. At my lodging.

Roderigo. I'll be with thee betimes.

Iago. Go to: farewell. Do you hear, Roderigo?

Roderigo. What say you?

Iago. No more of drowning, do you hear?

Roderigo. I am changed. I'll sell all my land.

Iago. Go to; farewell! put money enough in your purse.   *(Exit Roderigo.)*

Thus do I ever make my fool my purse;   360

For I mine own gain'd knowledge should profane,

---

[159] I.e., uncontrolled.   [160] Offshoot.   [161] Change thy appearance (for the worse?).   [162] Assumed. [163] Estrangement.   [164] Sweet-tasting fruits (perhaps the carob, the edible seedpod of an evergreen tree in the Mediterranean area).   [165] Purgative derived from a bitter apple.   [166] Vagabond.   [167] Exceedingly refined.   [168] Rely on the outcome.   [169] Allied.   [170] March.

If I would time expend with such a snipe[171]
But for my sport and profit. I hate the Moor,
And it is thought abroad[172] that 'twixt my sheets
He has done my office: I know not if 't be true,
But I, for mere suspicion in that kind,
Will do as if for surety.[173] He holds me well;[174]
The better shall my purpose work on him.
Cassio's a proper[175] man; let me see now:
To get his place; and to plume up[176] my will   370
In double knavery; how, how? Let's see:
After some time to abuse Othello's ear
That he[177] is too familiar with his wife:
He hath a person and a smooth dispose[178]
To be suspected; framed[179] to make women false,
The Moor is of a free and open nature,
That thinks men honest that but seem to be so,
And will as tenderly be led by the nose
As asses are.
I have 't; it is engender'd: hell and night   380
Must bring this monstrous birth to the world's light.   (Exit.)

ACT II

Scene 1.   A Sea-port Town in Cyprus. An open place near the Quay.

(Enter Montano and two Gentlemen.)

Montano. What from the cape can you discern at sea?
First Gentleman.   Nothing at all: it is a high-wrought flood;
    I cannot 'twixt the heaven and the main[180]
    Descry a sail.
Montano. Methinks the wind hath spoke aloud at land;
    A fuller blast ne'er shook our battlements;
    If it hath ruffian'd so upon the sea,
    What ribs of oak, when mountains melt on them,
    Can hold the mortise?[181] What shall we hear of this?
Second Gentleman.   A segregation[182] of the Turkish fleet;   10
    For do but stand upon the foaming shore,
    The chidden billow seems to pelt the clouds;

---

[171] Dupe.   [172] People think.   [173] As if it were certain.   [174] In high regard.   [175] Handsome.
[176] Make ready.   [177] I.e., Cassio.   [178] Bearing.   [179] Designed, apt.   [180] Ocean.   [181] Hold the joints together.   [182] Scattering.

The wind-shak'd surge, with high and monstrous mane,
Seems to cast water on the burning bear[183]
And quench the guards of the ever-fixed pole:[184]
I never did like[185] molestation view
On the enchafed[186] flood.

Montano.   If that[187] the Turkish fleet
Be not enshelter'd and embay'd, they are drown'd;
It is impossible they bear it out.

(Enter a Third Gentleman.)

Third Gentleman.   News, lad! our wars are done.   20
The desperate tempest hath so bang'd the Turks
That their designment halts;[188] a noble ship of Venice
Hath seen a grievous wrack and suffrance[189]
On most part of their fleet.

Montano. How! is this true?

Third Gentleman.   The ship is here put in,
A Veronesa;[190] Michael Cassio,
Lieutenant to the warlike Moor Othello,
Is come on shore: the Moor himself's at sea,
And is in full commission here for Cyprus.

Montano. I am glad on 't; 'tis a worthy governor.   30

Third Gentleman.   But this same Cassio, though he speak of comfort
Touching the Turkish loss, yet he looks sadly
And prays the Moor be safe; for they were parted
With foul and violent tempest.

Montano.   Pray heaven he be;
For I have serv'd him, and the man commands
Like a full soldier. Let's to the sea-side, ho!
As well to see the vessel that's come in
As to throw out our eyes for brave Othello,
Even till we make the main and the aerial blue
An indistinct regard.[191]   40

Third Gentleman.   Come, let's do so;
For every minute is expectancy
Of more arrivance.

(Enter Cassio.)

---

[183] Ursa Minor (the Little Dipper).   [184] Polaris, the North Star, almost directly above the Earth's axis, is part of the constellation of the Little Bear, or Dipper.   [185] Similar.   [186] Agitated.   [187] If.   [188] Plan is stopped.   [189] Damage.   [190] Probably a *type* of ship, rather than a ship from Verona—not only because Verona is an inland city but also because of "a noble ship of Venice" above.   [191] Till our (straining) eyes can no longer distinguish sea and sky.

Cassio. Thanks, you the valiant of this warlike isle,
    That so approve the Moor. O! let the heavens
    Give him defence against the elements,
    For I have lost him on a dangerous sea.
Montano. Is he well shipp'd?
Cassio. His bark is stoutly timber'd, and his pilot
    Of very expert and approv'd allowance;[192]   50
    Therefore my hopes, not surfeited to death,[193]
    Stand in bold cure.[194]

(Within, 'A sail!—a sail!—a sail!' Enter a Messenger.)

Cassio. What noise?
Messenger. The town is empty; on the brow o' the sea
    Stand ranks of people, and they cry 'A sail!'
Cassio. My hopes do shape him for the governor.

(Guns heard.)

Second Gentleman. They do discharge their shot of courtesy;
    Our friends at least.
Cassio.   I pray you, sir, go forth.
    And give us truth who 'tis that is arriv'd.
Second Gentleman. I shall.   *(Exit.)*   60
Montano. But, good lieutenant, is your general wiv'd?
Cassio. Most fortunately: he hath achiev'd a maid
    That paragons[195] description and wild fame;
    One that excels the quirks[196] of blazoning pens,
    And in th' essential vesture of creation[197]
    Does tire the ingener.[198]

(Re-enter Second Gentleman.)

                    How now! who has put in?
Second Gentleman. 'Tis one Iago, ancient to the general.
Cassio. He has had most favourable and happy speed:
    Tempests themselves, high seas, and howling winds,
    The gutter'd[199] rocks, and congregated sands,   70
    Traitors ensteep'd[200] to clog the guiltless keel,
    As having sense of beauty, do omit

---

[192] Admitted and proven to be expert.   [193] Overindulged.   [194] With good chance of being fulfilled.
[195] Exceeds, surpasses.   [196] Ingenuities.   [197] I.e., just as God made her; or: (even in) the (mere) essence of human nature.   [198] Inventor (i.e., of her praises?).   [199] Jagged; or: submerged.   [200] Submerged.

Their mortal[201] natures, letting go safely by
The divine Desdemona.

Montano.   What is she?

Cassio. She that I spake of, our great captain's captain,
Left in the conduct of the bold Iago,
Whose footing[202] here anticipates our thoughts
A se'nnight's[203] speed. Great Jove, Othello guard,
And swell his sail with thine own powerful breath,
That he may bless this bay with his tall[204] ship,   80
Make love's quick pants in Desdemona's arms,
Give renew'd fire to our extinced spirits,
And bring all Cyprus comfort!

(Enter Desdemona, Emilia, Iago, Roderigo, and Attendants.)

                                     O! behold,
The riches of the ship is come on shore.
Ye men of Cyprus, let her have your knees.
Hail to thee, lady! and the grace of heaven,
Before, behind thee, and on every hand,
Enwheel thee round!

Desdemona.   I thank you, valiant Cassio.
What tidings can you tell me of my lord?

Cassio. He is not yet arriv'd; nor know I aught   90
But that he's well, and will be shortly here.

Desdemona. O! but I fear—How lost you company?

Cassio. The great contention of the sea and skies
Parted our fellowship. But hark! a sail.

(Cry within, 'A sail—a sail!' Guns heard.)

Second Gentleman. They give their greeting to the citadel:
This likewise is a friend.

Cassio.   See for the news!   *(Exit Gentleman.)*
Good ancient, you are welcome:—*(To Emilia.)* welcome, mistress.
Let it not gall your patience, good Iago,
That I extend my manners; 'tis my breeding
That gives me this bold show of courtesy.   *(Kissing her.)*   100

Iago. Sir, would she give you so much of her lips
As of her tongue she oft bestows on me,
You'd have enough.

Desdemona.   Alas! she has no speech.

[201] Deadly.   [202] Landing.   [203] Week's.   [204] Brave.

Iago. In faith, too much;
  I find it still when I have list[205] to sleep:
  Marry, before your ladyship, I grant,
  She puts her tongue a little in her heart,
  And chides with thinking.[206]

Emilia. You have little cause to say so.

Iago. Come on, come on; you are pictures[207] out of doors, 110
  Bells[208] in your parlours, wild cats in your kitchens,
  Saints in your injuries, devils being offended,
  Players[209] in your housewifery,[210] and housewives[211] in your beds.

Desdemona. O! fie upon thee, slanderer.

Iago. Nay, it is true, or else I am a Turk:
  You rise to play and go to bed to work.

Emilia. You shall not write my praise.

Iago.   No, let me not.

Desdemona. What wouldst thou write of me, if thou shouldst praise me?

Iago. O gentle lady, do not put me to 't,
  For I am nothing if not critical. 120

Desdemona. Come on; assay. There's one gone to the harbour?

Iago. Ay, madam.

Desdemona *(aside).* I am not merry, but I do beguile
  The thing I am by seeming otherwise.
  (To Iago.) Come, how wouldst thou praise me?

Iago. I am about it; but indeed my invention
  Comes from my pate[212] as birdlime does from frize;[213]
  It plucks out brains and all: but my muse labours
  And thus she is deliver'd.
  If she be fair and wise, fairness and wit, 130
  The one's for use, the other useth it.

Desdemona. Well prais'd! How if she be black and witty?

Iago. If she be black,[214] and thereto have a wit,
  She'll find a white that shall her blackness fit.

Desdemona. Worse and worse.

Emilia. How if fair and foolish?

Iago. She never yet was foolish that was fair,
  For even her folly[215] help'd to an heir.

Desdemona. These are old fond[216] paradoxes to make fools laugh i' the alehouse.
  What miserable praise has thou for her that's foul and foolish? 140

Iago. There's none so foul and foolish thereunto,
  But does foul pranks which fair and wise ones do.

---

[205] Wish.   [206] I.e., without words.   [207] I.e., made up, "painted."   [208] I.e., jangly.   [209] Triflers, wastrels.
[210] Housekeeping.   [211] (1) Hussies, (2) (unduly) frugal with their sexual favors, (3) businesslike, serious.
[212] Head.   [213] Coarse cloth.   [214] Brunette, dark haired.   [215] Here also, wantonness.   [216] Foolish.

Desdemona. O heavy ignorance! thou praisest the worst best. But what praise couldst thou bestow on a deserving woman indeed, one that, in the authority of her merit, did justly put on the vouch[217] of very malice itself?

Iago. She that was ever fair and never proud,
    Had tongue at will and yet was never loud,
    Never lack'd gold and yet went never gay,
    Fled from her wish and yet said 'Now I may,'
    She that being anger'd, her revenge being nigh,   150
    Bade her wrong stay and her displeasure fly,
    She that in wisdom never was so frail
    To change the cod's head for the salmon's tail,[218]
    She that could think and ne'er disclose her mind,
    See suitors following and not look behind,
    She was a wight, if ever such wight were,—

Desdemona. To do what?

Iago. To suckle fools and chronicle small beer.[219]

Desdemona. O most lame and impotent conclusion! Do not learn of him, Emilia, though he be thy husband. How say you, Cassio? Is he not a most profane and liberal[220] counsellor?   161

Cassio. He speaks home,[221] madam; you may relish him more in the soldier than in[222] the scholar.

Iago (aside). He takes her by the palm: ay, well said, whisper; with as little a web as this will I ensnare as great a fly as Cassio. Ay, smile upon her, do; I will gyve[223] thee in thine own courtship. You say true, 'tis so, indeed. If such tricks as these strip you out of your lieutenantry, it had been better you had not kissed your three fingers so oft, which now again you are most apt to play the sir[224] in. Very good; well kissed! an excellent courtesy! 'tis so, indeed. Yet again your fingers to your lips? would they were clyster-pipes[225] for your sake! (A trumpet heard.) The Moor! I know his trumpet.[226]   171

Cassio. 'Tis truly so.

Desdemona. Let's meet him and receive him.

Cassio. Lo! where he comes.

(Enter Othello and Attendants.)

Othello. O my fair warrior!

Desdemona.   My dear Othello!

Othello. It gives me wonder great as my content
    To see you here before me. O my soul's joy!
    If after every tempest come such calms,

---

[217] Compel the approval.   [218] To make a foolish exchange (a bawdy secondary meaning is probable).   [219] I.e., keep petty household accounts.   [220] Free-spoken, licentious.   [221] To the mark, aptly.   [222] As . . . as.   [223] Entangle.   [224] Gentleman.   [225] Syringes, enema pipes.   [226] I.e., Othello's distinctive trumpet call.

May the winds blow till they have waken'd death!
And let the labouring bark climb hills of seas   180
Olympus-high, and duck again as low
As hell's from heaven! If it were now to die,
'Twere now to be most happy, for I fear
My soul hath her content so absolute
That not another comfort like to this
Succeeds in unknown fate.

Desdemona.   The heavens forbid
But that our loves and comforts should increase
Even as our days do grow!

Othello. Amen to that, sweet powers!
I cannot speak enough of this content;   190
It stops me here; it is too much of joy:
And this, and this, the greatest discords be   *(Kissing her.)*
That e'er our hearts shall make!

Iago *(aside)*.   O! you are well tun'd now,
But I'll set down[227] the pegs that make this music,
As honest as I am.

Othello.   Come, let us to the castle.
News, friends; our wars are done, the Turks are drown'd.
How does my old acquaintance of this isle?
Honey, you shall be well desir'd[228] in Cyprus;
I have found great love amongst them. O my sweet,
I prattle out of fashion, and I dote   200
In mine own comforts. I prithee, good Iago,
Go to the bay and disembark my coffers.
Bring thou the master to the citadel;
He is a good one, and his worthiness
Does challenge much respect. Come, Desdemona,
Once more well met at Cyprus.

(Exeunt all except Iago and Roderigo.)

Iago. Do thou meet me presently at the harbour. Come hither. If thou be'st valiant,
as they say base men being in love have then a nobility in their natures more
than is native to them, list[229] me. The lieutenant to-night watches on the court of
guard:[230] first, I must tell thee this, Desdemona is directly in love with him.   210

Roderigo. With him! Why, 'tis not possible.

Iago. Lay thy finger thus, and let thy soul be instructed. Mark me with what
violence she first loved the Moor but for bragging and telling her fantasti-
cal lies; and will she love him still for prating? let not thy discreet heart think

---

[227] Loosen.   [228] Welcomed.   [229] Listen to.   [230] Guardhouse.

it. Her eye must be fed; and what delight shall she have to look on the devil? When the blood is made dull with the act of sport, there should be, again to inflame it, and to give satiety a fresh appetite, loveliness in favour, sympathy in years, manners, and beauties; all which the Moor is defective in. Now, for want of these required conveniences, her delicate tenderness will find itself abused, begin to heave the gorge,[231] disrelish and abhor the Moor; very nature will instruct her in it, and compel her to some second choice. Now, sir, this granted, as it is a most pregnant[232] and unforced position, who stands so eminently in the degree of this fortune as Cassio does? a knave very voluble, no further conscionable[233] than in putting on the mere form of civil and humane seeming, for the better compassing of his salt[234] and most hidden loose affection? why, none; why, none: a slipper[235] and subtle knave, a finder-out of occasions, that has an eye can stamp and counterfeit advantages, though true advantage never present itself; a devilish knave! Besides, the knave is handsome, young, and hath all those requisites in him that folly and green minds look after; a pestilent complete knave! and the woman hath found him already.   231

Roderigo. I cannot believe that in her; she is full of most blessed condition.

Iago. Blessed fig's end! the wine she drinks is made of grapes;[236] if she had been blessed she would never have loved the Moor; blessed pudding! Didst thou not see her paddle with the palm of his hand? didst not mark that?

Roderigo. Yes, that I did; but that was but courtesy.

Iago. Lechery, by this hand! an index[237] and obscure prologue to the history of lust and foul thoughts. They met so near with their lips, that their breaths embraced together. Villainous thoughts, Roderigo! when these mutualities so marshal the way, hard at hand comes the master and main exercise, the incorporate[238] conclusion. Pish![239] But, sir, be you ruled by me: I have brought you from Venice. Watch you to-night; for the command, I'll lay 't upon you: Cassio knows you not. I'll not be far from you: do you find some occasion to anger Cassio, either by speaking too loud, or tainting[240] his discipline; or from what other course you please, which the time shall more favourably minister.   245

Roderigo. Well.

Iago. Sir, he is rash and very sudden in choler, and haply may strike at you: provoke him, that he may; for even out of that will I cause these of Cyprus to mutiny, whose qualification[241] shall come into no true taste again but by the displanting of Cassio. So shall you have a shorter journey to your desires by the means I shall then have to prefer[242] them; and the impediment most profitably removed, without the which there were no expectation of our prosperity.

Roderigo. I will do this, if I can bring it to any opportunity.

Iago. I warrant thee. Meet me by and by at the citadel: I must fetch his necessaries ashore. Farewell.

---

[231] Vomit.   [232] Obvious.   [233] Conscientious.   [234] Lecherous.   [235] Slippery.   [236] I.e., she is only flesh and blood.   [237] Pointer.   [238] Carnal.   [239] Exclamation of disgust.   [240] Disparaging.   [241] Appeasement.   [242] Advance.

Roderigo. Adieu. *(Exit.)*

Iago. That Cassio loves her, I do well believe it;
 That she loves him, 'tis apt,[243] and of great credit:[244]
 The Moor, howbeit that I endure him not,   260
 Is of a constant, loving, noble nature;
 And I dare think he'll prove to Desdemona
 A most dear[245] husband. Now, I do love her too;
 Not out of absolute lust,—though peradventure[246]
 I stand accountant[247] for as great a sin,—
 But partly led to diet my revenge,
 For that I do suspect the lusty Moor
 Hath leap'd into my seat; the thought whereof
 Doth like a poisonous mineral gnaw my inwards;
 And nothing can or shall content my soul   270
 Till I am even'd with him, wife for wife;
 Or failing so, yet that I put the Moor
 At least into a jealousy so strong
 That judgment cannot cure. Which thing to do,
 If this poor trash[248] of Venice, whom I trash[249]
 For his quick hunting, stand the putting-on,[250]
 I'll have our Michael Cassio on the hip;
 Abuse him to the Moor in the rank garb,[251]
 For I fear Cassio with my night-cap too,
 Make the Moor thank me, love me, and reward me   280
 For making him egregiously an ass
 And practising upon his peace and quiet
 Even to madness. 'Tis here, but yet confus'd:
 Knavery's plain face is never seen till us'd.   *(Exit.)*

Scene 2.   A Street.

(Enter a Herald with a proclamation; people following.)

Herald.   It is Othello's pleasure, our noble and valiant general, that, upon certain
 tidings now arrived, importing the mere[252] perdition of the Turkish fleet, every
 man put himself into triumph; some to dance, some to make bonfires, each man
 to what sport and revels his addiction leads him; for, besides these beneficial news,
 it is the celebration of his nuptial. So much was his pleasure should be proclaimed.
 All offices[253] are open, and there is full liberty of feasting from this present hour
 of five till the bell have told eleven. Heaven bless the isle of Cyprus and our noble
 general Othello!   *(Exeunt.)*

---

[243] Natural, probable.   [244] Easily believable.   [245] A pun on the word in the sense of expensive.
[246] Perchance, perhaps.   [247] Accountable.   [248] I.e., Roderigo.   [249] Check, control.   [250] Inciting.
[251] Gross manner.   [252] Utter.   [253] Kitchens and storehouses.

ISBN: 145760429

Place Inside the Box

1. Rental Returns

Items to Include	Quantity
Literature: The Human Experience: Reading and Writing	1

2. Packing Slip

Put the packing slip inside the box

FOR MERCHANT USE ONLY:

RNS-A9UWZA0MF5CR9

Customer ID: A2T0Y2IUPR46U5

Total Number of Items: 1

Item	Due Date
Literature: The Human Experience: Reading and Writing / ISBN-13: 9781457604294, ISBN-10: 1457604299	5/29/15

Scene 3. A Hall in the Castle.

(Enter Othello, Desdemona, Cassio, and Attendants.)

Othello. Good Michael, look you to the guard to-night:
  Let's teach ourselves that honourable stop,[254]
  Not to outsport discretion.
Cassio. Iago hath direction what to do:
  But, notwithstanding, with my personal[255] eye
  Will I look to 't.
Othello.   Iago is most honest.
  Michael, good-night; to-morrow with your earliest
  Let me have speech with you. *(To Desdemona.)* Come, my dear love,
  The purchase made, the fruits are to ensue;
  That profit's yet to come 'twixt me and you.   10
  Good-night.

                    (Exeunt Othello, Desdemona, and Attendants.)

(Enter Iago.)

Cassio. Welcome, Iago; we must to the watch.
Iago. Not this hour, lieutenant; 'tis not yet ten o' the clock. Our general casts us thus early for the love of his Desdemona, who let us not therefore blame; he hath not yet made wanton the night with her, and she is sport for Jove.
Cassio. She's a most exquisite lady.
Iago. And, I'll warrant her, full of game.
Cassio. Indeed, she is a most fresh and delicate creature.
Iago. What an eye she has! methinks it sounds a parley[256] of provocation.
Cassio. An inviting eye: and yet methinks right modest.   20
Iago. And when she speaks, is it not an alarum[257] to love?
Cassio. She is indeed perfection.
Iago. Well, happiness to their sheets! Come, lieutenant, I have a stoup of wine, and here without are a brace[258] of Cyprus gallants that would fain have a measure to the health of black Othello.
Cassio. Not to-night, good Iago: I have very poor and unhappy brains for drinking: I could well wish courtesy would invent some other custom of entertainment.
Iago. O! they are our friends; but one cup: I'll drink for you.   29
Cassio. I have drunk but one cup to-night, and that was craftily qualified[259] too, and, behold, what innovation[260] it makes here: I am unfortunate in the infirmity, and dare not task my weakness with any more.

---

[254] Discipline.   [255] Own.   [256] Conference.   [257] Call-to-arms.   [258] Pair.   [259] Diluted.   [260] Change, revolution.

Iago. What, man! 'tis a night of revels; the gallants desire it.

Cassio. Where are they?

Iago. Here at the door; I pray you, call them in.

Cassio. I'll do 't; but it dislikes me. *(Exit.)*

Iago. If I can fasten but one cup upon him,
    With that which he hath drunk to-night already,
    He'll be as full of quarrel and offence
    As my young mistress' dog. Now, my sick fool Roderigo,   40
    Whom love has turn'd almost the wrong side out,
    To Desdemona hath to-night carous'd
    Potations pottle-deep;[261] and he's to watch.
    Three lads of Cyprus, noble swelling spirits,
    That hold their honours in a wary distance,[262]
    The very elements[263] of this warlike isle,
    Have I to-night fluster'd with flowing cups,
    And they watch too. Now, 'mongst this flock of drunkards,
    Am I to put our Cassio in some action
    That may offend the isle. But here they come.   50
    If consequence[264] do but approve my dream,
    My boat sails freely, both with wind and stream.

(Re-enter Cassio, with him Montano, and Gentlemen. Servant following with wine.)

Cassio. 'Fore God, they have given me a rouse[265] already.

Montano. Good faith, a little one; not past a pint, as I am a soldier.

Iago. Some wine, ho!
    (Sings.) And let me the canakin[266] clink, clink;
        And let me the canakin clink:
        A soldier's a man;
        A life's but a span;
        Why then let a soldier drink.   60
    Some wine, boys!

Cassio. 'Fore God, an excellent song.

Iago. I learned it in England, where indeed they are most potent in potting; your Dane, your German, and your swag-bellied[267] Hollander,—drink ho!—are nothing to your English.

Cassio. Is your Englishman so expert in his drinking?

Iago. Why, he drinks you[268] with facility your Dane dead drunk; he sweats not to overthrow your Almain;[269] he gives your Hollander a vomit ere the next pottle can be filled.

---

[261] Bottoms-up.   [262] Take offense easily.   [263] Types.   [264] Succeeding events.   [265] Drink.   [266] Small cup.   [267] With a pendulous belly.   [268] The "ethical" dative, i.e., you'll see that he drinks.   [269] German.

Cassio. To the health of our general! 70

Montano. I am for it, lieutenant; and I'll do you justice.

Iago. O sweet England!

    (*Sings.*) King Stephen was a worthy peer,
        His breeches cost him but a crown;
    He held them sixpence all too dear,
        With that he call'd the tailor lown.[270]
    He was a wight of high renown,
        And thou art but of low degree:
    'Tis pride that pulls the country down,
        Then take thine auld cloak about thee. 80

  Some wine, ho!

Cassio. Why, this is a more exquisite song than the other.

Iago. Will you hear 't again?

Cassio. No; for I hold him to be unworthy of his place that does those things. Well, God's above all; and there be souls must be saved, and there be souls must not be saved.

Iago. It's true, good lieutenant.

Cassio. For mine own part,—no offence to the general, nor any man of quality,— I hope to be saved.

Iago. And so do I too, lieutenant. 90

Cassio. Ay; but, by your leave, not before me; the lieutenant is to be saved before the ancient. Let's have no more of this; let's to our affairs. God forgive us our sins! Gentlemen, let's look to our business. Do not think, gentlemen, I am drunk: this is my ancient; this is my right hand, and this is my left hand. I am not drunk now; I can stand well enough, and speak well enough.

All. Excellent well.

Cassio. Why, very well, then; you must not think then that I am drunk.

                                               (*Exit.*)

Montano. To the platform, masters; come, let's set the watch.

Iago. You see this fellow that is gone before;
He is a soldier fit to stand by Caesar 100
And give direction; and do but see his vice;
'Tis to his virtue a just equinox,[271]
The one as long as the other; 'tis pity of him.
I fear the trust Othello puts him in,
On some odd time of his infirmity,
Will shake this island.

Montano.   But is he often thus?

Iago. 'Tis evermore the prologue to his sleep;
He'll watch the horologe a double set,[272]
If drink rock not his cradle.

---

[270] Lout, rascal.   [271] Equivalent.   [272] Stand watch twice twelve hours.

Montano.   It were well
  The general were put in mind of it.   110
  Perhaps he sees it not; or his good nature
  Prizes the virtue that appears in Cassio,
  And looks not on his evils. Is not this true?

(Enter Roderigo.)

Iago *(aside to him).*   How now, Roderigo!
  I pray you, after the lieutenant; go.   *(Exit Roderigo.)*
Montano. And 'tis great pity that the noble Moor
  Should hazard such a place as his own second
  With one of an ingraft²⁷³ infirmity;
  It were an honest action to say
  So to the Moor.
Iago.   Not I, for this fair island: 120
  I do love Cassio well, and would do much
  To cure him of this evil. But hark! what noise?

(Cry within, 'Help! Help!' Re-enter Cassio, driving in Roderigo.)

Cassio. You rogue! you rascal!
Montano.   What's the matter, lieutenant?
Cassio. A knave teach me my duty!
  I'll beat the knave into a twiggen²⁷⁴ bottle.
Roderigo. Beat me!
Cassio.   Dost thou prate, rogue?

(Striking Roderigo.)

Montano *(staying him).*   Nay, good lieutenant;
  I pray you, sir, hold your hand.
Cassio.   Let me go, sir,
  Or I'll knock you o'er the mazzard.²⁷⁵
Montano.   Come, come; you're drunk.
Cassio. Drunk!   130

(They fight.)

Iago *(aside to Roderigo).*   Away, I say! go out, and cry a mutiny.

                                                        (Exit Roderigo.)

---

²⁷³ Ingrained.   ²⁷⁴ Wicker.   ²⁷⁵ Head.

Nay, good lieutenant! God's will, gentlemen!
Help, ho! Lieutenant! sir! Montano! sir!
Help, masters! Here's a goodly watch indeed!

(Bell rings.)

Who's that that rings the bell? Diablo, ho!
The town will rise: God's will! lieutenant, hold!
You will be sham'd for ever.

(Re-enter Othello and Attendants.)

Othello.   What is the matter here?
Montano. 'Zounds! I bleed still; I am hurt to the death.

(He faints.)

Othello. Hold, for your lives!   140
Iago. Hold, ho, lieutenant! Sir! Montano! gentlemen!
   Have you forgot all sense of place and duty?
   Hold! the general speaks to you; hold for shame!
Othello. Why, how now, ho! from whence ariseth this?
   Are we turn'd Turks, and to ourselves do that
   Which heaven hath forbid the Ottomites?
   For Christian shame put by this barbarous brawl;
   He that stirs next to carve for his own rage
   Holds his soul light; he dies upon his motion.
   Silence that dreadful bell! it frights the isle   150
   From her propriety. What is the matter, masters?
   Honest Iago, that look'st dead with grieving,
   Speak, who began this? On thy love, I charge thee.
Iago. I do not know; friends all but now, even now,
   In quarter[276] and in terms like bride and groom
   Devesting[277] them for bed; and then, but now,—
   As if some planet had unwitted men,—
   Swords out, and tilting one at other's breast,
   In opposition bloody. I cannot speak
   Any beginning to this peevish odds,[278]   160
   And would in action glorious I had lost
   Those legs that brought me to a part of it!
Othello. How comes it, Michael, you are thus forgot?
Cassio. I pray you, pardon me; I cannot speak.

---

[276] On duty.   [277] Undressing.   [278] Silly quarrel.

Othello. Worthy Montano, you were wont be civil;
The gravity and stillness of your youth
The world hath noted, and your name is great
In mouths of wisest censure:[279] what's the matter,
That you unlace[280] your reputation thus
And spend your rich opinion[281] for the name   170
Of a night-brawler? give me answer to it.

Montano. Worthy Othello, I am hurt to danger;
Your officer, Iago, can inform you,
While I spare speech, which something now offends[282] me,
Of all that I do know; nor know I aught
By me that's said or done amiss this night,
Unless self-charity be sometimes a vice,
And to defend ourselves it be a sin
When violence assails us.

Othello.   Now, by heaven,
My blood begins my safer guides to rule,   180
And passion, having my best judgment collied,[283]
Assays to lead the way. If I once stir,
Or do but lift this arm, the best of you
Shall sink in my rebuke. Give me to know
How this foul rout began, who set it on;
And he that is approv'd[284] in this offence,
Though he had twinn'd with me—both at a birth—
Shall lose me. What! in a town of war,
Yet wild, the people's hearts brimful of fear,
To manage private and domestic quarrel,   190
In night, and on the court and guard of safety!
'Tis monstrous. Iago, who began 't?

Montano. If partially affin'd,[285] or leagu'd in office,
Thou dost deliver more or less than truth,
Thou art not soldier.

Iago.   Touch me not so near;
I had rather[286] have this tongue cut from my mouth
Than it should do offence to Michael Cassio;
Yet, I persuade myself, to speak the truth
Shall nothing wrong him. Thus it is, general.
Montano and myself being in speech,   200
There comes a fellow crying out for help,
And Cassio following with determin'd sword
To execute upon him. Sir, this gentleman

---

[279] Judgment.   [280] Undo.   [281] High reputation.   [282] Pains, harms.   [283] Clouded.   [284] Proved (i.e., guilty).   [285] Favorably biased (by ties of friendship, or as Cassio's fellow officer).   [286] More quickly.

Steps in to Cassio, and entreats his pause;
Myself the crying fellow did pursue,
Lest by his clamour, as it so fell out,
The town might fall in fright; he, swift of foot,
Outran my purpose, and I return'd the rather
For that I heard the clink and fall of swords,
And Cassio high in oath, which till to-night   210
I ne'er might say before. When I came back,—
For this was brief,—I found them close together,
At blow and thrust, even as again they were
When you yourself did part them.
More of this matter can I not report:
But men are men; the best sometimes forget:
Though Cassio did some little wrong to him,
As men in rage strike those that wish them best,
Yet, surely Cassio, I believe, receiv'd
From him that fled some strange indignity,   220
Which patience could not pass.
Othello.   I know, Iago.
Thy honesty and love doth mince[287] this matter,
Making it light to Cassio. Cassio, I love thee;
But never more be officer of mine.

(Enter Desdemona, attended.)

Look! if my gentle love be not rais'd up;
(To Cassio.) I'll make thee an example.
Desdemona.   What's the matter?
Othello. All's well now, sweeting; come away to bed.
Sir, for your hurts, myself will be your surgeon.
Lead him off.   *(Montano is led off.)*
Iago, look with care about the town,   230
And silence those whom this vile brawl distracted.
Come, Desdemona; 'tis the soldier's life,
To have their balmy slumbers wak'd with strife.

(Exeunt all but Iago and Cassio.)

Iago. What! are you hurt, lieutenant?
Cassio. Ay; past all surgery.
Iago. Marry, heaven forbid!

---

[287] Tone down.

Cassio. Reputation, reputation, reputation! O! I have lost my reputation. I have lost the immortal part of myself, and what remains is bestial. My reputation, Iago, my reputation!

Iago. As I am an honest man, I thought you had received some bodily wound; there is more offence in that than in reputation. Reputation is an idle and most false imposition;[288] oft got without merit, and lost without deserving: you have lost no reputation at all, unless you repute yourself such a loser. What! man; there are ways to recover the general again; you are but now cast in his mood,[289] a punishment more in policy[290] than in malice; even so as one would beat his offenceless dog to affright an imperious lion. Sue to him again, and he is yours.

Cassio. I will rather sue to be despised than to deceive so good a commander with so slight, so drunken and so indiscreet an officer. Drunk! and speak parrot![291] and squabble, swagger, swear, and discourse fustian[292] with one's own shadow! O thou invisible spirit of wine! if thou hast no name to be known by, let us call thee devil!

Iago. What was he that you followed with your sword? What hath he done to you?

Cassio. I know not.

Iago. Is 't possible?

Cassio. I remember a mass of things, but nothing distinctly; a quarrel, but nothing wherefore. O God! that men should put an enemy in their mouths to steal away their brains; that we should, with joy, pleasance,[293] revel, and applause, transform ourselves into beasts.   260

Iago. Why, but you are now well enough; how came you thus recovered?

Cassio. It hath pleased the devil drunkenness to give place to the devil wrath; one unperfectness shows me another, to make me frankly despise myself.

Iago. Come, you are too severe a moraler. As the time, the place, and the condition of this country stands, I could heartily wish this had not befallen, but since it is as it is, mend it for your own good.

Cassio. I will ask him for my place again; he shall tell me I am a drunkard! Had I as many mouths as Hydra,[294] such an answer would stop them all. To be now a sensible man, by and by a fool, and presently a beast! O strange! Every inordinate cup is unblessed and the ingredient[295] is a devil.   270

Iago. Come, come; good wine is a good familiar creature if it be well used; exclaim no more against it. And, good lieutenant, I think you think I love you.

Cassio. I have well approved it, sir. I drunk!

Iago. You or any man living may be drunk at some time, man. I'll tell you what you shall do. Our general's wife is now the general; I may say so in this respect, for that he hath devoted and given up himself to the contemplation, mark, and denotement of her parts and graces: confess yourself freely to her; importune

---

[288] Something external.   [289] Dismissed because he is angry.   [290] I.e., more for the sake of the example or to show his fairness.   [291] I.e., without thinking.   [292] I.e., nonsense.   [293] Pleasure.   [294] Many-headed snake in Greek mythology.   [295] Contents.

her; she'll help to put you in your place again. She is of so free, so kind, so apt, so blessed a disposition, that she holds it a vice in her goodness not to do more than she is requested. This broken joint between you and her husband entreat her to splinter;[296] and, my fortunes against any lay[297] worth naming, this crack of your love shall grow stronger than it was before.

Cassio. You advise me well.

Iago. I protest, in the sincerity of love and honest kindness.

Cassio. I think it freely; and betimes in the morning I will beseech the virtuous Desdemona to undertake for me. I am desperate of my fortunes if they check me here.

Iago. You are in the right. Good-night, lieutenant; I must to the watch.

Cassio. Good-night, honest Iago!   *(Exit.)*

Iago. And what's he then that says I play the villain?   290
    When this advice is free I give and honest,
    Probal[298] to thinking and indeed the course
    To win the Moor again? For 'tis most easy
    The inclining Desdemona to subdue
    In any honest suit; she's fram'd as fruitful[299]
    As the free elements. And then for her
    To win the Moor, were 't to renounce his baptism,
    All seals and symbols of redeemed sin,
    His soul is so enfetter'd to her love,
    That she may make, unmake, do what she list,   300
    Even as her appetite shall play the god
    With his weak function.[300] How am I then a villain
    To counsel Cassio to this parallel[301] course,
    Directly to his good? Divinity of hell!
    When devils will the blackest sins put on,
    They do suggest at first with heavenly shows,
    As I do now; for while this honest fool
    Plies Desdemona to repair his fortunes,
    And she for him pleads strongly to the Moor,
    I'll pour this pestilence into his ear   310
    That she repeals[302] him for her body's lust;
    And, by how much she strives to do him good,
    She shall undo her credit with the Moor.
    So will I turn her virtue into pitch,
    And out of her own goodness make the net
    That shall enmesh them all.

(Re-enter Roderigo.)

---

[296] Bind up with splints.   [297] Wager.   [298] Provable.   [299] Generous.   [300] Faculties.   [301] Purposeful.   [302] I.e., seeks to recall.

Iago.   How now, Roderigo!

Roderigo. I do follow here in the chase, not like a hound that hunts, but one that
fills up the cry.[303] My money is almost spent; I have been to-night exceedingly
well cudgelled; and I think the issue will be, I shall have so much experience for
my pains; and so, with no money at all and a little more wit, return again to
Venice.

Iago. How poor are they that have not patience!
What wound did ever heal but by degrees?
Thou know'st we work by wit and not by witchcraft,
And wit depends on dilatory time.
Does 't not go well? Cassio hath beaten thee,
And thou by that small hurt hast cashiered Cassio.
Though other things grow fair against the sun,
Yet fruits that blossom first will first be ripe:
Content thyself awhile. By the mass, 'tis morning;   330
Pleasure and action make the hours seem short.
Retire thee; go where thou art billeted:
Away, I say; thou shalt know more hereafter:
Nay, get thee gone. *(Exit Roderigo.)* Two things are to be done,
My wife must move for Cassio to her mistress;
I'll set her on;
Myself the while to draw the Moor apart,
And bring him jump[304] when he may Cassio find
Soliciting his wife: ay, that's the way:
Dull not device by coldness and delay.   *(Exit.)*

ACT III

Scene 1.   Cyprus. Before the Castle.

(Enter Cassio, and some Musicians.)

Cassio. Masters, play here, I will content your pains;[305]
Something that's brief; and bid 'Good-morrow, general.'   *(Music.)*

(Enter Clown.)

Clown. Why, masters, have your instruments been in Naples, that they speak i'
the nose[306] thus?

---

[303] Pack (hunting term).   [304] At the exact moment.   [305] Reward your efforts.   [306] Naples was
notorious for venereal disease, and syphilis was believed to affect the nose.

First Musician. How, sir, how?

Clown. Are these, I pray you, wind-instruments?

First Musician. Ay, marry, are they, sir.

Clown. O! thereby hangs a tale.

First Musician. Whereby hangs a tale, sir?

Clown. Marry, sir, by many a wind-instrument that I know. But, masters, here's money for you; and the general so likes your music, that he desires you, for love's sake, to make no more noise with it.

First Musician. Well, sir, we will not.

Clown. If you have any music that may not be heard, to 't again; but, as they say, to hear music the general does not greatly care.

First Musician. We have none such, sir.

Clown. Then put up your pipes in your bag, for I'll away.
Go; vanish into air; away! *(Exeunt Musicians.)*

Cassio. Dost thou hear, mine honest friend?

Clown. No, I hear not your honest friend; I hear you. 20

Cassio. Prithee, keep up thy quillets.[307] There's a poor piece of gold for thee. If the gentlewoman that attends the general's wife be stirring, tell her there's one Cassio entreats her a little favour of speech: wilt thou do this?

Clown. She is stirring, sir: if she will stir hither, I shall seem to notify unto her.

Cassio. Do, good my friend. *(Exit Clown.)*

(Enter Iago.)

> In happy time, Iago.

Iago. You have not been a-bed, then?

Cassio. Why, no; the day had broke
Before we parted. I have made bold, Iago,
To send in to your wife; my suit to her
Is, that she will to virtuous Desdemona 30
Procure me some access.

Iago. I'll send her to you presently;
And I'll devise a mean to draw the Moor
Out of the way, that your converse and business
May be more free.

Cassio. I humbly thank you for 't. *(Exit Iago.)*
> I never knew
A Florentine more kind and honest.[308]

(Enter Emilia.)

Emilia. Good-morrow, good lieutenant: I am sorry

---

[307] Quibbles. [308] Cassio means that not even a fellow Florentine could behave to him in a friendlier fashion than does Iago.

For your displeasure,[309] but all will soon be well.
The general and his wife are talking of it,
And she speaks for you stoutly: the Moor replies   40
That he you hurt is of great fame in Cyprus
And great affinity,[310] and that in wholesome wisdom
He might not but refuse you; but he protests he loves you,
And needs no other suitor but his likings
To take the safest occasion by the front[311]
To bring you in again.[312]

Cassio.   Yet, I beseech you,
If you think fit, or that it may be done,
Give me advantage of some brief discourse
With Desdemona alone.

Emilia.   Pray you, come in:
I will bestow you where you shall have time   50
To speak your bosom[313] freely.

Cassio.   I am much bound to you.   *(Exeunt.)*

Scene 2. A Room in the Castle.

(Enter Othello, Iago, and Gentlemen.)

Othello. These letters give, Iago, to the pilot,
And by him do my duties to the senate;
That done, I will be walking on the works;
Repair there to me.

Iago.   Well, my good lord, I'll do 't.

Othello. This fortification, gentlemen, shall we see 't?

Gentlemen. We'll wait upon your lordship.   *(Exeunt.)*

Scene 3. Before the Castle.

(Enter Desdemona, Cassio, and Emilia.)

Desdemona. Be thou assur'd, good Cassio, I will do
All my abilities in thy behalf.

Emilia. Good madam, do: I warrant it grieves my husband,
As if the case were his.

Desdemona. O! that's an honest fellow. Do not doubt, Cassio,
But I will have my lord and you again
As friendly as you were.

---

[309] Disgrace.   [310] Family connection.   [311] Forelock.   [312] Restore you (to Othello's favor).
[313] Heart, inmost thoughts.

Cassio.   Bounteous madam,
   Whatever shall become of Michael Cassio,
   He's never any thing but your true servant.
Desdemona. I know 't; I thank you. You do love my lord;   10
   You have known him long; and be you well assur'd
   He shall in strangeness[314] stand no further off
   Than in a politic[315] distance.
Cassio.   Ay, but, lady,
   That policy may either last so long,
   Or feed upon such nice[316] and waterish diet,
   Or breed itself so out of circumstance,
   That, I being absent and my place supplied,
   My general will forget my love and service.
Desdemona. Do not doubt[317] that; before Emilia here
   I give thee warrant of thy place. Assure thee,   20
   If I do vow a friendship, I'll perform it
   To the last article; my lord shall never rest;
   I'll watch him tame,[318] and talk him out of patience;
   His bed shall seem a school, his board a shrift;[319]
   I'll intermingle every thing he does
   With Cassio's suit. Therefore be merry, Cassio;
   For thy solicitor shall rather die
   Than give thy cause away.[320]

(Enter Othello and Iago, at a distance.)

Emilia. Madam, here comes my lord.
Cassio. Madam, I'll take my leave.   30
Desdemona. Why, stay, and hear me speak.
Cassio. Madam, not now; I am very ill at ease,
   Unfit for mine own purposes.
Desdemona. Well, do your discretion.   *(Exit Cassio.)*
Iago. Ha! I like not that.
Othello.   What dost thou say?
Iago. Nothing, my lord: or if—I know not what.
Othello. Was not that Cassio parted from my wife?
Iago. Cassio, my lord? No, sure, I cannot think it,
   That he would steal away so guilty-like,
   Seeing you coming.
Othello.   I do believe 'twas he.   40
Desdemona. How now, my lord!

---

[314] Aloofness.   [315] I.e., dictated by policy.   [316] Slight, trivial.   [317] Fear.   [318] Outwatch him (i.e., keep him awake) till he submits.   [319] Confessional.   [320] Abandon your cause.

I have been talking with a suitor here,
A man that languishes in your displeasure.

Othello. Who is 't you mean?

Desdemona. Why, your lieutenant, Cassio. Good my lord,
If I have any grace or power to move you,
His present[321] reconciliation take;
For if he be not one that truly loves you,
That errs in ignorance and not in cunning,
I have no judgment in an honest face.   50
I prithee[322] call him back.

Othello.   Went he hence now?

Desdemona. Ay, sooth; so humbled,
That he hath left part of his grief with me,
To suffer with him. Good love, call him back.

Othello. Not now, sweet Desdemona; some other time.

Desdemona. But shall 't be shortly?

Othello.   The sooner, sweet, for you.

Desdemona. Shall 't be to-night at supper?

Othello.   No, not to-night.

Desdemona. To-morrow dinner, then?

Othello.   I shall not dine at home;
I meet the captains at the citadel.

Desdemona. Why, then, to-morrow night; or Tuesday morn;   60
Or Tuesday noon, or night; or Wednesday morn:
I prithee name the time, but let it not
Exceed three days: in faith, he's penitent;
And yet his trespass, in our common reason,—
Save that they say, the wars must make examples
Out of their best,—is not almost[323] a fault
To incur a private check.[324] When shall he come?
Tell me, Othello: I wonder in my soul,
What you could ask me, that I should deny,
Or stand so mammering[325] on. What! Michael Cassio,   70
That came a wooing with you, and so many a time,
When I have spoke of you dispraisingly,
Hath ta'en your part; to have so much to do
To bring him in! Trust me, I could do much,—

Othello. Prithee, no more; let him come when he will;
I deny thee nothing.

Desdemona.   Why, this is not a boon;
'Tis as I should entreat you wear your gloves,
Or feed on nourishing dishes, or keep you warm,

---

[321] Immediate.   [322] Pray thee.   [323] Hardly.   [324] (Even) a private reprimand.   [325] Shilly-shallying.

Or sue to you to do a peculiar profit
To your own person: nay, when I have a suit   80
Wherein I mean to touch your love indeed,
It shall be full of poise[326] and difficult weight,
And fearful to be granted.
Othello.   I will deny thee nothing:
Whereon, I do beseech thee, grant me this,
To leave me but a little to myself.
Desdemona. Shall I deny you? no: farewell, my lord.
Othello. Farewell, my Desdemona: I'll come to thee straight.
Desdemona. Emilia, come. Be as your fancies teach you;
Whate'er you be, I am obedient.   *(Exit, with Emilia.)*
Othello. Excellent wretch![327] Perdition catch my soul,   90
But I do love thee! and when I love thee not,
Chaos is[328] come again.
Iago. My noble lord,—
Othello.   What dost thou say, Iago?
Iago. Did Michael Cassio, when you woo'd my lady,
Know of your love?
Othello. He did, from first to last: why dost thou ask?
Iago. But for a satisfaction of my thought;
No further harm.
Othello.   Why of thy thought, Iago?
Iago. I did not think he had been acquainted with her.
Othello. O! yes; and went between us very oft.   100
Iago. Indeed!
Othello. Indeed! ay, indeed; discern'st thou aught in that?
Is he not honest?
Iago.   Honest, my lord?
Othello.   Honest! ay, honest.
Iago. My lord, for aught I know.
Othello. What dost thou think?
Iago.   Think, my lord!
Othello.   Think, my lord!
By heaven, he echoes me,
As if there were some monster in his thought
Too hideous to be shown. Thou dost mean something:
I heard thee say but now, thou lik'dst not that,
When Cassio left my wife; what didst not like?   110
And when I told thee he was of my counsel
In my whole course of wooing, thou criedst, 'Indeed!'
And didst contract and purse thy brow together,
As if thou then hadst shut up in thy brain

---

[326] Weight.   [327] Here, a term of endearment.   [328] Will have.

Some horrible conceit.[329] If thou dost love me,
Show me thy thought.

Iago. My lord, you know I love you.

Othello.   I think thou dost;
And, for[330] I know thou art full of love and honesty,
And weigh'st thy words before thou givest them breath,
Therefore these stops[331] of thine fright me the more;   120
For such things in a false disloyal knave
Are tricks of custom, but in a man that's just
They are close dilations,[332] working from the heart
That passion cannot rule.

Iago.   For Michael Cassio,
I dare be sworn I think that he is honest.

Othello. I think so too.

Iago.   Men should be what they seem;
Or those that be not, would they might seem none!

Othello. Certain men should be what they seem.

Iago. Why then, I think Cassio's an honest man.

Othello. Nay, yet there's more in this.   130
I pray thee, speak to me as to thy thinkings,
As thou dost ruminate, and give thy worst of thoughts
The worst of words.

Iago.   Good my lord, pardon me;
Though I am bound to every act of duty,
I am not bound to[333] that all slaves are free to.
Utter my thoughts? Why, say they are vile and false;
As where's that palace whereinto foul things
Sometimes intrude not? who has a breast so pure
But some uncleanly apprehensions[334]
Keep leets and law-days,[335] and in session sit   140
With meditations lawful?

Othello. Thou dost conspire against thy friend, Iago,
If thou but think'st him wrong'd, and mak'st his ear
A stranger to thy thoughts.

Iago.   I do beseech you,
Though I perchance am vicious in my guess,—
As, I confess, it is my nature's plague
To spy into abuses, and oft my jealousy[336]
Shapes faults that are not,—that your wisdom yet,
From one that so imperfectly conceits,
Would take no notice, nor build yourself a trouble   150

[329] Fancy.   [330] Because.   [331] Interruptions, hesitations.   [332] Secret (i.e., involuntary, unconscious) revelations.   [333] Bound with regard to.   [334] Conceptions.   [335] Sittings of the local courts.   [336] Suspicion.

Out of his scattering and unsure observance.
It were not for your quiet nor your good,
Nor for my manhood, honesty, or wisdom,
To let you know my thoughts.

Othello.   What dost thou mean?

Iago.   Good name in man and woman, dear my lord,
Is the immediate jewel of[337] their souls:
Who steals my purse steals trash; 'tis something, nothing;
'Twas mine, 'tis his, and has been slave to thousands;
But he that filches from me my good name
Robs me of that which not enriches him,   160
And makes me poor indeed.

Othello.   By heaven, I'll know thy thoughts.

Iago.   You cannot, if my heart were in your hand;
Nor shall not, whilst 'tis in my custody.

Othello.   Ha!

Iago.   O! beware, my lord, of jealousy;
It is the green-ey'd monster which doth mock
The meat it feeds on: that cuckold[338] lives in bliss
Who, certain of his fate, loves not his wronger;
But, O! what damned minutes tells[339] he o'er
Who dotes, yet doubts; suspects, yet soundly loves!   170

Othello.   O misery!

Iago.   Poor and content is rich, and rich enough,
But riches fineless[340] is as poor as winter
To him that ever fears he shall be poor.
Good heaven, the souls of all my tribe defend
From jealousy!

Othello.   Why, why is this?
Think'st thou I'd make a life of jealousy,
To follow still the changes of the moon
With fresh suspicions? No; to be once in doubt
Is once to be resolved. Exchange me for a goat   180
When I shall turn the business of my soul
To such exsufflicate[341] and blown[342] surmises,
Matching thy inference. 'Tis not to make me jealous
To say my wife is fair, feeds well, loves company,
Is free of speech, sings, plays, and dances well;
Where virtue is, these are more virtuous:
Nor from mine own weak merits will I draw
The smallest fear, or doubt of her revolt;
For she had eyes, and chose me. No, Iago;

---

[337] Jewel closest to.   [338] Husband of an adulterous woman.   [339] Counts.   [340] Boundless.
[341] Spat out (?).   [342] Fly-blown.

I'll see before I doubt; when I doubt, prove; 190
And, on the proof, there is no more but this,
Away at once with love or jealousy!

Iago. I am glad of it; for now I shall have reason
To show the love and duty that I bear you
With franker spirit; therefore, as I am bound,
Receive it from me; I speak not yet of proof.
Look to your wife; observe her well with Cassio;
Wear your eye thus, not jealous nor secure:
I would not have your free and noble nature
Out of self-bounty[343] be abus'd; look to 't: 200
I know our country disposition[344] well;
In Venice they do let heaven see the pranks
They dare not show their husbands; their best conscience
Is not to leave 't undone, but keep 't unknown.

Othello. Dost thou say so?

Iago. She did deceive her father, marrying you;
And when she seem'd to shake and fear your looks,
She lov'd them most.

Othello.   And so she did.

Iago.   Why, go to,[345] then;
She that so young could give out such a seeming,
To seel her father's eyes up close as oak, 210
He thought 'twas witchcraft; but I am much to blame;
I humbly do beseech you of your pardon
For too much loving you.

Othello.   I am bound to thee for ever.

Iago. I see, this hath a little dash'd your spirits.

Othello. Not a jot, not a jot.

Iago.   I' faith, I fear it has.
I hope you will consider what is spoke
Comes from my love. But I do see you're mov'd;
I am to pray you not to strain my speech
To grosser issues nor to larger reach
Than to suspicion. 220

Othello. I will not.

Iago.   Should you do so, my lord,
My speech should fall into such vile success
As my thoughts aim not at. Cassio's my worthy friend—
My lord, I see you're mov'd.

Othello.   No, not much mov'd:
I do not think but Desdemona's honest.[346]

---

[343] Innate generosity.   [344] I.e., that of Venice.   [345] Colloquialism; here, something like "all right."
[346] Chaste.

Iago. Long live she so! and long live you to think so!

Othello. And yet, how nature erring from itself,—

Iago. Ay, there's the point: as, to be bold with you,
    Not to affect many proposed matches
    Of her own clime,[347] complexion, and degree,[348]   230
    Whereto, we see, in all things nature tends;
    Foh! one may smell in such, a will most rank,
    Foul disproportion, thoughts unnatural.
    But pardon me; I do not in position[349]
    Distinctly[350] speak of her, though I may fear
    Her will, recoiling[351] to her better judgment,
    May fall to match you with her country forms
    And happily[352] repent.

Othello.   Farewell, farewell:
    If more thou dost perceive, let me know more;
    Set on thy wife to observe. Leave me, Iago.   240

Iago. My lord, I take my leave.   *(Going.)*

Othello. Why did I marry? This honest creature, doubtless,
    Sees and knows more, much more, than he unfolds.

Iago *(returning).* My lord, I would I might entreat your honour
    To scan this thing no further; leave it to time.
    Although 'tis fit that Cassio have his place,
    For, sure he fills it up with great ability,
    Yet, if you please to hold him off awhile,
    You shall by that perceive him and his means:
    Note if your lady strain his entertainment[353]   250
    With any strong or vehement importunity;
    Much will be seen in that. In the mean time,
    Let me be thought too busy[354] in my fears,
    As worthy cause I have to fear I am,
    And hold her free, I do beseech your honour.

Othello. Fear not my government.

Iago. I once more take my leave.   *(Exit.)*

Othello. This fellow's of exceeding honesty,
    And knows all qualities, with a learned spirit,
    Of human dealings; if I do prove her haggard,[355]   260
    Though that her jesses[356] were my dear heart-strings,
    I'd whistle her off and let her down the wind,[357]
    To prey at fortune. Haply, for I am black,
    And have not those soft parts of conversation

---

[347] Country.   [348] Social rank.   [349] In definite assertion.   [350] Specifically.   [351] Reverting.   [352] Perhaps.   [353] Urge his re-welcome (i.e., to Othello's trust and favor).   [354] Meddlesome.   [355] Wild hawk.   [356] Leather thongs by which the hawk's legs were strapped to the trainer's wrist.   [357] I'd let her go and take care of herself.

That chamberers[358] have, or, for I am declin'd
Into the vale of years—yet that's not much—
She's gone, I am abus'd;[359] and my relief
Must be to loathe her. O curse of marriage!
That we can call these delicate creatures ours,
And not their appetites. I had rather be a toad,   270
And live upon the vapour of a dungeon,
Than keep a corner in the thing I love
For others' uses. Yet, 'tis the plague of great ones;
Prerogativ'd[360] are they less than the base;
'Tis destiny unshunnable, like death:
Even then this forked plague[361] is fated to us
When we do quicken.[362]
                              Look! where she comes.
If she be false, O! then heaven mocks itself.
I'll not believe it.

(*Re-enter Desdemona and Emilia.*)

Desdemona.   How now, my dear Othello!
Your dinner and the generous[363] islanders   280
By you invited, do attend your presence.
Othello. I am to blame.
Desdemona.   Why do you speak so faintly?
Are you not well?
Othello. I have a pain upon my forehead here.[364]
Desdemona. Faith, that's with watching; 'twill away again:
Let me but bind it hard, within this hour
It will be well.
Othello.   Your napkin[365] is too little:

(*She drops her handkerchief.*)

Let it alone. Come, I'll go in with you.
Desdemona. I am very sorry that you are not well.

(*Exeunt Othello and Desdemona.*)

Emilia. I am glad I have found this napkin;   290
This was her first remembrance from the Moor;
My wayward husband hath a hundred times

---

[358] Courtiers; or (more specifically) gallants, frequenters of bed chambers.   [359] Deceived.
[360] Privileged.   [361] I.e., the cuckold's proverbial horns.   [362] Are conceived, come alive.   [363] Noble.
[364] Othello again refers to his cuckoldom.   [365] Handkerchief.

Woo'd me to steal it, but she so loves the token,
For he conjur'd her she should ever keep it,
That she reserves it evermore about her
To kiss and talk to. I'll have the work ta'en out,[366]
And giv 't Iago:
What he will do with it heaven knows, not I;
I nothing but[367] to please his fantasy.[368]

(Enter Iago.)

Iago. How now! what do you here alone?
Emilia. Do not you chide; I have a thing for you.
Iago. A thing for me? It is a common thing—
Emilia. Ha!
Iago. To have a foolish wife.
Emilia. O! is that all? What will you give me now
  For that same handkerchief?
Iago.   What handkerchief?
Emilia. What handkerchief!
  Why, that the Moor first gave to Desdemona:
  That which so often you did bid me steal.
Iago. Hath stol'n it from her?   310
Emilia. No, faith; she let it drop by negligence,
  And, to the advantage, I, being there, took 't up.
  Look, here it is.
Iago.   A good wench; give it me.
Emilia. What will you do with 't, that you have been so earnest
  To have me filch it?
Iago.   Why, what's that to you?   *(Snatches it.)*
Emilia. If it be not for some purpose of import
  Give 't me again; poor lady! she'll run mad
  When she shall lack it.
Iago. Be not acknown on 't;[369] I have use for it.
  Go, leave me.   *(Exit Emilia.)*
  I will in Cassio's lodging lose this napkin,
  And let him find it; trifles light as air
  Are to the jealous confirmations strong
  As proofs of holy writ; this may do something.
  The Moor already changes with my poison:
  Dangerous conceits are in their natures poisons,
  Which at the first are scarce found to distaste,[370]

---

[366] Pattern copied.   [367] I.e., only want.   [368] Whim.   [369] You know nothing about it.   [370] Scarce can be tasted.

But with a little act upon the blood,
Burn like the mines of sulphur. I did say so:
Look! where he comes!

(Enter Othello.)

         Not poppy,[371] nor mandragora,[372]   330
Nor all the drowsy syrups[373] of the world,
Shall ever medicine thee to that sweet sleep
Which thou ow'dst yesterday.
Othello.   Ha! ha! false to me?
Iago. Why, how now, general! no more of that.
Othello. Avaunt! be gone! thou hast set me on the rack;
 I swear 'tis better to be much abus'd
 Than but to know 't a little.
Iago.   How now, my lord!
Othello. What sense had I of her stol'n hours of lust?
 I saw 't not, thought it not, it harm'd not me;
 I slept the next night well, was free and merry;   340
 I found not Cassio's kisses on her lips;
 He that is robb'd, not wanting what is stol'n,
 Let him not know 't, and he's not robb'd at all.
Iago. I am sorry to hear this.
Othello. I had been happy, if the general camp,[374]
 Pioners[375] and all, had tasted her sweet body,
 So[376] I had nothing known. O! now, for ever
 Farewell the tranquil mind; farewell content!
 Farewell the plumed troop and the big wars
 That make ambition virtue! O, farewell!   350
 Farewell the neighing steed, and the shrill trump,
 The spirit-stirring drum, the ear-piercing fife,
 The royal banner, and all quality,
 Pride, pomp, and circumstance[377] of glorious war!
 And, O you mortal engines,[378] whose rude throats
 The immortal Jove's dread clamours counterfeit,
 Farewell! Othello's occupation's gone!
Iago. Is it possible, my lord?
Othello. Villain, be sure thou prove my love a whore,
 Be sure of it; give me the ocular proof;   360
 Or, by the worth of mine eternal soul,
 Thou hadst been better have been born a dog
 Than answer my wak'd wrath.

---

[371] Opium. [372] A soporific. [373] I.e., soporifics. [374] Whole army. [375] Lowest rank of manual laborers in the army. [376] As long as. [377] Pageantry. [378] Deadly artillery.

Iago. Is 't come to this?

Othello. Make me to see 't; or, at the least, so prove it,
  That the probation[379] bear no hinge nor loop
  To hang a doubt on; or woe upon thy life!

Iago. My noble lord—

Othello. If thou dost slander her and torture me,
  Never pray more; abandon all remorse;
  On horror's head horrors accumulate;
  Do deeds to make heaven weep, all earth amaz'd;
  For nothing canst thou to damnation add
  Greater than that.

Iago. O grace! O heaven forgive me!
  Are you a man! have you a soul or sense?
  God be wi' you; take mine office. O wretched fool!
  That liv'st to make thine honesty a vice.
  O monstrous world! Take note, take note, O world!
  To be direct and honest is not safe.
  I thank you for this profit,[380] and, from hence
  I'll love no friend, sith[381] love breeds such offence.

Othello. Nay, stay; thou shouldst be honest.

Iago. I should be wise; for honesty's a fool,
  And loses that it works for.

Othello. By the world,
  I think my wife be honest and think she is not;
  I think that thou art just and think thou art not.
  I'll have some proof. Her name, that was as fresh
  As Dian's[382] visage, is now begrim'd and black
  As mine own face. If there be cords or knives,
  Poison or fire or suffocating streams,
  I'll not endure it. Would I were satisfied!

Iago. I see, sir, you are eaten up with passion.
  I do repent me that I put it to you.
  You would be satisfied?

Othello. Would! nay, I will.

Iago. And may; but how? how satisfied, my lord?
  Would you, the supervisor,[383] grossly gape on;
  Behold her tupp'd?

Othello. Death and damnation! O!

Iago. It were a tedious[384] difficulty, I think,
  To bring them to that prospect; damn them then,
  If ever mortal eyes do see them bolster[385]

370

380

390

---

[379] Proof.   [380] Lesson.   [381] Since.   [382] Diana's, the goddess of the moon.   [383] Observer.   [384] Laborious.   [385] Lie together.

More[386] than their own! What then? how then?   400
What shall I say? Where's satisfaction?
It is impossible you should see this,
Were they as prime[387] as goats, as hot as monkeys,
As salt as wolves in pride,[388] and fools as gross
As ignorance made drunk; but yet, I say,
If imputation, and strong circumstances,
Which lead directly to the door of truth,
Will give you satisfaction, you may have it.

Othello. Give me a living reason she's disloyal.

Iago. I do not like the office;   410
But, sith I am enter'd in this cause so far,
Prick'd to 't by foolish honesty and love,
I will go on. I lay with Cassio lately;
And, being troubled with a raging tooth,
I could not sleep.
There are a kind of men so loose of soul
That in their sleeps will mutter their affairs;
One of this kind is Cassio.
In sleep I heard him say, 'Sweet Desdemona,
Let us be wary, let us hide our loves!'   420
And then, sir, would he gripe[389] and wring my hand,
Cry, 'O, sweet creature!' and then kiss me hard,
As if he pluck'd up kisses by the roots,
That grew upon my lips; then laid his leg
Over my thigh, and sigh'd, and kiss'd; and then
Cried, 'Cursed fate, that gave thee to the Moor!'

Othello. O monstrous! monstrous!

Iago.   Nay, this was but his dream.

Othello. But this denoted a foregone conclusion:[390]
'Tis a shrewd doubt,[391] though it be but a dream.

Iago. And this may help to thicken other proofs   430
That do demonstrate thinly.

Othello.   I'll tear her all to pieces.

Iago. Nay, but be wise; yet we see nothing done;
She may be honest yet. Tell me but this:
Have you not sometimes seen a handkerchief
Spotted with strawberries in your wife's hand?

Othello. I gave her such a one; 'twas my first gift.

Iago. I know not that; but such a handkerchief—
I am sure it was your wife's—did I to-day
See Cassio wipe his beard with.

---

[386] Other.   [387] Lustful.   [388] Heat.   [389] Seize.   [390] Previous consummation.   [391] (1) Cursed,
(2) Acute, suspicion.

Othello. If it be that,—

Iago. If it be that, or any that was hers, 440
It speaks against her with the other proofs.

Othello. O! that the slave had forty thousand lives;
One is too poor, too weak for my revenge.
Now do I see 'tis true. Look here, Iago;
All my fond love thus do I blow to heaven:
'Tis gone.
Arise, black vengeance, from the hollow hell!
Yield up, O love! thy crown and hearted throne
To tyrannous hate. Swell, bosom, with thy fraught,[392]
For 'tis of aspics'[393] tongues!

Iago. Yet be content.[394] 450

Othello. O! blood, blood, blood!

Iago. Patience, I say; your mind, perhaps, may change.

Othello. Never, Iago. Like to the Pontic sea,[395]
Whose icy current and compulsive course
Ne'er feels retiring ebb, but keeps due on
To the Propontic and the Hellespont,[396]
Even so my bloody thoughts, with violent pace,
Shall ne'er look back, ne'er ebb to humble love,
Till that a capable[397] and wide revenge
Swallow them up. *(Kneels.)*
Now, by yond marble heaven, 460
In the due reverence of a sacred vow
I here engage my words.

Iago. Do not rise yet. *(Kneels.)*
Witness, you ever-burning lights above!
You elements that clip[398] us round about!
Witness, that here Iago doth give up
The execution of his wit, hands, heart,
To wrong'd Othello's service! Let him command,
And to obey shall be in me remorse,[399]
What bloody business ever.[400] *(They rise.)*

Othello. I greet thy love,
Not with vain thanks, but with acceptance bounteous, 470
And will upon the instant put thee to 't:
Within these three days let me hear thee say
That Cassio 's not alive.

Iago. My friend is dead; 'tis done at your request:
But let her live.

---

[392] Burden. [393] Poisonous snakes. [394] Patient. [395] The Black Sea. [396] The Sea of Marmara, the Dardanelles. [397] Comprehensive. [398] Encompass. [399] Probably a corrupt line; the meaning appears to be: "to obey shall be my solemn obligation." [400] Soever.

Othello. Damn her, lewd minx! O, damn her!
  Come, go with me apart; I will withdraw.
  To furnish me with some swift means of death
  For the fair devil. Now art thou my lieutenant.
Iago. I am your own for ever. *(Exeunt.)*

Scene 4. Before the Castle.

(Enter Desdemona, Emilia, and Clown.)

Desdemona. Do you know, sirrah,[401] where Lieutenant Cassio lies?[402]
Clown. I dare not say he lies any where.
Desdemona. Why, man?
Clown. He is a soldier; and for one to say a soldier lies, is stabbing.[403]
Desdemona. Go to;[404] where lodges he?
Clown. To tell you where he lodges is to tell you where I lie.
Desdemona. Can anything be made of this?
Clown. I know not where he lodges, and for me to devise[405] a lodging, and say he
  lies here or he lies there, were to lie in mine own throat.
Desdemona. Can you inquire him out, and be edified by report? 10
Clown. I will catechize the world for him; that is, make questions, and by them
  answer.
Desdemona. Seek him, bid him come hither; tell him I have moved my lord in
  his behalf, and hope all will be well.
Clown. To do this is within the compass of man's wit, and therefore I will attempt
  the doing it. *(Exit.)*
Desdemona. Where should I lose that handkerchief, Emilia?
Emilia. I know not, madam.
Desdemona. Believe me, I had rather have lost my purse
  Full of cruzadoes;[406] and, but my noble Moor 20
  Is true of mind, and made of no such baseness
  As jealous creatures are, it were enough
  To put him to ill thinking.
Emilia. Is he not jealous?
Desdemona. Who! he? I think the sun where he was born
  Drew all such humours from him.
Emilia. Look! where he comes.
Desdemona. I will not leave him now till Cassio
  Be call'd to him.

(Enter Othello.)

---

[401] Common form of address to inferiors. [402] Lives. [403] I.e., is cause for stabbing. [404] Here
apparently: "Come on!" [405] Invent. [406] Portuguese gold coins.

Desdemona.   How is 't with you, my lord?

Othello. Well, my good lady. *(Aside.)* O! hardness to dissemble.
  How do you, Desdemona?

Desdemona.   Well, my good lord.

Othello. Give me your hand. This hand is moist,[407] my lady.   30

Desdemona. It yet has felt no age nor known no sorrow.

Othello. This argues fruitfulness and liberal[408] heart;
  Hot, hot, and moist; this hand of yours requires
  A sequester[409] from liberty, fasting and prayer,
  Much castigation, exercise devout;
  For here 's a young and sweating devil here,
  That commonly rebels. 'Tis a good hand,
  A frank one.

Desdemona. You may, indeed, say so;
  For 'twas that hand that gave away my heart.   40

Othello. A liberal hand; the hearts of old gave hands,
  But our new heraldry[410] is hands not hearts.

Desdemona. I cannot speak of this. Come now, your promise.

Othello. What promise, chuck?[411]

Desdemona. I have sent to bid Cassio come speak with you.

Othello. I have a salt and sorry rheum offends me.
  Lend me thy handkerchief.

Desdemona.   Here, my lord.

Othello. That which I gave you.

Desdemona.   I have it not about me.

Othello. Not?

Desdemona. No, indeed, my lord.

Othello.   That is a fault.   50
  That handkerchief
  Did an Egyptian[412] to my mother give;
  She was a charmer,[413] and could almost read
  The thoughts of people; she told her, while she kept it,
  'Twould make her amiable[414] and subdue my father
  Entirely to her love, but if she lost it
  Or made a gift of it, my father's eye
  Should hold her loathed, and his spirits should hunt
  After new fancies.[415] She dying gave it me;
  And bid me, when my fate would have me wive,
  To give it her. I did so; and take heed on 't;   60
  Make it a darling like your precious eye;

---

[407] A supposed symptom of a lustful nature.   [408] With overtones of: too free, loose.   [409] Separation.   [410] I.e., new heraldic symbolism (Othello means that the new way is not to give the heart together with the hand).   [411] Common term of endearment.   [412] Gypsy.   [413] Sorceress. [414] Lovable, desirable.   [415] Loves.

To lose 't or give 't away, were such perdition
As nothing else could match.
Desdemona. Is 't possible?
Othello. 'Tis true; there 's magic in the web of it;
A sibyl,[416] that had number'd in the world
The sun to course two hundred compasses,
In her prophetic fury sew'd the work;
The worms were hallow'd that did breed the silk,
And it was dy'd in mummy[417] which the skilful
Conserv'd of maidens' hearts.
Desdemona. Indeed! is 't true?   70
Othello. Most veritable; therefore look to 't well.
Desdemona. Then would to heaven that I had never seen it!
Othello. Ha! wherefore?
Desdemona. Why do you speak so startingly and rash?
Othello. Is 't lost? is 't gone? speak, is it out o' the way?
Desdemona. Heaven bless us!
Othello. Say you?
Desdemona. It is not lost; but what an if[418] it were?
Othello. How!
Desdemona. I say, it is not lost.
Othello. Fetch 't, let me see 't!   80
Desdemona. Why, so I can, sir, but I will not now.
This is a trick to put me from my suit:
Pray you let Cassio be receiv'd again.
Othello. Fetch me the handkerchief; my mind misgives.
Desdemona. Come, come;
You'll never meet a more sufficient[419] man.
Othello. The handkerchief!
Desdemona. I pray, talk[420] me of Cassio.
Othello. The handkerchief!
Desdemona. A man that all his time
Hath founded his good fortunes on your love,
Shar'd dangers with you,—   90
Othello. The handkerchief!
Desdemona. In sooth, you are to blame.
Othello. Away!   (*Exit.*)
Emilia. Is not this man jealous?
Desdemona. I ne'er saw this before.
Sure, there's some wonder in this handkerchief;
I am most unhappy in the loss of it.

---

[416] Prophetess.   [417] Drug (medicinal or magic) derived from embalmed bodies.   [418] If.   [419] Adequate.   [420] Talk to.

Emilia. 'Tis not a year or two shows us a man;
    They are all but stomachs, and we all but[421] food;
    They eat us hungerly, and when they are full   100
    They belch us. Look you! Cassio and my husband.

(Enter Iago and Cassio.)

Iago. There is no other way; 'tis she must do 't:
    And, lo! the happiness;[422] go and importune her.
Desdemona. How now, good Cassio! what 's the news with you?
Cassio. Madam, my former suit: I do beseech you
    That by your virtuous means I may again
    Exist, and be a member of his love
    Whom I with all the office[423] of my heart
    Entirely honour; I would not be delay'd.
    If my offence be of such mortal kind   110
    That nor my service past, nor present sorrows,
    Nor purpos'd merit in futurity,
    Can ransom me into his love again,
    But to know so must be my benefit;
    So shall I clothe me in a forc'd content,
    And shut myself up in some other course
    To fortune's alms.
Desdemona.   Alas! thrice-gentle Cassio!
    My advocation is not now in tune;
    My lord is not my lord, nor should I know him,
    Were he in favour[424] as in humour alter'd.   120
    So help me every spirit sanctified,
    As I have spoken for you all my best
    And stood within the blank of[425] his displeasure
    For my free speech. You must awhile be patient;
    What I can do I will, and more I will
    Than for myself I dare: let that suffice you.
Iago. Is my lord angry?
Emilia.   He went hence but now,
    And certainly in strange unquietness.
Iago. Can he be angry? I have seen the cannon,
    When it hath blown his ranks[426] into the air,   130
    And, like the devil, from his very arm
    Puff'd his own brother; and can he be angry?
    Something of moment[427] then; I will go meet him;
    There's matter in 't indeed, if he be angry.

[421] Only…only.   [422] "What luck!"   [423] Duty.   [424] Appearance.   [425] As the target for.   [426] I.e., his soldiers.   [427] Important.

Desdemona. I prithee, do so. *(Exit Iago.)* Something, sure, of state,[428]
    Either from Venice, or some unhatch'd[429] practice
    Made demonstrable here in Cyprus to him,
    Hath puddled[430] his clear spirit; and, in such cases
    Men's natures wrangle with inferior things,
    Though great ones are their object. 'Tis even so;   140
    For let our finger ache, and it indues[431]
    Our other healthful members even to that sense
    Of pain. Nay, we must think men are not gods,
    Nor of them look for such observancy[432]
    As fits the bridal.[433] Beshrew me much, Emilia,
    I was—unhandsome warrior as I am—
    Arraigning his unkindness with[434] my soul;
    But now I find I had suborn'd the witness,[435]
    And he 's indicted falsely.

Emilia. Pray heaven it be state matters, as you think,
    And no conception,[436] nor no jealous toy[437]   150
    Concerning you.

Desdemona. Alas the day! I never gave him cause.

Emilia. But jealous souls will not be answer'd so;
    They are not ever jealous for the cause,
    But jealous for they are jealous; 'tis a monster
    Begot upon itself, born on itself.

Desdemona. Heaven keep that monster from Othello's mind!

Emilia. Lady, amen.

Desdemona. I will go seek him. Cassio, walk hereabout;   160
    If I do find him fit, I'll move your suit
    And seek to effect it to my uttermost.

Cassio. I humbly thank your ladyship.

(Exeunt Desdemona and Emilia.)

(Enter Bianca.)

Bianca. Save you, friend Cassio!

Cassio.   What make you from home?
    How is it with you, my most fair Bianca?
    I' faith, sweet love, I was coming to your house.

---

[428] Public affairs.   [429] Abortive or budding plot.   [430] Muddied.   [431] Brings, leads.   [432] Attention. [433] Wedding.   [434] To.   [435] I.e., caused my soul to bring in wrong charges.   [436] Fancy, supposition. [437] Fancy.

Bianca. And I was going to your lodging, Cassio.
  What! keep a week away? seven days and nights?
  Eight score eight hours? and lovers' absent hours,
  More tedious than the dial eight score times?   170
  O weary reckoning!
Cassio.   Pardon me, Bianca,
  I have this while with leaden thoughts been press'd;
  But I shall, in a more continuate[438] time,
  Strike off[439] this score of absence. Sweet Bianca,

(Giving her Desdemona's handkerchief.)

  Take me this work out.
Bianca.   O Cassio! whence came this?
  This is some token from a newer friend;
  To the felt absence now I feel a cause;
  Is 't come to this? Well, well.
Cassio.   Go to, woman!
  Throw your vile guesses in the devil's teeth,
  From whence you have them. You are jealous now   180
  That this is from some mistress, some remembrance:
  No, in good troth, Bianca.
Bianca.   Why, whose is it?
Cassio. I know not, sweet; I found it in my chamber.
  I like the work well; ere it be demanded,—[440]
  As like enough it will,—I'd have it copied;
  Take it and do 't; and leave me for this time.
Bianca. Leave you! wherefore?
Cassio. I do attend here on[441] the general,
  And think it no addition,[442] nor my wish,
  To have him see me woman'd.
Bianca.   Why, I pray you?   190
Cassio. Not that I love you not.
Bianca.   But that you do not love me.
  I pray you, bring me on the way a little
  And say if I shall see you soon at night.
Cassio. 'Tis but a little way that I can bring you,
  For I attend here; but I'll see you soon.
Bianca. 'Tis very good; I must be circumstanc'd.[443]   *(Exeunt.)*

---

[438] Uninterrupted.   [439] Cancel (i.e., make up for).   [440] Asked for.   [441] Wait for.   [442] Advantage, credit.   [443] Governed by circumstances.

ACT IV

Scene 1.   Cyprus. Before the Castle.

(Enter Othello and Iago.)

Iago. Will you think so?
Othello.   Think so, Iago!
Iago.   What!
  To kiss in private?
Othello.   An unauthoriz'd kiss.
Iago. Or to be naked with her friend a-bed
  An hour or more, not meaning any harm?
Othello. Naked a-bed, Iago, and not mean harm?
  It is hypocrisy against the devil:[444]
  They that mean virtuously, and yet do so,
  The devil their virtue tempts, and they tempt heaven.
Iago. If they do nothing, 'tis a venial slip;
  But if I give my wife a handkerchief,—   10
Othello. What then?
Iago. Why, then, 'tis hers, my lord; and, being hers,
  She may, I think, bestow 't on any man.
Othello. She is protectress of her honour too;
  May she give that?
Iago. Her honour is an essence that 's not seen;
  They have it very oft that have it not:[445]
  But for the handkerchief,—
Othello. By heaven, I would most gladly have forgot it:—
  Thou said'st,—O! it comes o'er my memory,   20
  As doth the raven[446] o'er the infected house,
  Boding to all,—he had my handkerchief.
Iago. Ay, what of that?
Othello.   That's not so good now.
Iago.   What,
  If I had said I had seen him do you wrong?
  Or heard him say, as knaves be such abroad,[447]
  Who having, by their own importunate suit,
  Or voluntary dotage[448] of some mistress,
  Convinced or supplied them,[449] cannot choose
  But they must blab.

---

[444] I.e., by not committing the sin which the situation invites.   [445] I.e., some unchaste women are thought chaste.   [446] (1) A bad omen, (2) A carrier of the plague.   [447] As there are some such in the world.   [448] Foolish affection.   [449] Overcome (their reluctance) or satisfied (their desires).

Othello.   Hath he said any thing?

Iago. He hath, my lord; but be you well assur'd,   30
No more than he'll unswear.

Othello.   What hath he said?

Iago. Faith, that he did— I know not what he did.

Othello. What? what?

Iago. Lie—

Othello. With her?

Iago.   With her, on her; what you will.

Othello. Lie with her; lie on her! We say, lie on her, when they belie her. Lie with
her! that's fulsome. Handkerchief,—confessions,—handkerchief! To confess,
and be hanged for his labour. First, to be hanged, and then to confess: I tremble
at it. Nature would not invest herself in such shadowing passion without some
instruction.[450] It is not words that shake me thus. Pish! Noses, ears, and lips. Is it
possible?—Confess!—Handkerchief!—O devil!

(Falls in a trance.)

Iago. Work on,
My medicine, work! Thus credulous fools are caught;
And many worthy and chaste dames even thus,
All guiltless, meet reproach. What, ho! my lord!
My lord, I say! Othello!

(Enter Cassio.)

                    How now, Cassio!

Cassio. What's the matter?

Iago. My lord is fallen into an epilepsy;[451]
This is his second fit; he had one yesterday.

Cassio. Rub him about the temples.

Iago.   No, forbear;   50
The lethargy[452] must have his quiet course,
If not, he foams at mouth, and by and by
Breaks out to savage madness. Look! he stirs;
Do you withdraw yourself a little while,
He will recover straight; when he is gone,
I would on great occasion[453] speak with you.   *(Exit Cassio.)*
How is it, general? have you not hurt your head?

Othello. Dost thou mock me?[454]

Iago.   I mock you! no, by heaven.
Would you would bear your fortune like a man!

---

[450] I would not fall into such passion unless there were some real grounds for it.   [451] Seizure, fit.
[452] Coma.   [453] Important matter.   [454] Another allusion to the cuckold's horns.

Othello. A horned man's a monster and a beast. 60

Iago. There's many a beast then, in a populous city,
    And many a civil[455] monster.

Othello. Did he confess it?

Iago.   Good sir, be a man;
    Think every bearded fellow that's but yok'd
    May draw[456] with you; there's millions now alive
    That nightly lie in those unproper[457] beds
    Which they dare swear peculiar;[458] your case is better.
    O! 'tis the spite of hell, the fiend's arch-mock,
    To lip[459] a wanton in a secure[460] couch,
    And to suppose her chaste. No, let me know; 70
    And knowing what I am, I know what she shall be.

Othello. O! thou art wise; 'tis certain.

Iago.   Stand you awhile apart;
    Confine yourself but in a patient list.[461]
    Whilst you were here o'erwhelmed with your grief,—
    A passion most unsuiting such a man,—
    Cassio came hither; I shifted him away,
    And laid good 'scuse upon your ecstasy;[462]
    Bade him anon return and here speak with me;
    The which he promis'd. Do but encave yourself,
    And mark the fleers, the gibes, and notable scorns, 80
    That dwell in every region of his face;
    For I will make him tell the tale anew,
    Where, how, how oft, how long ago, and when
    He hath, and is again to cope[463] your wife:
    I say, but mark his gesture. Marry, patience;
    Or I shall say you are all in all in spleen,[464]
    And nothing of a man.

Othello.   Dost thou hear, Iago?
    I will be found most cunning in my patience;
    But—dost thou hear?—most bloody.

Iago.   That's not amiss:
    But yet keep time[465] in all. Will you withdraw?   *(Othello goes apart.)*
    Now will I question Cassio of Bianca,
    A housewife[466] that by selling her desires
    Buys herself bread and clothes; it is a creature
    That dotes on Cassio; as 'tis the strumpet's plague
    To beguile many and be beguil'd by one.

---

[455] Citizen.   [456] I.e., pull the burden of cuckoldom.   [457] Not exclusively their own.   [458] Exclusively their own.   [459] Kiss.   [460] I.e., without suspicion of having a rival.   [461] Bounds of patience.   [462] Derangement, trance.   [463] Close with.   [464] Completely overcome by passion.   [465] Maintain control.   [466] Hussy.

He, when he hears of her, cannot refrain
From the excess of laughter. Here he comes:

(Re-enter Cassio.)

As he shall smile, Othello shall go mad;
And his unbookish[467] jealousy must construe
Poor Cassio's smiles, gestures, and light behaviour   100
Quite in the wrong. How do you now, lieutenant?

Cassio. The worser that you give me the addition[468]
Whose want[469] even kills me.

Iago. Ply Desdemona well, and you are sure on 't.
(Speaking lower.) Now, if this suit lay in Bianca's power,
How quickly should you speed!

Cassio.   Alas! poor caitiff![470]

Othello. Look! how he laughs already!

Iago. I never knew woman love man so.

Cassio. Alas! poor rogue, I think i' faith, she loves me.

Othello. Now he denies it faintly, and laughs it out.   110

Iago. Do you hear, Cassio?

Othello.   Now he importunes him
To tell it o'er; go to; well said, well said.

Iago. She gives it out that you shall marry her;
Do you intend it?

Cassio. Ha, ha, ha!

Othello. Do you triumph, Roman?[471] do you triumph?

Cassio. I marry her! what? a customer?[472] I prithee, bear some charity to my
wit;[473] do not think it so unwholesome. Ha, ha, ha!

Othello. So, so, so, so. They laugh that win.[474]

Iago. Faith, the cry goes that you shall marry her.   120

Cassio. Prithee, say true.

Iago. I am a very villain else.

Othello. Have you scored me?[475] Well.

Cassio. This is the monkey's own giving out: she is persuaded I will marry her,
out of her own love and flattery, not out of my promise.

Othello. Iago beckons me;[476] now he begins the story.

Cassio. She was here even now; she haunts me in every place. I was the other
day talking on the sea-bank with certain Venetians, and thither comes this bau-
ble,[477] and, by this hand, she falls me thus about my neck;—

Othello. Crying, 'O dear Cassio!' as it were; his gesture imports it.   130

---

[467] Unpracticed, naive.   [468] Title.   [469] The want of which.   [470] Wretch.   [471] I.e., one who
triumphs (?).   [472] Courtesan, prostitute.   [473] Give me credit for some sense.   [474] "He who laughs
last laughs longest" (?).   [475] Wounded, defaced (?); or: settled my account (?).   [476] Signals.
[477] Plaything.

Cassio. So hangs and lolls and weeps upon me; so hales[478] and pulls me; ha, ha, ha!

Othello. Now he tells how she plucked him to my chamber. O! I see that nose of yours, but not the dog I shall throw it to.

Cassio. Well, I must leave her company.

Iago. Before me![479] look, where she comes.

Cassio. 'Tis such another fitchew![480] marry, a perfumed one.

(Enter Bianca.)

What do you mean by this haunting of me?

Bianca. Let the devil and his dam haunt you! What did you mean by that same handkerchief you gave me even now? I was a fine fool to take it. I must take out the work! A likely piece of work, that you should find it in your chamber, and not know who left it there! This is some minx's token, and I must take out the work! There, give it your hobby-horse;[481] wheresoever you had it I'll take out no work on 't.

Cassio. How now, my sweet Bianca! how now, how now!

Othello. By heaven, that should be[482] my handkerchief!

Bianca. An you'll come to supper to-night, you may; an you will not, come when you are next prepared[483] for. *(Exit.)*

Iago. After her, after her.

Cassio. Faith, I must; she'll rail in the street else. 150

Iago. Will you sup there?

Cassio. Faith, I intend so.

Iago. Well, I may chance to see you, for I would very fain[484] speak with you.

Cassio. Prithee come; will you?

Iago. Go to; say no more. *(Exit Cassio.)*

Othello *(advancing).* How shall I murder him, Iago?

Iago. Did you perceive how he laughed at his vice?

Othello. O! Iago!

Iago. And did you see the handkerchief?

Othello. Was that mine? 160

Iago. Yours, by this hand; and to see how he prizes the foolish woman your wife! she gave it him, and he hath given it his whore.

Othello. I would have him nine years a-killing. A fine woman! a fair woman! a sweet woman!

Iago. Nay, you must forget that.

Othello. Ay, let her rot, and perish, and be damned to-night; for she shall not live. No, my heart is turned to stone; I strike it, and it hurts my hand. O! the world

---

[478] Hauls.   [479] An exclamation of surprise.   [480] Polecat, noted both for its strong smell and for its lechery.   [481] Harlot.   [482] I.e., I think that is.   [483] Expected (Bianca means that if he does not come that night, she will never want to see him again).   [484] Gladly.

hath not a sweeter creature; she might lie by an emperor's side and command him tasks.

Iago. Nay, that's not your way.[485]   170

Othello. Hang her! I do but say what she is. So delicate with her needle! An admirable musician! O, she will sing the savageness out of a bear. Of so high and plenteous wit and invention!

Iago. She's the worse for all this.

Othello. O! a thousand, a thousand times. And then, of so gentle a condition![486]

Iago. Ay, too gentle.[487]

Othello. Nay, that's certain;—but yet the pity of it, Iago!
O! Iago, the pity of it, Iago!

Iago. If you are so fond over her iniquity, give her patent to offend; for, if it touch not you, it comes near nobody.

Othello. I will chop her into messes.[488] Cuckold me!

Iago. O! 'tis foul in her.

Othello. With mine officer!

Iago. That's fouler.

Othello. Get me some poison, Iago; this night: I'll not expostulate with her, lest her body and beauty unprovide my mind again.[489] This night, Iago.

Iago. Do it not with poison, strangle her in her bed, even the bed she hath contaminated.

Othello. Good, good; the justice of it pleases; very good.   170

Iago. And for Cassio, let me be his undertaker;[490] you shall hear more by midnight.

Othello. Excellent good. *(A trumpet within.)* What trumpet is that same?

Iago. Something from Venice, sure. 'Tis Lodovico,
Come from the duke; and see, your wife is with him.

(Enter Lodovico, Desdemona, and Attendants.)

Lodovico. God save you, worthy general!

Othello.   With all my heart, sir.

Lodovico. The duke and senators of Venice greet you.

(Gives him a packet.)

Othello. I kiss the instrument of their pleasures.

(Opens the packet, and reads.)

---

[485] Proper course.   [486] So much the high-born lady.   [487] I.e., yielding.   [488] Bits.   [489] Unsettle my intention.   [490] Dispatcher.

Desdemona. And what's the news, good cousin Lodovico?

Iago. I am very glad to see you, signior; 200
Welcome to Cyprus.

Lodovico. I thank you. How does Lieutenant Cassio?

Iago. Lives, sir.

Desdemona. Cousin, there's fall'n between him and my lord
An unkind⁴⁹¹ breach; but you shall make all well.

Othello. Are you sure of that?

Desdemona. My lord?

Othello (reads). 'This fail you not to do, as you will'—

Lodovico. He did not call; he's busy in the paper.
Is there division⁴⁹² twixt my lord and Cassio? 210

Desdemona. A most unhappy one; I would do much
To atone⁴⁹³ them, for the love I bear to Cassio.

Othello. Fire and brimstone!

Desdemona. My lord?

Othello. Are you wise?

Desdemona. What! is he angry?

Lodovico. May be the letter mov'd him;
For, as I think, they do command him home,
Deputing Cassio in his government.

Desdemona. Trust me, I am glad on 't.

Othello. Indeed!

Desdemona. My lord?

Othello. I am glad to see you mad.

Desdemona. Why, sweet Othello?

Othello. Devil! (Strikes her.)

Desdemona. I have not deserved this. 220

Lodovico. My lord, this would not be believ'd in Venice,
Though I should swear I saw 't; 'tis very much;
Make her amends, she weeps.

Othello. O devil, devil!
If that the earth could teem with woman's tears,
Each drop she falls⁴⁹⁴ would prove a crocodile.⁴⁹⁵
Out of my sight!

Desdemona. I will not stay to offend you. (Going.)

Lodovico. Truly, an obedient lady;
I do beseech your lordship, call her back.

Othello. Mistress!

Desdemona. My lord?

Othello. What would you with her, sir? 230

Lodovico. Why, I, my lord?

---

⁴⁹¹ Unnatural. ⁴⁹² Estrangement. ⁴⁹³ Reconcile. ⁴⁹⁴ Lets fall. ⁴⁹⁵ The crocodile's tears were
supposed to be hypocritical.

Othello. Ay; you did wish that I would make her turn:
  Sir, she can turn, and turn, and yet go on,
  And turn again; and she can weep, sir, weep;
  And she's obedient, as you say, obedient,
  Very obedient. Proceed you in your tears.
  Concerning this, sir—O well-painted passion!—
  I am commanded home. Get you away;
  I'll send for you anon. Sir, I obey the mandate,
  And will return to Venice. Hence! avaunt!⁴⁹⁶   *(Exit Desdemona.)*
  Cassio shall have my place. And, sir, to-night,
  I do entreat that we may sup together;
  You are welcome, sir, to Cyprus. Goats and monkeys!   *(Exit.)*
Lodovico. Is this the noble Moor whom our full senate
  Call all-in-all sufficient? is this the noble nature
  Whom passion could not shake? whose solid virtue
  The shot of accident nor dart of chance
  Could neither graze nor pierce?
Iago.   He is much chang'd.
Lodovico. Are his wits safe? is he not light of brain?
Iago. He's that he is; I may not breathe my censure.   250
  What he might be, if, what he might, he is not,
  I would to heaven he were!⁴⁹⁷
Lodovico.   What! strike his wife!
Iago. Faith, that was not so well; yet would I knew
  That stroke would prove the worst!
Lodovico.   Is it his use?
  Or did the letters work upon his blood,
  And new-create this fault?
Iago.   Alas, alas!
  It is not honesty in me to speak
  What I have seen and known. You shall observe him,
  And his own courses⁴⁹⁸ will denote him so
  That I may save my speech. Do but go after   260
  And mark how he continues.
Lodovico. I am sorry that I am deceiv'd in him.   *(Exeunt.)*

Scene 2.   A Room in the Castle.

(Enter Othello and Emilia.)

Othello. You have seen nothing, then?
Emilia. Nor ever heard, nor ever did suspect.

---

⁴⁹⁶ Begone!   ⁴⁹⁷ Another of Iago's gnomic speeches; perhaps approximately: "If now he is not himself, I wish he would be what he could be!"   ⁴⁹⁸ Actions.

Othello. Yes, you have seen Cassio and her together.

Emilia. But then I saw no harm, and then I heard
    Each syllable that breath made up between them.

Othello. What! did they never whisper?

Emilia.   Never, my lord.

Othello. Nor send you out o' the way?

Emilia. Never.

Othello. To fetch her fan, her gloves, her mask, nor nothing?[499]

Emilia. Never, my lord.   10

Othello. That's strange.

Emilia. I durst, my lord, to wager she is honest,
    Lay down my soul at stake: if you think other,
    Remove your thought; it doth abuse your bosom.
    If any wretch have put this in your head,
    Let heaven requite it with the serpent's curse!
    For, if she be not honest, chaste, and true,
    There's no man happy; the purest of their wives
    Is foul as slander.

Othello.   Bid her come hither; go.   *(Exit Emilia.)*
    She says enough; yet she 's a simple[500] bawd   20
    That cannot say as much. This is a subtle whore,
    A closet lock and key of villainous secrets;
    And yet she 'll kneel and pray; I have seen her do 't.

(Re-enter Emilia with Desdemona.)

Desdemona. My lord, what is your will?

Othello.   Pray, chuck, come hither.

Desdemona. What is your pleasure?

Othello.   Let me see your eyes;
    Look in my face.

Desdemona.   What horrible fancy 's this?

Othello *(to Emilia).* Some of your function,[501] mistress;
    Leave procreants alone and shut the door;
    Cough or cry 'hem' if any body come;
    Your mystery,[502] your mystery; nay, dispatch.   *(Exit Emilia.)*

Desdemona. Upon my knees, what doth your speech import?
    I understand a fury in your words.
    But not the words.

Othello. Why, what art thou?

Desdemona.   Your wife, my lord; your true
    And loyal wife.

---

[499] Anything.   [500] Simpleminded.   [501] To your duty, business.   [502] Trade.

Othello.　　　　Come, swear it, damn thyself;
　Lest, being like one of heaven, the devils themselves
　Should fear to seize thee; therefore be double-damn'd;
　Swear thou art honest.
Desdemona.　　　　Heaven doth truly know it.
Othello. Heaven truly knows that thou art false as hell.
Desdemona. To whom, my lord? with whom? how am I false?　　40
Othello. Ah! Desdemona; away, away, away!
Desdemona. Alas, the heavy day!—Why do you weep?
　Am I the motive of these tears, my lord?
　If haply you my father do suspect
　An instrument of this your calling back,
　Lay not your blame on me; if you have lost him,
　Why, I have lost him too.
Othello.　　　　Had it pleas'd heaven
　To try me with affliction, had he rain'd
　All kinds of sores and shames on my bare head,
　Steep'd me in poverty to the very lips,　　　　　　　　50
　Given to captivity me and my utmost hopes,
　I should have found in some part of my soul
　A drop of patience; but, alas! to make me
　The fixed figure for the time of scorn[503]
　To point his slow and moving finger at;
　Yet could I bear that too; well, very well:
　But there, where I have garner'd[504] up my heart,
　Where either I must live or bear no life,
　The fountain from the which my current runs
　Or else dries up; to be discarded thence!　　　　　　60
　Or keep it as a cistern for foul toads
　To knot and gender in![505] Turn thy complexion there,[506]
　Patience, thou young and rose-lipp'd cherubin;
　Ay, there, look grim as hell!
Desdemona. I hope my noble lord esteems me honest.
Othello. O! ay; as summer flies are in the shambles,[507]
　That quicken even with blowing. O thou weed!
　Who art so lovely fair and smell'st so sweet
　That the sense aches at thee, would thou hadst ne'er been born.
Desdemona. Alas! what ignorant sin have I committed?　　70
Othello. Was this fair paper, this most goodly book,
　Made to write 'whore' upon? What committed!
　Committed! O thou public commoner![508]
　I should make very forges of my cheeks,

---

[503] I.e., the scornful world.　[504] Stored.　[505] Bunch up and procreate.　[506] I.e., change your color to suit the "cistern for foul toads."　[507] Slaughterhouse.　[508] Harlot.

That would to cinders burn up modesty,
Did I but speak thy deeds. What committed!
Heaven stops the nose at it and the moon winks,[509]
The bawdy wind that kisses all it meets
Is hush'd within the hollow mine of earth,
And will not hear it. What committed!
Impudent strumpet!   80

Desdemona.   By heaven, you do me wrong.

Othello. Are not you a strumpet?

Desdemona.   No, as I am a Christian.
If to preserve this vessel for my lord
From any other foul unlawful touch
Be not to be a strumpet, I am none.

Othello. What! not a whore?

Desdemona.   No, as I shall be sav'd.

Othello. Is it possible?

Desdemona. O! heaven forgive us.

Othello.   I cry you mercy,[510] then;
I took you for that cunning whore of Venice
That married with Othello. You, mistress,   90
That have the office opposite to Saint Peter,
And keep the gate of hell!

(Re-enter Emilia.)

                     You, you, ay, you!
We have done our course; there's money for your pains.
I pray you, turn the key and keep our counsel.   *(Exit.)*

Emilia. Alas! what does this gentleman conceive?[511]
How do you, madam? how do you, my good lady?

Desdemona. Faith, half asleep.

Emilia. Good madam, what 's the matter with my lord?

Desdemona. With who?

Emilia. Why, with my lord, madam.   100

Desdemona. Who is thy lord?

Emilia.   He that is yours, sweet lady.

Desdemona. I have none; do not talk to me, Emilia;
I cannot weep, nor answer have I none,
But what should go by water.[512] Prithee, to-night
Lay on my bed my wedding sheets: remember:
And call thy husband hither.

Emilia.   Here is a change indeed!   *(Exit.)*

---

[509] Closes her eyes.   [510] Beg your pardon.   [511] Imagine.   [512] Be conveyed by means of tears.

Desdemona. 'Tis meet I should be us'd so, very meet.
How have I been behav'd, that he might stick
The small'st opinion on my least misuse?[513]

(Re-enter Emilia, with Iago.)

Iago. What is your pleasure, madam? How is it with you? 110
Desdemona. I cannot tell. Those that do teach young babes
Do it with gentle means and easy tasks;
He might have chid me so; for, in good faith,
I am a child to chiding.
Iago. What 's the matter, lady?
Emilia. Alas, Iago, my lord hath so bewhor'd her,
Thrown such despite[514] and heavy terms upon her,
As true hearts cannot bear.
Desdemona. Am I that name, Iago?
Iago. What name, fair lady?
Desdemona. Such as she says my lord did say I was.
Emilia. He call'd her whore; a beggar in his drink 120
Could not have laid such terms upon his callat.[515]
Iago. Why did he so?
Desdemona. I do not know; I am sure I am none such.
Iago. Do not weep, do not weep. Alas the day!
Emilia. Has she forsook so many noble matches,
Her father and her country and her friends,
To be call'd whore? would it not make one weep?
Desdemona. It is my wretched fortune.
Iago. Beshrew[516] him for it!
How comes this trick upon him?
Desdemona. Nay, heaven doth know.
Emilia. I will be hang'd, if some eternal villain, 130
Some busy and insinuating rogue,
Some cogging[517] cozening slave, to get some office,
Have not devis'd this slander; I'll be hang'd else.
Iago. Fie! there is no such man; it is impossible.
Desdemona. If any such there be, heaven pardon him!
Emilia. A halter pardon him, and hell gnaw his bones!
Why should he call her whore? who keeps her company?
What place? what time? what form? what likelihood?
The Moor 's abus'd by some most villainous knave,
Some base notorious knave, some scurvy fellow. 140
O heaven! that such companions[518] thou'dst unfold,

---

[513] The least suspicion on my slightest misconduct. [514] Abuse. [515] Slut. [516] Curse. [517] Cheating.
[518] Fellows (derogatory).

And put in every honest hand a whip
To lash the rascals naked through the world,
Even from the east to west!

Iago. Speak within door.

Emilia. O! fie upon them. Some such squire he was
That turn'd your wit the seamy side without,[519]
And made you to suspect me with the Moor.

Iago. You are a fool; go to.

Desdemona. O good Iago,
What shall I do to win my lord again?
Good friend, go to him; for, by this light of heaven,   150
I know not how I lost him. Here I kneel:
If e'er my will did trespass 'gainst his love,
Either in discourse of thought or actual deed,
Or that mine eyes, mine ears, or any sense,
Delighted them[520] in any other form;
Or that I do not yet,[521] and ever did,
And ever will, though he do shake me off
To beggarly divorcement, love him dearly,
Comfort forswear me! Unkindness may do much;
And his unkindness may defeat[522] my life,   160
But never taint my love. I cannot say 'whore':
It does abhor me now I speak the word;
To do the act that might the addition earn
Not the world's mass of vanity could make me.

Iago. I pray you be content, 'tis but his humour;
The business of the state does him offence,
And he does chide with you.

Desdemona. If 'twere no other,—

Iago. 'Tis but so, I warrant.   *(Trumpets.)*
Hark! how these instruments summon to supper;
The messengers of Venice stay the meat: 170
Go in, and weep not; all things shall be well.

               (Exeunt Desdemona and Emilia.)

(Enter Roderigo.)

How now, Roderigo!

Roderigo. I do not find that thou dealest justly with me.

Iago. What in the contrary?[523]

Roderigo. Every day thou daffest me[524] with some device, Iago; and rather, as
it seems to me now, keepest from me all conveniency,[525] than suppliest me

---

[519] Outward.   [520] Found delight.   [521] Still.   [522] Destroy.   [523] I.e., what reason do you have
for saying that?   [524] You put me off.   [525] Favorable circumstances.

with the least advantage of hope. I will indeed no longer endure it, nor am I yet persuaded to put up[526] in peace what already I have foolishly suffered.

Iago. Will you hear me, Roderigo?

Roderigo. Faith, I have heard too much, for your words and performances are no kin together.

Iago. You charge me most unjustly.

Roderigo. With nought but truth. I have wasted myself out of my means. The jewels you have had from me to deliver to Desdemona would half have corrupted a votarist;[527] you have told me she has received them, and returned me expectations and comforts of sudden respect[528] and acquaintance, but I find none.

Iago. Well; go to; very well.

Roderigo. Very well! go to! I cannot go to, man; nor 'tis not very well: by this hand, I say, it is very scurvy, and begin to find myself fobbed[529] in it.   190

Iago. Very well.

Roderigo. I tell you 'tis not very well. I will make myself known to Desdemona; if she will return me my jewels, I will give over my suit and repent my unlawful solicitation; if not, assure yourself I will seek satisfaction of you.

Iago. You have said now.[530]

Roderigo. Ay, and said nothing, but what I protest intendment of doing.

Iago. Why, now I see there's mettle in thee, and even from this instant do build on thee a better opinion than ever before. Give me thy hand, Roderigo; thou hast taken against me a most just exception; but yet, I protest, I have dealt most directly in thy affair.   200

Roderigo. It hath not appeared.

Iago. I grant indeed it hath not appeared, and your suspicion is not without wit and judgment. But, Roderigo, if thou hast that in thee indeed, which I have greater reason to believe now than ever, I mean purpose, courage, and valour, this night show it: if thou the next night following enjoy not Desdemona, take me from this world with treachery and devise engines for[531] my life.

Roderigo. Well, what is it? is it within reason and compass?

Iago. Sir, there is especial commission come from Venice to depute Cassio in Othello's place.   210

Roderigo. Is that true? why, then Othello and Desdemona return again to Venice.

Iago. O, no! he goes into Mauritania, and takes away with him the fair Desdemona, unless his abode be lingered here by some accident; wherein none can be so determinate[532] as the removing of Cassio.

Roderigo. How do you mean, removing of him?

Iago. Why, by making him uncapable of Othello's place; knocking out his brains.

---

[526] Put up with.   [527] Nun.   [528] Immediate consideration.   [529] Cheated.   [530] I.e., "I suppose you're through?" (?); or: "Now you're talking" (?).   [531] Devices against.   [532] Effective.

Roderigo. And that you would have me do?

Iago. Ay; if you dare do yourself a profit and a right. He sups to-night with a harlotry,[533] and thither will I go to him; he knows not yet of his honourable fortune. If you will watch his going thence,—which I will fashion to fall out between twelve and one,—you may take him at your pleasure; I will be near to second your attempt, and he shall fall between us. Come, stand not amazed at it, but go along with me; I will show you such a necessity in his death that you shall think yourself bound to put it on him. It is now high supper-time, and the night grows to waste; about it.

Roderigo. I will hear further reason for this.

Iago. And you shall be satisfied. *(Exeunt.)*

Scene 3. Another Room in the Castle.

(Enter Othello, Lodovico, Desdemona, Emilia, and Attendants.)

Lodovico. I do beseech you, sir, trouble yourself no further.

Othello. O! pardon me; 'twill do me good to walk.

Lodovico. Madam, good-night; I humbly thank your ladyship.

Desdemona. Your honour is most welcome.

Othello.   Will you walk, sir?
    O! Desdemona,—

Desdemona. My lord?

Othello. Get you to bed on the instant; I will be returned forthwith; dismiss your
    attendant there; look it be done.

Desdemona. I will, my lord.   *(Exeunt Othello, Lodovico, and Attendants.)*

Emilia. How goes it now? He looks gentler than he did.   10

Desdemona. He says he will return incontinent;[534]
    He hath commanded me to go to bed,
    And bade me to dismiss you.

Emilia.   Dismiss me!

Desdemona. It was his bidding; therefore, good Emilia,
    Give me my nightly wearing, and adieu:
    We must not now displease him.

Emilia. I would you had never seen him.

Desdemona. So would not I; my love doth so approve him,
    That even his stubbornness,[535] his checks[536] and frowns,—
    Prithee, unpin me,—have grace and favour in them.   20

Emilia. I have laid those sheets you bade me on the bed.

Desdemona. All's one.[537] Good faith! how foolish are our minds!
    If I do die before thee, prithee, shroud me
    In one of those same sheets.

---

[533] Harlot.   [534] At once.   [535] Roughness.   [536] Rebukes.   [537] I.e., it doesn't matter.

Emilia.   Come, come, you talk.
Desdemona. My mother had a maid call'd Barbara;
    She was in love, and he she lov'd prov'd mad[538]
    And did forsake her; she had a song of 'willow';
    An old thing 'twas, but it express'd her fortune,
    And she died singing it; that song to-night
    Will not go from my mind; I have much to do   30
    But to go hang my head all at one side,
    And sing it like poor Barbara. Prithee, dispatch.
Emilia. Shall I go fetch your night-gown?
Desdemona.   No, unpin me here.
    This Lodovico is a proper man.
Emilia. A very handsome man.
Desdemona. He speaks well.
Emilia. I know a lady in Venice would have walked barefoot to Palestine for a
    touch of his nether lip.
Desdemona *(sings).*
    The poor soul sat sighing by a sycamore tree,
        Sing all a green willow;
    Her hand on her bosom, her head on her knee,   40
        Sing willow, willow, willow:
    The fresh streams ran by her, and murmur'd her moans;
        Sing willow, willow, willow:
    Her salt tears fell from her and soften'd the stones;—

    Lay by these:—
        Sing willow, willow, willow:

    Prithee, hie thee;[539] he 'll come anon.—

        Sing all a green willow must be my garland.
            Let nobody blame him, his scorn I approve,—   50
    Nay, that's not next. Hark! who is it that knocks?
Emilia. It is the wind.
Desdemona.
    I call'd my love false love; but what said he then?
        Sing willow, willow, willow:
    If I court moe[540] women, you 'll couch with moe men.

    So, get thee gone; good-night. Mine eyes do itch;
    Doth that bode weeping?
Emilia.   'Tis neither here nor there.
Desdemona. I have heard it said so. O! these men, these men!

---

[538] Wild.   [539] Hurry.   [540] More.

Dost thou in conscience think, tell me, Emilia,
That there be women do abuse their husbands 60
In such gross kind?
Emilia.   There be some such, no question.
Desdemona. Wouldst thou do such a deed for all the world?
Emilia. Why, would not you?
Desdemona.   No, by this heavenly light!
Emilia. Nor I neither by this heavenly light;
    I might do 't as well i' the dark.
Desdemona. Wouldst thou do such a deed for all the world?
Emilia. The world is a huge thing; 'tis a great price
    For a small vice.
Desdemona.   In troth, I think thou wouldst not.
Emilia. In troth, I think I should, and undo 't when I had done. Marry, I would
    not do such a thing for a joint-ring,[541] nor measures of lawn,[542] nor for gowns,
    petticoats, nor caps, nor any petty exhibition;[543] but for the whole world, who
    would not make her husband a cuckold to make him a monarch? I should
    venture purgatory for 't.
Desdemona. Beshrew me, if I would do such a wrong
    For the whole world.
Emilia. Why, the wrong is but a wrong i' the world; and having the world for
    your labour, 'tis a wrong in your own world, and you might quickly make it
    right.
Desdemona. I do not think there is any such woman.
Emilia. Yes, a dozen; and as many to the vantage,[544] as 80
    Would store[545] the world they played for.
    But I do think it is their husbands' faults
    If wives do fall. Say that they slack their duties,
    And pour our treasures into foreign laps,
    Or else break out in peevish jealousies,
    Throwing restraint upon us; or say they strike us,
    Or scant[546] our former having[547] in despite;
    Why, we have galls;[548] and though we have some grace,
    Yet have we some revenge. Let husbands know
    Their wives have sense like them; they see and smell,
    And have their palates both for sweet and sour, 90
    As husbands have. What is it that they do
    When they change us for others? Is it sport?[549]
    I think it is; and doth affection breed it?
    I think it doth; is 't frailty that thus errs?
    It is so too; and have not we affections,
    Desires for sport, and frailty, as men have?

---

[541] Ring made in separable halves.   [542] Fine linen.   [543] Offer, gift.   [544] Over and above.
[545] Populate.   [546] Reduce.   [547] Allowance.   [548] Spirits, temper.   [549] Lust, sexual enjoyment.

Then, let them use us well; else let them know,
The ills we do, their ills instruct us so.

Desdemona. Good-night, good night; heaven me such usage[550] send,   100
Not to pick bad from bad, but by bad mend!   (*Exeunt.*)

ACT V

Scene 1.   Cyprus. A Street.

(*Enter Iago and Roderigo.*)

Iago. Here, stand behind this bulk,[551] straight will he come:
Wear thy good rapier bare, and put it home.
Quick, quick; fear nothing; I 'll be at thy elbow.
It makes us, or it mars us; think on that,
And fix most firm thy resolution.
Roderigo. Be near at hand; I may miscarry in 't.
Iago. Here, at thy hand: be bold, and take thy stand.   (*Retires.*)
Roderigo. I have no great devotion to the deed;
And yet he has given me satisfying reasons:
'Tis but a man gone: forth, my sword; he dies.   10
Iago. I have rubb'd this young quat[552] almost to the sense,[553]
And he grows angry. Now, whether he kill Cassio,
Or Cassio him, or each do kill the other,
Every way makes my gain: live Roderigo,
He calls me to a restitution large
Of gold and jewels that I bobb'd[554] from him,
As gifts to Desdemona;
It must not be: if Cassio do remain,
He hath a daily beauty in his life
That makes me ugly: and, besides, the Moor   20
May unfold me to him; there stand I in much peril.
No, he must die. But so;[555] I hear him coming.

(*Enter Cassio.*)

Roderigo. I know his gait; 'tis he. Villain, thou diest!

(*Makes a pass at Cassio.*)

---

[550] Habits (?), treatment (?).   [551] Jutting part of a wall.   [552] Pimple.   [553] To the quick.
[554] Swindled.   [555] I.e., that's the only way.

Cassio. That thrust had been mine enemy indeed
But that my coat is better than thou know'st;
I will make proof of thine.

(Draws, and wounds Roderigo.)

Roderigo.   O! I am slain.

(Iago from behind wounds Cassio in the leg, and exit.)

Cassio. I am maim'd for ever. Help, ho! murder! murder!   *(Falls.)*

(Enter Othello, at a distance.)

Othello. The voice of Cassio: Iago keeps his word.
Roderigo. O! villain that I am!
Othello.   It is e'en so.
Cassio. O, help, ho! light! a surgeon!   30
Othello. 'Tis he: O brave Iago, honest and just!
That hast such noble sense of thy friend's wrong;
Thou teachest me. Minion,[556] your dear lies dead,
And your unblest fate hies; strumpet, I come!
Forth of my heart those charms, thine eyes, are blotted;
Thy bed lust-stain'd shall with lust's blood be spotted.   *(Exit.)*

(Enter Lodovico and Gratiano, at a distance.)

Cassio. What ho! no watch? no passage?[557] murder! murder!
Gratiano. 'Tis some mischance; the cry is very direful.
Cassio. O, help!
Lodovico. Hark!   40
Roderigo. O wretched villain!
Lodovico. Two or three groans: it is a heavy[558] night;
These may be counterfeits; let 's think 't unsafe
To come in to the cry[559] without more help.
Roderigo. Nobody come? then shall I bleed to death.
Lodovico. Hark!

(Re-enter Iago, with a light.)

Gratiano. Here 's one comes in his shirt, with light and weapons.
Iago. Who 's there? whose noise is this that cries on murder?

---

[556] (Cassio's) darling, i.e., Desdemona.   [557] Passer-by.   [558] Dark.   [559] Where the cry comes from.

Lodovico. We do not know.

Iago.   Did not you hear a cry?

Cassio. Here, here! for heaven's sake, help me.

Iago.   What's the matter?   50

Gratiano. This is Othello's ancient, as I take it.

Lodovico. The same indeed; a very valiant fellow.

Iago. What are you here that cry so grievously?

Cassio. Iago? O! I am spoil'd, undone by villains!
   Give me some help.

Iago. O me, lieutenant! what villains have done this?

Cassio. I think that one of them is hereabout,
   And cannot make away.

Iago.   O treacherous villains!
   (To Lodovico and Gratiano.) What are you there? come in, and
   give some help.   60

Roderigo. O! help me here.

Cassio. That's one of them.

Iago.   O murderous slave! O villain!

(Stabs Roderigo.)

Roderigo. O damn'd Iago! O inhuman dog!

Iago. Kill men i' the dark! Where be these bloody thieves?
   How silent is this town! Ho! murder! murder!
   What may you be? are you of good or evil?

Lodovico. As you shall prove us, praise us.

Iago. Signior Lodovico?

Lodovico. He, sir.

Iago. I cry you mercy. Here 's Cassio hurt by villains.   70

Gratiano. Cassio!

Iago. How is it, brother?

Cassio. My leg is cut in two.

Iago.   Marry, heaven forbid.
   Light, gentlemen; I 'll bind it with my shirt.

(Enter Bianca.)

Bianca. What is the matter, ho? who is 't that cried?

Iago. Who is 't that cried!

Bianca. O my dear Cassio! my sweet Cassio!
   O Cassio, Cassio, Cassio!

Iago. O notable strumpet! Cassio, may you suspect
   Who they should be that have thus mangled you?   80

Cassio. No.

Gratiano. I am sorry to find you thus; I have been to seek you.

Iago. Lend me a garter. So. O! for a chair,
  To bear him easily hence!
Bianca. Alas; he faints! O Cassio, Cassio, Cassio!
Iago. Gentlemen all, I do suspect this trash[560]
  To be a party in this injury.
  Patience awhile, good Cassio. Come, come.
  Lend me a light. Know we this face, or no?
  Alas! my friend and my dear countryman,   90
  Roderigo? no: yes, sure, O heaven! Roderigo.
Gratiano. What! of Venice?
Iago. Even he, sir, did you know him?
Gratiano.   Know him! ay.
Iago. Signior Gratiano? I cry you gentle pardon;
  These bloody accidents must excuse my manners,
  That so neglected you.
Gratiano.   I am glad to see you.
Iago. How do you, Cassio? O! a chair, a chair!
Gratiano. Roderigo!

(A chair brought in.)

Iago. He, he, 'tis he,—O! that 's well said; the chair:
  Some good men bear him carefully from hence;   100
  I 'll fetch the general's surgeon. *(To Bianca.)* For you, mistress,
  Save you your labour. He that lies slain here, Cassio,
  Was my dear friend. What malice was between you?
Cassio. None in the world; nor do I know that man.
Iago *(to Bianca)*. What! look you pale? O! bear him out o' the air—

(Cassio and Roderigo are borne off.)

  Stay you, good gentlemen. Look you pale, mistress?—
  Do you perceive the gastness[561] of her eye?
  Nay, if you stare, we shall hear more anon.
  Behold her well; I pray you, look upon her.
  Do you see, gentlemen? nay, guiltiness will speak   110
  Though tongues were out of use.

(Enter Emilia.)

Emilia. 'Las! what 's the matter? what 's the matter, husband?
Iago. Cassio hath here been set on in the dark

---

[560] I.e., Bianca.   [561] Terror.

By Roderigo and fellows that are 'scaped:
He 's almost slain, and Roderigo dead.

Emilia. Alas! good gentleman; alas! good Cassio!

Iago. This is the fruit of whoring. Prithee, Emilia,
Go know of Cassio where he supp'd to-night.
(To Bianca.) What! do you shake at that?

Bianca. He supp'd at my house; but I therefore shake not.   120

Iago. O! did he so? I charge you, go with me.

Emilia. Fie, fie, upon thee, strumpet!

Bianca. I am no strumpet, but of life as honest
As you that thus abuse me.

Emilia.   As I! foh! fie upon thee!

Iago. Kind gentlemen, let 's go see poor Cassio dress'd.[562]
Come, mistress, you must tell 's another tale.
Emilia, run you to the citadel,
And tell my lord and lady what hath happ'd.
Will you go on afore? *(Aside.)* This is the night
That either makes me or fordoes[563] me quite.   *(Exeunt.)*

Scene 2. A Bedchamber in the Castle. Desdemona in bed asleep. A light
burning.

(Enter Othello.)

Othello. It is the cause,[564] it is the cause, my soul;
Let me not name it to you, you chaste stars!
It is the cause. Yet I 'll not shed her blood,
Nor scar that whiter skin of hers than snow,
And smooth as monumental alabaster.
Yet she must die, else she 'll betray more men.
Put out the light, and then put out the light:
If I quench thee, thou flaming minister,[565]
I can again thy former light restore,
Should I repent me; but once put out thy light,   10
Thou cunning'st[566] pattern of excelling nature,
I know not where is that Promethean[567] heat
That can thy light relume.[568] When I have pluck'd the rose,
I cannot give it vital growth again,
It needs must wither: I 'll smell it on the tree. *(Kisses her.)*
O balmy breath, that dost almost persuade

---

[562] Bandaged.   [563] Ruins.   [564] I.e., Desdemona's unchastity (Othello means that the severity of
the punishment is required by the nature of her sin).   [565] I.e., the candle.   [566] Most intricately
wrought.   [567] In Greek mythology the demigod Prometheus stole fire from the gods and gave it to
man.   [568] Relight.

Justice to break her sword! One more, one more.
Be thus when thou art dead, and I will kill thee,
And love thee after. One more, and this the last:
So sweet was ne'er so fatal. I must weep,   20
But they are cruel tears; this sorrow 's heavenly,
It strikes where it doth love. She wakes.
Desdemona. Who 's there? Othello?
Othello.   Ay, Desdemona.
Desdemona. Will you come to bed, my lord?
Othello. Have you pray'd to-night, Desdemona?
Desdemona.   Ay, my lord.
Othello. If you bethink yourself of any crime
  Unreconcil'd as yet to heaven and grace,
  Solicit for it straight.
Desdemona. Alas! my lord, what may you mean by that?
Othello. Well, do it, and be brief; I will walk by:[569]   30
  I would not kill thy unprepared spirit;
  No; heaven forfend![570] I would not kill thy soul.
Desdemona. Talk you of killing?
Othello.   Ay, I do.
Desdemona.   Then heaven
  Have mercy on me!
Othello.   Amen! with all my heart.
Desdemona. If you say so, I hope you will not kill me.
Othello. Hum!
Desdemona. And yet I fear you; for you are fatal then
  When your eyes roll so. Why I should fear I know not,
  Since guiltiness I know not; but yet I feel I fear.
Othello. Think on thy sins.
Desdemona.   They are loves I bear to you.   40
Othello. Ay, and for that thou diest.
Desdemona. That death's unnatural that kills for loving.
  Alas! why gnaw you so your nether lip?
  Some bloody passion shakes your very frame;
  These are portents,[571] but yet, I hope, I hope
  They do not point on me.
Othello.   Peace, and be still!
Desdemona. I will so. What 's the matter?
Othello. That handkerchief which I so lov'd and gave thee
  Thou gav'st to Cassio.
Desdemona.   No, by my life and soul!
  Send for the man and ask him.

---

[569] Nearby.   [570] Forbid.   [571] Omens.

Othello.   Sweet soul, take heed,   50
Take heed of perjury; thou 'rt on thy death-bed.
Desdemona. Ay, but not yet to die.
Othello.   Yes, presently;[572]
Therefore confess thee freely of thy sin;
For to deny each article with oath
Cannot remove nor choke the strong conception[573]
That I do groan withal. Thou art to die.
Desdemona. Then Lord have mercy on me!
Othello.   I say, amen.
Desdemona. And have you mercy too! I never did
Offend you in my life; never lov'd Cassio
But with such general warranty[574] of heaven   60
As I might love; I never gave him token.
Othello. By heaven, I saw my handkerchief in 's hand.
O perjur'd woman! thou dost stone[575] my heart,
And mak'st me call what I intend to do
A murder, which I thought a sacrifice:
I saw the handkerchief.
Desdemona.   He found it then;
I never gave it him. Send for him hither;
Let him confess a truth.
Othello.   He had confessed.
Desdemona. What, my lord?
Othello. That he hath us'd thee.
Desdemona.   How? Unlawfully?
Othello.   Ay.   70
Desdemona. He will not say so.
Othello.   No; his mouth is stopp'd:
Honest Iago hath ta'en order for 't.[576]
Desdemona. O! my fear interprets. What! is he dead?
Othello. Had all his hairs been lives, my great revenge
Had stomach[577] for them all.
Desdemona. Alas! he is betray'd and I undone.
Othello. Out, strumpet! Weep'st thou for him to my face?
Desdemona. O! banish me, my lord, but kill me not!
Othello. Down, strumpet!
Desdemona. Kill me to-morrow; let me live to-night!   80
Othello. Nay, if you strive,—
Desdemona. But half an hour!
Othello.   Being done, there is no pause.
Desdemona. But while I say one prayer!

---

[572] At once.   [573] Belief.   [574] Permission.   [575] Turn to stone.   [576] Taken steps.   [577] Appetite.

Othello.   It is too late.   *(He smothers her.)*

Emilia *(within).* My lord, my lord! what, ho! my lord, my lord!

Othello. What noise is this? Not dead? Not yet quite dead?
  I that am cruel am yet merciful;
  I would not have thee linger in thy pain.
  So, so.

Emilia *(within).* What, ho! my lord, my lord!

Othello.   Who's there?

Emilia *(within).* O! good my lord, I would speak a word with you!   90

Othello. Yes; 'tis Emilia: by and by.[578] She's dead.
  'Tis like[579] she comes to speak of Cassio's death;
  The noise was high. Ha! no more moving?
  Still as the grave. Shall she come in? were 't good?[580]
  I think she stirs again: no. What 's best to do?
  If she come in she'll sure speak to my wife:
  My wife! my wife! what wife? I have no wife;
  O, insupportable! O heavy hour!
  Methinks it should be now a huge eclipse
  Of sun and moon, and that the affrighted globe   100
  Should yawn[581] at alteration.

Emilia *(within).*   I do beseech you
  That I may speak with you, O! good my lord.

Othello. I had forgot thee: O! come in, Emilia:
  Soft, by and by: let me the curtains draw.
  Where art thou?   *(Unlocks the door.)*

(Enter Emilia.)

              What 's the matter with thee now?

Emilia. O! my good lord, yonder 's foul murder done.

Othello. What! now?

Emilia. But now, my lord.

Othello. It is the very error[582] of the moon;
  She comes more near the earth than she was wont,   110
  And makes men mad.

Emilia. Cassio, my lord, has kill'd a young Venetian
  Call'd Roderigo.

Othello.   Roderigo kill'd!
  And Cassio kill'd?

Emilia.   No, Cassio is not kill'd.

Othello. Not Cassio kill'd! then murder 's out of tune,
  And sweet revenge grows harsh.

---

[578] I.e., "just a moment."   [579] Likely.   [580] Would that be wise.   [581] Open up (as in an earthquake).
[582] Straying.

Desdemona. O! falsely, falsely murder'd.

Emilia. Alas! what cry is that?

Othello. That! what?

Emilia. Out, and alas! that was my lady's voice:
Help! Help, ho! help! O lady, speak again! 120
Sweet Desdemona! O! sweet mistress, speak.

Desdemona. A guiltless death I die.

Emilia. O! who hath done this deed?

Desdemona. Nobody; I myself; farewell:
Commend me to my kind lord. O! farewell! *(Dies.)*

Othello. Why, how should she be murder'd?

Emilia. Alas! who knows?

Othello. You heard her say herself it was not I.

Emilia. She said so; I must needs report the truth.

Othello. She 's like a liar gone to burning hell;
'Twas I that kill'd her.

Emilia. O! the more angel she, 130
And you the blacker devil.

Othello. She turn'd to folly, and she was a whore.

Emilia. Thou dost belie her, and thou art a devil.

Othello. She was false as water.

Emilia. Thou art rash as fire to say
That she was false! O! she was heavenly true.

Othello. Cassio did tup her; ask thy husband else.
O! I were damn'd beneath all depth in hell
But that I did proceed[583] upon just grounds
To this extremity. Thy husband knew it all.

Emilia. My husband! 140

Othello. Thy husband.

Emilia. That she was false to wedlock?

Othello. Ay, with Cassio. Nay, had she been true,
If heaven would make me such another world
Of one entire and perfect chrysolite,[584]
I'd not have sold her for it.

Emilia. My husband!

Othello. Ay, 'twas he that told me first:
An honest man he is, and hates the slime
That sticks on filthy deeds.

Emilia. My husband!

Othello. What needs this iterance,[585] woman? I say thy husband. 150

Emilia. O mistress! villany hath made mocks with love.
My husband say that she was false!

---

[583] Had I not proceeded.   [584] Topaz.   [585] Repetition.

Othello.   He, woman;
  I say, thy husband: dost understand the word?
  My friend, thy husband, honest, honest Iago.
Emilia. If he say so, may his pernicious soul
  Rot half a grain a day! he lies to the heart:
  She was too fond of her most filthy bargain.[586]
Othello. Ha!
Emilia. Do thy worst:
  This deed of thine is no more worthy heaven   160
  Than thou wast worthy her.
Othello.   Peace! you were best.[587]
Emilia. Thou hast not half the power to do me harm
  As I have to be hurt. O gull! O dolt!
  As ignorant as dirt! thou hast done a deed,—
  I care not for thy sword; I'll make thee known,
  Though I lost twenty lives. Help! help, ho! help!
  The Moor has kill'd my mistress! murder! murder!

(Enter Montano, Gratiano, Iago, and others.)

Montano. What is the matter? How now, general!
Emilia. O! are you come, Iago? you have done well,
  That men must lay their murders on your neck.   170
Gratiano. What is the matter?
Emilia. Disprove this villain if thou be'st a man:
  He says thou told'st him that his wife was false.
  I know thou didst not, thou 'rt not such a villain.
  Speak, for my heart is full.
Iago. I told him what I thought, and told no more
  Than what he found himself was apt and true.
Emilia. But did you ever tell him she was false?
Iago. I did.
Emilia. You told a lie, an odious damned lie;   180
  Upon my soul, a lie, a wicked lie;
  She false with Cassio! Did you say with Cassio?
Iago. With Cassio, mistress. Go to, charm[588] your tongue.
Emilia. I will not charm my tongue; I am bound to speak.
  My mistress here lies murder'd in her bed.
All. O heavens forfend!
Emilia. And your reports have set the murder on.
Othello. Nay, stare not, masters; it is true, indeed.
Gratiano. 'Tis a strange truth.
Montano. O monstrous act!

---

[586] I.e., Othello.   [587] You'd better be quiet.   [588] I.e., into silence.

Emilia.   Villany! villany! villany!   190
I think upon 't, I think, I smell 't; O villany!
I thought so then;[589] I'll kill myself for grief.
O! villany, villany!
Iago. What! are you mad? I charge you, get you home.
Emilia. Good gentlemen, let me have leave to speak:
'Tis proper I obey him, but not now.
Perchance, Iago, I will ne'er go home.
Othello. O! O! O!   *(Falls on the bed.)*
Emilia.   Nay, lay thee down and roar,
For thou hast kill'd the sweetest innocent
That e'er did lift up eye.
Othello.   O! she was foul.   *(Rises.)*
I scarce did know you, uncle. There lies your niece,
Whose breath, indeed, these hands have newly stopp'd:
I know this act shows terrible and grim.
Gratiano. Poor Desdemona! I am glad thy father's dead.
Thy match was mortal to him, and pure grief
Shore[590] his old thread in twain: did he live now,
This sight would make him do a desperate turn,
Yea, curse his better angel from his side,
And fall to reprobation.[591]
Othello. 'Tis pitiful; but yet Iago knows   210
That she with Cassio hath the act of shame
A thousand times committed; Cassio confess'd it:
And she did gratify[592] his amorous works
With that recognizance and pledge of love
Which I first gave her. I saw it in his hand:
It was a handkerchief, an antique token
My father gave my mother.
Emilia. O heaven! O heavenly powers!
Iago.   Come, hold your peace.
Emilia. 'Twill out, 'twill out; I hold my peace, sir? no;
No, I will speak as liberal as the north;[593]   220
Let heaven and men and devils, let them all,
All, all, cry shame against me, yet I'll speak.
Iago. Be wise, and get you home.
Emilia.   I will not.

(Iago threatens to stab Emilia.)

---

[589] *Cf.* "I will be hang'd, if some eternal villain, / Some busy and insinuating rogue, / Some cogging cozening slave, to get some office, / Have not devis'd this slander; . . ." (IV, 2, 130 ff.). Emilia means not that she guessed Iago's guilt but that she rightly guessed the slanderer's motive.   [590] Cut.   [591] Damnation.   [592] Reward.   [593] I.e., the north wind (?), the supposedly free-spoken people of north England (?).

Gratiano.   Fie!
    Your sword upon a woman!

Emilia.   O thou dull Moor! that handkerchief thou speak'st of
    I found by fortune and did give my husband;
    For often, with a solemn earnestness,
    More than, indeed, belong'd to such a trifle,
    He begg'd of me to steal it.

Iago.   Villainous whore!

Emilia.   She give it Cassio! no, alas! I found it,   230
    And I did give 't my husband.

Iago.   Filth, thou liest!

Emilia.   By heaven, I do not, I do not, gentlemen.
    O murderous coxcomb![594] what should such a fool
    Do with so good a wife?

Othello.   Are there no stones[595] in heaven
    But what serve for the thunder? Precious villain!

(He runs at Iago. Iago stabs Emilia.)

Gratiano.   The woman falls; sure, he has kill'd his wife.   *(Exit Iago.)*

Emilia.   Ay, ay; O! lay me by my mistress' side.

Gratiano.   He 's gone; but his wife 's kill'd.

Montano.   'Tis a notorious[596] villain. Take you this weapon,
    Which I have here recover'd from the Moor.   240
    Come, guard the door without; let him not pass,
    But kill him rather. I'll after that same villain,
    For 'tis a damned slave.   *(Exeunt Montano and Gratiano.)*

Othello.   I am not valiant neither,
    But every puny whipster[597] gets my sword.
    But why should honour outlive honesty?
    Let it go all.

Emilia.   What did thy song bode, lady?
    Hark, canst thou hear me? I will play the swan,
    And die in music:—
    (Sings.)   Willow, willow, willow.
    Moor, she was chaste; she lov'd thee, cruel Moor;
    So come my soul to bliss as I speak true;   250
    So speaking as I think, I die, I die.   *(Dies.)*

Othello.   I have another weapon in this chamber;
    It is a sword of Spain, the ice-brook's temper.[598]
    O! here it is. Uncle, I must come forth.

---

[594] Idiot.   [595] I.e., thunderbolts (to strike Iago down).   [596] Notable.   [597] I.e., a small boy whipping a top.   [598] Tempered in icy water (or the reference may be to Innsbruck, famed for the quality of its steel, but this hardly fits "a sword of Spain").

Gratiano *(within).* If thou attempt it, it will cost thee dear:
   Thou hast no weapon, and perforce must suffer.
Othello. Look in upon me then, and speak with me,
   Or, naked[599] as I am, I will assault thee.

(Re-enter Gratiano.)

Gratiano. What is the matter?
Othello.   Behold! I have a weapon;
   A better never did itself sustain   260
   Upon a soldier's thigh: I have seen the day,
   That with this little arm, and this good sword,
   I have made my way through more impediments
   Than twenty times your stop: but, O vain boast!
   Who can control his fate? 'tis not so now.
   Be not afraid, though you do see me weapon'd;
   Here is my journey's end, here is my butt,[600]
   And very sea-mark of my utmost sail.[601]
   Do you go back dismay'd? 'tis a lost fear;
   Man but a rush[602] against Othello's breast,   270
   And he retires. Where should Othello go?
   Now how dost thou look now? O ill-starr'd wench!
   Pale as thy smock! when we shall meet at compt,[603]
   This look of thine will hurl my soul from heaven,
   And fiends will snatch at it. Cold, cold, my girl!
   Even like thy chastity.
   O! cursed, cursed slave. Whip me, ye devils,
   From the possession of this heavenly sight!
   Blow me about in winds! roast me in sulphur!
   Wash me in steep-down gulfs of liquid fire!   280
   O Desdemona! Desdemona! dead!
   Oh! Oh! Oh!

(Enter Lodovico, Montano, Cassio carried in a chair, and Officers with Iago, prisoner.)

Lodovico. Where is this rash and most unfortunate man?
Othello. That's he that was Othello; here I am.
Lodovico. Where is that viper? bring the villain forth.
Othello. I look down towards his feet;[604] but that's a fable.
   If that thou be'st a devil, I cannot kill thee.   *(Wounds Iago.)*
Lodovico. Wrench his sword from him.   *(Othello is disarmed.)*

---

[599] Unarmed.   [600] Goal, end, limit.   [601] Destination of my farthest journey.   [602] Wield but a reed.
[603] On the day of judgment.   [604] I.e., for the Devil's cloven hoof.

Iago.   I bleed, sir; but not kill'd.

Othello. I am not sorry neither; I'd have thee live;
   For, in my sense,[605] 'tis happiness to die.   290

Lodovico. O thou Othello! that wert once so good,
   Fall'n in the practice[606] of a damned slave,[607]
   What shall be said to thee?

Othello.   Why, any thing:
   An honourable murderer, if you will;
   For nought did I in hate, but all in honour.

Lodovico. This wretch hath part confess'd his villany:
   Did you and he consent in Cassio's death?

Othello. Ay.

Cassio. Dear general, I never gave you cause.

Othello. I do believe it, and I ask your pardon.   300
   Will you, I pray, demand that demi-devil
   Why he hath thus ensnar'd my soul and body?

Iago. Demand me nothing: what you know, you know:
   From this time forth I never will speak word.

Lodovico. What! not to pray?

Gratiano.   Torments will ope[608] your lips.

Othello. Well, thou dost best.

Lodovico. Sir, you shall understand what hath befall'n,
   Which, as I think, you know not. Here is a letter
   Found in the pocket of the slain Roderigo,
   And here another; the one of them imports   310
   The death of Cassio to be undertook
   By Roderigo.

Othello. O villain!

Cassio.   Most heathenish and most gross!

Lodovico. Now here's another discontented paper,
   Found in his pocket too; and this, it seems,
   Roderigo meant to have sent this damned villain,
   But that, belike,[609] Iago in the interim[610]
   Came in and satisfied him.

Othello.   O the pernicious caitiff!
   How came you, Cassio, by that handkerchief
   That was my wife's?

Cassio.   I found it in my chamber;   320
   And he himself confess'd but even now
   That there he dropp'd it for a special purpose
   Which wrought to his desire.

Othello.   O fool! fool! fool!

---

[605] The way I feel. [606] Plot, machination. [607] I.e., Iago. [608] Open. [609] Most likely. [610] In the meantime.

Cassio. There is besides in Roderigo's letter
  How he upbraids Iago that he made him
  Brave me upon the watch; whereon it came
  That I was cast:[611] and even but now he spake,
  After long seeming dead, Iago hurt him,
  Iago set him on.
Lodovico. You must forsake this room and go with us;   330
  Your power and your command is taken off,
  And Cassio rules in Cyprus. For this slave,
  If there be any cunning cruelty
  That can torment him much and hold him long,
  It shall be his. You shall close prisoner rest,
  Till that the nature of your fault be known
  To the Venetian state. Come, bring him away.
Othello. Soft you; a word or two before you go.
  I have done the state some service, and they know 't;
  No more of that. I pray you, in your letters,   340
  When you shall these unlucky deeds relate,
  Speak of me as I am; nothing extenuate,
  Nor set down aught[612] in malice: then, must you speak
  Of one that lov'd not wisely but too well;
  Of one not easily jealous, but, being wrought,
  Perplex'd[613] in the extreme; of one whose hand
  Like the base Indian,[614] threw a pearl away
  Richer than all his tribe; of one whose subdu'd[615] eyes
  Albeit unused to the melting mood,
  Drop tears as fast as the Arabian trees   350
  Their med'cinable gum. Set you down this;
  And say besides, that in Aleppo once,
  Where a malignant and a turban'd Turk
  Beat a Venetian and traduc'd the state,
  I took by the throat the circumcised dog,
  And smote him, thus.   *(Stabs himself.)*
Lodovico. O bloody period![616]
Gratiano.   All that's spoke is marr'd.
Othello. I kiss'd thee ere I killed thee; no way but this.
                      (Falling upon Desdemona.)
  Killing myself to die upon a kiss.   *(Dies.)*
Cassio. This did I fear, but thought he had no weapon;   360
  For he was great of heart.
Lodovico *(to Iago).*   O Spartan dog!
  More fell[617] than anguish, hunger, or the sea.

---

[611] Dismissed.   [612] Anything.   [613] Distracted.   [614] The Folio reads "Iudean." Both readings denote the foolish infidel who fails to appreciate the treasure he possesses.   [615] Overcome (by grief).
[616] Ending.   [617] Grim, cruel.

Look on the tragic loading of this bed;
This is thy work; the object poisons sight;
Let it be hid. Gratiano, keep the house,
And seize upon the fortunes of the Moor,
For they succeed on you. To you, lord governor,
Remains the censure of this hellish villain,
The time, the place, the torture; O! enforce it.
Myself will straight aboard, and to the state   370
This heavy act with heavy heart relate.   (*Exeunt.*)

FOR ANALYSIS

1. In what sense might it be said that Othello is responsible for his own downfall?

2. Do you find the reasons that Iago gives for his actions consistent and convincing?

3. Discuss the functions of the minor characters, such as Roderigo, Bianca, and Emilia.

4. Is the rapidity of Othello's emotional collapse (act III, scene 3) plausible? Does his race contribute to his emotional turmoil? Explain.

5. The first part of act IV, scene 2 (until Othello exits), is sometimes called the "brothel" scene. What features of Othello's language and behavior justify this designation?

6. Why does Iago kill Roderigo?

7. What are the benefits of moving the main characters to Cyprus rather than setting the drama in Venice?

8. Compare the speeches of Cassio and Iago in act II, scene 1. What do the differences in language and **style** reveal about their characters?

9. Carefully review the play to determine how much time elapses between the arrival in Cyprus and the end of the action. Can you find narrated events that could not possibly have occurred within that time frame? What effect do the chronological inconsistencies have on you? Explain.

WRITING TOPICS

1. Write an analysis of the **figurative language** in Iago's soliloquies at the end of act I and at the end of act II, scene 1.

2. Choose a minor character, such as Roderigo, Emilia, or Bianca, and in a carefully reasoned essay, explain how the character contributes to the design of the play.

3. Discuss the relationship between love and hate in this **tragedy**.

JUAN LUIS VIVES (1493–1540)

FROM INSTRUCTION OF A CHRISTIAN WOMAN 1557

HOW THE MAID SHALL SEEK A HUSBAND

The wise poet Virgil, where he doth bring in king Latinus, and his wife Amata, talking together with Turnus, which should be their daughter's husband, their daughter also present, he maketh the maid to do no more but weep and blush, without speaking of words: whereby he signifieth, that it becometh not a maid to talk, where her father and mother be in communication about her marriage: but to leave all that care and charge wholly unto them which love her as well as her self doth. And let her think that her father and mother will provide no less diligently for her, than she would for herself: but much better, by the reason they have more experience and wisdom. Moreover it is not comely for a maid to desire marriage, and much less to show herself to long therefore. . . .

It is a great charge for a man to seek a husband for his daughter, neither it ought not to be gone about negligently. It is a knot that cannot be lightly loosed, only death undoeth it. Wherefore the fathers and mothers procure unto their daughters, either perpetual felicity, if they marry them to good men, or perpetual misery, marrying them unto ill. Here is much to be studied, and great deliberation to be taken, with good advisement and counsel, afore a man determine ought. For there is much weariness in marriage, and many pains must be suffered. There is nothing but one, that shall cause marriage to be easy unto a woman: that is, if she chance on a good and a wise husband. . . .

I thought it had been but a fable, that men tell, how Pasiphae[1] the queen of Candy,[2] did lie with a Bull: and other as ungracious deeds as that: which I have heard say, other women have done: but now me thinketh them all likely enough to be true, when I see women can find in their hearts, to tumble and lie with vicious and filthy men, and drunkards, and brawlers, and dawish,[3] and brainless, cruel and murderers. For what difference is between them and asses, swine, boars, bulls, or bears? What madness is it to have delight in such men, and to flee and eschew wise men, as Plutarch the Philosopher saith, and flee honest men and good men, as warily as they would flee from venomous beasts? Wherefore it was well and aptly spoken, that a countryman of mine said, that the nature of women was in choosing men, like to the female wolves: which among a great sort of males, take the foulest and worst favored. But men never cast any favor to a woman, but for some good property, either of substance, person, or wit. And women many times love some men, because

---

[1] Queen of Crete and mother of the Minotaur.   [2] From the Latin *Candia*, another name for Crete.
[3] Silly or sluttish.

there is nothing in them worthy to be beloved. Whereby they declare the more plainly, that they go without reason. Which things I say by some, that have nothing a do with their reason, but all given and applied unto their body. . . .

Now afore I make an end of this book, I will answer unto a mad and a frantic opinion, which both maidens and wives have, and all the common people in general, that think it is expedient for maids, that are come to lawful age of marriage, to be seen oft abroad among people, goodly and pickedly[4] arrayed, and to keep company and communication with men, to be eloquent in speech, and cunning in dancing and singing: yea and to love him aforehand, whom they intend to marry. For so (they say), they shall the more lightly meet with a bargain. . . . What wise man, I pray you, would ever counsel this thing, knowing, that ill is not to be done, that good may come thereof? And specially where the ill is evident enough, and the good neither certain nor customed to follow commonly upon the deed. Wherefore if the maid can get no marriage, except she infect her mind, and jeopardize her honesty on this fashion, it were better never to marry: or else to marry only Christ, than to marry first unto the devil, that she may be married to a man afterward.

Now two things there be, the most precious that a woman can bring with her to a man, honesty of body, and good fame. Nor there is no man so foolish and mad, neither so set upon beauty and covetous of goods, neither so ungracious and so unthrifty of living, but he will be content with any wife, having these two: which if she lack, how can he be content? Then would I wit, whether maid is the more likely to be of good fame and behavior, whether she that bideth most at home, or she that walketh much abroad? At home there is none occasion of evil, and forth abroad every place is full. And of her that tarrieth at home, no man maketh question or argument: but of her that walketh much about, every man will say his opinion. Where among so diverse sentences a maid shall soon catch a blot, which will stick in no place more sooner than on a maid, neither worse to get out. . . .

And as for those that keep much company with men, what man is there, that will not suspect ill by them? Or what husband shall she find so patient, that will be content to have his wife to company still and common with men? Or would not rather have such a one, as would more gladly company with her husband alone, than with a great multitude of men? Where one shall tempt her mind with eloquence, another with comeliness of person, some with beauty, some with liberty, and some with nobleness. For as for maids to be eloquent of speech, that is to say great babblers, is a token of a light mind and shrewd conditions. In so much that he that shall marry her, shall think he hath a serpent and no wife. For young men will praise her unto her face, that is full of talk, and a jolly dancer, and full of merry conceits, and play, and pleasant, and call her well mannered, and well brought up, all to have her at their pleasure, but none to marry her: and all believe that they may quickly obtain their purpose of such one. But never a one will be glad to have such one to his wife, that he seeth is applying[5] unto every man's will. They praise for the time all that

---

[4] Meticulously, tastefully.   [5] Seeking to gain the attentions of.

she doth, because they have delight therein. But and[6] the foolish maids could hear what men speak afterwards among themself one unto another, without dissimulation: then, should they know indeed how heartily they praised them and liked them. They should understand then, that when the men called her merry conceited, they meant they were babblers, and chatters: and when they called them lusty stirrers[7] they meant they were light minded: and where they called them well nurtured, they meant they were wanton. . . .

Now will I speak a few words of love, the which doteth all maids for the most part, and deceiveth them greatly, and bringeth to much mischief. For it doth not become a maid to make any sign, that she would fain be married, or that she love any young man to wed. For if she love him afore she have him, that it be known, what shall he think, but that she will as lightly love another as she hath done him, whom as yet she ought to show no love unto. Neither he will believe that she loveth him alone, seeing there is as great cause to love other. And if he should marry her, he will think she will have as good mind to other as himself, when she is so light of love.

Let everybody excuse the matter as they will, but in very deed every woman, that loveth any man beside her husband, is accursed, if she have ado with him: and though she have not, yet is she an harlot in mind. And there hath been many that have loved so outrageously, that they have been obedient unto the pleasure of those men, whom they hoped should be their husbands. And afterwards these men have despised and cast them up which in my mind was well and wisely done. For they be unworthy to be married, that dare show an example unto those men, whom they should have, how well they can find in their heart to lie with a man that is not their husband. For by likelihood they will both do that same with other men afore their marriage, and in their marriage with their adulterers. . . . And so it chanceth unto such women, even by the punishment of God, that all the love, which they ought to keep in their marriage, they spend it out afore. . . . Wherefore it is not expedient to make marriages by love aforehand, neither to couple and bind that most holy charity with so filthy and brittle bands. And yet much worse is it to make them to marry by striving, and hate, threatening, and suit,[8] as when they go to law together, the man for the woman, bearing her in hand, that she is his wife: and the woman in like manner for the man.

FOR ANALYSIS

1. What are the dangers the author sees in the practice among some young women of being seen in public and to consort with men?

2. What does the author think of love matches? How should a wife and husband be brought together instead?

3. From the start of this excerpt, it is clear that young women occupy a subordinate position in society. Do they have any power? Does the power to make what the author sees as bad decisions count?

---

[6] If.   [7] Active people ("stirrers").   [8] Lawsuit.

GEORGE BEST (D. CA. 1584)

FROM A TRUE DISCOURSE OF THE LATE VOYAGES OF DISCOVERY 1578

Also the Englishmen made another voyage very prosperous and gainful, Anno 1554, to the coasts of *Benin*, lying East from *Guinea*, being within three degrees of the Equinoctial. And yet it is reported of a truth, . . . all the whole Bay is more subject to many blooming and smothering heats, with infectious and contagious airs, than any other place in all *Torrida Zone*:[1] and the cause thereof is some accidents in the land. For it is most certain, that mountains, seas, woods, and lakes, etc. may cause through their sundry kind of situation sundry strange and extraordinary effects, which the reason of the clime otherwise would not give. I mention these voyages of our Englishmen not so much to prove that *Torrida Zone* may be, and is inhabited, as to show their readiness in attempting long and dangerous Navigations. We also among us in England, have black Moors, Ethiopians, out of all parts of Torrida Zone, which after a small continuance, can well endure the cold of our Country, and why should not we as well abide the heat of their Country? But what should I name any more experiences, seeing that all the coasts of Guinea and Benin are inhabited of Portugals, Spaniards, French, and some Englishmen, and there have built Castles and Towns. Only this I will say to the Merchants of London that trade yearly to Marochus,[2] it is very certain that the greatest part of the burning Zone is far more temperate and cool than the Country of Marochus, as shall appear by these reasons and experiences following. . . .

And first by the experience of sundry men, yea thousands, Travelers and Merchants, to the East and West *Indies* in many places both directly under and hard by the Equinoctial, they with one consent affirm that it aboundeth in the middle of *Torrida Zone* with all manner of grain, herbs, grass, fruit, wood, and cattle that we have here, and thousands other sorts, far more wholesome, delectable, and precious than any we have in these Northern climates, as very well shall appear to him that will read the Histories and Navigations of such as have traveled *Arabia, India,* . . . the Islands *Molucca, America,* etc., which all lie about the middle of the burning Zone, where it is truly reported that the great herbs, . . . do wax ripe, greater, more savory and delectable in taste than ours, within sixteen days after the seed is sown. . . .

Others again imagine the middle Zone to be extreme hot, because the people of *Africa*, especially the Ethiopians, are so coal black, and their hair like wool curled short, which blackness and crooked hair they suppose to come only by the parching heat of the Sun, which how it should be possible, I cannot see. For even under the Equinoctial in America, and in the East Indies, and in the

---

[1] Region of the earth between the Tropic of Cancer and the Tropic of Capricorn.   [2] Morocco.

Islands Malucca, the people are not black, but white, with long hair uncurled as we have, so that if the Ethiopians' blackness came by the heat of the Sun, why should not those Americans and Indians also be as black as they, seeing the Sun is equally distant from them both, they abiding in one Parallel . . . ?

. . . Therefore, to return again to the black Moors, I myself have seen an Ethiopian as black as a coal brought into England, who, taking a fair English woman to Wife, begat a son in all respects as black as the father was, although England were his native Country, and an English woman his Mother: whereby it seemeth this blackness proceedeth rather of some natural infection of that man, which was so strong that neither the nature of the Clime, neither the good complexion of the Mother concurring, could anything alter, and therefore we cannot impute it to the nature of the Clime. And for a more fresh example, our people of Meta Incognita[3] (of whom and for whom this discourse is taken in hand) that were brought this last year into England, were all generally of the same color that many Nations be, lying in the middle of the middle Zone. And this their color was not only in the face, which was subject to Sun and Air, but also in their bodies, which were still covered with garments, as ours are: yea, the very sucking child, of twelve months' age, had his skin of the very same color that most have under the Equinoctial, which thing cannot proceed by reason of the clime, for that they are at least ten degrees more toward the North than we in England are . . . where by it followeth that there is some other cause than the Climate, or the Sun's perpendicular reflection, that should cause the Ethiopians' great blackness. And the most probable cause to my judgment is that this blackness proceedeth of some natural infection of the first inhabitants of that Country, and so all the whole progeny of them descended are still polluted with the same blot of infection.

Therefore, it shall not be far from our purpose to examine the first original of these black men and how by lineal descent they have hitherto continued thus black. It manifestly and plainly appeareth by holy Scripture that after the general inundation and overflowing of the Earth,[4] there remained no more men alive, but Noah and his three sons, Shem, Ham, and Japheth, who only were left to possess and inhabit the whole face of the earth: therefore, all the land that until this day hath been inhabited by sundry descents must needs come of the offspring either of Shem, Ham, and Japheth, as the only sons of Noah, who, all three being white, and their wives also, by course of nature should have begotten and brought forth white children. But the envy of our great and continual enemy the wicked Spirit is such that, as he could not suffer our old Father Adam to live in the felicity and Angelic state wherein he was first created, but tempting him, sought and procured his ruin and fall. So again, finding at this flood none but a father and three sons living, he so

---

[3] Meta Incognita means *Of Limits unknown*. Best is alluding to three Inuit captives Martin Frobisher brought to England after his second voyage to the Artic, all of whom died within one month of arriving in England.   [4] The biblical flood.

caused one of them to transgress and disobey his father's commandment, that after him, all his posterity should be accursed.

The fact of disobedience was this: When Noah at the commandment of God had made and entered the Ark and the floodgates of Heaven were opened so that the whole face of the earth, every tree and mountain, was covered with abundance of water, he straightly commanded his sons and their wives that they should with reverence and fear behold the justice and mighty power of God, and that during the time of the flood, while they remained in the Ark, they should use continency and abstain from carnal copulation with their wives: and many other precepts he gave unto them, and admonitions, touching the justice of God in revenging sin and his mercy in delivering them, who nothing deserved it. Which good instructions and exhortations notwithstanding, his wicked son Ham disobeyed, and being persuaded that the first child born after the flood (by right and law of nature) should inherit and possess all the dominion of the earth, he, contrary to his father's commandment, while they were yet in the Ark, used company with his wife, and craftily went about, thereby to disinherit the offspring of his other two brethren. For the which wicked and detestable fact, as an example for contempt of Almighty God and disobedience of parents, God would a son should be born whose name was Chus, who, not only itself but all his posterity after him, should be so black and loathsome that it might remain a spectacle of disobedience to all the World.

And of this black and cursed Chus came all these black Moors which are in Africa, for after the water was banished from off the face of the earth, and that the land was dry, Shem chose that part of the land to inhabit in which now is called Asia, and Japheth had that which now is called Europe, wherein we dwell, and Africa remained for Cham [Ham], and his black son Chus, and was called Chamesis, after the father's name, being perhaps a cursed, dry, sandy, and unfruitful ground, fit for such a generation to inhabit in. Thus, you see that the cause of the Ethiopians' blackness is the curse and natural infection of blood, and not the distemperature of the climate, which also may be proved by this example: that these black men are found in all parts of Africa, as well without the Tropics, as within, even unto Capo d'buona Speranza Southward, where, by reason of the Sphere, should be the same temperature as is in Spain, Laddigna, and Sicilia, where all be of very good complexions. Wherefore I conclude that the blackness proceedeth not of the hotness of the Clime but, as I said, of the infection of blood, and therefore this their argument gathered of the Africans' blackness is not able to destroy the temperature of the middle Zone.

FOR ANALYSIS

1. With which explanations for black skin does Best engage? How does he evaluate each of these explanations?

2. While Best's tone is dispassionate, what are the probable effects of his argument on the treatment of these "black Moors"? Is this simply a disquisition on the facts?

ROBERT BURTON   (1577-1640)

FROM ANATOMY OF MELANCHOLY   1632

SYMPTOMS OF JEALOUSY

Of all passions . . . Love is most violent, and of those bitter potions which this
Love-Melancholy affords, this bastard jealousy is the greatest, as appears by
those prodigious Symptoms which it hath and that it produceth. For besides
Fear and *Sorrow*, which is common to all Melancholy, anxiety of mind, suspicion, aggravation, restless thoughts, paleness, meagerness, neglect of business,
and the like, these men are farther yet misaffected, and in an higher strain. 'Tis
a more vehement passion, a more furious perturbation, a bitter pain, a fire, a
pernicious curiosity, a gall corrupting the honey of our life, madness, vertigo,
plague, hell: they are more than ordinarily disquieted, they lose *bonum pacis*,[1]
as *Chrysostom*[2] observes, and though they be rich, keep sumptuous tables, be
nobly allied, yet *misserrimi omnium sunt*,[3] they are most miserable: they are
more than ordinarily discontent, more sad, . . . more than ordinarily suspicious. "Jealousy," saith Vives, "begets unquietness in the mind, night and day:
he hunts after every word he hears, every whisper, and amplifies it to himself,
(*as all melancholy men do in other matters*) with a most injust calumny of others, he misinterprets every thing [that] is said or done, most apt to mistake
or misconstrue," he pries in every corner, follows close, observes to a hair . . .
besides those strange gestures of staring, frowning, grinning, rolling of eyes,
menacing, ghastly looks, broken pace, interrupt, precipitate, half turns. He
will sometimes sigh, weep, sob for anger . . . swear and belie, slander any man,
curse, threaten, brawl, scold, fight and sometimes again flatter, and speak fair,
ask forgiveness, kiss and coll,[4] condemn his rashness and folly, vow, protest
and swear he will never do so again; and then eftsoons,[5] impatient as he is,
rave, roar, and lay about him like a mad man, thump her sides, drag her about
perchance, drive her out of doors, send her home, he will be divorced forthwith, she is a whore, &c. By and by with all submiss complement,[6] entreat her
fair, and bring her in again, he loves her dearly, she is his sweet, most kind and
loving wife, he will not change, nor leave her for a kingdom; so he continues
off and on, as the toy takes him, the object moves him, but most part brawling,
fretting, unquiet he is, accusing and suspecting not strangers only, but Brothers and Sisters, Father and Mother, nearest and dearest friends. . . .

And through fear, conceives unto himself things almost incredible and
impossible to be effected. As an Heron when she fishes, still prying on all sides;
or as a Cat doth a Mouse, his eye is never off hers, he glotes[7] on him, on her,
accurately observing on whom she looks, who looks at her, what she saith,

---

[1] The good of peace.   [2] John Chrysostom (347–407 A.D.), archbishop of Constantinople known
for his ascetic sensibilities.   [3] They are the most wretched of all.   [4] Hug.   [5] Soon after.   [6] Subtle
flattery.   [7] Looks askance.

doth, at dinner, at supper, sitting, walking, at home, abroad, he is the same, still enquiring, mandring,[8] gazing, listening, affrighted with every small object; why did she smile? Why did she pity him, commend him? Why did she drink twice to such a man? Why did she offer to kiss, to dance? &c. a whore, a whore, an arrant whore. . . . Though there be no danger at all, no cause of suspicion, she live in such a place, where *Messalina*[9] herself could not be dishonest if she would, yet he suspects her as much as if she were in a bawdy house, some Prince's Court, or in a common Inn, where all comers might have free access. He calls her on a sudden all to naught, she is a strumpet, a light huswife, a bitch, an arrant whore. No persuasion, no protestation can divert this passion, nothing can ease him, secure, or give him satisfaction. It is most strange to report what outrageous acts by men and women have been committed in this kind, by women especially, that will run after their husbands into all places, and companies. . . . But women are sufficiently curbed in such cases, the rage of men is more eminent, and frequently put in practice. See but with what rigor those jealous husbands tyrannize over their poor wives, in *Greece*, *Spain*, *Italy*, *Turkey*, *Africa*, *Asia*, and generally over all those hot countries. . . .

CURE OF JEALOUSY

I could willingly wink at Lady's faults, but that I am bound by the laws of history to tell the truth. I speak not of our times all this while, we have good, honest, virtuous men and women, whom fame, zeal, fear of God, religion and superstition contains, and yet for all that, we have too many knights of this order, so dubbed by their wives, many good women abused by dissolute husbands. In some places and such persons you may as soon enjoin them to carry water in a Sieve,[10] as to keep themselves honest. What shall a man do now in such a case? What remedy is to be had, how shall he be eased? By suing a divorce? That is hard to be affected . . . they carry the matter so cunningly, that though it be as common as Simony,[11] as clear and as manifest as the nose in a man's face, yet it cannot be evidently proved. . . . She will hardly be surprised by her husband, be he never so wary. Much better than to put it up, the more he strives in it, the more he shall divulge his own shame; make a virtue of necessity, and conceal it: Yea but the world takes notice of it, 'tis in every man's mouth, let them talk their pleasure, of whom speak they not in this sense? From the highest to the lowest they are thus censured all, there is no remedy then but patience.

FOR ANALYSIS

1. Why does Burton claim of those who are in love that "*miserrimi omnium sunt.*" What makes them so?

2. How do you read Burton's description of the jealous lover? Is it accurate? Is it cartoonish? Do you think it is supposed to be humorous?

---

[8] Grumbling.   [9] The third wife of the emperor Claudius (10 B.C.–54 A.D.). She was known for promiscuity and political manipulation.   [10] An allusion to the legend of a Roman vestal virgin who proved her chastity by carrying water in a sieve.   [11] Buying or selling church pardons or offices.

FRANCIS BACON   (1561–1626)

FROM THE ESSAYS OR COUNSELS, CIVIL AND MORAL   1625

CHAPTER 9

Of Envy

There be none of the *Affections* which have been noted to fascinate, or bewitch, but *Love* and *Envy*. They both have vehement wishes; they frame themselves readily into Imaginations and Suggestions; And they come easily into the Eye, especially upon the presence of the Objects, which are the Points that conduce to Fascination, if any such thing there be. We see, likewise, the Scripture calleth *Envy* an *Evil Eye*: and the Astrologers call the evil Influences of the Stars *Evil Aspects*; So that still there seemeth to be acknowledged in the Act of *Envy* an Ejaculation, or Irradiation of the Eye. Nay, some have been so curious as to note that the Times when the Stroke or Percussion of an *Envious Eye* doth most hurt are when the *Party envied* is beheld in Glory, or Triumph; For that sets an Edge upon *Envy*; And besides, at such times, the spirits of the *person Envied* do come forth, most into the outward Parts, and so meet the Blow. . . .

A man that hath no virtue in himself ever *envieth* Virtue in others. For Men's Minds will either feed upon their own Good or upon others' Evil; and who wanteth the one will prey upon the other; And who so is out of Hope to attain to another's Virtue will seek to come at even hand by Depressing another's Fortune.

A man that is Busy, and Inquisitive, is commonly *Envious*. Therefore, it must needs be that he taketh a kind of play-pleasure in looking upon the Fortunes of others; Neither can he that mindeth but his own Business find much matter for *Envy*. For *Envy* is a Gadding Passion, and walketh the Streets, and doth not keep home. . . .

Lastly, near Kinsfolks, and Fellows in Office, and those that have been bred together are more apt to *Envy* their Equals, when they are raised. For it doth upbraid unto them their own Fortunes; And pointeth at them, and cometh oftener into their remembrance, and incurreth likewise more into the note of others: And *Envy* ever redoubleth from Speech and Fame. *Cain's Envy* was the more vile and Malignant toward his brother *Abel* because when his Sacrifice was better accepted, there was no Body to look on. . . .

Concerning *those that are more or less subject to Envy*: First, Persons of eminent Virtue, when they are advanced, are less *envied*, for their fortune seemeth but due unto them; and no man *Envieth* the Payment of a Debt, but Rewards, and Liberality, rather. Again, *Envy* is ever joined with the Comparing of a Man's Self; And where there is no Comparison, no *Envy*; And therefore Kings are not *envied* but by Kings. . . .

Persons of Noble Blood are less *envied* in their Rising: For it seemeth but Right done to their Birth. Besides, there seemeth not much added to their Fortune; and *Envy* is as the Sunbeams that beat hotter upon a Bank or steep rising Ground than upon a flat. And for the same reason, those that are advanced by degrees are less *envied* than those that are advanced suddenly, and *per saltum*.[1]

Those that have joined with their Honor, great Travels, Cares, or Perils are less subject to *Envy*. For Men think that they earn their Honors hardly, and pity them sometimes; and *Pity* ever healeth *Envy*; Wherefore, you shall observe that the more deep and sober sort of Politic persons, in their Greatness, are ever bemoaning themselves, what a Life they lead; Chanting a *Quanta patimur*.[2] Not that they feel it so, but only to abate the Edge of *Envy*. . . . And nothing doth extinguish *Envy* more than for a great Person to preserve all other inferior Officers, in their full Rights and Preeminences of their Places, for by that means there be so many Screens between him and *Envy*.

. . . As we said in the beginning, that the Act of *Envy* had somewhat in it of *Witchcraft*; so there is no other Cure of *Envy* but the cure of *Witchcraft*. And that is to remove the *Lot* (as they call it) and to lay it upon another. For which purpose, the wiser Sort of great Persons bring in ever upon the Stage somebody upon whom to derive the *Envy* that would come upon themselves; Sometimes upon Ministers and Servants; Sometimes upon Colleagues and Associates; and the like. And for that turn, there are never wanting some Persons of violent and undertaking Natures who so they may have Power, and Business, will take it at any Cost.

Now to speak of Public *Envy*. There is yet some good in *Public Envy*; whereas in *Private*, there is none. For *Public Envy* is as an *Ostracism* that eclipseth Men when they grow too great. And therefore, it is a Bridle also to Great Ones to keep them within Bounds.

This *Envy*, being in the Latin word *Invidia*, goeth in the Modern languages by the name of *Discontentment*; Of which we shall speak in handling *Sedition*. It is a disease, in a State, like to Infection. For as Infection spreadeth upon that which is sound and tainteth it; So when envy is gotten once into a State, it traduceth[3] even the best Actions thereof and turneth them into an ill Odor. . . .

We will add this, in general, touching the Affection of *Envy*, that of all other Affections, it is the most importune and continual. For of other *Affections*, there is occasion given but now and then. And therefore, it was well said, *Invidia festos dies non agit*.[4] For it is ever working upon some or other. And it is also noted that *Love* and *Envy* do make a man pine, which other Affections do not, because they are not so continual. It is also the vilest Affection, and the most depraved; For which cause, it is the proper Attribute of the Devil, who is called *The Envious Man, that soweth tares amongst wheat by night.* As it always cometh to pass that *Envy* worketh subtly and in the dark; And to the prejudice of good things, such as is the *Wheat*.

---

[1] In one fell swoop.   [2] How much we suffer.   [3] Changes perverts.   [4] Envy takes no holidays.

FOR ANALYSIS

1. According to Bacon, does the existence of envy depend entirely on the envious party? Can the envied individual bear responsibility too?

2. How does Bacon connect envy and witchcraft?

MAKING CONNECTIONS

1. How do these different writers think about the effects of the passions? Do the passions affect only the individual in whom they work? Do they affect others? How do their ideas illuminate Othello's actions? Do they help you think about others' actions, too?

2. How does Best's attempt to understand the cause for the difference in complexion help you understand *Othello*? What might it say about how Othello is seen by other characters and even by himself? Do you think Shakespeare expresses any of his own ideas about the phenomenon of race in his play, or is he simply repeating the ideas expressed by people of his time and place?

3. How do these four perspectives on love, race, and gender in the Renaissance help you understand Desdemona? Do they help you think more or differently about her motivations, about how she sees the world or how the world sees her?

WRITING TOPICS

1. Write an analysis of the **figurative language** in Iago's soliloquies at the end of act I and at the end of act II, scene 1.

2. Choose a minor character, such as Roderigo, Emilia, or Bianca, and in a carefully reasoned essay, explain how the character contributes to the design of the play.

3. Discuss the relationship between love and hate in this **tragedy**.

SUSAN GLASPELL   (1882–1948)

TRIFLES   1916

CHARACTERS

George Henderson, county
  attorney
Henry Peters, sheriff

Lewis Hale, a neighboring farmer
Mrs. Peters
Mrs. Hale

Scene
The kitchen in the now abandoned farmhouse of John Wright, a gloomy kitchen, and left without having been put in order—the walls covered with a faded wall paper. Down right is a door leading to the parlor. On the right wall above this door is a built-in kitchen cupboard with shelves in the upper portion and drawers below. In the rear wall at right, up two steps is a door opening onto stairs leading to the second floor. In the rear wall at left is a door to the shed and from there to the outside. Between these two doors is an old-fashioned black iron stove. Running along the left wall from the shed door is an old iron sink and sink shelf, in which is set a hand pump. Down-stage of the sink is an uncurtained window. Near the window is an old wooden rocker. Center stage is an unpainted wooden kitchen table with straight chairs on either side. There is a small chair down right. Unwashed pans under the sink, a loaf of bread outside the breadbox, a dish towel on the table—other signs of incompleted work. At the rear the shed door opens and the Sheriff comes in followed by the County Attorney and Hale. The Sheriff and Hale are men in middle life, the County Attorney is a young man; all are much bundled up and go at once to the stove. They are followed by the two women—the Sheriff's wife, Mrs. Peters, first; she is a slightly wiry woman, with a thin nervous face. Mrs. Hale is larger and would ordinarily be called more comfortable looking, but she is disturbed now and looks fearfully about as she enters. The women have come in slowly, and stand close together near the door.

County Attorney (*at stove rubbing his hands*). This feels good. Come up to the
  fire, ladies.
Mrs. Peters (*after taking a step forward*). I'm not—cold.
Sheriff (*unbuttoning his overcoat and stepping away from the stove to right of table
  as if to mark the beginning of official business*). Now, Mr. Hale, before we move
  things about, you explain to Mr. Henderson just what you saw when you came
  here yesterday morning.
County Attorney (*crossing down to left of the table*). By the way, has anything been
  moved? Are things just as you left them yesterday?
Sheriff (*looking about*). It's just about the same. When it dropped below zero last
  night I thought I'd better send Frank out this morning to make a fire for us—
  (*sits right of center table*) no use getting pneumonia with a big case on, but I told
  him not to touch anything except the stove—and you know Frank.

County Attorney. Somebody should have been left here yesterday.

Sheriff. Oh—yesterday. When I had to send Frank to Morris Center for that man who went crazy—I want you to know I had my hands full yesterday. I knew you could get back from Omaha by today and as long as I went over everything here myself—

County Attorney. Well, Mr. Hale, tell just what happened when you came here yesterday morning.

Hale (*crossing down to above table*). Harry and I started to town with a load of potatoes. We came along the road from my place and as I got here I said, "I'm going to see if I can't get John Wright to go in with me on a party telephone." I spoke to Wright about it once before and he put me off, saying folks talked too much anyway, and all he asked was peace and quiet—I guess you know about how much he talked himself; but I thought maybe if I went to the house and talked about it before his wife, though I said to Harry that I didn't know as what his wife wanted made much difference to John———

County Attorney. Let's talk about that later, Mr. Hale. I do want to talk about that, but tell now just what happened when you got to the house.

Hale. I didn't hear or see anything; I knocked at the door, and still it was all quiet inside. I knew they must be up, it was past eight o'clock. So I knocked again, and I thought I heard somebody say, "Come in." I wasn't sure. I'm not sure yet, but I opened the door—this door (*indicating the door by which the two women are still standing*) and there in that rocker—(*pointing at it*) sat Mrs. Wright. (*They all look at the rocker down left.*)

County Attorney. What—was she doing?

Hale. She was rockin' back and forth. She had her apron in her hand and was kind of—pleating it.

County Attorney. And how did she—look?

Hale. Well, she looked queer.

County Attorney. How do you mean—queer?

Hale. Well, as if she didn't know what she was going to do next. And kind of done up.

County Attorney (*takes out notebook and pencil and sits left of center table*). How did she seem to feel about your coming?

Hale. Why, I don't think she minded—one way or another. She didn't pay much attention. I said, "How do, Mrs. Wright, it's cold, ain't it?" And she said, "Is it?"—and went on kind of pleating at her apron. Well, I was surprised; she didn't ask me to come up to the stove, or to set down, but just sat there, not even looking at me, so I said, "I want to see John." And then she—laughed. I guess you would call it a laugh. I thought of Harry and the team outside, so I said a little sharp: "Can't I see John?" "No," she says, kind o' dull like. "Ain't he home?" says I. "Yes," says she, "he's home." "Then why can't I see him?" I asked her, out of patience. " 'Cause he's dead," says she. "*Dead?*" says I. She just nodded her head, not getting a bit excited, but rockin' back and forth. "Why— where is he?" says I, not knowing what to say. She just pointed upstairs—like that. (*Himself pointing to the room above.*) I started for the stairs, with the idea of going up there. I walked from there to here—then I says, "Why, what did he die of?" "He died of a rope round his neck," says she, and just went on, pleatin' at her apron. Well, I went out and called Harry. I thought I might—need help. We went upstairs and there he was lyin'————

County Attorney. I think I'd rather have you go into that upstairs, where you can point it all out. Just go on now with the rest of the story.

Hale. Well, my first thought was to get that rope off. It looked . . . (stops; his face twitches) . . . but Harry, he went up to him, and he said, "No, he's dead all right, and we'd better not touch anything." So we went back downstairs. She was still sitting that same way. "Has anybody been notified?" I asked. "No," says she, unconcerned. "Who did this, Mrs. Wright?" said Harry. He said it business-like—and she stopped pleatin' of her apron. "I don't know," she says. "You don't *know*?" says Harry. "No," says she. "Weren't you sleepin' in the bed with him?" says Harry. "Yes," says she, "but I was on the inside." "Somebody slipped a rope round his neck and strangled him and you didn't wake up?" says Harry. "I didn't wake up," she said after him. We must 'a' looked as if we didn't see how that could be, for after a minute she said, "I sleep sound." Harry was going to ask her more questions but I said maybe we ought to let her tell her story first to the coroner, or the sheriff, so Harry went fast as he could to Rivers' place, where there's a telephone.

County Attorney. And what did Mrs. Wright do when she knew that you had gone for the coroner?

Hale. She moved from the rocker to that chair over there (pointing to a small chair in the down right corner) and just sat there with her hands held together and looking down. I got a feeling that I ought to make some conversation, so I said I had come in to see if John wanted to put in a telephone, and at that she started to laugh, and then she stopped and looked at me—scared. (The County Attorney, who has had his notebook out, makes a note.) I dunno, maybe it wasn't scared. I wouldn't like to say it was. Soon Harry got back, and then Dr. Lloyd came and you, Mr. Peters, and so I guess that's all I know that you don't.

County Attorney (rising and looking around). I guess we'll go upstairs first—and then out to the barn and around there. (To the Sheriff.) You're convinced that there was nothing important here—nothing that would point to any motive?

Sheriff. Nothing here but kitchen things.

(The County Attorney, after again looking around the kitchen, opens the door of a cupboard closet in right wall. He brings a small chair from right—gets on it and looks on a shelf. Pulls his hand away, sticky.)

County Attorney. Here's a nice mess. (The women draw nearer up center.)

Mrs. Peters (to the other woman). Oh, her fruit; it did freeze. (To the Lawyer.) She worried about that when it turned so cold. She said the fire'd go out and her jars would break.

Sheriff (*rises*). Well, can you beat the woman! Held for murder and worryin' about her preserves.

County Attorney (*getting down from chair*). I guess before we're through she may have something more serious than preserves to worry about. (*Crosses down right center.*)

Hale. Well, women are used to worrying over trifles. (*The two women move a little closer together.*)

County Attorney (*with the gallantry of a young politician*). And yet, for all their worries, what would we do without the ladies? (*The women do not unbend. He goes below the center table to the sink, takes a dipperful of water from the pail, and pouring it into a basin, washes his hands. While he is doing this the Sheriff and Hale cross to cupboard, which they inspect. The County Attorney starts to wipe his hands on the roller towel, turns it for a cleaner place.*) Dirty towels! (*Kicks his foot against the pans under the sink.*) Not much of a housekeeper, would you say, ladies?

Mrs. Hale (*stiffly*). There's a great deal of work to be done on a farm.

County Attorney. To be sure. And yet (*with a little bow to her*) I know there are some Dickson County farmhouses which do not have such roller towels.

(*He gives it a pull to expose its full length again.*)

Mrs. Hale. Those towels get dirty awful quick. Men's hands aren't always as clean as they might be.

County Attorney. Ah, loyal to your sex, I see. But you and Mrs. Wright were neighbors. I suppose you were friends, too.

Mrs. Hale (*shaking her head*). I've not seen much of her of late years. I've not been in this house—it's more than a year.

County Attorney (*crossing to women up center*). And why was that? You didn't like her?

Mrs. Hale. I liked her all well enough. Farmers' wives have their hands full, Mr. Henderson. And then———

County Attorney. Yes——— ?

Mrs. Hale (*looking about*). It never seemed a very cheerful place.

County Attorney. No—it's not cheerful. I shouldn't say she had the homemaking instinct.

Mrs. Hale. Well, I don't know as Wright had, either.

County Attorney. You mean that they didn't get on very well?

Mrs. Hale. No, I don't mean anything. But I don't think a place'd be any cheerfuller for John Wright's being in it.

County Attorney. I'd like to talk more of that a little later. I want to get the lay of things upstairs now.

(*He goes past the women to up right where steps lead to a stair door.*)

Sheriff. I suppose anything Mrs. Peters does'll be all right. She was to take in some clothes for her, you know, and a few little things. We left in such a hurry, yesterday.

County Attorney. Yes, but I would like to see what you take, Mrs. Peters, and keep an eye out for anything that might be of use to us.

Mrs. Peters. Yes, Mr. Henderson.

(The men leave by up right door to stairs. The women listen to the men's steps on the stairs, then look about the kitchen.)

Mrs. Hale *(crossing left to sink).* I'd hate to have men coming into my kitchen, snooping around and criticizing.

(She arranges the pans under sink which the Lawyer had shoved out of place.)

Mrs. Peters. Of course it's no more than their duty.

(Crosses to cupboard up right.)

Mrs. Hale. Duty's all right, but I guess that deputy sheriff that came out to make the fire might have got a little of this on. *(Gives the roller towel a pull.)* Wish I'd thought of that sooner. Seems mean to talk about her for not having things slicked up when she had to come away in such a hurry.

(Crosses right to Mrs. Peters at cupboard.)

Mrs. Peters *(who has been looking through cupboard, lifts one end of towel that covers a pan).* She had bread set.

(Stands still.)

Mrs. Hale *(eyes fixed on a loaf of bread beside the breadbox, which is on a low shelf of the cupboard).* She was going to put this in there. *(Picks up a loaf, abruptly drops it. In a manner of returning to familiar things.)* It's a shame about her fruit. I wonder if it's all gone. *(Gets up on the chair and looks.)* I think there's some here that's all right, Mrs. Peters. Yes—here; *(holding it toward the window)* this is cherries, too. *(Looking again.)* I declare I believe that's the only one. *(Gets down, jar in her hand. Goes to the sink and wipes it off on the outside.)* She'll feel awful bad after all her hard work in the hot weather. I remember the afternoon I put up my cherries last summer.

(She puts the jar on the big kitchen table, center of the room. With a sigh, is about to sit down in the rocking chair. Before she is seated realizes what chair it is; with a slow look at it, steps back. The chair which she has touched rocks back and forth. Mrs. Peters moves to center table and they both watch the chair rock for a moment or two.)

Mrs. Peters (*shaking off the mood which the empty rocking chair has evoked. Now in a businesslike manner she speaks*). Well I must get those things from the front room closet. (*She goes to the door at the right but, after looking into the other room, steps back.*) You coming with me, Mrs. Hale? You could help me carry them. (*They go in the other room; reappear, Mrs. Peters carrying a dress, petticoat, and skirt, Mrs. Hale following with a pair of shoes.*) My, it's cold in there.

(*She puts the clothes on the big table and hurries to the stove.*)

Mrs. Hale (*right of center table examining the skirt*). Wright was close. I think maybe that's why she kept so much to herself. She didn't even belong to the Ladies' Aid. I suppose she felt she couldn't do her part, and then you don't enjoy things when you feel shabby. I heard she used to wear pretty clothes and be lively, when she was Minnie Foster, one of the town girls singing in the choir. But that—oh, that was thirty years ago. This all you want to take in?

Mrs. Peters. She said she wanted an apron. Funny thing to want, for there isn't much to get you dirty in jail, goodness knows. But I suppose just to make her feel more natural. (*Crosses to cupboard.*) She said they was in the top drawer in this cupboard. Yes, here. And then her little shawl that always hung behind the door. (*Opens stair door and looks.*) Yes, here it is.

(*Quickly shuts door leading upstairs.*)

Mrs. Hale (*abruptly moving toward her*). Mrs. Peters?
Mrs. Peters. Yes, Mrs. Hale?

(*At up right door.*)

Mrs. Hale. Do you think she did it?
Mrs. Peters (*in a frightened voice*). Oh, I don't know.
Mrs. Hale. Well, I don't think she did. Asking for an apron and her little shawl. Worrying about her fruit.
Mrs. Peters (*starts to speak, glances up, where footsteps are heard in the room above. In a low voice*). Mr. Peters says it looks bad for her. Mr. Henderson is awful sarcastic in a speech and he'll make fun of her sayin' she didn't wake up.
Mrs. Hale. Well, I guess John Wright didn't wake when they was slipping that rope under his neck.
Mrs. Peters (*crossing slowly to table and placing shawl and apron on table with other clothing*). No, it's strange. It must have been done awful crafty and still. They say it was such a—funny way to kill a man, rigging it all up like that.
Mrs. Hale (*crossing to left of Mrs. Peters at table*). That's just what Mr. Hale said. There was a gun in the house. He says that's what he can't understand.
Mrs. Peters. Mr. Henderson said coming out that what was needed for the case was a motive; something to show anger, or—sudden feeling.

Mrs. Hale (*who is standing by the table*). Well, I don't see any signs of anger around
here. (*She puts her hand on the dish towel, which lies on the table, stands looking
down at table, one-half of which is clean, the other half messy.*) It's wiped to here.
(*Makes a move as if to finish work, then turns and looks at loaf of bread outside the
breadbox. Drops towel. In that voice of coming back to familiar things.*) Wonder
how they are finding things upstairs. (*Crossing below table to down right.*) I hope
she had it a little more red-up[1] up there. You know, it seems kind of *sneaking*.
Locking her up in town and then coming out here and trying to get her own
house to turn against her!

Mrs. Peters. But, Mrs. Hale, the law is the law.

Mrs. Hale. I s'pose 'tis. (*Unbuttoning her coat.*) Better loosen up your things, Mrs.
Peters. You won't feel them when you go out.

(*Mrs. Peters takes off her fur tippet, goes to hang it on chair back left of table, stands
looking at the work basket on floor near down left window.*)

Mrs. Peters. She was piecing a quilt.

(*She brings the large sewing basket to the center table and they look at the bright
pieces, Mrs. Hale above the table and Mrs. Peters left of it.*)

Mrs. Hale. It's a log cabin pattern. Pretty, isn't it? I wonder if she was goin' to
quilt it or just knot it?

(*Footsteps have been heard coming down the stairs. The Sheriff enters followed by
Hale and the County Attorney.*)

Sheriff. They wonder if she was going to quilt it or just knot it!

(*The men laugh, the women look abashed.*)

County Attorney (*rubbing his hands over the stove*). Frank's fire didn't do much
up there, did it? Well, let's go out to the barn and get that cleared up.

(*The men go outside by up left door.*)

Mrs. Hale (*resentfully*). I don't know as there's anything so strange, our takin'
up our time with little things while we're waiting for them to get the evidence.
(*She sits in chair right of table smoothing out a block with decision.*) I don't see as
it's anything to laugh about.

Mrs. Peters (*apologetically*). Of course they've got awful important things on
their minds.

(*Pulls up a chair and joins Mrs. Hale at the left of the table.*)

---

[1] A slang expression for "make attractive."

Mrs. Hale (*examining another block*). Mrs. Peters, look at this one. Here, this is the one she was working on, and look at the sewing! All the rest of it has been so nice and even. And look at this! It's all over the place! Why, it looks as if she didn't know what she was about!

(*After she has said this they look at each other, then start to glance back at the door. After an instant Mrs. Hale has pulled at a knot and ripped the sewing.*)

Mrs. Peters. Oh, what are you doing, Mrs. Hale?

Mrs. Hale (*mildly*). Just pulling out a stitch or two that's not sewed very good. (*Threading a needle.*) Bad sewing always made me fidgety.

Mrs. Peters (*with a glance at door, nervously*). I don't think we ought to touch things.

Mrs. Hale. I'll just finish up this end. (*Suddenly stopping and leaning forward.*) Mrs. Peters?

Mrs. Peters. Yes, Mrs. Hale?

Mrs. Hale. What do you suppose she was so nervous about?

Mrs. Peters. Oh—I don't know. I don't know as she was nervous. I sometimes sew awful queer when I'm just tired. (*Mrs. Hale starts to say something, looks at Mrs. Peters, then goes on sewing.*) Well, I must get these things wrapped up. They may be through sooner than we think. (*Putting apron and other things together.*) I wonder where I can find a piece of paper, and string.

(*Rises.*)

Mrs. Hale. In that cupboard, maybe.

Mrs. Peters (*crosses right looking in cupboard*). Why, here's a bird-cage. (*Holds it up.*) Did she have a bird, Mrs. Hale?

Mrs. Hale. Why, I don't know whether she did or not—I've not been here for so long. There was a man around last year selling canaries cheap, but I don't know as she took one; maybe she did. She used to sing real pretty herself.

Mrs. Peters (*glancing around*). Seems funny to think of a bird here. But she must have had one, or why would she have a cage? I wonder what happened to it?

Mrs. Hale. I s'pose maybe the cat got it.

Mrs. Peters. No, she didn't have a cat. She's got that feeling some people have about cats—being afraid of them. My cat got in her room and she was real upset and asked me to take it out.

Mrs. Hale. My sister Bessie was like that. Queer, ain't it?

Mrs. Peters (*examining the cage*). Why, look at this door. It's broke. One hinge is pulled apart.

(*Takes a step down to Mrs. Hale's right.*)

Mrs. Hale (*looking too*). Looks as if someone must have been rough with it.

Mrs. Peters. Why, yes.

(She brings the cage forward and puts it on the table.)

Mrs. Hale *(glancing toward up left door).* I wish if they're going to find any evidence they'd be about it. I don't like this place.

Mrs. Peters. But I'm awful glad you came with me, Mrs. Hale. It would be lonesome for me sitting here alone.

Mrs. Hale. It would, wouldn't it? *(Dropping her sewing.)* But I tell you what I do wish, Mrs. Peters. I wish I had come over sometimes when *she* was here. I—*(looking around the room)*—wish I had.

Mrs. Peters. But of course you were awful busy, Mrs. Hale—your house and your children.

Mrs. Hale *(rises and crosses left).* I could've come. I stayed away because it weren't cheerful—and that's why I ought to have come. I—*(looking out left window)*—I've never liked this place. Maybe because it's down in a hollow and you don't see the road. I dunno what it is, but it's a lonesome place and always was. I wish I had come over to see Minnie Foster sometimes. I can see now—

(Shakes her head.)

Mrs. Peters *(left of table and above it).* Well, you mustn't reproach yourself, Mrs. Hale. Somehow we just don't see how it is with other folks until—something turns up.

Mrs. Hale. Not having children makes less work—but it makes a quiet house, and Wright out to work all day, and no company when he did come in. *(Turning from window.)* Did you know John Wright, Mrs. Peters?

Mrs. Peters. Not to know him; I've seen him in town. They say he was a good man.

Mrs. Hale. Yes—good; he didn't drink, and kept his word as well as most, I guess, and paid his debts. But he was a hard man, Mrs. Peters. Just to pass the time of day with him—*(Shivers.)* Like a raw wind that gets to the bone. *(Pauses, her eye falling on the cage.)* I should think she would 'a' wanted a bird. But what do you suppose went with it?

Mrs. Peters. I don't know, unless it got sick and died.

(She reaches over and swings the broken door, swings it again, both women watch it.)

Mrs. Hale. You weren't raised round here, were you? *(Mrs. Peters shakes her head.)* You didn't know—her?

Mrs. Peters. Not till they brought her yesterday.

Mrs. Hale. She—come to think of it, she was kind of like a bird herself—real sweet and pretty, but kind of timid and—fluttery. How—she—did—change. *(Silence: then as if struck by a happy thought and relieved to get back to everyday things. Crosses right above Mrs. Peters to cupboard, replaces small chair used to stand on to its original place down right.)* Tell you what, Mrs. Peters, why don't you take the quilt in with you? It might take up her mind.

Mrs. Peters. Why, I think that's a real nice idea, Mrs. Hale. There couldn't possibly be any objection to it could there? Now, just what would I take? I wonder if her patches are in here—and her things.

(They look in the sewing basket.)

Mrs. Hale *(crosses to right of table).* Here's some red. I expect this has got sewing things in it. *(Brings out a fancy box.)* What a pretty box. Looks like something somebody would give you. Maybe her scissors are in here. *(Opens box. Suddenly puts her hand to her nose.)* Why———*(Mrs. Peters bends nearer, then turns her face away.)* There's something wrapped up in this piece of silk.

Mrs. Peters. Why, this isn't her scissors.

Mrs. Hale *(lifting the silk).* Oh, Mrs. Peters—it's———

(Mrs. Peters bends closer.)

Mrs. Peters. It's the bird.

Mrs. Hale. But, Mrs. Peters—look at it! Its neck! Look at its neck! It's all—other side *to.*

Mrs. Peters. Somebody—wrung—its—neck.

(Their eyes meet. A look of growing comprehension, of horror. Steps are heard outside. Mrs. Hale slips box under quilt pieces, and sinks into her chair. Enter Sheriff and County Attorney. Mrs. Peters steps down left and stands looking out of window.)

County Attorney *(as one turning from serious things to little pleasantries).* Well, ladies, have you decided whether she was going to quilt it or knot it?

(Crosses to center above table.)

Mrs. Peters. We think she was going to—knot it.

(Sheriff crosses to right of stove, lifts stove lid, and glances at fire, then stands warming hands at stove.)

County Attorney. Well, that's interesting, I'm sure. *(Seeing the bird-cage.)* Has the bird flown?

Mrs. Hale *(putting more quilt pieces over the box).* We think the—cat got it.

County Attorney *(preoccupied).* Is there a cat?

(Mrs. Hale glances in a quick covert way at Mrs. Peters.)

Mrs. Peters (*turning from window takes a step in*). Well, not *now*. They're superstitious, you know. They leave.

County Attorney (*to Sheriff Peters, continuing an interrupted conversation*). No sign at all of anyone having come from the outside. Their own rope. Now let's go up again and go over it piece by piece. (*They start upstairs.*) It would have to have been someone who knew just the——

(*Mrs. Peters sits down left of table. The two women sit there not looking at one another, but as if peering into something and at the same time holding back. When they talk now it is in the manner of feeling their way over strange ground, as if afraid of what they are saying, but as if they cannot help saying it.*)

Mrs. Hale (*hesitatively and in hushed voice*). She liked the bird. She was going to bury it in that pretty box.

Mrs. Peters (*in a whisper*). When I was a girl—my kitten—there was a boy took a hatchet, and before my eyes—and before I could get there—— (*Covers her face an instant.*) If they hadn't held me back I would have—(*catches herself, looks upstairs where steps are heard, falters weakly*)—hurt him.

Mrs. Hale (*with a slow look around her*). I wonder how it would seem never to have had any children around. (*Pause.*) No, Wright wouldn't like the bird—a thing that sang. She used to sing. He killed that, too.

Mrs. Peters (*moving uneasily*). We don't know who killed the bird.

Mrs. Hale. I knew John Wright.

Mrs. Peters. It was an awful thing was done in this house that night, Mrs. Hale. Killing a man while he slept, slipping a rope around his neck that choked the life out of him.

Mrs. Hale. His neck. Choked the life out of him.

(*Her hand goes out and rests on the bird-cage.*)

Mrs. Peters (*with rising voice*). We don't know who killed him. We don't *know*.

Mrs. Hale (*her own feeling not interrupted*). If there'd been years and years of nothing, then a bird to sing to you, it would be awful—still, after the bird was still.

Mrs. Peters (*something within her speaking*). I know what stillness is. When we homesteaded in Dakota, and my first baby died—after he was two years old, and me with no other then——

Mrs. Hale (*moving*). How soon do you suppose they'll be through looking for the evidence?

Mrs. Peters. I know what stillness is. (*Pulling herself back.*) The law has got to punish crime, Mrs. Hale.

Mrs. Hale (*not as if answering that*). I wish you'd seen Minnie Foster when she wore a white dress with blue ribbons and stood up there in the choir and sang. (*A look around the room.*) Oh, I *wish* I'd come over here once in a while! That was a crime! That was a crime! Who's going to punish that?

Mrs. Peters (*looking upstairs*). We mustn't—take on.

Mrs. Hale. I might have known she needed help! I know how things can be—for women. I tell you, it's queer, Mrs. Peters. We live close together and we live far apart. We all go through the same things—it's all just a different kind of the same thing. *(Brushes her eyes, noticing the jar of fruit, reaches out for it.)* If I was you I wouldn't tell her her fruit was gone. Tell her it *ain't.* Tell her it's all right. Take this in to prove it to her. She—she may never know whether it was broke or not.

Mrs. Peters *(takes the jar, looks about for something to wrap it in; takes petticoat from the clothes brought from the other room, very nervously begins winding this around the jar. In a false voice).* My, it's a good thing the men couldn't hear us. Wouldn't they just laugh! Getting all stirred up over a little thing like a— dead canary. As if that could have anything to do with—with—wouldn't they laugh!

(The men are heard coming downstairs.)

Mrs. Hale *(under her breath).* Maybe they would—maybe they wouldn't.

County Attorney. No, Peters, it's all perfectly clear except a reason for doing it. But you know juries when it comes to women. If there was some definite thing. *(Crosses slowly to above table. Sheriff crosses down right. Mrs. Hale and Mrs. Peters remain seated at either side of table.)* Something to show—something to make a story about—a thing that would connect up with this strange way of doing it———

(The women's eyes meet for an instant. Enter Hale from outer door.)

Hale *(remaining by door).* Well, I've got the team around. Pretty cold out there.

County Attorney. I'm going to stay awhile by myself. *(To the Sheriff.)* You can send Frank out for me, can't you? I want to go over everything. I'm not satisfied that we can't do better.

Sheriff. Do you want to see what Mrs. Peters is going to take in?

(The Lawyer picks up the apron, laughs.)

County Attorney. Oh, I guess they're not very dangerous things the ladies have picked out. *(Moves a few things about, disturbing the quilt pieces which cover the box. Steps back.)* No, Mrs. Peters doesn't need supervising. For that matter a sheriff's wife is married to the law. Ever think of it that way, Mrs. Peters?

Mrs. Peters. Not—just that way.

Sheriff *(chuckling).* Married to the law. *(Moves to down right door to the other room.)* I just want you to come in here a minute, George. We ought to take a look at these windows.

County Attorney *(scoffingly).* Oh, windows!

Sheriff. We'll be right out, Mr. Hale.

(Hale goes outside. The Sheriff follows the County Attorney into the room. Then Mrs. Hale rises, hands tight together, looking intensely at Mrs. Peters, whose eyes make a slow turn, finally meeting Mrs. Hale's. A moment Mrs. Hale holds her, then her own eyes point the way to where the box is concealed. Suddenly Mrs. Peters throws back quilt pieces and tries to put the box in the bag she is carrying. It is too big. She opens box, starts to take bird out, cannot touch it, goes to pieces, stands there helpless. Sound of a knob turning in the other room. Mrs. Hale snatches the box and puts it in the pocket of her big coat. Enter County Attorney and Sheriff, who remain down right.)

County Attorney *(crosses to up left door facetiously)*. Well, Henry, at least we found out that she was not going to quilt it. She was going to—what is it you call it, ladies?

Mrs. Hale *(standing center below table facing front, her hand against her pocket)*. We call it—knot it, Mr. Henderson.

Curtain.

FOR ANALYSIS

1. What is the meaning of the title? Glaspell titled a short-story version of the play "A Jury of Her Peers." Is that a better title than *Trifles*? Explain.

2. What are the major differences between Mrs. Hale and Mrs. Peters?

3. At one point, Mrs. Peters tells Mrs. Hale a childhood story about a boy who killed her kitten. Why is she reminded of this event? What does it tell us about her reaction to the Wrights' marriage?

4. Which of the two women undergoes the most noticeable character development? Explain.

5. In what ways do the relationships between the two couples—Mrs. Hale and Mrs. Peters, and Henry Peters and Lewis Hale—change by the end of the play?

6. Do Henry Peters and Lewis Hale change in the course of the play?

7. Why are the men unable to see the clues that become obvious to the women?

8. Can you suggest why Mrs. Wright is the only one identified by her birth name?

MAKING CONNECTIONS

1. What similarities in attitudes toward women do you find in this play and in Ibsen's *A Doll's House* (p. 228)?

2. Do you think it is fair to say that Mrs. Wright in this play and the **narrator** in Gilman's "The Yellow Wallpaper" (p. 551) are people whose lives have been blighted by a patriarchal society that confines women to narrow, stereotypical roles? Explain.

WRITING TOPICS

1. Show how the discussion of Mrs. Wright's quilt embodies the major **themes** of *Trifles*.

2. Argue for or against the proposition that Mrs. Hale and Mrs. Peters are morally obligated to tell the county attorney what they know about the murder.

LYNN NOTTAGE (B. 1964)

POOF! 1993

CHARACTERS

Samuel, Loureen's husband
Loureen, a demure housewife, early thirties
Florence, Loureen's best friend, early thirties

Time: *The present*

Place: *Kitchen*

A Note: *Nearly half the women on death row in the United States were convicted of killing abusive husbands. Spontaneous combustion is not recognized as a capital crime.*

Darkness.

Samuel *(In the darkness).* WHEN I COUNT TO TEN I DON' WANT TO SEE YA! I DON' WANT TO HEAR YA! ONE, TWO, THREE, FOUR—
Loureen *(In the darkness).* DAMN YOU TO HELL, SAMUEL!

A bright flash.
  Lights rise. A huge pile of smoking ashes rests in the middle of the kitchen. Loureen, a demure housewife in her early thirties, stares down at the ashes incredulously. She bends and lifts a pair of spectacles from the remains. She ever so slowly backs away.

  Samuel? Uh! *(Places the spectacles on the kitchen table)* Uh! . . . Samuel? *(Looks around)* Don't fool with me now. I'm not in the mood. *(Whispers)* Samuel? I didn't mean it really. I'll be good if you come back . . . Come on now, dinner's waiting. *(Chuckles, then stops abruptly)* Now stop your foolishness . . . And let's sit down. *(Examines the spectacles)* Uh! *(Softly)* Don't be cross with me. Sure I forgot to pick up your shirt for tomorrow. I can wash another, I'll do it right now. Right now! Sam? . . . *(Cautiously)* You hear me! *(Awaits a response)* Maybe I didn't ever intend to wash your shirt. *(Pulls back as though about to receive a blow; a moment)* Uh! *(Sits down and dials the telephone)* Florence, honey, could you come on down for a moment. There's been a . . . little . . . accident . . . Quickly please. Uh!

Loureen hangs up the phone. She gets a broom and a dust pan. She hesitantly approaches the pile of ashes. She gets down on her hands and knees and takes a closer

1063

look. A fatuous grin spreads across her face. She is startled by a sudden knock on the door. She slowly walks across the room like a possessed child. Loureen lets in Florence, her best friend and upstairs neighbor. Florence, also a housewife in her early thirties, wears a floral housecoat and a pair of oversized slippers. Without acknowledgment Loureen proceeds to saunter back across the room.

Florence. HEY!

Loureen *(Pointing at the ashes)*. Uh! . . . *(She struggles to formulate words, which press at the inside of her mouth, not quite realized)* Uh! . . .

Florence. You all right? What happened? *(Sniffs the air)* Smells like you burned something? *(Stares at the huge pile of ashes)* What the devil is that?

Loureen *(Hushed)*. Samuel . . . It's Samuel, I think.

Florence. What's he done now?

Loureen. It's him. It's him. *(Nods her head repeatedly)*

Florence. Chile, what's wrong with you? Did he finally drive you out your mind? I knew something was going to happen sooner or later.

Loureen. Dial 911, Florence!

Florence. Why? You're scaring me!

Loureen. Dial 911!

Florence picks up the telephone and quickly dials.

I think I killed him.

Florence hangs up the telephone.

Florence. What?

Loureen *(Whimpers)*. I killed him! I killed Samuel!

Florence. Come again? . . . He's dead dead?

Loureen wrings her hands and nods her head twice, mouthing "dead dead." Florence backs away.

No, stop it, I don't have time for this. I'm going back upstairs. You know how Samuel hates to find me here when he gets home. You're not going to get me this time. *(Louder)* Y'all can have your little joke, I'm not part of it! *(A moment. She takes a hard look into Loureen's eyes; she squints)* Did you really do it this time?

Loureen *(Hushed)*. I don't know how or why it happened, it just did.

Florence. Why are you whispering?

Loureen. I don't want to talk too loud—something else is liable to disappear.

Florence. Where's his body?

Loureen *(Points to the pile of ashes)*. There! . . .

Florence. You burned him?

Loureen. I DON'T KNOW! *(Covers her mouth as if to muffle her words; hushed)* I think so.

Florence. Either you did or you didn't, what you mean you don't know? We're talking murder, Loureen, not oven settings.

Loureen. You think I'm playing?

Florence. How many times have I heard you talk about being rid of him. How many times have we sat at this very table and laughed about the many ways we could do it and how many times have you done it? None.

Loureen (*Lifting the spectacles*). A pair of cheap spectacles, that's all that's left. And you know how much I hate these. You ever seen him without them, no! . . . He counted to four and disappeared. I swear to God!

Florence. Don't bring the Lord into this just yet! Sit down now . . . What you got to sip on?

Loureen. I don't know whether to have a stiff shot of scotch or a glass of champagne.

Florence takes a bottle of sherry out of the cupboard and pours them each a glass. Loureen downs hers, then holds out her glass for more.

He was . . .

Florence. Take your time.

Loureen. Standing there.

Florence. And?

Loureen. He exploded.

Florence. Did that muthafucka hit you again?

Loureen. No . . . he exploded. Boom! Right in front of me. He was shouting like he does, being all colored, then he raised up that big crusty hand to hit me, and poof, he was gone . . . I barely got words out and I'm looking down at a pile of ash.

Florence belts back her sherry. She wipes her forehead and pours them both another.

Florence. Chile, I'll give you this, in terms of color you've matched my husband Edgar, the story king. He came in at six Sunday morning, talking about he'd hit someone with his car, and had spent all night trying to outrun the police. I felt sorry for him. It turns out he was playing poker with his paycheck no less. You don't want to know how I found out . . . But I did.

Loureen. You think I'm lying?

Florence. I certainly hope so, Loureen. For your sake and my heart's.

Loureen. Samuel always said if I raised my voice something horrible would happen. And it did. I'm a witch . . . the devil spawn!

Florence. You've been watching too much television.

Loureen. Never seen anything like this on television. Wish I had, then I'd know what to do . . . There's no question, I'm a witch. (*Looks at her hands with disgust*)

Florence. Chile, don't tell me you've been messing with them mojo women again? What did I tell ya.

Loureen, agitated, stands and sits back down.

Loureen. He's not coming back. Oh no, how could he? It would be a miracle! Two in one day . . . I could be canonized. Worse yet, he could be . . . All that needs to happen now is for my palms to bleed and I'll be eternally remembered as Saint Loureen, the patron of battered wives. Women from across the country will make pilgrimages to me, laying pies and pot roast at my feet and asking the good saint to make their husbands turn to dust. How often does a man like Samuel get damned to hell, and go?

She breaks down. Florence moves to console her friend, then realizes that Loureen is actually laughing hysterically.

Florence. You smoking crack?
Loureen. Do I look like I am?
Florence. Hell, I've seen old biddies creeping out of crack houses, talking about they were doing church work.
Loureen. Florence, please be helpful, I'm very close to the edge! . . . I don't know what to do next! Do I sweep him up? Do I call the police? Do I . . .

The phone rings.

Oh God.
Florence. You gonna let it ring?

Loureen reaches for the telephone slowly.

Loureen. NO! *(Holds the receiver without picking it up, paralyzed)* What if it's his mother? . . . She knows!

The phone continues to ring. They sit until it stops. They both breathe a sigh of relief.

I should be mourning, I should be praying, I should be thinking of the burial, but all that keeps popping into my mind is what will I wear on television when I share my horrible and wonderful story with a studio audience . . . *(Whimpers)* He's made me a killer, Florence, and you remember what a gentle child I was. *(Whispers)* I'm a killer, I'm a killer, I'm a killer.
Florence. I wouldn't throw that word about too lightly even in jest. Talk like that gets around.
Loureen. You think they'll lock me up? A few misplaced words and I'll probably get the death penalty, isn't that what they do with women like me, murderesses?
Florence. Folks have done time for less.
Loureen. Thank you, just what I needed to hear!
Florence. What did you expect, that I was going to throw up my arms and congratulate you? Why'd you have to go and lose your mind at this time of day, while I got a pot of rice on the stove and Edgar's about to walk in the door and

wonder where his goddamn food is. *(Losing her cool)* And he's going to start in on me about all the nothing I've been doing during the day and why I can't work and then he'll mention how clean you keep your home. And I don't know how I'm going to look him in the eye without. . .

Loureen. I'm sorry, Florence. Really. It's out of my hands now.

She takes Florence's hand and squeezes it.

Florence *(Regaining her composure)*. You swear on your right tit?

Loureen *(Clutching both breasts)*. I swear on both of them!

Florence. Both your breasts, Loureen! You know what will happen if you're lying. *(Loureen nods; hushed)* Both your breasts Loureen?

Loureen. Yeah!

Florence *(Examines the pile of ashes, then shakes her head)*. Oh sweet, sweet Jesus. He must have done something truly terrible.

Loureen. No more than usual. I just couldn't take being hit one more time.

Florence. You've taken a thousand blows from that man, couldn't you've turned the cheek and waited? I'd have helped you pack. Like we talked about.

A moment.

Loureen. Uh! . . . I could blow on him and he'd disappear across the linoleum. *(Snaps her fingers)* Just like that. Should I be feeling remorse or regret or some other "R" word? I'm strangely jubilant, like on prom night when Samuel and I first made love. That's the feeling! *(The women lock eyes)* Uh!

Florence. Is it . . .

Loureen. Like a ton of bricks been lifted from my shoulders, yeah.

Florence. Really?

Loureen. Yeah!

Florence walks to the other side of the room.

Florence. You bitch!

Loureen. What?

Florence. We made a pact.

Loureen. I know.

Florence. You've broken it . . . We agreed that when things got real bad for both of us we'd . . . you know . . . together . . . Do I have to go back upstairs to that? . . . What next?

Loureen. I thought you'd tell me! . . . I don't know!

Florence. I don't know!

Loureen. I don't know!

Florence begins to walk around the room, nervously touching objects. Loureen sits, wringing her hands and mumbling softly to herself.

Florence. Now you got me, Loureen, I'm truly at a loss for words.

Loureen. Everybody always told me, "Keep your place, Loureen." My place, the silent spot on the couch with a wine cooler in my hand and a pleasant smile that warmed the heart. All this time I didn't know why he was so afraid for me to say anything, to speak up. Poof! . . . I've never been by myself, except for them two weeks when he won the office pool and went to Reno with his cousin Mitchell. He wouldn't tell me where he was going until I got that postcard with the cowboy smoking a hundred cigarettes . . . Didn't Sonny Larkin look good last week at Caroline's? He looked good, didn't he . . .

Florence nods. She nervously picks up Samuel's jacket, which is hanging on the back of the chair. She clutches it unconsciously.

NO! No! Don't wrinkle that, that's his favorite jacket. He'll kill me. Put it back!

Florence returns the jacket to its perch. Loureen begins to quiver.

I'm sorry. (*She grabs the jacket and wrinkles it up*) There! (*She then digs into the coat pockets and pulls out his wallet and a movie stub*) Look at that, he said he didn't go to the movies last night. Working late. (*Frantically thumbs through his wallet*) Picture of his motorcycle, Social Security card, driver's license, and look at that from our wedding. (*Smiling*) I looked good, didn't I? (*She puts the pictures back in the wallet and holds the jacket up to her face*) There were some good things. (*She then sweeps her hand over the jacket to remove the wrinkles, and folds it ever so carefully, and finally throws it in the garbage*) And out of my mouth those words made him disappear. All these years and just words, Florence. That's all they were.

Florence. I'm afraid I won't ever get those words out. I'll start resenting you, honey. I'm afraid won't anything change for me.

Loureen. I been to that place.

Florence. Yeah? But now I wish I could relax these old lines (*Touches her forehead*) for a minute maybe. Edgar has never done me the way Samuel did you, but he sure did take the better part of my life.

Loureen. Not yet, Florence.

Florence (*Nods*). I have the children to think of . . . right?

Loureen. You can think up a hundred things before . . .

Florence. Then come upstairs with me . . . we'll wait together for Edgar and then you can spit out your words and . . .

Loureen. I can't do that.

Florence. Yes you can. Come on now.

Loureen shakes her head no.

Well, I guess my mornings are not going to be any different.

Loureen. If you can say for certain, then I guess they won't be. I couldn't say that.

Florence. But you got a broom and a dust pan, you don't need anything more than that . . . He was a bastard and nobody will care that he's gone.

Loureen. Phone's gonna start ringing soon, people are gonna start asking soon, and they'll care.

Florence. What's your crime? Speaking your mind?

Loureen. Maybe I should mail him to his mother. I owe her that. I feel bad for her, she didn't understand how it was. I can't just throw him away and pretend like it didn't happen. Can I?

Florence. I didn't see anything but a pile of ash. As far as I know you got a little careless and burned a chicken.

Loureen. He was always threatening not to come back.

Florence. I heard him.

Loureen. It would've been me eventually.

Florence. Yes.

Loureen. I should call the police, or someone.

Florence. Why? What are you gonna tell them? About all those times they refused to help, about all those nights you slept in my bed 'cause you were afraid to stay down here? About the time he nearly took out your eye 'cause you flipped the television channel?

Loureen. No.

Florence. You've got it, girl!

Loureen. Good-bye to the fatty meats and the salty food. Good-bye to the bourbon and the bologna sandwiches. Good-bye to the smell of his feet, his breath and his bowel movements . . . (*A moment. She closes her eyes and, reliving a horrible memory, she shudders*) Good-bye. (*Walks over to the pile of ashes*) Samuel? . . . Just checking.

Florence: Good-bye Samuel.

They both smile.

Loureen. I'll let the police know that he's missing tomorrow . . .

Florence. Why not the next day?

Loureen. Chicken's warming in the oven, you're welcome to stay.

Florence. Chile, I got a pot of rice on the stove, kids are probably acting out . . . and Edgar, well . . . Listen, I'll stop in tomorrow.

Loureen. For dinner?

Florence. Edgar wouldn't stand for that. Cards maybe.

Loureen. Cards.

The women hug for a long moment. Florence exits. Loureen stands over the ashes for a few moments contemplating what to do. She finally decides to sweep them under the carpet, and then proceeds to set the table and sit down to eat her dinner.

End of Play

FOR ANALYSIS

1. What does the interplay between Loureen and her friend Florence add to the play?

2. Nottage's play is about a serious subject but is not itself always serious. How would you characterize *Poof!*'s **tone**? How do the play's attitudes and **moods** work with and/or against its subjects?

3. Would you describe *Poof!* as a realistic play? Is its subject "real"? Its **plot**? What does it mean to say a work of imaginative literature is realistic?

MAKING CONNECTIONS

1. Compare Nottage's depiction of violence to Theodore Roethke's in "My Papa's Waltz" (p. 937). Taking into account differences in genre, how do Roethke's and Nottage's choices compare? What are the effects of each?

2. Read *Poof!* against Zora Neale Hurston's "Sweat" (p. 840). How does each work treat its main character? How does each work treat the husbands? What does each have to say about their deaths, and about their wives' parts in those deaths?

WRITING TOPIC

Reimagine *Poof!* as told or seen from Samuel's **point of view**. Would you still have the play begin at the end of Samuel's life? Where would you set it? Would Samuel be alone? If not, with whom would you have him talk? Reflect on your choices: could you explore the same situations and **themes** that Nottage does in her version of the play, or would you be led in different directions?

NONFICTION

PAUL   (D. CA. 64 A.D.)

1 CORINTHIANS 13   CA. 56

If I speak in the tongues of men° and of angels, but have not love, I am a noisy gong or a clanging cymbal. ² And if I have prophetic powers, and understand all mysteries and all knowledge, and if I have all faith, so as to remove mountains, but have not love, I am nothing. ³ If I give away all I have, and if I deliver my body to be burned, but have not love, I gain nothing.

⁴ Love is patient and kind; love is not jealous or boastful; ⁵ it is not arrogant or rude. Love does not insist on its own way; it is not irritable or resentful; ⁶ it does not rejoice at wrong, but rejoices in the right. ⁷ Love bears all things, believes all things, hopes all things, endures all things.

⁸ Love never ends; as for prophesies, they will pass away; as for tongues, they will cease; as for knowledge, it will pass away. ⁹ For our knowledge is imperfect and our prophecy is imperfect; ¹⁰ but when the perfect comes, the imperfect will pass away. ¹¹ When I was a child, I spoke like a child, I thought like a child, I reasoned like a child; when I became a man, I gave up childish ways. ¹² For now we see in a mirror dimly, but then face to face. Now I know in part; then I shall understand fully, even as I have been fully understood. ¹³ So faith, hope, love abide, these three; but the greatest of these is love.

FOR ANALYSIS

1. How does Paul emphasize the significance of love in verses 1–3?

2. What does Paul mean by "now" and "then" in verse 12?

3. In verse 13, Paul mentions "faith, hope, love" as abiding values. What do you understand by "faith" and "hope"? What do you think "love" means to Paul? Why does he rank it above the others?

°Glossolalia, the ecstatic uttering of unintelligible sounds that some interpret as a deeply religious experience.

MAKING CONNECTIONS

How do you think the characters in Carver's "What We Talk About When We Talk About Love" (p. 850) would respond to Paul's definition of *love* or the absence of love?

WRITING TOPICS

1. Read Paul's First Epistle to the Corinthians (preferably in a well-annotated study Bible), and analyze the relationship of chapter 13 to the rest of the epistle.

2. This text, translated from the original Greek, is taken from the Revised Standard Version of the Bible. Read the same passage in two or three other versions (for example, the King James Version, the Douay Version, the New American Bible), and compare the translations in terms of **style** and effectiveness.

MAXINE HONG KINGSTON (B. 1940)

NO NAME WOMAN 1970

"Y ou must not tell anyone," my mother said, "what I am about to tell you. In China your father had a sister who killed herself. She jumped into the family well. We say that your father has all brothers because it is as if she had never been born.

"In 1924 just a few days after our village celebrated seventeen hurry-up weddings—to make sure that every young man who went 'out on the road' would responsibly come home—your father and his brothers and your grand-father and his brothers and your aunt's new husband sailed for America, the Gold Mountain. It was your grandfather's last trip. Those lucky enough to get contracts waved good-bye from the decks. They fed and guarded the stowa-ways and helped them off in Cuba, New York, Bali, Hawaii. 'We'll meet in California next year,' they said. All of them sent money home.

"I remember looking at your aunt one day when she and I were dressing; I had not noticed before that she had such a protruding melon of a stomach. But I did not think, 'She's pregnant,' until she began to look like other preg-nant women, her shirt pulling and the white tops of her black pants showing. She could not have been pregnant, you see, because her husband had been gone for years. No one said anything. We did not discuss it. In early summer she was ready to have the child, long after the time when it could have been possible.

"The village had also been counting. On the night the baby was to be born the villagers raided our house. Some were crying. Like a great saw, teeth strung with lights, files of people walked zigzag across our land, tearing the rice. Their lanterns doubled in the disturbed black water, which drained away through the broken bunds. As the villagers closed in, we could see that some of them, probably men and women we knew well, wore white masks. The people with long hair hung it over their faces. Women with short hair made it stand up on end. Some had tied white bands around their foreheads, arms, and legs.

"At first they threw mud and rocks at the house. Then they threw eggs 5 and began slaughtering our stock. We could hear the animals scream their deaths—the roosters, the pigs, a last great roar from the ox. Familiar wild heads flared in our night windows; the villagers encircled us. Some of the faces stopped to peer at us, their eyes rushing like searchlights. The hands flattened against the panes, framed heads, and left red prints.

"The villagers broke in the front and the back doors at the same time, even though we had not locked the doors against them. Their knives dripped with the blood of our animals. They smeared blood on the doors and walls. One woman swung a chicken, whose throat she had slit, splattering blood in red arcs about her. We stood together in the middle of our house, in the family hall with the pictures and tables of the ancestors around us, and looked straight ahead.

"At that time the house had only two wings. When the men came back, we would build two more to enclose our courtyard and a third one to begin a second courtyard. The villagers pushed through both wings, even your grandparents' rooms, to find your aunt's, which was also mine until the men returned. From this room a new wing for one of the younger families would grow. They ripped up her clothes and shoes and broke her combs, grinding them underfoot. They tore her work from the loom. They scattered the cooking fire and rolled the new weaving in it. We could hear them in the kitchen breaking our bowls and banging the pots. They overturned the great waist-high earthenware jugs; duck eggs, pickled fruits, vegetables burst out and mixed in acrid torrents. The old woman from the next field swept a broom through the air and loosed the spirits-of-the-broom over our heads. 'Pig.' 'Ghost.' 'Pig,' they sobbed and scolded while they ruined our house.

"When they left, they took sugar and oranges to bless themselves. They cut pieces from the dead animals. Some of them took bowls that were not broken and clothes that were not torn. Afterward we swept up the rice and sewed it back up into sacks. But the smells from the spilled preserves lasted. Your aunt gave birth in the pigsty that night. The next morning when I went for the water, I found her and the baby plugging up the family well.

"Don't let your father know that I told you. He denies her. Now that you have started to menstruate, what happened to her could happen to you. Don't humiliate us. You wouldn't like to be forgotten as if you had never been born. The villagers are watchful."

Whenever she had to warn us about life, my mother told stories that ran like this one, a story to grow up on. She tested our strength to establish realities. Those in the emigrant generations who could not reassert brute survival died young and far from home. Those of us in the first American generations have had to figure out how the invisible world the emigrants built around our childhoods fit in solid America. 10

The emigrants confused the gods by diverting their curses, misleading them with crooked streets and false names. They must try to confuse their offspring as well, who, I suppose, threaten them in similar ways—always trying to get things straight, always trying to name the unspeakable. The Chinese I know hide their names; sojourners take new names when their lives change and guard their real names with silence.

Chinese Americans, when you try to understand what things in you are Chinese, how do you separate what is peculiar to childhood, to poverty, insanities, one family, your mother who marked your growing with stories, from what is Chinese? What is Chinese tradition and what is the movies?

If I want to learn what clothes my aunt wore, whether flashy or ordinary, I would have to begin, "Remember Father's drowned-in-the-well sister?"

I cannot ask that. My mother has told me once and for all the useful parts. She will add nothing unless powered by Necessity, a riverbank that guides her life. She plants vegetable gardens rather than lawns; she carries the odd-shaped tomatoes home from the fields and eats food left for the gods.

Whenever we did frivolous things, we used up energy; we flew high kites. We children came up off the ground over the melting cones our parents brought home from work and the American movie on New Year's Day—*Oh, You Beautiful Doll* with Betty Grable one year, and *She Wore a Yellow Ribbon* with John Wayne another year. After the one carnival ride each, we paid in guilt; our tired father counted his change on the dark walk home.

Adultery is extravagance. Could people who hatch their own chicks and eat 15 the embryos and the heads for delicacies and boil the feet in vinegar for party food, leaving only the gravel, eating even the gizzard lining—could such people engender a prodigal aunt? To be a woman, to have a daughter in starvation time was a waste enough. My aunt could not have been the lone romantic who gave up everything for sex. Women in the old China did not choose. Some man had commanded her to lie with him and be his secret evil. I wonder whether he masked himself when he joined the raid on her family.

Perhaps she had encountered him in the fields or on the mountain where the daughters-in-law collected fuel. Or perhaps he first noticed her in the marketplace. He was not a stranger because the village housed no strangers. She had to have dealings with him other than sex. Perhaps he worked an adjoining field, or he sold her the cloth for the dress she sewed and wore. His demand must have surprised, then terrified her. She obeyed him; she always did as she was told.

When the family found a young man in the next village to be her husband, she had stood tractably beside the best rooster, his proxy, and promised before they met that she would be his forever. She was lucky that he was her age and she would be the first wife, an advantage secure now. The night she first saw him, he had sex with her. Then he left for America. She had almost forgotten what he looked like. When she tried to envision him, she only saw the black and white face in the group photograph the men had had taken before leaving.

The other man was not, after all, much different from her husband. They both gave orders: she followed. "If you tell your family, I'll beat you. I'll kill you. Be here again next week." No one talked sex, ever. And she might have separated the rapes from the rest of living if only she did not have to buy her oil from him or gather wood in the same forest. I want her fear to have lasted just as long as rape lasted so that the fear could have been contained. No drawn-out fear. But women at sex hazarded birth and hence lifetimes. The fear did not stop but permeated everywhere. She told the man, "I think I'm pregnant." He organized the raid against her.

On nights when my mother and father talked about their life back home, sometimes they mentioned an "outcast table" whose business they still seemed to be settling, their voices tight. In a commensal tradition, where food is precious, the powerful older people made wrongdoers eat alone. Instead of letting them start separate new lives like the Japanese, who could become samurais and geishas, the Chinese family, faces averted but eyes glowering sideways, hung on to the offenders and fed them leftovers. My aunt must have lived in the same house as my parents and eaten at an outcast table. My mother spoke about the raid as if she had seen it, when she and my aunt, a daughter-in-law to a different household, should not have been living together at all. Daughters-in-law lived with their husbands' parents, not their own; a synonym for marriage in Chinese is "taking a daughter-in-law." Her husband's parents could have sold her, mortgaged her, stoned her. But they had sent her back to her own mother and father, a mysterious act hinting at disgraces not told me. Perhaps they had thrown her out to deflect the avengers.

She was the only daughter; her four brothers went with her father, husband, and uncles "out on the road" and for some years became Western men. When the goods were divided among the family, three of the brothers took land, and the youngest, my father, chose an education. After my grandparents gave their daughter away to her husband's family, they had dispensed all the adventure and all the property. They expected her alone to keep the traditional ways, which her brothers, now among the barbarians, could fumble without detection. The heavy, deep-rooted women were to maintain the past against the flood, safe for returning. But the rare urge west had fixed upon our family, and so my aunt crossed boundaries not delineated in space.

The work of preservation demands that the feelings playing about in one's guts not be turned into action. Just watch their passing like cherry blossoms. But perhaps my aunt, my forerunner, caught in a slow life, let dreams grow and fade and after some months or years went toward what persisted. Fear at the enormities of the forbidden kept her desires delicate, wire and bone. She looked at a man because she liked the way the hair was tucked behind his ears, or she liked the question-mark line of a long torso curving at the shoulder and straight at the hip. For warm eyes or a soft voice or a slow walk—that's all—a few hairs, a line, a brightness, a sound, a pace, she gave up family. She offered us up for a charm that vanished with tiredness, a pigtail that didn't toss when the wind died. Why, the wrong lighting could erase the dearest thing about him.

It could very well have been, however, that my aunt did not take subtle enjoyment of her friend, but, a wild woman, kept rollicking company. Imagining her free with sex doesn't fit, though. I don't know any women like that, or men either. Unless I see her life branching into mine, she gives me no ancestral help.

To sustain her being in love, she often worked at herself in the mirror, guessing at the colors and shapes that would interest him, changing them frequently in order to hit on the right combination. She wanted him to look back.

On a farm near the sea, a woman who tended her appearance reaped a reputation for eccentricity. All the married women blunt-cut their hair in flaps about their ears or pulled it back in tight buns. No nonsense. Neither style blew easily into heart-catching tangles. And at their weddings they displayed themselves in their long hair for the last time. "It brushed the backs of my knees," my mother tells me. "It was braided, and even so, it brushed the backs of my knees."

At the mirror my aunt combined individuality into her bob. A bun could 25 have been contrived to escape into black streamers blowing in the wind or in quiet wisps about her face, but only the older women in our picture album wear buns. She brushed her hair back from her forehead, tucking the flaps behind her ears. She looped a piece of thread, knotted into a circle between her index fingers and thumbs, and ran the double strand across her forehead. When she closed her fingers as if she were making a pair of shadow geese bite, the string twisted together catching the little hairs. Then she pulled the thread away from her skin, ripping the hairs out neatly, her eyes watering from the needles of pain. Opening her fingers, she cleaned the thread, then rolled it along her hairline and the tops of her eyebrows. My mother did the same to me and my sisters and herself. I used to believe that the expression "caught by the short hairs" meant a captive held with a depilatory string. It especially hurt at the temples, but my mother said we were lucky we didn't have to have our feet bound when we were seven. Sisters used to sit on their beds and cry together, she said, as their mothers or their slave removed the bandages for a few minutes each night and let the blood gush back into their veins. I hope that the man my aunt loved appreciated a smooth brow, that he wasn't just a tits-and-ass man.

Once my aunt found a freckle on her chin, at a spot that the almanac said predestined her for unhappiness. She dug it out with a hot needle and washed the wound with peroxide.

More attention to her looks than these pullings of hairs and pickings at spots would have caused gossip among the villagers. They owned work clothes and good clothes, and they wore good clothes for feasting the new seasons. But since a woman combing her hair hexes beginnings, my aunt rarely found an occasion to look her best. Women looked like great sea snails—the corded wood, babies, and laundry they carried were the whorls on their backs. The Chinese did not admire a bent back; goddesses and warriors stood straight. Still there must have been a marvelous freeing of beauty when a worker laid down her burden and stretched and arched.

Such commonplace loveliness, however, was not enough for my aunt. She dreamed of a lover for the fifteen days of New Year's, the time for families to exchange visits, money, and food. She plied her secret comb. And sure enough she cursed the year, the family, the village, and herself.

Even as her hair lured her imminent lover, many other men looked at her. Uncles, cousins, nephews, brothers would have looked, too, had they been home between journeys. Perhaps they had already been restraining their curiosity, and they left, fearful that their glances, like a field of nesting birds, might be startled and caught. Poverty hurt, and that was their first reason for leaving. But another, final reason for leaving the crowded house was the never-said.

She may have been unusually beloved, the precious only daughter, spoiled 30 and mirror-gazing because of the affection the family lavished on her. When her husband left, they welcomed the chance to take her back from the in-laws; she could live like the little daughter for just a while longer. There are stories that my grandfather was different from other people, "crazy ever since the little Jap bayoneted him in the head." He used to put his naked penis on the dinner table, laughing. And one day he brought home a baby girl, wrapped up inside his brown Western-style greatcoat. He had traded one of his sons, probably my father, the youngest, for her. My grandmother made him trade back. When he finally got a daughter of his own, he doted on her. They must have all loved her, except perhaps my father, the only brother who never went back to China, having once been traded for a girl.

Brothers and sisters, newly men and women, had to efface their sexual color and present plain miens. Disturbing hair and eyes, a smile like no other, threatened the ideal of five generations living under one roof. To focus blurs, people shouted face to face and yelled from room to room. The immigrants I know have loud voices, unmodulated to American tones even after years away from the village where they called their friendships out across the fields. I have not been able to stop my mother's screams in public libraries or over telephones. Walking erect (knees straight, toes pointed forward, not pigeon-toed, which is Chinese-feminine) and speaking in an inaudible voice, I have tried to turn myself American-feminine. Chinese communication was loud, public. Only sick people had to whisper. But at the dinner table, where the family members came nearest one another, no one could talk, not the outcasts nor any eaters. Every word that falls from the mouth is a coin lost. Silently they gave and accepted food with both hands. A preoccupied child who took his bowl with one hand got a sideways glare. A complete moment of total attention is due everyone alike. Children and lovers have no singularity here, but my aunt used a secret voice, a separate attentiveness.

She kept the man's name to herself throughout her labor and dying; she did not accuse him that he be punished with her. To save her inseminator's name she gave silent birth.

He may have been somebody in her own household, but intercourse with a man outside the family would have been no less abhorrent. All the village were kinsmen, and the titles shouted in loud country voices never let kinship be forgotten. Any man within visiting distance would have been neutralized as a lover—"brother," "younger brother," "older brother"—115 relationship titles. Parents researched birth charts probably not so much to assure good fortune as to circumvent incest in a population that has but one hundred surnames. Everybody has eight million relatives. How useless then sexual mannerisms, how dangerous.

As if it came from an atavism deeper than fear, I used to add "brother" silently to boys' names. It hexed the boys, who would or would not ask me to dance, and made them less scary and as familiar and deserving of benevolence as girls.

But, of course, I hexed myself also—no dates. I should have stood up, both 35 arms waving, and shouted out across libraries, "Hey, you! Love me back." I had no idea, though, how to make attraction selective, how to control its direction and magnitude. If I made myself American-pretty so that the five or six Chinese boys in the class fell in love with me, everyone else—the Caucasian, Negro, and Japanese boys—would too. Sisterliness, dignified and honorable, made much more sense.

Attraction eludes control so stubbornly that whole societies designed to organize relationships among people cannot keep order, not even when they bind people to one another from childhood and raise them together. Among the very poor and the wealthy, brothers married their adopted sisters, like doves. Our family allowed some romance, paying adult brides' prices and providing dowries so that their sons and daughters could marry strangers. Marriage promises to turn strangers into friendly relatives—a nation of siblings.

In the village structure, spirits shimmered among the live creatures, balanced and held in equilibrium by time and land. But one human being flaring up into violence could open up a black hole, a maelstrom that pulled in the sky. The frightened villagers, who depended on one another to maintain the real, went to my aunt to show her a personal, physical representation of the break she had made in the "roundness." Misallying couples snapped off the future, which was to be embodied in true offspring. The villagers punished her for acting as if she could have a private life, secret and apart from them.

If my aunt had betrayed the family at a time of large grain yields and peace, when many boys were born, and wings were being built on many houses, perhaps she might have escaped such severe punishment. But the men—hungry, greedy, tired of planting in dry soil, cuckolded—had been forced to leave the village in order to send food-money home. There were ghost plagues, bandit plagues, wars with the Japanese, floods. My Chinese brother and sister had died of an unknown sickness. Adultery, perhaps only a mistake during good times, became a crime when the village needed food.

The round moon cakes and round doorways, the round tables of graduated size that fit one roundness inside another, round windows and rice bowls— these talismans had lost their power to warn this family of the law: a family must be whole, faithfully keeping the descent line by having sons to feed the old and the dead, who in turn look after the family. The villagers came to show my aunt and her lover-in-hiding a broken house. The villagers were speeding up the circling of events because she was too shortsighted to see that her infidelity had already harmed the village, that waves of consequences would return unpredictably, sometimes in disguise, as now, to hurt her. This roundness had to be made coin-sized so that she would see its circumference: punish her at the birth of her baby. Awaken her to the inexorable. People who refused fatalism because they could invent small resources insisted on culpability. Deny accidents and wrest fault from the stars.

After the villagers left, their lanterns now scattering in various directions 40 toward home, the family broke their silence and cursed her. "Aiaa, we're going to die. Death is coming. Death is coming. Look what you've done. You've killed us. Ghost! Dead ghost! Ghost! You've never been born." She ran out into the fields, far enough from the house so that she could no longer hear their voices, and pressed herself against the earth, her own land no more. When she felt the birth coming, she thought that she had been hurt. Her body seized together. "They've hurt me too much," she thought. "This is gall, and it will kill me." With forehead and knees against the earth, her body convulsed and then relaxed. She turned on her back, lay on the ground. The black well of sky and stars went out and out and out forever; her body and her complexity seemed to disappear. She was one of the stars, a bright dot in blackness, without home, without a companion, in eternal cold and silence. An agoraphobia rose in her, speeding higher and higher, bigger and bigger; she would not be able to contain it; there would be no end to fear.

Flayed, unprotected against space, she felt pain return, focusing her body. This pain chilled her—a cold, steady kind of surface pain. Inside, spasmodically, the other pain, the pain of the child, heated her. For hours she lay on the ground, alternately body and space. Sometimes a vision of normal comfort obliterated reality: she saw the family in the evening gambling at the dinner table, the young people massaging their elders' backs. She saw them congratulating one another, high joy on the mornings the rice shoots came up. When these pictures burst, the stars drew yet further apart. Black space opened.

She got to her feet to fight better and remembered that old-fashioned women gave birth in their pigsties to fool the jealous, pain-dealing gods, who do not snatch piglets. Before the next spasms could stop her, she ran to the pigsty, each step a rushing out into emptiness. She climbed over the fence and knelt in the dirt. It was good to have a fence enclosing her, a tribal person alone.

Laboring, this woman who had carried her child as a foreign growth that sickened her every day, expelled it at last. She reached down to touch the hot, wet, moving mass, surely smaller than anything human, and could feel that it was human after all—fingers, toes, nails, nose. She pulled it up on to her belly, and it lay curled there, butt in the air, feet precisely tucked one under the other. She opened her loose shirt and buttoned the child inside. After resting, it squirmed and thrashed and she pushed it up to her breast. It turned its head this way and that until it found her nipple. There, it made little snuffling noises. She clenched her teeth at its preciousness, lovely as a young calf, a piglet, a little dog.

She may have gone to the pigsty as a last act of responsibility: she would protect this child as she had protected its father. It would look after her soul, leaving supplies on her grave. But how would this tiny child without family find her grave when there would be no marker for her anywhere, neither in the earth nor the family hall? No one would give her a family hall name. She had taken the child with her into the wastes. At its birth the two of them had felt the same raw pain of separation, a wound that only the family pressing tight could close. A child with no descent line would not soften her life but only trail after her, ghostlike, begging her to give it purpose. At dawn the villagers on their way to the fields would stand around the fence and look.

Full of milk, the little ghost slept. When it awoke, she hardened her breasts 45 against the milk that crying loosens. Toward morning she picked up the baby and walked to the well.

Carrying the baby to the well shows loving. Otherwise abandon it. Turn its face into the mud. Mothers who love their children take them along. It was probably a girl; there is some hope of forgiveness for boys.

"Don't tell anyone you had an aunt. Your father does not want to hear her name. She has never been born." I have believed that sex was unspeakable and words so strong and fathers so frail that "aunt" would do my father mysterious harm. I have thought that my family, having settled among immigrants who had also been their neighbors in the ancestral land, needed to clean their name, and a wrong word would incite the kinspeople even here. But there is more to this silence: they want me to participate in her punishment. And I have.

In the twenty years since I heard this story I have not asked for details nor said my aunt's name; I do not know it. People who can comfort the dead can also chase after them to hurt them further—a reverse ancestor worship. The real punishment was not the raid swiftly inflicted by the villagers, but the family's deliberately forgetting her. Her betrayal so maddened them, they saw to it that she would suffer forever, even after death. Always hungry, always needing, she would have to beg food from other ghosts, snatch and steal it from those whose living descendants give them gifts. She would have to fight the ghosts massed at crossroads for the buns a few thoughtful citizens leave to decoy her away from village and home so that the ancestral spirits could feast unharassed. At peace, they could act like gods, not ghosts, their descent lines providing them with paper suits and dresses, spirit money, paper houses, paper automobiles, chicken, meat, and rice into eternity—essences delivered up in smoke and flames, steam and incense rising from each rice bowl. In an attempt to make the Chinese care for people outside the family, Chairman Mao encourages us now to give our paper replicas to the spirits of outstanding soldiers and workers, no matter whose ancestors they may be. My aunt remains forever hungry. Goods are not distributed evenly among the dead.

My aunt haunts me—her ghost drawn to me because now, after fifty years of neglect, I alone devote pages of paper to her, though not origamied into houses and clothes. I do not think she always means me well. I am telling on her, and she was a spite suicide, drowning herself in the drinking water. The Chinese are always very frightened of the drowned one, whose weeping ghost, wet hair hanging and skin bloated, waits silently by the water to pull down a substitute.

FOR ANALYSIS

1. In what sense did the **narrator** participate in her aunt's punishment?

2. Given the Chinese belief system, what is the No Name Woman's most significant punishment?

3. What evidence in the essay supports the view that the Chinese villagers favored males over females?

4. Why does the woman enter the pigsty to give birth?

5. What factors intensify the ferocity of the villagers' attack on the house?

6. Discuss the significance of the assertion in paragraph 49: "I alone devote pages of paper to her, though not origamied into houses and clothes."

7. Reread the essay, noting scenes the speaker seems to invent. What reasons might Kingston have for imagining the events that she could not have known?

MAKING CONNECTIONS

Some authors, such as Chopin in "The Storm" (p. 835), seem to treat sexual infidelity casually; others, such as Shakespeare in *Othello* (p. 947), treat it murderously. Give reasons to support each view.

WRITING TOPIC

Describe the No Name Woman's sin. Was it a sin against the absent husband of her hastily arranged marriage, against her extended family, against the village, against the gods?

WINTER COUNT, 1964 2005

When Sherri Luna rammed Jerry Kruger's crew-cut head into the hand-ball court wall at Kester Avenue Elementary School on February 15, 1964, I knew she loved him, a swirling, butch, embarrassed sort of love that denied itself even as it was expressed. She loved him the way a nine-year-old, beefy-ankled, white-socked, scuffed-up saddle-shoed, Valley girl chicana loves a drawly, red-necked, red-haired, red-freckled, cracker son of a Pentecostal preacher from Oklahoma who wouldn't let his kid slow dance in Miss Arling-ton's A4 class, not because Miss Arlington was a wafer-thin woman with a two-foot-high beehive hairdo that made her look like an alien from some planet of white-porcelain doll people with blood-red lips and fingernails long and sharp as steak knives, but because Jerry's preacher pa didn't believe nine-year-olds, much less anybody, should be cradling one another's bodies in their arms and breathing softly on their necks as they swayed to music. Nosiree, Sherri Luna didn't love Jerry that way, the slow dance, fandango way, where holding someone close is as sweet and natural as lying on your back in the backyard watching the clouds and letting the sunlight kiss your cheek, but she loved him just the same. I knew it when I first saw her rub her body up against Jerry's blue jeans as she slugged him in the arm by the water fountain the first day he came to class that winter. Plus, she didn't want to slow dance, not because she didn't believe in it, but because she was constitutionally against any request that curled out of Miss Arlington's pouty lips.

"Just do it, honey."

"No."

"Please?"

"No, I said!"   5

So, "Ka-Chunk," went Jerry's head, cradled in Sherri's gentle headlock when Miss Arlington was putting a scratchy waltz on the mono record player that Ricky LaConte had lugged out onto the playground after lunch. Ricky, a fat kid who liked to have us punch his stomach in the boys' room until his bubbly flesh was filled with blotches like lesions, liked to do such favors, his arm shooting up like a rocket ship out of its socket every time Miss Arlington asked with those pouty lips just who would like to do this or that for her. And that's a sort of love, too, don't get me wrong, only it wasn't Sherri Luna's sort of love. She needed to touch the someone she loved, even if she didn't under-stand what the yearning in her heart was asking her nine-year-old body to do.

So, "Ka-Chunk."

I was breathing my face into Melinda Coates's blond ringlets, getting hairs twisted in my glasses' hinges and imagining myself in heaven and then feeling embarrassed for even thinking such a slack-brained thing as that when I heard it.

"Ka-Chunk," echoing into the mauve plastic handball court wall that rose out of the blacktop playground surrounded by bungalows, chain-link fence, and honeysuckle rustling in the winter breeze like our breaths on one another's necks as we danced.

"Ka-Chunk." 10

"That was fun," Jerry laughed. "Do it again," with again drawled out so long, so slow, that it slobbered and dribbled out of his mouth into a dopey-grinned, three-syllabled, shrieky a-gaaa-in.

"Do it a-gaaa-in."

Poor Ricky. He was right next to me, swaying sort of sad-like, out of time and out of step with Louise Dolan. He wanted to be in that headlock, too, I guess. Maybe he thought that the bumps on his forehead would go with the blotches on his stomach. I don't know, but I know this. Sherri would have none of him. Ricky wasn't Jerry in any way, shape, or form, and Sherri Luna loved Jerry. That was that, end of the story. We were dancing that Strauss waltz you hear in *2001* when the ship docks with the space station, and I swear I saw her gently bend over as pretty as you please and nibble out a tongue-licked hickey on that sun-burnt, freckly red neck of his when she thought no one was looking. We stared and stared. Not even the creamy touch of Melinda Coates could keep me from it. No one in Miss Arlington's A4 class in 1964 had ever seen such a thing.

And then she counted to three. And then she did it again.

And then she did it again. And I swear she didn't miss a beat, not a one, not 15 a single one.

FOR ANALYSIS

1. Why does Sherri Luna bang Jerry's head into the wall? Why does he ask her to do it again?

2. Why does Ricky let people punch him in the stomach? What about the "blotches" left by the punches parallels the hickey Sherri leaves on Jerry's neck?

3. A *winter count* is a story or oral history used by certain Native American tribes to mark individual years in tribal history by retelling an event from that year that is memorable or significant. Why do you think the incident retold in this essay is significant enough to mark its year?

MAKING CONNECTIONS

1. Compare the juxtaposition of violence and attraction in "Winter Count, 1964" to the juxtaposition of sex and parental love in Kinnell's "After Making Love We Hear Footsteps" (p. 919). What do these perhaps unexpected combinations have in common? How do they work in each piece of writing?

2. The children (including the **narrator**) "stared and stared" at Sherri Luna and Jerry Kruger's love dance. Compare this moment to the children staring in Bambara's "The

Lesson" (p. 96). What are the children in each seeing? What does their seeing mean? What are they learning about?

WRITING TOPICS

1. In what other ways do people (of all ages) manifest the combination of desire for and fear of physical intimacy? Reflect on ways in which you and people you have observed or read about deal (or don't deal) with this tension.

2. "'Ka-chunk,' went Jerry's head" (para. 6). Write a short essay in which you relate an incident or a moment, using the vivid transcription of sound.

MY FATHER'S NOOSE   2007

When my father was a boy, his mother hung him.
   Enter Tondo, a Manila slum, and stand in the kitchen of his childhood home. Look up. The crusty knot is still there, tied around the light fixture.

I imagine my father, Totoy, at ten. He hasn't graduated yet to long pants and shoes; his shorts and T-shirt are faded and soft from the wear of three older brothers.

Totoy has done something to make his mother angrier than she's ever been. And now, Totoy balances on a stack of vegetable crates, his neck connected to the ceiling. He's wearing one rubber slipper, and after slapping him on the ears, his mother has tucked the other slipper under the bowtie of her apron. If Totoy becomes dizzy and loses balance, or if Inang kicks the crates away, he might save himself by curling his fingers around the rope and pulling against the noose as if it were the mouth on a drawstring bag.

But his mother plants his palms to his hips and she looks up at him. She 5
doesn't say a word, but Totoy hears, "Don't try to save yourself. Don't you dare."

He moves only his eyes and from this height, he notices his mother is balding. Her gray hair is loosely bunned and there are triangles of white flesh between the comb tracks. Her body is thick and intimidating, fleshy roll layered onto fat, souvenirs from eleven pregnancies. Totoy is number seven.

When she's angry, she makes noise and breaks things and stares until you look away. One by one, Totoy's siblings return from school and work, take a step into the kitchen, and right back out without a word.

With a pestle, she pounds garlic in the mortar bowl. She raises the butcher knife to her shoulder and chops heads from fish. She'll fry the bodies for dinner and save the heads and tails for soup the next day.

What does Totoy think as he stands there watching his mother prepare dinner? Does he believe he will taste that dinner? Perhaps his mother will remove the crates and watch him suffocate and kick until the knot is as tight as it will go; allow his siblings to play tetherball with his body; or keep him tied there, hanging from the kitchen.

His siblings are hiding, staying far away from the kitchen. Even if his father 10
could be found—perhaps he is playing pool in a neighborhood bar or perhaps he is earning money by taking a passenger from the market to their home on the sidecar of his tricycle—Totoy's father wouldn't save him. Mother knows best, and she tells him, "I'm doing this because you're my son. You need to learn right from wrong."

Totoy doesn't know this yet: he will survive. Fifteen years later, he will have me, a daughter. But he will never forgive his mother, and half a century later, he won't attend her funeral. Totoy will try his best not to abuse his children. But he's his mother's son. He will.

FOR ANALYSIS

1. What circumstances of Totoy's mother's life help to explain (if not justify) her actions? Do you judge her less harshly because of what you know about her life?

2. Why does Totoy's mother say she does this to him? Does it work? If so, how? If not, why not?

3. Part of the power of this brief essay comes from the way it ends. How does the ending extend the meaning of the event described?

MAKING CONNECTIONS

1. Compare "My Father's Noose" to one or more of the poems in "Connecting Poems: Remembering Fathers." How do the two (or more) works address the ways in which love expresses itself? How do they show how love can look similar to hate?

2. Though about quite different situations, Talusan's essay and Hayden's poem "Those Winter Sundays" (p. 937) both recognize the hard work parents do to care for their children, the love that motivates that work, and the toll that work sometimes takes on those who do it. How do the selections differ? What do the children in each poem learn from their experiences?

WRITING TOPICS

1. How would Totoy's mother justify her actions? Do you think she could put together a convincing argument for the necessity of her actions? What might she include in such an argument?

2. Write a brief arresting essay (or story) in which you use some of Talusan's techniques (such as a shocking opening or an ending with a twist).

CONNECTING NONFICTION:
LOVE IN THE DIGITAL AGE

Sometimes it is hard to see how the world has changed, living in the middle of it as we do. Many of us remember a time when people would meet each other in the flesh, and get to know each other face-to-face, or in long telephone conversations on phones that actually plugged into the wall, but so much in so many of our lives happens these days online. As a result of the ubiquity of wired activity, it is hard to recognize its effects on the way we interact with each other, the way we see things, the way we feel. As you read the two essays in this cluster, look for ways in which they both grapple with the effects of the Internet on relationships and their aftermath; keep an eye out also for the effects of their both appearing pretty early in the evolution of the Web.

KATHA POLLITT   (B. 1949)

WEBSTALKER   2004

After my lover left me, I went a little crazy for a while. By day, I could pass for normal, as that concept is broadly understood on the Upper West Side, where I live—I sat at my desk, I took long furious walks in Riverside Park rehearsing all the terrible things I would say to him as he lay stricken with something rare and painful, I wandered through Zabar's looking for kitchen things to replace the ones he took when he moved out. What kind of person walks out the door after seven years with a wooden spoon, a spatula, a whisk? For months, I would find myself in the middle of a recipe only to discover that some basic, necessary implement was missing. But at night, after my daughter was in bed, I would settle myself at the computer with a cup of coffee, and till one or two in the morning I would browse the Internet, searching for information about him. Except "browse" is much too placid and leisured a word—a cow browses in a meadow, a reader browses in a library for a novel to take home for the weekend. What I did fell between zeal and monomania. I was like Javert, hunting him through the sewers of cyberspace, moving from link to link in the dark, like Spider-Man flinging himself by a filament over the shadowy chasm between one roof and another. "Are you Webstalking him?" a friend in her twenties asked over coffee. I hadn't known there was a word for what I was doing.

At first, I felt guilty, as if somehow he could know. After all, if an e-mail program can tell you whether your message has been opened, maybe a search engine can tell you that someone is checking you out. Still, I would plug his name into Google, Lycos, HotBot, AltaVista, and up would pop, in distilled, allusive, elliptical form, like a haiku or a mathematical curve, everything I should have known: the life behind my life. Out of a soup or cloud composed of book reviews, publishers' notices, conference announcements, course assignments, Listserv postings, and tiny mentions and stray references embedded in documents devoted to some quite distant theme, a person would slowly condense, like someone approaching out of a fog who at first looks as if he were made out of fog, only darker. There on my screen glowed the programs of academic gatherings he had attended going back for a decade: the same female names appeared over and over entwined with his in panel announcements. Why hadn't it struck me as odd that his "best friend," a professor of English literature, was the respondent for papers he gave at conferences on art history and philosophy? Was I even aware that they attended these events together? And what about the philosopher he'd been seeing, I'd recently discovered, when we started dating, and the art historian who called all the time and then, one day, stopped calling? They were on those panels, too. I had been so out of it!

But of course I already knew that. After he left, I walked around my semi- 5 dismantled apartment and interrogated the ghost-squares on the empty walls. Were any of the pictures I had lived with gifts from women he had romanced? The cat cartoon? The charcoal of sad-looking trees? A splashy abstractionist painter, as a thank-you for writing about her work, had given him a big acrylic of black stripes laid over red swirls, like flames billowing behind an iron grille. He hung it in the living room and refused to take it down when I said I hated it, it reminded me of the gates of Hell. He had left only one art work behind—a colorful picture of two ambiguously sexed people embracing, by a jolly, tough-talking artist we had socialized with when her child and mine were small. I called her up and told her I had belatedly come to conclude that my lover had had affairs during our years together and I didn't want to keep her picture if she had slept with him. "I never saw his genitals," she said cheerfully—just mooned around with him in coffee shops. He had told her that I accepted his need for other women, so it didn't seem fair to hate her. Besides, she'd turned him down. I left her picture up in the bathroom, next to the towel rack.

Still, it astonished me that she believed that business about my permitting his philandering. The only people who seem to know such women firsthand are the men who are cheating on them. You never hear a woman say, "Whatever George wants is fine with me—I just want him to be happy!" No woman has ever passed on to another the riveting news that Miriam understands that Joe needs variety. It is only men who seem to possess that bit of intimate knowledge, which apparently is so instantly credible, so obviously true, that no one ever asks the woman herself about it. What was it about me, I wondered, that made people accept his story? Perhaps I emitted a sort of wan victim-aura, like someone sitting alone in a Greek diner. Or perhaps people just couldn't believe I was so oblivious. After all, I was intelligent, I was a New Yorker, I was alive.

But, then, how well does anyone really know anyone else? My lover used 5 to make fun of people who gave money to museums and universities—he claimed that they just wanted to feel important by connecting themselves to élite bourgeois institutions. Yet, according to Google, in 1995 he made a donation to the Weidner Center for the Performing Arts, at the University of

Wisconsin in Green Bay, a cultural venue that he never mentioned and that I was not even aware existed. Or was it someone else? After all, he was not the only person with his name. There was his father, the Marxist theoretician. Most of my search results were about him—fans from Canada to Korea posted his works far and wide. While living with his son, I had found his books impenetrably technical and Teutonic, but through sheer familiarity I was coming to enjoy his gloomy, sardonic turn of mind, his doom-laden pronouncements in which the certainty that he was right was given a poignant cast by his awareness that few were listening and fewer agreed. I found myself nodding in sympathy as I reencountered his work. "Capitalism," he wrote, "has nowhere to go but to its death." You can't argue with that. There were also numerous mentions of a property lawyer in Australia who was active in his children's school, and an accountant on the Isle of Wight who placed well in the 1999 North Drove Doddle amateur rowing competition, and who may or may not be the man of the same name who was an avid promoter of shove ha'penny, an old English game. It was barely possible, but most unlikely, that my lover, sometimes under his name and sometimes under assorted misspellings of it, posted brief rude messages in idiomatic French on a Web site devoted to the work of the "bad boy" filmmaker Leos Carax (*"bojarksi arrête de boire la tasse": "bah alors!"*). But that person did not sound like someone who cared about bringing culture to the Midwest. Perhaps the Weidner donor was one of those rare people who are unknown to the Net: someone with no e-mail, no Web site or Web page, no blog or—barring that one donation—connections with anyone who has. Perhaps he still wrote letters on a typewriter and posted them at the mailbox on the corner when he walked the dog in the crisp Wisconsin morning. If only I had met him instead of my lover! Unless, of course, he was my lover.

Mostly, though, I Webstalked him to find out what he was up to now. I knew when he went to Philadelphia for the College Art Association meeting, when his essay on eighteenth-century art-critical terminology was assigned in a class at Essex University, when he sent a flattering e-mail to the Web site of a conceptual artist whose work consisted of reading "Das Kapital" out loud in dozens of obscure foreign languages and invited this artist to be involved in a book he was "producing" with his new girlfriend. I don't know what made me saddest: that they were co-writing, or at least co-producing—whatever that is—a book? That he was seeking out this half-baked poseur? That he prefaced his girlfriend's name with "critic," the way it would appear in *Time*? Clearly, his prose style had deteriorated since he left me—the man I loved would surely have written "the critic," which is the correct and elegant usage.

I've always believed in the Nero Wolfe theory of knowledge. You can just sit quietly in your room—according to Pascal, the activity that if practiced more assiduously would free humanity from most of its troubles, but that was before e-mail—and through sheer mental effort force the tiniest snippets of information to yield the entire story of which they are a fragment, because the whole truth is contained in every particle of it, the way every human cell contains our DNA. Thus, each new search result drove me wild with excitement: maybe this would be the link that would, properly understood, reveal all. Late at night, sipping my cold coffee, I saw the Web as a parallel world, the verbal equivalent of the life we live, a shimmering net of information that exactly and completely corresponds to the world. It was like something a medieval rabbi might conjure up out of the Kabbalah: a magical set of propositions that acted as a mirror of reality and perhaps even allowed you to control it and change it. It was as if I would be able actually to watch him in real time—giving a talk, teaching a class, making dinner, making love—if I could only find that final link that would make the parallel proposition-world complete. Unfortunately, I wasn't very technologically adept. I kept running into the limits of my skills. What, for example, is a PDF? Some pieces of seemingly routine information I was unable to find, although I felt sure they had to be there, somewhere, behind the brick wall of my ineptitude: his course schedule (did it still match that of the "best friend"?), his new girlfriend's undergraduate college or home town or birth date. I knew where he lived, because his girlfriend was listed in the phone book, but did they have cats? Did he take her to the restaurants we had discovered together? I kicked myself for not having written down his Social Security and credit-card numbers. "You don't have those?" my young friend asked, surprised. She had a whole I.D. file on her boyfriend, "just in case."

How could I find out more? I considered replying to one of those spam ads advertising detective software, like the "Banned CD" that supposedly helps you turn up all sorts of hidden legal and financial information about people. But those e-mails had a threatening, paranoid tone: responding might connect me with sinister people who would show up at my apartment. Besides, it was one thing to stay up half the night going through the archives of obscure leftist Listservs and e-mailing this or that woman to ask if she had ever slept with my lover. (Amazingly, they all wrote back nice notes affirming that they had, except for one, who sent a huffy e-mail saying that it was none of my business. In other words, yes.) Then, too, the Banned CD cost $19.95, and to pay for information would be proof of serious dementia.

Instead, I tried to break into his e-mail. I had his password—"marxist"—or did I? When I asked him what his password was, a few months before he left, he had cleared his throat and paused. I attributed this hesitation to modesty—he was embarrassed to claim such a heroic identity, or to use such a large, noble, world-historical word for such a trivial purpose. But perhaps he hesitated because he was afraid I would use it and find out his secrets—or was thinking up a fake password so that I couldn't. In any case, "marxist" didn't work when I tried to access his mail through mail2web.com—nor did any of the other words I tried: "marxism," "karlmarx," "engels," "communist," "communism," "pannekoek," "korsch," "luxemburg," "luxembourg," "belguim," "chocolate," "godiva," "naked," "breast," "cunnilingus," "fellatio," or the names of our cats, his new girlfriend, his mother's dead golden retriever. My password is "secret," which is so obvious that e-mail programs cite it as the exact word not to choose, but which

I liked because it was a pun—"secret" as a secret password, the word that is also the thing itself. I noticed he didn't ask for my password, but I told him anyway.

He had accused me of being addicted to the Internet, and he was right. 10 I spent hours every day following the news, and surfing from one odd Web site to another. I joined Listservs all over the left, from Aut-Op-Sy, which focussed on the ideas of the Italian anarchist Toni Negri, to Women Leaders Online, for pro-choice Democratic feminists, and carried on intense discussions with people I came to feel I knew in some deep, ultimate way, although I had never met them and didn't want to. What I loved about the Internet was its purity and swiftness, I told him, the feeling of being without a body, of flying into space in all directions at once, of becoming a stream of words going into the blue, a mind touching other minds. I think he took this as a sexual rejection. "You would spend five hours e-mailing with the Women Leaders Online," he said accusingly the day he left, "but you wouldn't spend five hours in bed with me." My women friends all had the same response to this remark: "Five hours?"

When he left, I felt like an alcoholic who can finally put the bottle on the table and drink as much as she wants. He wasn't my only target; I Webstalked everyone in his world. His girlfriend, of course, whose prolific output of art journalism I was able to skim online: how apparent, once you looked for them, were the little signs of his growing influence over the past few years—his favorite tag from Nietzsche, a nod to Pierre Bourdieu. I knew what courses she taught and in what month her term on the faculty senate would expire. I followed the fortunes of her books on Amazon, where I did not post nasty anonymous readers' reviews ("Writes like a baton twirler with a Ph.D."— John Ruskin, Yale University; "The Worst!"—a reader from Colorado). That would be dishonorable, and, besides, what if she figured out it was me? A search for images turned up three magazine covers, a basket of kittens, and a darkly beautiful, radiantly smiling woman dressed in sequins and lifting a glass of champagne. Fortunately, further research suggested that this was not her but an Italian countess involved in animal rescue. Once, I even tried to listen to a lecture she gave on conceptual art at a remote Midwestern university, but I couldn't figure out how to make the audio work, and then suddenly out of the machine a kind of rushing-water sound welled up that could have been hands clapping, and I knew I was on the edge of true self-humiliation and quickly hit Restart, burning with shame.

I Googled his mother, his therapist, his former girlfriends, the members of the Marxist study group we had attended together. I spent a whole night trying to reconstruct, Web site by Web site, what he had told me about a widowed friend: had her husband really been a bigamist, with another wife and child, and did the admiring graduate student who wrote his online obituary know that? My lover had always defended this arrangement, which involved a certain amount of subterfuge: a false phone number and a secret studio reached through a hallway disguised as a closet. That should have told me something. My lover claimed that the friend—the bigamee?—had had numerous affairs while her semi-partner or half husband or whatever you call him was off with his other family. In fact, he claimed that she had told him she was unable to be friends with a man without sleeping with him. You'd never imagine it to meet her, a shy, trim woman in her seventies with a child's scrubbed face and the ethereal smile of an ex-nun. That should have told me something, too.

You think what people say is what matters, an older friend told me long ago. You think it's all about words. Well, that's natural, isn't it? I'm a writer, I can float for hours on a word like "amethyst" or "broom" or the way so many words sound like what they are: "earth" so firm and basic, "air" so light, like a breath. You can't imagine them the other way around: *she plunged her hands into the rich brown air.* Sometimes I think I would like to be a word— not a big important word, like "love" or "truth," just a small ordinary word, like "orange" or "inkstain" or "so," a word that people use so often and so unthinkingly that its specialness has all been worn away like the roughness on a pebble in a creekbed, but that has a solid heft when you pick it up, and if you hold it to the light at just the right angle you can glimpse the spark at its core. But of course what my friend meant was that I ignored inconvenient subtexts, the meaning behind the meaning: that someone might say he loved you, but what really mattered was the way he let your hand go after he said it. It did not occur to me, either, that somebody might just lie, that there are people who lie for pleasure, for the feeling of superiority and power. And yet it should have. When I was a magazine editor, I had an assistant who lied all the time. Once, on a slow spring day, he called up the N.Y.U. Jewish student center, pretended to be a British Jew stranded in New York, and wangled an invitation to its Seder. Finally, he went too far, insisting that he had checked the price of a book on Buddhism we had reviewed in the previous issue, and it really was $18.03. "I thought it was odd, too," he mused. "It must be a Zen thing." By the time I worked up the courage to fire him, he had already talked his way into a much better job, and somehow arranged it that his new employers never called me for a reference. Some people just land on their feet.

After the first burst of information, progress was slow. How thrilling was it, really, to discover that his name was mentioned in the abstract of a paper about religious iconography in a particular Catholic girls' school in Western Australia? And yet I kept on. After all, some people, mostly women, not all of them in the porn business, had Web sites hooked up to a camera in their home: you could watch them talking on the phone, eating toast, taking a shower, sleeping, and you could read the diaries in which they nattered on about their day, entries so unenlivened by wit or dash or passion or curiosity that you despaired for the human race. Perhaps if I persisted I would discover tucked away in a far corner of the Web a camera recording his new life: Did he and his new girlfriend stay up till 3 A.M. talking? Did she wake up at night and lie there brimming over with happiness? Of course, a camera couldn't tell you that; all you'd see would be a quilt with a lump under it. Still, I might have watched. It was so terrible to go from living with someone to never seeing him, never even glimpsing the top of his head bent over the art magazines at Barnes & Noble or catching sight of him through the window at the meat counter at Citarella. It was as if he had vanished in a puff of smoke.

Actually, the amazing thing was that, in a way, there was such a camera. 15 Leafing through the *Times* real-estate listings one Sunday, idly looking for that elusive "Classic 6 Riv Vu Needs TLC—Owner Anxious!," I came across an ad for an open house: they were selling her apartment. I wasn't surprised—I had heard they had gotten married. But was I correctly remembering her address? I went to the real-estate company's Web site and, sure enough, there was a list of open houses. I clicked on the address I had seen in the paper and up came a floor plan—a typical single-woman one-bedroom, small and boxy, with, I was pleased to note, only one good-sized closet. "Excellent FS building," chirped the accompanying text. "Great light—sun pours in!" I clicked again and slowly a photograph cranked into focus: the living room. It had obviously been edited and tidied for the buyer's eye, but you could see the inhabitants' taste: spare, contemporary, unencumbered—not his style at all. Still, there was his music stand in the corner, a pillow I had forgotten about was carefully deployed on a gray couch, and there on her wall were the pictures that had formerly hung on my wall—the cat cartoon, the sad trees, the gates of Hell. If only I could enlarge the photo enough times, perhaps I would make out my old spoon and spatula and whisk in the container on the countertop. It was as if the two of them had just left and would come back any minute, laden with groceries, laughing. I clicked on the bedroom photo, but it wouldn't come up. Perhaps they were in there, basking in the great light.

There wasn't any point going on after that. I had found the magic Web site, the one that was a secret window into reality, but what did it show me that I didn't already know? What diference did it make what color their sofa was? In fact, what had any of my researches revealed that mattered in the end? I had proved to myself that the Internet was indeed a verbal map of the world, the set of propositions that were all that was the case, thrown over the physical world like a medieval rabbi's invisible cloak. But that was all it was. It could mirror facts and events, but not only could it not control or change them, it could not answer my real question: Why? In the months to come, I would look back on this time in my life almost as a kind of out-of-body travel, from which I had returned with nothing but a sense memory of having been somewhere inexpressibly exciting and far away. It wasn't like a dream, exactly, although it had a dream's strange internal logic. It was like looking through the window of an airplane at night, the way the city below appears so near, yet untouchable beyond the glass—a network of lights, flames, stars.

FOR ANALYSIS

1. What does it feel like to read such intimate things about a writer's life? How does the fact that the writer tells you these things herself (rather than hearing about them from someone else) affect the experience?

2. How would Pollitt's reaction have been different if her breakup had happened, say, fifteen years earlier?

3. What does it mean to piece together a new picture of a person you used to know intimately from random facts found on the Internet? What does it say about the knowledge we think we have of those closest to us? What does it say about love?

WRITING TOPIC

Have you ever found yourself feeling the way Pollitt did during the time she describes here? If not, can you imagine such a feeling? For either case, reflect on the emotional state and ask yourself what you might be capable of doing along the lines of what Pollitt did on the Internet.

MEGHAN DAUM   (B. 1970)

VIRTUAL LOVE   1997

It was last November; fall was drifting away into an intolerable chill. I was at the end of my twenty-sixth year, and was living in New York City, trying to support myself as a writer, and taking part in the kind of urban life that might be construed as glamorous were it to appear in a memoir in the distant future. At the time, however, my days felt more like a grind than like an adventure: hours of work strung between the motions of waking up, getting the mail, watching TV with my roommates, and going to bed. One morning, I logged on to my America Online account to find a message under the heading "is this the real meghan daum?" It came from someone with the screen name PFSlider. The body of the message consisted of five sentences, written entirely in lower-case letters, of perfectly turned flattery: something about PFSlider's admiration of some newspaper and magazine articles I had published over the last year and a half, something about his resulting infatuation with me, and something about his being a sportswriter in California.

I was engaged for the thirty seconds that it took me to read the message and fashion a reply. Though it felt strange to be in the position of confirming that I was indeed "the real meghan daum," I managed to say, "Yes, it's me. Thank you for writing." I clicked the "Send Now" icon, shot my words into the void, and forgot about PFSlider until the next day, when I received another message, this one headed "eureka."

"wow, it is you," he wrote, still in lower case. He chronicled the various conditions under which he'd read my few-and-far-between articles—a boardwalk in Laguna Beach, the spring-training pressroom for a baseball team that he covered for a Los Angeles newspaper. He confessed to having a crush on me. He referred to me as "princess daum." He said he wanted to have lunch with me during one of his two annual trips to New York.

The letter was outrageous and endearingly pathetic, possibly the practical joke of a friend trying to rouse me out of a temporary writer's block. But the kindness pouring forth from my computer screen was bizarrely exhilarating, and I logged off and thought about it for a few hours before writing back to express how flattered and "touched"—this was probably the first time I had ever used that word in earnest—I was by his message.

I am not what most people would call a computer person. I have no interest in chat rooms, newsgroups, or most Web sites. I derive a palpable thrill from sticking a letter in the United States mail. But I have a constant low-grade fear of the telephone, and I often call people with the intention of getting their answering machines. There is something about the live voice that I have come to find unnervingly organic, as volatile as live television. E-mail provides a useful antidote for my particular communication anxieties. Though I generally send and receive only a few messages a week, I take comfort in their silence and their boundaries.

PFSlider and I tossed a few innocuous, smart-assed notes back and forth over the week following his first message. Let's say his name was Pete. He was twenty-nine, and single. I revealed very little about myself, relying instead on the ironic commentary and forced witticisms that are the conceit of so many E-mail messages. But I quickly developed an oblique affection for PFSlider. I was excited when there was a message from him, mildly depressed when there wasn't. After a few weeks, he gave me his phone number. I did not give him mine, but he looked it up and called me one Friday night. I was home. I picked up the phone. His voice was jarring, yet not unpleasant. He held up more than his end of the conversation for an hour, and when he asked permission to call me again I granted it, as though we were of an earlier era.

Pete—I could never wrap my mind around his name, privately thinking of him as PFSlider, "E-mail guy," or even "baseball boy"—began phoning me two or three times a week. He asked if he could meet me, and I said that that would be O.K. Christmas was a few weeks away, and he told me that he would be coming back East to see his family. From there, he would take a short flight to New York and have lunch with me.

"It is my off-season mission to meet you," he said.

"There will probably be a snowstorm," I said.

"I'll take a team of sled dogs," he answered.

We talked about our work and our families, about baseball and Bill Clinton and Howard Stern and sex, about his hatred for Los Angeles and how much he wanted a new job. Sometimes we'd find each other logged on simultaneously and type back and forth for hours.

I had previously considered cyber-communication an oxymoron, a fast road to the breakdown of humanity. But, curiously, the Internet—at least in the limited form in which I was using it—felt anything but dehumanizing. My interaction with PFSlider seemed more authentic than much of what I experienced in the daylight realm of living beings. I was certainly putting more energy into the relationship than I had put into many others. I also was giving Pete attention that was by definition undivided, and relishing the safety of the distance between us by opting to be truthful instead of doling out the white lies that have become the staple of real life. The outside world—the place where

I walked around avoiding people I didn't want to deal with, peppering my casual conversations with half-truths, and applying my motto "Let the machine take it" to almost any scenario—was sliding into the periphery of my mind.

For me, the time on-line with Pete was far superior to the phone. There were no background noises, no interruptions from "call waiting," no long-distance charges. Through typos and misspellings, he flirted maniacally. "I have an absurd crush on you," he said. "If I like you in person, you must promise to marry me." I was coy and conceited, telling him to get a life; baiting him into complimenting me further, teasing him in a way I would never have dared to do in person, or even on the phone. I would stay up until 3 A.M. typing with him, smiling at the screen, getting so giddy that when I quit I couldn't fall asleep. I was having difficulty recalling what I used to do at night. It was as if he and I lived together in our own quiet space—a space made all the more intimate because of our conscious decision to block everyone else out. My phone was tied up for hours at a time. No one in the real world could reach me, and I didn't really care.

Since my last serious relationship, I'd had the requisite number of false starts and five-night stands, dates that I wasn't sure were dates, and emphatically casual affairs that buckled under their own inertia. With PFSlider, on the other hand, I may not have known my suitor, but, for the first time in my life, I knew the deal: I was a desired person, the object of a blind man's gaze. He called not only when he said he would call but unexpectedly, just to say hello. He was protected by the shield of the Internet; his guard was not merely down but nonexistent. He let his phone bill grow to towering proportions. He told me that he thought about me all the time, though we both knew that the "me" in his mind consisted largely of himself. He talked about me to his friends, and admitted it. He arranged his holiday schedule around our impending date. He managed to charm me with sports analogies. He didn't hesitate. He was unblinking and unapologetic, all nerviness and balls to the wall.

And so PFSlider became my everyday life. All the tangible stuff fell away. My body did not exist. I had no skin, no hair, no bones. All desire had converted itself into a cerebral current that reached nothing but my frontal lobe. There was no outdoors, no social life, no weather. There was only the computer screen and the phone, my chair, and maybe a glass of water. Most mornings, I would wake up to find a message from PFSlider, composed in Pacific time while I slept in the wee hours. "I had a date last night," he wrote. "And I am not ashamed to say it was doomed from the start because I couldn't stop thinking about you." 15

I fired back a message slapping his hand. "We must be careful where we tread," I said. This was true but not sincere. I wanted it, all of it. I wanted unfettered affection, soul-mating, true romance. In the weeks that had elapsed since I picked up "is this the real meghan daum?" the real me had undergone some kind of meltdown—a systemic rejection of all the savvy and independence I had worn for years, like a grownup Girl Scout badge.

Pete knew nothing of my scattered, juvenile self, and I did my best to keep it that way. Even though I was heading into my late twenties, I was still a child, ignorant of dance steps and health insurance, a prisoner of credit-card debt and student loans and the nagging feeling that I didn't want anyone to find me until I had pulled myself into some semblance of an adult. The fact that Pete had literally seemed to discover me, as if by turning over a rock, lent us an aura of fate which I actually took half-seriously. Though skepticism seemed like the obvious choice in this strange situation, I discarded it precisely because it was the obvious choice, because I wanted a more interesting narrative than cynicism would ever allow. I was a true believer in the urban dream: the dream of years of struggle, of getting a break, of making it. Like most of my friends, I wanted someone to love me, but I wasn't supposed to need it. To admit to loneliness was to smack the face of progress, to betray the times in which we lived. But PFSlider derailed me. He gave me all of what I'd never even realized I wanted.

My addiction to PFSlider's messages indicated a monstrous narcissism, but it also revealed a subtler desire, which I didn't fully understand at the time. My need to experience an old-fashioned kind of courtship was stronger than I had ever imagined. And the fact that technology was providing an avenue for such archaic discourse was a paradox that both fascinated and repelled me. Our relationship had an epistolary quality that put our communication closer to the eighteenth century than to the impending millennium. Thanks to the computer, I was involved in a well-defined courtship, a neat little space in which he and I were both safe to express the panic and the fascination of our mutual affection. Our interaction was refreshingly orderly, noble in its vigor, dignified despite its shamelessness. It was far removed from the randomness of real-life relationships. We had an intimacy that seemed custom-made for our strange, lonely times. It seemed custom-made for me.

The day of our date, a week before Christmas, was frigid and sunny. Pete was sitting at the bar of the restaurant when I arrived. We shook hands. For a split second, he leaned toward me with his chin, as if to kiss me. He was shorter than I had pictured, though he was not short. He struck me as clean-cut. He had very nice hands. He wore a very nice shirt. We were seated at a very nice table. I scanned the restaurant for people I knew, saw none, and couldn't decide how I felt about that.

He talked, and I heard nothing he said. I stared at his profile and tried to figure out whether I liked him. He seemed to be saying nothing in particular, but he went on forever. Later, we went to the Museum of Natural History and watched a science film about storm chasers. We walked around looking for the dinosaurs, and he talked so much that I wanted to cry. Outside, walking along Central Park West at dusk, through the leaves, past the yellow cabs and the splendid lights of Manhattan at Christmas, he grabbed my hand to kiss me and I didn't let him. I felt as if my brain had been stuffed with cotton. Then, for some reason, I invited him back to my apartment. I gave him a few beers and finally let him kiss me on the lumpy futon in my bedroom. The radiator clanked. The phone rang and the machine picked up. A car alarm blared outside. A key turned in the door as one of my roommates came home. I had no sensation at all—only a clear conviction that I wanted Pete out of my apartment. I wanted to hand him his coat, close the door behind him, and fight the ensuing empti-ness by turning on the computer and taking comfort in PFSlider.

When Pete finally did leave, I berated myself from every angle: for not kiss-ing him on Central Park West, for letting him kiss me at all, for not liking him, for wanting to like him more than I had wanted anything in such a long time. I was horrified by the realization that I had invested so heavily in a made-up character—a character in whose creation I'd had a greater hand than even Pete himself. How could I, a person so self-congratulatingly reasonable, have been sucked into a scenario that was more akin to a television talk show than to the relatively full and sophisticated life I was so convinced I led? How could I have received a fan letter and allowed it to go this far?

The next day, a huge bouquet of FTD flowers arrived from him. No one had ever sent me flowers before. I forgave him. As human beings with actual flesh and hand gestures and Gap clothing, Pete and I were utterly incompatible, but I decided to pretend otherwise. He returned home and we fell back into the computer and the phone, and I continued to keep the real world safely away from the desk that held them. Instead of blaming him for my disappointment, I blamed the earth itself, the invasion of roommates and ringing phones into the immaculate communication that PFSlider and I had created.

When I pictured him in the weeks that followed, I saw the image of a plane lifting off over an overcast city. PFSlider was otherworldly, more a concept than a person. His romance lay in the notion of flight, the physics of gravity defiance. So when he offered to send me a plane ticket to spend the weekend with him in Los Angeles I took it as an extension of our blissful remoteness, a three-dimensional E-mail message lasting an entire weekend.

The temperature on the runway at J.F.K. was seven degrees Fahrenheit. Our DC-10 sat for three hours waiting for deicing. Finally, it took off over the fro-zen city, and the ground below shrank into a drawing of itself. Phone calls were made, laptop computers were plopped onto tray tables. The recirculating air dried out my contact lenses. I watched movies without the sound and told myself that they were probably better that way. Something about the plastic interior of the fuselage and the plastic forks and the din of the air and the engines was soothing and strangely sexy.

Then we descended into LAX. We hit the tarmac, and the seat-belt signs 25 blinked off. I hadn't moved my body in eight hours, and now I was walking through the tunnel to the gate, my clothes wrinkled, my hair matted, my hands shaking. When I saw Pete in the terminal, his face seemed to me just as blank and easy to miss as it had the first time I'd met him. He kissed me chastely. On the way out to the parking lot, he told me that he was being seriously considered for a job in New York. He was flying back there next week. If he got the job, he'd be moving within the month. I looked at him in astonishment. Something silent and invisible seemed to fall on us. Outside, the wind was warm, and the Avis and Hertz buses ambled alongside the curb of Terminal 5. The palm trees shook, and the air seemed as heavy and palpable as Pete's hand, which held mine for a few seconds before dropping it to get his car keys out of his pocket. He stood before me, all flesh and preoccupation, and for this I could not forgive him.

Gone were the computer, the erotic darkness of the telephone, the clean, single dimension of Pete's voice at 1 A.M. It was nighttime, yet the combination of sight and sound was blinding. It scared me. It turned me off. We went to a restaurant and ate outside on the sidewalk. We strained for conversation, and I tried not to care that we had to. We drove to his apartment and stood under the ceiling light not really looking at each other. Something was happening that we needed to snap out of. Any moment now, I thought. Any moment and we'll be all right. These moments were crowded with elements, with carpet fibers and automobiles and the smells of everything that had a smell. It was all wrong. The physical world had invaded our space.

For three days, we crawled along the ground and tried to pull ourselves up. We talked about things that I can no longer remember. We read the Los Angeles *Times* over breakfast. We drove north past Santa Barbara to tour the wine country. I felt like an object that could not be lifted, something that secretly weighed more than the world itself. Everything and everyone around us seemed imbued with a California lightness. I stomped around the countryside, an idiot New Yorker in my clunky shoes and black leather jacket. Not until I studied myself in the bathroom mirror of a highway rest stop did I fully realize the preposterousness of my uniform. I was dressed for war. I was dressed for my regular life.

That night in a tiny town called Solvang, we ate an expensive dinner. We checked into a Marriott and watched television. Pete talked at me and through me and past me. I tried to listen. I tried to talk. But I bored myself and irritated him. Our conversation was a needle that could not be threaded. Still, we played nice. We tried to care, and pretended to keep trying long after we had given up. In the car on the way home, he told me that I was cynical, and I didn't have the presence of mind to ask him just how many cynics he had met who would travel three thousand miles to see someone they barely knew.

Pete drove me to the airport at 7 A.M. so I could make my eight-o'clock flight home. He kissed me goodbye—another chaste peck that I recognized from countless dinner parties and dud dates. He said that he'd call me in a few days when he got to New York for his job interview, which we had discussed only in passing and with no reference to the fact that New York was where I happened to live. I returned home to frozen January. A few days later, he came to New York, and we didn't see each other. He called me from the plane taking him back to Los Angeles to tell me, through the static, that he had got the job. He was moving to my city.

PFSlider was dead. There would be no meeting him in distant hotel lobbies 30 during the baseball season. There would be no more phone calls or E-mail messages. In a single moment, Pete had completed his journey out of our mating dance and officially stepped into the regular world—the world that gnawed at me daily, the world that fostered those five-night stands, the world where romance could not be sustained, because so many of us simply did not know how to do it. Instead, we were all chitchat and leather jackets, bold proclaimers of all that we did not need. But what struck me most about this affair was the unpredictable nature of our demise. Unlike most cyber-romances, which seem to come fully equipped with the inevitable set of misrepresentations and false expectations, PFSlider and I had played it fairly straight. Neither of us had lied. We'd done the best we could. Our affair had died from natural causes rather than virtual ones.

Within a two-week period after I returned from Los Angeles, at least seven people confessed to me the vagaries of their own E-mail affairs. This topic arose, unprompted, in the course of normal conversation. I heard most of these stories in the close confines of smoky bars and crowded restaurants, and we all shook our heads in bewilderment as we told our tales, our eyes focussed on some point in the distance. Four of these people had met their correspondents, by travelling from New Haven to Baltimore, from New York to Montana, from Texas to Virginia, and from New York to Johannesburg. These were normal people, writers and lawyers and scientists. They were all smart, attractive, and more than a little sheepish about admitting just how deeply they had been sucked in. Mostly, it was the courtship ritual that had seduced us. E-mail had become an electronic epistle, a yearned-for rule book. It allowed us to do what was necessary to experience love. The Internet was not responsible for our remote, fragmented lives. The problem was life itself.

The story of PFSlider still makes me sad, not so much because we no longer have anything to do with each other but because it forces me to see the limits and the perils of daily life with more clarity than I used to. After I realized that our relationship would never transcend the screen and the phone—that, in fact, our face-to-face knowledge of each other had permanently contaminated the screen and the phone—I hit the pavement again, went through the motions of everyday life, said hello and goodbye to people in the regular way. If Pete and I had met at a party, we probably wouldn't have spoken to each other for more than ten minutes, and that would have made life easier but also less interesting. At the same time, it terrifies me to admit to a firsthand understanding of the way the heart and the ego are snarled and entwined like diseased trees that have folded in on each other. Our need to worship somehow fuses with our need to be worshipped. It upsets me still further to see how inaccessibility can make this entanglement so much more intoxicating. But I'm also thankful that I was forced to unpack the raw truth of my need and stare at it for a while. It was a dare I wouldn't have taken in three dimensions.

The last time I saw Pete, he was in New York, three thousand miles away from what had been his home, and a million miles away from PFSlider. In a final gesture of decency, in what I later realized was the most ordinary kind of closure, he took me out to dinner. As the few remaining traces of affection turned into embarrassed regret, we talked about nothing. He paid the bill. He drove me home in a rental car that felt as arbitrary and impersonal as what we now were to each other.

Pete had known how to get me where I lived until he came to where I lived: then he became as unmysterious as anyone next door. The world had proved to be too cluttered and too fast for us, too polluted to allow the thing we'd attempted through technology ever to grow in the earth. PFSlider and I had joined the angry and exhausted living. Even if we met on the street, we wouldn't recognize each other, our particular version of intimacy now obscured by the branches and bodies and falling debris that make up the physical world.

FOR ANALYSIS

1. As the author's online relationship picks up steam, did you have any expectations about where it was going and how it would end up? Were your expectations confirmed or confounded? Do you think the author intended you to have the reading experience you had?

2. Daum writes that the affair "died of natural causes" (para. 30). Based on the evidence of her essay, do you agree? Why or why not?

3. Note the essay's date of publication. Does anything feel dated about it? If so, does that change the effect of reading the essay? Do you evaluate its accuracy or applicability differently?

MAKING CONNECTIONS

1. The last sentence of Daum's essay ends with the phrase "the physical world." What relationship does the world in which most of the action of both essays takes place— the virtual world—have to the "real" physical world? In each of these essays, in what ways is the virtual world part of the real world? In what ways is it not?

2. In both essays, it seems likely that the lack of human contact with the partner, either the ex or a prospective lover, creates problems. While the cause of this absence of contact is different in each case—the breakup in Pollitt's, the Internet (and geography) in Daum's—do you think the effects might be similar? What do we get out of direct interaction with other people—that is, what about seeing people, hearing their voices, and watching their faces and posture is important to the way we get along with them?

3. Both of these essays focus in part on the phenomenon of Internet addiction. While this sounds like a psychological condition, there are ways in which many of us feel the attraction of being on the Internet in ways that feel less intense than a diagnosable syndrome might indicate. What do you think are the costs of this attraction? What are the benefits of being as wired as we are these days? What are the drawbacks?

WRITING TOPIC

Daum describes her "addiction" to her virtual lover's messages as indicating (among other things) what she calls "a monstrous narcissism" (para. 18). Do you agree? How much of "regular" romantic love could be said to involve the same condition?

FURTHER QUESTIONS
FOR THINKING AND WRITING

1. How do the works in this section support the contention that love and hate are closely related emotions? **Writing Topic:** Discuss the relationship between love and hate in Carver's "What We Talk About When We Talk About Love" and Shakespeare's *Othello*.

2. What images are characteristically associated with love in the prose and poetry of this section? What images are associated with hate? **Writing Topic:** Compare the image patterns in Shakespeare's Sonnets 18 and 130 or the image patterns in Donne's "A Valediction: Forbidding Mourning" and Marlowe's "The Passionate Shepherd to His Love."

3. The Greeks have three words that can be translated by the English word *love*: *eros*, *agape*, and *philia*. Describe the differences among these three types of love. **Writing Topic:** Find a story or poem that is representative of each type of love. In analyzing each work, discuss the extent to which the primary notion of love being addressed or celebrated is tempered by the other two types.

4. Blake's "A Poison Tree," Peacock's "Say You Love Me," Kizer's "Bitch," and Plath's "Daddy" all seem to describe aspects of hate. Distinguish among the different varieties of hatred expressed in each poem. **Writing Topic:** Compare and contrast the source of the speaker's hatred in two of these poems.

5. Which works in this section treat love and/or hate in a way that corresponds most closely with your own experience or conception of those emotional states? Which contradict your experience? **Writing Topic:** For each case, isolate the elements in the work that provoke your response, and discuss them in terms of their "truth" or "falsity."

LIFE AND DEATH

Death and Life, 1908–1916, by Gustav Klimt.

The inevitability of death is not implied in the biblical story of creation; it required an act of disobedience before an angry God passed a sentence of hard labor and mortality on humankind: "In the sweat of your face you shall eat bread till you return to the ground, for out of it you were taken; you are dust and to dust you shall return." These words, written down some 2,800 years ago, preserve one ancient explanation for a persistently enigmatic condition of life and a persistent awareness of the implications of our actions. From earliest times men and women have attempted to characterize death, to cultivate beliefs about it, and to let it inform how they spend their time among the living. The mystery and certainty of death, in every age, make it an important theme for literary art.

Beliefs about the nature of death vary widely. The ancient Jews of the Pentateuch reveal no conception of immortality. Ancient Buddhist writings describe death as a mere translation from one painful life to another in an ongoing process of atonement that only the purest can avoid. The Christians conceive of a soul, separate from the body, which at the body's death is freed for a disembodied eternal life. The speaker in Robert Frost's "Stopping by Woods on a Snowy Evening" gazes into the dark woods filling up with snow, momentarily drawn toward the peace it represents; but Frost's is a secular poem, and the speaker turns back to life. In much religious poetry—John Donne's sonnet "Death, Be Not Proud" is an outstanding example—death is celebrated as a release from a burdensome existence into the eternal happiness of the afterlife. More recently, attitudes about death have reflected the great intellectual revolutions that affected all thought. For example, the Darwinian revolution replaced humans, the greatest glory of God's creation, with upright primates whose days are likely to be numbered by the flux between the fire and ice of geological history; and the Freudian revolution robbed men and women of their proudest certainty—the conviction that they possessed a dependable and controlling rational mind. In the context of Western tradition, these ideas serve to diminish us, to mock our self-importance. And, inevitably, these shifts lead us to alter our conception of death.

Death often inspires evaluation, or re-evaluation. Another's death affords us the opportunity to look back on a life and judge its worth; it also impels us to look again at our own lives. Simple awareness of the fact of death is sometimes enough to make us worry about what we are doing with our lives—a theme explored by poets in the "Seizing the Day" cluster in this chapter—and reactions to such a realization can range from Rainer Maria Rilke's cautionary encouragement "You must change your life" to James Wright's resigned declaration "I have wasted my life."

The view that establishes death as the great leveler, bringing citizens and emperors to the selfsame dust, is apparent in such poems as Percy Bysshe Shelley's "Ozymandias" and A. E. Housman's "To an Athlete Dying Young." This leveling view of death leads easily to the tradition wherein life itself is made absurd by the fact of death. Shakespeare's Macbeth finally declares that life is "a tale / Told by an idiot, full of sound and fury, / Signifying nothing." And the contemplation of suicide, which the pain and absurdity of life would seem to commend, provokes responses such as Edwin Arlington Robinson's ironic "Richard Cory." Some rage against death, as Dylan Thomas does in "Do Not Go Gentle into That Good Night"; others caution a quiet resignation, like Frost in "After Apple-Picking" and Catherine Davis in "After a Time," her answer to Thomas. Much fine poetry on death is elegiac—it speaks the melancholy response of the living to the fact of death. And reminders of this fact do not arise only from the death of a solitary person or within a grieving community: we are faced with it when we recognize the lives and deaths of the animals with whom we share the planet, as we see in Lydia Millet's story "Girl and Giraffe" and William Greenway's poem "Pit Pony." These writers urge us to see that the animal world is an inextricable part of the human experience; it isn't there simply to help us think about our own deaths and lives, but exists in its own right as a world worthy of attention, one whose own cycle of life and death can be shaped, sometimes quite harmfully, by human actions.

In short, literary treatments of death and how it shapes life display immense diversity. In Leo Tolstoy's "The Death of Iván Ilých," dying leads to a redemptive awareness. Leslie Marmon Silko's "The Man to Send Rain Clouds" explores sacrificial death as a means to control nature. In Victor Hernández Cruz's "Problems with Hurricanes" the comic lightens the weight of death. And in "Joyas Voladores," Brian Doyle confronts the truth that one life is just that, and each of us "must live alone in the house of the heart." The inevitability of death and the way one confronts it paradoxically give life its meaning and its value.

QUESTIONS FOR THINKING AND WRITING

As you read the selections in this section, consider the following questions. You may want to write out your thoughts informally in a journal as a way of preparing to respond to the selections, or you may wish to make one of these questions the basis for a formal essay.

1. Has a close relative or friend of yours died? Was the person young or old, vigorous or in poor health? How did you feel? How might the circumstances of death alter one's feelings toward death or toward the person who died?

2. Do you believe that some essential part of you will survive the death of your body? On what do you base the belief? How does this belief alter your feelings about the death of people close to you? How does it alter your own behavior?

3. Are there any circumstances that justify suicide? Explain. If you believe that some suicides are justifiable, would it also be justifiable to help someone end his or her life? Explain.

4. Are there any circumstances that justify killing someone? Explain.

5. Imagine as best you can the circumstances of your own death. Describe them.

6. Write your own obituary. How would you like to be remembered? If you want, instead of the reserved, respectful tone characteristic of the genre, write something funny or satirical, but still take the exercise seriously. What are the important things you want people to remember about you, that you did or said? What kind of person were you really?

FICTION

EDGAR ALLAN POE   (1809–1849)

THE CASK OF AMONTILLADO   1846

The thousand injuries of Fortunato I had borne as I best could, but when he ventured upon insult, I vowed revenge. You, who so well know the nature of my soul, will not suppose, however, that I gave utterance to a threat. At *length* I would be avenged; this was a point definitely settled—but the very definitiveness with which it was resolved precluded the idea of risk. I must not only punish, but punish with impunity. A wrong is unredressed when retribution overtakes its redresser. It is equally unredressed when the avenger fails to make himself felt as such to him who has done the wrong.

It must be understood that neither by word nor deed had I given Fortunato cause to doubt my good will. I continued, as was my wont, to smile in his face, and he did not perceive that my smile *now* was at the thought of his immolation.

He had a weak point—this Fortunato—although in other regards he was a man to be respected and even feared. He prided himself on his connoisseurship in wine. Few Italians have the true virtuoso spirit. For the most part their enthusiasm is adopted to suit the time and opportunity to practise imposture upon the British and Austrian *millionnaires*. In painting and gemmary Fortunato, like his countrymen, was a quack, but in the matter of old wines he was sincere. In this respect I did not differ from him materially;—I was skillful in the Italian vintages myself, and bought largely whenever I could.

It was about dusk, one evening during the supreme madness of the carnival season, that I encountered my friend. He accosted me with excessive warmth, for he had been drinking much. The man wore motley. He had on a tight-fitting parti-striped dress, and his head was surmounted by the conical cap and bells. I was so pleased to see him, that I thought I should never have done wringing his hand.

I said to him—"My dear Fortunato, you are luckily met. How remarkably 5 well you are looking to-day! But I have received a pipe[1] of what passes for Amontillado, and I have my doubts."

---

[1] Large wine cask.

"How?" said he, "Amontillado? A pipe? Impossible! And in the middle of the carnival!"

"I have my doubts," I replied; "and I was silly enough to pay the full Amontillado price without consulting you in the matter. You were not to be found, and I was fearful of losing a bargain."

"Amontillado!"

"I have my doubts."

"Amontillado!" 10

"And I must satisfy them."

"Amontillado!"

"As you are engaged, I am on my way to Luchesi. If any one has a critical turn, it is he. He will tell me—"

"Luchesi cannot tell Amontillado from Sherry."

"And yet some fools will have it that his taste is a match for your own." 15

"Come, let us go."

"Whither?"

"To your vaults."

"My friend, no; I will not impose upon your good nature. I perceive you have an engagement. Luchesi—"

"I have no engagement;—come." 20

"My friend, no. It is not the engagement, but the severe cold with which I perceive you are afflicted. The vaults are insufferably damp. They are encrusted with nitre."

"Let us go, nevertheless. The cold is merely nothing. Amontillado! You have been imposed upon; and as for Luchesi, he cannot distinguish Sherry from Amontillado."

Thus speaking, Fortunato possessed himself of my arm. Putting on a mask of black silk, and drawing a *roquelaure*[2] closely about my person, I suffered him to hurry me to my palazzo.

There were no attendants at home; they had absconded to make merry in honor of the time. I had told them that I should not return until the morning, and had given them explicit orders not to stir from the house. These orders were sufficient, I well knew, to insure their immediate disappearance, one and all, as soon as my back was turned.

I took from their sconces two flambeaux, and giving one to Fortunato, 25 bowed him through several suites of rooms to the archway that led into the vaults. I passed down a long and winding staircase, requesting him to be cautious as he followed. We came at length to the foot of the descent, and stood together on the damp ground of the catacombs of the Montresors.

The gait of my friend was unsteady, and the bells upon his cap jingled as he strode.

"The pipe," said he.

"It is farther on," said I; "but observe the white web-work which gleams from these cavern walls."

[2] Short cloak.

He turned towards me, and looked into my eyes with two filmy orbs that distilled the rheum of intoxication.

"Nitre?" he asked, at length. 30

"Nitre," I replied. "How long have you had that cough?"

"Ugh! ugh! ugh!—ugh! ugh! ugh!—ugh! ugh! ugh!—ugh! ugh! ugh!—ugh! ugh! ugh!"

My poor friend found it impossible to reply for many minutes.

"It is nothing," he said, at last.

"Come," I said, with decision, "we will go back; your health is precious. You 35 are rich, respected, admired, beloved; you are happy, as once I was. You are a man to be missed. For me it is no matter. We will go back; you will be ill, and I cannot be responsible. Besides, there is Luchesi—"

"Enough," he said; "the cough is a mere nothing: it will not kill me. I shall not die of a cough."

"True—true," I replied; "and, indeed, I had no intention of alarming you unnecessarily—but you should use all proper caution. A draught of this Medoc will defend us from the damps."

Here I knocked off the neck of a bottle which I drew from a long row of its fellows that lay upon the mould.

"Drink," I said, presenting him the wine.

He raised it to his lips with a leer. He paused and nodded to me familiarly, 40 while his bells jingled.

"I drink," he said, "to the buried that repose around us."

"And I to your long life."

He again took my arm, and we proceeded.

"These vaults," he said, "are extensive."

"The Montresors," I replied, "were a great and numerous family." 45

"I forget your arms."

"A huge human foot d'or, in a field azure; the foot crushes a serpent rampant whose fangs are imbedded in the heel."

"And the motto?"

"*Nemo me impune lacessit.*"[3]

"Good!" he said. 50

The wine sparkled in his eyes and the bells jingled. My own fancy grew warm with the Medoc. We had passed through walls of piled bones, with casks and puncheons intermingling, into the inmost recesses of the catacombs. I paused again, and this time I made bold to seize Fortunato by an arm above the elbow.

"The nitre!" I said; "see, it increases. It hangs like moss upon the vaults. We are below the river's bed. The drops of moisture trickle among the bones. Come, we will go back ere it is too late. Your cough—"

"It is nothing," he said; "let us go on. But first, another draught of the Medoc."

---

[3] No one provokes me with impunity (the motto of Scotland).

I broke and reached him a flagon of De Grâve. He emptied it at a breath. His eyes flashed with a fierce light. He laughed and threw the bottle upwards with a gesticulation I did not understand.

I looked at him in surprise. He repeated the movement—a grotesque one. 55
"You do not comprehend?" he said.
"Not I," I replied.
"Then you are not of the brotherhood."
"How?"
"You are not of the masons."[4] 60
"Yes, yes," I said; "yes, yes."
"You? Impossible! A mason?"
"A mason," I replied.
"A sign," he said.
"It is this," I answered, producing a trowel from beneath the folds of my 65 *roquelaure.*

"You jest," he exclaimed, recoiling a few paces. "But let us proceed to the Amontillado."

"Be it so," I said, replacing the tool beneath the cloak, and again offering him my arm. He leaned upon it heavily. We continued our route in search of the Amontillado. We passed through a range of low arches, descended, passed on, and descending again, arrived at a deep crypt, in which the foulness of the air caused our flambeaux rather to glow than flame.

At the most remote end of the crypt there appeared another less spacious. Its walls had been lined with human remains piled to the vault overhead, in the fashion of the great catacombs of Paris. Three sides of this interior crypt were still ornamented in this manner. From the fourth the bones had been thrown down, and lay promiscuously upon the earth, forming at one point a mound of some size. Within the wall thus exposed by the displacing of the bones, we perceived a still interior recess, in depth about four feet, in width three, in height six or seven. It seemed to have been constructed for no especial use within itself, but formed merely the interval between two of the colossal supports of the roof of the catacombs, and was backed by one of their circum-scribing walls of solid granite.

It was in vain that Fortunato, uplifting his dull torch, endeavored to pry into the depths of the recess. Its termination the feeble light did not enable us to see.

"Proceed," I said; "herein is the Amontillado. As for Luchesi—" 70

"He is an ignoramus," interrupted my friend, as he stepped unsteadily forward, while I followed immediately at his heels. In an instant he had reached the extremity of the niche, and finding his progress arrested by the rock, stood stupidly bewildered. A moment more and I had fettered him to the granite. In its surface were two iron staples, distant from each other about two feet, horizontally. From one of these depended a short chain, from the other a

[4] A member of the Freemasons, an international secretive mutual aid society.

padlock. Throwing the links about his waist, it was but the work of a few seconds to secure it. He was too much astounded to resist. Withdrawing the key I stepped back from the recess.

"Pass your hand," I said, "over the wall; you cannot help feeling the nitre. Indeed it is *very* damp. Once more let me *implore* you to return. No? Then I must positively leave you. But I must first render you all the little attentions in my power."

"The Amontillado!" ejaculated my friend, not yet recovered from his astonishment.

"True," I replied; "the Amontillado."

As I said these words I busied myself among the pile of bones of which I have 75 before spoken. Throwing them aside, I soon uncovered a quantity of building-stone and mortar. With these materials and with the aid of my trowel, I began vigorously to wall up the entrance of the niche.

I had scarcely laid the first tier of the masonry when I discovered that the intoxication of Fortunato had in a great measure worn off. The earliest indication I had of this was a low moaning cry from the depth of the recess. It was *not* the cry of a drunken man. There was then a long and obstinate silence. I laid the second tier, and the third, and the fourth; and then I heard the furious vibrations of the chain. The noise lasted for several minutes, during which, that I might hearken to it with the more satisfaction, I ceased my labors and sat down upon the bones. When at last the clanking subsided, I resumed the trowel, and finished without interruption the fifth, the sixth, and the seventh tier. The wall was now nearly upon a level with my breast. I again paused, and holding the flambeaux over the masonwork, threw a few feeble rays upon the figure within.

A succession of loud and shrill screams, bursting suddenly from the throat of the chained form, seemed to thrust me violently back. For a brief moment I hesitated—I trembled. Unsheathing my rapier, I began to grope with it about the recess; but the thought of an instant reassured me. I placed my hand upon the solid fabric of the catacombs, and felt satisfied. I reapproached the wall. I replied to the yells of him who clamored. I re-echoed—I aided—I surpassed them in volume and in strength. I did this, and the clamorer grew still.

It was now midnight, and my task was drawing to a close. I had completed the eighth, the ninth, and the tenth tier. I had finished a portion of the last and the eleventh; there remained but a single stone to be fitted and plastered in. I struggled with its weight; I placed it partially in its destined position. But now there came from out the niche a low laugh that erected the hairs upon my head. It was succeeded by a sad voice, which I had difficulty in recognizing as that of the noble Fortunato. The voice said—

"Ha! ha! ha!—he! he! he!—a very good joke indeed—an excellent jest. We will have many a rich laugh about it at the palazzo—he! he! he!—over our wine—he! he! he!"

"The Amontillado!" I said. 80

"He! he! he!—he! he! he!—yes, the Amontillado. But is it not getting late? Will not they be awaiting us at the palazzo, the Lady Fortunato and the rest? Let us be gone."

"Yes," I said, "let us be gone."

"For the love of God, Montresor!"

"Yes," I said, "for the love of God!"

But to these words I hearkened in vain for a reply. I grew impatient. I called 85 aloud;

"Fortunato!"

No answer. I called again;

"Fortunato!"

No answer still. I thrust a torch through the remaining aperture and let it fall within. There came forth in return only a jingling of the bells. My heart grew sick—on account of the dampness of the catacombs. I hastened to make an end of my labor. I forced the last stone into its position; I plastered it up. Against the new masonry I reerected the old rampart of bones. For the half of a century no mortal has disturbed them. *In pace requiescat!*[5]

FOR ANALYSIS

1. We are not told how Fortunato insulted Montresor. Would the story be more effective if we knew? Explain.

2. Are there any clues that suggest when and to whom Montresor tells his tale? Explain.

3. How is Montresor able to lure Fortunato into the catacombs?

4. Describe the qualities that Montresor insists on as the characteristics of a successful vengeance.

5. Describe the **style** of this story, particularly the speech of the characters. What effect does the archaic flavor contribute to the tale?

MAKING CONNECTIONS

Compare this story with Jackson's "The Lottery" (p. 373), which also ends with an unexpected and horrible murder. What similarities do you find? What differences?

WRITING TOPICS

1. In an essay, imagine and describe the circumstances and the nature of Fortunato's insult.

2. Choose a short section of the story—say, three or four paragraphs—and carefully analyze the language line by line (particularly as it differs from ordinary colloquial English). How does the unusual language contribute to the story's effect?

[5] May he rest in peace.

THE DEATH OF IVÁN ILÝCH[1]   1886

CHAPTER I

During an interval in the Melvínski trial in the large building of the Law Courts the members and public prosecutor met in Iván Egórovich Shébek's private room, where the conversation turned on the celebrated Krasóvski case. Fëdor Vasílievich warmly maintained that it was not subject to their jurisdiction, Iván Egórovich maintained the contrary, while Peter Ivánovich, not having entered into the discussion at the start, took no part in it but looked through the *Gazette* which had just been handed in.

"Gentlemen," he said, "Iván Ilých has died!"

"You don't say so!"

"Here, read it yourself," replied Peter Ivánovich, handing Fëdor Vasílievich the paper still damp from the press. Surrounded by a black border were the words: "Praskóvya Fëdorovna Goloviná, with profound sorrow, informs relatives and friends of the demise of her beloved husband Iván Ilých Golovín, Member of the Court of Justice, which occurred on February the 4th of this year 1882. The funeral will take place on Friday at one o'clock in the afternoon."

Iván Ilých had been a colleague of the gentlemen present and was liked by 5 them all. He had been ill for some weeks with an illness said to be incurable. His post had been kept open for him, but there had been conjectures that in case of his death Alexéev might receive his appointment, and that either Vínnikov or Shtábel would succeed Alexéev. So on receiving the news of Iván Ilých's death the first thought of each of the gentlemen in that private room was of the changes and promotions it might occasion among themselves or their acquaintances.

"I shall be sure to get Shtábel's place or Vínnikov's," thought Fëdor Vasílievich. "I was promised that long ago, and the promotion means an extra eight hundred rubles a year for me besides the allowance."

"Now I must apply for my brother-in-law's transfer from Kalúga," thought Peter Ivánovich. "My wife will be very glad, and then she won't be able to say that I never do anything for her relations."

"I thought he would never leave his bed again," said Peter Ivánovich aloud. "It's very sad."

"But what really was the matter with him?"

"The doctors couldn't say—at least they could, but each of them said some- 10 thing different. When last I saw him I thought he was getting better."

[1] Translated by Aylmer Maude.

"And I haven't been to see him since the holidays. I always meant to go."

"Had he any property?"

"I think his wife had a little—but something quite trifling."

"We shall have to go to see her, but they live so terribly far away."

"Far away from you, you mean. Everything's far away from your place." 15

"You see, he never can forgive my living on the other side of the river," said Peter Ivánovich, smiling at Shébek. Then, still talking of the distances between different parts of the city, they returned to the Court.

Besides considerations as to the possible transfers and promotions likely to result from Iván Ilých's death, the mere fact of the death of a near acquaintance aroused, as usual, in all who heard of it the complacent feeling that, "it is he who is dead and not I."

Each one thought or felt, "Well, he's dead but I'm alive!" But the more intimate of Iván Ilých's acquaintances, his so-called friends, could not help thinking also that they would now have to fulfill the very tiresome demands of propriety by attending the funeral service and paying a visit of condolence to the widow.

Fëdor Vasílievich and Peter Ivánovich had been his nearest acquaintances. Peter Ivánovich had studied law with Iván Ilých and had considered himself to be under obligations to him.

Having told his wife at dinner-time of Iván Ilých's death, and of his con- 20 jecture that it might be possible to get her brother transferred to their circuit, Peter Ivánovich sacrificed his usual nap, put on his evening clothes, and drove to Iván Ilých's house.

At the entrance stood a carriage and two cabs. Leaning against the wall in the hall downstairs near the cloak-stand was a coffin-lid covered with cloth of gold, ornamented with gold cord and tassels, that had been polished up with metal powder. Two ladies in black were taking off their fur cloaks. Peter Ivánovich recognized one of them as Iván Ilých's sister, but the other was a stranger to him. His colleague Schwartz was just coming downstairs, but on seeing Peter Ivánovich enter he stopped and winked at him, as if to say: "Iván Ilých has made a mess of things—not like you and me."

Schwartz's face with his Piccadilly whiskers, and his slim figure in evening dress, had as usual an air of elegant solemnity which contrasted with the playfulness of his character and had a special piquancy here, or so it seemed to Peter Ivánovich.

Peter Ivánovich allowed the ladies to precede him and slowly followed them upstairs. Schwartz did not come down but remained where he was, and Peter Ivánovich understood that he wanted to arrange where they should play bridge that evening. The ladies went upstairs to the widow's room, and Schwartz with seriously compressed lips but a playful look in his eyes, indicated by a twist of his eyebrows the room to the right where the body lay.

Peter Ivánovich, like everyone else on such occasions, entered feeling uncertain what he would have to do. All he knew was that at such times it is always safe to cross oneself. But he was not quite sure whether one should make obeisances while doing so. He therefore adopted a middle course. On entering the room he began crossing himself and made a slight movement resembling a bow. At the same time, as far as the motion of his head and arm allowed, he surveyed the room. Two young men—apparently nephews, one of whom was a high-school pupil—were leaving the room, crossing themselves as they did so. An old woman was standing motionless, and a lady with strangely arched eyebrows was saying something to her in a whisper. A vigorous, resolute Church Reader, in a frock-coat, was reading something in a loud voice with an expression that precluded any contradiction. The butler's assistant, Gerásim, stepping lightly in front of Peter Ivánovich, was strewing something on the floor. Noticing this, Peter Ivánovich was immediately aware of a faint odour of a decomposing body.

The last time he had called on Iván Ilých, Peter Ivánovich had seen Gerásim in the study. Iván Ilých had been particularly fond of him and he was performing the duty of a sick nurse.

Peter Ivánovich continued to make the sign of the cross slightly inclining his head in an intermediate direction between the coffin, the Reader, and the icons on the table in a corner of the room. Afterwards, when it seemed to him that this movement of his arm in crossing himself had gone on too long, he stopped and began to look at the corpse.

The dead man lay, as dead men always lie, in a specially heavy way, his rigid limbs sunk in the soft cushions of the coffin, with the head forever bowed on the pillow. His yellow waxen brow with bald patches over his sunken temples was thrust up in the way peculiar to the dead, the protruding nose seeming to press on the upper lip. He was much changed and had grown even thinner since Peter Ivánovich had last seen him, but, as is always the case with the dead, his face was handsomer and above all more dignified than when he was alive. The expression on the face said that what was necessary had been accomplished, and accomplished rightly. Besides this there was in that expression a reproach and a warning to the living. This warning seemed to Peter Ivánovich out of place, or at least not applicable to him. He felt a certain discomfort and so he hurriedly crossed himself once more and turned and went out of the door—too hurriedly and too regardless of propriety, as he himself was aware.

Schwartz was waiting for him in the adjoining room with legs spread wide apart and both hands toying with his top-hat behind his back. The mere sight of that playful, well-groomed, and elegant figure refreshed Peter Ivánovich. He felt that Schwartz was above all these happenings and would not surrender to any depressing influences. His very look said that this incident of a church service for Iván Ilých could not be a sufficient reason for infringing the order of the session—in other words, that it would certainly not prevent his unwrapping a new pack of cards and shuffling them that evening while a footman placed four fresh candles on the table: in fact, there was no reason for supposing that this incident would hinder their spending the evening agreeably. Indeed he said this in a whisper as Peter Ivánovich passed him, proposing that they should meet for a game at Fëdor Vasílievich's. But apparently Peter Ivánovich was not destined to play bridge that evening. Praskóvya Fëdorovna (a short, fat woman who despite all efforts to the contrary had continued to broaden steadily from her shoulders downwards and who had the same extraordinarily arched eyebrows as the lady who had been standing by the coffin), dressed all in black, her head covered with lace, came out of her own room with some other ladies, conducted them to the room where the dead body lay, and said: "The service will begin immediately. Please go in."

Schwartz, making an indefinite bow, stood still, evidently neither accepting nor declining this invitation. Praskóvya Fëdorovna recognizing Peter Ivánovich, sighed, went close up to him, took his hand, and said: "I know you were a true friend to Iván Ilých . . ." and looked at him awaiting some suitable response. And Peter Ivánovich knew that, just as it had been the right thing to cross himself in that room, so what he had to do here was to press her hand, sigh, and say, "Believe me . . ." So he did all this and as he did it felt that the desired result had been achieved: that both he and she were touched.

"Come with me. I want to speak to you before it begins," said the widow.   30
"Give me your arm."

Peter Ivánovich gave her his arm and they went to the inner rooms, passing Schwartz who winked at Peter Ivánovich compassionately.

"That does for our bridge! Don't object if we find another player. Perhaps you can cut in when you do escape," said his playful look.

Peter Ivánovich sighed still more deeply and despondently, and Praskóvya Fëdorovna pressed his arm gratefully. When they reached the drawing-room, upholstered in pink cretonne and lighted by a dim lamp, they sat down at the table—she on a sofa and Peter Ivánovich on a low pouffe, the springs of which yielded spasmodically under his weight. Praskóvya Fëdorovna had been on the point of warning him to take another seat, but felt that such a warning was out of keeping with her present condition and so changed her mind. As he sat down on the pouffe Peter Ivánovich recalled how Iván Ilých had arranged this room and had consulted him regarding this pink cretonne with green leaves. The whole room was full of furniture and knick-knacks, and on her way to the sofa the lace of the widow's black shawl caught on the carved edge of the table. Peter Ivánovich rose to detach it, and the springs of the pouffe, relieved of his weight, rose also and gave him a push. The widow began detaching her shawl herself, and Peter Ivánovich again sat down, suppressing the rebellious springs of the pouffe under him. But the widow had not quite freed herself and Peter Ivánovich got up again, and again the pouffe rebelled and even creaked. When this was all over she took out a clean cambric handkerchief and began to weep. The episode with the shawl and the struggle with the pouffe had cooled Peter Ivánovich's emotions and he sat there with a sullen look on his face. This awkward situation was interrupted by Sokolóv, Iván Ilých's butler, who came to report that the plot in the cemetery that Praskóvya Fëdorovna had chosen would cost two hundred rubles. She stopped weeping and, looking at Peter Ivánovich with the air of a victim, remarked in French that it was very hard for her. Peter Ivánovich made a silent gesture signifying his full conviction that it must indeed be so.

"Please smoke," she said in a magnanimous yet crushed voice, and turned to discuss with Sokolóv the price of the plot for the grave.

Peter Ivánovich while lighting his cigarette heard her inquiring very circum- 35
stantially into the price of different plots in the cemetery and finally decide which she would take. When that was done she gave instructions about engaging the choir. Sokolóv then left the room.

"I look after everything myself," she told Peter Ivánovich, shifting the albums that lay on the table; and noticing that the table was endangered by his cigarette-ash, she immediately passed him an ashtray, saying as she did so: "I consider it an affectation to say that my grief prevents my attending to practical affairs. On the contrary, if anything can—I won't say console me, but— distract me, it is seeing to everything concerning him." She again took out her handkerchief as if preparing to cry, but suddenly, as if mastering her feeling, she shook herself and began to speak calmly. "But there is something I want to talk to you about."

Peter Ivánovich bowed, keeping control of the springs of the pouffe, which immediately began quivering under him.

"He suffered terribly the last few days."

"Did he?" said Peter Ivánovich.

"Oh, terribly! He screamed unceasingly, not for minutes but for hours. For the 40
last three days he screamed incessantly. It was unendurable. I cannot understand how I bore it; you could hear him three rooms off. Oh, what I have suffered!"

"Is it possible that he was conscious all that time?" asked Peter Ivánovich.

"Yes," she whispered. "To the last moment. He took leave of us a quarter of an hour before he died, and asked us to take Volódya away."

The thought of the sufferings of this man he had known so intimately, first as a merry little boy, then as a school-mate, and later as a grown-up colleague, suddenly struck Peter Ivánovich with horror, despite an unpleasant consciousness of his own and this woman's dissimulation. He again saw that brow, and that nose pressing down on the lip, and felt afraid for himself.

"Three days of frightful suffering and then death! Why, that might suddenly, at any time, happen to me," he thought, and for a moment felt terrified. But— he did not himself know how—the customary reflection at once occurred to him that this had happened to Iván Ilých and not to him, and that it should not and could not happen to him, and that to think that it could would be yielding to depression which he ought not to do, as Schwartz's expression plainly showed. After which reflection Peter Ivánovich felt reassured, and began to ask with interest about the details of Iván Ilých's death, as though death was an accident natural to Iván Ilých but certainly not to himself.

After many details of the really dreadful physical sufferings Iván Ilých 45
had endured (which details he learnt only from the effect those sufferings had produced on Praskóvya Fëdorovna's nerves) the widow apparently found it necessary to get to business.

"Oh, Peter Ivánovich, how hard it is! How terribly, terribly hard!" and she again began to weep.

Peter Ivánovich sighed and waited for her to finish blowing her nose. When she had done so he said, "Believe me . . ." and she again began talking and brought out what was evidently her chief concern with him—namely, to question him as to how she could obtain a grant of money from the government on the occasion of her husband's death. She made it appear that she was asking Peter Ivánovich's advice about her pension, but he soon saw that she already knew about that to the minutest detail, more even than he did himself. She knew how much could be got out of the government in consequence of her husband's death, but wanted to find out whether she could not possibly extract something more. Peter Ivánovich tried to think of some means of doing so, but after reflecting for a while and, out of propriety, condemning the government for its niggardliness, he said he thought that nothing more could be got. Then she sighed and evidently began to devise means of getting rid of her visitor. Noticing this, he put out his cigarette, rose, pressed her hand, and went out into the anteroom.

In the dining-room where the clock stood that Iván Ilých had liked so much and had bought at an antique shop, Peter Ivánovich met a priest and a few acquaintances who had come to attend the service, and he recognized Iván Ilých's daughter, a handsome young woman. She was in black and her slim figure appeared slimmer than ever. She had a gloomy, determined, almost angry expression, and bowed to Peter Ivánovich as though he were in some way to blame. Behind her, with the same offended look, stood a wealthy young man, an examining magistrate, whom Peter Ivánovich also knew and who was her fiancé, as he had heard. He bowed mournfully to them and was about to pass into the death-chamber, when from under the stairs appeared the figure of Iván Ilých's schoolboy son, who was extremely like his father. He seemed a little Iván Ilých, such as Peter Ivánovich remembered when they studied law together. His tear-stained eyes had in them the look that is seen in the eyes of boys of thirteen or fourteen who are not pure-minded. When he saw Peter Ivánovich he scowled morosely and shamefacedly. Peter Ivánovich nodded to him and entered the death-chamber. The service began: candles, groans, incense, tears, and sobs. Peter Ivánovich stood looking gloomily down at his feet. He did not look once at the dead man, did not yield to any depressing influence, and was one of the first to leave the room. There was no one in the anteroom, but Gerásim darted out of the dead man's room, rummaged with his strong hands among the fur coats to find Peter Ivánovich's and helped him on with it.

"Well, friend Gerásim," said Peter Ivánovich, so as to say something. "It's a sad affair, isn't it?"

"It's God's will. We shall all come to it some day," said Gerásim, displaying 50 his teeth—the even, white teeth of a healthy peasant—and, like a man in the thick of urgent work, he briskly opened the front door, called the coachman, helped Peter Ivánovich into the sledge, and sprang back to the porch as if in readiness for what he had to do next.

Peter Ivánovich found the fresh air particularly pleasant after the smell of incense, the dead body, and carbolic acid.

"Where to, sir?" asked the coachman.

"It's not too late even now. . . . I'll call round on Fëdor Vasílievich."

He accordingly drove there and found them just finishing the first rubber, so that it was quite convenient for him to cut in.

CHAPTER II

Iván Ilých's life had been most simple and most ordinary and therefore most terrible. 55

He had been a member of the Court of Justice, and died at the age of forty-five. His father had been an official who after serving in various ministries and departments in Petersburg had made the sort of career which brings men to positions from which by reason of their long service they cannot be dismissed, though they are obviously unfit to hold any responsible position, and for whom therefore posts are specially created, which though fictitious carry salaries of from six to ten thousand rubles that are not fictitious, and in receipt of which they live on to a great age.

Such was the Privy Councillor and superfluous member of various superfluous institutions, Ilyá Epímovich Golovín.

He had three sons, of whom Iván Ilých was the second. The eldest son was following in his father's footsteps only in another department, and was already approaching that stage in the service at which a similar sinecure would be reached. The third son was a failure. He had ruined his prospects in a number of positions and was now serving in the railway department. His father and brothers, and still more their wives, not merely disliked meeting him, but avoided remembering his existence unless compelled to do so. His sister had married Baron Greff, a Petersburg official of her father's type. Iván Ilých was *le phénix de la famille*[2] as people said. He was neither as cold and formal as his elder brother nor as wild as the younger, but was a happy mean between them—an intelligent, polished, lively and agreeable man. He had studied with his younger brother at the School of Law, but the latter had failed to complete the course and was expelled when he was in the fifth class. Iván Ilých finished the course well. Even when he was at the School of Law he was just what he remained for the rest of his life: a capable, cheerful, good-natured, and sociable man, though strict in the fulfilment of what he considered to be his duty: and he considered his duty to be what was so considered by those in authority. Neither as a boy nor as a man was he a toady, but from early youth was by nature attracted to people of high station as a fly is drawn to the light, assimilating their ways and views of life and establishing friendly relations with them. All the enthusiasms of childhood and youth passed without leaving much trace on him; he succumbed to sensuality, to vanity, and latterly among the highest classes to liberalism, but always within limits which his instinct unfailingly indicated to him as correct.

---

[2] The phoenix of the family, here meaning "rare bird" or "prodigy."

At school he had done things which had formerly seemed to him very horrid and made him feel disgusted with himself when he did them; but when
later on he saw that such actions were done by people of good position and
that they did not regard them as wrong, he was able not exactly to regard them
as right, but to forget about them entirely or not be at all troubled at remembering them.

Having graduated from the School of Law and qualified for the tenth rank 60
of the civil service, and having received money from his father for his equipment, Iván Ilých ordered himself clothes at Scharmer's, the fashionable tailor,
hung a medallion inscribed *respice finem*[3] on his watch-chain, took leave of
his professor and the prince who was patron of the school, had a farewell dinner with his comrades at Donon's first-class restaurant, and with his new and
fashionable portmanteau, linen, clothes, shaving and other toilet appliances,
and a travelling rug, all purchased at the best shops, he set off for one of the
provinces where, through his father's influence, he had been attached to the
Governor as an official for special service.

In the province Iván Ilých soon arranged as easy and agreeable a position
for himself as he had had at the School of Law. He performed his official
tasks, made his career, and at the same time amused himself pleasantly and
decorously. Occasionally he paid official visits to country districts, where he
behaved with dignity both to his superiors and inferiors, and performed the
duties entrusted to him, which related chiefly to the sectarians,[4] with an exact-
ness and incorruptible honesty of which he could not but feel proud.

In official matters, despite his youth and taste for frivolous gaiety, he was
exceedingly reserved, punctilious, and even severe; but in society he was often
amusing and witty, and always good-natured, correct in his manner, and *bon
enfant*, as the governor and his wife—with whom he was like one of the family—
used to say of him.

In the provinces he had an affair with a lady who made advances to the elegant
young lawyer, and there was also a milliner; and there were carousals with aides-
de-camp who visited the district, and after-supper visits to a certain outlying
street of doubtful reputation; and there was too some obsequiousness to his
chief and even to his chief's wife, but all this was done with such a tone of good
breeding that no hard names could be applied to it. It all came under the heading of the French saying: "Il faut que jeunesse se passe."[5] It was all done with
clean hands, in clean linen, with French phrases, and above all among people of
the best society and consequently with the approval of people of rank.

So Iván Ilých served for five years and then came a change in his official
life. The new and reformed judicial institutions were introduced, and new
men were needed. Iván Ilých became such a new man. He was offered the post

[3] Regard the end.
[4] A large sect, whose members were placed under many legal restrictions, which broke away from
the Orthodox Church in the seventeenth century.
[5] Youth must have its fling.

of Examining Magistrate, and he accepted it though the post was in another province and obliged him to give up the connections he had formed and to make new ones. His friends met to give him a send-off; they had a group-photograph taken and presented him with a silver cigarette-case, and he set off to his new post.

As examining magistrate Iván Ilých was just as *comme il faut*[6] and deco- 65 rous a man, inspiring general respect and capable of separating his official duties from his private life, as he had been when acting as an official on special service. His duties now as examining magistrate were far more interesting and attractive than before. In his former position it had been pleasant to wear an undress uniform made by Scharmer, and to pass through the crowd of petitioners and officials who were timorously awaiting an audience with the governor, and who envied him as with free and easy gait he went straight into his chief's private room to have a cup of tea and a cigarette with him. But not many people had then been directly dependent on him—only police officials and the sectarians when he went on special missions—and he liked to treat them politely, almost as comrades, as if he were letting them feel that he who had the power to crush them was treating them in this simple, friendly way. There were then but few such people. But now, as an examining magistrate, Iván Ilých felt that everyone without exception, even the most important and self-satisfied, was in his power, and that he need only write a few words on a sheet of paper with a certain heading, and this or that important, self-satisfied person would be brought before him in the role of an accused person or a witness, and if he did not choose to allow him to sit down, would have to stand before him and answer his questions. Iván Ilých never abused his power; he tried on the contrary to soften its expression, but the consciousness of it and of the possibility of softening its effect, supplied the chief interest and attraction of his office. In his work itself, especially in his examinations, he very soon acquired a method of eliminating all considerations irrelevant to the legal aspect of the case, and reducing even the most complicated case to a form in which it would be presented on paper only in its externals, completely excluding his personal opinion of the matter, while above all observing every prescribed formality. The work was new and Iván Ilých was one of the first men to apply the new Code of 1864.[7]

On taking up the post of examining magistrate in a new town, he made new acquaintances and connections, placed himself on a new footing, and assumed a somewhat different tone. He took up an attitude of rather dignified aloofness towards the provincial authorities, but picked out the best circle of legal gentlemen and wealthy gentry living in the town and assumed a tone of slight dissatisfaction with the government, of moderate liberalism, and of enlightened citizenship. At the same time, without at all altering the elegance of his toilet, he ceased shaving his chin and allowed his beard to grow as it pleased.

---

[6] Proper.

[7] Judicial procedures were reformed after the emancipation of the serfs in 1861.

Iván Ilých settled down very pleasantly in this new town. The society there, which inclined towards opposition to the Governor, was friendly, his salary was larger, and he began to play *vint*,[8] which he found added not a little to the pleasure of life, for he had a capacity for cards, played good-humouredly, and calculated rapidly and astutely, so that he usually won.

After living there for two years he met his future wife, Praskóvya Fëdorovna Míkhel, who was the most attractive, clever, and brilliant girl of the set in which he moved, and among other amusements and relaxations from his labours as examining magistrate, Iván Ilých established light and playful relations with her.

While he had been an official on special service he had been accustomed to dance, but now as an examining magistrate it was exceptional for him to do so. If he danced now, he did it as if to show that though he served under the reformed order of things, and had reached the fifth official rank, yet when it came to dancing he could do it better than most people. So at the end of an evening he sometimes danced with Praskóvya Fëdorovna, and it was chiefly during these dances that he captivated her. She fell in love with him. Iván Ilých had at first no definite intention of marrying, but when the girl fell in love with him he said to himself: "Really, why shouldn't I marry?"

Praskóvya Fëdorovna came of a good family, was not bad looking and 70 had some little property. Iván Ilých might have aspired to a more brilliant match, but even this was good. He had his salary, and she, he hoped, would have an equal income. She was well connected, and was a sweet, pretty, and thoroughly correct young woman. To say that Iván Ilých married because he fell in love with Praskóvya Fëdorovna and found that she sympathized with his views of life would be as incorrect as to say that he married because his social circle approved of the match. He was swayed by both these considerations: the marriage gave him personal satisfaction, and at the same time it was considered the right thing by the most highly placed of his associates.

So Iván Ilých got married.

The preparations for marriage and the beginning of married life, with its conjugal caresses, the new furniture, new crockery, and new linen, were very pleasant until his wife became pregnant—so that Iván Ilých had begun to think that marriage would not impair the easy, agreeable, gay and always decorous character of his life, approved of by society and regarded by himself as natural, but would even improve it. But from the first months of his wife's pregnancy, something new, unpleasant, depressing, and unseemly, and from which there was no way of escape, unexpectedly showed itself.

His wife, without any reason—*de gaieté de coeur*[9] as Iván Ilých expressed it to himself—began to disturb the pleasure and propriety of their life. She began to be jealous without any cause, expected him to devote his whole attention to her, found fault with everything, and made coarse and ill-mannered scenes.

---

[8] A card game similar to bridge.
[9] Of a joyous heart. Iván uses the expression ironically.

At first Iván Ilých hoped to escape from the unpleasantness of this state of affairs by the same easy and decorous relation to life that had served him heretofore: he tried to ignore his wife's disagreeable moods, continued to live in his usual easy and pleasant way, invited friends to his house for a game of cards, and also tried going out to his club or spending his evenings with friends. But one day his wife began upbraiding him so vigorously, using such coarse words, and continued to abuse him every time he did not fulfil her demands, so resolutely and with such evident determination not to give way till he submitted—that is, till he stayed at home and was bored just as she was—that he became alarmed. He now realized that matrimony—at any rate with Praskóvya Fëdorovna—was not always conducive to the pleasures and amenities of life but on the contrary often infringed both comfort and propriety, and that he must therefore entrench himself against such infringement. And Iván Ilých began to seek for means of doing so. His official duties were the one thing that imposed upon Praskóvya Fëdorovna, and by means of his official work and the duties attached to it he began struggling with his wife to secure his own independence.

With the birth of their child, the attempts to feed it and the various failures in doing so, and with the real and imaginary illnesses of mother and child, in which Iván Ilých's sympathy was demanded but about which he understood nothing, the need of securing for himself an existence outside his family life became still more imperative. 75

As his wife grew more irritable and exacting and Iván Ilých transferred the centre of gravity of his life more and more to his official work, so did he grow to like his work better and became more ambitious than before.

Very soon, within a year of his wedding, Iván Ilých had realized that marriage, though it may add some comforts to life, is in fact a very intricate and difficult affair towards which in order to perform one's duty, that is, to lead a decorous life approved of by society, one must adopt a definite attitude just as towards one's official duties.

And Iván Ilých evolved such an attitude towards married life. He only required of it those conveniences—dinner at home, housewife, and bed—which it could give him, and above all that propriety of external forms required by public opinion. For the rest he looked for lighthearted pleasure and propriety, and was very thankful when he found them, but if he met with antagonism and querulousness he at once retired into his separate fenced-off world of official duties, where he found satisfaction.

Iván Ilých was esteemed a good official, and after three years was made Assistant Public Prosecutor. His new duties, their importance, the possibility of indicting and imprisoning anyone he chose, the publicity his speeches received, and the success he had in all these things, made his work still more attractive.

More children came. His wife became more and more querulous and ill-tempered, but the attitude Iván Ilých had adopted towards his home life rendered him almost impervious to her grumbling. 80

After seven years' service in that town he was transferred to another province as Public Prosecutor. They moved, but were short of money and his wife did not like the place they moved to. Though the salary was higher the cost of living was greater, besides which two of their children died and family life became still more unpleasant for him.

Praskóvya Fëdorovna blamed her husband for every inconvenience they encountered in their new home. Most of the conversations between husband and wife, especially as to the children's education, led to topics which recalled former disputes, and those disputes were apt to flare up again at any moment. There remained only those rare periods of amorousness which still came to them at times but did not last long. These were islets at which they anchored for a while and then again set out upon that ocean of veiled hostility which showed itself in their aloofness from one another. This aloofness might have grieved Iván Ilých had he considered that it ought not to exist, but he now regarded the position as normal, and even made it the goal at which he aimed in family life. His aim was to free himself more and more from those unpleasantnesses and to give them a semblance of harmlessness and propriety. He attained this by spending less and less time with his family, and when obliged to be at home he tried to safeguard his position by the presence of outsiders. The chief thing however was that he had his official duties. The whole interest of his life now centered in the official world and that interest absorbed him. The consciousness of his power, being able to ruin anybody he wished to ruin, the importance, even the external dignity of his entry into court, or meetings with his subordinates, his success with superiors and inferiors, and above all his masterly handling of cases, of which he was conscious—all this gave him pleasure and filled his life, together with chats with his colleagues, dinners, and bridge. So that on the whole Iván Ilých's life continued to flow as he considered it should do—pleasantly and properly.

So things continued for another seven years. His eldest daughter was already sixteen, another child had died, and only one son was left, a schoolboy and a subject of dissension. Iván Ilých wanted to put him in the School of Law, but to spite him Praskóvya Fëdorovna entered him at the High School. The daughter had been educated at home and had turned out well: the boy did not learn badly either.

CHAPTER III

So Iván Ilých lived for seventeen years after his marriage. He was already a Public Prosecutor of long standing, and had declined several proposed transfers while awaiting a more desirable post, when an unanticipated and unpleasant occurrence quite upset the peaceful course of his life. He was expecting to be offered the post of presiding judge in a University town, but Happe somehow came to the front and obtained the appointment instead. Iván Ilých became irritable, reproached Happe, and quarreled both with him and with his immediate superiors—who became colder to him and again passed him over when other appointments were made.

This was in 1880, the hardest year of Iván Ilých's life. It was then that it became evident on the one hand that his salary was insufficient for them to live on, and on the other that he had been forgotten, and not only this, but that what was for him the greatest and most cruel injustice appeared to others a quite ordinary occurrence. Even his father did not consider it his duty to help him. Iván Ilých felt himself abandoned by everyone, and that they regarded his position with a salary of 3,500 rubles as quite normal and even fortunate. He alone knew that with the consciousness of the injustices done him, with his wife's incessant nagging, and with the debts he had contracted by living beyond his means, his position was far from normal.

In order to save money that summer he obtained leave of absence and went with his wife to live in the country at her brother's place.

In the country, without his work, he experienced *ennui* for the first time in his life, and not only *ennui* but intolerable depression, and he decided that it was impossible to go on living like that, and that it was necessary to take energetic measures.

Having passed a sleepless night pacing up and down the veranda, he decided to go to Petersburg and bestir himself, in order to punish those who had failed to appreciate him and to get transferred to another ministry.

Next day, despite many protests from his wife and her brother, he started for Petersburg with the sole object of obtaining a post with a salary of five thousand rubles a year. He was no longer bent on any particular department, or tendency, or kind of activity. All he now wanted was an appointment to another post with a salary of five thousand rubles, either in the administration, in the banks, with the railways, in one of the Empress Márya's Institutions,[10] or even in the customs—but it had to carry with it a salary of five thousand rubles and be in a ministry other than that in which they had failed to appreciate him.

And this quest of Iván Ilých's was crowned with remarkable and unexpected success. At Kursk an acquaintance of his, F. I. Ilyín, got into the first-class carriage, sat down beside Iván Ilých, and told him of a telegram just received by the Governor of Kursk announcing that a change was about to take place in the ministry: Peter Ivánovich was to be superseded by Iván Semënovich.

The proposed change, apart from its significance for Russia, had a special significance for Iván Ilých, because by bringing forward a new man, Peter Petróvich, and consequently his friend Zachár Ivánovich, it was highly favourable for Iván Ilých, since Zachár Ivánovich was a friend and colleague of his.

In Moscow this news was confirmed, and on reaching Petersburg Iván Ilých found Zachár Ivánovich and received a definite promise of an appointment in his former Department of Justice.

A week later he telegraphed to his wife: "Zachár in Miller's place. I shall receive appointment on presentation of report."

Thanks to this change of personnel, Iván Ilých had unexpectedly obtained an appointment in his former ministry which placed him two stages above

[10] A charitable organization founded in the late eighteenth century by the empress Márya.

his former colleagues besides giving him five thousand rubles salary and three thousand five hundred rubles for expenses connected with his removal. All his ill humour towards his former enemies and the whole department vanished, and Iván Ilých was completely happy.

He returned to the country more cheerful and contented than he had 95 been for a long time. Praskóvya Fëdorovna also cheered up and a truce was arranged between them. Iván Ilých told of how he had been fêted by everybody in Petersburg, how all those who had been his enemies were put to shame and now fawned on him, how envious they were of his appointment, and how much everybody in Petersburg had liked him.

Praskóvya Fëdorovna listened to all this and appeared to believe it. She did not contradict anything, but only made plans for their life in the town to which they were going. Iván Ilých saw with delight that these plans were his plans, that he and his wife agreed, and that, after a stumble, his life was regaining its due and natural character of pleasant lightheartedness and decorum.

Iván Ilých had come back for a short time only, for he had to take up his new duties on the 10th of September. Moreover, he needed time to settle into the new place, to move all his belongings from the province, and to buy and order many additional things: in a word, to make such arrangements as he had resolved on, which were almost exactly what Praskóvya Fëdorovna too had decided on.

Now that everything had happened so fortunately, and that he and his wife were at one in their aims and moreover saw so little of one another, they got on together better than they had done since the first years of marriage. Iván Ilých had thought of taking his family away with him at once, but the insistence of his wife's brother and her sister-in-law, who had suddenly become particularly amiable and friendly to him and his family, induced him to depart alone.

So he departed, and the cheerful state of mind induced by his success and by the harmony between his wife and himself, the one intensifying the other, did not leave him. He found a delightful house, just the thing both he and his wife had dreamt of. Spacious, lofty reception rooms in the old style, a convenient and dignified study, rooms for his wife and daughter, a study for his son—it might have been specially built for them. Iván Ilých himself superintended the arrangements, chose the wallpapers, supplemented the furniture (preferably with antiques which he considered particularly *comme il faut*), and supervised the upholstering. Everything progressed and progressed and approached the ideal he had set himself: even when things were only half completed they exceeded his expectations. He saw what a refined and elegant character, free from vulgarity, it would all have when it was ready. On falling asleep he pictured to himself how the reception-room would look. Looking at the yet unfinished drawing-room he could see the fireplace, the screen, the what-not, the little chairs dotted here and there, the dishes and plates on the walls, and the bronzes, as they would be when everything was in place. He was pleased by the thought of how his wife and daughter, who shared his taste in this matter, would be impressed by it. They were certainly not expecting as much.

He had been particularly successful in finding, and buying cheaply, antiques which gave a particularly aristocratic character to the whole place. But in his letters he intentionally understated everything in order to be able to surprise them. All this so absorbed him that his new duties—though he liked his official work—interested him less than he had expected. Sometimes he even had moments of absent-mindedness during the Court Sessions, and would consider whether he should have straight or curved cornices for his curtains. He was so interested in it all that he often did things himself, rearranging the furniture, or rehanging the curtains. Once when mounting a step-ladder to show the upholsterer, who did not understand, how he wanted the hangings draped, he made a false step and slipped, but being a strong and agile man he clung on and only knocked his side against the knob of the window frame. The bruised place was painful but the pain soon passed, and he felt particularly bright and well just then. He wrote: "I feel fifteen years younger." He thought he would have everything ready by September, but it dragged on till mid-October. But the result was charming not only in his eyes but to everyone who saw it.

In reality it was just what is usually seen in the houses of people of moderate means who want to appear rich, and therefore succeed only in resembling others like themselves: there were damasks, dark wood, plants, rugs, and dull and polished bronzes—all the things people of a certain class have in order to resemble other people of that class. His house was so like the others that it would never have been noticed, but to him it all seemed to be quite exceptional. He was very happy when he met his family at the station and brought them to the newly furnished house all lit up, where a footman in a white tie opened the door into the hall decorated with plants, and when they went on into the drawing room and the study uttering exclamations of delight. He conducted them everywhere, drank in their praises eagerly, and beamed with pleasure. At tea that evening, when Praskóvya Fëdorovna among other things asked him about his fall, he laughed and showed them how he had gone flying and had frightened the upholsterer. 100

"It's a good thing I'm a bit of an athlete. Another man might have been killed, but I merely knocked myself, just here; it hurts when it's touched, but it's passing off already—it's only a bruise."

So they began living in their new home—in which, as always happens, when they got thoroughly settled in they found they were just one room short—and with the increased income, which as always was just a little (some five hundred rubles) too little, but it was all very nice.

Things went particularly well at first, before everything was finally arranged and while something had still to be done: this thing bought, that thing ordered, another thing moved, and something else adjusted. Though there were some disputes between husband and wife, they were both so well satisfied and had so much to do that it all passed off without any serious quarrels. When nothing was left to arrange it became rather dull and something seemed to be lacking, but they were then making acquaintances, forming habits, and life was growing fuller.

Iván Ilých spent his mornings at the law court and came home to dinner, and at first he was generally in a good humour, though he occasionally became irritable just on account of his house. (Every spot on the tablecloth or the upholstery, and every broken window-blind string, irritated him. He had devoted so much trouble to arranging it all that every disturbance of it distressed him.) But on the whole his life ran its course as he believed life should do: easily, pleasantly, and decorously.

He got up at nine, drank his coffee, read the paper, and then put on his undress uniform and went to the law courts. There the harness in which he worked had already been stretched to fit him and he donned it without a hitch: petitioners, inquiries at the chancery, the chancery itself, and the sittings public and administrative. In all this the thing was to exclude everything fresh and vital, which always disturbs the regular course of official business, and to admit only official relations with people, and then only on official grounds. A man would come, for instance, wanting some information. Iván Ilých, as one in whose sphere the matter did not lie, would have nothing to do with him: but if the man had some business with him in his official capacity, something that could be expressed on officially stamped paper, he would do everything, positively everything he could within the limits of such relations, and in doing so would maintain the semblance of friendly human relations, that is, would observe the courtesies of life. As soon as the official relations ended, so did everything else. Iván Ilých possessed this capacity to separate his real life from the official side of affairs and not mix the two, in the highest degree, and by long practice and natural aptitude had brought it to such a pitch that sometimes, in the manner of a virtuoso, he would even allow himself to let the human and official relations mingle. He let himself do this just because he felt that he could at any time he chose resume the strictly official attitude again and drop the human relation. And he did it all easily, pleasantly, correctly, and even artistically. In the intervals between the sessions he smoked, drank tea, chatted a little about politics, a little about general topics, a little about cards, but most of all about official appointments. Tired, but with the feelings of a virtuoso—one of the first violins who has played his part in an orchestra with precision—he would return home to find that his wife and daughter had been out paying calls, or had a visitor, and that his son had been to school, had done his homework with his tutor, and was duly learning what is taught at High Schools. Everything was as it should be. After dinner, if they had no visitors, Iván Ilých sometimes read a book that was being much discussed at the time, and in the evening settled down to work, that is, read official papers, compared the depositions of witnesses, and noted paragraphs of the Code applying to them. This was neither dull nor amusing. It was dull when he might have been playing bridge, but if no bridge was available it was at any rate better than doing nothing or sitting with his wife. Iván Ilých's chief pleasure was giving little dinners to which he invited men and women of good social position, and just as his drawing-room resembled all other drawing-rooms so did his enjoyable little parties resemble all other such parties.

Once they even gave a dance. Iván Ilých enjoyed it and everything went off well, except that it led to a violent quarrel with his wife about the cakes and sweets. Praskóvya Fëdorovna had made her own plans, but Iván Ilých insisted on getting everything from an expensive confectioner and ordered too many cakes, and the quarrel occurred because some of those cakes were left over and the confectioner's bill came to forty-five rubles. It was a great and disagreeable quarrel. Praskóvya Fëdorovna called him "a fool and an imbecile," and he clutched at his head and made angry allusions to divorce.

But the dance itself had been enjoyable. The best people were there, and Iván Ilých had danced with Princess Trúfonova, a sister of the distinguished founder of the Society "Bear My Burden."

The pleasures connected with his work were pleasures of ambition; his social pleasures were those of vanity; but Iván Ilých's greatest pleasure was playing bridge. He acknowledged that whatever disagreeable incident happened in his life, the pleasure that beamed like a ray of light above everything else was to sit down to bridge with good players, not noisy partners, and of course to four-handed bridge (with five players it was annoying to have to stand out, though one pretended not to mind), to play a clever and serious game (when the cards allowed it) and then to have supper and drink a glass of wine. After a game of bridge, especially if he had won a little (to win a large sum was unpleasant), Iván Ilých went to bed in specially good humour.

So they lived. They formed a circle of acquaintances among the best people and were visited by people of importance and by young folk. In their views as to their acquaintances, husband, wife and daughter were entirely agreed, and tacitly and unanimously kept at arm's length and shook off the various shabby friends and relations who, with much show of affection, gushed into the drawing-room with its Japanese plates on the walls. Soon these shabby friends ceased to obtrude themselves and only the best people remained in the Golovíns' set.

Young men made up to Lisa, and Petríshchev, an examining magistrate and Dmítri Ivanovich Petríshchev's son and sole heir, began to be so attentive to her that Iván Ilých had already spoken to Praskóvya Fëdorovna about it, and considered whether they should not arrange a party for them or get up some private theatricals. 110

So they lived, and all went well, without change, and life flowed pleasantly.

CHAPTER IV

They were all in good health. It could not be called ill health if Iván Ilých sometimes said that he had a queer taste in his mouth and felt some discomfort in his left side.

But this discomfort increased and, though not exactly painful, grew into a sense of pressure in his side accompanied by ill humour. And his irritability became worse and worse and began to mar the agreeable, easy, and correct life that had established itself in the Golovín family. Quarrels between husband

and wife became more and more frequent, and soon the ease and amenity disappeared and even the decorum was barely maintained. Scenes again became frequent, and very few of those islets remained on which husband and wife could meet without explosion. Praskóvya Fëdorovna now had good reason to say that her husband's temper was trying. With characteristic exaggeration she said he had always had a dreadful temper, and that it had needed all her good nature to put up with it for twenty years. It was true that now the quarrels were started by him. His bursts of temper always came just before dinner, often just as he began to eat his soup. Sometimes he noticed that a plate or dish was chipped, or the food was not right, or his son put his elbow on the table, or his daughter's hair was not done as he liked it, and for all this he blamed Praskóvya Fëdorovna. At first she retorted and said disagreeable things to him, but once or twice he fell into such a rage at the beginning of dinner that she realized it was due to some physical derangement brought on by taking food, and so she restrained herself and did not answer, but only hurried to get the dinner over. She regarded this self-restraint as highly praiseworthy. Having come to the conclusion that her husband had a dreadful temper and made her life miserable, she began to feel sorry for herself, and the more she pitied herself the more she hated her husband. She began to wish he would die; yet she did not want him to die because then his salary would cease. And this irritated her against him still more. She considered herself dreadfully unhappy just because not even his death could save her, and though she concealed her exasperation, that hidden exasperation of hers increased his irritation also.

After one scene in which Iván Ilých had been particularly unfair and after which he had said in explanation that he certainly was irritable but that it was due to his not being well, she said that if he was ill it should be attended to, and insisted on his going to see a celebrated doctor.

He went. Everything took place as he had expected and as it always does. 115 There was the usual waiting and the important air assumed by the doctor, with which he was so familiar (resembling that which he himself assumed in court), and the sounding and listening, and the questions which called for answers that were foregone conclusions and were evidently unnecessary, and the look of importance which implied that "if only you put yourself in our hands we will arrange everything—we know indubitably how it has to be done, always in the same way for everybody alike." It was all just as it was in the law courts. The doctor put on just the same air towards him as he himself put on towards an accused person.

The doctor said that so-and-so indicated that there was so-and-so inside the patient, but if the investigation of so-and-so did not confirm this, then he must assume that and that. If he assumed that and that, then . . . and so on. To Iván Ilých only one question was important: was his case serious or not? But the doctor ignored that inappropriate question. From his point of view it was not the one under consideration, the real question was to decide between a floating kidney, chronic catarrh, or appendicitis. It was not a question of Iván Ilých's life or death, but one between a floating kidney and appendicitis. And that question the doctor solved brilliantly, as it seemed to Iván Ilých, in favour of the appendix, with the reservation that should an examination of the urine give fresh indications the matter would be reconsidered. All this was just what Iván Ilých had himself brilliantly accomplished a thousand times in dealing with men on trial. The doctor summed up just as brilliantly, looking over his spectacles triumphantly and even gaily at the accused. From the doctor's summing up Iván Ilých concluded that things were bad, but that for the doctor, and perhaps for everybody else, it was a matter of indifference, though for him it was bad. And this conclusion struck him painfully, arousing in him a great feeling of pity for himself and of bitterness towards the doctor's indifference to a matter of such importance.

He said nothing of this, but rose, placed the doctor's fee on the table, and remarked with a sigh: "We sick people probably often put inappropriate questions. But tell me, in general, is this complaint dangerous, or not? . . ."

The doctor looked at him sternly over his spectacles with one eye, as if to say: "Prisoner, if you will not keep to the questions put to you, I shall be obliged to have you removed from the court."

"I have already told you what I consider necessary and proper. The analysis may show something more." And the doctor bowed.

Iván Ilých went out slowly, seated himself disconsolately in his sledge, and 120 drove home. All the way home he was going over what the doctor had said, trying to translate those complicated, obscure, scientific phrases into plain language and find in them an answer to the question: "Is my condition bad? Is it very bad? Or is there as yet nothing much wrong?" And it seemed to him that the meaning of what the doctor had said was that it was very bad. Everything in the streets seemed depressing. The cabmen, the houses, the passers-by, and the shops, were dismal. His ache, this dull gnawing ache that never ceased for a moment, seemed to have acquired a new and more serious significance from the doctor's dubious remarks. Iván Ilých now watched it with a new and oppressive feeling.

He reached home and began to tell his wife about it. She listened, but in the middle of his account his daughter came in with her hat on, ready to go out with her mother. She sat down reluctantly to listen to this tedious story, but could not stand it long, and her mother too did not hear him to the end.

"Well, I am very glad," she said. "Mind now to take your medicine regularly. Give me the prescription and I'll send Gerásim to the chemist's." And she went to get ready to go out.

While she was in the room Iván Ilých had hardly taken time to breathe, but he sighed deeply when she left it.

"Well," he thought, "perhaps it isn't so bad after all."

He began taking his medicine and following the doctor's directions, which 125 had been altered after the examination of the urine. But then it happened that there was a contradiction between the indications drawn from the examination of the urine and the symptoms that showed themselves. It turned out that what was happening differed from what the doctor had told him, and that he had either forgotten, or blundered, or hidden something from him. He could not, however, be blamed for that, and Iván Ilých still obeyed his orders implicitly and at first derived some comfort from doing so.

From the time of his visit to the doctor, Iván Ilých's chief occupation was the exact fulfilment of the doctor's instructions regarding hygiene and the taking of medicine, and the observation of his pain and his excretions. His chief interests came to be people's ailments and people's health. When sickness, deaths, or recoveries were mentioned in his presence, especially when the illness resembled his own, he listened with agitation which he tried to hide, asked questions, and applied what he heard to his own case.

The pain did not grow less, but Iván Ilých made efforts to force himself to think that he was better. And he could do this so long as nothing agitated him. But as soon as he had any unpleasantness with his wife, any lack of success in his official work, or held bad cards at bridge, he was at once acutely sensible of his disease. He had formerly borne such mischances, hoping soon to adjust what was wrong, to master it and attain success, or make a grand slam. But now every mischance upset him and plunged him into despair. He would say to himself: "There now, just as I was beginning to get better and the medicine had begun to take effect, comes this accursed misfortune, or unpleasantness. . . ." And he was furious with the mishap, or with the people who were causing the unpleasantness and killing him, for he felt that this fury was killing him but could not restrain it. One would have thought that it should have been clear to him that this exasperation with circumstances and people aggravated his illness, and that he ought therefore to ignore unpleasant occurrences. But he drew the very opposite conclusion: he said that he needed peace, and he watched for everything that might disturb it and became irritable at the slightest infringement of it. His condition was rendered worse by the fact that he read medical books and consulted doctors. The progress of his disease was so gradual that he could deceive himself when comparing one day with another—the difference was so slight. But when he consulted the doctors it seemed to him that he was getting worse, and even very rapidly. Yet despite this he was continually consulting them.

That month he went to see another celebrity, who told him almost the same as the first had done but put his questions rather differently, and the interview with this celebrity only increased Iván Ilých's doubts and fears. A friend of a friend of his, a very good doctor, diagnosed his illness again quite differently from the others, and though he predicted recovery, his questions and suppositions bewildered Iván Ilých still more and increased his doubts. A homeopathist diagnosed the disease in yet another way, and prescribed medicine which Iván Ilých took secretly for a week. But after a week, not feeling any improvement and having lost confidence both in the former doctor's treatment and in this one's, he became still more despondent. One day a lady acquaintance mentioned a cure effected by a wonder-working icon. Iván Ilých caught himself listening attentively and beginning to believe that it had occurred. This incident alarmed him. "Has my mind really weakened to such an extent?" he asked himself. "Nonsense! It's all rubbish. I mustn't give way to nervous fears but having chosen a doctor must keep strictly to his treatment. That is what I will do. Now it's all settled. I won't think about it, but will follow the treatment seriously till summer, and then we shall see. From now there must be no more of this wavering!" This was easy to say but impossible to carry out. The pain in his side oppressed him and seemed to grow worse and more incessant, while the taste in his mouth grew stranger and stranger. It seemed to him that his breath had a disgusting smell, and he was conscious of a loss of appetite and strength. There was no deceiving himself: something terrible, new, and more important than anything before in his life, was taking place within him of which he alone was aware. Those about him did not understand or would not understand it, but thought everything in the world was going on as usual. That tormented Iván Ilých more than anything. He saw that his household, especially his wife and daughter who were in a perfect whirl of visiting, did not understand anything of it and were annoyed that he was so depressed and so exacting, as if he were to blame for it. Though they tried to disguise it he saw that he was an obstacle in their path, and that his wife had adopted a definite line in regard to his illness and kept to it regardless of anything he said or did. Her attitude was this: "You know," she would say to her friends, "Iván Ilých can't do as other people do, and keep to the treatment prescribed for him. One day he'll take his drops and keep strictly to his diet and go to bed in good time, but the next day unless I watch him he'll suddenly forget his medicine, eat sturgeon—which is forbidden—and sit up playing cards till one o'clock in the morning."

"Oh, come, when was that?" Iván Ilých would ask in vexation. "Only once at Peter Ivánovich's."

"And yesterday with Shébek."

"Well, even if I hadn't stayed up, this pain would have kept me awake."

"Be that as it may you'll never get well like that, but will always make us wretched."

Praskóvya Fёdorovna's attitude to Iván Ilých's illness, as she expressed it both to others and to him, was that it was his own fault and was another of the annoyances he caused her. Iván Ilých felt that this opinion escaped her involuntarily—but that did not make it easier for him.

At the law courts too, Iván Ilých noticed, or thought he noticed, a strange attitude towards himself. It sometimes seemed to him that people were watching him inquisitively as a man whose place might soon be vacant. Then again, his friends would suddenly begin to chaff him in a friendly way about his low spirits, as if the awful, horrible, and unheard-of thing that was going on within him, incessantly gnawing at him and irresistibly drawing him away, was a very agreeable subject for jests. Schwartz in particular irritated him by his jocularity, vivacity, and *savoir-faire,* which reminded him of what he himself had been ten years ago.

Friends came to make up a set and they sat down to cards. They dealt, bending the new cards to soften them, and he sorted the diamonds in his hand and

130

135

found he had seven. His partner said "No trumps" and supported him with two diamonds. What more could be wished for? It ought to be jolly and lively. They would make a grand slam. But suddenly Iván Ilých was conscious of that gnawing pain, that taste in his mouth, and it seemed ridiculous that in such circumstances he should be pleased to make a grand slam.

He looked at his partner Mikháil Mikháylovich, who rapped the table with his strong hand and instead of snatching up the tricks pushed the cards courteously and indulgently towards Iván Ilých that he might have the pleasure of gathering them up without the trouble of stretching out his hand for them. "Does he think I am too weak to stretch out my arm?" thought Iván Ilých, and forgetting what he was doing he over-trumped his partner, missing the grand slam by three tricks. And what was most awful of all was that he saw how upset Mikháil Mikháylovich was about it but did not himself care. And it was dreadful to realize why he did not care.

They all saw that he was suffering and said: "We can stop if you are tired. Take a rest." Lie down? No, he was not at all tired, and he finished the rubber. All were gloomy and silent. Iván Ilých felt that he had diffused this gloom over them and could not dispel it. They had supper and went away, and Iván Ilých was left alone with the consciousness that his life was poisoned and was poisoning the lives of others, and that this poison did not weaken but penetrated more and more deeply into his whole being.

With this consciousness, and with physical pain besides the terror, he must go to bed, often to lie awake the greater part of the night. Next morning he had to get up again, dress, go to the law courts, speak, and write; or if he did not go out, spend at home those twenty-four hours a day each of which was a torture. And he had to live thus all alone on the brink of an abyss, with no one who understood or pitied him.

CHAPTER V

So one month passed and then another. Just before the New Year his brother-in-law came to town and stayed at their house. Iván Ilých was at the law courts and Praskóvya Fëdorovna had gone shopping. When Iván Ilých came home and entered his study he found his brother-in-law there—a healthy, florid man—unpacking his portmanteau himself. He raised his head on hearing Iván Ilých's footsteps and looked up at him for a moment without a word. That stare told Iván Ilých everything. His brother-in-law opened his mouth to utter an exclamation of surprise but checked himself, and that action confirmed it all.

"I have changed, eh?"

"Yes, there is a change."

And after that, try as he would to get his brother-in-law to return to the subject of his looks, the latter would say nothing about it. Praskóvya Fëdorovna came home and her brother went out to her. Iván Ilých locked the door and began to examine himself in the glass, first full face, then in profile. He took

140

up a portrait of himself taken with his wife, and compared it with what he saw in the glass. The change in him was immense. Then he bared his arms to the elbow, looked at them, drew the sleeves down again, sat down on an ottoman, and grew blacker than night.

"No, no, this won't do!" he said to himself, and jumped up, went to the table, took up some law papers and began to read them, but could not continue. He unlocked the door and went into the reception-room. The door leading to the drawing room was shut. He approached it on tiptoe and listened.

"No, you are exaggerating!" Praskóvya Fëdorovna was saying.

"Exaggerating! Don't you see it? Why, he's a dead man! Look at his eyes— 145 there's no light in them. But what is it that is wrong with him?"

"No one knows. Nikoláevich (that was another doctor) said something, but I don't know what. And Leshchetítsky (this was the celebrated specialist) said quite the contrary . . ."

Iván Ilých walked away, went to his own room, lay down, and began musing: "The kidney, a floating kidney." He recalled all the doctors had told him of how it detached itself and swayed about. And by an effort of imagination he tried to catch that kidney and arrest it and support it. So little was needed for this, it seemed to him. "No, I'll go to see Peter Ivánovich again." (That was the friend whose friend was a doctor.) He rang, ordered the carriage, and got ready to go.

"Where are you going, Jean?" asked his wife, with a specially sad and exceptionally kind look.

This exceptionally kind look irritated him. He looked morosely at her.

"I must go to see Peter Ivánovich."   150

He went to see Peter Ivánovich, and together they went to see his friend, the doctor. He was in, and Iván Ilých had a long talk with him.

Reviewing the anatomical and physiological details of what in the doctor's opinion was going on inside him, he understood it all.

There was something, a small thing, in the vermiform appendix. It might all come right. Only stimulate the energy of one organ and check the activity of another, then absorption would take place and everything would come right. He got home rather late for dinner, ate his dinner, and conversed cheerfully, but could not for a long time bring himself to go back to work in his room. At last, however, he went to his study and did what was necessary, but the consciousness that he had put something aside—an important, intimate matter which he would revert to when his work was done—never left him. When he had finished his work he remembered that this intimate matter was the thought of his vermiform appendix. But he did not give himself up to it, and went to the drawing-room for tea. There were callers there, including the examining magistrate who was a desirable match for his daughter, and they were conversing, playing the piano and singing. Iván Ilých, as Praskóvya Fëdorovna remarked, spent that evening more cheerfully than usual, but he never for a moment forgot that he had postponed the important matter of the appendix. At eleven o'clock he said good-night and went to his bedroom. Since his illness he had slept alone in a small room next to his study.

He undressed and took up a novel by Zola, but instead of reading it he fell into thought, and in his imagination that desired improvement in the vermiform appendix occurred. There was the absorption and evacuation and the reestablishment of normal activity. "Yes, that's it!" he said to himself. "One need only assist nature, that's all." He remembered his medicine, rose, took it, and lay down on his back watching for the beneficent action of the medicine and for it to lessen the pain. "I need only take it regularly and avoid all injurious influences. I am already feeling better, much better." He began touching his side: it was not painful to the touch. "There, I really don't feel it. It's much better already." He put out the light and turned on his side . . . "The appendix is getting better, absorption is occurring." Suddenly he felt the old, familiar, dull, gnawing pain, stubborn and serious. There was the same familiar loathsome taste in his mouth. His heart sank and he felt dazed. "My God! My God!" he muttered. "Again, again! and it will never cease." And suddenly the matter presented itself in a quite different aspect. "Vermiform appendix! Kidney!" he said to himself. "It's not a question of appendix or kidney, but of life and . . . death. Yes, life was there and now it is going, going and I cannot stop it. Yes. Why deceive myself? Isn't it obvious to everyone but me that I'm dying, and that it's only a question of weeks, days . . . it may happen this moment. There was light and now there is darkness. I was here and now I'm going there! Where?" A chill came over him, his breathing ceased, and he felt only the throbbing of his heart.

"When I am not, what will there be? There will be nothing. Then where shall I be when I am no more? Can this be dying? No, I don't want to!" He jumped up and tried to light the candle, felt for it with trembling hands, dropped candle and candlestick on the floor, and fell back on his pillow.

"What's the use? It makes no difference," he said to himself, staring with wide-open eyes into the darkness. "Death. Yes, death. And none of them know or wish to know it, and they have no pity for me. Now they are playing." (He heard through the door the distant sound of a song and its accompaniment.) "It's all the same to them, but they will die too! Fools! I first, and they later, but it will be the same for them. And now they are merry . . . the beasts!" 155

Anger choked him and he was agonizingly, unbearably miserable. "It is impossible that all men have been doomed to suffer this awful horror!" He raised himself.

"Something must be wrong. I must calm myself—must think it all over from the beginning." And he again began thinking. "Yes, the beginning of my illness: I knocked my side, but I was still quite well that day and the next. It hurt a little, then rather more. I saw the doctors, then followed despondency and anguish, more doctors, and I drew nearer to the abyss. My strength grew less and I kept coming nearer and nearer, and now I have wasted away and there is no light in my eyes. I think of the appendix—but this is death! I think of mending the appendix, and all the while here is death! Can it really be death?" Again terror seized him and he gasped for breath. He leant down and began feeling for the matches, pressing with his elbow on the stand beside the bed. It was in his way and hurt him, he grew furious with it, pressed on it still harder, and upset it. Breathless and in despair he fell on his back, expecting death to come immediately.

Meanwhile the visitors were leaving. Praskóvya Fëdorovna was seeing them off. She heard something fall and came in.

"What has happened?"

"Nothing. I knocked it over accidentally."

She went out and returned with a candle. He lay there panting heavily, like a man who has run a thousand yards, and stared upwards at her with a fixed look.

"What is it, Jean?"

"No . . . o . . . thing. I upset it." ("Why speak of it? She won't understand," he thought.)

And in truth she did not understand. She picked up the stand, lit his candle, and hurried away to see another visitor off. When she came back he still lay on his back, looking upwards.

"What is it? Do you feel worse?"

"Yes."

She shook her head and sat down.

"Do you know, Jean, I think we must ask Leshchetítsky to come and see you here."

This meant calling in the famous specialist, regardless of expense. He smiled malignantly and said "No." She remained a little longer and then went up to him and kissed his forehead.

While she was kissing him he hated her from the bottom of his soul and with difficulty refrained from pushing her away.

"Good-night. Please God you'll sleep."

"Yes."

CHAPTER VI

Iván Ilých saw that he was dying, and he was in continual despair.

In the depth of his heart he knew he was dying, but not only was he not accustomed to the thought, he simply did not and could not grasp it.

The syllogism he had learnt from Kiezewetter's Logic:[11] "Caius is a man, men are mortal, therefore Caius is mortal," had always seemed to him correct as applied to Caius, but certainly not as applied to himself. That Caius—man in the abstract—was mortal, was perfectly correct, but he was not Caius, not an abstract man, but a creature quite, quite separate from all others. He had been little Ványa, with a mamma and a papa; with Mitya and Volódya, and the toys, a coachman and a nurse, afterwards with Kátenka and with all the joys, griefs, and delights of childhood, boyhood, and youth. What did Caius know

[11] Karl Kiezewetter (1766–1819), author of an outline of logic widely used in Russian schools at the time.

of the smell of that striped leather ball Ványa had been so fond of? Had Caius kissed his mother's hand like that, and did the silk of her dress rustle so for Caius? Had he rioted like that at school when the pastry was bad? Had Caius been in love like that? Could Caius preside at a session as he did? "Caius really was mortal, and it was right for him to die; but for me, little Ványa, Iván Ilých, with all my thoughts and emotions, it's altogether a different matter. It cannot be that I ought to die. That would be too terrible."

Such was his feeling.

"If I had to die like Caius I should have known it was so. An inner voice would have told me so, but there was nothing of the sort in me and I and all my friends felt that our case was quite different from that of Caius. And now here it is!" he said to himself. "It can't be. It's impossible! But here it is. How is this? How is one to understand it?"

He could not understand it, and tried to drive this false, incorrect, morbid thought away and to replace it by other proper and healthy thoughts. But that thought, and not the thought only but the reality itself, seemed to come and confront him.

And to replace that thought he called up a succession of others, hoping to find in them some support. He tried to get back into the former current of thoughts that had once screened the thought of death from him. But strange to say, all that had formerly shut off, hidden, and destroyed, his consciousness of death, no longer had that effect. Iván Ilých now spent most of his time in attempting to re-establish that old current. He would say to himself: "I will take up my duties again—after all I used to live by them." And banishing all doubts he would go to the law courts, enter into conversation with his colleagues, and sit carelessly as was his wont, scanning the crowd with a thoughtful look and leaning both his emaciated arms on the arms of his oak chair; bending over as usual to a colleague and drawing his papers nearer he would interchange whispers with him, and then suddenly raising his eyes and sitting erect would pronounce certain words and open the proceedings. But suddenly in the midst of those proceedings the pain in his side, regardless of the stage the proceedings had reached, would begin its own gnawing work. Iván Ilých would turn his attention to it and try to drive the thought of it away, but without success. *It* would come and stand before him and look at him, and he would be petrified and the light would die out of his eyes, and he would again begin asking himself whether *It* alone was true. And his colleagues and subordinates would see with surprise and distress that he, the brilliant and subtle judge, was becoming confused and making mistakes. He would shake himself, try to pull himself together, manage somehow to bring the sitting to a close, and return home with the sorrowful consciousness that his judicial labours could not as formerly hide from him what he wanted them to hide, and could not deliver him from *It*. And what was worst of all was that *It* drew his attention to itself not in order to make him take some action but only that he should look at *It*, look it straight in the face: look at it and without doing anything, suffer inexpressibly.

And to save himself from this condition Iván Ilých looked for consolations— 180
new screens—and new screens were found and for a while seemed to save him,
but then they immediately fell to pieces or rather became transparent, as if *It*
penetrated them and nothing could veil *It*.

In these latter days he would go into the drawing-room he had arranged—
that drawing-room where he had fallen and for the sake of which (how bitterly ridiculous it seemed) he had sacrificed his life—for he knew that his
illness originated with that knock. He would enter and see that something had
scratched the polished table. He would look for the cause of this and find that
it was the bronze ornamentation of an album, that had got bent. He would
take up the expensive album which he had lovingly arranged, and feel vexed
with his daughter and her friends for their untidiness—for the album was torn
here and there and some of the photographs turned upside down. He would
put it carefully in order and bend the ornamentation back into position. Then
it would occur to him to place all those things in another corner of the room,
near the plants. He could call the footman, but his daughter or wife would
come to help him. They would not agree, and his wife would contradict him,
and he would dispute and grow angry. But that was all right, for then he did
not think about *It. It* was invisible.

But then, when he was moving something himself, his wife would say: "Let
the servants do it. You will hurt yourself again." And suddenly *It* would flash
through the screen and he would see it. It was just a flash, and he hoped it would
disappear, but he would involuntarily pay attention to his side. "It sits there as
before, gnawing just the same!" And he could no longer forget *It,* but could distinctly see it looking at him from behind the flowers. "What is it all for?"

"It really is so! I lost my life over that curtain as I might have done when
storming a fort. Is that possible? How terrible and how stupid. It can't be true!
It can't, but it is."

He would go to his study, lie down, and again be alone with *It:* face to face
with *It.* And nothing could be done with *It* except to look at it and shudder.

CHAPTER VII

How it happened it is impossible to say because it came about step by step, 185
unnoticed, but in the third month of Iván Ilých's illness, his wife, his daughter,
his son, his acquaintances, the doctors, the servants, and above all he himself,
were aware that the whole interest he had for other people was whether he
would soon vacate his place, and at last release the living from the discomfort
caused by his presence and be himself released from his sufferings.

He slept less and less. He was given opium and hypodermic injections of
morphine, but this did not relieve him. The dull depression he experienced
in a somnolent condition at first gave him a little relief, but only as something
new, afterwards it became as distressing as the pain itself or even more so.

Special foods were prepared for him by the doctors' orders, but all those
foods became increasingly distasteful and disgusting to him.

For his excretions also special arrangements had to be made, and this was a torment to him every time—a torment from the uncleanliness, the unseemliness, and the smell, and from knowing that another person had to take part in it.

But just through this most unpleasant matter Iván Ilých obtained comfort. Gerásim, the butler's young assistant, always came in to carry the things out. Gerásim was a clean, fresh peasant lad, grown stout on town food and always cheerful and bright. At first the sight of him, in his clean Russian peasant costume, engaged on that disgusting task embarrassed Iván Ilých.

Once when he got up from the commode too weak to draw up his trousers, 190 he dropped into a soft armchair and looked with horror at his bare, enfeebled thighs with the muscles so sharply marked on them.

Gerásim with a firm light tread, his heavy boots emitting a pleasant smell of tar and fresh winter air, came in wearing a clean Hessian apron, the sleeves of his print shirt tucked up over his strong bare young arms; and refraining from looking at his sick master out of consideration for his feelings, and restraining the joy of life that beamed from his face, he went up to the commode.

"Gerásim!" said Iván Ilých in a weak voice.

Gerásim started, evidently afraid he might have committed some blunder, and with a rapid movement turned his fresh, kind, simple young face which just showed the first downy signs of a beard.

"Yes, sir?"

"That must be very unpleasant for you. You must forgive me. I am helpless." 195

"Oh, why, sir," and Gerásim's eyes beamed and he showed his glistening white teeth, "what's a little trouble? It's a case of illness with you, sir."

And his deft strong hands did their accustomed task, and he went out of the room stepping lightly. Five minutes later he as lightly returned.

Iván Ilých was still sitting in the same position in the armchair.

"Gerásim," he said when the latter had replaced the freshly-washed utensil. "Please come here and help me." Gerásim went up to him. "Lift me up. It is hard for me to get up, and I have sent Dmítri away."

Gerásim went up to him, grasped his master with his strong arms deftly but 200 gently, in the same way that he stepped—lifted him, supported him with one hand, and with the other drew up his trousers and would have set him down again, but Iván Ilých asked to be led to the sofa. Gerásim, without an effort and without apparent pressure, led him, almost lifting him, to the sofa and placed him on it.

"Thank you. How easily and well you do it all!"

Gerásim smiled again and turned to leave the room. But Iván Ilých felt his presence such a comfort that he did not want to let him go.

"One thing more, please move up that chair. No, the other one—under my feet. It is easier for me when my feet are raised."

Gerásim brought the chair, set it down gently in place, and raised Iván Ilých's legs on to it. It seemed to Iván Ilých that he felt better while Gerásim was holding up his legs.

"It's better when my legs are higher," he said. "Place that cushion under 205
them."

Gerásim did so. He again lifted the legs and placed them, and again Iván
Ilých felt better while Gerásim held his legs. When he set them down Iván
Ilých fancied he felt worse.

"Gerásim," he said. "Are you busy now?"

"Not at all, sir," said Gerásim, who had learnt from the townsfolk how to
speak to gentlefolk.

"What have you still to do?"

"What have I to do? I've done everything except chopping the logs for 210
tomorrow."

"Then hold my legs up a bit higher, can you?"

"Of course I can. Why not?" And Gerásim raised his master's legs higher
and Iván Ilých thought that in that position he did not feel any pain at all.

"And how about the logs?"

"Don't trouble about that, sir. There's plenty of time."

Iván Ilých told Gerásim to sit down and hold his legs, and began to talk to 215
him. And strange to say it seemed to him that he felt better while Gerásim held
his legs up.

After that Iván Ilých would sometimes call Gerásim and get him to hold
his legs on his shoulders, and he liked talking to him. Gerásim did it all easily, willingly, simply, and with a good nature that touched Iván Ilých. Health,
strength, and vitality in other people were offensive to him, but Gerásim's
strength and vitality did not mortify but soothed him.

What tormented Iván Ilých most was the deception, the lie, which for some
reason they all accepted, that he was not dying but was simply ill, and that
he only need keep quiet and undergo a treatment and then something very
good would result. He however knew that do what they would nothing would
come of it, only still more agonizing suffering and death. This deception tortured him—their not wishing to admit what they all knew and what he knew,
but wanting to lie to him concerning his terrible condition, and wishing and
forcing him to participate in that lie. Those lies—lies enacted over him on the
eve of his death and destined to degrade this awful, solemn act to the level
of their visitings, their curtains, their sturgeon for dinner—were a terrible
agony for Iván Ilých. And strangely enough, many times when they were going
through their antics over him he had been within a hairbreadth of calling out
to them: "Stop lying! You know and I know that I am dying. Then at least stop
lying about it!" But he had never had the spirit to do it. The awful, terrible act
of his dying was, he could see, reduced by those about him to the level of a
casual, unpleasant, and almost indecorous incident (as if someone entered a
drawing-room diffusing an unpleasant odour) and this was done by that very
decorum which he had served all his life long. He saw that no one felt for him,
because no one even wished to grasp his position. Only Gerásim recognized it
and pitied him. And so Iván Ilých felt at ease only with him. He felt comforted
when Gerásim supported his legs (sometimes all night long) and refused to go

to bed, saying, "Don't you worry, Iván Ilých. I'll get sleep enough later on," or when he suddenly became familiar and exclaimed: "If you weren't sick it would be another matter, but as it is, why should I grudge a little trouble?" Gerásim alone did not lie; everything showed that he alone understood the facts of the case and did not consider it necessary to disguise them, but simply felt sorry for his emaciated and enfeebled master. Once when Iván Ilých was sending him away he even said straight out: "We shall all of us die, so why should I grudge a little trouble?"—expressing the fact that he did not think his work burdensome, because he was doing it for a dying man and hoped someone would do the same for him when his time came.

Apart from this lying, or because of it, what most tormented Iván Ilých was that no one pitied him as he wished to be pitied. At certain moments after prolonged suffering he wished most of all (though he would have been ashamed to confess it) for someone to pity him as a sick child is pitied. He longed to be petted and comforted. He knew he was an important functionary, that he had a beard turning grey, and that therefore what he longed for was impossible, but still he longed for it. And in Gerásim's attitude towards him there was something akin to what he wished for, and so that attitude comforted him. Iván Ilých wanted to weep, wanted to be petted and cried over, and then his colleague Shébek would come, and instead of weeping and being petted, Iván Ilých would assume a serious, severe, and profound air, and by force of habit would express his opinion on a decision of the Court of Cassation and would stubbornly insist on that view. This falsity around him and within him did more than anything else to poison his last days.

CHAPTER VIII

It was morning. He knew it was morning because Gerásim had gone, and Peter the footman had come and put out the candles, drawn back one of the curtains, and begun quietly to tidy up. Whether it was morning or evening, Friday or Sunday, made no difference, it was all just the same: the gnawing, unmitigated, agonizing pain, never ceasing for an instant, the consciousness of life inexorably waning but not yet extinguished, that approach of that ever dreaded and hateful Death which was the only reality, and always the same falsity. What were days, weeks, hours, in such a case?

"Will you have some tea, sir?"   220

"He wants things to be regular, and wishes the gentlefolk to drink tea in the morning," thought Iván Ilých, and only said "No."

"Wouldn't you like to move onto the sofa, sir?"

"He wants to tidy up the room, and I'm in the way. I am uncleanliness and disorder," he thought, and said only:

"No, leave me alone."

The man went on bustling about. Iván Ilých stretched out his hand. Peter   225
came up, ready to help.

"What is it, sir?"

"My watch."

Peter took the watch which was close at hand and gave it to his master.

"Half-past eight. Are they up?"

"No, sir, except Vladímir Ivánich" (the son) "who has gone to school. Pra- 230
skóvya Fëdorovna ordered me to wake her if you asked for her. Shall I do so?"

"No, there's no need to." "Perhaps I'd better have some tea," he thought,
and added aloud: "Yes, bring me some tea."

Peter went to the door but Iván Ilých dreaded being left alone. "How can I
keep him here? Oh yes, my medicine." "Peter, give me my medicine." "Why
not? Perhaps it may still do me some good." He took a spoonful and swallowed it. "No, it won't help. It's all tomfoolery, all deception," he decided as
soon as he became aware of the familiar, sickly, hopeless taste. "No, I can't
believe in it any longer. But the pain, why this pain? If it would only cease just
for a moment!" And he moaned. Peter turned towards him. "It's all right. Go
and fetch me some tea."

Peter went out. Left alone Iván Ilých groaned not so much with pain, terrible
though that was, as from mental anguish. Always and for ever the same, always
these endless days and nights. If only it would come quicker! If only *what* would
come quicker? Death, darkness? . . . No, no! Anything rather than death!

When Peter returned with the tea on a tray, Iván Ilých stared at him for a
time in perplexity, not realizing who and what he was. Peter was disconcerted
by that look and his embarrassment brought Iván Ilých to himself.

"Oh, tea! All right, put it down. Only help me to wash and put on a clean shirt." 235

And Iván Ilých began to wash. With pauses for rest, he washed his hands
and then his face, cleaned his teeth, brushed his hair, and looked in the glass.
He was terrified by what he saw, especially by the limp way in which his hair
clung to his pallid forehead.

While his shirt was being changed he knew that he would be still more
frightened at the sight of his body, so he avoided looking at it. Finally he was
ready. He drew on a dressing-gown, wrapped himself in a plaid, and sat down
in the armchair to take his tea. For a moment he felt refreshed, but as soon as
he began to drink the tea he was again aware of the same taste, and the pain
also returned. He finished it with an effort, and then lay down stretching out
his legs, and dismissed Peter.

Always the same. Now a spark of hope flashes up, then a sea of despair rages,
and always pain; always pain, always despair, and always the same. When alone
he had a dreadful and distressing desire to call someone, but he knew beforehand
that with others present it would be still worse. "Another dose of morphine—to
lose consciousness. I will tell him, the doctor, that he must think of something
else. It's impossible, impossible, to go on like this."

An hour and another pass like that. But now there is a ring at the door bell.
Perhaps it's the doctor? It is. He comes in fresh, hearty, plump, and cheerful,
with that look on his face that seems to say: "There now, you're in a panic
about something, but we'll arrange it all for you directly!" The doctor knows
this expression is out of place here, but he has put it on once for all and can't

take it off—like a man who has put on a frock-coat in the morning to pay a round of calls.

The doctor rubs his hands vigorously and reassuringly. 240

"Brr! How cold it is! There's such a sharp frost; just let me warm myself!" he says, as if it were only a matter of waiting till he was warm, and then he would put everything right.

"Well now, how are you?"

Iván Ilých feels that the doctor would like to say: "Well, how are our affairs?" but that even he feels that this would not do, and says instead: "What sort of a night have you had?"

Iván Ilých looks at him as much as to say: "Are you really never ashamed of lying?" But the doctor does not wish to understand this question, and Iván Ilých says: "Just as terrible as ever. The pain never leaves me and never subsides. If only something . . ."

"Yes, you sick people are always like that. . . . There, now I think I am warm 245 enough. Even Praskóvya Fëdorovna, who is so particular, could find no fault with my temperature. Well, now I can say good-morning," and the doctor presses his patient's hand.

Then, dropping his former playfulness, he begins with a most serious face to examine the patient, feeling his pulse and taking his temperature, and then begins the sounding and auscultation.

Iván Ilých knows quite well and definitely that all this is nonsense and pure deception, but when the doctor, getting down on his knee, leans over him, putting his ear first higher then lower, and performs various gymnastic movements over him with a significant expression on his face, Iván Ilých submits to it all as he used to submit to the speeches of the lawyers, though he knew very well that they were all lying and why they were lying.

The doctor, kneeling on the sofa, is still sounding him when Praskóvya Fëdorovna's silk dress rustles at the door and she is heard scolding Peter for not having let her know of the doctor's arrival.

She comes in, kisses her husband, and at once proceeds to prove that she has been up a long time already, and only owing to a misunderstanding failed to be there when the doctor arrived.

Iván Ilých looks at her, scans her all over, sets against her the whiteness and 250 plumpness and cleanness of her hands and neck, the gloss of her hair, and the sparkle of her vivacious eyes. He hates her with his whole soul. And the thrill of hatred he feels for her makes him suffer from her touch.

Her attitude towards him and his disease is still the same. Just as the doctor had adopted a certain relation to his patient which he could not abandon, so had she formed one towards him—that he was not doing something he ought to do and was himself to blame, and that she reproached him lovingly for this—and she could not now change that attitude.

"You see he doesn't listen to me and doesn't take his medicine at the proper time. And above all he lies in a position that is no doubt bad for him—with his legs up."

She described how he made Gerásim hold his legs up.

The doctor smiled with a contemptuous affability that said: "What's to be done? These sick people do have foolish fancies of that kind, but we must forgive them."

When the examination was over the doctor looked at his watch, and then 255 Praskóvya Fëdorovna announced to Iván Ilých that it was of course as he pleased, but she had sent to-day for a celebrated specialist who would examine him and have a consultation with Michael Danílovich (their regular doctor).

"Please don't raise any objections. I am doing this for my own sake," she said ironically, letting it be felt that she was doing it all for his sake and only said this to leave him no right to refuse. He remained silent, knitting his brows. He felt that he was so surrounded and involved in a mesh of falsity that it was hard to unravel anything.

Everything she did for him was entirely for her own sake, and she told him she was doing for herself what she actually was doing for herself, as if that was so incredible that he must understand the opposite.

At half-past eleven the celebrated specialist arrived. Again the sounding began and the significant conversations in his presence and in another room, about the kidneys and the appendix, and the questions and answers, with such an air of importance that again, instead of the real question of life and death which now alone confronted him, the question arose of the kidney and appendix which were not behaving as they ought to and would now be attacked by Michael Danílovich and the specialist and forced to amend their ways.

The celebrated specialist took leave of him with a serious though not hopeless look, and in reply to the timid question Iván Ilých, with eyes glistening with fear and hope, put to him as to whether there was a chance of recovery, said that he could not vouch for it but there was a possibility. The look of hope with which Iván Ilých watched the doctor out was so pathetic that Praskóvya Fëdorovna, seeing it, even wept as she left the room to hand the doctor his fee.

The gleam of hope kindled by the doctor's encouragement did not last long. 260 The same room, the same pictures, curtains, wall-paper, medicine bottles, were all there, and the same aching suffering body, and Iván Ilých began to moan. They gave him a subcutaneous injection and he sank into oblivion.

It was twilight when he came to. They brought him his dinner and he swallowed some beef tea with difficulty, and then everything was the same again and night was coming on.

After dinner, at seven o'clock, Praskóvya Fëdorovna came into the room in evening dress, her full bosom pushed up by her corset, and with traces of powder on her face. She had reminded him in the morning that they were going to the theater. Sarah Bernhardt was visiting the town and they had a box, which he had insisted on their taking. Now he had forgotten about it and her toilet offended him, but he concealed his vexation when he remembered that he had himself insisted on their securing a box and going because it would be an instructive and aesthetic pleasure for the children.

Praskóvya Fëdorovna came in, self-satisfied but yet with a rather guilty air. She sat down and asked how he was, but, as he saw, only for the sake of asking and not in order to learn about it, knowing that there was nothing to learn—and then went on to what she really wanted to say: that she would not on any account have gone but that the box had been taken and Helen and their daughter were going, as well as Petríshchev (the examining magistrate, their daughter's fiancé) and that it was out of the question to let them go alone; but that she would have much preferred to sit with him for a while; and he must be sure to follow the doctor's orders while she was away.

"Oh, and Fëdor Petróvich" (the fiancé) "would like to come in. May he? And Lisa?"

"All right."   265

Their daughter came in in full evening dress, her fresh young flesh exposed (making a show of that very flesh which in his own case caused so much suffering), strong, healthy, evidently in love, and impatient with illness, suffering, and death, because they interfered with her happiness.

Fëdor Petróvich came in too, in evening dress, his hair curled *á la Capoul*, a tight stiff collar round his long sinewy neck, an enormous white shirt-front and narrow black trousers tightly stretched over his strong thighs. He had one white glove tightly drawn on, and was holding his opera hat in his hand.

Following him the schoolboy crept in unnoticed, in a new uniform, poor little fellow, and wearing gloves. Terribly dark shadows showed under his eyes, the meaning of which Iván Ilých knew well.

His son had always seemed pathetic to him, and now it was dreadful to see the boy's frightened look of pity. It seemed to Iván Ilých that Vásya was the only one besides Gerásim who understood and pitied him.

They all sat down and again asked how he was. A silence followed. Lisa asked   270 her mother about the opera-glasses, and there was an altercation between mother and daughter as to who had taken them and where they had been put. This occasioned some unpleasantness.

Fëdor Petróvich inquired of Iván Ilých whether he had ever seen Sarah Bernhardt. Iván Ilých did not at first catch the question, but then replied: "No, have you seen her before?"

"Yes, in *Adrienne Lecouvreur*."[12]

Praskóvya Fëdorovna mentioned some roles in which Sarah Bernhardt was particularly good. Her daughter disagreed. Conversation sprang up as to the elegance and realism of her acting—the sort of conversation that is always repeated and is always the same.

In the midst of the conversation Fëdor Petróvich glanced at Iván Ilých and became silent. The others also looked at him and grew silent. Iván Ilých was staring with glittering eyes straight before him, evidently indignant with them. This had to be rectified, but it was impossible to do so. The silence had to be

[12] A play by the French dramatist Eugène Scribe (1791–1861).

broken, but for a time no one dared to break it and they all became afraid that the conventional deception would suddenly become obvious and the truth become plain to all. Lisa was the first to pluck up courage and break that silence, but by trying to hide what everybody was feeling, she betrayed it.

"Well, if we are going it's time to start," she said, looking at her watch, 275 a present from her father, and with a faint and significant smile at Fëdor Petróvich relating to something known only to them. She got up with a rustle of her dress.

They all rose, said good-night, and went away.

When they had gone it seemed to Iván Ilých that he felt better; the falsity had gone with them. But the pain remained—that same pain and that same fear that made everything monotonously alike, nothing harder and nothing easier. Everything was worse.

Again minute followed minute and hour followed hour. Everything remained the same and there was no cessation. And the inevitable end of it all became more and more terrible.

"Yes, send Gerásim here," he replied to a question Peter asked.

CHAPTER IX

His wife returned late at night. She came in on tiptoe, but he heard her, opened 280 his eyes, and made haste to close them again. She wished to send Gerásim away and to sit with him herself, but he opened his eyes and said: "No, go away."

"Are you in great pain?"

"Always the same."

"Take some opium."

He agreed and took some. She went away.

Till about three in the morning he was in a state of stupefied misery. It seemed 285 to him that he and his pain were being thrust into a narrow, deep black sack, but though they were pushed further and further in they could not be pushed to the bottom. And this, terrible enough in itself, was accompanied by suffering. He was frightened yet wanted to fall through the sack, he struggled but yet co-operated. And suddenly he broke through, fell, and regained consciousness. Gerásim was sitting at the foot of the bed dozing quietly and patiently, while he himself lay with his emaciated stockinged legs resting on Gerásim's shoulders; the same shaded candle was there and the same unceasing pain.

"Go away, Gerásim," he whispered.

"It's all right, sir. I'll stay a while."

"No. Go away."

He removed his legs from Gerásim's shoulders, turned sideways onto his arm, and felt sorry for himself. He only waited till Gerásim had gone into the next room and then restrained himself no longer but wept like a child. He wept on account of his helplessness, his terrible loneliness, the cruelty of man, the cruelty of God, and the absence of God.

"Why hast Thou done all this? Why hast Thou brought me here? Why, why 290 dost Thou torment me so terribly?"

He did not expect an answer and yet wept because there was no answer and could be none. The pain again grew more acute, but he did not stir and did not call. He said to himself: "Go on! Strike me! But what is it for? What have I done to Thee? What is it for?"

Then he grew quiet and not only ceased weeping but even held his breath and became all attention. It was as though he were listening not to an audible voice but to the voice of his soul, to the current of thoughts arising within him.

"What is it you want?" was the first clear conception capable of expression in words, that he heard.

"What do you want? What do you want?" he repeated to himself.

"What do I want? To live and not to suffer," he answered.   295

And again he listened with such concentrated attention that even his pain did not distract him.

"To live? How?" asked his inner voice.

"Why, to live as I used to—well and pleasantly."

"As you lived before, well and pleasantly?" the voice repeated.

And in imagination he began to recall the best moments of his pleasant life. 300 But strange to say none of those best moments of his pleasant life now seemed at all what they had then seemed—none of them except the first recollections of childhood. There, in childhood, there had been something really pleasant with which it would be possible to live if it could return. But the child who had experienced that happiness existed no longer, it was like a reminiscence of somebody else.

As soon as the period began which had produced the present Iván Ilých, all that had then seemed joys now melted before his sight and turned into something trivial and often nasty.

And the further he departed from childhood and the nearer he came to the present the more worthless and doubtful were the joys. This began with the School of Law. A little that was really good was still found there—there was lightheartedness, friendship, and hope. But in the upper classes there had already been fewer of such good moments. Then during the first years of his official career, when he was in the service of the Governor, some pleasant moments again occurred: they were the memories of love for a woman. Then all became confused and there was still less of what was good; later on again there was still less that was good, and the further he went the less there was. His marriage, a mere accident, then the disenchantment that followed it, his wife's bad breath and the sensuality and hypocrisy: then that deadly official life and those preoccupations about money, a year of it, and two, and ten, and twenty, and always the same thing. And the longer it lasted the more deadly it became. "It is as if I had been going downhill while I imagined I was going up. And that is really what it was. I was going up in public opinion, but to the same extent life was ebbing away from me. And now it is all done and there is only death."

"Then what does it mean? Why? It can't be that life is so senseless and horrible. But if it really has been so horrible and senseless, why must I die and die in agony? There is something wrong!"

"Maybe I did not live as I ought to have done," it suddenly occurred to him. "But how could that be, when I did everything properly?" he replied, and immediately dismissed from his mind this, the sole solution of all the riddles of life and death, as something quite impossible.

"Then what do you want now? To live? Live how? Live as you lived in the 305 law courts when the usher proclaimed 'The judge is coming!'" "The judge is coming, the judge!" he repeated to himself. "Here he is, the judge. But I am not guilty!" he exclaimed angrily. "What is it for?" And he ceased crying, but turning his face to the wall continued to ponder on the same question: Why, and for what purpose, is there all this horror? But however much he pondered he found no answer. And whenever the thought occurred to him, as it often did, that it all resulted from his not having lived as he ought to have done, he at once recalled the correctness of his whole life and dismissed so strange an idea.

CHAPTER X

Another fortnight passed. Iván Ilých now no longer left his sofa. He would not lie in bed but lay on the sofa, facing the wall nearly all the time. He suffered ever the same unceasing agonies and in his loneliness pondered always on the same insoluble question: "What is this? Can it be that it is Death?" And the inner voice answered: "Yes, it is Death."

"Why these sufferings?" And the voice answered, "For no reason—they just are so." Beyond and besides this there was nothing.

From the very beginning of his illness, ever since he had first been to see the doctor, Iván Ilých's life had been divided between two contrary and alternating moods: now it was despair and the expectation of this uncomprehended and terrible death, and now hope and an intently interested observation of the functioning of his organs. Now before his eyes there was only a kidney or an intestine that temporarily evaded its duty, and now only that incomprehensible and dreadful death from which it was impossible to escape.

These two states of mind had alternated from the very beginning of his illness, but the further it progressed the more doubtful and fantastic became the conception of the kidney, and the more real the sense of impending death.

He had but to call to mind what he had been three months before and what 310 he was now, to call to mind with what regularity he had been going downhill, for every possibility of hope to be shattered.

Latterly during that loneliness in which he found himself as he lay facing the back of the sofa, a loneliness in the midst of a populous town and surrounded by numerous acquaintances and relations but that yet could not have been more complete anywhere—either at the bottom of the sea or under the earth—during that terrible loneliness Iván Ilých had lived only in memories of the past. Pictures of his past rose before him one after another. They always began with what was nearest in time and then went back to what was most remote—to his childhood—and rested there. If he thought of the stewed prunes that had been offered him that day, his mind went back to the raw shrivelled French plums of his childhood, their peculiar flavor and the flow of saliva when he sucked their stones, and along with the memory of that taste came a whole series of memories of those days: his nurse, his brother, and their toys. "No, I mustn't think of that. . . . It is too painful," Iván Ilých said to himself, and brought himself back to the present—to the button on the back of the sofa and the creases in its morocco. "Morocco is expensive, but it does not wear well: there had been a quarrel about it. It was a different kind of quarrel and a different kind of morocco that time when we tore father's portfolio and were punished, and mamma brought us some tarts. . . ." And again his thoughts dwelt on his childhood, and again it was painful and he tried to banish them and fix his mind on something else.

Then again together with that chain of memories another series passed through his mind—of how his illness had progressed and grown worse. There also the further back he looked the more life there had been. There had been more of what was good in life and more of life itself. The two merged together. "Just as the pain went on getting worse and worse so my life grew worse and worse," he thought. "There is one bright spot there at the back, at the beginning of life, and afterwards all becomes blacker and blacker and proceeds more and more rapidly—in inverse ratio to the square of the distance from death," thought Iván Ilých. And the example of a stone falling downwards with increasing velocity entered his mind. Life, a series of increasing sufferings, flies, further and further towards its end—the most terrible suffering. "I am flying. . . ." He shuddered, shifted himself, and tried to resist, but was already aware that resistance was impossible, and again with eyes weary of gazing but unable to cease seeing what was before them, he stared at the back of the sofa and waited—awaiting that dreadful fall and shock and destruction.

"Resistance is impossible!" he said to himself. "If I could only understand what it is all for! But that too is impossible. An explanation would be possible if it could be said that I have not lived as I ought to. But it is impossible to say that," and he remembered all the legality, correctitude, and propriety of his life. "That at any rate can certainly not be admitted," he thought, and his lips smiled ironically as if someone could see that smile and be taken in by it. "There is no explanation! Agony, death. . . . What for?"

CHAPTER XI

Another two weeks went by in this way and during that fortnight an event occurred that Iván Ilých and his wife had desired. Petríshchev formally proposed. It happened in the evening. The next day Praskóvya Fëdorovna came into her husband's room considering how best to inform him of it, but that very night there had been a fresh change for the worse in his condition. She found him still lying on the sofa but in a different position. He lay on his back, groaning and staring fixedly straight in front of him.

She began to remind him of his medicines, but he turned his eyes towards 315 her with such a look that she did not finish what she was saying; so great an animosity, to her in particular, did that look express.

"For Christ's sake, let me die in peace!" he said.

She would have gone away, but just then their daughter came in and went up to say good morning. He looked at her as he had done at his wife, and in reply to her inquiry about his health said dryly that he would soon free them all of himself. They were both silent and after sitting with him for a while went away.

"Is it our fault?" Lisa said to her mother. "It's as if we were to blame! I am sorry for papa, but why should we be tortured?"

The doctor came at his usual time. Iván Ilých answered "Yes" and "No," never taking his angry eyes from him, and at last said: "You know you can do nothing for me, so leave me alone."

"We can ease your sufferings." 320

"You can't even do that. Let me be."

The doctor went into the drawing-room and told Praskóvya Fëdorovna that the case was very serious and that the only resource left was opium to allay her husband's sufferings, which must be terrible.

It was true, as the doctor said, that Iván Ilých's physical sufferings were terrible, but worse than the physical sufferings were his mental sufferings which were his chief torture.

His mental sufferings were due to the fact that that night, as he looked at Gerásim's sleepy, good-natured face with its prominent cheek-bones, the question suddenly occurred to him: "What if my whole life has really been wrong?"

It occurred to him that what had appeared perfectly impossible before, 325 namely that he had not spent his life as he should have done, might after all be true. It occurred to him that his scarcely perceptible attempts to struggle against what was considered good by the most highly placed people, those scarcely noticeable impulses which he had immediately suppressed, might have been the real thing, and all the rest false. And his professional duties and the whole arrangement of his life and of his family, and all his social and official interests, might all have been false. He tried to defend all those things to himself and suddenly felt the weakness of what he was defending. There was nothing to defend.

"But if that is so," he said to himself, "and I am leaving this life with the consciousness that I have lost all that was given me and it is impossible to rectify it—what then?"

He lay on his back and began to pass his life in review in quite a new way. In the morning when he saw first his footman, then his wife, then his daughter, and then the doctor, their every word and movement confirmed to him the awful truth that had been revealed to him during the night. In them he saw himself—all that for which he had lived—and saw clearly that it was not real at all, but a terrible and huge deception which had hidden both life and death.

This consciousness intensified his physical suffering tenfold. He groaned and tossed about, and pulled at his clothing which choked and stifled him. And he hated them on that account.

He was given a large dose of opium and became unconscious, but at noon his sufferings began again. He drove everybody away and tossed from side to side.

His wife came to him and said:

"Jean, my dear, do this for me. It can't do any harm and often helps. Healthy people often do it."

He opened his eyes wide.

"What? Take communion? Why? It's unnecessary! However. . . ."

She began to cry.

"Yes, do, my dear. I'll send for our priest. He is such a nice man."

"All right. Very well," he muttered.

When the priest came and heard his confession, Iván Ilých was softened and seemed to feel a relief from his doubts and consequently from his sufferings, and for a moment there came a ray of hope. He again began to think of the vermiform appendix and the possibility of correcting it. He received the sacrament with tears in his eyes.

When they laid him down again afterwards he felt a moment's ease, and the hope that he might live awoke in him again. He began to think of the operation that had been suggested to him. "To live! I want to live!" he said to himself.

His wife came in to congratulate him after his communion, and when uttering the usual conventional words she added:

"You feel better, don't you?"

Without looking at her he said "Yes."

Her dress, her figure, the expression of her face, the tone of her voice, all revealed the same thing. "This is wrong, it is not as it should be. All you have lived for and still live for is falsehood and deception, hiding life and death from you." And as soon as he admitted that thought, his hatred and his agonizing physical suffering again sprang up, and with that suffering a consciousness of the unavoidable, approaching end. And to this was added a new sensation of grinding shooting pain and a feeling of suffocation.

The expression of his face when he uttered that "yes" was dreadful. Having uttered it, he looked her straight in the eyes, turned on his face with a rapidity extraordinary in his weak state and shouted:

"Go away! Go away and leave me alone!"

CHAPTER XII

From that moment the screaming began that continued for three days, and was so terrible that one could not hear it through two closed doors without horror. At the moment he answered his wife he realized that he was lost, that there was no return, that the end had come, the very end, and his doubts were still unsolved and remained doubts.

"Oh! Oh! Oh!" he cried in various intonations. He had begun by screaming 345
"I won't!" and continued screaming on the letter "o."

For three whole days, during which time did not exist for him, he struggled
in that black sack into which he was being thrust by an invisible, resistless
force. He struggled as a man condemned to death struggles in the hands of the
executioner, knowing that he cannot save himself. And every moment he felt
that despite all his efforts he was drawing nearer and nearer to what terrified
him. He felt that his agony was due to his being thrust into that black hole
and still more to his not being able to get right into it. He was hindered from
getting into it by his conviction that his life had been a good one. That very
justification of his life held him fast and prevented his moving forward, and it
caused him most torment of all.

Suddenly some force struck him in the chest and side, making it still harder
to breathe, and he fell through the hole and there at the bottom was a light.
What had happened to him was like the sensation one sometimes experiences
in a railway carriage when one thinks one is going backwards while one is
really going forwards and suddenly becomes aware of the real direction.

"Yes, it was all not the right thing," he said to himself, "but that's no matter.
It can be done. But what *is* the right thing?" he asked himself, and suddenly
grew quiet.

This occurred at the end of the third day, two hours before his death. Just
then his schoolboy son had crept softly in and gone up to the bedside. The
dying man was still screaming desperately and waving his arms. His hand fell
on the boy's head, and the boy caught it, pressed it to his lips, and began to cry.

At that very moment Iván Ilých fell through and caught sight of the light, 350
and it was revealed to him that though his life had not been what it should
have been, this could still be rectified. He asked himself, "What *is* the right
thing?" and grew still, listening. Then he felt that someone was kissing his
hand. He opened his eyes, looked at his son, and felt sorry for him. His wife
came up to him and he glanced at her. She was gazing at him open-mouthed,
with undried tears on her nose and cheek and a despairing look on her face.
He felt sorry for her too.

"Yes, I am making them wretched," he thought. "They are sorry, but it will
be better for them when I die." He wished to say this but had not the strength
to utter it. "Besides, why speak? I must act," he thought. With a look at his
wife he indicated his son and said: "Take him away . . . sorry for him . . .
sorry for you too. . . ." He tried to add, "forgive me," but said "forego" and
waved his hand, knowing that He whose understanding mattered would
understand.

And suddenly it grew clear to him that what had been oppressing him and
would not leave him was all dropping away at once from two sides, from
ten sides, and from all sides. He was sorry for them, he must act so as not to
hurt them: release them and free himself from these sufferings. "How good
and how simple!" he thought. "And the pain?" he asked himself. "What has
become of it? Where are you, pain?"

He turned his attention to it.

"Yes, here it is. Well, what of it? Let the pain be."

"And death . . . where is it?"   355

He sought his former accustomed fear of death and did not find it. "Where is it? What death?" There was no fear because there was no death.

In place of death there was light.

"So that's what it is!" he suddenly exclaimed aloud. "What joy!"

To him all this happened in a single instant, and the meaning of that instant did not change. For those present his agony continued for another two hours. Something rattled in his throat, his emaciated body twitched, then the gasping and rattle became less and less frequent.

"It is finished!" said someone near him.   360

He heard these words and repeated them in his soul.

"Death is finished," he said to himself. "It is no more!"

He drew in a breath, stopped in the midst of a sigh, stretched out, and died.

FOR ANALYSIS

1. Discuss the evidence that Ilých's death is a moral judgment—that is, a punishment for his life.

2. Discuss "The Death of Iván Ilých" from Paul's perspective revealed in 1 Corinthians 13 (p. 1071). What accounts for the change in Ilých's attitude toward his approaching death?

3. Discuss the fact that Gerásim, Ilých's peasant servant, is more sympathetic to his condition than Ilých's family is.

4. Suggest a reason for Tolstoy's decision to begin the story immediately after Ilých's death and then move back to recount the significant episodes of his life.

MAKING CONNECTIONS

Compare the significance of death to the characters in this story with the significance of death to the characters in one or both of the following works: Porter's "The Jilting of Granny Weatherall" (p. 1182) and Silko's "The Man to Send Rain Clouds" (p. 1173).

WRITING TOPICS

1. At the conclusion of the story, Ilých achieves peace and understanding, and the questions that have been torturing him are resolved. He realizes that "though his life had not been what it should have been, this could still be rectified" (para. 350). What does this mean?

2. In an essay, compare and contrast the attitudes of various characters to Ilých's mortal illness. How do his colleagues respond? His wife? His children? His servant Gerásim?

KATE CHOPIN (1850–1904)

THE STORY OF AN HOUR 1894

Knowing that Mrs. Mallard was afflicted with a heart trouble, great care was taken to break to her as gently as possible the news of her husband's death.

It was her sister Josephine who told her, in broken sentences; veiled hints that revealed in half concealing. Her husband's friend Richards was there, too, near her. It was he who had been in the newspaper office when intelligence of the railroad disaster was received, with Brently Mallard's name leading the list of "killed." He had only taken the time to assure himself of its truth by a second telegram, and had hastened to forestall any less careful, less tender friend in bearing the sad message.

She did not hear the story as many women have heard the same, with a paralyzed inability to accept its significance. She wept at once, with sudden, wild abandonment, in her sister's arms. When the storm of grief had spent itself she went away to her room alone. She would have no one follow her.

There stood, facing the open window, a comfortable, roomy armchair. Into this she sank, pressed down by a physical exhaustion that haunted her body and seemed to reach into her soul.

She could see in the open square before her house the tops of trees that were 5 all aquiver with the new spring life. The delicious breath of rain was in the air. In the street below a peddler was crying his wares. The notes of a distant song which some one was singing reached her faintly, and countless sparrows were twittering in the eaves.

There were patches of blue sky showing here and there through the clouds that had met and piled one above the other in the west facing her window.

She sat with her head thrown back upon the cushion of the chair, quite motionless, except when a sob came up into her throat and shook her, as a child who had cried itself to sleep continues to sob in its dreams.

She was young, with a fair, calm face, whose lines bespoke repression and even a certain strength. But now there was a dull stare in her eyes, whose gaze was fixed away off yonder on one of those patches of blue sky. It was not a glance of reflection, but rather indicated a suspension of intelligent thought.

There was something coming to her and she was waiting for it, fearfully. What was it? She did not know; it was too subtle and elusive to name. But she felt it, creeping out of the sky, reaching toward her through the sounds, the scents, and the color that filled the air.

Now her bosom rose and fell tumultuously. She was beginning to recognize 10 this thing that was approaching to possess her, and she was striving to beat it back with her will—as powerless as her two white slender hands would have been.

When she abandoned herself a little whispered word escaped her slightly parted lips. She said it over and over under her breath: "free, free, free!" The vacant stare and the look of terror that had followed it went from her eyes. They stayed keen and bright. Her pulses beat fast, and the coursing blood warmed and relaxed every inch of her body.

She did not stop to ask if it were or were not a monstrous joy that held her. A clear and exalted perception enabled her to dismiss the suggestion as trivial.

She knew that she would weep again when she saw the kind, tender hands folded in death; the face that had never looked save with love upon her, fixed and gray and dead. But she saw beyond that bitter moment a long procession of years to come that would belong to her absolutely. And she opened and spread her arms out to them in welcome.

There would be no one to live for her during those coming years: she would live for herself. There would be no powerful will bending hers in that blind persistence with which men and women believe they have a right to impose a private will upon a fellow-creature. A kind intention or a cruel intention made the act seem no less a crime as she looked upon it in that brief moment of illumination.

And yet she had loved him—sometimes. Often she had not. What did it matter! What could love, the unsolved mystery, count for in face of this posses-sion of self-assertion which she suddenly recognized as the strongest impulse of her being! 15

"Free! Body and soul free!" she kept whispering.

Josephine was kneeling before the closed door with her lips to the keyhole, imploring for admission. "Louise, open the door! I beg; open the door—you will make yourself ill. What are you doing, Louise? For heaven's sake open the door."

"Go away. I am not making myself ill." No; she was drinking in a very elixir of life through that open window.

Her fancy was running riot along those days ahead of her. Spring days, and summer days, and all sorts of days that would be her own. She breathed a quick prayer that life might be long. It was only yesterday she had thought with a shudder that life might be long.

She arose at length and opened the door to her sister's importunities. There was a feverish triumph in her eyes, and she carried herself unwittingly like a goddess of Victory. She clasped her sister's waist, and together they descended the stairs. Richards stood waiting for them at the bottom. 20

Some one was opening the front door with a latchkey. It was Brently Mal-lard who entered, a little travel-stained, composedly carrying his gripsack and umbrella. He had been far from the scene of accident, and did not even know there had been one. He stood amazed at Josephine's piercing cry; at Richards' quick motion to screen him from the view of his wife.

But Richards was too late.

When the doctors came they said she had died of heart disease—of joy that kills.

FOR ANALYSIS

1. How does Chopin's story begin? Are we introduced to **character**, **setting**, and **plot** first, or do we find things out gradually? Does all the important action happen in the story's present, or has some already happened? What are the effects of beginning the story this way?

2. How did you feel as you read of Mrs. Mallard's reactions to the news? Did your feelings change as hers did? How did all of this make you feel about her as a person?

3. How would you describe **point of view** in this story? From what perspective is the story told? How do we know what we know? What are the effects of this use of point of view?

MAKING CONNECTIONS

What do Mrs. Mallard and the main character in Charlotte Perkins Gilman's "The Yellow Wallpaper" (p. 551) have in common? How are the two characters different in terms of their situations and their reactions to them?

WRITING TOPIC

Write about a time in your own life when your reaction to an event was not what others might have expected it to be. What did this situation feel like? How did you deal with the fact that you were not meeting expectations? Were these expectations fair?

TIM O'BRIEN   (B. 1946)

THE THINGS THEY CARRIED   1986

First Lieutenant Jimmy Cross carried letters from a girl named Martha, a junior at Mount Sebastian College in New Jersey. They were not love letters, but Lieutenant Cross was hoping, so he kept them folded in plastic at the bottom of his rucksack. In the late afternoon, after a day's march, he would dig his foxhole, wash his hands under a canteen, unwrap the letters, hold them with the tips of his fingers, and spend the last hour of light pretending. He would imagine romantic camping trips into the White Mountains in New Hampshire. He would sometimes taste the envelope flaps, knowing her tongue had been there. More than anything, he wanted Martha to love him as he loved her, but the letters were mostly chatty, elusive on the matter of love. She was a virgin, he was almost sure. She was an English major at Mount Sebastian, and she wrote beautifully about her professors and roommates and midterm exams, about her respect for Chaucer and her great affection for Virginia Woolf. She often quoted lines of poetry; she never mentioned the war, except to say, Jimmy, take care of yourself. The letters weighed ten ounces. They were signed "Love, Martha," but Lieutenant Cross understood that "Love" was only a way of signing and did not mean what he sometimes pretended it meant. At dusk, he would carefully return the letters to his rucksack. Slowly, a bit distracted, he would get up and move among his men, checking the perimeter, then at full dark he would return to his hole and watch the night and wonder if Martha was a virgin.

The things they carried were largely determined by necessity. Among the necessities or near necessities were P-38 can openers, pocket knives, heat tabs, wrist watches, dog tags, mosquito repellent, chewing gum, candy, cigarettes, salt tablets, packets of Kool-Aid, lighters, matches, sewing kits, Military Payment Certificates, C rations, and two or three canteens of water. Together, these items weighed between fifteen and twenty pounds, depending upon a man's habits or rate of metabolism. Henry Dobbins, who was a big man, carried extra rations; he was especially fond of canned peaches in heavy syrup over pound cake. Dave Jensen, who practiced field hygiene, carried a toothbrush, dental floss, and several hotel-size bars of soap he'd stolen on R&R[1] in Sydney, Australia. Ted Lavender, who was scared, carried tranquilizers until he was shot in the head outside the village of Than Khe in mid-April. By necessity, and because it was SOP,[2] they all carried steel helmets that weighed five pounds including the liner and camouflage cover. They carried the standard

[1] Rest and recreation.
[2] Standard operating procedure.

1159

fatigue jackets and trousers. Very few carried underwear. On their feet they carried jungle boots—2.1 pounds—and Dave Jensen carried three pairs of socks and a can of Dr. Scholl's foot powder as a precaution against trench foot. Until he was shot, Ted Lavender carried six or seven ounces of premium dope, which for him was a necessity. Mitchell Sanders, the RTO, carried condoms. Norman Bowker carried a diary. Rat Kiley carried comic books. Kiowa, a devout Baptist, carried an illustrated New Testament that had been presented to him by his father, who taught Sunday school in Oklahoma City, Oklahoma. As a hedge against bad times, however, Kiowa also carried his grandmother's distrust of the white man, his grandfather's old hunting hatchet. Necessity dictated. Because the land was mined and booby-trapped, it was SOP for each man to carry a steel-centered, nylon-covered flak jacket, which weighed 6.7 pounds, but which on hot days seemed much heavier. Because you could die so quickly, each man carried at least one large compress bandage, usually in the helmet band for easy access. Because the nights were cold, and because the monsoons were wet, each carried a green plastic poncho that could be used as a raincoat or ground sheet or makeshift tent. With its quilted liner, the poncho weighed almost two pounds, but it was worth every ounce. In April, for instance, when Ted Lavender was shot, they used his poncho to wrap him up, then to carry him across the paddy, then to lift him into the chopper that took him away.

They were called legs or grunts.

To carry something was to "hump" it, as when Lieutenant Jimmy Cross humped his love for Martha up the hills and through the swamps. In its intransitive form, "to hump" meant "to walk," or "to march," but it implied burdens far beyond the intransitive.

Almost everyone humped photographs. In his wallet, Lieutenant Cross carried two photographs of Martha. The first was a Kodachrome snapshot signed "Love," though he knew better. She stood against a brick wall. Her eyes were gray and neutral, her lips slightly open as she stared straight-on at the camera. At night, sometimes, Lieutenant Cross wondered who had taken the picture, because he knew she had boyfriends, because he loved her so much, and because he could see the shadow of the picture taker spreading out against the brick wall. The second photograph had been clipped from the 1968 Mount Sebastian yearbook. It was an action shot—women's volleyball—and Martha was bent horizontal to the floor, reaching, the palms of her hands in sharp focus, the tongue taut, the expression frank and competitive. There was no visible sweat. She wore white gym shorts. Her legs, he thought, were almost certainly the legs of a virgin, dry and without hair, the left knee cocked and carrying her entire weight, which was just over one hundred pounds. Lieutenant Cross remembered touching that left knee. A dark theater, he remembered, and the movie was *Bonnie and Clyde,* and Martha wore a tweed skirt, and during the final scene, when he touched her knee, she turned and looked at him in a sad, sober way that made him pull his hand back, but he would always remember the feel of the tweed skirt and the knee beneath it and the sound of the gunfire that killed Bonnie and Clyde, how embarrassing it was, how slow and oppressive. He remembered kissing her good night at the dorm door. Right then, he thought, he should've done something brave. He should've carried her up the stairs to her room and tied her to the bed and touched that left knee all night long. He should've risked it. Whenever he looked at the photographs, he thought of new things he should've done.

What they carried was partly a function of rank, partly of field specialty.

As a first lieutenant and platoon leader, Jimmy Cross carried a compass, maps, code books, binoculars, and a .45-caliber pistol that weighed 2.9 pounds fully loaded. He carried a strobe light and the responsibility for the lives of his men.

As an RTO, Mitchell Sanders carried the PRC-25 radio, a killer, twenty-six pounds with its battery.

As a medic, Rat Kiley carried a canvas satchel filled with morphine and plasma and malaria tablets and surgical tape and comic books and all the things a medic must carry, including M&M's for especially bad wounds, for a total weight of nearly twenty pounds.

As a big man, therefore a machine gunner, Henry Dobbins carried the 10
M-60, which weighed twenty-three pounds unloaded, but which was almost always loaded. In addition, Dobbins carried between ten and fifteen pounds of ammunition draped in belts across his chest and shoulders.

As PFCs or Spec 4s, most of them were common grunts and carried the standard M-16 gas-operated assault rifle. The weapon weighed 7.5 pounds unloaded, 8.2 pounds with its full twenty-round magazine. Depending on numerous factors, such as topography and psychology, the riflemen carried anywhere from twelve to twenty magazines, usually in cloth bandoliers, adding on another 8.4 pounds at minimum, fourteen pounds at maximum. When it was available, they also carried M-16 maintenance gear—rods and steel brushes and swabs and tubes of LSA oil—all of which weighed about a pound. Among the grunts, some carried the M-79 grenade launcher, 5.9 pounds unloaded, a reasonably light weapon except for the ammunition, which was heavy. A single round weighed ten ounces. The typical load was twenty-five rounds. But Ted Lavender, who was scared, carried thirty-four rounds when he was shot and killed outside Than Khe, and he went down under an exceptional burden, more than twenty pounds of ammunition, plus the flak jacket and helmet and rations and water and toilet paper and tranquilizers and all the rest, plus the unweighed fear. He was dead weight. There was no twitching or flopping. Kiowa, who saw it happen, said it was like watching a rock fall, or a big sandbag or something—just boom, then down—not like the movies where the dead guy rolls around and does fancy spins and goes ass over teakettle—not like that, Kiowa said, the poor bastard just flat-fuck fell. Boom. Down. Nothing else. It was a bright morning in mid-April. Lieutenant Cross felt the pain. He blamed himself. They stripped off Lavender's canteens and ammo, all the heavy things, and Rat Kiley said the obvious, the guy's dead, and Mitchell Sanders used his radio to report one U.S. KIA and to request a chopper. Then they wrapped Lavender in his poncho. They carried him out to a dry paddy, established security, and sat smoking the dead man's dope until the chopper came. Lieutenant Cross kept to himself. He pictured Martha's smooth young face, thinking he loved her more than anything, more than his men, and now Ted Lavender was dead because he loved her so much and could not stop thinking about her. When the dust-off arrived, they carried Lavender aboard. Afterward they burned Than Khe. They marched until dusk, then dug their holes, and that night Kiowa kept explaining how you had to be there, how fast it was, how the poor guy just dropped like so much concrete. Boom-down, he said. Like cement.

In addition to the three standard weapons—the M-60, M-16, and M-79— they carried whatever presented itself, or whatever seemed appropriate as a means of killing or staying alive. They carried catch-as-catch-can. At various times, in various situations, they carried M-14s and CAR-15s and Swedish Ks and grease guns and captured AK-47s and Chi-Coms and RPGs and Simonov carbines and black-market Uzis and .38-caliber Smith & Wesson handguns and 66 mm LAWs and shotguns and silencers and blackjacks and bayonets and C-4 plastic explosives. Lee Strunk carried a slingshot; a weapon of last resort, he called it. Mitchell Sanders carried brass knuckles. Kiowa carried his grandfather's feathered hatchet. Every third or fourth man carried a Claymore antipersonnel mine—3.5 pounds with its firing device. They all carried fragmentation grenades—fourteen ounces each. They all carried at least one M-18 colored smoke grenade—twenty-four ounces. Some carried CS or tear-gas grenades. Some carried white-phosphorus grenades. They carried all they could bear, and then some, including a silent awe for the terrible power of the things they carried.

In the first week of April, before Lavender died, Lieutenant Jimmy Cross received a good-luck charm from Martha. It was a simple pebble, an ounce at most. Smooth to the touch, it was a milky-white color with flecks of orange and violet, oval-shaped, like a miniature egg. In the accompanying letter, Martha wrote that she had found the pebble on the Jersey shoreline, precisely where the land touched water at high tide, where things came together but also separated. It was this separate-but-together quality, she wrote, that had inspired her to pick up the pebble and to carry it in her breast pocket for several days, where it seemed weightless, and then to send it through the mail, by air, as a token of her truest feelings for him. Lieutenant Cross found this romantic. But he wondered what her truest feelings were, exactly, and what she meant by separate-but-together. He wondered how the tides and waves had come into play on that afternoon along the Jersey shoreline when Martha saw the pebble and bent down to rescue it from geology. He imagined bare feet. Martha was a poet, with the poet's sensibilities, and her feet would be brown and bare, the toenails unpainted, the eyes chilly and somber like the ocean in March, and though it was painful, he wondered who had been with her that afternoon. He imagined a pair of shadows moving along the strip of sand where things came together but also separated. It was phantom jealousy, he knew, but he couldn't help himself. He loved her so much. On the march, through the hot days of early April, he carried the pebble in his mouth, turning it with his tongue, tasting sea salts and moisture. His mind wandered. He had difficulty keeping his attention on the war. On occasion he would yell at his men to spread out the column, to keep their eyes open, but then he would slip away into daydreams, just pretending, walking barefoot along the Jersey shore, with Martha, carrying nothing. He would feel himself rising. Sun and waves and gentle winds, all love and lightness.

What they carried varied by mission.

When a mission took them to the mountains, they carried mosquito net- 15 ting, machetes, canvas tarps, and extra bug juice.

If a mission seemed especially hazardous, or if it involved a place they knew to be bad, they carried everything they could. In certain heavily mined AOs, where the land was dense with Toe Poppers and Bouncing Betties, they took turns humping a twenty-eight-pound mine detector. With its headphones and big sensing plate, the equipment was a stress on the lower back and shoulders, awkward to handle, often useless because of the shrapnel in the earth, but they carried it anyway, partly for safety, partly for the illusion of safety.

On ambush, or other night missions, they carried peculiar little odds and ends. Kiowa always took along his New Testament and a pair of moccasins for silence. Dave Jensen carried night-sight vitamins high in carotin. Lee Strunk carried his slingshot; ammo, he claimed, would never be a problem. Rat Kiley carried brandy and M&M's. Until he was shot, Ted Lavender carried the starlight scope, which weighed 6.3 pounds with its aluminum carrying case. Henry Dobbins carried his girlfriend's pantyhose wrapped around his neck as a comforter. They all carried ghosts. When dark came, they would move out single file across the meadows and paddies to their ambush coordinates, where they would quietly set up the Claymores and lie down and spend the night waiting.

Other missions were more complicated and required special equipment. In mid-April, it was their mission to search out and destroy the elaborate tunnel complexes in the Than Khe area south of Chu Lai. To blow the tunnels, they carried one-pound blocks of pentrite high explosives, four blocks to a man, sixty-eight pounds in all. They carried wiring, detonators, and battery-powered clackers. Dave Jensen carried earplugs. Most often, before blowing the tunnels, they were ordered by higher command to search them, which was considered bad news, but by and large they just shrugged and carried out orders. Because he was a big man, Henry Dobbins was excused from tunnel duty. The others would draw numbers. Before Lavender died there were seventeen men in the platoon, and whoever drew the number seventeen would strip off his gear and crawl in head first with a flashlight and Lieutenant Cross's

.45-caliber pistol. The rest of them would fan out as security. They would sit down or kneel, not facing the hole, listening to the ground beneath them, imagining cobwebs and ghosts, whatever was down there—the tunnel walls squeezing in—how the flashlight seemed impossibly heavy in the hand and how it was tunnel vision in the very strictest sense, compression in all ways, even time, and how you had to wiggle in—ass and elbows—a swallowed-up feeling—and how you found yourself worrying about odd things—will your flashlight go dead? Do rats carry rabies? If you screamed, how far would the sound carry? Would your buddies hear it? Would they have the courage to drag you out? In some respects, though not many, the waiting was worse than the tunnel itself. Imagination was a killer.

On April 16, when Lee Strunk drew the number seventeen, he laughed and muttered something and went down quickly. The morning was hot and very still. Not good, Kiowa said. He looked at the tunnel opening, then out across a dry paddy toward the village of Than Khe. Nothing moved. No clouds or birds or people. As they waited, the men smoked and drank Kool-Aid, not talking much, feeling sympathy for Lee Strunk but also feeling the luck of the draw. You win some, you lose some, said Mitchell Sanders, and sometimes you settle for a rain check. It was a tired line and no one laughed.

Henry Dobbins ate a tropical chocolate bar. Ted Lavender popped a tran- 20 quilizer and went off to pee.

After five minutes, Lieutenant Jimmy Cross moved to the tunnel, leaned down, and examined the darkness. Trouble, he thought—a cave-in maybe. And then suddenly, without willing it, he was thinking about Martha. The stresses and fractures, the quick collapse, the two of them buried alive under all that weight. Dense, crushing love. Kneeling, watching the hole, he tried to concentrate on Lee Strunk and the war, all the dangers, but his love was too much for him, he felt paralyzed, he wanted to sleep inside her lungs and breathe her blood and be smothered. He wanted her to be a virgin and not a virgin, all at once. He wanted to know her. Intimate secrets—why poetry? Why so sad? Why the grayness in her eyes? Why so alone? Not lonely, just alone—riding her bike across campus or sitting off by herself in the cafeteria. Even dancing, she danced alone—and it was the aloneness that filled him with love. He remembered telling her that one evening. How she nodded and looked away. And how, later, when he kissed her, she received the kiss without returning it, her eyes wide open, not afraid, not a virgin's eyes, just flat and uninvolved.

Lieutenant Cross gazed at the tunnel. But he was not there. He was buried with Martha under the white sand at the Jersey shore. They were pressed together, and the pebble in his mouth was her tongue. He was smiling. Vaguely, he was aware of how quiet the day was, the sullen paddies, yet he could not bring himself to worry about matters of security. He was beyond that. He was just a kid at war, in love. He was twenty-two years old. He couldn't help it.

A few moments later Lee Strunk crawled out of the tunnel. He came up grinning, filthy but alive. Lieutenant Cross nodded and closed his eyes while the others clapped Strunk on the back and made jokes about rising from the dead.

Worms, Rat Kiley said. Right out of the grave. Fuckin' zombie.

The men laughed. They all felt great relief. 25

Spook City, said Mitchell Sanders.

Lee Strunk made a funny ghost sound, a kind of moaning, yet very happy, and right then, when Strunk made that high happy moaning sound, when he went *Ahhooooo,* right then Ted Lavender was shot in the head on his way back from peeing. He lay with his mouth open. The teeth were broken. There was a swollen black bruise under his left eye. The cheekbone was gone. Oh shit, Rat Kiley said, the guy's dead. The guy's dead, he kept saying, which seemed profound—the guy's dead. I mean really.

The things they carried were determined to some extent by superstition. Lieutenant Cross carried his good-luck pebble. Dave Jensen carried a rabbit's foot. Norman Bowker, otherwise a very gentle person, carried a thumb that had been presented to him as a gift by Mitchell Sanders. The thumb was dark brown, rubbery to the touch, and weighed four ounces at most. It had been cut from a VC[3] corpse, a boy of fifteen or sixteen. They'd found him at the bottom of an irrigation ditch, badly burned, flies in his mouth and eyes. The boy wore black shorts and sandals. At the time of his death he had been carrying a pouch of rice, a rifle, and three magazines of ammunition.

You want my opinion, Mitchell Sanders said, there's a definite moral here.

He put his hand on the dead boy's wrist. He was quiet for a time, as if count- 30 ing a pulse, then he patted the stomach, almost affectionately, and used Kiowa's hunting hatchet to remove the thumb.

Henry Dobbins asked what the moral was.

Moral?

You know. *Moral.*

Sanders wrapped the thumb in toilet paper and handed it across to Norman Bowker. There was no blood. Smiling, he kicked the boy's head, watched the flies scatter, and said, It's like with that old TV show—Paladin. Have gun, will travel.

Henry Dobbins thought about it. 35

Yeah, well, he finally said. I don't see no moral.

There it *is,* man.

Fuck off.

They carried USO stationery and pencils and pens. They carried Sterno, safety pins, trip flares, signal flares, spools of wire, razor blades, chewing tobacco, liberated joss sticks and statuettes of the smiling Buddha, candles, grease pencils, *The Stars and Stripes,*[4] fingernail clippers, Psy Ops leaflets, bush hats, bolos, and much more. Twice a week, when the resupply choppers came in, they carried hot chow in green Mermite cans and large canvas

---

[3] Vietcong.
[4] The military's officially sanctioned overseas newspaper.

bags filled with iced beer and soda pop. They carried plastic water containers, each with a two-gallon capacity. Mitchell Sanders carried a set of starched tiger fatigues for special occasions. Henry Dobbins carried Black Flag insecticide. Dave Jensen carried empty sandbags that could be filled at night for added protection. Lee Strunk carried tanning lotion. Some things they carried in common. Taking turns, they carried the big PRC-77 scrambler radio, which weighed thirty pounds with its battery. They shared the weight of memory. They took up what others could no longer bear. Often, they carried each other, the wounded or weak. They carried infections. They carried chess sets, basketballs, Vietnamese-English dictionaries, insignia of rank, Bronze Stars and Purple Hearts, plastic cards imprinted with the Code of Conduct. They carried diseases, among them malaria and dysentery. They carried lice and ringworm and leeches and paddy algae and various rots and molds. They carried the land itself—Vietnam, the place, the soil—a powdery orange-red dust that covered their boots and fatigues and faces. They carried the sky. The whole atmosphere, they carried it, the humidity, the monsoons, the stink of fungus and decay, all of it, they carried gravity. They moved like mules. By daylight they took sniper fire, at night they were mortared, but it was not battle, it was just the endless march, village to village, without purpose, nothing won or lost. They marched for the sake of the march. They plodded along slowly, dumbly, leaning forward against the heat, unthinking, all blood and bone, simple grunts, soldiering with their legs, toiling up the hills and down into the paddies and across the rivers and up again and down, just humping, one step and then the next and then another, but no volition, no will, because it was automatic, it was anatomy, and the war was entirely a matter of posture and carriage, the hump was everything, a kind of inertia, a kind of emptiness, a dullness of desire and intellect and conscience and hope and human sensibility. Their principles were in their feet. Their calculations were biological. They had no sense of strategy or mission. They searched the villages without knowing what to look for, not caring, kicking over jars of rice, frisking children and old men, blowing tunnels, sometimes setting fires and sometimes not, then forming up and moving on to the next village, then other villages, where it would always be the same. They carried their own lives. The pressures were enormous. In the heat of early afternoon, they would remove their helmets and flak jackets, walking bare, which was dangerous but which helped ease the strain. They would often discard things along the route of march. Purely for comfort, they would throw away rations, blow their Claymores and grenades, no matter, because by nightfall the resupply choppers would arrive with more of the same, then a day or two later still more, fresh watermelons and crates of ammunition and sunglasses and woolen sweaters—the resources were stunning—sparklers for the Fourth of July, colored eggs for Easter. It was the great American war chest—the fruits of science, the smokestacks, the canneries, the arsenals at Hartford, the Minnesota forests, the machine shops, the vast fields of corn and wheat—they carried like freight trains; they carried it on their backs and shoulders—and for all the ambiguities of Vietnam, all the mysteries and unknowns, there was at least the single abiding certainty that they would never be at a loss for things to carry.

After the chopper took Lavender away, Lieutenant Jimmy Cross led his 40 men into the village of Than Khe. They burned everything. They shot chickens and dogs, they trashed the village well, they called in artillery and watched the wreckage, then they marched for several hours through the hot afternoon, and then at dusk, while Kiowa explained how Lavender died, Lieutenant Cross found himself trembling.

He tried not to cry. With his entrenching tool, which weighed five pounds, he began digging a hole in the earth.

He felt shame. He hated himself. He had loved Martha more than his men, and as a consequence Lavender was now dead, and this was something he would have to carry like a stone in his stomach for the rest of the war.

All he could do was dig. He used his entrenching tool like an ax, slashing, feeling both love and hate, and then later, when it was full dark, he sat at the bottom of his foxhole and wept. It went on for a long while. In part, he was grieving for Ted Lavender, but mostly it was for Martha, and for himself, because she belonged to another world, which was not quite real, and because she was a junior at Mount Sebastian College in New Jersey, a poet and a virgin and uninvolved, and because he realized she did not love him and never would.

Like cement, Kiowa whispered in the dark. I swear to God—boom-down. Not a word.

I've heard this, said Norman Bowker. 45

A pisser, you know? Still zipping himself up. Zapped while zipping.

All right, fine. That's enough.

Yeah, but you had to see it, the guy just—

I *heard,* man. Cement. So why not shut the fuck *up?*

Kiowa shook his head sadly and glanced over at the hole where Lieutenant 50 Jimmy Cross sat watching the night. The air was thick and wet. A warm, dense fog had settled over the paddies and there was the stillness that precedes rain.

After a time Kiowa sighed.

One thing for sure, he said. The Lieutenant's in some deep hurt. I mean that crying jag—the way he was carrying on—it wasn't fake or anything, it was real heavy-duty hurt. The man cares.

Sure, Norman Bowker said.

Say what you want, the man does care.

We all got problems. 55

Not Lavender.

No, I guess not, Bowker said. Do me a favor, though.

Shut up?

That's a smart Indian. Shut up.

Shrugging, Kiowa pulled off his boots. He wanted to say more, just to 60 lighten up his sleep, but instead he opened his New Testament and arranged

it beneath his head as a pillow. The fog made things seem hollow and unat-
tached. He tried not to think about Ted Lavender, but then he was thinking
how fast it was, no drama, down and dead, and how it was hard to feel anything except surprise. It seemed un-Christian. He wished he could find some
great sadness, or even anger, but the emotion wasn't there and he couldn't
make it happen. Mostly he felt pleased to be alive. He liked the smell of the
New Testament under his cheek, the leather and ink and paper and glue, whatever the chemicals were. He liked hearing the sounds of night. Even his fatigue,
it felt fine, the stiff muscles and the prickly awareness of his own body, a floating feeling. He enjoyed not being dead. Lying there, Kiowa admired Lieutenant Jimmy Cross's capacity for grief. He wanted to share the man's pain, he
wanted to care as Jimmy Cross cared. And yet when he closed his eyes, all he
could think was Boom-down, and all he could feel was the pleasure of having his boots off and the fog curling in around him and the damp soil and the
Bible smells and the plush comfort of night.

After a moment Norman Bowker sat up in the dark.

What the hell, he said. You want to talk, *talk*. Tell it to me.

Forget it.

No, man, go on. One thing I hate, it's a silent Indian.

For the most part they carried themselves with poise, a kind of dignity. 65
Now and then, however, there were times of panic, when they squealed
or wanted to squeal but couldn't, when they twitched and made moaning
sounds and covered their heads and said Dear Jesus and flopped around on
the earth and fired their weapons blindly and cringed and sobbed and begged
for the noise to stop and went wild and made stupid promises to themselves
and to God and to their mothers and fathers, hoping not to die. In different ways, it happened to all of them. Afterward, when the firing ended, they
would blink and peek up. They would touch their bodies, feeling shame,
then quickly hiding it. They would force themselves to stand. As if in slow
motion, frame by frame, the world would take on the old logic—absolute
silence, then the wind, then sunlight, then voices. It was the burden of being
alive. Awkwardly, the men would reassemble themselves, first in private,
then in groups, becoming soldiers again. They would repair the leaks in their
eyes. They would check for casualties, call in dust-offs, light cigarettes, try to
smile, clear their throats and spit and begin cleaning their weapons. After a
time someone would shake his head and say, No lie, I almost shit my pants,
and someone else would laugh, which meant it was bad, yes, but the guy had
obviously not shit his pants, it wasn't that bad, and in any case nobody would
ever do such a thing and then go ahead and talk about it. They would squint
into the dense, oppressive sunlight. For a few moments, perhaps, they would
fall silent, lighting a joint and tracking its passage from man to man, inhal-
ing, holding in the humiliation. Scary stuff, one of them might say. But then
someone else would grin or flick his eyebrows and say, Roger-dodger, almost
cut me a new asshole, *almost*.

There were numerous such poses. Some carried themselves with a sort of wistful resignation, others with pride or stiff soldierly discipline or good humor or macho zeal. They were afraid of dying but they were even more afraid to show it.

They found jokes to tell.

They used a hard vocabulary to contain the terrible softness. *Greased,* they'd say. *Offed, lit up, zapped while zipping.* It wasn't cruelty, just stage presence. They were actors and the war came at them in 3-D. When someone died, it wasn't quite dying, because in a curious way it seemed scripted, and because they had their lines mostly memorized, irony mixed with tragedy, and because they called it by other names, as if to encyst and destroy the reality of death itself. They kicked corpses. They cut off thumbs. They talked grunt lingo. They told stories about Ted Lavender's supply of tranquilizers, how the poor guy didn't feel a thing, how incredibly tranquil he was.

There's a moral here, said Mitchell Sanders.

They were waiting for Lavender's chopper, smoking the dead man's dope.   70

The moral's pretty obvious, Sanders said, and winked. Stay away from drugs. No joke, they'll ruin your day every time.

Cute, said Henry Dobbins.

Mind-blower, get it? Talk about wiggy—nothing left, just blood and brains.

They made themselves laugh.

There it is, they'd say, over and over, as if the repetition itself were an act 75 of poise, a balance between crazy and almost crazy, knowing without going. There it is, which meant be cool, let it ride, because oh yeah, man, you can't change what can't be changed, there it is, there it absolutely and positively and fucking well *is.*

They were tough.

They carried all the emotional baggage of men who might die. Grief, terror, love, longing—these were intangibles, but the intangibles had their own mass and specific gravity, they had tangible weight. They carried shameful memories. They carried the common secret of cowardice barely restrained, the instinct to run or freeze or hide, and in many respects this was the heaviest burden of all, for it could never be put down, it required perfect balance and perfect posture. They carried their reputations. They carried the soldier's greatest fear, which was the fear of blushing. Men killed, and died, because they were embarrassed not to. It was what had brought them to the war in the first place, nothing positive, no dreams of glory or honor, just to avoid the blush of dishonor. They died so as not to die of embarrassment. They crawled into tunnels and walked point and advanced under fire. Each morning, despite the unknowns, they made their legs move. They endured. They kept humping. They did not submit to the obvious alternative, which was simply to close the eyes and fall. So easy, really. Go limp and tumble to the ground and let the muscles unwind and not speak and not budge until your buddies picked you up and lifted you into the chopper that would roar and dip its nose and carry you off to the world. A mere matter of falling, yet no one ever fell. It was not courage, exactly; the object was not valor. Rather, they were too frightened to be cowards.

By and large they carried these things inside, maintaining the masks of composure. They sneered at sick call. They spoke bitterly about guys who had found release by shooting off their own toes or fingers. Pussies, they'd say. Candyasses. It was fierce, mocking talk, with only a trace of envy or awe, but even so, the image played itself out behind their eyes.

They imagined the muzzle against flesh. They imagined the quick, sweet pain, then the evacuation to Japan, then a hospital with warm beds and cute geisha nurses.

They dreamed of freedom birds.   80

At night, on guard, staring into the dark, they were carried away by jumbo jets. They felt the rush of takeoff. *Gone!* they yelled. And then velocity, wings and engines, a smiling stewardess—but it was more than a plane, it was a real bird, a big sleek silver bird with feathers and talons and high screeching. They were flying. The weights fell off, there was nothing to bear. They laughed and held on tight, feeling the cold slap of wind and altitude, soaring, think-ing *It's over, I'm gone!*—they were naked, they were light and free—it was all lightness, bright and fast and buoyant, light as light, a helium buzz in the brain, a giddy bubbling in the lungs as they were taken up over the clouds and the war, beyond duty, beyond gravity and mortification and global entan-glements—*Sin loi!* they yelled, *I'm sorry, motherfuckers, but I'm out of it, I'm goofed, I'm on a space cruise, I'm gone!*—and it was a restful, disencumbered sensation, just riding the light waves, sailing that big silver freedom bird over the mountains and oceans, over America, over the farms and great sleeping cities and cemeteries and highways and the golden arches of McDonald's. It was flight, a kind of fleeing, a kind of falling, falling higher and higher, spin-ning off the edge of the earth and beyond the sun and through the vast, silent vacuum where there were no burdens and where everything weighed exactly nothing. *Gone!* they screamed, *I'm sorry but I'm gone!* And so at night, not quite dreaming, they gave themselves over to lightness, they were carried, they were purely borne.

On the morning after Ted Lavender died, First Lieutenant Jimmy Cross crouched at the bottom of his foxhole and burned Martha's letters. Then he burned the two photographs. There was a steady rain falling, which made it difficult, but he used heat tabs and Sterno to build a small fire, screening it with his body, holding the photographs over the tight blue flame with the tips of his fingers.

He realized it was only a gesture. Stupid, he thought. Sentimental, too, but mostly just stupid.

Lavender was dead. You couldn't burn the blame.

Besides, the letters were in his head. And even now, without photographs,   85
Lieutenant Cross could see Martha playing volleyball in her white gym shorts and yellow T-shirt. He could see her moving in the rain.

When the fire died out, Lieutenant Cross pulled his poncho over his shoulders and ate breakfast from a can.

There was no great mystery, he decided.

In those burned letters Martha had never mentioned the war, except to say, Jimmy, take care of yourself. She wasn't involved. She signed the letters "Love," but it wasn't love, and all the fine lines and technicalities did not matter.

The morning came up wet and blurry. Everything seemed part of everything else, the fog and Martha and the deepening rain.

It was a war, after all.   90

Half smiling, Lieutenant Jimmy Cross took out his maps. He shook his head hard, as if to clear it, then bent forward and began planning the day's march. In ten minutes, or maybe twenty, he would rouse the men and they would pack up and head west, where the maps showed the country to be green and inviting. They would do what they had always done. The rain might add some weight, but otherwise it would be one more day layered upon all the other days.

He was realistic about it. There was that new hardness in his stomach.

No more fantasies, he told himself.

Henceforth, when he thought about Martha, it would be only to think that she belonged elsewhere. He would shut down the daydreams. This was not Mount Sebastian, it was another world, where there were no pretty poems or midterm exams, a place where men died because of carelessness and gross stupidity. Kiowa was right. Boom-down, and you were dead, never partly dead.

Briefly, in the rain, Lieutenant Cross saw Martha's gray eyes gazing back   95 at him.

He understood.

It was very sad, he thought. The things men carried inside. The things men did or felt they had to do.

He almost nodded at her, but didn't.

Instead he went back to his maps. He was now determined to perform his duties firmly and without negligence. It wouldn't help Lavender, he knew that, but from this point on he would comport himself as a soldier. He would dispose of his good-luck pebble. Swallow it, maybe, or use Lee Strunk's slingshot, or just drop it along the trail. On the march he would impose strict field discipline. He would be careful to send out flank security, to prevent straggling or bunching up, to keep his troops moving at the proper pace and at the proper interval. He would insist on clean weapons. He would confiscate the remainder of Lavender's dope. Later in the day, perhaps, he would call the men together and speak to them plainly. He would accept the blame for what had happened to Ted Lavender. He would be a man about it. He would look them in the eyes, keeping his chin level, and he would issue the new SOPs in a calm, impersonal tone of voice, an officer's voice, leaving no room for argument or discussion. Commencing immediately, he'd tell them, they would no longer abandon equipment along the route of march. They would police up their acts. They would get their shit together, and keep it together, and maintain it neatly and in good working order.

He would not tolerate laxity. He would show strength, distancing himself. 100

Among the men there would be grumbling, of course, and maybe worse, because their days would seem longer and their loads heavier, but Lieutenant Cross reminded himself that his obligation was not to be loved but to lead. He would dispense with love; it was not now a factor. And if anyone quarreled or complained, he would simply tighten his lips and arrange his shoulders in the correct command posture. He might give a curt little nod. Or he might not. He might just shrug and say Carry on, then they would saddle up and form into a column and move out toward the villages of Than Khe.

FOR ANALYSIS

1. What are the various meanings of "Things" in the title?

2. What is the **narrator's** attitude toward war? Does his attitude differ from the attitudes of the soldiers he is describing? Explain.

3. How do Lieutenant Cross's thoughts about Martha fit into the overall **thematic** pattern of the story?

4. What is the attitude of the men toward the enemy?

5. How effective do you find the cataloging of things as a way to tell this story? Explain.

MAKING CONNECTIONS

Compare and contrast O'Brien's perspective on war with Owen's in "Dulce et Decorum Est" (p. 462). Which do you find to be a more effective antiwar statement? Explain.

WRITING TOPICS

1. Discuss the meaning of heroism in this story.

2. Write an essay showing how Lieutenant Cross's thoughts and feelings about Martha reflect the changes he undergoes in the course of the narrative.

THE MAN TO SEND
RAIN CLOUDS   1981

They found him under a big cottonwood tree. His Levi jacket and pants were faded light blue so that he had been easy to find. The big cottonwood tree stood apart from a small grove of winterbare cottonwoods which grew in the wide, sandy arroyo. He had been dead for a day or more, and the sheep had wandered and scattered up and down the arroyo. Leon and his brother-in-law, Ken, gathered the sheep and left them in the pen at the sheep camp before they returned to the cottonwood tree. Leon waited under the tree while Ken drove the truck through the deep sand to the edge of the arroyo. He squinted up at the sun and unzipped his jacket—it sure was hot for this time of year. But high and northwest the blue mountains were still in snow. Ken came sliding down the low, crumbling bank about fifty yards down, and he was bringing the red blanket.

Before they wrapped the old man, Leon took a piece of string out of his pocket and tied a small gray feather in the old man's long white hair. Ken gave him the paint. Across the brown wrinkled forehead he drew a streak of white and along the high cheekbones he drew a strip of blue paint. He paused and watched Ken throw pinches of corn meal and pollen into the wind that fluttered the small gray feather. Then Leon painted with yellow under the old man's broad nose, and finally, when he had painted green across the chin, he smiled.

"Send us rain clouds, Grandfather." They laid the bundle in the back of the pickup and covered it with a heavy tarp before they started back to the pueblo.

They turned off the highway onto the sandy pueblo road. Not long after they passed the store and post office they saw Father Paul's car coming toward them. When he recognized their faces he slowed his car and waved them to stop. The young priest rolled down the car window.

"Did you find old Teofilo?" he asked loudly.   5

Leon stopped the truck. "Good morning, Father. We were just out to the sheep camp. Everything is O.K. now."

"Thank God for that. Teofilo is a very old man. You really shouldn't allow him to stay at the sheep camp alone."

"No, he won't do that any more now."

"Well, I'm glad you understand. I hope I'll be seeing you at Mass this week—we missed you last Sunday. See if you can get old Teofilo to come with you." The priest smiled and waved at them as they drove away.

Louise and Teresa were waiting. The table was set for lunch, and the coffee   10
was boiling on the black iron stove. Leon looked at Louise and then at Teresa.

"We found him under a cottonwood tree in the big arroyo near sheep camp. I guess he sat down to rest in the shade and never got up again." Leon walked toward the old man's bed. The red plaid shawl had been shaken and spread carefully over the bed, and a new brown flannel shirt and pair of stiff new Levi's were arranged neatly beside the pillow. Louise held the screen door open while Leon and Ken carried in the red blanket. He looked small and shriveled, and after they dressed him in the new shirt and pants he seemed more shrunken.

It was noontime now because the church bells rang the Angelus. They ate the beans with hot bread, and nobody said anything until after Teresa poured the coffee.

Ken stood up and put on his jacket. "I'll see about the gravediggers. Only the top layer of soil is frozen. I think it can be ready before dark."

Leon nodded his head and finished his coffee. After Ken had been gone for a while, the neighbors and clanspeople came quietly to embrace Teofilo's family and to leave food on the table because the gravediggers would come to eat when they were finished.

The sky in the west was full of pale yellow light. Louise stood outside with 15 her hands in the pockets of Leon's green army jacket that was too big for her. The funeral was over, and the old men had taken their candles and medicine bags and were gone. She waited until the body was laid into the pickup before she said anything to Leon. She touched his arm, and he noticed that her hands were still dusty from the corn meal that she had sprinkled around the old man. When she spoke, Leon could not hear her.

"What did you say? I didn't hear you."

"I said that I had been thinking about something."

"About what?"

"About the priest sprinkling holy water for Grandpa. So he won't be thirsty."

Leon stared at the new moccasins that Teofilo had made for the ceremonial 20 dances in the summer. They were nearly hidden by the red blanket. It was getting colder, and the wind pushed gray dust down the narrow pueblo road. The sun was approaching the long mesa where it disappeared during the winter. Louise stood there shivering and watching his face. Then he zipped up his jacket and opened the truck door. "I'll see if he's there."

Ken stopped the pickup at the church, and Leon got out; and then Ken drove down the hill to the graveyard where people were waiting. Leon knocked at the old carved door with its symbols of the Lamb. While he waited he looked up at the twin bells from the king of Spain with the last sunlight pouring around them in their tower.

The priest opened the door and smiled when he saw who it was. "Come in! What brings you here this evening?"

The priest walked toward the kitchen, and Leon stood with his cap in his hand, playing with the earflaps and examining the living room—the brown sofa, the green armchair, and the brass lamp that hung down from the ceiling by links of chain. The priest dragged a chair out of the kitchen and offered it to Leon.

"No thank you, Father. I only came to ask you if you would bring your holy water to the graveyard."

The priest turned away from Leon and looked out the window at the patio 25 full of shadows and the dining-room windows of the nuns' cloister across the patio. The curtains were heavy, and the light from within faintly penetrated; it was impossible to see the nuns inside eating supper. "Why didn't you tell me he was dead? I could have brought the Last Rites anyway."

Leon smiled. "It wasn't necessary, Father."

The priest stared down at his scuffed brown loafers and the worn hem of his cassock. "For a Christian burial it was necessary."

His voice was distant, and Leon thought that his blue eyes looked tired.

"It's O.K. Father, we just want him to have plenty of water."

The priest sank down into the green chair and picked up a glossy missionary 30 magazine. He turned the colored pages full of lepers and pagans without looking at them.

"You know I can't do that, Leon. There should have been the Last Rites and a funeral Mass at the very least."

Leon put on his green cap and pulled the flaps down over his ears. "It's getting late, Father. I've got to go."

When Leon opened the door Father Paul stood up and said, "Wait." He left the room and came back wearing a long brown overcoat. He followed Leon out the door and across the dim churchyard to the adobe steps in front of the church. They both stooped to fit through the low adobe entrance. And when they started down the hill to the graveyard only half of the sun was visible above the mesa.

The priest approached the grave slowly, wondering how they had managed to dig into the frozen ground, and then he remembered that this was New Mexico, and saw the pile of cold loose sand beside the hole. The people stood close to each other with little clouds of steam puffing from their faces. The priest looked at them and saw a pile of jackets, gloves, and scarves in the yellow, dry tumbleweeds that grew in the graveyard. He looked at the red blanket, not sure that Teofilo was so small, wondering if it wasn't some perverse Indian trick—something they did in March to ensure a good harvest—wondering if maybe old Teofilo was actually at sheep camp corraling the sheep for the night. But there he was, facing into a cold dry wind and squinting at the last sunlight, ready to bury a red wool blanket while the faces of his parishioners were in shadow with the last warmth of the sun on their backs.

His fingers were stiff, and it took him a long time to twist the lid off the holy 35 water. Drops of water fell on the red blanket and soaked into dark icy spots. He sprinkled the grave and the water disappeared almost before it touched the dim, cold sand; it reminded him of something—he tried to remember what it was, because he thought if he could remember he might understand this.

He sprinkled more water; he shook the container until it was empty, and the water fell through the light from sundown like August rain that fell while the sun was still shining, almost disappearing before it touched the wilted squash flowers.

The wind pulled at the priest's brown Franciscan robe and swirled away the corn meal and pollen that had been sprinkled on the blanket. They lowered the bundle into the ground, and they didn't bother to untie the stiff pieces of new rope that were tied around the ends of the blanket. The sun was gone, and over on the highway the eastbound lane was full of headlights. The priest walked away slowly. Leon watched him climb the hill, and when he had disappeared within the tall, thick walls, Leon turned to look up at the high blue mountains in the deep snow that reflected a faint red light from the west. He felt good because it was finished, and he was happy about the sprinkling of the holy water; now the old man could send them big thunderclouds for sure.

FOR ANALYSIS

1. Why do Leon and Ken not tell Father Paul that Teofilo is dead? Why do they later ask Father Paul to bring holy water to the funeral?

2. Two rituals associated with death—the Native American and the Roman Catholic— seem to conflict. Why does Teofilo's family seek the priest's help? Why does Father Paul agree to help them?

3. Although the story is mostly told from the **point of view** of an omniscient narrator, at one point we share two characters' thoughts. What effect does this shift generate?

4. Why do you think Silko included the detail (in the last paragraph) about the automobile lights on the highway?

5. Why does Leon feel good at the end of the story?

MAKING CONNECTIONS

1. Compare this story with Jackson's "The Lottery" (p. 373). What similarities do you find? What differences?

2. Contrast the narrative **style** of this story with the style of Poe's "The Cask of Amontillado" (p. 1108) and Tolstoy's "The Death of Iván Ilých" (p. 1114). Some writers use unusual language and sentence structure; some insist on close realistic detail; some use understatement and leave much unsaid. How would you describe the style of this story? Defend your response.

WRITING TOPIC

"The Man to Send Rain Clouds" remains silent about the characters' spirituality: there is no **narrator** commenting on whether their rituals and beliefs are effective or true. How did you respond to the different points of view on death and the natural world presented in the story? How might the characters respond to your points of view about the world? Where did you get them?

Helena María Viramontes   (B. 1954)

The Moths   1985

I was fourteen years old when Abuelita requested my help. And it seemed only fair. Abuelita had pulled me through the rages of scarlet fever by placing, removing, and replacing potato slices on the temples of my forehead; she had seen me through several whippings, an arm broken by a dare jump off Tío Enrique's toolshed, puberty, and my first lie. Really, I told Amá, it was only fair.

Not that I was her favorite granddaughter or anything special. I wasn't even pretty or nice like my older sisters and I just couldn't do the girl things they could do. My hands were too big to handle the fineries of crocheting or embroidery and I always pricked my fingers or knotted my colored threads time and time again while my sisters laughed and called me bull hands with their cute waterlike voices. So I began keeping a piece of jagged brick in my sock to bash my sisters or anyone who called me bull hands. Once, while we all sat in the bedroom, I hit Teresa on the forehead, right above her eyebrow and she ran to Amá with her mouth open, her hand over her eye while blood seeped between her fingers. I was used to the whippings by then.

I wasn't respectful either. I even went so far as to doubt the power of Abuelita's slices, the slices she said absorbed my fever. "You're still alive, aren't you?" Abuelita snapped back, her pasty gray eye beaming at me and burning holes in my suspicions. Regretful that I had let secret questions drop out of my mouth, I couldn't look into her eyes. My hands began to fan out, grow like a liar's nose until they hung by my side like low weights. Abuelita made a balm out of dried moth wings and Vicks and rubbed my hands, shaped them back to size and it was the strangest feeling. Like bones melting. Like sun shining through the darkness of your eyelids. I didn't mind helping Abuelita after that, so Amá would always send me over to her.

In the early afternoon Amá would push her hair back, hand me my sweater and shoes, and tell me to go to Mama Luna's. This was to avoid another fight and another whipping, I knew. I would deliver one last direct shot on Marisela's arm and jump out of our house, the slam of the screen door burying her cries of anger, and I'd gladly go help Abuelita plant her wild lilies or jasmine or heliotrope or cilantro or hierbabuena in red Hills Brothers coffee cans. Abuelita would wait for me at the top step of her porch holding a hammer and nail and empty coffee cans. And although we hardly spoke, hardly looked at each other as we worked over root transplants, I always felt her gray eye on me. It made me feel, in a strange sort of way, safe and guarded and not alone. Like God was supposed to make you feel.

On Abuelita's porch, I would puncture holes in the bottom of the coffee 5 cans with a nail and a precise hit of a hammer. This completed, my job was to fill them with red clay mud from beneath her rose bushes, packing it softly, then making a perfect hole, four fingers round, to nest a sprouting avocado pit, or the spidery sweet potatoes that Abuelita rooted in mayonnaise jars with toothpicks and daily water, or prickly chayotes that produced vines that twisted and wound all over her porch pillars, crawling to the roof, up and over the roof, and down the other side, making her small brick house look like it was cradled within the vines that grew pear-shaped squashes ready for the pick, ready to be steamed with onions and cheese and butter. The roots would burst out of the rusted coffee cans and search for a place to connect. I would then feed the seedlings with water.

But this was a different kind of help, Amá said, because Abuelita was dying. Looking into her gray eye, then into her brown one, the doctor said it was just a matter of days. And so it seemed only fair that these hands she had melted and formed found use in rubbing her caving body with alcohol and marihuana, rubbing her arms and legs, turning her face to the window so that she could watch the Bird of Paradise blooming or smell the scent of clove in the air. I toweled her face frequently and held her hand for hours. Her gray wiry hair hung over the mattress. Since I could remember, she'd kept her long hair in braids. Her mouth was vacant and when she slept, her eyelids never closed all the way. Up close, you could see her gray eye beaming out the window, staring hard as if to remember everything. I never kissed her. I left the window open when I went to the market.

Across the street from Jay's Market there was a chapel. I never knew its denomination, but I went in just the same to search for candles. I sat down on one of the pews because there were none. After I cleaned my fingernails, I looked up at the high ceiling. I had forgotten the vastness of these places, the coolness of the marble pillars and the frozen statues with blank eyes. I was alone. I knew why I had never returned.

That was one of Apá's biggest complaints. He would pound his hands on the table, rocking the sugar dish or spilling a cup of coffee and scream that if I didn't go to mass every Sunday to save my goddamn sinning soul, then I had no reason to go out of the house, period. Punto final. He would grab my arm and dig his nails into me to make sure I understood the importance of catechism. Did he make himself clear? Then he strategically directed his anger at Amá for her lousy ways of bringing up daughters, being disrespectful and unbelieving, and my older sisters would pull me aside and tell me if I didn't get to mass right this minute, they were all going to kick the holy shit out of me. Why am I so selfish? Can't you see what it's doing to Amá, you idiot? So I would wash my feet and stuff them in my black Easter shoes that shone with Vaseline, grab a missal and veil, and wave good-bye to Amá.

I would walk slowly down Lorena to First to Evergreen, counting the cracks on the cement. On Evergreen I would turn left and walk to Abuelita's. I liked her porch because it was shielded by the vines of the chayotes and I could get a good look at the people and car traffic on Evergreen without them knowing. I would jump up the porch steps, knock on the screen door as I wiped my feet and call Abuelita? mi Abuelita? As I opened the door and stuck my head in, I would catch the gagging scent of toasting chile on the placa. When I entered the sala, she would greet me from the kitchen, wringing her hands in her apron. I'd sit at the corner of the table to keep from being in her way. The chiles made my eyes water. Am I crying? No, Mama Luna, I'm sure not crying. I don't like going to mass, but my eyes watered anyway, the tears dropping on the tablecloth like candle wax. Abuelita lifted the burnt chiles from the fire and sprinkled water on them until the skins began to separate. Placing them in front of me, she turned to check the menudo. I peeled the skins off and put the flimsy, limp looking green and yellow chiles in the molcajete and began to crush and crush and twist and crush the heart out of the tomato, the clove of garlic, the stupid chiles that made me cry, crushed them until they turned into liquid under my bull hand. With a wooden spoon, I scraped hard to destroy the guilt, and my tears were gone. I put the bowl of chile next to a vase filled with freshly cut roses. Abuelita touched my hand and pointed to the bowl of menudo that steamed in front of me. I spooned some chile into the menudo and rolled a corn tortilla thin with the palms of my hands. As I ate, a fine Sunday breeze entered the kitchen and a rose petal calmly feathered down to the table.

I left the chapel without blessing myself and walked to Jay's. Most of the 10 time Jay didn't have much of anything. The tomatoes were always soft and the cans of Campbell soups had rusted spots on them. There was dust on the tops of cereal boxes. I picked up what I needed: rubbing alcohol, five cans of chicken broth, a big bottle of Pine Sol. At first Jay got mad because I thought I had forgotten the money. But it was there all the time, in my back pocket.

When I returned from the market, I heard Amá crying in Abuelita's kitchen. She looked up at me with puffy eyes. I placed the bags of groceries on the table and began putting the cans of soup away. Amá sobbed quietly. I never kissed her. After a while, I patted her on the back for comfort. Finally: "¿Y mi Amá?" she asked in a whisper, then choked again and cried into her apron.

Abuelita fell off the bed twice yesterday, I said, knowing that I shouldn't have said it and wondering why I wanted to say it because it only made Amá cry harder. I guess I became angry and just so tired of the quarrels and beatings and unanswered prayers and my hands just there hanging helplessly by my side. Amá looked at me again, confused, angry, and her eyes were filled with sorrow. I went outside and sat on the porch swing and watched the people pass. I sat there until she left. I dozed off repeating the words to myself like rosary prayers: when do you stop giving when do you start giving when do you. . . . and when my hands fell from my lap, I awoke to catch them. The sun was setting, an orange glow, and I knew Abuelita was hungry.

There comes a time when the sun is defiant. Just about the time when moods change, inevitable seasons of a day, transitions from one color to another, that hour or minute or second when the sun is finally defeated, finally sinks into the realization that it cannot with all its power to heal or burn, exist forever, there comes an illumination where the sun and earth meet, a final burst of burning red orange fury reminding us that although endings are inevitable, they are necessary for rebirths, and when that time came, just when I switched on the light in the kitchen to open Abuelita's can of soup, it was probably then that she died.

The room smelled of Pine Sol and vomit and Abuelita had defecated the remains of her cancerous stomach. She had turned to the window and tried to speak, but her mouth remained open and speechless. I heard you, Abuelita, I said, stroking her cheek, I heard you. I opened the windows of the house and let the soup simmer and overboil on the stove. I turned the stove off and poured the soup down the sink. From the cabinet I got a tin basin, filled it with lukewarm water and carried it carefully to the room. I went to the linen closet and took out some modest bleached white towels. With the sacredness of a priest preparing his vestments, I unfolded the towels one by one on my shoulders. I removed the sheets and blankets from her bed and peeled off her thick flannel nightgown. I toweled her puzzled face, stretching out the wrinkles, removing the coils of her neck, toweled her shoulders and breasts. Then I changed the water. I returned to towel the creases of her stretch-marked stomach, her sporadic vaginal hairs, and her sagging thighs. I removed the lint from between her toes and noticed a mapped birthmark on the fold of her buttock. The scars on her back which were as thin as the life lines on the palms of her hands made me realize how little I really knew of Abuelita. I covered her with a thin blanket and went into the bathroom. I washed my hands, and turned on the tub faucets and watched the water pour into the tub with vitality and steam. When it was full, I turned off the water and undressed. Then, I went to get Abuelita.

She was not as heavy as I thought and when I carried her in my arms, her body fell into a V, and yet my legs were tired, shaky, and I felt as if the distance between the bedroom and bathroom was miles and years away. Amá, where are you?

I stepped into the bathtub one leg first, then the other. I bent my knees slowly to descend into the water slowly so I wouldn't scald her skin. There, there, Abuelita, I said, cradling her, smoothing her as we descended, I heard you. Her hair fell back and spread across the water like eagle's wings. The water in the tub overflowed and poured onto the tile of the floor. Then the moths came. Small, gray ones that came from her soul and out through her mouth fluttering to light, circling the single dull light bulb of the bathroom. Dying is lonely and I wanted to go to where the moths were, stay with her and plant chayotes whose vines would crawl up her fingers and into the clouds; I wanted to rest my head on her chest with her stroking my hair, telling me about the moths that lay within the soul and slowly eat the spirit up; I wanted to return to the waters of the womb with her so that we would never be alone again. I wanted. I wanted my Amá. I removed a few strands of hair from Abuelita's face and held her small light head within the hollow of my neck. The bathroom was filled with moths, and for the first time in a long time I cried, rocking us, crying for her, for me, for Amá, the sobs emerging from the depths of anguish, the misery of feeling half born, sobbing until finally the sobs rippled into circles and circles of sadness and relief. There, there, I said to Abuelita, rocking us gently, there, there.

FOR ANALYSIS

1. Why do you think the observation that the **narrator** does not kiss people is repeated?

2. Why is it important that the old person with whom the narrator connects is a woman and not a man?

3. In what ways is the grandmother's death important to the narrator? Why, when the narrator holds her body at the end of the story, does she say that she rocks "us"?

MAKING CONNECTIONS

1. Compare the relationships between the two elderly women and their caregivers in "The Moths" and Katherine Anne Porter's "The Jilting of Granny Weatherall" (p. 1182). How are they similar? How are they different?

2. How does telling the story of an older woman's death from her **point of view** differ from telling it from the younger woman's point of view? What effects does each have? Why do you think the authors chose to tell their stories the way they did?

WRITING TOPICS

1. Reread "The Moths" and keep a reading log, tracking your emotions as you go. Then reflect on what elements of the story made you feel these ways.

2. Does the story read significantly differently if you do or don't believe that the moths at the end actually exist? How so? What do you choose to believe?

CONNECTING STORIES:
BETWEEN LIFE AND DEATH

The two stories in this unit share their subject—the moment of death—but regardless of the amount of action on the level of plot, their real focus is not on the event but on the minds of their main characters. As you read these unusual and emotionally affecting stories, consider the difficulties entailed in writing about something you and your readers can never have experienced—death itself—and also the possibilities such an absence of experience opens up.

KATHERINE ANNE PORTER (1890–1980)

THE JILTING OF
GRANNY WEATHERALL 1930

She flicked her wrist neatly out of Doctor Harry's pudgy careful fingers and pulled the sheet up to her chin. The brat ought to be in knee breeches. Doctoring around the country with spectacles on his nose! "Get along now, take your schoolbooks and go. There's nothing wrong with me."

Doctor Harry spread a warm paw like a cushion on her forehead where the forked green vein danced and made her eyelids twitch. "Now, now, be a good girl, and we'll have you up in no time."

"That's no way to speak to a woman nearly eighty years old just because she's down. I'd have you respect your elders, young man."

"Well, Missy, excuse me." Doctor Harry patted her cheek. "But I've got to warn you, haven't I? You're a marvel, but you must be careful or you're going to be good and sorry."

"Don't tell me what I'm going to be. I'm on my feet now, morally speaking. 5 It's Cornelia. I had to go to bed to get rid of her."

Her bones felt loose, and floated around in her skin, and Doctor Harry floated like a balloon around the foot of the bed. He floated and pulled down his waistcoat and swung his glasses on a cord. "Well, stay where you are, it certainly can't hurt you."

"Get along and doctor your sick," said Granny Weatherall. "Leave a well woman alone. I'll call for you when I want you. . . . Where were you forty years ago when I pulled through milk-leg and double pneumonia? You weren't even born. Don't let Cornelia lead you on," she shouted, because Doctor Harry appeared to float up to the ceiling and out. "I pay my own bills, and I don't throw my money away on nonsense!"

She meant to wave good-by, but it was too much trouble. Her eyes closed of themselves, it was like a dark curtain drawn around the bed. The pillow rose and floated under her, pleasant as a hammock in a light wind. She listened

to the leaves rustling outside the window. No, somebody was swishing newspapers: no, Cornelia and Doctor Harry were whispering together. She leaped
broad awake, thinking they whispered in her ear.

"She was never like this, *never* like this!" "Well, what can we expect?" "Yes,
eighty years old. . . ."

Well, and what if she was? She still had ears. It was like Cornelia to whis-   10
per around doors. She always kept things secret in such a public way. She was
always being tactful and kind. Cornelia was dutiful; that was the trouble with
her. Dutiful and good: "So good and dutiful," said Granny, "that I'd like to
spank her." She saw herself spanking Cornelia and making a fine job of it.

"What'd you say, Mother?"

Granny felt her face tying up in hard knots.

"Can't a body think, I'd like to know?"

"I thought you might want something."

"I do. I want a lot of things. First off, go away and don't whisper."   15

She lay and drowsed, hoping in her sleep that the children would keep out
and let her rest a minute. It had been a long day. Not that she was tired. It was
always pleasant to snatch a minute now and then. There was always so much
to be done, let me see: tomorrow.

Tomorrow was far away and there was nothing to trouble about. Things
were finished somehow when the time came; thank God there was always a
little margin over for peace: then a person could spread out the plan of life
and tuck in the edges orderly. It was good to have everything clean and folded
away, with the hair brushes and tonic bottles sitting straight on the white
embroidered linen: the day started without fuss and the pantry shelves laid
out with rows of jelly glasses and brown jugs and white stone china jars with
blue whirligigs and words painted on them: coffee, tea, sugar, ginger, cinnamon, allspice: and the bronze clock with the lion on top nicely dusted off. The
dust that lion could collect in twenty-four hours! The box in the attic with all
those letters tied up, well she'd have to go through that tomorrow. All those
letters—George's letters and John's letters and her letters to them both—lying
around for the children to find afterwards made her uneasy. Yes, that would
be tomorrow's business. No use to let them know how silly she had been once.

While she was rummaging around she found death in her mind and it felt
clammy and unfamiliar. She had spent so much time preparing for death
there was no need for bringing it up again. Let it take care of itself now.
When she was sixty she had felt very old, finished, and went around making farewell trips to see her children and grandchildren, with a secret in her
mind: this is the very last of your mother, children! Then she made her will
and came down with a long fever. That was all just a notion like a lot of
other things, but it was lucky too, for she had once and for all got over the
idea of dying for a long time. Now she couldn't be worried. She hoped she
had better sense now. Her father had lived to be one hundred and two years
old and had drunk a noggin of strong hot toddy on his last birthday. He told
the reporters it was his daily habit, and he owed his long life to that. He had

made quite a scandal and was very pleased about it. She believed she'd just
plague Cornelia a little.

"Cornelia! Cornelia!" No footsteps, but a sudden hand on her cheek. "Bless
you, where have you been?"

"Here, mother."

"Well, Cornelia, I want a noggin of hot toddy." 20

"Are you cold, darling?"

"I'm chilly, Cornelia. Lying in bed stops the circulation. I must have told
you that a thousand times."

Well, she could just hear Cornelia telling her husband that Mother was getting childish and they'd have to humor her. The thing that most annoyed her
was that Cornelia thought she was deaf, dumb, and blind. Little hasty glances
and tiny gestures tossed around her and over her head saying, "Don't cross
her, let her have her way, she's eighty years old," and she sitting there as if she
lived in a thin glass cage. Sometimes Granny almost made up her mind to pack
up and move back to her own house where nobody could remind her every
minute that she was old. Wait, wait, Cornelia, till your own children whisper
behind your back!

In her day she had kept a better house and had got more work done. She 25
wasn't too old yet for Lydia to be driving eighty miles for advice when one of
the children jumped the track, and Jimmy still dropped in and talked things
over: "Now, Mammy, you've a good business head, I want to know what you
think of this? . . ." Old Cornelia couldn't change the furniture around without
asking. Little things, little things! They had been so sweet when they were little.
Granny wished the old days were back again with the children young and everything to be done over. It had been a hard pull, but not too much for her. When
she thought of all the food she had cooked, and all the clothes she had cut and
sewed, and all the gardens she had made—well, the children showed it. There
they were, made out of her, and they couldn't get away from that. Sometimes
she wanted to see John again and point to them and say, Well, I didn't do so
badly, did I? But that would have to wait. That was for tomorrow. She used to
think of him as a man, but now all the children were older than their father, and
he would be a child beside her if she saw him now. It seemed strange and there
was something wrong in the idea. Why, he couldn't possibly recognize her. She
had fenced in a hundred acres once, digging the post holes herself and clamp-
ing the wires with just a negro boy to help. That changed a woman. John would
be looking for a young woman with the peaked Spanish comb in her hair and
the painted fan. Digging post holes changed a woman. Riding country roads in
the winter when women had their babies was another thing: sitting up nights
with sick horses and sick negroes and sick children and hardly ever losing one.
John, I hardly ever lost one of them! John would see that in a minute, that would
be something he could understand, she wouldn't have to explain anything!

It made her feel like rolling up her sleeves and putting the whole place to
rights again. No matter if Cornelia was determined to be everywhere at once,
there were a great many things left undone in this place. She would start

tomorrow and do them. It was good to be strong enough for everything, even if all you made melted and changed and slipped under your hands, so that by the time you finished you almost forgot what you were working for. What was it I set out to do? she asked herself intently, but she could not remember. A fog rose over the valley, she saw it marching across the creek swallowing the trees and moving up the hill like an army of ghosts. Soon it would be at the near edge of the orchard, and then it was time to go in and light the lamps. Come in, children, don't stay out in the night air.

Lighting the lamps had been beautiful. The children huddled up to her and breathed like little calves waiting at the bars in the twilight. Their eyes followed the match and watched the flame rise and settle in a blue curve, then they moved away from her. The lamp was lit, they didn't have to be scared and hang on to mother any more. Never, never, never more. God, for all my life I thank Thee. Without Thee, my God, I could never have done it. Hail, Mary, full of grace.

I want you to pick all the fruit this year and see that nothing is wasted. There's always someone who can use it. Don't let good things rot for want of using. You waste life when you waste good food. Don't let things get lost. It's bitter to lose things. Now, don't let me get to thinking, not when I am tired and taking a little nap before supper. . . .

The pillow rose about her shoulders and pressed against her heart and the memory was being squeezed out of it: oh, push down the pillow, somebody: it would smother her if she tried to hold it. Such a fresh breeze blowing and such a green day with no threats in it. But he had not come, just the same. What does a woman do when she has put on the white veil and set out the white cake for a man and he doesn't come? She tried to remember. No, I swear he never harmed me but in that. He never harmed me but in that . . . and what if he did? There was the day, the day, but a whirl of dark smoke rose and covered it, crept up and over into the bright field where everything was planted so carefully in orderly rows. That was hell, she knew hell when she saw it. For sixty years she had prayed against remembering him and against losing her soul in the deep pit of hell, and now the two things were mingled in one and the thought of him was a smoky cloud from hell that moved and crept in her head when she had just got rid of Doctor Harry and was trying to rest a minute. Wounded vanity, Ellen, said a sharp voice in the top of her mind. Don't let your wounded vanity get the upper hand of you. Plenty of girls get jilted. You were jilted, weren't you? Then stand up to it. Her eyelids wavered and let in streamers of blue-gray light like tissue paper over her eyes. She must get up and pull the shades down or she'd never sleep. She was in bed again and the shades were not down. How could that happen? Better turn over, hide from the light, sleeping in the light gave you nightmares. "Mother, how do you feel now?" and a stinging wetness on her forehead. But I don't like having my face washed in cold water!

Hapsy? George? Lydia? Jimmy? No, Cornelia, and her features were swollen 30 and full of little puddles. "They're coming, darling, they'll all be here soon." Go wash your face, child, you look funny.

Instead of obeying, Cornelia knelt down and put her head on the pillow. She seemed to be talking but there was no sound. "Well, are you tongue-tied? Whose birthday is it? Are you going to give a party?"

Cornelia's mouth moved urgently in strange shapes. "Don't do that, you bother me, daughter."

"Oh, no, Mother, Oh, no. . . ."

Nonsense. It was strange about children. They disputed your every word. "No what, Cornelia?"

"Here's Doctor Harry."   35

"I won't see that boy again. He just left five minutes ago."

"That was this morning, Mother. It's night now. Here's the nurse."

"This is Doctor Harry, Mrs. Weatherall. I never saw you look so young and happy!"

"Ah, I'll never be young again—but I'd be happy if they'd let me lie in peace and get rested."

She thought she spoke up loudly, but no one answered. A warm weight on   40
her forehead, a warm bracelet on her wrist, and a breeze went on whispering, trying to tell her something. A shuffle of leaves in the everlasting hand of God. He blew on them and they danced and rattled. "Mother, don't mind, we're going to give you a little hypodermic." "Look here, daughter, how do ants get in this bed? I saw sugar ants yesterday." Did you send for Hapsy too?

It was Hapsy she really wanted. She had to go a long way back through a great many rooms to find Hapsy standing with a baby on her arm. She seemed to herself to be Hapsy also, and the baby on Hapsy's arm was Hapsy and himself and herself, all at once, and there was no surprise in the meeting. Then Hapsy melted from within and turned flimsy as gray gauze and the baby was a gauzy shadow, and Hapsy came up close and said, "I thought you'd never come," and looked at her very searchingly and said, "You haven't changed a bit!" They leaned forward to kiss, when Cornelia began whispering from a long way off, "Oh, is there anything you want to tell me? Is there anything I can do for you?"

Yes, she had changed her mind after sixty years and she would like to see George. I want you to find George. Find him and be sure to tell him I forgot him. I want him to know I had my husband just the same and my children and my house like any other woman. A good house too and a good husband that I loved and fine children out of him. Better than I hoped for even. Tell him I was given back everything he took away and more. Oh, no, oh, God, no, there was something else besides the house and the man and the children. Oh, surely they were not all? What was it? Something not given back. . . . Her breath crowded down under her ribs and grew into a monstrous frightening shape with cutting edges; it bored up into her head, and the agony was unbelievable. Yes, John, get the doctor now, no more talk, my time has come.

When this one was born it should be the last. The last. It should have been born first, for it was the one she had truly wanted. Everything came in good time. Nothing left out, left over. She was strong. In three days she would be as well as ever. Better. A woman needed milk in her to have her full health.

"Mother, do you hear me?"

"I've been telling you—"

"Mother, Father Connolly's here."

"I went to Holy Communion only last week. Tell him I'm not so sinful as all that."

"Father just wants to speak to you."

He could speak as much as he pleased. It was like him to drop in and inquire about her soul as if it were a teething baby, and then stay on for a cup of tea and a round of cards and gossip. He always had a funny story of some sort, usually about an Irishman who made his little mistakes and confessed them, and the point lay in some absurd thing he would blurt out in the confessional showing his struggles between naive piety and original sin. Granny felt easy about her soul. Cornelia, where are your manners? Give Father Connolly a chair. She had her secret comfortable understanding with a few favorite saints who cleared a straight road to God for her. All as surely signed and sealed as the papers for the new Forty Acres. Forever . . . heirs and assigns forever. Since the day the wedding cake was not cut, but thrown out and wasted. The whole bottom dropped out of the world, and there she was blind and sweating with nothing under her feet and the walls falling away. His hand had caught her under the breast, she had not fallen, there was the freshly polished floor with the green rug on it, just as before. He had cursed like a sailor's parrot and said, "I'll kill him for you." Don't lay a hand on him, for my sake leave something to God. "Now, Ellen, you must believe what I tell you. . . ."

So there was nothing, nothing to worry about any more, except some- 50 times in the night one of the children screamed in a nightmare, and they both hustled out shaking and hunting for the matches and calling, "There, wait a minute, here we are!" John, get the doctor now, Hapsy's time has come. But there was Hapsy standing by the bed in a white cap. "Cornelia, tell Hapsy to take off her cap, I can't see her plain."

Her eyes opened very wide and the room stood out like a picture she had seen somewhere. Dark colors with the shadows rising towards the ceiling in long angles. The tall black dresser gleamed with nothing on it but John's picture, enlarged from a little one, with John's eyes very black when they should have been blue. You never saw him, so how do you know how he looked? But the man insisted the copy was perfect, it was very rich and handsome. For a picture, yes, but it's not my husband. The table by the bed had a linen cover and a candle and a crucifix. The light was blue from Cornelia's silk lampshades. No sort of light at all, just frippery. You had to live forty years with kerosene lamps to appreciate honest electricity. She felt very strong and she saw Doctor Harry with a rosy nimbus around him.

"You look like a saint, Doctor Harry, and I vow that's as near as you'll ever come to it."

"She's saying something."

"I heard you, Cornelia. What's all this carrying on?"

"Father Connolly's saying—"

Cornelia's voice staggered and bumped like a cart in a bad road. It rounded corners and turned back again and arrived nowhere. Granny stepped up in the cart very lightly and reached for the reins, but a man sat beside her and she knew him by his hands, driving the cart. She did not look in his face, for she knew without seeing, but looked instead down the road where the trees leaned over and bowed to each other and a thousand birds were singing a Mass. She felt like singing too, but she put her hand in the bosom of her dress and pulled out a rosary, and Father Connolly murmured Latin in a very solemn voice and tickled her feet. My God, will you stop that nonsense? I'm a married woman. What if he did run away and leave me to face the priest by myself? I found another a whole world better. I wouldn't have exchanged my husband for anybody except St. Michael himself, and you may tell him that for me with a thank you in the bargain.

Light flashed on her closed eyelids, and a deep roaring shook her. Cornelia, is that lightning? I hear thunder. There's going to be a storm. Close all the windows. Call the children in. . . . "Mother, here we are, all of us." "Is that you, Hapsy?" "Oh, no, I'm Lydia. We drove as fast as we could." Their faces drifted above her, drifted away. The rosary fell out of her hands and Lydia put it back. Jimmy tried to help, their hands fumbled together, and Granny closed two fingers around Jimmy's thumb. Beads wouldn't do, it must be something alive. She was so amazed her thoughts ran round and round. So, my dear Lord, this is my death and I wasn't even thinking about it. My children have come to see me die. But I can't, it's not time. Oh, I always hated surprises. I wanted to give Cornelia the amethyst set—Cornelia, you're to have the amethyst set, but Hapsy's to wear it when she wants, and, Doctor Harry, do shut up. Nobody sent for you. Oh, my dear Lord, do wait a minute. I meant to do something about the Forty Acres, Jimmy doesn't need it and Lydia will later on, with that worthless husband of hers. I meant to finish the altar cloth and send six bottles of wine to Sister Borgia for her dyspepsia. I want to send six bottles of wine to Sister Borgia, Father Connolly, now don't let me forget.

Cornelia's voice made short turns and tilted over and crashed. "Oh, Mother, oh, Mother, oh, Mother. . . ."

"I'm not going, Cornelia. I'm taken by surprise. I can't go."

You'll see Hapsy again. What about her? "I thought you'd never come." 60 Granny made a long journey outward, looking for Hapsy. What if I don't find her? What then? Her heart sank down and down, there was no bottom to death, she couldn't come to the end of it. The blue light from Cornelia's lampshade drew into a tiny point in the center of her brain, it flickered and winked like an eye, quietly it fluttered and dwindled. Granny lay curled down within herself, amazed and watchful, staring at the point of light that was herself; her body was now only a deeper mass of shadow in an endless darkness and this darkness would curl around the light and swallow it up. God, give a sign!

For the second time there was no sign. Again no bridegroom and the priest in the house. She could not remember any other sorrow because this grief wiped them all away. Oh, no, there's nothing more cruel than this—I'll never forgive it. She stretched herself with a deep breath and blew out the light.

FOR ANALYSIS

1. Characterize Granny Weatherall. What facts about her life does the story provide?

2. Why, after sixty years, does the jilting by George loom so large in Granny's mind? Should we accept her own strong statements that the pain of the jilting was more than compensated for by the happiness she ultimately found with her husband, her children, and her grandchildren? Defend your response.

3. Who is Hapsy? Why do you think she is not present?

4. Why doesn't the author present Granny's final thoughts in an orderly and sequential way?

5. Granny is revealed to us not only through her direct thoughts but also through the many images that float through her mind—a "fog" (para. 26), a "breeze blowing" (para. 29), a "whirl of dark smoke" (para. 29), and others. What do these images reveal about Granny?

WRITING TOPIC

The final paragraph echoes Christ's parable of the bridegroom (Matthew 25:1–3). If you are not familiar with this parable, find a copy of the New Testament in print or online and read it. Why does Granny connect this final, deep religious grief with the grief she felt when George jilted her? What does this biblical **allusion** add to the story?

TOBIAS WOLFF (B. 1945)

BULLET IN THE BRAIN 1995

The line was endless. Anders couldn't get to the bank until just before it closed and now he was stuck behind two women whose loud, stupid conversation put him in a murderous temper. He was never in the best of tempers anyway, Anders—a book critic known for the weary, elegant savagery with which he dispatched almost everything he reviewed.

With the line still doubled around the rope, one of the tellers stuck a Position Closed sign in her window and walked to the back of the bank, where she leaned against a desk and began to pass the time with a man shuffling papers. The women in front of Anders broke off their conversation and watched the teller with hatred. "Oh, that's nice," one of them said. She turned to Anders and added, confident of his accord, "One of those little human touches that keep us coming back."

Anders had conceived his own towering hatred of the teller, but he immediately turned it on the presumptuous crybaby in front of him. "Damned unfair," he said. "Tragic, really. If they're not chopping off the wrong leg, or bombing your ancestral village, they're closing their positions."

She stood her ground. "I didn't say it was tragic," she said. "I just think it's a pretty lousy way to treat your customers."

"Unforgivable," Anders said. "Heaven will take note." 5

She sucked in her cheeks but stared past him and said nothing. Anders saw that the other woman, her friend, was looking in the same direction. And then the tellers stopped what they were doing, and the customers slowly turned, and silence came over the bank. Two men wearing black ski masks and blue business suits were standing to the side of the door. One of them had a pistol pressed against the guard's neck. The guard's eyes were closed, and his lips were moving. The other man had a sawed-off shotgun. "Keep your big mouth shut!" the man with the pistol said, though no one had spoken a word. "One of you tellers hits the alarm, you're all dead meat. Got it?"

The tellers nodded.

"Oh, bravo," Anders said. "Dead meat." He turned to the woman in front of him. "Great script, eh? The stern, brass-knuckled poetry of the dangerous classes."

She looked at him with drowning eyes.

The man with the shotgun pushed the guard to his knees. He handed the 10
shotgun to his partner and yanked the guard's wrists up behind his back and locked them together with a pair of handcuffs. He then toppled him onto the floor with a kick between the shoulder blades. He took his shotgun back and went over to the security gate at the end of the counter. He was short and heavy and moved with peculiar slowness, even torpor. "Buzz him in," his partner said. The man with the shotgun sauntered along the line of tellers, handing each of them a Hefty bag. When he came to the empty position he looked over at the man with the pistol, who said, "Whose slot is that?"

Anders watched the teller. She put her hand to her throat and turned to the man she'd been talking to. He nodded. "Mine," she said.

"Then get your ugly ass in gear and fill that bag."

"There you go," Anders said to the woman in front of him. "Justice is done."

"Hey! Bright boy! Did I tell you to talk?"

"No," Anders said. 15

"Then shut your trap."

"Did you hear that?" Anders said. " 'Bright boy.' Right out of 'The Killers.' "

"Please be quiet," the woman said.

"Hey, you deaf or what?" The man with the pistol walked over to Anders. He poked the weapon into Anders' gut. "You think I'm playing games?"

"No," Anders said, but the barrel tickled like a stiff finger and he had to 20
fight back the titters. He did this by making himself stare into the man's eyes, which were clearly visible behind the holes in the mask: pale-blue and rawly red-rimmed. The man's left eyelid kept twitching. He breathed out a piercing, ammoniac smell that shocked Anders more than anything that had happened, and he was beginning to develop a sense of unease when the man prodded him again with the pistol.

"You like me, bright boy?" he said. "You want to suck my dick?"

"No," Anders said.

"Then stop looking at me."

Anders fixed his gaze on the man's shiny wing-tip shoes.

"Not down there. Up there." He stuck the pistol under Anders' chin and 25 pushed it upward until Anders was looking at the ceiling.

Anders had never paid much attention to that part of the bank, a pompous old building with marble floors and counters and pillars and gilt scrollwork over the tellers' cages. The domed ceiling had been decorated with mythological figures whose fleshy, toga-draped ugliness Anders had taken in at a glance many years earlier and afterward declined to notice. Now he had no choice but to scrutinize the painter's work. It was worse than he remembered, and all of it executed with the utmost gravity. The artist had a few tricks up his sleeve and used them again and again—a certain rosy blush on the underside of the clouds, a coy backward glance on the faces of the cupids and fauns. The ceiling was crowded with various dramas, but the one that caught Anders' eye was Zeus and Europa—portrayed, in this rendition, as a bull ogling a cow from behind a haystack. To make the cow sexy, the painter had canted her hips suggestively and given her long, droopy eyelashes, through which she gazed back at the bull with sultry welcome. The bull wore a smirk and his eyebrows were arched. If there'd been a bubble coming out of his mouth, it would have said, "Hubba hubba."

"What's so funny, bright boy?"

"Nothing."

"You think I'm comical? You think I'm some kind of clown?"

"No." 30

"You think you can fuck with me?"

"No."

"Fuck with me again, you're history. *Capeesh?*"

Anders burst out laughing. He covered his mouth with both hands and said, "I'm sorry, I'm sorry," then snorted helplessly through his fingers and said, "*Capeesh,* oh, God, *capeesh,*" and at that the man with the pistol raised the pistol and shot Anders right in the head.

The bullet smashed Anders' skull and plowed through his brain and exited 35 behind his right ear, scattering shards of bone into the cerebral cortex, the corpus callosum, back toward the basal ganglia, and down into the thalamus. But before all this occurred, the first appearance of the bullet in the cerebrum set off a crackling chain of ion transports and neurotransmissions. Because of their peculiar origin, these traced a peculiar pattern, flukishly calling to life a summer afternoon some forty years past, and long since lost to memory. After striking the cranium, the bullet was moving at nine hundred feet per second, a pathetically sluggish, glacial pace compared with the synaptic lightning that flashed around it. Once in the brain, that is, the bullet came under the mediation of brain time, which gave Anders plenty of leisure to contemplate the scene that, in a phrase he would have abhorred, "passed before his eyes."

It is worth noting what Anders did not remember, given what he did remember. He did not remember his first lover, Sherry, or what he had most madly loved about her, before it came to irritate him—her unembarrassed carnality, and especially the cordial way she had with his unit, which she called Mr. Mole, as in "Uh-oh, looks like Mr. Mole wants to play," and "Let's hide Mr. Mole!" Anders did not remember his wife, whom he had also loved, before she exhausted him with her predictability, or his daughter, now a sullen professor of economics at Dartmouth. He did not remember standing just outside his daughter's door as she lectured her bear about his naughtiness and described the truly appalling punishments Paws would receive unless he changed his ways. He did not remember a single line of the hundreds of poems he had committed to memory in his youth so that he could give himself the shivers at will—not "Silent, upon a peak in Darien," or "My God, I heard this day," or "All my pretty ones? Did you say all? O hell-kite! All?" None of these did he remember, not one. Anders did not remember his dying mother saying of his father, "I should have stabbed him in his sleep."

He did not remember Professor Josephs telling his class how the Spartans had released Athenian prisoners from their mines if they could recite Aeschylus, and then reciting Aeschylus himself, right there, in the Greek. Anders did not remember how his eyes had burned at those sounds. He did not remember the surprise of seeing a college classmate's name on the jacket of a novel not long after they graduated, or the respect he had felt after reading the book. He did not remember the pleasure of giving respect.

Nor did Anders remember seeing a woman leap to her death from the building opposite his own, just days after his daughter was born. He did not remember shouting, "Lord have mercy!" He did not remember deliberately crashing his father's car into a tree, or having his ribs kicked in by three policemen at an antiwar rally, or waking himself up with laughter. He did not remember when he began to regard the heap of books on his desk with boredom and dread, or when he grew angry at writers for writing them. He did not remember when everything began to remind him of something else.

This is what he remembered. Heat. A baseball field. Yellow grass, the whirr of insects, himself leaning against a tree as the boys of the neighborhood gather for a pickup game. The captains, precociously large boys named Burns and Darsch, argue the relative genius of Mantle and Mays. They have been worrying this subject all summer, and it has become tedious to Anders; an oppression, like the heat.

Then the last two boys arrive, Coyle and a cousin of his from Mississippi. 40 Anders has never met Coyle's cousin before and will never see him again. He says hi with the rest but takes no further notice of him until they've chosen sides and Darsch asks the cousin what position he wants to play. "Shortstop," the boy says. "Short's the best position they is." Anders turns and looks at him. He wants to hear Coyle's cousin repeat what he's just said, but he knows better than to ask. The others will think he's being a jerk, ragging the kid for his grammar. But that isn't it, not at all—it's that Anders is strangely roused, elated, by those final two words, their pure unexpectedness and their music. He takes the field in a trance, repeating them to himself.

The bullet is already in the brain; it won't be outrun forever, or charmed to a halt. In the end, it will do its work and leave the troubled skull behind, dragging its comet's tail of memory and hope and talent and love into the marble hall of commerce. That can't be helped. But for now Anders can still make time. Time for the shadows to lengthen on the grass, time for the tethered dog to bark at the flying ball, time for the boy in right field to smack his sweat-blackened mitt and softly chant, *They is, they is, they is.*

FOR ANALYSIS

1. How do you feel about the main **character** at the beginning of the story? How does Wolff establish our initial sense of him so quickly?

2. What does the main character do for a living? How does he feel about it? How does the rest of the story, even though it never explicitly mentions this profession again, depend on our being able to trace how he came to the profession and how he feels about it?

3. The "life flashing before the eyes" idea is an old standby in stories. How does Wolff use it? Does he follow the expectations we might have when we see this **plot** device used?

4. How do you feel about the main character by the story's end? Has your sense of him changed? If so, how?

MAKING CONNECTIONS

1. "The Jilting of Granny Weatherall" and "Bullet in the Brain" are both deeply affecting stories. What is the importance of our identification with the main character to the emotional impact each story has? How much depends on our liking them? How much depends on the way they bring us inside their minds?

2. Each of these stories takes the moment of death as an opportunity to look back on the main character's life. How does each do this? What does each focus on? Why?

3. Compare the representations of the moment of death in these two stories. How are they similar? How are they different? Do you find one more effective? If so, why?

WRITING TOPIC

One of the things that makes this story powerful is the way in which it gets inside the head—literally—of its main character, particularly because it does so at such an unusual moment. Imagine your own kind of story like this, where you as the writer get inside the head of a character at an unlikely moment. Describe this story, or write it if you want. How do you capitalize on an opportunity to present what's inside someone's mind at such a moment? What can you do to make it seem real? What can you do to make it emotionally affecting?

The stories in this cluster are about animals. That means they are about people, too, because—as these stories remind us—humans are only one species of the animal kingdom. Though humans are shown as having dominion over other animals in both of these stories, in many ways science and the power of rational thought, which we believe make us better than animals, seem to be less powerful than we assume and our irrationality, selfishness, and obtuseness seem more characteristic of how we approach our lives and the lives of others than we would wish. As you read these stories, think about the state of animal life on the planet and the precarious future for many of its species. And don't leave us humans out.

T. CORAGHESSAN BOYLE (B. 1948)

ADMIRAL 2007

She knew in her heart it was a mistake, but she'd been laid off and needed the cash, and her memories of the Strikers were mostly on the favorable side, so when Mrs. Striker called—*Gretchen, this is Gretchen? Mrs. Striker?*—she'd said yes, she'd love to come over and hear what they had to say. First, though, she had to listen to her car cough as she drove across town (fuel pump, that was her father's opinion, offered in a flat voice that said it wasn't his problem, not anymore, not now that she was grown and living back at home after a failed attempt at life), and she nearly stalled the thing turning into the Strikers' block. And then did stall it as she tried, against any reasonable expectation of success, to parallel park in front of their great rearing fortress of a house. It felt strange punching in the code at the gate and seeing how things were different and the same, how the trees had grown while the flowerbeds remained in a state of suspended animation, everything in perpetual bloom and clipped to within a millimeter of perfection. The gardeners saw to that. A whole battalion of them that swarmed over the place twice a week with their blowers and edgers and trimmers, at war with the weeds, the insects, the gophers and ground squirrels, and the very tendency of the display plants to want to grow outside the box. At least that was how she remembered it. The gardeners. And how Admiral would rage at the windows, showing his teeth and scrabbling with his claws—and if he could have chewed through glass he would have done it. "That's right, boy," she'd say, "that's right—don't let those bad men steal all your dead leaves and dirt. You go, boy. You go. That's right."

She rang the bell at the front door and it wasn't Mrs. Striker who answered it but another version of herself in a white maid's apron and a little white maid's cap perched atop her head, and she was so surprised she had to double-clutch to keep from dropping her purse. *A woman of color does not clean house,* that was what her mother always told her, and it had become a kind of mantra when she was growing up, a way of reinforcing core values, of promoting education and the life of the mind, but she couldn't help wondering how much higher a dog-sitter was on the socioeconomic scale than a maid. Or a sous-chef, waitress, aerobics instructor, ticket puncher, and tortilla maker, all of which she'd been at one time or another. About the only thing she hadn't tried was leech-gathering. There was a poem on the subject in her college text by William Wordsworth, the poet of daffodils and leeches, and she could summon it up whenever she needed a good laugh. She developed a quick picture of an old long-nosed white man rolling up his pant legs and wading into the murk, then squeezed out a miniature smile and said, "Hi, I'm Nisha? I came to see Mrs. Striker? And Mr. Striker?"

The maid—she wasn't much older than Nisha herself, with a placid expression that might have been described as self-satisfied or just plain vacant—held open the door. "I'll tell them you're here," she said.

Nisha murmured a thank-you and stepped into the tiled foyer, thinking of the snake brain and the olfactory memories that lay coiled there. She smelled dog—smelled Admiral—with an overlay of old sock and furniture polish. The great room rose up before her like something transposed from a cathedral. It was a cold room, echoing and hollow, and she'd never liked it. "You mind if I wait in the family room?" she asked.

The maid—or rather the girl, the young woman, the young woman in the 5 demeaning and stereotypical maid's costume—had already started off in the direction of the kitchen, but she swung round now to give Nisha a look of surprise and irritation. For a moment it seemed as if she might snap at her, but then, finally, she just shrugged and said, "Whatever."

Nothing had changed in the paneled room that gave onto the garden, not as far as Nisha could see. There were the immense old high-backed leather armchairs and the antique Stickley sofa rescued from the law offices of Striker and Striker, the mahogany bar with the wine rack and the backlit shrine Mr. Striker had created in homage to the spirits of single-malt scotch whisky, and overseeing it all, the oil portrait of Admiral with its dark heroic hues and golden patina of varnish. She remembered the day the painter had come to the house and posed the dog for the preliminary snapshots. Admiral uncooperative, Mrs. Striker strung tight as a wire, and the inevitable squirrel bounding across the lawn at the crucial moment. The painter had labored mightily in his studio to make his subject look noble, snout elevated, eyes fixed on some distant, presumably worthy, object, but to Nisha's mind an Afghan—any Afghan—looked inherently ridiculous, like some escapee from *Sesame Street,* and Admiral seemed a kind of concentrate of the absurd. He looked goofy, just that.

When she turned round, both the Strikers were there, as if they'd floated in out of the ether. As far as she could see, they hadn't aged at all. Their skin was flawless, they held themselves as stiff and erect as the Ituri carvings they'd picked up on their trip to Africa, and they tried hard to make small talk and avoid any appearance of briskness. In Mrs. Striker's arms—*Call me Gretchen, please*—was an Afghan pup, and after the initial exchange of pleasantries, Nisha, her hand extended to rub the silk of the ears and feel the wet probe of the tiny snout on her wrist, began to get the idea. She restrained herself from asking after Admiral. "Is this his pup?" she asked instead. "Is this little Admiral?" The Strikers exchanged a glance. The husband hadn't said, *Call me Cliff,* hadn't said much of anything, but now his lips compressed. "Didn't you read about it in the papers?"

There was an awkward pause. The pup began to squirm. "Admiral passed," Gretchen breathed. "It was an accident. We had him—well, we were in the park, the dog park . . . you know, the one where the dogs run free? You used to take him there, you remember, up off Sycamore? Well, you know how exuberant he was . . ."

"You really didn't read about it?" There was incredulity in the husband's voice.

"Well, I—I was away at college and then I took the first job I could find. 10 Back here, I mean. Because of my mother. She's been sick."

Neither of them commented on this, not even to be polite.

"It was all over the press," the husband said, and he sounded offended now. He adjusted his oversized glasses and cocked his head to look down at her in a way that brought the past rushing back. "*Newsweek* did a story, *USA Today*— we were on *Good Morning America,* both of us."

She was at a loss, the three of them standing there, the dog taking its spiked dentition to the underside of her wrist now, just the way Admiral used to when he was a pup. "For what?" she was about to say, when Gretchen came to the rescue.

"This is little Admiral. Admiral II, actually," she said, ruffling the blond shag over the pup's eyes.

The husband looked past her, out the window and into the yard, an ironic 15 grin pressed to his lips. "Two hundred and fifty thousand dollars," he said, "and it's too bad he wasn't a cat."

Gretchen gave him a sharp look. "You make a joke of it," she said, her eyes suddenly filling, "but it was worth every penny and you know it." She mustered a long-suffering smile for Nisha. "Cats are simpler—their eggs are more mature at ovulation than dogs' are."

"I can get you a cat for thirty-two thou."

"Oh, Cliff, stop. Stop it."

He moved into his wife and put an arm round her shoulders. "But we didn't want to clone a cat, did we, honey?" He bent his face to the dog's, touched noses with him, and let his voice rise to a falsetto: "Did we now, Admiral. Did we?"

* * *

At seven-thirty the next morning, Nisha pulled up in front of the Strikers' 20
house and let her car wheeze and shudder a moment before killing the engine.
She flicked the radio back on to catch the last fading chorus of a tune she liked,
singing along with the sexy low rasp of the lead vocalist, feeling good about
things—or better, anyway. The Strikers were giving her twenty-five dollars an
hour, plus the same dental and health-care package they offered the staff at
their law firm, which was a whole solid towering brick wall of improvement
over what she'd been making as a waitress at Johnny's Rib Shack, sans health
care, sans dental, and sans any tip she could remember above 10 percent of
the pretax total because the people who came out to gnaw ribs were just plain
cheap and no two ways about it. When she stepped out of the car, there was
Gretchen coming down the front steps of the house with the pup in her arms,
just as she had nine years ago when Nisha was a high school freshman taking
on what she assumed was going to be a breeze of a summer job.

Nisha took the initiative of punching in the code herself and slipping
through the gate to hustle up the walk and save Gretchen the trouble, because
Gretchen was in a hurry, always in a hurry. She was dressed in a navy-blue
suit with a double string of pearls and an antique silver pin in the shape of
a bounding borzoi that seemed eerily familiar—it might have been the exact
ensemble she'd been wearing when Nisha had told her she'd be quitting to
go off to college. *I'm sorry, Mrs. Striker, and I've really enjoyed the opportunity
to work for you and Mr. Striker,* she'd said, hardly able to contain the swell of
her heart, *but I'm going to college. On a scholarship.* She'd had the acceptance
letter in her hand to show her, thinking how proud of her Mrs. Striker would
be, how she'd take her in her arms for a hug and congratulate her, but the first
thing she'd said was, *What about Admiral?*

As Gretchen closed on her now, the pup wriggling in her arms, Nisha could
see her smile flutter and die. No doubt she was already envisioning the cream-
leather interior of her BMW (a 750i in Don't-Even-Think-About-It Black)
and the commute to the office and whatever was going down there, court sessions, the piles of documents, contention at every turn. Mr. Striker—Nisha
would never be able to call him Cliff, even if she lived to be eighty, but then
he'd have to be a hundred and ten and probably wouldn't hear her anyway—
was already gone, in his matching Beemer, his and hers. Gretchen didn't say
Good morning or *Hi* or *How are you?* or *Thanks for coming,* but just enfolded her
in the umbrella of her perfume and handed her the dog. Which went immediately heavy in Nisha's arms, fighting for the ground with four flailing paws
and the little white ghoul's teeth that fastened on the top button of her jacket.
Nisha held on. Gave Gretchen a big grateful-for-the-job-and-the-health-care
smile, no worries, no worries at all.

"Those jeans," Gretchen said, narrowing her eyes. "Are they new?"

The dog squirming, squirming. "I, well—I'm going to set him down a minute, okay?"

"Of course, of course. Do what you do, what you normally do." An impa- 25
tient wave. "Or what you used to do, I mean."

They both watched as the pup fell back on its haunches, rolled briefly in the grass, and sprang up to clutch Nisha's right leg in a clumsy embrace. "I just couldn't find any of my old jeans—my mother probably threw them all out long ago. Plus"—a laugh—"I don't think I could fit into them anymore." She gave Gretchen a moment to ruminate on the deeper implications here—time passing, adolescents grown into womanhood, flesh expanding, that sort of thing—then gently pushed the dog down and murmured, "But I *am* wearing—right here, under the jacket?—this T-shirt I know I used to wear back then."

Nothing. Gretchen just stood there, looking distracted.

"It's been washed, of course, and sitting in the back of the top drawer of my dresser where my mother left it, so I don't know if there'll be any scent or anything, but I'm sure I used to wear it because Tupac really used to drive my engine back then, if you know what I mean." She gave it a beat. "But hey, we were all fourteen once, huh?" Gretchen made no sign that she'd heard her— either that or she denied the proposition outright. "You're going to be all right with this, aren't you?" she said, looking her in the eye. "Is there anything we didn't cover?"

The afternoon before, during her interview—but it wasn't really an interview because the Strikers had already made up their minds, and if she'd refused them they would have kept raising the hourly till she capitulated—the two of them, Gretchen and Cliff, had positioned themselves on either side of her and leaned into the bar over caramel-colored scotches and a platter of ebi and maguro sushi to explain the situation.

Just so that she was clear on it. "You know what cloning is, right?" Gretchen 30 said. "Or what it involves? You remember Dolly?"

Nisha was holding fast to her drink, her left elbow pressed to the brass rail of the bar in the family room. She'd just reached out her twinned chopsticks for a second piece of the shrimp but withdrew her hand. "You mean the country singer?"

"The sheep," the husband said.

"The first cloned mammal," Gretchen put in. "Or larger mammal."

"Yeah," she said, nodding. "Sure. I guess."

What followed was a short course in genetics and the method of somatic- 35 cell nuclear transplant that had given the world Dolly, various replicated cattle, pigs, and hamsters, and now Admiral II, the first cloned dog made available commercially through SalvaPet, Inc., the genetic-engineering firm with offices in Seoul, San Juan, and Cleveland. Gretchen's voice constricted as she described how they'd taken a cell from the lining of Admiral's ear just after the accident and inserted it into a donor egg that had had its nucleus removed, stimulated the cell to divide through the application of an electric current, and then inserted the developing embryo into the uterus of a host mother— "The sweetest golden retriever you ever saw. What was her name, Cliff? Some flower, wasn't it?"

"Peony."

"Peony? Are you sure?"

"Of course I'm sure."

"I thought it was—oh, I don't know. You sure it wasn't Iris?"

"The point is," he said, setting his glass down and leveling his gaze at Nisha, 40 "you can get a genetic copy of the animal, a kind of three-dimensional Xerox, but that doesn't guarantee it'll be like the one you, well, the one you lost."

"It was so sad," Gretchen said.

"It's nurture that counts. You've got to reproduce the animal's experiences, as nearly as possible." He gave a shrug, reached for the bottle. "You want another?" he asked, and she held out her glass. "Of course we're both older now—and so are you, we realize that—but we want to come as close as possible to replicating the exact conditions that made Admiral what he was, right down to the toys we gave him, the food, the schedule of walks and play, and all the rest. Which is where you come in—"

"We need a commitment here, Nisha," Gretchen breathed, leaning in so close Nisha could smell the scotch coming back at her. "Four years. That's how long you were with him last time. Or with Admiral, I mean. The original Admiral."

The focus of all this deliberation had fallen asleep in Gretchen's lap. A single probing finger of sunlight stabbed through the window to illuminate the pale fluff over the dog's eyes. At that moment, in that light, little Admiral looked like some strange conjunction of ostrich and ape. Nisha couldn't help thinking of *The Island of Dr. Moreau*, the cheesy version with Marlon Brando looking as if he'd been genetically manipulated himself, and she would have grinned a private grin, fueled by the scotch and the thundering absurdity of the moment, but she had to hide everything she thought or felt behind a mask of impassivity. She wasn't committing to anything for four years—four years? If she was still living here in this crap-hole of a town four years from now she promised herself she'd go out and buy a gun and eliminate all her problems with a single, very personal squeeze of the trigger.

That was what she was thinking when Gretchen said, "We'll pay you twenty 45 dollars an hour," and the husband said, "With health care—and dental," and they both stared at her so fiercely she had to look down into her glass before she found her voice. "Twenty-five," she said.

And oh, how they loved that dog, because they never hesitated. "Twenty-five it is," the husband said, and Gretchen, a closer's smile blooming on her face, produced a contract from the folder at her elbow. "Just sign here," she said.

After Gretchen had climbed into her car and the car had slid through the gate and vanished down the street, Nisha sprawled out on the grass and lifted her face to the sun. She was feeling the bliss of déjà vu—or no, not déjà vu, but a virtual return to the past, when life was just a construct and there was nothing she couldn't have done or been and nothing beyond the thought of clothes and boys and the occasional term paper to hamper her. Here she was, gone back in time, lying on the grass at quarter of eight in the morning on a sunstruck June day, playing with a puppy while everybody else was going to work—it was hilarious, that's what it was. Like something you'd read about in the paper—a behest from some crazed millionaire. Or in this case, two crazed millionaires. She felt so good she let out a laugh, even as the pup came charging across the lawn to slam headfirst into her, all feet and pink panting tongue, and he was Admiral all right.

Admiral in the flesh, born and made and resurrected for the mere little pittance of a quarter million dollars. For a long while she wrestled with him, flipping him over on his back each time he charged, scratching his belly and baby-talking him, enjoying the novelty of it, but by quarter past eight she was bored and she pushed herself up to go on into the house and find something to eat. *Do what you used to do,* Gretchen had told her, but what she used to do, summers especially, was nap and read and watch TV and sneak her friends in to tip a bottle of the husband's forty-year-old scotch to their adolescent lips and make faces at one another before descending into giggles. Twice a day she'd take the dog to the doggy park and watch him squat and crap and run wild with the other mutts till his muzzle was streaked with drool and he dodged at her feet to snatch up mouthfuls of the Evian the Strikers insisted he drink. Now, though, she just wanted to feel the weight of the past a bit, and she went in the back door, the dog at her heels, thinking to make herself a sandwich—the Strikers always had cold cuts in the fridge, mounds of pastrami, capicolla, smoked turkey, and Swiss, individual slices of which went to Admiral each time he did his business outside where he was supposed to or barked in the right cadence or just stuck his goofy head in the door. She could already see the sandwich she was going to make—a whole deli's worth of meat and cheese piled up on Jewish rye; they always had Jewish rye—and she was halfway to the refrigerator before she remembered the maid.

There she was, in her maid's outfit, sitting at the kitchen table with her feet up and the newspaper spread out before her, spooning something out of a cup. "Don't you bring that filthy animal in here," she said, glancing up sharply.

Nisha was startled. There didn't used to be a maid. There was no one in the 50 house, in fact, till Mrs. Yamashita, the cook, came in around four, and that was part of the beauty of it. "Oh, hi," she said, "hi, I didn't know you were going to be—I just . . . I was going to make a sandwich, I guess." There was a silence. The dog slunk around the kitchen, looking wary. "What was your name again?"

"Frankie," the maid said, swallowing the syllables as if she weren't ready to give them up, "and I'm the one has to clean up all these paw marks off the floor—and did you see what he did to that throw pillow in the guest room?"

"No," Nisha said, "I didn't," and she was at the refrigerator now, sliding back the tray of the meat compartment. This would go easier if they were friends, no doubt about it, and she was willing, more than willing. "You want anything?" she said. "A sandwich—or, or something?"

Frankie just stared at her. "I don't know what they're paying you," she said, "but to me? This is the craziest shit I ever heard of in my life. You think I couldn't let the dog out the door a couple times a day? Or what, take him to the park—that's what you do, right, take him to the doggy park over on Sycamore?"

The refrigerator door swung shut, the little light blinking out, the heft of the meat satisfying in her hand. "It's insane, I admit it—hey, I'm with you. You think I wanted to grow up to be a dog-sitter?"

"I don't know. I don't know anything about you. Except you got your 55 degree—you need a degree for that, dog-sitting, I mean?" She hadn't moved, not a muscle, her feet propped up, the cup in one hand, spoon in the other.

"No," Nisha said, feeling the blood rise to her face, "no, you don't. But what about you—you need a degree to be a maid?"

That hit home. For a moment, Frankie said nothing, just looked from her to the dog—which was begging now, clawing at Nisha's leg with his forepaws— and back again. "This is just temporary," she said finally.

"Yeah, me too." Nisha gave her a smile, no harm done, just establishing a little turf, that was all. "Totally."

For the first time, Frankie's expression changed: she almost looked as if she were going to laugh. "Yeah, that's right," she said, "temporary help, that's all we are. We're the temps. And Mr. and Mrs. Striker—dog-crazy, plain crazy, two-hundred-and-fifty-thousand-dollar-crazy—they're permanent."

And now Nisha laughed, and so did Frankie—a low rumble of amusement 60 that made the dog turn its head. The meat was on the counter now, the cellophane wrapper pulled back. Nisha selected a slice of Black Forest ham and held it out to him. "Sit!" she said. "Go ahead, sit!" And the dog, just like his father or progenitor or donor or whatever he was, looked at her stupidly till she dropped the meat on the tile and the wet plop of its arrival made him understand that here was something to eat.

"You're going to spoil that dog," Frankie said.

Nisha went unerringly to the cabinet where the bread was kept, and there it was, Jewish rye, a fresh loaf, springy to the touch. She gave Frankie a glance over her shoulder. "Yeah," she said. "I think that's the idea."

A month drifted by, as serene a month as Nisha could remember. She was making good money, putting in ten-hour days during the week and half days on the weekends, reading through all the books she hadn't had time for in college, exhausting the Strikers' DVD collection and opening her own account at the local video store, walking, lazing, napping the time away. She gained five pounds and vowed to start swimming regularly in the Strikers' pool, but hadn't got round to it yet. Some days she'd help Frankie with the cleaning and the laundry so the two of them could sit out on the back deck with their feet up, sharing a bottle of sweet wine or a joint. As for the dog, she tried to be conscientious about the whole business of imprinting it with the past—or a past—though she felt ridiculous. Four years of college for this? Wars were being fought, people were starving, there were diseases to conquer, children to educate, good to do in the world, and here she was reliving her adolescence in the company of an inbred semi-retarded clown of a cloned Afghan hound because two childless rich people decreed it should be so. All right. She knew she'd have to move on. Knew it was temporary. Swore that she'd work up a new résumé and start sending it out—but then the face of her mother, sick from vomiting and with her scalp as smooth and slick as an eggplant, would rise up to shame her. She threw the ball to the dog. Took him to the park. Let the days fall round her like leaves from a dying tree.

And then one afternoon, on the way back from the dog park, Admiral jerking at the leash beside her and the sky opening up to a dazzle of sun and pure white tufts of cloud that made her feel as if she were floating untethered through the universe along with them, she noticed a figure stationed outside the gate of the Strikers' house. As she got closer, she saw that it was a young man dressed in baggy jeans and a T-shirt, his hair fanning out in rusty blond dreads and a goatee of the same color clinging to his chin. He was peering over the fence. Her first thought was that he'd come to rob the place, but she dismissed it—he was harmless; you could see that a hundred yards off. Then she saw the paint smears on his jeans and wondered if he was a painting contractor come to put in a bid on the house, but that wasn't it either. He looked more like an amateur artist—and here she had to laugh to herself—the kind who specializes in dog portraits. But she was nearly on him now, thinking to brush by him and slip through the gate before he could accost her, whatever he wanted, when he turned suddenly and his face caught fire. "Wow!" he said. "Wow, I can't believe it! You're her, aren't you, the famous dog-sitter? And this"—he went down on one knee and made a chirping sound deep in his throat—"this is Admiral. Right? Am I right?"

Admiral went straight to him, lurching against the leash, and in the next 65 instant was flopping himself down on the hot pavement, submitting to the man's caresses. The rope of a tail whapped and thrashed, the paws gyrated, the puppy teeth came into play. "Good boy," the man crooned, his dreads riding a wave across his brow. "He likes that, doesn't he? Doesn't he, boy?"

Nisha didn't say anything. She just watched, the smallest hole dug out of the canyon of her boredom, till the man rose to his feet and held out his hand even as Admiral sprang up to hump his leg with fresh enthusiasm. "I'm Erhard," he said, grinning wide. "And you're Nisha, right?"

"Yes," she said, taking his hand despite herself. She was on the verge of asking how he knew her name, but there was no point: she already understood. He was from the press. In the past month there must have been a dozen reporters on the property, the Strikers stroking their vanity and posing for pictures and answering the same idiotic questions over and over—*A quarter-million dollars: that's a lot for a dog, isn't it?*—and she herself had been interviewed twice already. Her mother had even found a fuzzy color photo of her and Admiral (couchant, lap) on the Web under the semi-hilarious rubric CLONE SITTER. So this guy was a reporter—a foreign reporter, judging from the faint trace of an accent and the blue-eyed rearing height of him, German, she supposed. Or Austrian. And he wanted some of her time.

"Yes," he said, as if reading her thoughts. "I am from *Die Weltwoche*, and I wanted to ask of you—prevail upon you, beg you—for a few moments? Is that possible? For me? Just now?"

She gave him a long slow appraisal, flirting with him, yes, definitely flirting. "I've got nothing but time," she said. And then, watching his grin widen: 70 "You want a sandwich?"

They ate on the patio overlooking the pool. She was dressed casually in shorts and flip-flops and her old Tupac tee, and that wasn't necessarily a bad thing because the shirt—too small by half—lifted away from her hips when she leaned back in the chair, showing off her navel and the onyx ring she wore there. He was watching her, chattering on about the dog, lifting the sandwich to his lips and putting it down again, fooling with the lens on the battered old Hasselblad he extracted from the backpack at his feet. The sun made sequins on the surface of the pool. Admiral lounged beneath the table, worrying a raw-hide bone. She was feeling good, better than good, sipping a beer and watching him back.

They had a little conversation about the beer. "Sorry to offer you Miller, but that's all we have—or the Strikers have, I mean."

"Miller High Life," he said, lifting the bottle to his mouth. "Great name. What person would not want to live the high life? Even a dog. Even Admiral. He lives the high life, no?"

"I thought you'd want a German beer, something like Beck's or something."

He set down the bottle, picked up the camera, and let the lens wander down 75 the length of her legs. "I'm Swiss, actually," he said. "But I live here now. And I like American beer. I like everything American."

There was no mistaking the implication, and she wanted to return the sentiment, but she didn't know the first thing about Switzerland, so she just smiled and tipped her beer to him.

"So," he said, cradling the camera in his lap and referring to the notepad he'd laid on the table when she'd served him the sandwich, "this is the most interesting for me, this idea that Mr. and Mrs. Striker would hire you for the dog? This is very strange, no?"

She agreed that it was.

He gave her a smile she could have fallen into. "Do you mind if I should ask what are they paying you?"

"Yes," she said. "I do." 80

Another smile. "But it is good—worth your while, as they say?"

"I thought this was about Admiral," she said, and then, because she wanted to try it out on her tongue, she added, "Erhard."

"Oh, it is, it is—but I find you interesting too. More interesting, really, than the dog." As if on cue, Admiral backed out from under the table and squatted on the concrete to deposit a glistening yellow turd, which he examined briefly and then promptly ate.

"Bad dog," she said reflexively.

Erhard studied the dog a moment, then shifted his eyes back to her. "But how do you feel about the situation, this concept of cloning a pet? Do you know anything about this process, the cruelty involved?"

"You know, frankly, Erhard, I haven't thought much about it. I don't know really what it involves. I don't really care. The Strikers love their dog, that's all, and if they want to, I don't know, bring him back—"

"Cheat death, you mean."

She shrugged. "It's their money."

He leaned across the table now, his eyes locked on hers. "Yes, but they must artificially stimulate so many bitches to come into heat, and then they must take the eggs from the tubes of these bitches, what they call 'surgically harvesting,' if you can make a guess as to what that implies for the poor animals"— she began to object but he held up a peremptory finger—"and that is nothing when you think of the numbers involved. Do you know about Snuppy?"

She thought she hadn't heard him right. "Snuppy? What's that?"

"The dog, the first one ever cloned—it was two years ago, in Korea? Well, this dog, this one dog—an Afghan, like your dog here—was the result of over a thousand embryos created in the laboratory from donor skin cells. And they put these embryos into one hundred and twenty-three bitches and only three clones resulted—and two died. So: all that torture of the animals, all that money—and for what?" He glanced down at Admiral, the flowing fur, the blunted eyes. "For this?"

A sudden thought came to her; "You're not really a journalist, are you?"

He slowly shook his head, as if he couldn't bear the weight of it.

"You're what—one of these animal people, these animal liberators or whatever they are. Isn't that right? Isn't that what you are?" She felt frightened suddenly, for herself, for Admiral, for the Strikers and Frankie and the whole carefully constructed edifice of getting and wanting, of supply and demand and all that it implied.

"And do you know why they clone the Afghan hound," he went on, ignoring her, "the very stupidest of all the dogs on this earth? You don't? Breeding, that is why. This is what they call an uncomplicated genetic line, a pure line all the way back to the wolf ancestor. Breeding," he said, and he'd raised his voice so that Admiral looked up at the vehemence of it, "so that we can have this purity, this stupid hound, this *replica* of nature."

Nisha tugged down her T-shirt, drew up her legs. The sun glared up off the water so that she had to squint to see him. "You haven't answered my question," she said. "Erhard. If that's even your name."

Again, the slow rolling of the head on his shoulders, back and forth in rhythmic contrition. "Yes," he said finally, drawing in a breath, "I am one of 'these animal people.'" His eyes went distant a moment and then came back to her. "But I am also a journalist, a journalist first. And I want you to help me."

That night, when the Strikers came home—in convoy, her car following his through the gate, Admiral lurching across the lawn to bark furiously at the shimmering irresistible discs of the wheels of first one car, then the other—Nisha was feeling conflicted. Her loyalties were with the Strikers, of course. And with Admiral too, because no matter how brainless and ungainly the dog was, no matter how many times he wet the rug or ravaged the flower-bed or scrambled up onto the kitchen table to choke down anything any-one had been foolish enough to leave untended even for thirty seconds, she'd bonded with him—she would have been pretty cold if she hadn't. And she wasn't cold. She was as susceptible as anyone else. She loved animals, loved dogs, loved the way Admiral sprang to life when he saw her walk through the door, loved the dance of his fur, his joyous full-throated bark, the feel of his wet whiskered snout in the cupped palm of her hand. But Erhard had made her feel something else altogether. What was it? A sexual stirring, yes, absolutely—after the third beer, she'd found herself leaning into him for the first of a series of deep, languid, adhesive kisses—but it was more than that. There was something transgressive in what he wanted her to do, something that appealed to her sense of rebellion, of anarchy, of applying the pin to the swollen balloon . . . but here were the Strikers, emerging separately from their cars as Admiral bounced between them, yapping out his ecstasy. And now Gretchen was addressing her, trying to shout over the dog's sharp vocaliza-tions, but without success. In the next moment, she was coming across the lawn, her face set.

"Don't let him chase the car like that," she called, even as Admiral tore round her like a dust devil, nipping at her ankles and dodging away again. "It's a bad habit."

"But Admiral—I mean, the first Admiral—used to chase cars all the time, remember?" 100

Gretchen had pinned her hair up so that all the contours of her face stood out in sharp relief. There were lines everywhere suddenly, creases and gouges, frown marks, little embellishments round her eyes, and how could Nisha have missed them? Gretchen was old—fifty, at least—and the realization came home to Nisha now, under the harsh sun, with the taste of the beer and of Erhard still tingling on her lips. "I don't care," Gretchen was saying, and she was standing beside Nisha now, like a figurine the gardeners had set down amid that perfect landscape.

"But I thought we were going to go for everything, the complete behavior, good or bad, right? Because otherwise—"

"That was how the accident happened. At the dog park. He got through the gate before Cliff or I could stop him and just ran out into the street after some idiot on a motorcycle. . . ." She looked past Nisha a moment, to where Admi-ral was bent over the pool, slurping up water as if his pinched triangular head worked on a piston. "So no," she said, "no, we're going to have to modify some behavior. I don't want him drinking that pool water, for one thing. Too many chemicals."

"Okay, sure," Nisha said, shrugging. "I'll try." She raised her voice and sang out, "Bad dog, bad dog," but it was halfhearted and Admiral ignored her.

The cool green eyes shifted to meet hers again. "And I don't want him eating 105 his own"—she paused to search for the proper word for the context, running through various euphemisms before giving it up—"shit."

Another shrug.

"I'm serious on this. Are you with me?"

Nisha couldn't help herself, and so what if she was pushing it? So what?

"Admiral did," she said. "Maybe you didn't know that."

Gretchen just waved her hand in dismissal. "But *this* Admiral," she said. 110 "He's not going to do it. Is he?"

Over the course of the next two weeks, as summer settled in with a succession of cloudless, high-arching days and Admiral steadily grew into the promise of his limbs, Erhard became a fixture at the house. Every morning, when Nisha came through the gate with the dog on his leash, he was there waiting for her, shining and tall and beautiful, with a joke on his lips and always some little treat for Admiral secreted in one pocket or another. The dog worshipped him. Went crazy for him. Pranced on the leash, spun in circles, nosed at his sleeves and pockets till he got his treat, then rolled over on his back in blissful submission. And then it was the dog park, and instead of sitting there wrapped up in the cocoon of herself, she had Erhard to sustain her, to lean into her so that she could feel the heat of him through the thin cotton of his shirt, to kiss her, and later, after lunch and the rising ride of the beer, to make love to her on the divan in the cool shadows of the pool house. They swam in the afternoons—he didn't mind the five pounds she'd put on; he praised her for them—and sometimes Frankie would join them, shedding the maid's habit for a white two-piece and careering through a slashing backstroke with a bottle of beer her reward, because she was part of the family too. Mama and Papa and Aunt Frankie, all there to nurture little Admiral under the beneficent gaze of the sun. Of course, Nisha was no fool. She knew there was a quid pro quo involved here, knew that Erhard had his agenda, but she was in no hurry, she'd committed to nothing, and as she lay there on the divan smoothing her hands over his back, tasting him, enjoying him, taking him inside her, she felt hope, real hope, for the first time since she'd come back home. It got so that she looked forward to each day, even the mornings that had been so hard on her, having to take a tray up to the ghost of her mother while her father trudged off to work, the whole house like a turned grave, because now she had Admiral, now she had Erhard, and she could shrug off anything. Yes. Sure. That was the way it was. Until the day he called her on it.

Cloudless sky, steady sun, every flower at its peak. She came down the walk with Admiral on his leash at the appointed hour, pulled back the gate, and there he was—but this time he wasn't alone. Beside him, already straining at the leash, was a gangling overgrown Afghan pup that could have been the twin of Admiral, and though she'd known it was coming, known the plan since the very first day, she was awestruck.

"Jesus," she said, even as Admiral jerked her forward and the two dogs began to romp round her legs in a tangle of limbs and leashes, "how did you—? I mean, he's the exact, he's totally—"

"That's the idea, isn't it?"

"But where did you find him?" Erhard gave her a look of appraisal, then his eyes jumped past her to sweep the street. "Let's go inside, no? I don't want that they should see us here, anyone—not right in the front of the house."

He hadn't talked her into it, not yet, not exactly, but now that the moment had come she numbly punched in the code and held the gate open for him. What he wanted to do, what he was in the process of doing with her unspoken complicity, was to switch the dogs—just for a day, two at the most—by way of experiment. His contention was that the Strikers would never know the differ- ence, that they were arrogant exemplars of bourgeois excess, even to the point of violating the laws of nature—and God, God too—simply to satisfy their own solipsistic desires. Admiral wouldn't be harmed—he'd enjoy himself, the change of scenery, all that. And certainly she knew how much the dog had come to mean to him. "But these people will not recognize their own animal," he'd insisted, his voice gone hard with conviction, "and so I will have my story and the world will know it."

Once inside the gate, they let the dogs off their leashes and went round back of the house where they'd be out of sight. They walked hand in hand, his fin- gers entwined with hers, and for a long while, as the sun rode high overhead and a breeze slipped in off the ocean to stir the trees, they watched as the two dogs streaked back and forth, leaping and nipping and tumbling in doggy rhapsody. Admiral's great combed-out spill of fur whipped round him in a frenzy of motion, and the new dog, Erhard's dog—the impostor—matched him step for step, hair for glorious hair. "You took him to the groomer, didn't you?" she said.

Erhard gave a stiff nod. "Yes, sure. What do you think? He must be exact."

She watched, bemused, for another minute, her misgivings buried deep under the pressure of his fingers, bone, sinew, the wedded flesh, and why shouldn't she go along with him? What was the harm? His article, or exposé, or whatever it was, would appear in Switzerland, in German, and the Strikers would never know the difference. Or even if they did, even if it was translated into English and grabbed headlines all over the country, they had it coming to them. Erhard was right. She knew it. She'd known it all along. "So what's his name?" she asked, the dogs shooting past her in a moil of fur and flashing feet. "Does he have a name?"

"Fred."

"Fred? What kind of name is that for a pedigree dog?"

"What kind of name is Admiral?"

She was about to tell him the story of the original Admiral, how he'd earned his sobriquet because of his enthusiasm for the Strikers' yacht and how they were planning on taking Admiral II out on the water as soon as they could, when the familiar rumble of the driveway gate drawing back on its runners startled her. In the next moment, she was in motion, making for the near corner of the house where she could see down the long macadam strip of the drive. Her heart skipped a beat: it was Gretchen. Gretchen home early, some crisis compelling her, mislaid papers, her blouse stained, the flu, Gretchen in her black Beemer, waiting for the gate to slide back so she could roll up the drive and exert dominion over her house and property, her piss-stained carpets, and her insuperable dog. "Quick!" Nisha shouted, whirling round. "Grab them. Grab the dogs!"

She saw Erhard plunge forward and snatch at them, the grass rising up to meet him and both dogs tearing free. "Admiral!" he called, scrambling to his knees. "Here, boy. Come!" The moment thundered in her ears. The dogs hesitated, the ridiculous sea of fur smoothing and settling momentarily, and then one of them—it was Admiral, it had to be—came to him, and he got hold of it even as the other pricked up its ears at the sound of the car and bolted round the corner of the house.

"I'll stall her," she called. 125

Erhard, all six feet five inches of him, was already humping across the grass in the direction of the pool house, the dog writhing in his arms.

But the other dog—it was Fred, it had to be—was chasing the car up the drive now, nipping at the wheels, and as Nisha came round the corner she could read the look on her employer's face. A moment and she was there, grabbing for the dog as the car rolled to a stop and the engine died. Gretchen stepped out of the car, heels coming down squarely on the pavement, her shoulders thrust back tightly against the grip of her jacket. "I thought I told you . . ." she began, her voice high and querulous, but then she faltered and her expression changed. "But where's Admiral?" she said. "And whose dog is *that*?"

In the course of her life, short though it had been, she'd known her share of embittered people—her father, for one; her mother, for another—and she'd promised herself she'd never go there, never descend to that hopeless state of despair and regret that ground you down till you were nothing but raw animus, but increasingly now everything she thought or felt or tasted was bitter to the root. Erhard was gone. The Strikers were inflexible. Her mother lingered. Admiral reigned supreme. When the car had come up the drive and Gretchen had stood there confronting her, she'd never felt lower in her life. Until Admiral began howling in the distance and then broke free of Erhard to come careening round the corner of the house and launch himself in one wholly coordinated and mighty leap right into the arms of his protector. And then Erhard appeared, head bowed and shoulders slumped, looking abashed.

"I don't think I've had the pleasure," Gretchen said, setting down the dog (which sprang right up again, this time at Erhard) and at the same time shooting Nisha a look before stepping forward and extending her hand.

"Oh, this is, uh, Erhard," she heard herself say. "He's from Switzerland, and I, well, I just met him in the dog park, and since he had an Afghan too—" 130

Erhard was miserable, as miserable as she'd ever seen him, but he mustered a counterfeit of his smile and said, "Nice to meet you," even as Gretchen dropped his hand and turned to Nisha.

"Well, it's a nice idea," she said, looking down at the dogs, comparing them. "Good for you for taking the initiative, Nisha . . . but really, you have to know that Admiral didn't have any—*playmates*—here on the property, Afghans or no, and I'm sure he wasn't exposed to anybody from *Switzerland*, if you catch my drift?"

There was nothing Nisha could do but nod her acquiescence.

"So," Gretchen said, squaring her shoulders and turning back to Erhard. "Nice to meet you," she said, "but I'm going to have to ask that you take your dog—what's his name?"

Erhard ducked his head. "Fred." 135

"Fred? What an odd name. For a dog, I mean. He does have papers, doesn't he?"

"Oh, yes, he's of the highest order, very well-bred."

Gretchen glanced dubiously down at the dog, then back at Erhard. "Yes, well, he looks it," she said, "and they do make great dogs, Afghans—we ought to know. I don't know if Nisha told you, but Admiral is very special, very, very special, and we can't have any other dogs on the property. And I don't mean to be abrupt"—a sharp look for Nisha—"but strangers of any sort, or species, just cannot be part of this, this . . ." She trailed off, fighting, at the end, to recover the cold impress of her smile. "Nice meeting you," she repeated, and there was nowhere to go from there.

It had taken Nisha a while to put it all behind her. She kept thinking Erhard was lying low, that he'd be back, that there had been something between them after all, but by the end of the second week she no longer looked for him at the gate or at the dog park or anywhere else. And very slowly, as the days beat on, she began to understand what her role was, her true role. Admiral chased his tail and she encouraged him. When he did his business along the street, she nudged the hard little bolus with the tip of her shoe till he stooped to take it up in his mouth. Yes, she was living in the past and her mother was dying and she'd gone to college for nothing, but she was determined to create a new future—for herself and Admiral—and when she took him to the dog park she lingered outside the gate, to let him run free where he really wanted to be, out there on the street where the cars shunted by and the wheels spun and stalled and caught the light till there was nothing else in the world. "Good boy," she'd say. "Good boy."

FOR ANALYSIS

1. Opening lines can be very important in modern short stories. What does Boyle establish with the story's very first sentence? What else about the main **character** and her situation do we learn in the story's first paragraph?

2. What was your reaction to the portrait of Admiral we see early in the story? Why do you think Boyle places it there?

3. How is race important in the story? Would it make sense without it? What about social class?

4. What is the "true role" Nisha realizes is hers in the last paragraph?

WRITING TOPICS

1. Erhard describes the cloning in this story as a way to "cheat death" (para. 87). What are your thoughts about cloning? Do you have objections—ethical, scientific, or otherwise—or not? Does it, in the story's words, violate the laws of nature and God (para. 117)? Explain your answer. Alternatively, write a story in which one or more of the characters are animal or human clones and which explains your thinking about cloning.

2. What do you envision doing for a living in five years? Imagine how you will feel if you find yourself doing something completely different from what you now envision. Describe it. Is your job just your job or is it tied up with your sense of yourself? What else is it tied up with?

LYDIA MILLET (B. 1968)

GIRL AND GIRAFFE   2007

Girl spent the first nine months of her life as a ward of one Ronald Ryves, a sergeant in the Scots Guards. This was the early nineteen-sixties in Kenya, where the Second Battalion of the Scots Guards was stationed to fight a mutiny in Dar-es-Salaam. It was the tail end of the British empire in East Africa.

A man who had adopted Kenya as his home, name of George Adamson, wrote about Girl in his autobiography. Girl was one of his success stories whereas her brother, Boy, was an extravagant failure; yet Boy was the one that Adamson deeply loved.

Adamson lived a long life, long and rough and mostly in a large tent in the bush, a tent with a thatch roof and dirt floor, full of liquor and books. He smoked a pipe with a long stem; he sported a white goatee and went around bare-chested in khaki shorts, a small, fit man, deeply tanned. He was murdered in his eighty-third year by Somali lion poachers.

Joy Adamson, his wife and the famous author of *Born Free*, had been stabbed to death a few years before. She bled out alone, on the road where she fell.

They were somewhat estranged by the time of Joy's death. They had cats 5 instead of children—George had raised scores of lions while Joy had moved on from lions to cheetahs to leopards—and lions and leopards could not cohabit, so George and Joy also lived apart. They maintained contact, but they were hundreds of miles distant.

When Girl and Boy were nine months old the Scots Guards brought them to the plains beneath Mount Kenya, to a farm where a British company was filming *Born Free*. Along with twenty-two other lions, Girl and Boy had roles in the movie. Afterward most of the lions were sent to zoos, where they would live out their lives in narrow spaces. But Girl and Boy were given to Adamson, and he took them to a place named Meru, where he made a camp. This was red-earth country, with reticulated giraffes browsing among the acacia and thornbush. Zebras roamed in families and the odd solitary rhino passed through the brush; there were ostriches and an aged elephant named Rudkin, who plundered tomatoes.

Girl had been fed all her life, but she took readily to the hunt. Her first kill was a jeering baboon, her second an eland with a broken leg, her third a baby zebra. From there she took down a full-grown cow eland and was soon accomplished. Meanwhile Boy did not feel moved to kill for himself; he merely feasted off the animals she brought down.

So Girl became a wild lion, but Boy did not. Boy remained close to Adamson all his life, often in camp, between two worlds. Though he made forays to the wild he did not vanish into it: and on one occasion, hanging around camp while people were visiting, he stuck his head into a jeep and bit the arm of a seven-year-old boy. This boy was the son of the local park warden; soon an order came down for Boy's execution.

But before Adamson could carry out the shooting—he was busy protesting to bureaucrats, who declined to listen—Boy was found under a bush with a porcupine quill through one eye and a broken leg. If not euthanized on the spot he would have to be moved; so Adamson sat on the ground beside him until the veterinarian could fly in, by turns sleeping, drinking whiskey, and brandishing his rifle.

After a surgery in camp Adamson prepared for an airlift. The two of them 10 would live on a private property of Joy's while Adamson nursed Boy back to health. And curiously, though Girl had barely seen her brother for a year, she emerged suddenly from the bush as they were loading him into Adamson's pickup to go to the airstrip. She jumped onto the back of the truck, where Boy lay sedated and wrapped in a blanket. No one was able to entice her away, so they began the drive to the airstrip with Girl along too.

But on the way she spotted a young giraffe by the road and was distracted. She jumped off the pickup. She had become a wild lion; wild lions are hungry.

This was the last time Adamson saw Girl and the last time she saw any of them. Afterward, when Adamson returned to Meru, he would search for her fruitlessly.

Boy grew irritable in temperament after the surgery, due to the steel rod in his leg; and who among us might not become cantankerous? Two years after he and Girl were parted he suddenly attacked a man named Stanley who had tended him with gentle care through illness and injury. Adamson heard a scream and went running with his rifle to find that Boy had bitten deep into Stanley's shoulder; he turned and shot his beloved lion through the heart and then tended to his friend, who bled to death from a severed jugular inside ten minutes.

In Adamson's autobiography the end of Boy is well-described while the end of Girl, who lived out her days in the wild, is invisible. Happy endings often are.

But there is one more report of Girl outside Adamson's published writ-ings. It was made by a man who claimed to have visited Adamson in his camp the year before his murder, one Stefan Juncker based in Tübingen, Germany. Juncker said he had made a pilgrimage to see Adamson at Kora, where he was living with his final lions. Since Adamson constantly welcomed guests to his camp such a visit would not have been uncommon.

The two men sat beside a fire one night and Adamson—in his cups, which the German implied was not rare—became melancholy. He remembered a time when he had not been alone, before his wife and his brother had died. He remembered his old companions, sitting there at the base of the hills among the boulders and the thornbush; he remembered all his lions, his women and men.

His brother Terence, who had lived with him at Kora, had in his dotage discovered that he had what Adamson called "a talent for divining." By wield-ing a swinging pendulum over a map he could determine the location of lost or wanted things. This included water, missing persons, and lions, which he correctly located about sixty percent of the time. Adamson was skeptical in theory, not being much given to magical thinking, but had to admit that his brother's method led him to his lions faster than spoor- or radio-based track-ing. It was inexplicable, he said, but there it was.

Since Terence had died of an embolism two years before, he no longer had a diviner.

At this point Adamson gestured toward a flower bush a few feet away. That was where Terence lay now, he said. And there, he said, turning, over there by a tree was Boy's grave; he had buried his dear lion himself, though others had dug up the corpse later to have proof he was dead. He had been forced to rebury him several times.

The German was disturbed. He did not like the fact that Adamson had laid his brother to rest a stone's throw from a killer.

There was much that science had not yet understood, went on Adamson, about the minds of lions and men and how they might meet. Divining was one example—had the lions somehow told Terence where they could be found?— but he had also known others. In fact, he said, he would tell of an odd event he had once witnessed. Over the years he had thought of it now and then, he said;

15

20

and at this point a warm, low wind sprang up from the Tana River and blew out the embers of their campfire, sinking them into darkness.

He had thought of it over the years, he repeated, but he had mentioned it to no one. He would tell it, if the German could keep a secret.

Of course, said the German.

It was when he was first taking Girl out to hunt. This was in Meru, he said, in the mid-nineteen-sixties. Of course now, more than twenty years later, Girl would have to be long dead.

All your stories end with someone dead, said the German.   25

All *my* stories? asked Adamson.

He and Girl had been walking through the forest together and had emerged into a clearing, where they surprised a herd of giraffes browsing. The herd quickly took off, galloping away before Adamson even had a chance to count them, but they left behind a gangly foal without the sense to run. Perfect prey. It should fall easily. It stood stupidly, blinking, backed up against a large tree.

Girl charged, with Adamson standing by proudly. She had made several kills in the preceding days and he considered her a prodigy.

But abruptly she stopped, pulling up short. Her ears were flat; then they pricked. She and the foal seemed to be studying each other. Adamson was shocked, bordering on indignant, but he remained in the copse. Possibly she sensed something wrong with the giraffe, he thought; or possibly there were other predators behind it, competition in the form of a clan of hyenas he could not see.

As he waited Girl stood unmoving, crouched a few feet from her quarry.   30
Then the giraffe reached up slowly and mouthed a branch with its mobile, rubbery lips. It chewed.

Adamson was flabbergasted. Possibly the animal recognized his lion as a neophyte hunter: but how could it? Giraffes were not insightful; they had the dullness of most placid grazers. Either way, the animal should be bolting. Girl would be on him in a second, fast as light.

He could only see Girl from the rear; her tail twitched, her shoulders hunched. He could not see her face, which frustrated him, he told the German, for a lion's face is extraordinary in its capacity for expression. What was she waiting for?

Then again, he thought as he watched the stillness between them and held his own breath, the foal was going nowhere. Maybe Girl was hypnotized by the future: maybe she saw the arc of her own leap, was already feeling the exhilaration of flight and the impact, the smell and weight of the foal as it crumpled beneath her, as she dragged and wrestled and tore it down, worried the tough hide and sweet flesh. Possibly she was waiting, pent up and ready.

But no. Girl straightened; she relaxed. She sniffed around the foal's long legs. She jumped onto a dry log. She yawned.

And the giraffe kept eating, munching and grunting softly. It shifted on its   35
feet; it stooped down, head dipping toward Girl and up again to the branches,

where it tore and chewed, tore and chewed with a complacent singularity of purpose.

There was sun on the log, glancing across the nape of the lion's neck so that her face was illuminated, the rest of her in shadow. She licked a paw and lay down.

Adamson, squatting in the bushes, stayed put. His body was still but his mind worked hard, puzzling. He considered giraffes. Terence had a weakness for elephants; himself he was strictly a lion man. But giraffes, though morphological freaks, had never interested either of them. Artiodactyla, for one thing: the order of camel, swine and bovids. Not suited for long-term relationships. Strictly for riding, eating or milking, really. He pitied them, but not much. There were no refrigerators in nature; meat and milk had to keep themselves fresh.

After years in the bush he saw all animals as predators or prey. The tourists that came through his camp wanting to pet the lions? Now those were strictly prey, he mused.

Then, recalled to the present after a pause: No offense.

None taken, said the German heartily.   40

In fact the German felt a prickle of annoyance. The flight in, on a single-engine Cessna in jolting turbulence, had made him squeeze his eyes shut and pray silently to a God in whom he did not believe. For this?

An old alcoholic, he thought angrily, with poor hygiene: that was all. He had been eight years of age when he saw *Born Free*, living in a claustrophobic bourgeois household in Stuttgart. His father was fat as blood sausage and his mother used a bottle of hairspray a week. He thought Adamson and his beautiful wife were like Tarzan and Jane.

But Kirsten had disapproved of this trip and she was probably right: nothing more than a mid-life crisis.

The smoke from Adamson's pipe was spicy. The German was disgusted by smoking—frankly any man fool enough to do it deserved what he got—but he had to admit the pipe smelled far better than cigarettes.

You were saying, the German reminded him. Girl and giraffe?   45

Yes, said Adamson softly.

The old man was frail, thought the German, with the ranginess of a hungry dog; his muscles had no flesh between them. He had nothing to spare.

So Girl had lain there on the log in the sun, dozing while the giraffe moved from tree to tree. The sun crossed the sky and clouds massed, casting a leaden grayness over the low hills. Adamson stayed seated in the scrub, drank from a flask and puffed on his pipe. There was a silver elegance to the day, which was unusually mild and breezy; he listened to the wind rattle the branches and whisper the dry grass. Birds alit in the trees and moved off—he noticed mostly black-headed weavers and mourning doves—and Girl and the giraffe ignored them. The shadows grew longer; the sun was sinking. Adamson began to feel impatient, pulled back to camp. He had things he should do before dark.

It was almost dusk when the giraffe moved. It ambled over and bent its head to Girl again, who stirred.

While it is not true, said Adamson solemnly to the German, that giraffes 50 never lie down, as legend has it, it *is* true that they do so rarely and for a very short time. And never, he said, in his experience, did they lie down at the feet of their predators.

And yet this was what the foal did.

It had been a good day, said Adamson, and raised his glass.

As he talked the German had built up the fire again and now he saw the flames reflecting off amber. He was regretting his choice. It had been this or Mallorca, where his wife was now tanning.

The foal lay down deliberately, said Adamson, right beside the dry log. It was deliberate.

And Girl stretched her legs, as a cat will do, luxurious and long, all four 55 straight out at their fullest reach like table legs. She stretched and rose, jumped languidly off the log, and paused. Then she leaned down over the foal and sank in her teeth.

The movement, said Adamson, was gentle. The foal barely struggled; its legs jerked reflexively but soon it was still.

Later, he said, he almost believed he had dreamed the episode. But came to believe, over the years, that a call and answer had passed between Girl and the giraffe: the foal had asked for and been granted reprieve. She had given him a whole afternoon in which to feel the thorny branches and leaves in his mouth, the sun and shade cross his neck, his heavy lashes blink in the air.

It was a free afternoon, because all afternoon the foal had been free of the past and free of the future. Completely free.

It was almost, said Adamson, as though the possibilities of the world had streamed through Girl and the giraffe: and he, a hunched-over primate in the bushes, had been the dumb one, with his insistent frustration at that which he could not easily fathom, his restless, churning efforts to achieve knowledge. Being a primate he watched; being a primate he was separate forever. The two of them opened up beyond all he knew of their natures, suspended: they were fluid in time and space, and between them flowed the utter acceptance of both of their deaths.

They had been together, said Adamson, closer than he had ever been to any- 60 one. They had given; they had given; they had shimmered with spirit.

Spirits, thought the German, glancing at the luminous dial of his watch: yes indeed. Bushmill's, J&B, Ballantine, Cutty Sark, and Glenlivet on special occasions.

This was in Kenya in the late nineteen-eighties, decades after the Mau Mau rebellion brought the deaths of two hundred whites and twenty thousand blacks. A new homespun corruption had replaced the old foreign repression; fewer and fewer lions roamed the grasslands of East Africa, and the British were long gone.

FOR ANALYSIS

1. What is so remarkable about George? How do you feel about him?

2. What is so remarkable about the story of Girl and the giraffe? Did it end the way you expected? What is so important about the ending?

3. George Adamson was a real person. Boy was a real lion who died in the way Millet describes. The story about Girl and the giraffe is imagined by Millet. Does knowing it is fictional change how you read the story?

4. What role does the German play in this story? Why did Millet include him?

MAKING CONNECTIONS

1. When the German in "Girl and Giraffe" tells Adamson that all of his stories end in death, Adamson responds, "All *my* stories?" (para. 26). In what sense do all stories end with death? What does that say about life? What does it say about stories?

2. Both stories are in part about animals being raised by people. What does this situation allow each of these stories to explore about the nature of animals? What does it allow them to say about human nature?

3. "There was much that science had not yet understood," Millet writes in "Girl and Giraffe" (para. 21). What does each story have to say about science? How does each story represent science?

WRITING TOPIC

Retell the story of Girl and the giraffe from the **point of view** of Girl, and reflect afterward on both the problems and possibilities of using such a point of view. Also, how is the central mystery of the story for George—what was going on in the two animals' minds—different if you're inside one of them?

POETRY

ANONYMOUS

EDWARD

1

"Why does your brand° sae° drap wi' bluid,   *sword/so*
    Edward, Edward,
Why does your brand sae drap wi' bluid,
    And why sae sad gang° ye, O?"   *go*
"O I ha'e killed my hawk sae guid,
    Mither, mither,
O I ha'e killed my hawk sae guid,
    And I had nae mair but he, O."

2

"Your hawke's bluid was never sae reid,°   *red*
    Edward, Edward,   10
Your hawke's bluid was never sae reid,
    My dear son I tell thee, O."
"O I ha'e killed my reid-roan steed,
    Mither, mither,
O I ha'e killed my reid-roan steed,
    That erst was sae fair and free, O."

3

"Your steed was auld, and ye ha'e gat mair,
    Edward, Edward,
Your steed was auld, and ye ha'e gat mair,
    Some other dule° ye drie,° O."   *grief/suffer* 20
"O I ha'e killed my fader dear,
    Mither, mither,
O I ha'e killed my fader dear,
    Alas, and wae° is me, O!"   *woe*

4

"And whatten penance wul ye drie for that,
      Edward, Edward?
And whatten penance wul ye drie for that,
   My dear son, now tell me, O?"
"I'll set my feet in yonder boat,
      Mither, mither,   30
I'll set my feet in yonder boat,
   And I'll fare over the sea, O."

5

"And what wul ye do wi' your towers and your ha',
      Edward, Edward?
And what wul ye do wi' your towers and your ha',
   That were sae fair to see, O?"
"I'll let them stand tul they down fa',
      Mither, mither,
I'll let them stand tul they down fa',
   For here never mair maun° I be, O."   must 40

6

"And what wul ye leave to your bairns° and your wife,   children
      Edward, Edward?
And what wul ye leave to your bairns and your wife,
   Whan ye gang over the sea, O?"
"The warlde's° room, let them beg thrae° life,   world's/through
      Mither, mither,
The warlde's room, let them beg thrae life,
   For them never mair wul I see, O."

7

"And what wul ye leave to your ain mither dear,
      Edward, Edward?   50
And what wul ye leave to your ain mither dear,
   My dear son, now tell me, O?"
"The curse of hell frae° me sall° ye bear,   from/shall
      Mither, mither,
The curse of hell frae me sall ye bear,
   Sic° counsels ye gave to me, O."   such

FOR ANALYSIS

1. Why does the mother reject Edward's answers to her first two questions?

2. Does the poem provide any clues to the murderer's motive?

3. Edward has murdered his father and then bitterly turns away from his mother, wife, and children. What basis is there in the poem for nevertheless sympathizing with Edward?

WRITING TOPIC

What effects are achieved through the question-and-answer technique and the repetition of lines?

WILLIAM SHAKESPEARE (1564–1616)

SONNET 1609

73

That time of year thou mayst in me behold
When yellow leaves, or none, or few, do hang
Upon those boughs which shake against the cold,
Bare ruined choirs, where late the sweet birds sang.
In me thou see'st the twilight of such day
As after sunset fadeth in the west;
Which by and by black night doth take away,
Death's second self, that seals up all in rest.
In me thou see'st the glowing of such fire,
That on the ashes of his youth doth lie,   10
As the deathbed whereon it must expire,
Consumed with that which it was nourished by.
This thou perceiv'st, which makes thy love more strong,
To love that well which thou must leave ere long.

FEAR NO MORE
THE HEAT O' THE SUN 1623

Fear no more the heat o' the sun,[1]
  Nor the furious winter's rages;
Thou thy worldly task hast done,
    Home art gone, and ta'en thy wages:

Fear No More the Heat o' the Sun
[1] From *Cymbeline*, act IV, scene 2.

Golden lads and girls all must,
As chimney-sweepers, come to dust.

Fear no more the frown o' the great;
   Thou art past the tyrant's stroke;
Care no more to clothe and eat;
   To thee the reed is as the oak:
The scepter, learning, physic,° must²   10
All follow this, and come to dust.   medicine

Fear no more the lightning flash,
   Nor the all-dreaded thunder stone;³
Fear not slander, censure rash;
   Thou hast finished joy and moan:
All lovers young, all lovers must
Consign to° thee, and come to dust.   agree with

No exorciser harm thee!
Nor no witchcraft charm thee!   20
Ghost unlaid forbear thee!
Nothing ill come near thee!
Quiet consummation have;
And renownéd be thy grave!

JOHN DONNE   (1572–1631)

DEATH, BE NOT PROUD   1633

Death be not proud, though some have calléd thee
Mighty and dreadful, for thou art not so;
For those whom thou think'st thou dost overthrow
Die not, poor Death, nor yet canst thou kill me.
From rest and sleep, which but thy pictures be,
Much pleasure; then from thee much more must flow,
And soonest our best men with thee do go,
Rest of their bones, and soul's delivery.
Thou art slave to fate, chance, kings, and desperate men,
And dost with poison, war, and sickness dwell,   10
And poppy or charms can make us sleep as well

Fear No More the Heat o' the Sun
  ² I.e., kings, scholars, and physicians.
  ³ It was believed that thunder was caused by falling meteorites.

And better than thy stroke; why swell'st thou then?
One short sleep past, we wake eternally
And death shall be no more; Death, thou shalt die.

PERCY BYSSHE SHELLEY   (1792–1822)

OZYMANDIAS[1]   1818

I met a traveller from an antique land
Who said: Two vast and trunkless legs of stone
Stand in the desert . . . Near them, on the sand,
Half sunk, a shattered visage lies, whose frown,
And wrinkled lip, and sneer of cold command,
Tell that its sculptor well those passions read
Which yet survive, stamped on these lifeless things,
The hand that mocked them, and the heart that fed:
And on the pedestal these words appear:
"My name is Ozymandias, king of kings: 10
Look on my works, ye Mighty, and despair!"
Nothing beside remains. Round the decay
Of that colossal wreck, boundless and bare
The lone and level sands stretch far away.

JOHN KEATS   (1795–1821)

ODE ON A GRECIAN URN   1820

I

Thou still unravished bride of quietness,
    Thou foster child of silence and slow time,
Sylvan historian, who canst thus express
    A flowery tale more sweetly than our rhyme:
What leaf-fringed legend haunts about thy shape
    Of deities or mortals, or of both,
        In Tempe or the dales of Arcady?[1]
    What men or gods are these? What maidens loath?

Ozymandias
    [1] Egyptian monarch of the thirteenth century B.C., said to have erected a huge statue of himself.
Ode on a Grecian Urn
    [1] Tempe and Arcady are valleys in Greece famous for their beauty. In ancient times, Tempe was regarded as sacred to Apollo.

What mad pursuit? What struggle to escape?
    What pipes and timbrels? What wild ecstasy?   10

II

Heard melodies are sweet, but those unheard
    Are sweeter; therefore, ye soft pipes, play on;
Not to the sensual ear, but, more endeared,
    Pipe to the spirit ditties of no tone:
Fair youth, beneath the trees, thou canst not leave
    Thy song, nor ever can those trees be bare;
      Bold Lover, never, never canst thou kiss,
Though winning near the goal—yet, do not grieve;
    She cannot fade, though thou hast not thy bliss,
    Forever wilt thou love, and she be fair!   20

III

Ah, happy, happy boughs! that cannot shed
    Your leaves, nor ever bid the Spring adieu;
And, happy melodist, unwearièd,
    Forever piping songs forever new;
More happy love! more happy, happy love!
    Forever warm and still to be enjoyed,
      Forever panting, and forever young;
All breathing human passion far above,[2]
    That leaves a heart high-sorrowful and cloyed,
      A burning forehead, and a parching tongue.   30

IV

Who are these coming to the sacrifice?
    To what green altar, O mysterious priest,
Lead'st thou that heifer lowing at the skies,
    And all her silken flanks with garlands dressed?
What little town by river or sea shore,
    Or mountain-built with peaceful citadel,
      Is emptied of this folk, this pious morn?
And, little town, thy streets forevermore
    Will silent be; and not a soul to tell
      Why thou art desolate, can e'er return.   40

---

[2] I.e., far above all breathing human passion.

V

O Attic[3] shape! Fair attitude! with brede
  Of marble men and maidens overwrought,
With forest branches and the trodden weed;
  Thou, silent form, dost tease us out of thought
As doth eternity: Cold Pastoral!
  When old age shall this generation waste,
    Thou shalt remain, in midst of other woe
  Than ours, a friend to man, to whom thou say'st,
"Beauty is truth, truth beauty,—that is all
    Ye know on earth, and all ye need to know."   50

FOR ANALYSIS

1. Describe the scene the poet sees depicted on the urn. Describe the scene the poet imagines as a consequence of the scene on the urn.

2. Why are the boughs, the piper, and the lovers happy in **stanza** III?

3. Explain the assertion of stanza II: "Heard melodies are sweet, but those unheard / Are sweeter."

4. Does the poem support the assertion of the last two lines? What do they mean?

WRITING TOPIC

Discuss Keats's view of the connection between art and life. With this in mind, consider the meaning of the phrase "Cold Pastoral!" (l. 45).

EMILY DICKINSON   (1830–1886)

AFTER GREAT PAIN, A FORMAL FEELING COMES   CA. 1862

After great pain, a formal feeling comes—
The Nerves sit ceremonious, like Tombs—
The stiff Heart questions was it He, that bore,
And Yesterday, or Centuries before?

The Feet, mechanical, go round—
Of Ground, or Air, or Ought—
A Wooden way

Ode on a Grecian Urn
  [3] Athenian, thus simple and graceful.

Regardless grown,
A Quartz contentment, like a stone—

This is the Hour of Lead—   10
Remembered, if outlived,
As Freezing persons, recollect the Snow—
First—Chill—then Stupor—then the letting go—

FOR ANALYSIS

Is this poem about physical or psychic pain? Explain.

WRITING TOPIC

What is the meaning of "stiff Heart" (l. 3) and "Quartz contentment" (l. 9)? What part do they play in the larger pattern of **images** in this poem?

I HEARD A FLY BUZZ—
WHEN I DIED   CA. 1862

I heard a Fly buzz—when I died—
The Stillness in the Room
Was like the Stillness in the Air—
Between the Heaves of Storm—

The Eyes around—had wrung them dry—
And Breaths were gathering firm
For that last Onset—when the King
Be witnessed—in the Room—

I willed my Keepsakes—Signed away
What portion of me be   10
Assignable—and then it was
There interposed a Fly—

With Blue—uncertain stumbling Buzz—
Between the light—and me—
And then the Windows failed—and then
I could not see to see—

APPARENTLY WITH NO SURPRISE CA. 1884

Apparently with no surprise
To any happy Flower,
The Frost beheads it at its play
In accidental power.
The blond Assassin passes on,
The Sun proceeds unmoved
To measure off another Day
For an Approving God.

BECAUSE I COULD NOT STOP
FOR DEATH CA. 1863, 1890

Because I could not stop for Death—
He kindly stopped for me—
The Carriage held but just Ourselves—
And Immortality.

We slowly drove—He knew no haste
And I had put away
My labor and my leisure too,
For his Civility—

We passed the School, where Children strove
At Recess—in the Ring—   10
We passed the Fields of Gazing Grain—
We passed the Setting Sun—

Or rather—He passed Us—
The Dews drew quivering and chill—
For only Gossamer, my Gown—
My Tippet—only Tulle—

We paused before a House that seemed
A Swelling of the Ground—
The Roof was scarcely visible—
The Cornice—in the Ground—   20

Since then—'tis Centuries—and yet
Feels shorter than the Day
I first surmised the Horses' Heads
Were toward Eternity—

GERARD MANLEY HOPKINS   (1844–1889)

GOD'S GRANDEUR   1918

The world is charged with the grandeur of God.
  It will flame out, like shining from shook foil°   metal foil
  It gathers to a greatness, like the ooze of oil
Crushed. Why do men then now not reck° his rod?   heed
Generations have trod, have trod, have trod;
  And all is seared with trade; bleared, smeared with toil;
  And wears man's smudge and shares man's smell: the soil
Is bare now, nor can foot feel, being shod.

And for all this, nature is never spent;
  There lives the dearest freshness deep down things;   10
And though the last lights off the black West went
  Oh, morning, at the brown brink eastward, springs—
Because the Holy Ghost over the bent
  World broods with warm breast and with ah! bright wings.

A. E. HOUSMAN   (1859–1936)

TO AN ATHLETE DYING YOUNG   1896

The time you won your town the race
We chaired you through the market place;
Man and boy stood cheering by,
And home we brought you shoulder-high.

Today, the road all runners come,
Shoulder-high we bring you home,
And set you at your threshold down,
Townsman of a stiller town.

Smart lad, to slip betimes away
From fields where glory does not stay,   10

And early though the laurel grows
It withers quicker than the rose.

Eyes the shady night has shut
Cannot see the record cut,
And silence sounds no worse than cheers
After earth has stopped the ears:

Now you will not swell the rout
Of lads that wore their honors out,
Runners whom renown outran
And the name died before the man.   20

So set, before its echoes fade,
The fleet foot on the sill of shade,
And hold to the low lintel up
The still-defended challenge cup.

And round that early-laureled head
Will flock to gaze the strengthless dead
And find unwithered on its curls
The garland briefer than a girl's.

WILLIAM BUTLER YEATS   (1865–1939)

SAILING TO BYZANTIUM[1]   1927

1

That is no country for old men. The young
In one another's arms, birds in the trees
—Those dying generations—at their song,
The salmon-falls, the mackerel-crowded seas,
Fish, flesh, or fowl, commend all summer long
Whatever is begotten, born, and dies.
Caught in that sensual music all neglect
Monuments of unaging intellect.

Sailing to Byzantium
[1] Capital of the ancient Eastern Roman Empire, Byzantium (modern Istanbul) is celebrated for
its great art, including mosaics (in ll. 17–18, Yeats addresses the figures in one of these mosaics). In
A Vision, Yeats cites Byzantium as possibly the only civilization that had achieved what he called "Unity
of Being"—a state where "religious, aesthetic, and practical life were one."

2

An aged man is but a paltry thing,
A tattered coat upon a stick, unless   10
Soul clap its hands and sing, and louder sing
For every tatter in its mortal dress,
Nor is there singing school but studying
Monuments of its own magnificence;
And therefore I have sailed the seas and come
To the holy city of Byzantium.

3

O sages standing in God's holy fire
As in the gold mosaic of a wall,
Come from the holy fire, perne in a gyre,[2]
And be the singing-masters of my soul.
Consume my heart away; sick with desire   20
And fastened to a dying animal
It knows not what it is; and gather me
Into the artifice of eternity.

4

Once out of nature I shall never take
My bodily form from any natural thing,
But such a form as Grecian goldsmiths make
Of hammered gold and gold enameling
To keep a drowsy Emperor awake;[3]
Or set upon a golden bough to sing   30
To lords and ladies of Byzantium
Of what is past, or passing, or to come.

FOR ANALYSIS

1. This poem incorporates a series of contrasts, among them "that" country and
Byzantium, and the real birds of the first **stanza** and the artificial bird of the final
stanza. What others do you find?

---

[2] I.e., whirl in a spiral motion. Yeats associated this motion with the cycles of history and the fate
of the individual. Here he entreats the sages represented in the mosaic to take him out of the natural
world described in the first stanza and into the eternal world of art.

[3] "I have read somewhere," Yeats wrote, "that in the Emperor's palace at Byzantium was a tree made
of gold and silver, and artificial birds that sang." The poet wishes to become an artificial bird (a work of
art) in contrast to the real birds of the first stanza.

2. What are the meanings of "generations" (l. 3)?

3. For what is the poet "sick with desire" (l. 21)?

4. In what sense is eternity an "artifice" (l. 24)?

WRITING TOPIC

In what ways are the **images** of bird and song used throughout this poem?

EDWIN ARLINGTON ROBINSON   (1869–1935)

RICHARD CORY   1897

Whenever Richard Cory went down town,
We people on the pavement looked at him:
He was a gentleman from sole to crown,
Clean favored, and imperially slim.

And he was always quietly arrayed,
And he was always human when he talked;
But still he fluttered pulses when he said,
"Good-morning," and he glittered when he walked.

And he was rich—yes, richer than a king—
And admirably schooled in every grace: 10
In fine, we thought that he was everything
To make us wish that we were in his place.

So on we worked, and waited for the light,
And went without the meat, and cursed the bread;
And Richard Cory, one calm summer night,
Went home and put a bullet through his head.

ROBERT FROST   (1874–1963)

AFTER APPLE-PICKING   1914

My long two-pointed ladder's sticking through a tree
Toward heaven still,
And there's a barrel that I didn't fill
Beside it, and there may be two or three

Apples I didn't pick upon some bough.
But I am done with apple-picking now.
Essence of winter sleep is on the night,
The scent of apples: I am drowsing off.
I cannot rub the strangeness from my sight
I got from looking through a pane of glass   10
I skimmed this morning from the drinking trough
And held against the world of hoary grass.
It melted, and I let it fall and break.
But I was well
Upon my way to sleep before it fell,
And I could tell
What form my dreaming was about to take.
Magnified apples appear and disappear,
Stem end and blossom end,
And every fleck of russet showing clear.   20
My instep arch not only keeps the ache,
It keeps the pressure of a ladder-round.
I feel the ladder sway as the boughs bend.
And I keep hearing from the cellar bin
The rumbling sound
Of load on load of apples coming in.
For I have had too much
Of apple-picking: I am overtired
Of the great harvest I myself desired.
There were ten thousand thousand fruit to touch,   30
Cherish in hand, lift down, and not let fall.
For all
That struck the earth,
No matter if not bruised or spiked with stubble,
Went surely to the cider-apple heap
As of no worth.
One can see what will trouble
This sleep of mine, whatever sleep it is.
Were he not gone,
The woodchuck could say whether it's like his   40
Long sleep, as I describe its coming on,
Or just some human sleep.

FOR ANALYSIS

1. What does apple-picking **symbolize**?

2. At the end of the poem, why is the speaker uncertain about what kind of sleep is coming on him?

CASE STUDY

POEMS ABOUT PAINTINGS

The works in this section offer a unique opportunity to reflect on the ways meaning can be conveyed through different media. Most of the poems here are linked with the paintings that inspired them; others appear with paintings thematically similar in their treatment of death. While all these groupings offer an opportunity for rich examination, the ones featuring poems inspired by a particular painting open up even more complex areas for analysis: not only can the painting and the poem be considered independently of each other, but the poem can also be analyzed as a reading of the painting—an interpretation in words of a visual object.

As you enter into a dialogue between the works of art and the poems, jot down your reactions to each painting in some detail before reading the accompanying poem. After you have read a poem, compare your reactions to the poet's. Did reading the poem clarify or in any other way alter your response to the painting? Are the poems successful or even comprehensible without reference to the paintings? How are the works alike or different? With paired works, why does the poet choose to emphasize certain details of a painting and ignore others? What accounts for the order in which the poet deals with the details of the painting? Is the poet attempting an accurate and neutral description of the painting or making some judgment about it?

If you wish to look beyond the individual work, you might consider researching one of the poets and investigating why he or she was so moved by the painting as to write about it. Or you might examine the historical context of both the poem and the painting for any illuminating connections.

W. H. AUDEN   (1907–1973)

MUSÉE DES BEAUX ARTS   1940

About suffering they were never wrong,
The Old Masters: how well they understood
Its human position; how it takes place
While someone else is eating or opening a window or just walking dully along;
How, when the aged are reverently, passionately waiting
For the miraculous birth, there always must be
Children who did not specially want it to happen, skating
On a pond at the edge of the wood:
They never forgot

That even the dreadful martyrdom must run its course   10
Anyhow in a corner, some untidy spot
Where the dogs go on with their doggy life and the torturer's horse
Scratches its innocent behind on a tree.

In Brueghel's *Icarus*,[1] for instance: how everything turns away
Quite leisurely from the disaster; the plowman may
Have heard the splash, the forsaken cry,
But for him it was not an important failure; the sun shone
As it had to on the white legs disappearing into the green
Water; and the expensive delicate ship that must have seen
Something amazing, a boy falling out of the sky,   20
Had somewhere to get to and sailed calmly on.

Landscape with the Fall of Icarus, ca. 1560, by Pieter Brueghel the Elder

[1] This poem describes and comments on Pieter Brueghel's painting *Landscape with the Fall of Icarus* (reproduced above). According to myth, Daedalus and his son Icarus made wings, whose feathers they attached with wax, to escape Crete. Icarus flew so near the sun that the wax melted and he fell into the sea.

FOR ANALYSIS

1. Look up the story of Icarus. What aspects of the human condition or human nature does the story embody? How does Brueghel interpret the story? What other interpretations are possible? Compare Sexton's interpretation of the legend in her poem "To a Friend Whose Work Has Come to Triumph," which can be found in her volume *All My Pretty Ones* (1962).

2. Does the poem offer an accurate interpretation of the painting? Explain.

3. Which details of the painting does the poem describe? Does the poet omit details you found important?

LAWRENCE FERLINGHETTI (B. 1919)

IN GOYA'S GREATEST SCENES   1958

In Goya's greatest scenes[1] we seem to see
                            the people of the world
    exactly at the moment when
        they first attained the title of
                'suffering humanity'
   They writhe upon the page
           in a veritable rage
               of adversity
   Heaped up
        groaning with babies and bayonets   10
               under cement skies
  in an abstract landscape of blasted trees
     bent statues bats wings and beaks
        slippery gibbets
    cadavers and carnivorous cocks
and all the final hollering monsters
    of the
        'imagination of disaster'
  they are so bloody real
          it is as if they really still existed   20

  And they do

---

[1] Francisco José de Goya (1746–1828), famous Spanish artist, celebrated for his representations of "suffering humanity."

Only the landscape is changed
They still are ranged along the roads
plagued by legionaires
false windmills and demented roosters

They are the same people
only further from home
on freeways fifty lanes wide
on a concrete continent
spaced with bland billboards   30
illustrating imbecile illusions of happiness
The scene shows fewer tumbrils[2]
but more maimed citizens
in painted cars
and they have strange license plates
and engines
that devour America

The Third of May, 1808, Madrid, 1814, by Francisco de Goya

[2] Carts in which prisoners were conducted to the place of execution.

FOR ANALYSIS

1. *While The Third of May, 1808, Madrid* commemorates the uprising of the Spanish people against the invading forces of Napoleon, it has come to be seen as a powerful and universal statement against the brutalities of war. Goya also created a series of eighty-five etchings entitled *The Disasters of War* (1810–1820), which shows how individuals are transformed into "suffering humanity" when they are savaged by war. Compare the painting and some of the etchings as views of the disasters of war. Does the use of color in the painting and of black and white in the etchings cause different responses in the viewer? Explain.

2. Goya represents suffering and death in their most elemental, physical sense. Do you find Ferlinghetti's transformation of suffering and death from the literal to the metaphoric in the second half of his poem successful? Explain.

ANNE SEXTON (1928-1974)

THE STARRY NIGHT 1961

That does not keep me from having a terrible need of—shall I say the word—religion. Then I go out at night to paint the stars.

        —Vincent van Gogh in a letter to his brother

The town does not exist
except where one black-haired tree slips
up like a drowned woman into the hot sky.
The town is silent. The night boils with eleven stars
Oh starry starry night! This is how
I want to die

It moves. They are all alive.
Even the moon bulges in its orange irons
to push children, like a god from its eye.
The old unseen serpent swallows up the stars.   10
Oh starry starry night! This is how
I want to die:

into that rushing beast of the night,
sucked up by that great dragon, to split
from my life with no flag,
no belly,
no cry.

The Starry Night, 1889, by Vincent van Gogh (1853–1890). Oil on canvas, 29″ × 36¼″. Acquired through the Lillie P. Bliss Bequest. (472.1941). The Museum of Modern Art, New York, NY, U.S.A. Digital image © The Museum of Modern Art/Licensed by SCALA/Art Resource, NY. Reproduced with permission.

FOR ANALYSIS

1. In what ways does your reaction to the painting agree with Sexton's? In what ways does it differ? Does her poem open your eyes to elements of the painting you had not initially seen? Explain.

2. The first two **stanzas** of the poem end with the refrain "This is how / I want to die." What does "This" refer to? In what sense might *The Starry Night* be described as a painting about death?

3. Around the time of this painting, van Gogh was much preoccupied with cypress trees. He wrote his brother, "The tree is as beautiful of line and proportion as an Egyptian obelisk. And the green has such a quality of distinction. It is a splash of black in a sunny landscape, but it is one of the most interesting black notes, and the most difficult to hit off exactly that I can imagine." How is Sexton's reference to the cypress tree in the opening lines of her poem related to her overall reading of the painting?

4. Describe the difference in brushstrokes van Gogh uses for the sky and those he uses for the village. How is this difference related to the painting's **theme**?

5. *The Starry Night* was painted in the town of Saint-Rémy. Later in the same year, van Gogh did another painting, this one in the town of Arles, to which he gave the same title. Look up this later painting, and compare the differences in the painter's handling of light, both natural and artificial.

6. Some of van Gogh's paintings have been described as mystical. Which of his two *Starry Night* paintings does the term best fit? Explain. What similarities and differences do you find between the depiction of the village and the sky in the two works?

DONALD FINKEL   (1929–2008)

THE GREAT WAVE: HOKUSAI   1959

But we will take the problem in its most obscure manifestation, and suppose that our spectator is an average Englishman. A trained observer, carefully hidden behind a screen, might notice a dilation in his eyes, even an intake of his breath, perhaps a grunt.

—Herbert Read, *The Meaning of Art*

It is because the sea is blue,
Because Fuji is blue, because the bent blue
Men have white faces, like the snow
On Fuji, like the crest of the wave in the sky the color of their
Boats. It is because the air
Is full of writing, because the wave is still: that nothing
Will harm these frail strangers,
That high over Fuji in an earthcolored sky the fingers
Will not fall; and the blue men
Lean on the sea like snow, and the wave like a mountain leans   10
Against the sky.

        In the painter's sea
All fishermen are safe. All anger bends under his unity.
But the innocent bystander, he merely
'Walks round a corner, thinking of nothing': hidden
Behind a screen we hear his cry.
He stands half in and half out of the world; he is the men,
But he cannot see below Fuji
The shore the color of sky; he is the wave, he stretches
His claws against strangers. He is   20
Not safe, not even from himself. His world is flat.
He fishes a sea full of serpents, he rides his boat
Blindly from wave to wave toward Ararat.

The Great Wave Off Kanagawa, 1831–1833, by Katsushika Hokusai

FOR ANALYSIS

1. The "average Englishman" or indeed any other eyewitness to the actual scene depicted in this print would reasonably assume that the men in the boats are in imminent danger of being drowned by the enormous, menacing wave about to crash down upon them. Yet that is not how the poet interprets the scene. On what basis does he declare "that nothing / Will harm these frail strangers" (ll. 6–7) and that "In the painter's sea / All fishermen are safe" (ll. 12–13)?

2. What does Finkel mean when he says, "In the painter's sea / All fishermen are safe. All anger bends under his unity" (ll. 12–13)? How has the artist's representation of nature changed its reality—that is, eliminated the danger and imposed unity?

3. What does the "innocent bystander" not understand that the poet does? Why is the bystander not safe from himself? In contrast to the world represented by the artist, what kind of world does the bystander inhabit? Why is his sea "full of serpents" (l. 22), and why is his boat headed for Ararat (l. 23)?

4. Finkel's epigraph is taken from a passage in section 1, paragraph 17, of Herbert Read's *The Meaning of Art* (1968). Read the passage, which defines "the problem," and explain why Finkel uses it to introduce his poem.

5. Compare Finkel's poem with Keats's "Ode on a Grecian Urn" (p. 1221), and discuss the similarities and differences in the way they interpret the visual work that has inspired them to poetry.

'OUT, OUT—'[1] 1916

The buzz-saw snarled and rattled in the yard
And made dust and dropped stove-length sticks of wood,
Sweet-scented stuff when the breeze drew across it.
And from there those that lifted eyes could count
Five mountain ranges one behind the other
Under the sunset far into Vermont.
And the saw snarled and rattled, snarled and rattled,
As it ran light, or had to bear a load.
And nothing happened: day was all but done.
Call it a day, I wish they might have said   10
To please the boy by giving him the half hour
That a boy counts so much when saved from work.
His sister stood beside them in her apron
To tell them 'Supper.' At the word, the saw,
As if to prove saws knew what supper meant,
Leaped out at the boy's hand, or seemed to leap—
He must have given the hand. However it was,
Neither refused the meeting. But the hand!
The boy's first outcry was a rueful laugh,
As he swung toward them holding up the hand   20
Half in appeal, but half as if to keep
The life from spilling. Then the boy saw all—
Since he was old enough to know, big boy
Doing a man's work, though a child at heart—
He saw all spoiled. 'Don't let him cut my hand off—
The doctor, when he comes. Don't let him, sister!'
So. But the hand was gone already.
The doctor put him in the dark of ether.
He lay and puffed his lips out with his breath.
And then—the watcher at his pulse took fright.   30
No one believed. They listened at his heart.
Little—less—nothing!—and that ended it.
No more to build on there. And they, since they
Were not the one dead, turned to their affairs.

---

[1] The title is taken from the famous speech of Macbeth upon hearing that his wife has died (*Macbeth*, act V, scene 5).

NOTHING GOLD CAN STAY   1923

Nature's first green is gold,
Her hardest hue to hold.
Her early leaf's a flower;
But only so an hour.
Then leaf subsides to leaf.
So Eden sank to grief,
So dawn goes down to day.
Nothing gold can stay.

FOR ANALYSIS

1. Does this poem protest or accept the transitoriness of things?

2. Why does Frost use the word *subsides* in line 5 rather than a word like *expands* or *grows*?

3. How are "Nature's first green" (l. 1), "Eden" (l. 6), and "dawn" (l. 7) linked together?

STOPPING BY WOODS ON A SNOWY EVENING   1923

Whose woods these are I think I know.
His house is in the village though;
He will not see me stopping here
To watch his woods fill up with snow.

My little horse must think it queer
To stop without a farmhouse near
Between the woods and frozen lake
The darkest evening of the year.

He gives his harness bells a shake
To ask if there is some mistake.
The only other sound's the sweep
Of easy wind and downy flake.

The woods are lovely, dark and deep,
But I have promises to keep,
And miles to go before I sleep,
And miles to go before I sleep.

10

FOR ANALYSIS

1. What does the description of the horse tell us about the speaker?
2. What function does the repetition in the last two lines of the poem serve?
3. Why does the speaker refer to the owner of the woods in the opening **stanza**?

DESIGN   1936

I found a dimpled spider, fat and white,
On a white heal-all, holding up a moth
Like a white piece of rigid satin cloth—
Assorted characters of death and blight
Mixed ready to begin the morning right,
Like the ingredients of a witches' broth—
A snow-drop spider, a flower like a froth,
And dead wings carried like a paper kite.

What had that flower to do with being white,
The wayside blue and innocent heal-all?   10
What brought the kindred spider to that height,
Then steered the white moth thither in the night?
What but design of darkness to appall?—
If design govern in a thing so small.

WRITING TOPIC

Compare this poem with Dickinson's "Apparently with no surprise" (p. 1225).

PABLO NERUDA   (1904–1973)

THE DEAD WOMAN   1972

If suddenly you do not exist,
if suddenly you are not living,
I shall go on living.

I do not dare,
I do not dare to write it,
if you die.

I shall go on living.

Because where a man has no voice,
there, my voice.

Where blacks are beaten,   10
I can not be dead.
When my brothers go to jail
I shall go with them.

When victory,
not my victory
but the great victory
arrives,
even though I am mute I must speak:
I shall see it come even though I am blind.

No, forgive me.   20
If you are not living,
if you, beloved, my love,
if you
have died,
all the leaves will fall on my breast,
it will rain upon my soul night and day,
the snow will burn my heart,
I shall walk with cold and fire and death and snow,
my feet will want to march toward where you sleep,
but   30
I shall go on living,
because you wanted me to be, above all things,
untamable,
and, love, because you know that I am not just one man
but all men.

DYLAN THOMAS (1914–1953)

DO NOT GO GENTLE INTO THAT GOOD NIGHT 1952

Do not go gentle into that good night,
Old age should burn and rave at close of day;
Rage, rage against the dying of the light.

Though wise men at their end know dark is right,
Because their words had forked no lightning they
Do not go gentle into that good night.

Good men, the last wave by, crying how bright
Their frail deeds might have danced in a green bay,
Rage, rage against the dying of the light.

Wild men who caught and sang the sun in flight,   10
And learn, too late, they grieved it on its way,
Do not go gentle into that good night.

Grave men, near death, who see with blinding sight
Blind eyes could blaze like meteors and be gay,
Rage, rage against the dying of the light.

And you, my father, there on the sad height,
Curse, bless, me now with your fierce tears, I pray.
Do not go gentle into that good night.
Rage, rage against the dying of the light.

FOR ANALYSIS

1. What do wise, good, wild, and grave men have in common?

2. Why does the poet use the adjective *gentle* rather than the adverb *gently* in the title?

3. What is the "sad height" (l. 16)?

WRITING TOPIC

This poem is a **villanelle,** which means that it contains only two rhymes and that the first and third lines alternate as the third lines in each stanza following and form a final **couplet.** Why do you think Thomas chose this form for his poem? How does it relate to the poem's subject and its treatment of that subject?

CATHERINE DAVIS   (1924–2002)

AFTER A TIME   1961?

After a time, all losses are the same.
One more thing lost is one thing less to lose;
And we go stripped at last the way we came.

Though we shall probe, time and again, our shame,
Who lack the wit to keep or to refuse,
After a time, all losses are the same.

No wit, no luck can beat a losing game;
Good fortune is a reassuring ruse:
And we go stripped at last the way we came.

Rage as we will for what we think to claim,   10
Nothing so much as this bare thought subdues:
After a time, all losses are the same.

The sense of treachery—the want, the blame—
Goes in the end, whether or not we choose,
And we go stripped at last the way we came.

So we, who would go raging, will go tame
When what we have we can no longer use:
After a time, all losses are the same;
And we go stripped at last the way we came.

FOR ANALYSIS

1. What is this poem's **tone**? How might the fourth **stanza** help you describe it?

2. What kind of losses is the poem talking about?

WRITING TOPIC

This poem is free of concrete **images** and situations. Reflect on how it might be different if the poet had included some. What might be gained? What lost?

DONALD HALL   (B. 1928)

AFFIRMATION   2002

To grow old is to lose everything.
Aging, everybody knows it.
Even when we are young,
we glimpse it sometimes, and nod our heads
when a grandfather dies.
Then we row for years on the midsummer
pond, ignorant and content. But a marriage,
that began without harm, scatters
into debris on the shore,
and a friend from school drops   10
cold on a rocky strand.
If a new love carries us
past middle age, our wife will die
at her strongest and most beautiful.
New women come and go. All go.
The pretty lover who announces
that she is temporary
is temporary. The bold woman,

middle-aged against our old age,
sinks under an anxiety she cannot withstand.　　　　20
Another friend of decades estranges himself
in words that pollute thirty years.
Let us stifle under mud at the pond's edge
and affirm that it is fitting
and delicious to lose everything.

FOR ANALYSIS

1. What exactly does this poem affirm?

2. The first and last lines of the poem end with "to lose everything." If the poem begins and ends the same way, does anything change in the middle? If so, what?

MAKING CONNECTIONS

The last sentence of the poem seems to allude to Wilfred Owens's "Dulce et Decorum Est" (p. 462). Why do you think Hall might have made this **allusion**?

WRITING TOPIC

Did you identify with the "we" in lines 3 through 5? Or lines 6 and 7? How aware are you of the fact that, as Hall puts it, "all go" (l. 15)? Reflect on the ways in which you do and don't think about the inevitable fact of death.

MARY OLIVER　(B. 1935)

WHEN DEATH COMES　1992

When death comes
like the hungry bear in autumn;
when death comes and takes all the bright coins from his purse

to buy me, and snaps the purse shut;
when death comes
like the measle-pox;

when death comes
like an iceberg between the shoulder blades,

I want to step through the door full of curiosity, wondering:
what is it going to be like, that cottage of darkness?　　　　10

And therefore I look upon everything
as a brotherhood and a sisterhood,

and I look upon time as no more than an idea,
and I consider eternity as another possibility,

and I think of each life as a flower, as common
as a field daisy, and as singular,

and each name a comfortable music in the mouth,
tending, as all music does, toward silence,

and each body a lion of courage, and something
precious to the earth.   20

When it's over, I want to say: all my life
I was a bride married to amazement.
I was the bridegroom, taking the world into my arms.

When it's over, I don't want to wonder
if I have made of my life something particular, and real.
I don't want to find myself sighing and frightened,
or full of argument.

I don't want to end up simply having visited this world.

For Analysis

1. This poem turns on a series of **images.** Describe each image associated with
approaching death, evaluating its effectiveness and appropriateness.

2. What is the "cottage of darkness" (l. 10)?

3. What images are associated with life and experience? Are they effective? Explain.

4. What is wrong with "simply having visited this world" (l. 28)?

Writing Topic

Lines 24–27 express the poet's attitude toward life as its end approaches. In an essay,
explain how a life that is "particular, and real" leads naturally to a death that does not
generate either sighing and fear, or argument.

Alicia Ostriker   (B. 1937)

Daffodils   2005

For David Lehman

Ten thousand saw I at a glance
Tossing their heads in sprightly dance.
            —William Wordsworth

> Going to hell so many times tears it
> Which explains poetry.
> —JACK SPICER

The day the war against Iraq begins
I'm photographing the yellow daffodils
With their outstretched arms and ruffled cups
Blowing in the wind of Jesus Green

Edging the lush grassy moving river
Along with the swans and ducks
Under a soft March Cambridge sky
Embellishing the earth like a hand

Starting to illustrate a children's book
Where people in light clothes come out   10
To play, to frisk and run about
With their lovers, friends, animals, and children

As down every stony back road of history
They've always done in the peaceful springs
—Which in a sense is also hell because
The daffodils do look as if they dance

And make some of us in the park want to dance
And breathe deeply and I know that
Being able to eat and incorporate beauty like this
I am privileged and by that token can   20

Taste pain, roll it on my tongue, it's good
The cruel wars are good the stupidity is good,
The primates hiding in their caves are very good,
They do their best, which explains poetry.

What explains poetry is that life is hard
But better than the alternatives,
The no and the nothing. Look at this light
And color, a splash of brilliant yellow

Punctuating an emerald text, white swans
And mottled brown ducks floating quietly along   30
Whole and alive, like an untorn language
That lacks nothing, that excludes

Nothing. Period. Don't you think
It is our business to defend it

Even the day our masters start a war?
To defend the day we see the daffodils?

FOR ANALYSIS

1. How does the physical **setting** of the poem and the way it is described contrast with the day on which it is set?

2. What is the effect of ending the poem with questions? What kind of questions are they?

3. By the end of the poem, it is clear what the speaker thinks "explains poetry." What is it? How does it explain poetry?

WRITING TOPIC

As the first **epigraph** makes plain, this poem alludes to William Wordsworth's 1807 poem "I Wandered Lonely as a Cloud" (often referred to as "Daffodils"). Find a copy of Wordsworth's poem and write a short essay explaining Ostriker's **allusion**. Why does she point to that poem in particular? What about the subject and spirit of her poem is illuminated by bringing to mind Wordsworth's?

SEAMUS HEANEY   (B. 1939)

MID-TERM BREAK   1966

I sat all morning in the college sick bay
Counting bells knelling classes to a close.
At two o'clock our neighbors drove me home.

In the porch I met my father crying—
He had always taken funerals in his stride—
And Big Jim Evans saying it was a hard blow.

The baby cooed and laughed and rocked the pram
When I came in, and I was embarrassed
By old men standing up to shake my hand

And tell me they were "sorry for my trouble,"   10
Whispers informed strangers I was the eldest,
Away at school, as my mother held my hand

In hers and coughed out angry tearless sighs.
At ten o'clock the ambulance arrived
With the corpse, stanched and bandaged by the nurses.

Next morning I went up into the room. Snowdrops
And candles soothed the bedside; I saw him
For the first time in six weeks. Paler now,

Wearing a poppy bruise on his left temple,
He lay in the four foot box as in his cot.   20
No gaudy scars, the bumper knocked him clear.

A four foot box, a foot for every year.

FOR ANALYSIS

1. Although it contains little **rhyme**, this poem is remarkably musical. Identify the
assonance and **alliteration** that permeate the poem.

2. What event does the poem describe?

3. How is the poem's title relevant?

WRITING TOPIC

Describe the family and the society revealed in this short poem.

JANICE MIRIKITANI (B. 1942)

SUICIDE NOTE 1987

*. . . An Asian-American college student was reported to have jumped to her death
from her dormitory window. Her body was found two days later under a deep cover
of snow. Her suicide note contained an apology to her parents for having received
less than a perfect four-point grade average. . . .*

How many notes written . . .
ink smeared like birdprints in snow.

not good enough   not pretty enough   not smart enough
dear mother and father.
I apologize
for disappointing you.
I've worked very hard,
                not good enough
harder, perhaps to please you.
If only I were a son, shoulders broad   10
as the sunset threading through pine,
I would see the light in my mother's
eyes, or the golden pride reflected

in my father's dream
of my wide, male hands worthy of work
and comfort.
I would swagger through life
muscled and bold and assured,
drawing praises to me
like currents in the bed of wind, virile   20
with confidence.
   not good enough not strong enough not good enough

I apologize.
Tasks do not come easily.
Each failure, a glacier.
Each disapproval, a bootprint.
Each disappointment,
ice above my river.
So I have worked hard.
    not good enough   30
My sacrifice I will drop
bone by bone, perched
on the ledge of my womanhood,
fragile as wings.
    not strong enough
It is snowing steadily
surely not good weather
for flying—this sparrow
sillied and dizzied by the wind
on the edge.   40
    not smart enough
I make this ledge my altar
to offer penance.
This air will not hold me,
the snow burdens my crippled wings,
my tears drop like bitter cloth
softly into the gutter below.
  not good enough not strong enough not smart enough
    Choices thin as shaved
    ice. Notes shredded   50
    drift like snow

on my broken body,
cover me like whispers
of sorries
sorries.

Perhaps when they find me
they will bury
my bird bones beneath
a sturdy pine
and scatter my feathers like   60
unspoken song
over this white and cold and silent
breast of earth.

FOR ANALYSIS

1. Would the speaker kill herself if she were male? Explain.

2. Why does the speaker kill herself? What assumptions about self-worth underlie her act?

3. What function does the bird **imagery** (beginning at l. 31) serve? Do you find these images effective? Explain.

4. Contrast the images associated with the imagined "son" she might have been with the images the speaker uses to display herself.

WRITING TOPICS

1. Argue that this poem should be placed in the thematic section "Culture and Identity" rather than in "Life and Death."

2. Is suicide ever justified? Explain.

JANE KENYON   (1947–1995)

LET EVENING COME   1996

Let the light of late afternoon
shine through chinks in the barn, moving
up the bales as the sun moves down.

Let the cricket take up chafing
as a woman takes up her needles
and her yarn. Let evening come.

Let dew collect on the hoe abandoned
in long grass. Let the stars appear
and the moon disclose her silver horn.

Let the fox go back to its sandy den.   10
Let the wind die down. Let the shed
go black inside. Let evening come.

To the bottle in the ditch, to the scoop
in the oats, to air in the lung
let evening come.

Let it come, as it will, and don't
be afraid. God does not leave us
comfortless, so let evening come.

FOR ANALYSIS

1. What does evening signify in this poem?

2. Why do you think Kenyon includes "air in the lung" (l. 14) as one of the things that evening should be allowed to come to?

3. How would you characterize the sounds and **rhythms** of this poem? How do they serve the subject?

WRITING TOPICS

1. "Let Evening Come" was published shortly after the death of its author. Reflect on how knowing this might change your reading experience or interpretation of the poem. Does it change your sense of what the poem is about? Does it change its emotional **tone**? Should it? Should knowing something about the life of a writer change how you read that writer's work?

2. Do you have an opinion on the poem's assertion that "God does not leave us / comfortless" (ll. 17–18)? What does it mean? Does your agreement or disagreement with that assertion change how you feel about the poem?

YUSEF KOMUNYAKAA (B. 1947)

FACING IT   1988

My black face fades,
hiding inside the black granite.
I said I wouldn't,
dammit: No tears.
I'm stone. I'm flesh.
My clouded reflection eyes me
like a bird of prey, the profile of night
slanted against morning. I turn
this way—the stone lets me go.
I turn that way—I'm inside
the Vietnam Veterans Memorial
again, depending on the light
to make a difference.
I go down the 58,022 names,

10

half-expecting to find
my own in letters like smoke.
I touch the name Andrew Johnson;
I see the booby trap's white flash.
Names shimmer on a woman's blouse
but when she walks away   20
the names stay on the wall.
Brushstrokes flash, a red bird's
wings cutting across my stare.
The sky. A plane in the sky.
A white vet's image floats
closer to me, then his pale eyes
look through mine. I'm a window.
He's lost his right arm
inside the stone. In the black mirror
a woman's trying to erase names: 30
No, she's brushing a boy's hair.

FOR ANALYSIS

1. What is the speaker in "Facing It" facing? Is it one thing? More than one thing? If more than one, does "facing" mean the same thing for each "it"?

2. In what ways does the poem refer to the war itself? Does it include direct represen-tation of the violence or the participants? Indirect representation? Why do you think Komunyakaa chose to refer to it in these ways?

WRITING TOPIC

The Vietnam Veterans Memorial was controversial when it first opened. (If you are not familiar with the memorial, refer to a picture of it.) How does "Facing It" engage how the memorial is experienced by people? What might it have to say to those who criticize the memorial as unpatriotic or disrespectful?

VICTOR HERNÁNDEZ CRUZ   (B. 1949)

PROBLEMS WITH HURRICANES   1991

A campesino looked at the air
And told me:
With hurricanes it's not the wind
or the noise or the water.
I'll tell you he said:
it's the mangoes, avocados
Green plantains and bananas
flying into town like projectiles.

How would your family
feel if they had to tell
The generations that you
got killed by a flying
Banana.   10

Death by drowning has honor
If the wind picked you up
and slammed you
Against a mountain boulder
This would not carry shame
But
to suffer a mango smashing
Your skull
or a plantain hitting your   20
Temple at 70 miles per hour
is the ultimate disgrace.

The campesino takes off his hat—
As a sign of respect
towards the fury of the wind
and says:
Don't worry about the noise
Don't worry about the water
Don't worry about the wind—   30
If you are going out
beware of mangoes
And all such beautiful
sweet things.

MARK HALLIDAY (B. 1949)

CHICKEN SALAD   2007

Three hours before he died,
my father felt he should have an answer
when I asked what he might like to eat.
He remembered a kind of chicken salad he liked
weeks ago when living was more possible
and he said, "Maybe that chicken salad"
but because of the blood in his mouth
and because of his shortness of breath

he had to say it several times before I understood.
So I went out and bought a container of chicken salad,   10
grateful for the illusion of helping,
but when I brought it back to the apartment
my father studied it for thirty seconds
and set it aside on the bed. I wasn't ready
to know what the eyes of the nurse at the hospice
had tried to tell me before dawn, so I said,
"Don't you want your chicken salad, Daddy?"
He glanced at it from a distance of many miles—
little tub of chicken salad down on the planet of
slaughtered birds and mastication, digestion, excretion—   20
and murmured. "Maybe later." He was in
the final austerity
which I was too frazzled to quite recognize
but ever since his death I see with stony clarity
the solitary dignity of
the totality of his knowing
how far beyond the pleasure of chicken salad
he had gone already and would go.

LINDA GREGERSON   (B. 1950)

SWEET   2007

> Linda,
Said my mother when the buildings fell,

before, you understand, we knew a thing
> about the reasons or the ways

> and means,
while we were still dumbfounded, still

bereft of likely narratives, *We cannot*
> *continue to live in a world where we*

> *have so much*
and other people have so little.   10

Sweet, he said.
> Your mother's wrong but sweet, the world

has never self-corrected,
you Americans break my heart.

Our possum—she must be hungry or
    she wouldn't venture out in so

      much daylight—has found
a way to maneuver on top of the snow.

Thin crust. Sometimes her foot breaks through.
    The edge   20

      of the woods for safety or
for safety's hopeful look-alike. *Di-*

delphis, "double-wombed," which is
    to say, our one marsupial:

      the shelter then
the early birth, then shelter perforce again.

Virginiana for the place. The place
    for a queen

      supposed to have her maidenhead.
He was clever.   30

He had moved among the powerful.
    Our possum—possessed

      of thirteen teats, or so
my book informs me, quite a ready-made

republic—guides
    her blind and all-but-embryonic

      young to their pouch
by licking a path from the birth canal.

Resourceful, no? Requiring
    commendable limberness, as does   40

      the part I've seen, the part
where she ferries the juveniles on her back.

Another pair of eyes above
    her shoulder. Sweet. The place

    construed as yet-to-be-written-upon-
by-us.

And many lost. As when
    their numbers exceed the sources of milk

    or when the weaker ones fall
by the wayside. There are   50

principles at work, no doubt:
    beholding a world of harm, the mind

    will apprehend some bringer-of-harm,
some cause, or course,

that might have been otherwise, had we possessed
    the wit to see.

    Or ruthlessness. Or what? Or heart.
My mother's mistake, if that's

the best the world-as-we've-made-it
    can make of her, hasn't   60

    much altered with better advice. It's
wholly premise, rather like the crusted snow.

FOR ANALYSIS

1. What event is referred to at the poem's start?

2. What does the possum stand for? How do you know?

3. Why does "he" say the mother is "sweet" (l. 11)? Does the speaker agree? Why or
why not?

WRITING TOPIC

What are your feelings about the events of September 11, 2001, and what came after?
How old were you then? How did you learn about what happened? What do you
think about how people reacted then? What do you think about the way people think
now of what happened that day and of what happened in response to what happened
that day? Reflect on these questions in a short essay.

MARIE HOWE (B. 1950)

WHAT THE LIVING DO   1998

Johnny, the kitchen sink has been clogged for days, some utensil
     probably fell down there.
And the Drano won't work but smells dangerous, and the crusty
     dishes have piled up

waiting for the plumber I still haven't called. This is the everyday
     we spoke of.
It's winter again: the sky's a deep, headstrong blue, and the sunlight
     pours through

the open living-room windows because the heat's on too high in
     here and I can't turn it off.
For weeks now, driving, or dropping a bag of groceries in the
     street, the bag breaking,

I've been thinking: This is what the living do. And yesterday,
     hurrying along those
wobbly bricks in the Cambridge sidewalk, spilling my coffee
     down my wrist and sleeve,

I thought it again, and again later, when buying a hairbrush:
     This is it.
Parking. Slamming the car door shut in the cold. What you
     called that yearning.   10

What you finally gave up. We want the spring to come and the
     winter to pass. We want
whoever to call or not call, a letter, a kiss—we want
     more and more and then more of it.

But there are moments, walking, when I catch a glimpse of myself
     in the window glass,
say, the window of the corner video store, and I'm gripped by a
     cherishing so deep

for my own blowing hair, chapped face, and unbuttoned coat
     that I'm speechless:
I am living. I remember you.

FOR ANALYSIS

1. Who do you think Johnny might be?

2. What is it that Johnny "finally gave up" (l. 11)?

3. What kinds of things make the speaker stop and think about Johnny? How does she characterize these thoughts?

WRITING TOPIC

Often we think of the dead in terms of loss—of who they were, of what they meant to us, of how they are gone. The speaker in "What the Living Do" thinks of them in terms of what the title names—what those of us still here do in our everyday lives. Write an essay in which you describe the ways in which you think of those who are no longer with us.

MARK TURPIN (B. 1953)

THE MAN WHO BUILT THIS HOUSE 2003

First realize he didn't build it for himself,
and that changes a man, and the way he thinks
about building a house. There is joy but
it's a colder type—he'd as easily joy in
tearing it down, as we have done, down
to the bare frame, loaded boxes of lath
and plaster, stirring a dust unstirred since
well, we know the date: Thursday, June 19, 1930.
Date on the newspaper stuffed between
the doorbell battery and the box it lodged in.   10
Not so long ago, seventy years, historical
only to a Californian. The headline: "Admiral Byrd
Given Welcome In N.Y." "Rear Admiral
Richard E. Byrd, conqueror of the South Pole."
Safe to say, the man who built this house
is gone or nearly gone by now—and we think
of the houses we have built, and the strangers
who will certainly, eventually come to change
or tear them down—that further event that
needs to happen. And there is a foulness   20
to this dust, dust locked in walls till
we arrived to release it to the world again.
So, maybe, all is as it should be. Still, the man
himself haunts me. I noticed it—especially

after my apprentice saw fit to criticize his work,
this neat but spindly frame of rough 2 × 4's—
2 × 4's for the walls, the rafters, even for the ceiling joists
(that he tied to the ridge to keep the ceiling from sagging)
that functioned adequately all these years
till we knocked it loose. And so, for reasons   30
my apprentice wouldn't understand, I admit
a liking, yes, for him and for this sketch
of a house, the lightness of his eye, as if
there might be something else to think about:
a sister taken sick, or maybe just a book or
a newspaper with a coffee and a smoke, as if
to say to the world: This is all you take from me.
Of course, having lived here a month already,
I know better—accustomed now to the
hieroglyphs of his keel marks, his red crayon   40
with an arrow denoting the sole plate of a wall,
imaginary, invisible lines that he
unknowing, passes on to me, numbers and lines
radiating from the corners and the eaves
—where the bird nests hide inside the vents—
all lining up, falling plumb, coming square and true
for me, and all his offhand easiness just a guise
for a mind too quick ever to be satisfied
—just moving quickly through the motions.
And, now, what he has to show for it, hauled away   50
in boxes and bags, and me about to alter
what's left—not like Byrd's Pole, fixed
forever. The pure radiating lines forever
flowing and unalterable—lines of mind only,
without a house attached. And yet, even a South Pole
doesn't seem much of an accomplishment to us—
to have merely found another place on Earth.
There is a special pity that we reserve
for the dead, trapped in their newspapers'
images of time, wearing what they wore,   60
doing what they did. I feel as much for this man here,
and for the force it took to pull a chalked string
off the floor, let it snap, and, make a wall.
Something apart from something else,
not forever but for a little while.
He must have felt it too, a man like him,
else why leave the newspaper for us?

CONNECTING POEMS: ANIMAL FATES

The poems in this unit focus on the ways in which our own reflections on mortality can involve the animal world beyond the human. They consider the decisions people must make when faced with the death of animals, the way such deaths can make us think about our own lives, and the thoughts about the mysteries of life itself that as innocent a gesture as playing with a cat can prompt.

ELIZABETH BISHOP (1911–1979)

THE FISH   1946

I caught a tremendous fish
and held him beside the boat
half out of water, with my hook
fast in a corner of his mouth.
He didn't fight.
He hadn't fought at all.
He hung a grunting weight,
battered and venerable
and homely. Here and there
his brown skin hung in strips   10
like ancient wallpaper,
and its pattern of darker brown
was like wallpaper:
shapes like full-blown roses
stained and lost through age.
He was speckled with barnacles,
fine rosettes of lime,
and infested
with tiny white sea-lice,
and underneath two or three   20
rags of green weed hung down.
While his gills were breathing in
the terrible oxygen
—the frightening gills,
fresh and crisp with blood,
that can cut so badly—
I thought of the coarse white flesh

packed in like feathers,
the big bones and the little bones,
the dramatic reds and blacks
of his shiny entrails,   30
and the pink swim-bladder
like a big peony.
I looked into his eyes
which were far larger than mine
but shallower, and yellowed,
the irises backed and packed
with tarnished tinfoil
seen through the lenses
of old scratched isinglass.   40
They shifted a little, but not
to return my stare.
—It was more like the tipping
of an object toward the light.
I admired his sullen face,
the mechanism of his jaw,
and then I saw
that from his lower lip
—if you could call it a lip—
grim, wet, and weaponlike,   50
hung five old pieces of fish-line,
or four and a wire leader
with the swivel still attached,
with all their five big hooks
grown firmly in his mouth.
A green line, frayed at the end
where he broke it, two heavier lines,
and a fine black thread
still crimped from the strain and snap
when it broke and he got away.   60
Like medals with their ribbons
frayed and wavering,
a five-haired beard of wisdom
trailing from his aching jaw.
I stared and stared
and victory filled up
the little rented boat,
from the pool of bilge
where oil had spread a rainbow
around the rusted engine   70
to the bailer rusted orange,
the sun-cracked thwarts,

the oarlocks on their strings,
the gunnels—until everything
was rainbow, rainbow, rainbow!
And I let the fish go.

FOR ANALYSIS

1. What is the nature of the speaker's "victory" (l. 66)?

2. Where does the poem turn—that is, where does the poem shift its attention to
something that changes what it is about and what it means?

WRITING TOPIC

"The Fish" is packed with details. List the details Bishop includes, breaking them
down into the groups in which they appear (for example, those describing the fish's
skin, those describing the boat). Then reflect on how the poem uses these details. How
do they create pictures, set moods, imply thoughts and feelings?

WILLIAM STAFFORD   (1914-1995)

TRAVELING THROUGH THE DARK   1962

Traveling through the dark I found a deer
dead on the edge of the Wilson River road.
It is usually best to roll them into the canyon:
that road is narrow; to swerve might make more dead.

By glow of the tail-light I stumbled back of the car
and stood by the heap, a doe, a recent killing;
she had stiffened already, almost cold.
I dragged her off; she was large in the belly.

My fingers touching her side brought me the reason—
her side was warm; her fawn lay there waiting,   10
alive, still, never to be born.
Beside that mountain road I hesitated.

The car aimed ahead its lowered parking lights;
under the hood purred the steady engine.
I stood in the glare of the warm exhaust turning red;
around our group I could hear the wilderness listen.

I thought hard for us all—my only swerving—,
then pushed her over the edge into the river.

FOR ANALYSIS

1. Why is it best to clear the dead deer off the road? Why does the speaker hesitate?

2. How is the speaker's car described? Why do you think Stafford describes it this way?

3. Stafford uses versions of the word *swerve* twice. Why do you think he uses them?

WRITING TOPIC

Stafford chose not to explain how the deer came to be dead, perhaps in part because it is obvious that cars kill deer on this road often. Why else might he not have mentioned it? What could this poem be saying about this unnamed cause?

WILLIAM GREENWAY (B. 1947)

PIT PONY 1987

There are only a few left, he says,
kept by old Welsh miners, souvenirs, like
gallstones or gold teeth, torn
from this "pit," so cold and wet my
breath comes out a soul up
into my helmet's lantern
beam, anthracite walls running,
gleaming, and the floors iron-rutted
with tram tracks, the almost pure
rust that grows and waves like   10
orange moss in the gutters of water
that used to rise and drown.
He makes us turn all lights off, almost
a mile down. While children scream
I try to see anything, my hand touching
my nose, my wife beside me—darkness palpable,
a velvet sack over our heads, even the glow
of watches left behind. This is where
they were born, into this nothing, felt
first with their cold noses for the shaggy   20
side and warm bag of black
milk, pulled their trams for twenty
years through pitch, past birds
that didn't sing, through doors
opened by five-year-olds who sat
in the cheap, complete blackness listening
for steps, a knock. And they
died down here, generation after

generation. The last one, when it
dies in the hills, not quite blind, the mines   30
closed forever, will it die strangely? Will it
wonder dimly why it was exiled from the rest
of its race, from the dark flanks of the soft
mother, what these timbers are that hold up
nothing but blue? If this is the beginning
of death, this wind, these stars?

FOR ANALYSIS

1. What are there only a few of left in the poem's first line?

2. While down in the mine, the speaker imagines life for the ponies that worked
there. How might the speaker's act of imagination be affected by the fact that he is
touring the mine with his family?

3. What is the **tone** of the poem's description of the pony's lives in the pits? How
about the tone of the description of life aboveground? Is it what you might expect?
Why or why not?

WRITING TOPIC

Write (or describe) a poem written in whole or in part from the **point of view** of an
animal, and reflect on what you've written. How is the animal's life like and unlike
human life? Can our imagination of an animal's interior life ever approach what it's
actually like?

EDWARD HIRSCH   (B. 1950)

WILD GRATITUDE   1986

Tonight when I knelt down next to our cat, Zooey,
And put my fingers into her clean cat's mouth,
And rubbed her swollen belly that will never know kittens,
And watched her wriggle onto her side, pawing the air,
And listened to her solemn little squeals of delight,
I was thinking about the poet, Christopher Smart,
Who wanted to kneel down and pray without ceasing
In everyone of the splintered London streets,

And was locked away in the madhouse at St. Luke's
With his sad religious mania, and his wild gratitude,   10
And his grave prayers for the other lunatics,
And his great love for his speckled cat, Jeoffry.
All day today—August 13, 1983—I remembered how

Christopher Smart blessed this same day in August, 1759,
For its calm bravery and ordinary good conscience.

This was the day that he blessed the Postmaster General
"And all conveyancers of letters" for their warm humanity,
And the gardeners for their private benevolence
And intricate knowledge of the language of flowers,
And the milkmen for their universal human kindness.   20
This morning I understood that he loved to hear—
As I have heard—the soft clink of milk bottles
On the rickety stairs in the early morning,

And how terrible it must have seemed
When even this small pleasure was denied him.
But it wasn't until tonight when I knelt down
And slipped my hand into Zooey's waggling mouth
That I remembered how he'd called Jeoffry "the servant
Of the Living God duly and daily serving Him,"
And for the first time understood what it meant.   30
Because it wasn't until I saw my own cat

Whine and roll over on her fluffy back
That I realized how gratefully he had watched
Jeoffry fetch and carry his wooden cork
Across the grass in the wet garden, patiently
Jumping over a high stick, calmly sharpening
His claws on the woodpile, rubbing his nose
Against the nose of another cat, stretching, or
Slowly stalking his traditional enemy, the mouse,
A rodent, "a creature of great personal valour,"   40
And then dallying so much that his enemy escaped.

And only then did I understand
It is Jeoffry—and every creature like him—
Who can teach us how to praise—purring
In their own language,
Wreathing themselves in the living fire.

For Analysis

1. What is the "wild gratitude" of the poem for? Why is it "wild"?

2. Is there any sense of death in this poem? Is there anything about the focus on praising life that relates to death?

3. Does the speaker consider Smart to have been mad? Why or why not? How do you know?

MAKING CONNECTIONS

1. How do these poems create moments in which the speakers think of animals as individual beings? How do they create personal (or emotional) connections with animals?

2. Some of these poems confront humans with a dilemma about killing animals. How does each resolve its dilemma? How does each poem present the decision that is made? Do any of them judge the decision?

3. What do humans do for animals in these poems? What do animals do for humans? Reflect on what these poems as a group say about the relationship between humans and nonhuman animals.

WRITING TOPIC

Animals often appear in poems as vehicles through which poets can express something about themselves, or more generally about human life—or even more broadly, about life itself. Sometimes animals appear as themselves, as the objects of fascination or affection, but other times their appearance can mirror the way humans tend to use animals for their own purposes. How would you describe Hirsch's use of Zooey? How do you feel about the way animals are used in poems, and in life?

CONNECTING POEMS:
SEIZING THE DAY

This section contains a range of poems, some quite similar, some very different; all could be said to fall in the line of poems that confront the idea that at some point in our lives, we feel as if we must seize the day, or that we have failed to do so. As you read, listen for the way in which these poets reflect on life's way of reminding us that we're not here forever.

RAINER MARIA RILKE   (1875–1926)

ARCHAIC TORSO OF APOLLO[1]   1908

We cannot know his legendary head
with eyes like ripening fruit. And yet his torso
is still suffused with brilliance from inside,
like a lamp, in which his gaze, now turned to low,

gleams in all its power. Otherwise
the curved breast could not dazzle you so, nor could

[1] Translated by Stephen Mitchell.

a smile run through the placid hips and thighs
to that dark center where procreation flared.

Otherwise this stone would seem defaced
beneath the translucent cascade of the shoulders   10
and would not glisten like a wild beast's fur:

would not, from all the borders of itself,
burst like a star: for here there is no place
that does not see you. You must change your life.

FOR ANALYSIS

1. Who was Apollo? Why can we not know his legendary head?
2. How would you describe the poem's **tone**? What is the experience it expresses?
3. Who utters the poem's last sentence? Who is "you"?
4. What motivates the poem's final statement? Were you expecting it?

WRITING TOPIC

Rilke worked for sculptor Auguste Rodin for a time, studying his sculptures and
sculpture in general because he wanted his poetry to be less **abstract** and more
concrete. Write or describe an alternative poem to this in which the ideas are
explored and the sentiments are expressed with less concrete **imagery**. How might
you do it? How would it compare to Rilke's?

JAMES WRIGHT   (1927–1980)

LYING IN A HAMMOCK AT WILLIAM DUFFY'S FARM IN PINE ISLAND, MINNESOTA   1990

Over my head, I see the bronze butterfly,
Asleep on the black trunk,
Blowing like a leaf in green shadow.
Down the ravine behind the empty house,
The cowbells follow one another
Into the distances of the afternoon.
To my right,
In a field of sunlight between two pines,
The droppings of last year's horses
Blaze up into golden stones.   10
I lean back, as the evening darkens and comes on.

A chicken hawk floats over, looking for home.
I have wasted my life.

FOR ANALYSIS

1. What is the speaker doing as he sees the things he describes in this poem?

2. What unites the different things the speaker sees? Is there anything more than the fact that he can see them from where he lies?

3. What might the last line mean? Does what the speaker has been doing constitute the wasting of his life, or has he wasted his life not doing more of it? Defend your answer.

4. Do you think there might be any special significance to the fact that the day is ending at the end of the poem? What might it be?

WRITING TOPIC

Poets sit around a lot, thinking and looking at things. Write an essay in which you honestly consider the writing of poetry as an activity, calling, or profession. Is it a noble profession? A necessary one? Is it a nice thing to have people doing? Is it a waste of time? Explain your answer(s).

BILLY COLLINS (B. 1941)

THE SANDHILL CRANES
OF NEBRASKA 2011

Too bad you weren't here six months ago,
was a lament I heard on my visit to Nebraska.
You could have seen the astonishing spectacle
of the sandhill cranes, thousands of them
feeding and even dancing on the shores of the Platte River.

There was no point in pointing out
the impossibility of my being there then
because I happened to be somewhere else,
so I nodded and put on a look of mild disappointment
if only to be part of the commiseration.   10

It was the same look I remember wearing
about six months ago in Georgia
when I was told that I had just missed
the spectacular annual outburst of azaleas,
brilliant against the green backdrop of spring

and the same in Vermont six months before that
when I arrived shortly after

the magnificent foliage had gloriously peaked,
Mother Nature, as she is called,
having touched the hills with her many-colored brush,   20

a phenomenon that occurs, like the others,
around the same time every year when I am apparently off
in another state, stuck in a motel lobby
with the local paper and a styrofoam cup of coffee,
busily missing God knows what.

FOR ANALYSIS

1. Why does the speaker miss the various events he mentions?
2. What do these events have in common?
3. How does the speaker feel about missing these things? How do you know?
4. What is important about the details Collins provides in the final **stanza**?

WRITING TOPIC

"Mother nature, as she is called," in Collins's words (l. 19), is the source of much
attention in poetry, from the pastoral poems of ancient Greece to the poems of the
British Romantics. Often the poems take nature as a topic in order to reflect on
human life or grand metaphysical questions about existence or religion. Write about
"Sandhill Cranes of Nebraska" as a nature poem. How does Collins represent nature
in this poem? Why does he take nature as a subject here?

BARBARA RAS   (B. 1949)

YOU CAN'T HAVE IT ALL   1997

But you can have the fig tree and its fat leaves like clown hands
gloved with green. You can have the touch of a single eleven-year-old finger
on your cheek, waking you at one a.m. to say the hamster is back.
You can have the purr of the cat and the soulful look
of the black dog, the look that says, If I could I would bite
every sorrow until it fled, and when it is August,
you can have it August and abundantly so. You can have love,
though often it will be mysterious, like the white foam
that bubbles up at the top of the bean pot over the red kidneys
until you realize foam's twin is blood.   10
You can have the skin at the center between a man's legs,
so solid, so doll-like. You can have the life of the mind,

glowing occasionally in priestly vestments, never admitting pettiness,
never stooping to bribe the sullen guard who'll tell you
all roads narrow at the border.
You can speak a foreign language, sometimes,
and it can mean something. You can visit the marker on the grave
where your father wept openly. You can't bring back the dead,
but you can have the words *forgive* and *forget* hold hands
as if they meant to spend a lifetime together. And you can be grateful   20
for makeup, the way it kisses your face, half spice, half amnesia, grateful
for Mozart, his many notes racing one another towards joy, for towels
sucking up the drops on your clean skin, and for deeper thirsts,
for passion fruit, for saliva. You can have the dream,
the dream of Egypt, the horses of Egypt and you riding in the hot sand.
You can have your grandfather sitting on the side of your bed,
at least for a while, you can have clouds and letters, the leaping
of distances, and Indian food with yellow sauce like sunrise.
You can't count on grace to pick you out of a crowd
but here is your friend to teach you how to high jump,   30
how to throw yourself over the bar, backwards,
until you learn about love, about sweet surrender,
and here are periwinkles, buses that kneel, farms in the mind
as real as Africa. And when adulthood fails you,
you can still summon the memory of the black swan on the pond
of your childhood, the rye bread with peanut butter and bananas
your grandmother gave you while the rest of the family slept.
There is the voice you can still summon at will, like your mother's,
it will always whisper, you can't have it all,
but there is this.   40

FOR ANALYSIS

1. Why is the first word of the poem "But"?

2. Who is "you"?

3. Do you ever have a sense of what "it all" means? Find the moments where the speaker says you can't have something. What connects those things?

WRITING TOPIC

Reread "You Can't Have It All" and record your reflections on these questions: What connects the different items in this poem? Where are their clear transitions or associations between two items, or phrases, or **images**? Where are there jumps without connection, logical or otherwise? Afterward, review your reflections and try to describe the method behind Ras's choices.

TONY HOAGLAND (B. 1953)

I HAVE NEWS FOR YOU   2010

There are people who do not see a broken playground swing
as a symbol of ruined childhood

and there are people who don't interpret the behavior
of a fly in a motel room as a mocking representation of their thought process.

There are people who don't walk past an empty swimming pool
and think about past pleasures unrecoverable

and then stand there blocking the sidewalk for other pedestrians.
I have read about a town somewhere in California where human beings

do not send their sinuous feeder roots
deep into the potting soil of others' emotional lives   10

as if they were greedy six-year-olds
sucking the last half-inch of milkshake up through a noisy straw;

and other persons in the Midwest who can kiss without
debating the imperialist baggage of heterosexuality.

Do you see that creamy, lemon-yellow moon?
There are some people, unlike me and you,

who do not yearn after fame or love or quantities of money as
            unattainable as that moon;
thus, they do not later
                have to waste more time
defaming the object of their former ardor.   20

Or consequently run and crucify themselves
in some solitary midnight Starbucks Golgotha.

I have news for you—
there are people who get up in the morning and cross a room

and open a window to let the sweet breeze in
and let it touch them all over their faces and bodies.

1272

FOR ANALYSIS

1. What kind of person is the speaker describing who does all these things he says others do not do?

2. What does the poem get out of describing the phenomenon on which it focuses in negative terms? That is, why does it talk about some people who don't do these things rather than people who do them?

3. Do you find this poem humorous? If so, what is the source of the humor? How does Hoagland convey it?

4. Does the poem say one kind of person is better than the other? Is it that simple? What do you think the poem might be saying about this question? Does it matter that the speaker is not one of those who can walk by one of these opportunities to muse without musing?

MAKING CONNECTIONS

1. The poems in this section are all in one way or another about opportunities taken or not taken, lives well spent or wasted, things noticed or ignored. Are there any poems that could be seen to have very different takes on these phenomena? Pick two and make the argument.

2. There is a long tradition of carpe diem poetry. The phrase originates with the Roman poet Horace. Find the original quote. What does the second half, after carpe diem, say about the source of the urgency to seize opportunities rather than let them pass by?

3. In these poems about how people choose to live their lives, there are a fair number of references to death. Find a few across the poems. What does each mean in the context of the poem?

WRITING TOPIC

Which kind of person are you? Or are you some combination? Do you have friends or family who seem to be one or the other? Write a short portrait of a person or people in light of Hoagland's distinction. How do you see this person (even if it's you)? How do others see him or her?

CONNECTING POEMS: INTO THE WORLD

The poems in this unit all recognize the intimate, unseverable connection between life and death, a connection many of us, much of the time, would sooner forget. The beauty of the cycle of life is only a small part of this connection; the fragility of life, the short time we have on earth, the danger in which new life and old often finds itself, the risk at which history puts us all—these are part of the life and death connection as well. As you read these poems, watch for the many different ways in which the poets reflect on this connection by focusing, either glancingly or at length, on the moment of birth.

GWENDOLYN BROOKS   (1917–2000)

THE MOTHER   1963

Abortions will not let you forget.
You remember the children you got that you did not get,
The damp small pulps with a little or with no hair,
The singers and workers that never handled the air.
You will never neglect or beat
Them, or silence or buy with a sweet.
You will never wind up the sucking-thumb
Or scuttle off ghosts that come.
You will never leave them, controlling your luscious sigh,
Return for a snack of them, with gobbling mother-eye.   10

I have heard in the voices of the wind the voices of my dim killed children.
I have contracted. I have eased
My dim dears at the breasts they could never suck.
I have said, Sweets, if I sinned, if I seized
Your luck
And your lives from your unfinished reach,
If I stole your births and your names,
Your straight baby tears and your games,
Your stilted or lovely loves, your tumults, your marriages, aches,
       and your deaths,
If I poisoned the beginnings of your breaths,   20
Believe that even in my deliberateness I was not deliberate.
Though why should I whine,
Whine that the crime was other than mine?—
Since anyhow you are dead.
Or rather, or instead,
You were never made.
But that too, I am afraid,
Is faulty: oh, what shall I say, how is the truth to be said?
You were born, you had body, you died.
It is just that you never giggled or planned or cried.   30

Believe me, I loved you all.
Believe me, I knew you, though faintly, and I loved, I loved you
All.

FOR ANALYSIS

1. Who is "you"? What is the effect of using this pronoun? What other choices could
Brooks have made?

2. What is the effect of the speaker's framing her loss in terms of what will never happen—what she and her unborn children will never do?

3. What two phrases are repeated in the final two lines? Why do you think Brooks decided to repeat each?

WRITING TOPIC

It would be too simple to call this an antiabortion poem, though it does not defend abortion, either. Imagine a conversation about this poem between two people with different opinions on this issue. What might each have to say about this poem? What points of agreement might they find? Where would it be harder for them to find common ground?

LISEL MUELLER   (B. 1924)

CURRICULUM VITAE   1996

1992

1) I was born in a Free City, near the North Sea.

2) In the year of my birth, money was shredded into
confetti. A loaf of bread cost a million marks. Of
course I do not remember this.

3) Parents and grandparents hovered around me. The
world I lived in had a soft voice and no claws.

4) A cornucopia filled with treats took me into a building
with bells. A wide-bosomed teacher took me in.

5) At home the bookshelves connected heaven and earth.   10

6) On Sundays the city child waded through pinecones
and primrose marshes, a short train ride away.

7) My country was struck by history more deadly than
earthquakes or hurricanes.

8) My father was busy eluding the monsters. My mother
told me the walls had ears. I learned the burden of secrets.

9) I moved into the too bright days, the too dark nights
of adolescence.

10) Two parents, two daughters, we followed the sun
and the moon across the ocean. My grandparents stayed
behind in darkness.   20

11) In the new language everyone spoke too fast. Eventually
I caught up with them.

12) When I met you, the new language became the language
of love.

13) The death of the mother hurt the daughter into poetry.
The daughter became a mother of daughters.

14) Ordinary life: the plenty and thick of it. Knots tying
threads to everywhere. The past pushed away, the future left
unimagined for the sake of the glorious, difficult, passionate
present.   30

15) Years and years of this.

16) The children no longer children. An old man's pain, an
old man's loneliness.

17) And then my father too disappeared.

18) I tried to go home again. I stood at the door to my
childhood, but it was closed to the public.

19) One day, on a crowded elevator, everyone's face was younger
than mine.

20) So far, so good. The brilliant days and nights are
breathless in their hurry. We follow, you and I.   40

FOR ANALYSIS

1. What is a curriculum vitae?

2. What is the most striking formal aspect of this poem? What does it have to do with
the title? What is the effect on your reading?

3. What about the speaker's early life was difficult? How has the rest of her life been?

4. What does it mean to be "hurt" into poetry? Does the speaker still seem hurt? How
is she at the end of the poem?

WRITING TOPIC

Write a poem in the form of a numbered list. Reflect on the form. Was it easy to use?
Was it difficult? Did the subject you chose fit the form?

SAM HAMILL (B. 1943)

THE ORCHID FLOWER 2002

Just as I wonder
whether it's going to die,
the orchid blossoms

and I can't explain why it
moves my heart, why such pleasure

comes from one small bud
on a long spindly stem, one
blood red gold flower

opening at mid-summer,
tiny, perfect in its hour.   10

Even to a white-
haired craggy poet, it's
purely erotic,

pistil and stamen, pollen,
dew of the world, a spoonful

of earth, and water.
Erotic because there's death
at the heart of birth,

drama in those old sunrise
prisms in wet cedar boughs,   20

deepest mystery
in washing evening dishes
or teasing my wife,

who grows, yes, more beautiful
because one of us will die.

FOR ANALYSIS

1. How old is the orchid blossom? How old is the speaker?

2. Versions of the words *birth* and *death*, or **images** representing them, appear
numerous times in the poem. Why do you think this is?

3. Though this poem is as much about birth as it is death, is it a sad poem? An angry poem? How would you describe its **mood**?

4. What do the last two lines of the poem mean?

WRITING TOPIC

Many poems feature flowers, and whether used as images of life or death, they are often described as beautiful. Imagine (and write!) a poem in which the symbol of natural processes is not conventionally attractive; it can be a plant or an animal, but make sure most people wouldn't instantly think of it as pretty. Reflect on this poem: what changes when the natural object isn't poetically pretty?

DAVID WOJAHN   (B. 1953)

AUGUST, 1953   2011

A nurse gathers up the afterbirth. My mother

⁎

had been howling but now could sleep.

⁎

By this time I am gone—also gathered up

⁎

& wheeled out. Above my jaundiced face the nurses hover.

⁎

Outside, a scab commands a city bus. The picketers battle cops

⁎

& ten thousand Soviet conscripts in goggles

⁎

kneel & cover their eyes. Mushroom cloud above the Gobi,

⁎

& slithering toward Stalin's brain, the blood clot

⁎

takes its time. Ethel Rosenberg has rocketed

⁎

to the afterlife, her hair shooting flame. The afterbirth   10

⁎

is sloshing in a pail, steadied by an orderly who curses

⁎

when the elevator doors stay shut: I am soul & body & medical waste

⁎

foaming to the sewers of St. Paul. I am not yet aware

⁎

of gratitude or shame.
                    I do know the light is everywhere.

FOR ANALYSIS

1. In what moment is this poem set?

2. What is unusual about the situation of this speaker? What verb tense is used? Does it mean what it usually means? What is the effect as you read?

3. What kinds of events does the speaker note? Are they all of the same kind, or of different kinds? If the latter, what are the different kinds, and how do they relate to one another?

4. How would you characterize this poem's **tone**? Is it uniform, or is there more than one emotional shading to it?

MAKING CONNECTIONS

1. How do these poems touch on birth? What does it mean to each?

2. In some of these poems, life and death are private; in others, they become public—no matter whether the anguish is personal or whether the circumstances or issues surrounding them are larger. How does the public intrude on or even help to shape what's private in these poems?

3. While some of these poems are matter-of-fact in their language and **imagery** and some are more dramatic or extreme, all of them are quite emotionally affecting. What are the different ways in which these poems achieve their effects?

WRITING TOPIC

Take a few minutes to look up what happened in the month of your birth. List the events, and then categorize them. What kinds of events turn up? Are they notable, serious, or famous? Are they obscure, absurd, or fun? Would they make for a good poem? If you want, write it.

DRAMA

WOODY ALLEN   (B. 1935)

DEATH KNOCKS   1968

The play takes place in the bedroom of Nat Ackerman's two-story house, somewhere in Kew Gardens.[1] The carpeting is wall-to-wall. There is a big double bed and a large vanity. The room is elaborately furnished and curtained, and on the walls there are several paintings and a not really attractive barometer. Soft theme music as the curtain rises. Nat Ackerman, a bald, paunchy fifty-seven-year-old dress manufacturer, is lying on the bed finishing off tomorrow's Daily News.[2] *He wears a bathrobe and slippers, and reads by a bed light clipped to the white headboard of the bed. The time is near midnight. Suddenly we hear a noise, and Nat sits up and looks at the window.*

Nat. What the hell is that?

(Climbing awkwardly through the window is a sombre, caped figure. The intruder wears a black hood and skintight black clothes. The hood covers his head but not his face, which is middle-aged and stark white. He is something like Nat in appearance. He huffs audibly and then trips over the windowsill and falls into the room.)

Death *(for it is no one else).* Jesus Christ. I nearly broke my neck.
Nat *(watching with bewilderment).* Who are you?
Death. Death.
Nat. Who?
Death. Death. Listen—can I sit down? I nearly broke my neck. I'm shaking like a leaf.
Nat. Who *are* you?
Death. *Death.* You got a glass of water?
Nat. Death? What do you mean, Death?

---

[1] A middle-class neighborhood in the New York City borough of Queens.   [2] The *Daily News* is a tabloid newspaper; the morning edition used to be distributed at about 10 P.M. the previous night.

Death. What is wrong with you? You see the black costume and the whitened face?

Nat. Yeah.

Death. Is it Halloween?

Nat. No.

Death. Then I'm Death. Now can I get a glass of water—or a Fresca?

Nat. If this is some joke—

Death. What kind of joke? You're fifty-seven? Nat Ackerman? One eighteen Pacific Street? Unless I blew it—where's that call sheet? *(He fumbles through pocket, finally producing a card with an address on it. It seems to check.)*

Nat. What do you want with me?

Death. What do I want? What do you think I want?

Nat. You must be kidding. I'm in perfect health.

Death *(unimpressed)*. Uh-huh. *(Looking around)* This is a nice place. You do it yourself?

Nat. We had a decorator, but we worked with her.

Death *(looking at picture on the wall)*. I love those kids with the big eyes.

Nat. I don't want to go yet.

Death. *You* don't want to go? Please don't start in. As it is, I'm nauseous from the climb.

Nat. What climb?

Death. I climbed up the drainpipe. I was trying to make a dramatic entrance. I see the big windows and you're awake reading. I figure it's worth a shot. I'll climb up and enter with a little—you know . . . *(Snaps fingers)* Meanwhile, I get my heel caught on some vines, the drainpipe breaks, and I'm hanging by a thread. Then my cape begins to tear. Look, let's just go. It's been a rough night.

Nat. You broke my drainpipe?

Death. Broke. It didn't break. It's a little bent. Didn't you hear anything? I slammed into the ground.

Nat. I was reading.

Death. You must have really been engrossed. *(Lifting newspaper Nat was reading)* "NAB COEDS IN POT ORGY." Can I borrow this?

Nat. I'm not finished.

Death. Er—I don't know how to put this to you, pal. . . .

Nat. Why didn't you just ring downstairs?

Death. I'm telling you, I could have, but how does it look? This way I get a little drama going. Something. Did you read "Faust"?

Nat. What?

Death. And what if you had company? You're sitting there with important people. I'm Death—I should ring the bell and traipse right in the front? Where's your thinking?

Nat. Listen, Mister, it's very late.

Death. Yeah. Well, you want to go?

Nat. Go where?

Death. Death. It. The Thing. The Happy Hunting Grounds. *(Looking at his own knee)* Y'know, that's a pretty bad cut. My first job, I'm liable to get gangrene yet.

Nat. Now, wait a minute. I need time. I'm not ready to go.

Death. I'm sorry. I can't help you. I'd like to, but it's the moment.

Nat. How can it be the moment? I just merged with Modiste Originals.

Death. What's the difference, a couple of bucks more or less.

Nat. Sure, what do you care? You guys probably have all your expenses paid.

Death. You want to come along now?

Nat *(studying him).* I'm sorry, but I cannot believe you're Death.

Death. Why? What'd you expect—Rock Hudson?

Nat. No, it's not that.

Death. I'm sorry if I disappointed you.

Nat. Don't get upset. I don't know, I always thought you'd be . . . uh . . . taller.

Death. I'm five seven. It's average for my weight.

Nat. You look a little like me.

Death. Who should I look like? I'm your death.

Nat. Give me some time. Another day.

Death. I can't. What do you want me to say?

Nat. One more day. Twenty-four hours.

Death. What do you need it for? The radio said rain tomorrow.

Nat. Can't we work out something?

Death. Like what?

Nat. You play chess?

Death. No, I don't.

Nat. I once saw a picture of you playing chess.

Death. Couldn't be me, because I don't play chess. Gin rummy, maybe.

Nat. You play gin rummy?

Death. Do I play gin rummy? Is Paris a city?

Nat. You're good, huh?

Death. Very good.

Nat. I'll tell you what I'll do—

Death. Don't make any deals with me.

Nat. I'll play you gin rummy. If you win, I'll go immediately. If I win, give me some more time. A little bit—one more day.

Death. Who's got time to play gin rummy?

Nat. Come on. If you're so good.

Death. Although I feel like a game . . .

Nat. Come on. Be a sport. We'll shoot for a half hour.

Death. I really shouldn't.

Nat. I got the cards right here. Don't make a production.

Death. All right, come on. We'll play a little. It'll relax me.

Nat *(getting cards, pad, and pencil).* You won't regret this.

Death. Don't give me a sales talk. Get the cards and give me a Fresca and put out something. For God's sake, a stranger drops in, you don't have potato chips or pretzels.

Nat. There's M&M's downstairs in a dish.

Death. M&M's. What if the President came? He'd get M&M's too?

Nat. You're not the President.

Death. Deal.

(Nat deals, turns up a five.)

Nat. You want to play a tenth of a cent a point to make it interesting?

Death. It's not interesting enough for you?

Nat. I play better when money's at stake.

Death. Whatever you say, Newt.

Nat. Nat, Nat Ackerman. You don't know my name?

Death. Newt, Nat—I got such a headache.

Nat. You want that five?

Death. No.

Nat. So pick.

Death *(surveying his hand as he picks).* Jesus, I got nothing here.

Nat. What's it like?

Death. What's what like?

(Throughout the following, they pick and discard.)

Nat. Death.

Death. What should it be like? You lay there.

Nat. Is there anything after?

Death. Aha, you're saving twos.

Nat. I'm asking. Is there anything after?

Death *(absently).* You'll see.

Nat. Oh, then I will actually see something?

Death. Well, maybe I shouldn't have put it that way. Throw.

Nat. To get an answer from you is a big deal.

Death. I'm playing cards.

Nat. All right, play, play.

Death. Meanwhile, I'm giving you one card after another.

Nat. Don't look through the discards.

Death. I'm not looking. I'm straightening them up. What was the knock card?

Nat. Four. You ready to knock already?

Death. Who said I'm ready to knock. All I asked was what was the knock card.

Nat. And all I asked was is there anything for me to look forward to.

Death. Play.

Nat. Can't you tell me anything? Where do we go?

Death. We? To tell you the truth, *you* fall in a crumpled heap on the floor.

Nat. Oh, I can't wait for that! Is it going to hurt?

Death. Be over in a second.

Nat. Terrific. *(Sighs)* I needed this. A man merges with Modiste Originals . . .

Death. How's four points?

Nat. You're knocking?

Death. Four points is good?

Nat. No, I got two.

Death. You're kidding.

Nat. No, you lose.

Death. Holy Christ, and I thought you were saving sixes.

Nat. No. Your deal. Twenty points and two boxes. Shoot. *(Death deals.)* I must fall on the floor, eh? I can't be standing over the sofa when it happens?

Death. No. Play.

Nat. Why not?

Death. Because you fall on the floor! Leave me alone. I'm trying to concentrate.

Nat. Why must it be on the floor? That's all I'm saying! Why can't the whole thing happen and I'll stand next to the sofa?

Death. I'll try my best. Now can we play?

Nat. That's all I'm saying. You remind me of Moe Lefkowitz. He's also stubborn.

Death. I remind you of Moe Lefkowitz. I'm one of the most terrifying figures you could possibly imagine, and him I remind of Moe Lefkowitz. What is he, a furrier?

Nat. You should be such a furrier. He's good for eighty thousand a year. Passementeries. He's got his own factory. Two points.

Death. What?

Nat. Two points. I'm knocking. What have you got?

Death. My hand is like a basketball score.

Nat. And it's spades.

Death. If you didn't talk so much.

(They redeal and play on.)

Nat. What'd you mean before when you said this was your first job?

Death. What does it sound like?

Nat. What are you telling me—that nobody ever went before?

Death. Sure they went. But I didn't take them.

Nat. So who did?

Death. Others.

Nat. There's others?

Death. Sure. Each one has his own personal way of going.

Nat. I never knew that.

Death. Why should you know? Who are you?

Nat. What do you mean who am I? Why—I'm nothing?

Death. Not nothing. You're a dress manufacturer. Where do you come to knowledge of the eternal mysteries?

Nat. What are you talking about? I make a beautiful dollar. I sent two kids through college. One is in advertising, the other's married. I got my own home.

I drive a Chrysler. My wife has whatever she wants. Maids, mink coat, vacations. Right now she's at the Eden Roc. Fifty dollars a day because she wants to be near her sister. I'm supposed to join her next week, so what do you think I am—some guy off the street?

Death. All right. Don't be so touchy.

Nat. Who's touchy?

Death. How would you like it if I got insulted quickly?

Nat. Did I insult you?

Death. You didn't say you were disappointed in me?

Nat. What do you expect? You want me to throw you a block party?

Death. I'm not talking about that. I mean me personally. I'm too short, I'm this, I'm that.

Nat. I said you looked like me. It's like a reflection.

Death. All right, deal, deal.

(They continue to play as music steals in and the lights dim until all is in total darkness. The lights slowly come up again, and now it is later and their game is over. Nat tallies.)

Nat. Sixty-eight . . . one-fifty . . . Well, you lose.

Death *(dejectedly looking through the deck)*. I knew I shouldn't have thrown that nine. Damn it.

Nat. So I'll see you tomorrow.

Death. What do you mean you'll see me tomorrow?

Nat. I won the extra day. Leave me alone.

Death. You were serious?

Nat. We made a deal.

Death. Yeah, but—

Nat. Don't "but" me. I won twenty-four hours. Come back tomorrow.

Death. I didn't know we were actually playing for time.

Nat. That's too bad about you. You should pay attention.

Death. Where am I going to go for twenty-four hours?

Nat. What's the difference? The main thing is I won an extra day.

Death. What do you want me to do—walk the streets?

Nat. Check into a hotel and go to a movie. Take a *schvitz*.[3] Don't make a federal case.

Death. Add the score again.

Nat. Plus you owe me twenty-eight dollars.

Death. *What?*

Nat. That's right, Buster. Here it is—read it.

Death *(going through pockets)*. I have a few singles—not twenty-eight dollars.

Nat. I'll take a check.

[3] Steam bath.

Death. From what account?

Nat. Look who I'm dealing with.

Death. Sue me. Where do I keep my checking account?

Nat. All right, gimme what you got and we'll call it square.

Death. Listen, I need that money.

Nat. Why should you need money?

Death. What are you talking about? You're going to the Beyond.

Nat. So?

Death. So—you know how far that is?

Nat. So?

Death. So where's gas? Where's tolls?

Nat. We're going by car!

Death. You'll find out. *(Agitatedly)* Look—I'll be back tomorrow, and you'll give me a chance to win the money back. Otherwise I'm in definite trouble.

Nat. Anything you want. Double or nothing we'll play. I'm liable to win an extra week or a month. The way you play, maybe years.

Death. Meantime I'm stranded.

Nat. See you tomorrow.

Death *(being edged to the doorway)*. Where's a good hotel? What am I talking about hotel, I got no money. I'll go sit in Bickford's.[4] *(He picks up the News.)*

Nat. Out. Out. That's my paper. *(He takes it back.)*

Death *(exiting)*. I couldn't just take him and go. I had to get involved in rummy.

Nat *(calling after him)*. And be careful going downstairs. On one of the steps the rug is loose.

(And, on cue, we hear a terrific crash. Nat sighs, then crosses to the bedside table and makes a phone call.)

Nat. Hello, Moe? Me. Listen, I don't know if somebody's playing a joke, or what, but Death was just here. We played a little gin . . . No, *Death.* In person. Or somebody who claims to be Death. But, Moe, he's such a *schlep!*[5]

Curtain

FOR ANALYSIS

1. Consider the stage direction that opens the play. What sort of household is described?

2. The stage direction describes Nat Ackerman as a dress manufacturer. If you were directing the play, how might you convey that information to your audience? Why do you suppose Allen included the information in a stage direction?

3. Reread the stage directions and identify any others that are literary rather than dramatic tools.

---

[4] Bickford's was a chain of inexpensive all-night cafeterias in New York City.   [5] Boring jerk.

4. Describe the speech patterns of the characters. How do they contribute to the play's effect?

MAKING CONNECTIONS

Both *Death Knocks* and Lynn Nottage's *Poof!* (p. 1063) handle the idea of sudden death with a degree of humor. Compare the ways in which Allen and Nottage use a light **tone** to address a serious **theme** like death.

WRITING TOPIC

Either read—or rent a DVD of—Ingmar Bergman's *The Seventh Seal*. In an essay, describe the effect of Allen's central **allusion** to *The Seventh Seal* in *Death Knocks*.

NONFICTION

JOHN DONNE   (1572–1631)

MEDITATION XVII, FROM DEVOTIONS UPON EMERGENT OCCASIONS   1623

Nunc lento sonitu dicunt morieris.
  Now this bell tolling softly for another says to me, Thou must die.

Perchance he for whom this bell tolls may be so ill as that he knows not it tolls for him; and perchance I may think myself so much better than I am, as that they who are about me and see my state may have caused it to toll for me, and I know not that. The church is catholic, universal, so are all her actions; all that she does belongs to all. When she baptizes a child, that 5 action concerns me; for that child is thereby connected to that head which is my head too, and ingrafted into that body whereof I am a member. And when she buries a man, that action concerns me: all mankind is of one author and is one volume; when one man dies, one chapter is not torn out of the book, but translated into a better language; and every chapter must be so translated. 10 God employs several translators; some pieces are translated by age, some by sickness, some by war, some by justice; but God's hand is in every translation, and his hand shall bind up all our scattered leaves again for that library where every book shall lie open to one another. As therefore the bell that rings to a sermon calls not upon the preacher only, but upon the congregation to come, 15 so this bell calls us all; but how much more me, who am brought so near the door by this sickness. There was a contention as far as a suit[1] (in which piety and dignity, religion and estimation, were mingled) which of the religious orders should ring to prayers first in the morning; and it was determined that they should ring first that rose earliest. If we understand aright the dignity of 20 this bell that tolls for our evening prayer, we would be glad to make it ours

---

[1] An argument settled by a lawsuit.

by rising early, in that application, that it might be ours as well as his whose indeed it is. The bell doth toll for him that thinks it doth, and though it intermit again, yet from that minute that that occasion wrought upon him, he is united to God. Who casts not up his eye to the sun when it rises? but who takes off his eye from a comet when that breaks out? Who bends not his ear to any bell which upon any occasion rings? but who can remove it from that bell which is passing a piece of himself out of this world? No man is an island, entire of itself; every man is a piece of the continent, a part of the main. If a clod be washed away by the sea, Europe is the less, as well as if a promontory were, as well as if a manor of thy friend's or of thine own were. Any man's death diminishes me, because I am involved in mankind; and therefore never send to know for whom the bell tolls; it tolls for thee. Neither can we call this a begging of misery or a borrowing of misery, as though we were not miserable enough of ourselves but must fetch in more from the next house, in taking upon us the misery of our neighbors. Truly it were an excusable covetousness if we did; for affliction is a treasure, and scarce any man hath enough of it. No man hath affliction enough that is not matured and ripened by it, and made fit for God by that affliction. If a man carry treasure in bullion, or in a wedge of gold, and have none coined into current moneys, his treasure will not defray him as he travels. Tribulation is treasure in the nature of it, but it is not current money in the use of it, except we get nearer and nearer our home, heaven, by it. Another man may be sick too, and sick to death, and this affliction may lie in his bowels as gold in a mine and be of no use to him; but this bell that tells me of his affliction digs out and applies that gold to me, if by this consideration of another's danger I take mine own into contemplation and so secure myself by making my recourse to my God, who is our only security.

FOR ANALYSIS

1. What does Donne mean when he says that the death bell "tolls for thee" (l. 33)?

2. Toward the end of his meditation, Donne states that "tribulation is treasure" (l. 41). What does he mean? What will that treasure purchase?

3. Donne is justly admired for his use of **figurative language**. What extended **metaphors** does he use to characterize humankind and death?

MAKING CONNECTIONS

Read this meditation with Donne's "Death, Be Not Proud" (p. 1220). What attitude does each have toward death? How does each offer alternatives to fear of death and sadness about death?

WRITING TOPICS

1. What does Donne mean by "affliction is a treasure" (l. 37)? Do you agree? Explain.

2. Identify and analyze the **figurative language** Donne uses to illuminate the human condition and his attitude toward death.

RACHEL CARSON   (1907–1964)

THE OBLIGATION TO ENDURE   1962

The history of life on earth has been a history of interaction between living things and their surroundings. To a large extent, the physical form and the habits of the earth's vegetation and its animal life have been molded by the environment. Considering the whole span of earthly time, the opposite effect, in which life actually modifies its surroundings, has been relatively slight. Only within the moment of time represented by the present century has one species—man—acquired significant power to alter the nature of his world.

During the past quarter century this power has not only increased to one of disturbing magnitude but it has changed in character. The most alarming of all man's assaults upon the environment is the contamination of air, earth, rivers, and sea with dangerous and even lethal materials. This pollution is for the most part irrecoverable; the chain of evil it initiates not only in the world that must support life but in living tissues is for the most part irreversible. In this now universal contamination of the environment, chemicals are the sinister and little-recognized partners of radiation in changing the very nature of the world—the very nature of its life. Strontium 90, released through nuclear explosions into the air, comes to earth in rain or drifts down as fallout, lodges in soil, enters into the grass or corn or wheat grown there, and in time takes up its abode in the bones of a human being, there to remain until his death. Similarly, chemicals sprayed on croplands or forests or gardens lie long in soil, entering into living organisms, passing from one to another in a chain of poisoning and death. Or they pass mysteriously by underground streams until they emerge and, through the alchemy of air and sunlight, combine into new forms that kill vegetation, sicken cattle, and work unknown harm on those who drink from once pure wells. As Albert Schweitzer has said, "Man can hardly even recognize the devils of his own creation."

It took hundreds of millions of years to produce the life that now inhabits the earth—eons of time in which that developing and evolving and diversifying life reached a state of adjustment and balance with its surroundings. The environment, rigorously shaping and directing the life it supported, contained elements that were hostile as well as supporting. Certain rocks gave out dangerous radiation; even within the light of the sun, from which all life draws its energy, there were short-wave radiations with power to injure. Given time—time not in years but in millennia—life adjusts, and a balance has been reached. For time is the essential ingredient; but in the modern world there is no time.

The rapidity of change and the speed with which new situations are created follow the impetuous and heedless pace of man rather than the deliberate pace of nature. Radiation is no longer merely the background radiation of rocks, the bombardment of cosmic rays, the ultraviolet of the sun that have existed before there was any life on earth; radiation is now the unnatural creation of man's tampering with the atom. The chemicals to which life is asked to make its adjustment are no longer merely the calcium and silica and copper and all the rest of the minerals washed out of the rocks and carried in rivers to the sea; they are the synthetic creations of man's inventive mind, brewed in his laboratories, and having no counterparts in nature.

To adjust to these chemicals would require time on the scale that is nature's; 5 it would require not merely the years of a man's life but the life of generations. And even this, were it by some miracle possible, would be futile, for the new chemicals come from our laboratories in an endless stream; almost five hundred annually find their way into actual use in the United States alone. The figure is staggering and its implications are not easily grasped—500 new chemicals to which the bodies of men and animals are required somehow to adapt each year, chemicals totally outside the limits of biologic experience.

Among them are many that are used in man's war against nature. Since the mid-1940s over 200 basic chemicals have been created for use in killing insects, weeds, rodents, and other organisms described in the modern vernacular as "pests"; and they are sold under several thousand different brand names.

These sprays, dusts, and aerosols are now applied almost universally to farms, gardens, forests, and homes—nonselective chemicals that have the power to kill every insect, the "good" and the "bad," to still the song of birds and the leaping of fish in the streams, to coat the leaves with a deadly film, and to linger on in soil—all this though the intended target may be only a few weeds or insects. Can anyone believe it is possible to lay down such a barrage of poisons on the surface of the earth without making it unfit for all life? They should not be called "insecticides," but "biocides."

The whole process of spraying seems caught up in an endless spiral. Since DDT was released for civilian use, a process of escalation has been going on in which ever more toxic materials must be found. This has happened because insects, in a triumphant vindication of Darwin's principle of the survival of the fittest, have evolved super races immune to the particular insecticide used, hence a deadlier one has always to be developed—and then a deadlier one than that. It has happened also because, for reasons to be described later, destructive insects often undergo a "flareback," or resurgence, after spraying, in numbers greater than before. Thus the chemical war is never won, and all life is caught in its violent crossfire.

Along with the possibility of the extinction of mankind by nuclear war, the central problem of our age has therefore become the contamination of man's total environment with such substances of incredible potential for harm—

substances that accumulate in the tissues of plants and animals and even penetrate the germ cells to shatter or alter the very material of heredity upon which the shape of the future depends.

Some would-be architects of our future look toward a time when it will be 10 possible to alter the human germ plasm by design. But we may easily be doing so now by inadvertence, for many chemicals, like radiation, bring about gene mutations. It is ironic to think that man might determine his own future by something so seemingly trivial as the choice of an insect spray.

All this has been risked—for what? Future historians may well be amazed by our distorted sense of proportion. How could intelligent beings seek to control a few unwanted species by a method that contaminated the entire environment and brought the threat of disease and death even to their own kind? Yet this is precisely what we have done. We have done it, moreover, for reasons that collapse the moment we examine them. We are told that the enormous and expanding use of pesticides is necessary to maintain farm production. Yet is our real problem not one of *overproduction*? Our farms, despite measures to remove acreages from production and to pay farmers *not* to produce, have yielded such a staggering excess of crops that the American taxpayer in 1962 is paying out more than one billion dollars a year as the total carrying cost of the surplus-food storage program. And is the situation helped when one branch of the Agriculture Department tries to reduce production while another states, as it did in 1958, "It is believed generally that reduction of crop acreages under provisions of the Soil Bank will stimulate interest in use of chemicals to obtain maximum production on the land retained in crops."

All this is not to say there is no insect problem and no need of control. I am saying, rather, that control must be geared to realities, not to mythical situations, and that the methods employed must be such that they do not destroy us along with the insects.

The problem whose attempted solution has brought such a train of disaster in its wake is an accompaniment of our modern way of life. Long before the age of man, insects inhabited the earth—a group of extraordinarily varied and adaptable beings. Over the course of time since man's advent, a small percentage of the more than half a million species of insects have come into conflict with human welfare in two principal ways: as competitors for the food supply and as carriers of human disease.

Disease-carrying insects become important where human beings are crowded together, especially under conditions where sanitation is poor, as in time of natural disaster or war or in situations of extreme poverty and deprivation. Then control of some sort becomes necessary. It is a sobering fact, however, as we shall presently see, that the method of massive chemical control has had only limited success, and also threatens to worsen the very conditions it is intended to curb.

Under primitive agricultural conditions the farmer had few insect problems. 15 These arose with the intensification of agriculture—the devotion of immense acreages to a single crop. Such a system set the stage for explosive increases in specific insect populations. Single-crop farming does not take advantage of the principles by which nature works; it is agriculture as an engineer might conceive it to be. Nature has introduced great variety into the landscape, but man has displayed a passion for simplifying it. Thus he undoes the built-in checks and balances by which nature holds the species within bounds. One important natural check is a limit on the amount of suitable habitat for each species. Obviously then, an insect that lives on wheat can build up its population to much higher levels on a farm devoted to wheat than on one in which wheat is intermingled with other crops to which the insect is not adapted.

The same thing happens in other situations. A generation or more ago, the towns of large areas of the United States lined their streets with the noble elm tree. Now the beauty they hopefully created is threatened with complete destruction as disease sweeps through the elms, carried by a beetle that would have only limited chance to build up large populations and to spread from tree to tree if the elms were only occasional trees in a richly diversified planting.

Another factor in the modern insect problem is one that must be viewed against a background of geologic and human history: the spreading of thousands of different kinds of organisms from their native homes to invade new territories. This worldwide migration has been studied and graphically described by the British ecologist Charles Elton in his recent book *The Ecology of Invasions*. During the Cretaceous Period, some hundred million years ago, flooding seas cut many land bridges between continents and living things found themselves confined in what Elton calls "colossal separate nature reserves." There, isolated from others of their kind, they developed many new species. When some of the land masses were joined again, about 15 million years ago, these species began to move out into new territories—a movement that is not only still in progress but is now receiving considerable assistance from man.

The importation of plants is the primary agent in the modern spread of species, for animals have almost invariably gone along with the plants, quarantine being a comparatively recent and not completely effective innovation. The United States Office of Plant Introduction alone has introduced almost 200,000 species and varieties of plants from all over the world. Nearly half of the 180 or so major insect enemies of plants in the United States are accidental imports from abroad, and most of them have come as hitchhikers on plants.

In new territory, out of reach of the restraining hand of the natural enemies that kept down its numbers in its native land, an invading plant or animal is able to become enormously abundant. Thus it is no accident that our most troublesome insects are introduced species.

These invasions, both the naturally occurring and those dependent on 20 human assistance, are likely to continue indefinitely. Quarantine and massive chemical campaigns are only extremely expensive ways of buying time. We are faced, according to Dr. Elton, "with a life-and-death need not just to find new technological means of suppressing this plant or that animal"; instead we need the basic knowledge of animal populations and their relations to their surroundings that will "promote an even balance and damp down the explosive power of outbreaks and new invasions."

Much of the necessary knowledge is now available but we do not use it. We train ecologists in our universities and even employ them in our governmental agencies but we seldom take their advice. We allow the chemical death rain to fall as though there were no alternative, whereas in fact there are many, and our ingenuity could soon discover many more if given opportunity.

Have we fallen into a mesmerized state that makes us accept as inevitable that which is inferior or detrimental, as though having lost the will or the vision to demand that which is good? Such thinking, in the words of the ecologist Paul Shepard, "idealizes life with only its head out of water, inches above the limits of toleration of the corruption of its own environment. . . . Why should we tolerate a diet of weak poisons, a home in insipid surroundings, a circle of acquaintances who are not quite our enemies, the noise of motors with just enough relief to prevent insanity? Who would want to live in a world which is just not quite fatal?"

Yet such a world is pressed upon us. The crusade to create a chemically sterile, insect-free world seems to have engendered a fanatic zeal on the part of many specialists and most of the so-called control agencies. On every hand there is evidence that those engaged in spraying operations exercise a ruthless power. "The regulatory entomologists . . . function as prosecutor, judge and jury, tax assessor and collector and sheriff to enforce their own orders," said Connecticut entomologist Neely Turner. The most flagrant abuses go unchecked in both state and federal agencies.

It is not my contention that chemical insecticides must never be used. I do contend that we have put poisonous and biologically potent chemicals indiscriminately into the hands of persons largely or wholly ignorant of their potentials for harm. We have subjected enormous numbers of people to contact with these poisons, without their consent and often without their knowledge. If the Bill of Rights contains no guarantee that a citizen shall be secure against lethal poisons distributed either by private individuals or by public officials, it is surely only because our forefathers, despite their considerable wisdom and foresight, could conceive of no such problem.

I contend, furthermore, that we have allowed these chemicals to be used 25 with little or no advance investigation of their effect on soil, water, wildlife, and man himself. Future generations are unlikely to condone our lack of prudent concern for the integrity of the natural world that supports all life.

There is still very limited awareness of the nature of the threat. This is an era of specialists, each of whom sees his own problem and is unaware of or intolerant of the larger frame into which it fits. It is also an era dominated by industry, in which the right to make a dollar at whatever cost is seldom challenged. When the public protests, confronted with some obvious evidence of damaging results of pesticide applications, it is fed little tranquilizing pills of half truth. We urgently need an end to these false assurances, to the sugar coating of unpalatable facts. It is the public that is being asked to assume the risks that the insect controllers calculate. The public must decide whether it wishes to continue on the present road, and it can do so only when in full possession of the facts. In the words of Jean Rostand, "The obligation to endure gives us the right to know."

FOR ANALYSIS

1. What are the two greatest threats Carson sees to the survival of life on earth?

2. "Future historians may well be amazed by our distorted sense of proportion," Carson writes (para. 11). How does Carson think our sense of proportion is out of whack?

3. There are two kinds of timelines in this essay that operate on radically different scales. What are they? What does Carson achieve by bringing them together?

4. In what year did this selection appear? What were many Americans afraid of at that time? How might the threat in this essay have compared to that one?

MAKING CONNECTIONS

1. Knowledge is very important to Carson here—what it tells us and how we respond to it. Compare this sense of human knowledge to that in Millet's "Girl and Giraffe" (p. 1210). How do they differ?

2. Compare Carson's treatment of fatalism to Alicia Ostriker's in "Daffodils" (p. 1246). How does each describe it, and how does each respond?

WRITING TOPICS

1. How do you feel about the state of our planet today, environmentally or ecologically? Write an account of what you know and what you think and feel about it.

2. Many people don't think of *Silent Spring*, the book by Carson from which this selection is drawn, as literature. Yet it is beautifully written and quite powerful in its ability to capture the world and make the reader think and feel. Do you think this essay is literature? Why or why not? What definition of literature are you depending on for your answer?

JILL CHRISTMAN (B. 1969)

THE SLOTH 2002

There is a nothingness of temperature, a point on the body's mercury where our blood feels neither hot nor cold. I remember a morning swim on the black sand eastern coast of Costa Rica four months after my twenty-two-year-old fiancé was killed in a car accident. Walking into the water, disembodied by grief, I felt no barriers between my skin, the air, and the water.

Later, standing under a trickle of water in the wooden outdoor shower, I heard a rustle, almost soundless, and looking up, expecting something small, I saw my first three-toed sloth. Mottled and filthy, he hung by his meat-hook claws not five feet above my head in the cecropia tree. He peered down at me, his flattened head turned backwards on his neck. Here is a fact: a sloth cannot regulate the temperature of his blood. He must live near the equator.

I thought I knew slow, but this guy, this guy was *slow*. The sound I heard was his wiry-haired blond elbow, brushed green with living algae, stirring a leaf as he reached for the next branch. Pressing my wet palms onto the rough wooden walls, I watched the sloth move in the shadows of the canopy. Still reaching. And then still reaching.

What else is this slow? Those famous creatures of slow—the snail, the tortoise—they move faster. Much. This slow seemed impossible, not real, like a trick of my sad head. Dripping and naked in the jungle, I thought, *That sloth is as slow as grief.* We were numb to the speed of the world. We were one temperature.

FOR ANALYSIS

1. What emotion other than grief is present in this essay?

2. How does the author approach the subject of her grief? What are the effects of writing about it in this way? Would representing it and discussing it more directly have been more or less effective for you?

MAKING CONNECTIONS

Read "The Sloth" with any or all of the selections in "Connecting Poems: Animal Fates" (p. 1261). How does Christman's use of the sloth compare to the way these other writers use animals in their work?

WRITING TOPIC

Write about a time when you felt something strongly. Is there an animal you could have compared yourself to? How?

These essays explore the ways we think about death and the ways in which death makes us think about life. Life's fragility can sometimes act as a reminder to seize the day, and at other times it sends a chill down our spines. Sometimes it does both, and sometimes it does other things that we don't expect. As you read these essays, note the variety of ways death—even just the idea of it—causes reflection. And note the variety of ways these writers, master stylists all, convey these reflections.

E. B. WHITE   (1899–1985)

ONCE MORE TO THE LAKE   1941

One summer, along about 1904, my father rented a camp on a lake in Maine and took us all there for the month of August. We all got ringworm from some kittens and had to rub Pond's Extract on our arms and legs night and morning, and my father rolled over in a canoe with all his clothes on; but outside of that the vacation was a success and from then on none of us ever thought there was any place in the world like that lake in Maine. We returned summer after summer—always on August 1st for one month. I have since become a salt-water man, but sometimes in summer there are days when the restlessness of the tides and the fearful cold of the sea water and the incessant wind which blows across the afternoon and into the evening make me wish for the placidity of a lake in the woods. A few weeks ago this feeling got so strong I bought myself a couple of bass hooks and a spinner and returned to the lake where we used to go, for a week's fishing and to revisit old haunts.

I took along my son, who had never had any fresh water up his nose and who had seen lily pads only from train windows. On the journey over to the lake I began to wonder what it would be like. I wondered how time would have marred this unique, this holy spot—the coves and streams, the hills that the sun set behind, the camps and the paths behind the camps. I was sure that the tarred road would have found it out and I wondered in what other ways it would be desolated. It is strange how much you can remember about places like that once you allow your mind to return into the grooves which lead back. You remember one thing, and that suddenly reminds you of another thing. I guess I remembered clearest of all the early mornings, when the lake was cool and motionless, remembered how the bedroom smelled of the lumber it was made of and of the wet woods whose scent entered through the screen. The partitions in the camp were thin and did not extend clear to the top of the rooms, and as I was always the first up I would dress softly so as not to wake the others, and sneak out into the sweet outdoors and start out in the canoe, keeping close along the shore in the long shadows of the pines. I remembered being very careful never to rub my paddle against the gunwale for fear of disturbing the stillness of the cathedral.

The lake had never been what you would call a wild lake. There were cottages sprinkled around the shores, and it was in farming country although the shores of the lake were quite heavily wooded. Some of the cottages were owned by nearby farmers, and you would live at the shore and eat your meals at the farmhouse. That's what our family did. But although it wasn't wild, it was a fairly large and undisturbed lake and there were places in it which, to a child at least, seemed infinitely remote and primeval.

I was right about the tar: it led to within half a mile of the shore. But when I got back there, with my boy, and we settled into a camp near a farmhouse and into the kind of summertime I had known, I could tell that it was going to be pretty much the same as it had been before—I knew it, lying in bed the first morning, smelling the bedroom, and hearing the boy sneak quietly out and go off along the shore in a boat. I began to sustain the illusion that he was I, and therefore, by simple transposition, that I was my father. This sensation persisted, kept cropping up all the time we were there. It was not an entirely new feeling, but in this setting it grew much stronger. I seemed to be living a dual existence. I would be in the middle of some simple act, I would be picking up a bait box or laying down a table fork, or I would be saying something, and suddenly it would be not I but my father who was saying the words or making the gesture. It gave me a creepy sensation.

We went fishing the first morning. I felt the same damp moss covering the 5 worms in the bait can, and saw the dragonfly alight on the tip of my rod as it hovered a few inches from the surface of the water. It was the arrival of this fly that convinced me beyond any doubt that everything was as it always had been, that the years were a mirage and there had been no years. The small waves were the same, chucking the rowboat under the chin as we shed at anchor, and the boat was the same boat, the same color green and the ribs broken in the same places, and under the floor-boards the same freshwater leavings and débris—the dead helgramite, the wisps of moss, the rusty discarded fishhook, the dried blood from yesterday's catch. We stared silently at the tips of our rods, at the dragonflies that came and went. I lowered the tip of mine into the water, tentatively, pensively dislodging the fly, which darted two feet away, poised, darted two feet back, and came to rest again a little farther up the rod. There had been no years between the ducking of this dragonfly and the other one—the one that was part of memory. I looked at the boy, who was silently watching his fly, and it was my hands that held his rod, my eyes watching. I felt dizzy and didn't know which rod I was at the end of.

We caught two bass, hauling them in briskly as though they were mackerel, pulling them over the side of the boat in a businesslike manner without any landing net, and stunning them with a blow on the back of the head. When we got back for a swim before lunch, the lake was exactly where we had left it, the same number of inches from the dock, and there was only the merest suggestion of a breeze. This seemed an utterly enchanted sea, this lake you could leave to its own devices for a few hours and come back to, and find that it had not stirred, this constant and trustworthy body of water. In the shallows, the dark, water-soaked sticks and twigs, smooth and old, were undulating in clusters on the bottom against the clean ribbed sand, and the track of the mussel was plain. A school of minnows swam by, each minnow with its small, individual shadow, doubling the attendance, so clear and sharp in the sunlight. Some of the other campers were in swimming, along the shore, one of them with a cake of soap, and the water felt thin and clear and insubstantial. Over the years there had been this person with the cake of soap, this cultist, and here he was. There had been no years.

Up to the farmhouse to dinner through the teeming, dusty field, the road under our sneakers was only a two-track road. The middle track was missing, the one with the marks of the hooves and the splotches of dried, flaky manure. There had always been three tracks to choose from in choosing which track to walk in; now the choice was narrowed down to two. For a moment I missed terribly the middle alternative. But the way led past the tennis court, and something about the way it lay there in the sun reassured me; the tape had loosened along the backline, the alleys were green with plantains and other weeds, and the net (installed in June and removed in September) sagged in the dry noon, and the whole place steamed with midday heat and hunger and emptiness. There was a choice of pie for dessert, and one was blueberry and one was apple, and the waitresses were the same country girls, there having been no passage of time, only the illusion of it as in a dropped curtain—the waitresses were still fifteen; their hair had been washed, that was the only difference—they had been to the movies and seen the pretty girls with the clean hair.

Summertime, oh summertime, pattern of life indelible, the fade proof lake, the woods unshatterable, the pasture with the sweetfern and the juniper forever and ever, summer without end; this was the background, and the life along the shore was the design, the cottages with their innocent and tranquil design, their tiny docks with the flagpole and the American flag floating against the white clouds in the blue sky, the little paths over the roots of the trees leading from camp to camp and the paths leading back to the outhouses and the can of lime for sprinkling, and at the souvenir counters at the store the miniature birch-bark canoes and the post cards that showed things looking a little better than they looked. This was the American family at play, escaping the city heat, wondering whether the newcomers at the camp at the head of the cove were "common" or "nice," wondering whether it was true that the people who drove up for Sunday dinner at the farmhouse were turned away because there wasn't enough chicken.

It seemed to me, as I kept remembering all this, that those times and those summers had been infinitely precious and worth saving. There had been jollity and peace and goodness. The arriving (at the beginning of August) had been so big a business in itself, at the railway station the farm wagon drawn up, the first smell of the pineladen air, the first glimpse of the smiling farmer, and the great importance of the trunks and your father's enormous authority in such matters, and the feel of the wagon under you for the long ten-mile haul, and at the top of the last long hill catching the first view of the lake after eleven months of not seeing this cherished body of water. The shouts and cries of the other campers when they saw you, and the trunks to be unpacked, to give up their rich burden. (Arriving was less exciting nowadays, when you sneaked up in your car and parked it under a tree near the camp and took out the bags and in five minutes it was all over, no fuss, no loud wonderful fuss about trunks.)

Peace and goodness and jollity. The only thing that was wrong now, really, was the sound of the place, an unfamiliar nervous sound of the outboard motors. This was the note that jarred, the one thing that would sometimes break the illusion and set the years moving. In those other summertimes, all motors were inboard; and when they were at a little distance, the noise they made was a sedative, an ingredient of summer sleep. They were one-cylinder and two-cylinder engines, and some were make-and-break and some were jump-spark, but they all made a sleepy sound across the lake. The one-lungers throbbed and muttered, and the twin-cylinder ones purred and purred, and that was a quiet sound too. But now the campers all had outboards. In the daytime, in the hot mornings, these motors made a petulant, irritable sound; at night, in the still evening when the afterglow lit the water, they whined about one's ears like mosquitoes. My boy loved our rented outboard, and his great desire was to achieve singlehanded mastery over it, and authority, and he soon learned the trick of choking it a little (but not too much), and the adjustment of the needle valve. Watching him I would remember the things you could do with the old one-cylinder engine with the heavy flywheel, how you could have it eating out of your hand if you got really close to it spiritually. Motor boats in those days didn't have clutches, and you would make a landing by shutting off the motor at the proper time and coasting in with a dead rudder. But there was a way of reversing them, if you learned the trick, by cutting the switch and putting it on again exactly on the final dying revolution of the flywheel, so that it would kick back against compression and begin reversing. Approaching a dock in a strong following breeze, it was difficult to slow up sufficiently by the ordinary coasting method, and if a boy felt he had complete mastery over his motor, he was tempted to keep it running beyond its time and then reverse it a few feet from the dock. It took a cool nerve, because if you threw the switch a twentieth of a second too soon you could catch the flywheel when it still had speed enough to go up past center, and the boat would leap ahead, charging bull-fashion at the dock.

We had a good week at the camp. The bass were biting well and the sun shone endlessly, day after day. We would be tired at night and lie down in the accumulated heat of the little bedrooms after the long hot day and the breeze would stir almost imperceptibly outside and the smell of the swamp drift in through the rusty screens. Sleep would come easily and in the morning the red squirrel would be on the roof, tapping out his gay routine. I kept remembering everything, lying in bed in the mornings—the small steamboat that had a long rounded stern like the lip of a Ubangi, and how quietly she ran on the moonlight sails, when the older boys played their mandolins and the girls sang and we ate doughnuts dipped in sugar, and how sweet the music was on the water in the shining night, and what it had felt like to think about girls then. After breakfast we would go up to the store and the things were in the same place—the minnows in a bottle, the plugs and spinners disarranged and pawed over by the youngsters from the boys' camp, the fig newtons and the Beeman's gum. Outside, the road was tarred and cars stood in front of the store. Inside, all was just as it had always been, except there was more Coca-Cola and not so much Moxie and root beer and birch beer and sarsaparilla. We would walk out with a bottle of pop apiece and sometimes the pop would backfire up our noses and hurt. We explored the streams, quietly, where the turtles slid off the sunny logs and dug their way into the soft bottom; and we lay on the town wharf and fed worms to the tame bass. Everywhere we went I had trouble making out which was I, the one walking at my side, the one walking in my pants.

One afternoon while we were there at that lake a thunderstorm came up. It was like the revival of an old melodrama that I had seen long ago with childish awe. The second-act climax of the drama of the electrical disturbance over a lake in America had not changed in any important respect. This was the big scene, still the big scene. The whole thing was so familiar, the first feeling of oppression and heat and a general air around camp of not wanting to go very far away. In mid-afternoon (it was all the same) a curious darkening of the sky, and a lull in everything that had made life tick; and then the way the boats suddenly swung the other way at their moorings with the coming of a breeze out of the new quarter, and the premonitory rumble. Then the kettle drum, then the snare, then the bass drum and cymbals, then crackling light against the dark, and the gods grinning and licking their chops in the hills. Afterward the calm, the rain steadily rustling in the calm lake, the return of light and hope and spirits, and the campers running out in joy and relief to go swimming in the rain, their bright cries perpetuating the deathless joke about how they were getting simply drenched, and the children screaming with delight at the new sensation of bathing in the rain, and the joke about getting drenched linking the generations in a strong indestructible chain. And the comedian who waded in carrying an umbrella.

When the others went swimming my son said he was going in too. He pulled his dripping trunks from the line where they had hung all through the shower, and wrung them out. Languidly, and with no thought of going in, I watched him, his hard little body, skinny and bare, saw him wince slightly as he pulled up around his vitals the small, soggy, icy garment. As he buckled the swollen belt suddenly my groin felt the chill of death.

FOR ANALYSIS

1. How is the lake the same as it was in the past? How has it changed?
2. Why is it important that White brings his son along on this trip?
3. What does the trip remind White of? What does that reminiscence make him aware of?

WRITING TOPICS

1. Note the kinds of details White selects in painting his portrait of the lake. Reflect on his choices: Why is the lake "fade-proof," the woods "unshatterable"?

2. Write a short narrative of a trip you took or a visit you made that brought you back to when you were younger. Try to include as much descriptive detail as you can, and try to make that detail work to express the feelings you had.

BRIAN DOYLE (B. 1956)

JOYAS VOLADORES 2004

Consider the hummingbird for a long moment. A hummingbird's heart beats ten times a second. A hummingbird's heart is the size of a pencil eraser. A hummingbird's heart is a lot of the hummingbird. *Joyas voladores,* flying jewels, the first white explorers in the Americas called them, and the white men had never seen such creatures, for hummingbirds came into the world only in the Americas, nowhere else in the universe, more than three hundred species of them whirring and zooming and nectaring in hummer time zones nine times removed from ours, their hearts hammering faster than we could clearly hear if we pressed our elephantine ears to their infinitesimal chests.

Each one vists a thousand flowers a day. They can dive at sixty miles an hour. They can fly backwards. They can fly more than five hundred miles without pausing to rest. But when they rest they come close to death: On frigid nights, or when they are starving, they retreat into torpor, their metabolic rate slowing to a fifteenth of their normal sleep rate, their hearts sludging nearly to a halt, barely beating, and if they are not soon warmed, if they do not soon find that which is sweet, their hearts grow cold, and they cease to be. Consider for a moment those hummingbirds who did not open their eyes again today, this very day, in the Americas: bearded helmet-crests and booted racket-tails, violet-tailed sylphs and violet-capped wood-nymphs, crimson topazes and purple-crowned fairies, red-tailed comets and amethyst woodstars, rainbow-bearded thornbills and glittering-bellied emeralds, velvet-purple coronets and golden-bellied star-frontlets, fiery-tailed awlbills and Andean hillstars, spatuletails and pufflegs, each the most amazing thing you have never seen, each thunderous wild heart the size of an infant's fingernail, each mad heart silent, a brilliant music stilled.

Hummingbirds, like all flying birds but more so, have incredible enormous immense ferocious metabolisms. To drive those metabolisms they have race-car hearts that eat oxygen at an eye-popping rate. Their hearts are built of thinner, leaner fibers than ours. Their arteries are stiffer and more taut. They have more mitochondria in their heart muscles—anything to gulp more oxygen.

Their hearts are stripped to the skin for the war against gravity and inertia, the mad search for food, the insane idea of flight. The price of their ambition is a life closer to death; they suffer heart attacks and aneurysms and ruptures more than any other living creature. It's expensive to fly. You burn out. You fry the machine. You melt the engine. Every creature on earth has approximately two billion heartbeats to spend in a lifetime. You can spend them slowly, like a tortoise, and live to be two hundred years old, or you can spend them fast, like a hummingbird, and live to be two years old.

The biggest heart in the world is inside the blue whale. It weighs more than seven tons. It's as big as a room. It *is* a room, with four chambers. A child could walk around in it, head high, bending only to step through the valves. The valves are as big as the swinging doors in a saloon. This house of a heart drives a creature a hundred feet long. When this creature is born it is twenty feet long and weighs four tons. It is waaaaay bigger than your car. It drinks a hundred gallons of milk from its mama every day and gains two hundred pounds a day and when it is seven or eight years old it endures an unimaginable puberty and then it essentially disappears from human ken, for next to nothing is known of the mating habits, travel patterns, diet, social life, language, social structure, diseases, spirituality, wars, stories, despairs, and arts of the blue whale. There are perhaps ten thousand blue whales in the world, living in every ocean on earth, and of the largest mammal who ever lived we know nearly nothing. But we know this: The animals with the largest hearts in the world generally travel in pairs, and their penetrating moaning cries, their piercing yearning tongue, can be heard underwater for miles and miles.

Mammals and birds have hearts with four chambers. Reptiles and turtles   5 have hearts with three chambers. Fish have hearts with two chambers. Insects and mollusks have hearts with one chamber. Worms have hearts with one chamber, although they may have as many as eleven single-chambered hearts. Unicellular bacteria have no hearts at all; but even they have fluid eternally in motion, washing from one side of the cell to the other, swirling and whirling. No living being is without interior liquid motion. We all churn inside.

So much held in a heart in a lifetime. So much held in a heart in a day, an hour, a moment. We are utterly open with no one, in the end—not mother and father, not wife or husband, not lover, not child, not friend. We open windows to each but we live alone in the house of the heart. Perhaps we must. Perhaps we could not bear to be so naked, for fear of a constantly harrowed heart. When young we think there will come one person who will savor and sustain us always; when we are older we know this is the dream of a child, that all hearts finally are bruised and scarred, scored and torn, repaired by time and will, patched by force of character, yet fragile and rickety forevermore, no matter how ferocious the defense and how many bricks you bring to the wall. You can brick up your heart as stout and tight and hard and cold and impregnable as you possibly can and down it comes in an instant, felled by a woman's second glance, a child's apple breath, the shatter of glass in the road, the words

I have something to tell you, a cat with a broken spine dragging itself into the forest to die, the brush of your mother's papery ancient hand in the thicket of your hair, the memory of your father's voice early in the morning echoing from the kitchen where he is making pancakes for his children.

FOR ANALYSIS

1. What is the organ Doyle focuses on in "Joyas Voladores"? What does it usually symbolize in poetry and in life?

2. How would you characterize Doyle's description of the hummingbird? What is he expressing?

3. What connects Doyle's observations about the incredible and incredibly fragile body of the hummingbird and the subject of his final paragraph?

WRITING TOPIC

Why might someone be tempted to call this a poem instead of an essay? What about it is poetic? What does it mean to say something is poetic—is it the same as saying it's poetry? Reflect on these questions, decide what you think, and finally, say if it matters, and why.

CHANG-RAE LEE   (B. 1965)

COMING HOME AGAIN   1995

When my mother began using the electronic pump that fed her liquids and medication, we moved her to the family room. The bedroom she shared with my father was upstairs, and it was impossible to carry the machine up and down all day and night. The pump itself was attached to a metal stand on casters, and she pulled it along wherever she went. From anywhere in the house, you could hear the sound of the wheels clicking out a steady time over the grout lines of the slate-tiled foyer, her main thoroughfare to the bathroom and the kitchen. Sometimes you would hear her halt after only a few steps, to catch her breath or steady her balance, and whatever you were doing was instantly suspended by a pall of silence.

I was usually in the kitchen, preparing lunch or dinner, poised over the butcher block with her favorite chef's knife in my hand and her old yellow apron slung around my neck. I'd be breathless in the sudden quiet, and, having ceased my mincing and chopping, would stare blankly at the brushed sheen of the blade. Eventually, she would clear her throat or call out to say she was fine, then begin to move again, starting her rhythmic *ka-jug*; and only then could I go on with my cooking, the world of our house turning once more, wheeling through the black.

I wasn't cooking for my mother but for the rest of us. When she first moved downstairs she was still eating, though scantily, more just to taste what we were having than from any genuine desire for food. The point was simply to sit together at the kitchen table and array ourselves like a family again. My mother would gently set herself down in her customary chair near the stove. I sat across from her, my father and sister to my left and right, and crammed in the center was all the food I had made—a spicy codfish stew, say, or a casserole of gingery beef, dishes that in my youth she had prepared for us a hundred times.

It had been ten years since we'd all lived together in the house, which at fifteen I had left to attend boarding school in New Hampshire. My mother would sometimes point this out, by speaking of our present time as being "just like before Exeter," which surprised me, given how proud she always was that I was a graduate of the school.

My going to such a place was part of my mother's not so secret plan to 5 change my character, which she worried was becoming too much like hers. I was clever and able enough, but without outside pressure I was readily given to sloth and vanity. The famous school—which none of us knew the first thing about—would prove my mettle. She was right, of course, and while I was there I would falter more than a few times, academically and otherwise. But I never thought that my leaving home then would ever be a problem for her, a private quarrel she would have even as her life waned.

Now her house was full again. My sister had just resigned from her job in New York City, and my father, who typically saw his psychiatric patients until eight or nine in the evening, was appearing in the driveway at four-thirty. I had been living at home for nearly a year and was in the final push of work on what would prove a dismal failure of a novel. When I wasn't struggling over my prose, I kept occupied with the things she usually did—the daily errands, the grocery shopping, the vacuuming and the cleaning, and, of course, all the cooking.

When I was six or seven years old, I used to watch my mother as she prepared our favorite meals. It was one of my daily pleasures. She shooed me away in the beginning, telling me that the kitchen wasn't my place, and adding, in her half-proud, half-deprecating way, that her kind of work would only serve to weaken me. "Go out and play with your friends," she'd snap in Korean, "or better yet, do your reading and homework." She knew that I had already done both, and that as the evening approached there was no place to go save her small and tidy kitchen, from which the clatter of her mixing bowls and pans would ring through the house.

I would enter the kitchen quietly and stand beside her, my chin lodging upon the point of her hip. Peering through the crook of her arm, I beheld the movements of her hands. For *kalbi*, she would take up a butchered short rib in her narrow hand, the flinty bone shaped like a section of an airplane wing and deeply embedded in gristle and flesh, and with the point of her knife cut so that the bone fell away, though not completely, leaving it connected to the meat by the barest opaque layer of tendon. Then she methodically butterflied the flesh, cutting and unfolding, repeating the action until the meat lay out on her board, glistening and ready for seasoning. She scored it diagonally, then sifted sugar into the crevices with her pinched fingers, gently rubbing in the crystals. The sugar would tenderize as well as sweeten the meat. She did this with each rib, and then set them all aside in a large shallow bowl. She minced a half-dozen cloves of garlic, a stub of gingerroot, sliced up a few scallions, and spread it all over the meat. She wiped her hands and took out a bottle of sesame oil, and, after pausing for a moment, streamed the dark oil in two swift circles around the bowl. After adding a few splashes of soy sauce, she thrust her hands in and kneaded the flesh, careful not to dislodge the bones. I asked her why it mattered that they remain connected. "The meat needs the bone nearby," she said, "to borrow its richness." She wiped her hands clean of the marinade, except for her little finger, which she would flick with her tongue from time to time, because she knew that the flavor of a good dish developed not at once but in stages.

Whenever I cook, I find myself working just as she would, readying the ingredients—a mash of garlic, a julienne of red peppers, fantails of shrimp—and piling them in little mounds about the cutting surface. My mother never left me any recipes, but this is how I learned to make her food, each dish coming not from a list or a card but from the aromatic spread of a board.

I've always thought it was particularly cruel that the cancer was in her stom- 10 ach, and that for a long time at the end she couldn't eat. The last meal I made for her was on New Year's Eve, 1990. My sister suggested that instead of a rib roast or a bird, or the usual overflow of Korean food, we make all sorts of finger dishes that our mother might fancy and pick at.

We set the meal out on the glass coffee table in the family room. I prepared a tray of smoked-salmon canapes, fried some Korean bean cakes, and made a few other dishes I thought she might enjoy. My sister supervised me, arranging the platters, and then with some pomp carried each dish in to our parents. Finally, I brought out a bottle of champagne in a bucket of ice. My mother had moved to the sofa and was sitting up, surveying the low table. "It looks pretty nice," she said. "I think I'm feeling hungry."

This made us all feel good, especially me, for I couldn't remember the last time she had felt any hunger or had eaten something I cooked. We began to eat. My mother picked up a piece of salmon toast and took a tiny corner in her mouth. She rolled it around for a moment and then pushed it out with the tip of her tongue, letting it fall back onto her plate. She swallowed hard, as if to quell a gag, then glanced up to see if we had noticed. Of course we all had. She attempted a bean cake, some cheese, and then a slice of fruit, but nothing was any use.

She nodded at me anyway, and said, "Oh, it's very good." But I was already feeling lost and I put down my plate abruptly, nearly shattering it on the thick glass. There was an ugly pause before my father asked me in a weary, gentle voice if anything was wrong, and I answered that it was nothing, it was the last night of a long year, and we were together, and I was simply relieved. At midnight, I poured out glasses of champagne, even one for my mother, who took a deep sip. Her manner grew playful and light, and I helped her shuffle to her mattress, and she lay down in the place where in a brief week she was dead.

My mother could whip up most anything, but during our first years of living in this country we ate only Korean foods. At my haranguelike behest, my mother set herself to learning how to cook exotic American dishes. Luckily, a kind neighbor, Mrs. Churchill, a tall, florid young woman with flaxen hair, taught my mother her most trusted recipes. Mrs. Churchill's two young sons, palish, weepy boys with identical crewcuts, always accompanied her, and though I liked them well enough, I would slip away from them after a few minutes, for I knew that the real action would be in the kitchen, where their mother was playing guide. Mrs. Churchill hailed from the state of Maine, where the finest Swedish meatballs and tuna casserole and angel-food cake in America are made. She readily demonstrated certain techniques—how to layer wet sheets of pasta for a lasagna or whisk up a simple roux, for example. She often brought gift shoeboxes containing curious ingredients like dried oregano, instant yeast, and cream-of-mushroom soup. The two women, though at ease and jolly with each other, had difficulty communicating, and this was made worse by the often confusing terminology of Western cuisine ("corned beef," "devilled eggs"). Although I was just learning the language myself, I'd gladly play the interlocutor, jumping back and forth between their places at the counter, dipping my fingers into whatever sauce lay about.

I was an insistent child, and, being my mother's firstborn, much too prized. 15
My mother could say no to me, and did often enough, but anyone who knew us—particularly my father and sister—could tell how much the denying pained her. And if I was overconscious of her indulgence even then, and suffered the rushing pangs of guilt that she could inflict upon me with the slightest wounded turn of her lip, I was too happily obtuse and venal to let her cease. She reminded me daily that I was her sole son, her reason for living, and that if she were to lose me, in either body or spirit, she wished that God would mercifully smite her, strike her down like a weak branch.

In the traditional fashion, she was the house accountant, the maid, the launderer, the disciplinarian, the driver, the secretary, and, of course, the cook. She was also my first basketball coach. In South Korea, where girls' high-school basketball is a popular spectator sport, she had been a star, the point guard for the national high-school team that once won the all-Asia championships. I learned this one Saturday during the summer, when I asked my father if he would go down to the school yard and shoot some baskets with me. I had just finished the fifth grade, and wanted desperately to make the middle-school team the coming fall. He called for my mother and sister to come along. When we arrived, my sister immediately ran off to the swings, and I recall being annoyed that my mother wasn't following her. I dribbled clumsily around the

key, on the verge of losing control of the ball, and flung a flat shot that caromed wildly off the rim. The ball bounced to my father, who took a few not so
graceful dribbles and made an easy layup. He dribbled out and then drove to
the hoop for a layup on the other side. He rebounded his shot and passed the
ball to my mother, who had been watching us from the foul line. She turned
from the basket and began heading the other way.

"*Um-mah*," I cried at her, my exasperation already bubbling over, "the basket's over *here*!"

After a few steps she turned around, and from where the professional three-
point line must be now, she effortlessly flipped the ball up in a two-handed set
shot, its flight truer and higher than I'd witnessed from any boy or man. The
ball arced cleanly into the hoop, stiffly popping the chain-link net. All afternoon, she rained in shot after shot, as my father and I scrambled after her.

When we got home from the playground, my mother showed me the photograph album of her team's championship run. For years, I kept it in my room,
on the same shelf that housed the scrapbooks I made of basketball stars, with
magazine clippings of slick players like Bubbles Hawkins and Pistol Pete and
George (the Iceman) Gervin.

It puzzled me how much she considered her own history to be immaterial, 20
and if she never patently diminished herself, she was able to finesse a kind
of self-removal by speaking of my father whenever she could. She zealously
recounted his excellence as a student in medical school and reminded me,
each night before I started my homework, of how hard he drove himself in his
work to make a life for us. She said that because of his Asian face and imperfect
English, he was "working two times the American doctors." I knew that she
was building him up, buttressing him with both genuine admiration and her
own brand of anxious braggadocio, and that her overarching concern was that
I might fail to see him as she wished me to—in the most dawning light, his
pose steadfast and solitary.

In the year before I left for Exeter, I became weary of her oft-repeated
accounts of my father's success. I was a teenager, and so ever inclined to be
dismissive and bitter toward anything that had to do with family and home.
Often enough, my mother was the object of my derision. Suddenly, her life
seemed so small to me. She was there, and sometimes, I thought, *always* there,
as if she were confined to the four walls of our house. I would even complain
about her cooking. Mostly, though, I was getting more and more impatient
with the difficulty she encountered in doing everyday things. I was afraid for
her. One day, we got into a terrible argument when she asked me to call the
bank, to question a discrepancy she had discovered in the monthly statement.
I asked her why she couldn't call herself. I was stupid and brutal, and I knew
exactly how to wound her.

"Whom do I talk to?" she said. She would mostly speak to me in Korean,
and I would answer in English.

"The bank manager, who else?"

"What do I say?"

"Whatever you want to say." 25

"Don't speak to me like that!" she cried.

"It's just that you should be able to do it yourself," I said.

"You know how I feel about this!"

"Well, maybe then you should consider it *practice*," I answered lightly, using the Korean word to make sure she understood.

Her face blanched, and her neck suddenly became rigid, as if I were throt- 30 tling her. She nearly struck me right then, but instead she bit her lip and ran upstairs. I followed her, pleading for forgiveness at her door. But it was the one time in our life that I couldn't convince her, melt her resolve with the blandishments of a spoiled son.

When my mother was feeling strong enough, or was in particularly good spirits, she would roll her machine into the kitchen and sit at the table and watch me work. She wore pajamas day and night, mostly old pairs of mine.

She said, "I can't tell, what are you making?"

"*Mahn-doo* filling."

"You didn't salt the cabbage and squash."

"Was I supposed to?" 35

"Of course. Look, it's too wet. Now the skins will get soggy before you can fry them."

"What should I do?"

"It's too late. Maybe it'll be O.K. if you work quickly. Why didn't you ask me?"

"You were finally sleeping."

"You should have woken me." 40

"No way."

She sighed, as deeply as her weary lungs would allow.

"I don't know how you were going to make it without me."

"I don't know, either. I'll remember the salt next time."

"You better. And not too much." 45

We often talked like this, our tone decidedly matter-of-fact, chin up, just this side of being able to bear it. Once, while inspecting a potato-fritter batter I was making, she asked me if she had ever done anything that I wished she hadn't done. I thought for a moment, and told her no. In the next breath, she wondered aloud if it was right of her to have let me go to Exeter, to live away from the house while I was so young. She tested the batter's thickness with her finger and called for more flour. Then she asked if, given a choice, I would go to Exeter again.

I wasn't sure what she was getting at, and I told her that I couldn't be certain, but probably, yes, I would. She snorted at this and said it was my leaving home that had once so troubled our relationship. "Remember how I had so much difficulty talking to you? Remember?"

She believed back then that I had found her more and more ignorant each time I came home. She said she never blamed me, for this was the way she knew it would be with my wonderful new education. Nothing I could say seemed to quell the notion. But I knew that the problem wasn't simply the *education*; the first time I saw her again after starting school, barely six weeks later, when she and my father visited me on Parents Day, she had already grown nervous and distant. After the usual campus events, we had gone to the motel where they were staying in a nearby town and sat on the beds in our room. She seemed to sneak looks at me, as though I might discover a horrible new truth if our eyes should meet.

My own secret feeling was that I had missed my parents greatly, my mother especially, and much more than I had anticipated. I couldn't tell them that these first weeks were a mere blur to me, that I felt completely overwhelmed by all the studies and my much brighter friends and the thousand irritating details of living alone, and that I had really learned nothing, save perhaps how to put on a necktie while sprinting to class. I felt as if I had plunged too deep into the world, which, to my great horror, was much larger than I had ever imagined.

I welcomed the lull of the motel room. My father and I had nearly dozed 50 off when my mother jumped up excitedly, murmured how stupid she was, and hurried to the closet by the door. She pulled out our old metal cooler and dragged it between the beds. She lifted the top and began unpacking plastic containers, and I thought she would never stop. One after the other they came out, each with a dish that travelled well—a salted stewed meat, rolls of Korean-style sushi. I opened a container of radish kimchi and suddenly the room bloomed with its odor, and I revelled in the very peculiar sensation (which perhaps only true kimchi lovers know) of simultaneously drooling and gagging as I breathed it all in. For the next few minutes, they watched me eat. I'm not certain that I was even hungry. But after weeks of pork parmigiana and chicken patties and wax beans, I suddenly realized that I had lost all the savor in my life. And it seemed I couldn't get enough of it back. I ate and I ate, so much and so fast that I actually went to the bathroom and vomited. I came out dizzy and sated with the phantom warmth of my binge.

And beneath the face of her worry, I thought, my mother was smiling.

From that day, my mother prepared a certain meal to welcome me home. It was always the same. Even as I rode the school's shuttle bus from Exeter to Logan airport, I could already see the exact arrangement of my mother's table.

I knew that we would eat in the kitchen, the table brimming with plates. There was the *kalbi*, of course, broiled or grilled depending on the season. Leaf lettuce, to wrap the meat with. Bowls of garlicky clam broth with miso and tofu and fresh spinach. Shavings of cod dusted in flour and then dipped in egg wash and fried. Glass noodles with onions and shiitake. Scallion-and-hot-pepper pancakes. Chilled steamed shrimp. Seasoned salads of bean sprouts, spinach, and white radish. Crispy squares of seaweed. Steamed rice with barley and red beans. Homemade kimchi. It was all there—the old flavors I knew, the beautiful salt, the sweet, the excellent taste.

After the meal, my father and I talked about school, but of course I could never say enough for it to make any sense. My father would often recall his high-school principal, who had gone to England to study the methods and traditions of the public schools, and regaled students with stories of the great Eton man. My mother sat with us, paring fruit, not saying a word but taking everything in. When it was time to go to bed, my father said good night first. I usually watched television until the early morning. My mother would sit with me for an hour or two, perhaps until she was accustomed to me again, and only then would she kiss me and head upstairs to sleep.

During the following days, it was always the cooking that started our con- 55 versations. She'd hold an inquest over the cold leftovers we ate at lunch, discussing each dish in terms of its balance of flavors or what might have been prepared differently. But mostly I begged her to leave the dishes alone. I wish I had paid more attention. After her death, when my father and I were the only ones left in the house, drifting through the rooms like ghosts, I sometimes tried to make that meal for him. Though it was too much for two, I made each dish anyway, taking as much care as I could. But nothing turned out quite right—not the color, not the smell. At the table, neither of us said much of anything. And we had to eat the food for days.

I remember washing rice in the kitchen one day, and my mother's saying in English, from her usual seat, "I made a big mistake."

"About Exeter?"

"Yes. I made a big mistake. You should be with us for that time. I should never let you go there."

"So why did you?" I said.

"Because I didn't know I was going to die." 60

I let her words pass. For the first time in her life, she was letting herself speak her full mind, so what else could I do?

"But you know what?" she spoke up. "It was better for you. If you stayed home, you would not like me so much now."

I suggested that maybe I would like her even more.

She shook her head. "Impossible."

Sometimes I still think about what she said, about having made a mis- 65 take. I would have left home for college, that was never in doubt, but those years I was away at boarding school grew more precious to her as her illness progressed. After many months of exhaustion and pain and the haze of the drugs, I thought that her mind was beginning to fade, for more and more it seemed that she was seeing me again as her fifteen-year-old boy, the one she had dropped off in New Hampshire on a cloudy September afternoon.

I remember the first person I met, another new student, named Zack, who walked to the welcome picnic with me. I had planned to eat with my parents—my mother had brought a coolerful of food even that first day—but I learned of the cookout and told her that I should probably go. I wanted to go, of course. I was excited, and no doubt fearful and nervous, and I must have thought I was only thinking ahead. She agreed wholeheartedly, saying I certainly should. I walked them to the car, and perhaps I hugged them, before saying goodbye. One day, after she died, my father told me what happened on the long drive home to Syracuse.

He was driving the car, looking straight ahead. Traffic was light on the Massachusetts Turnpike, and the sky was nearly dark. They had driven for more than two hours and had not yet spoken a word. He then heard a strange sound from her, a kind of muffled chewing noise, as if something inside her were grinding its way out.

"So, what's the matter?" he said, trying to keep an edge to his voice.

She looked at him with her ashen face and she burst into tears. He began to cry himself, and pulled the car over onto the narrow shoulder of the turnpike, where they stayed for the next half hour or so, the blank-faced cars droning by them in the cold, onrushing night.

Every once in a while, when I think of her, I'm driving alone somewhere on   70
the highway. In the twilight, I see their car off to the side, a blue Olds coupe
with a landau top, and as I pass them by I look back in the mirror and I see
them again, the two figures huddling together in the front seat. Are they sleeping? Or kissing? Are they all right?

FOR ANALYSIS

1. Why is it "particularly cruel" (para. 10) that Lee's mother dies of stomach cancer? How does the moment when he tells us this provide emotional impact?

2. Much of the essay is concerned about Lee's feelings for his mother, but how does he feel about himself? What kind of picture of himself does he paint?

3. Lee describes his and his mother's tone while talking together as "just this side of being able to bear it" (para. 46). Would you say that **tone** applies to the way he writes this essay? If so, what do you think of his use of this tone for an essay with this subject?

4. Food plays a major role in "Coming Home Again." What is its significance?

MAKING CONNECTIONS

1. The presence of death can make itself felt in many different ways. How do these essays show it appearing? How do they show the different ways we react?

2. While all of these essays are in part about death and the pain that attends loss, none is without pleasure. How does each balance pain and pleasure, and to what ends?

3. How does the natural or physical, earthly world appear in each of these essays? How is it used? How is it part of the human experience?

WRITING TOPIC

The end of this essay is very sad; it is especially affecting because of the twists and turns of feeling in the essay that lead up to it. Review the essay and keep a log of these twists and turns. Describe as precisely as you can where Lee takes us over the course of the essay, and then reflect on why this journey ends so powerfully.

FURTHER QUESTIONS
FOR THINKING AND WRITING

1. Although Housman's "To an Athlete Dying Young" and Neruda's "The Dead Woman" employ different poetic forms, they both embody a poetic mode called **elegy.** Define *elegy* in terms of the characteristic **tone** of these poems. Compare the elegiac tone of these poems. **Writing Topic:** Compare the elegiac tone of one of these poems with the tone of Owen's "Dulce et Decorum Est" or Thomas's "Do Not Go Gentle into That Good Night."

2. What **figurative language** in the prose and poetry of this section is commonly associated with death? With dying? Contrast the characteristic **imagery** of this section with the characteristic imagery of love poetry. **Writing Topic:** Compare the imagery in Shakespeare's Sonnet 18 with the imagery in Sonnet 73.

3. In Tolstoy's "The Death of Iván Ilých" and Donne's **sonnet** "Death, Be Not Proud," death and dying are considered from a religious viewpoint. **Writing Topic:** Discuss whether these works develop a similar attitude toward death or whether the attitudes they develop differ.

4. State the argument against resignation to death made in Thomas's "Do Not Go Gentle into That Good Night." State the argument of Davis's reply, "After a Time." **Writing Topic:** Using these positions as the basis of your discussion, select for analysis two works that support Thomas's argument and two works that support Davis's.

5. Viramontes, a Mexican American, and Silko, an American Indian, both treat death as a ritualistic event. How are their stories similar? How do they differ? **Writing Topic:** Contrast the ritualistic elements in these stories with the religious elements in Tolstoy's "The Death of Iván Ilých."

6. Which works in this section treat death and dying in a way that corresponds most closely to your own attitude toward mortality? Which contradict your attitude? **Writing Topic:** Choose two works, each of which affects you differently, and discuss the elements responsible for your response.

APPENDICES

GLOSSARY OF CRITICAL APPROACHES

INTRODUCTION

This glossary attempts to define, briefly and in general terms, some major critical approaches to literature. Because literary criticism has to do with the value of literature—not with its history—judgments tend to be subjective, and disagreements frequent and even acrimonious. The truth of a work of art is very different from the truth of a mathematical formula. Certainly one's attitudes toward war, religion, sex, and politics are irrelevant to the truth of a formula but quite relevant to one's judgment of a literary work.

Most critical approaches can, in a general sense, be placed into one of three categories:

1. those that focus exclusively on the work itself, including the internal connections between its various parts and elements

2. those that approach a work with certain preconceived assumptions against which the work is evaluated

3. those that reject any "pure" approach and instead encourage an eclecticism that draws from whatever sources seem best suited to the work and the predilections of the critic.

Most of us are likely to find the third approach most congenial.

Yet any examination of the broad range of literary criticism reveals that groups of critics (and all readers are ultimately critics) share certain assumptions about literature. These assumptions govern the way critics approach a work, the elements they tend to look for and emphasize, the details they find significant or insignificant, and finally, the overall value they place on the work.

We do not suggest that one approach is more valid than another or that the lines dividing the various approaches are always clear and distinct. Readers will perhaps discover one approach more congenial to their temperament, more "true" to their sense of the world, than another. More likely, they will find themselves using more than one approach in dealing with a single work. Many of the diverse approaches described here actually overlap, and even those critics who champion a single abstract theory often draw on a variety of useful approaches when they write about a particular work.

Formalist critics assume that a literary text remains independent of the writer who created it. The function of the critic, then, is to discover how the author has deployed language to create (or perhaps failed to create) a formal and aesthetically satisfying structure. The influential American formalists of the 1940s and 1950s (the New Critics) were fond of describing literary texts as "autonomous," meaning that political, historical, biographical, and other considerations were always secondary if not irrelevant to any discussion of their merits.

Furthermore, formalist critics argue that the various elements of a "great" work interweave to create a seamless whole that embodies "universal" values. Unsurprisingly, the "universal" values formalist critics praise, on close analysis, tend to parallel the moral, political, and cultural ideals of the critics' social class. This tendency becomes even more problematic and complex in dealing with the literature of formerly colonized people.

But the formalist point of view, cherishing the artwork's structure, spawned its own antithesis—a group of theorists called *deconstructionists*. These writers argued that language itself was too shifty to support the expectations of formalist criticism. One reader might read a sentence literally, while another might read it ironically. Hence, their "understanding" of the text would be diametrically opposed.

The deconstructionists believe that intelligent readers cannot be expected to ignore those responses that interfere with some "correct" or "desirable" reading of the piece. Given what they see as the notoriously ambiguous and unstable nature of language, deconstructionist critics argue that a literary text can never have a fixed meaning.

While the formalists and deconstructionists wrestle over the philosophy of language and its implications for the nature of literary texts, other critics pursue quite different primary interests. The term *ethical criticism* describes a variety of approaches, all of which argue that literature, like any other human activity, connects to the real world and, consequently, influences real people. If that is so, our appraisal of a work must take into account the ethical and moral values it embodies. Though it sounds simple enough, in reality the task is difficult and often quite controversial. Ethical criticism is the very opposite of the "art for art's sake" approach, best represented by formalist criticism. The formalist critic tries to isolate the work in a timeless world of universal aesthetic considerations; the ethical critic insists on making judgments about whether a work serves values that are "good" or encourages values that are "bad."

Other critical approaches analyze literary works from still other perspectives. *Reader-response* critics assert that a work of art is created as much by its audience as by the artist. For these critics, art has no significant abstract existence: a reader's experience of the work gives birth to it and contributes crucially to its power and value. Further, since each reader embodies a unique set of experiences and values, each reader's response to the work will in some respects be uniquely personal. *Psychoanalytic* criticism, similar to reader-response, is nevertheless distinctive in its application of psychoanalytic principles to works of art. Those principles, originally derived from the work of Sigmund Freud (1856–1939), now often reflect the views of more recent theorists such as Jacques Lacan (1901–1981). There is, finally, the recently emergent approach called *new historical* criticism, which brings historical knowledge to bear on the analysis of literary works in new and sophisticated ways. The result is a sometimes dizzying proliferation of analyses that argue for the relationship between literature and life.

The glossary that follows reveals the widely diverse and often contradictory views expressed by professional theorists and critics.

Deconstruction This approach grew out of the work of certain twentieth-century European philosophers, notably Jacques Derrida (1930–2004), whose study of language led to the conclusion that since we can know only through the medium of language, and language is unstable and ambiguous, it is impossible to talk about truth and knowledge and meaning in any absolute sense. Verbal structures, these critics maintained, inevitably contained within themselves oppositions. Derrida asserted that in the Western world, language leads us to think in terms of opposites (for example, soul/body, man/woman, master/slave) that imply what he called "a violent hierarchy," with one of the terms (the first) always being superior to the other (the second). The aim of deconstruction is to show that this hierarchy of values cannot be permanent and absolute.

Readers therefore cannot be expected to ignore the oppositions and contradictions in a text just because they do not contribute to some "correct" or "desirable" reading of the piece that might uphold a particular political, social, or cultural view.

Formalism assures us that the successful artist is the master of language and that he or she consciously deploys all its resources to achieve a rich and unified work. Sensitive readers can aspire to a complete understanding of a work undistorted by their own idiosyncrasies, subjective states, or ideological biases.

Rejecting the formalist assumption about authorial control and conscious design, deconstruction attempts to show that by its very nature, language is constantly "saying" more than the writer can control or even know. Thus, a close study of any text (literary or otherwise) will reveal contradictory and irreconcilable elements.

Deconstructionist critics do not necessarily reject the validity of feminist, Marxist, formalist, and other critical approaches. In fact, they often draw on the insights furnished by them. But the deconstructionist critic says that any discourse or critical approach that fails to recognize the inherently shifting and unstable nature of language is bound to produce only a partial if not misleading interpretation. For example, in his study *America the Scrivener: Deconstruction and the Subject of Literary Studies* (1990), Gregory S. Jay finds Emily Grierson, the protagonist of William Faulkner's story "A Rose for Emily" (p. 649), a "puzzle" and warns against simplistic interpretations:

> As feminist subject, her story speaks of a revolutionary subversion of patriarchy; as herself, a figure of racial and class power, Emily also enacts the love affair of patriarchy with its own past, despite all the signs of decline and degradation. She is a split subject, crossed by rival discourses. What the text forces us to think, then, is the complex and ironic alliances between modes of possession and subjection, desire and ownership, identity and position.

Like Marxism and feminism, deconstruction defines itself both as a critical theory of literature and as a philosophy of human values. Hence, it is applicable not only to literature but also to an understanding of the power relations among humans and the societies they create. In insisting that we recognize the way language embodies and supports class, gender, and other biases, deconstruction challenges both the ethnocentrism of political structures and the idea of "universal values" in literary works.

Ethical Criticism   Ethical criticism may range from a casual appraisal of a work's moral content to the more rigorous and systematic analysis driven by a coherent set of stated beliefs and assumptions. A *religious* critic (committed to certain moral positions) might attack a work (regardless of its artfulness or brilliance) because it does not condemn adultery. A *feminist* critic might focus on the way literary works devalue women; a *black* critic, on the way they stereotype blacks; a *Marxist* critic, on the way they support class divisions; and a *new historicist* critic, on the way a dominant class interprets history to protect its own interests. But all of them agree that literary works invite ethical judgments. Most of them also agree that literary works must be judged as another means by which a society both defines and perpetuates its political institutions and cultural values. The feminist critic, the black critic, and the Marxist critic would also agree that the political institutions and cultural values of most Western societies have been carefully designed to serve the interests of a dominant class: white, male, and wealthy.

Ethical criticism takes us out of the comparatively calm, academic world of aesthetic values into the larger world of moral judgments. If a literary work's capacity to promote good or bad behavior becomes the criterion for judging its value, then surely some people will try to suppress works they perceive as morally threatening. It is here that ethical criticism encounters its most vexing and dangerous problem: censorship. The literary critic Wayne Booth, who advocates ethical criticism in his book *The Company We Keep: An Ethics of Fiction* (1988), concedes the danger but notes that teaching itself is a form of censorship in that "we impose our ethical choices on our students when we choose our reading lists."

Feminist Criticism   Feminist critics hold that literature is merely one of many expressions of a patriarchal society with a vested interest in keeping women subordinate to men. Thus literature, in the way it portrays gender roles, helps to condition women to accept as normal a society that directs them to become nurses rather than doctors, secretaries rather than attorneys or corporate executives, sex symbols rather than thinkers, elementary school teachers rather than university professors. Beyond this general critique of patriarchy, feminists differ in their detailed analyses. Some have re-examined history to show that a literary canon created by males has slighted and ignored female authors. Others, studying canonical works from a feminist perspective, have come up with fresh readings that challenge conventional interpretations, focusing on how women are empowered in literary texts or through writing literary texts. Some, believing that language itself allows men to impose their power, use literary analyses to expose the gender bias of language. Why, they ask, is the English language so rich in words to describe a quarrelsome, abusive woman (*shrew, harridan, termagant*) but so lacking in comparable terms for men? Some feminists believe that the male bias of language, far deeper than mere words, is actually structural. The constellation of qualities connoted by *masculine* and *feminine*, they say, reveals how deeply the positive (male) and negative (female) values are embedded in the language.

While a psychoanalytic critic might use Freud's Oedipal theories to explain Emily's relationship to Homer Barron in William Faulkner's "A Rose for Emily" (p. 649), the feminist critic Judith Fetterley maintains that the explanation is to be found in the fact that a patriarchal culture instills in us the notion "that men and women are made for each other" and that " 'masculinity' and 'femininity' are the natural reflection of that divinely ordained complement." In a society where there is "a massive differentiation of everything according to sex, one sees that in reality a sexist culture is one in which men and women are not simply incompatible but murderously so. . . . Emily murders Homer Barron because she must at any cost get a man" (*The Resisting Reader: A Feminist Approach to American Fiction*, 1978).

Formalist Criticism   Like deconstruction, formalism focuses on the ambiguous and multilayered nature of language but does so to achieve the precisely opposite effect. Formalism assures us that the successful artist is the master of language and consciously deploys all its resources to achieve a rich and unified work. Careful readers can aspire to a complete understanding of a work undistorted by their own idiosyncrasies or subjective states or ideological biases. The formalist rejects the central tenet of the reader-response critic—that a work comes into existence, so to speak, through the interaction of the reader with the work. For the formalist, the work exists independent of any particular reader. The work is a structured and formal aesthetic object comprising such elements as symbol, image, and sound patterns. Political, biographical, or historical considerations not embodied in the work itself are irrelevant.

The formalist sees literature as a sort of Platonic ideal form—immutable and objective. Works close to that ideal are praised for their aesthetic energy and their universality (a characteristic of the greatest literature). Works that do not exhibit this prized formal coherence are dispraised and often dismissed as neither universal nor important. Because formalism focuses on the internal structure of literature above all else, it rejects didactic works—those intended to teach or convey moral observations. During the 1940s and 1950s, when the New Critics (as the formalists were called) dominated academic literary criticism, social protest writing was generally dismissed as subliterary because it lacked the "universality" of great literature. What was important in a work of art was not that it might change people's behavior but that its parts coalesced into a beautiful whole. Consider the following comment by two formalist critics (Caroline Gordon and Allen Tate, *The House of Fiction*, 1950) on Nathaniel Hawthorne's "Young Goodman Brown" (p. 79):

> *The dramatic impact would have been stronger if Hawthorne had let the incidents tell their own story: Goodman Brown's behavior to his neighbors and finally to his wife show us that he is a changed man. Since fiction is a kind of shorthand of human behavior and one moment may represent years in a man's life, we would have concluded that the change was to last his entire life. But Hawthorne's weakness for moralizing and his insufficient technical equipment betray him into the anticlimax of the last paragraph.*

African American writers and critics, for example, complained that the criterion of universality was merely a way of protecting white, conservative social and political dominance. The New Critics dismissed African American literature that sought to deal with racism and the struggle for equality as mere didacticism or agitprop, not to be compared with the great white literary productions that achieved universal import. In a major work of New Criticism published in 1952, the influential critic R. P. Blackmur dismissed *Native Son*, a powerful and now classic novel about white racism, as "one of those books in which everything is undertaken with seriousness except the writing."

Marxist Criticism   The Marxist critic sees literature as one activity among many to be studied and judged in terms of a larger and all-encompassing ideology derived from the economic and political doctrines of Karl Marx (1818–1883). Marxism offers a comprehensive theory about the nature of humans and the way in which a few of them manage to seize control of the means of production and thereby exploit the masses of working people. But Marxism is about more than analysis. As Karl Marx himself said, "It is not enough to analyze society; we must also change it."

The Marxist critic analyzes literary works to show how, wittingly or unwittingly, they support the dominant social class or how they, in some way, contribute to the struggle against oppression and exploitation. And since the Marxist critic views literature as just one among the variety of human activities that reflect power relations and class divisions, he or she is likely to be more interested in what a work says than in its formal structure.

The Marxist argues that one cannot properly understand a literary work unless one understands how it reflects the relationship between economic production and social class. Further, this relationship cannot be explored adequately without examining a range of questions that other critical approaches, notably formalism, deem irrelevant. How does the work relate to the profit-driven enterprise of publishing? What does the author's biography reveal about his or her class biases? Does the work accurately portray the class divisions of society? Does the work expose the economic bases of oppression and advance the cause of liberation?

And since Marxist critics see their duty—indeed, the duty of all responsible and humane people—as not merely to describe the world but to change it, they judge literature by the contribution it makes to bringing about revolution or in some way enlightening its readers about oppression and the necessity for class struggle.

For example, a Marxist critic's analysis of Matthew Arnold's poem "Dover Beach" (p. 909) might see it not as a brilliantly structured pattern of images and sounds but as the predictable end product of a dehumanizing capitalist economy in which a small class of oligarchs is willing, at whatever cost, to protect its wealth and power. The Marxist critic, as a materialist who believes that humans make their own history, would find Arnold's reference to the "eternal note of sadness" (l. 14) a mystic evasion of the real sources of his alienation and pain: Arnold's misery can be clearly and unmystically explained by his fearful responses to the socioeconomic conditions of his time.

Arnold's refusal to face this fact leads him to the conclusion typical of a bourgeois artist-intellectual who cannot discern the truth. But the cure for Arnold's pain, the Marxist would argue, cannot be found in a love relationship because relations between people are determined crucially by socioeconomic conditions. The cure for the pain he describes so well will be found in the world of action, in the struggle to create a society that is just and humane. "Dover Beach," the Marxist critic would conclude, is both a brilliant evocation of the alienation and misery caused by a capitalist economy and a testimony to the inability of a bourgeois intellectual to understand what is responsible for his feelings.

New Historical Criticism There is nothing "new" about historians drawing on literary works as significant documents to support and illuminate historical analysis; nor is there anything "new" about literary critics drawing on history to illuminate literary works. For the historian, Sophocles' *Antigonê* (p. 468) tells us much about the conflict between the old-time religion and the new secularism in fifth-century B.C. Athens. The literary critic of *Othello* (p. 947) goes to the historian to understand the way in which Shakespeare and his contemporaries viewed black Africans. But until recently, the provinces of the historian and of the literary critics were pretty much mutually exclusive.

The new historians (influenced by modern theories of language and literature) began to question the very idea of history as it had been practiced. The historians of the past tended, for the most part, to think of history in terms of overarching themes and theses, and attempted to understand it in terms of some perceived *Zeitgeist*, or "spirit of the times." This kind of history was often linked to nationalism. Hence (for one example), nineteenth-century Americans created the idea of manifest destiny and then used it to explain and justify eastern settlers' movement west and their attendant atrocities against the Native Americans who resided there. When the Nazis came to power in Germany, they developed the idea that true Germans were descended from a superior Aryan race and then used that idea to deprive "inferior races" of civil rights, of property, and finally, of life.

More abstractly, the purpose of writing history was to articulate and reinforce the values and beliefs that gave a culture unity. By that means, some new historians note, history became the story (and the ideas and beliefs and culture) of the rich, the powerful, the privileged, the victorious. The new historians see history not as the search for some grand, unifying thesis but as the articulation of the various kinds of discourse that compete with, contradict, overlap, and modify one another in the constant struggle for dominance. Indeed, the new historians, influenced by deconstructionist views of language, came to question the very idea of historical truth.

The new historians also reject the traditional division between history and other disciplines, appropriating to historical studies many kinds of texts—including literary texts—that traditional historians left to others. These critics assert that without an understanding of the historical context that produced it, no work of literature can really be understood; therefore, in their eyes, literature belongs as much to the historian as to the literary critic. Such critics aim at what they call a "thick" description of a literary work, one that applies to a text as much information as can be gathered about every aspect of the author, his work, and his times. While its practitioners generally share the fundamental ideas outlined here, they can differ widely in the tools and methodologies they use to analyze a literary text. That is to say, a new historian may also be a Marxist, feminist, or deconstructionist.

Postcolonial Criticism Postcolonial criticism belongs to the larger field of postcolonial studies, which evolved in the wake of the liberation of many nations from the domination of the European powers of the nineteenth century. It is distinguished not so much by any singular approach as by its subject: the examination of postcolonial writings that explore the way in which the colonizers imposed their culture and values on native peoples and thus distorted or suppressed their past.

One prominent purpose of postcolonial criticism is to explain and expose the mechanisms the colonizer used—from brute force to subtle psychological techniques—to gain and maintain control. It becomes, in effect, a new lens through which the literature of the colonizing culture can be examined in order to expose its biased judgments about the society it has dominated, its distortions of native culture as compared with the colonizing culture. This kind of analysis will lead the critic away from narrowly defined literary concerns to examine the colonized culture's past, including its precolonial past. Thus postcolonial critics (and historians), by uncovering the past, may give their newly liberated compatriots the means of re-creating an identity and may give its imaginative writers the material for a national literature.

Because postcolonial criticism is a relatively new field, it is still developing its distinctive areas of interest and techniques of analysis. By its nature it is eclectic, drawing on any other literary approach (as well as academic discipline) that seems relevant to a critic's purpose.

Psychoanalytic Criticism Psychoanalytic criticism always proceeds from a set of principles that describes the inner life of men and women. Though differing psychological theorists argue for diverse views, all analysts and all psychoanalytic critics assume that the development of the psyche is analogous to the development of the body. Doctors can provide charts indicating physical growth stages; analysts can supply similar charts indicating stages in the growth of the psyche. Sigmund Freud, for all practical purposes, invented psychoanalysis by creating a theoretical model for the (mostly male) human psyche.

The Oedipus complex is a significant element in that model. Freud contends that everyone moves through a childhood stage of erotic attachment to the parent of the opposite sex and an accompanying hostility and aggression against the parent of the same sex, who is seen as a rival. Such feelings, part of the natural biography of the psyche, pass or are effectively controlled in most cases. But sometimes the child grown to adulthood is still strongly gripped by the Oedipal mode, which then may result in neurotic or even psychotic behavior. Freud did not invent the Oedipus complex—he simply described it. It was always there, especially noticeable in the work of great literary artists who, in every era, demonstrate a special insight into the human condition.

Along with Oedipal feelings, the psyche inevitably embodies aggressive feelings—the urge to attack those who exercise authority, who deny us our primal desires. For the young, the authority figure is frequently a parent. Adults must deal with police, government officials, the boss. As far back as the Hebrew Bible story of the tower of Babel and the old Greek myths in which the giant Titans, led by Cronus, overthrow their father, and Zeus and the Olympians subsequently overthrow Cronus, there is evidence of the rebellion against the parent-authority figure. Freud views that aggressive hostility as another component of the developing psyche. But, in the interest of civilization, society has developed ways to control that aggressiveness.

Freud saw us as divided selves. An unconscious *id* struggles to gratify aggressive and erotic primal urges, while a *superego* (roughly what society calls *conscience*), by producing guilt feelings, struggles to control the id. The *ego* (the self) is defined by the struggle. Thus the Freudian psychoanalytic critic is constantly aware that authors and their characters suffer and resuffer a primal tension that results from the conflict between psychic aggressions and social obligations.

Freud has been succeeded by a number of psychological theorists who present quite different models of the psyche, and recent literary theory has responded to these post-Freudian views. Among the most important are Carl Gustav Jung (1875–1961), who argued that there exists a collective (as well as a racial and individual) unconscious. Residing there are archetypes—original patterns—that emerge into our consciousness in the form of shadowy images that persistently appear and reappear in such literary themes as the search for the father, death and resurrection, the quest, and the double.

The psychoanalytic critic understands literature in terms of the psychic models that Freud and others defined. Originally, such critics tended to analyze literature in an attempt to identify the author's neuroses. More recently, psychoanalytic critics have argued that the patterns they discover in works allow us to tap into and, perhaps, resolve our own neuroses.

Reader-Response Criticism   Reader-response criticism (also called *transactional theory*) emerged in the 1970s as one of the many challenges to formalist principles. Reader-response critics focus on the interaction between the work and the reader, holding that, in a sense, a work exists only when it is experienced by the reader. If the work exists only in the mind of the reader, the reader becomes an active participant in the creative process rather than a passive receptacle for an autonomous work. The creation of a work thus becomes a dynamic enterprise between the reader and the text, each acting on the other. The study of the affective power of a work becomes not a fallacy, as formalism holds, but the central focus of criticism. The task of the critic is to investigate this dynamic relationship between reader and text in order to discover how it works.

We know that various readers respond differently to the same text. In fact, the same reader might respond to the text quite differently at a different time. The reader-response critic wants to know why. In what ways do such conditions as age, gender, upbringing, and race account for differing responses? Does the reader's mood at the time of reading make a difference? If you accept the principles of reader-response criticism, the inevitable conclusion—*reductio ad absurdum*, its critics would say—is that there is no limit to the possible readings of any text. Consequently, many reader-response critics qualify the intense subjectivity of their approach by admitting that an "informed" or "educated" reader is likely to produce a more "valid" reading than an "uninformed" or "uneducated" one.

Gaps or blanks in literary texts provide particular opportunities to readers. Every narrative work omits, for example, periods of time that the reader must fill in. In Nathaniel Hawthorne's "Young Goodman Brown" (p. 79), the author omits all the years of Brown's life between his emergence from the forest and his death. The reader is free to imagine that history. The filling in of these blanks enables readers to participate in "creating" a text and reinforces the arguments of reader-response theorists.

BIOGRAPHICAL NOTES ON THE AUTHORS

CHIMAMANDA NGOZI ADICHIE (b. 1977) Adichie was born in Enugu, Nigeria, and raised in the town of Nsukka. Her parents were very accomplished: Her father was the University of Nigeria's first professor of statistics and later served as deputy vice-chancellor of the university, and her mother was the first female registrar there. Adichie completed her secondary education at the university's school and later studied medicine and pharmacy at the university. At the age of nineteen, she moved to the United States and attended Drexel university on a scholarship to study communication. She then went on to pursue a degree in communication and political science at Eastern Connecticut State University, from which she graduated summa cum laude. She later earned her M.A. in creative writing at Johns Hopkins University. Her first novel, *Purple Hibiscus* (2003), won the Commonwealth Writers' Prize and the Hurston/Wright Legacy Award. Her second novel, *Half of a Yellow Sun* (2006), was awarded the 2007 Orange Prize for Fiction. Her latest work is a collection of short stories, *The Thing Around Your Neck* (2009). Her short fiction has appeared in such publications as *The New Yorker, Virginia Quarterly Review, Fiction, Granta, Prospect, Iowa Review,* and others. Adichie received an O. Henry Prize in 2003 for her short story "The American Embassy," and her story "Ceiling" was included in *Best American Short Stories* 2011. Of her fiction, fellow Nigerian author Chinua Achebe has said that "Adichie knows what is at stake and what to do about it."

ANNA AKHMATOVA (1889–1966) Akhmatova was born Anna Andreevna Gorenko in Odessa, Ukraine. She started writing poems as a very young woman; her father's disapproval led her to assume a pen name. Her first collection of poems, *Evening,* was published in 1912; her second collection, *Rosary,* appeared in 1914. Her work was banned under Stalin from 1925 to 1940, but she had become so popular with the Russian people that they shared her work illicitly. Although Akhmatova and her family suffered at the hands of the Bolsheviks, she remained in Russia rather than flee like many of her contemporaries. After Stalin's death in 1953, she was celebrated as a symbol of survival of the repression. Several volumes of her poems were collected and published beginning in the late 1950s. A well-respected figure, she was visited at her villa by the likes of Joseph Brodsky and Robert Frost. Akhmatova died in St. Petersburg in 1966. What is perhaps her greatest poem, *Requiem,* about the suffering of the Russian people under Stalin, was not published in its entirety in the Soviet Union until 1987.

SHERMAN ALEXIE (b. 1966) A Spokane/Coeur d'Alene Indian, Sherman Alexie was born on the Spokane Indian Reservation in Wellpinit, Washington. In 1981, he left the reservation school and enrolled in a predominantly white high school, where, according to Alexie, he "kept [his] mouth shut and became a good white Indian." He enrolled at Gonzaga University in Spokane and began to discover his love for literature and his talent for writing. After two years at Gonzaga, he transferred to Washington State University in Pullman, where he began to write seriously. A year after he received his degree, he published two collections of poetry, *The Business of Fancydancing* (1992) and *I Would Steal*

Horses (1992), followed the next year by another poetry collection, *First Indian on the Moon* (1993). Alexie then turned to prose, publishing a volume of loosely related stories dealing with life on the reservation, *The Lone Ranger and Tonto Fistfight in Heaven* (1993). One of the stories in this collection, "This Is What It Means to Say Phoenix, Arizona," provided the basis for the film *Smoke Signals* (1998), which Alexie produced and for which he wrote the screenplay. He went on to write two more films: *The Business of Fancydancing* (2002), which he also directed, and *49?* (2003). He has published two other collections of short stories, *The Toughest Indian in the World* (2000) and *Ten Little Indians* (2003), along with a number of collections of poetry, including *Dangerous Astronomy* (2005). Alexie has also penned several novels, among them *Reservation Blues* (1995), *Indian Killer* (1996), and *Flight* (2007). His novel for young adults, *The Absolutely True Diary of a Part-Time Indian* (2007), won the National Book Award for Young People's Literature. He recently published *War Dances* (2009), a collection of stories, poems, and question-and-answer sequences that explore generational and artistic complexities. About the criticism he has received from members of his reservation, who find his portrayals of Native Americans and reservation life demeaning, Alexie replied, "I write what I know, and I don't try to mythologize myself, which is what some seem to want, and which some Indian women and men writers are doing, this Earth Mother and Shaman Man thing, trying to create these 'authentic, traditional' Indians. We don't live our lives that way."

WOODY ALLEN (b. 1935)   After being dismissed from both City College of New York and New York University, this precocious and prototypical New Yorker became a television comedy writer at the age of eighteen. He wrote two successful Broadway plays; his first screenplay, *What's New Pussycat?*, appeared in 1965. A dozen years in show business gave him the confidence to set out on his own, and he began performing as a stand-up comic. Soon after, he embarked on the filmmaking career—writing, performing, directing, and producing—for which he is famous. His talents, and those of the actors and technical group he brought together as a kind of filmmaking repertory company, account for his reputation as an innovative contributor to cinema history. His 1977 film, *Annie Hall*, won four Academy Awards, and Allen has received lifetime achievement awards from the Venice Film Festival (1995), the Directors Guild of America (1996), and the Cannes Film Festival (2002). In his spare time he plays the clarinet in a Dixieland jazz group at a New York nightspot, and continues to write occasional pieces such as *Death Knocks*. His recent films include *Vicky Cristina Barcelona* (2008), *Whatever Works* (2009), *You Will Meet a Tall Dark Stranger* (2010), and *Midnight in Paris* (2011).

JULIA ALVAREZ (b. 1950)   Alvarez was born in New York City to Dominican parents. Her family moved to the Dominican Republic when she was three months old and remained there until she was ten, when her father's involvement in a political uprising forced them to flee to the United States. Her struggle to assimilate into American culture and forge an identity informs much of her work. She published a volume of poetry, *Homecoming* (1984), before writing three novels that brought her great acclaim: *How the García Girls Lost Their Accents* (1991), *In the Time of the Butterflies* (1994), and *¡Yo!* (1997). She went on to publish more poetry, a children's book, and several novels. Among the places Alvarez has taught are the University of Vermont, George Washington College, and the University of Illinois, Urbana; she is now a writer-in-residence at Middlebury College. Some of her most recent publications are a work of nonfiction, *Once upon a Quinceañera: Coming of Age in the USA* (2007), and a novel for children about migrant workers, *Return to Sender* (2009). Alvarez has said, "When I'm asked what made me into a writer, I point to the watershed experience of coming to this country. Not understanding the language, I had to pay close attention to each word. . . . I also discovered the welcoming world of the imagination and books. There, I sunk my new roots."

MAGGIE ANDERSON (b. 1948) Anderson was born in New York and has dedicated her life to creating and promoting poetry. In 1971, she co-founded the poetry journal *Trellis* and served as its editor until 1981. In 1989, Anderson took a position teaching creative writing at Kent State University, where she became coordinator of the Wick Poetry Program in 1992. She was also part of the founding committee of the Northeast Ohio Master of Fine Arts in Creative Writing and served as Kent's campus coordinator from 2003 to 2006 and as director of the Northeast Ohio M.F.A. Consortium from 2006 to 2009. When she retired from Kent State in 2009, the university created the Maggie Anderson Endowment Fund to honor her contributions to the college. Anderson's poetry collections include *The Great Horned Owl* (1979), *Years That Answer* (1980), *Cold Comfort* (1986), *A Space Filled with Moving* (1992), and *Windfall: New and Selected Poems* (2000). Recently, her poems have been published in the *Alaska Quarterly*, *Georgia Review*, and *American Poetry Review*. She has received a National Endowment for the Arts Fellowship in Poetry, a West Virginia Commission on the Arts Fellowship in Poetry, an Ohio Arts Council Fellowship, a Pennsylvania Council on the Arts Fellowship, and a MacDowell Colony Fellowship.

MATTHEW ARNOLD (1822–1888) Born in Middlesex, England, Arnold attended Rugby School, where his father was headmaster, and studied classics at Oxford University. Following his graduation in 1844, he became a fellow at Oxford and a master at Rugby. In 1851, he was appointed inspector of schools in England and was sent by the government to observe educational systems in Europe. He remained in that post for some thirty-five years. As a poet, Arnold took inspiration from Greek tragedies, Keats, and Wordsworth. His collections include *Empedocles on Etna and Other Poems* (1852). An eminent social and literary critic in his later years, Arnold lectured in the United States in 1883 and 1886. His essay "The Function of Criticism" sheds light on his transition from poet to critic. Much of his work is collected in *Complete Prose Works* (11 volumes, 1960–1977).

HANAN MIKHA'IL 'ASHRAWI (b. 1946) 'Ashrawi was born to a wealthy Christian Palestinian family just two years before Israel became a country—an event the Palestinians call *al-nakba* (the disaster). She grew up in Ramallah, a West Bank town outside Jerusalem. She was a student of literature at the American University in Beirut, Lebanon, when the 1967 Six Days' War broke out. When the fighting ended, her hometown, along with significant additional territory west of the river Jordan was occupied by Israel, and for six years the occupying forces refused to allow Palestinians who had been absent during the war to return to the West Bank. During that period, 'Ashrawi traveled and continued her studies, earning a Ph.D. from the University of Virginia in medieval and comparative literature. She returned to Palestine in 1973, where she established and chaired the department of English at Birzeit University in the West Bank, rose to the position of dean of the Faculty of Arts, and remained a faculty member through 1995. She produced several works on literary theory and on contemporary Palestinian literature. She served on numerous commissions on education and politics in the region and is recognized as an eloquent spokesperson for Palestinian civil, economic, and political rights. Her publications include *Intifada to Independence* (1989) and her autobiography, *This Side of Peace: A Personal Account* (1995).

W. H. AUDEN (1907–1973)   A poet, playwright, translator, librettist, critic, and editor, Wystan Hugh Auden was born in York, England, son of a medical officer and a nurse. He attended Oxford University from 1925 to 1928, then taught, traveled, and moved from faculty to faculty of several universities in the United States, becoming a naturalized citizen in 1946. He won the Pulitzer Prize in 1948 for his collection *The Age of Anxiety*, an expression he coined to describe the 1930s. While his early writing exhibited Marxist sympathies and reflected the excitement of new Freudian psychoanalytic thought, he later embraced Christianity and produced sharply honed verse in the rhyme and meter of traditional forms.

FRANCIS BACON (1561–1626)   Bacon was many things—including an English statesman, historian, intellectual reformer, and philosopher—but his most important role was as a champion of modern science. Born at York House in the Strand, he was sent at the age of thirteen to Trinity College, Cambridge, with his elder brother Anthony. While at Trinity, he met Queen Elizabeth I, who was impressed by his precocious nature and sharp intellect. Around this time Bacon also began to form the foundations of his life's work, claiming "all knowledge as his province" and starting to form his now-renowned inductive methodologies for learning. Bacon favored an educational system where the ultimate goal was practical knowledge for "the use and benefit of men," and he believed that empirical evidence gathered from the natural world should be the basis for study and the development of new ideas. Bacon advanced his governmental aspirations somewhat under Queen Elizabeth's rule, but he truly climbed the political ladder once King James I took the throne. Bacon was knighted in 1603 and then went on to serve as solicitor general (1607), attorney general (1613), and eventually lord chancellor (1618). His time in public office was cut short when he was indicted on charges of bribery, after which he retired to his estate and continued his literary, scientific, and philosophical work. He died in 1626, but the legacy of his inductive methodologies laid the groundwork for many of the scientific and technological achievements of the modern world.

JAMES BALDWIN (1924–1987)   Born in New York City, the son of a Harlem minister, Baldwin began preaching as a young teenager. Some years later, he experienced a religious crisis, left the church, and moved to New York City's bohemian Greenwich Village, where he began his career as a writer, supporting himself with menial jobs and publishing occasional articles in journals such as the *Nation* and *Commentary*. By the end of the 1940s, Baldwin's anger over the treatment of African Americans led him into exile in France. There, Baldwin completed his acclaimed first novel, *Go Tell It on the Mountain* (1953), a work focusing on a minister's son for which he drew heavily on his own childhood. His next work, *Notes of a Native Son* (1955), a collection of personal, literary, and social essays, secured Baldwin's reputation as a major American writer. Two later collections of essays, *Nobody Knows My Name* (1961) and *The Fire Next Time* (1963), established Baldwin as one of the most powerful voices of the turbulent civil rights movement of the 1960s. But as riots, bombings, and other violence grew more frequent, Baldwin grew increasingly pessimistic over the prospect that white America could ever overcome its racism. That pessimism was deepened by two traumatic events: the 1963 bombing of the Sixteenth Street Baptist Church in Birmingham, Alabama, that killed four young girls attending a Sunday school class, and the assassination of the Reverend Martin Luther King Jr. in 1968. Baldwin began making periodic trips to France, settling there permanently in 1974.

TONI CADE BAMBARA (1939–1995)   Born in New York City, Bambara was educated there as well as in Italy and Paris. Early in her career she worked as an investigator for the New York State Department of Social Welfare, but she later devoted herself to teaching and writing. One of the best representatives of a group of African American writers who emerged in the 1960s, Bambara was a consistent civil rights activist, involved both politically and culturally in African American life. Much of her writing focuses on African American women, particularly as they confront experiences that force them to new awareness. She authored several collections of short stories, including *Gorilla, My Love* (1972) and *The Sea Birds Are Still Alive: Collected Stories* (1977), and two novels, *The Salt Eaters* (1980) and *If Blessing Comes* (1987). She also edited a groundbreaking collection of African American women's writing, *The Black Woman: An Anthology* (1970). Two works, *Deep Sightings and Rescue Missions: Fiction, Essays, and Conversations* (1996) and the novel *These Bones Are Not My Child* (1999), were published posthumously.

AIMEE BENDER (b. 1969)   Bender attended the University of California at San Diego and taught elementary school in San Francisco for three years before getting her M.F.A. from the University of California at Irvine. She cites Oscar Wilde, Hans Christian Andersen, and the Brothers Grimm as influences on her writing. Her first collection of short stories, *The Girl in the Flammable Skirt* (1998), was a *New York Times* notable book of the year. Bender then published a novel, *An Invisible Sign of My Own* (2000), and another collection of short stories, *Willful Creatures* (2005). Her most recent novel is *The Particular Sadness of Lemon Cake* (2011). Her work has also appeared in magazines such as *Granta*, *GQ*, and *Harper's*, among others. She won the Pushcart Prize twice. Bender currently lives in Los Angeles and teaches creative writing at the University of Southern California. Her writing has been described as contemporary fairy tales, and she has said about fiction, "There are no rules. You're absolutely free."

BRUCE BENNETT (b. 1940)   Bennett was born in Philadelphia, Pennsylvania, and began writing poems when he was eight years old. He attended Harvard University as an undergraduate and graduate student, receiving a Ph.D. in English (1967). From 1967 to 1970 he taught at Oberlin College, where he co-founded *Field: Contemporary Poetry and Poetics*. In 1971 he co-founded and co-edited the literary journal *Ploughshares*. In that year he married Renaissance art historian Bonnie Apgar; the couple lived in Florence, Italy, for two years, and return there often. Since 1973, Bennett has taught English and directed creative writing at Wells College in Aurora, New York; in 1993 he also became director of the Wells College Book Arts Center. He has published numerous books and chapbooks, including *Navigating the Distances* (1999), which was selected by *Booklist* as "one of the Top Ten Poetry Books of 1999." Some of his recent publications include *Subway Figure* (2009), *Something Like Karma* (2009), and *The Holding Stone* (2010). Bennett writes in a variety of forms and moods, and regards storytelling as a key element of his work. He believes poetry should be accessible, a part of everyone's life, and approvingly quotes William Carlos Williams: "If it ain't pleasure, it ain't a poem." Through public readings and visits to schools, he encourages young people to write poems. X. J. Kennedy has called Bennett a "master fabulist and satirist" and a "parodist *par excellence*," who "often compresses realms of wisdom into tight, economical packages."

GEORGE BEST (d. ca. 1584)   George Best was an Elizabethan scientist and explorer who chronicled the expeditions led by Martin Frobisher in search of the Northwest Passage. The scope and accuracy of Best's observations from the voyages have made his work of enduring importance, though little else is known about his life. He reportedly died in a duel with Oliver St. John, an English soldier, around 1584.

ELIZABETH BISHOP (1911–1979)   Bishop was born in Worcester, Massachusetts. Her father died before she was a year old; four years later, when her mother suffered a mental breakdown, Bishop was taken to live with her grandmother in Nova Scotia. Although her mother lived until 1934, Bishop saw her for the last time in 1916, a visit recalled in one of her rare autobiographical stories, "In the Village." Bishop planned to enter Cornell Medical School after graduating from Vassar, but was persuaded by poet Marianne Moore to become a writer. For the next fifteen years, she was a virtual nomad, traveling in Canada, Europe, and North and South America. In 1951, she finally settled in Rio de Janeiro, where she lived for almost twenty years. During the final decade of her life, Bishop continued to travel, but she resumed living in the United States and taught frequently at Harvard University. She was an austere writer, publishing only four slim volumes of poetry: *North and South* (1946); *A Cold Spring* (1955), which won the Pulitzer Prize; *Questions of Travel* (1965); and *Geography III* (1976), which won the National Book Critics Circle Award. *The Complete Poems, 1927–1979* (1984) was published after her death, as was a collection of her prose. Despite her modest output, she has earned an enduring place of respect among twentieth-century poets.

WILLIAM BLAKE (1757–1827)   Born in London to an obscure family, Blake was educated at home until he was ten and then enrolled in a drawing school, advancing ultimately to a formal apprenticeship as an engraver. At an early age, Blake exhibited talent as both an artist and a poet. Throughout his life, he read widely among modern philosophers and poets and experienced mystical visions that provided him with the inspiration for many of his poems. Blake devised a process he called illuminated printing, which involved the preparation of drawings and decorative frames to complement his poems. He published *Songs of Innocence* (1789) and *Songs of Experience* (1794) in this fashion. These books, as well as the many subsequent works he wrote and illustrated, earned him a reputation as one of the most important artists of his day. Many of Blake's works assert his conviction that the established church and state hinder rather than nurture human freedom and the sense of divine love.

ADRIAN BLEVINS (b. 1964)   Adrian Blevins received her B.A. in English from Virginia Intermont College, her M.A. in fiction from Hollins University, and her M.F.A. in poetry from Warren Wilson College in 2002. She then taught at Roanoke College and Hollins University, and she is currently an associate professor of creative writing at Colby College in Waterville, Maine. Her first full-length collection of poetry, *The Brass Girl Brouhaha* (2003), won the 2004 Kate Tufts Discovery Award. Blevins has also received the Rona Jaffe Writers Foundation Award for poetry, the Lamar York Prize for Nonfiction, and a 1996 Bright Hill Press award for her first chapbook, *The Man Who Went Out for Cigarettes* (1997). Her most recent collection is *Live from the Homesick Jamboree* (2009), which Tawnysha Green of the *Southern Humanities Review* called "Blevins's most haunting work yet." Her poems have also appeared in the *American Poetry Review*, *Poetry*, *Southern Review*, *Ploughshares*, *North American Review*, and the *Georgia Review*, among other renowned literary journals.

T. CORAGHESSAN BOYLE (b. 1948)   Tom Coraghessan Boyle grew up in Peekskill, New York. He received a B.A. in history and English from the State University of

New York at Potsdam, his M.F.A. from the University of Iowa, and his Ph.D. in nineteenth-century British literature from the University of Iowa Writer's Workshop. He is the author of twenty-two books of fiction, the most recent of which have included *The Human Fly* (2005), *Talk Talk* (2006), *The Women* (2009), *Wild Child* (2010), and *When the Killing's Done* (2011). His work has been translated into over two dozen languages and been featured in such publications as *The New Yorker, Harper's, Esquire, Atlantic Monthly, Playboy, Paris Review, GQ, Antaeus, Granta,* and *McSweeney's.* He has won numerous literary awards, including the PEN/Faulkner Prize for best novel of the year for *World's End* (1988), the PEN/Malamud Prize for *T.C. Boyle Stories* (1999), and the Prix Médicis Étranger for best foreign novel in France for *The Tortilla Curtain* (1997). He currently lives near Santa Barbara with his family and is Distinguished Professor of English at the University of Southern California.

ANNE BRADSTREET (1612–1672) The first notable poet in American literature, Bradstreet was born in England, where her father, a Puritan, managed the business affairs of the estate of the earl of Lincoln. Unlike most women of her time, Bradstreet received a good deal of formal education. At age sixteen she married Simon Bradstreet, a graduate of Cambridge University, who, like her father, was a Puritan. Two years later, Bradstreet, her husband, and her parents set sail for the Massachusetts Bay Colony, where her father and husband became governors. Anne and Simon Bradstreet settled on a farm near Andover, on the Merrimac River, where the primitive conditions of life left her unhappy and unsatisfied for a period. Ultimately, she reconciled to this new life and her role as a wife, giving birth to eight children. But despite the demands of domestic life in a frontier village, she read a great deal and wrote poetry, which she circulated among family and friends. One of her relatives, who preserved copies of her poems without her knowledge, took them to England, where they were published in 1650 under the title *The Tenth Muse Lately Sprung Up in America . . . By a Gentlewoman of Those Parts.* The first volume of poetry by an English colonist, it was to be the only volume of Bradstreet's poetry published during her lifetime. She continued to write new poems and to revise her older ones; these later poems were included in the second edition of *The Tenth Muse,* published posthumously in 1678.

ROBERT H. BRINKMEYER JR. (b. 1951) Brinkmeyer earned his B.A. from Duke University and his M.A. and Ph.D. from the University of North Carolina at Chapel Hill. His extensive, renowned scholarship on Southern literature has appeared in publications such as *Southern Quarterly* and *Mississippi Quarterly,* and he has published several books, including *Three Catholic Writers of the Modern South* (1985), *The Art and Vision of Flannery O'Connor* (1993), and *Remapping Southern Literature: Contemporary Southern Writers and the West* (2000). His most recent book, *The Fourth Ghost: White Southern Writers and European Fascism, 1930–1950* (2009), won the 2008 Warren-Brooks Award for Academic Excellence and the 2010 Prose Award from the Association of American Publishers. He has won several awards from the National Endowment for the Humanities and was awarded a Guggenheim Fellowship in 2004. He has held teaching positions at North Carolina Central University, Tulane University, the University of Mississippi, and the University of Arkansas, as well as visiting appointments to the University of Vienna and the University of Helsinki. He is currently the Emily Brown Jeffries Professor of English and Professor of Southern Studies at the University of South Carolina.

GWENDOLYN BROOKS (1917–2000) Brooks, who was born in Topeka, Kansas, attended public schools in Chicago and graduated from Wilson Junior College in 1936.

She received early recognition for her talent when she attended a poetry workshop at Chicago's Southside Community Art Center. Shortly after, she published her first book of poems, *A Street in Bronzeville* (1945). She quickly established her reputation as a major poet with *Annie Allen* (1949), which received the Pulitzer Prize for Poetry, making Brooks the first African American to receive this distinction. Her many honors include her designation as poet laureate of Illinois (1968) and as poetry consultant to Congress (1985–1986). Although her poetry always focused on the hardships and joys of being poor and black, she steadily moved away from the apolitical integrationist views of her early years. By the 1960s, she had become a passionate advocate of African American consciousness and activism. In addition to reworking traditional forms such as the ballad and sonnet, Brooks achieved greater power in many poems by juxtaposing formal speech with black vernacular. Her other collections of poems include *The Bean Eaters* (1960), *In the Mecca* (1968), *To Disembark* (1981), and *Children Coming Home* (1992). She also published a novel, *Maude Martha* (1953), and an autobiography, *Report from Part One* (1972). Her final volume of poetry, *Montgomery and Other Poems*, was published posthumously in 2003. Its title is taken from the Alabama city that one critic describes as "one of those iconic sites of the Civil Rights Movement, in large part because of the yearlong bus boycotts from 1955 to 1956."

ROBERT BROWNING (1812–1889)   Born in London, Browning attended a private school and was later tutored at home. After one year as a student of Greek at the University of London, he moved with his family to Hatcham, where he studied, wrote poetry, and practiced writing for the theater. In 1845, he began exchanging poems and letters with the already famous poet Elizabeth Barrett; they eloped in 1846. They moved to Italy, where Browning completed most of his work. When Elizabeth died in 1861, he returned to England and began to establish his own reputation. He is noted especially for his fine dramatic monologues in which a wide range of characters reveal the complexity of human belief and passion. His many volumes of poetry include *Dramatis Personae* (1864) and *The Ring and the Book* (1868–1869)

HALLMAN B. BRYANT (b. ?)   Bryant's literary criticism has appeared in *Literature/ Film Quarterly* and *Studies in Short Fiction* as well as many edited collections. His article "Reading the Map in 'A Good Man Is Hard to Find'" is among the most famous essays on Flannery O'Connor's renowned short story.

ROBERT BURNS (1759–1796)   Born in Scotland to a family of poor tenant farmers, Burns was working in the fields with his father by age twelve. During these early years, the family moved often, in fruitless attempts to improve their lot. Although Burns received formal education only intermittently, he read widely on his own. After the death of his father, Burns and his brother worked vainly to make their farm pay, an effort Burns was able to abandon when his first volume of poetry, *Poems, Chiefly in the Scottish Dialect* (1786) brought him overnight fame. One result of this fame was his appointment as an excise officer, a position that gave him some financial security while he continued to write poetry. Burns's humble origins instilled in him a lifelong sympathy for the poor and downtrodden, the rebels and iconoclasts, as well as a disdain for religion, particularly Calvinism and what he considered the hypocrisy of its "devout" ministers.

ROBERT BURTON (1577–1640)   Burton was prominent English scholar at Oxford University during the early seventeenth century. While many of his contemporaries, such as Francis Bacon, championed natural science and its importance to humanity, Burton argued that knowledge of psychology was humans' greatest need. It was this focus on the self that informed his landmark work, *The Anatomy of Melancholy* (1621). During Burton's time, a person's every ecstasy and anguish—from laymen to scholars, from lovers to clergy—was attributed to "melancholy," and Burton used a tongue-in-cheek approach to dissect this mysterious malady in exhaustive detail. The book's winking tone has delighted critics and readers for centuries and remained Burton's defining work; as Nick Lezard, critic for *The Guardian*, said in 2000 (over three and a half centuries after the book was first published), *Anatomy of Melancholy* "survives among the cognoscenti" of the literary world.

REBECCA R. BUTLER (b. 1943)   Butler is a literary critic and the author of *The Fifty-Minute Essay and Other Timed Writing* (2000).

RACHEL CARSON (1907–1964)   Carson was a marine biologist and conservationist whose bold writing helped to advance the 1960s global environmental movement. Carson graduated from Pennsylvania College for Women (now Chatham College) in 1929, studied at the Woods Hole Marine Biological Laboratory, and received her M.A. in zoology from Johns Hopkins University in 1932. She then worked as a biologist for the U.S. Bureau of Fisheries and became a full-time nature writer in the 1950s. Carson made herself a household name with the publication of *The Sea Around Us* (1951), a best seller that was praised by critics and readers alike. It won both the 1952 National Book Award for Nonfiction and a Burroughs Medal in nature writing. Her next book, *The Edge of the Sea* (1955), was also well received. In the late 1950s, Carson turned her attention to the environmental problems caused by the irresponsible use of synthetic chemical pesticides after World War II. She chronicled these concerns in *Silent Spring* (1962), a groundbreaking book that made an unprecedented call for a change in the way that humans treated the natural world and prompted the grassroots environmental movement that led to the creation of the Environmental Protection Agency. Carson died in 1964 from breast cancer, but the impact of her work has proved indelible. In 1980, she was posthumously awarded the Presidential Medal of Freedom by President Jimmy Carter.

RAYMOND CARVER (1938–1988)   Carver was born in Clatskanie, Oregon, the son of a sawmill worker and a mother who did odd jobs. He graduated from high school at age eighteen, and was married and the father of two children before he was twenty. The following years were difficult as he struggled to develop a writing career while supporting a family. While at Chico State College (now California State University at Chico), Carver took a creative writing course that profoundly affected him. He went on to earn a B.A. (1963) from Humboldt State College in Eureka and spent the following year studying writing at the University of Iowa. As he became known, he began to lecture on English and creative writing at various universities, including the University of Iowa's Writers' Workshop. He taught at Goddard College in Vermont and was professor of English at Syracuse University from 1980 to 1983. In 1983, he received the Mildred and Harold Strauss Living Award, which allowed him to devote the next five years to writing. His first collection of short stories, *Will You Please Be Quiet, Please?* (1976), was nominated for the National Book Award. Other short-story collections include *What We Talk About When We Talk About Love* (1981) and *Cathedral* (1984). He also published five volumes of poems, among them *Near Klamath* (1968), *Ultramarine* (1986), and *A New Path to the Waterfall* (1989); *No Heroics, Please* (1992) was published posthumously. During the last ten years of his life, Carver lived with the poet and short-story writer Tess Gallagher, whom he married shortly before his death.

SANDRA M. CASTILLO (b. 1962)   Castillo was born in Havana, Cuba, and moved to Miami, Florida, with her family in 1970. Her poetry draws heavily from her early experience of emigrating to the United States as well as from her family's relationships, frequently looking back on the life her family left behind when they fled Cuba. Castillo received both her B.A. and M.A. in creative writing from Florida State University. Her first published collection was the chapbook *Red Letters* (1991), and her first full-length collection was *My Father Sings to My Embarrassment* (2002), which Cornelius Eady selected for the White Pine Press Poetry Prize. Her poems have been published in *Cimarron Review, Midway Journal, Borderlands: Texas Poetry Review, PALABRA: A Magazine of Chicano & Latino Literary Art*, and the anthology *Cool Salsa: Bilingual Poems on Growing Up Latino in the United States* (1994). She currently teaches at Miami Dade College in Florida.

CATULLUS (ca. 84–ca. 54 B.C.)   Relatively little is known about the Latin poet Gaius Valerius Catullus. He is believed to have been born into an influential family in Verona, and his father was said to be a friend to Julius Caesar. The Roman philosopher Cicero described Catullus as a "neoteric" poet who rejected the epic poems characteristic of his time, opting instead to compose poems in plain language mainly about personal experiences. All knowledge of Catullus's poetry has been gleaned from a single extant manuscript of 116 poems, or *carmina*, and the majority of what is known about Catullus's short life has been gathered from the experiences and observations presented in these poems.

MARILYN CHIN (b. 1955)   Chin emigrated with her family from Hong Kong, grew up in Portland, Oregon, and earned degrees from the University of Massachusetts and the University of Iowa. She is the author of three volumes of poetry—*Dwarf Bamboo* (1987), *The Phoenix Gone, the Terrace Empty* (1994), and *Rhapsody in Plain Yellow* (2002)—as well as a novel, *Revenge of the Mooncake Vixen* (2009). She has received two grants from the National Endowment for the Arts as well as a Stegner Fellowship, the PEN/Josephine Miles Award, four Pushcart Prizes, and a Fulbright scholarship. She is codirector of the M.F.A. program at San Diego State University. About her work, Chin says, "My poetry both laments and celebrates my 'hyphenated' identity. . . . I am an American poet, a hyphenated American poet, to be precise; and what is American about my poetry is my muse's indomitable conviction to hammer the rich virtues and contradictions of my adopted country into a fusionist's delight."

KATE CHOPIN (1851–1904)   Born Kate O'Flaherty in St. Louis, Missouri, Chopin was raised by her mother, grandmother, and great-grandmother, all widows, after her father's death when she was four. In 1870, following her graduation from Sacred Heart Convent, she married Oscar Chopin and moved to New Orleans, where she became a housewife and eventually had six children. After her husband's death in 1882, she returned to her mother's home in St. Louis and began her career as a writer. Her first novel, *At Fault* (1890), and her stories, collected in *Bayou Folk* (1894) and *A Night in Acadie* (1897), gained her a reputation as a vivid chronicler of the lives of Creoles and Acadians (Cajuns) in Louisiana. Many of these stories explore a female protagonist's attempts to achieve self-fulfillment. Her novel *The Awakening* (1899) is probably her most ambitious exploration of this theme. It is the story of a woman whose awakening to her passion and inner self leads her to adultery and suicide. The storm of controversy with which this work was met virtually ended Chopin's literary career.

JILL CHRISTMAN (b. 1969) Christman earned her M.F.A. at the University of Alabama and is currently a professor at Ball State University, where she teaches courses in creative nonfiction. Her memoir, *Darkroom: A Family Exposure* (2002), which chronicles her difficult childhood and a string of family tragedies, won the Associated Writing Programs Award for Creative Nonfiction. More recently, Christman's essays have appeared in journals such as *Brevity*, *Harpur Palate*, and *Mississippi Review*. She lives with her husband and daughter in Muncie, Indiana.

SANDRA CISNEROS (b. 1954) Cisneros, the daughter of a Mexican father and a Mexican American mother, grew up in poor neighborhoods of Chicago, where she attended public schools. The only daughter among seven children, Cisneros recalled that because her brothers attempted to control her and expected her to assume a traditional female role, she grew up feeling as if she had "seven fathers." The family's frequent moves, many of them between the United States and Mexico to visit a grandmother, left Cisneros feeling alone and displaced. She found refuge both in reading and in writing poems and stories. In the late 1970s, Cisneros's writing talent earned her admission to the University of Iowa's Writers' Workshop. There, Cisneros observed, "Everyone seemed to have some communal knowledge which I did not have. . . . My classmates were from the best schools in the country. They had been bred as fine hothouse flowers. I was a yellow weed among the city's cracks." This realization led Cisneros to focus her writing on the conflicts and yearnings of her own life and culture. Her writings include four volumes of poetry—*Bad Boys* (1980), *The Rodrigo Poems* (1985), *My Wicked, Wicked Ways* (1987), and *Loose Woman* (1994)—and three volumes of fiction—*The House on Mango Street* (1983), *Woman Hollering Creek and Other Stories* (1991), and *Caramelo* (2002). She is also the author of a bilingual children's book, *Hairs = Pelitos* (1994). She received a prestigious MacArthur Fellowship in 1995. Her most recent work, *Vintage Cisneros* (2004), includes excerpts from her novels as well as previously published poems and short stories.

LUCILLE CLIFTON (b. 1936–2010) Born in Depew, New York, Clifton attended Howard University (1953–1955) and Fredonia State Teachers College. She worked as a claims clerk in the New York State Division of Employment in Buffalo (1958–1960), and as literature assistant in the Office of Education in Washington, D.C. (1960–1971). In 1969, she received the YM-YWHA Poetry Center Discovery Award, and her first collection, *Good Times*, was selected as one of the ten best books of 1969 by the *New York Times*. From 1971 to 1974 she was poet-in-residence at Coppin State College in Baltimore, and in 1979 she was named poet laureate of the state of Maryland. She has written many collections for children and a free-verse chronicle of five generations of her family, *Generations: A Memoir* (1976). Her final publication was *Voices* (2008). In 2007, Clifton was awarded the Ruth Lilly Poetry Prize, a prestigious honor given to living U.S. poets "whose lifetime accomplishments warrant extraordinary recognition." Noted for celebrating ordinary people and everyday things, Clifton was quoted as saying, "I am a black woman poet, and I sound like one."

JOSHUA CLOVER (b. 1962) Clover was born in Berkeley, California; he grew up there and just outside of Boston. He graduated from Boston University and the University of Iowa's Writers' Workshop and is currently a professor at the University of California at Davis. Clover has been a regular contributor to the *New York Times Sunday Book Review*, the *Village Voice*, the *Nation*, and *Spin* magazine. He has won two Pushcart Prizes and received a grant from the National Endowment for the Arts. His two volumes of poetry are

Madonna anno domini (1997), which won the Academy of American Poets' Walt Whitman Award, and *The Totality for Kids* (2006). His most recent book, a cultural study titled *1989: Bob Dylan Didn't Have This to Sing About*, was published in 2010.

JUDITH ORTIZ COFER (b. 1952) Cofer was born in Hormigueros, Puerto Rico. She earned a B.A. (1974) from Augusta College and an M.A. (1977) from Florida Atlantic University and briefly attended Oxford University. She began her teaching career as a bilingual instructor in Florida public schools and taught at a number of schools, including the University of Miami and the University of Georgia. Her first volume of poems, *Latin Women Pray*, appeared in 1981, and she has since published poetry collections, essays, and a novel. Her recent work includes several multigenre collections of stories, poems, and essays about coming of age in the barrio, including *The Year of Our Revolution: New and Selected Stories and Poems* (1998) and *Woman in Front of the Sun: On Becoming a Writer* (2000). More recently, she published a novel, *Call Me María* (2004), and a collection of poetry, *A Love Story Beginning in Spanish* (2005). Cofer points out that her family is an important source for her writing: "The place of birth itself becomes a metaphor for the things we must all leave behind; the assimilation of a new culture is the coming into maturity by accepting the terms necessary for survival."

BILLY COLLINS (b. 1941) Collins was born in New York City and earned a B.A. (1963) from the College of the Holy Cross and a Ph.D. (1971) from the University of California at Riverside. He has been teaching at the City University of New York since 1971. *Pokerface*, the first of his several books of poetry, was published in 1977. Collins's later work attracted so much attention that his early poetry books became economically valuable. Consequently, the University of Pittsburgh Press, publisher of *The Art of Drowning* (1995) and *Picnic, Lightning* (1998), at first withheld permission from Random House to reprint earlier poems in Collins's *Sailing around the Room: New and Selected Poems* (2000). The matter was settled, and Random House published his next collection of poems, *Nine Horses* (2002). The struggle between Random House and the University of Pittsburgh Press over the rights to Collins's work made him sufficiently notorious. He has since published *The Trouble with Poetry and Other Poems* (2005), *Ballistics: Poems* (2008), and *Horoscopes for the Dead: Poems* (2012). He has won several poetry prizes as well as fellowships from the New York Foundation for the Arts, the National Endowment for the Arts, and the Guggenheim Foundation. Collins was the poet laureate of the United States from 2001 to 2003 and the poet laureate for New York State from 2004 to 2006. In 2005, he was the first recipient of the Mark Twain Prize for Humor in Poetry. He commented to one journalist: "I think my work has to do with a sense that we are attempting, all the time, to create a logical, rational path through the day. To the left and right there are an amazing set of distractions that we usually can't afford to follow. But the poet is willing to stop anywhere."

RICHARD CRASHAW (1612–1649) Crashaw was the only son of William Crashaw, a fervently anti-Catholic preacher. Crashaw did not share his father's religious views, however; he was a Catholic sympathizer. He attended Pembroke College, Cambridge, where he earned his B.A. in 1634. He went to Peterhouse in 1636 and became a fellow of the college in 1637, earning his M.A. there in 1638. However, in 1644 he was ejected from the college for his religious leanings, after which he fled to France and became a Catholic sometime around 1645. His friend Abraham Cowley later found him destitute in Paris and helped him regain his footing, introducing Crashaw to Charles I's queen, Henrietta Maria, who sent Crashaw to Rome with a recommendation to the Pope. Crashaw died in 1649 while serving in the Cathedral of Santa Casa in Loreto. He wrote throughout his life, and his poetry came to be known for its brilliant use of extravagant baroque imagery. His works were first collected by an anonymous friend and published as *Steps to the Temple* in 1646.

VICTOR HERNÁNDEZ CRUZ (b. 1949) Cruz was born in Aguas Buenas, Puerto Rico, and immigrated with his family to New York City in 1954. He recalls, "My family life was full of music, guitars and conga drums, maracas and songs. . . . Even when it was five below zero in New York [my mother] sang warm tropical ballads." By 1966, he had already completed a collection of verse, *Papa Got His Gun, and Other Poems*, and in 1969 he published *Snaps*. He has edited *Umbra* magazine in New York, lectured at the University of California, Berkeley, and taught at San Francisco State University. Cruz says he writes in three languages: Spanish, English, and Bilingual. "From the mixture a totally new language emerges, an intense collision, not just of words, but of attitudes." His other works include *Mainland* (1973), *Tropicalizations* (1976), *Red Beans: Poems* (1991), *Panoramas* (1997), *Maraca: New and Selected Poems, 1965–2000* (2001), *The Mountain in the Sea* (2006), and, most recently, *In the Shadow of Al-Andalus* (2011). Cruz is also co-editor of the poetry anthology *Paper Dance: 55 Latino Poets* (2008).

COUNTEE CULLEN (1903–1946) Born Countee L. Porter in New York City, Cullen was adopted by the Reverend and Mrs. Cullen in 1918 and raised in Harlem. He was extraordinarily precocious, and by 1920 his poems had been published in *Poetry*, the *Nation*, and *Harper's*. He published his famous poem "Heritage" in 1925, the year he graduated from New York University. After earning an M.A. in English from Harvard in 1926, he taught French in a junior high school and was assistant editor of the National Urban League's *Opportunity: Journal of Negro Life*. Cullen, along with Langston Hughes and Jean Toomer, was a central figure in the Harlem Renaissance of the 1920s. He received a Guggenheim Fellowship in 1929. In addition to five volumes of poetry, he published a novel, *One Way to Heaven* (1932), which deals with the interaction between upper- and lower-class African Americans in Harlem in the 1920s.

E. E. CUMMINGS (1894–1962) Born in Cambridge, Massachusetts, Edward Estlin Cummings attended Harvard University (B.A., 1915; M.A., 1916), served as a volunteer ambulance driver in France during World War I, was imprisoned for three months in a French detention camp, served in the U.S. Army (1918–1919), and then studied art and painting in Paris (1920–1924). His prose narrative *The Enormous Room* (1922), a recollection of his imprisonment, brought instant acclaim. Several volumes of poetry followed. His experiments with punctuation, line division, and capitalization make his work immediately recognizable. In a letter to young poets published in a high school newspaper, Cummings said, "[N]othing is quite so easy as using words like somebody else. We all of us do exactly this nearly all the time—and whenever we do it, we're not poets."

MEGHAN DAUM (b. 1970) Daum was born in California but grew up on the East Coast. She is a graduate of Vassar College and the M.F.A. writing program at Columbia University's School of the Arts. In 1999, while working as a reporter and an essayist, Daum moved to Lincoln, Nebraska—an experience that inspired her debut novel *The Quality of Life Report* (2003), which tells the story of a New York City reporter who moves to Prairie City, USA, to fulfill her "heartland fantasy." Daum is also the author of a collection of essays, *My Misspent Youth* (2001), and another novel, *Life Would Be Perfect If I Lived in That House* (2010). Her work has appeared in *The New Yorker*, *Harper's*, *GQ*, *Vogue*, *Self*, *New*

York, Travel & Leisure, BlackBook, Harper's Bazaar, the *Village Voice*, and the *New York Times Book Review*, and she writes a weekly column for the *Los Angeles Times*. She lives in Los Angeles with her husband, Alan Zarembo, and their sheepdog, Rex.

DONALD DAVIE (1922–1995)   Davie was an esteemed poet renowned not only for his poems, but also for his criticism on poetry. Born in Barnsley, Yorkshire, he received his early education at Barnsley Holgate Grammar School. He went on to attend St. Catharine's College in Cambridge, though his studies there were interrupted when he joined the navy in 1941. After spending time in northern Russia, Davie retuned to Cambridge in 1944 and completed his studies, earning his B.A., M.A., and Ph.D. He then went on to teach English at the University of Essex, at Stanford University, and at Vanderbilt University. Throughout his life, Davie displayed a keen interest in poetic technique as well as the ethical implications of poetic subject matter, which he felt many contemporary poets had lost sight of; his *Purity of Diction in English Verse* (1952) is among the best-known volumes of poetic criticism. Along with poets like Philip Larkin, D. J. Enright, and John Wain, Davie was part of a group known as The Movement, who considered "amoral" poetry unworthy of attention. He published many collections of poetry, the best known of which include *Essex Poems* (1969), *In the Stopping Train* (1977), and *To Scorch or Freeze* (1988). He also penned eighteen volumes of criticism across literary, social, religious, and political subjects. Davie considered himself first and foremost a poet, but he claimed to write criticism "in order to explain to myself the sort of thing I've been doing." He became an active editor, editing the newly launched *PN Review* in 1972 and such collections as *The Late Augustans: Longer Poems of the Eighteenth Century* (1958), *Russian Literature and Modern English Fiction* (1965), and *The New Oxford Book of Christian Verse* (1981), among other titles. He also co-edited and supplied the verse translations for *Pasternak: Modern Judgements* (1969) and wrote introductions to Elizabeth Daryush's *Collected Poems* (1976) and the *Collected Poems of Yvor Winters* (1978). When Davie passed away in 1995 at the age of 73, Karl Miller, the former editor of the *London Review of Books*, said of the late poet, "He will be remembered as a man who stood up for poetry at a time when it needed defending."

CATHERINE DAVIS (1924–2002)   Davis studied poetry with Allen Tate at the University of Minnesota and with J. V. Cunningham at the University of Chicago before going to Stanford University on a Stegner Creative Writing Fellowship in 1950. She studied with Yvor Winters, worked for the Stanford University Press as a copy editor, and won several poetry prizes. Winters praised her work in *Forms of Discovery* (1967), and included seven of her poems in *Quest for Reality* (1969). In 1953, Winters wrote to Louise Bogan, *New Yorker* poetry editor, asking her help in finding editorial work in New York, saying that she "grew up in extreme poverty and in pretty rough surroundings and has had a hard life all the way." Davis lived in New York in the early 1950s and moved to Alexandria, Virginia, in the late 1950s to work in Washington and study at George Washington University. During this time she purchased a handpress and self-published two pamphlets of her work: *The Leaves: Lyrics and Epigrams* (1960) and *Second Beginnings and Other Poems* (1961). She also published widely in periodicals such as *Poetry, Paris Review*, and *Southern Review* and in the anthology *The New Poets of England and America* (1957). In the early 1960s, she studied at the Creative Writing Workshop, University of Iowa, where she published another fine press book, *Under This Lintel* (1962), while working in the University of Iowa Typographic Laboratory under the distinguished printer Harry Duncan. She taught at various schools throughout the country and spent her later years teaching at the University of Massachusetts–Boston. She died after suffering from Alzheimer's disease for two years. In a

1973 *Southern Review* essay, Helen Pinkerton Trimpi wrote that Davis's contribution to the classical epigram is "her adaptation of it to her own subject matter: physical, mental, and moral destitution."

CARL DENNIS (b. 1939)   Dennis was born in St. Louis, Missouri. He received his B.A. from the University of Minnesota and his Ph.D. in English literature from the University of California, Berkeley. In 1966, he became assistant professor of English at the University at Buffalo and has since spent the majority of his career there; he became one of the school's artists in residence in 2002. He has published numerous volumes of poetry, including *House of My Own* (1974), *The Outskirts of Troy* (1988), *Meetings with Time* (1992), and *Practical Gods* (2001), for which he won the Pulitzer Prize. His most recent collections are *Unknown Friends* (2007) and *Callings* (2010). He has also published a volume of criticism, *Poetry as Persuasion* (2001), and contributed to many literary journals and magazines, such as the *Atlantic Monthly*, *American Poetry Review*, *Ironwood*, *Kenyon Review*, *The New Yorker*, *New Republic*, *Paris Review*, *Poetry*, and *Salmagundi*. Dennis has been awarded a fellowship at the Rockefeller Study Center, a National Endowment for the Arts Fellowship in Poetry, a Guggenheim Fellowship, and the Ruth Lilly Poetry Prize.

EMILY DICKINSON (1830–1886)   Dickinson, one of three children, was born in Amherst, Massachusetts. Her father was a prominent lawyer. Except for one year away at a nearby college and a trip with her sister to Washington, D.C., to visit her father when he was serving in Congress, she lived out her life, unmarried, in her parents' home. During her trip to Washington, she met the Reverend Charles Wadsworth, a married man, whom she came to characterize as her "dearest earthly friend." Little is known of this relationship except that Dickinson's feelings for Wadsworth were strong. In 1862 Wadsworth moved to San Francisco, an event that coincided with a period of Dickinson's intense poetic creativity. Also in that year, she initiated a literary correspondence with the critic T. W. Higginson, to whom she sent some of her poems for his opinion. Higginson, although he recognized her talent, was puzzled by her startling originality and urged her to write more conventionally, advice she was unable to follow. Only seven of her poems were published while she was alive, none of them with her consent. After her death, the extraordinary richness of her imaginative life came to light with the discovery of her more than 1,000 poems.

E. L. DOCTOROW (b. 1931)   Doctorow was born and raised in New York City, where he attended the Bronx High School of Science. After earning an A.B. degree with honors at Kenyon College, Ohio, he returned to New York for a year of graduate studies and then served in the U.S. Army. On his return to New York, he worked as senior editor for New American Library from 1959 to 1964. During this period, he also worked as a script reader for Columbia Pictures, a job which he said required him "to suffer one lousy Western after another, and it occurred to me that I could lie about the West in a much more interesting way than any of these people were lying." The result was his first novel, *Welcome to Hard Times* (1961), a dark, symbolic novel about the West. Among his subsequent novels are *The Book of Daniel* (1971), a fictionalized account of the lives of Julius and Ethel Rosenberg, executed for conspiracy to commit treason during the Cold War (adapted in 1983 into the film *Daniel*, directed by Sidney Lumet). This novel was followed by *Ragtime* (1975), a sprawling historical novel about early twentieth-century America (adapted in 1981 into the film *Ragtime*, directed by Milos Forman). *Ragtime* was named by the editorial board of the Modern Library as one of the 100 best English-language novels of the twentieth century. Doctorow's novel *The March* (2005) won the PEN/Faulkner Award and the National Book

Critics Circle Award, and he then published *Creationists: Selected Essays 1993–2006*. His most recent work is *Homer & Langley* (2009). He has received numerous awards and prizes, among them the National Book Award and the National Humanities Medal. Since 1982, Doctorow has taught at New York University, where he holds the Lewis and Loretta Brennan Glucksman Chair of English and American Letters.

JOHN DONNE (1572–1631)   Born in London into a prosperous Roman Catholic family of tradespeople at a time when England was staunchly anti-Catholic, Donne was forced to leave Oxford University without a degree because of his religion. He studied law and at the same time read widely in theology in an attempt to decide whether the Roman or the Anglican Church was the true Catholic Church, a decision he was not able to make for many years. In the meantime, he became known as a witty man of the world and the author of original, often dense, erotic poems. Donne left his law studies, participated in two naval expeditions, and then became secretary to a powerful noble, a job he lost when he was briefly sent to prison for secretly marrying his patron's niece. In 1615, at the age of forty-two, Donne accepted ordination in the Anglican Church. He quickly earned a reputation as one of the greatest preachers of his time. He was dean of St. Paul's from 1621 until his death. In his later years, Donne repudiated the poetry of his youth.

RITA DOVE (b. 1952)   Dove was born in Akron, Ohio, the daughter of an African American research chemist who broke the color barrier in the tire industry. She began writing and staging plays at an early age. In 1970, she was named a Presidential Scholar, an annual award given to the top 100 high school graduates in the country. She attended Miami University in Ohio on a National Merit Scholarship, graduating Phi Beta Kappa in 1973. After completing a Fulbright fellowship at the University of Tübingen, Germany, she returned to the United States and earned an M.F.A. at the University of Iowa's Writers' Workshop. Her earliest poems appeared in two chapbooks, followed by her first volume of poems, *The Yellow House on the Corner* (1980). Since then, she has published more than a half-dozen volumes of poetry, including the Pulitzer Prize–winning *Thomas and Beulah* (1987). In recognition of her poetic achievement, she was appointed poet laureate of the United States in 1993. *On the Bus with Rosa Parks* (1999), inspired by a bus trip the author shared with the celebrated heroine of the civil rights movement, was nominated for a National Book Critics Circle Award. Her most recent volumes are *American Smooth* (2004) and *Sonata Mulattica* (2009), and she edited *The Penguin Anthology of Twentieth-Century American Poetry* (2011). Dove is also the author of a collection of short stories, *Fifth Sunday* (1990); a novel, *Through the Ivory Gate* (1992); and a play, *The Darker Face of the Earth* (1997). Among her many other honors, she has received the National Association for the Advancement of Colored People's Great American Artist Award (2003) and the Duke Ellington Lifetime Achievement Award (2001). Most recently, President Barack Obama presented her with the 2011 National Medal of Arts. She is Commonwealth Professor of Creative Writing at the University of Virginia.

BRIAN DOYLE (b. 1956)   Doyle, the son of a journalist and a teacher, was born in New York City and graduated from the University of Notre Dame. He was an editor at *U.S. Catholic* magazine and a writer at *Boston College Magazine* before becoming the editor of *Portland Magazine* at the University of Portland. He is the author of several books, among them *Credo: Essays on Grace, Altar Boys, Bees, Kneeling, Saints, the Mass, Priests, Strong Women, Epiphanies, a Wake, and the Haunting Thin Energetic Dusty Figure of Jesus the Christ* (1999); *The Wet Engine: Exploring the Mad Wild Miracle of the Heart* (2005);

Epiphanies and Elegies: Very Short Stories (2006); and *Mink River* (2010). His work has also appeared in anthologies, such as *The Best Spiritual Writing* and *The Best American Essays,* and a number of periodicals, among them *Atlantic Monthly, American Scholar, Harper's, Gourmet,* and the *London Times.* Doyle served as editor of the Best Catholic Writing series from Loyola Press from 2004 to 2006. He lives with his wife and three children.

PAUL LAURENCE DUNBAR (1872–1906) The son of former slaves, Dunbar was born in Dayton, Ohio, where he graduated from Dayton High School (1891) and worked for two years as an elevator operator. In 1893, he worked in Chicago at the World's Columbian Exhibition. His first verse collection, *Oak and Ivy,* was published in 1893. William Dean Howells—an eminent editor, author, and critic—encouraged him to write and had him join a lecture bureau in 1896. While Dunbar maintained that African American poetry was not much different from white poetry—and wrote many poems in standard English—he often wrote poems in black dialect that seemed to cater to the racial stereotypes of his white audience. He died of tuberculosis in 1906. His complete works appear in *The Dunbar Reader* (1975).

STEVE EARLE (b. 1955) Earle was born in Fort Monroe, Virginia, the son of an air traffic controller, and grew up in Schertz, Texas. At fourteen, he left home for Houston to live with an uncle, who encouraged Earle's guitar playing. By the time he graduated from high school, Earle was launched on a career in music. At age nineteen he was in Nashville, playing in rockabilly bands and trying to get well-known artists to record his songs. From 1975 to 1978, he was a staff writer for a music division of RCA. His first album, *Guitar Town* (1986), was an instant critical and commercial success, garnering him two Grammy nominations. But after his fourth album, *Shut Up and Die Like an Aviator* (1991), MCA refused to renew his contract because of his severe drug addiction. In 1994, he was arrested and sent to prison for narcotics possession and later paroled after successfully completing a drug rehabilitation program. He resumed his career with *The Hard Way* (1996), an album he said he "almost died in the process of making." The albums that have followed reveal Earle's growing sense of social and political outrage. His album *The Revolution Starts Now* (2004) is comprised wholly of protest songs, and won a Grammy for best contemporary folk album. In the liner notes, Earle writes that the album grew out of his sense of urgency in responding to what was happening both at home and abroad: "The prisoner scandal had just broken and the Bush administration, still reeling from the 9/11 commission hearings, was circling the wagons. The Democrats, for their part, were carefully (sometimes, in my opinion, too carefully) trying to sort out how best to press the advantage. Meanwhile, back here in Tennessee, me and my boys had a deadline to meet." Most recently, Earle released his Grammy-winning album *Washington Square Serenade* (2007), produced an album for Joan Baez, appeared as a recovering drug addict in several episodes of HBO's series *The Wire,* and hosted a show on Sirius Satellite Radio. He also recently published his first novel, *I'll Never Get Out of This World Alive* (2011), which is titled after a Hank Williams song.

T. S. ELIOT (1888–1965) Thomas Stearns Eliot was born in St. Louis, Missouri. His father was president of the Hydraulic Press Brick Company, and his mother was a teacher, social worker, and writer. Educated at private academies, Eliot earned two philosophy degrees at Harvard University (B.A., 1909; M.A., 1910). After graduate study in Paris and England, he worked for eight years as a clerk in Lloyd's Bank in London and became a naturalized British citizen in 1927. He was editor, then director, of Faber & Gwyer Publishers (later Faber & Faber) from 1925 to 1965 and spent time in the United States as a visiting lecturer and scholar. Admirers and detractors alike agree that Eliot was the most imposing and influential poet writing between the world wars. His poems "The Love Song of J. Alfred Prufrock" (1917) and *The Waste Land* (1922) are among his earliest and most famous. Acknowledging his dependence on a preexisting cultural tradition, Eliot explained: "The existing order is complete before the new work arrives; for order to persist after the supervention of novelty, the whole existing order must be altered." Eliot also wrote plays, including *Murder in the Cathedral* (1935) and *The Cocktail Party* (1950). The long-running Broadway musical *Cats* is based on his 1939 verse collection, *Old Possum's Book of Practical Cats.* He won the Nobel Prize for Literature in 1948.

HARLAN ELLISON® (b. 1934)   Born in Cleveland, Ohio, Ellison published his first story when he was thirteen. He left Ohio State University after two years and worked at a variety of odd jobs while establishing himself as a writer. In a career spanning over sixty years, he has written or edited a hundred books and more than 1,700 stories, essays, reviews, articles, motion picture scripts, and teleplays. He has won the Hugo Award ten and a half times; the Nebula Award five times, as well as a Grandmaster Nebula Award (basically a lifetime achievement award); the Edgar Allan Poe Award of the Mystery Writers of America twice; the Bram Stoker Award from the Horror Writers Association six times, including the Lifetime Achievement Award in 1996; the Georges Méliès fantasy film award twice; the World Fantasy Award twice, the second time for lifetime achievement; two Audie Awards (for the best in audio recordings); the British Fantasy Award; and the Silver Pen for journalism from PEN. He was presented with the first Living Legend award by the International Horror Critics at the 1995 World Horror Convention, and in March 1998, the National Women's Committee of Brandeis University honored him with their Words, Wit, Wisdom Award. He is the only scenarist in Hollywood ever to have won the Writers Guild of America award for Most Outstanding Teleplay four times for solo work. His latest books are *Bugf#ck: The Useless Wit & Wisdom of Harlan Ellison* (2011) and a new series with the Publishing 180 program. These books are a mixture of classic stories and essays and original never-before-available teleplays: *Brain Movies: The Original Teleplays of Harlan Ellison* (Volumes One and Two), *Harlan 101: Encountering Ellison,* and *Harlan 101: The Sound of a Scythe Plus Three Classic Novellas.* For the first time, Ellison's collections of essays on television, *The Glass Teat* and *The Other Glass Teat,* have been published in one volume as the complete *Omnibus.* He has also written numerous short stories for various magazines, most recently "How Interesting: A Tiny Man," which garnered Ellison his fourth Nebula Award. In celebration of Ellison's seventy-fifth birthday, documentarian Erik Nelson produced a feature-length film that looks at Ellison's life and work. The documentary, *Dreams with Sharp Teeth,* was released on DVD in May 2009. Ellison currently lives with his wife, Susan, in the Los Angeles area.

RALPH ELLISON (1914–1994)   Ellison was born in Oklahoma City, Oklahoma. He studied music, specifically trumpet and piano, and sculpture before embarking on a writing career. In New York City, encouraged by his friend and fellow writer Richard Wright, Ellison began writing book reviews, essays, and short stories. He also earned money as a freelance photographer. His first novel, *Invisible Man* (1952), for which he is best known, won the National Book Award in 1953. He published two collections of essays, *Shadow and Act* (1964) and *Going to the Territory* (1986). He taught at Bard College, Rutgers University, the University of Chicago, and New York University before dying of pancreatic cancer in

1994. His short stories were collected and published posthumously in *Flying Home and Other Stories* (1996). Ellison wrote more than 2,000 pages for a second novel, *Juneteenth*, over the span of forty years; it was edited down to 368 pages and published five years after his death, in 1999.

"EPHELIA" (fl. ca. 1679)   The identity of the writer and poet known as "Ephelia" has been long disputed by scholars. Maureen E. Mulvihill, a scholar in Restoration and eighteenth-century English literature who is widely considered the leading authority on the enigmatic author, claims that "Ephelia" was actually Mary Villiers Stuart, Duchess of Richmond and Lennox. While there has been no definitive counterargument to this claim, many scholars consider Mulvihill's arguments too speculative to accept as fact. Indeed, some hypothesize that "Ephelia" may even have been a hoax perpetrated by male authors of the period. Her most famous work is a poetry collection called *Female Poems on Several Occasions* (1679), though she is also credited with numerous political broadsides, a play (*The Pair-Royal of Coxcombs*), several songs, and a series of reproving verse-epistles to high-ranking members of English society. Whoever "Ephelia" was, her body of work created the impression of an outspoken author who was not afraid to acknowledge and criticize the political and social shortcomings of her time.

LOUISE ERDRICH (b. 1954)   Erdrich was born in Little Falls, Minnesota, and grew up in North Dakota. Her father was German American and her mother was French and Anishinaabe; Erdrich is a member of the Native American Anishinaabe Nation. She earned degrees from Dartmouth College and Johns Hopkins University. Before fully embarking on her writing career, she worked as a lifeguard, waitress, prison poetry teacher, construction flagger, and newspaper editor. She began by publishing poems and short fiction and won the Nelson Algren Prize for her short story "The World's Greatest Fisherman" in 1982. Her first novel, *Love Medicine* (1984), won the National Book Critics Circle Award. She went on to write more than ten other novels, notably *The Beet Queen* (1986), *Tracks* (1988), *The Antelope Wife* (1998), and *The Painted Drum* (2005). In addition to having written five novels for adolescents and three works of nonfiction, Erdrich has published three books of poetry: *Jacklight* (1984), *Baptism of Desire* (1989), and *Original Fire: Selected and New Poems* (2003). Her most recent works are *The Plague of Doves* (2008), a novel; *The Red Convertible: Collected and New Stories 1978–2008* (2009); and *Shadow Tag: A Novel* (2010). She has won several awards including an O. Henry Award, a Pushcart Prize, and a Guggenheim Fellowship. Erdrich owns a bookstore in Minneapolis, Minnesota, and hosts annual writing workshops on the Turtle Mountain Indian Reservation in North Dakota.

WILLIAM FAULKNER (1897–1962)   Faulkner was born in New Albany, Mississippi, and lived most of his life in Oxford, the seat of the University of Mississippi. Although he did not graduate from high school, he attended the university as a special student from 1919 to 1921. During this period, he also worked as a janitor, a bank clerk, and a postmaster. His southern forebears had held slaves, served during the Civil War, endured the deprivations of Reconstruction, fought duels, and even wrote the occasional romance of the old South. Faulkner mined these generous layers of history in his work. He created the mythical Yoknapatawpha County in northern Mississippi and traced the destinies of its inhabitants from the colonial era to the middle of the twentieth century in such novels as *The Sound and the Fury* (1929), *Light in August* (1932), and *Absalom, Absalom!* (1936). Further, Faulkner described the decline of the pre–Civil War aristocratic families and the rise of mean-spirited money-grubbers in a trilogy: *The Hamlet* (1940), *The Town* (1957), and *The Mansion* (1959). Recognition came late, and Faulkner fought a constant battle to keep afloat financially. During the 1940s, he wrote screenplays in Hollywood, but his achievements brought him the Nobel Prize in 1950.

ALAN FELDMAN (b. 1945)   Feldman's poetry has appeared in many top literary publications throughout his career, including the *Atlantic, The New Yorker, Nation, Poetry, Kenyon Review, Southern Review, Ploughshares, Iowa Review, Threepenny Review, Virginia Quarterly Review,* and others. His work has also been included in many anthologies, including *To Woo and To Wed: Poets on Love and Marriage* (1992), *The Best American Erotic Poems 1800-Present,* and *The Best American Poetry* 2001 and 2011, and Feldman has also been honored with poetry fellowships from the National Endowment for the Arts and the Massachusetts Artists Foundation. In 1979, his collection *The Happy Genius* (1978) won the Elliston Book Award, and his most recent full-length collection, *A Sail to Great Island* (2004), won the 2004 Felix Pollak Prize in Poetry. Feldman lives in Framingham, Massachusetts, and is married to Nan Hass Feldman, an artist.

LAWRENCE FERLINGHETTI (b. 1919)   Born Lawrence Ferling, this irreverent writer assumed his original family name in 1954. He earned a B.A. in journalism from the University of North Carolina in 1941, served as lieutenant commander in the U.S. Naval Reserve during World War II, and then received graduate degrees from Columbia University and the University of Paris. He worked briefly as a translator of French before rising to prominence in the San Francisco–based Beat literary movement of the 1950s, composed of a group of writers who felt strongly that art should be accessible to all, not just to a small group of intellectuals. Ferlinghetti received great praise from many readers and some critics for his attempts to incorporate American vernacular speech and the rhythms of modern jazz into his writings, while he was roundly attacked by defenders of the status quo. Ferlinghetti has been a prolific writer in all genres. In addition, he co-founded the San Francisco bookstore City Lights and two publishing enterprises, City Lights Books and the Pocket Book Series. In 1998 Ferlinghetti was named San Francisco's first poet laureate. He won the Poetry Society of America's Robert Frost Medal and the Authors Guild Lifetime Achievement Award, and was elected to the American Academy of Arts and Letters in 2003. In 2005, he received the National Book Foundation's first Literarian Award for outstanding service to the American literary community. He has published two novels, many plays, and over two dozen volumes of poetry including *Americus, Book I* (2004) and *Poetry as Insurgent Art* (2007). His early work, *A Coney Island of the Mind* (1958), remains his most popular and best-selling poetry collection.

ANNIE FINCH (b. 1956)   Finch was born in New Rochelle, New York, and earned degrees from Yale University, the University of Houston, and Stanford University. She taught at the University of Northern Iowa and Miami University of Ohio before assuming her current role as director of the M.F.A. program at the University of Southern Maine. Among her several books of poetry are *The Encyclopedia of Scotland* (1982), *Eve* (1997), *Calendars* (2003), and *Annie Finch's Greatest Hits* (2007). She has also written two opera librettos, translated the poems of French Renaissance poet Louise Labé, and edited several anthologies of poetry and essays. Her most recent work is an intertwined feminist poem and opera libretto called *Among the Goddesses: An Epic Libretto in Seven Dreams* (2010). About the influence of other poets on her own work, Finch has said, "I love the way bits of poems I've read, maybe years ago, will find their way subtly, secretly, into the poems

I write and surprise me when I find them there. And I love to consciously invoke or copy the form or some other aspect of poems I've read in my own work; it's a wonderful way to pay tribute."

DONALD FINKEL (1929–2008)   Donald Finkel was born in New York City, the son of an attorney. He earned a B.S. (1952) and an M.A. (1953) from Columbia University. In 1956 he married the writer Constance Urdang. Shortly thereafter, Finkel began a university teaching career at the University of Iowa and in 1960 moved to Washington University in St. Louis where he became poet-in-residence. His interest in Antarctica and exploration produced *Endurance: An Antarctic Idyll* and *Going Under* (1978). The first describes the shipwreck and rescue of Ernest Shackleton's 1914 expedition. The second examines two men who explored Kentucky's Mammoth Cave. His many books, including *Selected Shorter Poems* (1987), *A Splintered Mirror: Chinese Poetry from the Democracy Movement* (1991), and *A Question of Seeing: Poems* (1998), have earned him abundant awards and honors, among them a Guggenheim Fellowship (1967), nomination for a National Book Award (1970), and two nominations for the National Book Critics Circle Award (1975, 1981). His final volume was *Not So the Chairs: Selected and New Poems* (2003).

CAROLYN FORCHÉ (b. 1950)   Born in Detroit, Forché earned a B.A. in international relations and creative writing at Michigan State University in 1972. After graduate study at Bowling Green State University in 1975, she taught at a number of schools, including the University of Arkansas, Vassar College, Columbia University, and George Mason University. She won the Yale Series of Younger Poets Award in 1976 for her first collection, *Gathering the Tribes*. Other honors include a Guggenheim Fellowship and the Lamont Award (1981). Forché was a journalist for Amnesty International in El Salvador in 1983 and Beirut correspondent for the National Public Radio program *All Things Considered*. Her works include the collections of poetry *The Country between Us* (1981) and *The Angel of History* (1994), both embodying her passionate preoccupation with the dehumanizing effects of political repression. Among her most recent publications are a book of poems, *Blue Hour* (2003), and a memoir, *The Horse on Our Balcony* (2009). She currently teaches and directs the creative writing center at Skidmore College.

CARRIE FOUNTAIN (b. ?)   Carrie Fountain hails from Las Cruces, New Mexico. She has served as a fellow at University of Texas's Michener Center for Writers, has written for the *Texas Observer*, and was a poetry columnist for the *Austin American-Statesman*. Her poems have been published in *32 Poems Magazine, Cimarron Review, Black Warrior Review, Crazyhorse, Cream City Review*, and *Southwestern American Literature*. Her first collection, *Burn Lake* (2010), won the 2009 National Poetry Series Award. Fountain also received *Swink Magazine*'s Award for Emerging Writers and the Marlboro Poetry Prize. She lives in Austin, Texas, with her husband, the playwright Kirk Lynn, and teaches at St. Edward's University.

DAISY FRIED (b. 1967)   Fried has taught creative writing at Villanova University, Haverford College, the University of Pennsylvania, in Warren Wilson College's low-residency M.F.A. program, and as the Grace Hazard Conkling Writer-in-Residence at Smith College. She has been the recipient of Guggenheim, Hodder, and Pew Fellowships, a Pushcart Prize, and the Cohen Award from *Ploughshares*. Her poetry has been featured in such publications as the *Nation, Poetry, New Republic, American Poetry Review, Antioch Review, Threepenny Review, Ploughshares*, and elsewhere. She has published two books of poetry: *She Didn't Mean to Do It* (2000), which won the Agnes Lynch Starrett Prize, and *My Brother Is Getting Arrested Again* (2006), a finalist for the National Book Critics Circle Award. In 2009, she was awarded *Poetry*'s Editors Prize for Feature Article for her essay "Sing, God-Awful Muse," which discusses *Paradise Lost* and breastfeeding. She lives in South Philadelphia with her husband and daughter.

ROBERT FROST (1874–1963)   Frost was born in San Francisco but from the age of ten lived in New England. He attended Dartmouth College briefly and then became a teacher, but soon decided to resume his formal training and enrolled at Harvard University. He left Harvard after two years without a degree and for several years supported himself and his growing family by tending a farm his grandfather bought for him. When he was not farming, he read and wrote intensively, though he received little recognition. Discouraged by his lack of success, he sold the farm and moved his family to England, where he published his first volumes of poetry, *A Boy's Will* (1913) and *North of Boston* (1914). After three years in England, Frost returned to the United States a recognized poet. Later volumes, notably *Mountain Interval* (1916), *New Hampshire* (1923), *West-Running Brook* (1928), and *A Further Range* (1936), won Frost wide popularity and numerous awards, including two Pulitzer Prizes. By the time he delivered his poem "The Gift Outright" at the inauguration of President John F. Kennedy in 1961, Frost had achieved the status of unofficial poet laureate of the United States, widely revered and beloved for his folksy manner and seemingly artless, accessible poems.

RIVKA GALCHEN (b. 1976)   Galchen was born in Toronto, though she moved with her parents to the United States when she was just a baby. She matriculated to Princeton University in 1994 to study English, but during her sophomore year she applied to an early-admissions program at the Mount Sinai School of Medicine. She received her M.D. from Mount Sinai in 2003 and went on to earn an M.F.A. from Columbia University. Her work has appeared in *The New Yorker*, *Harper's*, the *New York Times*, *The Believer*, and elsewhere. She has received many literary honors, including the 2006 Rona Jaffe Foundation Writers' Award, and she was included in *The New Yorker*'s 2010 "20 Under 40" list. She was also the 2011 Mary Ellen von der Heyden Fiction Fellow at the American Academy in Berlin. Her first novel, *Atmospheric Disturbances* (2008), has been translated into over twenty languages and won the William J. Saroyan International Prize for Fiction. Galchen currently teaches writing at Columbia University and is a contributing editor for *Harper's Magazine*.

TESS GALLAGHER (b. 1943)   Gallagher was born in Port Angeles, Washington, the eldest of five children of a logger and longshoreman. She earned degrees from the University of Washington in Seattle and the University of Iowa. She has been married three times, most recently to writer Raymond Carver. She has taught at a number of institutions, among them St. Lawrence University; the University of Montana, Missoula; the University of Arizona, Tucson; Syracuse University; and Willamette University. Her many awards include an Elliston Award, multiple grants from the National Endowment for the Arts, and a Guggenheim Fellowship. Gallagher has written two collections of short stories, *The Lover of Horses* (1986) and *At the Owl Woman Saloon* (1996), as well as two collections of essays, *A Concert of Tenses* (1983) and *Soul Barnacles* (2003). She has penned more than ten volumes of poetry, including *Instructions to the Double* (1976), *Moon Crossing Bridge* (1992), *I Stop Writing the Poem* (1992), *Dear Ghosts* (2006), and, most recently, *Midnight Lantern: New and Selected Poems* (2011).

RICHARD GARCIA (b. 1941) Garcia was born in San Francisco, California, and earned his M.F.A. in creative writing at Warren Wilson College in Asheville, North Carolina. He is the author of four volumes of poetry: *Selected Poems* (1972), *The Flying Garcias* (1991), *Rancho Notorious* (2001), and *The Persistence of Objects* (2006). In addition, his poems have appeared in a number of periodicals, including *Ploughshares*, *Antioch Review*, *Blue Moon Review*, *Slope*, and *Diode*. He is also the author of a bilingual book for children titled *My Aunt Otilia's Spirits* (1978). Among Garcia's awards are a Pushcart Prize and a fellowship from the National Endowment for the Arts. He has served as poet-in-residence at the Long Beach Museum of Art and at the Children's Hospital in Los Angeles. Before assuming his current role as faculty member in the M.F.A. program at Antioch University in Los Angeles, he taught at the University of Southern California and at numerous writing festivals, conferences, and workshops. He lives with his wife and dog on James Island in South Carolina.

DEBORAH GARRISON (b. 1965) Garrison was born in Ann Arbor, Michigan, and earned degrees from Brown University and New York University. She worked for *The New Yorker* magazine, as part of the editorial staff and as the senior nonfiction editor, for over fifteen years before taking on her current roles as poetry editor at Alfred A. Knopf and senior editor at Pantheon Books. Her poems have appeared in a number of periodicals, among them *Elle*, *The New Yorker*, the *New York Times*, and *Slate*. Her first book of poetry, *A Working Girl Can't Win, and Other Poems* (1998), is considered a poetry best seller. Her second volume of poetry is *The Second Child* (2007). Garrison lives with her husband and three children in Montclair, New Jersey. About her work, both as a poetry editor and a writer, she has said, "There's a real yearning for authenticity. It's just such a pure thing. Poetry isn't being optioned to the movies for $3 million. Poetry is immune to all that stuff. It's a haven."

DAGOBERTO GILB (b. 1950) Gilb was raised by his mother in Los Angeles. He graduated from the University of California, Santa Barbara in 1974 with a double major in philosophy and religious studies, and went on to earn his M.A. in religious studies in 1976. His work has appeared in many magazines, most recently *Harper's*, *The New Yorker*, and *Callaloo*, and has been widely anthologized and translated. Gilb also received a Guggenheim Fellowship and has been a finalist for the National Book Critics Circle Award. Some of his publications include *The Magic of Blood* (1993), which won the PEN/Hemingway Award and was a finalist for the PEN/Faulkner Award; *The Last Known Residence of Mickey Acuña* (1994), a *New York Times* Notable Book; *Woodcuts of Women* (2001); *Gritos* (2003), a finalist for the 2004 National Book Critics Circle Award; and *The Flowers* (2008). His most recent work is *Before the End, After the Beginning* (2011), a collection of stories that Gilb wrote while recovering from a stroke in 2009. He lives in Austin, Texas, and teaches in the M.F.A. program at Southwest Texas State University.

CHARLOTTE PERKINS GILMAN (1860–1935) Gilman was born in Hartford, Connecticut. Shortly after her birth, her father deserted the family. Left with two children to support and scant help from their father, her mother was unable to provide her children with a secure and stable childhood. Gilman attended the Rhode Island School of Design for a time and went on to work as a commercial artist and teacher. In 1884 she married Charles Stetson, an artist. Following the birth of her only child the next year, Gilman was immobilized by a deep depression. At the urging of her husband, she became the patient of S. Weir Mitchell, a physician celebrated for his treatment of female nervous disorders.

Gilman found the treatment intolerable and finally abandoned it. In 1888, convinced that her marriage threatened her sanity, she moved with her daughter to California and began her productive career as writer and feminist. In 1900, after her divorce, she married her first cousin George Houghton Gilman, enjoying a happy relationship that lasted until his sudden death thirty-four years later. Among Gilman's many works are *Women and Economics* (1899), *The Home: Its Work and Influence* (1903), and *The Man-Made World* (1911), whose thesis is that war and injustice will be eliminated only when women assume a larger role in national and international affairs. Gilman's fiction includes the novels *Moving the Mountain* (1911), *Herland* (1915), and *With Her in Ourland* (1916). Her autobiography, *The Living of Charlotte Perkins Gilman,* was published posthumously in 1935, the year she committed suicide to avoid suffering the final stages of breast cancer.

ALLEN GINSBERG (1926–1997)   Born in Newark, New Jersey, Ginsberg was among the foremost members of the Beat Generation. He matriculated to Columbia University in 1943, where he met Lucien Carr—the man who introduced him to William S. Burroughs, Neal Cassady, John Clellon Holmes, and Jack Kerouac, who would all eventually become renowned Beat poets: writers whose poetry conveyed a sense of spiritual exhaustion and rebellion against the hypocrisy and unprecedented materialism that overtook America in the wake of World War II. In his journal, Ginsberg described the "new vision" to which the Beats led him: "Since art is merely and ultimately self-expressive, we conclude that the fullest art, the most individual, uninfluenced, unrepressed, uninhibited expression of art is true expression and the true art." In 1954, Ginsberg moved to San Francisco where his mentor, William Carlos Williams, introduced him to Kenneth Rexroth, a prominent figure in the San Francisco Renaissance. Rexroth helped to establish Ginsberg as part of the San Francisco poetry scene, a task that came to a head when Ginsberg organized a reading for the Six Gallery on October 7, 1955. This was the first public reading of Ginsberg's "Howl"—a poem that attracted worldwide attention for the poet and his colleagues—and came to be known as the birth of the Beat Generation. Ginsberg labored tirelessly thereafter to promote his work and that of his peers, traveling throughout America and Europe to give readings. Ginsberg's first full-length poetry collection, *Howl and Other Poems* (1956), was widely banned for obscenity when it was first published, but over time "Howl" became one of the most read poems of the century. Ginsberg published nearly two dozen other poetry collections, including *Kaddish and Other Poems* (1961), *Planet News* (1968), *Iron Horse* (1972), and *The Fall of America: Poems of These States* (1973), which won the National Book Award. Ginsberg was also involved in many political activities throughout the 1960s and 1970s, including Vietnam War protests and speaking out in defense of the North American Man/Boy Love Association (NAMBLA). In 1973, he co-founded and directed the Jack Kerouac School of Disembodied Poetics at the Naropa Institute in Colorado. In his later years, Ginsberg became a Distinguished Professor at Brooklyn College, and in 1993 he was named a *Chevalier des Arts et des Lettres* (Knight of the Order of Arts and Letters) by the French Minister of Culture. He continued to travel throughout his life despite developing both diabetes and Reynaud's disease and suffering two minor strokes in the 1970s. He died in New York in 1997 after a battle with liver cancer.

NIKKI GIOVANNI (b. 1943)   Born Yolande Cornelia Giovanni Jr. in Knoxville, Tennessee, daughter of a probation officer and a social worker, Giovanni graduated with honors from Fisk University in 1967. She attended the University of Pennsylvania School of Social Work and Columbia School of the Arts, was assistant professor of black studies at Queens College (1968), and associate professor of English at Rutgers University (1968–1970). She is currently Distinguished Professor of English at Virginia Tech. Giovanni's early work reflects her social activism as an African American college student in the 1960s, while her later works focus on the individual struggle for fulfillment rather than the collective struggle for black empowerment. Her books include *Black Feeling, Black Talk, Black Judgment* (1970), *My House* (1972), and *The Women and the Men* (1975). Among her most recent publications are *Acolytes* (2007), *Hip Hop Speaks to Children* (2008), and *Bicycles: Love Poems* (2009). She was nominated for a Grammy in 2004 for her spoken-word album, *The Nikki Giovanni Poetry Collection*, and in 2009 she was commissioned by National Public Radio's *All Things Considered* to create an inaugural poem for President Barack Obama.

SUSAN GLASPELL (1882–1948) Born and raised in Davenport, Iowa, Glaspell began her career as a novelist and author of sentimental short stories for popular magazines. By 1915, she had turned her energies to the theater, becoming one of the founders of the Provincetown Players, a group devoted to experimental drama. In 1916, Glaspell moved with the company, now called the Playwright's Theatre, to Greenwich Village in New York, where for two seasons—as writer, director, and actor—she played an important role in a group that came to have a major influence on the development of American drama. *Trifles* was written to be performed with a group of one-act plays by Eugene O'Neill at the company's summer playhouse on Cape Cod. Among her longer plays that embody a feminist perspective are *The Verge* (1921) and *Allison's House* (1931), a Pulitzer Prize–winning drama based on the life of Emily Dickinson. Among more than forty short stories, some twenty plays, and ten novels, Glaspell's best works deal with the theme of the new woman, presenting a protagonist who embodies the American pioneer spirit of independence and freedom.

LOUISE GLÜCK (b. 1943) Glück was born in New York City and raised on Long Island. She attended Sarah Lawrence College and Columbia University and has taught at over a dozen institutions, among them the University of Iowa, Columbia University, the University of California at Berkeley, and Harvard University; she is currently a faculty member at Boston University and a writer-in-residence at Yale University. Her numerous awards include an Academy of American Poets Prize, a National Book Critics Circle Award, a Pulitzer Prize, and most recently the Wallace Stevens Award in 2008. She is also the recipient of fellowships from the Guggenheim Foundation, the Rockefeller Foundation, and the National Endowment for the Arts. Glück was poet laureate of the United States from 2003 to 2004. She is the author of one nonfiction book, *Proofs and Theories: Essays on Poetry* (1994), and a dozen volumes of poetry, including *Firstborn* (1968), *The Triumph of Achilles* (1985), *Ararat* (1990), *The Wild Iris* (1992), *Vita Nova* (1999), *Averno* (2006), and *A Village Life: Poems* (2009), her latest, which was shortlisted for the 2010 International Griffin Poetry Prize.

WILLIAM GREENWAY (b. 1947) Greenway was born and raised in Atlanta, Georgia, and earned his B.A. from Georgia State University in 1970. After being drafted by the U.S. Navy as an electronics technician in New Orleans, he went on to earn his Ph.D. in modern literature and poetry from Tulane University. Greenway has taught English at Youngstown State University since 1986, where he has been awarded three Distinguished Professorships in both teaching and scholarship. Greenway has also been honored with the Larry Levis Editors' Prize from *Missouri Review*, the Open Voice Poetry Award from *The Writer's Voice*, the Helen and Laura Krout Memorial Poetry Award, an Academy of American Poets Prize, and an Ohio Arts Council Grant, and he was named the 1994 Georgia

Author of the Year. In addition to having published over six hundred poems in various top literary journals, Greenway has written nine full-length poetry collections, including *Ascending Order* (2003), winner of the 2004 Ohioana Poetry Book of the Year Award; *Fishing at the End of the World* (2005); and *Everywhere at Once* (2008), which was nominated for the 2008 Ohioana Poetry Book of the Year Award. In a 2010 interview with the YSU Student Literary Arts Association, Greenway said of his poems that "though they are often set in a real and particular place, the place is changed, almost surrealistically, as in a dream, to a place which, though still recognizable as a particular place, is now universal, an Everywhere which I hope is accessible to everyone."

LINDA GREGERSON (b. 1950) Gregerson grew up in Illinois and received her B.A. from Oberlin College, her M.A. from Northwestern University, her M.F.A. from the University of Iowa Writers' Workshop, and her Ph.D. from Stanford University. She has written several books of poetry, including *Fire in the Conservatory* (1982); *The Woman Who Died in Her Sleep* (1996), a finalist for the Poet's Prize and the Lenore Marshall Award; *Waterborne* (2002), which won the Kingsley Tufts Poetry Award; and, most recently, *Magnetic North* (2007), a National Book Award finalist. She has also written two volumes of literary criticism, *The Reformation of the Subject: Spenser, Milton, and the English Protestant Epic* (1995) and *Negative Capability: Contemporary American Poetry* (2001). She has been awarded the American Academy of Arts and Letters Award in Literature, the Levinson Prize from *Poetry* magazine, the Consuelo Ford Award from the Poetry Society of America, the Isabel MacCaffrey Award from the Spenser Society of America, a Guggenheim Fellowship, and three Pushcart Prizes. Gregerson currently lives in Michigan with her husband and two daughters and directs the M.F.A. Program in Creative Writing at the University of Michigan.

MARILYN HACKER (b. 1942) Hacker, the only child of two chemists, was born and raised in the Bronx and graduated from the Bronx High School of Science at age fifteen. She immediately enrolled at New York University, dropped out, got married, and worked as an editor for a time before returning to NYU to earn a bachelor's degree in Romance languages. Hacker's poems appeared in *Epoch, London Magazine, Ambit,* and *New American Review* before her first book of poetry, *Presentation Piece,* was published in 1974 and won the National Book Award. Among her numerous other volumes of poetry are *Separations* (1976), *Taking Notice* (1980), *Winter Numbers: Poems* (1995), *Desesperanto: Poems 1999–2002* (2003), and *Essays on Departure: New and Selected Poems* (2006). She has served as editor of the *Kenyon Review* and taught at the City College of New York. Hacker is known for her use of traditional poetic forms, including the sonnet and villanelle, to explore subjects such as feminism, anti-Semitism, AIDS, suffering, lesbianism, and her own battle with breast cancer.

DONALD HALL (b. 1928) Hall grew up in Hamden, Connecticut, and attended Phillips Exeter Academy in New Hampshire. He went on to earn his B.A. from Harvard in 1951, a B.Litt. from Oxford, and an honorary Ph.D. in literature from Bates College. In 1957, he took a position as an assistant professor of English at the University of Michigan, which is where he met his future wife, the poet Jane Kenyon. After they married, the couple moved to Eagle Pond Farm in rural New Hampshire and led a quiet, harmonious life that both poets recounted in many of their poems. But that quiet life was interrupted in 1989 when Hall was diagnosed with colon cancer. Despite unfavorable odds, he eventually went into remission. In 1994, however, Kenyon was diagnosed with leukemia and died fifteen months later. Her death struck Hall hard, and he attempted to work through his grief in writing. In 1998, on the third anniversary of his wife's death, Hall published *Without: Poems* (1998), a volume *Publishers Weekly* called "a heartbreaking portrait of a marriage that has not quite ended." Hall also wrote a memoir about his and Kenyon's twenty-three-year marriage called *The Best Day the Worst Day: Life with Jane Kenyon* (2005). In addition to these works, some of Hall's most notable collections are *Exiles and Marriages* (1955), which was the Academy of American Poets' Lamont Poetry Selection for 1956; *The Happy Man* (1986), winner of the Lenore Marshall Poetry Prize; *The One Day* (1988), which won the National Book Critics Circle Award and the *Los Angeles Times* Book Prize, and was nominated for a Pulitzer Prize. His more recent collections include *The Painted Bed* (2002) and *White Apples and the Taste of Stone: Selected Poems 1946–2006* (2006). Among Hall's many literary honors are two Guggenheim Fellowships, the Poetry Society of America's Robert Frost Medal, a Lifetime Achievement award from the New Hampshire Writers and Publishers Project, and the Ruth Lilly Prize for poetry. Hall also served as poet laureate of New Hampshire from 1984 to 1989 and was appointed the Library of Congress's fourteenth Poet Laureate Consultant in Poetry in 2006. He still resides in New Hampshire.

MARK HALLIDAY (b. 1949) Halliday earned bachelor's and master's degrees from Brown University before earning a doctorate in English literature from Brandeis University. He taught at Wellesley College, the University of Pennsylvania, Western Michigan University, and Indiana University before joining the faculty at Ohio University. He is the author of five volumes of poems: *Little Star* (1987), *Tasker Street* (1992), *Selfwolf* (1999), *Jab* (2002), and *Keep This Forever* (2008). He was awarded the Rome Prize of the American Academy of Arts and Letters in 2001 and a fellowship from the Guggenheim Foundation in 2006. About the colloquial style of his poetry, Halliday has said, "I love the analogy between a poem and a speech that you might actually hear in real life. . . . People do, over a few beers, let's say, if they're having trouble in their marriage or they're trying to change their lives, they do go from anecdote to meditation to comic speculation and then back to the beer, back to a joke—the movement of thought has those different levels. I love poems that show a speaker living through those moves."

SAM HAMILL (b. 1943) Hamill grew up on a farm in Utah in the care of foster parents. His discovery of Albert Camus's essays on pacifism—which Hamill came across during a judge-ordained enlistment in the Marine Corps—helped him to overcome the violence and instability he had faced as a child, and his ensuing commitment to Zen practices greatly informed his poetry. He studied with Kenneth Rexroth at the University of California, Santa Barbara, but left UCSB to co-found with Tree Swenson the Copper Canyon Press. Hamill served as editor there from 1972 through 2004. He also founded Poets Against the War in 2003 to protest America's invasion of Iraq, a movement that inspired the 2004 documentary *Voices in Wartime* and spawned the collection *Poets Against the War* (2003), which Hamill edited. Hamill has written more than a dozen volumes of poetry, including *Destination Zero: Poems 1970–1995* (1995), *Gratitude* (1998), *Dumb Luck* (2002), *Almost Paradise: New and Selected Poems and Translations* (2005), and *Measured by Stone* (2007). He has received fellowships from the National Endowment for the Arts, the Guggenheim Foundation, and the Woodrow Wilson Foundation, the U.S.-Japan Friendship Commission; two Washington Governor's Arts Awards; the Stanley Lindberg Lifetime Achievement Award for Editing; and the Washington Poets Association Lifetime Achievement Award for poetry.

LORRAINE HANSBERRY (1930–1965) Lorraine Hansberry was born into a prosperous, middle-class African American family on the South Side of Chicago. When she was seven, her family went to court over an attempt to deny them the right to buy a home in a restricted white neighborhood. Their lawsuit challenging the restrictive covenant was finally decided in their favor by the U.S. Supreme Court. Hansberry later recalled, "Both of my parents were strong-minded, civic-minded, exceptionally race-minded people who made enormous sacrifices on behalf of the struggle for civil rights throughout their lifetimes." After graduating from the segregated public school system of Chicago, she attended the University of Wisconsin and studied at the Art Institute of Chicago and abroad. She soon gave up her artistic plans and moved to New York City to pursue a writing career. She also became politically active in liberal causes. During a protest demonstration at New York University, she met Robert Nemiroff, a white writer and political activist. They married in 1953. Encouraged by her husband, Hansberry finally completed *A Raisin in the Sun*, a play she had been working on for some time. It opened in 1959, becoming the first play written by a black woman to be produced on Broadway. An immediate success, the play won the New York Drama Critics' Circle Award. A film version, for which she wrote the screenplay, was released in 1961. Her next play, *The Sign in Sidney Brustein's Window* (1964), met with less success. She was working on another play, *Les Blancs*, when she died of cancer (the play was produced in 1970). Although Nemiroff and Hansberry divorced in 1964, he was appointed her literary executor and assembled, from his former wife's writings and words, a dramatic autobiography titled *To Be Young, Gifted, and Black* (1969).

THOMAS HARDY (1840–1928) Hardy was born near Dorchester in southeastern England, on which he based the Wessex of many of his novels and poems. Hardy worked for the ecclesiastical architect John Hicks from 1856 to 1861. He then moved to London to practice architecture and took evening classes at King's College for six years. In 1867, he gave up architecture to become a full-time writer, and after writing short stories and poems, he found success as a novelist. *The Mayor of Casterbridge* (1886) and *Tess of the d'Urbervilles* (1891) reveal Hardy's concern for victims of circumstance and his appeal to humanitarian sympathy in readers. After his novel *Jude the Obscure* (1896) was strongly criticized, Hardy set aside prose fiction and returned to poetry—a genre in which he was most prolific and successful after he reached the age of seventy.

ROBERT HASS (b. 1941) Hass was born in San Francisco, California. He attended St. Mary's College and received both his M.A. and Ph.D. in English from Stanford University. Among his many books of poetry are *Field Guide* (1973), which was selected by Stanley Kunitz for the Yale Younger Poets Series; *Praise* (1979), for which he received the William Carlos Williams Award; *Human Wishes* (1989); *Sun Under Wood: New Poems* (1996), which won the National Book Critics Circle Award; and *Time and Materials* (2007), which won the National Book Award and the 2007 Pulitzer Prize for Poetry. His most recent collection is *The Apple Trees at Olema: New and Selected Poems* (2010). Hass served two terms as poet laureate of the United States (1995–1997) and was a chancellor of the Academy of American Poets from 2001 to 2007. In addition to his poetry, Hass is also a prolific critic and translator, most notably of the Polish poet Czeslaw Milosz and of Japanese haiku masters Basho, Buson, and Issa. In an interview with the *Chicago Review*, Hass once said that "Poetry is a way of living . . . a human activity like baking bread or playing basketball." He lives in California with his wife, the poet Brenda Hillman, and teaches at the University of California, Berkeley.

TERRANCE HAYES (b. 1971)   Hayes was born in Columbia, South Carolina. He studied at Coker College and later earned his M.F.A. from the University of Pittsburgh. He has received many literary honors including a Whiting Writers Award, three Best American Poetry selections, a Pushcart Prize, and fellowships from the National Endowment for the Arts and the Guggenheim Foundation. His collections of poetry include *Muscular Music* (1999), winner of the Kate Tufts Discovery Award; *Hip Logic* (2002), which won the 2001 National Poetry Series and was a finalist for the *Los Angeles Times* Book Award; *Wind in a Box* (2006); and *Lighthead* (2010), which won the National Book Award for Poetry. In praise of Hayes's work, Cornelius Eady has said, "First you'll marvel at his skill, his near-perfect pitch, his disarming humor, his brilliant turns of phrase. Then you'll notice the grace, the tenderness, the unblinking truth-telling just beneath his lines, the open and generous way he takes in our world." Hayes teaches creative writing at Carnegie Mellon University and lives in Pittsburgh with his wife, the poet Yona Harvey, and their children.

NATHANIEL HAWTHORNE (1804–1864)   The son of a merchant sea captain who died in a distant port when Nathaniel was four, Hawthorne grew up in genteel poverty in Massachusetts and Maine. His earliest American ancestor, the magistrate William Hathorne, ordered the whipping of a Quaker woman in Salem. William's son John was one of the three judges at the Salem witch trials of 1692. Aware of his family's role in colonial America, Hawthorne returned to Salem after graduating from Bowdoin College (where future president Franklin Pierce was a friend and classmate), determined to be a writer. He recalled and destroyed copies of his first novel, the mediocre *Fanshawe* (1828). His short stories, often set in Puritan America, revealed a moral complexity that had not troubled his righteous ancestors William and John. His success as an author allowed him to marry Sophia Peabody in 1842, after a four-year engagement. Though his stories were critically praised, they did not earn much money, and in 1846 he used his political connections with the Democratic Party to obtain a job at the Salem custom house. His dismissal in 1849 (when the Democrats lost) produced both anger and resolve. The result was a great American novel, *The Scarlet Letter* (1850), which made him famous and improved his fortune. Although he was friendly with Emerson and his circle of optimistic transcendentalists, some of whom established the utopian socialist community at Brook Farm, Hawthorne's vision of the human condition was considerably darker. Herman Melville dedicated *Moby-Dick* to Hawthorne and characterized him as a man who could say "No" in thunder.

ROBERT HAYDEN (1913–1980)   Born in Detroit, Hayden studied at Wayne State University and the University of Michigan (M.A., 1944). In 1946, he joined the faculty of Fisk University. He left Fisk in 1968 for a professorship at the University of Michigan, where he remained until his death. He produced some ten volumes of poetry but did not receive the acclaim many thought he deserved until late in life, with the publication of *Words in the Mourning Time: Poems* (1971). In the 1960s, he aroused some hostility from African Americans who wanted him to express more militancy. But Hayden did not want to be part of what he called a "kind of literary ghetto." He considered his own work "a form of prayer—a prayer for illumination, perfection."

SEAMUS HEANEY (b. 1939)   Heaney, the eldest of nine children, was born on his family's farm near Belfast in County Derry, Northern Ireland. He attended local schools, earned a degree in English with first-class honors from Queen's University, Belfast, and received a teacher's certificate in English from St. Joseph's College in Belfast. He published his first writings while a student at St. Joseph's and began a career as a teacher. His first volume of poetry, *Death of a Naturalist* (1966), won several prizes and launched Heaney's distinguished career as a poet. He has produced several volumes of essays, most recently *Finders Keepers: Selected Prose 1971–2001* (2002). Among his numerous volumes of poetry are *The Spirit Level* (1996), *Opened Ground: Poems 1966–1996* (1998), *The Riverbank Field* (2007), and *Articulations* (2008). His 2006 volume, *District and Circle,* won the T. S. Eliot Prize, and his most recent volume, *Human Chain* (2010), won the Forward Poetry Prize Best Collection 2010 award and the Irish Times Poetry Now Award for 2011. Other recent publications include *Beowulf: A New Verse Translation* (2002) and *The Burial at Thebes: A Version of Sophocles'* Antigone (2004). He has taught at Oxford University, the University of California at Berkeley, and Harvard University. An immensely popular poet, he enjoys the support of a host of "Heaneyboppers" who attend his readings. Several modern critics characterize him as "the most important Irish poet since Yeats." When asked "about his abiding interest in memorializing the people of his life, he replied, 'The elegiac Heaney? There's nothing else.'" In 1995, Heaney was awarded the Nobel Prize for Literature.

ERNEST HEMINGWAY (1899–1961) Born in Oak Park, Illinois, Hemingway became a cub reporter after high school. After World War I—during which he was seriously wounded while serving as an ambulance driver—he lived in Paris, a member of a lively and productive expatriate community characterized by Gertrude Stein as "a lost generation." He lived an active life, not only as a writer but also as a war correspondent, big-game hunter, and fisherman. In such novels as *The Sun Also Rises* (1926), *A Farewell to Arms* (1929), and *For Whom the Bell Tolls* (1940), his fictional characters exhibit a passion for courage and integrity, for grace under pressure. Hemingway's spare, unembellished style reinforced his central theme that one must confront danger and live honorably. He won the Nobel Prize for Literature in 1954. In 1961, unable to write because treatment for mental instability affected his memory, he killed himself with the shotgun he had so often used when hunting.

JUAN FELIPE HERRERA (b. 1948) Herrera was born in Fowler, California, to Mexican migrant farmworkers. He earned a bachelor's degree in social anthropology at the University of California at Los Angeles, a master's degree in social anthropology from Stanford University, and an M.F.A. from the University of Iowa. He taught at California State University at Fresno before assuming his current role as the Tomás Rivera Endowed Chair in the Creative Writing Department at the University of California, Riverside. Herrera describes himself as an educator, poet, writer, artist, performer, and musician. In addition to writing children's books, novels for young adults, prose, and short stories, he is the author of more than a dozen volumes of poetry. Among his most recent publications are *Cinnamon Girl: Letters Found Inside a Cereal Box* (2005), *Downtown Boy* (2005), *187 Reasons Mexicanos Can't Cross the Border: Undocuments 1971–2007* (2007), and *Half of the World in Light: New and Selected Poems* (2008).

ROBERT HERRICK (1591–1674) Born in London, Herrick was apprenticed to his uncle, a goldsmith, for ten years until at age twenty-two he was sent to Cambridge University in recognition of his academic talents. Little is known of the decade following his graduation from Cambridge, although it seems certain that he associated with a circle of literary artists. In 1629, he was appointed vicar at Dean Prior, Devonshire, a rural parish that the sophisticated and cosmopolitan Herrick looked upon as a kind of exile. Yet, he was fascinated by the pagan elements of local songs and dances, and often drew upon pre-Christian writers for inspiration. His chief work, *Hesperides* (1648), is a collection of some twelve hundred poems—mostly written in Devonshire—about local scenery, customs, and people.

EDWARD HIRSCH (b. 1950)   Hirsch was born and raised in Chicago, Illinois. He attended Grinnell College and the University of Pennsylvania, where he received a Ph.D. in folklore. Hirsch's first poetry collection, *For the Sleepwalkers* (1981), received the Lavan Younger Poets Award from the Academy of American Poets and the Delmore Schwartz Memorial Award from New York University. His second collection, *Wild Gratitude* (1986), also received acclaim, garnering the National Book Critics Circle Award. Among Hirsch's more recent collections are *Lay Back the Darkness* (2003), *Special Orders* (2008), and *The Living Fire: New and Selected Poems* (2010). He has also written several volumes of prose about the act of reading, including *Responsive Reading* (1999), *The Demon and the Angel: Searching for the Source of Artistic Inspiration* (2002), and the surprise national bestseller *How to Read a Poem: And Fall in Love with Poetry* (1999). Critic Kerry Fried praises Hirsch's awareness as an author: "Many of his fellow poets have suffered for their art, have been imprisoned and killed—but above all, Hirsch makes us realize that, no matter what the artist's circumstances, subject, or theme, 'the stakes are always high' in this game that writer and reader alike must keep playing." Hirsch has received many awards and fellowships, including from the Guggenheim and MacArthur foundations and from the National Endowment for the Arts, and in 2008, Hirsch was elected a chancellor of the Academy of American Poets. He is currently president of the John Simon Guggenheim Memorial Foundation.

TONY HOAGLAND (b. 1953)   Hoagland was born in Fort Bragg, North Carolina, and educated at the University of Iowa and the University of Arizona. He has taught at many institutions, including Kalamazoo College, University of Michigan, Warren Wilson College, and Colby College. He now teaches in the creative writing program at the University of Houston. His poems and critical writings have appeared in such publications as *Ploughshares*, *American Poetry Review*, and the *Pushcart Prize Anthology* (1991). Hoagland's first three collections of poems were chapbooks: *A Change in Plans* (1985), *Talking to Stay Warm* (1986), and *History of Desire* (1990). His first full-length volume of poetry, *Sweet Ruin* (1992), won the Brittingham Prize in poetry as well as the Zacharas Award from Emerson College. His most recent collections of poetry are *What Narcissism Means to Me* (2003), *Hard Rain* (2005), and *Unincorporated Persons in the Late Honda Dynasty: Poems* (2010). In 2005, he won the Poetry Foundation's Mark Twain Award and the Folger Shakespeare Library's O. B. Hardison Jr. Poetry Prize, which honors excellence in teaching as well as in writing. In 2006, Hoagland published *Real Sofistikashun: Essays on Poetry and Craft*, which explores "how poems behave and how they are made."

GERARD MANLEY HOPKINS (1844–1889)   Raised in London, Hopkins won a scholarship to Balliol College, Oxford University, where he studied classical literature. He converted to Roman Catholicism in 1866 and two years later entered the Jesuit novitiate. In 1877, he was ordained a Jesuit priest and served in missions in London, Liverpool, Oxford, and Glasgow until 1882. From 1884 to his death in 1889, he was professor of Greek at University College, Dublin. A technically innovative poet, Hopkins saw only three of his poems published during his lifetime. He gained posthumous recognition in 1918 when a friend, the poet laureate Robert Bridges, published Hopkins's complete works. His early poems celebrate the beauty of God's world, but later works reflect his poor health and depression.

A. E. HOUSMAN (1859–1936)   Born in Fockbury, England, and an outstanding student, Alfred Edward Housman nonetheless failed his final examinations at Oxford University in 1881, possibly due to emotional chaos caused by his love for a male classmate. Working as a clerk in the patent office in London, he pursued classical studies on his own, earned an M.A., and was appointed chair of Latin at University College, London. In 1910 he became professor of Latin at Cambridge, where he remained until his death in 1936. As a poet, Housman was concerned primarily with the fleetingness of love and the decay of youth. After his first collection, *A Shropshire Lad*, was rejected by several publishers, Housman published it at his own expense in 1896. It gained popularity during World War I, and his 1922 collection, *Last Poems*, was well received. In his lecture "The Name and Nature of Poetry" (1933), Housman argued that poetry should appeal to emotions rather than intellect. *More Poems* (1936) was published posthumously.

MARIE HOWE (b. 1950)   Howe was born in Rochester, New York, and received her M.F.A. from Columbia University in 1983. Her first poetry collection, *The Good Thief* (1988), was selected by Margaret Atwood for the National Poetry Series, and that same year, Stanley Kunitz also selected Howe for a Lavan Younger Poets Award from the Academy of American Poets. Kunitz called Howe's poetry "luminous, intense, and eloquent, rooted in an abundant inner life." Howe's second collection of poetry was *What the Living Do* (1998), which she wrote something of an elegy for her brother John, who died of AIDS in 1989; Howe was also co-editor of the anthology *In the Company of My Solitude: American Writing from the AIDS Pandemic* (1995). Her most recent poetry collection, *The Kingdom of Ordinary Time: Poems* (2009), was a finalist for the *Los Angeles Times* Book Prize. Among Howe's other honors are grants from the Guggenheim Foundation, the Bunting Institute, and the National Endowment for the Arts. Howe currently lives in New York City and teaches at Sarah Lawrence College, New York University, and Columbia University.

LANGSTON HUGHES (1902–1967)   Hughes was born in Joplin, Missouri. His father was a businessman and lawyer; his mother, a teacher. Hughes attended Columbia University, graduated from Lincoln University in 1929, traveled throughout the world, and held many odd jobs as a young man. While Hughes had a long and prolific career as a writer in all genres, he is still remembered as the central figure of the Harlem Renaissance of the 1920s, a movement that committed itself to the examination and celebration of black life in America and its African heritage. He was the Madrid correspondent for the Baltimore *Afro-American* (1937) and a columnist for the Chicago *Defender* (1943–1967) and the New York *Post* (1962–1967). His poems of racial affirmation and protest are often infused with the rhythms of blues and jazz music. He wrote over two dozen plays (many musicalized) and founded the Suitcase Theater (Harlem, 1938), the New Negro Theater (Los Angeles, 1939), and the Skyloft Players (Chicago, 1941). His works include *The Weary Blues* (1926), *Montage of a Dream Deferred* (1951), and *The Panther and the Lash: Poems of Our Times* (1969).

ZORA NEALE HURSTON (1891–1960)   Born in Eatonville, Florida, an African American town, Hurston enjoyed a happy early childhood in a town that spared her from racism and with a mother who instilled a strong sense of self-worth in her. With the death of her mother, she was sent off to boarding school but was forced to give up her formal education when her father remarried and refused to give her further financial help. She supported herself with odd jobs, managing to earn a high school diploma and enter Howard University in Washington, D.C. Unable to support herself as a full-time student,

Hurston quit college after five years, having earned only a year and a half of college credits. She moved to Harlem, determined to pursue a writing career. In New York, she was hired as a personal secretary by the novelist Fannie Hurst, who arranged a scholarship for her at Barnard College. There, she studied with the famous anthropologist Franz Boas and became interested in black folk traditions. She earned her degree from Barnard in 1927 and received a fellowship to study the oral traditions of her hometown. She wrote her first novel, *Jonah's Gourd Vine* (1934), while doing fieldwork in Eatonville. *Mules and Men* (1935), based on the material her fieldwork had produced, was attacked by African American intellectuals and writers for its refusal to acknowledge and confront racism. Nevertheless, Hurston was awarded a Guggenheim Fellowship to study voodoo in the Caribbean, which gave her the material for her second and most celebrated novel, *Their Eyes Were Watching God* (1937). During the last two decades of her life, she continued to write novels, plays, and an autobiography, *Dust Tracks on the Road* (1942), but drew increasing criticism from the African American press for her refusal to publicly condemn segregation. In 1950, she was the subject of a *Miami Herald* news story that carried the headline: "Famous Negro Author Working as a Maid Here 'Just to Live a Little.'" She claimed that she needed a break from writing and that she was busy making plans for writing projects and for a national magazine devoted to domestics. Her last years were troubled by poor health, emotional fatigue, and lack of money. She died of a stroke, penniless, in a welfare home in Fort Pierce, Florida.

DAVID HENRY HWANG (b. 1957)   Hwang was born in Los Angeles, California, earned a degree from Stanford University, and attended the Yale University School of Drama for one year. His first play, *F.O.B.* (for "fresh off the boat") won an OBIE for best New American Off-Broadway Play of 1980. Hwang has written a number of plays, musicals, operas, and screenplays but is best known for *M. Butterfly*, for which he won a Tony Award in 1988 and received a Pulitzer Prize nomination in 1989. His other awards include fellowships from the Guggenheim Foundation and the National Endowment for the Arts; an OBIE for best playwriting in 1997 and a Tony Award nomination for best Broadway play in 1998 for *Golden Child*; and a Tony Award nomination for his adaptation of the musical *Flower Drum Song* in 2003. Although Hwang once called his Chinese American heritage "a minor detail, like having red hair," cultural conflict and Asian themes are hallmarks of his most acclaimed works.

HENRIK IBSEN (1828–1906)   Ibsen was born in the seaport of Skien, Norway, the son of a wealthy merchant. When Ibsen was eight, his father's business failed, and at fifteen he was apprenticed to an apothecary in the tiny town of Grimstad. He hated this profession. To solace himself, he read poetry and theology and began to write. When he was twenty-two, he became a student in Christiania (now Oslo) and published his first play. In 1851, his diligent though unremarkable writing earned him an appointment as theater-poet at a new theater in Bergen, where he remained until 1857, learning both the business and the art of drama. He wrote several plays based on Scandinavian folklore, held positions at two theaters in Christiania, and married. When he was thirty-six, he applied to the government for a poet's pension—a stipend that would have permitted him to devote himself to writing. The stipend was refused. Enraged, he left Norway and, though he was granted the stipend two years later, spent the next twenty-seven years in Italy and Germany, where he wrote the realistic social dramas that established his reputation as the founder of modern theater. Such plays as *Ghosts* (1881), *An Enemy of the People* (1882), and *A Doll's House* (1878) inevitably generated controversy as Ibsen explored venereal disease, the stupidity and greed of the "compact majority," and the position of women in society. In 1891, he returned to live in Christiania, where he was recognized and honored as one of Norway's (and Europe's) finest writers.

SHIRLEY JACKSON (1919–1965) Born in San Francisco, Jackson moved with her family to Rochester, New York, in her teens. An episode of severe depression (a recurrent problem during her life) forced her out of the University of Rochester, but she later graduated from Syracuse University. She married the eminent critic Stanley Edgar Hyman, had four children, and kept to a rigid writing schedule. Although her major work tends toward the ominous, she contributed humorous pieces to popular magazines on the problems of house-keeping and raising children. These were collected in *Life among the Savages* (1953) and *Raising Demons* (1957). She wrote four novels, and her short stories are collected in three volumes: *The Lottery* (1949), *The Magic of Shirley Jackson* (1966), and *Come Along with Me* (1968).

HA JIN (b. 1956) Jin is the pen name of Ji-n Xuĕfe-i. Born in Liaoning, China, he grew up under the communist regime and was enlisted in the People's Liberation Army for six years. He earned two degrees in China before completing his doctorate at Brandeis University near Boston. Jin taught at Emory University and currently teaches at Boston University, where he is a professor in the English department. He has written three books of poetry: *Between Silences* (1990), *Facing Shadows* (1996), and *Wreckage* (2001). He is also the author of three books of short stories and five novels, most recently *War Trash* (2004), *A Free Life* (2007), and *A Good Fall* (2009). He is the recipient of numerous awards, including the Flannery O'Connor Prize for Short Fiction, a PEN/Hemingway Award, two PEN/Faulkner Awards, a National Book Award, and fellowships from the Guggenheim Foundation and the American Academy of Arts and Sciences. His latest work is *Nanjing Requiem: A Novel* (2011). Jin, who writes entirely in English about thorny Chinese-related themes, has said, "When a writer adopts another language there are a lot of motivations: necessity, ambition, estrangement. Estrangement is a big part of it. . . . It creates a kind of distance. In a way, it enables me to write more objectively."

GEORGIA DOUGLAS JOHNSON (1880–1966) Johnson was born in Atlanta, Georgia, to parents of African American, Native American, and English descent. She graduated from Atlanta University's Normal School in 1896, eventually going on to study music at the Oberlin Conservatory and the Cleveland College of Music. On September 28, 1903, Johnson married Henry Lincoln Johnson, an Atlanta-based lawyer and a prominent supporter of the Republican Party. When her husband accepted an appointment as the recorder of deeds from President William Howard Taft in 1910, the Johnsons moved to Washington, D.C. It was during this time that Johnson began to write. She published her first poems in 1916 in the NAACP's magazine *Crisis*, and her first volume of poetry, *The Heart of a Woman*, two years later. She also wrote a weekly column called "Homely Philosophy" from 1926 to 1932. She traveled widely during the 1920s to give poetry readings and published three additional collections during her lifetime: *Bronze* (1922), *An Autumn Love Cycle* (1928), and *Share My World* (1962). She also wrote numerous plays, including *A Sunday Morning in the South* (1925), *Blue Blood* (1926), and *Plumes* (1927). Her house at 1461 S Street Northwest—known as site of the S Street Salon—was a principal meeting place for Harlem Renaissance writers in Washington, D.C., and she often held open houses and readings there. Johnson received an honorary doctorate in literature from Atlanta University in 1965, one year before she passed away. She was also inducted posthumously into the Georgia Writers Hall of Fame in 2010.

JAMES WELDON JOHNSON (1871–1938) Johnson was born in Jacksonville, Florida, where from a young age he was encouraged by his parents to study English literature and the European musical tradition—an exception for most African Americans at the time. He later attended Atlanta University, during which time he taught for two summers in the rural, poor town of Hampton, Georgia. This experience exposed him to hardships from which he had been previously sheltered and ignited what became an enduring desire to help the black community. In 1901, Johnson and his brother Rosamond—a talented composer—moved to New York City to pursue a life writing songs for the musical theater. The brothers collaborated on the song "Lift Ev'ry Voice and Sing," which swiftly gained popularity and was adopted by the NAACP as the "Negro National Anthem." Johnson also studied creative literature at Columbia University for three years and became an active member of the Republican Party. He served as treasurer of New York's Colored Republican Club and helped compose songs for Republican candidate Theodore Roosevelt's presidential campaign. In 1906, Johnson was appointed to a job as U.S. consul to Venezuela, where he had poems published in the *Century Magazine* and *The Independent*. In 1912, he pseudonymously published *The Autobiography of an Ex-Colored Man*, the story of a biracial musician who rejects his African American heritage in favor of living a life of leisure among whites. In 1916, Johnson became the national organizer for the NAACP and served as its executive secretary for ten years starting in 1920. He also remained an active literary figure, editing *The Book of American Negro Poetry* (1922), which is to this day a landmark text in African American literature; *The Book of American Negro Spirituals* (1925); and *The Second Book of American Negro Spirituals* (1926). He also published *God's Trombones* (1927), a book of poetry that was greatly influenced by his time spent in Hampton, and *Black Manhattan* (1930), a survey of African American contributions to the artistic scene in New York. In 1934 he published *Negro Americans, What Now?*, an extended political argument in favor of racial integration. Of the adversities that he and other African Americans had faced, he declared, "I will not allow one prejudiced person or one million or one hundred million to blight my life. I will not let prejudice or any of its attendant humiliations and injustices bear me down to spiritual defeat. My inner life is mine, and I shall defend and maintain its integrity against all the powers of hell."

LACY M. JOHNSON (b. 1978) Johnson earned her Ph.D. from the University of Houston's Creative Writing Program. Her work has appeared in *Sentence, Nimrod, Memoir (and), Gulf Coast, Pebble Lake Review,* and *Irish Studies Review*. Her first book, *Trespasses: A Memoir* (2012), explores identity as it is associated with region, and region as it is experienced through memory, history, and theory. Author and critic Nick Flynn said of *Trespasses*: "Utterly hip, while at the same time a voice from another era, *Trespasses* is about 'growing up in a poor farming town in the Great Plains,' an examination of the term 'white trash' through interviews, research, and memory, and an evocation of a place many of us will never see. Yet, at its heart, it is a lyric evocation of self. Plainspoken, tattooed, and brilliant, Lacy Johnson pushes the boundaries of what memoir—and, perhaps more importantly, what *any of us*—can be."

BEN JONSON (1572–1637) Jonson was born in Westminster, England, and after leaving school, began earning his living as a bricklayer, the trade of his stepfather. Though he never attended college, he taught himself enough to be considered learned. He soon abandoned construction work and earned his reputation as one of the preeminent playwrights of his period. A contemporary of Shakespeare, he also wrote poetry and translations of classical Roman authors for his English Renaissance audience. Among other works, Jonson is the author of the satirical plays *Volpone, The Alchemist,* and *Bartholemew Fair*; his best known poems include "On My First Sonne," "To Celia," and "To Penshurst."

JUNE JORDAN (1936–2002)   Jordan was born in Harlem, New York, and attended Barnard College (1953–1955) and the University of Chicago (1955–1956). A poet, novelist, and writer of children's books, she taught widely at university campuses, including the City College of the City University of New York (1966–1968) and Connecticut College (1969–1974), where she taught English and served as director of Search for Education, Elevation and Knowledge (SEEK). She was later professor of English at the State University of New York, Stony Brook. In addition to many appointments as visiting professor, she served as chancellor's distinguished lecturer, University of California at Berkeley (1986). Her numerous honors include the Prix de Rome in Environmental Design (1970–1971), the Nancy Bloch Award (1971) for her reader *The Voice of the Children,* and the achievement award from the National Association of Black Journalists (1984). Her many books include *His Own Where* (1971), *Dry Victories* (1972), and *Kimako's Story* (1981), all for juvenile and young adult readers. Her collections of poetry include *Things That I Do in the Dark* (1977), *Living Room: New Poems, 1980–1984* (1985), *Naming Our Destiny: New and Selected Poems* (1989), *Poetic Justice* (1991), *Haruko: Love Poems* (1994), and *Kissing God Goodbye: Poems 1991–1997* (1997). Jordan is also the author of *Technical Difficulties: African-American Notes on the State of the Union* (1992) and *Affirmative Acts: Political Essays* (1998). *Some of Us Did Not Die: New and Selected Essays* (2002) was published shortly after her death.

JAMES JOYCE (1882–1941)   Though educated in Jesuit schools, Joyce came to reject Catholicism; and though an expatriate living in Paris, Trieste, and Zurich for most of his adult life, he wrote almost exclusively about his native Dublin. Joyce's rebelliousness, which surfaced during his university career, generated a revolution in modern literature. His novels *Ulysses* (1922) and *Finnegan's Wake* (1939) introduced radically new narrative techniques. "Araby"—from his first collection of short stories, *Dubliners* (1914)—is one of a series of sharply realized vignettes based on Joyce's experiences in Ireland, the homeland he later characterized as "a sow that eats its own farrow." Joyce lived precariously on earnings as a language teacher and also modest contributions from wealthy patrons, support that he justified by becoming one of the most influential novelists of the twentieth century. Because *Ulysses* dealt frankly with sexuality and used coarse language, the U.S. Post Office charged that the novel was obscene and forbade its importation. A celebrated 1933 court decision lifted the ban.

FRANZ KAFKA (1883–1924)   Born into a middle-class, German-speaking Jewish family in Prague, Kafka earned a law degree in 1906 and worked as a claims investigator for an insurance company for most of his adult life. He remained in constant conflict with his domineering father, who belittled his literary aims. He became engaged to a woman in 1912 but broke with her after five years. In 1917, he contracted the tuberculosis that was to kill him at age forty-one. Despite the deadening monotony of his job and his personal anguish, he created a remarkable and original body of work during his short life, including the masterful novels *The Trial* (1925) and *The Castle* (1926). His starkly realistic stories and novels take place in nightmarish dreamworlds where stifling bureaucracy chokes his protagonists and diminishes their dignity and their lives. A fierce perfectionist, Kafka published little during his life and left written instructions to his friend and executor, Max Brod, to destroy his unpublished manuscripts. Fortunately, Brod could not bring himself to comply.

JOHN KEATS (1795–1821)   Keats was born in London, the eldest son of a stablekeeper who died in an accident in 1804. His mother died of tuberculosis shortly after remarrying, and the grandmother who raised Keats and his siblings died in 1814. At eighteen, Keats wrote his first poem, "Imitation of Spenser," inspired by Edmund Spenser's long narrative poem *The Faerie Queene.* The thirty-three poems he wrote while training to be a surgeon were published in a collection in 1817, and Keats then gave up medicine for writing. After more traumatic losses in 1818, including the departure of one brother for the United States and the death of his other brother of tuberculosis, Keats wrote his second collection, *Lamia, Isabella, The Eve of St. Agnes, and Other Poems* (1820). Ill with tuberculosis himself, Keats was sent to Rome to recover. He died at twenty-six, but despite his short career he is a major figure of the romantic period.

JANE KENYON (1947–1995)   Kenyon was born in Ann Arbor, Michigan, and attended the University of Michigan, where she received a B.A. (1970) and M.A. (1972). While at Michigan she studied under Donald Hall, the eminent poet and teacher, whom she married in the year she received her master's. The couple moved to Eagle Pond Farm in rural New Hampshire, living a quiet life that Kenyon celebrated in many of her early poems. They became well known not only through her poems but also through the books Hall wrote about life on their farm. In her last poems, Kenyon wrote about her struggle with leukemia, which claimed her life at age forty-eight. At the time of her death, she was New Hampshire's poet laureate. During her lifetime, she published four collections of poems, *From Room to Room* (1978), *The Boat of Quiet Hours* (1986), *Let Evening Come* (1990), and *Constance* (1993). Since her death, two additional volumes have been published, *Otherwise: New and Selected Poems* (1996) and *A Hundred White Daffodils: Essays, Interviews, the Akhmatova Translations, Newspaper Columns, and One Poem* (1999). In 1998, on the third anniversary of Kenyon's death, Donald Hall published *Without: Poems,* a volume *Publishers Weekly* called "a heartbreaking portrait of a marriage that has not quite ended."

JAMAICA KINCAID (b. 1949)   Kincaid was born Elaine Potter Richardson in St. Johns, Antigua, in the West Indies, then a British colony. At age seventeen, she left home to become an au pair in New York. Determined to make something of her life, Kincaid took night classes and ultimately earned a high school diploma. She went on to take classes at the New School for Social Research in New York, and attended college in New Hampshire on a scholarship. When she returned to New York, she changed her name to Jamaica Kincaid and began writing. Of her life up to this point, Kincaid told a reporter: "Everyone thought I had a way with words, but it came out as a sharp tongue. No one expected anything from me at all. Had I just sunk in the cracks it would not have been noted. I would have been lucky to be a secretary somewhere." Her first publication, a collection of short stories titled *At the Bottom of the River* (1983), earned her wide critical praise and recognition as a new voice in American fiction. That was followed by three novels, including *The Autobiography of My Mother* (1995). *My Brother* (1997) deals with the death of her brother from AIDS. Her most recent publication is *Among Flowers: A Walk in the Himalaya* (2005). The recipient of many literary honors, Kincaid served as a staff writer for *The New Yorker* (1976–1995) and visiting professor at Harvard University.

MARTIN LUTHER KING JR. (1929–1968)   King was born in Atlanta, Georgia, where his father was pastor of the Ebenezer Baptist Church. He attended public schools (skipping the ninth and twelfth grades) and entered Morehouse College in Atlanta. He was ordained as a Baptist minister just before his graduation in 1948. He then enrolled in

Crozer Theological Seminary in Pennsylvania and after earning a divinity degree there, attended graduate school at Boston University, where he earned a Ph.D. in theology in 1955. At Boston University he met Coretta Scott; they were married in 1953. King's rise to national and international prominence began in 1955 in Montgomery, Alabama, when Rosa Parks, an African American woman, was arrested for refusing to obey a city ordinance that required African Americans to sit or stand at the back of municipal buses. The African American citizens of the city, one of the most thoroughly segregated in the South, organized a bus boycott in protest and asked King to serve as their leader. Thousands boycotted the buses for more than a year, and despite segregationist violence against them, King grounded their protests in his deeply held belief in nonviolence. In 1956, the U.S. Supreme Court ordered Montgomery to provide integrated seating on public buses. In the following year, King and other African American ministers founded the Southern Christian Leadership Conference (SCLC) to carry forward the nonviolent struggle against segregation and legal discrimination. As protests grew, so did the unhappiness of King and his associates with the unwillingness of the president and Congress to support civil rights. The SCLC, therefore, organized massive demonstrations in Montgomery (King wrote "Letter from Birmingham Jail" during these demonstrations). With the civil rights movement now in the headlines almost every day, President Kennedy proposed to Congress a far-reaching civil rights bill. On August 28, 1963, over 200,000 blacks and whites gathered at the Lincoln Memorial in Washington, D.C., where King delivered his now famous speech, "I Have a Dream." In the following year, Congress passed the Civil Rights Act of 1964, prohibiting racial discrimination in public places and calling for equal opportunity in education and employment. In that year, King received the Nobel Peace Prize. In 1965, King and others organized a march to protest the blatant denial of African Americans' voting rights in Selma, Alabama, where the march began. Before the protesters were able to reach Birmingham, the state capital, they were attacked by police with tear gas and clubs. This outrage, viewed live on national television, led President Johnson to ask Congress for a bill that would eliminate all barriers to voting rights. Congress responded by passing the landmark Voting Rights Act of 1965. King remained committed to nonviolence, but his conviction that economic inequality—not just race—was one of the root causes of injustice led him to begin organizing a Poor People's Campaign that would unite all poor people in the struggle for justice. These views also led him to criticize the role played by the United States in the Vietnam War. The Poor People's Campaign took King to Memphis, Tennessee, to support a strike of African American sanitation workers, where on April 4, 1968, he was shot and killed while standing on the balcony of his hotel room. Riots immediately erupted in scores of cities across the nation. A few months later, Congress enacted the Civil Rights Act of 1968, banning discrimination in the sale and rental of housing. King is the author of *Stride toward Freedom* (1958), dealing with the Montgomery bus boycott; *Strength to Love* (1953), a collection of sermons; and *Why We Can't Wait* (1964), a discussion of his general views on civil rights.

MAXINE HONG KINGSTON (b. 1940)   Kingston was born in Stockton, California. She earned a bachelor's degree from the University of California, Berkeley (1962), and a teaching certificate (1965). After teaching English and mathematics at a California high school, she moved to Hawaii and taught language arts and English as a second language at a number of schools. She became a visiting associate professor of English at the University of Hawaii after winning the National Book Critics Circle Award for *The Woman Warrior: Memoirs of a Girlhood among Ghosts* (1976). In that volume, she fashioned a new sort of genre—essays with substantial fictive elements. Her next book, *China Men* (1980), further developed that form. Her most recent works include *To Be the Poet* (2002), *The Fifth Book of Peace* (2003), and *I Love a Broad Margin to My Life* (2011), a free-verse memoir informed by the wide page margins in the Chinese editions of her work. An early critic characterized Kingston's work as the blending of "myth, legend, history, and autobiography into a genre of her own invention." Another argued that though Kingston's works are classified as non-fiction, "in a deeper sense, they are fiction at its best—novels, fairytales, epic poems." In 1993, Kingston founded the Veteran's Writing Group; she compiled and edited a collection of the group's writings in *Veterans of War, Veterans of Peace* (2006).

GALWAY KINNELL (b. 1927)   Born in Providence, Rhode Island, Kinnell graduated summa cum laude from Princeton University, served in the navy during World War II, and returned to earn a master's degree from the University of Rochester. He traveled extensively and lectured in France and Iran before returning to the United States. In 1963, he was a field-worker for the Congress of Racial Equality (CORE) and his involvement in the American civil rights movement informed what is perhaps his most famous collection of poetry, *Body Rags* (1968). Another of his prominent works, *The Book of Nightmares* (1971), is a book-length poem about the Vietnam War. He is the author of more than twenty additional volumes of poetry, the most recent being *Strong Is Your Hold* (2006). Kinnell taught at a large number of institutions, earned numerous awards, and served as chancellor of the Academy of American Poets from 2001 to 2007 before retiring to his home in Vermont.

CAROLYN KIZER (b. 1925)   Kizer was born in Spokane, Washington. Her father was a lawyer, her mother a biologist and professor. After graduating from Sarah Lawrence College in 1945, Kizer pursued graduate study at Columbia University and the University of Washington. From 1959 to 1965, she was editor of *Poetry Northwest* (which she founded in 1959 in Seattle) and spent 1964 and 1965 as a State Department specialist in Pakistan, where she taught at a women's college and translated poems from Urdu into English. She chose to leave early, after the U.S. decision to bomb North Vietnam in 1965. Later, she joined archaeological tours in Afghanistan and Iran. She has worked as director of literary programs for the National Endowment for the Arts in Washington, D.C.; has taught at several universities; and was poet-in-residence at the University of North Carolina and Ohio University. Her volumes of poetry include *Yin* (1984), which won a Pulitzer Prize the following year; *Mermaids in the Basement: Poems for Women* (1984); *The Nearness of You* (1986); *Harping On: Poems 1985–1995* (1996); *Pro Femina: A Poem* (2000); and *Cool, Calm & Collected: Poems 1960–2000* (2001). She has also published two collections of essays—*Proses: On Poems and Poets* (1993) and *Picking and Choosing: Essays on Prose* (1995)—and edited *100 Great Poems by Women: A Golden Ecco Anthology* (1995).

MARVIN KLOTZ (b. 1930)   Born in New York City, Klotz earned a Ph.D. from New York University and, in 1959, joined the faculty at what later became California State University, Northridge. He taught literature in five countries, retired in 1992, and began writing verse about fractured neighborhoods and a bi-polar world that can be found at www.marvinklotz.com.

ETHERIDGE KNIGHT (1931–1991)   Knight was born in Corinth, Mississippi, attended two years of public high school in Kentucky, and served in the U.S. Army from 1948 to 1951. After being convicted on a robbery charge and sentenced in 1960 to twenty years in Indiana State Prison, he discovered poetry; his first collection is entitled *Poems* *from Prison* (1968). Knight was paroled after eight years. From 1968 to 1971 he was poet-in-residence at several universities. An important African American voice in the 1960s and 1970s, Knight rejected the American and European aesthetic tradition, arguing that "the red of this esthetic rose got its color from the blood of black slaves, exterminated Indians, napalmed Vietnamese children." His collection *Belly Song and Other Poems* was nominated for the National Book Award and the Pulitzer Prize in 1973. His awards include National Endowment for the Arts and Guggenheim grants and the 1987 American Book Award for *The Essential Etheridge Knight* (1986).

YUSEF KOMUNYAKAA (b. 1947)   Born and raised in Bogalusa, Louisiana, James Willie Brown Jr. later took the surname of his great-grandparents who had come from Trinidad on a slave ship. His work often explores themes related to his life in the American south, the civil rights movement in America, and his tour of duty as a soldier during the Vietnam War. He began composing poetry even before he earned degrees from the University of Colorado, Colorado State University, and the University of California at Irvine. He taught at the University of New Orleans, Indiana University at Bloomington, and Princeton University before assuming his current role as a professor in the Creative Writing Program at New York University. He is the author of over a dozen books of poetry but gained attention for *Copacetic* (1984), *I Apologize for the Eyes in My Head* (1986), and *Dien Cai Dau* (1988). His most recent collection is *The Chameleon Couch: Poems* (2012). He is best known for *Neon Vernacular: New and Selected Poems* (1993), for which he won the Kingsley Tufts Poetry Award and a Pulitzer Prize. He also received the 2001 Ruth Lilly Poetry Prize, a prestigious honor given to living U.S. poets "whose lifetime accomplishments warrant extraordinary recognition."

HARI KUNZRU (b. 1969)   Kunzru was born in London to a Kashmiri Indian doctor and an English nurse. He grew up in Essex and earned degrees from Oxford University and the University of Warwick in Coventry, England. He worked as a journalist for a number of periodicals and as a decorator, disc jockey, juggler, promotions coordinator, telemarketer, van driver, and waiter. It was while working as a satellite-television host that he began writing his first novel, *The Impressionist* (2002), about a character who, like Kunzru himself, is a biracial Indian Englishman. The book was widely praised and a best seller, short-listed for a number of awards and named one of the best novels of 2002 by *Publishers Weekly*. His second novel, *Transmission* (2004), was a *New York Times* notable book of the year. He followed that with a collection of short stories, *Noise* (2005), and *My Revolutions: A Novel* (2007). His most recent work is *Gods without Men: A Novel* (2012).

JHUMPA LAHIRI (b. 1967)   Lahiri was born to Bengalese parents in London and was raised in Rhode Island before she earned multiple degrees from Barnard College and Boston University. Her time spent visiting extended family in Calcutta, India, and her immigrant identity informs her work. Her first book, a collection of stories titled *Interpreter of Maladies* (1999), won the Pulitzer Prize and the PEN/Hemingway Award, and was the *New Yorker* Debut of the Year. Her second work, the novel *The Namesake* (2003), was a *New York Times* notable book and was selected as one of the best books of the year by a number of publications, including *USA Today* and *Entertainment Weekly*. She has also received an O. Henry Award and a Guggenheim Fellowship and was named one of the twenty best young writers in America by *New Yorker* magazine. Her most recent work, a collection of stories, is *Unaccustomed Earth* (2008).

PHILIP LARKIN (1922–1985)   Born in Coventry, Larkin attended St. John's College, Oxford University (B.A., 1943; M.A., 1947). He was appointed librarian at the University of Hull in 1955, wrote jazz feature articles for the London *Daily Telegraph* from 1961 to 1971, and won numerous poetry awards, including the Queens Gold Medal (1965) and the Benson Medal (1975). His first collection, *The North Ship* (1945), was not well received, but he gained recognition after publication of *The Less Deceived* (1960). Larkin once said, "Form holds little interest for me. Content is everything."

EVELYN LAU (b. 1971)   Lau was born in Vancouver, Canada, to Chinese Canadian parents. Driven by an unhappy family life, she ran away from home and wound up living on the streets of Vancouver working as a prostitute to support her drug addiction. During these turbulent early years, Lau kept a diary, and she published poems in Canadian and American journals even before she ran away. Throughout the years of living on the edge, during which she made a number of suicide attempts and was confined in a psychiatric ward, Lau continued to write. With the help of a sympathetic psychiatrist and her commitment to writing, she managed to pull herself out of the chaos and turn herself into a professional and very successful writer. Her first published work was an autobiographical account of her early years, *Runaway: Diary of a Street Kid* (1989). An immediate success, it was filmed as *The Diary of Evelyn Lau* and aired on the Canadian Broadcasting Corporation in 1994. *Runaway* was followed by three volumes of poems, *You Are Not Who You Claim* (1990); *Oedipal Dreams*, nominated for the prestigious Governor General's Award for poetry (1993); and *In the House of Slaves* (1993). Lau is also the author of a novel, *Other Women* (1995), and a collection of short stories, *Choose Me* (1999). Her most recent publications are *Inside Out: Reflections on a Life So Far* (2001), *Treble* (2005), and *Living Under Plastic* (2010). Asked by an interviewer if she had acquired her "beautiful, clear" writing style in school, Lau replied, "Nope. All self-taught. In my teens I took some one-day writers' workshops and things like that. But I've never gone properly back to school."

CHANG-RAE LEE (b. 1965)   Lee was born in South Korea and emigrated to the United States with his family at the age of three. He received his B.A. in English from Yale University and an M.F.A. in writing from the University of Oregon. Lee's experiences of bridging a cultural divide inform much of his writing. Lee's first novel, *Native Speaker* (1995), which explores themes of identity and assimilation through the story of a Korean-American outsider turned spy, won him the PEN/Hemingway Award. His second book, *A Gesture Life* (1999), was also well-received, garnering Lee the Asian American Literary Award. His third novel, *Aloft* (2004), was his first book not to feature an Asian American protagonist, instead telling the story of an Italian American suburbanite who feels estranged from his surroundings. *Aloft* won the 2006 Asian/Pacific American Award for Literature in the Adult Fiction category. Lee's latest novel, *The Surrendered* (2010), won the 2011 Dayton Literary Peace Prize and was a finalist for the 2011 Pulitzer Prize for Fiction. Lee has said of his stories, "The characters may not always be Asian Americans, but they will always be people who are thinking about the culture and how they fit or don't fit into it." Lee currently teaches creative writing at Princeton University.

LI-YOUNG LEE (b. 1957)   Lee was born in Jakarta, Indonesia, to Chinese parents. While there, his father was imprisoned for his religious beliefs, and further anti-Chinese sentiment caused the entire family to flee the country. They traveled in exile for six years before finally settling in the United States. Lee earned a degree from the University of Pittsburgh and attended the University of Arizona and the State University of New York

College at Brockport for brief periods. He began writing in earnest in college and is the author of four books of poetry: *Rose* (1986), *The City in Which I Love You* (1990), *Book of My Nights* (2001), and *Behind My Eyes* (2008). He also penned a memoir, *The Winged Seed: A Remembrance* (1995), in which he recounts his family's troubled history and his turbulent youth. Lee has received awards from the Lannan and Whiting foundations, as well as fellowships from the Guggenheim Foundation and the National Endowment for the Arts.

URSULA K. LE GUIN (b. 1929)   The daughter of distinguished University of California at Berkeley anthropologists, Le Guin graduated from Radcliffe College and earned an M.A. from Columbia University. She enjoyed early success writing for science fiction and fantasy magazines (a genre often stigmatized as subliterary popular fiction), but she quickly established a reputation that places her in the tradition of earlier writers who used fantastic circumstances to shape their understanding of the human condition, such as Jonathan Swift, Edgar Allan Poe, and H. G. Wells. A prolific writer of fantasy fiction, Le Guin's latest works include *The Other Wind* (2001), *Tales from Earthsea* (2001), and the *Annals of the Western Shore* trilogy (2004–2007). Her most recent novel is *Lavinia* (2008). Among her collections of short stories are *The Birthday of the World* (2002), *Changing Planes* (2003), and most recently *The Wild Girls* (2011). Her latest book of poetry is *Incredible Good Fortune* (2006).

JONATHAN LETHEM (b. 1964)   Born in Brooklyn, New York, Lethem attended Bennington College in Vermont, dropped out during sophomore year, hitchhiked across the country, and landed in California, where he worked as a clerk in a bookstore for over a decade. He published his first short story in 1989. A prolific writer of novels, short stories, and essays, Lethem is widely considered by some to be a science fiction author, while others think his work much harder to categorize. A profile about Lethem in *Publishers Weekly* noted that his writing "exists somewhere in the previously uncharted interstices between science fiction, western, and coming-of-age novels." His notable novels include his first book, *Gun, with Occasional Music*, published in 1994; *Motherless Brooklyn* (1999), which won a National Book Critics Circle Award; and *The Fortress of Solitude*, which was a *New York Times* best seller. His most recent publication is *The Ecstasy of Influence: Nonfictions, Etc.* (2011). His work has appeared in numerous periodicals, among them *Entertainment Weekly*, *Esquire*, *GQ*, *Harper's*, the *New York Times*, *The New Yorker*, *Rolling Stone*, *Salon*, and the *Village Voice*. In 2010, he was named Disney Professor of Writing at Pomona College in Claremont, California.

PHILIP LEVINE (b. 1928)   The son of Russian Jewish immigrants, Levine was born in Detroit, Michigan, into a household where debates and discussions about radical politics instilled in him a political sensibility and an abiding sympathy for the poor and the powerless. After receiving his B.A. from Wayne State University (1950), he returned to Detroit and worked at various industrial jobs in the auto industry before enrolling in the University of Iowa in 1955, where he received his M.F.A. (1957). He earned his living teaching poetry, primarily at California State University at Fresno and Tufts University in Massachusetts, and is now retired. Since his first collection of poems, *On the Edge* (1961), Levine has published more than twenty volumes of poetry, many of them exhibiting his radical political consciousness. Among them are *They Feed They Lion* (1972); *Ashes* (1979); *What Work Is* (1991), which received the National Book Award; and *The Simple Truth* (1995), for which he received the Pulitzer Prize. His most recent volumes of poetry are *Breath* (2004) and *News of the World* (2011). In 1997, Levine was elected to the American Academy of Arts and Letters. He has summed up his aspirations as an artist with the remark, "My hope is to write poetry for people for whom there are no poems." He is 2011–2012 poet laureate of the United States.

YIYUN LI (b. 1972) Li grew up in Beijing and emigrated to the United States in 1996 after earning her B.S. at Peking University. Her work has been published in *The New Yorker*, *Best American Short Stories*, *O. Henry Prize Stories*, and elsewhere, and she has received awards and grants from the Lannan Foundation, the Whiting Foundation, and the MacArthur Foundation. Her debut short story collection, *A Thousand Years of Good Prayers* (2006), won the 2005 Frank O'Connor International Short Story Award, the PEN/Hemingway Award, a Guardian First Book Award, and a California Book Award for first fiction. Her novel *The Vagrants* (2010) won the gold medal of California Book Award for fiction. Her most recent work is *Gold Boy, Emerald Girl: Stories* (2010). *The New Yorker* named her to its "20 Under 40" list, a group of "young writers who capture the inventiveness and the vitality of contemporary American fiction," and she was selected by *Granta* as one of the 21 Best Young American Novelists under 35. She is also a contributing editor to the Brooklyn-based literary magazine *A Public Space*. She lives with her family in Oakland, California, and teaches at University of California, Davis.

SHIRLEY GEOK-LIN LIM (b. 1944) Lim was born in Malacca, Malaysia, and received her Ph.D. from Brandeis University in 1973. Lim's first collection of poems, *Crossing the Peninsula* (1980), won the Commonwealth Poetry Prize, a first both for an Asian author and a female author. She has written four other books of poetry; three books of short stories; a novel, *Joss and Gold* (2001); and two books of criticism: *Nationalism and Literature* (1993) and *Writing South/East Asia in English: Against the Grain* (1994). Her memoir *Among the White Moon Faces: An Asian-American Memoir of Homelands* (1996) received the 1997 American Book Award. She has edited and co-edited several scholarly collections, including *The Forbidden Stitch: An Asian American Women's Anthology* (1989), *Power, Race, and Gender in Academe: Strangers in the Tower?* (1999), and *The Columbia Companion to the Twentieth-Century American Short Story* (2001). She has taught abroad at the National University of Singapore, NIE of Nanyang Technological University, and the University of Hong Kong, and she currently teaches English at the University of California, Santa Barbara.

STUART LISHAN (b. 1955) Lishan is currently an associate professor of English at Ohio State University, where he teaches courses in creative writing, poetry, and literature. An author of both poetry and fiction, his work has appeared in numerous periodicals, including *American Literary Review*, *Antioch Review*, *Arts & Letters*, *Barrow Street*, *Kenyon Review*, and *Smartish Pace*. His chapbook manuscript, *Body Tapestries*, was a finalist in the 2000 Walt Whitman award competition and was published in the e-journal *Mudlark* in 2001. About "Winter Count, 1964," Lishan has said that he was inspired by "the deep need for intimacy among these kids, for physical contact, and the hostility and fear of it, as well. I love the edge and dramatic tension that creates. Basically, these kids don't know what to do with these desires. This piece explores that territory."

AUDRE LORDE (1934–1992) Born to middle-class West Indian immigrant parents in New York City, Lorde grew up in Harlem and attended the National University of Mexico (1954), Hunter College (B.A., 1959), and Columbia University (M.L.S., 1961). Her marriage in 1962, which produced two children, ended in divorce in 1970. During these early years, she worked as a librarian, but in 1968 her growing reputation as a writer led to her appointment as lecturer in creative writing at City College in New York. The following year, she was named lecturer in the education department at Herbert H. Lehman College. In 1970 she joined the English department at John Jay College of Criminal Justice, and in 1980 returned to Hunter College as professor of English. Besides teaching, Lorde raised a son and a daughter in an interracial lesbian relationship and was involved in political organizing of other black feminists and lesbians. In the early 1980s, Lorde helped to start Kitchen Table: Women of Color Press, and in 1991 she was named New York State Poet. Lorde is probably best known for her prose writings, among them two collections of essays, *Sister Outsider* (1984) and *Burst of Light* (1988), and the autobiographical *Zami: The Cancer Journals* (1980), a chronicle of her struggle with the breast cancer that ultimately claimed her life. Her poetry publications include *The First Cities* (1968), *The Black Unicorn* (1978), and *Undersong: Chosen Poems Old and New* (1993). Near the end of her life, Lorde made her home on St. Croix, U.S. Virgin Islands, and adopted the African name Gamba Adisa (Warrior—She Who Makes Her Meaning Known).

KATHARYN HOWD MACHAN (b. 1952) Machan grew up in Woodbury, Connecticut, and Pleasantville, New York. She studied creative writing and literature at the College of Saint Rose and at the University of Iowa, taught college for five years, then returned to graduate school for a Ph.D. in interpretation (performance studies) at Northwestern University. She is on the faculty of the Writing Program of Ithaca College, New York. For eight years she coordinated the Ithaca Community Poets and directed the national Feminist Women's Writing Workshops. Since 1967, more than 1,200 of her poems have appeared in numerous magazines, such as *Yankee, Nimrod, South Coast Poetry Journal, Hollins Critic, Seneca Review,* and *Louisiana Literature,* and in literature anthologies. She has published more than twenty-five collections of poetry, the most recent of which include *Sleeping with the Dead* (2004), *Redwing: Voices from 1888* (2005), and *Flags* (2007).

CHRISTOPHER MARLOWE (1564–1593) Born in Canterbury, Marlowe was educated at Cambridge University, where he embarked on a career of writing and political activity, eventually giving up his original intention of entering the priesthood. He was arrested in 1593 on a charge of atheism, but before he could be brought to trial he was murdered in a brawl apparently involving a wealthy family that had reason to want him silenced. Marlowe's literary reputation rests primarily on his plays, powerful in their own right and the most significant precursors of Shakespeare's poetic dramas. The most important are *Tamburlaine, Parts I and II* (ca. 1587–1588; published 1590), *The Jew of Malta* (1589; published 1633), and *The Tragical History of the Life and Death of Dr. Faustus* (1592; published 1604).

ANDREW MARVELL (1621–1678) Born in Yorkshire and educated at Cambridge University, Marvell received an inheritance on his father's death that allowed him to spend four years traveling the Continent. Though not a Puritan himself, Marvell supported the Puritans' cause during the English Civil War and held a number of posts during the Puritan regime, including that of assistant to the blind John Milton, Oliver Cromwell's Latin secretary. In 1659, a year before the Restoration, Marvell was elected to Parliament, where he served until his death. Soon after the Restoration, Marvell expressed strong disagreements with the government in a series of outspoken and anonymously printed satires. It was for these satires, rather than for his many love poems, that he was primarily known in his own day.

KATHERINE MCALPINE (b. 1948)   Katherine McAlpine grew up in western New Jersey. She studied voice with Leon Kurzer of the Vienna Opera and worked for a number of years as a singer and voice teacher. She now lives in Maine, where she works as a freelance writer. Her poetry has appeared in a wide variety of magazines and in several anthologies, and she is co-editor of *The Muse Strikes Back: A Poetic Response by Women to Men* (1997). She was a 1992 winner of the *Nation*'s Discovery Award and the Judith's Room Award for emerging women poets. Her latest chapbook of poetry is *Past and Present* (2004).

CLAUDE MCKAY (1890–1948)   Born in Sunny Ville, Jamaica, McKay had already completed two volumes of poetry before coming to the United States in 1912 at the age of twenty-three (the two volumes earned him awards, which paid his way). The racism he encountered as a black immigrant brought a militant tone to his writing. His popular poem "If We Must Die" (1919) helped to initiate the Harlem Renaissance of the 1920s. Between 1922 and 1934 he lived in Great Britain, Russia, Germany, France, Spain, and Morocco. His writings include four volumes of poems, many essays, an autobiography (*A Long Way from Home* [1937]), a novel (*Home to Harlem* [1928]), and a sociological study of Harlem. His conversion to Roman Catholicism in the 1940s struck his audience as an ideological retreat. McKay wrote in a letter to a friend: "[T]o have a religion is very much like falling in love with a woman. You love her for her . . . beauty, which cannot be defined."

PETER MEINKE (b. 1932)   Born in Brooklyn, New York, the son of a salesman, Meinke served in the U.S. Army from 1955 to 1957, attended Hamilton College (B.A., 1955) and the University of Michigan (M.A., 1961), and earned his Ph.D. at the University of Minnesota (1965). He taught English at a New Jersey high school, Hamline University, Presbyterian College (now Eckerd College), and Old Dominion University, where he held the Darden Chair in Creative Writing. His reviews, poems, and stories have appeared in periodicals such as the *Atlantic*, *The New Yorker*, and the *New Republic*. The latest of his published books include *Zinc Fingers: Poems A to Z (2000)*, *The Contracted World: New & More Selected Poems* (2006), and *Unheard Music: Stories* (2007). His collection of stories, *The Piano Tuner*, won the 1986 Flannery O'Connor Award. He has also been the recipient of a National Endowment for the Arts Fellowship in poetry.

HERMAN MELVILLE (1819–1891)   The death of his merchant father when Melville was twelve shattered the economic security of his family. The financial panic of 1837 reduced the Melvilles to the edge of poverty, and at age nineteen, Melville went to sea. Economic conditions on his return were still grim, and after a frustrating stint as a country schoolteacher, he again went to sea—this time on a four-year whaling voyage. He deserted the whaler in the South Pacific, lived for some time with cannibals, made his way to Tahiti and Hawaii, and finally joined the navy for a return voyage. He mined his experiences for two successful South Sea adventure books, *Typee* (1846) and *Omoo* (1847). On the strength of these successes he married, but his next novel, *Mardi* (1849), was too heavy-handed an allegory to succeed. Driven by the obligation to support his growing family, Melville returned to sea-adventure stories, with moderate success. But neither his masterpiece, *Moby-Dick* (1851), nor his subsequent short stories and novels found much of an audience, and in 1886 he accepted an appointment as customs inspector in Manhattan, a job he held until retirement. He continued to write, mostly poetry, and lived to see himself forgotten as an author. *Billy Budd*, found among his papers after his death and published in 1924, led to a revival of interest in Melville, now recognized as one of America's greatest writers.

W. S. MERWIN (b. 1927)   Merwin was born in New York City and raised in Union City, New Jersey, and Scranton, Pennsylvania. His parents' lives had a profound impact on Merwin's writing: His mother was an orphan who lost her brother and her first child, and his father—a Presbyterian minister—had grown up in a home plagued by domestic violence. Anger, inherited violence, and the poverty that can be bred by such conditions became prominent themes in Merwin's poetry. He attended Princeton University on a scholarship and, after graduating in 1948, spent an additional year there studying Romance language—the origin of his later work as a prolific translator of Spanish, Latin, and French poetry. After college, Merwin married his first wife, Dorothy Jeanne Ferry, and moved to Majorca to tutor the children of wealthy families. There he met Dido Milroy and collaborated with her on a play; they eventually married and moved to London. The couple moved to Boston in 1956 so Merwin could serve as playwright-in-residence at the Poet's Theatre in Cambridge, Massachusetts, but soon returned to Europe. They soon met and became close friends with Sylvia Plath and Ted Hughes, witnessing the brutal collapse of the couple's marriage and Plath's eventual suicide. In 1968, Merwin moved to New York City and separated from Milroy, who stayed at their home in France. In the late 1970s, Merwin moved to Hawaii and eventually divorced Milroy, marrying Paula Schwartz in 1983. Throughout his lengthy career, Merwin has published over twenty books of poetry, most notably *The Carrier of Ladders* (1971), which won the 1971 Pulitzer Prize for Poetry; *Travels* (1993), which received the Lenore Marshall Poetry Prize; *The River Sound* (1999), a *New York Times* Notable Book of the Year; *Migration: New & Selected Poems* (2005), which won the 2005 National Book Award; and *The Shadow of Sirius* (2008), which won the Pulitzer Prize for Poetry in 2009. Among Merwin's copious literary awards and honors are fellowships from the Academy of American Poets, the Guggenheim Foundation, the National Endowment for the Arts, and the Rockefeller Foundation. In 2010, the Library of Congress named Merwin the seventeenth U.S. poet laureate. Merwin currently lives on a former pineapple plantation built atop a dormant volcano in Maui, Hawaii.

ROBERT MEZEY (b. 1935)   Born in Philadelphia, Mezey attended Kenyon College and served a troubled hitch in the U.S. Army before earning his B.A. from the University of Iowa in 1959. He worked as a probation officer, advertising copywriter, and social worker; did graduate study at Stanford University; and began teaching English at Case Western Reserve University in 1963. After a year as poet-in-residence at Franklin and Marshall College, he joined the English department of California State University at Fresno, spent three years at the University of Utah, and settled in 1976 at Pomona College in Claremont, California. Mezey won the Lamont Award for *The Lovemaker* in 1960 and has published many other poetry collections. In addition, he co-edited *Naked Poetry* (1969) and was one of several translators for *Poems from the Hebrew* (1973). His recent work includes *Collected Poems: 1952–1999* (2000), for which he was awarded the 2002 Poet's Prize.

LYDIA MILLET (b. 1969)   Millet was born in Boston, Massachusetts, and raised in Toronto. She received her B.A. in creative writing from the University of North Carolina at Chapel Hill and her M.A. in environmental policy from Duke University. Her short story collection *Love in Infant Monkeys* (2009) was a finalist for the Pulitzer Prize. She has also written seven novels: *Omnivores* (1996); *George Bush: Dark Prince of Love* (2000); *My Happy Life* (2002), the 2003 winner of the PEN-USA Award for Fiction; *Everyone's Pretty* (2005); *Oh Pure and Radiant Heart* (2005); *How the Dead Dream* (2008), the first book of a trilogy; and *Ghost Lights* (2011), the second book of a trilogy. Millet is also working on a trilogy of children's books called *The Dissenters*, which so far includes The *Fires Beneath the Sea* (2011) and *The Shimmers in the Night* (2012).

JANICE MIRIKITANI (b. 1942)   Mirikitani, a third-generation Japanese American, was born in Stockton, California, a year after the Japanese attack on Pearl Harbor, which drew the United States into World War II. She was not yet two when she and her family, like thousands of other American citizens of Japanese descent, were rounded up and sent to an internment camp as security risks. After the war, her parents divorced; her mother's remarriage took her back to northern California, and there she endured years of sexual abuse. Despite these difficult years, Mirikitani graduated from the University of California at Los Angeles (cum laude, 1962). In the midst of pursuing a master's degree at San Francisco State University, she was drawn to the civil rights movement. She quit school, divorced her husband, and devoted a decade to raising her daughter Tianne and collaborating with other writers in Third World Communications, a literary collective. During this time, she began working at San Francisco's Glide Memorial United Methodist Church in the Tenderloin District. In 1982, she married the church's minister, Cecil Williams. The church has been the focus of Mirikitani's many community activities, and she currently serves as executive director of its foundation. She and her husband were awarded the Chancellor's Medal of Honor, University of California (1988). Among her other awards and honors are the American Book Lifetime Achievement Award for Literature (1996) and appointment as San Francisco's poet laureate (2000). She is the author of four collections of poems, most recently *Love Works* (2002).

LISEL MUELLER (b. 1924)   Born in Hamburg, Germany, to parents who were both teachers, Mueller moved to the United States in 1939 and became a citizen in 1945. Shortly before earning a B.A. from the University of Evansville (1944), she married. Later, she bore two children, pursued graduate studies at Indiana University, and held a number of positions, among them receptionist, caseworker, and library assistant. She served as an instructor in poetry writing at Elmhurst College (1969–1972) and later as an instructor in the Master of Fine Arts Writing Program at Goddard College, Vermont. She has received numerous awards, including the Robert M. Ferguson Memorial Award for her first book of poems, *Dependencies* (1965), the Pulitzer Prize for Poetry (1997) for *Alive Together: New and Selected Poems*, and a National Book Award for *The Need to Hold Still* (1980). Commenting on the nature of her verse in *The Private Life* (1976), one critic noted that "she goes after our secrets, this poet; often she finds them." In 2002, Mueller was awarded the Ruth Lilly Poetry Prize, a prestigious honor given to living U.S. poets "whose lifetime accomplishments warrant extraordinary recognition."

BHARATI MUKHERJEE (b. 1940)   Born in Calcutta, India, Mukherjee attended the University of Calcutta (B.A., 1959), the University of Baroda (M.A., 1961), and the University of Iowa, where she earned an M.F.A. (1963) and a Ph.D. (1969). In 1963 she married Clark Blaise, a Canadian writer and professor, and joined the faculty at McGill University in Montreal. In 1973, Mukherjee and her husband visited India and kept separate diaries of the trip, published as *Days and Nights in Calcutta* (1977). The diaries reveal marked differences in their responses: Mukherjee found her home environs, especially the status of women, worse than she remembered, while Blaise, after an initial revulsion at the squalor and poverty, found India a fascinating and attractive culture compared to the West. Mukherjee "left Canada after fifteen years due to the persistent effects of racial prejudice against people of my national origin." Her fiction frequently explores the tensions inevitable in intercultural relationships. Her first novel, *The Tiger's Daughter* (1972), deals with the disappointment of an expatriate's return to India. In her second novel, *Wife* (1975), a psychologically abused woman finally kills her husband. *The Middleman and Other Stories* (1988) won the National Book Critics' Award. *Desirable Daughters* (2003) and *The Tree Bride* (2004) are the first two novels in a projected trilogy dealing with Indian expatriates in America. Mukherjee currently teaches at the University of California at Berkeley.

TASLIMA NASRIN (b. 1962) Born and educated in Mymensingh, Bangladesh, Nasrin began writing poetry in her childhood, her earliest works appearing in a literary journal edited by her eldest brother. Following in the footsteps of her father, a doctor, she earned a degree in medicine from Mymensingh Medical College and for a few years practiced as a government doctor. Her study of modern science, Nasrin has written, "made me a rationalist." While practicing medicine, she continued her writing, publishing poems and novels. These works, along with the essays she penned as a syndicated columnist in Bangladesh, earned her a number of important literary prizes in 1992 and 1993. However, her rationalism and her feminism, as well as her 1993 novel *Shame*, enraged Islamic fundamentalists. Forced into hiding by death threats, Nasrin fled to Europe in 1994; she returned to India in 2007 only to flee again after facing further threats and physical violence. She entered India once again in 2008 and lives in hiding under tight security. Nasrin has won several humanitarian awards, among them the UNESCO-Madanjeet Singh Prize in 2004 for the promotion of tolerance and nonviolence and the Simone de Beauvoir feminist award in 2008 in recognition of her writing on women's rights. In an essay titled "Women's Rights," Nasrin writes, "My poetry, my prose, my entire output expresses the deprivation of women who have been exploited for centuries." She has written a multivolume autobiography which includes *Meyebela, My Bengali Girlhood: A Memoir of Growing Up Female in a Muslim World* (2002) and *Ka* (*Speak Up*, 2003), which was banned in Bangladesh. Among her other publications are an essay collection, *Narir Kono Desh Nei* (*A Woman Has No Country*, 2007), and several volumes of poetry, most recently *Bondini* (*Prisoner*, 2008).

MAGGIE NELSON (b. 1973) Nelson has taught in the CalArts M.F.A. writing program since 2005. Before then, she lived in New York City where she received her PhD from the Graduate Center of the City University of New York and taught literature and writing at Wesleyan University, at the Pratt Institute of Art, and at the New School Graduate Writing Program. She has also taught on the faculty of the Tinhouse Summer Writers Workshop and been a Distinguished Guest of the New School's Summer Writers Colony. Her essays and reviews have appeared in many publications, including the *New York Times Book Review*, *Artforum*, *Bookforum*, and *Cabinet*. She has written several books of poetry, including *Shiner* (2001), a finalist for the Poetry Society of America's Norma Farber First Book Award; *The Latest Winter* (2003); *Jane: A Murder* (2005), a finalist for the PEN/Martha Albrand Award for the Art of Memoir; and *Something Bright, Then Holes* (2007). She has also published four books of nonfiction: *The Red Parts: A Memoir* (2007), an "autobiographical book about sexual violence and media spectacle" that was named a Notable Book of the Year by the State of Michigan; *Women, the New York School, and Other True Abstractions* (2007), a critical study of poetry and painting that won the Susanne M. Glasscock Award for Interdisciplinary Scholarship and a Creative Capital/Andy Warhol Foundation Arts Writers Grant; *Bluets* (2009), a reflection on the color blue; and *The Art of Cruelty: A Reckoning* (2011). Most recently, Nelson has been awarded a 2010 Guggenheim Fellowship in Nonfiction and a 2011 National Endowment for the Arts Grant in Poetry.

PABLO NERUDA (1904–1973)   Neruda was born in Parral, Chile, the son of a rail-road worker. Shortly after leaving college, he joined the Chilean foreign service to begin a distinguished career as consul and ambassador at a variety of posts around the world, including Burma, Ceylon, Indonesia, Siam, Cambodia, Spain, France, and Mexico. He was elected to the Chilean senate as a communist. But when he published letters attacking the policies of Gabriel González Videla, the president of Chile, he was forced into exile. He returned to Chile after the victory of anti-Videla forces and rejoined the foreign service. His vast literary output won many prizes and honors. And, although American readers found it difficult to separate his poetry from his politics, he was, at his prime, generally considered to be the greatest poet writing in Spanish. One critic pointed out that Neruda "never both-ered his head about the state of poetry. He has just gone on exuding it as he draws breath." In an essay on impure poetry, Neruda wrote: "Let [this] be the poetry we search for: worn with the hand's obligations, as by acids, steeped in sweat and in smoke, smelling of lilies and urine, spattered diversely by the trades that we love by, inside the law or beyond it. A poetry impure as the clothing we wear, or our bodies, soup-stained, soiled with our shame-ful behavior, our wrinkles and vigils and dreams, observations and prophecies, declarations of loathing and love, idylls and beasts, the shocks of encounter, political loyalties, denials and doubts, affirmation and taxes." *Five Decades, a Selection: Poems, 1925–1970* appeared in 1974. He was awarded the Nobel Prize for Literature in 1971.

JOHN FREDERICK NIMS (1913–1999)   Nims was born in Muskegon, Michigan, and earned degrees from De Paul University, the University of Notre Dame, and the University of Chicago. He taught at a number of institutions, including the University of Toronto; the University of Illinois, Urbana; Harvard University; and Williams College. He wrote two works of nonfiction, *Western Wind: An Introduction to Poetry* (1974) and *A Local Habitation: Essays on Poetry* (1985). In addition to serving as the editor of *Poetry* magazine from 1978 to 1984, Nims was a talented poet in his own right. He was the author of more than eight collections of poems, including *The Iron Pastoral* (1947), *Of Flesh and Bone* (1967), *The Kiss: A Jambalaya* (1982), and *The Six-Cornered Snowflake* (1990). He was also known as an astute translator, publishing translations of the poetry of Sappho and St. John of the Cross, as well as *Andromache,* a Greek tragedy. His work appeared in a num-ber of periodicals, such as *American Scholar, Atlantic, Harper's, Kenyon Review, Mademoi-selle,* and *New Republic.* Among Nims's many awards were fellowships from the Academy of American Poets, the Guggenheim Foundation, and the University of Illinois Institute of the Humanities, as well as grants from the American Academy of Arts and Letters and the National Foundation for the Arts and Humanities.

JEAN NORDHAUS (b. 1939)   Nordhaus earned her B.A. in philosophy from Barnard College and her Ph.D. in German literature from Yale University. Her work includes a poetry chapbook, *A Language of Hands* (1982), as well as the full-length collections *A Brace-let of Lies* (1987), *My Life in Hiding* (1991), and *The Porcelain Apes of Moses Mendelssohn* (2002), and her latest work, *Innocence* (2006). Nordhaus's poetry has appeared in *The American Poetry Review, Hudson Review, Poetry, Prairie Schooner, Washington Review,* and *West Branch,* and was included in *The Best American Poetry* for 2000. She has served as coordinator for the Folger Shakespeare Library's poetry programs and as president of Washington Writers' Publishing House. She has also taught at the Writer's Center in Bethesda, Maryland. She lives in Washington, D.C.

LYNN NOTTAGE (b. 1964)   Nottage was born in Brooklyn, New York. She attended New York's High School of Music and Art and went on to graduate from Brown University and the Yale School of Drama. The MacArthur Foundation, which honored Nottage with a Genius Grant in 2007, called her "an original voice in American theater, a playwright whose entertaining and thought-provoking works address contemporary issues with empathy and humor." Nottage's plays include *Poof!* (1993), which won the Heideman Award; *Por'Knockers* (1994); *Crumbs from the Table of Joy* (1995); *Mud, River, Stone* (1998), a Blackburn Prize finalist; *Las Meninas* (2002); *Intimate Apparel* (2003), which won New York Drama Critics Circle awards, the 2004 Francesca Primus Prize, and the American Steinberg Theatre Critics New Play Award; *Fabulation, or the Re-Education of Undine* (2004); and *Ruined* (2008), which won the Pulitzer Prize for Drama in 2009. Other honors include a 2005 Guggenheim Fellowship, an OBIE Award for playwriting, two AUDELCO awards, and the 2010 Steinberg Distinguished Playwright Award. Her most recent play is *By the Way, Meet Vera Stark* (2011). Her plays have been produced throughout the United States and Europe at such venues as the Second Stage Theatre in New York, the Tricycle Theatre in London, and the Steppenwolf Theatre in Chicago, among many others. Nottage is currently a visiting lecturer at the Yale School of Drama.

JOYCE CAROL OATES (b. 1938)   Born in Lockport, New York, Oates majored in English at Syracuse University (B.A., 1960) as a scholarship student and earned an M.A. in English (1961) from the University of Wisconsin. While still an undergraduate, she won the *Mademoiselle* college fiction award (1959), beginning an enormously prolific career as a writer and editor. She publishes an average of two books a year, to date well over fifty volumes including novels, short story collections, poetry, drama, and critical essays. Her numerous awards and honors include the 1970 fiction National Book Award for her novel *Them* (1969). She taught at the universities of Detroit and Windsor (Canada) before joining the faculty at Princeton University, where she is the Roger S. Berlind Distinguished Professor. Among her many recent publications are the short story collection *Wild Nights!* (2008) and the novels *The Gravedigger's Daughter* (2007), *My Sister, My Love* (2008), and *A Fair Maiden* (2010).

TIM O'BRIEN (b. 1946)   O'Brien was born in Austin, Minnesota, attended public schools, and received a B.A. summa cum laude from Macalester College. Immediately following graduation, he was drafted into the U.S. Army (1968–1970), earning a Purple Heart. On his return to civilian life, he pursued graduate work at Harvard University and worked as a national affairs reporter for the *Washington Post*. His first novel, *If I Die in a Combat Zone, Box Me Up and Ship Me Home* (1973), is a semi-fictionalized account of his own Vietnam experiences. Many of O'Brien's novels either are set in Vietnam or focus on characters haunted by the war: *Northern Lights* (1975); *Going After Cacciato* (1978), which won a National Book Award; *The Nuclear Age* (1985); *The Things They Carried* (1990); and *In the Lake of the Woods* (1994). In an interview, O'Brien explained that his preoccupation with the Vietnam War was part of his need to write with "passion." Writing "good" stories, he went on to say, "requires a sense of passion, and my passion as a human being and as a writer intersect in Vietnam, not in the physical stuff but in the issues of Vietnam—of courage, rectitude, enlightenment, holiness, trying to do the right thing in the world." O'Brien wrote a comic novel, *Tomcat in Love* (1998), about a womanizing professor's midlife crisis, before returning to his earlier themes in his most recent book, *July, July* (2002).

FLANNERY O'CONNOR (1925–1964)   O'Connor, afflicted with lupus erythematosus, spent most of her short life in Milledgeville, Georgia. She began writing while a student at Georgia State College for Women in her hometown, and in 1947 earned an M.F.A. from the University of Iowa. Back in Milledgeville, she lived on a farm with her mother, raised peacocks, and endured the indignity of constant treatment for her progressive and incurable disease. She traveled and lectured when she could. She wrote two novels, *Wise Blood* (1952) and *The Violent Bear It Away* (1960), and two collections of stories, *A Good Man Is Hard to Find* (1955) and *Everything That Rises Must Converge* (1965). She was deeply religious and wrote numerous book reviews for Catholic newspapers. Her southern gothic tales often force readers to confront physical deformity, spiritual depravity, and the violence they often engender.

FRANK O'HARA (1926–1966)   Born in Baltimore, Maryland, O'Hara was raised in Massachusetts and from 1941 to 1944 studied piano at the New England Conservatory in Boston. Shortly after graduating from high school, O'Hara enlisted in the U.S. Navy and served as a sonarman on the USS *Nicholas*. After receiving an honorable discharge in 1946 he enrolled at Harvard University, where he met fellow poet John Ashbery. O'Hara soon began publishing poems in the *Harvard Advocate* and earned his B.A. in English in 1950. Thanks to a recommendation from his teacher John Ciardi, O'Hara received a graduate fellowship in comparative literature at the University of Michigan. He earned his M.A. there in 1951 and published his first collection of poems, *A City in Winter*, the following year. O'Hara then went with Ashbery to New York and became a renowned member of the New York School of poets, which included such authors as Ashbery, James Schuyler, Kenneth Koch, and Barbara Guest. O'Hara's poetry was widely praised for its refreshing originality and playful informality. His poems often recounted everyday activities— frequently from around his beloved New York—in conversational tones (O'Hara referred to these as "I do this I do that" poems). He sought to capture the immediacy and joy of life in the city in the same way that other poets sought to capture the beauty of nature. In his poem "Meditations in an Emergency," O'Hara wrote, "One need never leave the confines of New York to get all the greenery one wishes—I can't even enjoy a blade of grass unless I know there's a subway handy, or a record store or some other sign that people do not totally *regret* life." He published several volumes of poetry, including *Meditations in an Emergency* (1956), *Lunch Poems* (1964), and *Love Poems (Tentative Title)* (1965). In 1966, his life was cut short in a sand buggy accident on Fire Island. Further volumes of O'Hara's poems were published after his death, most notably *The Collected Poems of Frank O'Hara* (1971), *The Selected Poems of Frank O'Hara* (1974), and *Poems Retrieved: 1950–1966* (1977).

JOSEPH O'NEILL (b. 1964)   O'Neill was born in Cork, Ireland. He is the author of three novels, including *This Is the Life* (1991), *The Breezes* (1995), and *Netherland* (2008), which was included in the *New York Times* list of the 10 Best Books of 2008. He has also written a nonfiction book, *Blood-Dark Track: A Family History* (2001), which chronicles the mysterious imprisonment of both his grandfathers during World War II. O'Neill also writes literary and cultural criticism, most regularly for the *Atlantic* but also for the *New York Times* and *New York* magazine. He lives with his family in New York City.

SHARON OLDS (b. 1942)   Born in San Francisco, Olds attended Stanford University (B.A., 1964) and Columbia University (Ph.D., 1972). She joined the faculty of Theodor Herzl Institute in 1976 and has given readings at many colleges. She currently teaches at the Graduate Creative Writing Program at New York University. She won the Madeline Sadin Award from the *New York Quarterly* in 1978 for "The Death of Marilyn Monroe." Often compared to confessional poets Sylvia Plath and Anne Sexton, Olds published her first collection, *Satan Says*, in 1980, and won both the National Book Critics' Circle Award and the

Lamont Award for *The Dead and the Living* in 1983. She was poet laureate of New York State from 1998 to 2000. Her most recent volumes of poetry are *The Unswept Room* (2002), *Strike Sparks: Selected Poems, 1980–2002* (2004), and *One Secret Thing* (2008).

MARY OLIVER (b. 1935)   Mary Oliver was born in Cleveland, Ohio. She spent one year at Ohio State University and a second year at Vassar. Her distinctive poetic talent led to an appointment as the chair of the writing department of the Fine Arts Workshop in Provincetown, Massachusetts (1972–1973). Though she never graduated from college, she was awarded the Mather Visiting Professorship at Case Western Reserve University for 1980 and 1982, and among her many awards and honors, she received a National Endowment for the Arts Fellowship (1972–1973) and a Guggenheim Fellowship (1980–1981). The first of her several volumes of poems, *No Voyage and Other Poems*, appeared in 1963. Other books include *New and Selected Poems* (1992), *A Poetry Handbook* (1995), and *Blue Pastures* (1995), a collection of prose nature writing. Her most recent volumes are *Red Bird* (2008), *Evidence* (2009), and *Swan: Poems and Prose Poems* (2012).

DANIEL OROZCO (b. 1942)   Orozco earned his B.A. from Stanford University and his M.F.A. from the University of Washington. His work has appeared in *Harper's Magazine*, *McSweeney's*, *Zoetrope: All Story*, and other literary magazines, and has been anthologized in *Best American Essays*, *Best American Mystery Stories*, and *Best American Short Stories*. He was also awarded a Pushcart Prize for his story "The Bridge," wherein a rookie bridge painter is awakened from the monotony of his everyday routine by a face-to-face encounter with a woman who has just jumped. "The Bridge" is included in Orozco's collection *Orientation and Other Stories* (2011), which was named a Best of 2011 Short Story Collection by *Kirkus Reviews*. Fellow author Yiyun Lee has said that Orozco "has both the relentlessness and the compassion of a truly great writer." Orozco currently teaches in the Creative Writing Program at the University of Idaho.

GEORGE ORWELL (1903–1950)   Born Eric Blair in India, the son of a minor British colonial officer, Orwell was raised in England. His education at good grammar schools, culminating with a stay at Eton College, introduced him to what he later called the snobbish world of England's middle and upper classes. Denied a university scholarship, he joined the Indian Imperial Police in 1922 and served in Burma until he resigned in 1927, disgusted with the injustice of British imperialism in India and Burma. He was determined to be a writer and, living at the edge of poverty, deliberately mingled with social outcasts and impoverished laborers. These experiences produced *Down and Out in Paris and London* (1933). Although he was a socialist, his experiences while fighting alongside the leftists during the Spanish Civil War disillusioned him, and he embodied his distaste for any totalitarian system in *Animal Farm* (1945)—a satirical attack on the leadership of the Soviet Union. In his pessimistic novel *1984* (1949), he imagined a social order shaped by a propagandistic perversion of language, in which the government, an extension of "Big Brother," uses two-way television to control the citizenry. Orwell succumbed to tuberculosis at the age of forty-seven, but not before he produced six novels, three documentary works, over seven hundred newspaper articles and reviews, and a volume of essays.

ALICIA OSTRIKER (b. 1937)   Ostriker is a Professor Emerita of Rutgers University and a faculty member of the New England College Low-Residency Poetry M.F.A. Program. A major American poet and critic for decades, her poems have appeared in *The New*

Yorker, Paris Review, Antaeus, Nation, Poetry, American Poetry Review, Kenyon Review, Atlantic, MS, Tikkun, and many other literary journals, and have been translated into French, German, Italian, Chinese, Japanese, Hebrew, and Arabic. She has lectured and given performances of her work throughout the United States as well as in Europe, Australia, Israel, Japan, and China. In recognition of her tremendous contribution to the world of poetry, Ostriker has received awards from the National Endowment for the Arts, the Poetry Society of America, the San Francisco State Poetry Center, the Judah Magnes Museum, the New Jersey Arts Council, the Rockefeller Foundation, and the Guggenheim Foundation. She has written twelve volumes of poetry, most recently *The Book of Seventy* (2009), which won the Jewish Book Award for Poetry. She has also authored two seminal critical volumes on women's poetry: *Writing Like a Woman* (1983) and *Stealing the Language: The Emergence of Women's Poetry in America* (1987). Her most recent book of criticism is *Dancing at the Devil's Party: Essays on Poetry, Politics and the Erotic* (2000). She lives in Princeton, New Jersey, with her husband.

WILFRED OWEN (1893–1918)   Born in the Shropshire countryside of England, Owen began writing verse before he matriculated at London University, where he was known as a quiet and contemplative student. After some years of teaching English in France, Owen returned to England and joined the army. Wounded in 1917, he was killed in action leading an attack a few days before the armistice was declared in 1918. Owen's poems, published only after his death, along with his letters from the front to his mother, are perhaps the most powerful and vivid accounts of the horror of war to emerge from World War I.

DOROTHY PARKER (1893–1967)   Parker was born in West End, New Jersey, to a Scottish Presbyterian mother and a Jewish father as "a late unexpected arrival in a loveless family." She was educated in private schools and moved in 1911 to New York, where she lived in a boardinghouse and earned her living by playing piano at a dancing school. In 1915, one of the verses she sent around was accepted by *Vogue* magazine, and the editor later hired her to write captions for fashion illustrations. Her native wit captivated the editor, and he persuaded her to join *Vanity Fair* as drama critic, although she was fired when she wrote unfavorable reviews of several plays. She became the first woman among the regulars of the Algonquin Round Table—a group of writers who met regularly at the Algonquin Hotel in New York City that included Alexander Woollcott, George S. Kaufman, Robert Benchley, and Edna Ferber, among others. A master of irony and scathing wit, Parker, despite a troubled personal life that led to suicide attempts, flourished as a humorist, poet, short story writer, playwright, and screenwriter.

SUZAN-LORI PARKS (b. 1963)   Parks was born in Fort Knox, Kentucky. The daughter of an army colonel, she moved frequently and attended school in Germany. After earning a degree from Mount Holyoke College, where she began writing plays, and studying at the Yale University School of Drama, she moved to London to study acting. Her first play, *Betting on the Dust Commander,* was produced in New York City in 1987. Her second play, *Imperceptible Metabolites in the Third Kingdom,* won an OBIE for being one of the best new American Off-Broadway plays of 1989. Among her other plays are *Venus* (1996); *In the Blood* (1999); *Topdog/Underdog* (2001), winner of a Pulitzer Prize; and *The Book of Grace* (2010). Parks is also the author of three plays for radio; a novel, *Getting Mother's Body* (2003); and three screenplays, *Girl 6* (1996), *Their Eyes Were Watching God* (2005), and *The Great Debaters* (2007). Her numerous awards include a Whiting Writer's Award, a Guggenheim Fellowship, and grants from the Rockefeller Foundation, the National

Endowment for the Arts, and the MacArthur Foundation. Parks has taught at Yale University, the University of Michigan, and the Pratt Institute for the Arts. In November 2008, she became the first recipient of the Master Writer Chair at the Public Theater. Parks also serves as a visiting arts professor in dramatic writing at New York University's Tisch School of the Arts.

PAUL (d. ca. 64 A.D.) Paul was born Saul in Tarsus of Cilicia (located near the Mediterranean Sea in south-central Turkey, near Syria). He was an important Jerusalem Pharisee who, according to the Acts of the Apostles (Chapter 9), vigorously attacked both intellectually and physically those who proclaimed the deity of Jesus. The same source provides an account of Saul's conversion. Traveling to Damascus to arrest followers of Jesus, he experienced an intense light that blinded him and heard a voice that declared, "I am Jesus, whom you are persecuting." In Tarsus, his blindness was cured by Ananias, a follower of Jesus, and Paul became, arguably, the most important disciple of Jesus in the early church: his letters, and those attributed to him, constitute a quarter of the New Testament. His attempts to preach the new Way in the synagogues of the region were rebuffed, sometimes violently, and Paul was frequently jailed. He became the apostle to the Gentiles, traveling throughout the Mediterranean region to establish churches. His epistles to those young and fragile congregations helped formulate the political, legal, and spiritual institutions of the early church. His final arrest brought him to Rome to answer charges, and after two years of imprisonment, he died about 64 A.D.

MOLLY PEACOCK (b. 1947) Born in Buffalo, New York, Peacock was educated at the State University of New York at Binghamton and at Johns Hopkins University, where she received an M.A. with honors in 1977. From 1970 to 1973, she was the director of academic advising at Binghamton. She was appointed honorary fellow at Johns Hopkins in 1977 and, in the following year, poet-in-residence at the Delaware State Arts Council in Wilmington. Since 1979, she has directed the Wilmington Writing Workshops. She has published in many magazines, including the *Southern Review*, the *Ohio Review*, and the *Massachusetts Review*. She has published several books of poems including *And Live Apart* (1980); *Raw Heaven* (1984); *Take Heart* (1989), which deals with her father's alcoholism and the mental and physical abuse she endured while growing up; and *Original Love* (1995). She was also co-editor of *Poetry in Motion: 100 Poems from the Subways and Buses* (1996), a collection of the popular poems displayed on placards in New York City's subways and buses. *Paradise, Piece by Piece* (1998), which she calls a "hybrid memoir," blends real and invented characters and explains why she decided not to have children. Her most recent collections are *Cornucopia: New and Selected Poems 1975–2002* (2002) and *The Second Blush* (2008). She also recently published *The Paper Garden: An Artist Begins Her Life's Work at 72*, a book about life and work of famous eighteenth-century collage artist Mary Delany.

KATHERINE PHILIPS (1632–1664) Philips was born Katherine Fowler in London. She became fluent in several languages as a child and developed an interest in poetry during her early years at boarding school. In 1651, Philips founded the Society of Friendship, a semi-literary correspondence circle composed primarily of women who assumed pseudonyms from classical literature; Philips was known as "the Matchless Orinda." Much of Philips's poetry documents the relationships within the society, particularly her own with Mary Aubrey, "Rosania," and later with Anne Owen, or "Lucasia." Her contemporaries frequently compared Philips's work to that of Aphra Behn and Sappho, praising the for the modest and appropriately feminine subjects she chose. Yet only two of Philips's books were printed during her lifetime: a translation of Pierre Corneille's play *La Mort de Pompée* (1663) and *Poems by the Incomparable Mrs. K.P.* (1664), which Philips insisted be withdrawn just days after its publication because the text had been inadequately printed. Philips died later that year from smallpox. After her death, the "authorized" edition of her *Poems* appeared in 1667, with subsequent editions in 1669, 1678, and 1710.

CARL PHILLIPS (b. 1959) Phillips is a professor of English and of African and Afro-American Studies at Washington University. He has published many volumes of acclaimed poetry, including *In the Blood* (1992), winner of the Samuel French Morse Poetry Prize; *Cortége* (1995), a finalist for the National Book Critics Circle Award; *From the Devotions* (1998), a finalist for the National Book Award; *Pastoral* (2000), winner of the Lambda Literary Award; *The Tether* (2001), winner of the Kingsley Tufts Poetry Award; and *The Rest of Love* (2004), winner of the Theodore Roethke Memorial Foundation Poetry Prize and the Thom Gunn Award for Gay Male Poetry, and a finalist for the National Book Award. Among his most recent collections are *Riding Westward* (2006), *Speak Low* (2009), and *Double Shadow* (2011), a finalist for the 2011 National Book Award for poetry and winner of the *Los Angeles Times* Book Prize for poetry. Phillips also received the 2006 Academy of American Poets Fellowship, an Award in Literature from the American Academy of Arts and Letters, a Pushcart Prize, the Academy of American Poets Prize, and fellowships from the Guggenheim Foundation and the Library of Congress. He is currently a chancellor of the Academy of American Poets.

MARGE PIERCY (b. 1936) Born in Detroit, Marge Piercy was the first of her family to attend college. In 1957, she graduated from the University of Michigan (where she won prizes for poetry and fiction) and earned an M.A. from Northwestern University (1958). She was active in social and political causes and fought for equal treatment of women and minorities while opposing the Vietnam War. She supported herself with odd jobs in Chicago as she pursued a writing career, but her first novel was not published until after her 1969 move to Wellfleet, Massachusetts, where she still lives. She is an extraordinarily prolific writer. Among her more than a dozen novels are *He, She and It* (1991), *The Longings of Women* (1994), and *City of Darkness, City of Lights* (1996). Her many volumes of poetry include *My Mother's Body* (1985), *Available Light* (1988), *The Earth Shines Secretly: A Book of Days* (1990), and *Mars and Her Children* (1992). She has also written plays and several volumes of nonfiction and has edited the anthology *Early Ripening: American Women's Poetry Now* (1987). In the introduction to a volume of selected poems, *Circles on the Water* (1982), Piercy asserted that she wanted her poems to be "useful." "What I mean by useful is simply that readers will find poems that speak to and for them, will take those poems into their lives and say them to each other and put them up on the bathroom wall and remember bits and pieces of them in stressful or quiet moments. . . . To find ourselves spoken for in art gives dignity to our pain, our anger, our lust, our losses." Most recently, she has published two novels, *The Third Child* (2003) and *Sex Wars: A Novel of Gilded Age in New York* (2005), and three collections of poetry, *Colors Passing through Us* (2003), *The Crooked Inheritance* (2006), and *The Hunger Moon: New and Selected Poems, 1980–2010* (2011).

SYLVIA PLATH (1932–1963) Plath was born in Boston, Massachusetts, where her parents taught at Boston University. She graduated summa cum laude in English from Smith College (1955); earned an M.A. as a Fulbright scholar at Newnham College, Cambridge (1955–1957); and married British poet Ted Hughes (1956). Plath's poetry reveals the anger and anxiety that would eventually lead to her suicide. Her view that all relationships were in some way destructive and predatory surely darkened her life. Yet in 1963, during the month between the publication of her only novel, *The Bell Jar* (about a suicidal college student), and her death, Plath was extraordinarily productive; she produced finished poems every day. Her *Collected Poems* was published in 1981.

EDGAR ALLAN POE (1809–1849)   Poe, the son of traveling actors, was born in Boston, Massachusetts. Within a year, his alcoholic father deserted his mother and their three infant children. When his mother died of tuberculosis in Richmond, Virginia, three-year-old Edgar was adopted by John Allan and his wife. Allan, a prosperous businessman, spent time in England, where Poe began his education at private schools. Back in the United States, Allan forced Poe to leave the University of Virginia in 1826, when Poe incurred gambling debts he could not pay. Poe served in the U.S. Army from 1827 to 1829, eventually attaining the rank of sergeant major, and then attended West Point, hoping for further military advancement. Shortly thereafter, Mrs. Allan died of tuberculosis. Poe angrily confronted his foster father about his extramarital affairs, and for this candor he was disowned. Believing that Allan would never reinstate him as heir, Poe deliberately violated rules to provoke his dismissal from the academy. In 1835, Poe began his career as editor, columnist, and reviewer, earning a living he could not make as a writer of stories and poems. He married his thirteen-year-old cousin, Virginia Clemm, in 1836, and lived with her and her mother during a period marked by illness and poverty. Virginia died of tuberculosis in 1847. Poe died, delirious and under mysterious circumstances, in 1849. He perfected the gothic horror story ("Fall of the House of Usher") and originated the modern detective story ("The Gold Bug," "The Murders in the Rue Morgue"). Poe's work fascinated the French poet Baudelaire, who translated it into French.

KATHA POLLITT (b. 1949)   Pollitt has been a regular contributor to the *Nation* since 1980, and the *Washington Post* called her bimonthly column "Subject to Debate" "the best place to go for original thinking on the left." Pollitt was born into a socially and politically active family in Brooklyn Heights, New York. Her father, Basil Pollitt, was a lawyer and advocate for liberal causes, and her mother, Leonora Levine, was a real estate agent; both boasted lengthy F.B.I. files for everything from protesting segregation to making pro-communist speeches. Both parents were voracious readers and encouraged their daughter to pursue her interest in writing. Pollitt attended Harvard and the Columbia School of the Arts and has published prolifically throughout her career. In addition to *The Nation*, Pollitt's poetry and essays have appeared in *The New Yorker, Atlantic, Harper's, Ms.,* the *New York Times, New Republic, Glamour, Mother Jones,* the *London Review of Books,* and other publications. On top of copious other awards and honors, Pollitt received a grant from the National Endowment for the Arts and a Guggenheim Fellowship for her poetry, and her collection of poems *Antarctic Traveller* (1982) won the National Book Critics Circle Award. She has also published much prose, including *Reasonable Creatures: Essays on Women and Feminism* (1995), *Subject to Debate: Sense and Dissents on Women, Politics, and Culture* (2001), *Virginity or Death!: And Other Social and Political Issues of Our Time* (2006), and *Learning to Drive: And Other Life Stories* (2007). She lives in Manhattan.

DEBORAH POPE (b. ?)   Born in Cincinnati, Ohio, Pope graduated from Denison University and earned a Ph.D. from the University of Wisconsin. At present she teaches at Duke University, where she co-founded the Duke Writers Conference. Using her doctoral thesis as a basis, she published a study in criticism, *Separate Vision: Isolation in Contemporary Women's Poetry* (1984). In 1990, she co-edited *Ties That Bind: Essays on Mothering and Patriarchy*. Her first volume of poetry, *Frantic Heart* (1992), was followed by several others, including *Falling Out of the Sky* (1999). Doubtless, some of her poems are generated by the challenges and joys of a home life that includes two young sons. In an interview, she summed up her enthusiasm for teaching: "There is nothing like the joy and exhilaration that comes to me . . . when [students] have been able to bring some kind of formless chaotic experience into a balance in language."

KATHERINE ANNE PORTER (1890–1980)   Born in Texas and educated mostly at small convent schools, Porter traveled widely in her early years, living for some time in Mexico and, more briefly, in Germany. She gained a reputation primarily as a writer of finely crafted stories, gathered in *The Collected Stories of Katherine Anne Porter* (1965). She published one novel, *Ship of Fools*, in 1962. Porter's output of fiction was small, and she earned her livelihood mostly as a reporter, lecturer, scriptwriter, speaker, and writer-in-residence. Her achievement in fiction was recognized by a National Book Award and Pulitzer Prize for Fiction, both in 1966. Her final work, *The Never-Ending Wrong* (1977), is a memoir about her involvement in the celebrated Sacco-Vanzetti case.

KEVIN C. POWERS (b. ?)   Powers is a poet, a writer, and a veteran of the Iraq war. His poems have appeared in the *New Orleans Review*, *Poetry*, and the *New York Quarterly*. He is currently pursuing an M.F.A. at the University of Texas at Austin. According to his 2010 biography in *The Sun Magazine*, "When not thinking about poetry or Italy (where he hopes to live someday)," Powers can be found "riding his Royal Enfield motorcycle through the Texas hill country."

WYATT PRUNTY (b. 1947)   Prunty was born in Humboldt, Tennessee. After earning a B.A. from the University of the South in Sewanee, he went on to earn an M.A. from Johns Hopkins University and a Ph.D. (1979) from Louisiana State University. His poetry chapbook, *Domestic of the Outer Banks*, was published in 1980. Several volumes followed, among them *Since the Noon Mail Stopped* (1997) and *Unarmed and Dangerous* (2000). His poetry has been anthologized in *Anthology of Magazine Verse and Yearbook of American Poetry* for both 1979 and 1980. He was awarded a poetry prize by *Sewanee Review* (1969) and has been a fellow at the Bread Loaf Writers' Conference. He has taught in the graduate program of the Johns Hopkins Writing Seminars, where he was Elliott Coleman Professor of Poetry. Currently, he serves as Carlton Professor of English at the University of the South, where he teaches poetry, and where he founded and now directs the Sewanee Writers' Conference. His most recent work is a collection of poetry and fiction, *The Lover's Guide to Trapping* (2009).

SIR WALTER RALEIGH (1554–1618)   Born in Devonshire, England, into the landed gentry, Raleigh attended Oxford University but dropped out after a year to fight for the Huguenot cause in France. He returned to England, began the study of law, but again was drawn to a life of adventure and exploration. Through the influence of friends he came to the attention of Elizabeth I, after which his career flourished: he was knighted, given a number of lucrative commercial monopolies, made a member of Parliament, and, in 1587, named captain of the Yeomen of the Guard. During these years he invested in various colonies in North America, but all his settlements failed. He was briefly imprisoned in the Tower of London for offending the queen but was soon back in favor and in command of an unsuccessful expedition to Guiana (now Venezuela) in 1595. In 1603, he was again imprisoned in the tower, this time on a probably trumped-up charge of treason, where he remained until 1616, spending part of his time writing *A History of the World* (1614). After his release, he undertook yet another expedition to Guiana but again returned empty-handed. As a consequence of more political intrigue, James I ordered him executed. Although Raleigh epitomized the great merchant adventurers of Elizabethan England, he was also a gifted poet.

DUDLEY RANDALL (1914–2000)   Born in Washington, D.C., Randall worked during the Depression in the foundry of the Ford Motor Company in Dearborn, Michigan, and then as a carrier and clerk for the U.S. Post Office in Detroit. He served in the U.S. Army Signal Corps (1942–1946) and graduated from Wayne State University (B.A., 1949) and the University of Michigan (M.A.L.S., 1951). He was a librarian at several universities and founded the Broadside Press in 1965 "so black people could speak to and for their people." Randall told *Negro Digest*, "Precision and accuracy are necessary for both white and black writers. . . . 'A black aesthetic' should not be an excuse for sloppy writing." He urged African American writers to reject what was false in white poetry but not to forsake universal concerns in favor of a racial agenda. His works include *On Getting a Natural* (1969) and *A Litany of Friends: New and Selected Poems* (1981). He edited *For Malcolm: Poems on the Life and Death of Malcolm X* (1969) and *The Black Poets* (1971), an extensive anthology of poetry, from slave songs to the present.

BARBARA RAS (b. 1949)   Barbara Ras was born in New Bedford, Massachusetts, and has traveled extensively, living in Costa Rica, Colombia, and Athens, Georgia. Her work has appeared in many literary journals and magazines, including *The New Yorker, Boulevard, Massachusetts Review, Prairie Schooner, American Scholar*, and *Spoon River Poetry Review*. Her debut poetry collection *Bite Every Sorrow* (1998) was selected by C. K. Williams for the Walt Whitman Award in 1997. Her most recent collections are *One Hidden Stuff* (2006) and *The Last Skin* (2010). Ras has been honored with numerous literary awards, including the Kate Tufts Discovery Award, a Guggenheim Fellowship, and the Georgia Author of the Year Award for poetry. She has taught and worked across the country, including at the Warren Wilson M.F.A. Program for Writers and the University of Georgia Press. Currently, she serves as director of Trinity University Press in San Antonio, Texas.

SPENCER REECE (b. 1963)   Reece was born in Hartford, Connecticut. He attended Wesleyan University and received an M.A. from the University of York and an M.T.S. from the Harvard Divinity School. At Wesleyan, the Pulitzer Prize-winning writer Annie Dillard was one of Reece's poetry teachers: Reece describes her as "an early encourager" along with James Merrill, another poet with whom he corresponded. Reece's poetry collection *The Clerk's Tale* (2004), the title poem of which describes an ordinary day at a store in the Mall of America and was inspired by Reece's own experience working as a sales associate at Brooks Brothers, won the Bread Loaf Writers' Conference Bakeless Prize. Reece has also won the 2005 Whiting Writers' Award for poetry, a 2009 Pushcart Prize, a Guggenheim Fellowship, and a fellowship from the National Endowment for the Arts. His work has appeared in *Boulevard, The New Yorker*, and *American Poetry Review*. Reece was ordained as a minister in 2011 and is currently a chaplain to Bishop Carlos Lopez-Lozano of the Reformed Episcopal Church in Spain.

HENRY REED (1914–1986)   Reed was born in Birmingham, England; earned a B.A. from the University of Birmingham (1937); worked as a teacher and freelance writer (1937–1941); and served in the British Army (1941–1942). His early poetry dealt with political events before and during World War II. "Naming of Parts" was based on his frustrating experience in cadet training. His collection of poetry, *A Map of Verona* (1946), revealed a formal, reverent, but also humorous and ironic voice. Another collection of poetry, *Lessons of War*, was published in 1970. Reed began writing radio plays in 1947 and generated as many as four scripts a year. His best-known satirical work is the *Hilda Tablet* series, a 1960s BBC Radio production that parodied British society of the 1930s.

ADRIENNE RICH (1929–2012)   Born to a middle-class family, Rich was educated by her parents until she entered public school in the fourth grade. She graduated Phi Beta Kappa from Radcliffe College in 1951, the same year her first book of poems, *A Change of World*, appeared. That volume, chosen by W. H. Auden for the Yale Series of Younger Poets Award, and her next, *The Diamond Cutters and Other Poems* (1955), earned her a reputation as an elegant, controlled stylist. In the 1960s, however, Rich began a dramatic shift away from her earlier mode as she took up political and feminist themes and stylistic experimentation in such works as *Snapshots of a Daughter-in-Law* (1963), *The Necessities of Life* (1966), *Leaflets* (1969), and *The Will to Change* (1971). In *Diving into the Wreck* (1973) and *The Dream of a Common Language* (1978), she continued to experiment with form and to deal with the experiences and aspirations of women from a feminist perspective. In addition to her poetry, Rich published many essays on poetry, feminism, motherhood, and lesbianism. She also won numerous awards, most recently the National Book Foundation's Medal for Distinguished Contribution to American Letters in 2006. Her recent collections include *Telephone Ringing in the Labyrinth: Poems: 2004–2006* (2007), *A Human Eye: Essays on Art in Society, 1997–2008* (2009), and *Tonight No Poetry Will Serve: Poems 2007–2010* (2011).

RAINER MARIA RILKE (1875–1926)   Rilke is widely considered one of the most masterful and lyrically intense German-language poets. Born into an unhappy family in Prague, his parents shipped him away to military school when he was a child. He released his first collection of poetry, *Leben und Lieder* (1894), while enrolled at Charles-Ferdinand University, with two additional collections—*Larenopfer* (*Sacrifice to the Lares,* 1895) and *Traumgekrönt* (*Dream-Crowned,* 1896)—following soon after. During his lifetime Rilke authored hundreds of poems that garnered him an ardent following in European literary circles, and over time his poetry has been translated into many other languages. His best-known works among English-language readers are the collection *Duino Elegies* (1923) and his loosely autobiographical novel *The Notebooks of Malte Laurids Brigge* (1910). Rilke also became known for *Letters to a Young Poet,* a series of correspondence between Rilke and Franz Kappus, a nineteen-year-old cadet at the Vienna Military Academy who was discouraged by the prospect of army life. Kappus assembled and published the letters in 1929, three years after Rilke's death.

EDWIN ARLINGTON ROBINSON (1869–1935)   Robinson grew up in Gardiner, Maine; attended Harvard University; returned to Gardiner as a freelance writer; and then settled in New York City in 1896. His various odd jobs included a one-year stint as subway-construction inspector. President Theodore Roosevelt, a fan of his poetry, had him appointed to the United States Customs House in New York, where he worked from 1905 to 1909. Robinson wrote about people rather than nature, particularly New England characters remembered from his early years. Describing his first volume of poems, *The Torrent and the Night Before* (1896), he told a friend there was not "a single red-breasted robin in the whole collection." Popular throughout his career, Robinson won three Pulitzer prizes (1921, 1924, and 1927).

THEODORE ROETHKE (1908–1963)   Born in Saginaw, Michigan, Roethke was the son of a greenhouse owner, and greenhouses figure prominently in the imagery of his poems. He graduated magna cum laude from the University of Michigan in 1929, where he also earned an M.A. in 1936 after graduate study at Harvard University. He taught at several universities, coached two varsity tennis teams, and settled at the University of Washington in 1947. Intensely introspective and demanding of himself, Roethke was renowned as a great teacher, though he was sometimes incapacitated by bipolar disorder. His collection *The Waking: Poems 1933–1953* won the Pulitzer Prize in 1954. Other awards include Guggenheim Fellowships in 1945 and 1950, and a National Book Award and the Bollingen Prize in 1959 for *Words for the Wind* (1958).

SALMAN RUSHDIE (b. 1947)   Rushdie was born in Bombay into a family of Indian Muslims just two months before Indian independence and four months before South Asia was partitioned into a principally Muslim Pakistan and Hindu India. That process resulted in the murder of hundreds of thousands of people in the fighting that accompanied the vast migration of Hindus to the south and Muslims to the north. Some years later, Rushdie's upper-middle-class family sent him first to a British-style private school in Bombay and then to the elite Rugby School in England. There, Rushdie told an interviewer, he was miserable: "I was suddenly an Indian . . . and at the schoolboy level that was no fun." His Islamic family finally moved from Bombay to Karachi, Pakistan, while Rushdie completed an M.A. with honors in history at Cambridge University (1968). But shortly after his return to Pakistan, the government prohibited the performance of a television play he had produced and the publication of an article he had written about Pakistan. This numbing experience of official censorship convinced him to return to Britain in late 1968. There he supported himself as an actor and freelance advertising copywriter until he began his successful career as a writer. His second novel, *Midnight's Children* (1981), won three awards, including the prestigious Booker Prize, and was honored as the best Booker Prize novel in the prize's forty-year history. But his eminence seriously affected the conduct of his life when his novel *The Satanic Verses* (1988) profoundly offended Muslim sensibilities in some quarters and resulted in a *fatwa* issued by the Iranian ayatollah Khomeini, who offered a million dollars to the person who would execute Rushdie for blasphemy. Though Iran renounced the *fatwa* in 1998, in some Islamic quarters Rushdie remains a marked man. In 2007 Rushdie was knighted by Queen Elizabeth II of England, causing another outcry among Muslims; Al Qaeda called the knighthood "an insult to Islam" and threatened to retaliate. Rushdie has been elected to many prestigious positions in the world of letters, including the Royal Society of Literature, and he has served as president of the PEN American Center. His most recent novels are *Shalimar the Clown* (2005) and *The Enchantress of Florence* (2008). Bharati Mukherjee once characterized Rushdie as "up there with Joyce and Solzhenitsyn, an educated, implacable, remorseless dissenter from deep inside the family." And Rushdie characterized himself as one who has "spent my entire life as a writer in opposition, and had indeed conceived the writer's role as including the function as antagonist to the state."

KAY RYAN (b. 1945)   Ryan was born in San Jose and grew up in central and southern California. She attended Antelope Valley College in Lancaster, California, before earning two degrees from UCLA. For over thirty-five years, she was a part-time instructor of English at the College of Marin. Ryan is the author of eight volumes of poetry: *Dragon Acts to Dragon Ends* (1983), *Strangely Marked Metal* (1985), *Flamingo Watching* (1994), *Elephant Rocks* (1997), *Say Uncle* (2000), *The Niagara River* (2005), *The Jam Jar Lifeboat and Other Novelties Exposed* (2008), and *The Best of It: New and Selected Poems* (2011). Her poems have also appeared in a number of periodicals, including *American Scholar, Atlantic, The New Yorker, Paris Review,* and *Poetry* magazine. Among her many awards are fellowships from the Guggenheim Foundation and the National Endowment for the Arts, and the 2004 Ruth Lilly Poetry Prize, a prestigious honor given to living U.S. poets "whose lifetime accomplishments warrant extraordinary recognition." Ryan served two terms as poet laureate of the United States, from 2008 through 2010.

CARL SANDBURG (1878–1967)   H. L. Mencken once described Carl Sandburg as "indubitably an American in every pulse-beat." Sandburg came from humble beginnings in Galesburg, Illinois. His parents had emigrated to America from northern Sweden and were very poor. Sandburg spent much of his youth working odd jobs to earn money, from driving a milk truck to bricklaying. In 1989 he voluntarily joined the military, serving eight months in Puerto Rico during the Spanish-American War. After leaving the military, he returned to his hometown and enrolled in Lombard College, though he dropped out in 1903 before receiving his degree. He then moved to Milwaukee, and joined the Socialist Party of America, where he met his future wife, Lilian Steichen. The couple moved around frequently in their early years together, eventually settling in Elmhurst in 1919. During that time, Sandburg became an editor for the *Chicago Daily News* and came to be known as a part of the Chicago literary renaissance. In 1919, he won the Pulitzer Prize for Poetry for his collection *Cornhuskers* (1918), which celebrated the ordinary working people of the Midwest. The celebration of America became a trademark of Sandburg's poetry and was reflected in his subsequent poetry collections, some of which include *Smoke and Steel* (1920), *Slabs of the Sunburnt West* (1922), *Good Morning, America* (1928), *The People, Yes* (1936), *Harvest Poems* (1950), *Sandburg's Complete Poems* (1951, which also won a Pulitzer Prize), and *Honey and Salt* (1963). The 1920s also saw Sandburg tap into American folklore. He made brief yearly tours across America with a banjo or guitar, singing folk songs and reciting poems, and thereafter put those uniquely American experiences into songbooks: *The American Songbag* (1927) and *The New American Songbag* (1950). He also wrote a series of children's books called *Rootabaga Stories* (1922), *Rootabaga Pigeons* (1923), and *Potato Face* (1930), which grew out of his desire to have "American fairy tales" match actual American childhood. Sandburg spent years researching and writing a definitive, two-volume biography of Abraham Lincoln, the second volume of which—*Abraham Lincoln: The War Years* (1939)—also won Sandburg a Pulitzer Prize. He recorded excerpts from the biography for Caedmon Records in New York City in 1957 and made a recording of Aaron Copland's *Lincoln Portrait* with the New York Philharmonic, for which he won a 1959 Grammy Award. In 1945, Sandburg and his wife moved to an estate in Flat Rock, North Carolina, where they lived until Sandburg's death in 1967.

SAPPHO (ca. 610–ca. 580 B.C.)   Almost nothing certain is known of the finest woman lyric poet of the ancient world. Sappho was born to an aristocratic family and had three brothers, one of whom was a court cupbearer, a position limited to the sons of good families. She is associated with the island of Lesbos, set in the Aegean Sea. She married and had a daughter. For over 2,000 years, her reputation depended on fragments of her work quoted by other ancient authors. However, in the late nineteenth century a cache of papyrus and vellum codices, dating from the second to the sixth centuries A.D. and containing authentic transcriptions of a few of her lyrical poems, was discovered in Egypt. Unlike other ancient Greek poets, she wrote in ordinary Greek rather than in an exalted literary dialect; her lyrics, despite their simple language, conveyed women's concerns with intense emotion.

DAVID SEDARIS (b. 1956) Sedaris was born in Binghamton, New York, and raised in Raleigh, North Carolina. He attended Kent State University before working odd jobs and eventually earning a degree from the School of the Art Institute of Chicago. Sedaris garnered fame when he began reading essays based on his diary on National Public Radio, first on *Morning Edition* and then, at the behest of host Ira Glass, as a regular contributor to *This American Life*. His first book of humorous stories and autobiographical essays, *Barrel Fever*, was published in 1994. All seven of his other collections—*Naked* (1997), *Holidays on Ice* (1997), *Me Talk Pretty One Day* (2000), *Dress Your Family in Corduroy and Denim* (2004), *When You Are Engulfed in Flames* (2008), *Squirrel Seeks Chipmunk: A Modest Bestiary* (2010)—have appeared on the New York Times best-seller list. He has also contributed regularly to the *New Yorker* and *Esquire* magazines; has coauthored several plays with his sister Amy; and has been nominated for two Grammys for audio recordings of his own work.

ANNE SEXTON (1928–1974) Born in Newton, Massachusetts, Sexton attended Garland Junior College and Boston University, where she studied under Robert Lowell. She worked for a year as a fashion model in Boston and later wrote her first poetry collection, *To Bedlam and Part Way Back* (1960), while recovering from a nervous breakdown. Writing a poem almost every day was successful therapy for her. From 1961 to 1963, Sexton was a scholar at the Radcliffe Institute for Independent Study. A confessional poet, Sexton acknowledged her debt to W. D. Snodgrass, whose collection of poetry, *Heart's Needle* (1959), influenced her profoundly. Her second collection, *All My Pretty Ones* (1962), includes a quote from a letter by Franz Kafka that expresses her own literary philosophy: "A book should serve as the axe for the frozen sea within us." *Live or Die* (1967), her third collection of poems, won a Pulitzer Prize. She committed suicide in 1974.

WILLIAM SHAKESPEARE (1564–1616) Shakespeare was born at Stratford-on-Avon in April 1564. His father became an important public figure, rising to the position of high bailiff (equivalent to mayor) of Stratford. Although we know practically nothing of Shakespeare's personal life, we may assume that he received a decent grammar school education in literature, logic, and Latin (though not in mathematics or natural science). When he was eighteen he married Anne Hathaway, eight years his senior; six months later their son was born. Two years later, Anne bore twins. We do not know how the young Shakespeare supported his family, and we do not hear of him again until 1592, when a rival London playwright sarcastically refers to him as an "upstart crow." Shakespeare seems to have prospered in the London theater world. He probably began as an actor and earned enough as author and part owner of his company's theaters to acquire property. His sonnets, which were written during the 1590s, reveal rich and varied interests. Some are addressed to an attractive young man (whom the poet urges to marry); others to the mysterious dark lady; still others suggest a love triangle of two men and a woman. His dramas include historical plays based on English dynastic struggles; comedies, both festive and dark; romances such as *Pericles* (1608) and *Cymbeline* (1611) that cover decades in the lives of their characters; and the great tragedies *Hamlet* (1602), *Othello* (1604), *King Lear* (1605), and *Macbeth* (1606). About 1611, at age forty-seven, he retired to the second largest house in Stratford. He died in 1616, leaving behind a body of work that still stands as a pinnacle in world literature.

PERCY BYSSHE SHELLEY (1792–1822)   Born near Horsham, England, Shelley was the son of a wealthy landowner who sat in Parliament. At University College, Oxford University, he befriended Thomas Jefferson Hogg. Both became interested in radical philosophy and quickly became inseparable. After one year at Oxford they were both expelled for writing and circulating a pamphlet entitled "The Necessity of Atheism." Shelley married Harriet Westbrook soon after leaving Oxford. Though they had two children, the marriage was unsuccessful, and in 1814, Shelley left Harriet for Mary Wollstonecraft Godwin, the author of *Frankenstein*. After Harriet's apparent suicide, Shelley and Godwin were married. Escaping legal problems in England, he settled in Pisa, Italy, in 1820, and died in a sailing accident before his thirtieth birthday. A playwright and essayist as well as a romantic poet, Shelley is admired for his dramatic poem "Prometheus Unbound" (1820).

LESLIE MARMON SILKO (b. 1948)   Born in Albuquerque, New Mexico, Silko grew up on the Laguna Pueblo Reservation. She was educated in Bureau of Indian Affairs schools and at the University of New Mexico, where she graduated with highest honors. After three semesters in the American Indian Law program, Silko decided to devote her talents to writing about Native Americans. Her short stories quickly earned her a reputation; in 1974, she published a volume of poems, *Laguna Woman*. Her novel *Ceremony* (1977) was widely acclaimed and revived interest in her earlier short stories. *Storyteller* (1981) is a semi-autobiographical collection of stories and poems. In 1991 the novel *Almanac of the Dead* appeared, and a collection of essays on contemporary Native American life, *Yellow Woman and a Beauty of the Spirit*, followed in 1996. Silko has taught at the University of Arizona and the University of New Mexico, but with a large award from the prestigious MacArthur Foundation, she has been, in her words, "a little less beholden to the everyday world." Her other work includes the novel *Gardens in the Dunes* (1999) and *The Turquoise Ledge* (2010), a memoir that was the first book Silko had published in ten years.

STEVIE SMITH (1902–1971)   Born Florence Margaret Smith in Hull, England, Stevie Smith was a secretary at Newnes Publishing Company in London from 1923 to 1953 and occasionally worked as a writer and broadcaster for the BBC. Though in the 1930s she began publishing verse, which she often illustrated herself, Smith did not reach a wide audience until 1962, with the publication of *Selected Poems* and her appearance in the Penguin Modern Poets series. She is noted for her eccentricity and mischievous humor, often involving an acerbic twist on nursery rhymes, common songs, or hymns. Force-fed with what she considered lifeless language in the New English Bible, she often aimed satirical barbs at religion. Smith won the Queen's Gold Medal for poetry in 1969, two years before her death. She published three novels in addition to her eight volumes of poetry.

SOPHOCLES (496?–406 B.C.)   Born into a wealthy family at Colonus, a village just outside Athens, Sophocles distinguished himself early in life as a performer, musician, and athlete. Our knowledge of him is based on a very few ancient laudatory notices, but he certainly had a brilliant career as one of the three great Greek classical tragedians (the other two are Aeschylus, an older contemporary, and Euripides, a younger contemporary). He won the drama competition associated with the Dionysian festival (entries consisted of a tragic trilogy and a farce) at least twenty times, far more often than his two principal rivals. However, *Oedipus Rex*, his most famous tragedy, and the three other plays it was grouped with, took second place (ca. 429 B.C.). He lived during the golden age of Athens, when architecture, philosophy, and the arts flourished under Pericles. In 440 B.C. Sophocles was elected as one of the ten *strategoi* (military commanders), an indication of his stature in Athens. But his long life ended in sadder times, when the Peloponnesian War (431–404 B.C.), between the Athenian empire and an alliance led by Sparta, darkened the region. Though Sophocles wrote some 123 plays, only seven have survived; nonetheless, these few works establish him as the greatest of the ancient Western tragedians.

GARY SOTO (b. 1952)   Soto was born in Fresno, California, to working-class Mexican American parents. He grew up in the San Joaquin Valley and worked as a migrant laborer in California's rich agricultural regions. Uncertain of his abilities, he began his academic career at Fresno City College, moving on to California State University at Fresno and the University of California at Irvine, where he earned an M.F.A. (1976). In 1975, he married Carolyn Oda, a woman of Japanese ancestry. Although his work earned him recognition as early as 1975 (an Academy of American Poets Prize), his first book of poems—*The Elements of San Joaquin*, portraying grim pictures of Mexican American life in California's central valley—didn't appear until 1977. In 1985, he joined the faculty at the University of California at Berkeley, where he taught in both the English and Chicano studies departments. He gave up teaching in 1993 to become a full-time writer but returned to teaching in 2003, at the University of California at Riverside. His prolific output of poetry, memoirs, essays, and fiction continues unabated and has earned him numerous prizes, including an American Book Award from the Before Columbus Foundation for *Living up the Street* (1985). Soto's novel *Buried Onions* (1999) deals with the struggle and discomfort of a teenage boy's life in Fresno, California. *Nickel and Dime* (2000) is a fictional exploration of the interlocking lives of three Mexican American men in California. His latest publications are a novel for teenagers, *Accidental Love* (2006); a collection of stories for adolescents, *Facts of Life: Stories* (2008); and two collections of poems, *Partly Cloudy: Poems of Love and Longing* (2009) and *Human Nature* (2010). One critic points out that Soto has transcended the social commentary of his early work and shifted to "a more personal, less politically motivated poetry." Another argues that "Gary Soto has become not an important Chicano poet but an important American poet."

WOLE SOYINKA (b. 1934)   One of the most prolific and versatile writers of our time, and the first African to receive the Nobel Prize for Literature (1986), Soyinka was born in Akinwande, Nigeria, to Yoruba parents. After attending Nigerian schools, including the University of Obada, he moved to England, where he earned a B.A. (1958) in English literature. For the next few years he worked at the Royal Court Theatre in London, where his first works were performed. He returned to Nigeria in 1960, teaching drama in several universities and working on the creation of a Nigerian national theater. Because of his political opposition to the governing military dictatorship during the Nigerian civil war, he was twice arrested and jailed during the 1960s. Following his release almost two years after his second arrest, he went into voluntary exile in England, where he lectured and continued to write. This pattern of exile and return continued, depending on the political situation in his home country. He again went into exile in 1994, declaring, "Some people think the

Nobel Prize makes you bulletproof. I never had that illusion." Following the death of the military dictator Sani Abacha in 1998, Soyinka returned to Nigeria, where he now lives and teaches. Among his many plays are *The Lion and Jewel* (1959), *The Strong Breed* (1963), *The Trials of Brother Jero* (1964), *A Scourge of Hyacinths* (1992), and *King Baabu* (2001). *The Man Died* (1972) is an account of his first arrest and imprisonment. His volumes of poetry include *Mandela's Earth and Other Poems* (1988), *Early Poems* (1997), *Outsiders* (1999), and *Samarkand and Other Markets I Have Known* (2002). *The Burden of Memory, the Muse of Forgiveness* (1999) comprises Soyinka's reflections on the politics, government, and literature of Africa. His latest publications include his nonfiction work *Climate of Fear: The Quest for Dignity in a Dehumanized World* (2005) and his memoirs, *You Must Set Forth at Dawn* (2006).

WILLIAM STAFFORD (1914–1993)   Born in Hutchinson, Kansas, Stafford earned his bachelor's and master's degrees from the University of Kansas and his doctorate from the University of Iowa. Drafted during World War II, he declared himself pacifist and conscientious objector and spent several years doing forestry and soil-conservation work instead. He taught at a small number of institutions around the country before settling on Lewis & Clark College and the Pacific Northwest. Stafford did not publish a collection of poetry until he was forty-eight years old; his first volume, *Traveling through the Dark* (1962), won the National Book Award in 1963. An astonishingly prolific writer, he kept a journal for fifty years and composed almost twenty-two thousand poems, three thousand of which were published in nearly sixty volumes of poetry. Among his many titles are *The Rescued Year* (1966), *Stories That Could Be True: New and Collected Poems* (1977), *Writing the Australian Crawl: Views on the Writer's Vocation* (1978), and *An Oregon Message* (1987). Stafford also contributed to numerous periodicals; authored a memoir, essays, reviews, and a children's book; and edited and translated the works of others. His many awards include a Guggenheim Fellowship, a grant from the National Endowment for the Arts, a Shelley Memorial Award, and a Western States Lifetime Achievement Award in Poetry.

WALLACE STEVENS (1879–1955)   Born in Reading, Pennsylvania, Stevens graduated from Harvard University in 1900, worked for a year as a reporter for the New York *Herald Tribune*, graduated from New York University Law School in 1903, and practiced law in New York for twelve years. From 1916 to 1955, Stevens worked for the Hartford Accident and Indemnity Company, where he was appointed vice president in 1934. He was in his forties when he published his first book of poetry, *Harmonium, Ideas of Order* (1923). Stevens argued that poetry is a "supreme fiction" that shapes chaos and provides order to both nature and human relationships. He illuminates his philosophy in *Ideas of Order* (1935) and *Notes toward a Supreme Fiction* (1942). His *Collected Poems* (1954) won the Pulitzer Prize and established him as a major American poet.

JONATHAN SWIFT (1667–1745)   Born in Dublin, Ireland, of English parents, Swift moved to England following his graduation from Trinity College, Dublin. In 1695 he was ordained minister of the Anglican Church of Ireland and five years later became a parish priest in Laracor, Ireland. The conduct of church business took Swift to England frequently, where his wit and skill in defense of Tory politics made him many influential friends. He was rewarded for his efforts in 1713, when Queen Anne appointed him dean of St. Patrick's Cathedral in Dublin. The accession of George I to the throne in the following year, followed by the Tory's loss of the government to Whig control, ended the political power of

Swift and his friends. He spent the rest of his life as dean of St. Patrick's, writing during this period his most celebrated satirical narrative, *Gulliver's Travels* (1726), and his most savage essay, "A Modest Proposal" (1729). Among his many other works are *A Tale of a Tub* and *The Battle of the Books* (both 1704), and many poems.

WISLAWA SZYMBORSKA (b. 1923–2012)   Born in Pozna, Poland, Szymborska was eight when her family moved to Krakow, where she has lived ever since. After earning a degree from the University of Krakow, she worked as an editor on literary publications and as a newspaper columnist. Her attempt to publish a volume of poems in 1949 was thwarted by Communist censors. Her first collection was finally published in 1952, and a second appeared in 1954. She later renounced these first two collections, which conformed to the socialist realism dogma of the Stalinist era. Her first collection to appear in English, *Sounds, Feelings, Thoughts: Seventy Poems,* was published in 1981. By this time Poland was under martial law, and she had to assume a pseudonym and publish her works in exile, but through it all her fame in her native country remained undiminished. With the fall of the Soviet Union, Szymborska became more popular than ever. Little known outside Poland, she gained worldwide recognition when she was awarded the Nobel Prize for Literature in 1996. Among her other works available in English translation are *People on a Bridge* (1986, trans. 1990) and an anthology from earlier collections, *The End and the Beginning* (1993). Her later volumes in English are *Miracle Fair: Selected Poems* (2001), *Nonrequired Reading: Prose Pieces* (2002), and *Monologue of a Dog* (2005).

GRACE TALUSAN (b. 1972)   At age three, Talusan emigrated with her family from the Philippines to the United States. She was raised near Boston and earned degrees from Tufts University and the University of California at Irvine. Talusan taught at the University of Oregon and now teaches at Tufts. Her work, both fiction and memoir, has appeared in a number of periodicals, including *Asiaweek, Brevity,* the *Boston Globe, Creative Nonfiction,* the *Del Sol Review,* and the *San Diego Reader.*

AMY TAN (b. 1952)   Tan's parents emigrated from China to Oakland, California, before she was born, and she grew up in a rather traditional Chinese household. She earned a B.A. (1973) and an M.A. (1974) from San Jose State University and spent an additional two years in postgraduate study at the University of California at Berkeley. Her shift from a premed program to English and linguistics caused a serious break with her mother, and they didn't speak for two years. She was a writer from the outset and earned her living for several years as a medical and freelance technical writer. But her interest in fiction led her to the Squaw Valley Community of Writers, and shortly after returning from a trip to China, she published her first novel, *The Joy Luck Club* (1989), consisting of sixteen interwoven stories that reveal the struggles of four Chinese mothers with their sometimes rebellious daughters. Four more novels followed: *The Kitchen God's Wife* (1991), *The Hundred Secret Senses* (1995), *The Year of No Flood* (1995), and *The Bonesetter's Daughter* (2001). Her most recent publications are *The Opposite of Fate* (2003), a collection of essays; *Saving Fish from Drowning* (2005), a novel; and *Rules for Virgins* (2012), a novel.

SHEILA ORTIZ TAYLOR (b. 1939)   Taylor was born into a Mexican American family in the Silver Lake area of Los Angeles; she grew up between there and Toonerville. Taylor has said, "In every Mexican-American family there is an inscriber of stories, the keeper of the family fictions," a role that she filled within her own family. Taylor earned her B.A. from California State University, Northridge and her M.A. and Ph.D. from the University of California, Los Angeles. In 1973 she began teaching literature and creative writing at Florida State University, which is where she taught until retiring in 2006. She has been honored with a Fulbright Scholarship, a State of Florida Individual Artist Fellowship, a National Endowment for the Arts creative writing fellowship, the Alice B. Reader's Appreciation Medal, and holds memberships in the Modern Language Association, the Authors' Guild, and the Lambda Literary Foundation. She has written six novels, a memoir, and a volume of poetry. Her most recent work is a novel, *Homestead* (2011).

ALEXANDRA TEAGUE (b. 1974) Teague was born in Fort Worth, Texas, and has since lived many places across the United States, including Arkansas, Missouri, Montana, Florida, Hawaii, California, and Idaho. She earned an M.F.A. from the University of Florida in 1998 and was a 2006–2008 Stegner Fellow at Stanford University. She has also taught at the University of Miami and at City College of San Francisco, and she served as a Visiting Professor of Poetry at the University of Arkansas in the fall of 2010. Teague is currently an assistant professor of poetry at the University of Idaho and was the recipient of a 2011 National Endowment for the Arts Fellowship. Her poetry has appeared in *Best New Poets 2008* and *Best American Poetry 2009* as well as such literary journals as the *Missouri Review, Iowa Review, Southern Poetry Review, New England Review*, and others. Her first book of poetry, *Mortal Geography* (2010), won the 2009 Lexi Rudnitsky Prize and the 2010 California Book Award.

ALFRED, LORD TENNYSON (1809–1892) Tennyson was born in Lincolnshire and attended Trinity College, Cambridge (1828–1831), where he won the Chancellor's Medal for poetry in 1829. His 1842 collection, *Poems*, was not well received, but he gained prominence and Queen Victoria's favor with the 1850 publication of *In Memoriam*, an elegy written over seventeen years and inspired by the untimely death of his friend Arthur Hallam in 1833. That same year he married Emily Sellwood, after what had been a fourteen-year engagement. In 1850, he was named poet laureate of England after Wordsworth's death. His works include *Maud and Other Poems* (1855) and *Idylls of the King* (1859), based on the legendary exploits of King Arthur and the knights of the Round Table.

DYLAN THOMAS (1914–1953) Born in Swansea, Wales, Thomas decided to pursue a writing career directly after grammar school. At age twenty he published his first collection, *Eighteen Poems* (1934), but his lack of a university degree deprived him of most opportunities to earn a living as a writer in England. Consequently, his early life (as well as the lives of his wife and children) was darkened by a poverty compounded by his free spending and heavy drinking. A self-proclaimed romanticist, Thomas called his poetry a "record of [his] struggle from darkness towards some measure of light." *The Map of Love* appeared in 1939 and *Deaths and Entrances* in 1946. Later, as a radio playwright and screenwriter, Thomas delighted in the sounds of words, sometimes at the expense of sense. *Under Milk Wood* (produced in 1953) is filled with his private, onomatopoetic language. He suffered from alcoholism and lung ailments and died in a New York hospital in 1953. Earlier that year, he noted in his *Collected Poems*: "These poems, with all their crudities, doubts and confusions are written for the love of man and in Praise of God, and I'd be a damn fool if they weren't."

LEO TOLSTOY (1828–1910) Born in Russia into a family of aristocratic landowners, Tolstoy cut short his university education and joined the army, serving among the primitive

Cossacks, who became the subject of his first novel, *The Cossacks* (1863). Tolstoy left the army and traveled abroad, but was disappointed by Western materialism and returned home. After a brief period in St. Petersburg, he became bored with the life of literary celebrity and returned to his family estate. There he wrote his two greatest novels, *War and Peace* (1869) and *Anna Karenina* (1877). Around 1876, Tolstoy experienced a spiritual crisis that ultimately led him to reject his former beliefs, way of life, and literary works. He adopted the simple life of the Russian peasants, rejecting orthodoxy in favor of a rational Christianity that disavowed private property, class divisions, secular and institutional religious authority, as well as all art (including his own) that failed to teach the simple principles he espoused.

NATASHA TRETHEWEY (b. 1966) Trethewey was born in Gulfport, Mississippi. She earned a B.A. in English from the University of Georgia, an M.A. in English and creative writing from Hollins University, and an M.F.A in poetry from the University of Massachusetts. She has published three collections of poetry: *Domestic Work* (2000), *Bellocq's Ophelia* (2002), and *Native Guard* (2006), for which she won the 2007 Pulitzer Prize for Poetry. Her fourth collection, *Thrall* (2012), is forthcoming. Trethewey has also written a book of creative nonfiction, *Beyond Katrina: A Meditation on the Mississippi Gulf Coast* (2010). In addition to several fellowships from the Guggenheim Foundation, the Rockefeller Foundation, and elsewhere, she was awarded the 2008 Mississippi Governor's Award for Excellence in the Arts. She was also was named the 2008 Georgia Woman of the Year and was inducted into the Fellowship of Southern Writers in 2009. Most recently, she was inducted into the Georgia Writers Hall of Fame in 2011. She currently holds the Phillis Wheatley Distinguished Chair in Poetry at Emory University.

MARK TURPIN (b. 1953) Turpin, the son of a Presbyterian minister, spent twenty-five years working construction before graduating from Boston University with an M.A. in poetry at the age of forty-seven. His poems have appeared in the *Threepenny Review, Paris Review, Slate, Boston Review,* and *Ploughshares,* among other publications. In 1997, he received the prestigious Whiting Award for a book of poems in the new poets series, *Take Three.* He also won the 2004 Ploughshares John C. Zacharis First Book Award for his collection *Hammer* (2003). He teaches poetry and works as a carpenter in the San Francisco Bay area.

JOHN UPDIKE (1932–2009) Updike was born in Shillington, Pennsylvania, and graduated from Harvard University before attending the Ruskin School of Drawing and Fine Arts in Oxford. In England, he made the acquaintance of E. B. White, who offered Updike a job at *The New Yorker.* After two years at the magazine, he left to pursue his writing. His first book of poetry, *The Carpentered Hen and Other Tame Creatures,* was published in 1958. Updike was a prolific short story writer, poet, novelist, and critic, having written over sixty books, among them *A & P* (short stories, 1961), *Self-Consciousness: Memoirs* (1989), *Collected Poems 1953–1993* (1993), *Still Looking: Essays on American Art* (2005), and the novels *The Poorhouse Fair* (1959), *Rabbit, Run* (1960), *The Centaur* (1963), *The Witches of Eastwick* (1984), and *In the Beauty of the Lilies* (1996). His recent works include *Terrorist* (2006), *Due Considerations: Essays and Criticism* (2007), and *The Widows of Eastwick* (2008). Until he lost his battle with cancer in 2009, he was a regular contributor to *The New Yorker* and the *New York Review of Books.* His countless awards include a Guggenheim Fellowship, a National Book Award, an O. Henry Award, a Fulbright Fellowship, a Pulitzer Prize, a National Book Critics Circle Award, a PEN/Faulkner

Award, a National Medal of Arts, and a Caldecott Medal. Updike said that it was his aim to "give the mundane its beautiful due."

HELENA MARÍA VIRAMONTES (b. 1954)   Viramontes was one of nine children born to a construction worker and a homemaker in East Los Angeles, California. She earned degrees from Immaculate Heart College and the University of California at Irvine and currently teaches at Cornell University. Her work has appeared in a number of anthologies; in addition, she co-edited *Chicana Creativity and Criticism: Charting New Frontiers in American Literature* (1988) and *Chicana (w)rites: On Word and Film* (1995). She received a first prize for fiction from *Statement Magazine* and a fellowship from the National Endowment for the Arts. Viramontes, who writes about Chicano culture and women, is the author of three books: *The Moths and Other Stories* (1985); *Under the Feet of Jesus* (1995); and *Their Dogs Came with Them* (2007), which took her seventeen years to complete.

JUAN LUIS VIVES (1493–1540)   Vives was a Spanish humanist who was among the first scholars to envision and put forth a comprehensive theory of education. Besides his interest in and works on education, he wrote on such subjects as philosophy, psychology, politics, social reform, and religion. His best-known works are *De concordia et discordia in humano genere* (*On Concord and Discord in Humankind*, 1529), a social criticism that condemned war and called for peace; *De disciplinis* (*On the Disciplines*, 1531), a critique of contemporary education and a proposal for changes to the system; and *De anima et vita* (*On the Soul and Life*, 1538), an examination of how the soul interacts with the body. Vives's *De veritate fidei Christianae* (*On the Truth of the Christian Faith*), a treatise on his religious views, was published posthumously in 1543.

ALICE WALKER (b. 1944)   Born in Eatonton, Georgia, the eighth child of sharecroppers, Walker was educated at Spelman College and Sarah Lawrence College. She has been deeply involved in the civil rights movement, working to register voters in Georgia and on behalf of welfare rights and Head Start in Mississippi. She also worked for the Welfare Department of New York City. She has taught at Wellesley College and Yale University and been an editor of *Ms.* Her nonfiction works include a biography for children, *Langston Hughes: American Poet* (1973); numerous contributions to anthologies about African American writers; and a collection of essays, *In Search of Our Mothers' Gardens: Womanist Prose* (1983). Her novels, all dealing with the African American experience, include *The Third Life of Grange Copeland* (1973); *Meridian* (1976); *The Color Purple* (1982), which won both the Pulitzer Prize and the National Book Award; *The Temple of My Familiar* (1989); and *Possessing the Secret of Joy* (1992). Her short stories are collected in three volumes, *In Love and Trouble: Stories of Black Women* (1973), *You Can't Keep a Good Woman Down* (1981), and *The Way Forward Is with a Broken Heart* (2000). Her recent publications include *Devil's My Enemy* (2008), a novel; *Hard Times Require Furious Dancing: New Poems* (2010); and *The Chicken Chronicles: Sitting with the Angels Who Have Returned with My Memories: Glorious, Rufus, Gertrude Stein, Splendor, Hortensia, Agnes of God, The Gladyses, & Babe: A Memoir* (2011).

DAVID FOSTER WALLACE (1962–2008)   Wallace, the son of college professors, was born in Ithaca, New York, and grew up in the cities of Champaign and Urbana in Illinois. He attended Amherst College in Massachusetts where he majored in English and philosophy, with a focus on modal logic and mathematics. He earned his M.F.A. from the University of Arizona; he then went on to teach at Pomona College in Claremont, California. His first novel, *The Broom of the System*, was published in 1987. His second novel, *Infinite Jest* (1996), earned him praise from both critics and readers. Among his short fiction collections are *Girl with Curious Hair* (1989), *Brief Interviews with Hideous Men* (1999), and *Oblivion: Stories* (2004). His nonfiction work includes *A Supposedly Fun Thing I'll Never Do Again* (1997), *Everything and More: A Compact History of Infinity* (2003), and *Consider the Lobster* (2005). His work also appeared in a great number of periodicals, including the *Boston Globe, Los Angeles Times, Nation, The New Yorker, New York Times,* and *Time* magazine. Among his numerous honors were a writer's award from the Whiting Foundation, a fellowship from the National Endowment for the Arts, and a grant from the MacArthur Foundation. Wallace, who was widely considered one of the best young writers in the United States, battled depression for many years before committing suicide in 2008.

JAMES WELCH (1940–2003)   Welch was born in Browning, Montana. His father was a member of the Blackfeet tribe and his mother a member of the Gros Ventre tribe; growing up, Welch attended schools on the Blackfoot and Fort Belknap reservations. He earned his B.A. from the University of Montana, which is where he launched his writing career under the tutelage of Richard Hugo. Welch later taught at the University of Washington and at Cornell University and also served on the Parole Board of the Montana Prisons Systems and on the board of directors of the Newberry Library D'Arcy McNickle Center. Welch's first book was a collection of poetry entitled *Riding the Earthboy 40* (1971), which centered on the Native American experience. His first novel, *Winter in the Blood* (1974), also explored this theme. While teaching at Cornell, Welch wrote *The Death of Jim Loney* (1979) and *Fools Crow* (1986), which won the American Book Award, the Pacific Northwest Book Award, and the Los Angeles Times Book Prize. In 1997 Welch received a Lifetime Achievement Award from the Native Writers Circle, and in 2000 he was named a *Chevalier des Arts et des Lettres* (Knight of the Order of Arts and Letters) by the French Minister of Culture. His novel *The Heartsong of Charging Elk* (2000) garnered another Pacific Northwest Book Award in 2001. Welch and Paul Stekler cowrote the documentary *Last Stand at Little Bighorn* (1992), which aired on PBS and won an Emmy Award. They also coauthored *Killing Custer: The Battle of Little Bighorn and the Fate of the Plains Indians* (1994).Welch died of a heart attack in Missoula, Montana, in 2003.

PHILLIS WHEATLEY (1753–1784)   Wheatley was abducted from her home in Africa by slave traders and brought to Boston. There, according to an advertisement on August 3, 1761, in the *Boston Evening Post*, "A parcel of likely Negroes, imported from Africa" was offered "cheap for cash." One of them, a seven- or eight-year-old child, was bought as a house servant for Susannah Wheatley, the wife of a prosperous Boston tailor. The Wheatley family, impressed by the young African's quickness of intellect, taught her English and Christianity as well as Latin, ancient history, and classical literature. As Phillis Wheatley's formidable talents developed, the family allowed her time to study and to write. Her early poems, the first of them published when she was a young teenager, appeared in local broadside sheets sold on the streets of Boston. In 1773, her fame as a poet growing, she was taken by the Wheatley's son to London, where thirty-nine of her poems were published as *Poems on Various Subjects Religious and Moral*. The book was an instant success, and Phillis Wheatley was widely honored and lionized. The "Sable Muse," as the English dubbed her, received a visit from Benjamin Franklin, America's colonial agent in Britain; the Lord Mayor of London honored her with a gift; and even Voltaire praised her poems. As arrangements were being made to present her to George III, she was recalled to America to tend to her ailing mistress. In the following years, upon the deaths of the Wheatleys, she gained her freedom; married another freed slave, John Peters; and bore three children, all of whom died in childhood. During her final years, which were marked by failing health and the burdens of menial work, she did not publish any poems. Her attempt to revive her fortunes by advertising a three-hundred-page volume titled "Poems & Letters on various subjects dedicated to the Right Hon. Benjamin Franklin, Esq." failed to attract enough subscribers. She died, obscure and destitute, when she was about thirty.

E. B. WHITE (1899–1985)   Elwyn Brooks White was born in Mount Vernon, New York, a suburb of Manhattan. He served in the U.S. Army before earning a degree from Cornell University and then worked as a journalist at the *Seattle Times* and *Seattle Post-Intelligencer* and in advertising, jobs he loathed. In 1925, White submitted his first article to *The New Yorker*; he joined the staff two years later and contributed to the magazine for nearly sixty years. He was also a columnist for *Harper's* magazine from 1938 to 1943. Although White wrote poetry and published letters, he is perhaps best known for his essays, which varied widely in subject matter but always incorporated his amiable wit. He also took to writing children's literature for a beloved niece, and his books—*Stuart Little* (1945), *Charlotte's Web* (1952), and *Trumpet of the Swan* (1970)—became unqualified classics. Among White's countless awards are a Newbery Honor, a gold medal from the National Institute of Arts and Letters, a Laura Ingalls Wilder Award for "a lasting contribution to children's literature," a National Medal for Literature, and a Pulitzer Prize special citation for the body of his work. He spent most of his life at his home in Maine, where he died at age eighty-six.

WALT WHITMAN (1819–1892)   One of nine children, Whitman was born in Huntington, Long Island, in New York, and grew up in Brooklyn, where his father worked as a carpenter. At age eleven, after five years of public school, Whitman took a job as a printer's assistant. He learned the printing trade and, before his twentieth birthday, became editor of the *Long Islander*, a Huntington newspaper. He edited several newspapers in the New York area and one in New Orleans before leaving the newspaper business in 1848. He then lived with his parents, worked as a part-time carpenter, and began writing *Leaves of Grass*, which he first published at his own expense in 1855. After the Civil War (during which he was a devoted volunteer, ministering to the wounded), Whitman was fired from his job in the Department of the Interior by Secretary James Harlan, who considered *Leaves of Grass* obscene. Soon, however, he was rehired in the attorney general's office, where he remained until 1874. In 1881, after many editions, *Leaves of Grass* finally found a publisher willing to print it uncensored. Translations were enthusiastically received in Europe, but Whitman remained relatively unappreciated in the United States; not until after his death would a large audience come to admire his original and innovative expression of American individualism.

OSCAR WILLIAMS (1900–1964)   Williams was born in Brooklyn, New York, and worked at various advertising agencies between 1921 and 1937. His first book of poetry, *The Golden Darkness*, won the Yale Series of Younger Poets Award in 1921. Although his own poetic productivity was modest, he carved himself a special niche as an editor and anthologizer. Since his anthologies were frequently used as textbooks in university courses, he exercised significant influence on the mainstream of Western poetry from the 1940s until his death.

DAVID WOJAHN (b. 1953)   David Wojahn teaches poetry at Virginia Commonwealth University—where he has also directed the Creative Writing Program—and in the low-residency M.F.A. program at the Vermont College of Fine Arts. He has published eight collections of poetry: *Icehouse Lights* (1982), winner of the Yale Younger Poets Award; *Glassworks* (1987), which won the Society of Midland Authors Award; *Mystery Train* (1990); *Late Empire* (1994); *The Falling Hour* (1997); *Spirit Cabinet* (2002); *Interrogation Palace: New and Selected Poems 1982–2004* (2006); and, most recently, *World Tree* (2011). In addition to his poetry collections, he has written a collection of essays on contemporary verse *called Strange Good Fortune* (2001); co-edited *A Profile of Twentieth Century American Poetry* (1991); and edited a posthumous collection of his wife Lynda Hull's poetry, *The Only World* (1995). His work has been featured in many journals and anthologies, including the *Paris Review*, *The New Yorker*, *Best American Poetry* series, *American Poetry Review*, *New York Times Book Review*, *Chicago Tribune*, *Kenyon Review*, *New England Review*, *Georgia Review*, *TriQuarterly*, and others. Among his many literary honors are fellowships from the John Simon Guggenheim Memorial Foundation, the National Endowment for the Arts, the Fine Arts Work Center in Provincetown, the Illinois Arts Council, the Indiana Arts Commission, and the Bread Loaf Writers' Conference, as well as writing residencies from the Yaddo and McDowell colonies. He lives in Richmond, Virginia.

TOBIAS WOLFF (b. 1945)   Wolff was born in Birmingham, Alabama. He holds a First Class Honors degree in English from Hertford College, Oxford, and an M.A. from Stanford University. He contributes regularly to *The New Yorker*, *Atlantic*, *Harper's*, and other literary publications, and his work has been recognized with such honors as the PEN/Malamud Award, the Rea Award, the *Los Angeles Times* Book Prize, and the PEN/Faulkner Award. He has written two novels, *The Barracks Thief* (1984) and *Old School* (2003), the memoirs *This Boy's Life* (1989) and *In Pharaoh's Army* (1994), and the short story collections *In the Garden of the North American Martyrs* (1981), *Back in the World* (1985), *The Night in Question* (1997), and *Our Story Begins* (2008), which won the Story Prize. Wolff taught at Syracuse University from 1980 to 1997 and currently teaches English at his alma mater, Stanford University.

VIRGINIA WOOLF (1882–1941)   Woolf was born in London, where she spent most of her life. Because of her frail health and her father's Victorian attitudes about the proper role of women, she received little formal education. Nevertheless, the advantages of an upper-class family (her father, Sir Leslie Stephen, was a distinguished scholar and man of letters who hired tutors for her) and an extraordinarily powerful and inquiring mind allowed Woolf to educate herself. She began keeping a regular diary in her early teens. After moderate success with her first novels, the publication of *To the Lighthouse* (1927) and *Orlando* (1929) established her as a major novelist. While Woolf's reputation rests primarily on her novels, which helped revolutionize fictional technique, she was also a distinguished literary and social critic. A strong supporter of women's rights, she expressed her views on the subject in a series of lectures published as *A Room of One's Own* (1929) and in a collection of essays, *Three Guineas* (1938). Her reputation grew with the publication of her letters and diaries following her suicide by drowning.

WILLIAM WORDSWORTH (1770–1850)   Born in Cockermouth in the Lake District of England, Wordsworth was educated at Cambridge University. During a summer tour in France in 1790, Wordsworth had an affair with Annette Vallon that resulted in the birth of a daughter. The tour also made Wordsworth an ardent defender of the French Revolution of 1789 and kindled his sympathies for the plight of the common person. Wordsworth's acquaintance with Samuel Taylor Coleridge in 1795 began a close friendship that led to the collaborative publication of *Lyrical Ballads* in 1798. Wordsworth supplied a celebrated preface to the second edition in 1800, in which he announced himself a nature poet of pantheistic leanings, committed to democratic equality and the language of common people. He finished *The Prelude* in 1805, but it was not published until after his death. As he grew older, Wordsworth grew increasingly conservative, and though he continued to write prolifically, little that he wrote during the last decades of his life attained the heights of his earlier work. In 1843, he was appointed poet laureate.

JAMES WRIGHT (1927–1980)   Wright was born in Martins Ferry, Ohio, into a family afflicted by poverty and misfortune. His parents had never attended school beyond the eighth grade, and Wright himself graduated from high school a year late due to a nervous breakdown that forced him to take time off. After high school he joined the army and was stationed in Japan during the American occupation. After serving, he attended Kenyon College on the G.I. Bill, from where he graduated cum laude and Phi Beta Kappa in 1952. Wright went on to earn his M.A. and Ph.D. at the University of Washington, where he studied with Theodore Roethke and Stanley Kunitz. While Wright was a graduate student, W. H. Auden selected Wright's manuscript *The Green Wall* (1957) for publication in the Yale Younger Poets Series. Wright also contributed to many literary journals during this time, such as the *Sewanee Review*, *The New Yorker*, and *New Orleans Poetry Review*. He went on to teach at the University of Minnesota, Macalester College, and New York City's Hunter College. The subjects of Wright's earlier books, *The Green Wall* and *Saint Judas* (1959), focus on profound, isolating human issues such as lost love and marginalization from society, which Wright had witnessed firsthand during his childhood. Whereas his earlier work is mostly conventional in form, Wright's later works are more open and looser in structure, as seen in *The Branch Will Not Break* (1963) and *Shall We Gather at the River* (1968). In 1971, Wright was elected a fellow of The Academy of American Poets, and his *Collected Poems* (1972) received the Pulitzer Prize for Poetry the following year. He wrote actively during this period, publishing the collections *Two Citizens* (1973), *I See the Wind* (1974), *Old Booksellers and Other Poems* (1976), *Moments of the Italian Summer* (1976), and *To a Blossoming Pear Tree* (1978). He died in New York City in 1980. Three posthumous collections of his work have been published, including *This Journey* (1982), *The Temple in Nîmes* (1982), and *Above the River: The Complete Poems* (1992).

LADY MARY WROTH (1587–1651 or 1653)   Wroth's mother was a wealthy heiress from Wales and Sir Walter Raleigh's first cousin; her father was appointed the first Earl of Leicester by King James I. In 1604, it was arranged that Mary would marry Sir Robert Wroth, who turned out to be an alcoholic, a philanderer, and a compulsive gambler. Although Lady Wroth became a fixture in Queen Anne's court and was a close friend, and perhaps lover, of playwright, poet, and actor Ben Jonson, her husband's death in 1614 saddled her with considerable debt. Perhaps in an attempt to earn money to satisfy her creditors, she published *The Countesse of Montgomeries Urania* (1621). Credited as the first substantial work of fiction written by an Englishwoman, it included sonnets interspersed throughout the romantic prose. The work, however, was highly controversial as royal society believed that it bore a striking resemblance to real life and revealed the court's secrets; King James ordered that it be withdrawn. Among her other works, all unpublished during her lifetime, are *The Second Part of the Countesse of Montgomeries Urania*, a few poems, and an unfinished play titled *Love's Victory*. Scholars believe that her financial circumstances and the scandal surrounding *Urania* led to Wroth's departure from royal societal circles; thus, very little about her later life, including the exact date of her death, is known.

SIR THOMAS WYATT (1503–1542) Though people generally think of William Shakespeare when they hear the word "sonnet," Sir Thomas Wyatt is the poet generally credited as the "father of the English sonnet." Wyatt's father, Henry Wyatt, was one of Henry VII's Privy Councillors and remained a friend to the court when Henry VIII assumed the throne in 1509. Wyatt was educated at St. John's College at the University of Cambridge and followed his father to court in 1515 to be an ambassador for Henry VIII. In 1522 he married Elizabeth Brooke, sister of George Brooke—a baron—and later traveled to Rome as part of the delegation that petitioned the pope to annul Henry VIII's marriage to his first wife, Catherine of Aragon. Wyatt was knighted in 1535 but came to disgrace the following year when he was imprisoned in the Tower of London after quarrelling with the Duke of Suffolk (and possibly for committing adultery with Anne Boleyn, Henry VIII's wife at the time). Excepting a handful of poems included in the miscellany *The Court of Venus*, none of Wyatt's poems were printed during his lifetime; fifteen years after Wyatt's death his poetry finally appeared alongside that of Henry Howard, Earl of Surrey, in printer Richard Tottel's *Songs and Sonnets written by the Right Honorable Lord Henry Howard late Earl of Surrey and other*. Wyatt's poetry often reflects classical and Italian models, especially the Petrarchan sonnet, and he was also adept at other new forms in English. His poetry helped to establish the poetic convention of a cruel mistress who abuses her lover—a form that flourished in the English canon thereafter.

WILLIAM BUTLER YEATS (1865–1939) Yeats was born in Ireland and educated in both Ireland and London. Much of his poetry and many of his plays reflect his fascination with the history of Ireland—particularly the myths and legends of its ancient, pagan past—as well as his interest in the occult. As Yeats matured, he turned increasingly to contemporary subjects, expressing his nationalism in poems about the Irish struggle for independence from England. In 1891 he became one of the founders of an Irish literary society in London, the Rhymers' Club, and of another in Dublin the following year. Already a recognized poet, Yeats helped to establish the Irish National Theater in 1899; its first production was his play *The Countess Cathleen*, written in 1892. His contribution to Irish cultural and political nationalism led to his appointment as a senator when the Irish Free State was formed in 1922. Yeats's preeminence as a poet was recognized in 1923, when he received the Nobel Prize for Literature. Among his works are *The Wanderings of Oisin and Other Poems* (1889), *The Wind among the Reeds* (1899), *The Green Helmet and Other Poems* (1910), *Responsibilities: Poems and a Play* (1914), *The Tower* (1928), and *Last Poems and Two Plays* (1939).

YEVGENY YEVTUSHENKO (b. 1933) The son of two geologists, Yevtushenko was born in Siberia. He attended Gorky Literary Institute from 1951 to 1954 and worked on a geological expedition while establishing himself as an influential Soviet poet. During the 1950s his books were published regularly, and he was allowed to travel abroad. In 1960 he gave readings in Europe and the United States but was criticized by Russians for linking them with anti-Semitism in his poem "Babi Yar," the name of a ravine near Kiev where 96,000 Jews were killed by Nazis during World War II. Although considering himself a "loyal revolutionary Soviet citizen," he elicited official disapproval by opposing the 1968 occupation of Czechoslovakia (a performance of his play *Bratsk Power Station* [1967] was cancelled as a result) and for sending a telegram to then-Premier Brezhnev expressing concern for Aleksandr Solzhenitsyn after his arrest in 1974. His works include *A Precocious Autobiography* (1963); *From Desire to Desire* (1976); *Fatal Half Measures: The Culture of Democracy in the Soviet Union* (1991), an analysis of recent Russian history; and *Don't Die before You're Dead* (1995), an autobiographical novel.

DEAN YOUNG (b. 1955)   Young was born in Columbia, Pennsylvania, and currently lives in Berkeley, California. He teaches at the University of Iowa's Writers' Workshop and in the M.F.A. program at Warren Wilson College. He has been the recipient of fellowships from the Guggenheim Foundation, the National Endowment for the Arts, and Stanford University. He is the author of eight books of poetry, most recently *Skid* (2002), *Elegy on Toy Piano* (2005), *Embryoyo* (2007), and *Primitive Mentor* (2008). About his poems, Young has said, "I think they're very much about misunderstanding. . . . I wrote my first book to be understood, to be accepted. . . . And I realized that the poems in the first book weren't by me—they were instilled in my head. And that not being understood, not being accepted, was my subject." His recent volumes include *The Art of Recklessness: Poetry as Assertive Force and Contradiction* (2010) and *Fall Higher* (2011).

KEVIN YOUNG (b. 1970)   Young was born in Lincoln, Nebraska, and earned degrees from Harvard University and Brown University. He was a Stegner Fellow at Stanford University in the interim. Before taking on his current position as the William Livingston Chair of Poetry at the University of Texas at Austin in 2008, he taught at the University of Georgia, Indiana University, and Emory University. He has edited two collections in the Everyman's Library, *Blues Poems* (2003) and *Jazz Poems* (2006), and has published six volumes of his own poetry: *Most Way Home* (1998), *To Repel Ghosts: Five Sides in B Minor* (2002), *Jelly Roll: A Blues* (2003), *Black Maria: Poems Produced and Directed* (2005), *For the Confederate Dead* (2007), and *Dear Darkness* (2008). His work has also appeared in a number of periodicals, including *The New Yorker*, the *Paris Review*, *Ploughshares*, and *Poetry* magazine.

TIMOTHY YU (b. 1974)   Yu earned his B.A. from Harvard University and his Ph.D. from Stanford University. He is the author of *Race and the Avant-Garde: Experimental and Asian American Poetry Since 1965* (2009), which "delves into the 1960s social upheaval to trace how language and Asian American writing emerged as parallel poetics of the avant-garde, each with its own distinctive form, style, and political meaning." He has contributed poems and criticism to numerous publications, including *Interlope*, *Chicago Review*, *The Poetry Project Newsletter*, *Shampoo*, and *Cordite*. Yu is associate professor of English and Asian-American Studies at the University of Wisconsin-Madison.

GLOSSARY OF LITERARY TERMS

Abstract language   Language that describes ideas, concepts, or qualities, rather than particular or specific persons, places, or things. *Beauty, courage, love* are abstract terms, as opposed to such concrete terms as *man, stone, woman.* George Washington, the Rosetta stone, and Helen of Troy are particular concrete terms. Characteristically, literature uses *concrete* language to animate *abstract* ideas and principles. When Robert Frost, in "Provide, Provide," describes the pain of impoverished and lonely old age, he doesn't speak of an old, no longer beautiful female. He writes: "The witch that came (the withered hag) / To wash the steps with pail and rag, / Was once the beauty Abishag."

Alexandrine   In poetry, a line containing six iambic feet (iambic hexameter). Alexander Pope, in "An Essay on Criticism," reveals his distaste for the forms in a couplet: "A needless Alexandrine ends the song, / That, like a wounded snake, drags its slow length along." *See* Meter.

Allegory   A narrative in verse or prose, in which abstract qualities (*death, pride, greed,* for example) are personified as characters. In Nathaniel Hawthorne's story "Young Goodman Brown" (p. 79), Brown's wife personifies faith and the old man in the forest personifies Satan.

Alliteration   The repetition of the same consonant sounds, usually at the beginning of words in close proximity. The *w* sounds in these lines from Robert Frost's "Provide, Provide" alliterate: "The witch that came (the withered hag) / To wash the steps with pail and rag, / Was once the beauty Abishag."

Allusion   A reference in a literary work to something outside the work, usually to some famous person, place, thing, event, or other literary work.

Ambiguity   A phrase, statement, or situation that may be understood in two or more ways. In literature, ambiguity is used to enrich meaning or achieve irony by forcing readers to consider alternative possibilities. When the duke in Robert Browning's "My Last Duchess" (p. 179) says that he "gave commands; / Then all smiles stopped together. There she stands / As if alive," the reader cannot know exactly what those commands were or whether the last words refer to the commands (as a result of which she is no longer alive) or merely refer to the skill of the painter (the painting is extraordinarily lifelike).

Analogy   A comparison that uses a known thing or concept to explain something unfamiliar. *See* Metaphor; Simile.

Anapest   A three-syllable metrical foot consisting of two unaccented syllables followed by an accented syllable. *See* Meter.

Antagonist   A character in a story, play, or narrative poem who stands in opposition to the hero (*see* Protagonist). The conflict between antagonist and protagonist often generates the action or plot of the story.

Antistrophe   *See* Strophe.

Apostrophe   A direct address to a person who is absent or to an abstract or inanimate entity. In one of his sonnets (p. 1220), John Donne admonishes: "Death, be not proud!" And in "Lines Composed a Few Miles above Tintern Abbey," Wordsworth speaks to a river in Wales: "How oft, in spirit, have I turned to thee, / O sylvan Wye! thou wanderer through the woods."

Archaism   The literary use of obsolete language. When Keats, in "Ode on a Grecian Urn" (p. 1221), writes: "with brede / Of marble men and maidens overwrought," he uses an archaic word for *braid* and intends an obsolete definition, "worked all over" (that is, "ornamented"), for *overwrought*.

Archetype   Themes, images, and narrative patterns that are universal and thus embody some enduring aspects of human experience. Some of these themes are the death and rebirth of the hero, the underground journey, and the search for the father.

Assonance   The repetition of vowel sounds in a line, stanza, or sentence: *road nowhere*. By using assonance that occurs at the end of words—*my, pie*—or a combination of assonance and consonance (the repetition of final consonant sounds—*fish, wish*), poets create rhyme. Some poets use assonantial and consonantial off rhymes (*see* Near rhyme). W. H. Auden, in a celebrated verse from "Five Songs," writes: "That night when joy began / Our narrowest veins to flush, / We waited for the flash / Of morning's levelled gun." *Flush* and *gun* are assonantial, *flush* and *flash* are consonantial (and, of course, alliterative).

Atmosphere   The general feeling or mood created in the reader by a work. *See* Mood.

Aubade   A love song or lyric to be performed at sunrise.

Ballad   A narrative poem, originally of folk origin, usually focusing on a climactic episode and told without comment. The most common ballad form consists of quatrains of alternating four- and three-stress iambic lines, with the second and fourth lines rhyming. Often, the ballad will employ a *refrain*—that is, the last line of each stanza will be identical or similar. "Bonny Barbara Allan" (p. 897) is a traditional ballad. Dudley Randall's "Ballad of Birmingham" (p. 444) is a twentieth-century example of the ballad tradition.

Blank verse   Lines of unrhymed iambic pentameter. Shakespeare's dramatic poetry is written principally in blank verse. *See* Meter.

Caesura   A strong pause within a line of poetry. Note the caesuras indicated by a double vertical line (‖) in these lines from Robert Browning's "My Last Duchess" (p. 179): "That's my last Duchess painted on the wall, / Looking as if she were alive, ‖ I call / That piece a wonder, now: ‖ Frà Pandolf's hands / Worked busily a day, ‖ and there she stands."

Carpe diem   Latin, meaning "seize the day." A work, usually a lyric poem, in which the speaker calls the attention of the auditor (often a young woman) to the shortness of youth and life and then urges the auditor to enjoy life while there is time. Andrew Marvell's "To His Coy Mistress" (p. 944) is among the best of the *carpe diem* tradition in English. The opening stanza of a famous Robert Herrick poem nicely illustrates *carpe diem* principles: "Gather ye rosebuds while ye may, / Old Time is still a-flying / And this same flower that smiles today, / Tomorrow will be dying."

Catharsis   A key concept in the *Poetics* of Aristotle that attempts to explain why representations of suffering and death in drama paradoxically leave the audience feeling relieved rather than depressed. According to Aristotle, the fall of a tragic hero arouses in the viewer feelings of "pity" and "terror"—pity because the hero is an individual of great moral worth and terror because the viewer identifies with and, consequently, feels vulnerable to the hero's tragic fate. Ideally, the circumstances within the drama allow viewers to experience a catharsis that purges those feelings of pity and terror and leaves them emotionally purified.

Central intelligence   *See* Point of view.

Character   A person or figure in a literary work, sometimes classified as either *flat* (quickly describable) or *round* (more developed, complex). *See* Protagonist *and* Antagonist.

Characterization The means of presenting and developing a character, shown through the author's description, the character's actions or thoughts, or other characters' actions or thoughts.

Chorus Originally, a group of masked dancers who chanted lyric hymns at religious festivals in ancient Greece. In the plays of Sophocles, the chorus, while circling around the altar to Dionysus, chants the odes that separate the episodes. These odes, in some respects, represented an audience's reaction to, and comment on, the action in the episodes. In Elizabethan drama, and even, on occasion, in modern drama, the chorus appears, usually as a single person who comments on the action.

Comedy In drama, the representation of situations that are designed to delight and amuse and that end happily. Comedy often deals with ordinary people in their human condition, while tragedy deals with the ideal and heroic and, until recently, embodied only the high born as tragic heroes. *Compare* Tragedy.

Conceit A figure of speech that establishes an elaborate parallel between unlike things. The *Petrarchan conceit* (named for the fourteenth-century Italian writer of love lyrics) was often imitated by Elizabethan sonneteers until the device became so hackneyed that Shakespeare mocked the tendency in Sonnet 130 (p. 900): "My mistress' eyes are nothing like the sun; / Coral is far more red than her lips' red; / If snow be white, why then her breasts are dun; / If hairs be wires, black wires grow on her head." The *metaphysical conceit* employs strange, even bizarre, comparisons to heighten the wit of the poem. Perhaps the most famous metaphysical conceit is John Donne's elaborate and extended parallel of a drawing compass to the souls of the couple in "Valediction: Forbidding Mourning" (p. 902).

Concrete language *See* Abstract language.

Conflict The struggle of a protagonist, or main character, with forces that threaten to destroy him or her. The struggle creates suspense and is usually resolved at the end of the narrative. The force opposing the main character may be another person—the antagonist—or society (as in Harlan Ellison's "'Repent, Harlequin!' Said the Ticktockman," p. 401), or natural forces (as in Katherine Anne Porter's "The Jilting of Granny Weatherall," p. 1182). A fourth type of conflict reflects the struggle of opposing tendencies within an individual (as in Tolstoy's "The Death of Iván Ilých," p. 1114).

Connotation The associative and suggestive meanings of a word, in contrast to its literal or *denotative* meaning. One might speak of an *elected official*, a relatively neutral term without connotative implications. Others might call the same person a *politician*, a more negative term; still others might call him or her a *statesman*, a more laudatory term. *Compare* Denotation.

Consonance Repetition of the final consonant sounds in stressed syllables. In the second poem of W. H. Auden's "Five Songs," lines 1 and 4 illustrate consonance, as do lines 2 and 3. "That night when joy began / Our narrowest veins to flush, / We waited for the flash / Of morning's levelled gun."

Couplet A pair of rhymed lines—for example, these from A. E. Housman's "Terence, This Is Stupid Stuff" (p. 183). "Why, if 'tis dancing you would be, / There's brisker pipes than poetry."

Dactyl A three-syllable metrical foot consisting of an accented syllable followed by two unaccented syllables. *See* Meter.

Denotation The literal dictionary definition of a word, without associative and suggestive meanings. *See* Connotation.

Denouement The final revelations that occur after the main conflict is resolved; literally, the "untying" of the plot following the climax.

Deus ex machina Latin for "god from a machine." Difficulties were sometimes resolved in ancient Greek and Roman plays by a god, who was lowered to the stage by means of machinery. The term is now used to indicate unconvincing or improbable coincidences that are used to advance or resolve a plot.

Dialect A variety of a language distinguished by its pronunciation, vocabulary, rhetoric, and grammar. When used in dialogue, dialect reveals a character's membership in certain groups or communities.

Dialogue The exchange of words between characters in a drama or narrative.

Diction The choice of words in a work of literature and hence an element of style crucial to the work's effectiveness. The diction of a story told from the point of view of an inner-city child (as in Toni Cade Bambara's "The Lesson," p. 96) will differ markedly from a similar story told from the point of view of a mature and educated adult, like the narrator of James Joyce's "Araby" (p. 122).

Didactic A term applied to works with the primary and avowed purpose of persuading the reader that some philosophical, religious, or moral doctrine is true.

Dimeter A line of poetry consisting of two metrical feet. *See* Meter.

Distance The property that separates an author or a narrator from the actions of the characters he or she creates, thus allowing a disinterested, or aloof, narration of events. Similarly, distance allows the reader or audience to view the characters and events in a narrative dispassionately.

Dramatic irony *See* Irony.

Dramatic monologue A type of poem in which the speaker addresses another person (or persons) whose presence is known only from the speaker's words. During the course of the monologue, the speaker (often unintentionally) reveals his or her own character. Such poems are dramatic because the speaker interacts with another character at a specific time and place; they are monologues because the entire poem is uttered by the speaker. Robert Browning's "My Last Duchess" (p. 179), Matthew Arnold's "Dover Beach" (p. 909), and T. S. Eliot's "The Love Song of J. Alfred Prufrock" (p. 675) are dramatic monologues.

Elegy Usually, a poem that laments the death of a particular person. The term often is used to describe meditative poems on the subject of human mortality. A. E. Housman's "To an Athlete Dying Young" (p. 1226) is an elegy.

End-rhyme *See* Rhyme.

End-stopped line A line of verse that embodies a complete logical and grammatical unit. A line of verse that does not constitute a complete syntactic unit is called *run-on*. For example, in the opening lines of Robert Browning's "My Last Duchess" (p. 179): "That's my last Duchess painted on the wall, / Looking as if she were alive. I call / That piece a wonder, now . . . ," the opening line is end-stopped while the second line is run-on, because the direct object of *call* runs on to the third line.

English sonnet Also called *Shakespearean sonnet. See* Sonnet.

Enjambment The use of run-on lines. *See* End-stopped line.

Epigraph In literature, a short quotation or observation related to the theme and placed at the head of the work. T. S. Eliot's "The Love Song of J. Alfred Prufrock" (p. 675) has an epigraph.

Epiphany In literature, a showing forth, or sudden manifestation. James Joyce used the term to indicate a sudden illumination that enables a character (and, presumably, the reader) to understand his situation. The narrator of Joyce's "Araby" (p. 122) experiences an epiphany toward the end of the story, as does Leo Tolstoy's Iván Ilých (p. 1114).

Epode *See* Strophe.

Euphony Language embodying sounds pleasing to the ear.

Exposition Information supplied to readers and audiences that enables them to understand narrative action. Often, exposition establishes what has occurred before the narrative begins, or informs the audience about relationships among principal characters. The absence of exposition from some modern literature, particularly modern drama, contributes to the unsettling feelings sometimes experienced by the audience.

Farce A type of comedy, usually satiric, that relies on exaggerated character types, ridiculous situations, and often horseplay.

Feminine rhyme A two-syllable rhyme in which the second syllable is unstressed, as in the second and fourth lines of these verses from James Fenton's "God, A Poem": "A nasty surprise in a sandwich, / A drawing-pin caught in your sock, / The limpest of shakes from a hand which / You'd thought would be firm as a rock."

Figurative language A general term covering the many ways in which language is used nonliterally. *See* Hyperbole, Irony, Metaphor, Metonymy, Paradox, Simile, Symbol, Synecdoche, Understatement.

First-person narrator *See* Point of view.

Foot *See* Meter.

Free verse Poetry, usually unrhymed, that does not adhere to the metrical regularity of traditional verse. Although free verse is not metrically regular, it is nonetheless clearly more rhythmic than prose and makes use of other aspects of poetic discourse to achieve its effects.

Heroic couplet Iambic pentameter lines that rhyme *aa*, *bb*, *cc*, and so on. Usually, heroic couplets are *closed*—that is, the couplet's end coincides with a major syntactic unit so that the line is end-stopped. These lines from Alexander Pope's "Essay on Man" illustrate the form: "And, spite of pride, in erring reason's spite, / One truth is clear; Whatever IS, IS RIGHT."

Hexameter A line of verse consisting of six metrical feet. *See* Meter.

Hubris In Greek tragedy, arrogance resulting from excessive pride.

Hyperbole Figurative language that embodies overstatement or exaggeration. The boast of the speaker in Robert Burns's "A Red, Red Rose" (p. 909) is hyperbolic: "And I will luve thee still, my dear, / Til a' the seas gang dry."

Iamb A metrical foot consisting of an unstressed syllable followed by a stressed syllable. *See* Meter.

Imagery Language that embodies an appeal to a physical sense, usually sight, although the words may invoke sound, smell, taste, and touch as well. The term is often applied to all figurative language. *Images* illustrate a concept, thing, or process by appealing to the senses.

Internal rhyme *See* Rhyme.

Irony Figurative language in which the intended meaning differs from the literal meaning. *Verbal irony* includes overstatement (hyperbole), understatement, and opposite statement. The following lines from Robert Burns's "A Red, Red Rose" (p. 909) embody overstatement: "As fair art thou, my bonnie lass, / So deep in luve am I; / And I will luve thee still, my dear, / Til a' the seas gang dry." These lines from Andrew Marvell's "To His Coy Mistress" (p. 944) understate: "The grave's a fine and private place, / But none, I think, do there embrace." W. H. Auden's ironic conclusion to "The Unknown Citizen" (p. 443) reveals opposite statement: "Was he free? Was he happy? The question is absurd: / Had anything been wrong, we should certainly have heard." *Dramatic irony* occurs when a reader or an audience knows things a character does not and, consequently, hears things differently. For example, in Shakespeare's *Othello* (p. 947), the audience knows that Iago is Othello's enemy, but Othello doesn't. Hence, the audience's understanding of Iago's speeches to Othello differs markedly from Othello's.

Italian sonnet   Also called *Petrarchan sonnet*. *See* Sonnet.

Lyric   Originally, a song accompanied by lyre music. Now, a relatively short poem expressing the thought or feeling of a single speaker. Almost all the nondramatic poetry in this anthology is lyric poetry.

Metaphor   A figurative expression consisting of two elements in which one element is provided with special attributes by being equated with a second, unlike element. *See* Simile.

Meter   Refers to recurrent patterns of accented and unaccented syllables in verse. A metrical unit is called a *foot*, and there are four basic accented patterns. An *iamb*, or *iambic foot*, consists of an unaccented syllable followed by an accented syllable (bĕfóre, tŏdáy). A *trochee*, or *trochaic foot*, consists of an accented syllable followed by an unaccented syllable (fúnnў, phántŏm). An *anapest*, or *anapestic foot*, consists of two unaccented syllables followed by an accented syllable (in the line "If ĕv ‖ erўthĭng háp ‖ pĕns thăt cán't ‖ bĕ dóne," the second and third metrical feet are anapests). A *dactyl*, or *dactylic foot*, consists of a stressed syllable followed by two unstressed syllables (sýllăblĕ, métrĭcăl). One common variant, consisting of two stressed syllables, is called a *spondee*, or *spondaic foot* (dáybréak, moónshíne).

Lines are classified according to the number of metrical feet they contain (an iambic hexameter line is an *alexandrine*):

one foot	monometer
two feet	dimeter
three feet	trimeter
four feet	tetrameter
five feet	pentameter
six feet	hexameter

Here are some examples of various metrical patterns:

Tŏ eách ‖ hĭs súff ‖ erĭngs: áll ‖ ăre mén,	*iambic tetrameter*
Cŏndemnéd ‖ ăliké ‖ tŏ groán;	*iambic trimeter*
Ónce ŭp ‖ ón ă ‖ mídnĭght ‖ dréarў, ‖ whĭle Ĭ ‖	
póndĕred ‖ wéak ănd ‖ wéarў	*trochaic octameter*
Thĕ Ăssýr ‖ iăn căme dówn ‖ likĕ ă wólf ‖ ŏn thĕ fóld	*anapestic tetrameter*
Iš thís ‖ thĕ rég ‖ iŏn, thís ‖ thĕ soíl, ‖ thĕ clíme,	*iambic pentameter*
Fóllŏw ĭt ‖ úttĕrlў,	*dactylic dimeter*
Hópe bĕ ‖ yónd hópe:	*dimeter line—trochee and spondee*

Metonymy   A figure of speech in which a word stands for a closely related idea. In the expression "The pen is mightier than the sword," *pen* and *sword* are metonyms for written ideas and physical force.

Monologue   A long, uninterrupted speech by a character.

Mood   The atmosphere or general feeling of a work. *See* Atmosphere.

Muses   The nine daughters of Zeus and Mnemosyne (memory) who preside over various humanities. Although there are some variations, generally they may be assigned as follows: Calliope, epic poetry; Clio, history; Erato, lyric poetry; Euterpe, music; Melpomene, tragedy; Polyhymnia, sacred poetry; Terpsichore, dance; Thalia, comedy; and Urania, astronomy.

Narrator   The speaker of the story, not to be confused with the author. For kinds of narrators, *see* Point of view.

Near rhyme   Also called *off rhyme*, *slant rhyme*, or *oblique rhyme*. Usually the occurrence of consonance where rhyme is expected, as in *pearl*, *alcohol*, or *heaven*, *given*. *See* Rhyme.

Octave   An eight-line stanza. More often, the opening eight-line section of an Italian sonnet, rhymed *abbaabba*, followed by the sestet that concludes the poem. *See* Sonnet.

Ode   Usually, a long, serious poem on exalted subjects, often in the form of an address. Keats's "Ode on a Grecian Urn" (p. 1221) is representative. In Greek dramatic poetry, odes consisting of three parts—the *strophe*, the *antistrophe*, and the *epode*—were sung by the chorus between the episodes of the play. *See* Strophe.

Off rhyme   *See* Near rhyme.

Omniscient narrator   *See* Point of view.

Onomatopoeia   Language that sounds like what it means. Words like *buzz*, *bark*, and *hiss* are onomatopoetic. Also, sound patterns that reinforce the meaning may be designated onomatopoetic. Alexander Pope illustrates such onomatopoeia in this passage from "An Essay on Criticism":

> 'Tis not enough no harshness gives offense,
> The sound must seem an echo to the sense:
> Soft is the strain when Zephyr gently blows,
> And the smooth stream in smoother numbers flows;
> But when loud surges lash the sounding shore,
> The hoarse, rough verse should like the torrent roar:
> When Ajax strives some rock's vast weight to throw,
> The line too labors, and the words move slow;
> Not so, when swift Camilla scours the plain,
> Flies o'er the unbending corn, and skims along the main.

Opposite statement   *See* Irony.

Ottava rima   An eight-line, iambic pentameter stanza rhymed *abababcc*. Originating with the Italian poet Boccaccio, the form was made popular in English poetry by Milton, Keats, and Byron, among others.

Oxymoron   Literally, "acutely silly." A figure of speech in which contradictory ideas are combined to create a condensed paradox: *thunderous silence*, *sweet sorrow*, *wise fool*.

Paean   In classical Greek drama, a hymn of praise, usually honoring Apollo. Now, any lyric that joyously celebrates its subject.

Paradox   A statement that seems self-contradictory or absurd but is, somehow, valid. The conclusion of Donne's "Death, Be Not Proud" (p. 1220) illustrates: "One short sleep past, we wake eternally / And death shall be no more; Death, thou shalt die." In Holy Sonnet 14, Donne, speaking of his relationship with God, writes: "Take me to You, imprison me, for I, / Except You enthrall me, never shall be free, / Nor ever chaste, except You ravish me."

Parody   An imitation of a work using the original's form or content as a model, meant to criticize or create a humorous effect.

Pastoral   *Pastor* is Latin for "shepherd," and the pastoral is a poetic form invented by ancient Roman writers that deals with the complexities of the human condition as if they exist in a world peopled by idealized rustic shepherds. Pastoral poetry suggests that country life is superior to urban life. In the hands of such English poets as Marlowe and Milton, the pastoral embodies highly conventionalized and artificial language and situations. Christopher

Marlowe's "The Passionate Shepherd to His Love" (p. 943) is a famous example, as is Sir Walter Raleigh's mocking response, "The Nymph's Reply to the Shepherd" (p. 942).

Pentameter   A line containing five metrical feet. *See* Meter.

Persona   Literally, "actor's mask." The term is applied to a first-person narrator in fiction or poetry. The persona's views may differ from the author's.

Personification   The attribution of human qualities to nonhuman things, such as animals, aspects of nature, or even ideas and processes. When Donne exclaims in "Death, Be Not Proud" (p. 1220), "Death, thou shalt die," he uses personification.

Petrarchan sonnet   Also called *Italian sonnet*. *See* Sonnet.

Plot   A series of events in a story or drama that bear a significant relationship to each other. E. M. Forster illuminates the definition: "'The King died, and then the Queen died,' is a story. 'The King died, and then the Queen died of grief,' is a plot."

Poetic license   Variation from standard word order to satisfy the demands of rhyme and meter.

Point of view   The person or intelligence a writer of fiction creates to tell the story to the reader. The major techniques are: (1) *first person*, where the story is told by someone (often, though not necessarily, the principal character) who identifies himself or herself as "I," as in James Joyce's "Araby" (p. 122); (2) *third person*, where the story is told by someone (not identified as "I") who is not a participant in the action and who refers to the characters by name or as "he," "she," and "they," as in Harlan Ellison's "'Repent, Harlequin!' Said the Ticktockman" (p. 401); (3) *omniscient*, a variation on the third person, where the narrator knows everything about the characters and events, can move about in time and place as well as from character to character at will, and can, whenever he or she wishes, enter the mind of any character, as in Tolstoy's "The Death of Iván Ilých" (p. 1114); (4) *central intelligence*, another variation on the third person, where narrative elements are limited to what a single character sees, thinks, and hears, as in Toni Cade Bambara's "The Lesson" (p. 96). *See also* Unreliable narrator.

Prose   Ordinary written or spoken expression, resembling everyday language or speech.

Prosody   The study of the elements of versification, such as *rhyme, meter, stanzaic patterns*, and so on.

Protagonist   Originally, the first actor in a Greek drama. In Greek, *agon* means "contest." Hence, the protagonist is the hero, the main character in a narrative, in conflict either with his or her situation or with another character. *See* Antagonist.

Quatrain   A four-line stanza.

Refrain   The repetition within a poem of a group of words, often at the end of ballad stanzas.

Rhyme   The repetition of the final stressed vowel sound and any sounds following (*cat, rat; debate, relate; pelican, belly can*) produces perfect rhyme. When the last stressed syllable rhymes, the rhyme is called masculine (*cat, rat*). Two-syllable rhymes with unstressed last syllables are called feminine (*ending, bending*). When rhyming words appear at the end of lines, the poem is *end-rhymed*. When rhyming words appear within one line, the line contains *internal rhyme*. When the correspondence in sounds is imperfect (*heaven, given; began, gun*), *off rhyme, slant rhyme*, or *near rhyme* is produced.

Rhythm   The quality created by the relationship between stressed and unstressed syllables. A regular pattern of alternation between stressed and unstressed syllables produces *meter*. Irregular alternation of stressed and unstressed syllables produces *free verse*. Compare the rhythm of the following verses from Robert Frost's "Stopping by Woods on a Snowy Evening" (p. 1240) and Walt Whitman's "Out of the Cradle Endlessly Rocking":

> Whose woods these are I think I know.
> His house is in the village though;
> He will not see me stopping here
> To watch his woods fill up with snow.

> Out of the cradle endlessly rocking,
> Out of the mocking-bird's throat, the musical shuttle,
> Out of the Ninth-month midnight,
> Over the sterile sands and the fields beyond, where the child leaving his bed
>   wander'd alone, bareheaded, barefoot,
> Down from the shower'd halo.

Run-on line   *See* End-stopped line.

Satire   Writing in a comic mode that holds a subject up to scorn and ridicule, often with the purpose of correcting human vice and folly. Harlan Ellison's "'Repent, Harlequin!' Said the Ticktockman" (p. 401) satirizes a society obsessed with time and order.

Scansion   The analysis of patterns of stressed and unstressed syllables to establish the metrical or rhythmical pattern of a poem.

Sestet   The six-line resolution of a Petrarchan sonnet. *See* Sonnet.

Setting   The place, time, and social context in which a work occurs. Often the setting contributes significantly to the story; for example, the tawdry gloom at the fair in James Joyce's "Araby" (p. 122) destroys the narrator's expectations.

Shakespearean sonnet   Also called *English sonnet*. *See* Sonnet.

Simile   Similar to metaphor, the simile is a comparison of unlike things introduced by the words *like* or *as*. For example, Robert Burns, in "A Red, Red Rose" (p. 909), exclaims, "O My Luve's like a red, red rose," and Shakespeare mocks extravagant similes when he admits in Sonnet 130, "My mistress' eyes are nothing like the sun" (p. 900).

Slant rhyme   *See* Rhyme.

Soliloquy   A dramatic convention in which an actor, alone on the stage, speaks his or her thoughts aloud. Iago's speech that closes act I of Shakespeare's *Othello* (p. 947) is a soliloquy, as is Othello's speech in act III, scene 3, lines 258–79.

Sonnet   A lyric poem of fourteen lines, usually of iambic pentameter. The two major types are the Petrarchan (or Italian) and Shakespearean (or English). The Petrarchan sonnet is divided into an octave (the first eight lines, rhymed *abbaabba*) and sestet (the final six lines, usually rhymed *cdecde* or *cdcdcd*). The Shakespearean sonnet consists of three quatrains and a concluding couplet, rhymed *abab cdcd efef gg*. In general, the sonnet establishes some issue in the octave or three quatrains and then resolves it in the sestet or final couplet. Robert Frost's "Design" (p. 1241) is a Petrarchan sonnet; several Shakespearean sonnets appear in the text.

Spondee   A metrical foot consisting of two stressed syllables, usually a variation within a metrical line. *See* Meter.

Stanza   The grouping of a fixed number of verse lines in a recurring metrical and rhyme pattern. Keats's "Ode on a Grecian Urn" (p. 1221), for example, employs ten-line stanzas rhymed *ababcdecde*.

Stream-of-consciousness technique   The narrative technique that attempts to reproduce the full and uninterrupted flow of a character's mental process, in which ideas, memories, and sense impressions may intermingle without logical transitions. Writers using this technique sometimes abandon conventional rules of syntax and punctuation.

Strophe In Greek tragedy, the unit of verse the chorus chanted as it moved to the left in a dance rhythm. The chorus sang the *antistrophe* as it moved to the right and the *epode* while standing still.

Style The way an author expresses his or her matter. Style embodies, and depends upon, all the choices an author makes—the diction, syntax, figurative language, and sound patterns of the piece.

Subplot A second plot, usually involving minor characters. The subplot is subordinate to the principal plot but is often resolved by events that figure in the main plot. For example, Iago's manipulation of Roderigo in Shakespeare's *Othello* (p. 947) is a subplot that enters the main plot and figures prominently in the play's climax.

Symbol An object, an action, or a person that represents more than itself. The urn in Keats's "Ode on a Grecian Urn" (p. 1221) symbolizes the cold immortality of art. The symbolism arises from the *context*. *Public symbols*, in contrast to these *contextual symbols*, are objects, actions, or persons that history, myth, or legend has invested with meaning—the cross, Helen of Troy, a national flag.

Synecdoche A figure of speech in which a part is used to signify the whole. In "Elegy Written in a Country Churchyard," Thomas Gray writes of "Some heart once pregnant with celestial fire; / Hands that the rod of empire might have swayed." That heart, and those hands, of course, refer to whole persons who are figuratively represented by significant parts.

Synesthesia An image that uses a second sensory impression to modify the primary sense impression. When one speaks of a "cool green," for example, the primary *visual* evocation of green is combined with the *tactile* sensation of coolness. Keats, in "Ode to a Nightingale," asks for a drink of wine "Tasting of Flora and the country green, / Dance, and Provençal song, and sunburnt mirth!" Here, the *taste* of wine is synesthetically extended to the sight of flowers and meadows, the movement of dance, the sound of song, and the heat of the sun.

Tetrameter A verse line containing four metrical feet. *See* Meter.

Theme The statement or underlying idea of a literary work, advanced through the concrete elements of character, action, and setting. The theme of Harlan Ellison's "'Repent, Harlequin!' Said the Ticktockman" (p. 401), in which an ordinary person defies an oppressive system, might be that to struggle against dehumanizing authority is obligatory.

Third-person narrator A voice telling a story who refers to characters by name or as "he," "she," or "they." *See* Point of view.

Tone The attitude embodied in the language a writer chooses. The tone authors take in a work toward readers, the subject matter, or themselves might be sad, joyful, ironic, solemn, playful. Notice, for example, the somber tone of Matthew Arnold's "Dover Beach" (p. 909).

Tragedy The dramatic representation of serious and important actions that culminate in catastrophe for the protagonist, or chief actor, in the play. Aristotle saw tragedy as the fall of a noble figure from a high position and happiness to defeat and misery as a result of *hamartia*, some misjudgment or frailty of character. *Compare* Comedy.

Trimeter A verse line consisting of three metrical feet. *See* Meter.

Triplet A sequence of three verse lines that rhyme.

Trochee A metrical foot consisting of a stressed syllable followed by an unstressed syllable. *See* Meter.

Understatement   A figure of speech that represents something as less important than it really is—hence, a form of irony. When in Robert Browning's "My Last Duchess" (p. 179) the duke asserts, "This grew; I gave commands; / Then all smiles stopped together," the words ironically understate what was likely an order for his wife's execution.

Unreliable narrator   The speaker or voice of a work who is not able to accurately or objectively report events, as in Charlotte Perkins Gilman's "The Yellow Wallpaper" (p. 551).

Verse   A stanza of a poem. More generally, verse can be used interchangeably with the term *poetry*.

Villanelle   A French verse form of nineteen lines (of any length) divided into six stanzas—five tercets and a final quatrain—employing two rhymes and two refrains. The refrains consist of lines 1 (repeated as lines 6, 12, and 18) and 3 (repeated as lines 9, 15, and 19). Dylan Thomas's "Do Not Go Gentle into That Good Night" (p. 1242) and Catherine Davis's response "After a Time" (p. 1243) are villanelles.

Acknowledgments (continued from p. ii)

Text Credits

Chimamanda Ngozi Adichie. "Birdsong" by Chimamanda Ngozi Adichie, originally published in *The New Yorker*. Copyright © 2010 by Chimamanda Ngozi Adichie, used by permission of The Wylie Agency LLC.

Anna Akhmatova. From "Requiem" from *Anna Akhmatova: Poems* by Anna Akhmatova, translated by Lyn Coffin. Copyright © 1983 by Lyn Coffin. Used by permission of W. W. Norton & Company, Inc.

Sherman Alexie. "War Dances" from *War Dances*. Copyright © 2009 by Sherman Alexie. Used by permission of Grove/Atlantic, Inc.

Woody Allen. "Death Knocks" from *Getting Even* by Woody Allen. Copyright © 1966, 1967, 1968, 1969, 1970, 1971 by Woody Allen.

Julia Alvarez. "Woman's Work" from *Homecoming*. Copyright © 1984, 1996 by Julia Alvarez. Published by Plume, an imprint of Penguin Group (USA); originally published by Grove Press. By permission of Susan Bergholz Literary Services, New York, NY and Lamy, NM. All rights reserved.

Maggie Anderson. "Long Story" from *A Space Filled with Moving*, by Maggie Anderson. Copyright © 1992. Reprinted by permission of the University of Pittsburgh Press.

Anonymous. 56 lines from "Edward" from *The First Poems in English* translated and edited by Michael Alexander (translations first published 1966, revised and expanded 1991. This edition first published in 2008). Copyright © Michael Alexander 1966, 1977, 1991, 2008.

Hanan Mikha'il Ashrawi. Excerpt from the "Diary of an Almost Four-Year-Old" and "Night Patrol" from *Anthology of Modern Palestinian Literature* edited by Salma Khadra Jayyusi. Copyright © 1992 by Columbia University Press. Reprinted with the permission of the publisher.

W. H. Auden. "Musée des Beaux Arts" and "The Unknown Citizen." Copyright © 1940 and renewed 1968 by W.H. Auden, from *Collected Poems of W.H. Auden* by W.H. Auden. Used by permission of Random House, Inc.

James Baldwin. "Sonny's Blues." Copyright © 1957 by James Baldwin was originally published in *Partisan Review*. Copyright renewed. Collected in *Going to Meet the Man*, published by Vintage Books. Used by arrangement with the James Baldwin Estate.

Toni Cade Bambara. "The Lesson" from *Gorilla, My Love* by Toni Cade Bambara. Copyright © 1972 by Toni Cade Bambara. Used by permission of Random House, Inc.

Aimee Bender. "Tiger Mending" from *Black Book Magazine*. Reprinted by permission of the author.

Bruce Bennett. "The True Story of Snow White" from *Navigating the Distance: Poems New and Old Selected* by Bruce Bennett. Copyright © 1999 by Bruce Bennett. Reprinted with permission of the author.

Elizabeth Bishop. "One Art" and "The Fish" from *The Complete Poems 1927–1979* by Elizabeth Bishop. Copyright © 1979, 1983 by Alice Helen Methfessel. Reprinted by permission of Farrar, Straus and Giroux, LLC.

Adrian Blevins. "The Case Against April" from *The Brass Girl Brouhaha*. Copyright © 2003 by Adrian Blevins. Reprinted with the permission of The Permissions Company, Inc. on behalf of Copper Canyon Press, www.coppercanyonpress.org.

T. Coraghessan Boyle. "Admiral" from *Wild Child and Other Stories* by T. Coraghessan Boyle. Copyright © 2010 by T. Coraghessan Boyle. Used by permission of Viking Penguin, a division of Penguin Group (USA) Inc.

Robert H. Brinkmeyer. "Flannery O'Connor and Her Readers" from *The Art and Vision of Flannery O'Connor* by Robert H. Brinkmeyer (Louisiana State University Press, 1989). Reprinted by permission of Louisiana State University Press.

Gwendolyn Brooks. "The Mother" and "We Real Cool." Reprinted by consent of Brooks Permissions.

Hallman B. Bryant. "Reading the Map in 'A Good Man Is Hard to Find'" from *Studies in Short Fiction* 18.3 (Summer 1981): 301–07.

Rebecca R. Butler. "What's So Funny about Flannery O'Connor?" Reprinted from *The Flannery O'Connor Bulletin*.

Rachel Carson. "The Obligation to Endure" from *Silent Spring* by Rachel Carson. Copyright © 1962 by Rachel L. Carson. Copyright © renewed 1990 by Roger Christie. Reprinted by permission of Houghton Mifflin Harcourt Publishing Company. All rights reserved.

Raymond Carver. "What We Talk About When We Talk About Love" from *What We Talk About When We Talk About Love* by Raymond Carver. Copyright © 1974, 1976, 1978, 1980, 1981 by Raymond Carver. Used by permission of Alfred A. Knopf, a division of Random House, Inc.

Sandra M. Castillo. "Christmas, 1970" from *My Father Sings, To My Embarrassment.* Copyright © 2002 by Sandra M. Castillo. Reprinted with the permission of The Permissions Company, Inc., on behalf of White Pine Press, www.whitcpinc.org.

Marilyn Chin. "How I Got That Name" from *The Phoenix Gone, The Terrace Empty* by Marilyn Chin (Minneapolis: Milkweed Editions, 1994). Copyright © 1994 by Marilyn Chin. Reprinted with permission from Milkweed Editions. www.milkweed.org.

Kate Chopin. "The Storm" from *The Complete Works of Kate Chopin* (Louisiana State University Press, 1969). Reprinted by permission of Louisiana State University Press.

Jill Christman. "The Sloth" by Jill Christman. Copyright © 2008 by Jill Christman. First published in *Brevity* 26, Winter 2008. Reprinted by permission of Brandt & Hochman Literary Agents, Inc. All rights reserved.

Sandra Cisneros. "My Wicked, Wicked Ways" from *My Wicked, Wicked Ways.* Copyright © 1987 by Sandra Cisneros, published by Third Woman Press and in hardcover by Alfred A. Knopf. By permission of Third Woman Press and Susan Bergholz. All rights reserved.

Lucille Clifton. "There Is a Girl Inside." Copyright © 1977, 1980 by Lucille Clifton. First appeared in American Poetry Review. Now appears in *good woman: poems and a memoir 1969–1980*, published BOA Editions Ltd. Reprinted by permission of Curtis Brown, Ltd.

Joshua Clover. "The Nevada Glassworks" from *Madonna Anno Domini* by Joshua Clover. Copyright © 1997. Reprinted by permission of Louisiana State University Press.

Judith Ortiz Cofer. "American History" from *The Latin Deli: Prose and Poetry* by Judith Ortiz Cofer. Copyright © 1993 by Judith Ortiz Cofer. Reprinted with the permission of The University of Georgia Press.

———. "Latin Women Pray" from *Reaching for the Mainland and Selected New Poems* by Judith Ortiz Cofer; Bilingual Press/Editorial Bilingüe, 1995, Tempe, Arizona.

Billy Collins. "Monday" from *The Trouble with Poetry* by Billy Collins. Copyright © 2005 by Billy Collins. Used by permission of Random House, Inc.

———. Chris Calhoun Agency for the poem "Sandhill Cranes of Nebraska" by Billy Collins, copyright © Billy Collins.

———. "Sonnet." Copyright © 2001 by Billy Collins, from *Sailing Alone Around the Room* by Billy Collins. Used by permission of Random House, Inc.

Countee Cullen. "Incident." Copyrights held by Amistad Research Center, Tulane University. Administered by Thompson and Thompson, Brooklyn, NY.

e. e. cummings. "in Just-" and "the Cambridge ladies who live in furnished souls," copyright © 1923, 1951, 1991 by the Trustees for the E. E. Cummings Trust. Copyright © 1976 by George James Firmage. "she being Brand." Copyright © 1926, 1954, 1991 by the Trustees for the E. E.Cummings Trust. Copyright © 1985 by George James Firmage. From *Complete Poems: 1904–1962* by E. E. Cummings, edited by George J. Firmage. Used by permission of Liveright Publishing Corporation.

Meghan Daum. "Virtual Love." Reprinted by permission of International Creative Management, Inc. Copyright © 1997 by Meghan Daum.

Donald Davie. "The Nonconformist." *Selected Poems* (Carcanet, 1985).

Catherine Davis. "After a Time." Reprinted with permission of the author.

Carl Dennis. "Thanksgiving Letter from Harry" from *Unknown Friends* by Carl Dennis. Copyright © 2007 by Carl Dennis. Used by permission of Penguin, a division of Penguin Group (USA) Inc.

Emily Dickinson. "I felt a Funeral, in my Brain," "Much Madness is divinest Sense," "She rose to His Requirement," "I'm Nobody! Who are you?," "What Soft—Cherubic Creatures—," "After great pain, a formal feeling comes," "I heard a Fly buzz—when I died," "Apparently with no surprise," and "Because I could not stop for Death." Reprinted by permission of the publishers and the Trustees of Amherst College from *The Poems of Emily Dickinson*, Thomas H. Johnson, ed., Cambridge, Mass.: The Belknap Press of Harvard University Press. Copyright © 1951, 1955, 1979, 1983 by the President and Fellows of Harvard College.

E. L. Doctorow. "Why We Are Infidels" reprinted by permission of the publisher from *Reporting the Universe* by E. L. Doctorow, pp. 8388, Cambridge, Mass.: Harvard University Press, Copyright © 2003 by E. L. Doctorow.

Rita Dove. "My Mother Enters the Work Force" from *On the Bus with Rosa Parks*, W.W. Norton & Company, New York, N. Copyright © 1999 by Rita Dove. Reprinted by permission of the author.

Brian Doyle. "Joyas Voladores." Reprinted from *The American Scholar*, Volume 73, No. 4, Autumn 2004. Copyright © 2004 by the author.

William Greenway. "Pit Pony." Reprinted by permission of the author.

Linda Gregerson. "Sweet" from *Magnetic North: Poems* by Linda Gregerson. Copyright © 2007 by Linda Gregerson. Reprinted by permission of Houghton Mifflin Harcourt Publishing Company. All rights reserved.

Marilyn Hacker. "Conte" from *Taking Notice* by Marilyn Hacker. Copyright © 1976, 1978, 1979, 1980 by Marilyn Hacker. Reprinted by permission of Frances Collin, Literary Agent.

Donald Hall. "Affirmation" from *The Painted Bed: Poems* by Donald Hall. Copyright © 2002 by Donald Hall. Reprinted by permission of Houghton Mifflin Harcourt Publishing Company. All rights reserved.

Mark Halliday. "Chicken Salad," from *The Gettysburg Review* and *Keep This Forever* (Tupelo Press, 2008). Reprinted by permission of the author.

Sam Hamill. "The Orchid Flower" from *Dumb Luck* (Rochester: BOA Editions, 2002). Copyright © 2002 by Sam Hamill. Reprinted by permission of The Permissions Company, Inc., on behalf of Sam Hamill.

Lorraine Hansberry. *A Raisin in the Sun* by Lorraine Hansberry. Copyright © 1958 by Robert Nemiroff, as an unpublished work. Copyright © 1959, 1966, 1984 by Robert Nemiroff. Copyright renewed 1986, 1987 by Robert Nemiroff. Used by permission of Random House, Inc.

Robert Hass. "Meditation at Lagunitas" from *Praise* by Robert Hass. Copyright © 1979 by Robert Hass. Reprinted by permission of HarperCollins Publishers.

Robert Hayden. "Those Winter Sundays." Copyright © 1966 by Robert Hayden, from *Collected Poems of Robert Hayden* by Robert Hayden, edited by Frederick Glaysher. Used by permission of Liveright Publishing Corporation.

Terrance Hayes. "Root" from *Wind in a Box* by Terrance Hayes. Copyright © 2006 by Terrance Hayes. Used by permission of Penguin, a division of Penguin Group (USA) Inc.

Seamus Heaney. "Valediction" and "Mid-Term Break" from *Opened Ground: Selected Poems 1966–1996* by Seamus Heaney. Copyright © 1998 by Seamus Heaney. Reprinted by permission of Farrar, Straus and Giroux, LLC and Faber & Faber Ltd.

Ernest Hemingway. "Hills Like White Elephants," reprinted with the permission of Scribner, a Division of Simon & Schuster, Inc., from *The Short Stories of Ernest Hemingway* by Ernest Hemingway. Copyright © 1927 by Charles Scribner's Sons. Copyright renewed © 1955 by Ernest Hemingway. All rights reserved.

Juan Felipe Herrera. "187 Reasons Mexicanos Can't Cross the Border (Remix)." From *187 Reasons Mexicanos Can't Cross the Border: Undocuments* by Juan Felipe Herrera. Copyright © 2007. Reprinted by permission.

Edward Hirsch. "Wild Gratitude" from *Wild Gratitude* by Edward Hirsch. Copyright © 1985 by Edward Hirsch. Used by permission of Alfred A. Knopf, a division of Random House, Inc.

Tony Hoagland. "I Have News for You" from *Unincorporated Persons in the Late Honda Dynasty*. Copyright © 2010 by Tony Hoagland. Reprinted with the permission of The Permissions Company, Inc., on behalf of Graywolf Press, Minneapolis, Minnesota, www.graywolfpress.org.

Marie Howe. "What the Living Do" from *What the Living Do* by Marie Howe. Copyright © 1997 by Marie Howe. Used by permission of W. W. Norton & Company, Inc.

Langston Hughes. "Mother to Son," "Harlem (2)," and "I, Too," from *The Collected Poems of Langston Hughes*. Copyright © 1994 by the Estate of Langston Hughes. Reprinted by permission of Alfred A. Knopf, Inc., a division of Random House Inc. Used by permission of Alfred A. Knopf, a division of Random House, Inc.

———. "Salvation" from *The Big Sea* by Langston Hughes. Copyright © 1940 by Langston Hughes. Copyright renewed 1968 by Arna Bontemps and George Houson Bass. Reprinted by permission of Hill and Wang, a division of Farrar, Straus and Giroux, LLC.

David Henry Hwang. *Trying to Find Chinatown* by David Henry Hwang from *Trying to find Chinatown: The Selected Plays of David Henry Hwang*. Copyright © 2000 by David Henry Hwang. Published by Theatre Communications Group. Used by permission of Theatre Communications Group.

Shirley Jackson. "The Lottery" from *The Lottery* by Shirley Jackson. Copyright © 1948, 1949 by Shirley Jackson. Copyright renewed 1976, 1977 by Laurence Hyman, Barry Hyman, Mrs. Sarah Webster and Mrs. Joanne Schnurer. Reprinted by permission of Farrar, Straus and Giroux, LLC.

Ha Jin. "The Bridegroom." Copyright © 2000 by Ha Jin, from *The Bridegroom* by Ha Jin. Used by permission of Pantheon Books, a division of Random House, Inc.

James Weldon Johnson. "A Poet to His Baby Son" from *James Weldon Johnson: Complete Poems* by James Weldon Johnson, edited by Sondra Kathryn Wilson. Copyright © 2000 Sondra Kathryn Wilson, Literary Executor of the Estate of James Weldon Johnson. Used by permission of Penguin, a division of Penguin Group (USA) Inc.

Lacy M. Johnson. "White Trash Primer." First appeared in *Memoir Journal*; adapted for inclusion in *Trespasses: A Memoir*. Copyright © 2012 University of Iowa Press.

June Jordan. "Memo." Copyright © 1983 by June Jordan. Reprinted with permission of The June M. Jordan Literary Estate. www.junejordan.com.

Franz Kafka. "A Hunger Artist" from *Franz Kafka: The Complete Stories* by Franz Kafka, edited by Nahum N. Glatzer. Copyright © 1946, 1947, 1948, 1949, 1954, 1958, 1971 by Schocken Books. Used by permission of Schocken Books, a division of Random House, Inc.

Jane Kenyon. "Let Evening Come" from *Collected Poems*. Copyright © 2005 by the Estate of Jane Kenyon. Reprinted with the permission of The Permissions Company, Inc. on behalf of Graywolf Press, Minneapolis, Minnesota, www.graywolfpress.org.

Jamaica Kincaid. "Girl," from *At the Bottom of the River*. Copyright © 1983 by Jamaica Kincaid. Reprinted by permission of Farrar, Straus and Giroux, LLC.

———. "On Seeing England for the First Time" by Jamaica Kincaid, *Transition*, 1991 (Indiana University Press).

Martin Luther King Jr. "Letter from Birmingham Jail." Reprinted by arrangement with The Heirs to the Estate of Martin Luther King Jr., c/o Writers House as agent for the proprietor New York, NY. Copyright 1963 Dr. Martin Luther King Jr; copyright renewed 1991 Coretta Scott King.

Maxine Hong Kingston. "No Name Woman" from *The Woman Warrior* by Maxine Hong Kingston. Copyright ©1975, 1976 by Maxine Hong Kingston. Used by permission of Alfred A. Knopf, a division of Random House, Inc.

Galway Kinnell. "After Making Love We Hear Footsteps" from *Mortal Acts, Mortal Words* by Galway Kinnell. Copyright © 1980 by Galway Kinnell. Reprinted by permission of Houghton Mifflin Harcourt Publishing Company. All rights reserved.

Carolyn Kizer. "Bitch" from *Cool, Calm, and Collected: Poems 1960–2000*. Copyright © 2001 by Carolyn Kizer. Reprinted with the permission of The Permissions Company, Inc. on behalf of Copper Canyon Press, www.coppercanyonpress.org.

Etheridge Knight. "Hard Rock Returns to Prison from the Hospital for the Criminal Insane" from *The Essential Etheridge Knight* by Etheridge Knight. Copyright © 1986. Reprinted by permission of the University of Pittsburgh Press.

Yusef Komunyakaa. "Facing It" from *Pleasure Dome: New and Collected Poems*. Copyright © 2001 by Yusef Komunyakaa. Reprinted with permission of Wesleyan University Press.

Hari Kunzru. "Raj, Bohemian." Reproduced with permission of Curtis Brown Group Ltd, London on behalf of Hari Kunzru. Copyright © Hari Kunzru 2008.

Jhumpa Lahiri. "Hell-Heaven" from *Unaccustomed Earth* by Jhumpa Lahiri. Copyright © 2008 by Jhumpa Lahiri. Used by permission of Alfred A. Knopf, a division of Random House, Inc.

Philip Larkin. "A Study of Reading Habits" and "This Be the Verse" from *Collected Poems* by Philip Larkin. Copyright © 1988, 2003 by the Estate of Philip Larkin. Reprinted by permission of Farrar, Straus and Giroux, LLC. and Faber and Faber Ltd.

Evelyn Lau. "Solipsim," from *In the House of Slaves* by Evelyn Lau. Copyright © 1994 (Coach House Press, 1994). Reprinted by permission of the author.

Ursula K. Le Guin. "The Ones Who Walk Away from Omelas" fom *The Wind's Twelve Quarters*. Originally published in *New Dimensions 3*. Copyright © 1973, 2001 by Ursula K. Le Guin.

Chang-rae Lee. "Coming Home Again" originally published in *The New Yorker*, October 16, 1995.

Li-Young Lee. "Eating Alone" from *Rose*. Copyright © 1986 by Li-Young Lee. Reprinted with the permission of The Permissions Company, Inc. on behalf of BOA Editions, Ltd., www.boaeditions.org.

Jonathan Lethem. "Super Goat Man" originally published in *The New Yorker,* April 5, 2004. Copyright © 2004 by Jonathan Lethem.

Philip Levine. "What Work Is" from *What Work Is* by Philip Levine. Copyright © 1992 by Philip Levine. Used by permission of Alfred A. Knopf, Inc., a division of Random House, Inc.

Yiyun Li. "The Science of Flight" by Yiyun Li, originally published in *The New Yorker*. Copyright © 2010 by Yiyun Li, used by permission of The Wylie Agency LLC.

Shirley Geok-lin Lim. "Learning to Love America" from *What the Fortune Teller Didn't Say*. Copyright © 1998 by Shirley Geok-lin Lim. Reprinted with the permission of The Permissions Company, Inc., on behalf of West End Press, Albuquerque, New Mexico, http://www.westendpress.org.

Stuart Lishan. "Winter Count, 1964." Reprinted by permission of the author.

Audre Lorde. "Hanging Fire" from *The Black Unicorn* by Audre Lorde. Copyright © 1978 by Audre Lorde. Used by permission of W. W. Norton & Company, Inc.

Katharyn Howd Machan. "Hazel Tells Laverne" from *Light Year 1985* by Katharyn Howd Machan. Reprinted with the permission of the author.

Katherine McAlpine. "Plus C'est la Même Chose" originally published in *The Nation*. Copyright © 1994 by Katherine McAlpine. Reprinted with permission of the author.

Peter Meinke. "Advice to My Son" from *Liquid Paper: New and Selected Poems* by Peter Meinke. Copyright © 1991. Reprinted by permission of the University of Pittsburgh Press.

W. S. Merwin. "Thanks" from *Rain in the Trees* by W.S. Merwin. Copyright © 1988 by W.S. Merwin. Used by permission of Alfred A. Knopf, a division of Random House, Inc.

Robert Mezey. "My Mother" from *The Door Standing Open* (London: Oxford University Press, 1970). Reprinted with permission of the author.

Lydia Millet. "Girl and Giraffe" originally published in *McSweeney's* Issue 22 (2006).

Janice Mirikitani. "Suicide Note" from *Shedding Silence: Poetry and Prose* by Janice Mirikitani. Copyright © 1987 by Janice Mirikitani. Used by permission of Celestial Arts, an imprint of the Crown Publishing Group, a division of Random House, Inc.

Lisel Mueller. "Happy and Unhappy Families" and "Curriculum Vitae" from *Alive Together* by Lisel Mueller. Copyright © 1996 by Lisel Mueller. Reprinted with the permission of Louisiana State University Press.

Bharati Mukherjee. "Two Ways to Belong in America" from *The New York Times*, September 22, 1996. Copyright © 1996 *The New York Times*. Reprinted by permission.

Taslima Nasrin. "Things Cheaply Had" from *The New Yorker*, October 9, 1995. Translated from the Bengali by Carolyne Wright, with Mohammad Nurul Huda and the author. Copyright © 1995 by Carolyne Wright. Reprinted with the permission of Carolyne Wright.

Maggie Nelson. Copyright © 2007 by Maggie Nelson from *Something Bright, Then Holes*. Reprinted by permission of Counterpoint.

Pablo Neruda. "The Dead Woman" by Pablo Neruda, from *The Captain's Verses*. Copyright ©1972 by Pablo Neruda and Donald D. Walsh. Reprinted by permission of New Directions Publishing Corp.

John Frederick Nims. "Love Poem" from *Selected Poems* by John Frederick Nims. Copyright © 1982 John Frederick Nims. University of Chicago Press.

Jean Nordhaus. "A Dandelion for My Mother." Reprinted by permission of The Ohio State University Press.

Lynn Nottage. *Poof!* by Lynn Nottage. Copyright © 1993, 2004 by Lynn Nottage. Published by Theatre Communications Group. Used by permission of Theatre Communications Group.

Joyce Carol Oates. "Where Are You Going, Where Have You Been?" Copyright © 1970 Ontario Review, Inc. Reprinted by permission of John Hawkins & Associates, Inc.

Tim O'Brien. "The Things They Carried" from *The Things They Carried* by Tim O'Brien. Copyright © 1990 by Tim O'Brien. Reprinted by permission of Houghton Mifflin Harcourt Publishing Company. All rights reserved.

Flannery O'Connor. "A Good Man Is Hard to Find" from *A Good Man Is Hard to Find and Other Stories*. Copyright 1953 by Flannery O'Connor and renewed 1981 by Regina O'Connor, reprinted by permission of Houghton Mifflin Harcourt Publishing Company. All rights reserved.

———. Excerpt from *Mystery and Manners* by Flannery O'Connor, edited by Sally and Robert Fitzgerald. Copyright © 1969 by the Estate of Mary Flannery O'Connor. Reprinted by permission of Farrar, Straus & Giroux, LLC.

Frank O'Hara. "My Heart" from *The Collected Poems of Frank O'Hara* by Frank O'Hara, edited by Donald Allen. Copyright © 1971 by Maureen Granville-Smith, Administratrix of the Estate of Frank O'Hara, copyright renewed 1999 by Maureen O'Hara Granville-Smith and Donald Allen. Used by permission of Alfred A. Knopf, a division of Random House, Inc.

Sharon Olds. "Sex Without Love" from *The Dead and the Living* by Sharon Olds. Copyright © 1987 by Sharon Olds. Used by permission of Alfred A. Knopf, a division of Random House, Inc.

———. "My Father's Diary" from *Blood, Tin, Straw* by Sharon Olds. Copyright © 1999 by Sharon Olds. Used by permission of Alfred A. Knopf, a division of Random House, Inc.

Mary Oliver. "When Death Comes" from *New and Selected Poems* by Mary Oliver. Published by Beacon Press, Boston. Copyright © 1992 by Mary Oliver. Reprinted by permission of The Charlotte Sheedy Literary Agency Inc.

Joseph O'Neill. "Touched by Evil." Reprinted by permission of the author. Originally published in *The Atlantic*.

Daniel Orozco. "Orientation." Reprinted by permission of *The Seattle Review*.

George Orwell. "Shooting an Elephant" from *Shooting an Elephant and Other Essays* by George Orwell. Copyright 1950 by Sonia Brownell Orwell and renewed 1978 by Sonia Pitt-Rivers, reprinted by permission of Houghton Mifflin Harcourt Publishing Company. All rights reserved.

Alicia Suskin Ostriker. "Daffodils" from *No Heaven* by Alicia Suskin Ostriker. Copyright © 2005. Reprinted by permission of the University of Pittsburgh Press.

———. "The Starry Night" from *All My Pretty Ones* by Anne Sexton. Copyright © 1962 by Anne Sexton, renewed 1990 by Linda G. Sexton. Reprinted by permission of Houghton Mifflin Harcourt Publishing Company. All rights reserved.

Leslie Marmon Silko. "The Man to Send Rain Clouds" from *Storyteller* by Leslie Marmon Silko. Copyright © 1969, 1981 by Leslie Marmon Silko, used by permission of The Wylie Agency LLC.

Stevie Smith. "Not Waving but Drowning" by Stevie Smith. Copyright ©1957 by Stevie Smith, and "To Carry the Child" by Stevie Smith, copyright ©1972 by Stevie Smith, from *Collected Poems of Stevie Smith*. Reprinted by permission of New Directions Publishing.

Sophocles. "Antigone" from *Sophocles, the Oedipus Cycle: An English Version* by Dudley Fitts and Robert Fitzgerald. Copyright 1939 by Houghton Mifflin Harcourt Publishing Company. Copyright © renewed 1967 by Dudley Fitts and Robert Fitzgerald. Reprinted by permission of Houghton Mifflin Harcourt Publishing Company. All rights reserved. All professional, amateur, motion picture, recitation, lecturing, performance, public reading, radio, and television rights are strictly reserved. Inquiries on all rights should be sent to Houghton Mifflin Harcourt at 215 Park Avenue South, New York, NY 10003.

Gary Soto. "Behind Grandma's House." From *New and Selected Poems* © 1995 by Gary Soto. Used with permission of Chronicle Books LLC, San Francisco. Visit ChronicleBooks.com.

Wole Soyinka. "Telephone Conversation." Copyright © 1962, 1990 by Wole Soyinka. Reprinted with permission by Melanie Jackson Agency, LLC.

William Stafford. "Traveling through the Dark" from *The Way It Is: New and Selected Poems*. Copyright © 1962, 1998 by William Stafford and the Estate of William Stafford. Reprinted with the permission of The Permissions Company, Inc. on behalf of Graywolf Press, Minneapolis, Minnesota, www.graywolfpress.org.

Wallace Stevens. "Sunday Morning" from *The Collected Poems of Wallace Stevens* by Wallace Stevens. Copyright 1954 by Wallace Stevens and renewed 1982 by Holly Stevens. Used by permission of Alfred A. Knopf, a division of Random House, Inc.

Wislawa Szymborska. "A Happy Love." Krynski, Magnus J. (trans.); *Sounds, Feelings, Thought*. Copyright © 1981 Princeton University Press. Reprinted by permission of Princeton University Press.

Grace Talusan. "My Father's Noose" originally published in *Brevity: A Journal of Concise Literary Nonfiction*, Winter 2007 Issue Twenty-Three. Reprinted by permission of the author.

Amy Tan. "Two Kinds" from *The Joy Luck Club* by Amy Tan. Copyright © 1989 by Amy Tan. Used by permission of G.P. Putnam's Sons, a division of Penguin Group (USA) Inc.

Sheila Ortiz Taylor. "The Way Back" from *Slow Dancing at Miss Polly's* (Naiad Press, 1989). Reprinted by permission of the author.

Alexandra Teague. "Adjectives of Order" from *Slate*. Copyright © 2007 The Slate Group. All rights reserved. Used by permission and protected by the Copyright Laws of the United States. The printing, copying, redistribution, or retransmission of the Material without express written permission is prohibited.

Dylan Thomas. "Fern Hill." Copyright ©1945 by The Trustees for the Copyrights of Dylan Thomas, and "Do Not Go Gentle Into That Good Night," copyright ©1952 by Dylan Thomas, from *The Poems of Dylan Thomas*. Reprinted by permission of New Directions Publishing Corp.

Natasha Trethewey. "Flounder" from *Domestic Work*. Copyright © 2000 by Natasha Trethewey. Reprinted with the permission of The Permissions Company, Inc., on behalf of Graywolf Press, Minneapolis, Minnesota, www.graywolfpress.org.

Mark Turpin. "The Man Who Built This House" from *Hammer*. Copyright © 2003 by Mark Turpin. Reprinted with the permission of The Permissions Company, Inc. on behalf of Sarabande Books, www.sarabandebooks.org.

John Updike. "A & P" from *Pigeon Feathers and Other Stories* by John Updike. Copyright © 1962 and renewed 1990 by John Updike. Used by permission of Alfred A. Knopf, Inc., a division of Random House, Inc.

Helena María Viramontes. "The Moths" is reprinted with permission from the publisher of *The Moths and Other Stories* by Helena Maria Viramontes. Copyright ©1985 Arte Público Press- University of Houston.

Alice Walker. "Everyday Use" from *In Love & Trouble: Stories of Black Women*. Copyright © 1973 by Alice Walker, reprinted by permission of Houghton Mifflin Harcourt Publishing Company. All rights reserved.

David Foster Wallace. "Commencement Speech, Kenyon College." Copyright Guardian News & Media Ltd 2008.

———. "Good People." Copyright 2007, David Foster Wallace. Used by permission of the David Foster Wallace Literary Trust. Originally published in *The New Yorker* in the February 5, 2007 issue.

James Welch. "Christmas Comes to Moccasin Flat" from *Riding the Earthboy 40* by James Welch. Copyright © 1971, 1976, 1990 by James Welch. Used by permission of Penguin, a division of Penguin Group (USA) Inc.

E. B. White. "Once More to the Lake" from *One Man's Meat* by E. B. White. Text copyright © 1941 by E. B. White, renewed. Reprinted by permission of Tilbury House Publishers, Gardiner, Maine.

Oscar Williams. "A Total Revolution" from *That's All That Matters* by Oscar Williams. Reprinted with permission.

David Wojahn. "August, 1953" from *World Tree*, by David Wojahn. Copyright © 2011. Reprinted by permission of the University of Pittsburgh Press.

Tobias Wolff. "Bullet in the Brain" from *The Night in Question* by Tobias Wolff. Copyright © 1996 by Tobias Wolff. Used by permission of Alfred A. Knopf, a division of Random House, Inc.

Virginia Woolf. "Shakespeare's Sister" from *A Room of One's Own* by Virginia Woolf. Copyright 1929 by Houghton Mifflin Harcourt Publishing Company and renewed 1957 by Leonard Woolf, reprinted by permission of the publisher. All rights reserved.

James Wright. "Lying in a Hammock at William Duffy's Farm in Pine Island, Minnesota" from *Collected Poems*. Copyright © 1971 by James Wright. Reprinted with permission of Wesleyan University Press.

W. B. Yeats. "Lead and the Swan" and "Sailing to Byzantium." Copyright © 1928 by The Macmillan Company, renewed 1956 by Georgie Yeats, and "The Great Day," copyright © 1940 by Georgie Yeats, renewed 1968 by Bertha Georgie Yeats, Michael Butler Yeats, and Anne Yeats. Reprinted with the permission of Scribner, a Division of Simon & Schuster, Inc., from *The Collected Works of W.B. Yeats, Volume I: The Poems, Revised* by W. B. Yeats, edited by Richard J. Finneran. All rights reserved.

Yevgeny Yevtushenko. "I Would Like" from *Yevgeny Yevtushenko: The Collected Poems 1952–1990*, edited by Albert C. Todd. Copyright © 1991 by Henry Holt and Company, LLC.

Dean Young. "Winged Purpose" from *Fall Higher*. Copyright © 2011 by Dean Young. Reprinted by permission of The Permissions Company, Inc. on behalf of Copper Canyon Press, www.coppercanyonpress.org.

Kevin Young. "Negative." Reprinted from *To Repel Ghosts* by permission of Steerforth Press L.L.C.

Timothy Yu. "Chinese Silence No. 22." Reprinted by permission of the author.

Art Credits

p. 18. The Dionysius Theatre in Athens. © Bettmann/CORBIS.

p. 19. Interior of the Swan Theatre, London, 1596. © Culver Pictures, Inc.

p. 20. Hypothetical reconstruction of the interior of the Globe Theatre in the days of Shakespeare. © Bettmann/CORBIS.

p. 21. A seventeenth-century French box stage. © Bettmann/CORBIS.

p. 76. *The Grandmother* (*La Abuela*), 1974, by Fernando Botero. © Fernando Botero courtesy Marlborough Gallery, New York. Art Resource, NY.

p. 322. *Untitled*, 1985, by Keith Haring. © Keith Haring Foundation. Used by permission.

p. 548. *This Is Harlem* (detail), 1943, by Jacob Lawrence. © 2012 The Jacob and Gwendolyn Lawrence Foundation, Seattle/Artists Rights Society (ARS), New York.

p. 832. *Two Lovers*, 1630, by Safavid, Riza 'Abbasi (ca. 1565-1635), Isfahan, Iran. Tempera and gilt paint on paper; 7 1/8 × 4 11/16 in. (18.1 × 11.9 cm). The Metropolitan Museum of Art, Purchase, Francis M. Weld Gift, 1950. (50.164). Image © The Metropolitan Museum of Art. Reproduced with permission.

p. 1104. *Death and Life*, 1910–1916, by Gustav Klimt. Oil on canvas, 178 × 198 cm. Photo credit: Erich Lessing/Art Resource, NY. Reproduced with permission.

p. 1232. *Landscape with the Fall of Icarus*, ca. 1560, by Pieter Brueghel the Elder. Musée d'Art Ancien, Musées Royaux des Beaux-Arts, Brussels, Belgium. Photo credit: Scala/Art Resource, NY. Reproduced with permission.

p. 1234. *The Third of May*, 1808, by Francisco de Goya y Lucientes. Painted in 1814. Oil on canvas, 266 × 345 cm. Museo del Prado, Madrid, Spain. Photo credit: Erich Lessing/Art Resource, NY. Reproduced with permission.

p. 1236. *The Starry Night*, 1889, by Vincent van Gogh (1853–1890). Oil on canvas, 29 × 36 1/4 in. Acquired through the Lillie P. Bliss Bequest. (472.1941). The Museum of Modern Art, New York, NY, U.S.A. Digital image © The Museum of Modern Art/Licensed by SCALA/Art Resource, NY. Reproduced with permission.

p. 1238. *The Great Wave off Kanagawa* (from a series of "Thirty-six Views of Mount Fuji"), Edo period (1615–1868), ca. 1831–33, Katsushika Hokusai (Japanese, 1760–1849); Published by Eijudo, polychrome ink and color on paper; 10 1/8 × 14 15/16 in. (25.7 × 37.9 cm) (Oban size). The Metropolitan Museum of Art, H. O. Havemeyer Collection. Bequest of Mrs. H. O. Havemeyer, 1929, (JP 1847). Image © The Metropolitan Museum of Art. Photo credit: Art Resource, NY. Reproduced with permission.

INDEX OF AUTHORS AND TITLES